THE PAPERS OF

Andrew Johnson

Sponsored by

The University of Tennessee

The National Historical Publications Commission

The Tennessee Historical Commission

A likeness of Andrew Johnson.
Copyrighted 1899 by James D. Richardson.
From photogravure, *courtesy Pierpont Morgan Library*.

THE PAPERS OF
Andrew Johnson

Volume 3, 1858-1860

EDITORS
LEROY P. GRAF AND RALPH W. HASKINS

ASSISTANT EDITOR, PATRICIA P. CLARK

1972
THE UNIVERSITY OF TENNESSEE PRESS
KNOXVILLE

Library of Congress Catalog Card Number: 67–25733

International Standard Book Number 0–87049–141–5

Manufactured in the United States of America

TO

Our Families

RUTH, CHRISTINA, MELISSA, JEREMY GRAF

FLORENCE AND JIM HASKINS

Contents

1859

1860

Illustrations

Introduction

The life of an individual offers a case study in one of history's eternally fascinating themes: the interplay between continuity and change. Now and then the fundamental thread is obscured by the superficial strand, a truism amply demonstrated by the career of Andrew Johnson and reflected here in his early senatorial years. Ostensibly his move from the state to the national scene meant a significant break with the past; yet this latest stage in his progress from tailor shop to White House, like his elevation from congressman to governor, represented a remarkable degree of continuity. The Johnson who entered the Senate in the waning months of 1857 was essentially the Johnson of old, in personality, in commitment to the common man, in dedication to cherished goals—homestead legislation, economy in government, and constitutional amendments designed to further the democratic process. During his decade in Congress, he had promoted these "Andyjohnsonisms" in the House; as Tennessee's chief executive, he had urged them upon the General Assembly.[1]

Thrust into the governorship inadequately prepared for the task,[2] he now returned to the Washington milieu where, ironically, he was more at home than in the statehouse. Had he engaged in a cursory study of the Senate in 1857, just as he once had evaluated the House,[3] he would have found that one-third of the membership—fifteen on the Democratic side and seven of varying political hue across the aisle—had been colleagues at some time during his congressional career. With some, notably Thomas L. Clingman of North Carolina, Jacob Collamer of Vermont, Jefferson Davis of Mississippi, and John P. Hale of New Hampshire, he had locked horns in caustic debate; others, erstwhile Democrats like Preston King of New York and Hannibal Hamlin of Maine, had by now embraced the Republican cause. Although the older generation of national statesmen—Calhoun, Clay, and Webster—was gone, the roster contained many names which would figure prominently in war and Reconstruction. Few indeed were those laboring to reconcile sectional differences and avert the dissolution of the Union—men like John Bell of Tennessee, John J. Crittenden of Kentucky, Stephen A. Douglas of Illinois, and

1. See *Johnson Papers*, II, 205–6, 334–36.
2. *Ibid.*, xix.
3. *Ibid.*, 506.

Sam Houston of Texas. Far more numerous were those responsive to the siren call of sectionalism: from the South, Judah P. Benjamin and John Slidell of Louisiana, James Henry Hammond of South Carolina, James M. Mason of Virginia, Alfred Iverson and Robert Toombs of Georgia, and James Green of Missouri; from the North, Simon Cameron of Pennsylvania, Zachariah Chandler of Michigan, William H. Seward of New York, Benjamin F. Wade of Ohio, and Henry Wilson of Massachusetts. Some would play significant roles during his years in the White House: Seward as his secretary of state and King as his confidant, Chandler, Wade, and Wilson as his bitter antagonists. Johnson's own position in the growing crisis was for some time uncertain; not until December, 1860, would he clearly become one of the voices of moderation.

He had left Congress in 1853, at a time when compromise appeared to have solved a great national dilemma. When he returned four years later, the artificial calm had been broken by the Kansas-Nebraska Act and "Bleeding Kansas," by the stern enforcement of the Fugitive Slave Act and the ensuing personal liberty laws, by the advent of a sectional Republican party and the waging of a tumultuous presidential campaign. The Dred Scott decision, coming only a few days after Buchanan's inauguration, further exacerbated the national temper. In Congress the pronounced aversion to compromise, the indiscriminate use of epithet and innuendo, the occasional resort to mayhem, whether of fisticuffs or the caning of Charles Sumner, made that body at times almost a parody of a legislature.

Although the senator from Tennessee eventually added his strident tones to the discordant voices reverberating through the chamber, he did not immediately become involved in the vitriolic debate on slavery. On record as a proponent of the peculiar institution—a normal condition of mankind "in perfect harmony" with democracy[4] —he soon clarified his position on the Kansas-Nebraska question during a heated exchange with his colleague John Bell. But if he did not always speak out directly on some of the great national issues, he referred to them obliquely while concentrating on his pet propositions, the enactment of a homestead law and stringent economy in federal spending.

As governor he had had little opportunity to advance national land reform, though he did make some recommendations to the legislature. In Congress itself, the homestead question had remained comparatively quiescent from 1855 to 1858, reflecting southern dominance of the Democratic party and Republican uncertainty as to the issue's political appeal. Neither Pierce nor Buchanan, "dough-

4. *Ibid.*, 355.

faces" in the parlance of the day, inclined toward a measure unpopular with the planter interests; but Johnson, never especially close to his fellow southerners, stubbornly resumed the fight and not only introduced a homestead measure soon after the Senate convened but got it considered during the spring of 1858. He soon became a channel through which individuals and groups, largely from the North and West, registered their interest in the pending legislation.

His homestead manifesto of May 20 occupied more than eight pages of the *Congressional Globe*'s microscopic print. Rambling and discursive, it represented a catchall—a kind of omnium-gatherum of the major arguments revolving around the homestead. He denied categorically that it was unconstitutional, that it was a donation and wasteful of the revenue, that it held out a novel and dangerous idea, that it smacked of demagoguery, agrarianism, and sectionalism. On the contrary, it was national in its interest. To demonstrate the antiquity of the homestead principle, he conducted his listeners on an historical excursion which began with Moses, continued with Vattel, and ended with Andrew Jackson. Marshaling the inevitable phalanx of statistics, he asserted that, far from being a drain on the treasury, it would yield revenue. Yet there was much more than money involved, added Johnson, sounding like an Alexander Hamilton of the common man. If you "provide a man with a home . . . you make him a better man. You give him an interest in the country." Urging the diffusion of a growing population, he echoed Jefferson's strictures on the urban way of life. "Do we want cities to take control of this Government?" No! Interest men in the soil and build up the middle class, "the mechanical and agricultural portions of this community . . . the very salt of it." Let political power remain with that class and thus avoid a "miserable city rabble on the one hand" and a "pampered, bloated, corrupted aristocracy on the other." Alleging that opponents of the homestead displayed a deep distrust of "popularizing our institutions," Johnson reaffirmed the divinity of man and delivered a lengthy discourse on the superiority of democracy. Why such reluctance to appropriate lands for the people, when we so gladly grant land to states and corporations? Why spend for armies on the frontier, when we could have an army of men who would "defend their own firesides?" Affirming the dignity of labor, he denied that all "mudsills" were slaves; if one accepted this premise, the world had seen many distinguished slaves—Socrates, who "wielded the chisel and the mallet," Paul, a "tent-maker," and Adam, "a tailor by trade." Yet Johnson stood shoulder to shoulder with the apologists for the peculiar institution and anticipated the day when northerners, recognizing that certain staples could be produced only with slave labor, would advocate slavery in the North. The homestead policy would be a great national panacea—reconcile North and South and "strengthen the bonds of the Union."

That his multifarious arguments won converts remains a moot question; nevertheless, congressional attitudes changed sufficiently during the ensuing two years to allow the passage of a measure. Two new ingredients had been added. The first was Republican espousal of homestead legislation, "a great principle advocated by the Democratic party for years," said Johnson, speaking in April, 1860, and now, as he ironically observed—conveniently overlooking a long-standing free-soil element in the West, bastion of the new party— taken up after "the public judgment is recorded for it." In reality, southern acceptance was requisite to passage, and it was perforce to the South that he must primarily direct his appeal. A second ingredient making for success lay in the modification of the bill during a protracted debate, much of it centering around a question of semantics: was this a homestead bill, a graduation bill, or simply public lands legislation? Whatever its nature, Albert Gallatin Brown of Mississippi identified Johnson as "the parent," insisting that he "has a right to give the baptismal name to his offspring."[5] This ado about nomenclature was not without significance. In its ramifications, the bill under consideration was scarcely Johnson's proposal in its pristine state; on the contrary, argued some of its quondam followers, the original had been watered down by amendment—so much so that James Green of Missouri, reflecting a stance characteristic of those southern proslavery men adamantly opposed to the homestead principle, could lend his support, inasmuch as "the original cheat, fraud, and trick has been eviscerated; its bowels have been taken out."[6] To politicians of this persuasion, the act of June, 1860, had become "a proposition simply to dispose of the public lands,"[7] and they could vote without qualms of conscience for a measure no longer redolent of agrarianism.

In his unrelenting struggle for the homestead, the "parent" acted like the predictable Andrew Johnson. With a lack of tact displayed so often during his career, he not only flayed Republican opportunism but jeopardized his appeal for southern support by strictures on southern leaders, living and dead: on Mason, "an unworthy and unfaithful sentinel," and on Calhoun, "more of a politician than a statesman." The speech of May 20 was essentially a reiteration of arguments advanced over the years to an indifferent or antagonistic Congress; as always, there was the ubiquitous statistical evidence

5. *Cong. Globe*, 36 Cong., 1 Sess., 2044.
6. *Ibid.*, 1992.
7. *Ibid.*

designed to disarm the skeptical and convince the intractable. Calling attention to that portion of Buchanan's inaugural which dealt with land policy, he expressed the hope that the veto would not be invoked—this despite the fact that the "old public functionary" had already registered his opposition to "giving away" the public lands.[8]

But Johnson's hopes were attended by grave misgivings. As early as June 2, seventeen days before the bill passed and three weeks before its veto, he was accumulating evidence which he would employ to counter the President's objections.[9] When the blow fell, the principal burden of the plebeian's impassioned response was the intrinsic merit of the measure—sound in principle, reflecting "the high behest of the American people." He castigated the message as hastily prepared and highly distorted, "more like the *ad captandum* of the mere politician or demagogue, than a grave and sound reason to be offered by the President in a veto message upon so important a measure." Refuting at length Buchanan's position, he inveighed against the arbitrary use of the veto power and indulged himself in invidious comparison between the incumbent and his great predecessors Washington, Jefferson, and Jackson, all of whom Johnson cavalierly enlisted in the cause of the homestead. Moreover, his bitterness led him into a personal attack upon the perpetrator of the veto. Alluding to Buchanan's confirmed bachelorhood, he speculated "Whether considerations so national, so humane, so Christian, have ever penetrated the brain of one whose bosom has never yet swelled with emotions for wife or children, is for an enlightened public to determine." But logical reasoning, emotional appeal, and personal recrimination were all in vain; the veto stood, and ironically, in the eyes of contemporaries and their posterity, credit for the Homestead would accrue not to Andrew Johnson but to the Republican party.

Though land reform was the Tennessean's principal cause, "retrenchment" and "economy" were also recurrent themes during these first two years in the Senate, just as they had been in the House. Whether it involved salaries for additional Washington police, school funds for the District of Columbia, an aqueduct to bring water to the capital, furniture for new committee rooms, or messengers for the Senate, Johnson was ever a spokesman for keeping expenditures down, or better still, eliminating them entirely. Whenever possible he drew his arguments from his favorite source—the Constitution strictly construed. He entertained strong reservations about congressional prerogative in internal improvements, pronouncing it a doctrine of "the latitudinarians." Thus he could say characteristically

8. See Buchanan's veto of "the agricultural-college bill," February 24, 1859, in Richardson, *Messages*, V, 548–50.
9. See Letters from Joseph Wilson, June 2, 15, 1860.

"You have no more power to take money from the Federal Treasury and appropriate it to local improvements in the District of Columbia, than you have to appropriate it for such improvements in St. Louis— not a single scintilla of power more." When he raised his voice in outspoken opposition to Jefferson Davis' Pacific Railroad bill during the winter of 1859, he was merely being consistent. Could the latitudinarians expect a single scintilla of sympathy from a onetime state legislator who had viewed railroad charters as monopolies and had allegedly prophesied that the roads would "violate the laws of nature in pulling down hills and filling up hollows?"[10] This doughty champion of economy, seizing upon Buchanan's invitation to Congress to "institute a rigid scrutiny" of federal spending, introduced a resolution, eventually passed, placing a $50,000,000 limit on estimates of annual expenditures. But retrenchment was not to be achieved, a reality perhaps sensed by Johnson when he argued on behalf of this resolution, "It can do no earthly harm, and may do a great deal of good."

Yet there was an even starker reality to be confronted. As the decade drew to a close, the nation was shocked by John Brown's October raid on Harper's Ferry. Not only the event and its implications but the public reaction as well would be hotly argued as soon as Congress convened early in December, 1859. Johnson's views were aired in the course of the week-long debate prompted by a resolution calling for a complete investigation. While denying any partisan intent, the southerner blamed the Republicans and their predecessors for propounding ideas such as the bloody overthrow of slavery and the dissolution of the Union that led logically, nay inevitably, to the violence which had occurred. In a typically digressive speech, he denied that Congress had any sovereign power over the territories, charged the Republicans with demanding for the slave rights denied free Negroes in the North, and refuted to his own satisfaction Seward's "irrepressible conflict" between free and slave labor, finding instead an irrepressible conflict in the North between capital and labor. "The southern man, with his capital invested in slaves," he announced, "is the best and most reliable advocate that the free laboring man at the North has."

Quoting Seward at some length, Johnson charged him and his ilk with scheming to amend the Constitution so as to "obliterate" slavery. No wonder southerners were alarmed! In fervid language he inveighed against Brown, who stood "before the country a murderer," arraigned his senatorial apologists, and condemned those who went so far as to compare John Brown with Jesus Christ and the gallows with the cross. Intermittently during the speech, as well

10. Nashville *True Whig*, May 14, 1853.

as in a resounding peroration, he denounced those who would twist the Constitution or threaten the Union. Forecasting his subsequent course, he vowed to "place my feet upon that Constitution which I have sworn to support, and to stand there and battle for all its guarantees," in the unshakable faith that it was "the common altar" around which all should rally to preserve the Union, and under which all might have "peace and harmony" and "unexampled prosperity." It was a stirring oration and, except for the homestead speech, his most extended during his first years in the Senate, but, unlike his Union speech of twelve months later, it created no especial furor in or out of Congress. Two days later the resolution on Harper's Ferry was adopted and the Senate turned to other matters.

Though a variety of business occupied the Senate during the final six months of the session, Johnson did not participate in the principal debates centering around the issue of slavery in the territories and highlighted by Jefferson Davis' resolutions which, by directly opposing popular sovereignty, in effect constituted a southern ultimatum in this critical election year. Instead, the Tennessean concentrated on the homestead question, now reaching its climax; inevitably, too, he became embroiled with personalities. In March, he took exception to a campaign speech in which Daniel Clark of New Hampshire, comparing New England, with its sterile soil and free men, and Tennessee, with its rich resources and blight of slavery, observed that he had "seen copper taken from the mines there and sent to New York to be smelted by the 'mud-sills' of society, because there were not energy and enterprise enough in Tennessee to do it." Here was a challenge to a hardy provincial, and Johnson rose to the occasion. Summoning an imposing array of figures, he set out to prove that "the energy and enterprise" of Tennesseans in agriculture, mining, and even manufacturing equalled, and in some respects far surpassed, that of New Hampshire. In the face of this statistical onslaught, Clark solemnly promised to say nothing disparaging about Tennessee; certainly he would "not dispute but that they raise more horses, asses, and mules than we do."[11]

But the major reason for Johnson's comparative detachment was an increasing absorption with presidential politics. In the light of his driving ambition and his slow but steady climb to higher office, it is not strange that he regarded himself as a distinct possibility for the nomination in 1860. Four years earlier he had fancied the role of favorite son at the Cincinnati convention. Although nothing came of this maneuver and few Democrats took him seriously, the idea of the presidency remained a bright and even tangible vision. After all, Jackson and Polk had occupied the White House: why not another

11. *Cong. Globe*, 36 Cong., 1 Sess., 1368.

Tennessean? Yet it was not a vision that Johnson proposed to reveal immediately to the public eye; indeed, to the casual observer of that day, he might have seemed to scorn the chief magistracy. "I would rather be an honest man, an honest representative, than be President of the United States forty times," he declared on the Senate floor in early 1859, intimating that his old foil Jefferson Davis openly coveted the nomination. Let the ambitious, the self-seeking, pursue the highest office in the land; Andrew Johnson remained content to serve the people and the state. "I say damn the Presidency; it is not worthy of a man who believes in doing good, and is in a position to serve his country by popularizing her free institutions." But these asperities, uttered in the heat of the moment, should not be taken out of context: he was saying, in so many words, leave president-making to the people and not to Congress. Indeed this public stance toward the office belies his real position, best expressed in a letter written to a Chattanooga editor in August, 1859. At first glance the statement appears to be another disclaimer; but upon closer scrutiny, it proves to be a clear invitation. Remarking that "I never was and never expect to be an aspirant to the presidency," he observed that some men, regarding the office as "the Summit of all human greatness," had sacrificed principle to expedience in its pursuit. This *he* would never do! Generally cynical about the national nominating process, he averred that "the man who has most merit and strength before the people has the least chance befor [*sic*] the Convention," adding that he would take no steps to place his name before the Democracy at Charleston. "If it goes there it must be the act of others not mine— If presidential honors ever *beset* my *path* it must be upon the principles laid down in . . . this letter *and none other*—" Concluding on an equivocal note, he thanked the editor for his interest "in promoting my presidential aspirations if I had any—." However much he might cavil about terminology, Johnson certainly harbored "aspirations," a fact made abundantly clear in his correspondence during the winter and spring of 1860.

Patently, his prospects at Charleston would hinge upon backing from Tennessee. As the state Democratic convention approached, not only Johnson but also his old, but now lukewarm, friend Senator A. O. P. Nicholson and his open rival, Governor Isham G. Harris, were prominent possibilities. While some Nashville and Memphis organs suggested Harris' name for the presidential ticket, other papers endorsed Johnson's candidacy; the Fayetteville *Lincoln Journal* urged his supporters "to speak out in their conversations, in primary meetings and through the press."[12] When the convention met in

12. Mary R. Campbell, *The Attitude of Tennesseans toward the Union, 1847–1861* (New York, 1961), 105.

Nashville on January 18, Johnson's partisans, especially his Greeneville lieutenant William Lowry, maneuvered so adroitly behind the scenes that the senator's name alone was presented to the delegates. The fact that another close personal friend, former Congressman George W. Jones, was the presiding officer facilitated the endorsement, despite the presence of "some wild men in the Convention." The resolution declaring that Johnson "possesses in an eminent degree the high qualifications demanded by the exigencies of the times," and "combines in his character, history and political antecedents more of the elements of success" than any other leading presidential aspirant, was greeted "with old fashioned, Shouts, and applause." An observer thought he saw "two or three men, whose faces looked twisted, and resembled a boy who had been eating green parcimons"; but the Nashville *Union and American*, itself not particularly enthusiastic about the choice, confessed that "the devotion of the Democratic masses in Tennessee to this unflinching champion of their rights, amounts almost to idolatry."[13]

Perhaps as significant as the convention's endorsement was its selection of delegates. The Tennessee contingent could scarcely be described as "packed" with Johnson men, and his friend Hu Douglas called it an "unfortunate selection." Indeed there is reason to believe that a number preferred Stephen A. Douglas and intended no more than a complimentary vote for their favorite son. Nevertheless, the group included such good friends as Sam Milligan, Washington C. Whitthorne, John K. Howard, William Henry Maxwell, and W. E. B. Jones; two of the four Tennessee representatives on committees were Johnson supporters; and in addition to his sons Charles and Robert, such old cronies as William Lowry and Hu Douglas were at Charleston lobbying for his nomination. Except for minor defections, the delegation, representing virtually his sole support, stayed with him through thirty-six ballots, then switched to James Guthrie of Kentucky, whom it supported for the remainder of the voting. Meanwhile one delegate, William H. Carroll, telegraphed, "We have withdrawn you. Douglas has majority ought we support him," to which Johnson, who in 1852 had called the Little Giant "the candidate of the *cormorants* of our party,"[14] replied evasively, "The delegation present, with all the facts before them are better prepared to determine what Course to pursue than I am." Thus in the final analysis he declined responsibility for the decision.

When the Democratic convention reassembled in Baltimore, he continued to stand aloof, requesting that Tennessee refrain from

13. Letter from Samuel R. Anderson, January 21, 1860; Nashville *Union and American*, January 19, 20, 1860.
14. Letter to David T. Patterson, April 4, 1852, in *Johnson Papers*, II, 30.

presenting his name to that body. Possibly his flaccid approach to the proceedings at Charleston and Baltimore stemmed from his inherent dislike for the convention process; on the other hand, it may have been the timing which militated against his fullest involvement in the nominating race. In Congress the months of April and May, 1860, were crucial times for the homestead measure, by now a veritable obsession with the Tennessee senator. To play a leading part in the climactic scenes of a drama to which he had devoted himself intermittently for a decade and a half was far more intriguing, far more rewarding, than the distant arena in which his prospects of emerging in the leading role were at best meagre.

One can only speculate about Johnson's thoughts at this time. Did he really believe he had a chance for the nomination? Did he hope for the consolation prize of second place? Or did he regard the events of 1860 as prologue to the presidency four years hence? There is no conclusive evidence that contemporaries saw him as a front runner; nor have historians thought otherwise. Although he may have contemplated the role of dark horse—a southern moderate standing somewhere between Douglas and a deep-South "ultra"—there is substantial evidence that, as the convention approached, he had become reconciled to the nomination of Douglas. As early as January he cautioned his son against any criticism of the Illinois senator, "for at present he is the Strong man in the free States and will go into the convention the strong man of the party." With a calculating eye to his own future, Johnson refrained from a public stand; but he remarked privately that "There Could be no Safer positin [sic] to Secure the first place four years hence than Second place on the ticket now," adding that Tennessee could thus "pass one of her Citizens through all the gradations of office from the lowest to highest which would be a very remarkable fact to record in history—." Clio would chronicle the unwavering ascent of a tailor from alderman to President! But mingled with personal considerations lay concern for the survival of the party and, transcending all else, the preservation of the nation itself. Thus in June, with the Baltimore convention past, he pleaded, "in this hour of peril to the harmony and integrity of the Democratic party—in this hour of serious apprehension for the future welfare and perpetuity of our government," for a closing of the ranks, to the end that "the Union, with the blessings, guaranties, and protection of its constitution be perpetuated forever."

For a campaigner ordinarily unable to resist the lure of the hustings and a man gravely concerned about the impending crisis of the Union, Johnson remained strangely inactive during the summer of 1860, restricting himself to one speech at Greeneville prior to entering the canvass at Nashville late in September. To importunities from Democrats throughout the state, he pleaded the precarious state of his health without precisely identifying the complaint. Given the stance he ultimately assumed, his illness may have been both bona fide and a reflection of the malaise from which the Democracy, particularly in the border states, suffered—the trauma of a divided party with two candidates, neither likely to be successful. Although earlier inclined toward Douglas as the standard-bearer of a united party, Johnson made a southern decision when confronted with the irreparable cleavage which produced the Breckinridge candidacy. At the time, he regarded the Kentuckian as "the strongest man south"; subsequently, he rationalized this choice by observing that "I believed he was a better Union man than any other candidate in the field."[15] Yet he was hardly more than a lukewarm Breckinridge supporter. Even when active in the campaign, he devoted himself primarily to bringing the party together against "Lincoln a Black Republican, and Bell nearly one." Perhaps with a thought to his own reelection in 1863, he was especially concerned with the preservation of the Democracy in Tennessee: why divide on minor differences and give the state away to Bell? Thus Johnson became identified with the abortive Britton proposal—there were those who called him its instigator—a fusion scheme which would concentrate Democratic electoral support on the candidate most likely to win in Tennessee. Essentially Johnson viewed himself as "not so much the advocate of any particular man or candidate, as of measures and principles." In the end his gloomiest forebodings were realized; John Bell carried the state and Abraham Lincoln won the presidency.

Indeed, 1860 had been a year of bitter disappointment. He had witnessed at long last the passage of his cherished homestead, only to have victory snatched from his grasp by a Democratic President. He saw his immediate presidential aspirations frustrated, the Democracy dissevered, and a sectional party triumphant. Once again Tennessee had been lost by the Democrats, and the defeat rankled the more because the state went to his old antagonist John Bell. And at year's end the lowering cloud of secession stood starkly on the horizon.

Despite his nominal support of the party wing most commonly identified with disunionist sentiment, Johnson had long avowed his devotion to the Union and his faith in the constitutional process. He was not one to yield on the question of southern rights; yet he never brandished the threat of secession. Now that the nation faced the prospect of disunion, he sought a formula by which the South might safely remain within the Union. How better could this be achieved

15. Speech at Memphis, October 16, 1860; *Cong. Globe*, 37 Cong., 1 Sess., 295.

than by amending that palladium of American liberties, the Constitution? To popular election of senators and limited tenure for all federal judges, he now added proposals reminiscent of Calhoun's concurrent voice: the rotation of the presidential office between slaveholding and nonslaveholding states and an equal balance of supreme court justices between North and South. Concerned, like many of his southern contemporaries, with safeguarding slavery and the interests of the slave states, he also offered a series of unamendable amendments which, with a host of similar proposals, would shortly come under the scrutiny of the newly formed Committee of Thirteen.

In the meantime, speaking at Greeneville on November 24, he urged the South to pursue "a course of moderation," to steer clear of northern fanaticism and southern secessionism—in short, to "demand her rights in the Union and not out of it."[16] This wise counsel anticipated his speech of December 18–19—a ringing defense of the Union which catapulted the champion of the common man and apostle of the homestead onto the national scene, his name a household word honored in the North, excoriated in the South. Emergence as a Union symbol seemed to presage a fundamental departure in the career of Andrew Johnson; yet the future, like the past, would hold more of continuity than of change.

THIS VOLUME

The materials of the first half of Johnson's senatorial term—letters and telegrams, speeches and remarks, exchanges and resolutions, miscellaneous business papers—provide evidence of his continuing progress toward national recognition. As is characteristic of the Johnson papers in the antebellum period, there is a dearth of correspondence with national figures, indicative of his comparative isolation from the mainstream of political leadership. As in previous volumes, most of the letters herein were addressed *to* the Tennessean; out of a total of 288 items, only forty-four were written by Johnson himself. Yet these are of great value. Many, directed to his son Robert and other intimates, represent his assessment of the state and national political scene; others relate to family affairs; a comparative few are concerned with routine matters. Letters *to* Johnson —ranging from a disquisition on Welsh customs to a gossipy report on the Charleston convention to a medium's prediction that he would be the Democratic presidential nominee—tell us much about the man and his milieu. This correspondence, coming not only from his sons and close political friends but from total strangers as well, offers

16. Greeneville *Democrat*, November 27, 1860.

a broad spectrum of opinions concerning public issues and policies as the nation struggled with the onrushing sectional controversy. Such communications remind us once again that the common man continued to feel at ease writing to his self-appointed spokesman.

The speeches printed here largely depict Johnson in the Senate rather than on the hustings, for the very nature of his office precluded extensive speaking in Tennessee. Chosen for a full term in 1857, he would not soon be seeking reelection; thus during these years he spent most of his time addressing fellow senators rather than fellow Tennesseans. These speeches, remarks, and exchanges document his views on such current issues as federal authority in the West, popular sovereignty, government expenditures, homestead legislation, transcontinental railroads, and the Harper's Ferry episode. Seen *in toto*, they exhibit Johnson's salient characteristics—not only his unlimited faith in the wisdom of the people and his "industry, courage and unswerving perseverance," but also his "inveterate prejudices or preconceptions,"[17] often vented on his colleagues, whether northern Republicans or southern Democrats. It should be noted that these three years in the Senate, when compared with his earlier decade in the House, show rather less attention to the personal problems of his constituents and a greater preoccupation with questions of national concern.

Although Johnson's primary attention was focused on the national scene, his eye was never far from Tennessee, the base of his political power. Kept apprised of state affairs by Robert and sundry Democratic friends, he turned his attention more closely to Tennessee after his son was elected to the lower house in August, 1859. This correspondence reveals his opinions of state affairs as conveyed to Robert and hence to the legislature. "Bank democrats and democrats who have Banks to control," he wrote on one occasion, perhaps fusing political with parental advice, "are very much like putting virtuous females in houses of illfame to protect their honesty and purity of character— They may enter virtuous women: but they never fail to come out prostitutes of the most accomplished order—"

During the early months of 1860, as he and his supporters eyed the nomination at Charleston, Johnson's links with the state became stronger. Once the conventions were over, aside from a few postmortems, the most significant material comes from his speeches late in the campaign. The final items revert to the national scene as the Tennessee senator, back in Washington, launched a last desperate effort to preserve the Union.

Interspersed throughout are documents which illuminate Johnson

17. John J. Craven, *Prison Life of Jefferson Davis* (New York, 1905), 263.

the man: senatorial exchanges revealing the insecurity which arose from humble origins and acute class consciousness; accounts, deeds, and letters supplying some evidence of his business transactions; a receipt for whiskey and occasional missives from female friends—both reminders of a "social" Andrew Johnson.

Notwithstanding an abundance of information about the last years of the decade, this volume has important lacunae. Once again significant family correspondence, particularly from his wife and daughters, is missing—a lack the more striking because Johnson spent so much of his time in Washington. Missing, with one or two important exceptions, are the letters he must have written to old political cronies like Milligan, Lowry, and McDannel. Moreover, many questions remain unanswered. Who were his Washington political associates? What were his connections with the Republican supporters of the homestead measure? How did he pass his leisure hours in the national capital? Queries might also be raised about his relations with Governor Harris and the state party, as well as his ties with the national Democracy.

Inadequacies in the record there may be, but the fact remains that the 288 letters, the forty-four congressional and newspaper selections, and the several miscellaneous documents contribute substantially to the picture of the maturing politician about to emerge into the full glare of the national spotlight, transformed from "a southern spokesman for democracy"[18] into a staunch defender of the Union.

ACKNOWLEDGMENTS

A volume of this kind must inevitably rest upon the contributions of many people. Once again we owe much to several persons who have assisted us in the past: Mrs. Margaret Johnson Patterson Bartlett, great-granddaughter of Andrew Johnson; Oliver W. Holmes, executive secretary of the National Historical Publications Commission, and the Commission staff, particularly Roger Bruns; Eleanor E. Goehring, Olive H. Branch, and John H. Dobson of the University of Tennessee Library; and the personnel of the Tennessee State Library and Archives.

Fortunate indeed is the editorial project which possesses a staff as able and dedicated as that of the Andrew Johnson Papers. Under the capable supervision of Patricia Clark, a number of workers helped in the preparation of this volume: Edith Landis, research assistant; Eileen Cave and Tina Ellstrom, secretaries; Edwin Hardison and Fred Bailey, graduate assistants; and Jane Terry Brown

18. *Johnson Papers*, II, xxxii.

and Denise Smith, work-study students. Preliminary preparation of the Appendix was done by Barbara Bennett Solymos and Edwin Hardison.

A list of repositories to which we are gratefully indebted may be found in Editorial Method, Symbols List A. We are under special obligation to Mrs. Margaret Bartlett of Greeneville and Nathaniel Stein of New York City for their kindness in making available materials from their private holdings.

The three agencies most significantly involved in support of the Andrew Johnson Papers continue to be the University of Tennessee, which provides housing for the Project and released time for the editors; the National Historical Publications Commission, which makes generous annual grants; and the Tennessee Historical Commission, which supports some of the costs of publication. Without them this volume would not have been possible. As always, we are grateful for the cooperation and assistance of the University of Tennessee Press.

LeRoy P. Graf
Ralph W. Haskins

Knoxville, Tennessee
February 29, 1972

Editorial Method

Once again Washington materials—from the Library of Congress, the National Archives, and the *Congressional Globe*—constitute the principal source for *The Papers of Andrew Johnson*. As compared with previous volumes, fewer of the items printed herein come from scattered repositories, private collections, and newspapers; yet the Huntington Library contributed five significant letters from Johnson to his son, the Nathaniel Stein Collection provided a lengthy disquisition on the Tennessean's presidential aspirations, and Tennessee newspapers supplied the chief evidence of Johnson's activities on the stump.

This volume includes all significant correspondence, speeches, exchanges, resolutions, and business records which are available. Except for representative samples, it omits routine correspondence relating to recommendations, pensions, petitions, requests for speeches and public documents, letters of introduction, and appointments to the service academies.

In general, the sources of information found in footnotes have been indicated. The absence of a citation may indicate that the subject is a matter of general knowledge, that the person has been previously identified (as reference to the Index will show), or that information is unavailable. Extended identifications provided in Volumes I and II are referenced in the footnotes; birth and death dates for some Nashvillians are taken from the *Index to Interments in the Nashville City Cemetery, 1846–1962* (Nashville, 1964). Most city and business directories are to be found in the microfiche collection produced by New Haven Research Publications, Inc.

In transcribing documents the editors have sought to combine fidelity to the original text with consideration for the reader. The writer's spelling is reproduced without change, except where confusion might occur; in such cases the bracketing of letters, words, or *sic* is designed to clarify the meaning. Aside from the insertion of bracketed periods, the original punctuation has been retained. Repetitious phrases, obviously a slip of the pen, have been eliminated. Although information added by the editors is normally bracketed, exceptions are made when a correspondent's location or the date of a document are beyond doubt. Cities and towns without a state designation are in Tennessee.

SYMBOLS

A. Repositories

CSmH	Henry E. Huntington Library, San Marino, California
DLC	Library of Congress, Washington, D. C.
DNA	National Archives, Washington, D. C.

RECORD GROUPS USED

RG15	Records of the Veterans Administration
RG29	Records of the Bureau of the Census
RG45	Naval Records Collection of the Office of Naval Records and Library
RG46	Records of the United States Senate
RG49	Records of the Bureau of Land Management
RG59	General Records of the Department of State
RG60	General Records of the Department of Justice
RG84	Records of the Foreign Service Posts of the Department of State
RG92	Records of the Office of the Quartermaster General
RG94	Records of the Adjutant General's Office
RG107	Records of the Office of the Secretary of War

MB	Boston Public Library, Boston, Massachusetts
MWiW-C	Williams College, Chapin Library, Williamstown, Massachusetts
NN	New York Public Library, New York, New York
NNPM	Pierpont Morgan Library, New York, New York
NjMoW	Washington Headquarters Library, Morristown, New Jersey
PHi	Historical Society of Pennsylvania, Philadelphia, Pennsylvania
THi	Tennessee Historical Society, Nashville, Tennessee
TKL	Knoxville Public (Lawson McGhee) Library, Knoxville, Tennessee
TxDaHi	Dallas Historical Society, Dallas, Texas

B. Manuscripts

AL	Autograph Letter
ALS	Autograph Letter Signed
ANS	Autograph Note Signed
Copy	Copy not by writer
D	Document
DS	Document Signed
LS	Letter Signed
Pet.	Petition
PI	Printed Invitation
RS	Receipt Signed
Tel	Telegram
Tel, draft	Telegram, draft

ABBREVIATIONS

A.; App.	Appendix
Adj. Gen.	Adjutant General
Appl. & Recomm.	Applications and Recommendations
Appt.	Appointment
c	About
Ch.	Chapter
Col.	Collection
Com.	Committee
Cong.	Congress, congressional
Corres.	Correspondence
fl	Flourishing
Gen. Let. Bk.	General Letter Book
H. R.	House of Representatives
LC	Library of Congress
Let.	Letter, letters
Let. Recd.	Letter Received
Let. Sent	Letter Sent
M	Microcopy
Misc.	Miscellaneous
S.	Senate
Sec.	Secretary, section
Ser.	Series
Sess.	Session
Tr.	Transcriber

SHORT TITLES

Annals of Cong.

The Debates and Proceedings in the Congress . . . from First to Eighteenth Congresses [March 3, 1789–May 27, 1824] (Washington, D. C., 1834–56).

Appleton's Cyclopedia

James G. Wilson and John Fiske, eds., Appleton's Cyclopedia of American Biography (6 vols., New York, 1887–89).

BDAC

Biographical Directory of the American Congress, 1774–1961 . . . (House Document No. 442, 85 Congress, 2 Session, Washington, D. C., 1961).

1860 Census, Tenn., Greene

U. S. Bureau of the Census, Eighth Census, 1860, Population, Tennessee, Greene County (original schedules on microfilm).

Clayton, Davidson County

W. Woodford Clayton, History of Davidson County, Tennessee (Philadelphia, 1880).

Cong. Dir. (1878)

Ben: Perley Poore, comp., The Political Register and Congressional Directory . . . of the United States of America, 1776–1878 (Boston, 1878).

Cong. Dir. (1903)

A Biographical Congressional Directory, 1774 to 1903 . . . Washington, D. C., 1903).

Cong. Globe

U. S. Congress, The Congressional Globe . . . (23 Congress to the 42 Congress, Washington, D. C., 1834–73).

DAB

Allen Johnson and Dumas Malone, eds., Dictionary of American Biography (20 vols., supplements, and index, New York, 1930–   ).

Documentary History of the Capitol

History of the . . . United States Capitol Building and Grounds (House Report No. 646, 58 Congress, 2 Session, Washington, D. C., 1904).

ETHS *Publications*   East Tennessee Historical Society's
                           Publications

Goodspeed's Bedford
Goodspeed's East
  Tennessee
Goodspeed's Gibson
Goodspeed's Hamilton   Goodspeed Publishing Company,
Goodspeed's Haywood   *History of Tennessee, from the*
Goodspeed's Knox   *Earliest Time to the Present*
Goodspeed's Maury   . . . (Chicago and Nashville,
Goodspeed's Montgomery   1887).
Goodspeed's Robertson
Goodspeed's Shelby
Goodspeed's Williamson
Hesseltine, *Three against*   William B. Hesseltine, ed., *Three*
  Lincoln   *against Lincoln: Murat Hal-*
                              stead Reports the Caucuses of
                              1860 (Baton Rouge, 1960).

House Ex. Doc.   *House Executive Document*
House Misc. Doc.   *House Miscellaneous Document*
JP   Andrew Johnson Papers, Library
                             of Congress. JP refers to the first
                             series only; JP2, etc., to suc-
                             ceeding series.
Johnson Papers   LeRoy P. Graf and Ralph W.
                             Haskins, eds., *The Papers of*
                             Andrew Johnson (2 vols., Knox-
                             ville, 1967–   ).
Johnson-Bartlett Col.   Andrew Johnson materials in pos-
                             session of Mrs. Margaret John-
                             son Patterson Bartlett, Greene-
                             ville, Tennessee.
McGavock, *Pen and*   Randal W. McGavock, *Pen and*
  Sword   *Sword: The Life and Journals*
                             of Randal W. McGavock, Her-
                             schel Gower and Jack Allen,
                             eds. (Nashville, 1959).
Milton, *Eve of Conflict*   George F. Milton, *Eve of Conflict:*
                             Stephen A. Douglas and the
                             Needless War (Cambridge,
                             Mass., 1934).
Nashville Bus. Dir.   John P. Campbell, comp., *Nash-*
  (1860–61)   *ville City and Business Direc-*
                             tory, 1860–61 (Vol. V, Nash-
                             ville, 1860).

NCAB	*National Cyclopedia of American Biography* . . . (48 vols., New York, 1965 ed.)
Nevins, *Emergence of Lincoln*	Allan Nevins, *The Emergence of Lincoln* (2 vols., New York, 1950).
OR	*War of the Rebellion: A Compilation of the Official Records of the Union and Confederate Armies* (70 vols. in 128, Washington, D. C., 1880–1901).
RG	Record Group, National Archives (see DNA symbol)
Richardson, *Messages*	James D. Richardson, *A Compilation of the Messages and Papers of the Presidents, 1789–1902* (10 vols., New York, 1903).
Robison Biog. Data	Dan M. Robison, Biographical Data concerning Tennessee Legislators (Tennessee State Library and Archives, Nashville, Tennessee).
Robison, *Preliminary Directory,* Bedford Franklin Lincoln Montgomery Rutherford	Dan M. Robison, *Biographical Directory (Preliminary) of Tennessee General Assembly, 1796–1967* (Nashville, 1967–).
Senate Doc.	*Senate Document*
Senate Ex. Doc.	*Senate Executive Document*
Senate Ex. Journal	*Senate Executive Journal*
Senate Misc. Doc.	*Senate Miscellaneous Document*
Stevenson, *Quotations*	Burton Stevenson, *Home Book of Quotations* (New York, 1964).
Tenn. Acts	*Acts of the State of Tennessee*
Tenn. Hist. Quar.	*Tennessee Historical Quarterly*
Tenn. House Journal	*Tennessee House Journal*
Tenn. Official Manual (1890)	Charles A. Miller, comp., *The Official and Political Manual of the State of Tennessee* (Nashville, 1890).
Tenn. Senate Journal	*Tennessee Senate Journal*

Tennesseans in the Civil War	Civil War Centennial Commission, *Tennesseans in the Civil War: A Military History of Confederate and Union Units with Available Rosters of Personnel* (2 pts., Nashville, 1964).
U. S. Official Register	*Register of the Officers and Agents, Civil, Military and Naval in the Service of the United States . . .* (Washington, D. C., 1851ff.).
U. S. Statutes	*United States Statutes at Large*
Webster's Third International	*Webster's Third New International Dictionary of the English Language Unabridged* (Springfield, Mass., 1968).
West Tenn. Hist. Soc. *Papers*	West Tennessee Historical Society *Papers*
White, East Tenn. Journalism	Moses White, East Tennessee Journalism (Typescript, University of Tennessee Library).
White, *Messages*	Robert H. White, *Messages of the Governors of Tennessee* (7 vols., Nashville, 1952–).
WPA	U. S. Works Project Administration, Historical Records Survey (Nashville, 1936–41).

Chronology

1808, December 29	Born at Raleigh, Wake County, North Carolina
1812, January 4	Death of father, Jacob Johnson
1822, February 18	Bound as a tailor's apprentice to James J. Selby, Raleigh
1826, September	Arrived in Greeneville, Tennessee
1827, May 17	Married Eliza McCardle, daughter of John and Sarah Phillips McCardle
1828, October 25	Birth of daughter, Martha
1829–35	Served as alderman, then mayor, of Greeneville
1830, February 19	Birth of son, Charles
1832, May 8	Birth of daughter, Mary
1834, February 22	Birth of son, Robert
1835–37; 1839–41	State representative
1841–43	State senator
1843–53	Congressman, first district
1852, August 5	Birth of son, Andrew, Jr. (Frank)
1853, August 4	Elected governor of Tennessee, defeating Gustavus A. Henry, Whig
1855, August 2	Reelected governor, defeating Meredith P. Gentry, Know-Nothing
1857, October 8	Elected to U. S. Senate, defeating Neill S. Brown, Opposition
1857, December 22	Introduced Homestead Bill
1858, May 20	Speech on Homestead Bill
1859, January 25	Speech on Transcontinental Railroads
1859, August	Robert Johnson elected to legislature
1859, December 12	Speech on Harper's Ferry Incident
1859, December 21	Named chairman of committee on contingent expenses and member of committees on public lands and the District of Columbia, 36 Congress, 1 Session
1860, January 18	Received Democratic State Convention favorite son endorsement
1860, April 11	Speech on Amendment to Homestead Bill

2

1860, May 1	Nominated presidential candidate at Democratic national convention, Charleston
1860, June 18	Withdrew name from presidential nomination at Baltimore convention
1860, June 23	Speech on Homestead Veto
1860, June 28	36 Congress, 1 Session adjourned; returned to Greeneville
1860, September–October	Participated in Democratic presidential campaign
1860, December 10	Renamed to committee assignments of previous Congress
1860, December 18–19	Senate speech for the Union
1862, March 4	Appointed military governor of Tennessee
1864, November 8	Elected vice president
1865, April 15	Became President following Lincoln's assassination
1866, August 28–September 15	Made "swing around the circle" campaign
1868, February 24	Impeachment voted by House of Representatives
1868, May 16, 26	Acquitted by Senate
1869, March	Returned to Greeneville
1869, October 22	Defeated for Senate by Henry Cooper, Radical
1872, November 5	Ran unsuccessfully for congressman-at-large against Horace Maynard, Republican, and Benjamin F. Cheatham, Conservative Democrat
1875, January 26	Elected to Senate
1875, March 5–24	Served in extra session of Congress
1875, July 31	Died at Mary Johnson Stover's home in Carter County

THE PAPERS OF

Andrew Johnson

1858

To Rae Burr,[1] *Philadelphia, Pa.*

Washington City Jan 3d 1858

Miss Rae Burr,

My dear friend,

Your favor of the 29th ult; but post marked the 31st was received on the morning of the 1st inst— My letter was written under the impression that there would be ample time for a reply before the 1st Jan— I had strong hopes that you would come to Washington and spend the christmas holidays and as New Years day approached and no answer to my letter, my hope was almost reduced to a certainty that you would be here by that time— Notwithstanding I received no letter from you saying that you would be here, I went to the Depot on Thursday evening believing that I would meet you there; but sure enough there was no Rae— I returned to my quarters and went to reading and reflecting on the past and so put in the night— On the morning of the first I received your letter and read it with interest and deeply regretted that I could not be in Philadelphia and [spend?] the day with you and the children or that you were not here and spend the day in visting the white house and the Heads of Dep't— The day was a lovely one, the air was mild and balmy the sun shown forth with unusual brilliancy & all seemed to be favorable [for] the reception of visitors— There was no immense concourse in attendence on the President on the first as well as at the other places of reception— It would have afforded me much pleasure to have waited on Miss Rae while visiting the President and others— Congress will meet on monday and at [that time] it is thought that there will be some important questions brought before both houses in a few days and I do not like to absent myself until I see what direction things may take—[2] But the first day that will admit of my paying you a visit I will do so— I cannot say now what day it will be— I hope though that you may find it convenient to pay Washington a visit in the mean time and see Congress in session and by that time I can arrange my matters so as to accompey you home and then go on to New York— I hope you will find it convenient to come to Washington and if you do, write a line

in advance informing me what day I may look for you and I will
meet you at the Depot and see that you have the proper attention
&c— My intention is now to stop a few days in Phila' and have my
arm eximned by Dr Mott[3] and then go to New York— I regret that
I could not be with the family on the first, and must hold you in
part responsible for it for it was too late after receiving your letter
notifying me that you could not visit Washington at present— But
that is neither here nor there[.] I will see you all as soon as I can—
It is with great difficulty that I write and will conclude this incoherent scrawl— The last three days have been all that heart could
wish at this season of the year and delightfully you could have
whiled away a few days here and then have returned home— This
sunday is one of the most delightful days I ever witnessed[.] Give
my love to all—kiss the children[4] and tell them I will see [them?]
before long and accept for your *owne noble* self assurances of my
high esteem and sincere regard[.]

Andrew Johnson

ALS, National Park Service, Andrew Johnson National Monument,
Greeneville.

1. Rachael Burr (b. c1836), allegedly a cousin of Aaron Burr, was a
member of a Philadelphia family—some of whom were tailors—with which
Johnson was on intimate terms, an intimacy which seems to have evolved
during the period when he was a congressman in Washington without his
family. In the course of the year following this letter, Rae married A. Nelson
Batten. 1860 Census, Pa., Philadelphia, 10th Ward, 74. See also Letter from
Rae Batten, November 23, 1859.

2. Scarcely a month old, this session had seen the introduction of bills
concerning Kansas statehood, the establishment of Arizona Territory, and
federal aid for Pacific railroad construction. While these issues might all be
regarded as in one way or another important, it is probable, given the bent of
his interest, that Johnson had in mind the possibility that the Senate, as it
resumed its activity on the morrow, might take up one of the several measures
related to the public land question: S. 2, introduced by Solomon Foot of Vermont on December 17, to make grants of public lands to actual settlers; S. 24,
introduced by Henry Wilson of Massachusetts on December 21, to secure
land to actual settlers in the alternate sections of lands reserved for railroads;
or, most important of all, S. 25, Johnson's own homestead bill, introduced
December 22, the day before the recess began. *Cong. Globe*, 35 Cong., 1 Sess.,
62, 65, 135.

3. Johnson's arm, broken and crushed in a Georgia train wreck on his
way home from Washington in January, 1857, continued to cause him great
pain. His hope for relief through a visit to Dr. Valentine Mott (1785–1865)
is understandable, since the physician, born on Long Island and trained at
Columbia (1806), was a pioneer in the field, with a worldwide reputation
both as a practicing surgeon and as a lecturer. In this latter capacity, he may
have been in Philadelphia, speaking at one of its well-known medical schools
or societies and therefore available for consultation. *Johnson Papers*, II, 482n,
525; *DAB*, XIII, 290–91.

4. Rae's recently orphaned nieces, Helen (b. c1845) and Cecelia Morton
(b. c1847), who lived in the Burr household. 1860 Census, Pa., Philadelphia,
10th Ward, 74; *McElroy's Philadelphia Directory* (1860), 46, 121.

From John B. Floyd[1]

Hon. Andrew Johnson   War Department
Senate.   Washington, January 7, 1858.
My dear Sir:
I have had the honor to receive from your hands the following
named papers, which I beg to assure you shall be carefully filed, and
duly considered when the time arrives for action upon the subject[2]
to which they refer:
Letter from several officers of the army dated Detroit, Sept. 26, 1857
"   "   Robert B. Maclin   "   "   Dec. 11, 1857.
"   "   Maj. E. Backus   "   "   5,   "
"   "   Sackfield Maclin   "   "   11   "
"   "   Several citizens of Athens, Tenn.   7   "
"   "   John L. Bridges   "   "   5   "
"   "   Wm. Horace Briant   "   "   7   "
"   "   John C. Vaughn of Knoxville, Tenn.   Nov. 28   "
"   "   J. T. Council   "   "   Dec. 4   "
"   "   Wm. G. Newman   "   "   "   "   "
"   "   do   enclosing muster rolls of a volunteer
company dated Knoxville, Dec. 4, 1857.
                          I remain, my dear Sir   Yours very truly
                                                     John B. Floyd
                                                     Secretary of War.

Copy, DNA–RG107, Copies Let. Sent, Vol. 40, p. 5.
1. John B. Floyd (1806–1863), Virginia-born Democrat, served in the
General Assembly (1847, 1848, 1855), as governor (1849–52), and as
secretary of war under Buchanan (1857–60). In the course of a reorganization of the cabinet, Floyd and other southern sympathizers resigned late in
1860; he was subsequently a Confederate general. DAB, VI, 482–83.
2. These letters concerned the organization of volunteer military companies to serve in the West. In his annual report (December 5, 1857), Floyd
had recommended five new regiments because of "the menacing attitude of
affairs in Utah, and of the importance of prompt and thorough suppression of
the spirit of rebellion reigning there. . . ." House Ex. Doc. No. 2, 35 Cong.,
1 Sess., 9.

From Thomas A. Hendricks[1]

                             General Land Office   Jany 11 1858
Hon Andrew Johnson,
U S Senate
Sir,
I have the honor to enclose herewith pursuant to your oral request
of the 9 inst statements showing the estimated quantities of unsold
and unappropriated lands in each of the States, on the 30 June

1856, the estimated quantities of lands which will enure to the States and Railroad grants to the 30 June 1857, and the quantity of Swamp lands approved to the States on the 30 June 1857.[2]

Very respectfully   You[r] obt Svt   Tho A. Hendricks
Commr

Copy, DNA-RG49, Misc. Let. Sent (M25).

1. Thomas A. Hendricks (1819–1885), an Indiana Democrat currently commissioner of the general land office (1855–59), had been a congressman (1851–55); subsequently he served as U. S. senator (1863–69), governor (1872–77), and vice president (1885). *BDAC*, 1041.

2. Johnson used this information in his Speech on the Homestead Bill, May 20, 1858.

From Blackston McDannel

January 20, 1858, Greeneville; ALS, DNA–RG15, War of 1812 Pensions, William Brown.

Requests Johnson's aid for William Brown of Lick Creek, Greene County, who is filing "for an Invalid Pension on account of Rheumatism contracted while in the service of the U. States in 1814" and has been applying unsuccessfully since 1845. The letter records in detail these previous efforts. [Forwarded by Johnson to the commissioner of pensions with a personal request that the case be examined.]

To Robert Johnson, Greeneville

Washington City   Jan 23d 1858

My dear Son,

Your letter of the 8th inst was recieved some two or three days since and would have been answered before this time; but for the fact of being unprepared to answer it satisfactorily to myself and am Compelled to confess that I do not now know what to Say in reference to your determination to remove to the Territory of Arizona— As it will be some time before final action will be had by Congress on the Subject I will decline making any answer at the present time and will therefore leave it an open question to be determined hereafter as Circumstances m[a]y require— As to my throwing any obstacles in the way of your getting an appointment, you of Course, know and feel that I would do nothing but what I might believe would in the end result in your advancement in whatever it might Chance to be— Any thing that I Can do that will promote Milligans interest will be done with much pleasure— What the Chances will be for obtaining an appointment in Arizona I Cannot tell at the present writing—

Inclosed you will find a lettere from F. C Dunnington[2] which I

wish you to read and then Show that portion of it which relats to
Milligan and here what he has to say— Dunnington Says in his
letter as you will perceive Says that he will sell out his interest
in the Union upon very favorable terms and seems to thinks that
Milligan would be the man to be assocatate with it at the present
time— How would Milligan do to be associated at the present time
and in view of Coming events— Nicholson would I think favor the
idea of his Connection with the Union, and furthermore how would
you like to turn in yourself to an arrangement of that kind— If Milligan thinks well of the Suggestion do you write and let me know—
I will write to night to Dunnington and inform him that I have taken
Steps to have Milligan Consulted on the subject and will let him
know as Soon as I hear from him[.] If I was Satisfied that Milligan
was the right man for the position I would take some trouble to have
the arrangement made and turn him in and see what he would do—
Think this matter all over and give me the benefit of your Conclusions— Suppose you Consult Judge Patterson on the Subject and
See what he has to Say on the Subject— Dunnington Seems to have
rather a poor opinion of the Legislature generally and especially So
of Some few of the members— I shall regret to See him Cut loose
from the Union for Eastman as the matter Stands is Compelled to
be the mere tool of Brown— When surrounded by the most favorable Circumstances there is a great want of independence and as
now related to the P. O. Dept[3] would be the mere echo of the Pillow
and Brown regency— He Cant help it[.] it is his misfortune and not
his fault; it is natural with him and he Cannot help it—
Mr Buchanan, has but few friends in either house of Congress who
are willing to Stand firmly and Closely by him— He Seems to have
no personal Strength with the members and is powerless beyond the
mere force of party organization and has not a Sufficient hold upon
the popular heart to force Congress up to a decided Support of his
measure; I fear his administration will be a failure[.]
it is too timid to venture upon any thing new or risk much upon
any thing old— His administration will be I think *eminently Conservative* with a pretty fair proportion of grannyism— To hear him
talk one would think that he was quite bold and decided; but: in
practice he is timid and hesitating—

Douglas' name will be a failure in the end with Henry A. Wise
thrown in—[4] Douglas was of the opinion that his bolt upon the
admission of Kansas into the Union as a State with the Lacompton
Constitution as it is Called, would bring all the antislavry men north
up to his Support and that he Could hold on to what Strength he had
in the South, which will in the end do him more harm than it will the
democratic party— For he has lost the confidence of the South

while he has gained none north, So in the effort to gain both he has lost both and at present is perfectly flat and might be considered a dead cock in the pit— It may be that he may recupirate after a while, time must determin— He has been a very precocious politician and I think has had groth and will now decay as all other premature things— If it was his (D) intention to bolt and I think it was & leave the democratic party he Could not have Selected a better time for doi[n]g the party as little harm as possible—

I say let him go and the party will very Soon recover from the shock and move on as though it had never occured— I have no news of interest to write more than to Say that on thursday last the Committee on public lands were unanimous in recommendg the passage of the Homestead bill and instructed me to report it to the Senate with the recommendation that it do pass which I did—[5] I am of the opinon; it will pass without difficulty— I will be Compelled to bring this letter to a Close for my arm pains me So that Can Scarcely hold it upon the table— The winter So far has been mild and open and I was inhopes it would Continue So; but to dy looks like winter intended to Set in and has turned much Colder— Tell Charles I am alwys proud to receive a letter from him and that he will write Soon—

Your devoted father
Andrew Johnson

ALS, DLC–JP.

1. In his first annual message, December 8, 1857, Buchanan asked Congress to establish a territorial government for Arizona, but, as Johnson anticipated, Congress was slow to act and the territory was not set up until 1863; thus Robert never had a chance to apply for an appointment. In late December he had written Congressman George W. Jones, a family friend, asking for support in obtaining an Arizona post. Richardson, *Messages*, V, 456–57; *U. S. Statutes*, XII, 664–65; George W. Jones to Robert Johnson, January 10, 1857, Johnson Papers, LC.

2. Francis C. Dunnington (1826–1875), lawyer, editor, and state legislator (1855–57) of Maury County, bought into the Nashville *Union and American* in 1856. Neither Milligan nor Robert acquired Dunnington's interest in the paper; in May, 1858, he sold one-half of it to G. G. Poindexter. As *Union* editor, Dunnington was a leading Johnson supporter; however, in the secession crisis he embraced the Confederate cause. Later his bitter political enmity climaxed in a widely disseminated speech attacking Johnson during the congressional canvass of 1872. Clayton, *Davidson County*, 240; White, *Messages*, VI, 255–67.

3. Aaron V. Brown, one of the leaders of the anti-Johnson Democrats, was postmaster general in Buchanan's cabinet.

4. Wise, an antagonist of the antislavery faction and a longtime Buchanan supporter, was nevertheless strongly and verbally opposed to the Lecompton Constitution and was the one southern Democrat to give "hearty approbation" to Douglas' anti-Lecompton stand. Barton H. Wise, *The Life of Henry A. Wise* (New York, 1899), 236; George Fort Milton, *The Eve of Conflict: Stephen A. Douglas and the Needless War* (Boston, 1934), 280.

5. Johnson reported the bill from committee on January 21, 1858.

With remarks, amendments, comments, and a speech, he tried unsuccessfully for the next four months to push the bill through the Senate. Finally, on May 27, he was forced to move postponement of the homestead question until the next session. *Cong. Globe*, 35 Cong., 1 Sess., 354, 2102, 2239, 2265–73, 2306–7, 2422–24. See also Appendix II.

To Lewis Cass, Washington, D. C.

January 27, 1858, Washington, D. C.; LS, DNA–RG59, Corres. *re*Publication of Laws.

Johnson and other southern Democrats request that the Knoxville *Southern Citizen* "may be favoured with the publication of the Laws of the United States."

From Thomas A. Hendricks

General Land Office   Feby 5th 1858

Hon A. Johnson
U. S. Senate
Sir

I have the honor to return herewith H R Bill 7, May 13 1852, with the amendment H R 7, May 26 1853 "to encourage agriculture commerce" &c which you left at this Office, for examination; and in answer to your oral inquiry as to whether the machinery contemplated by this Bill would operate in case the Bill should be matured into an Act of Congress. I have the honor to report that so far as I can forsee the working of the measure, I am of opinion that it would subserve the purpose contemplated thereby[.]

Very respectfully,   Your obt Sert,
Tho A. Hendricks   Commr

Copy, DNA–RG49, Misc. Let. Sent (M25).

From Finley Bigger[1]

Treasury Department
Registers Office, Feby 9th./58

Sir:

In accordance with the request contained in your letter of the 17th. ult. I have the honor to transmit, enclosed, a Statement showing the amount expended by the U. States for improvements in the District of Columbia up to June 30th. 1857.[2]

It may be that there are items included in it, which you would not regard as expenditures for *improvements*, and, vice versa; it may be also possible that expenditures for the Government and expenditures for the District are included, occasionally, in one item, and, therefore, inseparable: but these instances are few, and it is believed that all the sums given are strictly, and properly, chargeable as improvements, and that the statement is as complete as is possible to make it from the records of this Office.

I am, Very Respectfully
F. Bigger,   Register.

Hon. Andrew Johnson
U. S. Senate

ALS, DLC–JP.

    1. Finley Bigger of Indiana served as register of the treasury (1853–61). *Cong. Dir.* (1878), 229.
    2. Johnson used this information in his Speech on School Funds for District of Columbia, May 15, 1858.

From John Commerford[1]

New York Feby 9th 1858.

Dear Sir

    I understand that Mr Devyr[2] of Brooklyn has sent you a letter disapproving of the Bill introduced by you. Mr D came to our meeting of the Committee last week and endeavoured to get us to pass a Resolution to this effect, but we refused to do it for the reason that I was instructed at a former meeting to leave the matter at your disposal; believing that you would obtain all that you could for us[.] Mr D is a sincere & good man but he is rather impracticable, and would forfeit all rather [than] take up with what he denominates as a half way measure[.] I send you One Hundred & fifty names[.][3] Principaly they are business men who have been injured in their financial transactions by having their customers appropriate the money that was due them for speculation in lands[.] I have never before seen such a disposition manifested in favor of giving the people a Homestead[.] We could procure One Hundred Thousand names if our Members had the time to obtain them[.]

Very Respectfully   Your Obd St
John Commerford

Hon A Johnson
P S I wrote a Circular[4] and have sent a copy to each Member of Congress. I was somewhat doubtful about the propriety & policy of it, but I was overruled by my associates. When you think proper to write I hope you will give your opinion in relation to the effect & policy of what we have done in this particular[.]

JC

ALS, DNA–RG46, 35 Cong., Pet. Homestead Legislation, 35A–J1.

1. John Commerford (*fl*1874), a chairmaker and labor leader, had been an early advocate of land and prison reform. Politically active but not personally ambitious, he had served as secretary of the National Trades Union (1834), president of the General Trades' Union of New York (1835), and had become one of George Henry Evans' principal lieutenants in organizing the National Reform Association to agitate for a homestead law. Leaving the Democratic party in 1859 because of its failure to espouse homestead legislation, he was a Republican candidate for Congress in 1860. Helene S. Zahler, *Eastern Workingmen and National Land Policy, 1829–1862* (New York, 1941), 25n, 27, 28n, 30; Walter Hugins, *Jacksonian Democracy and the Working Class: A Study of the New York Workingman's Movement 1829–1837* (Stanford, 1960), 72–74.

2. Thomas Ainge Devyr (*c*1808–*fl*1875), Irish Chartist and fugitive from English justice, was the owner-editor of the Williamsburgh (N. Y.) *Morning Post* and the associate editor of the *Irish World* (N. Y.). An advocate of land reform, he helped organize the National Reform Association. *NCAB*, VIII, 440; Zahler, *Eastern Workingmen*, 36, 77.

3. Like others of its kind, this petition, which Johnson presented on February 10, was tabled.

4. Commerford's circular, enclosed with this letter, was apparently not presented to the Senate until January 31, 1859.

From Isham G. Harris

February 15, 1858, Nashville; Copy, DNA–RG46, 35 Cong., Post Office Pet., 35A–H13.

Encloses copy of resolution, passed by the Tennessee General Assembly, instructing U. S. senators "to use all possible means to so amend the Postage Laws, as to allow any person to endorse his or her name on any public document or newspaper" for purpose of forwarding same to someone else.

Speech on Maintaining Federal Authority in Utah[1]

February 17, 1858

Mr. JOHNSON, of Tennessee. I wish to present an amendment to this bill, which I ask the Senator from Massachusetts to accept in lieu of his proposition. My amendment is, to strike out all of the bill after the enacting clause, and insert:

That the President, for the purpose of enforcing the laws of the United States and protecting the citizens on the route of emigration in the Territory of Utah,[2] and to be employed in said Territory, be, and he is hereby, authorized to call for and accept the services of any number of volunteers, not exceeding in all four thousand officers and men, who may offer their services as infantry to serve for and during the pending difficulties with the Mormons in said Territory, and no longer; and that the sum of ___ dollars be, and the same is hereby, appropriated out of any money in the Treasury not otherwise appropriated, for the purpose of carrying the provisions of this act into effect.

SEC. 2. *And be it further enacted*, That the volunteers so offering their services shall be accepted by the President in companies, battalions, or regiments; and that each company shall consist of the same number of officers and men as now prescribed by law for the infantry arm of the Army; and that the companies, battalions, and regiments, shall be each respectively authorized to elect their own officers, and when so elected shall be commissioned by the President of the United States.

SEC. 3. *And be it further enacted*, That said volunteers, when mustered into the service, shall be armed and equipped at the expense of the United States, and until discharged therefrom, be subject to the rules and articles of war, and shall be organized in the same manner and shall receive the same pay and allowances as the infantry arm of the Army of the United States.

SEC. 4. *And be it further enacted*, That the volunteers who may be received into the service of the United States by virtue of this act, and who shall be wounded or otherwise disabled in the service, shall be entitled to all the benefits which may be conferred upon persons wounded or disabled in the service of the United States.

SEC. 5. *And be it further enacted*, That the said officers, musicians, and privates, authorized by this act, shall immediately be disbanded at the termination of the pending difficulties with the Mormons in the Territory of Utah.

I merely present the amendment now for the purpose of having it understood that I shall offer it at the proper time, if the Senator from Massachusetts does not accept it in lieu of his proposition.

[After Wilson accepts the substitution, a brief discussion ensues on the order of pending business.]

Mr. JOHNSON, of Tennessee. The application to the Congress of the United States for an increased military force is made in the name of the President of the United States; and we are called upon to sustain it as an Administration measure. I have offered this amendment for the purpose of setting myself right; for the purpose of showing how far I am willing to go; and to enable me, if I can, to act understandingly on what is presumed to be the measure of the Administration. I do not, however, sustain this simply and alone because it is an Administration measure, but I offer the proposition which I have presented because I believe it is right in itself, and at the same time will come up to the views of the Adminstration, in regard to the request it has made to Congress to increase the military force of the country.

I set out with the proposition that I am against an increase of the standing Army.[3] I am against adding another man to it. Standing armies are contrary to the genius of this Government; they are contrary to the temperament of our people; and, so far as I am concerned, I shall go against adding another soldier to our regular Army. I think, when we come to examine the subject, we shall find that the Committee on Military Affairs, in the bill reported by its chairman,[4] has not represented the Administration in its true character before the country. The bill of the committee, in the first instance, provides for an increase of the rank and file of the Army, to the extent of about four thousand men. In addition to this, it provides for thirty additional companies, as a permanent part of the standing Army. I do not understand the President as asking for a permanent increase of the standing Army. I understand him to have asked us to grant him an imposing force, that will enable him to correct the rebellious condition of affairs in Utah. For the purpose of setting myself right, and showing that my proposition covers the idea of the Administration, I propose to read a single paragraph. The President, in his annual message, after speaking for some considerable length upon the difficulties in Utah, and the declarations of Brigham Young, states:

A great part of all this may be idle boasting; but yet no wise Government will lightly estimate the efforts which may be inspired by such frenzied fanaticism as exists among the Mormons in Utah. This is the first rebellion which has existed in our Territories; and humanity itself requires that we should put it down in such a manner that it shall be the last. To trifle with it would be to encourage it and to render it formidable. We ought to go there with such an imposing force as to convince these deluded people that resistance would be vain, and thus spare the effusion of blood. We can in this manner best convince them that we are their friends, not their enemies. In order to accomplish this object, it will be necessary, according to the estimate of the War Department, to raise four additional regiments.[5]

Here the President tells us expressly that these troops are wanted to quell a rebellion which it is said exists among the Mormons in Utah. Is that asking Congress to make a permanent increase of the standing Army? Does he come before the country in such a position? He says that for the purpose of settling the difficulties in Utah we should give him an imposing force to quell rebellion, and thereby save the shedding of blood. Is this asking us to add six thousand or seven thousand men to the Army, to be salaried permanently at a great expense? Does the President ask any such thing? He does not. Why, then, should we be driven into an increase of the standing Army in compliance with the recommendation of the Committee on Military Affairs? We are not called upon by the Administration, as I understand it, to increase the standing Army by the addition of six or seven thousand men, as proposed by the committee.

I have said thus much for the purpose of showing that I am opposing no request of the Administration. Nor do I wish to be understood as being very squeamish and particular in the support of every measure that may come before the Senate as an Administration measure. If I support any measures that come before this body, I do so because I believe them to be right in principle and right in policy. I shall not support them on the mere dictum or recommendation of an Executive, without regard to their being right in themselves and correct in principle.

Then, as I understand the President, he asks for no additional force in the shape of an increase of the standing Army. He asks you to give him an imposing force to send to Utah, and thereby to prevent the shedding of blood, and put down the insurrection that is alleged to exist there. Why not employ volunteers for this emergency? Will not that answer the call of the President? I know it has been said that volunteers will cost more than regulars; but how can that be? I think it is evident that it will cost no more to call out volunteers than to call out regulars. We pay them the same amount, officers and men; and the volunteers are to be dismissed when the difficulties cease; whereas, regulars are a continual expense.

There seems to be a discrepancy between the President, the Secretary of War, and the Committee on Military Affairs. The Secretary of War asks for five regiments. The President tells us in his message that four will be necessary. There is a difference of one thousand men; and a difference in expense of $1,000,000, according to the estimates of the Senator from Georgia [Mr. TOOMBS] and the Senator from Maine, [Mr. HAMLIN.] It seems to me that we ought to act understandingly; we ought to know the exact effect of all the propositions that are before us. One reason why I have said what I have in reference to the Administration, that we were called upon by the chairman of the Committee on Military Affairs to act upon the bill when it was last before the Senate, so as to let the Administration know what it had to depend upon. The inference is that all those who are opposed to increasing the standing Army must be set down as opponents to the Administration and the recommendations of the executive.

[Since Davis is absent, his colleague, Albert G. Brown, interrupts to say that Johnson has misunderstood Davis.]

Mr. JOHNSON, of Tennessee. In the first instance, I have stated what I understood the chairman to say at the time; and in the next place, I shall show that statement to be substantially correct by the report of what took place here on last Thursday; for usually the reports are very accurate, and most speeches, if they have any method and order in them, are given with the fidelity of the daguerreotype. But this does not state it as strongly as the chairman stated it. I heard it with my own ears as I have stated it. The report is:

Mr. DAVIS. Let us pass the bill or reject it, and let the Administration know it.

Then it would seem that it is principally to be urged on the ground of an Administration measure. If we are to act on it as an Administration measure, let us see whether we cannot agree to a proposition that covers the ground the Administration really occupies.

It is agreed on all hands that the cost of the regular Army is about a million dollars to each thousand men. By one statement made by the Senator from Georgia—and I am free to say that I always hear him speak on this subject with great pleasure, and rely much on his statements—it appears that the cost is about a thousand dollars per man. That being so, each thousand men will cost $1,000,-000. By another statement, made by the Senator from Maine, [Mr. HAMLIN,] who seems to be accurate, and I presume is so, it appears that, including all expenses, the Army costs about fifteen hundred dollars a man, or a fraction less. If the force to be raised be five thousand men at $1,500 per man, they will cost $7,500,000; and that is to become a permanent expenditure, because the men being raised are a part of the permanent military establishment of the country, and must continue a charge on the Treasury of the United States.

I wish to ask Democratic Senators if this is a time to increase the expenditures of the Government? You are responsible for the expenses of the Government; you have the majority; you have the control of the Treasury in your hands. It is idle to go before the country, and talk before the people about the expenditures of the Administration. Who holds the purse-strings of this nation? When we run through the appropriations of this Government, from its origin to the present time, we find that the appropriations have generally outgone the expenditures. Who makes the expenditures? The President may recommend for this and for that, and he may make extravagant recommendations; but the query comes up, is Congress bound to appropriate? You, the appropriating power, hold the purse-strings of this nation in your hands; and if the expenditures of this Government go on increasing as they have been going on for a considerable number of years back, you are responsible, not the Administration.

Then I would ask, when we take up this question of expenditure, where is it going to carry us to? Is it not time to consult our log-book, and get a new reckoning? It seems to me that it is. At this point I wish to say to the chairman of the Committee on Finance[6] of this body, that I shall look to him with great interest in reference to his moves in retrenching the expenditures of the Government. I will follow him as an humble volunteer, for I favor the volunteer system; it is more in accordance with the genius of the Government, and the patriotic impulses of the American people. Let us go into the unnecessary and extraordinary expenditures of this Government, and reduce them down to what is reasonable and right. Is there no place at which we can begin this work? Cannot the expenditures be arrested? When we talk about retrenching upon this bill, it is said, "this is not the place; let this go; this is not the bill." This is allowed to pass, and soon we find another bill before us for the civil or naval department, or the West Point Academy, or the military establishment; and then we are told, "this is not the bill either; we cannot get along without this." Well, where is the bill? What measure is it? Some how or other, we cannot find any. "This is not the place; this is not the bill; this is not the department to which to lay the pruning-knife. Oh! no; we must not begin here." That is the constant cry.

Then if war happens to exist, and we talk about retrenching and reducing the expenditures in time of war, the answer is, "Oh! you cannot do it now; the public mind is occupied about something else; the public mind is engaged in carrying on the war." I ask, when will the time come? When are the foul, reeking corruptions of the Government to be stopped? Your newspapers are filled with the details of them every day, and men are confined in prison for refusing to tell the truth in reference to the corruptions of the Government.[7] What do those corruptions grow out of? The unnecessary and improper expenditures of the Government. It seems to me the time has come, and I think it is the duty of the Democratic party to commence the work of retrenchment. We have preached it in theory a long time. Let us commence to reduce our theory to practice.

I came into the Senate of the United States as a Democrat; and, if I know myself, I intend to be one in practice as well as in theory. I know it is against the taste, the refined and the peculiar notions of some men who get into high places, to talk about curtailing or reducing the expenditures of the Government. That, with them, is all cant; that is all for Buncombe; that amounts to nothing! Some may talk about it in that light, and some may act upon that principle, if it is a principle, but I intend to act in good faith, if I know myself. It may be said "Oh! he is a pence-calculating politician; he talks about the pence; he talks about the shillings; and consequently he is not to be regarded as being a statesman expanded in his views, liberal in his feelings, that grasps and takes in the scope of his mind all the nations of the earth, and the rest of mankind." [Laughter.] I wish to quote what a very distinguished man once said in reference to public revenue, and I do it with no desire to speak disparagingly of American Senators, for I put a very high estimate on their character and position, and especially so since I have got here. [Laughter.] Mr. Burke was a man of no mean consideration—I do not mean Edmund Burke, of New Hampshire, but the distinguished British statesman—and what does he say on this subject of revenue? He says "the revenue of the State is the State." That is a book; it is a text worth preaching from, that the revenue of the State is the State; and that Government which manages its revenue best operates most lightly and best for the people:

The revenue of the State is the State in effect; all depends upon it, whether for support or reformation. Through the revenue alone the body-politic can act in its true genius and character; and therefore it will display just as much of its collective virtue as it is possessed of a just revenue.[8]

That is what Edmund Burke said. He was one of your pence-calculating politicians. He was one of those demagogues who talk about the interests and the rights of the people. He, who was not only a statesman but a philosopher, declared that the revenue of a State is the State, and the virtue of the Government is indicated in the very same proportion that it collects a just revenue from the people.

Again, on this idea of the revenue of a Government, Lord Bacon, who was not the most virtuous it is true, but who wrote well, and said a great many good things, declared:

Above all things, good policy is to be used that the treasure and moneys in a State be not gathered into few hands; for otherwise a State may have a good stock and yet starve: and money is like muck, no good unless it is spread.[9]

What does he mean by that? Do not collect large sums of money from the people and appropriate them among the few; revenue, like muck, does no good unless it is spread; but how spread? Let the industrious portion of the community, the producers, spend their own money; let it be in their own pockets; appropriate it in such way as their interests, their happiness, and their prosperity may suggest: but we have reversed that proposition. We go on gathering muck from the barn-yards of the nation; we go on gathering revenue from the industry of the whole people, and we bring it here and squander it in appropriations, as I believe, wholly unnecessary to promote the interests and happiness of the people. As the cant is very common about demagogues, I desire to lay down as a text what was preached by Edmund Burke, one of the most distinguished of British statesmen.

Now, let us see where we are going on this subject of expenditure. And first as to the Army. I will divide our history into decades. At the end of the first decade, in 1800, the expense of the Army was $2,560,000. In 1810, it cost $2,294,000. In 1820, it cost $2,630,-

000. In 1830, the War Department cost $4,767,000. From 1820 to 1830 it jumped up to double. In 1840 it cost $7,695,000, nearly double again. It ran up from $7,695,000 in 1840, to $9,687,000 in 1850. You will mark that at the end of all these decades, in the year for which the calculation is made, no war existed; but these sums embrace all the expenditures of the War Department. In 1857 what do we find them to be? They reach the pretty little sum of $19,-159,000! This is the way we are traveling. Whither are we going? What destination shall we reach at this rate?

Then, suppose we take the aggregate expenditures of the Government, and how does the matter stand? We find that in the year 1800 the entire expenses of the Government were $7,411,000; in the year 1810, $5,592,000—there was a decrease; in the year 1820, $10,723,000. In the year 1830, the entire expenses of the Government were $13,864,000. So we find that from 1800 to 1830 the expenses never got above $13,000,000 [sic]. Then we find in 1840 the entire expenses of the Government were $26,196,000; in 1850 $44,049,000. Now, in 1857, before the end of another decade, the expenses run up from $44,049,000 to $65,032,000. In the year 1858 the expenses are estimated at $74,963,000. Here is an increase of ten millions in one year. At this rate where shall we go? At this rate of increasing the expenditures ten millions per annum, in another decade to the enormous sum of $175,000,000. If we increase them five millions per annum, in ten years we shall run the expenditures of the Government up to $125,000,000.

Is it not time to pause? It it not time to inquire where we are going; and how much we are spending? We find a corresponding increase to that which I have traced in the War Department running into the Navy, running into the civil department, running through all the expenditures of the Government. I have added together all the expenditures of your Government since 1790, embracing the Army, the Navy, the civil department, and all the other objects of appropriation; and I find the sum total to be $1,313,658,000. This is the large sum which has been drawn from the people since this Government was established. How much of that has been expended upon the Army and Navy? In a country where the prejudices of the people and the genius of the Government are against a standing army, in a country where the standing army has been put down to the lowest possible point, how much of this $1,313,658,000 have been consumed for military purposes? Here where you say your Army is in miniature, where your Navy has not got out of its swaddling clothes, how much has been expended on these two departments? Eight hundred and sixty-seven million five hundred and seventy-three thousand dollars have been expended on these two arms of the public service; and that, too, while your standing Army has been kept down to the lowest point, as we are told. Two thirds of the entire revenue collected from the people of the United States has been expended upon this Army and Navy in miniature. Let them grow until they become men; let them get matured; let them get full strength, and how much of the people's substance will it take to sustain this Army and Navy? As I remarked it has already taken the sum of $867,573,000, leaving $446,085,000 to be applied to all the other purposes of the Government.

This should, I think, teach us a very important lesson. What lesson? here where they have been kept in miniature, where they have been kept down, where their influence has been felt less than in other Governments, the Army and Navy have consumed two thirds of the revenue drawn from the people. Go to the Governments that have risen and fallen before us, and what has been the cause of their downfall and decline? It has resulted from the influence of armies and navies. Standing armies and navies sustained by money drawn from the people, are the two arteries that have bled the nations before us to death. They are the two arteries that are now bleeding our people more freely than any others in the body-politic. Shall we not profit by experience? Shall we not stop and consider?

I know it is very easy for Senators, and those who are not Senators, to speak disparagingly of those who count the dollars and cents when an appropriation is proposed for this or for that purpose; but we see where our appropriations have brought us. They have brought us just where we are—in the midst of extravagance, in the midst of profligacy, in the midst of corruption, in the midst of improper applications of the people's money. Is there no way to arrest it? I tell the Democratic party, especially when they find the Opposition willing to unite with them on this question, now is the time to curtail the expenditures of this Government. If it is not done now, when you get up a sufficient stir here, and go on constantly increasing the governmental expenses, the people will hear the noise. They will hear the struggle, and now and then a few of them will come up and look in and ascertain, if they can, what is going on; and when they do ascertain that there is a considerable struggle going on to reduce the enormous expenditures of this Government, to enable the people to retain the product of their honest labor in their own pockets, to be expended in their own way, they will come to the rescue of the party that is for arresting the extravagant expenditures of this Government. I now admonish those who have charge of the Government to commence the work in time, to commence it now.

But, sir, I come back to the more immediate question before the

Senate, and that is as to calling out an additional military force. We are told by the friends of the committee's bill that we do not want volunteers. General Washington, in 1794, ordered out fifteen thousand of the militia to suppress the insurrection of what were called the whisky boys in Pennsylvania, and General Washington at that time acted upon what he understood to be the theory of the Government, as contained in the Constitution.

In the enumerated powers of the Constitution, we find the grant to Congress of power—

To declare war, grant letters of marque and reprisal, and make rules concerning captures on land and water.

To raise and support armies; but no appropriation of money to that use shall be for a longer term than two years.

What is meant there? Does the Constitution contemplate a large standing army? Congress has power to declare war; and the body on which this power is conferred is authorized to raise and maintain an army. This is given as an incident as necessary to the express grant to carry out the war-making power. Does that imply that you can keep fixed on the people a large and expensive standing army? Proceeding with the Constitution, we find that Congress has power—

To provide for calling forth the militia to execute the laws of the Union, suppress insurrections, and repel invasions. To provide for organizing, arming, and disciplining the militia, and for governing such part of them as may be employed in the service of the United States, reserving to the States respectively the appointment of the officers, and the authority of training the militia according to the discipline prescribed by Congress.

Do we not see that the militia was considered the proper force to sustain the strong arm of the Government? It never was contemplated to have a standing army. But it is said we do not want this description of force. When we look into the Constitution further, we find that the States are prohibited from keeping a standing army. Our Federal and State Constitutions were made by our fathers, who were familiar with the oppressions of the Old World, who had witnessed the encroachments and dangers of standing armies in those old Governments. Hence we find in all our bills of rights— perhaps not in all of them, but certainly in most of them—that standing armies are dangerous, and shall not be allowed; and the Constitution of the United States provides for calling forth the militia to suppress rebellion or insurrection against the Government. What does this contemplate? It contemplates most clearly that the power of this Government is to be vested in the citizen soldiery, that they are to be called forth when the Government needs them, and to answer the purpose for which the Government calls them into service. I am for that description of force; I am for confiding in and relying upon the volunteers of the country. They are the citizen soldiery in the proper acceptation of the term. I am for that description of soldiers that go when war comes. I am for that description of soldiers that come when war goes, who are not willing to enter the Army for a livelihood, and depend upon the Army for their support. General Washington gives us, in his message of 1794, an illustrious example in what he said on this subject. He says of the fifteen thousand men who were called out to suppress and put down the whisky boys in Pennsylvania:

It has been a spectacle displaying to the highest advantage the value of republican Government to behold the most and the least wealthy of our citizens standing in the same ranks as private soldiers, preëminently distinguished by being the army of the Constitution.

That was what Washington thought. He would be considered a demagogue, a pence calculator, a narrow-minded politician if he were to live and speak that language now; but he thought the true army of a republican Government should be composed of the most respectable and the least respectable, of the most wealthy and the least wealthy, fighting together when an occasion required them to tender their services. This was the army that Washington presented as an admirable spectacle of a republican Government; but when we come to modern times and to more distinguished men, we find a different doctrine preached. The honorable chairman of the Military Committee—I am sorry he is not in his seat—in speaking of the citizen soldiery, or of volunteers, makes use of the following language:

Nothing would be more unjust than to call people from their peaceful avocations, and keep them for a long period at frontier posts to guard frontier settlements. It would take lower material, too, than compose the volunteers who turn out in time of war. Among my objections to the employment of volunteers for such service, is the very elevated character of the young men who are often induced thus to enter the service; men who are worthy of better employment; whose habits are injured, whose train of thought or pursuit of some profession is broken in upon by this temporary service where a cheaper man would do as well.[10]

General Washington presented it as a noble spectacle that the force which he had ordered out, in obedience to the wants of the Government, was composed of the most and the least wealthy and respectable. That was the idea that General Washington had, and he presents it as an illustrious example in a republican form of Government. But hear the chairman of the committee:

If I may be permitted, without an appearance of egotism, to refer to my own observation, I would say that when I have traveled among the people from whom the volunteers were drawn who went to Mexico, I have had this fact more deeply impressed upon me by the sad countenance of some father, the tears of some mother, over the fate of a promising young man, who fell in performing the duties of a private soldier. The material is too high, except when the honor of the country demands it.

This carries us back to the condition and material of which armies are composed in European countries. What is the material of which they are composed? There is a broken-down and brainless-headed aristocracy, members of decaying families that have no energy by which they can elevate themselves, relying on ancestral honors and their connection with the Government. On the other hand there is a rabble, in the proper acceptation of the term—a miserable lazzaroni, lingering, and hanging, and wallowing about their cities, that have no employment; and they are ready and anxious to enter the service of the Government at any time for a few sixpences to buy their grog and a little clothing to hide their state of nudity. Such is the material of which their armies are composed—the rabble on the one hand, and the broken-down, decaying aristocracy on the other. Where does the middle man stand? Where does the industrious bee that makes the honey stand, from whose labor all is drawn? Where is he? He is placed between the upper and the nether millstone, and is ground to death by the office-hunter on the one hand, and the miserable rabble in the shape of soldiery on the other. I want no rabble here on the one hand, and I want no aristocracy on the other. Let us elevate the masses, and make no places in our Government for the rabble, either in your Army or the Navy; but let us pursue those great principles of government and philanthropy that elevate the masses on the one hand, and dispense with useless offices on the other. Do this, and you preserve the great masses of the people, on whom all rests; without whom your Government would not have an entity.

Cheaper men and lower priced men! Are these the men that a great Republic like this is to depend upon when danger is upon us? Think of it, Mr. President! An army composed of a rabble like this! You have heard much from the honorable Senator from Georgia [Mr. TOOMBS] as to military despotism; but think of the result that will ensue if you increase your standing Army a regiment now and a regiment then, until it runs up to fifty or a hundred thousand men, with all power concentrated here, composed of these "cheap" men— of this miserable rabble. Suppose then a difficulty should arise between one of the States and the Federal head here; these cheap men would feel it to be their duty and their highest pride to obey the commands and dictates of some daring military adventurer; and we might not have to wait for dextrous moves or for *coups d'état* by a Louis Napoleon. No; you would have some man to make the move here. What high pride, what high patriotism, what high sentiment in reference to Government can these "cheap" men entertain? They will feel it to be their duty to obey orders when commanded to charge on one of the sovereign States of this Union.

Already the military spirit and patriotism of the States are diminishing; the militia system is giving way; all eyes are turned to the Federal Government, this great central head that is collecting its millions annually from the people. Your State officers, and your States themselves, are sinking into insignificance. Here is the great center; here is the great attractive power. Abandon your military systems in your States, do away with the military ardor that exists among the several States of this Confederacy, and where are you? States that are now sovereign and independent, will revolve around this great central orb as so many dependants or satellites, receiving from the great center their light, their heat, and their motion. Let him advocate a standing army who will—to give another direction to the language of the Senator from Georgia, at the conclusion of his speech, when he said, "I tell Senators to beware," I vary the language, and tell the States to beware, for their sovereignty is at an end, if you persist in your career.

If we do not commence the work and arrest the expenditures and corruptions of this Government, the time will come when this Government will be overthrown; the time will come when the sound from the hoof of the cavalry horse will announce to the sovereign States the approach of a usurper; the legions of the Government, in advancing column, announce a despotism; when the goddess which presides in the temple of liberty will descend, and the last expiring hope of free Government go staggering from our land through carnage and through blood.

A standing army is an incubus, a canker—a fungus on the body-politic. Rely on the citizen soldier—the man that loves his country. When you call for volunteers, the lowest man in the company does not start out with the feelings or subdued spirit of a common soldier; but each man that goes, goes as a hero—and with the expectation of distinguishing himself, even as a private, before he returns to his home.

But it would seem from reading the speech of the honorable Senator—and you can see that old European idea of standing armies, commanders, and subjects, sticking out—that when he returned to Mississippi, and met the mothers and the brothers and the sisters and the fathers of those gallant men who had gone to Mexico, many of whom now sleep in a foreign grave, with not even a rude stone to mark their burial place, and many of them, perhaps, without a winding sheet save the blanket they slept upon in the tented field, and it saturated with their blood—they had tears, they had sympathies, they had some one they cared for. Those men who entered the service, and went into a foreign land as volunteers, had somebody to care for too. They had their country that they loved, and were willing to defend, and in whose cause they were willing to perish. Notwithstanding the tears that trickled down the mother's cheek, her heart would expand with patriotism when she reflected that her son had fallen in a glorious cause, defending his country's rights. He could not have died a more glorious death.

But to return to the idea suggested by the chairman of the Committee on Military Affairs; that we want some cheap man, I suppose, that has no mother, no father, no sister, nobody to care for him or to shed a tear over him. Oh no; that is not the man we want. We do not want the Army filled up with a rabble that have no country, no friends, nobody to care for, but are ready and willing to obey the order of their commander whatever it may be! I do not want such cheap men. I am opposed to such an army. I do not want to provide a place in the Government for them. I want men who have homes, who have mothers, who have fathers and friends and relations to care for them. I want them to feel that they have something to defend, and that they have a country which is worth defending.

In the course of the discussion on this bill, there were occasionally some strange developments. The eloquent chairman, who sustained the bill with so much ability all the way through, whenever he came to notice a man who had distinguished himself, seemingly had prepared a standing eulogy to pronounce on his character. As to everything that pertained to the standing Army proper, he seemed to be *au fait*. He was ready at every point to present them and to identify them with the Army, and especially with West Point. He commenced with Washington, and pronounced a eulogy upon him, the great and good, "first in war, first in peace, and first in the hearts of his countrymen." My heart responds to all that. He spoke of Jackson, from my own State; and if there is any man that ever lived that I venerate, it is the illustrious Andrew Jackson. He spoke of Colonel Johnston,[11] who has command of your forces now away in the region of Utah, and he pronounced a eulogy upon him; of General Taylor, distinguished and brave, (and I have not aught to say against him,) and he pronounced a long eulogy upon him, his courage, his valor, his chivalry; and last, though not least, of my distinguished friend from Texas, [Mr. HOUSTON,] on whom he pronounced a eulogy, and I say amen to all of it.

I will not undertake to add anything to what he said on that occasion; but in this brilliant galaxy of military chieftains, men who have been in the thickest and hottest of battle; men over whose efforts your gallant banner has triumphantly waved, upon whose standard the eagle of liberty has again and again perched, did it not occur to you that there was another man who was somewhat distinguished? I understand that that man too concurs with the Secretary of War in asking for regiments; not to fill up the rank and file with cheap men, but to have regiments, not companies. Who is that man? It occurred to me as being somewhat strange that nothing was said of him. I am no admirer of the individual to whom I allude, in a political point of view; but his military reputation is a part of the history of this country, and his military renown is only bounded by the limits of the civilized world. Who is he? When you come to look to him exclusively in a military point of view, he stands up in this great cluster of military chiefs like some projecting cliff from a lofty mountain. Did we never hear of Winfield Scott? Has he no place in the military annals of our country? Has he fought no battles? Has he shed no blood? Has he not shown himself to be illustrious as a soldier, as well as a tactician? Why was he omitted? Why was he excluded from the category of great men? Why was there an omission to pronounce a eulogy upon him? I know there is nothing I could say that would add one gem to the brilliant chaplet that encircles his illustrious brow, and therefore I will not undertake to say anything in reference to that distinguished man. As a military chieftain, he belongs to the nation; his success in the battle-field, to the history of the world.

I do not understand the proposition before the Senate, as presented by the Military Committee, to be an Administration measure. When I turn to the report[12] of the Secretary of War, in what terms does he recommend an increase of the Army? The principal idea in his mind seems to be that because his predecessor had recommended an increase of the standing Army, he too should recommend it. Who was his predecessor? The illustrious chairman of the Committee on Military Affairs. I say it not in disparagement of him; but I refer to it as a fact that we all have pride of character, and anything which emanates from us is, in our opinion, better than that which emanates from anybody else. It was recommended by him as Secretary of War. He comes into the Senate as chairman of the Committee on Military Affairs to execute and carry out his own recommendation; and then we are told that it is an Administration measure. We see how this matter stands. It is so of human character. Notwithstanding it emanates from that distinguished committee, (for all of whom I have the most profound respect, for their talents and their integrity,) I must say that committee, distinguished as it is, is not infallible, and may originate measures that are not perfect. We are all attached to our offspring. When we claim paternity, though the infant be imperfect, crippled, deformed, not capable of taking care of itself, such are the affections of the parental heart that it clings with more tenacity to its crippled and dependent and imperfect offspring than it does to those who can go alone and take care of themselves. It may be so in this instance.

In reference to the volunteer service, the amendment I have offered proposes to raise four regiments of volunteers in the very language of the President himself, and for the purposes for which he states in his message that he wants them. The officers and men are to be paid precisely the same amount that you propose to pay to these "cheap" men who have no home, or country, or friends, to care for them. I state here now, in my place, that it is estimated the cost will be about a million dollars per regiment. I state here, in my place, that if you will enter into a contract with me, I will guaranty that Tennessee, the volunteer State, will take your $4,000,000 and acquit you of every claim hereafter, and will settle all your difficulties in Utah in less than six months. I was going to add, yes, we will do it for half the money. Tennessee has her companies and her regiments ready; and all the Government has to do is to say, "we will receive you into service and commission your officers," and the work is done. Volunteers are the very men to send there. Send them; and when Brigham Young has come to terms, when he has reached a state of subordination, when he has complied with the law, our volunteers will not only stop there, but if you will grant the boys homesteads, they will break up that rookery of polygamy, and Brigham will move to some other place. As a matter of economy, as a matter of expedition, as the most effectual means of restoring peace to the country, accept the proposition, and we will perform the work.

But there has been a great deal said on this subject; and especially the remarks of the Senator from New York, [Mr. SEWARD,] struck me with some force. In speaking of Brigham Young, and the institutions established under his government, if I remember right—I have not the speech before me, and it is not in any unkind spirit I refer to him; it is not my intention to make a wrong quotation—he said that they were a kind of Judaism; that they were deluded and fanatical; and the whole tenor of his speech was, that the power of the Government should be brought down upon them, and the anathemas of all Christian people should be hurled against them. The gentleman informed us that the Mormons had their origin in New York; that they went from there to Missouri, from Missouri to Illinois, and from there they took up their line of march, and located themselves at the Salt Lake, where they are now.

When we allude to Salt Lake and Brigham Young, there are many associations that come up with them, all of which were thrown out in the honorable Senator's speech. He is pronounced to be a deluded man, and his followers fanatics; it is said they are all laboring under a delusion. Suppose this be so: in what does this delusion consist? In the establishment of polygamy. Let us talk of things as they are.

In reference to the religion or delusion of these people, we should be a little careful in the advances we make upon them. We have a very striking illustration, admonishing us upon this subject. Charles V., the Emperor of Germany, when tired of the cares of State, resigned the possession of his dominions to his son, and retired to a monastery. While there, to amuse the evening of his life, he undertook to regulate the movement of watches; but after repeated efforts he found that it was impossible to make any two of them keep precisely the same time. He was thus led to reflect upon the crime or folly and wickedness he had committed in attempting to make men think alike. It is as natural for men to differ in their religious and political notions as it is in the complexion of their hair and their skins.

Does polygamy exist nowhere else? We are wonderfully alarmed at a little polygamy at Salt Lake; yet no longer ago than yesterday a resolution was reported by the honorable chairman of the Committee on Foreign Relations[13] which may result in the expenditure of thirty or forty thousand dollars to receive—whom? To receive the representative of the Grand Turk of Constantinople. [Laughter.] The first song I ever heard in my life used to run:

"The turban'd Turk who scorns the world."[14]

We all know the lines that follow. It is said that he has his harem of six hundred wives; and yet we are almost agonizing ourselves to appropriate the money of the people of this country, who are so much opposed to polygamy, to receive the representative of polygamy of the grand harem itself. Have we forgotten when Amin Bey[15] went through the country representing the Grand Turk and his harem, that he was escorted by the Secretary of State through the House of Representatives? An appropriation of money was made to defray his expenses. What all those expenses were, I shall not undertake to say.

Go to China; does not polygamy exist there? How long have we been trying to open commercial relations and intercourse with the Emperor of China? We have appointed a Minister[16] and we pay him a large salary to represent us at the court of that country, which tolerates polygamy. I think it ought to be a little excusable in Brigham Young, who is said to be a deluded fanatic, living and moving and acting under his delusion, and his poor, blind followers, too. If they are laboring under a delusion, let us act as Christians. I fear that all those suggestions have been thrown out to excite the prejudice, not to say the anger, of the American people, against these misguided, and, I was going to say, abominable people.

Why, Mr. President, have we forgotten the accounts we read about the Crusades? That was a delusion got up by the simple power of speech. Three million people were moved by a delusion. Richard I., the lion-hearted Richard, who was alluded to here the other day— the great conqueror of the East, engaged the embattled hosts that were led by Saladin, in carrying out a delusion. It is very easy to say that one man is a maniac, that another is deluded, that this or that man is not in his right mind. Of that are we to be the judges? They may say that we are deluded, that we are misguided, that we are misdirected; and who shall judge between us? Sir, in the midst of all this delusion, while we pursue the career upon which we intend to enter against the Mormons, we should act as Christians; and with the light of Christianity, with the Bible before us, we should endeavor to correct and reform that deluded and misguided people.

But suppose we come a little nearer home. Does polygamy exist nowhere else? I intend to speak of things as they are; and I will venture to say that there is more practical polygamy in the city of New York than there is in all Salt Lake, with this marked difference: at Salt Lake it is according to their religion, according to their delusion, according to the law and custom of the place; it is tolerated and made a matter of conscience: while in New York and many other places, practical polygamy exists in violation of our standard of morals, in violation of the law, in violation of what a sound virtuous community consider to be right. There is more practical polygamy now in many of the cities of this Confederacy than there is in all Salt Lake. Then, before we get so fierce, so rampant, and so willing to run these misguided and deluded people into the mountains, into the caverns and the gorges, as hiding places, I think we should be a little considerate, and see if we cannot correct the evil which lies at our own door.

I have occupied much more time, Mr. President, than I intended; but I desired to set myself right in the vote I should give in reference to the increase of the Army of the United States. The proposition I have introduced as a substitute for that of the Senator from Massachusetts, which is substantially his proposition with a little variation, covers, I think, what the President asks. I am willing to call out whatever number of volunteers is necessary to meet the emergency and answer the purposes of the Government; but I want to call out that description of men that have a country and care for somebody, and for whom somebody cares. I do not want to fill up the Army of this nation with a rabble. I do not want to fill up the Army of this nation with those who feel and have no responsibility. I want the men upon whom our liberties are to depend in time of battle to be men who have a country, and who feel an interest in that country. Stating these as my views for voting against the original bill and in favor of the proposition I offer, I conclude by expressing the hope that the Senate will adopt the volunteer proposition. If they think proper afterwards to authorize the War Department to do so, we will make a contract to do the work for half the money you propose to pay your "cheap" men.[17]

Cong. Globe, 35 Cong., 1 Sess., 737–41.

1. This speech, Johnson's first in the Senate, came during a debate over an administration request that the standing army be increased in order to deal with the insurrectionary situation in Utah. Henry Wilson of Massachusetts had proposed instead that volunteer, rather than regular, troops be used. *Cong. Globe*, 35 Cong., 1 Sess., 497, 737.

2. Upon the organization of Deseret as Utah Territory (1850), Fillmore had appointed Brigham Young governor. The Mormon leader, concentrating power in his own hands, ousted judges, forbade troops to come into the territory, and generally defied federal authority. Although removed from office in 1857, he continued to control the territory; in 1858, Albert Sidney Johnston with 1,500 regular troops achieved only nominal submission. Since the Utah settlements lay in the path of westward migration and since the Mormons were rumored to be instigating Indian hostilities, Buchanan asked for additional troops. Samuel Eliot Morison and Henry S. Commager, *The Growth of the American Republic* (2 vols., New York, 1962), I, 593; Richardson, *Messages*, V, 454–55; *Senate Ex. Doc.* No. 2, 35 Cong., 1 Sess., *passim*.

3. While the army fluctuated in size, it was at this time over 17,000. *Ibid.*, 4; *Cong. Globe*, 35 Cong., 1 Sess., 407.

4. Jefferson Davis.

5. Richardson, *Messages*, V, 456.

6. R. M. T. Hunter.

7. During the winter of 1858 charges of fraud and corruption were rife; according to *Harper's Weekly*, six congressional committees were currently investigating irregularities ranging from the war department's purchase of land at Willett's Point, New York, to the perennial issue of the public printing. On the previous day, J. W. Wolcott, a "contumacious witness" before a House committee concerned with vote-buying in the passage of the Tariff of 1857, had been sent to the county jail until he disclosed what had been done with $58,000 of the alleged "bribery fund." *Harper's Weekly*, March 13, 1858, p. 166; Washington *Evening Star*, February 16, 1858.

8. Without benefit of ellipsis, Johnson has lifted two sentences from Burke's "Reflections on the Revolution in France." See Edmund Burke, *The Works of* . . . (12 vols., Boston, 1865–67), III, 534, 535.

9. From "Of Seditions and Troubles," in Bacon's *Essays or Counsels* . . . , B. Montagu, ed. (London, 1845), 52.

10. These remarks, and those immediately following, appear in a debate between Davis and Fessenden of Maine on February 11. *Cong. Globe*, 35 Cong., 1 Sess., 676.

11. Albert Sidney Johnston (1803–1862) of Kentucky, graduate of West Point (1826), had served as Texas secretary of war (1838–40) and colonel of the Texas volunteers (1846–48). A U. S. cavalry officer in Utah and California prior to the Civil War, he became a Confederate general and was mortally wounded at Shiloh. *DAB*, X, 135–36; Charles P. Roland, *Albert Sidney Johnston* (Austin, 1964).

12. *Senate Ex. Doc.* No. 2, 35 Cong., 1 Sess., 2–6.

13. James M. Mason (1798–1871), Virginia Democrat, had served in the house of delegates (1826–32), in Congress (1837–39), and in the Senate (1847–61). Resigning at the beginning of the Civil War, he acted as Confederate commissioner to Great Britain (1862–65). *BDAC*, 1272; *DAB*, XII, 364–65.

14. Popular around 1810, this song, "The Irishman," had numerous stanzas, of which the following is one version of the first:

> "The turban'd Turk, who scorns the world,
> May strut about with his whiskers curl'd,
> Keep a hundred wives under lock and key,
> For nobody else but himself to see;
> Yet long may he pray with his Alcoran,
> Before he can love like an Irishman."

Notes and Queries (London, 1871), XLIV, 285, 350, 357.

15. Amin Bey, a special agent of the Sultan of Turkey, came to the U. S. in 1850 to study civil and social institutions, especially those related to the navy. Our minister in Constantinople and Secretary of State Webster had recommended that Congress receive the Bey as an official visitor and that his expenses be paid out of the public purse. *Cong. Globe*, 31 Cong., 1 Sess., 1985–86.

16. William B. Reed (1806–1876), a former Pennsylvania Whig legislator and attorney general, was given the China post as a reward for campaigning for Buchanan. During his mission (1857–59) he negotiated the Treaty of Tientsin giving the U. S. most-favored-nation treatment. Opposed to the Civil War, he suffered financial losses in his legal practice and turned to journalism. *DAB*, XV, 461–62.

17. The Senate adjourned without taking action. On February 25, Johnson's substitute was rejected, 26–23. A House bill to raise mounted volunteers for border service in Texas with a provision for two volunteer regiments for service in Utah, ultimately passed. *Cong. Globe*, 35 Cong., 1 Sess., 876, 1433; *U. S. Statutes*, XI, 262–63.

Exchanges Concerning Volunteer Forces[1]

February 18, 1858

Mr. JOHNSON, of Tennessee. I do not wish to detain the Senate, but I desire to make a few brief remarks in answer to some objections which have been urged to this proposition. It has been objected by some, for instance, that the substitute offered by me confines the President, in making his appointments, to particular persons, and that under the Constitution of the United States we have no such power. I wish to call the attention of the Senate to the fact that the law confines all appointments of midshipmen to the Naval School at Annapolis, and all appointments of cadets to the West Point Academy, to congressional districts. If you can confine the appointment of a cadet, or midshipman, or any other appointment to be made by the President of the United States, to a district, cannot you confine him to the appointment of particular persons? If the power is clear in the one case, it is equally clear in the other.

The objection is that my substitute confines the President in his appointments of officers to particular persons—those chosen by the companies. Well, sir, in 1846, when we passed what we called the ten regiment bill, it was provided:

That the President of the United States be, and he is hereby, authorized, by and with the advice and consent of the Senate, to appoint one additional major in each of the regiments of dragoons, artillery, infantry, and riflemen in the Army of the United States, who shall be taken from the captains in the Army.

This law confined the President, in appointing majors, to the captains then in the Army. If that was constitutional, and Congress had power in that instance to designate whom the President should appoint, how do the provisions of the substitute, confining the President in the appointment of officers to the persons indicated by the companies, battalions, and regiments, conflict with the Constitution? If you can compel him to select majors from a particular class—the captains of the Army—can you not compel the President to take as colonels, majors, and captains, the persons elected by the regiments, battalions, and companies, when organized? The power is as clear in the one case as it is in the other.

Let us see how the Constitution stands on that point, for I want this question made clear. I do not want the idea to go out to the country that this proposition has been rejected on the ground that it came in conflict with the Constitution, or invaded any power conferred on the President of the United States by the Constitution. I know that whenever you come to popularizing the institutions of this country, and especially when you come to popularizing the Army of the United States, there is always some pretext, some excuse, for interposing an objection to the exercise of power on the part of the people. Why should not the regiments, the battalions, and the companies be authorized to elect their own officers when it does not come in conflict with the Constitution of the United States?

But it has been intimated or suggested to me, that such a provision is not constitutional. I do not pretend to understand a great deal about the Constitution; but I am very much inclined to think that if it was read a little more than it is, it would be better understood by a great many of us throughout the country. We find that the Consitution provides:

The President shall have power, by and with the advice and consent of the Senate, to make treaties, provided two thirds of the Senators present concur; and he shall nominate, and, by and with the advice and consent of the Senate, shall appoint embassadors [sic], other public ministers and consuls, judges of the Supreme Court, and all other officers of the United States whose appointments are not herein otherwise provided for, and which shall be established by law.

We may go on and establish the office of head of a Department; he is a superior officer; but the query now comes up, cannot the head of that Department appoint the inferior officers? I say he can, and such has been the practice. The Constitution further provides in the same clause:

But the Congress may by law vest the appointment of such inferior officers as they think proper, in the President alone, in the courts of law, or in the heads of Departments.

I should like to know if the power is not clear. Does not my substitute vest the power absolutely in the President to appoint these colonels? It is as clear as the Constitution itself. The great objection to the exercise of this power is that it is a confirmation of the will of the regiments in the selection of their officers. Let the men choose those who are to guide them in battle. Let the men choose those who are to sleep with them on the tented field. Why this great dread that you cannot get along in making these appointments unless they are taken away from the people? It is clear that the first section of the substitute is constitutional. It provides for the appointment of officers in the way pointed out by the Constitution itself, practically. It prevents delay. It does not even make it necessary to send such nominations to this body; but I shall have no objection to that if it be insisted on. These regiments can be organized, the officers commissioned, and put into the field, if the exigencies of the country require it, and whatever the Government wants to be accomplished can be accomplished at once.

I have made these remarks merely to remove the objections that have been intimated to me against the first section of the substitute.

[Hannibal Hamlin offers an amendment, later adopted, that the force so raised be continued in service for no more than two years. A brief exchange follows between R. M. T. Hunter and Johnson, with the Virginia senator maintaining that Johnson's proposition to add 4,000 volunteers would in the end be more expensive than adding 2,200 to 2,300 regulars for temporary duty.]

Mr. JOHNSON, of Tennessee. I think the gentleman's argument, with due respect to him, has but very little in it. In the first instance, he presses his proposition on the ground of economy; and he seemed to congratulate himself and the country that there was so able a champion here in advocacy of the cause of economy; but he says he would have preferred to see my practice conform to my precepts. Let us take the Senator's argument and see if my practice does not conform to my precepts.

What was the proposition reported by the Committee on Military Affairs? It was to make a permanent addition to the standing Army, which was variously estimated here to cost from five to seven million dollars. The honorable chairman told us two or three times in his speech that he did not expect to live to see the day when the Army would be reduced; that the proposed addition was to be permanent. Then what is the issue? Between the original proposition and the one which I have offered. But the gentleman sees great expense in that, and he comes forward with a favorite idea of his own; and what is it? He says his proposition is to make a certain increase of the forces of the United States to the extent of some twenty-four or twenty-five hundred men—that is certain. Then what is the proposition with which he contrasts it? What do I propose? It leaves the number to be raised at the discretion of the President and the War Department, it is true, but it is not to exceed four thousand men. If the gentleman's twenty-five hundred men will answer the purpose of the Government—will be sufficient, and no more needed, will he impugn the President and Secretary of War[2] by saying that if we confer this discretion they will call more men into service than are required? That is the issue he makes: his issue is with them that they will abuse this privilege. They say they may want four thousand, and the issue is with the Secretary of War and the President, not with me. The Senator's idea is they cannot be trusted as to the number of men it will be necessary to raise to meet the emergency which may take place, or may not take place in Utah.

But again, the substitute I have offered proceeds on the idea that if troops are not necessary for service in Utah, the President is not to raise a man; and that if he does call out any, the number shall be in proportion to the wants of the Government; but he is not to go beyond the maximum of four thousand. Will the honorable chairman of the Committee on Finance deny the President and Secretary of War the discretion of calling out what they may deem sufficient between four thousand and the amount suggested by him, or not calling out any to meet the emergency? Is he not willing to trust them that far?

Mr. HUNTER. Let me ask the Senator if he is not willing to trust them so far as to give them the five regiments which the Secretary asks? Will he limit their discretion in that regard?

Mr. JOHNSON, of Tennessee. I do limit them; my proposition limits them. They may raise any number of men from one to four thousand. If there is no Utah war or difficulty, they need not raise any. That is my proposition. Your proposition is to raise some twenty-five hundred or three thousand men certainly. Do you not make a certain addition to the Army?

Mr. HUNTER. I have stated that it is a temporary addition, like the other.

Mr. JOHNSON, of Tennessee. Exactly; the other is a temporary addition. So I meet you on that point; and mine may not make any addition whatever. We understand that. I proceed more on the idea that these men will not be needed at all. I do not believe there will be any Utah war. I believe that these people will submit to the laws of the United States; and that there will be no necessity for this Government to shed the blood of what we conceive to be a misguided and deluded people; for when it is understood that the President has sufficient military force placed at his discretion to quell and subdue any resistance they may make, I believe they will desist; and especially so if the President of the United States proceeds on that humane and parental feeling which was pursued by General Washington when he issued two proclamations urging the whisky boys to submission to the laws of the United States. I think it meets the precise case.

The gentleman says this force is to cost more than an addition to the regular Army. The substitute provides that they shall receive the same pay and allowances; that they shall be subject to the rules and articles of war; that they shall receive the same clothing as regulars, and that they shall be equipped at the expense of the Government. There will be no claim for volunteers' horses—the horses are to be furnished. If these men are to enter the service of the United States and receive the same pay that the regulars do, will it cost any more to transport them than to transport regular soldiers? In many instances they can be raised almost in sight of the place, from the neighboring State you can send the men into the service of the Government. The substitute provides that they shall receive the same pay; and will transportation cost any more for volunteers than for regular soldiers?

What then becomes of the gentleman's argument about economy? The issue is made up as to the difference between precept and practice. I am glad that the honorable chairman has embraced the theory. I trust and hope we shall have many evidences, before the close of this session of Congress, of the theory being reduced to practice, so far as he and others are concerned. I repeat here, I will go with him in retrenching the expenditures and reforming the abuses of this Government, as far as he who goes furthest. I am glad that I have such a leader, such a captain in the cause of economy; and I give him the assurance that I shall never shrink while he stands to his post.

[At the suggestion of James F. Simmons of Rhode Island, Johnson accepts an amendment limiting the increase to three regiments in lieu of 4,000 men. Alfred Iverson of Georgia speaks at some length in behalf of expanding the regular army—"I am opposed entirely to the use of volunteers"—and observes that "one would suppose that a few regiments of Tennessee militia could go to Utah and swallow the Mormons at a single mouthful; eat them up at once . . . but my opinion is, that in eating up the Mormons, they will eat up the Treasury, and instead of an annual expense of seventy millions, we shall have a bill of a hundred millions a year, if we send four thousand volunteers to Utah." In the ensuing discussion, Seward inclines toward Johnson's position favoring volunteers, while Asa Biggs of North Carolina supports the Hunter–Iverson preference for regulars.]

Mr. JOHNSON, of Tennessee. I regret, Mr. President, to find myself situated as I am, to be compelled to make a reply to the Senator from Georgia, in consequence, as I think, of some unkind allusions that have been made to my State. But before I approach that portion of the subject—and I shall look at some one or two, or perhaps more, of the positions assumed by the Senator from Georgia—it occurs to me, that perhaps I had better answer a single point to which the Senator from North Carolina has called my attention. He, in the conclusion of his remarks, stated that I had, in the *debut* I had made in the Senate yesterday, laid down as a text, or called the attention of the country to the great fact enunciated by Edmund Burke, one of England's greatest statesmen, that "the revenue of the State is the State." I now promise and assure that Senator that I intend to act on that principle; and when the measure comes up, to which he has alluded, I pledge myself now, in advance, if there is truth in figures or sound argument, that I will demonstrate that the measure to which he alludes,[3] instead of being a waste of the public revenue, is a revenue measure, and will increase the revenues of the country instead of diminishing them. I will demonstrate to him, also, that it is not my intention gratuitously to give away the public lands. I do not believe that the Government has the power to make gratuities to give away the public lands. I do not believe that the Government has the power to make gratuities in the general acceptation of the term; but I will show, when the time comes, that the man who takes one hundred and sixty acres of land under the homestead bill, and goes to a frontier country to cultivate it, pays the highest consideration in reclaiming the land and reducing it to cultivation.

I will demonstrate still further, that if we grant one hundred and sixty acres of land to a man on condition that he occupy and cultivate it for a period of years, in the process of time it will yield twenty times the revenue to the Federal Government that it will while you permit a man to enter it and let it lie without cultivation for a series of years, or while you permit it to remain uncultivated without being entered at all. I will redeem every intimation of principle or position that is given out in what I stated yesterday in reference to the revenue of a State being the State. But I will let that pass.

The Senator from Georgia, it seems to me, has manifested more feeling than he has displayed sound argument and judgment on this occasion. I remarked yesterday, and I repeat now, that it is natural for a parent who has a deformed offspring to feel concerned for its fate; and his sensibilities are easily touched when there is an unkind remark made about the deformity. I did not intend that any allusions I made to the bill reported by the Military Committee should have this effect. My reference was to it as a measure.

The gentleman congratulates me upon indicating some distinguished ability in the assault I have made upon the bill reported by the Military Committee, and then he qualifies and corrects that by saying, no, it was not upon that bill. He says the argument I have made was against the bill which they reported, and not against the measure before the Senate. What is the illustration he gives of the great ability I manifested? It was that I had manufactured a man of straw, and then, to show my extraordinary gladiatorial powers, physical or intellectual, had crushed the man I had created. To what man of straw is it that the gentleman alludes? The bill reported by the Committee on Military Affairs? If I have demolished a man of straw, it is a man of your manufacture, not mine. If I have not shown any very great ability in the assault I have made on this man of straw, I have shown all that I could show in a contest with such an adversary as I had to contend with. It was at least sufficient for the occasion. I think I have nailed this man of straw, torn him to pieces, and exposed him to the country and the Senate. So much for the gentleman's man of straw.

But the Senator seems to pride himself on some calculations he has made, and he speaks sneeringly and disdainfully of volunteer forces. He says they are not the proper force to use for the service required by the Government. He reads from documents furnished by the War Department to prove that volunteer forces cost more than regulars. I imagine that if the gentleman will analyze that report, (and sometimes it is best for us to analyze documents that we use, and go into their details before we use the aggregate figures,) he will find that it embraces the additional expense incurred by calling out the militia for short periods, and then dismissing them. I imagine the great item of increase has been brought about by calling out the militia for very short periods of time.

[At this point Johnson and Iverson engage in a brief debate in which the latter claims that Johnson's amendment, which calls for twelve–month volunteers, would necessitate new enlistments should the affair last longer, thus adding to the expense. Johnson obliges the Georgian to admit he is actually reading from a substitute proposal by Henry Wilson of Massachusetts.]

Mr. JOHNSON, of Tennessee. Ah! that is another matter. So the Senate will discover that the Senator from Georgia has made a speech without a subject. He has missed the subject entirely. He shows that his argument was made upon another amendment. If a certain number of volunteers, say two thousand, be called out to serve during the pending difficulties in Utah, and in no event to serve longer than two years, can they cost more than two thousand regulars called out for two years specifically? In no event can they cost more, but they may cost less. It strikes me that that is just as clear as that two and two make four. What, then, becomes of the Senator's argument? what becomes of all the feeling he manifested? The feeling manifested was as unnecessary as the argument was absurd.

But the Senator, in another portion of his speech, said there were only two kinds of troops known to this Government—militia and regulars. I wish to refresh the Senator's recollection on that point. No longer ago than 1846, we passed a law providing that,

for the purpose of enabling the Government of the United States to prosecute said war to a speedy and successful termination, the President be, and he is hereby, authorized to employ the militia and naval and military forces of the United States, and to call for and accept the services of any number of volunteers, not exceeding fifty thousand.[4]

It seems to me that that looks as if we had had volunteer service. I do not know anything about the technicalities of military affairs, for I know but little about military matters; and I am free to say that if I belonged to any party as a general thing, I should belong to the peace party. As Lucius exclaimed when consulted, in the play of Cato, I must confess that about this time "my thoughts are turned on peace."[5] I am not quite so belligerent in my nature as some other gentlemen. My thoughts are turned upon the arts of peace. I want the energies, the talents, the physical power of this country directed to developing the resources of the nation. I want the power of the Government employed in adding to its wealth, instead of being wasted in armies, whether in the shape of volunteers or regulars.

After having met these positions of the gentleman, let me refer to the President's message. Certainly if the President had any distinct description of troops in his mind when he penned his message, we shall answer the purpose by placing volunteers at his discretion, to be used by him in suppressing the rebellion that is existing, or that is anticipated in Utah. It most clearly meets his idea. Why, then, this great resistance to volunteer service? Why these sneers at volunteers? If I had time to gather up the many gallant incidents of the brave volunteers of the many wars we have had, and to present them in regular train before the gentleman, I think he would be almost horror-stricken with regret at what he said today in reference to the volunteer service of the country. In the war of 1812, where is there a battle-field in which volunteer ability was not displayed, and volunteer blood shed? Go from Maine to Louisiana, go from the Atlantic coast to the golden shores of California, where is there a battle-field on which volunteer blood has not been poured out as an evidence of their high appreciation of their country? Are these men, who have rallied to your country's standard in all her perilous conflicts, and upon whose efforts victory has uniformly perched, to be regarded as occupying an inferior position to the regular soldiery, composed out of this lower, "cheaper material," of which you want your Army composed?

Let me ask the Senate, let me ask the country, if the destinies of this Government were at issue upon a single military contest, what service would you most rely upon? Would you not rely upon the volunteer who went at his country's first call; who responded to the first sound of the tocsin; who went to fight his country's cause; who went to fight for wife, for children, and for home? Would you rely upon the man that has an interest in his country, that has somebody to care for, and somebody to care for him; or the rabble soldier, that has no home, that has no country, whose highest ambition is a few sixpences and a little grog? These are the men that are eulogized and extolled, in comparison with the volunteers of these United States. God save the mark![6]

But, not content with that invidious comparison between regular and volunteer troops, the State which I represent must be arraigned; she must be attacked. It is true that I am not her native son, but I am her adopted son. She took me by the hand, and that generous, that brave, that patriotic people, have made me all that I am, be that much or little. Having placed me here, I intend to stand by her through evil and through good report. Come weal or come woe, I will be found standing by her interests, her honor—her sacred honor—let the consequences be what they may. Yes, I love her. The tenderest sympathies of my soul are entwined with her. There is where I live; there is where I hope to die; and beneath the clods of some of her valleys I hope my remains will be deposited. It is the home of my children; it is the home of all that is sacred to me. There upon her soil, and beneath her sky, the infant vision of those that are bone of my bone and flesh of my flesh, first saw the light; and I will stand up and defend her.

The gentleman being hard pressed, must needs lug in an unkind allusion. I will not be invidious to the citizens of the different States. I will not go to Georgia and arraign her prowess. I feel that my position is too elevated for that. I love Georgia; I love her people, and I admire many of her institutions; and if I should be hard pressed here or elsewhere in discussion, by way of covering a retreat, even were it in my power to do so, I would make no unkind allusion to her as a State, or to her people. The prowess, the valor of Tennessee is arraigned; and it is said that I, speaking in behalf of the volunteer State, have indicated some predilections for Mormonism. I ask those who heard me yesterday, the first time I attempted to make a little effort in this Chamber, whether that inference can fairly be drawn from what I said. Perhaps I spoke hurriedly and crudely, and I may have said something by inadvertence; but take the tenor and scope of what I said, and can the gentleman, even with magnifying glasses, discover the slightest hint or word that favored the institution of Mormonism? He says that if that is my theory and if my people entertain the same views, they might, when they got to Utah as volunteers, unite with Young and desert the standard of their country. So far as the honorable Senator's allusion is concerned, I am willing to compare theory with him on the subject of Mormonism, and I would not care much to compare practice. I will take him in theory or in practice, just which ever dilemma suits him best. I spurn the imputation as being unfounded and untrue in reference to my State or myself.

I remarked in the little speech I made yesterday, that we need not be so squeamish, or have our tender sensibilities so extraordinarily shocked at the Mormons, when the honorable chairman of the Committee on Foreign Relations, (and I intended it as no imputation on him,) had just reported a resolution—doing what? Providing for receiving, entertaining, and conferring extraordinary privileges upon the representative of the Grand Turk of Constantinople. History informs us that polygamy exists in Turkey to a very great extent, but because I alluded to it, did I say I justified it? I alluded to it as a palliating circumstance, and to show why we should not be so eager, in hot pursuit of the Mormons, either in reference to their religion or the institutions which they may have among them.

I intended to say then what I shall say now, that we have a striking illustration of the doctrine of our fathers, in regard to religious freedom, by the provision which is ingrafted in every constitution of the States of the Federal Union, that all men have a natural and indefeasible right to worship Almighty God according to the dictates of their own conscience. I act upon this great principle of civil liberty. Charles V., the Emperor of Germany, when he became tired of the cares of State, resigned his vast possessions to his son, and, to amuse the evening of his life, retired to a monastery, and there undertook to regulate the movement of watches; but finding it impossible to make any two of them keep precisely the same time, he was led to reflect on the crime, the folly, the wickedness he had committed in attempting to make men think alike. I am willing to be tolerant. Standing upon those great principles laid down and inculated in the constitutions of all the States, I think that we should adopt other means, we should act towards the Mormons as Christians ought to act—go with the Bible in one hand and the torch of reason in the other, and dissuade them if we could from their course.

I might refer to the various instances of impostors who have sprung up from the body of mankind, and raised organized communities, from the beginning of the world to the present time. They have had their day; they have risen and fallen. They are past and gone. But how do the honorable Senator and myself compare in practice? When the vote came up on the proposition to appropriate money to entertain, I suppose in magnificent style, the representative of the Turk, by way of expressing our high appreciation of the institutions of Turkey, how did the Senator vote? My recollection is, he will correct me if I am wrong, that he voted for that resolution, which is to take out of the Treasury the money of the people of the United States, who have such a great abhorrence of Mormonism, to be spent in entertaining the representative of the Grand Turk?

Mr. IVERSON. Does the Senator allude to me?

Mr. JOHNSON, of Tennessee. Yes, sir; I ask whether the Senator voted for that resolution?

Mr. IVERSON. I am sorry to spoil the eloquent rhapsody the Senator has delivered by saying that I voted in the negative on that proposition.

Mr. JOHNSON, of Tennessee. I am very happy to hear it; that is some evidence that the Senator is getting right. I referred to it to show why we should not run into extremes on questions of this kind. As to "rhapsody," that is a thing I do not know anything about. When I deal with figures, they are not figures of speech, but the figures used in the arithmetic; and as far as we have gone in this matter, I think we have shown that the gentlemen who urge this bill here are wholly wanting and at fault in their figures.

But, sir, the Senator has referred to my State. I ask the Senate, I ask the people of this nation, if it is any part of Tennessee's history that her people have ever been wanting in prowess or in courage. She needs no vindication from me. It exists in her own history. I could recite many of her military deeds that would be ample, if her reputation was not beyond the assaults of the Senator. I could begin with the battle of King's Mountain, which was fought before Tennessee was a State. It was then a portion of the territory of North Carolina, but the people went from the eastern counties of Tennessee to the battle of King's Mountain; and there, amidst the din and the dust and the heat of battle, they showed themselves to be brave men. Is it necessary to allude to the Seviers, the Shelbys, the Hardings, and the long list of those gallant patriots who participated in that battle? When you examine the history of the country carefully, you will find that it was that battle which turned the tide of the Revolution. The country had been laid waste; disaster had attended our arms; but from the battle of King's Mountain down to the surrender of Cornwallis our troops triumphed everywhere.

How was it in the war of 1812? Go to the cold regions of the North, and do you not find Tennessee soldiers, in connection with their compatriots in arms, traversing the frozen ground, and pouring out their blood freely in defense of the northern frontier? Go to your southern campaigns, in an inclement climate, beneath a burning sun, where disease and death cut them down; and were not Tennessee's sons there? Go through your Indian campaigns, and were they not there? Go to the battles of Talladega, Emuckfau, Horse-shoe, and Hickory-ground, and wherever it was necessary to make a display of bravery and gallantry were they not there? I could hardly undertake to name her gallant sons who have distinguished themselves in your military service, because they are so numerous that their names do not now occur to me. Where is your Carroll?[7] Where is your Houston, that was wounded in the battle of the Horse-shoe? I claim him as a Tennesseean.

How was it in the Mexican war? Go to Monterey; go to any point where there was fighting to be done, and were not Tennesseans there? Where was your Campbell? Where was your Anderson?[8] Were they not at Monterey, leading on their gallant followers in the thickest and the hottest of the fight? On what occasion is it that the sons of Tennessee have faltered? Was it at the battle of New Orleans? There were Jackson and Carroll, and a long list of others. On the 23d of December, 1814, they were gallantly engaged in the contest with the enemy, in the swamps and the lagoons; and on the memorable 8th of January, 1815, the sons of Tennessee, in connection with those of Kentucky and other States, distinguished themselves. When the embattled host was advancing, when the rockets were going up, indicating the commencement of battle, Tennessee's gallant leader, her own noble and glorious Jackson, who stands in this great forest of men the admiration of the American people—where was he? In the thickest and hottest of the battle his stern voice could be heard rising above the roar of artillery, urging his men on to the encounter.

Is this the State, is this the people that is to be taunted? Are taunts to be thrown out upon her volunteer forces? And now to be more direct and pointed, I ask does the Senator from Georgia intend to impute cowardice either to Haskell[9] or General Pillow, or the gallant men who were led on to that bitter, to that desperate, to that fatal charge which was made on Cerro Gordo?

[Iverson denies charging Tennesseans with cowardice but cites from General Pillow's report of the Cerro Gordo action that raw troops were unable to attack as seasoned troops attacked.]

Mr. JOHNSON, of Tennessee. I am very glad to hear the Senator make the explanation, disclaiming any intention to impute cowardice either to General Pillow, Colonel Haskell, or the men whom they led up to this masked battery. There are no troops on the face of the earth who could have stood it. Those who are familiar with the position say that the only alternative was to fall back or to be mowed down where they stood. It was the most impregnable point of the whole Mexican line. There is no man, taking the history of Tennessee and the facts connected with this particular transaction, who is disposed to be impartial, who can entertain, for a moment, the belief that there was a want of bravery on the part of the officers or men at this particular part of the battle of Cerro Gordo.

I will now say, what I was going to state in the absence of the gentleman's explanation, in which he has entered a disclaimer, that if his intention was to pass an imputation of cowardice on the people of Tennessee, or her officers or men, I must pronounce the imputation as wanton, unjust, and unfounded in truth; but I am not reduced to that alternative. In the absence of the explanation in which he has entered his disclaimer, and which I was proud to hear, I should have pronounced the imputation as false, absolutely false; and then as to the bravery of General Pillow and Colonel Haskell and others who were engaged in that contest, should have turned the Senator over to them for demonstrations that might have taken place in the future entirely satisfactory to him.

Yes, Mr. President, I am proud of my adopted State; and while here, or elsewhere if need be, I will vindicate her interest and her honor, let the consequences be what they may. I love her institutions; I am devoted to her people; and I will speak in strong language and upon high authority that "Whither thou goest, I will go; and where thou lodgest, I will lodge; thy people shall be my people, and thy God my God."[10] I will stand by her here, I will stand by her at home, as I have already said, come weal or come woe.

I now offer the Senate an apology for the remarks I have made on this subject; but I have felt, under the circumstances, that I was called upon to say this much in reference to the character, the reputation, and the military renown of the people of Tennessee.[11]

Cong. Globe, 35 Cong., 1 Sess., 757–58, 766–68.

1. The bill to increase the army (S. 79), together with Johnson's substitute offered the previous day, was under consideration.
2. John B. Floyd.
3. The homestead bill.
4. "An Act providing for the Prosecution of the existing War between the United States and the Republic of Mexico," May 13, 1846. *U. S. Statutes*, IX, 9.
5. Addison's *Cato*, Act II, sc. 1.
6. Shakespeare, *King Henry IV*, Pt. I, Act I, sc. 3.
7. William Carroll. See *Johnson Papers*, I, 57n.
8. William B. Campbell and Samuel R. Anderson were officers in the 1st Tennessee volunteer infantry. Francis B. Heitman, *Historical Register and Dictionary of the United States Army . . . 1789–1903* (2 vols., Washington, D. C., 1903), II, 43, 46.
9. William T. Haskell (1818–1859) of Murfreesboro, a state legislator

(1840–41) and Whig congressman (1847–49), had been a colonel in the Mexican War. *BDAC*, 1021.

10. Ruth 1:16.

11. Johnson's substitute bill was rejected, 26–23, on February 25. *Cong. Globe*, 35 Cong., 1 Sess., 876.

Speech on Popular Sovereignty and the Right of Instruction[1]

February 23, 1858

Mr. JOHNSON, of Tennessee. I regret, sir, that the remarks which have been made on this occasion compel me to say a few words in vindication of the State which I have the honor, in part, to represent. It is a very delicate thing to be compelled to make an issue with a colleague, on this floor or elsewhere; but I do not feel that I should be doing justice to what is commonly denominated the Democratic party of the State of Tennessee, if I were to remain silent and abstain from any reply to, or explanation of, what has been said by my colleague.

In making his remarks, my colleague has taken a course by which he intended to justify himself; and the conclusion of it was that he felt that the instructions of the Legislature of Tennessee were not binding upon him. He acknowledges no obligation of obedience to their instructions. He endeavored to prove, by a history of parties and events there, that the Legislature was not reflecting the popular sentiment. When we come to examine the history of parties in Tennessee, going no further back than 1854, we find that the Kansas-Nebraska question was then a matter of discussion throughout the State of Tennessee. I again repeat that I regret that this discussion has been imposed upon me; but, painful as it may be, I shall not shrink from a duty when it is imposed upon me. But for the remarks made by the Senator himself on the resolutions which have been presented, I should have been spared the performance of this painful duty.

The honorable gentleman undertakes to show that the Legislature of Tennessee, or the people of the State through their Legislature, have slept too long, that the Kansas-Nebraska bill was passed in 1854, and that it is strange, remarkably strange, that they should have waited until the present period of time before they instructed him. When we go back to the proceedings of the Legislature in 1854, we find that the subject was then before the Legislature prior to the passage of the bill in this House; and the Senate of Tennessee then passed the following resolution:

Resolved by the General Assembly of the State of Tennessee, That the bill now pending before Congress, called the Nebraska bill, the leading principle of which is that Congress has no right to legislate on the subject of slavery, but that the same is an institution over which the people alone, in forming their organic law, have full power and control, meets our cordial approval and is sanctioned clearly by the principles of the bills creating territorial governments for New Mexico and Utah, and we earnestly request our Senators and Representatives to give it their hearty support.[2]

This resolution passed the Senate with but only one dissenting voice: it went to the House of Representatives; and there Mr. Lamb,[3] a member of the Legislature, introduced a resolution in substance the same. Mr. McKnight,[4] a representative from the county of Rutherford, moved a resolution in lieu of Mr. Lamb's, as follows:

Resolved by the General Assembly of the State of Tennessee, That we cordially approve of the amendment proposed by the Hon. Archibald Dixon, of Kentucky, to the bill reported to the Senate of the United States by the Committee on Territories, for the organization and government of the Territories of Kansas and Nebraska. That we believe the principle involved in said amendment—that is, the extension of the principles of the compromise to those Territories—just and equitable in itself, and that it is in conformity with the Federal Constitution, with the treaty by which those Territories were acquired, and with the compromise of 1850.[5]

This was introduced by a Whig member of the House of Representatives, and voted for by every Whig in that body. In 1854, while the Kansas-Nebraska act was pending before Congress, the instructing resolution which I first read was passed in the State Senate. The resolution went to the House of Representatives, and there a substitute was offered by Mr. McKnight, who was a Whig member, and every Whig in the Legislature voted for that amendment, which expressed approval of the proposition of Mr. Dixon,[6] of Kentucky, to repeal the Missouri compromise. When we take these two resolutions together, one passed by the Senate of Tennessee in 1854, and the other voted for by every member of the Whig party, to which my honorable colleague belongs, in the House of Representatives of Tennessee, can there be any mistake about public opinion there? Can we pause, for a single moment, in reference to public opinion on that question? It seems to me not.

But my honorable colleague spoke of the contest of 1855. He will pardon me for making the allusion, but I was engaged in that contest. I was one of the candidates for Governor. I canvassed the State from the mountains of Johnson county to the Chickasaw Bluffs in Shelby county. I was in nearly every county in the State; and well do I recollect the exciting events that took place during that canvass. I had a competitor[7] who was eloquent, who is known to many members of this House, who was with me on every stump in the State. One of the leading issues in that canvass was the Kansas-Nebraska bill. I pressed my competitor upon it before every audience, and there were scarcely ever such turn outs in the State as during that canvass. It was one of the main issues between him and me. I pressed him upon it in every single speech I made in the State; and he uniformly declined to take ground. He was afraid to take ground against it or for it, as was then believed, for fear it would injure him in the canvass. He was afraid of coming in conflict with my honorable colleague and others in the State. There was no doubt, in fact, that he harmonized and agreed with the Democratic party on this point; yet he shrank from the responsibility with a view of getting many votes by taking a noncommittal course. If he had taken bold ground against the Kansas-Nebraska bill, with the other issues pending in that canvass, he would have been beaten thousands and thousands throughout the State; but from the fact of his taking a noncommittal position on the Kansas-Nebraska act, he was enabled to get many votes which he would not have received if he had taken bold ground on that question.

So far as the canvass of 1855 is concerned, can there be a doubt as to what the popular sentiment was? Can there be any mistake about it? After one of the most bitter and vindictive, and I may say malignant canvasses ever conducted in any State of this Confederacy, the Democratic party were triumphant throughout the State of Tennessee; the popular vote decided that the Democratic party was right. Then there can be no mistake in the history of the question thus far.

In November, 1856, we had another election. Prior to that election, however, the respective parties laid down a platform, and they took ground upon that platform. At Cincinnati, in June, 1856, upon the Kansas-Nebraska question, the Democratic party passed the following resolution:

Resolved, That we recognize the right of the people of all the Territories, including Kansas and Nebraska, acting through the legally and fairly expressed will of a majority of actual residents; and whenever the number of their inhabitants justifies it, to form a constitution with or without domestic slavery, and be admitted into the Union upon terms of perfect equality with the other States.[8]

This was laid down as one of the tenets in the Democratic creed. Mr. Buchanan, in his letter accepting the nomination, referred to this question, and placed himself upon that precise issue. In the fall of 1856 the canvass came on, with this as one of the main issues discussed in every district, in every county, in every town throughout the State. Mr. Buchanan's committal to the resolution adopted in 1856, in the Cincinnati convention, was well known, and it was the main issue throughout the State. We had carried the State in 1855, by a handsome majority under the circumstances; and with this the main issue in that canvass of 1856, the electors in the fields, and hundreds of other speakers throughout the State, Tennessee was carried for Mr. Buchanan, on the Kansas-Nebraska issue, by 7,500 votes. In our elections which took place last summer, following the popular impulse, and the decision made by the people of the State in the preceding year, the majority of the Democratic party was increased, and our present Governor,[9] after canvassing the State from one extreme to the other, was elected by a majority of 10,000 votes.[10]

Then can there be any sort of doubt, can there be the slightest semblance of a doubt, as to the opinion of the people of Tennessee on the Kansas-Nebraska question? Can we hesitate for one moment? Can we hesitate as to the opinion on this great question that has distracted and divided the public mind from one extreme of the country to the other? Can we believe for a moment that the people of Tennessee have not made up their minds on this subject? In addition to that, after the recent election for Governor, in which the Democratic candidate triumphed by ten thousand majority, we find both branches of the Legislature reflecting that popular sentiment, and sending it here in the shape of resolutions.

It is of this that my honorable colleague seems most to complain. The Legislature, having a majority of Democrats in both Houses, have by resolutions undertaken to reflect what they conceive to be the will of the people; and to this he objects. Can the Legislature be mistaken as to the will of the people? Have they misrepresented the people? Have they done any injustice in declaring that the will of the people of Tennessee is in favor of the Kansas-Nebraska act, and the admission of Kansas into the Union under the Lecompton constitution?

But my honorable colleague states that these resolutions contain a garbled extract of his speech, and he complains of that. Whether he intends it or not, his remarks are calculated to make the impression that there has been some portion of his speech taken from its context, and that by the separation of some material part he has been represented as meaning something that he did not mean. When we turn to the speech and examine it, we find that no injustice has been done to the honorable Senator. I have before me a pamphlet copy of his speech on the Kansas-Nebraska bill, revised and corrected by himself, I presume, and circulated all over the State of Tennessee, in which I find this declaration:

I was told, by some of my friends, that if I opposed the bill, such a course would be utterly destructive to me; that it would lead to a disruption of the Whig party in Tennessee, and furnish a plausible ground for imputations upon my motives. And those friendly warnings were given me up to the time of the final vote in the Senate. I said to some of those who thus kindly interposed their counsel frankly, that if my course, whatever it should be, was not approved by the Whigs of Tennessee, I was ready to retire from the Senate—that I would do it most cheerfully.[11]

On referring to the resolution introduced by Mr. McKnight, in the House of Representatives of Tennessee, we find that it was introduced by a Whig, voted for by Whigs, and that party as a party in the House of Representatives declared that they approved of the gist, the main point incorporated in the Kansas-Nebraska bill. That is no garbled extract. They did not recite this in the resolution. They did not go as far as they might have gone. But what they did recite will be found in the speech which has been read by the honorable gentleman, and I think the Legislature have done him no injustice in the extract they have quoted:

A noble, generous, and high-minded Senator from the South, within the last few days before the final vote was taken on the bill, appealed to me in a manner which I cannot narrate, and which affected me most deeply; the recollection of it affects and influences my feelings now, and ever will. I told that honorable Senator that there was one feature in the bill which made it impossible that I should vote for it, if I waived all other objections. I said to him, and I said to others who had made appeals to me on the subject, that, while it would afford me great pleasure to be sustained by my constituents, yet if I was not, I would resign my seat here the moment I found that my course upon this subject was not acceptable to them. As for my standing as a public man, and whatever prospects a public man of long service in the councils of the country might be supposed to have, I would resign them all with pleasure. I told that gentleman that if, upon this or any other great question affecting the interest of the South, I should find my views conflicting materially with what should appear to be the settled sentiment of that section, I should feel it my imperative duty to retire.[12]

My honorable colleague said, in another portion of his speech, that he would not be seen in the Senate another day after it was ascertained that his course was not acceptable to the people of Tennessee. Why, then, should the Legislature be complained of? The honorable gentleman says he looks upon the resolutions as an insult. An insult to recite his own language and address it to him in respectful terms, and present it to the Senate of the United States! That is no garbled extract. It is the speech as it is in its context, and reads just as it is. There is the fair, unequivocal declaration, that if his course came in conflict with the views of the people of Tennessee, he would not be seen in the Senate another day. Where is there anything wrong or insulting in reciting that? It seems to me that it is an improper construction put upon the resolutions, and great injustice has been done to those who passed them.

I have shown that the Whigs in the Legislature of the State of Tennessee, in 1854, voted to instruct their Senator to go for Mr. Dixon's amendment, or in other words, the repeal of the Missouri compromise. Now, the honorable gentleman says that repeal has produced agitation and confusion and strife throughout the country; has led to those mischievous influences that have been exerted from one end of the country to the other. As that subject has been introduced, I think we may just as well go into it understandingly and put it right. The query comes up, who is responsible for the passage, in the language of my honorable colleague, "of this most unfortunate act," as he says to-day "that was ever passed by the Congress of the United States?" If its consequences have been mischievous and dangerous, if it has caused a sectional division of parties, and if, as some infer, it may lead to a dissolution of the Union, I ask who is responsible? Where did the repeal of the Missouri compromise begin? In 1850 there was a bill passed establishing a territorial government in New Mexico. One of the provisions of that bill declared that New Mexico, "when admitted as a State, or any portion of the same, shall be received into the Union with or without slavery, as their constitution may prescribe at the time of admission." In what condition was New Mexico at that time? New Mexico ran up to the forty-second degree of north latitude. You went on to fix the southern boundary, and embraced a certain area as the Territory of New Mexico. Prior to the establishment of the territorial government in 1850, what was the condition of that Territory between 36°30′ and 42°?

In 1845, on the motion of the honorable Senator from Illinois, [Mr. DOUGLAS,] the Missouri compromise was extended to the western boundary of Texas, along the line of 36°30′.[13] The Missouri compromise was in existence to the western boundary of Texas in 1850, when we passed the bill establishing a territorial government for New Mexico. When was the Missouri compromise repealed? Without the incorporation of that provision in the bill establishing a territorial government for New Mexico, the people north of the line of 36°30′ would have been excluded from the introduction of slavery; but in the bill, you say that when they are admitted into the Union, they shall be admitted with or without slavery, as they may prescribe in their constitution. This is clearly a repeal of the Missouri compromise restriction, and enables the people, if they think proper, in the formation of their constitution, to establish slavery in that Territory. The Missouri compromise extended to the western boundary of Texas, along the line of 36°30′, and excluded slavery in the Territory between 36°30′ and 42°. The incorporation of that provision into the New Mexico bill, providing for their admission into the Union with or without slavery, removed the slavery restriction from 36°30′ up to 42°. That is the gist, that is the point, that is the great thing which was gained in 1850; that is what was understood to be the pivot on which all the compromise measures of 1850 turned. It was the removal of the slavery restriction, in fact, from

New Mexico, and the establishment of a principle[14] on which all future Territories were to come into the Union as States. We cannot misunderstand this.

Then, who voted for that repeal in 1850? And was not the Missouri compromise then repealed? It was to that extent, and the principle was established of admitting all future States into the Union on the policy of non-interference with slavery, allowing the people to have it or not, as they might prescribe in their constitution. Who voted for the repeal—that most unfortunate act? Who voted for the repeal—a measure which has resulted in bringing on the country so many mischievous consequences? Did not my honorable colleague stand up in 1850 and say "repeal it?"[15] Then we get a beginning-point. Now what extent of territory was that? Some may think there was none there; but what extent of territory is there between 36°30′ and 42° in New Mexico, from which the restriction was removed in 1850? I have taken the trouble to look at the map, and I find that there is enough of territory from which the slavery restriction was removed in 1850 by the repeal of the Missouri compromise to make eight States: in other words, there is enough to make a State larger than eight States in this Confederacy. There are 20,050 square miles in New Mexico, above the line of 36°30′, from which the slavery restriction was removed by the act of 1850, for which my colleague voted. New Hampshire has only 9,280 square miles; Vermont, 10,-212; Rhode Island, 1,306; Connecticut, 4,674. Even the State of Massachusetts has only 7,800 square miles; New Jersey, 8,320; Maryland, 11,120; Delaware, 2,120. This Territory was ten times larger than some of these sovereign States of the Confederacy. In 1850 the slavery restriction was removed from this extent of territory; for it was free territory then, and it was made discretionary with the people to have slavery or not afterwards in forming their State constitution.

Then we come to 1854. The Kansas-Nebraska territorial bill was first reported by the chairman of the Committee on Territories, the Senator from Illinois, and it came before this body. It was then sent back to the committee, and they reported it with a provision—doing what? Making no new law, but simply interpreting what was meant by the act which was intended as a repeal of the Missouri compromise, for they refer to the act of 1850, and establish that as a principle. Then they incorporate another provision in the following words, which are familiar to every member of the Senate:

It being the true intent and meaning of this act not to legislate slavery into any Territory or State, nor to exclude it therefrom, but to leave the people thereof perfectly free to form and regulate their domestic institutions in their own way, subject only to the Constitution of the United States.

Another provision of the Kansas-Nebraska act is in identically the same words as are contained in the bill establishing the territorial government of New Mexico. What are they? That when they are admitted into the Union as a State they shall be admitted with or without slavery as the people may prescribe in their constitution. The words are the same in the New Mexico bill as in the Kansas bill. All you did in 1854 was simply to interpret what you meant by the act of 1850, and that was that the people should come into the Union as a State with or without slavery as they might prescribe in their constitution; that it was not the intention of the act to legislate slavery in or out of the Territory, but to leave the people free to act upon the subject, and it is nothing more nor less than an interpretation of the act of 1850. In this body this identical proposition came up on a motion to strike out a portion of the bill. Mr. Dixon's amendment substantially was incorporated into the bill and perfected a little more by the chairman. A motion was made to strike out that clause, and upon it the yeas and nays were taken. That involved the very measure that my honorable colleague says has resulted in so much mischief, has produced agitation, and may bring about a dissolution of the Union; but he, under the solemn sanction of an oath, with all the lights before him, said "no; let it remain in the bill; repeal the Missouri compromise; that is the correct interpretation of the act of 1850; that is what I voted for then, and that is what I affirm now."[16] If this has been the most unfortunate act—if it has produced agitation, if it has produced distraction, and in the end should bring about a dissolution of the Union, my worthy colleague voted to put that very thing in the bill which has brought about all this agitation throughout this country.

But when the bill was put on its passage, after this provision was incorporated in it, it is true my honorable colleague voted against it; but the point, the gist of the thing, was voted for in 1850, and retained in the act of 1854. On a naked, clean proposition to exclude it from the bill, my honorable colleague said "no, let it remain there;" and now he tells the country that the repeal of the Missouri compromise was an unfortunate act—the most unfortunate that ever passed the Congress of the United States!

I know that, in my own State, and I have no doubt it is the case in most of the States of the Union, there is one party who deny obedience to popular sentiment, and who are always ready and willing, when they can do so plausibly and successfully, to evade the popular sentiment, especially when it comes in conflict with their peculiar notions. I know that there is a party in this country who have a great dread of popular sentiment; and hence may assume the position that the Senate of the United States is placed beyond the reach of the popular will, and should be so. I hold to no such doctrine. I hold that the popular sentiment, when fairly and fully expressed, should be obeyed by public agents in this Government. We assume here that all power is in the people, that they are sovereign; and when the sovereign expresses his will the agent is bound to obey. I know, as well as my honorable colleag[u]e, that there is nothing in the Constitution which requires or compels a Senator or Representative to obey instructions, further than what is acknowledged by the respective parties of the country. The Democratic party, as I understand, lay down the doctrine that their public servants are always bound to obey the popular will when it is fairly and fully understood and expressed. Take the expression of the Legislature of Tennessee in 1854; take the expression of the people in 1855; take the expression of the people in 1856, take their expression in 1857; and in every step we find that the popular sentiment is directed to one unerring point; and the people are in favor of the great principle laid down in the Kansas-Nebraska bill. What principle is that? That the people are the source of power; that when they come to form their organic law, it is for them to determine the nature and character of their institutions, without interference on the part of the Federal Government. The Democratic party hold that Governments are instituted for the good of the people; that a Government derives all its just powers from the consent of the governed; that government is made and organized and established for the people's convenience, and not the people for the Government; that the Government should always feel itself under the control of the popular sentiment, instead of the people feeling that they are under the control of the sentiment of the Government; that the Government should always be dependent on the people for support, instead of the people looking up to the Government to be protected and supported by it.

There are two parties in this Government, as there have been in all Governments, since men were organized into communities, and the Kansas-Nebraska bill tests the fundamental principle of the two parties in this country. The Kansas-Nebraska bill proclaims the great principle which was incorporated into the Declaration of Independence in 1776, when it issued forth from the old Congress Hall in Philadelphia, as a blaze of light and as a beacon to the patriots of the Revo[lu]tion. It asserts the great principle which was established by the successful Revolution of our fathers. What was that? That these Colonies are free and independent, and have a right to form their own constitutions, to regulate their own domestic institutions; that they are not dependent on Parliament; that they are not dependent on the Crown. Reversing the old notion of the divine right of kings; reversing the notion that an aristocracy, or a particular class of the community, has a right to govern contrary to the popular sentiment, they established the great principle that the people are sovereign; that the people are the source of power; that all government must be derived from the consent of the governed.

What, however, is the principle set up by those who opposed the Kansas-Nebraska bill? It is that sovereignty must reside somewhere; that it must have a lodgment; that it must have an abiding place; and they say this sovereignty resides in Congress. If Congress, by the passage of an organic law, can determine the nature and character of the institutions of the Territories in the formation of their State governments, do not the Territories occupy, towards the Congress of the United States, the same relation that the Colonies occupied to the Crown and Parliament of Great Britain? The Kansas-Nebraska bill proclaimed, in unmistakable language, that sovereignty resides in the people. That is the difference between the principles of the friends and opponents of that measure.

Nowadays we hear men talk about enabling acts on the part of Congress, as it would seem to develop sovereignty; and some tells us that Congress has sovereignty over the Territories vested in it as a trustee. I say this is reasserting the old doctrine which our fathers repudiated, and on account of which the separation of this Government was brought about from the mother-country. What, sir, an enabling act to authorize those who are sovereign to make a State? Opposition to the Kansas-Nebraska bill is a denial of the exercise of the great principle that man is capable of self-government and has a right to make his own government. My honorable colleague, while he voted to incorporate the mischievous and unfortunate part in the bill, then turned round and recorded his vote against it, thus denying the exercise of that great principle by the people in their original, organic character.

Some gentlemen who argue this question do not seem to be aware of the conclusions that naturally result from their premises. I have laid it down as a rule for myself that where I cannot see results clearly, where I cannot see all the collateral issues that may be brought up; where there is a principle involved, in the language of that philosopher and statesman, Mr. Jefferson, in all doubtful questions I will pursue principles. In the pursuit of correct principle, you can never reach a wrong conclusion. In this discussion there is involved a great principle—a principle of free government. We started in the revolution on the great idea that the people are sovereigns, that the people are capable of self-government, that the people have a right to originate their governments and determine the nature and character of their own institutions. When men get into Congress, however, removed from the people, their view becomes circumscribed; their vision is not quite so acute; they do not discriminate so nicely in reference to the power of the people; they become timid; they dread popular sentiment; they do not discover the true location of sovereign power. A distinguished gentleman of this body has informed us that Congress holds the sovereignty of the Territories as trustee, that it is here in a state of abeyance.[17] The idea of a man who can reason from cause to effect, who can discover the relation and dependencies of one thing on another, who understands something of that great law which observes the relation of things, talking about sovereignty being vested in the Congress of the United States, strikes me as very singular. What is this Federal Government? It is a government of derived, of limited powers, not possessing a single original power. Can we by any process of reasoning convert the derivative into the primitive? Can we convert the creature into the creator? Whence does this Government derive its power? From the States. It is the agent of the States, exercising delegated but not sovereign power. Where do the States derive their power? From the people. The people are the source, the original lodgment of power. Power is inherent in man now as in the Revolution. When a State is to be formed you must go back to this original power. Congress cannot impart it.

We are told by some that when a Territory has assumed the shape of an inchoate State, it may petition. I am noticing these objections in connection with the bold position taken by my colleague in opposition to the people making their own government, and in opposition to the Kansas-Nebraska bill. It is said that after the people of a Territory have organized themselves, not as a State, but in somewhat of an embryo condition, as a State in incipiency, an inchoate State, they may come here with a constitution in the shape of a petition, and that Congress, by a subsequent act, may cure the defects, may overlook the informalities or irregularities, and admit them.

Now, when we come to examine this proposition, it seems to me its absurdity is so striking, that those who wish to be right cannot fail to see it. What can Congress do on this subject? The Congress may—it is not compelled to do so—admit new States. The grant of power to admit a State does not confer on Congress power to make a State. The Congress may admit new States, but it has no power to make one. The idea of a community coming before Congress as petitioners, and Congress, by an act of admission overlooking irregularities and converting that community into a State, is an absurdity; it is a contradiction of terms that cannot be reconciled. Congress cannot admit anything but a State; and it must be a State in the technical and proper sense of that term before Congress can admit it; so that it is not the act of admission that makes it a State.

The simple act of admission merely makes it a member of this Union of States. It must be a State before. Congress cannot admit anything but a State; and it is not the act of admission that makes the State.

I see that some of the opponents of the Kansas-Nebraska bill, when hard pressed, when hunting for power in the Constitution in reference to legislation by Congress in regard to new States, abandon that old clause they used to rely upon that "Congress shall have power to dispose of and make all needful rules and regulations respecting the territory or other property belonging to the United States," and consequently can pass laws in reference to territorial governments. They have given that up; they have abandoned that idea; and when hard pressed, they now say that Congress, under the power to admit new States, may make a State. That is reversing all the rules of construction. It is making the incident a much greater power than the express grant. The argument is that the power to admit a State implies that you may make it; but it must be a State before you can admit it, so that there is nothing in that argument.

When we get back to the original meaning of the Constitution, properly speaking Congress has no right to legislate in the Territories, beyond making laws for the disposition of the public lands; but precedent and custom have gone on from time to time, until we have worn into it, and come to regard it as a part of the Constitution. My colleague, with others in taking their stand against the Kansas-Nebraska bill, did so against that great principle which lies at the foundation of this Government, that the people are the true source of power, that the people have the right and ought to determine the nature and character of their institutions in the formation of their constitution. Suppose an honest emigrant goes from the State of North Carolina, or Tennessee, or any of the older States, to Kansas, or any other Territory; he was a source of power in the State from which he emigrated, and the State derived all its legitimate functions from him as an item or part of the aggregation. I should like to know, when he goes into a Territory, if he does not carry sovereignty with him? Sovereignty is inherent in man. Man carries sovereignty into the Territories with him. Congress may give its assent that a certain number of individuals may erect a government upon its soil—the fee being here, the power existing on the part of the Federal Government to expel or eject intruders and trespassers. That is all the assent they need have from Congress. Man carries sovereignty with him; and sovereignty is the essential necessary to constitute a State. When the people in a Territory come to form their organic law, it is for them to combine their will in the shape of a constitution; and when they get there, I might say each is a part of one entire whole—the people's will the sovereign and soul.

Government emanates from them. They are the source of power. A government might be itinerant; yet it would be with the people though it might have no abiding place. All that is necessary is the assent of Congress, the fee being here and Congress having the power and the right to eject and expel intruders from its public domain; but that which is essential and necessary to constitute a government and make a State. Such a State as should be admitted into this Confederacy, must emanate from the people—not from enabling acts, not from laws curing defects. Sovereignty is inherent in man. He carries it with him as an item or part of the aggregate community that forms an organic law.

> What constitutes a State?
> Not high rais'd battlement or labor'd mound,
>   Thick wall or moated gate;
> Not cities proud with spires and turrets crowned;
>   Not bays and broad arm'd ports,
> Where, laughing at the storm, rich navies ride;
>   Not starr'd and spangled courts,
> Where low-brow'd baseness wafts perfume to pride.
>   No:—men, high-minded men,
> With powers as far above dull brutes endued,
>   In forest, brake, or den,
> As beasts excel cold rocks and brambles rude;
>   Men, who their duties know,
> But know their rights, and knowing dare maintain,
>   Prevent the long aim'd blow,
> And crush the tyrant, while they rend the chain:—
>   These constitute a State.[18]

Not your enabling acts, not your acts curing defects, not authority from Congress, but authority from the people; and the voice of the people, when it comes up here, even to the Senate, this august, dignified, and intelligent body, far removed from the people as it is, through their Legislatures, should be potential, and should be observed and obeyed.

Where does resistance to the Kansas-Nebraska act and to the principles laid down in it carry us? Let me address Democrats from the South on this question; we may as well come up to it like men. Some of us are a little timid and afraid when the sentiments of our hearts are known and understood, to trust the people on this great question of slavery. If we concede on the one hand that sovereignty is here, and that Congress has absolute control over the Territories, where is the South? Have not your opponents got the power both as to States and numbers of Representatives, and if you concede that sovereign power is lodged here to control, and that sovereignty emanates from the Federal Government, have you any hope? None. But according to the principle laid down in the Kansas-Nebraska act, the principle established in 1850, of leaving the people perfectly free to determine the nature and character of their own institutions, let us take our chances as to this institution of slavery as the people may determine. Here it is against us; there is some chance for us if we leave the question to the people. If they say "no slavery," exclude it from every Territory in the Union; but if they say "slavery," in the organic law which they may form, and come here for admission, let it remain; it is no business of Congress. It is for the people, and not the Congress of the United States, to decide. Where, I ask, does opposition to this principle lead? Where are those of you that deny this power and say it shall be exercised by Congress instead of the people in the formation of their constitutions, going? I find a resolution, adopted in Philadelphia, in June, 1856, which declares—

That the Constitution confers upon Congress sovereign power over the Territories of the United States for their government, and that in the exercise of this power it is both the right and the duty of Congress to prohibit in the Territories those twin relics of barbarism—polygamy and slavery.[19]

I ask our southern friends as well as our northern friends, where does this principle carry us? I know those in hot pursuit of the slavery question are willing to assume, and have assumed, because they have the power, that Congress is sovereign, and therefore has jurisdiction of the question of slavery in the Territories; but the time will come when negroes get out of the way, when a large portion of that party will abandon that principle, and deny that any such power is conferred on the Congress of the United States as sovereignty over the Territories. Every man who denies the exercise of power by the people, and claims it on the part of the Federal Government, is led naturally to the platform of the Black Republicans adopted in 1856, in the nomination of Mr. Frémont. Where else does it carry you? It carries you back to that position which was maintained and exercised by the Parliament and Crown of Great Britain in reference to the colonies. We might as well get right in reference to first principles. The time will come when a large portion of the Republican party, when negroes get out of the way, when the question of slavery is removed, and they begin to analyze the great principles of free government, will repudiate the doctrine that Congress is sovereign in the Territories. I deny it wholly. It comes in conflict with the first principles of free government. I care not whether it is exercised or claimed by the Black Republicans of the North, or any other description of party, North or South, East or West.

I have said more than I intended, Mr. President, but I have been induced to speak at this length because we have before us the subject of the admission of Kansas under the Lecompton constitution, and the doctrine of instructions, which together embrace the first principles of this Government. I did not hear my honorable colleague state what would be his position as to the last resolution. He will not understand me as improperly asking the question, what is his position in regard to it?

[Bell replies, as he did earlier, that he "did not acknowledge the instructions of the Legislature . . . as imposing . . . the obligation of obedience," though he would defer to their sentiments whenever in his opinion the legislators based their instructions on a full knowledge of the subject, and no constitutional issues were involved. Pushed by Johnson as to his intended vote on the Lecompton issue, Bell equivocates by declaring that he is not disregarding the legislature's instructions but is merely disagreeing with them. This somewhat lengthy exchange is made in an atmosphere of elaborate politeness and formality, with Johnson's observing at one point, "I am very much obliged to my colleague for the courteous and lucid manner in which he has some two or three times defined his position; and I must conclude that there is nothing wanting on his [Bell's] part, but it is obtuseness on the part of myself that I cannot comprehend clearly and distinctly all his positions."]

Mr. Johnson, of Tennessee. Without being egotistical or vain, I sometimes believe that I know when I have an issue, and when I know that I have one which will hold. Now, to save the multiplication of words, or any further explanation on this subject, I will try to make myself understood. The resolutions of the Legislature declare:

Be it resolved by the General Assembly of the State of Tennessee, That we fully concur with the Hon. John Bell as to the duty of a Senator when the voice of his constituency has decided against him on a question materially affecting their interest.

Be it further resolved, That, in our opinion, the voice of Mr. Bell's countrymen of Tennessee, in the recent elections, has declared against his course on the Kansas Nebraska bill, a question of vital importance to the South.[20]

Here are two resolutions about which there can be no mistake; but the point of my honorable colleague is, that in reference to these two resolutions there has not been sufficient time to mature public opinion. Let us look at this point in a proper spirit, and see whether we cannot come to a full understanding of the matter. In 1854, the Legislature, in both branches, expressed an opinion on the course he took at that time. He seems to think they then did not understand the question. Well, sir, in 1855, an election came off in the State, which was canvassed from one extreme to the other. This identical question was discussed, and a majority of the people, by their vote, decided against him.

[Interrupting once again, Bell asks how the legislature voted on the 1854 resolution and forces Johnson to admit that a joint resolution failed to pass.]

Mr. Johnson, of Tennessee. But a majority of both bodies expressed their opinion emphatically and unequivocally. This was the

Legislature of 1854. Then, in 1856, in the presidential election, the State was carried upon this identical issue by a majority of seven thousand votes. One of the electors, General Harris, who discussed this identical Kansas-Nebraska question as an elector for the State at large, succeeded by a majority of seven thousand five hundred, and in 1857 he was elected Governor by ten thousand majority. In 1856 the majority was seven thousand five hundred, and in 1857 it was ten thousand; but still the honorable gentleman cannot understand that the views of the people of Tennessee on this subject have been matured. I do not wish to be unkind or personal, for if I know myself I have the kindest feelings for my colleague. The Legislature have merely recited his own language, which he used in the Senate Chamber. He declared in the speech which they quote, that if any respectable portion of the people of Tennessee disagreed with him he would not be seen in the Senate a day longer. That is the substance of what he said. In the name of common sense, what process could be adopted to ascertain the popular sentiment of Tennessee on this great and important question if it has not already been ascertained? The Legislature, in 1858, has passed these resolutions. There have been four years for deliberation and consideration, and at the end of that time they come to the honorable Senator in his own language. He considers it as gratuitous, and as having originated with plotters. There may be plotters there; I know not; I know it is the voice of the people of Tennessee, and they have spoken on this subject in language not to be misunderstood; yet the honorable Senator says to that portion of it he acknowledges no obligation of obedience.

But, then, in the colloquy that has taken place here, he gives us to understand that the last resolution, instructing him to vote for the admission of Kansas into the Union, under the Lecompton constitution, he will obey; but I wish to test whether he feels the moral force and power of instructions emanating from the people, through their State Legislature. I think I understand him. He tells the Senate and the country, after repudiating the doctrine of instruction, and refusing to acknowledge obedience to it, that if left to himself he would vote against it; but as the same Legislature instructed him on this point which instructed him on the other, he will obey. If an honorable gentleman were disposed—I will not insinuate it—to play a bold game for the Presidency, I think he would want to play a bolder game than that. "I am going to vote for Lecompton; but I give you to understand the reason why I do it. It is because my Legislature has instructed me; I am against it; I am with you North; but the Legislature is at the South."

We find a very similar course to this on the passage of the Kansas-

Nebraska bill; and what is it? When the very gist of the bill, the point that is agitating the whole country, was in 1854 incorporated into the Nebraska bill, there stands his vote to retain it. "That will do in the South for my Whig friends in the Legislature who are for the amendment of Mr. Dixon, of Kentucky. I voted to put in that; and when the bill came to its passage I voted against it. Hence I can say to the South, I stood for the repeal of the Missouri compromise; I can say to the North, I resisted the passage of that act which has been so mischievous in its consequences to the country!" That looks a little like going North and a little like going South. I allude to it in no disparaging spirit—and only for the sake of illustrating my idea—but it is a good deal like the language we used to hear when I was a boy; and I suppose most of us heard it:

> He wires in and wires out,
>   Leaving the people all in doubt
> Whether the snake that made the track,
>   Is going North or coming back.[21]

We can understand that. To one set of resolutions passed by the Legislature, he acknowledges no obedience; repudiates and denies the right, the great doctrine of instruction; and in the next place says, "I will vote to let Lecompton in; yet I will tell the North I am against it"—in the one instance disregarding instructions, in the next instance acknowledging and obeying them. The reason why this great doctrine of instruction is to be disregarded is, that his own language has been couched in the resolutions and presented to him. Here I must disclaim, on the part of the members of the Legislature who passed the resolutions, any intention to insult the honorable Senator, or wound his feelings by using his own declaration, which is strong language, that if his course here should fail to meet the approbation of the people of Tennessee, he would not be seen here one day longer. I do not refer to this in the spirit of boasting or demagogism. I know that with some it is considered to be the great error of my life that I stand forth the advocate of popular sovereignty, and of the lodgment of power being with the people. If I err in this, I shall err where I have always been, and wish always to be. I have become too old, I have gone too far in the advocacy of this great doctrine of free government, and man being the source of power and capable of governing himself, now to retrace my steps. Whenever that great principle is attacked, if it comes within my sphere, or involves my duty in the slightest degree, humble and poor as my ability may be, the people shall have the benefit of this great principle to the extent of my power.

We see, in this instance, and there may be others, honorable Senators and members of Legislatures setting themselves up, and bidding defiance to popular sentiment. Would to God the voice of the people could be heard and felt more than it is throughout the land. If it could, we should be relieved from a great deal of improper, improvident, and extravagant legislation; and a large portion of it is fixed upon them in violation of their will. I know there are many who are brought up, raised in a sphere far removed from the mass of the people—men who have no confidence in the great mass. I think I know their prejudices; I think I know their points of honor; I think I know the leading principles that control the great mass of the people; and they are far higher, far more honorable, than those that actuate the leaders and rulers. I do not say it out of disparagement or disrespect; I speak of it as a fact. It is the interest of the mass of the people to do right in all governmental affairs; and they are more to be relied upon than those whose interest it is to violate great principles. This being so, they can be trusted and relied upon. Hence, as far as I am concerned, I always feel anxious to see popular sentiments, when fairly and fully expressed, obeyed and complied with.

But my honorable colleague, some how or other—I was going to say in covering a retreat on this subject, and apologizing or excusing his position—lugs in the idea of slavery, and makes the remark (I will not infer that he intends anything by it) that he has a great and deep interest in slaves, and intimates that he may be relied upon more than one who has not quite such a deep interest in slaves. I can only speak for myself, Mr. President. I will not say that his insinuation or his allusion was to me. I have not got many slaves;[22] I have got a few; but I made them by the industry of these hands. Can the Senator say as much? What I own cost me more labor and toil than some who own thousands, and got them because they were the sons of moneyed people. Upon the question of slavery, I should like to compare notes to discover who is the soundest in principle and in votes on this great question? Who is it that has cooperated with the North in the inroads and advances they have made on this institution which is so vital to the South? Who is it that has been constantly throwing out, as it were, tubs to the whale,[23] lures to the North? holding on to the South with one hand and throwing out inducements to the North with the other? Have I ever done that? Have I ever given any vote or made any speech in the Congress of the United States that indicates any such thing?

Pardon me if I am inclined to be egotistical. Though I may not own quite so many slaves as some others, though I may not have quite so deep an interest in the subject as some others when you measure interest by dollars and cents, yet I claim to understand the philosophy and the basis of the institution of slavery as well as, and I do not know that it would be very vain in me to say better than some who own their hundreds. My position is more defensible, if it required defense. I think it is the most unfortunate thing that ever befell Senators here that they become candidates for the Presidency. Whenever a Senator fixes his eyes upon the presidential mansion as the acme of his ambition, nineteen times out of twenty he falls by the way side. It has been so with the most distinguished men that have ever gone before us, who have participated in the most trying scenes and struggles of the country—bidding for northern and southern votes. I avow my sentiments here; I have avowed them in the other end of the Capitol; I have avowed them at home in reference to the great question of slavery; and I will say, as my honorable colleague has lugged it in, or thrown it in, that I think I understand the basis on which the institution of slavery rests. We may make our speeches to please the North, or please the South, as may suit us best, and subserve our interest most; but just so long as men are organized as they are, physically and mentally, one having more brains and more intellectual power than another, there will be different classes in society. Take the physical man alone, without reference to the intellectual, and force him in contact with the principles of production, and you will see that, under certain circumstances, one is enabled to produce more than another. This results from our organic structure.

Let me illustrate my meaning by an example: Here are two men, one of whom has double the physical strength of the other. Let us talk about things plainly and homely. I know this may be considered in bad taste by some; but sometimes the simplest similies best explain a subject. Take these two men, the one having twice the physical strength of the other, and put them to making rails. I know that is not a senatorial term, but it is a common thing in this country. The man of double physical strength will make twice as many rails in the course of a day as the other. Is not that a difference between men? The man of double the physical strength will increase in wealth, in anything to which you apply his labor, twice as rapidly as the other man. So it is with the exercise of his brain. This grows out of the organic structure of mankind. When you form a community out of individuals, they commence the work of production, intellectual and physical; and, as society moves on through time, we find some occupying the lower places and some occupying the higher places. I do not care whether you call it slavery or servitude; the man who has menial offices to perform is the slave or the servant, I care not whether he is white or black. Servitude or slavery grows out of the organic structure of man. All the talk which we hear in deprecation of the existence of slavery is idle, and a great portion of it mere twaddle. Slavery exists; it is an ingredient of society, growing out of man's mental and physical organization; and the only question for us to discuss is, what kind of slavery we shall have; not the existence of slavery, for it is in society; it is an element, an ingredient that you cannot get rid of so long as man's organic structure is what it is. Will you have white or black slavery? Shall it be voluntary or involuntary? These are the only questions. As to the great thing itself, about which there seems to be so much difficulty, it exists beyond the reach and the control of man, unless he can reconstruct society, and, after he has done that, reorganize the material of which society is composed.

I know where I stand on this question. I know what I could have done if I had been disposed to pander and appeal to the fanaticism that exists on this question, even in my own State. Shall it be given out here to the country that, because I do not own quite so many slaves, because my interest in the institution is not quite so deep as that of some others, my position is not as sound on the question as that of any other member of the Senate? Where has my honorable colleague been on the question of slavery? He assaults the Democratic party and charges it with being the cause of the agitation that has occurred on this subject. Who has been looking in that direction; the Democratic party or my honorable colleague? Go back to his course in reference to abolition petitions, and where does he stand?[24] Looking North. Who that lives at the South has ever gone further North than my honorable colleague on this subject? I should like to know the man who has ever bid higher? I want the North to know what a good candidate they would have had if they had been disposed to select my honorable colleague. On all questions connected with slavery, beginning with the abolition petitions, his leaning has been to the North; and in 1850, when the compromise measures were before the country, I ask my friend from Alabama to read a few paragraphs of what he then said.

Mr. CLAY[25] read the following extracts from a speech made by Mr. BELL on the 14th of September, 1850:

With regard to the constitutional power of Congress over this subject, I would say that the only doubt I have of the existence of the power either to suppress the slave trade or to abolish slavery in this District, is inspired by the respect I have for the opinions of so many distinguished and eminent men, both in and out of Congress, who hold that Congress has no such power. Reading the Constitution for myself, I believe that Congress has all the power over the subject in this District which the States have within their respective jurisdictions.   *   *   *   *   *   *
But, however great my respect may be for the opinions of others on the question of power, there are some considerations of such high account as, in my judgment, to make it desirable that, unless by common consent the project of abolition shall be wholly given up and disbanded,

the remnant of slavery existing in the District should be abolished at once; at the present moment, however, the excited state of public sentiment in the South, growing out of territorial questions, seems to forbid such a course. For myself, if the sentiment of the adjacent States and of the South generally were less inflamed, I would prefer that course to keeping it an open question. Slavery in the District of Columbia is now the only remaining ground of contention, the only remaining point of objection and assault, on the part of the anti-slavery North. I do not include the fanatics. They will be satisfied with nothing short of the extinction of slavery in the States; but all others at the North disclaim any intention, or design, or any constitutional power, to interfere with slavery anywhere but in the District of Columbia. I would be glad to see all cause of disturbance and contention in the District wholly removed; but let me say that this can never be done by the abolition of slavery, unless it be accompanied by some adequate provision for the removal or the effective control of the slaves after they shall have been emancipated. With this qualification, and in order to test the determination of the North in regard to any further and continued aggression upon southern feelings and the security of southern property, I would be content to see slavery in the District abolished to-day. In one aspect of the subject, I am not sure that it would not be a great conservative measure, both as regards the Union and the interests of the South: this District once relieved of all sources of dissension, we should be speedily enlightened upon the question whether the North would stop there, or raise new and more dangerous issues?

Mr. JOHNSON, of Tennessee. Connecting that speech, which was made on the bill before the Senate to abolish the slave trade in this District, with his uniform course on the reception of petitions on the subject of slavery, we find that my colleague makes greater concessions than I know of any other southern man ever having made. After throwing in a good many conditions and provisoes, and *ifs* and *ands*, he concludes that he would be willing to see the institution of slavery abolished in the District of Columbia to-day. First, he would concede the power to abolish slavery in the District of Columbia; and second, he was willing to see that power exercised, and then he could test how far the North would go in reference to southern institutions. You concede the abolition of slavery in the District of Columbia for the sake of making a test how far the North will go; you will concede the constitutional power for the sake of seeing how far they will go! If he concedes it here, would it not be reasonable to infer that he would favor the abolition of slavery in the Territories? Most clearly.

Who then has been compromising with the North? Who has been holding out inducements to the North to encroach upon the South? Is it the Democratic party? Have they been doing it? Have not southern men been catering for northern strength until the whole northern wing of their own party has been abolitionized? I have no unkind things to say towards the Abolitionists. I am speaking of them as a party. Who has held out inducements? Who has invited them to encroach? My honorable colleague. Then he talks about the deep interest, the great interest that men feel in slaves. Who has been throwing his banner to the North to get northern votes and northern strength, and then talks about the Democratic party producing all this agitation? The bill to abolish the slave trade in this District was one of the compromise measures of 1850. I voted for most of those compromise measures; but I want it understood now, as it was then, that I did not vote for them because they were compromise measures. Those for which I voted (for I voted for each measure by itself) I voted for because they were right in themselves; those I voted against I voted against because I believed they were wrong in themselves.[26] Compromise! Ah, yes; compromise with the North, and abolish slavery in the District of Columbia, and exercise the constitutional power in the Territories, and all for what? In the language of my honorable colleague—to see how far the North will go!

I was no compromise man then. I was for each of those measures which I sustained because I believed it to be right. I think it is time for the North and the South to abandon the idea of compromise. You have a Constitution which guaranties certain rights to all the States composing this Confederacy. Stand by the Constitution. Make no compromise by which the North will concede its rights to the South, or the South concede its rights to the North, but maintain the Constitution as it is, and thereby secure to each and all the States of this Confederacy their constitutional rights. Was there ever a compromise made in which some one was not wronged, in which some one of the parties did not lose? There is a great principle of right somewhere; let us ascertain where the right is and let the North and the South maintain it, neither making concessions.

What has been the history of compromises in this Government? In 1820 we had a compromise. The nation was agitated; dissolution was threatened before the compromise was made; and after the compromise was made, it became a fixed, permanent subject of contention and agitation and discussion, until it was repealed. You get up a great agitation, and settle it by a compromise; and then you keep up an agitation as to what the compromise means, or what is the extent of its obligation. I think it is time to quit compromising. In 1850 several measures were passed as compromise measures. They produced a great agitation. A dissolution of the Union was threatened; and in 1851 some great pacificators came forward—men who were willing to be sacrificed upon the altar of their country on another compromise.[27] That compromise has since been a continual and unceasing source of agitation. Is it not time for the North and the South to quit compromising? There is a great principle of right somewhere. Let us find out what is the right, and abide by it.

Whenever there is a difficulty between vice and virtue, vice can get up an agitation, an issue with virtue, and of course vice is always ready to compromise; but whenever virtue compromises with vice, vice obtains the ascendency. Whenever there is a contest between truth and falsehood, and it is settled by a compromise, truth gives way and falsehood triumphs. Is it not time to stop compromising? I think we have compromised enough, and I will say here in my place to-day, that I believe the agitation which has taken place, first, in getting up compromises, and then upon the compromises after they are made, has done more to make the institution of slavery permanent than all the other action of the Federal Government. The constant outside pressure, the agitation of the question in the free States, has done more to give the institution of slavery strength and solidity in the southern States than anything else that has taken place in the country. Among southern men the philosophy, the nature, the character of the institution of slavery are better understood than formerly. The southern mind, to-day, is more reconciled to the institution of slavery, and better satisfied with it, than it ever has been since the institution has existed. This is the fact, and it is not worth while to disguise it.

Then let us agree, North and South, to abide by the Constitution of the country, and have no more compromises. We have been compromised and conservatised until there is hardly any Constitution left. We first compromise and settle a question wrong, and then we must all turn conservatives and stand by the wrong that has been accomplished by the compromise. Compromise! I almost wish the term was stricken out of the English language. Conservatism! It is the argument of despots and tyrants, one that entails an existing institution in its present form, whether it be right or wrong. We must compromise, and inflict great wrong on the country; and then all are to turn conservatives, and stand by the wrong that has been inflicted on the country. So we see where this compromising spirit has carried us. We see the lure that has been thrown out by my honorable colleague and others, to induce northern men to encroach on the South. Notwithstanding his allusions to his deep interest in slavery, and all that, we see where he stands.

The Legislature of Tennessee have manifested no disrespect in these resolutions. They have exercised the privilege and power that has been exercised by most of the States of this Confederacy.

But, my honorable colleague would seem, in his concluding remarks, to have a desire to draw me off from his pursuit by throwing out a compliment, with the remark that I had made one of the most powerful arguments against the Lecompton constitution he had heard. I am at fault here again. It is my misfortune, I presume, not his fault. I did not understand myself that way, and how he can make such an application of my argument is a matter of profound astonishment to me. What was it, I said, that could convey, in the slightest degree, the idea that I was against the Lecompton constitution; or what position did I take that would demonstrate that I was against the Lecompton constitution? It would require a man with magnifying glasses, it would take a microscope that would multiply millions of times, to discover anything in the remarks I have made to-day which would seem to indicate opposition to the admission of Kansas under the Lecompton constitution. No, sir; and in continuation of what I was saying on that point—I will occupy the Senate but a few moments longer, for I have spoken three times as long as I intended—I shall vote to let Lecompton in; not because my Legislature has instructed me to do so,[28] but because I believe it is right, and the most effectual means to settle and put down the agitation that is now pervading the whole country.

What is it that I have said which would come in conflict with my going for the admission of Kansas into the Union as a State? Because I argued that power was with the people? Does that make an issue with the admission of Kansas? Not in the slightest degree. The only question for Congress to determine when Kansas applies for admission is, is it a State? Whether it has got to be a State by a regular process or by irregular process, so the end is reached that it is a State and has a republican form of government, it is entirely competent for Congress to admit her without reference to her irregularities or informalities. Many States have been admitted into the Union in this way, and the chances are that others will be.

What is there that I have said as to sovereignty abiding with man that comes in conflict with the admission of Kansas now? Go to the organic law and you find that the power is conferred on the people of Kansas to legislate. Was the passing of a law under the territorial government in conflict with the Constitution of the United States, which provided for the calling of a convention? Go back to the bill reported to the Senate during the last Congress, omitting the provision that the constitution should be submitted to the people. Who reported that bill? The honorable Senator from Illinois, chairman of the Committee on Territories.[29] He reported a bill to the Senate authorizing the adoption of a constitution without being submitted to the people. That bill when it first went to the committee had in it a clause providing that the constitution should be submitted, and it was reported back without that clause. Was it not intended by this enabling act, or whatever name you may properly call it, that the people may meet in convention, and when in convention may form a constitution, and may or may not, as circumstances may require, submit it to a popular vote at the polls, or adopt it as a constitution, without submission? That is what the committee must have intended. We find the Minnesota enabling act requiring the constitution to be submitted to the people. That bill came from the same committee. The committee must have understood the subject. They reported one bill requiring it to go to the people; the other bill came back from the committee with that clause out of it. The bill was lost in the other House, and then Kansas proceeded, through her Legislature, to pass a law authorizing the convention to be called, and the people elected delegates. I know the question is to come up here, and when it does, I will show gentlemen who make these insinuations, whether there is any conflict with my position.[30]

Whence does the convention derive its power? Some say from the Legislature, and some trace it to one source, and some to another. I say the Legislature took the regular steps, in an orderly, peaceable manner, for the election of delegates to the convention. The people elected delegates. The delegates being elected, met in convention, deriving their power from the people that elected them, and not from the Territorial Legislature. The convention was the representative of the sovereignty of the people; it was, in fact, the people assembled in their highest political attitude, acting in convention to prescribe the nature and character of their institutions. That convention being the people assembled in their highest political attitude, had the power to submit a constitution back to the people for ratification, or the power to adopt it at once, or to submit part of it. This was discretionary with them. If I had been a member of that convention, I am free to say I should have been in favor of the submission of the whole constitution to the popular vote; but the people were present in convention, and they determined this point for themselves. In that constitution they have made an express reservation of the right to alter or amend. In my judgment, without that reservation, they would have, in the language of the Declaration of Independence, the power to alter, amend, or abolish, their form of government at any time, in such manner as they may prescribe. But to make the point clear, the constitution of Kansas, in the bill of rights, expressly reserves to the people the right of alteration.

Then I should like to know how anything I have said conflicts in the slightest degree with the admission of Kansas into the Union as a State? I contend that the only question for Congress to determine is, whether a State has been formed, and whether it has a republican form of government. That being settled, Congress is either to admit it or keep it out. If Congress can assume as cause for sending the constitution back to the people, that the proceedings have been irregular and informal, Congress may assume as a cause that this provision, or that provision, or the other provision, is not right, and send it back to the people; and the result is, that Congress makes the constitution; Congress, not the people, exercises the power. When the State is admitted, the subject of her local policy belongs to her people. There may perhaps now be a majority of the actual persons in Kansas against some of the provisions of the constitution; but, if so, they have power, at any time they may think proper, to change that constitution, and change the institutions established by it. Here I desire to inquire what will be gained by keeping Kansas out of the Union? Do you thereby expedite the proceedings of the people there in reforming or altering the constitution? Can they not proceed as readily and as speedily after they are admitted into the Union to change the constitution if it is wrong, as they can proceed before its admission? The idea of Congress forcing a constitution on the people of a State is an absurdity. Congress does not force it on them at all; Congress does not make it; Congress takes the constitution as an evidence that a State has been formed, and says to her, "Walk in with your constitution, and afterwards change it in your own way, and at such time as you may select and prescribe."

What can be the objection to the admission of Kansas? This question is more clear as to a State than as to a Territory. No one has a right to interfere with the people of a State in regard to their institutions; but now the idea is suggested that when the people of a Territory have taken the necessary steps towards becoming a State, the constitution they may make is to be regarded as a petition, and that they do not become a State until Congress gives its assent. What does this imply? If it is not a State until Congress gives its assent, is not this an admission that sovereignty is here? If it cannot be a State until assent is given by Congress, Congress has the sovereignty, and must impart it to the State. I say it does not reside here; I say Congress cannot make a State; Congress cannot impart sovereignty, for it does not possess it. A State must emanate from the people; and whether they act regularly or irregularly, all that is necessary for us to do is to ascertain that a State has been formed, and has a republican constitution, and then to admit it into the Union, or keep it out.

I am as unfortunate in understanding gentlemen's notions in this respect as I was in not understanding precisely the definition which my honorable colleague gave of his position; but I think I understand myself. There is a principle in this matter; and if you will pursue principle, you will arrive at a proper conclusion.

Mr. President, I have said all that I intended to say upon the resolutions of the Legislature of Tennessee, and a great deal more on other matters. I did not intend to take the range which I have taken; but I have been led off into saying thus much without great order or method. I think I understand the principle which lies at the bottom of this controversy. I wish to act on that great principle. I desire to admit Kansas and allay agitation and strife. I want the North and the South alike to stand upon the Constitution. Let us make no compromises; but let us stand by the Constitution as it is. Though we may differ in reference to a local institution here and another there, let us act as lovers of the Constitution, in the North and in the South, neither conceding its rights, but both standing by the great principles of free government. Let us admit States into the Union, recognizing the great source of power by which States are made. Let us admit Kansas and Minnesota, whether they come hand in hand or separately, I care not. I stand ready to receive them both. I shall vote for the admission of Minnesota[31] because I believe it is right in principle, because I believe it is for the interest of the Confederacy. I shall vote for the admission of Kansas because I believe it is right to do so. As other States may be formed in the progress of this Government, I shall vote for their admission when I am satisfied that States have been formed, and that their constitutions are republican. I hope that I have succeeded in making myself understood by my competitor—

Mr. Bell. No competitor in any respect or in any way.

Mr. Johnson, of Tennessee. My colleague says he is not my competitor in any respect. When we are in the habit of particular kinds of discussions we are accustomed to use certain remarks; and by a slip of the tongue we sometimes use them inadvertently. Having had a good many competitors to contend with, the term has become familiar to me in speaking in opposition to another; and when one gets in the habit of using such terms, they are repeated sometimes unconsciously.

Mr. Bell. I excuse it.

Mr. Johnson, of Tennessee. My colleague says he is not my competitor in any respect.

Mr. Bell. I do not mean it in any offensive sense.

Mr. Johnson, of Tennessee. When the Democratic State convention met in our State the gauntlet was thrown out, and we could have had a fuller demonstration, if one was needed or could be had, of the opinion of the people of Tennessee on these questions. My honorable colleague, with all his power, with all his information, and all his tact as a debater in Congress and out of it, was invited to participate in that struggle; and if public opinion was wrong, the opportunity was tendered to him to go before the people and make public opinion right. Here, as it occurs to me, I will remark that when the convention nominating the opposition candidate for Governor sat, it was given out that he had made a speech in that convention, in which he declared that he was going forth, trident in hand; that he was going to put down everything that came in contact with him—yes, that the Hon. JOHN BELL was to be in the field, and the smaller aspirants had better get out of the way.

He was to be in the field with his armor on; and it was given out in a boasting and taunting manner that it made no odds whom he met, whether it was Richard or Saladin, whether it was Saxon or Saracen; if he came in contact with the Hon. JOHN BELL, his casque was sure to be crushed. These things were all given out; public opinion was to be set right. The gauntlet was taken up, contests were solicited and sought, and, in fact, the Democracy tried to provoke their opponent so as to get him into a fight. How many Democrats did he meet before the people of Tennessee in that canvass to set public opinion right? We have not many Richards and Saladins, or Saxons, or Saracens there. We have some few who try, and I think most of them do understand most of the questions that are discussed generally, and can take care of themselves. Who was crushed? I know some that were anxious to meet the honorable Senator on the stump in regular set-tos, if necessary, though they would have been crushed in the first tilt, but they were never afforded that opportunity. I have had competitors again and again, and many of them not inferior in ability and reputation even to the honorable Senator's own conception of himself. I will not refer to the result of the issues that took place between those competitors and myself. I leave that for the history of the country to tell. I have had competitors who were foemen worthy of my steel, and they have met their fate like honorable men, and recognized me as such. A gentleman and well-bred man will respect me, and all others I will make do it.

> Upon what meat doth this our Caesar feed,
> That he is grown so great? [32]

Is he beyond the reach of popular sentiment? In rather a taunting and sneering manner he says he is not my competitor in any sense. If you have never been my competitor, your equals have; and in the conclusion of their contest they adjusted their robes and prepared themselves for their fate; and, I repeat again, fell like honorable men. I stand here to-day not as the competitor of any Senator; but I stand here, in a senatorial sense, the compeer of any Senator. I know my rights, and I intend to try to learn the proprieties of the

Senate; and in compliance with those proprieties, my rights, and the rights of the State which I have the honor in part to represent, shall be maintained (to use terms very familiar with us) at all hazards and to the last extremity. So much for "competitors."

In the first place, we have gone over these instructions; in the next place, we have gone over the proper lodgment of sovereign power; and in the third place, we have gone over the idea thrown out about "competitors." I must say, in conclusion of these desultory remarks, that I have been forced before the Senate more and oftener than I intended to have been, under any reasonable circumstances, for the first twelve months or two years of my service here. My intention was to come here and pass through that probation which older and more experienced men and Senators more talented than myself should assign and prescribe for me. I have, however, been forced thus often before the Senate. It has been contrary to my inclination; but I believe that duty to myself, duty to my State, duty to principle, required me to do so; and acting under this impression I have ventured to trespass on the patience and time of the Senate. I did not intend to trespass on the Senate. I have come here to vote and act, and shall try to do so. I thank the Senate for the attention they have paid me.

Cong. Globe, 35 Cong., 1 Sess., 806–13.

1. Just prior to this speech, John Bell had addressed the Senate in answer to the legislature's instructions urging Tennessee's senators to support the admission of Kansas under the Lecompton Constitution. These instructions had been accompanied by a castigation of Bell for failure to support the Kansas-Nebraska bill and by a reminder of his avowed intention to resign should his course be contrary to Tennessee sentiments. In rebuttal, Bell denied that his position on the Kansas-Nebraska bill had ever been repudiated by Tennessee voters. *Tenn. Senate Journal*, 1857–58, p. 151; Joseph Parks, *John Bell of Tennessee* (Baton Rouge, 1950), 320–22; *Cong. Globe*, 35 Cong., 1 Sess., 804–6.

2. This resolution, introduced March 3, 1854, passed the next day. *Tenn. Senate Journal*, 1853–54, pp. 695, 713.

3. James B. Lamb.

4. William George McKnight (1824–1888), a Whig lawyer of Rutherford County, was president of Irving College in Warren County (1850–52) and a member of the lower house (1853–55). Moving to Texas, he served as a member of the house (1857) and as a representative to the state's secession convention. He returned to Tennessee after the war and was editor of the Nashville *Daily World* (1880–81).

5. *Tenn. House Journal*, 1853–54, pp. 1094–95.

6. Archibald Dixon (1802–1876), a Whig, served in the Kentucky legislature (1830, 1841), in the state senate (1836), as lieutenant governor (1843), and following Henry Clay's resignation was elected to the U. S. Senate (1852–55). *BDAC*, 815.

7. Meredith P. Gentry.

8. Kirk H. Porter and Donald B. Johnson, *National Party Platforms, 1840–1956* (Urbana, 1961), 25–26.

9. Isham G. Harris.

10. The majority was actually 11,371. Campbell, *Tenn. Attitudes*, 274.

11. *Cong. Globe*, 33 Cong., 1 Sess., App. 948.

12. *Ibid.*

13. Although Douglas' original resolutions (December 23, 1844) for "the reannexation of Texas" had affirmed in general terms the applicability of the Missouri Compromise to the area in question, it was the final measure (March 1, 1845), considerably amended, which incorporated the provisions of the Compromise as they related to the 36°30′ line. *Ibid.*, 28 Cong., 2 Sess., 65; *U. S. Statutes*, V, 798.

14. There is no conclusive evidence in the debates over the Utah and New Mexico measures that any significant number of congressmen conceived of those measures as repealing any or all of the Missouri Compromise. The great bulk of the area involved in New Mexico Territory lay west of the Louisiana Purchase, which alone was affected by the Compromise. Yet one student of this period has pointed out that "There is considerable evidence tending to prove that the extremists in the South took it for granted that the Missouri Compromise was repealed by the Compromise of 1850." Johnson in his statements clearly embraces this "extremist" southern view. P. Orman Ray, *The Repeal of the Missouri Compromise* (Cleveland, 1909), 93n, 191ff.

15. On February 28, 1850, Bell, in the course of offering compromise resolutions to be considered in place of Clay's recent proposals, argued that the South had made too much of the Missouri Compromise line as a defense of slavery. Like Webster, who spoke a week later, Bell saw geography and climate as factors more decisive than legislative fiat in limiting the spread of the peculiar institution. While he seems not to have specifically said "repeal it," as Johnson asserts, he did avow that "In every point of view . . . I regard the establishment of the Missouri compromise line as a thing of no value—a working of benefit of no kind," thus implying that it could be abandoned without harm to southern interests. *Cong. Globe*, 31 Cong., 1 Sess., 436–39; Parks, *John Bell*, 244–47, 257.

16. Once again, Johnson introduces a "quotation" which can only be described as a rhetorical figure. There is no evidence that Bell used these words, but there is some evidence that he reluctantly—but for a limited time only—during the debate on the Kansas-Nebraska Bill agreed to the Dixon amendment specifically repealing the Missouri Compromise. Ultimately he voted against the measure, the only southern Whig to do so. *Ibid.*, 284–301 *passim*.

17. This may possibly be a reference to Seward's famous "Higher Law" speech of March 11, 1850, in which he alluded to Congress' "stewardship" for the national domain. *Cong. Globe*, 31 Cong., 1 Sess., App. 265.

18. Sir William Jones, "An Ode in Imitation of Alcoeus." Stevenson, *Quotations*, 1917.

19. A plank in the platform of the first Republican National Convention. Porter and Johnson, *National Party Platforms*, 27.

20. *Tenn. Senate Journal*, 1857–58, p. 151.

21. Traditional political doggerel reputed to have been written by a Missouri editor commenting on Henry Clay's statements about the annexation of Texas; yet if we are to believe Johnson, it antedates the 1840's in popular usage. Charles G. Sellers, *James K. Polk, Continentalist, 1843–1846* (Princeton, 1966), 148.

22. According to census records, Johnson at this time owned four slaves—two adults and two children. 1860 Census, Tenn., Greene, 5.

23. Jonathan Swift, in the preface to *A Tale of a Tub*, refers to this practice.

24. While in Congress, Bell had revealed his "unsound" position on slavery when he opposed suspending the rules in 1836 in order to permit a vote on the series of resolutions which had included the Gag Resolution; moreover, both in 1836 and again in 1837 he refrained from voting on it. In 1838 he favored tabling the proposed Gag Resolution. Parks, *John Bell*, 171–72.

25. Clement C. Clay, Jr. (1816–1882), served in the Alabama legisla-

ture (1842, 1844, 1845), the U. S. Senate (1853–61), the Confederate Senate (1861–63), and was later a Confederate diplomatic agent. *BDAC*, 703; *DAB*, IV, 170–71.

26. Except for abolition of the slave trade in the District of Columbia, Johnson had voted in favor of the various compromise measures. *Cong. Globe*, 31 Cong., 1 Sess., 1764, 1772, 1776, 1807, 1837.

27. It appears that "1851" is a clerk's error for "1854," since Johnson seems clearly to refer to the Kansas-Nebraska bill in this statement.

28. Johnson's reasoning at this point appears somewhat ambivalent. He asserts that in voting for the Lecompton Constitution he would be acting from principle rather than instruction, but he implies that had he disagreed with the instruction, he would have ignored it and acted on principle—a course for which he had severely arraigned Bell in this very speech. It should be remembered that as recently as February 10, the Tennessee legislature had instructed Johnson and Bell to vote for the admission of Kansas under the Lecompton Constitution. *Tenn. Senate Journal*, 1857–58, pp. 150–51, 520; *Tenn. House Journal*, 1857–58, pp. 549–51.

29. Stephen A. Douglas.

30. As might be anticipated from the tenor of this speech, Johnson was among the majority in favor of admitting Kansas with the Lecompton Constitution when the final vote was taken on March 23. *Cong. Globe*, 35 Cong., 1 Sess., 1264.

31. *Ibid.*, 1516.

32. Shakespeare, *Julius Caesar*, Act I, sc. 2.

Exchange with John Bell[1]

February 24, 1858

Mr. JOHNSON, of Tennessee. By the permission of my colleague, I wish to make a single remark in this connection. The introduction my colleague seems now about making to his speech, and the manner in which he concluded his remarks yesterday evening, and what he said in the commencement of his speech then, have made the impression on my mind that he supposes it was my intention to attack his motives or his private character. I want to state to my colleague, so that we can proceed understandingly, that my intention was to have nothing to do with, and make no reference to, his motives as a man. My business with him was as a Senator, as an agent of the people, representing a State, and not with his personal integrity or his private character. I am inclined to think that when the gentleman's feelings subside, and he looks over my speech, he will find that there is nothing in it that makes any assault upon his integrity personally, or his private character. I want to comply with the courtesies of the Senate. I have said thus much for the purpose of making this discussion proceed understandingly. My business is not with him in any other character than as a Senator and an agent of the people.

We have many cases of this kind in the history of the British Parliament. I do not pretend to understand much about parliamentary law, but I have tried to make myself familiar with it to that extent which would enable me to conduct myself here with reasonable propriety. One one occasion, Colonel Barré in the British Parliament, declared the conduct of Lord North to be indecent and scandalous, to which Lord North replied with great severity, denouncing it as brutal and invidious.[2] The British Parliament called him to order, and made him observe order. It led to an explanation that Colonel Barré had the right to arraign him as a minister; that he might be arraigned as a minister, and his conduct denounced as indecent and scandalous when it was no attack on his personal integrity or his private character.

It has not been my intention to make use of anything that would impugn the motives of my colleague. It has not even been my intention to make use of language that was disrespectful even in relation to his course as a public man, and a public servant. If I can, I intend to keep myself in the right; I do not intend to be thrown in the wrong; and if, upon examination of my speech, there is anything that impugns the integrity or private character of my colleague, I disclaim it. I have not had time to read it. I did not even visit the reporters last night. I find it here on my table. I have not had time to examine it. I have felt it due to my colleague, seeing that he was laboring under some misapprehensions of this sort from his manner and one or two expressions that escaped him, to say thus much so that we could proceed understandingly hereafter.

[Bell, characterizing Johnson's remarks of the previous day as "the most offensive and insulting charge that can be made against me or any member of the Senate," defends at length his course in the Kansas–Nebraska question. Quoting from Johnson's statements of the day before, Bell insists—not inaccurately—that the main issue in the canvass of 1855 was not Kansas–Nebraska but Americanism, and he taxes his colleague with inconsistency on popular sovereignty. Referring to a speech in the campaign of 1856 (Speech at Nashville, July 15, 1856), Bell intimates that not only was there a discrepancy between the written and spoken word but also that Johnson had shifted ground even in the printed version. "Governor Johnson has a potent influence in Tennessee, even if you have not heard of him before," Bell asserts, alluding to the junior senator's relationship with the state Democracy in contrast to his relative national obscurity; "He controls his party on many questions. If their opinions . . . do not correspond with his generally, he lets them understand that they shall conform to his views."]

Mr. JOHNSON, of Tennessee. By permission of my honorable colleague, I will say that he seems to be predicating a position from which, I presume, he expects to draw some conclusions, on a conversation that he had had with some individuals, either Democrats or somebody else, in reference to a speech I made at Nashville.[3] My views as delivered at that meeting are published and printed in that speech, and I am responsible for them as there. I would prefer my colleague to make a quotation from the speech, and not a quotation from his memory of what somebody said about it. It is very easy, we all know, for persons on both sides to misrepresent a speech. Sometimes one understands it one way, and sometimes another. A sentence is quoted, and a particular expression is left out. My speech was published in that same community, and circulated by thousands. For that speech I am responsible.

Mr. BELL. I understand, then, that speech was a *retraxit* of any former opinions he had, if he had any such former opinions. I mean it was a withdrawal, a change of opinion from any he had entertained in the canvass of 1855.

Mr. JOHNSON, of Tennessee. That speech contained the opinions I expressed that night, written out and published—no withdrawal, no alteration.

[In continuing his rebuttal of Johnson's assertions made on February 23, Bell disclaims sympathy with antislavery, rationalizing his earlier stands on the reception of abolitionist petitions and on abolition of slavery in the District of Columbia; he denies that the state canvass of 1855 constituted a repudiation of his position on the Kansas–Nebraska issue, and insists that Tennesseans did not fully understand "the true bearings . . . of the Kansas–Nebraska bill until 1856;" he charges that Johnson, by quoting out of context, has garbled the meaning of Bell's 1854 speech.]

Mr. JOHNSON, of Tennessee. It is always proper to have the facts right, and after we get the facts right we can draw our own conclusions from them. By turning to the Journal of the Senate for 1854, page 162, we find that Senate bill No. 22, with the amendments submitted by Mr. Douglas, from the Committee on Territories, was under consideration; and then:

On motion by Mr. Chase, to amend the same by striking out, in section fourteen, the words "was superseded by the principles of the legislation of 1850, commonly called the compromise measures,"
It was determined in the negative—yeas 13, nays 30.
On motion by Mr. Dawson,
The yeas and nays being desired by one fifth of the Senators present.
Those who voted in the affirmative are—
Messrs. Allen, Cass, Chase, Everett, Fish, Foot, Hamlin, Seward, Smith, Stuart, Sumner, Wade, Walker.
Those who voted in the negative are—
Messrs. Adams, Atchison, Badger, Bayard, *Bell*, Benjamin, Bright, Brodhead, Butler, Clay, Dawson, Dixon, Dodge, of Iowa, Douglas, Evans, Fitzpatrick, Geyer, Hunter, Jones of Tennessee, Mallory, Mason, Norris, Pettit, Sebastian, Shields, Slidell, Thompson of Kentucky, Toucey, Weller, Williams.

Here the motion was to strike out that portion of the bill which declared that the Missouri compromise was superseded by the compromise measures of 1850; and my colleague voted against striking it out. If it had been striken out, the clause repealing the Missouri restriction would not have remained in the bill; but my colleague said no.

Mr. BELL. My colleague can correct me in facts if he pleases.

Mr. JOHNSON, of Tennessee. I state what is on the Journal. At page 188 of the Journal of the same year, we find, the same bill being under consideration, another amendment was offered:

On motion of Mr. Douglas, to amend the amendment by striking out, in section fourteen, the words "which was superseded by the principles of the legislation of 1850, commonly called the compromise measures," and inserting, "Which, being inconsistent with the principle of non-intervention by Congress with slavery in the States and Territories, as recognized by the legislation of 1850, commonly called the compromise measures, is hereby declared inoperative and void; it being the true intent and meaning of this act not to legislate slavery into any Territory or State, nor to exclude it therefrom, but to leave the people thereof perfectly free to form and regulate their domestic institutions in their own way, subject only to the Constitution of the United States."

My colleague voted against striking out that clause of the bill which repealed the Missouri compromise; and on this amendment offered by the Senator from Illinois, he recorded his vote to retain in the bill the repeal of the Missouri restriction.

[Bell, denying any inconsistency in his votes, argues that he was trying to perfect a bill which southerners could accept and which would be passed. Accusing his colleague of "wiring in and wiring out" like the windings of the snake, Bell declares that Johnson gave him "no notice whatever of the course he intended to pursue"—a course calculated "to hold me up as an unprincipled and profligate statesman."]

Mr. JOHNSON, of Tennessee. My statement was this, that it was said in the Patriot,[4] one of their papers, that the Hon. John Bell, in their convention, had indicated his willingness to enter the canvass; and that he would go into the canvass, and he would meet Saxon or Saracen, Richard or Saladin, and that whoever came in contact with him his casque would be crushed. It was never contradicted. It was taken up and republished in the newspapers, and the Democratic party sought through their papers, and in fact attempted to provoke the honorable Senator into a discussion in the canvass then going on throughout the State.

[The presiding officer, Asa Biggs, interrupts to say that he regrets very much the character of the debate. Though Johnson's remarks of the previous day were not strictly in order, Biggs had "felt too much embarrassed to interpose . . . under the circumstances"; but Bell's reply, being "of a character well calculated to excite personal feelings," is also out of order.]

Mr. JOHNSON, of Tennessee. I merely wish to say to the Senate that I have no disposition to continue a discussion out of order. I stated this morning in the explanation I made, that my intention was to confine myself strictly within the rules of the Senate, and that if I had traveled beyond them, so far as the Senate was concerned, I was prepared to make any apology that was necessary. I felt it due to place the allusions I have made to my honorable colleague on the proper ground. It was the furthest thing from my purpose or intention to violate any rule of this body or the common courtesies of private life. My colleague made an opening speech on these resolutions, and the allusions which he made to the Democratic party, and the connection I have with them, and the Legislature I have the honor to represent here, I thought made it my duty to reply as I did. In consequence of the announcement made by the Chair, I shall not persist in going on unless by the consent of the body. My colleague has made a speech of two hours, prepared and conned and got by rote, going off this morning in the most advantageous manner, as he believes, to himself and his party. All that I ask is to be heard within the rules of the Senate and the rules of common courtesy and propriety.

[With the reminder that the question is on Bell's motion to print the Tennessee resolutions, Biggs allows Johnson to proceed.]

Mr. JOHNSON, of Tennessee. I shall occupy the attention of the Senate but a short time. I will not make a long speech on this occasion, for I do not deem it necessary; because when the reply made by my honorable colleague, this morning, is reviewed, it will be found that he has not controverted a single fact that I stated yesterday; he has not answered a single argument that I presented. He has, in the run of his remarks, attempted to extenuate or apologize for some of the facts I presented, and some of the arguments I urged; but there has been no answer, and his speech furnishes the most conclusive evidence of the correctness and force of what I stated yesterday. In the little reply that I intend to make on this occasion, perhaps I had better invert the order of proceedings, and commence where my colleague concluded.

He seems, in the conclusion of his remarks, to work himself up into somewhat of an excitement. I thought the remarks I made this morning, when he commenced his speech, would place this matter upon proper grounds. I said that my business was with him as a Senator, as a public agent, that I did not attack his personal integrity or his private character as a man and a gentleman. The conduct of the agents of the people can be scrutinized, and it is parliamentary to scrutinize it with severity, without reference to their course as private citizens, or their integrity as gentlemen. I made no allusion to him as a private man; I made no assault on his personal integrity. I attacked him as a public man, and as a public agent.

But my colleague has said that his statements, just made, will stand until I take back what I have said in reference to him as a public man and as a Senator. I made the distinction here clearly this morning. I have stated facts in connection with the course of my colleague. From those facts I have drawn some conclusions and expressed some opinions. Those opinions as given, and those conclusions as drawn from the facts I stated in connection with his course as a public man, stand now just as they stood then. I have no other apology to make than the one I made this morning. That apology, I believe, and I know, according to my understanding of parliamentary law, makes the true, proper distinction, and brings what I said within the courtesies and proprieties of this Chamber.

My honorable colleague, however, has thought proper to introduce into the discussion here private conversations. I never lug in private conversations with an individual with whom I may be in contest, in addressing the people or in a deliberative body. Since the honorable gentleman and myself have met here as Senators, we have occasionally, without design, I presume, on the part of either, fallen in with each other; we have had casual conversations, and in those casual conversations it has been said that we were here as Senators representing the same State, and though we might disagree fundamentally in reference to the principles upon which the Government should be administered, yet personally we should cultivate those relations that should characterize representatives of the same State. I responded to my colleague. I told him I had no disposition to be on other than friendly terms, in a personal point of view; that it was always my pride and pleasure to cultivate relations of personal friendship with those amongst whom I lived, who differed with me politically in sentiment; and that, so far as I was concerned, in social intercourse he would find that I would not depart from these principles. I think I have not done so. It was my intention not to depart from them. In reference to the question now before the Senate, my colleague attempted to elicit from me, as I thought, a statement as to what my course would be when these resolutions were introduced. I replied to him, frankly, that I did not know; that it would depend on circumstances; and that I should be controlled by the tenor of his remarks and the circumstances that came up on their presentation. Was there any violation of that courtesy and comity which should subsist between gentlemen, in this? He presented the resolutions; he made his speech; he attacked the party with which I am associated; he spoke about their mischievous course in putting these measures upon the country; and hence I deemed it right and proper to show that he had been instrumental in doing this precise thing which he attributed to the Democratic party, and thence his inconsistency.

But in the conclusion of his remarks, he tells the Senate and the country that until I withdraw certain expressions in reference to his public course or opinions, he will not respect me. I repeat that in all that intercourse that brings man in contact with man, I will make him respect me. I will leave that right there, making a full period.

I quoted some lines that the boys sometimes repeat, and about which my colleague seems to have been thinking somewhat; for they appear to have made an impression on his mind. I did it in the sense applied to a politician. How common is it to speak of politicians being wiry? While they seem to be with one set of interests South, they are playing a game for strength at the North. It is an every-day expression. It is found in all your newspapers. Is there anything personal in that? I undertook to show from my colleague's course on the Kansas-Nebraska bill, in connection with his course in 1850, that he had voted for the repeal of the Missouri compromise; that he had voted for its confirmation and correct interpretation in 1854. I then showed that when the bill was put on its passage, he voted against it. I thus sought to show that on the main proposition in the bill his vote identified him with the South; but he voted against the whole bill, thereby identifying himself with the North; and then I drew the conclusion: might not a politician taking a course of this kind, look a little to the North and a little to the South?

If I were disposed to enlarge on this subject, (but I intend to be brief,) I could go back to 1850, and refer to the proceedings in the Senate when the compromise measures came up. We all remember the part taken by the distinguished statesman of Kentucky on that occasion. Notwithstanding it had been part of my teaching and a part of my education to oppose that distinguished man, yet I always looked upon him as a gallant, talented, and daring leader. In 1850, when I witnessed his efforts here in the Senate, when he was struggling for what many believed to be the peace and harmony of the country, when he threw himself into the breach, when he was standing here receiving assaults from all quarters, and defending those measures, where did my honorable colleague stand? Up to the time when God, in the exercise of his inscrutable Providence, called General Taylor to—

> The undiscover'd country, from whose bourn
> No traveler returns,[5]

and Mr. Fillmore was called into power, where did my colleague stand? Was it not understood that he was in opposition to the course taken by the distinguished statesman of Kentucky, whom I came here to listen to with delight and pleasure every day? The gallant bearing, the noble sentiments uttered by that great man during that contest, brought me up nearer to him and removed many of the prejudices I had contracted in early life, in reference to him. General Taylor, with all the patronage of the Administration, took his stand in favor of what was called the non-action policy, leaving the country and the questions to take care of themselves, though dissolution might come, though the country was bleeding. He was for letting in California, and leaving all the other questions unsettled. Have we forgotten that strong simile that was presented in the Senate, by Mr. Clay holding up his hand, extending his fingers, and saying that there were five bleeding wounds,[6] and that the Administration only proposed to stop one, leaving the other four bleeding profusely?

In this condition of things, and when that man was appealing to the country, where did the great compromiser—I mean my honorable colleague—stand? He stood here sustaining the Administration, and against Mr. Clay. Until General Taylor died, in July, 1850, here he stood, opposing all those measures, giving the weight of his reputation, and the benefit of his talents, in opposition to that distinguished man who has acquired some reputation as a compromiser, and deservedly so. Where did he stand while those five wounds were bleeding? After the President passed from time to eternity, and Mr. Fillmore came in, and action must ultimately be had, and his leader was gone then he came up to support the compromise. When you take my honorable colleague's course on all the measures with which he has been connected, you find a disposition rather to go along on both sides. It is his history. Take his speeches, with all his power to refine and double-distill, and they run along carrying arguments on both sides; it is hard to tell where he will locate until his vote is given.

My honorable colleague yesterday evening, in the midst of his excitement, (which was so great that he refused to allow anybody to move an adjournment,) in referring to what I had done, said that I had my documents dog-eared; and I had made a terrible onslaught. Why, sir, a portion of the things that were used by me were gotten up after the discussion commenced. In the very same remarks he told the Senate that he had studied his speech; that he had conned it; that he had memorized it; but that he had not delivered it in the Senate as he had prepared it; that he was careful in selecting the terms he used. I have no fault to find with that; but where is the force of the objection that I should have had a document ready to quote? I did have some references. I can inform my honorable colleague, if he does not know it, that I try to imitate; sometimes I am an imitator; and I remember reading the old maxim "always keep your powder dry."[7] It was a great maxim with Cromwell. I did not know but that he might come in here on the presentation of these resolutions, or on some other occasion, and make an onslaught on Democracy and the principles I advocated, and I wanted to be prepared, come when he might, to meet his assaults; for I knew they could be met and answered successfully. Dog-eared! I think if my colleague had dog-eared some of his documents a little more than he has done, he would have been more fortunate in some particulars than he has been.

The most of the speech that has been made today has been an attempt to show that public opinion in Tennessee has not come in conflict with his. He repeats what I stated yesterday, that I had canvassed the State from Johnson to Shelby, and that I made the issue upon every stump. That is true. I did make the issue with my competitor, Colonel Gentry,[8] who was a man popular in manners, of fine personal address, and as fine declamatory powers as any man in the country, and I pressed it upon him every day, with scarcely an exception. I pressed upon him to know how he was on the Kansas-Nebraska question? My honorable colleague's course was known. It was known that a portion of the delegation here had voted against him, and the inference was, that Colonel Gentry, if he had taken ground, would be with those colleagues in the other House who voted for the bill. That was the opinion; I will not say it was the fact; but it is well known that if he had taken ground against it, he would have been beaten many more thousand votes in the State than he was. He saved himself, and tried to save some of his friends, by withholding an avowal of his sentiments on the subject; but even with Know Nothingism on hand, with all their plans and the appliances that were brought to bear on that contest, the State was carried by a decisive Democratic majority. Look at the election of members of Congress, if you want to see how public opinion has been expressed. I see some of the members not far from me. The issue was made on this identical question, and every man who voted against that bill has been consigned to the tomb of the Capulets.[9] My honorable colleague is holding on to his place by the tenure of a six-years' term.

He says that the American party commenced the canvass of 1855 in the State of Tennessee with the confident hope of carrying the State by an overwhelming majority. That is very true. They did set out with the belief that they would carry it by a large majority. What they believed, and what they set out with, is one thing; but what they did, is another and a very different thing. The result turned out differently from their anticipation. They were disappointed, and we carried the State by an overwhelming majority. How is it possible, then, that my honorable colleague can be deceived in reference to public opinion there?

Then, in 1856, followed another contest, with identically the same issues involved, discussed by the electors throughout the State; and what was the result of that canvass? An increase of the popular majority for Democracy to seven thousand five hundred votes. In 1857 the same issues were before the country, and one of the electors who was on the ticket for the State at large the preceding fall was the candidate for Governor, and he carried the State by a majority of ten thousand votes. Yet my honorable colleague, in the face of all this, gets up here and tells the Senate that he does not believe there are five hundred men in the State of Tennessee who understand the question. That is very complimentary to the people of Tennessee! In 1854 the question was before the Legislature; it has since been discussed in two gubernatorial elections, in congressional and presidential elections; and yet my honorable colleague has the hardihood to give it as his opinion here that there are not five hundred men in the State who understand the question.

Now, when the Legislature are in session fresh from the people, elected at the same time with the Governor, who received ten thousand majority, they pass resolutions, after discussing the subject, in which they instruct their Senators to do certain things, in which they express their opinions, and in those resolutions they recite the language of my honorable colleague, in which he declared in substance, that if public opinion was against him in his own State he would not be seen one day longer in the Senate. Yesterday he declared that these extracts were garbled. What do we mean by a garbled extract? It is an extract taken from a paragraph, or a writing, or a speech, which taken by itself, means something different from what it would when read in connection with the whole context. Is not that so? He said it was garbled, thereby making him mean something that he did not state. Did my honorable colleague show to-day that by reading these paragraphs in connection with anything else, they meant anything but just what the Legislature has stated? He did not; and he leaves them untouched with the simple declaration that the extracts are garbled. How? They are there; every part that would make them mean just what they are; and what does he say? In his place here he declared that if the voice of the people of Tennessee was against him, he would not be seen in the Senate another day. How does he stand? Go to Mr. Etheridge's[10] district, now represented by General Atkins,[11] and to Nathaniel G. Taylor's district, now represented by the honorable Albert G. Watkins, and how does the matter stand? In Mr. Etheridge's district, where it was stated by my colleague the issue was directly made, and upon this question the election turned, and how does it stand there? Take the isolated case he presents. Mr. Etheridge, a man of talent and ability, was borne down by public opinion, and General Atkins sent here in his place. If all this evidence, when summed up and presented to my honorable colleague, is not a proof of popular sentiment, in the name of high Heaven, what will convince him as to the opinion of the people of Tennessee! If these proofs will not convince him, one rising from the dead would not convince him.

He says, though, that recently in arguing the question of squatter sovereignty, the people have begun to understand the subject. Then you see, that just in proportion as they began to understand the question, the Democratic majority increased. In the first race, we had say two thousand; in the next, seven thousand five hundred; in the next, ten thousand, carrying the Legislature by an overwhelming majority. Just as we understand it more and more, in the very same proportion the majority increases, running up, where they will continue to go until this question is settled.

He speaks of his course on the right of petition, and says I have referred to his course in reference to petitions. I did, and he does not controvert what I said. That stands just as it did before. The first speech I ever made in the Congress of the United States was on the right of petition.[12] I do not look upon that right in the light some do. I do not assume that the people of this Confederacy should approach the Congress of the United States in the humiliating and humble attitude of petitioners. It is not in accordance with the genius of the Government. It will do in monarchical and kingly Governments. It is true, we have in the Constitution a provision that the people have the right peaceably at all times to assemble and petition for redress of grievances; but we assume here that the people are sovereign. When the sovereign, the great mass of the nation, expresses its will, it is the duty of Congress to obey their master, not to receive their master in the humble character of petitioner. That is the difference between us on that point.

But by way of making a set-off and exonerating himself from the position that I had assigned him, when, going upon inference, I gave it as an opinion, that he might, if he were disposed, play a game for strength at the North and at the South; he says that I stated yesterday that I knew on this question of slavery what even I, humble as I am, could have done in my own State. I did not state it to show that I was actuated by principle. I understand the principles on which this great institution of slavery stands; and in the section of the State of Tennessee where I live, where there are but few slaves, I took the bold ground which I stated yesterday, in reference to the nature of the institution itself, and have continued to maintain it. But the gentleman here, has attempted to lug in on this occasion some things, that are understood at home, in an undercurrent. It was the reason and cause of my reply to his remarks yesterday on the subject of slavery. The idea with some is, and it is industriously cultivated—"Oh, he lives in Eastern Tennessee; there are not many slaves there; he does not own many," and hence the inference is "that he is to be doubted, and we will try to array all the slave feeling in the strong slaveholding counties against him." That is the game they play.

I wish he would bring here the speech he refers to, instead of relating it on some kind of conversation picked up from itinerants here and there, and read the speech itself, which he says was made on Broad street, in which I threw out some strange doctrines about squatter sovereignty and in reference to slavery. In that very speech my views are laid down on the question of slavery, and I argued on the principle upon which slavery stands. If I had been disposed to play the demagogue, I might have done so; but is there any evidence of it? In regard to my speech on Broad street,[13] he says that his friends, or somebody else, told him so and so, and gave him this version or that version of it. Now, if you let a man go about privateering, and picking up a little scrap of information here, a loose remnant there, and a sentence somewhere else, and put all this together and make a position of it, you can demonstrate anything on the face of the earth. I disclaim and deny that sort of process of reasoning. It is not legitimate; it is not according to the rules of the logician; it is far from the character of a statesman.

I did make a speech in Broad street, and I published it all. It was read, and I thought, when I got it down, to speak rather in the language of the schoolmaster, that there was some right good reading in it. It took pretty well; it was read, and sought for. My colleague made a speech in the market-house. He made one of those moving speeches; he commenced with a good large crowd, and he spoke it all away.[14] [Laughter] A few days afterwards he published half of it, but the other half has never been published yet. That is what he did.

But he refers to my course in the Legislature by way of relief; but in all that he has said, has he shown that I was inconsistent in anything? I do not claim to belong to the stiff-necked family that never change an opinion; but has he shown any inconsistency? Not the slightest. But take my competitor's course, before I come to the negro idea involved in this reference to my course in the Tennessee Legislature, and what is it? The lines I presented yesterday are a clear and good illustration of it. He was for the compromise awhile and then for the non-action policy; for the repeal of the Missouri compromise and against it. He voted to repeal it in 1850, and voted against its repeal in 1854. Take his course and his speech. We are getting to be sort of poetic here, and I think of two other little lines; they are from negro melodies, and they may be pardoned, as negroes seem to be the great subject in these times, like Aaron's rod,[15] swallowing up all other questions. What is his speech? Here is one point and there is another point; here is one inconsistency and there is another inconsistency, and I know nothing better to illustrate it by than the negro's melody:

> There's Point Look-out and Point Look-in,
> There's Point-no-Point, and Point Agin.[16]

That is about a good illustration and representation of his speeches here and elsewhere, and of his course, speaking on both sides, seeming to be with both parties, going along between wind and water. I am speaking of him as a politician. Has he shown my inconsistency? Not at all. What was the main thing he relied upon? That, in the Legislature, I had been somewhat strange in my proceedings or course in reference to the question of slavery. I dislike, in a discussion with an honorable colleague, to follow him along, step by step, and remove his arguments or statements piece by piece; and after having removed them all, when we march up to this last position, it is almost painful to me. I see him standing like a cripple, resting upon a crutch; and it appears to be somewhat unkind, after having driven him to his crutch, to walk up and kick the crutch from under him; and I am almost inclined, on this point, to let the cripple go.

But what is it that I did in the Legislature? He thinks it is the first Legislature I was ever in. It seems to be all conjecture, a mysterious, incomprehensible, indefinable sort of mass that is floating along through his cranium. There is nothing distinct or tangible; but it is all confusion, somehow or other—I cannot exactly tell how. You have seen that illustrated in the effort to-day to extricate himself from the votes I pinned upon him in the Journal; and even after he got the document and was reading from it, I showed that the position I assumed yesterday was true to the letter. But in the Legislature I introduced some resolutions; and what were they? Did he show that I was inconsistent? Did he show that I had backed out from them, that I had disavowed any opinion I had ever entertained? I was a member of the Legislature in 1842, after Congress had made the apportionment of the number of representatives to which the several States were entitled according to the existing ratio. Tennessee was entitled to eleven members in Congress under that ratio.

The number was settled. Three fifths of the slaves were added to the whole number of whites. In making the apportionment under the Constitution, to whom is it made? Is it made to particular districts? Is it made to particular localities, or is the apportionment made to the States? The apportionment is made to the States; and Tennessee, under the Constitution, received eleven members, getting the benefit of three fifths of the slaves. That point was settled; that was over; that was done.

In the Legislature of 1842, I introduced two resolutions.[17] There seems to be a contrariety of opinion about them; and I will state just what occurred, so that my colleague can readily remember it the next time he undertakes to tell it. What were those two resolutions? Some said elect by general ticket, some by districts, some one way, and some another. I said: "Gentlemen, if you elect by general ticket, the qualified voters will elect all the members. How do you elect members, now? Do you not elect by general ticket? And who does elect them? The voting population. Your State, in making up this electoral college, has the benefit of three fifths of the slaves, because that college consists of a number of electors equal to the whole number of Senators and Representatives. That is the basis of the college." Then in the Legislature of 1842, after my State had the benefit of the three-fifths principle in the apportionment of members of Congress, I introduced a resolution, that if the State were laid off into districts, the districts shall be composed of the several counties in the State, without regard to slave population. Another resolution was that the one hundred and twenty thousand qualified voters of the State should be divided by eleven, and that each eleventh of the qualified voters of the State should elect one Representative. I was for it then, and I am for it now. It is right, and it is correct. In the States, we hold that slaves are property. We hold, in laying our States off into senatorial and representative districts, that property is not an element of representation. These resolutions were substantially in the words of the constitution of the State, that the representatives shall be apportioned according to the number of qualified voters.

Is there any abolition in that? Coming back to the idea I have ever entertained since I formed an opinion in reference to sovereignty, what is it that constitutes a State? Is it not the qualified voters? Is it not the thinking, living, active, producing, intelligent, portion of the population who have the right of suffrage? If they constitute the State, are they not all equals? And where do you derive the right, in apportioning your representatives, to discriminate between sovereigns in the same State, and to give one a larger representation than you do another?

Does the Senator show any inconsistency in this? I was attacked upon it, and it was discussed from one extreme of the State to the other. I had to discuss the question in the strongest slaveholding county in the State of Tennessee—Fayette. I discussed it with Augustus Henry,[18] who is called the eagle orator—the lineal descendant of the forest-born Demosthenes, Patrick Henry. He, with all his eloquence and the attachment and devotion the Whig party had for him, pressed the question with all the power that was in him; and in the strongest slaveholding county in the State I increased the Democratic vote; and the State, which was understood then to be directly Whig in its complexion, was carried by the Democracy by a handsome majority.

Do none of the other southern States do what I proposed then? I think some of them do. I believe Louisiana has incorporated, to some extent, the same principle into her policy; and so have Mississippi and Alabama.[19] Where is the difference between this principle and electing the members by general ticket? Suppose you put all your members on one ticket: do not the whole number of qualified voters elect them? Suppose you divide the State into districts: does not each division elect its own member? So we see what that amounts to; but the gentleman has relied upon it as the main thing, as a set-off.

I know the Senate are tired of this dish of politics relating exclusively to the State of Tennessee, and I have no disposition to press it upon them. If my colleague, on introducing these resolutions, had made such remarks as I thought would not have called for reply, not one word would have been uttered by me.

But, Mr. President, in conclusion, how does this matter stand? I repeat again, by way of asking the question, has my honorable colleague refuted, or successfully met one single fact stated by me, or one single argument I have made? Does not my position stand untouched in the slightest degree? I feel now that I have pursued my colleague almost too far; for, from the contortions and restlessness manifested by him, I am not mistaken about the result. I know (and I say it not in the spirit of boast) when I have issues that will hold; I know when I have my victim that I can grip; I know when I have got the argument, and the fact that will sustain me, and upon which I can rely; and I have no disposition to pursue my colleague still further. I could enumerate many other inconsistencies of his; but, if I know myself, I am humane. I look, politically speaking, on my honorable colleague as now being down. He is now out of power, and he that is down can fall no lower. I am a humane man. I look upon him in his prostrate condition with all the tender sympathies of humanity. I have no disposition to pursue my colleague further. I will not mutilate the dead, nor add one additional pang to the tortures of the already-condemned.[20]

Cong. Globe, 35 Cong., 1 Sess., 830–39.

1. This discussion continues the preceding day's debate, in which Johnson had sought to make political capital of Bell's position on the Kansas-Nebraska bill and his failure to respond to the instructions of the Tennessee legislature.

2. In February, 1782, during debates on the course of the American war, Lord North, the prime minister, lost his temper while trying to convince the Commons that the ministry was working for peace. When Isaac Barré accused him of deviousness, North characterized Barré's remarks as "uncivil, brutal, and insolent," and "A long wrangle followed before North regained some of his aplomb and ended with what the opposition chose to interpret as an apology." Alan Valentine, *Lord North* (2 vols., Norman, Okla., 1967), II, 302.

3. See Speech at Nashville, July 15, 1856. *Johnson Papers,* II, 395–433.

4. Bell had attended the American party convention and made the closing speech "in response to the demands of his friends." According to the *Patriot,* which presented a paraphrased version, Bell announced that he intended to participate in the canvass: "The Democracy will find that he is prepared to give as well as receive blows; and, we will add, when one of their champions shall encounter him, that 'be he Saxon or Saracen, Richard or Saladin,' Bell will 'crash his casque.'" Nashville *Patriot,* May 4, 1857.

5. Shakespeare, *Hamlet,* Act III, sc. 1.

6. In speaking on the compromise bill May 21, 1850, Clay had asked: "Now what is the plan of the President? I will describe it by simile. . . . Here are five wounds—one, two, three, four, five—bleeding and threatening the well being, if not the existence of the body politic." Taylor's proposal for the admission of California, asserted the Kentuckian, would dress only one of these wounds. *Cong. Globe,* 31 Cong., 1 Sess., App. 615.

7. A statement attributed to Oliver Cromwell, who admonished his men: "Put your trust in God, my boys, and keep your powder dry." Stevenson, *Quotations,* 1650.

8. Johnson and Meredith P. Gentry, opposing gubernatorial candidates, had jointly canvassed the state during the summer of 1855.

9. A currently commonplace reference to death, taken from Shakespeare's *Romeo and Juliet,* Act IV, sc. 1, and used here to describe those politically dead by virtue of their stand on the Kansas-Nebraska Bill.

10. Emerson Etheridge (1819–1902), Tennessee Whig congressman (1853–57, 1859–61), had served in the state legislature (1845–47), and subsequently became clerk of the House of Representatives (1861–63) and a member of the state senate (1869–71). A Unionist associate of Johnson during the war, Etheridge bitterly opposed him during Reconstruction. *BDAC,* 866–67.

11. John D. C. Atkins (1825–1908), Henry County Democrat and graduate of East Tennessee University, had served in the Tennessee house (1849–51) and senate (1855–57), and was now in Congress (1857–59, 1873–83), having replaced the Whig Emerson Etheridge as representative from northwestern Tennessee. A lieutenant colonel in the Confederate army (1861) and a member of the Confederate Congress (1861–65), he became Indian commissioner (1885–88) under Cleveland. *Ibid.,* 494.

12. See Speech on the Gag Resolution, January 31, 1844. *Johnson Papers,* I, 133–46.

13. See Speech at Nashville, July 15, 1856. *Ibid.,* II, 395–433.

14. In reporting this speech, delivered on the night of July 21, 1857, the Nashville *Republican Banner* pictured Bell as addressing "an immense crowd" —a Bell who "seemed reanimated with the fire of youth, and nerved with the vigor of other days." Johnson's characterization of the address as "one of those moving speeches" in which Bell spoke his audience "all away" would seem to

reflect nothing more than Democratic partisanship. The speech, which dealt with the issues of distribution and alien suffrage, was published in the *Banner*'s August 1 issue. Printed in full but reduced to concise form, it appears to have been prepared for the press; thus Johnson was perhaps complaining that the later version excluded material which had appeared in the original speech. Nashville *Republican Banner*, July 23, August 1, 1857.

15. Exod. 7:12.

16. The source of this quotation has not been located.

17. These resolutions were introduced October 5, 1842. *Johnson Papers*, I, 85–86.

18. A clerk's mistake, this should be Gustavus Henry, Johnson's opponent for governor in 1853. Johnson erred, however, in referring to him as a lineal descendant of Patrick Henry.

19. Johnson's reference to Louisiana is puzzling. Though the constitutions of 1845 and 1852 were liberalizing instruments in keeping with the Jacksonian spirit, legislative apportionment had been changed in 1852 so as to rest upon the total population rather than on qualified voters. This Whig-inspired provision gave more power to planter interests, for, as its critics complained, "one Whig master with 1000 slaves possessed representation in the General Assembly equal to 1001 free, white Democrats." Perhaps Johnson was not aware of the 1852 apportioning action. Only Alabama seems to have used the white basis formula in allotting her congressional representation. In both Mississippi and Tennessee the white basis, *i.e.*, qualified voters, was the criterion for state legislative apportionment. Percy H. Howard, *Political Tendencies in Louisiana, 1812–1852* (Baton Rouge, 1957), 55; Lewy Dorman, *Party Politics in Alabama from 1850 through 1860* (Wetumpka, Ala., 1935), 96–98; Percy Rainwater, *Mississippi: Storm Center of Secession, 1856–1861* (Baton Rouge, 1938), 9.

20. After Bell briefly summarized the issues in a somewhat more conciliatory tone, the Senate agreed to print the Tennessee resolutions.

Remarks on State Representation in Congress[1]

March 25, 1858

Mr. JOHNSON, of Tennessee. I wish merely to make a single statement in relation to my vote. I doubt very much whether any of these amendments will improve the section that we have now under consideration. The Constitution of the United States provides, in the organization of the two bodies, that each House shall be judge of the election, returns, and qualifications of its own members. It also provides that each State shall be entitled to at least one Representative. The section, as I now understand it in the bill, gives to the State of Minnesota one Representative, and it then goes on to provide that she shall be entitled to as many other Representatives as her population shall justify. That settles the whole question. The House of Representatives is the arbiter. It is for that House to determine, and for them to determine it upon such evidence as will satisfy the House, what number of members she is entitled to; and, it seems to me, that section, as it now stands, will not be improved by the amendments proposed. The House of Representatives must determine the elections, returns, and qualifications of its own members. We say, in compliance with the Constitution, that Minnesota shall have one member certainly, and as many others as her population may entitle her to; and it is for the House to determine that question. It seems to me that the section is better than the amendments proposed will make it; and for that reason I shall vote to retain it in its present shape, and get it through as soon as we can.

While I am up, I desire to enter my protest against a doctrine which may be supposed to be advanced here in reference to the qualification of the voters of a State. This Government has no power under the Constitution of the United States to fix the qualification of voters in any sovereign State of this Confederacy. I want to enter my protest against the doctrine being indulged in or cultivated to any extent, that this Government has power to go inside a sovereign State, and prescribe the qualification of her voters at the ballotbox. It is for the State, and not for this Government, to do that. If the doctrine be once conceded that the Federal Government has the power to fix the qualifications of voters in a State, the idea of State sovereignty is utopian. There is no such thing as State sovereignty, if this Government can fix the qualification of voters. We have no right to inquire into it. There are simply two things to be ascertained here: first, have we evidence that a State has been formed? Second, have we evidence that it is republican in its character? These two things being ascertained, everything else is for the State that applies for admission into the Union.

[Mason of Virginia, whose amendment is on the floor, has a brief exchange with Stuart of Michigan before Johnson asks Mason's permission to pose a question.]

Mr. JOHNSON, of Tennessee. In 1843, after Congress had passed a law, or rather issued a *mandamus* to each State to lay off the State into congressional districts, many of the States refused to do so, but proceeded to elect their Representatives by general ticket, in violation of the law. They presented their credentials to the House of Representatives, and the House determined that they should take their seats,[2] that body having the power to do so under the clause of the Constitution making it the judge of the elections, returns, and qualifications of its members. That is a fact; and it does seem to me that the Senator from Virginia has made an unanswerable argument in favor of the provision of the bill as it now stands. First, the Constitution gives to each State one member, without reference to the number of her population. Next comes in this provision of the enabling act. That is the law of the case. It gives to Minnesota one Representative, and as many more as she can show herself to be entitled to under the Federal census. The law, as it now stands upon the statute-book, fixes the ratio at ninety-three thousand four hundred and twenty, and each State is entitled to one member of the House of Representatives for every ninety-three thousand four hundred and twenty Federal population that it contains. The House of Representatives is the proper tribunal to determine that question. The ratio being fixed by law, when the members present themselves it is for the House of Representatives to determine whether the State is entitled to as many as claim admission. I thank the Senator for the argument—for I think it is an unanswerable argument—in favor of the provision as it stands.[3]

Cong. Globe, 35 Cong., 1 Sess., 1326–27.

1. When Johnson rose to speak, the admission of Minnesota was under consideration; the debate and suggested amendments dealt with the number of representatives to which Minnesota should be entitled until the next decennial census and apportioning act.

2. By act of June 25, 1842, Congress had made provision for the apportioning of representatives on the basis of the sixth census; however, by the time the 28th Congress convened in November, 1843, Georgia, Mississippi, Missouri, and New Hampshire still had not complied with the law. After a running debate over a period of several days, the House seated the representatives of these states, despite an abortive minority protest designed "to vindicate the law, to purge the House, and bring it back to a condition of constitutional soundness." *U. S. Statutes*, V, 491–93; *Cong. Globe*, 28 Cong., 1 Sess., 2–3, 9–16, 23–27.

3. No action was taken at this time, but the bill admitting Minnesota as a state was passed May 11, 1858, with the provision that the new state was entitled to two representatives until the next apportioning act. *U. S. Statutes*, XI, 285.

Remarks on Amendment to Washington Police Bill[1]

April 5, 1858

Mr. JOHNSON, of Tennessee. I hope the Senate will postpone the consideration of this bill. It involves principles of no ordinary character. In connection with the remarks made by the Senator from Illinois,[2] I will say that I freely concur that there is a very bad state of morals here; that police regulations are needed, and that they ought to be rigidly enforced. I am fully aware and satisfied in my own mind that many persons around this city are not safe. But, while these matters are pressing themselves on our attention, it seems to me that there is another consideration immediately and strictly connected with it, and that is: who is responsible for them; where is the fault; where is the cause of this inefficiency of police regulations in Washington city? Is it because they want to force the expense and management of their police on Congress, and to get clear of them themselves? When we look at the statements in the morning papers of the outrages that are committed night after night, what a commentary is it upon the city of Washington, that the civil authority and the police regulations here are not sufficient even to preserve order and to prevent the recurrence of such acts as are published in the papers every morning! If we take upon ourselves the expense and trouble of forming a corps of police, establishing their officers, and fixing the number of buttons on their coats, and relieve the city authorities from it, of course they will be happy to have us do it.

But, while we admit that the police ought to be more efficient, what is the proper authority to enforce it and establish it? Suppose men are shot down here every night. They are shot down in Baltimore too; they are shot down in Cincinnati; they are shot down in New Orleans; they are shot down in New York. Pockets are picked, men are garroted or robbed in those cities as well as here; but because there is a man shot down in New York, must the Congress of the United States appoint a police regulation for them? Because a man is robbed in Baltimore must Congress take up the subject? It is legitimate and necessary that the city of Washington should establish and enforce its own police regulations as well as any other city. If we are to do it for them everything will be pushed upon Congress. I see a proposition to give up their charter; that the Senate, the House of Representatives, the President, and the Secretary of the Interior[3] are all to be engaged, and their time occupied attending to the police regulations of the city of Washington. If the act of incorporation does not give the city authorities here sufficient power, let Congress give them whatever power they need, to raise a sufficient number of policemen; give them power to pass laws to punish crimes; give them power to collect taxes to defray the expenses of police officers. They have not got enough policemen; there is great inefficiency here; something ought to be done; but I think Congress ought not to incur the expense of taking up the police regulation of the city of Washington, and devolving them on the Secretary of the Interior. I hope the bill will be postponed. I think it ought to be looked into.

[Brown of Mississippi agrees that city authorities are charged with responsibility for keeping the peace but insists that, in the absence of an adequate force, Congress must now do something to protect public and private property and persons.]

Mr. JOHNSON, of Tennessee. So far as the public property here is concerned, there is already a guard appointed by the Government to take care of and protect it; and I see no accounts of depredation committed on the public property. That now is in charge of guards appointed and paid by the Government. So far as outrages are concerned, they will increase; they are continuing to increase. The accounts of them in the city papers will be swelled every morning, until this bill is passed or rejected. I hope the bill will not be passed.

[Following a lengthy discussion, Brown proposes an appropriation of $75,000 for salaries and contingencies.]

Mr. JOHNSON, of Tennessee. I have an amendment to offer as an additional section; but I present it now, as it will affect the preceding section containing the blank proposed to be filled by the Senator from Mississippi. The amendment which I propose is:

And be it further enacted, That a tax sufficient to pay two thirds of the annual expense incurred by carrying this act into effect, shall be annually assessed upon the real and personal property and polls of the city of Washington, under the direction of the Secretary of the Interior, who is hereby authorized and directed to make such rules and regulations as shall be necessary for the collection of said taxation; and the same shall be assessed and collected in the manner now provided by law for the annual collection of the municipal taxes of said city.

There seems, sir, to be a perfect agreement on one point—that the city of Washington ought to incur the expense, and ought to be held responsible for the efficiency of its police; and then the inquiry is presented, how are we to enforce this duty upon them? how can we compel the city of Washington to establish an efficient police? It is very clear, that if we go on and establish a police force for their protection, we can lay a tax on them sufficient to defray the expense of that police.[4]

One main argument relied upon for the passage of this bill is the necessity for protecting the persons who come to the seat of Government—foreign ministers, members of Congress, and others; and on this account it is said to be the duty of the Government to aid to some extent in establishing an efficient police at this point. If this bill be passed, the result will be that the city will dispense with its police, and rely entirely upon the police established by the Federal Government. Then, it seems to me, if the Government incurs one third of the expense of this police, and thereby imparts efficiency to it, the city property, polls, and personality [*sic*] ought to pay the other two thirds of the expense. This seems to me to be fair and just. All the other cities of the Confederacy impose taxes upon the property of their citizens to defray the expenses of the city for keeping up a police force, and for other municipal purposes. Why should Washington city be exempt from the burden of taxation for such purposes? If you adopt this amendment requiring them to pay two thirds of the expense, we can enforce it; and when it is understood that the city of Washington must incur a large proportion of the expense incurred by the creation of this police force, they will be more efficient, and they will come up to the aid of the Government in the execution of the law.

Several gentlemen have suggested to me to change the proportion which my amendment proposes to lay upon the city and the Government, and to divide the expense half and half. To accommodate gentlemen, I will change it so as to provide that half of the expenses shall be borne by the city of Washington. Then it will be necessary to change the preceding section, so as to read:

That the sum of money necessary to carry this act into effect, not to exceed one half of the annual expense to be incurred in consequence of raising said auxiliary guard, be, and the same hereby is, appropriated.

And then will come in the additional section which I have proposed, and this, it seems to me, will place the matter on a fair basis.

While I am up, I cannot help stating that I concur in the principle enunciated by the Senator from Kentucky[5] in regard to the creation of offices, and conferring additional appointments on the President of the United States. So far as the Secretary of the Interior and the President of the United States are concerned, there is no one here or elsewhere that has more confidence in them than I have. I have no sort of doubt that they would execute the law faithfully and efficiently; but there is a principle involved in this matter. I am opposed to increasing executive patronage in any shape, if it can be avoided; but here is a provision not only for one hundred officers, but for two hundred, at the discretion of the Executive. The Senator from Texas[6] seemed to have his fears alarmed, and I agree with him on that point, at the idea of bringing any portion of the standing Army to suppress riots or put down mobs. What is the force you now propose to raise? I suppose it should be more properly called an auxiliary to your standing Army. It is to have captains and lieutenants appointed by the Executive, responsible directly to him for the manner in which they discharge their duty. I am for building up no pretorian bands here, either under a Democratic or any other Administration, I care not by what name they may be called. I am for building up no military guard here, to be placed at the discretion of the Executive. Everything must have a beginning: you begin now with two hundred at discretion, one hundred absolutely. Where will it end?

It is said that party has got into the appointment of the members of the present auxiliary guard,[7] and that party influences have rendered them inefficient. In the name of common sense, and all that is sacred and right, will you ever have an Administration here that is not a party Administration? Will you remove the difficulty that is complained of? Will not appointments always be fashioned by party? Unquestionably; and the very difficulty which you desire to avoid will be fastened upon the country by this bill. If it is to pass, let us impose half the expense, at least, upon the city of Washington, and thereby make it feel its responsibility. If the citizens here have to pay taxes for this force, they will impart more efficiency to the execution of the law.

I had hoped that this bill would be postponed, but I am prepared to act upon it now. I have no unkind feelings towards the citizens of Washington, more than I have towards the citizens of any other city; but I must say that there is a disposition manifested here which must be apparent to all, even the most unobservant, to put the entire expenses of this District on the Government of the United States. An avenue cannot be graded unless Congress does it;[8] streets cannot be lighted up unless Congress pays for doing it. There is a continual pressure on Congress to appropriate public money to sustain the District of Columbia. I have had some tables prepared which, at an appropriate time, when the proper measure shall come before the Senate, I will present, showing the amount that has been expended in this District for Government purposes.[9] Over twelve million dollars drawn from the people of the different States have been poured out at this capital, expended here. The city of New York, or St. Louis, or Baltimore, or Philadelphia, or New Orleans, or Cincinnati, instead of asking you to give them donations out of the Treasury, would pay your Treasury a bonus if you would locate the seat of Government there. Is it no benefit to a community to have large sums of money, which are drawn from the great mass of the people, poured out in its midst? Do we not know that the expenditure of large sums of money at this point is beneficial to this portion of the community at the expense of other portions of the community?

The Senator from Texas has alluded to the fact that the Government has property here which is exempt from taxation; but how did the Government get that property? A donation was made to the Government on condition that Congress would locate the seat of Government here. Parties said, we will give you so many lots, and thereby realize immense fortunes by bringing the seat of Government here; and now they turn round and talk about taxing the property of the United States, when it was speculation on their part that got the seat of Government here. In what State or county in the Union do you ever hear of the capitol of a State or the court-house of a county being taxed, or any other public buildings? Every locality that gets a location of this kind considers that the benefits conferred by the location go far beyond any advantage that would result from the little tax that would be imposed upon its property. Which is worth most to the citizens of Washington, the large amounts expended by you on public buildings and the large appropriations made for local improvements here, or the little money which they would derive from the privilege of taxing the Government property? Twelve million dollars, as I remarked before, have been expended here, drawn from the States; and of this sum, over six million dollars have been given for the local improvements of this District, for the especial and particular benefit of the people here.

I am merely looking into this matter on principle. I have no objection to the citizens of Washington getting all they can; but while they are guarding their interests, it is our duty, as representatives of the States and of the people, to guard their interests, and see that their money is not taken from them and improperly expended in local improvements in this particular locality. What authority have we to make appropriations in the District of Columbia more than we have in any other section of the country? I know that it is argued by some that we have exclusive legislative powers here. That may be true; but because we have the power of exclusive legislation, does that prove that we have unlimited legislation? I know there is no other authority that can legislate for the District of Columbia but Congress. But because Congress has exclusive legislation, it does not follow that your power of legislation is unlimited, and that you can appropriate money here under the Constitution of the United States that you cannot appropriate elsewhere. You have no more power to take money from the Federal Treasury and appropriate it to local improvements in the District of Columbia, than you have to appropriate it for such improvements in St. Louis—not a single scintilla of power more. The argument on this point results from confounding a power of exclusive legislation with unlimited legislation. We have no power to appropriate money in the District of Columbia for local purposes more than we have elsewhere.

It is said that the people of the District have no representation in Congress. Well, suppose they had a Delegate in Congress, the same as the Territories have: what would it be worth to them? Give them a Delegate; I am for giving them one; I would rather they had one; it would stop clamor, so far as that goes. They are now better represented, and get larger appropriations, than they would if they had a Delegate in the Congress of the United States.

I am willing to confer all the power that Congress possesses upon the municipal authorities here; to give them power to lay and collect taxes; to give them power, if they have it not already, to establish that description of police which will be efficient to sustain the reputation and character of the populations, so that the laws may be enforced, and persons be protected in life, liberty, and property.

I make these remarks out of no unkind feeling of prejudice to the people of the District, but I have seen how these appropriations have gone on from year to year. I have seen the feeling and the disposition that are manifested here. The public mind, in this locality, seems to be exercised in one particular channel: that is not in mechanics; it is not in agriculture; it is not in commerce; it is not in the improvement of the soil; it is not in producing and bringing the products of labor here and selling them in one of the best markets in the world; but the whole mind here is occupied and employed in devising ways and means by which we can get into the people's Treasury, divide it among ourselves, at our own discretion, for our particular benefit. If you refuse any appropriation they may ask or demand, it is very common to say: Why, you have exclusive legislation; the District belongs to Congress! I do not countenance any such idea. They are freemen. I assume that they are capable of self-government. I assume that they have got resources, as much so as the people have in other portions of the country, to pay their own taxes to enforce their own laws; and if they have not, what a commentary it is upon the population crowded around the Federal Government of the United States, that there is not enough moral power, that there is not enough capacity here to govern themselves, but they must call upon Congress to govern them—must go out to the States and bring in somebody here to govern them! Is it not a commentary on the Federal Government, on the population surrounding Congress and coming in contact with the *élite*, not only of the United States, but of all parts of the civilized world?

I shall vote against the bill, whether the amendment is adopted or not; but it seems to me that it is nothing but fair and just that one half or two thirds of the expense incurred in raising and sustaining this auxiliary, little standing army, whose appointment and control are under the Federal head, shall be incurred by this population. I am in hopes the Senate will adopt the amendment. After that, I am in hopes they will reject the bill.

The PRESIDING OFFICER, (Mr. BIGGS.) [10] Did the Chair understand the Senator from Tennessee as moving his proposition as an amendment to the amendment of the Senator from Mississippi? [11]

Mr. JOHNSON, of Tennessee. I wanted to suggest the amendment, and show the necessity of making the eighth section correspond with my amendment when added as an additional section.

[After Brown withdraws his previous motion pending disposal of Johnson's amendment, James S. Green of Missouri speaks in support of the bill. Brown then objects to Johnson's proposal to divide the cost of the auxiliary guard equally between city and federal government.]

Mr. JOHNSON, of Tennessee. I desire the Senator from Mississippi to understand my idea in offering the amendment. I am not influenced by the amount of money involved at all, but by imposing a part of this additional expense on the population here, you will give efficiency and effect to the bill, and you will impart more efficiency by reaching them through the taxing power, than in any other way.

[Brown remarks that the city is already bearing more than its proportionate share of expense in assuming the cost of the day police force. Following other objections by Houston, Johnson's amendment is read and rejected. Further discussion of the bill leads to Johnson's return to the debate.]

Mr. JOHNSON, of Tennessee. Then I move to recommit the bill to the Committee on the District of Columbia, with instructions to report a bill retroceding the District of Columbia to the State of Maryland, reserving the public buildings and public grounds, &c., and that said committee report at the earliest moment practicable.

I have but one object in view. It is, if I can, to impart some efficiency to the police of this city. There is great complaint here that we do not make sufficient appropriations, that Congress has exclusive power of legislation over the District; that we are their guardians, and that we should appropriate whatever they ask. They have no Representative in Congress. Now, if we retrocede this District to the State of Maryland, they can be represented in her Legislature, and have the power to tax themselves, and appropriate the money raised by taxation for all the necessary purposes of the community. The people of that portion of the District ceded by Virginia were anxious to go back to her jurisdiction, and they were retroceded to Virginia by a law passed some years since, and we have never heard any complaints from them since. Pass this District back to Maryland, reserving the public buildings and grounds, and we get clear of all this trouble.[12] I venture to predict now, that if you send this bill back to the committee, with these instructions, with a probability that the Senate will pass a bill of that kind, in four weeks from to-day, there will be an efficient, energetic police in this city, and you will not hear of another murder, or robbery, or assassination during the session of Congress.[13]

Cong. Globe, 35 Cong., 1 Sess., 1462, 1467–71.

1. The Senate had under discussion S. 232, designed "to establish an auxiliary police for the protection of public and private property in the City of Washington," and reported four days previously by Albert G. Brown, chairman of the committee on the District of Columbia, of which Johnson was a member. The idea of an auxiliary force was scarcely new, inasmuch as such a guard, employed strictly for night duty and paid for by federal funds, had been maintained since 1842. Yet the inefficiency of both this guard and the Washington police had been rendered the more glaring by occurrences during the previous summer, when it had been necessary for the President to call out the marines to quell an election riot, and by continuing disorder described as "a lasting reproach upon this Federal city." In its accompanying remarks—which pictured a situation strongly reminiscent of the present day—the committee observed: "Riot and bloodshed are of daily occurrence. Innocent and unoffending persons are shot, stabbed, and otherwise shamefully maltreated,

and not unfrequently the offender is not even arrested." Since local officials were unable to maintain order, "the obligation is thus thrown upon Congress." Moreover, the committee pointed out, Baltimore, a more compact city of 260,000, boasted a police force of 400; whereas Washington, with a larger geographic area and a population of 60,000, had only 57 policemen. Constance M. Green, *Washington: Village and Capital, 1800–1878* (2 vols., Princeton, 1962), I, 215–17; Wilhelmus B. Bryan, *History of the National Capital* (2 vols., Washington, D. C., 1916), II, 273–74, 428–30; *Cong. Globe*, 35 Cong., 1 Sess., 1460.

2. Stephen A. Douglas, who a few minutes earlier had waived consideration of the Minnesota bill to discuss the police bill, asserted that "life is not safe in this city at present. . . . Something must be done in order to restore the government of law." *Ibid.*, 1461–62.

3. Jacob Thompson of Mississippi was secretary of the interior (1857–61).

4. Johnson's colleagues objected strenuously to his suggestion that the people of Washington be taxed for the auxiliary police. The bill under discussion was never passed; not until August, 1861, did Congress provide for a metropolitan police system. *U. S. Statutes*, XII, 320–26.

5. John J. Crittenden.

6. Sam Houston.

7. The auxiliary guard, although paid by Congress, was under the supervision and control of the mayor and city council. The new bill would place responsibility for appointment of its major officers with the President and the secretary of the interior. Those who favored this arrangement argued that under the existing system the most active political partisans were appointed and the police chief was changed with each new city administration. Bryan, *Washington*, II, 430; *Cong. Globe*, 35 Cong., 1 Sess., 1465.

8. For Johnson's opinions on the issue of paving Washington streets, see *Johnson Papers*, I, 441–43.

9. See Speech on School Funds for District of Columbia, May 15, 1858.

10. Asa Biggs (1811–1878), Democratic senator from North Carolina, had served in the state senate (1844, 1854) and Congress (1845–47). Elected to the U. S. Senate in 1855, he resigned in 1858 to serve as a district judge and later as a Confederate judge (1861–65). *BDAC*, 553; *DAB*, II, 262.

11. Albert G. Brown (1813–1880), born in South Carolina, moved to Mississippi, where he studied law and at the age of twenty was admitted to the bar. A member of the Mississippi house (1835–39), circuit court judge (1842–43), governor (1844–48), congressman (1847–53) and senator (1854–61), he later withdrew from the Senate and served in the Confederate army and Congress (1862–65). *BDAC*, 605–6; *DAB*, III, 100–101.

12. The Virginia portion of the District of Columbia had been retroceded in 1846. In 1850, while he was in the House, Johnson had made a similar proposal of retrocession to Maryland. *Johnson Papers*, I, 529, 539.

13. Hale of New Hampshire successfully moved to strike the phrase relating to public buildings and grounds. After Johnson's motion to recommit was rejected, the final bill passed, 34–9, with Johnson voting nay.

Remarks on Voting Qualifications[1]

April 6–7, 1858

Mr. JOHNSON, of Tennessee. Before the Senator from Maryland[2] closes, in order to understand rightly a very important question involved in his argument, I wish to propound an inquiry to him. The

Congress of the United States, having the power, under the Constitution, pass a uniform rule of naturalization. Do I understand him as contending that when a man has been made a citizen of the United States by the naturalization law of Congress, any State into which he may emigrate is compelled to allow him to vote?

[Kennedy reiterates, "If a man has been naturalized in conformity with the law of Congress, he clearly has the right then to vote in any State"—the franchise to be exercised "In conformity always with the municipal laws of the State."]

Mr. JOHNSON, of Tennessee. Has not each State the power to fix the qualifications of its voters? Has it not a right to impose any prohibition it pleases? Some of the States of this Confederacy have required a man to be a property-holder before he could exercise the elective franchise. If a State cannot permit a man to vote until he is a citizen, is not the converse of the proposition equally true—that, when he is a citizen, no State can prevent him from voting? I say this, not for the purpose of confusing the Senator, or interfering with his argument, but in order to be instructed and informed on this subject; for I desire to understand his views. If it be true that, when an individual is once made a citizen of the United States, any State into which he goes is compelled to allow him to vote, what will be the consequence of such a principle? A free negro coming here from Africa could be naturalized, if your laws allowed it. As the naturalization laws now stand, none but white persons can be naturalized; but suppose those laws should be amended by striking out the word "white:" could you not make every negro who should emigrate from Africa to the United States a citizen? and, on being made a citizen, would not the southern States, according to this doctrine, be compelled to let him vote? What would become of southern rights and interests under such a system? Free negro emigrants from Africa, being naturalized, might flood the southern States.

[Kennedy reaffirms his belief that U. S. citizenship is the paramount qualification for voting, and for this reason he will "vote against the admission of Minnesota with her present constitution."]

Mr. JOHNSON, of Tennessee. It is not my object to consume the time of the Senate, or to delay the passage of the bill; but there is one point which has been suggested on which I have pretty well made up my mind, and if I am in error, I desire to be corrected. It is due in sincerity to the Senator from Maryland, that I should enter my protest against the doctrine enunciated by him on this occasion. I have no doubt about his sincerity and the correctness of his purpose in the great objects which he wishes to accomplish; but I think if the doctrine he has announced be sanctioned and obtain an ascendency in this Government, the very idea of State sovereignty will be at an end, and the existence of the State governments will be set at naught. He has read from pretty high authority as to the qualifications of voters in the States, but there is still higher authority, in my opinion, and it is made by the Constitution, the highest authority in this Government, the Supreme Court of the United States, which has decided this question.[3] My mind is influenced quite as much by that able, that distinguished, that discreet, that profound court, as by the opinion of Mr. Calhoun,[4] though he was a very great man. The Supreme Court has decided that the qualification of a voter in a sovereign State is a matter to be fixed by the State, and not to be controlled by the Congress of the United States in the passage of naturalization laws. If it be true that the Congress of the United States can fix the qualification of a voter in a State, where is your State sovereignty? Where does sovereignty begin according to the theory of this Government? Is it not with the people? If Congress can fix the qualifications of a voter in a State, does it not control the sovereignty of the State? If you can fix the qualifications to entitle a man to go to the ballot-box, from which law and order emanate, from which the State itself emanates, is not that taking control of the sovereignty of the State into the hands of the Congress of the United States. If it be true that Congress can fix the qualification of a voter in a State, of course the moment Congress, by making a man a citizen, qualifies him for a voter, it follows, his qualification being fixed, that every State is bound, under the Constitution, to let him vote. To this I cannot consent.

The courts have decided that free negroes are not citizens. Now suppose you should pass a naturalization law authorizing free negroes to become citizens of the United States: is there any one here in the Senate of the United States who will assert, or who, having asserted, will sustain on sound reason the proposition that a State could not pass a law excluding a free negro from the ballot-box, because you had made him a citizen of the United States? Suppose a State requires a voter to be a property holder; has it not a right to do so? I mention this merely to test the principle. I am myself in favor of the fullest extension of the elective franchise on correct principles. But take your own State, Mr. President, (Mr. BIGGS[5] in the chair,) my native State: how long has it been since you have seen citizens coming up to the ballot-box voting at one poll for Senators by property holders, and all the citizens voting at another poll for the Commons?[6] They were all citizens of the United States; and if this doctrine be true, North Carolina had no right, either by her constitution or her laws, to fix any qualification preventing a citizen from voting.

The Senator from Maryland wants to purify the ballot-box; a

great object with him is to restrain foreigners, to require them to live in the country a certain number of years, and be familiar with the nature and character and genius of the Government, before becoming citizens. With a view of purifying the ballot-box he is now striking at foreigners; but suppose the opposite idea to that which he entertains should obtain the ascendency; what then? If we can require them to stay here five years or twenty years before being naturalized, can we not allow them to be naturalized in twenty-five minutes or in twenty-five days? Can we tell where a desire for ascendency may carry a dominant party? It may be the policy of a party in the ascendency at one time to make men who come to the United States citizens in twenty-five days after they get here. It may be the policy of a party in power at some time to encourage the immigration of natives of Africa, to naturalize them, to make them citizens, and push them into the States, to take charge of the ballot-box throughout the South. I protest against this doctrine. It is a blow at State sovereignty; it is the assertion of a power that will sweep away forever every vestige of State sovereignty. It ought to be repudiated and put down. I care not whether it comes in the name of Know Nothingism, or Americanism, or under any other plausible name, in which you think proper to present it. It is a heresy, in my honest opinion, to talk about the Federal Government fixing the qualification of a voter in a State.

When you turn to the Constitution of the United States, do you not find that it proceeds on the very idea that it is a matter within the control of the States to fix the qualifications of voters? The Constitution provides that members of the House of Representatives shall be elected by those persons in each State who are qualified by the laws of the State to vote for members of the most numerous branch of its Legislature; thus conceding the exclusive power of the States to fix the qualification of voters within their limits. We make the issue upon Minnesota or any other State; but do we not see where the doctrine would carry us? In all doubtful questions, in the language of the illustrious Jefferson, let us pursue principles. There is a great principle of State sovereignty involved in this matter; let us pursue it. What becomes, let me ask, of the resolutions of the Old Dominion of 1798 and 1799, when she took bold ground against the alien law? Was it not because that was an assertion of power on the part of the Federal Government to go inside of a State and interfere with rights of citizenship secured under State authority? One of the main points covered by those resolutions was a denial of the exercise of the power to go inside of a sovereign State and interfere with the privileges conferred upon its citizens by the States. How can we object to admitting a State into the Union because she chooses to allow foreigners who have lived there six or twelve months to vote? If I were in a body fixing the qualification of voters, I would allow none to vote in the United States, in the States or Territories, until they were citizens; but that is a question to be fixed by each State for itself. My own State, in her constitution, requires all her voters to be citizens of the United States; but we claim the power to fix that matter, and deny it to the Federal Government. We say that Congress has no such right; that it belongs to us, not to you.

I do not want to consume time or protract this discussion, or keep Minnesota out of the Union; but I repeat again, if this doctrine be carried out, and the Opposition in principle get the ascendency, they might, if they were so disposed—I do not impute it to them—change the naturalization laws from five years to one month, or six months, or as soon as the process could be gone through with, and allow every free negro in the United States, every emigrant from Africa, to be made a citizen; and he being a citizen, the States would be compelled to admit him to the ballot-box, and allow him to exercise the elective franchise. I do not want such a doctrine sent to the country seemingly tacitly indorsed by the Senate of the United States. I merely got up to enter my protest against it.

So far as the view of the distinguished Senator from South Carolina, Mr. Calhoun, on this matter is concerned, I think it was one of those peculiar crotchets into which his mind fell. He was a great man, a distinguished man, a great logician, and could lay down propositions, and argue from premises to conclusions. His conclusions were clear; and from his premises no one could resist his conclusions. But I think this was one of the peculiarities of his mind. The courts have said differently. The opinion of the Supreme Court is entitled to at least as much respect, I think, as that of Mr. Calhoun. That is made the supreme arbiter by the Constitution of the United States, and it has decided and settled the question that the State is the competent authority to fix the qualification of a voter.

[Here the Senate adjourns; the remainder of Johnson's remarks are made on the following day, April 7, during a continuing discussion of the admission of Minnesota.]

Mr. JOHNSON, of Tennessee. I do not wish to occupy the time of the Senate, but I desire to say a few words on this subject. The Constitution of the United States provides that Congress shall have power "to establish an uniform rule of naturalization." Of course, when a foreigner comes into the United States, he cannot, until he is naturalized and becomes a citizen of the United States, claim protection of this Government. After being naturalized and becoming a citizen of the United States, it makes no odds where he goes, no matter in what part of the globe he may be, he can claim the protection of the United States. We have a striking illustration of this in the Koszta case,[7] where Mr. Marcy gave an able opinion that when an individual had only declared his intention to become a citizen, the United States took cognizance of the case and gave him protection. We see, then, the importance of becoming a citizen of the United States, though the individual may not have the privileges conferred upon a voter in any one of the several States. But it seems to me we run the thing into confusion; it may be that I am confused myself. The Constitution further provides:

The citizens of each State—
not of the United States

shall be entitled to all privileges and immunities of citizens in the several States.

Now what has that to do with conferring upon a foreigner the privilege of going into any one of the sovereign States and voting, unless he possesses the qualifications required by that State? I think one meaning of that clause of the Constitution is this: it was intended to prevent the States from discriminating between each other. For instance, take North Carolina; it was intended that she should not pass a law conferring privileges upon the citizens of New York or Pennsylvania that the citizens of the other States would not be entitled to exercise upon coming into her borders. It is to prevent one State from discriminating between citizens of the different States; in fact, it has no reference to a citizen of the United States. It was to prevent Tennessee, for instance, from passing a law saying that Massachusetts should not bring her articles into Tennessee, and that Pennsylvania might bring hers. This provision of the Constitution covers the case, and provides that the citizens of Pennsylvania and Massachusetts coming into Tennessee shall exercise privileges alike. It does not say that they shall come into Tennessee and exercise all the privileges of citizens of Tennessee in reference to voting, or anything else, but that they shall be treated alike in Tennessee if they go there.

The distinction is clear. There are many reasons why a man may be a citizen of the United States, and strong reasons, too, and yet not be admitted as a qualified voter of a State. This provision of the Constitution is often quoted inaccurately, and still more inaccurately understood. It is said that citizens going out of their own State are entitled to all the privileges and immunities of citizens of the State to which they go. That is not the Constitution, but it is that citizens of the different States shall all exercise the same privileges in a State into which they may go. So we see that does not cover the idea now presented, that if a citizen of the United States emigrates into one of the States, he is entitled to go to the polls and vote, unless he has the qualifications prescribed by that State.

There were scarcely any two States composing the Confederacy at the formation of the Government, in which the qualification of voters was exactly alike. This shows that it was not intended to bring about uniformity. Some States required a man to be a freeholder; others required a certain amount of personal property. The States even differed as to the age at which persons should be qualified to vote. But if the doctrine now advanced be true, when a man is once a citizen of the United States, every State into which he goes is compelled to let him vote, regardless of every other qualification which its laws may prescribe.

Upon this point I will say that I am not in favor of admitting everybody to vote without the requisite qualifications; but I desire it to be distinctly understood, at the same time, that I do not sanction the doctrines which are promulgated by a party that recently sprang up in the country and has as rapidly passed away.[8] I disclaim all power on the part of the Congress of the United States to interfere with the right of a State to fix the qualification of its voters; and although I might object to the qualification fixed in the constitution of Minnesota, that is a matter to be determined, not by Congress, but by the people of Minnesota. Repeating the language of my honorable friend from Texas,[9] but making a somewhat different application of it, I hold the doctrine that power resides with the people, and it is for the people of each State to fix the qualifications of voters in that State, and not for the Congress of the United States.

A great deal has been said in reference to foreigners. Some of them are unfortunate; some of them drift upon our shores, and they are not exactly the description of population we should like; but it seems to me that we might find a better, a higher, a loftier theme on which to let forth our eloquence than to abuse and appeal to the prejudices of the country about a few foreigners who may come to our land. The whole idea seems to be that if they were kept here twenty-one years in a degraded condition, degraded from the fact of being excluded from the exercise of the privileges of a citizen, you would thereby improve them and qualify them much better to go to the ballot-box. Mr. President, when you examine the true philosophy of that question, the converse of that proposition is precisely true. Your naturalization law, as it now stands, cannot be much bettered. It requires a man to file his declaration of intention three years before he becomes a citizen, and he must remain in the United States five years; he must furnish proof before one of the courts of the country that he is a man of good moral character; that he is attached to your institutions, and to your republican form of government. He must give such evidence of his attachment to the country, and of his moral character, as the court will be satisfied with, and upon being satisfied with it, the court administers to him the proper oaths, and he becomes a citizen of the United States. If a man, coming into this country, cannot show to your courts that he is of good moral character, that he is devoted to the institutions of your country, if he is a bad man, if he is an immoral man, if he is in favor of despotism and opposed to the institutions of this country, is not five years long enough to keep him here? Oh! no, say this new party, let us keep him twenty-one years. I say that as soon as a man can furnish evidence that he is qualified to become a citizen, both as to his character and his devotion to our free institutions, the better for him, and the better for the country to let him be a citizen. Five years is too long to keep a bad man; twenty-one years is a great deal worse. Instead of keeping them here twenty-one years before they should become citizens of the United States, the true doctrine would be to compel them, in five years, to show that they were men of good moral character, devoted to the institutions of the country, and fit to become citizens, and if they are not, they should leave the country. I would make them citizens at the earliest moment. There is really nothing in the question of time when squared by sound philosophy. One man may remain here one hundred years and never be qualified, while another, from a knowledge of your institutions, from an admiration of your government, from his good moral character, may be qualified for citizenship the instant he places his foot upon our shores. I think the five years fixed by the naturalization laws now is a reasonable time, and gives an opportunity for the ascertainment of the fact upon which the issuing of his naturalization papers depends. That fact is that he is of good moral character and devoted to the institutions of the country, and when the court is satisfied of that fact with reference to any man, I say let him become a citizen; and if he cannot show that he is fit to become a citizen at the end of five years, that is long enough to keep him here.

I shall vote for the admission of Minnesota into the Union, because I believe her constitution, taking its leading features, is republican in its character; and considering that all power resides with the people, it is for them in their own States, and not for Congress, to fix the qualification of their voters.

Cong. Globe, 35 Cong., 1 Sess., 1491–92, 1513–14.

1. The bill for the admission of Minnesota was before the Senate committee of the whole when Anthony Kennedy of Maryland announced his intention of voting against the bill. He opposed the state constitution not only because it

conferred suffrage upon every male twenty-one and over, regardless of race, but also because it granted suffrage to aliens who had declared their intention to become citizens.

2. Anthony Kennedy (1810–1892), Maryland-born Whig, had moved to Charles Town, Virginia (now West Virginia), and served in the Virginia House of Delegates and as a Jefferson County magistrate. Returning to Baltimore in 1851, he was a member of the Maryland legislature (1856) when elected to the Senate as a Unionist (1857–63). *BDAC*, 1155.

3. In the Dred Scott decision, handed down one year earlier, on March 6, 1857, the Court had ruled that suffrage rights are granted by the states and are not subject to citizenship, which is defined by the Constitution. Henry S. Commager, ed., *Documents of American History* (New York, 1963), 343.

4. Kennedy had quoted Calhoun to the effect that a state did not have the right either to confer citizenship upon aliens or to permit them to vote.

5. Asa Biggs of North Carolina.

6. The amendment establishing white manhood suffrage for all elections in North Carolina was less than a year old, having been added to the constitution in 1857. Previously, on the basis of the state Constitution of 1776 and subsequent amendments in 1835, the vote for state senators was confined to white freeholders of at least fifty acres; whereas all freemen, twenty-one and older, elected the lower house. Hugh T. Lefler, *History of North Carolina* (2 vols., New York, 1956), I, 227, 347, 380.

7. The Hungarian patriot Martin Koszta, who had fled to Turkey and then to the United States after the abortive revolution of 1848, was seized by agents of the Austrian government when he returned to Turkey on a business trip. Since he had taken out first citizenship papers and had obtained a safe-conduct pass from the American consulate, American officials demanded his release. An American naval vessel, arriving quite opportunely in Smyrna harbor, challenged the Austrian warship which held Koszta and obtained his release. An exchange of notes ensued between Chevalier Hülsemann, the Austrian *chargé* in Washington, and Secretary of State Marcy, who emphasized Koszta's residence in the United States, together with his filed declaration of intention to become a citizen, as bases for diplomatic protection. Koszta was released and returned to the United States. Samuel F. Bemis, ed., *American Secretaries of State and Their Diplomacy* (17 vols. to date, New York, 1927–67), VI, 268–73.

8. A reference to the American party.

9. Sam Houston had declared his intention of supporting the bill but qualified his support with a protest against the provision allowing aliens to vote.

Warranty Receipt to Jonathan Meredith[1]

Baltimore   April 7th 1858.

I have this day received from Jonathan Meredith, a pair of carriage horses, valued at Two hundred & fifty dollars, and one sum of Four hundred & fifty dollars in money, which I acknowledge to be full payment for a pair of Brown Horses sold to him, about 16 hands high, which I hereby warrant to be, not more than seven years old, sound in wind, limb, & every respect, and free from vice. And I hereby engage and agree, that should either of said horses prove unsound

APRIL 1858   108

or vicious, upon further trial, within six months from this date, I will on notice thereof pay to said Meredith the sum of Seven hundred dollars.[2]

Millers Hotell   Balt   A Johnson
Witness.
Gilmor Meredith[3]

RS, DLC-William Taylor Papers.
    1. Jonathan Meredith (c1785–1872), a native of Philadelphia, was a Baltimore attorney. J. Thomas Scharf, *The Chronicles of Baltimore* (Baltimore, 1874), 687–88.
    2. The endorsement reads, "A. Johnson Receipt with Warranty for a pair of Brown Horses/ 450 and old horses valued at $250/ April 7, 1858."
    3. Gilmor Meredith, a Baltimore commission merchant, shared a business address with Jonathan Meredith at 28 N. Calvert Street. *Woods' Baltimore Directory* (1858), 288.

From Josiah R. Hubbard[1]

Centreville Tennessee Apl 13th/58

Hon Andrew Johnson
My dear Sir.
    You will please to excuse this. I write you to obtain from the Department of the Interior Some information relative to the transfer made by the holder of a land warrant obtained for services rendered &c. The Warrant for 80 acres issued to Ann Vanlandingham minor child of Graves Thurmond decd. 8th November 1856. The assignment is in the following words— "For Value received I Ann Vanlandingham *minor child of Graves Thurmond decd*, to whom the within Warrant No 43.719 &c" Signed Ann Vanlandingham & FA Vanlandingham. You will readyily See that the assignment is void as She was a minor at the time of the assignment which is made 12th day of January 1857[.] The purchaser Jesse K. McMinn Esq of my County requests me to have the error So amended that he can either locate it or Sell it—. Will you be so kind as to make Such enquiries of the Commissioners of Pensions, as you may think proper to effect the object. Could not this Warrant No 43,719 be returned & cancelled & a duplicate issued? If so what will be required if any thing?
    I cannot close this Sir without a Congratulation to you for the very able & patriot efforts you have already made in behalf of our State & your constituents & as one of them I return you my acknowledgments of my high appreciation of both your effort in reply to Mr Iverson of Georgia & the Hon John Bell.[2] I have no right to impune the motives of any man but Sir I trust you will permit me to say can not picture for my life any honesty of purpose upon the part of the

Hon gentleman (Mr Bell) in the position he has assumed upon the Kansas question when he must know & feel of what vital importance Such a position must be to his Southern bretheren in times like these—. I often think of how much room he must give those who are the enemies of our institution to Complain of those of you who are Standing by your homes; Yea what Comfort he gives them;— & Sir it must afford a pretext to those who are *a little tender* on these exciting questions to leave us & join the "wild Shriekers" in their furious and blind opposition to truth & priciple.

I have as yet only met one full report of your Speech in this County which is in the possession of our Representative in the State Legislature[3] who furnished me with it to read & return it being to highly prized by him to part with as he also did your Speech in reply to the Georgia Senator— I can only Say of your last Sir that you have done far more for Some gentlemen than they would have done for you under like circumstances—. You will permit me to say to you that I have never feared to see you clothed with a *little power* as some of the pretended democracy are. I have ever felt that your highest pride would ever be to protect the rights of those whose interests you held in your own hands for I have met with you in times & at places & under circumstances that convinced me Sir of your powers & your moral worth—. You may perhaps have overlooked me among the multiplicity of your acquaintances but Sir I never think of victories without my mind calls to recollection the day of your triumph over Col Gentry at Perryville[4] which Caused the Counties of Perry & Decatur to wheel into ranks & Stand up in favor of truth in opposition to the follies of Know Nothingism—

You will I trust excuse thise. I had no idea of what an amount I had written but believing that you will accept it as it is offered—,

With my best wishes for your health & Success I remain very truly your obedient Servant and friend   Josiah R. Hubbard
                               Centreville   Hickman Co.   Tennessee
To   Hon Andrew Johnson
Washington City   D. C.

Should you feel disposed to circulate any documents in this Section I will at any time furnish you a list of names such as will appreciate your kindness &C[.][5]

ALS, DLC-JP2.

1. Josiah R. Hubbard, lawyer and native of Centerville, was a captain and later major in the Confederate service. W. Jerome Spence and David L. Spence, *A History of Hickman County, Tennessee* (Nashville, 1900), 73, 76.

2. Two months earlier, in the face of Iverson's strictures on "raw militia," Johnson had defended the fortitude of Tennessee volunteers; soon after, he had chided Bell for his indifference to the repeal of the Missouri Compromise.

See Exchanges Concerning Volunteer Forces, February 18, 1858; Speech on Popular Sovereignty and the Right of Instruction, February 23, 1858; and Exchange with John Bell, February 24, 1858. Alfred S. Iverson (1798–1873), Georgia-born Democratic congressman (1847–49) and judge of the state superior court (1849–53), was a radical states' righter, who served in the U. S. Senate from 1855 to January 28, 1861, when he withdrew to return to the practice of law in Columbus. *BDAC*, 1108; *DAB*, IX, 517–18.

3. John J. Williams (1829–1891), a native of Hickman County who moved to Franklin County, served in the legislature (1857–61, 1887–91), in the Confederate army, and as a circuit court judge (1877).

4. In the course of the 1855 canvass, Johnson and Gentry had spoken in Perryville on Friday, May 18. No report of this encounter, so significant in Hubbard's opinion, has been found. Murry B. Measamer, A History of the Know-Nothing Party in Tennessee (M. A. thesis, University of Tennessee, 1931), App. G.; Nashville *True Whig*, May 2, 1855.

5. Johnson's endorsement, dated Washington City, April 20, 1858, reads: "Hon Geo. C. Whiting   Sir   Will you be kind enough to furnish this gentleman with the information he desires and in so doing you will much oblige— Andrew Johnson   P. S.   please return this letter"

Remarks on Senate Calendar[1]

May 3, 1858

Mr. JOHNSON, of Tennessee. I really hope that we shall proceed with business in its regular order. The fishing bounties bill has been standing on the Calendar for a considerable length of time, and I understand the gentleman[2] who reported the bill is prepared to go on with its consideration at present. If that is to be waived, and these motions are to intervene, here comes forward another Senator,[3] who proposes to admit Oregon into the Union as a State. When we see that, is it not better for us to proceed in regular order and take up the business as it stands on the Calendar, and dispose of it?

I can see no great necessity for pressing the Indian appropriation bill at this time. All the appropriation bills will go through. They have a sufficient weight and influence always to take them through. I do not think the country will suffer a great deal by the delay of a few days in the passage of the appropriation bills; I do not think the Treasury will suffer by that; and I doubt very much whether we shall hear any complaints throughout the country in consequence of appropriation bills not being pressed through in such hot haste. I am willing to give gentlemen all the aid I can to take up bills in their proper order.

I wish to say, in this connection, that if I understand the Calendar aright, the homestead bill comes up next after the fishing bounties bill. The friends of that measure have been here quietly, patiently— or perhaps I ought to say impatiently—waiting for a considerable length of time to have that bill reached. I am in hopes that business will go on in its proper order, and that that bill will be taken up and disposed of. The gentleman from Alabama is now ready, and I understand the Senator from Maine[4] is ready, to go into the consideration of the first special order. Why not take it up, and let the Indian appropriation come up in its proper place, and be disposed of in due time? Let us take up first the fishing bounty bill, which is the first special order; next, the homestead bill, and dispose of it as we reach it. I am inclined to think that the great mass of the American people are as deeply interested in the proper distribution of the public lands, particularly when the proposition is to provide homes for the people, as in the appropriation of thousands and millions out of the Treasury, especially when the condition of the Treasury is, to say the least, not at all plethoric. I hope we shall go on with business in its proper order. I do not intend to be importunate; I do not intend to be obtrusive on the Senate; but I have the homestead bill, as I know many others have, deeply at heart, and I intend to press it earnestly on the consideration of the Senate from this time until it shall be disposed of.

[R. M. T. Hunter of Virginia and Asa Biggs of North Carolina urge consideration of the appropriation bills rather than the special orders, with Biggs observing: "If there is a measure before Congress that proposes to squander the public treasure in a worse direction than any other it seems to me it is the favorite *projet* of the Senator from Tennessee."]

Mr. JOHNSON, of Tennessee. In answer to the gentleman from North Carolina I will say, as I said on a former occasion, that I shall be able to prove that instead of the homestead bill diminishing the receipts into the Treasury, it will have precisely the contrary effect. I pledge him that, if he will unite with the friends of the bill to bring it up, and give it a fair consideration, and pass it, instead of its depleting the Treasury or squandering the public revenue, I shall demonstrate as clearly and conclusively as figures can demonstrate anything, that it will increase the public revenue, and, in fact, it ought to be pressed on the country, at this time, as a revenue measure, calculated, when carried into full and successful operation, to increase the resources of the nation.

Now, sir, I understand the remark of the President in his message, which has been alluded to, to be general; that he will not sign any bill which is passed at a later period than two days prior to the close of the session. Then, it is just as important to have the homestead bill passed two days before the close of the session as any other bill, if we expect the signature of the President, and of that I have no doubt. When the bill is passed, I have no doubt it will be signed by the President.[5] I feel satisfied that the public mind is made up in reference to the measure. I think the sense of the community is very decided upon the subject. If the Senate will now reflect the sense of the country, as it has been reflected on various occasions by the other House, this bill will soon become the law of the land. I hope we shall proceed with business in regular order. But if we are not to do so, I shall press this measure earnestly on the consideration of the Senate from day to day, till the close of the session.

[Biggs trusts that this measure "will be strangled in the two Houses of Congress." If, however, it passes both Houses, he entertains "a confident hope" that the President will veto the measure.]

Mr. JOHNSON, of Tennessee. I am in hopes that the President of the United States will have a fair opportunity to approve or disapprove of this measure; and I trust we shall not resort to strategy and legislative maneuver to strangle an important bill like this, which is to provide homes for the people. Sir, the measure has already been strangled twice. It passed the popular branch of Congress twice by overwhelming majorities, and it was sent to this body, and here it was strangled. Let us have fair, full, explicit action of the Senate upon the measure, and if the two Houses pass it, let the President have an unincumbered [sic] opportunity to approve or disapprove it. I predict now that the President of the United States, when the bill is presented him, will not withhold his signature.

[Several others, including Charles E. Stuart of Michigan and John Slidell of Louisiana, continue to discuss the calendar.]

Mr. JOHNSON, of Tennessee. In connection with what the Senator from Louisiana has said, I desire to remark that if it is understood that we shall afterwards take up the Calendar and go on with business in regular order, I am willing to consent, if it is more agreeable to the Senate, to take up the Indian bill first, as it is only to occupy a short time.

Cong. Globe, 35 Cong., 1 Sess., 1912–13.

1. The bill to repeal fishing bounties had priority on the calendar when proposals to consider the Indian appropriation bill and the admission of Oregon were put forward.

2. Clement C. Clay, Jr., of Alabama.

3. Stephen A. Douglas.

4. Hannibal Hamlin (1809–1891) had served in the Maine legislature (1836–40, 1847), in the House (1843–47), and in the Senate (1848–57). Elected governor in 1856, he served less than two months before resigning to return to the Senate (1857–61). An Anti-slavery Democrat, he became a Republican, served as Lincoln's first vice president (1861–65), returned to the Senate (1869–81), and was appointed minister to Spain (1881–82). BDAC, 998; DAB, VIII, 196–98.

5. Johnson was doomed to disappointment. Although his homestead bill did not get through the 35th Congress, an amended version which passed in June, 1860, was vetoed by Buchanan.

Remarks on Taking up Homestead Bill[1]

May 13, 1858

Mr. JOHNSON, of Tennessee. To accommodate the Senator from Georgia, and for the purpose of preventing hair-splitting questions of order under the Manual, I will simply make a motion to postpone this appropriation bill; and I will give, as a reason for making the motion to postpone, that my purpose is to take up the homestead bill. I presume that is legitimate and in order.

It is not often, Mr. President, that I obtrude myself upon this body; but when prompted to do so by principles of right, I shall do it with that respect and courtesy to which the Senate is entitled. This homestead proposition has been standing on your Calendar, as a special order, since the 19th of January, now nearly four months. I have been waiting patiently, with a view to have the business of the Senate taken up in its proper order, and disposed of, so that we might reach it. It is a proposition that has been determined in the public mind. It is a proposition that the country has decided should have been passed by the Congress of the United States long ago. It is a proposition that comes home to every man in the Confederacy; and it is strange that a measure calculated to promote the interests of the great mass of the people can scarcely get a hearing in this deliberative body.

Now, does not every Senator here know, and does not the country know, that appropriation bills have a specific weight that always carries them through? Who ever heard of an appropriation bill being lost? We know that the combination of influences interested in appropriations that take the people's money from the Treasury is such that there is no chance of their being stopped by the wayside. Why this great press for the appropriation bills? There is always a great press, and the necessity is said to be great and crying when the object is to put the hand into the people's pockets and take out their money; but when legislation is brought forward to advance and promote the common weal of the great mass of the people, there is not so much anxiety to consider them. Then, some contractor, some stockjobber, is pressing his claims before Congress. Suppose some one of these Departments was to run out of money for a short time: do you think the great mass of the people would suffer much? Suppose some of these Departments were fed on bread and water, as they used to feed the jurors in olden time:[2] I think it would bring about a state of depletion, and lead to economical appropriations and economy in sending their estimates to the Congress of the United States, that would be beneficial to, and approved by, the people.

When we come to legislate upon measures that promote the common weal, and that carry themselves home to the great mass of the people, they can have no hearing; but appropriation bills, to get money out of the people's pockets, are urged as required to be passed immediately, on account of some pressing necessity. For whom, sir, is three fourths of the legislation of this country done? Even go to your State Legislatures, and there nineteen twentieths of it is for monopolies, for classes, for stock-jobbers, for bankers, for corporations. The people are scarcely heard, nor are their interests understood or felt. When you come to the Congress of the United States, how is it? For whom is the legislation here done? How much of it is done for the country? That which is to take money out of the Treasury, to transfer it from the pockets of the many to the few, can always get a hearing; their bills and measures are of the most urgent necessity!

Why cannot the homestead bill get a hearing? Why cannot it be taken up and considered? Why cannot it be disposed of? I had determined not to be obtrusive; I had determined not to be offensive to the Senate in pressing it pertinaciously upon the body; but here it is standing as a special order, waiting and waiting for action. When we approach one measure that is to cut off bounties, and relieve the people from taxation on their salt, that is shoved out of the way to take up an appropriation bill. We have no salt manufactories in my State, but we live in their immediate vicinity. Our people are interested in having cheap salt; but when there is a proposition pending that is likely to take a bounty away from the salt manufactories of the country, you cannot get a sufficient combination to postpone the bill that withholds bounties from them. We can see how these combinations are effected. Here is a proposition to retain money in the Treasury on one hand and save the people that much tax, and here is another proposition to take away bounty from the manufacture of salt, which is a measure that comes home to every man throughout the whole country; and that must give way to an appropriation bill; and now the homestead is to yield.

I do not intend to consume the time of the Senate; I have not done so since I have been a member of this body; but I intend to press this measure every morning, I hope not offensively or disagreeably. I intend to press it every day from this time until the termination of the session, until it is disposed of by the Senate in a proper way. I hope the Senate will postpone this appropriation bill. The people's money will be got out of the Treasury fast enough by this or any other Administration. Let us do a little legislation for the country, for the great mass of the people. Let them be heard; let their influence be felt, and let their will be obeyed. I hope the Senate will postpone the appropriation bill and take up the homestead bill.[3]

Cong. Globe, 35 Cong., 1 Sess., 2102.

1. Johnson had moved postponement of a discussion on the appropriation bill in order to consider the homestead bill. When Alfred Iverson of Georgia raised a point of order, Vice President Breckinridge ruled in Johnson's favor.

2. Beginning in the later Middle Ages, English juries had customarily been incarcerated without sustenance until they returned a unanimous verdict. Frederick Pollack and Frederic W. Maitland, *The History of English Law: Before the Time of Edward I* (2 vols., Cambridge, 1952), II, 626.

3. Following a brief discussion, Johnson's motion was defeated, 35–18.

To David T. Patterson, Greeneville

Washington City
May 14th 1858

Hon D. T. Patterson,

Dear Sir,

Your letter was receivd and laid before Judge Merrick[1] and his answer forwarded a few days since— Inclosed you will find his second letter and you will understand from it what they require to be done— If you will have the idenity made out as required and send it to me I will have it placed in the hands of some one who will attend to it at once— Judge M seems to be disposed to have the matter Settled without any trouble to the parties—[2] I have no news of interest to write more than what you see in the newspapers of the day— Congress will adjourn on the 7th of June I think— Give my love to Martha and babe and accept for youself assurances of my high esteem[.]

Andrew Johnson

ALS, NNPM.

1. William M. Merrick (1818–1889), born near Faulkner, Maryland, was associate justice of the United States circuit court for the District of Columbia (1854–63) and served as a Democratic congressman from Maryland (1871–73). *BDAC*, 1322.

2. It has not been possible to uncover the specific "matter" to which this cryptic note refers, though it may relate to a dispute over land warrants held by Patterson. See Patterson to Robert Johnson, February 24, 1857, Johnson Papers, LC.

Speech on School Funds for District of Columbia[1]

May 15, 1858

Mr. JOHNSON, of Tennessee. I move to strike out the following words in the second section of the bill:

And that whenever the Secretary of the Treasury shall be officially notified by the Mayor that the said tax has been levied and collected, it shall be his duty to pay from the Treasury of the United States, to the persons legally authorized to receive school funds for the city of Washington, a sum equal to the amount thus raised by taxation: *Provided*, that not more than $20,000 per annum shall be paid by the United States, and that the payments shall continue for five years, unless Congress shall otherwise order.

It seems to me that this is a plain and distinct proposition for the Government of the United States to take charge of the public schools in this District. I think, sir, that we have really reached a point where we ought to stop. There is no Senator here who will go further than myself in promoting common schools and the cause of education. I have given evidence, in my own State, of my views in that regard. I may also remark, in this connection, that there is scarcely any one in the Senate or throughout the country who knows and feels the wants of educational advantages in early life more than I do. While I admit the great importance of educating all the children of the country, as far as they can be educated in the common schools and in higher schools, I want it done on correct principles; and I want those to pay the expense who are justly chargeable with it. In this case, why should the Government of the United States be taxed to educate the children of the people of the District of Columbia any more than the children in Mississippi, or Tennessee, or Georgia, or New York, or the New England States? If we look to our own States, we find that there is a great want of education there; we find that there are many children there who are not going to school; but is it, therefore, proper for us to ask the Federal Government to take money out of the Treasury of the United States to educate children in the different States? If it is not right in regard to the States, surely it is not right in regard to the District of Columbia. If we have not the power to educate children in the States, at the expense of the Federal Treasury, how can we have the power to educate children in the District of Columbia, at the national expense? Where do you derive the power any more in the one case than in the other? Where does the right exist more in the one case than in the other? This is a common Treasury; and have we any more authority, or any greater claim in right to use it for the education of children here, than for their education in the States?

I repeat there is no one who has higher regard for the children of the District of Columbia than I have, or who will go further to educate the great mass of the children throughout the whole country; but is it right, is it constitutional, to place the expense of their education upon the Federal Treasury? Should not this community bear the tax of educating its own children as well as other communities? Is it right to tax the people of the States, and devote the fund which you raise from them to educate the children in this District? Is there any justice in it? This is simply a proposition to fasten permanently on the Treasury an expense of $20,000 annually, and as much more as can be got, for the education of children in the District of Columbia. Where do you get the power? From what clause of the Constitution is it derived? I know that, at this late day, it is considered antiquated and rather old-fogyish to talk about constitutional restraints, and we are constantly met with the argument that, in the District of Columbia, Congress has exclusive power of legislation, and that, therefore, we can go into the Treasury of the United States and appropriate sums without limit for the purposes of the District. When we examine that subject closely, I think we shall find that we have no more authority to appropriate money from the national Treasury for the education of children in the District of Columbia than for the education of children in the State of Massachusetts or the State of Louisiana. It is true, Congress has exclusive power of legislation in the District of Columbia, but that does not mean unlimited legislation. Because Congress legislates exclusively for this District, Congress has no power to take money out of the Treasury of the United States and appropriate it in this District to purposes for which it could not appropriate it in the States. It has no such power. I admit that, while Congress is acting as a Legislature for the District of Columbia over the revenue or taxes derived from the District, it can appropriate them to any purposes to which the Legislature of the State of Maryland could have appropriated them; but that legislation must be in reference to taxes collected from the people of the District—not to taxes collected from the people of the whole Union. You have no more power to appropriate money out of the Treasury of the United States, for educational purposes in this District, than in the several States of this Confederacy. We not only violate right and justice, in taking a fund which properly belongs to others for the education of children here, but we violate a plain and fundamental principle of the Constitution.

I know it is stated in the report of the chairman of the District Committee[2]—and I am a member of the committee, and know something about the reporting of this bill—that the District of Columbia has had no public lands for this purpose, and therefore we can appropriate money for it. I am free to admit that, in my judgment, Congress can appropriate the public lands to some purposes to which it cannot appropriate money out of the Federal Treasury. Congress may appropriate the public lands to aid the cause of education in the States where the lands lie, or even, perhaps, in other places. There, I think, the power is clear, and the object is national; but I do not see what power Congress has to take money out of the Treasury, and appropriate it to school purposes in this District.

If the relation that exists between the District and the Congress of the United States is simply that which exists between the people of a State and their Legislature, then, while acting as a Legislature for the District of Columbia, we have no power to appropriate the money of the people of the United States for educational purposes in this District; and where is your authority for the passage of this bill? The first section of this bill, I think, is very liberal, because it proposes to appropriate, for the benefit of the schools in this city, all the money collected by the Government from fines and forfeitures here. In my opinion, that is going far enough, and they should not, in addition to that, ask Congress to give them $20,000 annually to sustain common schools here. We already pay the expenses of their judges and jurors; we build their jails, erect their penitentiaries, and feed their convicts. What more shall we do? The States tax their citizens for these purposes, and do not call upon the Treasury of the United States to pay these expenses. This community is as much bound in justice, under the Constitution, to pay all expenses of this character as are the respective communities in the several States. It is not right, decent, and just to impose all the expenses of this community upon the people of the United States.

There is another bill to which I may allude in this connection, proposing to appropriate money for the benefit of an asylum here for the deaf and dumb.[3] There is no one who has more sympathy for that unfortunate class of our fellow-citizens than myself, but where do we derive the power to appropriate for them? I think the appropriation contained in the bill to which I have alluded amounts to some two hundred or three hundred dollars per scholar for the deaf and dumb. This community, after asking an appropriation of that amount to take care of the deaf and dumb here, now want an appropriation for the education of the thousands of children who are placed in the world with all their faculties—hearing, smell, sight, taste, and touch. They come to Congress for an appropriation of two or three hundred dollars a head to take care of those who are unable to speak, those whose faculties are impaired, while at the same time there are hundreds of children born with all their faculties whom they are permitting to become deaf and dumb. Their sympathies are keenly alive to restore those who have lost their faculties, and who never can be restored. It is a strange kind of philanthropy. If one portion of the community is to be lost or thrown away, I think we had better throw away that portion who cannot be restored, and try to save those who are placed in the world with all their faculties.

I do not make these remarks out of any unkind feeling toward the District of Columbia, for I will go as far to promote their interests, on proper principles, as any one can go; but I am not willing to tax my constituents, or the people of the several States, to do here those

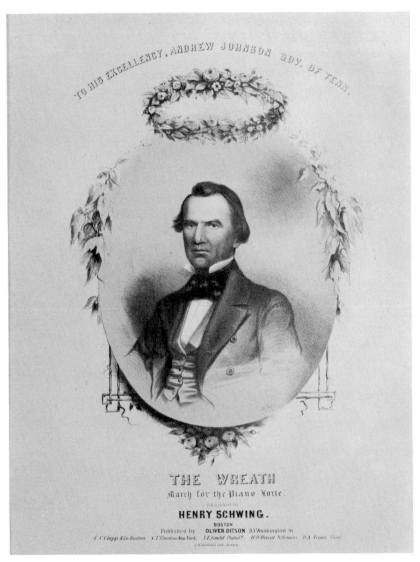

A lithograph of Andrew Johnson (c1856). By Winslow Homer, after engraving by T. D. Booth [see *Johnson Papers*, II, facing p. 276].
Courtesy Boston Museum of Fine Arts.

S. 25.

IN THE SENATE OF THE UNITED STATES,

DECEMBER 22, 1857.

Agreeably to notice, Mr. Johnson, of Tennessee, asked and obtained leave to bring in the following bill; which was read twice and referred to the Committee on Public Lands.

JANUARY 21, 1858.

Reported without amendment, considered as in Committee of the Whole, and postponed to, and made the special order for, Monday, the 8th of February next.

A BILL

To grant to any person who is the head of a family, and a citizen of the United States, a homestead of one hundred and sixty acres of land out of the public domain, upon condition of occupancy and cultivation of the same for the period herein specified.

1   *Be it enacted by the Senate and House of Representa-*

2 *tives of the United States of America in Congress assembled,*

3   That any person who is the head of a family, and a citizen of

4   the United States at the date of the passage of this act, shall,

5   from and after the passage of this act, be entitled to enter one-

6   quarter section of vacant and unappropriated public lands, or

7   a quantity equal thereto, to be located in a body, in conformity

8   with the legal subdivisions of the public lands, and after the

9   same shall have been surveyed.

Johnson's first Homestead Bill in the Senate, December 27, 1857.
Courtesy Library of Congress.

things which the people in the States are taxed to do for themselves. Let this community educate its own children; let it take care of its own deaf and dumb; let it punish its own offenders, build its own prisons, pay its own jurors and judges, as all other communities in this Confederacy do. Sir, the Congress of the United States has been exceedingly partial, to use no stronger term, toward this District from the beginning of the Government. Since this District has been under the charge of the General Government, up to 1857, we have paid to it, for purposes not connected with any Federal expenditures, $5,120,000, and this does not include all the items—over five million dollars for the local improvements, and to promote the individual interests of the people of the District of Columbia. Of this sum $1,150,000 was paid under an act for the relief of the several cities in the District. We have assumed debts that they created, and ought to have paid out of their own funds. Have there been no other benefits conferred on the District of Columbia by the Government being located here? As I have stated, we have expended for their individual benefit, and for the promotion of their local improvements, and the payment of their debts, $5,120,000; and while we have been doing this, we have also gathered from the different States of the Confederacy the taxes of the people, and poured out $12,748,000, like a fertilizing stream on this particular locality, for the erection of public buildings, and improvements of various kinds. I have obtained from the Treasury Department a statement showing the amount expended by the United States for improvements in the District of Columbia up to June 30, 1857:

During what time.	Improvements in the District for the Government.	Improvements for the District.
From 1800 to 1848............	$ 6,530,814 42	$2,708,253 88
" 1848 to 1849............	63,045 99	189,000 00
" 1849 to 1850............	69,945 01	195,126 03
" 1850 to 1851............	157,370 78	279,901 08
" 1851 to 1852............	403,265 69	158,869 03
" 1852 to 1853............	882,223 05	154,630 03
" 1853 to 1854............	429,884 03	954,910 81
" 1854 to 1855............	1,074,749 65	129,165 58
" 1855 to 1856............	1,278,230 35	200,495 26
" 1856 to 1857............	1,859,313 36	250,073 77
	$12,748,842 33	*$5,120,435 47
		[5,220,425 47][4]

*Of this sum $1,152,857 57 was paid under an act for the relief of the several corporate cities of the District, and $1,612,249 68 for the redemption of the debt contracted by said cities, and assumed by the United States.

F. BIGGER, *Register.*

TREASURY DEPARTMENT, REGISTER'S OFFICE,
February 9, 1858

Now, a community which has had $5,000,000 given to it, and which, besides, has enjoyed the profit and benefit which must result from an expenditure of $12,000,000 in its midst, comes to the Congress of the United States, and says it cannot educate its children. Though you pour out millions gathered from the whole people of the United States, for local improvements here and for public buildings, still they cannot educate their children; they cannot take care of the deaf and the dumb; they cannot take care of those who are born with all their faculties; they cannot pay their own jurors and judges; and the cry is, give, give to the District of Columbia, and tax the people of the States; pour it out here; and he who does it, he who votes for these appropriations, is a liberal and expansive statesman—enlarged in his views, comprehensive in his policy! Sir, let us be just before we are liberal. Let us go upon the Constitution, and the great principle of right which requires each community to defray the expenses incident to its own organization.

It seems to me that we are doing a great deal in granting to the school fund here the fines and forfeitures. I am willing to let them have them, if they be any inducement to prosecute suits and bring persons to justice. Anything that will impart efficiency and vigor to their system, and especially to their criminal code, I am willing to go for if it comes within the scope and design of the Constitution.

But, sir, I am getting tired of the talk about their exempting the Government property from taxation. What would the city of Washington be worth without the Government being here? Remove the seat of Government, and property of her citizens here would wither faster than Jonah's gourd, and I believe that withered in a night.[5] The cry is, appropriate for the District of Columbia. Sir, recipients always cry aloud and press their claims earnestly and vigorously when they seek to get that which they have not earned, and which does not belong to them. I say that the people of this District, like the other citizens of the Confederacy, ought to rely on their own resources, content with the great incidental advantages which flow to them from the location of the seat of Government here. As I have said, $12,000,000 have been poured out here for the erection of public buildings and similar works, on which laborers of every description have received employment at high prices, and in addition $5,000,000 have been expended for the individual benefit of the citizens of the District.

I know that sometimes persons become insane altogether, and now and then become insane on a particular subject, and are called monomaniacs. Well, I may perhaps be insane on this, and perhaps on all subjects; but I desire to see where this is carrying us. Here is a proposition to increase the annual expenditures of the Federal Government, which already amount to $70,000,000. New charges are being put upon the Treasury, and every step we advance they accumulate strength and power. The cry is, "give! give! give!" like the daughters of the horse-leech[6]—give still. It seems to me that their own self-respect, their own appreciation of themselves as citizens of the Federal city, ought to preclude them from coming here and asking Congress to educate their children.

I have already given you the items of some expenditures in this District; but they are hardly the commencement—no more than the A B C. How much will it take to complete the improvements now in progress here? Five or six million dollars will not complete them. There are your water works, and your extensive wings of the Capitol. Appropriation after appropriation is being made, and still we have applications for more. We have already expended $12,000,000 for public buildings and improvements here; and by the time we complete those now in progress, $20,000,000 will not foot the bill. Where, then, may we expect the expenditures of this Government to be carried? As long as I have a place here I intend to iterate and re-iterate these things. I have Shakespearean authority,[7] at least, for such a course; and after awhile, perhaps, I shall get the people to understand me. If iterating and reiterating the facts as to the expenditures of this Government will bring the attention of the country to them, I intend to do it if I stand here solitary and alone; but I think there is a disposition in the Senate to help such movements.

In 1790 the population of the United States was a fraction less than four millions, and the expenditures of the Government in 1791 were a fraction less than two million dollars. In 1858 the population is estimated to be twenty-eight millions, and what are the expenditures? Seventy-five million dollars. From 1790 to 1858, a period of sixty-eight years, the population of the United States has doubled seven times, while the expenditures have doubled thirty-five times, showing an increase of expenditures twenty-eight hundred per cent. greater than the increase of population in the same period.[8] When we see such results, is it not time to pause; is it not time for us to ascertain, if we can, where we are going, and what is the maximum we are to reach? If, as the Senator from Georgia [Mr. TOOMBS] remarked the other day, ours be the most corrupt Government upon the face of the earth, this is the most corrupt part of it. It is in the power of Congress to prevent these enormous expenditures; and if we do not interpose we are responsible for them. This Government, sixty-nine years of age, scarcely out of its swaddling-clothes, is making more corrupt uses of money in proportion to the amount collected from the people, as I honestly believe, than any other Government now on the face of the habitable globe. Just in proportion as you increase the amount collected and expended by the Federal Government, in the same proportion corruption goes along with it; and when you run the expenditures of this Government up to one hundred millions or one hundred and fifty millions a year, the Treasury of the United States will control the whole nation, and the people of the respective States will have very little part in the Government except to foot its bills in the shape of taxes.

It may be said that this is only a small amount, $20,000 per annum, which is to be voted to the District of Columbia, and that this is not the place to commence the work of reform; we cannot get the wedge in here; it will not do to stop this expenditure; oh, no, this is not the place. If we happen to get the place, then we are told it is not exactly the time, but the effort should be postponed to some other time. We always miss either the place or the time. When will the time come? It is suggested by my friend from Mississippi that this appropriation is to last only five years. Let them get it for five years; let their system be organized, and their teachers employed, depending for payment on the appropriation from the Treasury, and who will cut it off? Who will break it up? The appeal will be made that the Government is committed to the cause of education here, and will you now stop your appropriations, turn these children out, and deprive them of the benefit of schools? Once get the Government committed to the scheme, and at the end of the five years, instead of the appropriation being stopped, the probability is that it will be continued and increased to forty or fifty thousand dollars, on the plea that they have erected their schools and employed their teachers and want more money. I ask the Senate and the country if we have not reached a point at which we should pause and see whether an effort may not be made to introduce retrenchment and reform into some of the departments of the Government? In sixty-nine years your people have doubled seven times, while your expenditures have doubled thirty-five times. The one has quintupled the other. Where will the end be? I hope that some effort will be made to stop this downward career. I think this is a fit occasion for such an effort, and I hope the Senate will agree to my amendment. I do not wish to consume time, though much might be said on this subject.

[Brown, chairman of the committee on the District of Columbia, restates his argument that the government, as a nontaxpaying landholder, must bear some responsibility for municipal expenses and challenges Johnson's figures of money appropriated for the special benefit of Washington. Picturing "five thousand children, who come to-day . . . bearing their humble petition," Brown sneers that Johnson's "old friends, those who have gloried in his being an advocate of the poor, will think at least that his mind, since he got to the Senate, is a little unbalanced." Henry Wilson of Massachusetts, also objecting to the amendment, draws a parallel between the relationship of the federal government to the District, and of the state governments to the people of the states. In a third rebuttal, Seward argues that Congress has constitutional authority both to legislate for the District of Columbia and to appropriate from the treasury whatever may be necessary for public welfare.]

Mr. JOHNSON, of Tennessee. I do not wish to consume more than a few minutes' time, but I desire to say a few words to set myself right. I do not know whether I heard the Senator from New York correctly or not in his constitutional argument, but what I am about to say can as well be said in the absence of a correct understanding of his remarks as otherwise. If I understood him correctly, he seemed to think the power was clear beyond doubt. I know that on all propositions to take money out of the Treasury, it is very hard to make a constitutional question, and really, in these latter days, the Constitution practically has almost ceased to exist. It scarcely means anything. It is an antiquated affair, a mere paper wall, to make use of an old remark, that a man who wishes to violate can push his finger through wherever he thinks proper, or a piece of gum elastic that can be expanded or contracted at pleasure. That is about the shape the Constitution has got into, and most persons interpret it to suit their own peculiar notions. I know it is getting ancient and out of date to talk about constitutional questions, but I am rather old-fashioned on such points.

The Senator from Massachusetts says that the Congress of the United States occupies to the District of Columbia the same relation that the Legislatures of the States do to the people of the States. Let us take that proposition and see where it brings us[.] Before the cession of this District to the United States, Maryland had full power to legislate for it; it could lay taxes; it could collect taxes and appropriate them to common schools. That is clear. Where did it get the taxes from? From what source did it collect revenue? Was it not from the people of Maryland? Then if the Legislature ceded all the jurisdiction that Legislature had to the Federal Government, can this Government exercise any greater power than the Legislature of Maryland exercised over it? The fact that Congress has exclusive power of legislation here does not confer any additional power at all. Does the fact that the Congress of the United States takes the place of the Legislature of Maryland, give Congress, while acting in the capacity of a Legislature for the District, control over the Federal Treasury? I say it does not, and the proposition cannot be sustained in sound logic. While Congress occupies the relation of a Legislature, it can exercise the functions of a Legislature and none other. This would give it control over the fund collected from these people, to appropriate it to their own purposes, and not control over the Federal Treasury of the nation.

Let us take another case. Suppose you go to the constitution of the State of Maryland, and it says that the Legislature shall pass no law to abolish slavery. When the Legislature ceded the territory to the United States, did it confer any greater power than it had? It could not abolish slavery, and could it concede to or confer upon Congress the power to abolish slavery here? Not at all. If exclusive legislation gave unlimited power, Congress could abolish slavery in violation of the fundamental law of the State of Maryland. Suppose, for instance, the State of Maryland could grant titles of nobility. The Constitution of the United States expressly prohibits your granting them, but because you have exclusive legislation can you confer titles of nobility in the District of Columbia? Not at all.

Then, when we test this matter by principle, we find that simply those powers which might be exercised by the Legislature that ceded the territory to the Federal Government, can be exercised by the Federal Government. Can you not confer power on the people of the District to collect taxes for common schools and educate their children, as they should be educated, in every proper manner? But the argument seems to dwindle, and the views of some gentlemen to diminish and become very small when they talk about taking twenty or fifty or one hundred thousand dollars out of the Federal Treasury for purposes of education in the District of Columbia.

My friend, the chairman of the District Committee, makes rather a pathetic appeal. He says that I have acquired, to some extent in the country, the reputation of being the poor man's friend. Whether I have acquired that reputation or not, I know how the fact is; I know that the finger cannot be pointed to any vote I ever gave in the Congress of the United States for ten long years, or in my own State Legislature, or any recommendation I ever made to the Legislature as Executive of the State, that comes in conflict with the interests of the great mass of the people. In advocating the proposition I have moved to-day, I feel that I am standing on precisely the same ground. I am for ameliorating, for alleviating the condition of the great mass of the people. I am in favor of each community doing that out of its own resources, and upon its own responsibility. Let the States provide their systems of education, and educate their children and tax their people to a sufficient extent to enable them to do it. Each community should be taxed to that extent which will enable every child within its limits to be educated. I have advocated that in my own Legislature. How do I now come in conflict with that principle? When I go to the State which I have the honor in part to represent, I find there—I regret that it is so, but the truth should be told, and I know it is so in other States as well as my own—thousands of children who need education, whose parents have not the means to educate them, and who are suffering for the want of education. Many of them, if they received it, might be brilliant stars—boys of talent, girls of genius, who would profit as much by education as any children here could. What does this bill propose? It proposes to tax that very community who need money for educational purposes, and to use their taxes for educating children in this District; to filch money from them, as it were, by the operation of your revenue system; to take money away from gaunt and haggard poverty. You lay a tax on their salt, on their sugar, on their iron, on their leather, on their flannel, on their calico; you lay a tax on all the necessaries of life, and then bring the money here, and then it is statesmanlike, then we are the poor man's friends, if we shovel it out by thousands and millions to this particular community!

My honorable friend from Mississippi appeals to me as the poor man's friend and says, here are two thousand five hundred little boys on bended knees petitioning the Congress of the United States to educate them. Well, sir, how many little boys are there in the State of Mississippi who have no education; how many of them there would come before the Senator on bended knees, asking him to provide means to educate them? What is the proposition here? It is to take money from the parents of the two thousand five hundred or, perhaps, twenty-five thousand children in his own State who need education, and bring it to Washington city to lavish it on children here. If that is what the gentleman calls being the poor man's friend, I confess I do not understand it. I know his sympathies are excited. His heart is patriotic; he is benevolent and kind; and every emotion of his is generous. People in this community get around him and excite his sympathies. He sees the distress about him here. How many thousands, ay, millions, are there throughout the States whose children are suffering as much for the want of education? Is it right to tax them and still let them want and suffer, and bring their money here and pour it out for education in this District? All I ask is, that each community shall educate its own children and sustain its own poor.

Sir, no one prizes education more highly than I do. I felt the smart of a want of it in early life. I know what it is to have been excluded from the benefit of schools. I have my sympathies with the destitute boy who is cast upon the world without a farthing to sustain him. I know all about his condition; I know his wants; and there is no one here, my honorable friend from Mississippi not excepted, who would go further to relieve his condition than I would; but while I should be willing to relieve him, is it right to put my hands into the pockets of those suffering in the States, and take money away from them? It is very easy to talk of being generous, and of establishing a perfect system of common schools in the District of Columbia. The Senator from Massachusetts gets very pathetic about it. If I know anything of his history, he understands how to appreciate the advantages of education; but standing as we do, at different ends of the line, he and I reason differently on the subject. He is for being very liberal here. Well, sir, just in proportion as you increase the expenses of this Government, you increase the necessity for high protective tariffs. If you increase the expenditures and cause that necessity, a portion of his constituents would reap a benefit in the return of taxes in the shape of protection.

But the Senator from Massachusetts is for being very liberal. Now, I will make a proposition to him, and I do it in a spirit of kindness. I assume that we have no authority under the Constitution to take money out of the Federal Treasury for educational purposes in the District of Columbia. I assume that it violates a great principle of justice and of right to take it away from the people of any other communities to appropriate it here. Then we have no control of this fund; it is not ours. Let us be liberal with our own means; let us be generous with what is ours, what we have acquired by honest industry in our vocation, whatever it may be. I make this proposition to the Senator from Massachusetts: let the people's money alone; let us keep our hands off the money of the little boys and girls that has been gathered here from all the States, that is not ours; but let us now contribute out of our own private means; and I will give as much to aid the cause of education in the District of Columbia as the Senator from Massachusetts. That is a fair proposition. It is very easy to be generous and liberal with other people's money, but it is a different matter when it comes to handling our own cash for benevolent purposes. What I am for in theory, I will promote, as far as my means will permit me to do, out of my own individual funds.

But the Senator from Mississippi seems to think, and he presents it strongly and forcibly as an argument having much plausibility in it, that we own the public property here, and therefore we ought to pay a reasonable amount of taxes. Sir, you may go out through the country and find plenty of men not making over three, or four, or five hundred dollars a year, who are educating their own children. Even the lowest laborers on the public buildings are receiving more money in the course of a year than many respectable farmers throughout the country who educate their own children; but he says our public buildings are here, and consequently the Government ought to be taxed. Who ever heard of a county town or the capital of a State taxing its public buildings located there?

[Brown again interrupts to aver that county seats and state capitals belong to the people in the town or state who choose not to tax properties owned in common; because the people of the District have no choice, it behooves the federal government to put itself in the relationship of a property-holder.]

Mr. JOHNSON, of Tennessee. The gentleman's case almost illustrates itself. He says the public property in a county belongs to the people of the county, and the public buildings in a State belong to the people of the State. That is a very good illustration, and I thank him for it. Take a State that is composed of one hundred counties. Those counties, as counties, contribute to the erection of public buildings at the seat of the government; and when they are about to be built, there is always a great struggle as to where they shall be located, because of the many benefits conferred upon the community where they are located. The expenditure of money upon them brings persons to the place, adding value to property, and causing the city to improve. Is there a State in this Confederacy that permits the county in which the public buildings are located to tax them? There is not a county in the thirty-three States we have now that does it—I believe thirty-three is the number.

Mr. DURKEE.[9] Thirty-two and a half.[10]

Mr. JOHNSON, of Tennessee. The counties of a State own the public buildings, and they are exempt from taxation. All the people of the States of the Union own the public buildings here in the District of Columbia. The principle is identically the same. What would the people here say if you were to make a proposition to take away the public buildings? Instead of talking about releasing the Government from taxation on their property, they would be willing to pay you a bonus to remain. Is not this the property of all the people, those of the District included? Do not the public buildings in a State belong to the people of a State? This property belongs to the people of all the States, and there is no sort of difference in the cases. It is a tax upon other communities to sustain this community. We find a proposition to surrender their city charter; they want to throw everything upon Congress. Some time ago they had a proposition to make us raise a police force[11] for them, and a proposition to take care of the deaf and dumb. Everything is to be put on the Federal Treasury; and that is so much clear gain for them got out of the industry and earnings of others.

I do not wish to consume the time of the Senate. I think this is one of the clearest propositions I ever saw. First, we have no right to appropriate money for educational purposes here; next, it violates principles of justice to the people of the various States. My opposition to his measure, instead of coming in conflict with the positions and feelings of my whole public life, is perfectly consonant with them, and is in fact but another instance in which I carry out the policy I have advocated ever since I have been a public man. I am for the children of the District of Columbia being educated; I want to see them all educated, and I will contribute as much, in proportion to my individual means, as any other Senator to accomplish that object; but I will not take the money out of the pockets of my constituents whose children need education, and many of whom have not the means to educate them. There is no one who places a higher estimate on education than I do. It is an advantage to the community, to the child, to the man, in every possible position in which he can be placed. To use the eloquent language of another, in private life, education is a solace and a comfort; in public life it is an introduction and an ornament; abroad, a friend; it sustains a man in every position in which he may be placed; it will benefit a man in every possible position that he may be placed in; it lessens vice, it guides virtue, gives grace and dignity to genius.[12] The Senator from Massachusetts, the Senator from Mississippi, the Senator from any other State, will not go further in promoting the great cause of education than I will, but this is the wrong direction. This is taking money from one portion of the community and giving it to another. I am not for that policy, and I hope the section will be stricken out.

[John Crittenden, objecting to this reasoning as "not very pertinent" to the issue, suggests that the Senate consider two points only—does Congress have the power to make this appropriation, and if so, is it expedient to do so? Elaborating on the first point, he concludes that it does; as to expediency, he asserts that it is cheaper to educate than to pay the cost of ignorance.]

Mr. JOHNSON, of Tennessee. The Senator, I understand, assumes that we can exercise here all power which the State of Maryland could have exercised over the territory before it was ceded; and that we may, besides, exercise all the power conferred on the Federal Government by the Constitution of the United States. Putting these two together, he draws the conclusion that our power over this District is absolute. Well, sir, the constitution of Maryland, when she ceded the District to the Federal Government, provided, in the forty-third article, "The Legislature shall not pass any law abolishing the relation of master and slave as it now stands in the State." Now, all the power that is conferred on the Federal Government by the Constitution it can exercise here, together with whatever the State of Maryland could exercise. I desire, then, to ask the honorable Senator whether, that being the provision of the constitution of Maryland, Congress has power to abolish slavery in the District of Columbia? I put this by way of illustration of the principle.

[Crittenden maintains that congressional power over territories is a matter of generality rather than of specifics; he adds that a state has the right to establish any constitution or laws it may choose, as long as they conform to the federal Constitution, and that Congress stands in that same relationship to the territories.]

Mr. JOHNSON, of Tennessee. I confess—but I presume it is my fault—that my difficulty is not altogether removed on the question of power. In the first place, in making the cession of territory by the Legislature of the State of Maryland to the Federal Government, all that could be done was to confer on the Federal Government the power which the Legislature of Maryland could exercise before the act of cession. Could the Legislature of Maryland, in ceding the territory, confer upon the Congress of the United States any power over the Federal Treasury, when acting as a Legislature for the District of Columbia? That is the question. If not, and if the Constitution of the United States confers no power on the Congress of the United States to appropriate the revenues of the General Government for the purposes of the District, it has derived the power from neither source. If, however, the same absolute power is conferred upon the Federal Government in regard to the District that exists in a State which may alter and abolish its constitution, that is a different thing; but if the Federal Government does not derive the power, by the act of cession from the State of Maryland to this Government, over the subject of slavery, it has no power to abolish slavery—no more in that case than in the other, to appropriate money out of the Federal Treasury for the purposes of the District of Columbia. It derives no power from the Constitution of the United States, in general terms, to appropriate money for this particular locality. The State of Maryland, in ceding the territory, could confer no power over the Federal Treasury, because that belongs to the people of all the States. If, when acting as a Legislature for the District of Columbia, we occupy the same relation that we should if we were a State Legislature, we have no control over the revenue of the nation for local purposes here. The Maryland act of cession did not and could not confer any such power. If the constitution of that State said that their Legislature should never legislate on the subject of slavery, the Legislature being inhibited by the constitution from legislation on the relations of master and servant, could confer no such power upon Congress. The power in one case is as clear as in the other.[13]

Cong. Globe, 35 Cong., 1 Sess., App. 372–77.

1. S. 191, a bill for the benefit of the Washington City schools, was before the Senate. An all-encompassing measure, it included provisions to appropriate to the school fund the fines and forfeitures collected in the District of Columbia courts, to allow the corporate authorities "with the consent of owners of real estate in the City [to] levy a special tax of ten cents on each hundred dollars' worth of taxable property," and to provide matching funds from the U. S. treasury. The latter seemed warranted because about one-half the taxable real estate in Washington, as federal government property, was exempt. Just before Johnson spoke, the Senate, as a result of the objections of Hale of

New Hampshire, agreed to exempt Negro property from school taxation, inasmuch as Negroes were not educated in the public schools.

2. Albert G. Brown.

3. In February, 1857, Congress had chartered the Columbia Institution for the Deaf, Dumb, and Blind, endowed by former postmaster general Amos Kendall, and had provided a yearly grant of $150 for support of each handicapped child in the District of Columbia. Having opened in August, 1857, under Edward Gallaudet (son of Thomas Gallaudet, who introduced the sign-language method in America), the school was at this time seeking further financial support. Its efforts were successful when in May, 1858, Congress added $3,000 per annum for salaries and incidental expenses and also extended services to the handicapped children of military personnel. Green, *Washington*, I, 220–21; Edward M. Gallaudet, "A History of the Columbia Institution for the Deaf and Dumb," Columbia Historical Society *Records*, XV (1912), 1–3; *U. S. Statutes*, XI, 161–62, 293–94.

4. The discrepancy in addition reflects an error in printing. The correct figure for improvements for the District for 1848 to 1849 is $189,010.00 rather than $189,000.00, and for 1850 to 1851, $179,901.08 rather than $279,901.08. See "Statement showing the amount expended by the United States for improvements in the District of Columbia up to June 30th 1857." Johnson Papers, LC, Ser. 18; see also Letter from Finley Bigger, February 9, 1858.

5. Jon. 4:6–7.

6. Prov. 30:15.

7. Perhaps an allusion to *Henry IV*, Pt. I, Act I, sc. 2: "O, thou has damnable iteration."

8. Johnson's unconventional method of describing an increase is incorrect as to the "doubling" of expenditures; the figure should be thirty-seven and one-half times rather than thirty-five. Based, however, on the latter figure, his twenty-eight hundred percent is probably accurate.

9. Charles Durkee (1805–1870) of Wisconsin, a farmer and businessman, had served in the territorial legislature (1836–38, 1847, 1848), in Congress as a Free-Soiler (1849–53), was now serving in the Senate as a Republican (1855–61), and was later governor of Utah Territory (1865–70). *BDAC*, 839.

10. This is probably a reference to Minnesota, which had been admitted to the Union four days previously. *U. S. Statutes*, XI, 285.

11. See Remarks on Amendment to Washington Police Bill, April 5, 1858.

12. Joseph Addison, *The Spectator*, November 6, 1711. A similar paean to education concluded the section relating to that subject in Johnson's first Biennial Legislative Message, December 19, 1853. *Johnson Papers*, II, 195–96.

13. After Johnson's amendment was defeated, 26–13, the bill passed by an identical vote, the same senators supporting Johnson in both instances.

Amendments to Homestead Bill[1]

May 19, 1858

Mr. JOHNSON, of Tennessee. I wish now to indicate an amendment to the second and fifth sections of the bill, which will improve them and make them more acceptable to some of the friends of the bill. In section two, I propose to strike out all after the enacting clause and insert:

That the person applying for the benefit of this act shall, upon application to the register of the land office in which he or she is about to make such entry, make affidavit before the said register that he or she is the head of a family, or is twenty-one years of age, and that such application is made for his or her exclusive use and benefit, and those specially mentioned in this act, and not either directly or indirectly for the use or benefit of any other person or persons whomsoever; and on making the affidavit as above required, and filing the affidavit with the register, he or she shall thereupon be permitted to enter the quantity of land already specified: *Provided, however,* That no certificate shall be given, or patent issued therefor, until the expiration of five years from the date of such entry; and if, at the expiration of such time, the person making such entry, or if he be dead, his widow, or in case of her death, his heirs or devisee, or in case of a widow making such entry, her heirs or devisee, in case of her death, shall prove by two credible witnesses that he, she, or they have continued to reside upon and cultivate said land, and still reside upon the same, and have not alienated the same, or any part thereof; then in such case, he, she, or they shall be entitled to a patent, as in other cases provided for by law: *And provided, further,* In case of the death of both father and mother, leaving an infant child or children under twenty-one years of age, the right and the fee shall inure to the benefit of said infant child or children; and the executor, administrator, or guardian may, at any time within two years after the death or [sic] the surviving parent, and in accordance with the laws of the State in which such children for the time being have their domicile, sell said land for the benefit of said infants, but for no other purpose; and the purchaser shall acquire the absolute title by the purchase and be entitled to a patent from the United States.

I also propose, in section five, to strike out all after the enacting clause, and insert:

That if, at any time after filing the affidavit as required in the second section of this act, and before the expiration of the five years aforesaid, it shall be proven, after due notice to the settler, to the satisfaction of the register of the land office, that the person having filed such affidavit shall have actually changed his or her residence, or abandoned the said entry, for more than six months at any time, then, and in that event, the lands so entered shall revert back to the Government, and be disposed of as other public lands are now by law, subject to an appeal to the General Land Office.

I offer these two amendments as an improvement on the sections as they now stand in the bill; and I will remark in this connection, that the bill has been submitted to the Commissioner of the General Land Office,[2] with a view to have the sections made as practicable as possible when brought into operation. It has undergone a thorough scrutiny there; all the sections have been examined, and he thinks that the bill, with the amendments proposed in the second and fifth sections, can be put into successful practical operation.

Cong. Globe, 35 Cong., 1 Sess., 2239.

1. Discussion of the homestead bill (S. 25), pending since January, had been made the business of the current day, only to have David Yulee of Florida move its postponement in order to take up a patent office bill. Although John-

son was at first amenable to waiting until the next day, both Seward and Hamlin advised him not to acquiesce, whereupon Yulee withdrew his motion, and Johnson took the floor.

2. See Letter from Thomas A. Hendricks, February 5, 1858.

Speech on Homestead Bill[1]

May 20, 1858

Mr. JOHNSON, of Tennessee. The immediate proposition before the Senate is an amendment offered by the honorable Senator from North Carolina, [Mr. Clingman,] which provides that there shall be a land warrant issued to each head of a family, by the Secretary of the Interior, and distributed among those who do not emigrate to the public domain and take possession of and cultivate the land for the term of years specified in the bill. I have something to say in reference to that amendment, but I will not say it in this connection. I will take it up in its order. I propose, in the first place, to explain briefly the provisions of the bill.

The first section provides for granting one hundred and sixty acres of land to every head of a family who will emigrate to any of the public domain and settle upon it, and cultivate it for a term of five years. Upon those facts being made known to the register of the land office, he is to be entitled to obtain a patent. The second section provides that he shall make an affidavit, and show to the satisfaction of the officer that his entry is made in good faith, and that his intention is to cultivate the soil and become an actual settler. The sixth section of the bill provides that any person who is now an inhabitant of the United States, but not a citizen, if he makes application, and in the course of five years becomes a citizen of the United States, shall be placed on a footing of equality with the native-born citizens of the country in this respect. The third section provides that those entries shall be confined to land that has been in market, and subjected to private entry; and that the person entering the land shall be confined to each alternate section.

These are substantially the leading provisions of this bill. It does not proceed upon the idea, as some suppose, of making a donation or gift of the public land to the settler. It proceeds upon the principle of consideration, and, as I conceive, and I think many others do, the individual who emigrates to the West, and reclaims and reduces to cultivation one hundred and sixty acres of the public domain, subjecting himself to all the privations and hardships of such a life, pays the highest consideration for his land.

But, before I say more on this portion of the subject, I desire to premise a little by giving the history of this homestead proposition.

Some persons from my own region of the country, or, in other words, from the South, have thrown out the intimation that this is a proposition which partakes, to some extent, of the nature of the Emigrant Aid Society, and is to operate injuriously to the southern States. For the purpose of making the starting point right, I want to go back and show when this proposition was first introduced into the Congress of the United States. I am not so sure but that the Presiding Officer [Mr. Foot in the chair] remembers well the history of this measure.[2]

In 1846, on the 27th day of March, long before we had any emigrant aid societies, long before we had any compromises in 1850 in reference to the slavery question, long before we had any agitation on the subject of slavery in 1854, long before we had any agitation upon it in 1858, this proposition made its advent into the House of Representatives. It met with considerable opposition. It scarcely received serious consideration for a length of time; but the measure was pressed until the public mind took hold of it; and it was still pressed until the 12th day of May, 1852, when it passed that body by a two-third vote. Thus we see that its origin and its consummation, so far as the House of Representatives was concerned, had nothing to do with North or South, but it was proceeding upon that great principle which interests every man in this country, and which, in the end, secures and provides for him a home. By putting these dates together it will be perceived that it was just six years five months and fifteen days from the introduction of this bill until its passage by the House of Representatives.[3]

I shall not detain the Senate by any lengthy remarks on the general principles of the bill; for I do not intend to be prolix, or to consume much of the Senate's time. What is the origin of the great idea of a homestead of land? We find, on turning to the first law-writer—and I think one of the best, for we are informed that he wrote by inspiration—that he advances the first idea on this subject. Moses made use of the following language:

The land shall not be sold forever; for the land is mine—for ye are strangers and sojourners with me.—*Leviticus*, chapter XXV., verse 23.

We begin, then, with Moses.[4] The next writer to whom I will call the attention of the Senate is Vattel—one of the ablest, if not the ablest writer upon the laws of nations. He lays down this great principle, (book 1, chapter 7:)

[Vattel expatiates on the virtues of agriculture—"the nursing father of the State"— and its pursuit—"the natural employment of man." Citing examples from the pages of history and the countries of the world, he stresses the government's responsibility for the cultivation of the soil.]

I propose next to cite the authority of General Jackson, who was believed to be not only a friend to the South, but a friend to the Union. He inculcated this great doctrine in his message of 1832:

[In his Fourth Annual Message (December 4, 1832), Jackson urged the "speedy settlement" of public lands, with the goal of increasing population in the West rather than producing revenue.]

Then we have standing before us, in advocacy of this great principle, the first writer of laws, Moses; next we have Vattel; and in the third place we have General Jackson. Now, let us see whether there has been any homestead policy in the United States. By turning to our statutes, we find that the first homestead bill ever introduced into the Congress of the United States, was in 1791. I know that it is said by some, and it is sometimes cantingly and slurringly reiterated in the newspapers, that this is a demagogical movement, and that some person has introduced and advocates this policy purely for the purpose of pleasing the people. I want to see who some of these demagogues are; and before I read the section of this statute, I will refer, in connection with Jackson and these other distinguished individuals, to the fact that Mr. Jefferson, the philosopher and statesman, recognized and appreciated this great doctrine. In 1791, the first bill passed by the Congress of the United States recognizing the homestead principle, is in the following words:

That four hundred acres of land be given—that is the language of the statute. We do not assume in this bill to give land. We assume that a consideration passes; but here was a law that was based on the idea that four hundred acres of land were to be given
—to each of those persons who, in the year 1783, were heads of families at Vincennes, or the Illinois country, or the Mississippi, and who, since that time, have removed from one of the said places to the other; but the Governor of the Territory northwest of the Ohio is hereby directed to cause the same to be laid out for them at their own expense, &c.

Another section of the same act provides:

That the heads of families at Vincennes, or in the Illinois country, in the year 1783, who afterwards removed without the limits of said Territory, are nevertheless entitled to the donation of four hundred acres of land made by the resolve of Congress, &c.[5]

That act recognized the principle embraced in the homestead bill. If this is the idea of a demagogue, if it is the idea of one catering or pandering to the public sentiment to catch votes, it was introduced into Congress in 1791, and received the approval of Washington, the father of his country. I presume that if he lived at this day, and were to approve the measure, as he did in 1791, he would be branded, and put in the category of those persons who are denominated demagogues. Under his administration there was another bill passed of a similar import, recognizing and carrying out the great homestead principle. So we find that this policy, so far as legislation is concerned, commenced with Washington, and received his approval as early as 1791. From General Washington's administration there are forty-four precedents running through every administration of this Government, down to the present time, in which this principle has been recognized and indorsed.

We discover from this historical review that this is no new idea; that it is no recent invention; that it is no new movement for the purpose of making votes; but it is a principle well nigh as old as the Government itself, which was indorsed and approved by Washington himself.

This would seem, Mr. President, to settle the question of power. I know it has been argued by some that Congress had not the power to make donations of land; but even the statute, to which I have referred, makes use of the world "give" without consideration. It was considered constitutional by the early fathers to give away land. We proceed in this bill upon the principle that there is a consideration. If I were disposed to look for precedents, even for the donations of the public lands, I could instance the bounty land act. I could take you through other acts donating land, showing that the principle has been recognized again and again, and that there is not now a question as to its constitutionality.

I believe there is a clear difference in the power of the Federal Government in reference to its appropriations of money and its appropriations of the public land. The Congress of the United States has power to lay and collect taxes, duties, imposts, and excises, to pay the debts and provide for the common defense and general welfare. I believe it has the power to lay and collect duties for these legitimate purposes; but when taxes have been laid, collected, and paid into the Treasury, I do not think it has that general scope or that latitude in the appropriations of money that it has over the public lands. Once converted into revenue, Congress can only appropriate the revenue to the specific objects of the Constitution. It may derive revenue from the public lands, and being revenue, it can only be appropriated to the purposes for which revenue is raised under the Constitution.

But when we turn to another provision of the Constitution, we find that Congress has power "to dispose of and make all needful rules and regulations respecting the territory or other property belonging to the United States." Congress has, in the organization of all the Territories and in the admission of new States, recognized the principle most clearly of appropriating the public lands for the benefit of schools, colleges, and academies. It has granted the sixteenth and thirty-sixth sections in every township for school purposes; it has granted lands for their public buildings and various other improvements. I am very clear on this point, that in the disposition of the public lands they should be applied to national purposes. If we grant the public lands to actual settlers so as to induce them to settle upon and cultivate the public lands, can there be anything more national in its character? What is the great object of acquiring territory? Is it not for settlement and cultivation? We may acquire territory by the exercise of the treaty-making power. We may be engaged in a war, and as terms or conditions of peace, we may make large acquisitions of territory to the United States. But what is the great idea and principle on which you acquire territory? Is it not to settle and cultivate it?

I am aware that the argument is used, if you can dispose of the public lands for this purpose or that purpose, cannot you sell the public lands and apply the proceeds to the same purpose? I think there is a clear distinction between the two cases. It is equally clear to me that, if the Federal Government can set apart the public lands for school purposes in the new States, it can appropriate lands to enable the parent to sustain his child whilst enjoying the benefits conferred upon him by the Government in the shape of education. The argument is as sound in the one case as it is in the other. If we can grant lands in the one case we can in the other. If, without making a contract in advance, you can grant your public lands as gratuities, as donations to men who go out and fight the battles of their country, after the services have been rendered, is it not strange, passing strange, that you cannot grant land to those who till the soil and make provision to sustain your Army while it is fighting the battles of the country? It seems to me that the argument is clear. I do not intend to argue the constitutional question, for I think there can be really no doubt on that point. I do not believe any one at this day will seriously make any point on that ground against this bill. Is its purpose a national one? The great object is to induce persons to cultivate the land and thereby make the soil productive. By doing this, you induce hundreds of persons throughout the United States, who are now producing but little, to come in contact with the soil and add to the productive capacity of the country, and thereby promote the national weal.

I come now to the amendment offered by the Senator from North Carolina. I have not looked over the Globe this morning to read his remarks of yesterday; but if I understood him correctly, he advocated the proposition of issuing a warrant for a hundred and sixty acres of land to each head of a family in the United States. I am inclined to think the Senator is not serious in this proposition. It has been offered on some occasions heretofore, and rejected by very decided votes. Let us compare it with the proposition of the bill. The idea of the honorable Senator seems to be that this bill was designed to force or compel, to some extent, the citizens of other States to go to the new States. Why, sir, there is no compulsory process in the bill. It leaves each man at his own discretion, at his own free will, either to go or to stay, just as it suits his inclinations.

The Senator seems to think too—and the same idea was advanced by his predecessor[6]—that at this time such a measure would have a tendency to diminish the revenue. He intimates that the nation is now bankrupt, that we are borrowing money, that the receipts from customs have been greatly diminished, and that therefore it would be dangerous to pass this bill, because it would have a tendency to diminish the revenue. Let us compare the Senator's proposition, and that of the bill in this respect. His amendment is to issue warrants to each head of a family. The population of the United States is now estimated at about twenty-eight millions. Let us assume, for the sake of illustration, that there are three million heads of families in the United States. His proposition, then, is to issue and throw upon the market three million of warrants, each warrant entitling the holder to one hundred and sixty acres of land. If that were done, and those warrants were thrown upon the market, what would they sell for? Little or nothing. If such land warrants were thrown broadcast over the country, who would enter another acre of land at $1 25? Would not the warrants pass into the hands of land speculators and monopolists at a merely nominal price? Would they bring more than a quarter of a dollar an acre? If you were to throw three million of land warrants into the market at one time, would they bring anything? Then the effect of that proposition would be to do but little good to those to whom the warrants were issued, and by throwing them into the market, it would cut off the revenue from public lands entirely, for no one would enter land for cash as long as warrants could be bought. That proposition, then, is to aid and feed speculation. I do not say that is the motive or intention, but it is the tendency and effect of the Senator's proposition, to throw a large portion of the public lands into the hands of speculators, and to cut them off from the Treasury as a source of revenue.

But what does this bill propose? Will it diminish the receipts into the Treasury from the public lands? The bill provides that the entries under it shall be confined to the alternate sections, and that the person who obtains the benefit of the bill must be an actual settler and cultivator. In proportion as you settle and cultivate any portion of the public lands, do you not enhance the value of the remaining sections, and bring them into the market much sooner, and obtain a better price for them than you would without this bill? What is the principle upon which you have proceeded in all the railroad grants you have made? They have been defended upon the ground that by granting alternate sections for railroads, you thereby brought the remaining lands into the market, and enabled the Government to realize its means at a much earlier period, making the remainder of the public lands more valuable than they were before. This bill proceeds upon the same idea. You have granted an immense amount of lands to railroads on this principle,[7] and now why not do something for the people?

I say that instead of wasting the public lands, instead of reducing the receipts into the Treasury, this bill would increase them. In the first place, it will enhance the value of the reserved quarter sections. This may be illustrated by an example. In 1848 we had nine million quarter sections; in 1858 we have about seven millions. Let us suppose that our population is twenty-eight millions, and that under the operation of this bill one million heads of families who are now producing but very little, and who have no land to cultivate, and very scanty means of subsistence, shall each have a quarter section of land, what will the effect be? At present these persons pay little or nothing for the support of the Federal Government, under the operation of our tariff system, for the reason that they have not got much to buy with. How much does the land yield to the Government while it is lying in a state of nature, uncultivated? Nothing at all. At the rate we have been selling the public lands, about three million dollars' worth a year, estimating them at $1 25 an acre, it will take a fraction less than seven hundred years to dispose of the public domain.

I want to take a case that will demonstrate as clearly as the simplest sum in arithmetic that this is a revenue measure. Let us take a million families who can now hardly procure the necessaries of life, and place them each on a quarter section of land—how long will it be before their condition will be improved so as to make them able to contribute something to the support of the Government? Now, here is soil producing nothing, here are hands producing but little. Transfer the man from the point where he is producing nothing, bring him in contact with a hundred and sixty acres of productive soil, and how long will it be before that man changes his condition? As soon as he gets upon the land, he commences to make his improvements, he clears out his field, and the work of production is commenced. In a short time he has a crop, he has stock and other things that result from bringing his physical labor in contact with the soil. He has the products of his labor and his soil, and he is enabled to exchange them for articles of consumption. He is enabled to buy more than he was before, and thus he contributes more to the support of his Government, while, at the same time, he becomes a better man, and a more reliable man for all governmental purposes, because he is interested in the country in which he lives.

To illustrate the matter further, let us take a family of seven persons in number who now have no home, no abiding place that they can call their own, and transfer them to a tract of one hundred and sixty acres of land which they are to possess and cultivate. Is there a Senator here who does not believe, that, by changing their position from the one place to the other, they would produce at least a dollar more than they did before? I will begin at a point scarcely visible—a single dollar. Is there a man here or anywhere else who does not know the fact to be, that you increase a man's ability to buy when he produces more by bringing his labor in contact with the soil. The result of that contact is production; he produces something that he can convert and exchange for the necessities of his family. Suppose the increase was only a dollar a head for a million of families, each family consisting of seven persons. By transferring a million of families from their present dependent condition to the enjoyment and cultivation of the public domain, supposing it would only increase their ability to buy foreign imports to the extent of a dollar each, you would create a demand for seven millions' worth of imports. Our rates of duties, under the tariff act of 1846, are about thirty per cent., and thus, at the almost invisible beginning of a single dollar a head, you, in this way, increase the pecuniary and financial means of the Government to the extent of $2,100,000.

This would be the result, supposing that there would only be an addition of one dollar per head to the ability of each family by being taken from a condition of poverty and placed upon one hundred and sixty acres of land. This is the result, supposing them to have seven dollars more, with which to buy articles of consumption, than they had when they had no home, no soil to cultivate, no stimulant, no inducement to labor. If you suppose the effect would be to increase their ability two dollars per head, you would increase their consumption to the amount of $14,000,000, which, at thirty per cent. duty, would yield $4,200,000. If you supposed it increased the ability of a family four dollars per head, the total amount would be $28,000,000, which would yield a revenue of $8,400,000. I think that this would be far below the truth, and if you gave a family one hundred and sixty acres of land to cultivate, the effect would be to increase the ability of that family so as to buy fifty-six dollars' worth more than they bought before—seven dollars a head. That would be a small increase to a family who had a home, compared with the condition of that family when it had none. The effect of that would be to run up the amount they buy to $56,000,000, which, at a duty of thirty per cent., would yield the sum of $16,800,000.

I show you, then, that, by taking one million families, consisting of seven persons each, and putting them each upon a quarter section of land, making the soil productive, if you thereby only added to their capacity to buy goods to the amount of fifty-six dollars per family, you would derive a revenue of nearly seventeen million dollars. When you have done this, how much of the public lands would you have disposed of? Only one million quarter sections, and you would have nearly six million quarter sections left. By disposing of one sixth of your public domain in this way, upon this little miniature estimate, you bring into the coffers of the Federal Government by this bill $16,800,000.

Does this look like diminishing the revenue? Does it not rather show that this bill is a revenue measure? I think it is most clearly a revenue measure. Not only is this the case in a money point of view, so far as the imports are concerned, but, by settling the alternate sections with actual cultivators, you make the remaining sections more valuable to the Government, and you bring them sooner into market. In continuation of this idea, I will read a portion of the argument which I made upon this subject when I first introduced the bill into the other House.[8] I read from the report of my speech on that occasion:

Mr. J. said, it will be remembered by the House that he had already shown, that by giving an individual a quarter section of the land, the Government would receive back, in the shape of a revenue, in every seven years, more than the Government price of the land; and, upon this principle, the Government would, in fact, be realizing two hundred and ten dollars every subsequent term of seven years. The whole number of acres of public land belonging to the United States at this time, or up to the 30th of September, 1848, is one billion four hundred and forty two million two hundred and sixteen thousand one hundred and sixty eight acres. This amount, estimated at $1 25 per acre, will make $1,802,770,-000. To dispose of $3,000,000 worth per annum, which is more than an average sum, would require seven hundred years, a fraction less, to dispose of the entire domain. It will not be perceived at once the immense advantage the Government would derive by giving the land to the cultivator, instead of keeping it on hand this length of time. We find by this process the Government would derive from each quarter section in six hundred years, (throwing off the large excess of nearly one hundred years,) $17,000—seven going into six hundred eighty-five times. This, then, shows on the one hand what the Government would gain by giving the land away.

Now let us see what it will lose by retaining the land on hand this length of time. Time operates upon value as distance does upon magnitude. A ball of very large size, when close to the eye, is seen in its fullest extent; but when removed to a certain distance, dwindles to the human vision, or disappears altogether. So with the largest planets, removed from the eye to the position they now occupy in the heavens, they diminish to a mere point. To the business, practical world, a hundred dollars at the present time is just worth a hundred dollars. A hundred dollars twelve months hence, is worth just six per cent. less, and so on every twelve months, until sixteen years and eight months, when it has lost an amount equal to the principal; so it will be perceived that, in every sixteen years and eight months, the Government loses an amount equal to the price asked for each quarter section, which is $200, by keeping it on hand. Sixteen will go into six hundred thirty-seven times, which would make $7,400 the Government will lose. Now, I conceive that it would be fair and rational to the business world to set the loss down on the one hand and the gain on the other, and then add them together, which would show the difference to be $24,400 in the present system and the one proposed. This will hold good in principle, and will apply to each quarter section, as well as to the aggregate.

He repeated that by giving a quarter section of land to the honest cultivator, in six hundred years the Government would derive twenty-four thousand and four hundred dollars, ($24,400.) Upon this basis of calculation, the Government, in six hundred years, would draw from this source, by the operation of its revenue system, into the Treasury, two hundred and nineteen billions six hundred million dollars, ($219,-600,000,000,) which would be an amount sufficient, estimating the expenses of the Government at fifty millions of dollars annually, to carry it on for four thousand three hundred and ninety-two years. He said that this exposé ought to satisfy every one that instead of violating the plighted faith of the Government, it was enlarging and making more valuable, and enabling the Government to derive a much larger amount of revenue to meet all its liabilities, and thereby preserving its faith inviolate.

I do not think there can be any question as to the revenue part of this proposition. We show that by granting a million quarter sections you derive more revenue upon the public lands than you do by your entire land system, as it now stands. In 1850, it was estimated that each head of a family consumed $100 worth of home manufactures. If we increase the ability of the cultivator and occupier of the soil fifty-six dollars in the family, of course it is reasonable to presume that he would consume a corresponding proportion of home manufactures. Can that proposition be controverted? I think not. Then we see on the one hand that we should derive more revenue from granting the land, on the principle laid down in the bill, and also that we should open a market for articles manufactured in our own country. Then taking both views of the subject we see that it is an advantage to the manufacturing interest, and that it is also an advantage to the Government, so far as imports are concerned. I should like to know, then, where can the objection be, upon the score of revenue?

I am in hopes that the Senator from North Carolina will withdraw his amendment, for I cannot think he is serious. His proposition would have a tendency to cut off all the revenue from the public lands—to flood the market with land warrants to be sold at nominal prices, bringing scarcely anything even to those to whom the warrants would be issued.

Mr. CLINGMAN. I will say to the Senator that when he is through I shall offer a short explanation of the reasons why I offered the amendment. I do not desire to interrupt him now.

Mr. JOHNSON, of Tennessee. But, Mr. President, the question of dollars and cents is of no consideration to me. The money view of this subject does not influence my mind by the weight of a feather. I think it is clear, though; and this view has been presented to prove to Senators that this bill will not diminish, but, on the contrary, will increase the revenue.

But this is not the important view of the subject. When you look at our country as it is, you see that it is important that the great mass of the people should be interested in the country. By this bill you provide a man with a home, you increase the revenue, you increase the consumption of home manufactures, and you make him a better man. You give him an interest in the country. His condition is better. There is no man so reliable as he who is interested in the welfare of his country; and who are more interested in the welfare of their country than those who have homes? When a man has a home, he has a deeper, a more abiding interest in the country, and he is more reliable in all things that pertain to the Government. He is more reliable when he goes to the ballot-box; he is more reliable in sustaining the stability of our free institutions.

It seems to me that this, without the other consideration, would be a sufficient inducement. When we see the population that is accumulating about some of our cities, I think it behooves every man who is a statesman, a patriot, and a philanthropist, to turn his attention to this subject. I have lately seen some statistics with reference to the city of New York,[9] in which it is assumed that one sixth of the population are paupers; that two sixths of the population are barely able to sustain themselves; leaving one pauper to be sustained by every two persons in the city of New York. Does not that present a frightful state of things? Suppose the population of that city to be one million: you would have in the single city of New York, one hundred and sixty-six thousand paupers.

I do not look upon the growth of cities and the accumulation of population about cities, as being the most desirable object in this country. Here I will remark that I do not believe a large portion of this population, if you were to grant them homesteads, would ever go to them. I have no idea that they would; for a man who has spent most of his life about a city, and has sunk into a pauperized condition, is not a man to go West, reclaim one hundred and sixty acres of land, and reduce it to cultivation. He will not go there on that condition. Though we are satisfied of this, may not our policy be such as to prevent, as far as practicable, the accumulation of such an unproductive population about your cities? Let us try to prevent their future accumulation; let these live, have their day, and pass away—they will ultimately pass away—but let our policy be such as to induce men to become mechanics and agriculturists. Interest them in the country; pin them to the soil, and they become more reliable and sustain themselves, and you do away with the pauperism in the country. The population of the United States being twenty-eight millions, if the proportion of paupers in the city of New York existed in the country, you would have four million six hundred and sixty-six thousand paupers in the United States. Do we want all our population to become of that character? Do we want cities to take control of this Government? Unless the proper steps be taken, unless the proper direction be given to the future affairs of this Government, the cities are to take charge of it and control it. The rural population, the mechanical and agricultural portions of this community, are the very salt of it. They constitute the "mudsills,"[10] to use a term recently introduced here. They constitute the foundation upon which the Government rests; and hence we see the state of things before us. Should we not give the settlement of our public lands and the population of our country that direction which will beget and create the best portion of the population? Is it not fearful to think of four million six hundred and sixty-six thousand paupers in the United States, at the rate they have them in the city of New York? Mr. Jefferson never said a truer thing than when he declared that large cities were eye-sores in the body-politic;[11] in Democracies they are consuming cancers.

I know the idea of some is to build up great populous cities, and that thereby the interests of the country are to be promoted. Sir, a city not only sinks into pauperism, but into vice and immorality of every description that can be enumerated; and I would not vote for any policy that I believed would build up cities upon this principle. Build up your villages, build up your rural districts, and you will have men who rely upon their own industry, who rely upon their own efforts, who rely upon their own ingenuity, who rely upon their own economy and application to business for a support; and these are the people whom you have to depend upon. Why, Mr. President, how was it in ancient Rome? I know there has been a great deal said in denunciation of agrarianism and the Gracchi. It has been said that a doctrine something like this led to the decline of the Roman Empire; but the Gracchi never had their day until a cancerous influence had destroyed the very vitals of Rome; and it was the destruction of Rome that brought forth Tiberius Gracchus. It was to prevent land monopoly, not agrarianism, in the common acceptation of the term—which is dividing out lands that had been acquired by individuals. They sought to take back and put in the possession of the great mass of the people that portion of the public domain which had been assumed by the capitalists, who had no title to it in fact. The Gracchi tried to carry out this policy; to restore that which had been taken from the people. The population had sunk into the condition of large proprietors on the one hand, and dependents on the other; and when this dependent condition was brought about, as we find from Niebuhr's History,[12] the middle class of the community was all gone; it had left the country; there was nothing but an aristocracy on the one hand, and dependents upon that aristocracy on the other; and when this got to be the case, the Roman Empire went down.

Having this illustrious example before us, we should be warned by it. Our true policy is to build up the middle class; to sustain the villages; to populate the rural districts, and let the power of this Government remain with the middle class; I want no miserable city rabble on the one hand. I want no pampered, bloated, corrupted aristocracy on the other; I want the middle portion of society built up and sustained, and let them have the control of the Government. I am as much opposed to agrarianism[13] as any Senator on this floor, or any individual in the United States, and this bill does not partake in the slightest degree of agrarianism; but, on the contrary, it commences with a man at the precise point where agrarianism ends, and it carries him up in an ascending line, while that carries him down. It gives him an interest in his country, an interest in public affairs; and when you are involved in war, in insurrection, or rebellion, or danger of any kind, they are the men who are to sustain you. If you should have occasion to call volunteers into the service of the country, you will have a population of men having homes, having wives and children to care for, who will defend their hearthstones when invaded. What a sacred thing it is to a man to feel that he has a hearthstone to defend; a home, and a wife and children to care for, and to rest satisfied that they have an abiding place. Such a man is interested individually in repelling invasion; he is interested individually in having good Government.

I know there are many, and even some in the Democratic ranks, whose nerves are a little timid in regard to trusting the people with too much power. Sir, the people are the safest, the best, and the most reliable lodgment of power, if you have a population of this kind. Keep up the middle class, lop off an aristocracy on the one hand, and a rabble on the other; let the middle class maintain the ascendency, let them have the power, and your Government is always secure. Then you need not fear the people. I know, as I have just remarked, that some are timid in regard to trusting the people; but there can be no danger from a people who are interested in their Government, who have homes to defend, and wives and children to care for. Even if we test this proposition by that idea of self-interest which is said to govern and control man, I ask you if a man, who has an interest in his country, is not more reliable than one who has none? Is not a man who is adding to the wealth of his country more reliable than one who is simply a consumer, and has no interest in it? If we suppose a man to be governed only by the principle of self-interest, is he not more reliable when he has a stake in the country, and is it not his interest to promote and advance his own condition? Is it not to the interest of the great mass to have everything done rightly in reference to Government. The great mass of the people hold no office; they expect nothing from the Government. The only way they feel, and know, and understand the operations of the Government is in the exactions it makes from them. When they are receiving from the Government protection in common, it is their interest to do right in all governmental affairs; and that being their interest they are to be relied upon, even if you suppose men to be actuated altogether by the principle of self-interest. It is the interest of the middle class to do right in all governmental affairs; and hence they are to be relied upon. Instead of requiring you to keep up your armies, your mounted men, and your footmen on the frontier, if you will let the people go and possess this public land on the conditions proposed in this bill, you will have an army on the frontier composed of men who will defend their own firesides, who will take care of their own homes, and will defend the other portions of the country, if need be, in time of war.

I would remark in this connection, that the public lands have paid for themselves. According to the report[14] of Mr. Stuart, of Virginia, the Secretary of the Interior in 1850, it was shown that then the public lands had paid for themselves, and sixty millions over. We have received into the Treasury since that time about thirty-two million dollars from the public lands. They have, therefore, already paid the Government more than they cost, and there can be no objection to this bill on the ground that the public lands have been bought with the common treasure of the whole country. Besides, this bill provides that each individual making an entry shall pay all the expenses attending it.

We see then, Mr. President, the effect this policy is to have on population. Let me ask here, looking to our popular elections, looking to the proper lodgment of power, is it not time that we had adopted a policy which would give us men interested in the affairs of the country to control and sway our elections? It seems to me that this cannot long be debated; the point is too clear. The agricultural and mechanical portion of the community are to be relied upon for the preservation and continuance of this Government. The great mass of the people, the great middle class, are honest. They toil for their support, accepting no favor from Government. They live by labor. They do not live by consumption, but by production; and we should consume as small a portion of their production as it is possible for us to consume, leaving the producer to appropriate to his own use and benefit as much of the product of his own labor as it is possible in the nature of things to do. The great mass of the people need advocates—men who are honest and capable, who are willing to defend them. How much legislation is done for them? How much is done for classes? How little care seems to be exercised for the great mass of the people? When we are among our constituents, it is very easy to make appeals to the people and professions of patriotism, and then—I do not mean to be personal or invidious—it is very easy when we are removed from them a short distance, to forget the people and legislate for classes, neglecting the interest of the great mass. The mechanics and agriculturists are honest, industrious, and economical. Let it not be supposed that I am against learning or education, but I might speak of the man in the rural districts, in the language of Pope:

> Unlearned, he knew no schoolman's subtle art,
> No language but the language of the heart;
> By nature honest, by experience wise;
> Healthy by temperance and exercise.[15]

This is the kind of men whom we must rely upon. Let your public lands be settled; let them be filled up; let honest men become cultivators and tillers of the soil. I do not claim to be prophetic, but I have sometimes thought that if we would properly direct our legislation in reference to our public lands and our other public policy, the time would come when this would be the greatest Government on the face of the earth. Go to the great valley of the Mississippi; take the western slope of the mountain to the Pacific ocean; take the whole area of this country, and we find that we have over three million square miles. Throw off one fourth as unfit for cultivation, reducing the area of the United States to fifteen hundred million acres, and by appropriating three acres to a person, it will sustain a population of over five hundred million people; and I have no doubt, if this continent was strained to its utmost capacity, it could sustain the entire population of the world. Let us go on and carry out our destiny; interest men in the soil; let your vacant land be divided equally so that men can have homes; let them live by their own industry; and the time will come when this will be the greatest nation on the face of the earth. Let agriculture and mechanism maintain the ascendency, other professions and pursuits being subordinate to them, for on these two all others rest.

Since the crucifixion of our Savior, emigration has been westward; and the poetic idea might have started long before it did—

"Westward the star of empire takes its way."[16]

It has been taking its way westward. The United States are filling up. We are going on to the Pacific coast. Let me raise the inquiry here, when, in the history of mankind, in the progress of nations, was there any nation that ever reached the point we now occupy? When was there a nation in its progress, in its settlement, in its advance in all that constitutes and make a nation great, that occupied the position we now occupy? When was there any nation that could look to the East and behold the tide of emigration coming, and, at the same time, turn around and look to the mighty West, and behold the tide of emigration approaching from that direction. The waves of emigration have usually been running in one direction, but we find the tide of emigration now changed, and we are occupying a central position on the globe. Emigration is coming to us from the East and from the West, and when our vacant territory shall be filled up, when it shall reach a population of one hundred and fifty or five hundred millions, who can say what will be our destiny?

When our railroad system shall progress on proper principles, extending from one extreme of the country to the other, like so many arteries; when your telegraphic wires shall be stretched along them as the tendons in the human arm, and they shall run in parallel lines, and be crossed at right angles, until the whole globe, as it were, and especially in this great center, shall be covered like a network with these arteries and tendons; when the face of the globe shall flash intelligence like the face of man; when it shall become sensitive to touch—we, occupying this important point, receiving acquisitions from the East and from the West, may find our institutions more perfect, science may be advanced so that instead of receiving immigration, instead of receiving nations from abroad, this will be the great sensorium from which our notions of religion, our notions of government, our improvements in works of every description shall radiate from this as a common center, and revolutionize the whole world.

Who dares say that this is not our destiny, if we will only permit it to be fulfilled? Then let us go on with this great work of interesting men in becoming connected with the soil; interesting them in remaining in your mechanic shops; prevent their accumulation in the

streets of your cities; and in doing this, you will dispense with the
necessity for all your pauper system. By doing this you enable each
community to take care of its own poor. By doing this you destroy
and break down the great propensity that exists with men to hang
and loiter and perish about the cities of the Union, as is done now
in the older countries.

It is well enough, Mr. President, to see where our public lands
have been going. There seems to be a great scruple now in reference
to the appropriation of lands for the benefit of the people; but the
Federal Government has been very liberal heretofore in granting
lands to the States for railroad purposes. We can pass law after law,
making grant after grant of the public lands to corporations, without
alarming any one here. We have already granted to railroad monopolies, to corporations, twenty-four million two hundred and forty-
seven thousand acres. Those grants hardly meet with opposition in
Congress; but it seems to be very wrong, in the estimation of some,
to grant lands to the people on the conditions proposed in the bill
before us. We find, furthermore, that there have been granted to
the States, as swamp lands—and some of these lands will turn out
to be the most productive on the globe—forty million one hundred
and thirty-three thousand five hundred and sixty-five acres.

In relation to the public lands, and the grants which have been
made by the Government, I have obtained from the Commissioner
of the General Land Office several tables,[17] which I now submit.

Estimate of the quantities of land which will inure to the States
under grants for railroads, up to June 30, 1857.

States.	Acres.	Date of Law.
Illinois	2,595,053	September 20, 1850.
Missouri	1,815,435	June 10, 1852, Feb. 9, 1853.
Arkansas	1,465,297	February 9, 1853.
Michigan	3,096,000	June 3, 1856.
Wisconsin	1,622,800	June 3, 1856.
Iowa	3,456,000	May 15, 1856.
Louisiana	1,102,560	June 3, and Aug. 11, 1856.
Mississippi	950,400	August 11, 1856.
Alabama	1,913,390	May 17, June 3, and Aug. 11, 1856, March 3, 1857.
Florida	1,814,400	May 17, 1856.
Minnesota	4,416,000	March 3, 1857.
Total	24,247,335	

Statement showing the quantity of swamp land approved to the several
States, up to 30th June, 1857:

States.	Acres.
Ohio	25,650.71
Indiana	1,250,937.51
Illinois	1,369,140.72
Missouri	3,615,966.57
Alabama	2,595.51
Mississippi	2,834,796.11
Louisiana	7,601,535.46
Michigan	5,465,232.41

States.	Acres.
Arkansas	5,920,024.94
Florida	10,396,982.47
Wisconsin	1,650,712.10
Total	40,133,564.51

Estimate of unsold and unappropriated lands in each of the States and Territories, including surveyed and unsurveyed, offered and unoffered lands, on the 30th June, 1856:

States and Territories.	Acres.	Number of quarter sections.
Ohio	43,553.34	272
Indiana	36,307.41	227
Illinois	511,662.85	3,198
Missouri	13,365,319.81	83,533
Alabama	9,459,367.74	59,121
Mississippi	5,519,390.69	34,496
Louisiana	5,933,373.83	37,083
Michigan	10,056,298.06	62,852
Arkansas	15,609,542.84	97,560
Florida	18,067,072.75	112,919
Iowa	6,237,661.03	38,985
Wisconsin	15,222,549.50	95,141
California	113,682,436.00	710,515
Minnesota Territory	82,502,608.33	515,641
Oregon "	118,913,241.31	743,208
Washington "	76,444,055.25	477,775
New Mexico "	155,210,804.00	970,067
Utah "	134,243,733.00	839,023
Nebraska "	206,984,747.00	1,293,655
Kansas "	76,361,058.00	477,256
Indian "	42,892,800.00	268,080
Total	1,107,297,572.74	6,920,607

The table giving the estimated quantity of all our public lands, shows the feasibility of the plan in favor of which I have been speaking. I know that some gentlemen from the southern States object to this bill because they fear that it will carry emigrants from the free States into those States. Well, sir, on this point I have drawn some conclusions from figures, which I will present to the Senate. In the State of Alabama there are now undisposed of fifty-nine thousand one hundred and twenty-one quarter sections of land. I ask my southern friends, would it not be better if a man in the State of Alabama would select a quarter section there, and take the two hundred dollars it would have cost him, and expend it there, even though it might be inferior land, than to compel him to pay $1 25 an acre, and emigrate from the State of Alabama to a place where he could get better land? If you compel him to pay the higher price, it becomes his interest to leave his native State; but by permitting him to take the land and expend on its improvement what he would otherwise have to pay, and what it would cost him to move, the chances are that he will remain where he is. In the State of Mississippi there are thirty-four thousand four hundred and ninety-six quarter sections; in Louisiana, thirty-seven thousand; in Arkansas, ninety-seven thousand; in Florida, one hundred and twelve thousand. Altogether, the quarter sections of public lands belonging to the Government amount to six million nine hundred and twenty thousand. How feasible the plan is. I have shown, too, that it would take over six hundred years to dispose of the public lands at the rate we have been disposing of them, and that if you take one million quarter sections and have them settled and cultivated, you will obtain more revenue, and you will enhance the remaining public lands more than the value of those the Government gives.

I live in a southern State; and, if I know myself, I am as good a southern man as any one who lives within the borders of the South. It seems to be feared that by this bill we compel men to go on the lands. I want to compel no man to go. I want to leave each and every man to be controlled by his own inclination, by his own interest, and not to force him; but is it statesmanlike, is it philanthropic, is it Christian, to keep a man in a State, and refuse to let him go, because, it he does go, he will tend to populate some other portion of the country? If a man lives in the county in which I live, and he can, by crossing the line into another county, better his condition, I say let him go. If, by crossing the boundary of my State and going into another, he can better his condition, I say let him go. If a man can go from Tennessee into Illinois, or Louisiana, or Mississippi, or Arkansas, or any other State, and better his condition, let him go. I care not where he goes, so that he locates himself in this great area of freedom, becomes attached to our institutions, and interested in the prosperity and welfare of the country. I care not where he goes, so that he is under the protection of our stars and stripes. I say let him go where he can better the condition of himself, his wife, and children; let him go where he can receive the greatest remuneration for his toil and for his labor. What kind of a policy is it to say that a man shall be locked up where he was born, and shall be confined to the place of his birth? Take the State of North Carolina, represented by the honorable Senator before me, [Mr. Clingman]—and I have no doubt it is his intention to represent that people to their satisfaction—would it have been proper to require the people of North Carolina, from her early settlement to the present time, to be confined within her boundaries? Would they not have looked upon it as a hard sentence? Would they not have looked upon it as oppressive and cruel? North Carolina has supplied the western States with a large proportion of her population, for the reason that by going West they could better their condition.[18] Who would prevent them from doing it? Who would say to the poor man in North Carolina, that has no land of his own to cultivate, that lives upon some barren angle, or some piny plain, or in some other State upon some

New Senate Chamber, 1859. From Ben: Perley Poore, *Perley's Reminiscences of Sixty Years in the National Metropolis* (2 vols., Philadelphia, 1886), I, 491.

Washington City
Jany 12th 1860

My dear Son,

On last night I was much gratified by the receipt of four phials of Arnold's remon pills and at once took two of them and this morning feel somewhat relieved and hope to be entirely so in a few days — There is no election for Speaker as yet and in fact there seems to be but little prospect of one at present — I hope there will be a change for the better before long or it will look like there is a dead lock in the Government.

I see in the dision of the 7th inst that Barksdale has offered an amendment to his bill expelling free negroes from the State which I think from a cursory reading puts the measure in a pretty good

Nostrums and politics: a letter to son Robert, January 12, 1860 (pages 379–81). *Courtesy Henry E. Huntington Library.*

stony ridge, that he must plow and dig the place appointed to him by his landlord, and that he is not to emigrate where he can better his condition? What is his prospect? He has to live poor; he has to live hard; and, in the end, when he dies, poverty, want, is the only inheritance he can leave his children. There is no one who has a higher appreciation of North Carolina than I have; she is my native State. I found it to be my interest to emigrate, and I should have thought it cruel and hard if I had been told that I could not leave her boundary. Although North Carolina did not afford me the advantages of education, though I cannot speak in the language of the schoolmen, and call her my cherishing mother, yet, in the language of Cowper, "with all her faults, I love her still."[19] She is still my mother; she is my native State; and I love her as such, and I love her people, too. But what an idea is it to present, as influencing the action of a statesman, that people may not emigrate from one State to another! Sir, I say let a man go anywhere within the boundaries of the United States where he can better his condition.

Mr. President, if I entertained the notions that some of my friends who oppose this bill do, I should be a more ardent advocate of the policy than I am now, if that were possible. My friend from Alabama [Mr. Clay] entertains some strange notions in reference to Democracy and the people; and in his speech on the fisheries bill, he gave this proposition a kind of side blow, a lick by indirection.[20] I do not object to that; but if I entertained his opinions I should be a more determined and zealous advocate of the policy of this bill than I am now, if that were possible. In his speech upon the Lecompton constitution that Senator, in speaking of the powers of the convention which framed the constitution, said:

> In my opinion, they would have acted in stricter accordance with the spirit and genius of our institutions if they had not submitted it in whole or in part to the popular vote. Our governments are Republics, not democracies. The people exercise their sovereignty not in person at the ballot-box, but through agents, delegates, or representatives. Our fathers founded republican Governments in preference to Democracies, not so much because it would be impracticable as because it would be unwise and inexpedient for the people themselves to assemble and adopt laws.[21]

I have always thought the general idea had been that it was not practicable to do everything in a strict democratic sense, and that it was more convenient for the people to appear through their delegates. But the Senator said further:

> [Johnson continues to quote from Clement C. Clay's Lecompton speech of March 19, in which the Alabamian maintained that the constitution-makers knew that the majority was an irresponsible voice more often "swayed by passion than by reason . . . [and] might sacrifice public good or private rights to any ruling passion or interest of the hour,

with impunity." Clay regretted the growing tendency "to democratize our Government; to submit every question . . . to the vote of the people. This is sheer radicalism," not the Republicanism of our founders. Elsewhere he alluded to "Property . . . as the foundation of every social fabric"; society and government exist to "preserve, protect, and perpetuate rights of property."]

Now, if I entertained these notions, I should unquestionably go for the homestead bill. I am free to say, here, that I do not hold the doctrine advanced by the honorable gentleman from Alabama, to the extent that he goes. I believe the people are capable of self-government. I think they have demonstrated so most clearly; and I do not think the Senator's history of democracy states the case as it should be. I presume in the Senator's own State the people acted directly upon their constitution at the ballot-box.[22] That is the organic law. If they did not there, they have done so in most of the States of the Union; not, perhaps, in their original formation of their governments, but as the people have gone on and advanced in popular government. The honorable Senator seems to be opposed to democratizing; in other words, he is opposed to popularizing our institutions; he is afraid to trust the control of things to the people at the ballot-box. Why, sir, the organic law which confers all the power upon your State Legislatures, creates the different divisions, different departments of the State. The government are controlled at the ballot-box, and the doctrine set forth in the constitution of Alabama is, that the people have a right to abolish and change their form of government when they think proper. The principle is clearly recognized; and on this my honorable friend and myself differ essentially. I find a similar doctrine laid down in a pamphlet which I have here:

In the convention that framed the Constitution of the United States, Gouverneur Morris said, that "Property is the primary object of society." Mr. King said, "Property is the primary object of society." Mr. Butler contended strenuously that "Property was the only just measurer of representation. This was the great object of government; the great cause of war; the great means of carrying it on." Mr. Madison said, that "In future times a great majority of the people will not only be without landed, but any other sort of property. These will either combine under the influence of their common situation—in which case the right of property and the public liberty will not be secure in their hands—or, what is more probable, they will become the tools of opulence and ambition." Gouverneur Morris again said, "give the votes to the people who have no property, and they will sell them to the rich who will be able to buy them. We should not confine our attention to the present moment. The time is not far distant when this country will abound with mechanics and manufacturers, who will receive their bread from their employers. Will such men be the secure and faithful guardians of liberty?" Madison remarks, that those who opposed the property basis of representation, did so on the ground that numbers of people was a fair index to the amount of property in any district.[23]

These are not notions entertained by me; but they are important as the notions of some of our public men at the early formation of our Government. I entertain no such notions. If, however, the Senator from Alabama holds that property is the main object and basis of society, he, above all other men, ought to go for this bill, so as to place every man in the possession of a home and an interest in his country. The very doctrine that he lays down appeals to him trumpet-tongued, and asks him to place these men in a condition where they can be relied upon. His argument is unanswerable, if it be true, in favor of the homestead bill. It is taking men out of a dependent condition; it is preventing this Government from sinking into that condition that Rome did in her decline. I ask him now, if he entertains these opinions, as promulgated in his speech, to come up and join with us in the passage of this bill, and make every man, if possible, a property-holder, interested in his country; give him a basis to settle upon, and make him reliable at the ballot-box.

His speech is a fine production. I heard it with interest at the time it was delivered. I hold the opposite to him. Instead of the voice of the people being the voice of a demon, I go back to the old idea, and I favor the policy of popularizing all our free institutions. We are Democrats, occupying a position here from the South; we start together, but we turn our backs upon each other very soon. His policy would take the Government further from the people. I go in a direction to popularize it, and bring it nearer to the people. There is no better illustration of this than that old maxim, which is adopted in all our ordinary transactions, that "if you want a thing done, send somebody to do it; if you want it well done, go and do it yourself." It applies with great force in governmental affairs as in individual affairs; and as we can advance and make the workings and operation of our Government familiar to and understood by the people, the better for us. I say, when and wherever it is practicable, let the people transact their own business; bring them more in contact with their Government, and then you will arrest expenditure, you will arrest corruption, you will have a purer and better Government.

I hold to the doctrine that man can be advanced; that man can be elevated; that man can be more exalted in his character and condition. We are told, on high authority, that he is made in the image of his God; that he is endowed with a certain amount of divinity. And I believe man can be elevated; man can become more and more endowed with divinity; and as he does he becomes more God-like in his character and capable of governing himself. Let us go on elevating our people, perfecting our institutions, until democracy shall reach such a point of perfection that we can exclaim with truth that the voice of the people is the voice of God.

As I said, I have entertained different notions from those inculcated by the honorable Senator. If I entertained his notions, then I
should be for the homestead. I hold in my hand a document that was
proclaimed in 1776:

We hold these truths to be self-evident: that all men are created equal;
that they are endowed by their Creator with certain inalienable rights;
that among these are life, liberty, and the pursuit of happiness; that to
secure these rights governments are instituted among men, deriving
their just powers from the consent of the governed.

Is property laid down there as the great element and the great
basis of society? It is only one; and Mr. Jefferson laid it down in the
Declaration of Independence, that it was a self-evident truth that
government was instituted—for what? To protect men in life, liberty,
and the pursuit of happiness. That is what Mr. Jefferson said. And
who indorsed it? The men who framed the Declaration of Independence, not going upon the property idea, that that was the only element of society. This was the doctrine established by those who
proclaimed our independence. Life, liberty, and the pursuit of happiness were three great elements of government, and not property
exclusively. When the declaration came forth from the old Congress
hall, it came forth as a column of fire and light.[24] It declared that
the security of life and liberty and the pursuit of happiness, were the
three great elements of government. Mr. Jefferson, in his first inaugural address, which is the greatest paper that has ever been
written in this Government, and I commend it to the reading of those
who say they are Democrats, by way of refreshing their memories,
that they may understand what are correct Democratic principles,
says:

Sometimes it is said that man cannot be trusted with the government
of himself. Can he, then, be trusted with the government of others? Or
have we found angels in the form of kings to govern him? Let history
answer this question.[25]

Mr. Jefferson seems to think man can be trusted with the government of himself. In the Declaration of Independence he does not
embrace property; in fact, it is not referred to. But I am willing to
concede that it is one of the primary and elementary principles in
government. Mr. Jefferson declares the great truth that man is to
be trusted; that man is capable of governing himself, and that he
has a right to govern himself. In the same inaugural adresss of Mr.
Jefferson, we find the passage usually attributed to Washington's
Farewell Address, which has got universal circulation—that we
should pursue our own policy; that we should promote our own institutions, maintaining friendly relations with all, entangling alliances with none. Let us carry out the doctrines of the inaugural

address of Mr. Jefferson; let us carry out the great principles laid down in the Declaration of Independence, which this homestead bill embraces.

But I wish to call attention to some other authority on this subject. As contradistinguished from the views of the Senator from Alabama, I present the views of a recent writer[26] as in accordance with my own notions of Democracy:

The Democratic party represents the great principle of progress. It is onward and outward in its movements. It has a heart for action, and motives for a world. It constitutes the principles of diffusion, and is to humanity what the centrifugal force is to the revolving orbs of a universe. What motion is to them, Democracy is to principle. It is the soul in action. It conforms to the providence of God. It has confidence in man, and an abiding reliance in his high destiny. It seeks the largest liberty, the greatest good, and the surest happiness. It aims to build up the great interests of the many, to the least detriment of the few. It remembers the past, without neglecting the present. It establishes the present, without fearing to provide for the future. It cares for the weak, while it permits no injustice to the strong. It conquers the oppressor, and prepares the subjects of tyranny for freedom. It melts the bigot's heart to meekness, and reconciles his mind to knowledge. It dispels the clouds of ignorance and superstition, and prepares the people for instruction and self-respect. It adds wisdom to legislation, and improved judgment to government. It favors enterprise that yields a reward to the many and an industry that is permanent. It is the pioneer of humanity—the conservator of nations. It fails only when it ceases to be true to itself. *Vox populi vox Dei*, has proved to be both a proverb and a prediction.

It is a mistake to suppose that Democracy may not be advanced under different forms of government. Its own, it should be remembered, is the highest conventional form, that which precedes the lofty independence of the individual spoken of by the Apostle to the Hebrews, who will need government but from the law which the Lord has placed in his heart.

In one respect, all nations are governed upon the same principle; that is, each adopts the form which it has the understanding and the power to sustain. There is in all a greater or lesser power, and it requires no profound speculation to decide which will control. A tyrannical dictator may do more to advance the true interests of Democracy than a moderate sovereign who is scrupulously guarded by an antiquated constitution; for the tyrant adds vigor to his opponents by his deeds of oppression.

The frequent question as to what form of government is best, is often answered without any reference to condition or application of principles. There can be properly but one answer, and yet the application of that answer may lead to great diversity of views.

When it is asserted that the democratic form of government is unquestionably the best, it must be considered that the answer not only designates the form preferred, but implies a confident belief in the advanced condition of the people who are to be the subjects of it. It premises the capacity for self control, and a corresponding degree of knowledge in regard to the rights, balances, and necessities, of society. It involves a discriminating appreciation of the varied duties of the man, the citizen, and the legislator. It presupposes a reasonable knowledge of the legitimate means and ends of government, enlarged views of humanity, and of the elements of national existence.

The democratic form of government is the best, because its standard of moral requisition is the highest. It claims for man a universality of interest, liberty and justice[.] It is Christianity, with its mountain beacons and guides. It is the standard of Deity based on the eternal principles of truth, passing through and rising above the yielding clouds of ignorance, into the regions of infinite wisdom. As we live on, this "pillar of the cloud by day, and the pillar of fire by night," will not be taken from before the people, but stand immovable, immeasurable, and in the brightness of its glory continue to shed increasing light on a world and a universe.

The great objects of knowledge and moral culture of the people are among its most prominent provisions. Practical religion and religious freedom are the sunshine of its growth and glory. It is the sublime and mighty standard spoken of by the Psalmist, who exclaims, in the beautiful language of poetical conception:

"The Lord is high above all nations, and his glory above the heavens. Who is like unto the Lord our God, who dwelleth on high; who humbleth himself to behold the things that are in heaven and in the earth? He raiseth up the poor out of the dust, and lifteth the needy out of the dunghill, that he may set him with princes, even with the princes of the people."

Democracy is a permanent element of progress, and is present everywhere, whatever may be the temporary form of the ruling power. Its inextinguishable fires first burst forth in an empire, and its welcome lights cheer the dark domains of despotism. While tyrants hate the patriot and exile him from their contracted dominions, the spirit of Democracy invests him as a missionary of humanity, and inspires him with an eloquence which moves a world. Its lightning rays cannot be hidden; its presence cannot be banished. Dictators, kings, and emperors, are but its servants; and, as man becomes elevated to the dignity of self-knowledge and control, their administration ceases. Their rule indicates an imperfect state of society, and may be regarded as the moral props of the builder, necessary only to sustain a people in their different periods of growth. One cannot speak of them lightly, nor indulge in language that should seem to deny their fitness as the instruments of good in the hands of Providence. Their true position may be best gathered from the prediction which is based upon a knowledge of the past and present condition of man—that all kingdoms and empires must cease, whenever a people have a knowledge of their rights, and acquire the power of a practical application of principles. This is the work of time. It is the work of constant, repeated trial. The child that attempts to step an hundred times and falls; the new fledged bird that tries its feeble wings again and again before it is able to sweep the circle of the sky with its kindred flock, indicate the simple law upon which all strength depends, whether it be the strength of an insect, or the strength of a nation.

Because a people do not succeed in changing their form of government, even after repeated trials, we are not to infer that they are indulging in impracticable experiments, nor that they will be disappointed in ultimately realizing the great objects of their ambition. Indeed, all failures of this class are indicative of progressive endeavor. They imply an increasing knowledge of the true dignity of man, and a growing disposition to engage in new and more and more difficult endeavors. These endeavors are but the exercise of a nation, and without them, no people can ever command the elements of national existence and of self control. But inquiries in regard to so extensive a subject should be shaped within more practical limits.   *   *   *   *   *   *   *   *   *   *   *   *

The triumphs of Democracy constitute the way-marks of the world. They demand no extraneous element of endurance for permanency, no fictitious splendor for embellishment, no borrowed greatness for glory.

Originating in the inexhaustible sources of power, moved by the spirit of love and liberty, and guided by the wisdom which comes from the instincts and experience of the immortal soul, as developed in the people, Democracy exists in the imperishable principle of progress, and registers its achievements in the institutions of freedom, and in the blessings which characterize and beautify the realities of life. Its genius is to assert and advance the true dignity of mind, to elevate the motives and affections of man, and to extend, establish, protect, and equalize the common rights of humanity.

"Condorcet, although an aristocrat by genius and by birth, became a Democrat from philosophy."—*Lamartine.*

A few years since, a Whig member of the United States Senate sneeringly asked Senator Allen, of Ohio, the question, "what is Democracy?" The following was the prompt reply: "Democracy is a sentiment not to be appalled, corrupted, or compromised. It knows no baseness; it cowers to no danger; it oppresses no weakness; destructive only of despotism, it is the sole conservator of liberty, labor, and property. It is the sentiment of freedom, of equal rights, of equal obligations—the law of nature pervading the law of the land."

"What, sir," asked Patrick Henry, in the Virginia convention of 1778, "is the genius of Democracy? Let me read that clause of the bill of rights of Virginia which relates to this, (third clause:) That government is or ought to be instituted for the common benefit, protection, and security of the people, nation, or community; of all the various modes and forms of government, that is best which is capable of producing the greatest degree of happiness and safety, and is most effectually secured against the dangers of mal-administration; and that whenever any Government shall be found inadequate, or contrary to those principles, or contrary to those purposes, a majority of the community hath an indubitable, inalienable, and indefeasible right to reform, alter, or abolish it, in such manner as shall be judged the most conducive to the public weal."—*Elliot's Debates,* vol. 3, page 77.

In the same convention, Judge Marshall, said:

What are the favorite maxims of Democracy? A strict observance of justice and public faith, and a steady adherence to virtue—these, sir, are the principles of a good government.—*Ibid.,* vol. 3, page 223.

"Democracy," says the late Mr. Legaré, of South Carolina, in an article published in the New York Review, "in the high and only true sense of that much abused word, is the destiny of nations, because it is the spirit of Christianity."—Vol. 5, page 297.

I have referred to the remarks of the Senator from Alabama to show that if his doctrines were true, he should go for the passage of the homestead bill, because, in order to sustain the Government on the principles laid down by him, every man should be a property-holder. I want it understood that I enter a disclaimer to the doctrine presented by him, and merely present his argument to show why he, above all others, ought to go for the homestead policy. I refer to Mr. Legaré, Judge Marshall, and the author of the history of Democracy, as laying down my notions of Democracy, as contradistinguished from those laid down by the distinguished Senator from Alabama. We are both members of the Democratic party. I claim to be a Democrat, East, West, North, or South, or anywhere else.

I have nothing to disguise. I have referred to the Declaration of Independence, and to Mr. Jefferson's inaugural address, for the purpose of showing that Democracy means something very different from what was laid down by the distinguished Senator from Alabama. I furthermore refer to these important documents to show that property is not the leading element of government and of society. Mr. Jefferson lays down, as truths to be self-evident, that life, liberty, and the pursuit of happiness are the leading essentials of government.

But it is not my purpose to dwell longer on that; and I wish to pass to the speech of the Senator from South Carolina, [Mr. Hammond.] I disagree in much that was said by that distinguished Senator; and I wish to show that he ought to go for the homestead policy, so as to interest every man in the country. If property is the leading and principal element on which society rests; if property is the main object for which government was created, the gentlemen who are the foremost, the most zealous, and most distinguished advocates of that doctrine should sustain the homestead policy. The honorable Senator from South Carolina, in his speech on the Lecompton constitution, by innuendo or indirection, had a hit at the homestead—a side blow. He said:

Your people are awaking. They are coming here. They are thundering at our doors for homesteads, one hundred and sixty acres of land for nothing; and southern Senators are supporting them. Nay, they are assembling, as I have said, with arms in their hands, and demanding work at $1,000 a year for six hours a day. Have you heard that the ghosts of Mendoza and Torquemada are stalking in the streets of your great cities? That the Inquisition is at hand? [27]

If this be true, as assumed by the distinguished Senator from South Carolina, is it not an argument why men should be placed in a condition where they will not clamor, where they will not raise mobs to threaten Government, and demand homesteads? Interest these men in the country; give them homes, or let them take homes; let them become producers; or let them become better citizens; let them be more reliable at the ballot-box. I want to take them on their ground, their principle, that property is the main element of society and of government; and if their doctrine be true, the argument is still stronger in favor of the homestead than the position I assume. But the distinguished Senator from South Carolina goes on:

In all social systems there must be a class to do the menial duties, to perform the drudgery of life. That is, a class requiring but a low order of intellect, and but little skill. Its requisites are vigor, docility, fidelity. Such a class you must have, or you would not have that other class which leads progress, civilization, and refinement. It constitutes the very mud sill of society and of political government; and you might as well attempt to build a house in the air, as to build either the one or the other, except on this mud sill.

"The poor ye always have with you"; for the man who lives by daily labor, and scarcely lives at that, and who has to put his labor in the market, and take the best he can get for it—in short, your whole hireling class of manual laborers and "operatives," as you call them, are essentially slaves. The difference between us is, that our slaves are hired for life and well compensated; there is no starvation, no begging, no want of employment among our people; and not too much employment either. Yours are hired by the day, not cared for, and scantily compensated, which may be proved in the most painful manner, at any hour, in any street in any of your large towns. Why, you meet more beggars in one day, in any single street of the city of New York, than you would meet in a lifetime in the whole South. We do not think that whites should be slaves either by law or necessity.

In this portion of the Senator's remarks I concur. I do not think whites should be slaves; and if slavery is to exist in this country, I prefer black slavery to white slavery. But what I want to get at is, to show that my worthy friend from South Carolina should defend the homestead policy, and the impolicy of making the invidious remarks that have been made here in reference to a portion of the population of the United States. Mr. President, so far as I am concerned, I feel that I can afford to speak what are my sentiments. I am no aspirant for anything on the face of God Almighty's earth. I have reached the summit of my ambition. The acme of all my hopes has been attained, and I would not give the position I occupy here to-day for any other in the United States. Hence, I say, I can afford to speak what I believe to be true.

In one sense of the term we are all slaves. A man is a slave to his ambition; he is a slave to his avarice; he is a slave to his necessities; and, in enumerations of this kind, you can scarcely find any man, high or low in society, but who, in some sense, is a slave; but they are not slaves in the sense we mean at the South, and it will not do to assume that every man who toils for his living is a slave. If that be so, all are slaves; for all must toil more or less, mentally or physically. But in the other sense of the term, we are not slaves. Will it do to assume that the man who labors with his hands, every man who is an operative in a manufacturing establishment or a shop, is a slave? No, sir; that will not do. Will it do to assume that every man who does not own slaves, but has to live by his own labor, is a slave? That will not do. If this were true, it would be very unfortunate for a good many of us, and especially so for me. I am a laborer with my hands, and I never considered myself a slave, in the acceptation of the term slave in the South. I do own some; I made them by my industry, by the labor of my hands. In that sense of the term I should have been a slave while I was earning them with the labor of my hands.

Mr. HAMMOND. Will the Senator define a slave?

Mr. JOHNSON, of Tennessee. What we understand to be a slave in the South, is a person who is held to service during his or her natural life, subject to, and under the control of, a master who has the right to appropriate the products of his or her labor to his own use. The necessities of life, and the various positions in which a man may be placed, operated upon by avarice, gain, or ambition, may cause him to labor; but that does not make a slave. How many men are there in society who go out and work with their own hands, who reap in the field, and mow in a meadow, who hoe corn, who work in the shops? Are they slaves? If we were to go back and follow out this idea, that every operative and laborer is a slave, we should find that we have had a great many distinguished slaves since the world commenced. Socrates, who first conceived the idea of the immortality of the soul, Pagan as he was, labored with his own hands;—yes, wielded the chisel and the mallet, giving polish and finish to the stone; he afterwards turned to be a fashioner and constructor of the mind. Paul, the great expounder, himself was a tent-maker, and worked with his hands: was he a slave? Archimedes, who declared that, if he had a place on which to rest the fulcrum, with the power of his lever he could move the world: was he a slave? Adam, our great father and head, the lord of the world, was a tailer by trade: I wonder if he was a slave?

When we talk about laborers and operatives, look at the columns that adorn this Chamber, and see their finish and style. We are lost in admiration at the architecture of your buildings, and their massive columns. We can speak with admiration. What would it have been but for hands to construct it? Was the artizan who worked upon it a slave? Let us go to the South and see how the matter stands there. Is every man that is not a slaveholder to be denominated a slave because he labors? Why indulge in such a notion? The argument cuts at both ends of the line, and these kind of doctrines do us infinite harm in the South. There are operatives there; there are laborers there; there are mechanics there. Are they slaves? Who is it in the South that gives us title and security to the institution of slavery? Who is it, let me ask every southerner around me? Suppose, for instance, we take the State of South Carolina; and there are many things about her and her people that I admire: we find that the 384,984 slaves in South Carolina are owned by how many whites?[28] They are owned by 25,556. Take the State of Tennessee, with a population of 800,000; 239,000 slaves are owned by 33,864 persons. The slaves in the State of Alabama are owned by 29,295 whites. The whole number of slaveholders in all the slave States, when summed up, makes 347,000, owning three and a half million slaves. The white population in South Carolina is 274,000; the slaves greater than the whites. The aggregate population of the State is 668,507.

The operatives in South Carolina are 68,549. Now, take the 25,000 slave-owners out, and a large proportion of the people of South Carolina work with their hands. Will it do to assume that, in the State of South Carolina, the State of Tennessee, the State of Alabama, and the other slaveholding States, all those who do not own slaves are slaves themselves? Will this assumption do? What does it do at home in our own States? It has a tendency to raise prejudice, to engender opposition to the institution of slavery itself. Yet our own folks will do it.

[Mason interrupts to point out that Johnson's figures represent only heads of families and that any numerical comparison of slaveholders and slaves should consider not only the owner but also his family.]

Mr. JOHNSON, of Tennessee. The Senator says I have not made an exhibit of the fact. The Senator interrupted me before I had concluded. I gave way as a matter of courtesy to him. Perhaps his speech would have had no place, if he had waited to hear me a few moments longer.

Mr. MASON. I shall wait. I thought the Senator had passed that point.

Mr. JOHNSON, of Tennessee. I was stating the fact, that according to the census tables three hundred and forty-seven thousand white persons owned the whole number of slaves in the southern States. I was about to state that the families holding these slaves might average six or eight or ten persons, all of whom are interested in the products of slave labor, and many of these slaves are held by minors and by females. I was not alluding to the matter for the purpose the Senator from Virginia seems to have intimated, and I should have been much obliged to him if he had waited until he heard my application of these figures. I was going to show that expressions like those to which I have alluded, operate against us in the South, and I was following the example of no one. I was taking these facts from the census tables, which were published by order of Congress, to show the bad policy and injustice of declaring that the laboring portion of our population were slaves and menials. Such declarations should not be applied to the people either North or South. I wished to say in that connection, that, in my opinion, if a few men at the North and at the South, who entertain extreme views on the subject of slavery, and desire to keep up agitation, were out of the way, the great mass of the people, North and South, would go on prosperously and harmoniously under our institutions.

Nor, sir, am I a conservative; but I am for administering this

Government on correct principles. I believe the time will come when the northern States will be the advocates of the institution of slavery in the South. I believe the time will come which we heard announced on the other side of the House, when Massachusetts will be for free trade. How long is it since she was standing here advocating protection, high tariffs, and bounties? Yesterday her Senator told us she was for free trade, and the abolition of all custom-houses.[29] I am not a prophet, nor the son of a prophet, but I predict here that the time will come when the northern States will be the advocates of the institution of slavery as it exists in the South. Why? The whole difficulty, in my judgment, in regard to slavery, has arisen from a jealousy of political power in the Congress of the United States. The people of the North have been told that the South obtain an undue proportion of power in the councils of the nation because of the three fifths representation of slaves; that on the three million slaves they get eighteen Representatives. Now, if the question were looked at properly, it would be found that, instead of slavery being an element of political power, it is an element of political weakness. If slavery were abolished in the South, and her slaves made free men, instead of the South having eighteen Representatives for her three million slaves, she would have thirty Representatives. But for this provision of the Constitution, all the negroes in the South would be counted, and we should have a larger representation in the councils of the nation.

This is what I was going to show; and the time will come when the South will have the North advocating the institution of slavery. Why do I say so? Let us go on with the policy I am proposing, settle and cultivate these lands, reduce them to cultivation, widen the demand for cotton, widen the demand for rice, widen the demand for sugar and tobacco, widen the demand for the products of slave labor; and just in proportion as you do that, you reconcile the North to the institution of slavery. Let us populate our public lands, and reduce them to cultivation; let us embrace Cuba; and when we shall have a sufficient amount of country adapted to the production of sugar, and to the production of cotton, we shall supply the demands at home. Taking four hundred thousand bales of cotton as the amount consumed in the United States, and run your population to one hundred and fifty millions, and you create a demand at home for every pound of cotton that can be grown in the United States. Run it up to five hundred millions, and there will be more demand for rice, cotton, and sugar at home than you can produce.

When the northern people come to see and know that sugar, cotton, and rice, cannot be produced by any other kind of labor than slave labor, they will become reconciled to the institution. The demand becoming great, they will see and feel the necessity of having those articles. Cotton must be had; sugar must be had; rice must be had. Then present that other great idea, that slave labor is the only labor adapted to the production of these articles, and the non-slaveholding States will become reconciled to the institution. Especially will this be so when the northern mind comes to understand that the man who has his capital invested in labor is the surest and most reliable friend and advocate. Let us understand this idea.

The Senator from Virginia mistook where I was driving. He mistook the direction of the conclusion I was coming too. Look at the three million slaves owned by three hundred and forty-seven thousand white persons, and those interested.[30] Counting them at $500 a head, how much will they come to? Fifteen hundred million dollars invested in what? In labor. The time will come when slave labor will be more productive in sugar, cotton, and rice, than any other; when the demand increases at home and abroad. You will find that slaves will be confined to that description of labor which is more productive, and the production of those articles which are most needed by the country. Then, do we not see and understand that just in proportion as you foster the one you protect and foster the other?

[Mason again interrupts to reiterate his previous objections.]

Mr. JOHNSON, of Tennessee. The gentleman, in his former remarks, gave the explanation of it, and I told him I had not reached that point, and if he had waited a few moments I would have made the same explanation he put in my mouth. But I was going to show, Mr. President, that the people of the non-slaveholding States would ultimately become the advocates of the institution of slavery. Why? Is the South no market for the productions of the non-slaveholding States? Where does their pork, where do their horses, where do the mules, where do the large proportion of all the articles of our consumption come from? From Ohio, Indiana, and Illinois, a large proportion is furnished. Well, then, just in proportion as you create a demand in the South for those articles the northern producers become interested in the institutions of the South, and just in proportion as the South can get a high price for her cotton, she will pay a high price for every hog, every mule, and every horse she buys. Just so with the North in the manufacture of articles. They go on manufacturing, and the South is a market for them. Cotton is the great staple they consume. Hence, they become interested in the production of cotton. The South is interested in the articles consumed by the North, and, in return, the South is a market for their manufactured articles.

I have said that the three hundred and forty-seven thousand slave-holders in the South having an interest in slaves to the amount of $1,500,000,000, were the best friends, instead of being antagonists, to northern labor. Why do I say so? Their capital is invested in labor; and just in proportion as their capital is invested in labor, they become interested in hunting up new markets, in devising ways and means for the consumption of the products of slave labor; and therefore, obtaining a higher price for those productions, and just in proportion as they realize a higher price for labor, in the very same proportion they are protecting the labor of the white man in the non-slaveholding States. The necessity of the production of cotton and rice, when population reaches a certain point, and its consumption comes up to the product, will cause the northern mind to be reconciled to the institution of slavery.

Why is Great Britain so much opposed to the institution of slavery here? She sees and knows there are $1,500,000,000 invested in labor. That labor brings about an influence advocating high prices for labor. In what does the capital of Great Britain consist? It is in stocks and in money. It occupies a position that arrays it against high prices for labor. The capital of Great Britain is in the field against the world in opposition to high prices of labor. Her object is to reduce labor down to the lowest point she can get it. The interest of the southern man, his capital being in labor, is to bring it up to the highest price. If Great Britain can succeed in inducing the United States to change or to withdraw her capital out of labor, and put it in stocks or money, what would be the effect? The entire capital in the United States would at once be arrayed on the side of Great Britain, and on the side of the aristocracy of wealth against high prices for labor.

This number of persons and this immense amount of capital and talent connected with slave labor, make the South the surest and the most reliable advocate the northern man has for high prices for labor; and the time will come when there will be a perfect reciprocity in this country. The time will come, if we act as brethren and members of the same great Confederacy, when the northern man will see it to be his interest to stand by the institution of slave labor; when the southern man will see it to be his interest to stand by the Union, to stand by the agriculturists, and by the manufacturer. Then, let us all go on harmoniously and gloriously together, and fill up and carry out our destiny.

Take a simple illustration. A man at the South has a thousand dollars invested in labor. Does not that man try to get the highest price he can for the products of that labor? Take another man who has a thousand dollars in money. He has labor to buy, and does he not try to get labor as cheap as he can for his thousand dollars? Most unquestionably he does. The law is unerring and well established, and if it were well understood throughout the whole country, all the strife and turmoil with reference to the institution of slavery would be swept away, and the country everywhere reconciled. The Senator from Virginia, I think, interrupted me too soon in supplying what he supposed to be a deficiency in my statement.

Sir, carry out the homestead policy, attach the people to the soil, induce them to love the Government, and you will have the North reconciled to the South, and the South to the North, and we shall not have invidious doctrines preached to stir up bad feelings in either section. I know that in my own State, and in the other southern States, the men who do not own slaves are among the first to take care of the institution. They will submit to no encroachment from abroad, no interference from other sections.

I have said, Mr. President, much more than I intended to say, and, I fear, in rather a desultory manner, but I hope I have made myself understood on the subject of slavery. I heard that some gentlemen were going to offer an amendment to this bill, providing that the Government should furnish every man with a slave. So far as I am concerned, if it suited him, and his inclination led him that way, I wish to God every head of a family in the United States had one to take the drudgery and menial service off his family. I would have no objection to that; but this intimation was intended as a slur upon my proposition. I want that to be determined by the people of the respective States, and not by the Congress of the United States. I do not want this body to interfere by innuendo or by amendment, prescribing that the people shall have this or the other. I desire to leave that to be determined by the people of the respective States, and not by the Congress of the United States.

I hope, Mr. President, that this bill will be passed. I think it involves the very first principles of the Government: it is founded upon statesmanship, humanity, philanthropy, and even upon Christianity itself. I know the argument has been made, why permit one portion of the people to go and take some of this land and not another? The law is in general terms; it places it in the power of every man who will go to take a portion of the land. The Senator from Alabama suggests to me that a person, in order to get the benefit of this bill, must prove that he is not the owner of other land. An amendment was yesterday inserted in the bill striking out that provision.[31] Then it places all on an equality to go and take. Why should this not be done? It was conceded yesterday that the land was owned by the people. There are over three million heads of families in the United States; and if every man who is the head of a family were to take a quarter section of public land, there would still be nearly four million quarter sections left. If some people go and take quarter sections, it does not interfere with the rights of others, for he who goes takes only a part of that which is his, and takes nothing that belongs to anybody else. The domain belongs to the whole people; the equity is in the great mass of the people; the Government holds the fee and passes the title, but the beneficial interest is in the people. There are, as I have said, two quarter sections of land for every head of a family in the United States, and we merely propose to permit a head of a family to take one half of that which belongs to him.

I believe the passage of this bill will strengthen the bonds of the Union. It will give us a better voting population, and just in proportion as men become interested in property, they will become reconciled to all the institutions of property in the country in whatever shape they may exist. Take the institution of slavery, for instance: would you rather trust it to the mercies of a people liable to be ruled by the mobs of which my honorable friend from South Carolina spoke, or would you prefer an honest set of landholders? Which would be the most reliable? Who would guaranty the greatest security to our institutions, when they come to the test of the ballot-box?

Mr. President, I hope the Senate will pass this bill. I think it will be the beginning of a new state of things—a new era.

So far as I am concerned—I say it not in any spirit of boast or egotism—if this bill were passed, and the system it inaugurates carried out, granting a reasonable quantity of land for a man's family, looking far into the distance to see what is to result from it—a stable, an industrious, a hardy, a Christian, a philanthropic community growing out of it, I should feel that the great object of my little mission was fulfilled. All that I desire is the honor and the credit of being one of the American Congress to consummate and to carry out this great scheme that is to elevate our race and to make our institutions more permanent. I want no reputation as some have insinuated. You may talk about Jacobinism, Red Republicanism, and so on. I pass by such insinuations as the idle wind which I regard not.

I know the motives that prompt me to action. I can go back to that period in my own history when I could not say I had a home. This being so, when I cast my eyes from one extreme of the United States to the other, and behold the great number that are homeless, I feel for them. I believe this bill would put them in possession of homes; and I want to see them realizing that sweet conception when each man can proclaim, "I have a home; an abiding place for my wife and for my children; I am not the tenant of another; I am my own ruler; and I will move according to my own will, and not at the dictation of another." Yes, Mr. President, if I should never be heard of again on the surface of God's habitable globe, the proud and conscious satisfaction of having contributed my little aid to the consummation of this great measure is all the reward I desire.

The people need friends. They have a great deal to bear. They make all; they do all; but how little they participate in the legislation of the country? All, or nearly all, of our legislation is for corporations, for monopolies, for classes, and individuals; but the great mass who produce all, who make all while we do nothing but consume, are little cared for; their rights and interests are neglected and overlooked. Let us, as patriots, let us as statesmen, let us as Christians, consummate this great measure which will exert an influence throughout the civilized world in fulfilling our destiny. I thank the Senate for their attention.[32]

Cong. Globe, 35 Cong., 1 Sess., 2265–73; pamphlet printed at the *Congressional Globe* office.

1. Following Johnson's remarks of the preceding day, Senators Collamer and Clingman offered amendments. With Johnson's acquiescence, Collamer's amendments were adopted, as were Johnson's amendments to the second and fifth sections. Clingman, an opponent of the bill, proposed changing the first section, which offered a homestead "upon condition of occupancy and cultivation . . . for the period herein specified," so as to provide any head of family a warrant for one hundred and sixty acres "to be located in the same manner as that under which the bounty land warrants heretofore issued have been located on any of the public lands of the United States subject to entry." It was upon Clingman's amendment that the discussion continued. *Cong. Globe*, 35 Cong., 1 Sess., 2240; S. 25, Johnson Papers, LC, Ser. 2.
2. Solomon Foot (1802–1866) of Vermont, state legislator (1833–38, 1847–48) and Whig congressman (1843–47), was a Whig–Republican senator (1851–66). Though in Congress when Johnson first proposed homestead legislation (March 12, 1846), he did not take an active interest in the project. *BDAC*, 901; *DAB*, VI, 498–99.
3. The elapsed time was six years, *one month*, and fifteen days.
4. The reference to Moses and the subsequent quotations from Vattel and Jackson come virtually verbatim from Johnson's Speech on the Homestead Bill [Appendix Version], July 25, 1850. *Johnson Papers*, I, 563–64.
5. "An Act for granting lands to the Inhabitants and settlers of Vincennes and the Illinois country," March 3, 1791. *U. S. Statutes*, I, 221–22.
6. Asa Biggs had recently resigned to become a federal judge.
7. After modest grants (8,198,593 acres) to assist railroads during the first three years of the decade, Congress had recently, in 1856 and 1857, in "a perfect flood" authorized the transfer of 19,678,179 acres of public land to the railroads. It is no wonder that Johnson and his homestead associates felt that ample and recent precedent had been set for the gift of land without payment. Lewis H. Haney, *A Congressional History of Railways in the United States* (2 vols. in 1, New York, 1968 [1908, 1910]), II, 14–18.
8. Johnson is inaccurate in this statement. When he first introduced a homestead bill on March 27, 1846, he made no comments which were recorded by the House reporter. The passage quoted is from his Speech on the Homestead Bill [Appendix Version], July 25, 1850. *Johnson Papers*, I, 300–301, 568–69.

9. Due to the financial crisis of 1857, both pauperism and crime were on the rise in New York City. By 1858, according to the *Annual Report* of the New York Association for Improving the Conditions of the Poor, some 130,000 persons, or approximately one-seventh of the city's population, received relief of some kind. Samuel Rezneck, "The Influence of Depression upon American Opinion, 1857–1859," *Journal of Economic History,* II (May, 1942), 18.

10. In his famous speech of March 4, 1858, James H. Hammond of South Carolina asserted that "Cotton is King" and referred to the social necessity of an inferior class—"the mud-sills of society and of political government." *Cong. Globe,* 35 Cong., 1 Sess., 962.

11. "The mobs of great cities add just so much to the support of pure government as sores do to the strength of the human body." Thomas Jefferson, *Notes on the State of Virginia,* William Peden, ed. (Chapel Hill, 1955), 165.

12. Ten days earlier Johnson had borrowed from the Library of Congress Volumes II and IV of Niebuhr's *Rome.* He seems to have drawn particularly upon Lecture LXXVII. Borrower's Ledger, 1857–59, Library of Congress Archives, 146; Barthold G. Niebuhr, *Lectures on the History of Rome . . .* Leonard Schmitz, ed. (3 vols., London, 1849), II, 275–85 *passim.*

13. For respectable middle-class Americans of the mid-nineteenth century, "agrarianism" had a pejorative meaning, conveying the idea of "levelling," or forced distribution to the landless of the property of the landed. See *Johnson Papers,* I, 572n.

14. *House Ex. Doc.* No. 1, 31 Cong., 2 Sess., 26.

15. Alexander Pope, *Epistle to Dr. Arbuthnot,* l. 398. Stevenson, *Quotations,* 238.

16. A common misquotation of "Westward the course of empire takes its way." George Berkeley, *On the Prospects of Planting Arts and Learning in America. Ibid.,* 520.

17. Evidently these tables were included in the Letter from Thomas A. Hendricks, January 11, 1858.

18. The seventh and eighth censuses had dramatically revealed the migration of Tarheels from their native state. In 1850 nearly 300,000 North Carolinians were living in other states; ten years later the figure exceeded 400,000. Hugh T. Lefler and Albert R. Newsome, *North Carolina* (Chapel Hill, 1954), 306.

19. This is a paraphrase of "England, with all thy faults I love thee still, / My country!" William Cowper, *The Task,* Bk. II.

20. Opposing bounties for the New England codfisheries, Clement C. Clay, in an extended speech on May 4, 1858, inveighed against "a sentiment already too pervading in the country, of dependence on the Government for support." Johnson undoubtedly refers to the peroration: "Suppose it were possible for this Government to supply all the wants and satisfy all the desires of its citizens—to give lands to the landless, houses to the shelterless, food to the hungry, and clothing to the naked: how long would science, art, literature, freedom, religion, anything that ennobles man, and elevates him above the beast, survive such an experiment? How long would we have a Government worth preserving, or freemen to preserve it? Such a Government would prove a greater curse than that of Adam, and more intolerable than the vilest tyranny of barbaric autocrats." *Cong. Globe,* 35 Cong., 1 Sess., 1935.

21. *Ibid.,* App. 145.

22. The Alabama Constitution of 1819 provided that all political power resided in the people, who "have at all times an inalienable and indefeasible right to alter, reform, or abolish their form of government, in such manner as they may think expedient." *The Constitutions of the Several States of the Union and United States in the Year 1859* (New York, [1879?]), 307–8.

23. Although the pamphlet from which Johnson quotes cannot be identified, the several extracts come from James Madison's record of the constitu-

tional convention. See Max Farrand, ed., *The Records of the Federal Convention* (3 vols., New Haven, 1911), I, 541–42; II, 202, 203.

24. Exod. 40:38.

25. Richardson, *Messages*, I, 322.

26. The writer and pamphlet have not been identified.

27. *Cong. Globe*, 35 Cong., 1 Sess., 962.

28. With the exception of Tennessee's population, here rounded out from 756,836, Johnson has relied on the 1850 census figures. J. D. B. DeBow, *Statistical View of the United States . . . Compendium of the Seventh Census* (Washington, D. C., 1854), 45, 82, 95, 102.

29. This is a remarkable oversimplification, not to say distortion, of Henry Wilson's position in the previous day's debate. Although the specific discussion concerned placing a duty on salt and sugar, Wilson was expatiating upon the larger question of the respective fairness of direct and indirect taxation for raising revenue. Interpreting Jefferson Davis' position as favoring tariff duties as the sole source of revenue for support of the government, Wilson, protesting his concern for the laborer who, he averred, would under such a policy bear an undue tax burden, intemperately proclaimed, "then I say abolish your custom-houses altogether, and give us a system of direct taxation—taxation upon the property of the country, instead of taxation upon the labor of the country. Rather than adopt the policy indicated by the Senator from Mississippi . . . I would go for the entire abolition of your revenue system, and resort to direct taxation for the support of the Government." Obviously, such a statement, made in the course of a heated debate, has far less significance than Johnson claims for it. *Cong. Globe.*, 35 Cong., 1 Sess., 2234.

30. The 1850 census lists 3,204,313 slaves and 347,525 slave owners. DeBow, *1850 Census, Compendium*, 82, 95.

31. The previous day Johnson himself had offered this amendment. See Amendments to Homestead Bill, May 19, 1858.

32. The Senate proceeded with executive business before adjourning. On May 27, over Johnson's protest, a decision to postpone further consideration of the homestead bill until the next session was approved, 30–22. *Cong. Globe*, 35 Cong., 1 Sess., 2273, 2424–26.

To Committee of Tennessee Legislature,[1] *Nashville*

Washington City,
May 25th, 1858.

Gentlemen: —Your letter of —inst. making inquiry in regard to the Secretary of State making a bond to the Governor, as required by the act referred to, was received by last night's mail. My recollection is that the Secretary of State did execute a bond as required by law, and that the bond was filed in the office of the Secretary of State, with the bonds of the Comptroller. At this moment I do not remember the names of the securities, upon the bonds of either Secretary or Comptroller; at the time they were deemed good and sufficient. I will add, it may be possible that these bonds were filed with the bonds of the Clerks from the different counties, which are deposited in the Secretary's office for safe keeping.

I have the honor to be, most respectfully,

Your obedient ser'vt,   Andrew Johnson.

Hons. J. D. Goodpasture, A. F. Goff, T. W. Newman, M. Vaughn, *Committee.*

Nashville *Union and American*, June 8, 1858.

1. A joint select committee of the General Assembly was appointed in May, 1858, to investigate defalcations of state internal improvement bonds. Secretary of State F. N. W. Burton, who by virtue of office (under the Internal Improvement Act of 1846) served as commissioner of internal improvements, was implicated in the scandal. His personal bond of $20,000, as required by the act, could not be located. Burton resigned as secretary of state on May 29. *Tenn. Acts*, 1845–46, Ch. XXIII; McGavock, *Pen and Sword*, 470–72.

Remarks on Public Works Appropriations for Washington[1]

June 1, 1858

Mr. JOHNSON, of Tennessee. There is a great deal of talk here about economy, and curtailing public expenditures, and the necessity of appropriations merely for the continuance of works, to prevent the dilapidation of works already commenced, and all that. If you will examine this bill, you will find that from line two hundred and thirty-one to line two hundred and forty, there is an appropriation of $1,000,000 for the completion of the aqueduct, to bring water to Washington city. I do not intend to make a speech; but the engineer—Mr. Meigs,[2] I believe he is commonly called—told me the other day, before our committee, that of the whole amount of water to be brought into this city by the construction of the aqueduct, the Government would not require more than one fifth or one tenth of it for its purposes. Its cost will amount to some four or six millions by the time it is completed. I want to know where is the great necessity for the construction of this work at this particular period? The Treasury is bankrupt; we are borrowing money in order to meet the necessary expenses of the Government;[3] and yet here is a simple proposition to appropriate $1,000,000 to bring water to Washington city. The Government does not need one tenth of the water intended to be brought by the aqueduct, and if it should not be brought at all, we should still have plenty of water here to supply all the wants of the Government.

In addition to that, in the construction of our buildings here, we appropriate large sums and pay extravagant prices to make them all fire-proof; and after we have constructed them and made them fire-proof, it seems we must expend six or eight or ten million dollars to bring water into the city to preserve them from destruction by fire! So far as the consumption of water is concerned, for ordinary purposes, there is plenty of it here. As this is a time to retrench, as the Treasury is bankrupt and we are borrowing money and paying six per cent. on it, it seems to me that this expenditure might be gotten clear of. I therefore move to strike it out of the bill. I have no idea that the motion will be agreed to—none in the world; but I want to make a record on it; and I am in hopes that those gentlemen who are for it, and who intend to continue it, will have the moral courage to give us the yeas and nays upon my motion, if they intend to sustain it in the bill.

[The yeas and nays are ordered; Jefferson Davis, speaking against the motion, maintains that it is useless to argue the propriety of continuing the project and points out benefits which will accrue from the finished aqueduct. No vote is taken.]

Mr. JOHNSON, of Tennessee. Sometimes the construction of terms is brought about by very different considerations. If the term "economy" is abused in the sense in which I use it, I might be censured for the use of that term. I think it would be economy here to-night for the Government to abandon this work, and throw away every dollar it has expended upon it. After it has expended this $1,000,000 in the completion of the work, there will still be a continued expense in keeping it up, and keeping this city supplied with water. The idea of the Federal Government dealing out water to those who may want it, with a view of making a profit on it, is rather utopian to my mind. It seems to me there is no economy in that construction of the term. The idea of the Government erecting waterworks and selling water out to the different cities, with a view of making money! Did the Government ever commence a speculation of that kind but what resulted in total loss of the expenditure? Can there be a single instance found? The idea of the Government speculating in water-works and making a profitable investment, seems to me to be a very strange notion of economy. My own honest conviction here to-night is, that it would be better for the Government to abandon this whole concern. It will take a long time before the pipes rot; they would not decay much while the Treasury is exhausted and we are talking about the revenues; the aqueduct is constructed of brick and substantial material that will not rot. We might suspend the work upon it for a short time, until we see what the receipts into the Treasury amount to; and whether it will be necessary to increase the taxes on the people to carry on the Government. I do not think, if we were to suspend it until that could be ascertained, that it would cause any great delay or any great expenditure. I believe it would be profitable, and the safest investment for the Government, to appropriate a certain amount of money to get clear of the whole work, and authorize it to be sold. If we had been so disposed, it would have been very easy for us to have constructed machinery somewhere on the Potomac, of sufficient capability to supply all the water the Government might want. Such a work could have been constructed and kept up for one tenth or one twentieth, or perhaps one thirtieth, the amount the present plan will cost.

Sir, this appropriation is not based on the interests of the Government, but on the convenience and wants of the people of Georgetown and Washington. We might as well talk about the thing seriously. What amount of water do we need here? Is it necessary to construct water works, to cost some six or eight or ten million dollars before they are finished, to supply the Government with what water it wants about the public buildings in Washington city? Can anybody think so? While we are talking about economy, while the Government is in great straits, while we are talking about half a dozen wars with all the southern Republics, and Great Britain thrown in,[4] (which, by the by, has heretofore been considered a nation of some importance,) while we are borrowing $35,000,000, while the receipts are falling off, the people complaining, the expenditures of the Government, still increasing—yet, when it is proposed to cut off a simple item of a million dollars for water-works, the stoppage of which can injure nobody, and especially the Government, it is said, "oh, this is not the place; that is a bad notion of economy." I refer to this, not with any feelings of personal unkindness; and the Senator from Mississippi knows it. It is a mere difference in construction. He thinks that to strike out this item would be an abuse of the term "economy." Now, it seems to me that we could get clear of that single clause of a million dollars. That is something. If we should cut down a million dollars here, and five hundred thousand dollars somewhere else, and two hundred and fifty thousand dollars somewhere else, and if we should go on at that rate, in a short time we can bring down the expenditure of this Government within the receipts under the operation of the present tariff.

While I am up, I will call attention to another item which has been reported by the Committee on Finance:

For continuing the grading and planting with trees the unimproved portions of the Mall, $10,000.

That is a very great work of necessity, is it not? I want to know whether the Senate referred that subject to the Committee on Finance? The question was considered here to-day whether a committee had any authority to report anything to the Senate, unless the subject-matter was first referred by the Senate to the committee. When did the Senate refer the question of the improvement of the

Mall to the Committee on Finance? Here are $10,000 appropriated for continuing the grading and planting of trees on the Mall. How long has the Mall been in its present condition? Very nearly since God Almighty created the globe. It has, at least, been in that condition very nearly since this Government commenced; and now, all at once, we have got into a great strait for grading and planting trees, and continuing the improvement of the Mall. This is the way we are going along with economy and retrenchment!

Well, sir, here is another little item. I know the Senator from Mississippi and myself will not agree upon that, for he offered an amendment, the other day, to make it $1,100,000 instead of $750,000:

For the United States Capitol extension, $750,000.

That is a work of great necessity, is it not? With three wars in prospect, Great Britain to come along in the lead, the Treasury exhausted, your tariff too low, here are $750,000 appropriated for the extension of the Capitol. We have expended a large sum already upon that extension. In this connection, I will say that I would vote more cheerfully this night for an appropriation of money to pull down these extensions and haul them away, than I would vote for a single dollar to continue them. Look at that old Hall of the Representatives, which comports with our ancient notions of republican simplicity, plainness, and grandeur; compare it with that new Hall which you have constructed, and how does it compare? I expect, for convenience of the times, that we shall have to convert that old Hall —a representation of the fathers of the country—into a grocery,[5] or make a saloon of it, or something of the kind. There is that Hall lying waste which would have answered the purposes of this Government, and which corresponded, too, with our notions of republican simplicity, for the next one hundred years. By a little remodeling and taking out some of these partition walls, this Senate Chamber could have been made capacious enough to have contained everybody that desired to witness and hear what was transpiring in the Senate Chamber. But there are a set of cormorants, contractors, stock-jobbers—I will not stop there—plunderers of the Federal Treasury, that hang around, and can make programmes, and draughts, and drawings, and all that description of things, and who appeal to members—Senators and Representatives—to do this and do that by way of maintaining the national dignity and character. You must do something in the way of sculpture, something in the way of architecture, something in the way of magnificent buildings, to keep up our importance and maintain our character abroad, so that they can obtain jobs, contracts, speculations, and make employment out of the Government, and swindle it of thousands, from which no real good can result.

Look at that new Hall of the House of Representatives, and then recall the description given of it by my distinguished friend on my left, [Mr. Houston,] in his remarks on the subject the other day.[6] He was speaking about the goddess of Liberty. I did not know he was such a critic before. I do not make any pretensions of that sort, but it struck me with some force that he was a critic. He was speaking about the unnatural attitude and the position of the figure intended to represent the goddess of Liberty. He disclaimed, however, very gallantly, taking any undue liberties with the goddess; but his criticism, I thought, was merited upon all the gorgeous gilt thrown about the new Chambers, that it does not comport with our character and dignity as a free people. We talk about republican simplicity. Our public buildings should be erected upon a plan that should combine utility, while, at the same time, consulting appearance, to some extent.

Here are three appropriations, of $1,000,000 for water-works; $10,000 for the Mall—a work of great necessity—and $750,000 for the extension of the Capitol. Let me ask every Senator here, and every one that hears me, does the Government need the expenditure of this money now? Would it not be better, coming up to the strict meaning of the term "economy," so far as that is concerned, to dispense with these extensions, to omit this improvement of the Mall, and let the water-works go where they may, or pay something to get clear of them, than continue them, and make these appropriations at the present time? But even if we are disposed to continue these works, would it not be prudent and judicious to suspend them for the present, until we can see what receipts will be in the Treasury under the operation of the reduced tariff?[7] If we go on making these heavy appropriations, the argument will come in upon us, with tenfold force, to increase the tariff, and make the duties higher. We know this will be so.

We now see that the expenditures of the Government have run up to $75,000,000. Let me say to Democrats, Know Nothings, and Black Republicans, in the Senate Chamber of the United States, to-night, if the expenditures of this Government are not arrested, in 1860 the party that stands by and maintains them will be run over by the same irresistible avalanche that swept over the country in 1840. I am no prophet, nor the son of a prophet; but if these things are not arrested, like causes will produce like effects; and I tell you, when agitation ceases in the country, in reference to Kansas and negroes South and negroes North, and the public mind can be brought to consider these vast expenditures of the Federal Government, the party that stands by them and maintains them will be run over with an irresistible current, in 1860. I intend, so far as I am concerned, that my skirts shall be clear of these unnecessary, extravagant, and profligate appropriations of the people's money by the Federal Government. I believe them to be so. I do not intend to be personal to anybody; but I believe them to be so; I know them to be so. Here, then, are three little items, by the striking out of which, we can bring down the expenditures of this Government over a million and three quarters of dollars. When it is proposed to do so, however, we are told that this is not the place for retrenchment; these works should go on; we are committed to them. You may even go into the States and find works for which the Government have commenced unnecessary appropriations; but if there is an attempt made to discontinue them, you are told the work has been commenced, and you must not stop it, or you will lose all that which has been done. Nine times out of ten, it would be better to lose it and go no further with the thing. Here we have commenced the erection of water-works. Do not stop that. Oh, no; that must go on. Then we come to the Mall, and propose to strike out that item, and it will not do to stop that. You come to the appropriation for the extension of the Capitol, and it will not do to apply retrenchment there.

If you propose to reduce or strike out any of the appropriations for these improvements, you will have to meet the argument—I have been expecting it for some time—here are a great many men employed, and they will be turned out of employment if the proposition should be agreed to. The mere statement of the argument shows you where we are driving and tending, that the Government must make improvements in the shape of extensions of the Capitol, or the adornment of the Mall, or the erection of water-works, or the construction of a harbour, or something else—and for what? To give employment to the people—the most dangerous doctrine that ever was sustained in any government: that the Government must be the undertaker, that the Government must be the giver out of jobs for the sake of giving employment to the great mass of the people! The theory is wrong. Why do I say so? You are making the people look to the Government for employment; and just in proportion as you make the people dependent on the Government, the Government controls the people, instead of the people controlling the Government. Let the Government be dependent on the people, and let the people fall back on their own resources, on their own avocations, and not look to the Government of the United States, or even to the State governments, for employment; for just in proportion as the people look here for employment, and become dependent on the Government, State or

Federal, for employment, in the very same proportion they cease to be freemen; the Government becomes paramount and the people inferior.

But we will be met here, as we are met in every attempt of this kind to reduce our expenditures, by the plea that this is not the place. Oh, no; do not touch that appropriation. When we come along to another item, and propose to reduce that, that is not the place; do not touch that. You come along to another appropriation, and propose to reduce that, and you are told, do not touch that; it is not the place to reform. Mr. President, where is the place? Has anybody ever yet found out the right place? If you happen to find the right place, the next argument you are met with is, that this is not the time to retrench. The term is unmeaning. We go along in time of peace, but that is not the time, that is not the place, and that is not the occasion. When war breaks out, and we talk about retrenchment, it is said it is no time to talk about retrenchment in time of war. Well, when will it come? It is not the time of peace, it is not the proper time in war. I wish we could get an interval between peace and war, to see if that would be the time. I do not think the time will ever come. It never will come until the voice of the people comes in upon the Congress of the United States, and speaks to them in unmistakable language what their feelings and their sentiments are on this subject. I move that from line two hundred and thirty-one down to two hundred and forty be stricken out, and then I shall move that these two other propositions be stricken out; or I would prefer that the vote should be taken on all together, if it would suit, to save time.

[Davis takes issue on several points, including Homestead grants, and defends the new House wing as utilitarian; whereas the old House, although aesthetically more attractive, was acoustically a failure. Iverson calls attention to the fact that previous failure to appropriate money for the preservation of work already begun has resulted in damage suits by contractors whose work has been suspended; several such cases are pending in the committee on claims. If Johnson's motion prevails, more damage suits will result.]

Mr. JOHNSON, of Tennessee. I think the Senator from Mississippi misunderstood what I said in reference to the Senator from Texas. I understood the remarks of the Senator from Texas to be made in reference to the new Senate Hall, and I thought I so stated. It was not my intention to locate his criticism, but as I understood it I rather approved it. I pretend not to understand anything about sculpture or paintings, or the construction of halls; I do not pretend to have any taste for matters of that kind. If I come into a splendid hall, and look at it, I can tell whether it strikes me as of proper dimensions, and as being properly constructed, taken as a whole.

There is something in it that pleases or displeases me. I confess that, when I went into the new Hall of the House of Representatives, it did not strike me as being so imposing, and of a style of architecture so well adapted to the American character, as the old Hall of Representatives.

Mr. DAVIS. It is not as beautiful as the old Hall.

Mr. JOHNSON, of Tennessee. The old Hall is not guady; there are about it no unnecessary flourishes in guilding and painting; but there is a grandeur, a dignity, a republican simplicity about it, with which the new structure cannot at all compare. I do not care whether you call it beauty or not. I think it is much better adapted to our character. I know an objection was made that it was difficult to hear the Speaker when he was putting a question in the old Hall, and that it was difficult to hear members who were addressing the House; but it seems to me that the same means which have been resorted to in the new Hall to prevent that could have been applied as a remedy in the old Hall. The structure of the ceiling might have been altered, and in that way a remedy applied. Be that as it may, however, I do not think the reply of the Senator from Mississippi, on that point, has much to do with the remarks I made as to what had been said by the Senator from Texas.

The Senator from Mississippi seems to admit that there is one item of the bill to which I object that might be stricken out—the $10,000 for the improvement of the Mall. I infer from his remarks, though he did not say so expressly, that he thinks that is not necessary. He is, however, in favor of giving the citizens of Washington, and those persons who visit Washington, plenty of water—good, pure water, unadulterated, unmixed. Well, sir, if he were to pass a law of that character, and appropriate ten times the cost of the water-works to complete them, with a distinct understanding that the water is not to be adulterated, this city, and the comers to it, would vote down such a proposition at once, for pure water is the last thing they want. [Laughter.] That is not the article they desire. If that was to be the result of the completion of these water-works, the people of Washington would come here *en masse*, at least two thirds or three fourths of them, and three fourths of all the visitors here, and protest most zealously, earnestly, and emphatically, against the passage of any such law that would give them water without dilution. So, I do not think there is much in that portion of the argument.

But, in reply to what I said as to the Government giving employment to the people, the honorable Senator from Mississippi wants to know if the Government might not as well give employment to its citizens as give them land. Let me ask him how much the expenditure of $10,000 for the Mall, $750,000 for the Capitol extension, and $1,000,000 for the Washington aqueduct, will add to the productive capacity, or to the revenue, of the country? Do they bring one cent into the Treasury of the United States? Do they add anything to the productive capacity of the country? You may give a man employment on the work; you may pay him for days and months and years, while he labors on it; but he appropriates what he gets from the Government to his own support, and does not add anything to the production of the country. So far as he is concerned, I have no objection to the benefit done to him; my objection is on other grounds.

But, here is an indirect attack upon the homestead policy. The Senator speaks of it as giving away land. I do not admit that proposition. You have a large amount of public domain—fifteen hundred million acres—that has been acquired by the blood and treasure of the nation. To whom does it belong? The Federal Government, it is true, holds it in trust for the great mass of the people; and the proposition of the homestead bill is not to give land away, but to permit the head of a family to settle upon and take a part of that which is his, and for which he or his ancestors, or some connected with him, shed their blood and expended their money. Yes, sir; and many of them were with my honored friend on the field of battle. I prize him much higher when I call him Colonel Davis than Senator Davis, for the brightest and most imperishable laurels that encircle his brow were won under the appellation of Colonel. Many of those gallant men who, in Mexico, fought the battles of their country by his side, now sleep in a foreign grave. The result of that war was a large acquisition of territory. That domain was acquired by the United States as a consequence of their bravery, their patriotism, and their valor, in the battle-field with him. When I propose that the descendants of those men may go upon, settle, and occupy, a part of that which was won by the blood and the valor of their fathers, live upon it, and cultivate it, so as to make a support for their wives and their children, I am told that I propose to give away the public property; that these men are here asking charities in land. No, sir; they do not ask you to give them anything; but I demand, in the name of their valor, their blood, their patriotism, and their suffering widows and children, that you let them go and take that which belongs to them, which is the price of their blood and treasure.

[Mason asks, "If the lands belong to the people, why should they require a law to allow them to use them?"]

Mr. JOHNSON, of Tennessee. The Senator is a lawyer, and I will put a case to him. Suppose there was a trustee to hold an estate in his hands for the benefit of heirs: there are certain legal processes required to be gone through with before they can obtain possession of the estate, and use it. The Federal Government is the trustee of the public domain; but is it the owner of the soil? Is not the equity in the people? The Government being the trustee, we propose a mode according to the forms of law, of permitting the people to take that which belongs to them. Does not this Government belong to the people? Does not all the public domain belong to the people? The Government holds it in trust for the whole; and all we ask is, that you prescribe a mode by which each individual may possess himself of that which is his. Is there anything wrong in that? You have nearly seven million quarter sections of public lands; there are three million heads of families in the United States; and if you permit every head of a family to take a quarter of a section, you would still have half the domain left in the hands of the trustee to be disposed of. Is that giving? No; it is simply permitting each individual to go and possess himself of a part of that which is his, and not what belongs to anybody else. Who does he take it away from? Who is deprived of anything by permitting a man to go forward, and take a portion of that domain which is actually his? Who is deprived of any right, who is deprived of any soil by it? Nobody. But what is the effect? Leave the land as it is, and it is wholly unproductive; allow it to be occupied, and you increase its production, and of course increase the capacity of the settler upon it for consumption, and thereby increase the Federal revenue. While you do this for the Treasury, what do you do for the man himself? You give him an interest in the country; you make him a better man and a better voter; he goes to the ballot-box, and votes his own will, not that of his landlord or his master. So much for the land; so much for the pure water. I hope we shall have a vote.[8]

Cong. Globe, 35 Cong., 1 Sess., 2588–89, 2590.

1. The Senate, in an evening session, was considering the civil appropriation bill. A number of amendments, mostly for local or regional projects to please constituents, had been offered and rejected when Johnson obtained the floor.

2. Montgomery Meigs (1816–1892), a West Point graduate (1836), was the officer in charge of the army engineer corps detailed to Washington for the Capitol extension (1853–59) and for constructing an enormous aqueduct running from the Great Falls of the Potomac to a reservoir in the city. A major general in the quartermaster corps during the Civil War, he returned in 1866 to supervise construction on federal installations in Washington. DAB, XII, 507–8.

3. Following the Panic of 1857, the treasury was faced with new deficits, making imperative a revision of the revenue system. From 1858 to 1860 the accumulated deficits ran to $50,000,000; the government was living a hand-to-mouth existence. Federal income, which had amounted to $68,000,000 annually during the Pierce years, dropped to $46,500,000 in 1858. Davis R. Dewey, Financial History of the United States (New York, 1907), 262–66.

4. Although filibustering activities in Nicaragua and Cuba, along with British protectorate claims in Central America, had been causing international tension, Johnson may also refer to a recent incident involving visitation and search. In the spring of 1858, British warships which, in an effort to stamp out illegal slave trading, had been detaining and searching American vessels off the African coast, moved their activities into the Gulf of Mexico. With the principle of freedom of the seas thus in jeopardy, the Senate foreign affairs committee had recommended on May 28 that the President be authorized to dispatch American gunboats to the area; on June 16, in a special two-day session before final adjournment, resolutions to this effect were adopted. Nevins, *Emergence of Lincoln*, II, 483–86; *Cong. Globe*, 35 Cong., 1 Sess., 2451–52, 3061.

5. A "grocery," in nineteenth-century parlance, was a "whiskey shop or tavern." Mitford Mathews, *A Dictionary of Americanisms* (2 vols., Chicago, 1951), I, 747.

6. Four days earlier, amid the laughter of his colleagues, Houston had satirized the posture of the goddess of Liberty, "drawn back in the most ungraceful and ungainly attitude for a lady. It appears to be in torment; and had it been physical, I should have imagined that it really had a boil under the arm." The statue in question was the work of Thomas Crawford of New York. *Cong. Globe*, 35 Cong., 1 Sess., 2463.

7. In March, 1857, Congress had passed a tariff bill which greatly reduced import duties and added items to the free list. Dewey, *Financial History*, 262–65.

8. After several attempts at adjournment and a motion to reduce the appropriation from $800,000 to $400,000 were rejected, Johnson's amendment was defeated with only six votes in its favor.

To James Buchanan, Washington, D. C.

Washington, June 8' 1858

To His Excellency,
President Buchanan

Sir: We ask leave to present to the President Washington D Miller,[1] Esq of Texas, for Executive confidence & favor. In so doing, we beg leave to present a sketch of what we believe to be his claims upon public confidence. Mr. Miller was educated at Tuscaloosa College in Alabama. He then studied the profession of the Law, and in 1839, emigrated to Texas. Though very young, so highly was he appreciated by the citizens, that he was elected to the Congress of the Republic of Texas. As a member he was not surpassed by any one in the body, for talents and business qualifications. When an Executive[2] who had served with Mr. Miller in Congress was elected President in 1841, he selected Mr. Miller for his Private Secretary, who remained with him throughout his Presidential term, and rendered the most perfect satisfaction. During his Secretaryship, he was appointed Secretary to negotiate the Treaty of Annexation in 1843. When Texas became a Sovreign State of the Union by annexation, he remained in the employment of the State. When the second Governor[3] was elected, he was appointed Secretary of State, and subsequently elected Secretary of the Senate, and then Chairman of the Democratic Committee of the State, and an efficient and ardent democrat to this day.

The appointment which we solicit your Excellency to confer upon him, is not such an one as his merits and accomplishments might claim, but as he is desirous to obtain it, we sincerely hope your Excellency may think proper to confer it upon him feeling assured as we do, that he will be faithful to the trust confided to him.

The situation desired by Mr. Miller, is that of "Consul or Commercial Agent for the Port of St Paul de Loando, in the Portuguese Possessions in Africa."[4]

With great respect,

G. N Fitch	Sam Houston
Guy M Bryan	C. C. Clay, Jr.
John H. Reagan	Ben Fitzpatrick
J. L. M. Curry	Eli S. Shorter
David S. Reid	J F Dowdell
J. H. Hammond.	*R W Johnson*
J. Letcher	T. L. Clingman
Trusten Polk	J A. Pearce
A. Iverson	Wm M Gwin
J. F. Simmons	W K Sebastian
S. R. Mallory	A. G. Brown
Andrew Johnson	Geo W Jones
A Kennedy	W Wright
Jno B. Thompson	W. R. W. Cobb
James S. Green	Sydenham Moore
Geo S Houston	Wm. T. Avery
J A Stallworth	

LS, DNA-RG59, Appl. & Recomm., 1853–61, Washington D. Miller.

1. Washington D. Miller (1814–1866), South Carolina native, was active as a clerk and secretary in Texas government positions from his arrival in 1837 until his death. Amelia W. Williams and Eugene C. Barker, eds., *Writings of Sam Houston* (8 vols., Austin, 1938–43), II, 389n.

2. Sam Houston.

3. George T. Wood (1795–1858), a Georgian, moved to Texas in 1839, serving in the house of representatives of the Texas Republic, and in the state senate (1846). Commander of the 2nd Texas Mounted Volunteers in the Mexican War, he was afterward elected governor (1847–51). Walter P. Webb, ed., *The Handbook of Texas* (2 vols., Austin, 1952), II, 929–30.

4. Although Buchanan's endorsement reads "If Gen: Cass has no objection, he will please to appoint Mr. Miller," the *U. S. Official Register* (1859), 5, lists John G. Willis as agent at St. Paul.

Exchange on Widows' Pensions[1]

June 12, 1858

Mr. JOHNSON, of Tennessee. I have an amendment to offer:

And be it further enacted, That there be paid to Mrs. Mary Kirby Smith, widow of the late Captain E. Kirby Smith, of the United States Army, a sum, which, added to the pay to which she is entitled under the pension act as widow of a captain, will equal the half pay of a lieutenant colonel, this latter rank being the capacity in which said Captain Smith was serving at the time he received a mortal wound in leading on his battalion to the decisive charge at the battle of Molino del Rey, in Mexico.[2]

Mr. PUGH.[3] Let us take the question. I hope the Senate understands this business of putting one bill on to another.

Mr. JOHNSON, of Tennessee. I understand that the bill is a proposition to pension the widow of an officer of the Army who served his country for a long time, and perhaps very faithfully and efficiently, with high rank, at a large salary; but there is a good deal in the way these cases are stated. The argument is general, that the individual to whom you propose to give a pension served the country. Now, there is no one who will hear me say aught against the services and patriotism of General Jones; but there is another way to state the case. A man may serve his country, and his country may serve him; and sometimes if you keep a correct account, and credit the individual with all the services he rendered, and then charge him with the length of time the Government has supported him, there may be some doubt as to which way the balance would fall. General Jones served his country faithfully no doubt, and it is equally true that the country served him faithfully for some thirty-five or forty years, sustained him, paid him a large salary. He died in his bed, as I understand, at a green old age. I present you the case of a man who went out to fight the battles of his country, and who fell in fighting the battles of his country most gloriously and gallantly. When the widow of that captain comes here you put her on the pension roll at twenty dollars a month, in the first instance for only five years, but under the recent law it is continued for life. There does not seem to be any great sympathy for a widow of that description. Then look at the widows of the soldiers. They receive a half-pay pension for five years, which is only sixty dollars a year, and the whole five years would come to $300, just half the amount you propose to give in this bill for one year. It is strange that the widow of a gallant soldier, a private, a lieutenant, or captain, should not be entitled to receive the same amount of comfort and attention as the widow of an officer of higher rank, who always obtained large pay from the Government while alive. Mrs. Smith has three children, whom she supports by her own exertions as a teacher. If Mrs. Jones is entitled to fifty dollars a month as a gratuity, when her husband died at a ripe age, not from disease or wounds contracted in the line of duty, how much more is Mrs. Smith entitled to a like monthly allowance?

I do not intend to consume much time, but when there is such a great anxiety to do justice at this late hour of the session, I do not see why we should not embrace all the cases within the scope of justice. I do not see why individual cases should be selected and pressed at this unpropitious time, at the heel of the session, to the exclusion of all others. I desire to secure equality. In the case covered by the bill, the man died in his bed after his country had served him for a number of years. In the case for which my amendment provides, the man fell on the battlefield, left his wife and children to mourn his loss, unprovided for. I send up the report and ask to have it read at the clerk's table, as part of the speech I intend to make in the widow's behalf.

[Pugh of Ohio objects to the reading, but when Johnson insists, the clerk reads the report made by the House committee on invalid pensions, July 19, 1856, recommending that Mrs. Smith's petition be granted and that she be pensioned at the rate of one-half the salary of a lieutenant colonel, since Captain Smith was acting in that rank at the time of his death. Stuart of Michigan, while acknowledging the validity of the claim, nevertheless suggests that Johnson submit it separately and not encumber the present bill with this addition.]

Mr. JOHNSON, of Tennessee. An appeal from the Senator from Michigan would have as much influence with me as from any other Senator. I think he understands that always, when gentlemen have a favorite case, they want to get it through stripped of all incumbrances. This case is meritorious, and I think more so than the original bill.

[Stuart reiterates his advice that Mrs. Smith's bill be kept separate from that of Mrs. Jones.]

Mr. JOHNSON, of Tennessee. My object is to advance the great principle of justice; and while we are dealing out justice to one, I want to present another case stronger than the one we propose to provide for; and I hope we shall have the yeas and nays.

[Anthony Kennedy of Maryland has a case similar to Johnson's, but plans "to bring it in at the proper time as a separate, and distinct bill."]

Mr. JOHNSON, of Tennessee. I will simply say to the honorable Senator from Maryland that this is no constituent of mine. There never has been an appeal to me in this case. No interested or hired persons have made appeals to me in behalf of this widow. I accidentally came upon the case, and was made familiar with the facts. It is for no constituent of mine. I never saw any of the parties; I know nothing about them; but I was interested in it from the clear, strong appeal that is made by a simple recitation of the facts. Gentlemen call on us to pass the bill as an act of justice; I look upon it as a gratuity; and I think, in such matters, we should act equally. One appeal is just as strong as the other. I am in hopes the Senate will act favorably upon my amendment. It is not a case from my State. I think it is more meritorious than the original bill.[4]

Cong. Globe, 35 Cong., 1 Sess., 3000–3001.

1. Among a number of private bills, the Senate was considering a pension for Mary A. M. Jones, widow of Major General Roger Jones. The bill, as approved by the House, had been amended by the Senate, and a vote to reconsider that amendment was on the floor when Johnson spoke.

2. Ephraim Kirby Smith (1806–1847), older brother of Confederate General Edmund Kirby Smith, had graduated from West Point in 1826; a career officer, he was fatally wounded in the Mexican War. His widow, Mary Jerome Smith, of Syracuse, New York, opened a private school for young children to support herself and her three children. Joseph H. Parks, *General Edmund Kirby Smith* (Baton Rouge, 1954), *passim*.

3. George E. Pugh (1822–1876), Ohio Democrat, had served in the Mexican War, the state legislature (1848–50), as state attorney general (1852–54), and was now in the U. S. Senate (1855–61). Failing reelection, he resumed his law practice in Cincinnati. *BDAC*, 1486; *DAB*, XV, 258–59.

4. Before the Senate could vote on Johnson's amendment, the original amendment had to be disposed of, to avoid resubmitting an amended version to the House. Following its rejection, the discussion returned to Johnson's proposal. During the subsequent exchange, it was revealed that the House had voted a pension bill for Mrs. Smith which Johnson opposed, for it gave her a regular pension of only $20 a month, instead of half-pay, or $52 monthly. When the yeas and nays were ordered, Johnson's amendment was rejected, 25–9. *Cong. Globe*, 35 Cong., 1 Sess., 3001–2.

Remarks on Origin of Homestead Bill[1]

June 14, 1858

Mr. JOHNSON, of Tennessee. I do not intend to consume the time of the Senate, and I should not say a word now if I thought the time would be occupied more profitably; but I deem the homestead bill one of great importance to the country; and I wish to set right some statements which were made in reference to the origin and history of the measure on the discussion which took place upon its postponement a few weeks ago. On that occasion, my friend from Alabama, [Mr. Clay,] in assigning some reasons why the bill should be postponed, made the following statement:

I wish to make a remark or two in reply to what has fallen from the Senator from Tennessee, before the vote is taken on this bill. He argues that public opinion is in favor of this measure, and therefore it ought to be passed; but, admitting his premises, I do not agree that his conclusion is necessary. I do not think it is the business of this Senate, or of the House of Representatives, merely to reflect public opinion, whether right or wrong. I do not think it becomes us, as representatives of sovereign States, to run after public opinion; but I think we should rather lead it; we should correct it when it is wrong, and should only follow it when it accords with our judgment, and when it is right.

Now, in respect to this homestead policy, which the Senator says has been approved by public opinion. I dissent from him as to that conclusion. I deny that it is approved by public judgment. Why, sir, fourteen years ago, an unfortunate son of genius, who represented one of the districts in my own State, originated the idea in this country of giving homes to the homeless. Felix G. McConnell, of the State of Alabama, was in the habit, I believe, on all occasions when he arose to address the Speaker of the House of Representatives, of suggesting his proposition for a homestead for every man, matron, and maid in the United States, who was the head of a family. [Laughter.]

Mr. HAMLIN. And widow.

Mr. CLAY. Then it was treated with derision. About eight years ago, the Senator from New York, who perhaps is entitled to the credit of originating this measure in the Senate, offered a bill, of which this is a substantial copy, perhaps a literal one, and it received but two votes.[2]

It was stated by my friend from Alabama—and a former Senator from Mississippi (Mr. Adams)[3] fell into the same error—that Felix G. McConnell,[4] with whom I served in the House of Representatives, and for whom I entertained a great deal of respect, originated this homestead policy in that House. It is as far from me as it would be from any one, to detract aught from that individual. The Senator from Alabama calls him an unfortunate son of genius, from his own State. Sir, if there ever was a man who was a Democrat by instinct and by nature, it was Felix Grundy McConnell. Even when he was in one of those unfortunate moods—one of those unfortunate spells that he occasionally fell into—you might wake him up out of a reverie and present to him a question that involved Democracy on the one hand, and its opposite on the other, and by instinct or intuition he was always on the side of Democracy.

But I wish to set the facts right, as there seems to have been some controversy as to who was the originator of this great measure. So far as I am concerned, whenever I have alluded to this subject, from first to last, I have never claimed its paternity. In the speech which I made a short time since, I showed that the policy was inaugurated by Washington, that it had been approved and indorsed by the most distinguished men of the country, from that period down to the present time. As, however, there seems to have been some contest as to the origin of the measure in this particular form, I intend to state the facts without regard to what may be said in reference to myself.

It appears from the Journal of the House of Representatives, that on March 12, 1846,

Mr. A. Johnson asked leave to introduce a bill entitled "A bill to authorize every poor man in the United States who is the head of a family to enter one hundred and sixty acres of the public domain, without money and without price." Objection being made, it was not introduced.

On March 27, 1846,

Mr. A. Johnson, in pursuance of previous notice, asked and obtained leave to introduce "A bill to authorize every poor man in the United States to enter one hundred and sixty acres of land," &c.; which bill was read twice, and committed.

In the House of Representatives, August 5, 1846, the French spoliation bill being under consideration,

Mr. McConnell moved to add to the bill a section granting one hundred and sixty acres of land to every man, maid, or widow, in the United States. Ruled out of order.

August 6, 1846, the Oregon bill being under consideration

Mr. McConnell wished to offer as an amendment, an additional section authorizing every man, maid, or widow, &c., to enter one hundred and sixty acres of land in any portion of the territory of the United States. The Chairman decided the amendment out of order at that time.

Thus I find that on the 12th of March, 1846, notice of the bill was given, and on the 27th of March, 1846, the bill was introduced and committed; and on the 5th of August, 1846, Mr. McConnell offered it as an amendment to some other bill. My friend from Alabama was disposed to give the credit of it, if any credit attached to it, to a former Representative from Alabama, and he spoke of him as an unfortunate son of genius. If he was entitled to it, I should have no objection. He was for the measure; he was a Democrat; he loved his country; and if there was ever a man devoted to the people, it was Felix Grundy McConnell.

My honorable friend in arguing why it should be postponed, said that this measure had its origin in the Senate about eight years ago, when it was introduced by the honorable Senator from the State of New York, [Mr. Seward,] and said that his bill only received two votes in 1850. When we come to examine the facts, it seems a little strange that my friend from Alabama should fix upon the honorable Senator from New York as the introducer of his proposition. Why the Senator from New York was selected as the introducer of the bill, and the allegation made that then it only received two votes, I cannot tell, unless it was to convey prejudice to the South, on the supposition that owing to his peculiar relations to some of the States, his name would be calculated to prejudice, in the southern section of the country, a measure he introduced. A reference to the Journal of the Senate for 1850, will show that Daniel Webster and General

Houston introduced the proposition then. Stephen A. Douglas—I call him not as a Senator, but as Stephen A. Douglas from the State of Illinois, introduced two homestead bills, one in 1850 and 1851. Thus the proposition was brought forward by various distinguished individuals at about the same period of time; but somehow or other my friend from Alabama has the idea that the measure was then presented by the Senator from New York. It is not strange, when it was introduced by so many distinguished men, that my honorable friend did not think that some of them had introduced it; but how does the fact stand? I call on my honorable friend from Alabama to make his statement good. I want him to show when the Senator from New York ever introduced a homestead bill at all. I have examined the Journal and I cannot find it. If he has the reply ready, I will take it.

Mr. CLAY. I refer to the Senator from New York himself. I learned what I stated from him.

Mr. SEWARD. The honorable Senator from Tennessee, I suppose, will state the result of his researches. He knows more about it than I do.

Mr. JOHNSON, of Tennessee. Upon a bill to establish a surveyor general's office in the Territory of Oregon, there was an amendment offered preventing the land that was granted in that bill to actual settlers from forced sale of one hundred and sixty or three hundred and twenty acres, and upon that the yeas and nays were called, and there were only two votes for the amendment—not this proposition at all—the vote of the honorable Senator from New York and the honorable Senator from Wisconsin, (Mr. Walker.) The honorable Senator from New York never introduced a homestead bill; but he did in 1850 introduce a bill grounded partially on the same principles, granting land to the Hungarian refugees who were coming to this country, as will be seen by referring to the Journal of that year, page 119. True, the distinguished Senator from New York—and I think him for the argument he made; it did his heart and head credit—made a speech on the bill granting the overflowed lands to the States in which they lie, in which he argued this whole policy, and argued it ably and well before the whole country; but he never introduced a homestead proposition in the shape it is here, though he covered the whole subject in his speech.

Then, in the first instance, it is seen, on an examination of the Journals, that notice was given of the homestead bill. It was introduced and committed in the House of Representatives before my respected friend from Alabama (Mr. McConnell) ever offered his proposition as an amendment to the spoliation bill. In 1850, the period to which the Senator from Alabama carries us back in the Senate, the Senator from New York never introduced a homestead bill at all; but half a dozen others did shadow forth a proposition in its broadest sense. None of them were to be referred to by the Senator from Alabama; but the Senator from New York must be brought into connection with it. I do not say that my friend from Alabama intended to be unfair; I do not say that he intended to excite any improper prejudice by this connection; but I will say that his remarks, left as they were, were calculated to do that.

In the first place, we find the Senator from Alabama mistaken in his statement of fact as to the origin of the bill; in the second place, we find him mistaken as to the fact of Mr. Seward introducing the proposition eight years ago; in fact, he introduced no such measure at all. The remarkable accuracy with which the Senator from Alabama stated his facts seemed to indicate that he had made himself thoroughly acquainted with the history of the subject. If he had made himself acquainted with all the facts connected with the homestead proposition, I feel assured that he would not have made the statement he did; and not having made himself acquainted with the facts, he was not authorized in making the statement he did.

The Senator denies that this proposition has been approved by the public judgment. Let us see how the facts stand in regard to that statement. The measure, in its present form, was introduced in 1846; it was discussed in and out of Congress up to the 12th of May, 1852; and on that day the bill passed the popular branch of the national Legislature by a two-thirds vote. The bill was then lost in the Senate. Again, in 1854, it was originated in the House of Representatives by the Hon. John L. Dawson, of Pennsylvania, and was again passed by an overwhelming majority of that body, and was sent to the Senate, and lost. If we are to rely upon evidences like these, it is clear and manifest that the public judgment has been recorded in favor of the homestead proposition, the Senator's opinion to the contrary notwithstanding. We can have no safer guide, no better test, than the will of the people reflected through their representatives in their representative capacity.

But the gentleman went on to state that the Senate should not obey the popular will; that it should rather lead it; but in this particular case we find the Senator unwilling to lead, or to follow, either, what we conceive to be the public judgment; but sets himself up in opposition to it. If I were disposed to give another evidence of the popular judgment on this subject, I might mention that the Presiding Officer of this House, the Vice President of the United States,[5] recorded his vote in favor of the homestead bill in 1854; he

was placed upon the ticket for the Vice Presidency in 1856, with Mr. Buchanan, and his whole public course was scrutinized; his claims were submitted to the public consideration, and after a full and thorough investigation of his whole public course, there was not an objection urged against him for the Vice Presidency on account of having supported this policy in the Congress of the United States, that I am aware of; but, on the contrary, in many places it was one of the strongest arguments in his favor. Even in the gentleman's own State he received an overwhelming vote, after having supported the homestead measure.

The Senator, in the course of his remarks, admitted that the public judgment of his own State was once for it; but he does not condescend to give us any evidence that that public judgment has been changed. There have been no public meetings, no public demonstrations, no memorial or petition sent to the Congress of the United States against the passage of this measure; but in truth the evidences are all the other way; and so soon as the popular judgment can be brought to bear upon this body, the measure will be consummated and passed here. The Senator assumes, in bold terms, that the Senate should not obey the public judgment; that it should rather lead it. I hold that the Senate should obey the popular judgment, and that a majority of the States should rule in the Senate, as much so as the majority of the congressional districts in the House of Representatives. I hold it to be sound Democratic doctrine that a majority of the States should rule in the Senate; as much so as that a majority should rule in the House of Representatives; and then in a disagreement between the two Houses, measures are lost as contemplated by the Constitution; but in cases of this kind the Democratic party hold, that where a Senator cannot, consistently with his views of right or the Constitution, obey the will of the people of his State, it is his duty to resign, and give his place to some one who will faithfully and honestly obey the high behest of the people.[6]

Sir, I hope the period is not distant when the Senate will have to come down from its present proud and obstinate position, and pass more under the influence of the popular judgment of the respective States. I hope the time will come when the people of the several States will have the constitutional power restored to them of electing their Senators at the ballot-box,[7] as they now elect their Representatives, if not every two years, at least once in six years, thereby creating an immediate responsibility between them and the people. This would be one great step in popularizing our Government. I will say, in this connection, that I am anxious to see the election of President and Vice President made by the electors of each congressional district directly, by the people, in preference to the present mode. Wherever it is practicable, I desire to have the people to do their own public business by themselves, instead of through agents. There is an old and trite adage which I think holds good in public as in private affairs—"whenever you have anything to do, send somebody to do it; but if you want it well done, go and do it yourself." It will hold good in every department of human affairs, public as well as private. Hence, I repeat, I am in favor of popularizing our Government, and, wherever it is practicable, letting the people elect their agents, instead of having their agents selected by other agents, as Senators now are by the Legislatures—in some instances by intrigue and other anti-Democratic appliances. Let the people be heard, and let their mature judgment be final.

I have felt it my duty to say this much in setting the history of this great measure right, as I humbly conceive the greatest measure of the age or of modern times; and it will ultimately be spread upon your statute-book as the law of the land.

Cong. Globe, 35 Cong., 1 Sess., 3042–44.

1. The Senate had briefly adjourned from an executive session when Johnson moved a reconsideration of the vote which had postponed action on the homestead bill until the next January. An argument ensued between Johnson and Virginia Senator James Mason over a point of order, with Mason maintaining that Johnson could only move a reconsideration of the bill itself—not the vote to postpone. After Johnson indicated that his remarks would not extend beyond twenty minutes—the time at which the Senate would reconvene for executive session—the chair allowed him to proceed.

2. Clay had made these observations on May 27. *Cong. Globe*, 35 Cong., 1 Sess., 2425.

3. Stephen Adams (1807–1857), native of South Carolina, had served as a Democrat in the Tennessee senate (1833–34) before moving to Mississippi. A circuit court judge (1837–45), he sat in Congress (1845–47) and in the Mississippi legislature (1850), and was elected as a Union Democrat to the U. S. Senate (1852–57) to fill the vacancy caused when Jefferson Davis became secretary of war. *BDAC*, 460–61.

4. Felix Grundy McConnell (1809–1846), a Tennessee-born Democrat of limited education, had been a saddler before migrating to Alabama, where he had studied law, been admitted to the bar (1836), and served in both houses of the legislature (1838, 1839–43) before election to Congress (1843–46). *Ibid.*, 1287.

5. John C. Breckinridge.

6. The legislature's "right" to instruct senators how to vote on bills was not legally binding. A holdover from early forms of representative governments and embodied in some state constitutions, the practice had evolved in Tennessee through custom; by the late 1850's it had become an anachronism. Andrew C. McLaughlin and Albert B. Hart, *Encyclopedia of American Government* (3 vols., New York, 1914), II, 186.

7. In an effort to make direct election of senators—one of his perennial reforms—more acceptable, Johnson suggests that such a change would merely restore to the people a right which, presumably, they had yielded to the state legislatures in Art. I, Sec. 3, of the Constitution.

To Robert Johnson, Greeneville

Senate Chamber   June 15th 1858

My dear son,

I have determind to go to Philadelphia and See Dr Groce[1] and get his opin[i]on in regard to having my arm operated upon— I Shall not Stay there but a Short time and will then return home— The Executive Session will not hold but a few days— My intention is now to Stop and See Mary[2] as I come home which will take a few days— I have but little to Communicate and will pospone that until I come home— The administration is at present flat and infact has but few frinds— I hope Somthing will tu[r]n up that will give it Some vitality— I hope you have been attending to those money matters and that they are all in proper train— I want you to being [*sic*] thinking about your future and take some definite Course this summer and fall— I hope that you have matured Some Course that will Suit you whethe[r] it suits me or not— I will help you all that I can when I get home— Tell your mother what [it] is that Causes my detention[.] I will be there in a Short time[.] I hope that Charls has been doing well— I See from the Nashvill union that the Greenevill dinner[3] went off very well which I was glad to he[a]r—For I had been lead to think that it would be a failure— I hope that you [and] Charles contributed your full part in the matte[r] and that you done [it] willingly— The session will adjourn on to morrow I think and then I will Start to Phila and will return Soon—

Your father   Andrew Johnson

Robert Johnson Esqr

ALS, DLC-JP.

1. Samuel David Gross (1805–1884), born near Easton, Pennsylvania, began the practice of medicine in Philadelphia in 1828 and was thereafter professor of surgery in several American medical schools, including Jefferson Medical College, Philadelphia, where he was located after 1856. Regarded as the outstanding surgeon of his day, he was honored after his death by a monument in Washington, D. C. Morris Fishbein, *A History of the American Medical Association 1847 to 1947* (Philadelphia and London, 1947), 610–13.

2. Mary Johnson (Mrs. Daniel) Stover, Johnson's daughter, who was living at Carter's Depot in Carter County.

3. Johnson refers to a celebration staged on June 3, 1858, in honor of the completion of the East Tennessee and Virginia Railroad. Unlike the Knoxville celebration of 1855 marking the completion of the East Tennessee and Georgia Railroad, the Greeneville fete was a great success. James W. Holland, "The Building of the East Tennessee and Virginia Railroad," ETHS *Publications*, No. 4 (1932), 100; Nashville *Union and American*, June 8, 1858.

From Joseph Hedrick[1]

[U. S. Senate] July 21, 1858

Documents Due the Hon. A. Johnson

147 Finance Report for 1857
210 Mess & Documents for 1857–8
55 Armies Europe by Capt. McClelan[2]
40 Agrl. Patent office Rept for /56
20 Mechl.   do.   do.   do.   ./56
70 Coast Survey Rept for /56
60 Emory's Rept. vol 1 Mexican boundy
20 Espy's Report on Rain[3]
65 Commerce & Navigation for 1857
145 Pacific R. R. Rept. vols 5 6 7 & 8 each
70 Commercial Relations vols 2 & 4   "
70 Consumption of Cotton in Europe[4]
290 Dred Scott decision

The above Docs are all ready for delivery and Subject to your order[.][5]

July 21 1858   Yours truly   Jos Hedrick

ANS, DLC-JP.

1. Joseph Hedrick was superintendent of the Senate folding room. Joan M. Corbett (National Historical Publications Commission) to Andrew Johnson Project, June 30, 1966.
2. "Report of the Secretary of War communicating the report of Captain George B. McClellan, one of the officers sent to the Seat of War in Europe in 1855 and 1856," *Senate Ex. Doc.* No. 1, 34 Cong., Special Sess.
3. James P. Espy, "Fourth Meteorological Report," *Senate Ex. Doc.* No. 65, 34 Cong., 3 Sess.
4. Perhaps "Letter from the Secretary of State . . . transmitting a statement respecting . . . tabular comparative statements relative to the import and export of cotton," *House Ex. Doc.* No. 108, 34 Cong., 1 Sess.
5. This memorandum is endorsed by Johnson, "A List of documts at Washington City—to be sent for—"

From William Hickey[1]

Office of Secretary of the Senate,
August 27h, 1858.

The Hon'ble Andrew Johnson,
    Senator U. States,
Dr. Sir,

In accordance with the request contained in your note endorsed upon the letter of Mr. G. Magennis,[2] of Paterson, New Jersey, I

have this day prepared a copy of your Homestead Bill, and sent it
to him with a note from you, in the third person, giving him your
respects, as you have requested in your note.—

I have also prepared, and have now the pleasure to enclose to
you, two other copies of your Bill, as it now stands on the files, or
docket of the Senate;[3] supposing that it might be convenient to you
to have a copy of it by you, for your own use, and another for a
friend. Indeed, should you think it adviseable, I could very easily
have this bill printed in the Union and National Intelligencer
also.— The people would see it and understand it, and their Representatives at the next session, perhaps, would be better prepared to
conform to the wishes of the people upon the subject.— Should
you desire to have it so printed, or with modifications, be pleased to
return one of these copies to me, in the form in which you would
wish to see it published, and I will have it inserted in one or both of
those papers as you may desire.—[4]

I shall be here all the time, and will always be happy to attend
to any matter for your service or convenience, and hope you will
always freely command my services.—

With great respect & esteem, Dr. sir, Your obedient Servant
W. Hickey

ALS, DLC-JP.
1. William Hickey was chief clerk in the office of the secretary of the Senate, a position he held until 1867. *U. S. Official Register* (1859), 190.
2. George Magennis was listed in his local 1859 directory as an editor,
though there is no indication of the paper with which he was associated.
Boyd's Paterson City Directory (1859), 73.
3. The bill (S. 25), introduced by Johnson on December 22, 1857, would
"grant to every person who is the head of a family and a citizen of the United
States, a homestead of one hundred and sixty acres of land out of the public
domain." *Cong. Globe*, 35 Cong., 1 Sess., 135.
4. Johnson seems not to have taken advantage of Hickey's offer.

From Benjamin Price[1]

N. Y Aug 27, 1858

Dear Sir
Your favor of 26 July came duly to hand and was answered by
me Aug 7.
At last the Editor[2] of the Daily News (the organ of the Democratic
party in this city) has published your speech[3] which you will find
on page 6 of his paper (which I herewith send you) also a notice
of the same on page 4.
We want some copies of your speech of May 20 very much and
hope you will send us 500 copies.

Mr. Commerford[4] had an interview with a leading Democrat of Penn. last week who says he will see Senator Bigler[5] and thinks his vote can be secured for the Homestead Bill.

We are quite sanguine of success next winter and mean to push on the work[.] Let us hear from you soon & oblige.

Yours truly   Ben Price
48 King St.   N. Y

Hon Andrew Johnson U S S.

ALS, DLC-JP.

1. Price, an accountant, was evidently a worker in the cause of land reform. *Trow's New York City Directory* (1858), 671.
2. Presumably W. Drake Parsons, owner (1855–60) of the New York *Daily News*, an organ of Tammany Democracy. Frank L. Mott, *American Journalism: A History* (New York, 1962), 352.
3. Speech on Homestead Bill, May 20.
4. John Commerford.
5. William Bigler (1814–1880), Pennsylvania Democrat, had served as state senator (1841–47) and governor (1852–55) before being elected U. S. senator (1856–61). A supporter of the Crittenden Compromise and a member of the Senate Committee of Thirteen, he held no public office after the war, though he continued to be active in Democratic politics. That Commerford's "leading Democrat" had any influence on Bigler's attitude toward the homestead bill cannot be verified, but in any case the Pennsylvania senator voted with the majority both on the original passage of the bill, May 10, 1860, and subsequently in agreeing to the report of the conference committee. Along with many of his colleagues, he was absent when the unsuccessful effort was made to pass the measure over the President's veto. *BDAC*, 553; *DAB*, II, 264; *Cong. Globe*, 36 Cong., 1 Sess., 2043, 3159, 3272.

From Isham G. Harris

Nashville   Sept 7th 1858

Private

Hon Andrew Johnson
Dear Sir,

Many of our democratic friends have suggested the propriety [of] Calling a meeting of a few leading democrats from the different parts of the state to Consult as to *the precise and practical issue* which shall be presented by the Democratic party on the question of Currency in the next canvass.

With the hope that such consultation may Contribute to the harmony and success of the party and thereby promote the best interests of the country, I have ventured to suggest to several of our friends the propriety of meeting here on wednsday the 22nd Inst,[1] when and where we shall be much pleased to see you and such friends as you may see proper to bring with you,

Very truly   Your friend
Isham G. Harris

ALS, DLC-JP.

1. For results of this meeting, which Johnson attended, see The Tennessee Democracy on Banks and Currency, September 22, 1858.

The Tennessee Democracy on Banks and Currency[1]

[September 22, 1858]

The Committee have agreed to the following propositions for the adoption of the meeting:

1. That, it would be unwise policy to re-charter any of the existing Banks.

2. That such reforms should be made in our currency during the existence of the present Banks as will insure a sound circulating medium, convertible at all times into gold and silver.

3. That the several Banks as their respective charters shall expire, should to [sic] go out of existence, and such steps should be taken, consistently with the public interest, as will secure the liquidation of the Bank of Tennessee at the expiration of its charter.[2]

S. A. Smith.	Edwin A. Keeble.
Andrew Johnson.	John K. Howard.
A. O. P. Nicholson.	Committee.[3]

Nashville *Union and American*, September 23, 1858.

1. As a result of the Panic of 1857, Tennessee banks had suspended specie payments, leaving paper money the sole circulating medium. In January, 1858, the General Assembly ordered banks to resume specie payments on November 1, but some resumed on July 1, thereby causing considerable difficulty and confusion to the financial community and the public, as well as embarassment to the politicians. In an effort to bring together divergent Democratic views on banking and currency, a meeting was held in Nashville on September 22; out of it came these somewhat bland recommendations. Johnson was, in general, a "hard-money" Democrat. Claude A. Campbell, *The Development of Banking in Tennessee* (Nashville, 1932), 140–47.

2. One wonders whether Johnson may not have welcomed the opportunity which this crisis presented to further his long-standing desire to get rid of the Bank of Tennessee.

3. In his account of the session, the editor of Nashville's Democratic newspaper observed: "After a full and fair comparison of views the following report was adopted as embodying the sense of a majority of the meeting. It is moderate and conservative in tone, and we doubt not will meet the general acquiescence of our party throughout the State." Nashville *Union and American*, September 23, 1858.

To A. O. P. Nicholson, Columbia

Private   Greeneville Tenn
                                                             Novem 22d 1858

Dear Sir

Your letter of the 16th was received in due course of mail— The democrat will prepare an article on the subject of Banks as requested by you— I have understood the Editor[1] heretofore as agreeing in opinion with the views of the Union and thought they have been so expressed— However they will be more fully set forth in a short time— What course will the democratic party take in this state in the event Douglas should be the Candidate of the democratic party for the Presidency 1860— After all that has been said in reference to the course of Bell Crittenden and others on the Lecompton Constitution— It is a question we should begin to consider in time—For really it looks like it might be brought about frome the moves being made by the ultra souther[n] men— Will we then wheel about and sustain Mr Douglas who voted with Mr Bell & Crittenden— Can we repudidate the instructions of the Legislature[2] and the course of the whole delegation in Congress— I hope that you will begin to think about it in time so that we can have some concert of action when the time for acting comes— My opinion is that Douglas' fixed purpose is at this time to force himself upon the party as the nominee or to be an independent Candidate[.] I have no doubt of he and Seward having made an arrangmt either expressed or implied that they are to be the two candidates and that they are to keep themselves prominently before the public mind— Seward making the impression on the Republicans that he is the only man who can unite all the free states against the democratic party— Douglas on the other hand making the impression that he is the only man who can carry any of the free states against Seward, hence the issue between Douglas & Seward, and the two parties will be compelled to fight the battle under their respective banners— Are we in Tennessee prepared to submit to a state of things so humiliating as this— I hope not; but it is not an improvable [*sic*] result; hence the importance of preparing for it in time— I have always had one guide in doubtful questions of this kind and that was to pursue principle and intend to [do] so in the future let the consquines be what they m[a]y— I merly intended to acknowledge the receipt of your letter, noth[in]g more— I think all is right here on the Bank question so far as the democrats are concerned—

Accept assurances of my high esteem and sincere friendship
                                                             Andrew Johnson

P.S Give my respect to Genl Anderson—[3] I would like to here from him[.] Let me hear from you often this winter[.]

ALS, THi-Misc. Col.

1. H. G. Robertson (b. c1816) was editor of the Greeneville *Democrat,* established in the fall of 1858, which became the Greeneville *Banner* the following year. *Goodspeed's East Tennessee,* 889; White, East Tenn. Journalism, 16; 1860 Census, Tenn., Greene, 88.
2. In a resolution of February 10, 1858, the Tennessee legislature endorsed the Kansas-Nebraska bill, with the reminder that Senator John Bell had failed to support the measure and had promised in May, 1854, that, since he could not support the bill, "if my countrymen of Tennessee shall declare against my course on this subject . . . I will not be seen in the Senate a day afterwards." The resolution respectfully requested Bell "to redeem the pledge so solemnly made by him" and urged the senators and representatives to support the Lecompton Constitution. *Tenn. Senate Journal,* 1857–58, pp. 150–51.
3. Samuel R. Anderson.

Statement of Bonds[1]

Bonds owned by Andrew Johnson on the 1st day of December 1858

Nashville & Chattanooga Rail Road Company Bond No 136— Letter C. dated January 1st 1854—due 25 years after date for $1000— interest payable at Phenix Bank New York, semi-annually, at the rate of 6 per cent per annum—
V. K. Stevenson President
W. A. Gleaves Secretary—   Endorsed by the State of Tennessee 28th February 1854—by Andrew Johnson, Governor, W. B. A. Ramsey Secretary of State—

Do—No 109—Letter C—dated Jany 1st 1854 due 25 years after date—$1000—interest payable at Phenix Bank New York, semi-annually 6 per cent per annum—V. K. Stevenson, President W. A. Gleaves, Secretary— Endorsed as above

Do No 194—Letter C—same date—$1000—interest as above— signed as above— Endorsed as the above—

Do No 164—Letter C—same date—$1000—interest as above— signed as above— Endorsed as the above

Do No 172—Letter C—same date—$1000—interest as above— signed as above— Endorsed as the above

Do No 484—Letter C—same date—interest as above—signed as above Endorsed as the above on 20th Feby 1854

Do No 650—Letter C—same date—$1000—interest as above—signed as above— Endorsed as the above on 15th Feby 1854—

Do No 555—Letter C—Same date—$1000—interest as above—signed as above— endorsed as the above 15th Feby 1854

Do No 267—Letter B—dated 1st July 1852, due 30 years after date—$1000 interest as above—signed as above— Endorsed by State of Tennessee 5th of May 1853 W. B. Campbell, Governor, W. B. A. Ramsey, Secretary of State

Do No 275—Letter B—same date as last $1000—interest as the last—signed as the last—endorsed as the last
Do No 273—Letter B—same date—$1000—interest same—signed as last—endorsed as last—
Do No 314—Letter B—same date—$1000—interest same—signed as last—endorsed as last—
Interest payable on the above Bonds 1st Jany & July

East Tennessee & Virginia Rail Road Company Bonds 1861—$1000—dated May 1st 1856—due May 1st 1886—interest semi-annually—6 per cent per annum payable in New York—signed Saml B. Cunningham President—Wm G. Gammon, Treasurer—Endorsed by State of Tennessee, 2nd June 1856—by Andrew Johnson Governor—F. N. W. Burton, Secretary of State

Do No 94—$1000—Dates, signatures, & endorsement as the last—Interest payable on two last 1st May & November—

Treasury Notes—

Four Treasury notes of the United States $500 each—payable one year after date, to the order of Andrew Johnson—interest 3 per cent per Annum—dated 28th January 1858—Letters A-B-C & A—No's 259—260—261—262—signed Sam Casey Treasurer, U. S.—C. F. Jones, Acting Register of U. S. Treasury—

List of Bonds loaned to E. T. & Va Rail Road Company
Dec 1st 1860[2]
Regular Sixes

No 517	Due 1898	No 10086	Due 1898
" 536	" 1898	" 9860	" 1898
" 533	" 1898	" 90047	" 1898
" 535	" 1898	" 90048	" 1898
" 534	" 1898	" 9861	" 1898

Endorsed Bonds

No. 126 ET. & Va. R.R.   No. 131 ET. & Va. R.R.
"   86   "   "   "   132   "   "
"   113   "   "   "   117   "   "

D, DLC-JP18.

1. A notation at the top of the page reads: "List of Bonds loaned to
E. T. & Va R R Company Dec 1st 1860."

2. This heading and the lists of United States and endorsed East Tennessee and Virginia Railroad bonds were clearly a later addition. One may
speculate that these represent investments made during the intervening two
years, though the amount seems rather large.

To Robert Johnson, Greeneville

Washington city   Dec 16th 1858

My dear Son

Since my last I have had quite a time with our old friend Nimrod—[1] I have been to the post office Some four or five times to have
his draft Corrected.— It seems that the draft in the first place had
been issued to John Harold[2] in payment of his services as route
agent—. At first the auditor was willing to make the correction as
to the Spelling of the name: but upon examination it was found that
there had been an error committed in the amount of the draft and
that John Harold had been informed of the fact and drawn upon for
$75, the excess— After this was ascertained the Auditor Seemed
determined to Stop the draft and Send Nimrod back upon the persons of whom he obtained it— Against I[sic] which I took ground
allidging that the Gov[ernme]nt had no right to take an advantage
of its own wrong and inflict an injury upon an innocent party—That
if the goverment had paid Mr Harold too much that the govermet
must look to him and not to the innocent holder of its draft— After
h[a]ving it round and round for Some days they Came to terms after
a threat that it woul[d] be exposed by a resolution Setting forth all
the facts and directing the Auditor to pay it— So it is Nimrod to
night has his money in his pocket and the goverment and Harold
can arrange it in their own way— The rout agents wrote to me last
winter that they disired John appointed as an assistant and that
they would pay him out of their own pockets &c[.] I presented the
application to the P. M. Genl[3] my Self and induced him to make the
appointment for four months at $10 per month in addition to what
the other rout agents wer to give him and it is so endorsed on the
papers now on file in the department— It Seems that he only Served
about one month and a half— Precise amount due him from the gov-
ermnt at the rate of ten dollars per month the sum agreed to be paid
by the Govt when the appointment was made, was $14 98— The

Clerk who Stated the account and made out the draft estimated his pay at the Same the other rout agents were receiv[in]g overlooking the terms upon which he was appointed and issued a warrant for $90.00—75 2/100 more than he was entitled to—In a very Short time afterwards the Clerk discovered the error and by letter informed John of it and drew upon him for the excess— To this letter John replied that he had received the draft and transferred it to Some one: and that he had Settled with the other agents and that the Goverment might look to some other quarter for the excess and not to him and at this point the matter has rested up to the present time— I think John will be Called upon again as the whole affair was brought up in getting old man Kelly's warrant Corrected— It would have been better for John to have Corrected it at the time— If the other agents have paid him what they agreed to do and then to retain the draft of the Gov't for the whole amount also, it will look Somwhat dishonest in him and will do him more harm than the money will do him good— With these facts on record it will preclude him alw[a]ys here-after from getting any appointment from goverment— These things are better understood than m[an]y suppose, there is always Som one to bring them up in judgement against any one wanting favors from the governt— I have written this Statement of the facts so that you may know how [the] matter stands in the event John is Called on for the excess— It will make him and his father angry no doubt— They knew that there was Som[e]th[in]g wrong when they received the draft and then was the time to have Corrected it—

I have nothing Since my last of interest to write— The weather is now warm and pleasant— It has rained nearly ever Since I left home—   As ever your devoted father
                                                                Andrew Johnson

Robert Johnson Esqr

ALS, DLC-JP.

1. Nimrod O. Kelly. See Letter to Robert Johnson, December 23, 1858.

2. On the eve of the Civil War, John W. Harold (b. c1839), the elder son of Greeneville tailor James W. Harold, was described as a law student. 1860 Census, Tenn., Greene, 95.

3. Aaron V. Brown.

To Robert Johnson, Greeneville

                                    Washington City   Dec. 21st 1858
My dear Son

Your of the 16th inst was recieved last night— You Can say to Mr Sevier[1] that I offered more for the property than my Judgment dic-

tated by $250 a[t] least if not more— I thought then and think now
that $2500 is an outside price considering the Condition the House &
lot is in at this time— In fact I mad the offer I did more to please
Charles than any wish on my part to own the property— If the property Could be had for about $2000 it Could be made to do, and not
much more— To put the lot and House in good repair will Cost a
good deal of money, which would have to be done if we were to purchase it— If you Can buy it for $2,000, I will furnish the money to
pay for it— There is no use in buying property unless there is a bargain [in] it— If Mr Sevier will give you the precise amount of the
debt on the property to be sold and what property it is, if it is not too
much I will bid the amount of the debt— Howeve, I will determin
that when I see the [sic] how much it is— Send me the amount and
then I will write to you what to do— If Mr Sevier Could put off the
sale until after the 4th day of March I would be at home then and
would help them to run it up to a reasonable price— Sixty or Seventy
days is not too much time to give in the advertisement— That though
is a matter to be determi[n]ed by him and not me or the parties in
Greeneville— There Seems to be So much Capital about Greenevill
Seeking an investment in landed estate, it Can now have a chance—
The money has to be paid it is not Credit— There are alwys plenty
of buyers when there is Credit to be given— Ask Mr Sevier whether
he has written to Col Watkins[2] in reference to the Claim presented
by his father to Congress, and if he has not for him to do so— The
pension bill will pass the House of Reps to morrow I think without
doubt— What its fate will be in the Senate I do not know: but think
that it will pass if a direct vote Can be had— But there are various
ways to give it the go by—and it may be disposed of for the present
by indirection—[3] I am of opinion at this time that it will be passed
into a law befo the Close of the present session— But I would make
no moves until I Saw a little more about it; a very Short time after it
reach the Senate, there will be Some developement which will indicate the result— I will try and give you timely information and thats
all that you need in the premises— I [sic] have you heard any thing
fr[om] J Harold Since my last— He and father both no doubt are
Cursing the Gomnt and the Democracy &c— It is now rain[in]g and
warm and Seems as though it would Continue to rain all the time—
Tell your mother I have this moment received her letter and will
write So[o]n[.]   As ever
                                                    Andrew Johnson
I do hope your brother is attending to his business—

ALS, DLC-JP.
    1. David Deaderick Sevier.
    2. Albert G. Watkins, congressman from the first district.

3. Johnson refers to a bill granting pensions to soldiers who had participated in the War of 1812 and in the Indian wars of that period. Although
it passed the House, as he predicted, it was shunted aside in the Senate, even
as he suggested might happen, largely through the efforts of Clement C. Clay
of Alabama. *Cong. Globe*, 35 Cong., 2 Sess., 173, 1141–43.

To Robert Johnson, Greeneville

Washington City
Dec 23d 1858

My dear Son

Enclosed you will find an advertisement of N. O. Kelly in reference to a land warrant which he says was lost— Tell Robertson that
he must put [it] in the paper and take his Chances for getting the
pay out of the old man— This man who appears as his atty so far has
done all the wr[i]t[i]ng for nothing and of Course Cannot be expected to pay for the advertisement— I lear[n] too that the Same
man drew up his papers for him in the first instance without charge—
He must be sure to forward the advertisement with a certificate that
the advertisement appeared six times in the paper— With all Nimrod's insanity he Seems to understand how to take Care of his money
and to get along at as little Cost as most persons— While we had his
draft hung up before the P. O. Dept he pretended that he was out of
money altogether: but immediately after it was passed and he got
the money he Came to my room and Stated that it would not do to
tell his business to any body— He then Stated that he wanted me
to take his money and keep it for him— He then gave me the $90
the amoumt of his draft and then handed me $80 more making
$170— I took his money and locked it up in my trunk[.] he then
told me good bye and Stated that I would not See him for four or
five days— This morning Nimrod Came in and informed me that
he was going to New York and would write from there to me—
So Nimrod is now on his way to the great imporium[.] I do not
know what to think of the old man—

The pension bill[1] passed the House on yesterday as anticipated by
57 majority and is now before the Senate— I do not know what its
fate will be there— It Can pass on a direct vote if that can be had—
I will keep you posted up of its progress &c[.] The weather this
morning is Clear and frostey not to Say very Cold— I am rejoiced to
See one more fair day for it did really Seem that we were in the
midst of a rainey Season— Watkins left for home this mor[n]ing in-
tending to Stay at home during the holy days— He had as well be
there as a[n]y where else for the good he is doing here— I Can See
no good in getting on the road and riding one half the time on the

road at an increased expense— I have more business to attend to than I can get along with well and will bring all up as near as [I] Can while the rest of them are gadding about—

I have no news of interest to [report] more than what you see in the papers— Attend to Nimrods Case—

Your father   Andrew Johnson

Robert Johnson Esqr

ALS, DLC-JP.

1. H. R. 259, granting pensions to veterans of the War of 1812 and the Indian wars, passed, 130–74, but failed in the Senate. *Cong. Globe*, 35 Cong., 2 Sess., 172–73; see also Letter from Samuel Rhea, April 13, 1859.

To Robert Johnson, Greeneville

Washington City   Dec 26th 1858

My Son,

Your letter of the 22d inst was received in due Course of mail— I am free to say to you that I am not posted up in reference to the appointments to be made by the president— I have not as yet been to the *white house*: but intend to go in a few days and See how the old man looks and hear what he has to say about matters and things— I have seen Genl Cass two or three times and he Called to see me— You will see ere this reaches you that there is no war between Mexico and Spain and my opin[i]on is there will be none— Great Britain and France will not permit a war to take place between Mexico and Spain—[1] For the reason that it would open the way for the United States to take a part in the Contest and perhaps result in the loss of Cuba to Spain— You seem to have been in a belligerent mood when you wrote your letter, for it is full of fight all the w[a]y through and I must Say it is one of the best letters you have written to me in a long time[.] Let this all pass, for there will be no war for the present or at least that is my opinion at this time— You speak about Coming on to Washington in Janauy, that is if you could raise the money— If you want to Come, there will be some mony due on them Coupons on the first of Janury which you Can use if you desire to [do] so.— There will be enough to pay Burch[2] and answer your purpose I presume— At present I am at the St Charles[3] and perhaps will Continue here for this short session— Washington is duller than I ever Saw it I think and there are fewer persons in the City than I ever knew during the sitting of Congress. From present indications I do not think there will be much excitement this winter— Both parties seem to be waiting for developements and at a loss how to move— The chances are that there will not be much don until the meeting of the next congress in the way of President making except in an under Current— I have just received a letter from Genl Milligan in reference to the moves in that Congressional district and he Seems to think that Watkins is not thought of atall— He has not mentioned the Subject to me this winter— I presum he is now at home and had better stay there for the good he is doing here— He does not seem to have a[n]y thing to do or feel any interest in what is going on— He is nothing but an animal and Cares for nothi[n]g but the gratification of his appetites— I am inclined to think that his business at home in part is to see how matters are moving off in his district[.] He seems about as friendly with me as usual: but as before stated has never mentioned the election to me. I do hope, hope that Charles is at his business and Sober—   It is cold to day—   Geo Howard[4] is here on a visit—   As ever

                                                   Andrew Johnson

ALS, CSmH-Misc. #8204.

1. Relations between Spain and Mexico were strained and diplomatic ties severed as a result of the murder of Spanish subjects during the recent War of the Reform and because Juárez' *de facto* government had failed to pay debts due Spanish creditors. New York *Times*, December 23, 1858; Carl H. Bock, *Prelude to Tragedy* (Philadelphia, 1966), 34.

2. John C. Burch (1827–1881), a native of Georgia and a close friend and supporter of Johnson, was a leading figure in the Tennessee Democracy, serving in the house from Chattanooga (1855–57), as speaker of the state senate (1857–59), and as editor of the Nashville *Union and American* (1859–61, 1869–73, 1875–79). A Confederate officer, he was subsequently state comptroller (1873–75); in 1879 he became secretary of the U. S. Senate. Clayton, *Davidson County*, 407–8; McGavock, *Pen and Sword*, 352n.

3. The St. Charles Hotel, located at the northeast corner of Pennsylvania Avenue and Third Street, had been built in 1844. Bryan, *National Capital*, II, 445.

4. George A. Howard (1840–1900) of Carthage, the son of former Greenevillian Jacob Howard, and Sam Milligan's future brother-in-law, had entered the U. S. Naval Academy in 1858. On April 19, 1861, he resigned his commission to serve in the Confederate navy and later in the 10th Tennessee Infantry, CSA. Wounded and captured at Gettysburg, he settled in Davidson County after the war and was clerk of the Tennessee house (1869–75), U. S. postoffice clerk (1877–87), and sixth auditor (1893). *Register of the Officers of the Confederate States Navy* (Washington, 1931), 93; James Porter, *Tennessee*, Vol. VIII of *Confederate Military History*, Clement A. Evans, ed. (12 vols., Atlanta, 1899), 542–43.

1859

From Mrs. Henry Schoolcraft[1]

[January, 1859]   Washington etc. etc.

Hon Andrew Johnson
Tennessee.

Mrs Schoolcraft, whose philosophy of life,[2] Mr Johnson so much approves, is now in the gallery, & from thence forwards the wish that he may live a thousand years, as an illustration of the irresistable power of native genius, energy, and enterprize. Will Mr. Johnson, kindly advocate among his friends in the Senate, the passage of an act, to give Mrs S, the old plates, of her husbands "Indian History?" The Government has already made all the use it designs to, of these said plates, so that they will now be consigned to the sepulchral vaults, of the Capitol. Mr. Sebastian,[3] introduced a bill, last session, to give these plates, to the author, but the sudden adjournment of Congress prevented its passage. Please ask him, to bring it up this week.

Very Respectfully &C &C

Please speak to Mr. Polk.[4]

ALS, DLC-JP2.

1. Mary Howard Schoolcraft (1812–1878), a South Carolina native, was the second wife of Henry Rowe Schoolcraft (1793–1864), a New Yorker who wrote voluminously on Indian ethnology. The work alluded to is his six-volume *Historical and Statistical Information Respecting the History, Condition, and Prospects of the Indian Tribes of the United States*, subsidized by the government and published between 1851 and 1857. In 1860 Mrs. Schoolcraft published a volume of her own, *The Black Gauntlet: A Tale of Plantation Life in South Carolina*, a largely autobiographical proslavery narrative. *DAB*, XVI, 457; Chase S. and Stellanova Osborn, *Schoolcraft, Longfellow, Hiawatha* (Lancaster, Pa., 1942), 542, 571, 610.

2. We may speculate that this obvious flattery reflects a previous social encounter between Mrs. Schoolcraft and the senator.

3. William K. Sebastian (1812–1865), Arkansas senator (1848–61), had been circuit judge (1840–43), associate justice of the state supreme court (1843–45), and a member of the state senate (1846–47). As chairman of the committee on Indian affairs, Sebastian had presented on June 8, 1858, a bill which passed second reading before adjournment. Originally a relief bill for H. R. Schoolcraft, now infirm, the measure designated Mrs. Schoolcraft recipient of the plates. Reintroduced by Sebastian on January 19, 1859. it passed the Senate on January 21, and was signed into law three days later. *BDAC*, 1578; *Cong. Globe*, 35 Cong., 1 Sess., 2775; 2 Sess., 440, 512, 621.

4. Trusten Polk (1811–1876), Delaware-born and Yale-educated lawyer,

had been a delegate to the Missouri state constitutional convention (1845), presidential elector (1848), governor (1857), and was now Democratic senator (1857–62). A colonel in the Confederate army, he returned to St. Louis and his law practice after the war. *BDAC*, 1467.

Remarks on Retrenchment

January 4, 1859

Mr. JOHNSON, of Tennessee. I submit the following resolution, and ask for its consideration at the present time:

Resolved, That so much of the President's second annual message as relates to a reduction of the expenditures of the Government of the United States, which is in the following words, to wit: "I invite Congress to institute a rigid scrutiny to ascertain whether the expenses in all the Departments cannot be still further reduced; and I promise them all the aid in my power in pursuing the investigation," be referred to the Committee on Finance, and that said committee are hereby instructed, after first conferring with, and obtaining all "aid" and information from the President and heads of the Departments, as indicated in the President's message, to report a bill reforming, as far as possible, all abuses in the application of the appropriations made by Congress for the support of the various Departments, and which will reduce the expenditures to an honest, rigid, economical administration of the Government.[1]

Mr. HUNTER.[2] I should like to have that resolution lie over until to-morrow. I see that it instructs the committee.

Mr. JOHNSON, of Tennessee. I hope the Senator will make no objection to the resolution. It is merely directed to the committee, and instructs them, after obtaining the information, to do what the President himself says can be done. It seems to me this is a very auspicious time for such a movement.

[After hearing the resolution read again, Hunter suggests that the reduction of department expenditures should be considered by the appropriate Senate departmental committee rather than the finance committee.]

Mr. JOHNSON, of Tennessee. I am in hopes that the Senator from Virginia will withdraw his opposition to this resolution. The House of Representatives, under their rules, appoint committees to investigate and examine the expenditures of the respective Executive Departments. I served in that House ten years, and never knew any of those committees to make a report on the expenditures of any of the Departments. If we divide the labor here between these various committees, or appoint a special committee on the expenditures of the various Departments, there will never be anything done. I would prefer to have the labor and efforts of the Finance Committee first, to see if something cannot be done in the way of retrenching the expenditures of the Government, as indicated by the President of the United States. I think there can be no objection to this. If the Finance

Committee find it impossible for them to perform the labor, they can report that fact to the Senate. They are efficient; they are a working committee; and I hope the resolution will be referred to them.

While I am up, Mr. President, I must be permitted to make one other remark. I have been waiting a long time, and looking a good while for a favorable opportunity to commence the work of retrenchment.[3] I have long been satisfied in my own mind that it cannot be done unless the movement be headed by the Administration of the country. One member may come into the Senate Chamber, and a few others into the House of Representatives, and they may talk about retrenchment, and introduce resolutions, and propose propositions, and all that kind of thing, but it results in nothing; the effort fails; there is no retrenchment commenced, and there is no reform brought about. But now we have a favorable opportunity. It is in time of peace. A Democratic President now proposes, in his annual message, to lead in this work of retrenchment. He tells us in the message that the expenses of some of the Departments have been reduced below what they were last year;[4] and the suggestion is clear that if Congress will commence this work, the expenditures can be still further reduced. The President almost asks it. The President proposes to lead in the work of retrenchment, and why shall we not join him in the effort? It never will be done until this or some other Administration places itself in the lead of this great work. The President, it is true, says, in the message, that it is unreasonable to expect that the expenditures of the Government can now be as small as they were some years ago; that as the business of the country, and the country itself, increase, and become more extensive in everything that pertains to a Government, we must expect the expenditures of the Government to correspondingly increase. That is reasonable and right, and in that I concur with the President; but the question is whether the expenditures of the Government are not running far ahead of a corresponding increase of the population and business of the country. There are one or two facts that I think will go far to show the necessity of commencing this work of retrenchment and reform with the President at its head.

In 1790, the population of the United States was a fraction less than four million; and the expenditures, in 1791, were $2,000,000. At that time the amount required to carry on the Government for four million people was only $2,000,000. In 1858, we find that the population was twenty-eight million, and the expenditures of the Government for the last year were about seventy-five million dollars. At least, $75,000,000 was the estimate; but the actual expenditures, as we are told, were $81,000,000, and the amount we appropriated at the last Congress was $83,000,000. Confine it to the estimates made last year, and assume the expenditures to be $75,000,000. From 1790 up to the present period of time the population has increased seven fold; but the expenditures of the Government have increased thirty-five fold. I ask you if this ratio is not too great, if the expenditures of the Government have not gone too far ahead of the population and business of the country. Can we take any better data to get at what should be the expenditures of the Government than the population? There may be other things which may enable us to reach a correct conclusion; but this is near enough to show the country that the expenditures are outrunning our population and business in too great a ratio.

Our population has increased seven-fold, while our expenditures have multiplied thirty-five-fold. Thus it appears that, from 1790 to the present time, the expenditures of the Government have gone twenty-eight hundred per cent. in advance of the population. With that ratio going on in the future, how long will it be until the expenditures of the Government go beyond the ability of the people to pay the expenses of it?

I hope this resolution will go to the Committee on Finance. I think that is the appropriate committee. It is the committee that reports all the bills providing for the expenditures of the Government, and it is the appropriate committee, as I conceive, that should look into the expenditures and report to this House whether those expenditures cannot be reduced. I hope that the resolution will be referred to the Committee on Finance.

[Hunter and Fessenden observe that it would be physically impossible for their committee to make the thorough examination of department expenditures that the resolution requires.]

Mr. JOHNSON, of Tennessee. Mr. President, I hope the Committee on Finance will withdraw their opposition to this resolution going to them for consideration. It seems to be a proposition that everybody is for; yet there can be no agreement as to the proper disposition of the resolution. The Committee on Finance—not speaking disparagingly of the other committees—is an able, an industrious, a working committee, and that committee is necessarily compelled to make all the investigations that would be needed in order to frame a bill or bills of the description mentioned in the resolution. All the appropriations for the Navy, all the appropriations for the Army, all the appropriations for the civil department, all the appropriations for the judiciary, have to pass under the consideration of that committee. They, of course, must determine as to the propriety or impropriety of making the appropriations. They then, in fact, are compelled to make the investigation necessary to enable them to say how much is necessary. Why should they make the investigation without it being their duty to report a bill? We have most conclusive proof furnished to-day of the propriety of sending it to that committee. Just before its introduction we saw the honorable chairman of the Committee on Naval Affairs[5] reporting a bill increasing the expenditures of that Department. That does not seem likely to be a very appropriate committee at this time to bring about a reduction of expenditures in that Department. We see indicated, too, from the chairman of the Committee on Finance, his coöperation in this work of reduction; and he thinks it ought to be commenced, and is willing to commence it, but the greatest difficulty that seems to be in the way is the labor it imposes on that committee. As I before remarked, that committee, in fact, practically performs all the labor necessary to the ascertainment of the correct information which should be embodied in a bill of this description. If you refer this subject to the various committees of the Senate, the result will be no report and no reduction. I do not mean to cast any improper imputation on any of the committees; but when you call upon the Committee on Military Affairs to make a reduction in the expenditures of the War Department, they are fortified with all the arguments and reasons why those expenditures should be kept up or increased. When you call on the Naval Committee, it is the same thing; and so on with all the committees having charge of particular departments. Hence the Committee on Finance is the proper committee. It is their duty to supervise and look into the appropriations for all the departments, and see whether they are right or wrong, and report accordingly. I hope the chairman of the Committee on Finance will withdraw his opposition, and let the resolution go to his committee. Let them commence the work, and if they cannot go through with it during this session, let them report how far they have gone, and indicate how much can be done. You will find, too, when that committee commence the work, as I believe they will commence it in good earnest, if the duty is imposed upon them by a resolution, that war will be made upon them in many instances from other committees of this House. To my mind, the conclusion is clear and strong that that is the proper committee to commence this work of retrenchment.

But the Senator from Maine[6] throws out a doubt, in his remarks, as to the sincerity of the President in recommending retrenchment. I believe the President is in earnest, and that he has made the recommendation in good faith; but, if he is not in earnest, let us put him to the test. He has agreed to give aid to this committee, or any committee that Congress may institute, in prosecuting their investigations in the various Departments, and has recommended a reduction. Now, let us test his sincerity; and I ask the Senator from Maine to go with me, and put the President to the test. I know, so far as I am concerned—and I say it in no spirit of egotism—that my acts, my votes, and my speeches in the Congress of the United States for a number of years, correspond with my professions; and I am willing now to reduce my professions to practice. I am satisfied that the expenditures of this Government are too great; I am satisfied that they are unnecessary and profligate. I do honestly believe that millions of the people's money are collected and squandered here for improper purposes. It is our duty as faithful sentinels, as faithful representatives of the sovereign States, to commence the work of reduction and retrenchment of the expenses of the Government. Then let us unite in this movement. All agree that it is right; all agree that it should be done; all agree that the expenses are too great; all agree that there is extravagance and profligacy, and some insinuate that there is even corruption; but if we are all satisfied that this ought to be done, should we now be diverted from the object by a simple disinclination on the part of the Committee on Finance to go into the investigation?

Mr. President, (Mr. Fitzpatrick[7] in the chair,) you have been a member of this body a long time; I see many faces here that I served with in the House of Representatives;[8] and, from the time I took my seat there up to the present moment, whenever this subject was mooted the cry has been "this is not the time." There was always something in the way. An appropriation was needed for this, or an appropriation was needed for that, or the session was too short; it was not time to commence the work. When will the time come? When can we commence this work? In the estimation of some, it will never come; and, even amongst the friends of retrenchment and reform, when you present a proposition, it is not exactly in the right shape, its reference is not to the right committee, or the session is too short for anything to be done. If we are in earnest in this matter, if (following the intimation of the honorable Senator from Maine) we are sincere, let us give the public some evidence of our sincerity. Let us not talk about expenditure; let us not talk about extravagance; but let us reduce our professions and our talk and theories to practice.

I hope the Senate will send this resolution to the Committee on Finance. That is the committee whose duty it is to pass upon all the appropriations; and even if they were not favorably disposed, I say again, that, in preparing bills for the expenses of the different Departments they obtain all the information that is necessary to enable them to propose a general measure of economy. As to the suggestion that we should appoint a select committee, that would not be a proper committee. The Finance Committee is in possession of the real information, and that is the committee which should perform the work.

I hope the resolution will be sent to the Committee on Finance, and let them progress as far as they can. I believe if we pass a resolution of this kind, they will report a bill, and the work can be commenced in good earnest.[9]

Cong. Globe, 35 Cong., 2 Sess., 205–6, 208–9.

1. Buchanan's concern with the costs of government reflects the fiscal stringency which confronted the administration in the wake of the Panic of 1857.

2. Robert M. T. Hunter, chairman of the finance committee.

3. While a member of the House, Johnson had vigorously denounced government extravagance, demanding reductions in the number and salaries of federal employees as well as an accounting of John Quincy Adams' funeral expenses, and opposing a "pension" for Dolley Madison, the establishment of the Smithsonian, and the purchase of Washington's "Farewell Address." See Johnson Papers, I, 157, 302–5, 427–28, 440, 524–28, 585.

4. Buchanan had reported that the treasury, war, navy, and interior departments had reduced their estimates for the next fiscal year. Richardson, Messages, V, 524.

5. Stephen R. Mallory (c1813–1873), a lawyer born in Trinidad and reared in Key West, Florida, had been collector of the port of Key West (1845). Elected to the U. S. Senate over David T. Yulee in 1851, and re-elected in 1857, he withdrew in 1861 and became Confederate secretary of the navy. At the end of the war he resumed his law practice. DAB, XII, 224–25; Joseph T. Durkin, Stephen R. Mallory: Confederate Navy Chief (Chapel Hill, 1954).

6. William Pitt Fessenden (1806–1869), New Hampshire-born Whig lawyer and public financier, had served intermittent terms in the Maine lower house and in Congress (1841–43); a senator (1854–64), he later resigned to become Lincoln's secretary of the treasury. In 1865 he gave up his cabinet post to serve again in the Senate until his death. BDAC, 884; DAB, VI, 348–50; Charles A. Jellison, Fessenden of Maine: Civil War Senator (Syracuse, N. Y., 1962), passim.

7. Benjamin Fitzpatrick (1802–1869), Alabama lawyer, had served as Democratic governor (1841–45) before becoming senator (1848–49, 1853–61). BDAC, 893.

8. Twenty-four of Johnson's sixty-five senatorial colleagues had served with him in the House during the decade from 1843 to 1853: Albert G. Brown of Mississippi (1847–53), Thomas L. Clingman of North Carolina (1843–45), Jacob Collamer of Vermont (1843–49), Jefferson Davis of Mississippi (1845–46), James Dixon of Connecticut (1845–49), Stephen A. Douglas of Illinois (1843–47), Charles Durkee of Wisconsin (1849–53), Graham N. Fitch of Indiana (1849–53), Solomon Foot of Vermont (1843–47), James S. Green of Missouri (1847–51), John P. Hale of New Hampshire (1843–45), Hannibal Hamlin of Maine (1843–47), Robert M. T. Hunter of Virginia (1845–47), Alfred Iverson of Georgia (1847–49), Robert Johnson of Arkansas (1847–53), Preston King of New York (1843–47, 1849–53), Joseph Lane of Oregon (delegate, 1851–59), David S. Reid of North Carolina (1843–47), John Slidell of Louisiana (1843–45), Charles E. Stuart of Michigan (1851–53), John B. Thompson of Kentucky (1847–51), Robert Toombs of Georgia (1845–53), William Wright of New Jersey (1843–47), and David Yulee of Florida (delegate, 1841–45). Ibid., passim.

9. During the ensuing debate, Stuart of Michigan offered an amendment striking "all abuses in the application of the appropriations made by Congress" and substituting "the expenditures." Johnson objected, claiming that

such a change would be equivalent to rejecting the resolution; nonetheless, the proposal, with Stuart's amendment, received the Senate's unanimous consent. *Cong. Globe*, 35 Cong., 2 Sess., 211, 213; *Senate Ex. Journal*, 36 Cong., 2 Sess., 104.

From George C. Whiting

January 5, 1859, Washington, D. C.; Copy, DNA-RG15, War of 1812 Pensions, Anthony Rankins.

Commissioner of pensions finds that Anthony Rankin, ensign in 1st regiment of Tennessee militia, has not substantiated his claim for an invalid pension, inasmuch as he has not proved that the "fever" from which he suffered at the time of his discharge "is to be ascribed solely to exposure while he was in discharge of military duty . . . and is the cause of his present disability." [A Senate committee report of March, 1850, had recommended that Rankin be reimbursed thirty dollars, which he had paid for medical service in 1814 as a result of illness during his regiment's march to Knoxville.]

Remarks on Governmental Expenditures

January 17, 1859

Mr. JOHNSON, of Tennessee. I hope the Senate will take up a resolution which was left as the unfinished business some days ago, in reference to retrenchment and reform in the expenses of the Government. It will meet with no opposition, I think, and will not consume time.

[The motion agreed to, the Senate resumes consideration of Johnson's resolution submitted on January 4, calling for the Senate finance committee to investigate expenditures by the several departments. After Johnson accepts Michigan Senator Charles E. Stuart's amendment allowing the committee to continue its investigation beyond the current session, R. M. T. Hunter withdraws his amendment, which would replace "Committee on Finance" with "a select committee." William M. Gwin of California, another member of the finance committee, "renews" Hunter's amendment and calls for yeas and nays.]

Mr. JOHNSON, of Tennessee. I do not see that the modification of my resolution at all affects the right of the Senator from California to move his amendment. As the resolution now stands, it proposes to make it the duty of the Committee on Finance to make this inquiry and report to the Senate. I understand that simply a motion to strike out the Committee on Finance and appoint a select committee would attain the Senators's end.

Mr. GWIN. I make that motion.

Mr. JOHNSON, of Tennessee. I hope the Senate will not agree to it. The Finance Committee is the committee that has the moral influence to carry its measures; it has the power and can present measures to the Senate that will receive its consideration, and no doubt its sanction; and I hope the Senate will not strike out "the Finance Committee" and insert "a select committee." It is not worth while to repeat the arguments urged the other day on this point. They were cogent; they were clear and conclusive that the Committee on Finance was the proper committee to make this invesitgation, and report to the Senate. I hope the investigation will not be committed to a select committee.

[Gwin's amendment is approved, 34–24. He then moves to strike out the Stuart amendment, which seems not to have come to a vote.]

Mr. JOHNSON, of Tennessee. In the discussion of this resolution, it has been conceded, I think, by pretty much every Senator who has spoken upon it, that a great deal cannot be done during the present session. The provision now proposed to be stricken out was submitted to me by the Senator from Michigan, and I thought it was the best under the circumstances; that whether a select committee or the Committee on Finance undertook the investigation, the work could be commenced; but had no idea that it could be completed during the present session. Hence the amendment, as the resolution now stands, was accepted. I think it would be best to continue it in that shape.

I wish to say in this connection—and I rose more for that purpose than any other—that I have introduced no resolution to create a select committee. I am not the mover of a proposition of that sort, and if my proposition has been taken out of my hands by others, of course they entitle themselves to the courtesy that the mover of the resolution is always entitled to in selecting the chairman of the committee. I am satisfied in my own mind that the appointment of a select committee will result in doing no good. The Committee on Finance today, is in possession of more information necessary to an investigation of this sort, and the accomplishment of an end of this kind, than a select committee could be possessed of in the course of the next twelve months. If that committee could not complete their labors with the information they have, they could commence the work, and the Senate could indicate a determination that it was to be continued. I am in hopes that the Senate will not strike out what is now proposed to be stricken out by the Senator from California. In the event of the adoption of the resolution in its present form, that Senator has entitled himself to the honorable distinction of being chairman of the committee. I have introduced no resolution to appoint a select committee.[1]

Cong. Globe, 35 Cong., 2 Sess., 402–3, 405.

1. To the suggestion that he serve as chairman of the select committee, Johnson responded, "I cannot serve, because I believe it will do no good. I am in earnest in the proposition, and I want to give it that direction which will make it beneficial to the country." Further debate was discontinued upon notice of the death of Illinois Representative Thomas L. Harris. *Cong. Globe*, 35 Cong., 2 Sess., 406.

Speech on Transcontinental Railroads[1]

January 25, 1859

Mr. JOHNSON, of Tennessee. It was not my intention, Mr. President, to consume a single moment of the time of the Senate in the discussion of this bill. Every vote that I have given, every motion that I have made since the discussion of the subject commenced, has been with the view of having speedy action, by the Senate, upon this bill; but perhaps I may as well, at this time, state two or three reasons why I shall vote against the bill upon its final passage. The question has assumed a shape which makes it incumbent on me to do so.

The amendment[2] offered by the Senator from Mississippi [Mr. Davis] does not come up to what I would require in many particulars; but if that amendment were out of the way, I understand there is a proposition before the Senate to be acted upon, which was merely withdrawn for the purpose of testing the Senate upon the proposition of the Senator from Mississippi. The Senator from Tennessee [Mr. Bell] comes forward with a proposition in lieu of the original bill,[3] authorizing the Secretary of the Interior to receive proposals for the construction of three roads from the Atlantic to the Pacific side of the continent. This proposition is so enormous, it proposes to fix upon the country so great an expenditure, that, situated as I am, I feel called upon to give some reasons why I shall vote against it. There are other considerations in connection with the original bill, and some positions said to have been assumed by the party to which I belong, that I think untenable and unauthorized; hence I shall assign some few reasons, not consuming much of the time of the Senate, why I shall vote against these propositions at the present session.

Mr. President, to the extent that I have been instructed in the doctrines of either of the parties of this country, I have been trained in the school of the strict constructionists; and, according to my understanding of the Constitution of the country, I look upon this measure as being clearly unconstitutional. I know, in reference to works of internal improvement to be constructed by the Federal Government, it is difficult to determine where the power of the Federal Government begins and where it ends. It is somewhat difficult to determine what character of improvement is clearly within the Constitution, or, in other words, to determine what particular character of improvement is national and what is local. I know the distinction is hard to draw in many instances; for local works approach national works so closely that the line of division is scarcely within the reach of the human intellect; but there are some things which are certain. We cannot tell exactly when the light of day terminates, and the shades of night begin; but we can tell when it is mid-day, when the sun is at his meridian, and when midnight darkness is upon us. So we can determine the character of some of the works of internal improvement; we can tell when they are glaringly unconstitutional.

I have been taught, and it is my settled conviction, that in all questions of doubt, (admitting even that it was a doubtful question,) as to the constitutional power of Congress in reference to internal improvements, Congress should desist from the exercise of a doubtful power; and before its exercise Congress should look to the source of all our power to define specially the extent of the authority to be exercised by the legislative body. I have also learned that in doubtful questions of this kind we should pursue principle. Mr. Jefferson laid it down as a fundamental rule, in all doubtful questions, to pursue principle; and in the pursuit of a correct principle, you can never reach a wrong conclusion. What is the principle involved here? We assume, placing it upon the best ground on which it can be placed, that it is a doubtful power at least. Then, falling back upon the rule laid down by Mr. Jefferson, what is the principle? It is to call upon the source of all power before you exercise a doubtful authority.

If we continue the course of exercising doubtful constitutional powers, the Constitution will, in a very short time, cease, as it has, in a great measure, already ceased, to exist. I confess that I was somewhat refreshed the other day when the Senator from Louisiana [Mr. Benjamin][4] took up this question. I really felt gratified that the fact, the great fact, that a Constitution exists in this country, had not been altogether lost sight of, and that there was here and there a member of this body who still had a knowledge of the existence of the Constitution, and was disposed to recur to its provisions, and call the country to their proper exercise.

The Senator from Mississippi [Mr. Davis] congratulated himself upon the Senator from Louisiana coming over to the school of the strict constructionists; he congratulated himself upon the acquisition the Democratic party had made in receiving the accession of so distinguished an individual to the doctrines of a strict construction of the Constitution. Well, sir, I think we may congratulate the country on it; I think we may feel proud of the acquisition; but if the same rule laid down by the Senator, as applied to the Senator from Louisiana, be applied to himself, it would seem that when he is contending for the opposite construction of the Constitution, he is becoming a little latitudinous, and he is about to occupy the former position of the Senator from Louisiana. While I was gratified on the one hand to welcome the Senator from Louisiana into our ranks as a strict constructionist, I regretted extremely on the other to lose the Senator from Mississippi by his going over to the doctrines of the latitudinarians.

The power to construct this road is placed, by the friends of the bill, upon that provision of the Constitution which says that Congress shall have power to declare war. Because the power is conferred upon Congress to declare war, does the inference follow that Congress even has the right to declare war unless it is necessary and proper to do so? Does the fact that we have the power to declare war, imply that we must improperly exercise the power because it is conferred? Not at all.

But when it says that Congress shall have power to declare war, the Constitution goes on to say that Congress shall have power to raise an army. Why? Admitting that this is an express grant, it sinks into and becomes an incident to the power to declare war. The raising and maintaining of armies is a necessary incident to a declaration of war; but it should be necessary and proper to declare war first, and then to raise your armies as incident to a declaration of war when made. When you raise your armies, the Constitution says that all appropriations for their maintenance shall not exist more than two years. Why? Because it was looked upon as a dangerous power. In the event of a declaration of war, the Constitution of the country makes the President of the United States commander of the Army and Navy; in other words, it places the sword in the Executive hand, but it gives Congress the power to control appropriations, and prohibits Congress from making any appropriations for the support of the Army beyond two years.

Now, the question comes up, is it necessary and proper to declare war? Is it necessary and proper to raise and maintain an army in consequence of a declaration of war? If it is not necessary to exercise the war power, is it necessary to exercise any of the incidents that flow from the exercise of the war power? In the first place, we assume that it is not necessary to exercise the war power. It not being necessary to exercise the war power, of course it is not necessary or proper to carry the warmaking power into effect. Let me read the provisions of the Constitution on this subject in connection:

The Congress shall have power to declare war, * * * * to raise and support armies; but no appropriation of money to that use shall be for a longer term than two years, * * * * to provide for calling forth the militia to execute the laws of the Union, suppress insurrections, and repel invasions.

These are all express grants of power. Then the Constitution declares, in reference to the enumerated powers, that Congress shall have authority

To make all laws which shall be necessary and proper for carrying into execution the foregoing powers.

In the first place, it is not necessary to declare war; it is not necessary now to exercise the war power. It not being necessary to exercise any one of these powers at the present time, it is not necessary and proper to construct the Pacific railroad as an incident to carry into effect the war power, when it is not necessary to exercise it. The President of the United States says on this subject, in his late annual message:

Whilst disclaiming all authority to appropriate money for the construction of this road, [the Pacific railroad,] except that derived from the war-making power of the Constitution, there are important collateral considerations urging us to undertake the work as speedily as possible.[5]

The President himself then disclaims all power on the part of the Federal Government to make this road, unless it is under the war power; but he says there are other reasons why this road should be made. Now, let me ask every man who is a strict constructionist, and is willing to abide by the spirit as well as the letter of the Constitution, if you restrict this measure to the war power, and the President of the United States disclaims the power to exist anywhere else, is it necessary and proper now to construct a railroad that is to cost $200,000,000, in order to carry out the war-making power of the Constitution? What great emergency is upon the country? What great exigency exists? Why is it necessary to expend two, or six, or eight hundred million dollars in the construction of a road that is not essential to carry out the war-making power?

I cannot consent, that because the road will be a convenience in the event of a war, for carrying troops and munitions of war and all that pertains to an army, we have therefore the power to construct it, or to appropriate land and money to secure its construction as this bill provides, and then give it to the Territories through which the road may pass when they become States. If we can do it, why may we not begin at Maine on our extreme northeastern boundary, and construct a line of railroad to Boston, and from Boston to New York, and from New York to Philadelphia, and from Philadelphia to Baltimore, and from Baltimore to Washington, and from Washington to Richmond, and from Richmond to Lynchburg, and from Lynchburg to Knoxville, and from Knoxville to Chattanooga, and from Chattanooga to Memphis, and thence to Little Rock in Arkansas, a direct connection over a line stretching through the country?

Would not such a line of road be just as much a war measure, and be just as necessary and proper, as an exercise of the war power, as it is to construct a road from here to the Pacific ocean? If we have the power in the one case to construct a road from Little Rock or any place on the western boundary of Missouri, or any other point, to the Pacific ocean, and pay out money and public lands for it, is it not just as constitutional, is it not just as necessary and proper for the Government to come forward and relieve those States who are now groaning under the heavy debts that they have contracted for the construction of the roads I have mentioned? Can it not just as well do that as continue these roads to the Pacific, and surrender the line to the States through which it may be constructed? If we can make the road and surrender it in the one case, we can appropriate for one that is already constructed in the other.

I shall not undertake on this occasion to give any learned disquisition on the Constitution; I claim to understand it for myself. I shall exercise my privileges here according to my understanding of the Constitution of the country. I do not think the Constitution authorizes the construction of this road by the Federal Government. If, however, we now construct this road as a war measure, let me ask, after the road is constructed, what defense have you given to California by it? That appears to be the great object in view; and the idea is kept before the Senate and the country that our Pacific coast is in great danger, and that those of our citizens who have emigrated there will never be in a condition to protect themselves. It is said we must have a road by which men, munitions of war, and all those things necessary to the defense of a free people can be taken to California. Is there no gallantry, is there no patriotism, is there no love of country and the Union in the State of California as in the other States? I should think there was some there as well as here. I will not do that people injustice. I believe California is competent to defend herself. Give her the same means, the same instrumentalities that are exercised by the other States, and California will defend herself.

But suppose the road was constructed to California: our great danger, it is said, lies in apprehended descents from some great maritime Power. Some foreign Power is to attack our Pacific coast, and therefore a railroad is necessary to its defense. Suppose your road was constructed to day: would it protect California from any maritime Power? What would protect her from a British, or a French, or any other fleet that might be prepared to make a descent on her coast? Why, after your road is constructed, you must have forts, you must have harbors, you must have arsenals, you must have dock-yards, or else you have no defense. But suppose you pass to the other end of the line, and, without the road, construct forts and arsenals and dock-yards on the Pacific coast, as you have done on the Atlantic: are not the people of California as competent to defend themselves as we are? By the time we construct this road, which will not be less than twenty-five or perhaps a much greater number of years, they will be more competent to defend themselves against any foreign aggressions than we were when we succeeded in achieving the independence that we now enjoy.

It is not necessary, it is not proper to carry into effect any one of the expressly granted powers in the Constitution. If they need forts, if they need arsenals, if they need dock-yards, coming within the meaning and purview of the Constitution, as it has been acted on again and again, give them to California. The Senator from Rhode Island [Mr. Simmons][6] stated the other day that, if an army of thirty-five thousand men were placed on the Pacific coast, and they had to be supplied by means of this road from the Atlantic States, it would cost us over one hundred million dollars per annum to sustain them. Then we shall expend a much larger sum per annum for sustaining that force than your whole War Department costs, going upon the idea that California and the Pacific coast are never to be in a condition to defend themselves. I think the time will come, and long before this railroad is completed, when, on the other side of the mountains, on the great slope that leads to the Pacific coast, the people there will know how to make cannon as well as we do here; they will know how to manufacture powder, ball, and all the other implements necessary and proper for a people to carry on a war successfully. We seem to go on the idea, in making arguments for this road, that they are never to be competent there to the construction of any of the implements necessary successfully to carry on a war.

The President disclaims the power existing in the Constitution unless it is derived from the war power. This is an honest difference of opinion. I do not believe it can be derived from that power. There have been some others who claim the power as arising from the power in the Constitution to regulate commerce. I do not think that provision in the Constitution which provides for the regulation of commerce, confers power on Congress to make or to create commerce. Some derive the power from that provision of the Constitution which authorizes Congress to establish post offices and post roads. I do not believe the language employed in the Constitution to be so meant. The debates of the convention do not show that Congress was to make and construct roads through the country. It meant, I think, simply and plainly, that where there were lines of communication, Congress might establish them as the governmental channels through which communications of this kind might go, but not to construct roads. They may establish and recognize them as post roads, but not construct them.

It seems, from the multifarious views taken of the constitutional power to pass this measure by its friends, that it has no specific or definite location. It is a kind of migratory power that is wandering about in the Constitution, seeking some place to make a location. Then I come back to the text that I started with: placing it upon the best ground possible, it is a doubtful question; and being a doubtful question, I, as a Democrat, favoring a strict construction of the Constitution, say Congress should desist from the exercise of the power; and before the power is exercised, if this Government is to be preserved a free Government, let us go to the States that made the Constitution, and ask them for an enlargement of our authority or to definitely and distinctly define what power Congress shall exercise in reference to works of internal improvement.

But to make this road a little more plausible, and, as it were, to hang it as a millstone around the neck of the Democratic party, the distinguished Senator from California [Mr. Gwin] referred to the national convention which sat at Cincinnati in 1856. He says that that convention passed a resolution favoring the construction of this road as a part of the Democratic platform; that it was laid down as a tenet of the Democratic party; that it was adhered to by the party, and recommended by the President; and hence all the Senators on this side of the Chamber are considered bound to go for this measure. In the first place, Mr. President, I do not understand the resolution alluded to, as the Senator from California understands it. On the first day of the sitting of that convention, Mr. Hallett,[7] who by-the-by is generally a considerable man at gatherings of this kind, and is very expert as well as talented in the preparation of resolutions, introduced the following resolution:

Resolved, That a committee of one delegate from each State, to be selected by the delegation thereof, be appointed to report resolutions, and that all resolutions in relation to the platform of the Democratic party be referred to said committee, on presentation, without debate.[8]

On the third day of the convention, Mr. Hallett, as chairman of that committee, made this report:

I have been instructed, as the chairman of the committee on resolutions, to report to this convention the platform of resolutions which they have adopted. I am also instructed by the committee to say, that the portion of the resolutions which relates to Kansas and Nebraska, and those propositions concerning the administration of the General Government, have been adopted by the committee with entire unanimity, every member from every State having signified his perfect acquiescence in these resolutions. There is another and very important class of resolutions, relating to the foreign policy of the country. While these resolutions have been recommended by the committee as a portion of the platform, it is proper to state, that they were not adopted with entire unanimity.

Mark this; and then he adds:

I am also instructed to report a resolution, as recommended by the committee, concerning communication between the Atlantic and Pacific oceans.[9]

He reports the resolutions in regard to the Pacific railroad, not as part of the platform. Then comes the platform of resolutions reported, signed by "B. F. Hallett, chairman;" and this is added:

The following is the resolution with respect to overland communication with the Pacific.[10]

Then comes the resolution, an outside measure, not laid down as a tenet or article of faith, which was adopted by the Democratic party in that convention. This resolution was taken up, and Mr. H. Saulsbury,[11] of Delaware, moved to lay it on the table. When we come to read this resolution, all that it did was to assert the duty of Congress to exercise all its constitutional power on the subject. It did not even assume that Congress had any power in the matter. If they had none, it was a nullity and meant nothing at all. The resolution was taken up, and Mr. Saulsbury, of Delaware, moved to lay it on the table. This motion prevailed—yeas 154, nays 120; and the resolution was laid upon the table. The convention then, after having completed the Democratic platform, proceeded to the nomination of their candidate for the Presidency of the United States. Mr. Buchanan was nominated. The nomination was over, the platform complete; the creed of the Democratic party, so far as that convention went, was finished. In the evening session, after the candidate for the Presidency was nominated, Mr. Shields,[12] of Missouri, presented the following resolution:

Resolved, That it is the duty of the Federal Government to construct, so far as it has constitutional power so to do, a safe overland communication within our own territory between the Pacific and Atlantic States.[13]

Then the original resolution, which had been rejected, was offered in lieu of this, at the request of the Wisconsin delegation. The original resolution was adopted, in these words:

Resolved, That the Democratic party recognizes the great importance, in a political and commercial point of view, of a safe and speedy communication through our own territory between the Atlantic and Pacific coasts of the Union, and that it is the duty of the Federal Government to exercise all its constitutional power to the attainment of that object, thereby binding the Union of these States in indissoluble bonds, and opening to the rich commerce of Asia an overland transit from the Pacific to the Mississippi river and the great lakes of the North.[14]

Mark you, the President was nominated at this time, and this resolution was adopted merely as suggestive, it having once been rejected by a decided vote. It was not adopted as part of the platform, but simply as an outside, straggling resolution in the convention. The Vice President[15] was then nominated; and in the acceptance of his nomination, hear what his language is, and this goes to show that he did not understand that resolution as being a part of the platform:

The platform you have so unanimously adopted—

not the resolution that had been once rejected, and taken up and adopted as an outside measure; but—

—The platform you have so unanimously adopted, I need not, as a State-rights man, say I cordially approve and indorse.[16]

What construction does the Vice President put upon this resolution? What construction does everybody else put upon a resolution which has been sent forth to the country as being a Democratic measure, as an article of the Democratic faith? I say, according even to the proceedings of that convention, it is no article of the faith of the party to which I belong. It is no tenet of my creed, and I consider myself a Democrat, and do not look on it as adopted by the convention. It is merely thrown out as suggestive; it is nothing more than mere apocrypha; it is no tenet, no article of our faith. I remember very well, that after the nomination was made, the question came up as to whether this plank had been laid down as part of our creed, and I know that in the section of country where I was during the canvass, it was repudiated and condemned by all as not being part of the Democratic faith. I know that Mr. Buchanan was not understood in that region as entertaining opinions favorable to the Pacific railroad and admitting its constitutionality. Although the opinion may have been expressed, and it may have lain hidden somewhere else, yet during that canvass it was not before the public mind as a measure of the Democratic party. On the contrary, I well remember the surprise with which, in my section, the people received news from the State of California, after the election was over, after victory had perched upon the Democratic standard, that Mr. Buchanan had written a letter to California,[17] committing himself to the Pacific railroad; and it was so surprising that some even looked upon that letter, being published after the election was over, as a hoax, as not authentic, as gotten up for the occasion. But let that be as it may, the letter was written in September, went to California and did its work there, if it did any. I do not know whether it influenced the election there or not, but it was not known in the region of country from which I come until after the election was over, and it took us by surprise. I know there are some in my section of the country who are for a Pacific railroad, without regard to the Constitution, without regard to the existence of the power anywhere, and who look upon it as a great measure. For myself, however, I prefer, on such questions, to consult the Constitution of my country.

Mr. President, even if the Cincinnati convention had laid it down as an article of the Democratic faith, as a tenet in our creed, I should like to know of what binding force resolutions and tenets and articles of faith laid down by conventions in modern times, are upon any party, whatever? I think about this convention as I have thought about all conventions, from my earliest advent into public life to the present time. We know how these conventions are gotten up. We know the objection that was urged against the congressional caucus system in 1824, and we know that Andrew Jackson, being the people's man and a great advocate of popular rights, was brought forward as the most fit and suitable individual to break up the old congressional caucus system. Experience and observation, however, have satisfied my mind that the old congressional caucus system was infinitely preferable to your recent national convention system. In the one case, the members of Congress who made the nomination felt that they had some responsibility resting upon them, and when they went to their congressional districts they were responsible for the nominee who was put upon the country as a candidate for the Presidency. How have your national conventions been gotten up? I do not say it out of any disrespect, but I refer to it as a historical fact, that a large proportion of the persons who attend national conventions, go there without representing anybody. Little meetings, irresponsible caucuses get together, and appoint delegates to go to the conventions. They are men who, when they look to their congressional district, see that somebody represents it in Congress; when they look to their legislative district, they see that somebody represents it in the Legislature; they find the various places filled at home, and they go into a convention with their little amount of stock, to make the best and safest investment of it they can, and the candidate who can come forward, and, through his friends, hold out the greatest amount of appliances, fair or unfair, is the one who secures their support, and obtains a nomination.

Mr. President, I most sincerely hope the time will come when the people of the United States will have the constitutional right to elect their own President. Do they elect him now? No; they do not. Packed conventions are got up, and they, by the means to which I refer, make a nomination either on one side or the other. Democrats or Black Republicans, Democrats or Whigs, Democrats or Americans, make their nominations in conventions, and submit them to the

American people. Although our people are in theory a free people, and are supposed to elect their President, the fact is that in practice, the conventions have made the choice before they are called upon to vote; and after these conventions, on the one side and on the other, have chosen a President, the freemen of this country are brought up to the ballot-box and taken through the ridiculous mockery of voting for electors for President. I have gone for the nominees of conventions, and I have been in conventions; but need I stultify myself; need I deceive myself; do I not see their tendency—an alarming, corrupting, and dangerous tendency? There was one distinguished man whom I greatly admired; whose remains now repose in a neighboring State to my own; who has a permanent abiding place in the affections of his countrymen, and especially of his own State. I allude to Mr. Calhoun; and his State is selected as the place for the action of another convention[18] in direct opposition to the views which he entertained in reference to those conventions which have been fixing Presidents on the country. Mr. Calhoun fought the caucus system; he fought the convention system; he contended for the great principle that the people should elect the President themselves, or that he should be elected in the manner pointed out by the Constitution. How is it done now? Have the people the constitutional power? No. We talk about free Government, and the exercise of the elective franchise; but the people have no power to elect a President. The Constitution of the United States confers the power upon the States to appoint a certain number of electors, in such manner as the Legislature may prescribe. All the States give the election of electors to the people save one, and that is South Carolina; and I regret that she has not done it; but the privilege of voting for electors is exercised by the people at the mere grace and favor and condescension of the State Legislature.

I hope the time will come when the American people can for themselves, in a constitutional way, settle who shall be their Chief Magistrate. Would it not be better that the organic law of the land should be so changed as never to take the election before the House of Representatives in the event of no one of the candidates receiving a majority of all the votes? If a dozen candidates run, and no one receives a majority of all the votes, yet the people have indicated at the ballot-box whom they prefer. Every State of the Union might run a candidate; the people might vote for few or many, as they saw proper; and the preference of the people would be indicated in reference to men, whom, by service, by association, by merit, and by their public acts, had got their esteem and confidence, even though in particular localities. Suppose a dozen should run, and no one should have a majority. Change your organic law, send the two highest back to the people, and let it be settled by them just as it is now settled by the House of Representatives. I would to-morrow prefer to see an election made by the House of Representatives, much as I repudiate that provision of our Constitution, rather than by an irresponsible convention. They do settle it; they do make Presidents; and we know it is practically so. It is not worth while to discuss the point, which will be the safest—men who have merit in their districts, and have found their way as Representatives of a free people to the other Hall, and there voting by States, or irresponsible national conventions.

I have gone thus far to show that I do not recognize everything that may emanate from an irresponsible convention, as having a binding force upon me as an article of the Democratic faith. I look on these conventions, in fact, as in violation of the spirit, if not the letter, of the Constitution of the United States. Why do I say so? One convention of one party meets and nominates its man, and the other convention meets and nominates its candidate. There are only two candidates before the country, and the people, as I remarked before, come forward and ratify what the conventions have done; but when we come to look at the Constitution of the United States and the views of those who framed it, we find that that instrument, after declaring the mode in which the President shall be chosen by the electors, goes on to provide:

> The President of the Senate shall, in the presence of the Senate and House of Representatives, open all the certificates, and the votes shall then be counted. The person having the greatest number of votes for President shall be the President, if such number be a majority of the whole number of electors appointed; and if no person have such majority, then, from the persons having the highest numbers, not exceeding three, on the list of those voted for as President, the House of Representatives shall choose.

The original provision was, that in the event of a failure to elect by the electors, no more than five names should go before the House of Representatives. The Constitution was amended, and the number narrowed down to three. What does this contemplate? What is the idea held out? What is the theory inculcated? It is, that you shall have a greater number to vote for than two; at one time five, and at another time three, according to the Constitution. But the convention system says no, the people shall only have two to choose from. I look upon the proceedings of conventions, especially when there are only two, as coming directly in conflict with the spirit, if not the letter, of the Constitution, by depriving the people of the benefit of choice from five or three, as the case may be, when an election goes before the House of Representatives.

I repeat, I have acted with conventions because there have generally been but two in the country. Sometimes, to be sure, we have had an outside candidate nominated; but I have acted with my party and gone for the nominee of its convention. I do not, however, admit the correctness of the principle, nor do I admit the orthodoxy of the resolution laid down at the Cincinnati convention, which I look upon as irresponsible to a very great extent, and as being a resolution to control the Democratic party.

Mr. President, after this digression, I will return to the line of my argument. I shall go against the original bill, and against all the amendments. I may vote for some of them in lieu of the original bill, as a preference between the two. First, I conceive, under the war-making power, it not being necessary to exercise that power, it is not necessary to exercise any one of the incidents necessary and proper to carry it into effect. In the next place, when you attempt to impose it upon me as a measure of the Democratic party, I do not recognize it as a measure of the Democratic party. I do not recognize it as a tenet or article of faith of the Democratic party as laid down by the Cincinnati convention.

But, if these two grounds were out of the way, I should be opposed to it on the ground of expediency. Instead of reading the sections of the bill, I shall read from the remarks of the distinguished Senator from California, in which he explains the sections of his bill,[19] and take them as being more lucid and conclusive than the sections themselves. He says, in his speech made during the last session of Congress, in explanation of this bill:

> The fifth section requires the contracting party to proceed without delay to locate the general route of the road, and to furnish the President with a map of the same, who shall cause the public lands for forty miles on each side of the road to be surveyed, and the Indian titles thereto, if any, extinguished. It also gives the right of preëmption to the lands not granted to the contracting party, but withholds them from settlement until the lands granted are selected.

Now, I propose in my way to examine that proposition. The President is authorized first to make a contract with a corporation or individuals, and then he is to cause all lands to be surveyed within forty miles on each side of the road. On this point, let me advert to some other features of the Cincinnati Democratic platform, if I may dignify it with that appellation. There are some things laid down in it which I approve heartily and cordially. It admonishes the country against monopolies; it admonishes the country against class legislation, in substance; it admonishes the country against corporations, and against the exercise of doubtful powers. Well, what do we find here? According to this interpretation of the fifth section of the bill, what does it provide? That you shall make a contract with parties, and if the contract is made, forty miles on each side of the road shall be surveyed.

Another provision of the bill grants to the party with whom the contract is made, each alternate section for twenty miles on each side of the road. It further guaranties that even where the Indian titles are not yet extinguished, this Government is to go forward and extinguish the Indian titles to promote and advance the interests of the company with whom a contract may be made. Is not this a monopoly? Is it not an enormous grant? If the land is of no account, they cannot make the road; if the land is good, it is too much to grant. What is the supposed length of this road? According to some surveys it is twenty-five hundred miles; but I believe by none is it less than two thousand. Let us take the shortest distance—two thousand miles. We are to set apart and commence extinguishing the Indian titles to the land for twenty miles on each side, giving each alternate section to the company. A grant of the alternate sections for twenty miles on each side would make a solid belt twenty miles wide and two thousand miles long. Well, if it is of no account; if it is barren, sterile, arid, unproductive land, they cannot make the road with it. If it is rich, fertile, good land, fit for the habitation of man, it is too much to grant. Two thousand miles long and twenty miles wide of the public land, are to go at one single sweep! Here is a grant to a company of forty thousand square miles of territory, equal to twenty-five million six hundred thousand acres—think of it. We would go to war; we would fight France, England, and every other maritime Power upon God's habitable globe, if they were to make a demand on us for any of our territory; and here we propose to give away forty thousand square miles. There is not much difference between monopolies and corporations at home, and foreign Powers abroad, especially if they are monarchical. Here is a grant of country two thousand miles long and twenty miles wide—forty thousand square miles. Go to the State from which I come, with a population of a million, and what is the area of her territory? It is only forty-five thousand square miles.[20] Go to the great State of New York, with a population of three millions, and what is her area? Forty-seven thousand square miles. Go to Ohio, with a population of two and a half millions, and her number of square miles is only thirty-nine thousand. Here, at a single grant, at a single dash of the pen, the Congress of the United States is to grant to a corporation a monopoly of enough territory to make a sovereign State larger than the great State of Ohio, and nearly as large as Tennessee or New York.

But, does the enormity of the thing stop here? No. After you have granted to them absolutely forty thousand square miles—and some portion of it is said to be the best land on the face of the earth, but other portions, I suppose, are not good—you grant them the preëmption of the remaining sections. So says the Senator from California, in his interpretation of the sections of this bill. Think of it! Forty thousand square miles absolutely, and a preëmption right to as much more! Take England, with her powerful navy, the great Power of the commercial world, and the principal Power of Europe, France and Austria not excepted, and the basis for her action is only fifty thousand square miles. England, proud and potent as she is, with a navy that keeps in terror the civilized world, has only an area of fifty thousand square miles upon which she operates; but, at a single grant, the Congress of the United States is prepared to give away the foundation of an empire to a railroad company, or a party with whom the Government may make a contract.

We see, then, Mr. President, how we are going on; we see where the legislation of this country is tending. I know that when I refer to such things, my strictures are attributed to early prejudice and training; but I speak great truths. The tendency of the legislation of this country is to build up monopolies. The tendency of the legislation of this country is to build up the money power. The tendency of the legislation of this country is to concentrate power in the hands of the few. The tendency of the legislation of this country is for classes, and against the great mass of the people. How much legislation is done here for the people? How much is done for individuals and classes? How much is done in all the States for classes, and how much for the people? Sir, of all your legislation here, a very small proportion is for the great mass of the people, while four fifths of it is for individuals and for classes.

But the bill does not stop with grants of land and a preëmption right; it goes further. Here I may remark that I prefer the bill of the Senator from Mississippi to the original bill. The original bill merely proposes a beginning; the end no mortal man now sees or understands. The Senator from California, in his explanation of the bill, says:

The seventh section provides that so soon as one section of twenty-five miles of the road is completed, the President shall cause to be issued to the contracting party $12,500 per mile of said section in United States bonds bearing five per cent. interest, payable nineteen years from date; and in like manner to cause the same amount of bonds per mile to be issued for each succeeding section of twenty-five miles, when completed, until the whole road is built; provided that the aggregate amount of bonds issued shall not exceed the sum of $25,000,000.

Will $25,000,000 be a beginning, if the Government once embarks in a work of this sort? Does not every man here know that it will not? and then after you have given the benefit of the Government obligations for $25,000,000, how are they to be paid? On this point the Senator from California says:

It also provides that the amount of bonds thus issued, with the interest on the same, shall be paid to the United States by the transportation and service provided for in this act. The committee were of the opinion that the amount due for such service within nineteen years would be fully adequate to pay the bonds, principal and interest, and hence they inserted that date for their payment; I may also be permitted to observe, that nineteen years being supposed to be the term of life of one generation, it was not inappropriate to apply, in the building of this great work, the old Jeffersonian doctrine, that each generation should provide for the payment of its own debts.

When we examine the letter of Mr. Jefferson here referred to,[21] we find that he had been looking at some of the tables of mortality in Europe, and he found that of the adult persons existing at any particular period of time, in nineteen years the majority of those adult persons would have passed from time to eternity. Hence he fixed nineteen years as the duration of a generation of adults. These bonds are to fall due in nineteen years, presuming that by that time the price we are to pay for carrying the mail will more than liquidate the interest and the principal.

Well, suppose the road pays it; suppose we take the interest and the principal both out of the mail service: does not the Government still owe the money on the bonds? When your nineteen years have expired, the other doctrine that Mr. Jefferson wished to warn his countrymen against, leaving debts to posterity, stands untouched. Cannot we understand this thing? We may bamboozle each other if we will; we may attempt to bamboozle the people; but when we bring our minds to the proposition, we cannot be mistaken. The proposition is to give the $25,000,000, and the Government is to be paid in mail service, interest and principal; but how is the Government to pay the bonds? Have you any clause in this bill saying where the Government is to get the $25,000,000 from? You issue bonds, create debts, and provide no way in which the debts are to be paid. Is that Mr. Jefferson's doctrine? If that was the doctrine taught by the illustrious Jefferson, I confess that I have been so obtuse that I have not understood it; but precisely the reverse was the doctrine taught by him. We are doing the precise thing he admonished us against, even in this miniature proposition to expend $25,000,000. Most of the estimates to construct the road put its cost at over one hundred million dollars. Does not every Senator here know, does not every man in the country know, that if the Government undertakes to construct this road, it will not stop at $100,000,000, even if it stops at $200,000,000?

But, Mr. President, this is not all. After taking out your $25,-

000,000 in mail service, the duty on the iron for a railroad twenty-five hundred miles long, weighing sixty-eight or seventy-five pounds to the yard, is not to be paid; but the first service the road performs is to be used to liquidate the duty on the iron, instead of creating revenue on which the Government can subsist. Let me give you the explanation of that provision by the Senator from California:

This section also provides, that if the railroad iron used in the construction of the road shall be imported, the duties of the same will not be required to be paid in advance, but the amount shall be deducted from the first service performed for the Government under the act.

Here is an absorption of the means that ought to be derived by the Treasury from the iron used in this road. Well, look at it. Forty millions of square miles are granted absolutely; forty millions more preëmpted; $25,000,000 thrown out, and all the duty on iron taken from the Treasury of the United States, and yet you say it is no enormous proposition; it is going to save expenditure!

In another portion of the speech of the Senator from California, he says it is going to reduce the expenses of the War Department. From eighteen to twenty-five million dollars are now required for the War Department, putting it at the outside limit, and we think that is extravagant; but if the Government constructs this road, what will be the cost of it? Look at the history of railroads in the United States, and be not impatient in reference to the construction of railroads. Since 1828, the States have constructed about thirty thousand miles of railroad. We ought not to be impatient. I am a progressive Democrat, but I am for progressing within the prescribed limits of the Constitution and the law. Ought we to be impatient, when your States since 1828 have constructed thirty thousand miles of railroad? I believe the globe is only twenty-seven thousand miles round [sic], and we, from 1828 up to the present time, have constructed enough railroad to bound the globe, and to start a tunnel through the center; and still we are impatient at our slow progress in the construction of railroads. There is some talk about breaking the bands of the Union, and dissolving the Confederacy; but if the globe was cracked, and about to fall apart, we have constructed enough railroad to bind it clear around, and hold it together, if a railroad would do it. But it is said this road will reduce the expenses of the War Department.

If this road were constructed now—if it were laid down in the course of a night by enchantment, so that it would cost you nothing to construct it, it would cost you more than the entire expenses of the War Department to run the road. If you had a company that would construct the road in a night's time, and give it to you free of cost the next day, it would cost you more to run the road than it costs you to carry on the War Department now. Why, sir, you cannot protect the railroad. Suppose you put five men per mile on the road two thousand miles long; it would require ten thousand men. You might not want them equally dispersed, but average them at five men to the mile for two thousand miles, and you require ten thousand men; and in the manner in which we have been raising and supporting regiments by this Government, it has cost us $1,000,000 for each thousand men. That was the estimate at the last session. Then you must take into the account the interest of the money, and the other expenses of keeping it up without way travel or way freight, relying on through travel to sustain the line along such a trunk of railroad as that will be, if ever constructed; and all the railroad statistics of the country prove that railroads must rely on way travel, and way freight to be sustained. You must have people, and you must have country, you must have commerce to sustain the road, and not arid and sterile deserts.

Mr. President, the true policy to secure the construction of a road from here to the Pacific is the one we have been pursuing elsewhere in the country. Encourage settlement; encourage the cultivation of the soil; and as your settlements advance, carrying along with them the arts of agriculture, mechanics, and science of every description, as they want these improvements, they will follow as a legitimate incident. Let your settlements go on progressively, and as these improvements are wanted, your settlements will build them. Do not be afraid of California. The Californians are a brave and gallant people; and if you put the question to them to-day—I think I might speak authoritatively—they will tell you they can defend themselves; they will tell you, if you put the construction of this road exclusively on the war power, that they do not ask it for that. When you leave out the commercial reasons, when you leave out the other reasons for the construction of this road, and put it on the war power, California will tell you that she can defend herself. If she wants a fort, an arsenal, or a dockyard, give it to California, as you have to the other States.

In many instances, when this question has come up, the Union has been introduced, and we are told this road is to be a bond of union. California and Washington city are nearly as close to each other as Georgia and Maine were in the revolutionary war, in point of time, and closer than New Orleans would have been to Washington, if she had been a part of the Confederacy in the Revolution. This road is to be constructed as a bond of union—a road running through a desert—a road to bring us a little tea, to bring us some silks. This is a great bond of union; and one powerful reason I heard given on this floor, why this road should not [sic] be constructed at this immense expense was, that the flavor of the tea we get from China, passing through the torrid zone, was not quite so good as it ought to be, and therefore we must have a railroad to cost two or three hundred million dollars to get our tea with a little better flavor.[22] I do not think the people of this country will be injured much by the present flavor of the tea. There is enough of it used for all useful and wholesome purposes. But if this Union hangs together by no stronger tenure than the construction of a railroad which, as has been demonstrated, must go through an arid desert, I tell you it will go; and if California's remaining in the Union depends upon the construction of this railroad by the States on this side of the continent, I say, and I say it in good nature, let California go.

I do not believe any such thing of her. I believe she will stay. It is her interest to stay; and she will stay. Where would she go? Who would she take for a protector if she cannot protect herself? The Union—the Union is the constant cry, sir. I am for the Union; but in every little speech I have to make I do not deem it necessary to sing paeans and hosannas to the Union. I think the Union will stand uninterrupted; it will go on, as it has gone on, without my singing paeans to it; and this thing of saving the Union, I will remark here, has been done so often that it has got to be entirely a business transaction. Every now and then, as Addison used to say, great men come up in clusters; and there seems to come up a cluster of individuals who are exceedingly anxious for immortality, either in this or the other world; perhaps in both; and they must get up a great crisis; the different portions of the Union must be arrayed against each other; and it becomes necessary to save the Union. Hence there are compromises on one side and on the other; and they all come up and seem to make a sacrifice on the altar of their common country, and the Union is once more saved.

Well, sir, I have never considered the Union yet in danger. I do not believe all the factionists in this Government can pull it to pieces. I do not believe they possess power enough to dissolve the bands that bind this Government together—the bands of mutual interest, the bands of patriotism, the idea and association of a common suffering, the feeling of interest, to narrow it down to that sordid principle by which it is said most men are controlled, the sordid principle of self-interest. It cannot be dissolved. It is the interest of the States to stay in the Union; it is the interest of the States to keep the Union together; and when it gets [to be?] their interest, they will go out, and you cannot keep them here.

Mr. President, I never intended, until one day this week, to say a single word on this subject; and I have spoken in a very desultory manner. I am against this railroad for three reasons. The first two I have enumerated; the last one is understood.

I come now to the proposition offered by the distinguished Senator from Tennessee, [Mr. Bell.] The Senate, I hope, will pardon me for making use of a figure which used to be very familiar in my State, and had name and credit and authority with the citizens of that State. When we look on that proposition, it is to receive proposals for the construction of three roads, and after they are received they are to be opened and transmitted to the Congress of the United States. One section provides, that they must indicate in their bids how much money, how much lands, or how much of both, they will take to construct these roads; and there it ends. We start out with a bill to construct a road absolutely. The Senator from Mississippi, at the very outset, reports a bill in lieu of it. While we work along upon various propositions, we consume two sessions of Congress; and now we have reached the conclusion—and this is merely withheld to test the sense of the Senate on the proposition of the distinguished Senator from Mississippi. It is now withdrawn for the time being; but we are soon to have action on it; and what does it propose? Years ago it was thought necessary to make an appropriation to have surveys and explorations made. These explorations and surveys have been made; you have them all before you, of the different routes, costing in amount more than a million dollars. Now, having spent two sessions, and sessions before, in the discussion of this subject; after all this, we have reached the conclusion, that we will receive proposals and submit them to Congress, which amounts to just nothing at all. Does that seem to be disposing of the matter seriously?

It reminds me of the story related of Crockett and one of the judges of my State. How true it is, I do not know. In one of their canvasses, Judge Fitzgerald[23]—not a judge at that time—got up and made a speech; and about the time he was concluding his speech, Crockett, in his ironical way, got him just by the edge of his coat, and said, "Look here, Fitzgerald; you are coming out at precisely the same hole you went in at." [Laughter.] I think this proposition brings us out just precisely where we commenced. Proposals and estimates are to be received, and then the subject is to come here the next session with propositions to build three railroads.

We are to build three railroads. No one will pretend to say that if the Government constructs all these roads they will cost less than $200,000,000 apiece. Then we are to have three, which will amount to $600,000,000. Where will the end be? What will it come to? Does not the President himself tell you in his own message, that if the Government saw fit to undertake these roads, it will result in corruption, fraud, peculation, and speculation; hence he thinks it ought to be done by a company incorporated by the States? I will read his language from his message:

It is freely admitted that it would be inexpedient for this Government to exercise the power of constructing the Pacific railroad by its own immediate agents. Such a power would increase the patronage of the Executive to a dangerous extent, and introduce a system of jobbing and corruption which no vigilance on the part of Federal officials could either prevent or detect. This can only be done by the keen eye and active and careful supervision of individual and private interest. The construction of this road ought, therefore, to be committed to companies incorporated by the States, or other agencies whose pecuniary interests would be directly involved. Congress might then assist them in the work by grants of land, or of money, or both, under such conditions and restrictions as would secure the transportation of troops and munitions of war free from any charge, and of the United States mail at a fair and reasonable price.

The proposition of which I am now speaking, however, looks to the expenditure of $600,000,000 on three railroads running from the Atlantic to the Pacific coast, the southern one going as far south as the western boundary of Arkansas and Texas. Two of them are to be north. I do not object to them on that account. I object to the enormousness of the proposition—$600,000,000! Do you remember the history of the legislation in reference to the Cumberland road? That was a miniature, a mere minnow, compared with this leviathan measure. Look at the legislation of that time; look at the corruption, the endless legislation, I was going to say, that took place on that subject. Now, you are to begin three roads two thousand miles long, six thousand miles in all, to cost $600,000,000, and the Government is to embark in that. What will it cost? How much corruption, how much speculation, how much fraud, will ensue? Can any one tell? If we undertake a work of this kind, it will be nothing but a series of endless corrupting legislation; it will be a bottomless pit into which you may empty the revenues of this nation for the next fifty years, and you will still increase the centralizing power here.

What is now the debt of the Federal Government? Sixty-five millions; and we have a heavy public debt existing in another shape, not quite so centralizing in its influence. How much do your States now owe for railroads and other improvements? Go to your statistical tables, and see what your States owe. The people are burdened now. Municipal corporations are even taxed to death. How much do they owe? Take the States, and their indebtedness now runs up to over three hundred million dollars. Add to that the indebtedness of your various corporations, and it is over four hundred million dollars. It is true this is not quite so centralizing in its influence; but it is a great national debt that is imposed on the people, and the people have the interest and the principal to pay. After the States have exhausted their resources; after they have accumulated as much debt as they can bear, then the resort is from the States to the Federal Government, and the Federal Government is to be involved in a corresponding amount with just as much as the people can bear here. Do we not see where we are going? Do we not see the tendency of legislation?

Talk about dissolution of the Union! I never had any fears of a dissolution. My great apprehensions—and I think they are well founded when I look at the tendency of our whole policy—are that everything is tending to the center, and just in proportion as you increase the amount of money collected and disbursed by this Government, in the very same proportion you increase the centralizing power here. All parts of the nation look up to the Federal Government for contracts; they look up here for jobs; they look up here for cases of speculation and fraud; and the Government furnishes the means for them; while your States, instead of becoming more distinct and integral in their character, are sinking into mere petty corporations, sinking into insignificance, mere satellites of an inferior character, revolving around the great central power here at Washington. There is where your danger is. It is not in the centrifugal power being too great, but the centripetal influence is drawing all here.

I recur back to my proposition: let the States go on as they have been going on, settling up the new lands, making settlement after settlement, making improvement after improvement, as the wants of the country demand, and in the process of time our populations on each slope will reach each other, they will come together, and a union can be made without this Government being involved in bringing it about. If the time should come, as some have anticipated, when these States will be dissolved, so far from such a road as this being a cohesive tie, or having any adhesion in it, it would be no more than a rope of sand; its own weight would tumble it to pieces. Instead of being a tie, it would almost operate in the opposite direction. But, on the other hand, while it would not hold the States together if they were disposed to go off, we see in the expenditure of money for contracts, leading to frauds, the danger in reference to the power of the Federal Government.

I have occupied more time, Mr. President, than I intended, for my intention was not to have said a single word on this subject; but as the proposition has been brought forward, and assumed the shape it has, and especially as one seems designed for my own latitude, have no disguises to make about it. I did not care about the bill passing without indicating what my course is; and, so far as the various propositions are concerned, I have, in my way, pointed out their dangers; but I do not think there is any probability of accomplishing the proposition offered by the honorable Senator from Tennessee. I think it is merely thrown in as a kind of safety-valve by which the question can pass off, and nothing be done with it; but if it is to be treated seriously, and fixed on the country, I think I have pointed out, to some extent, the consequences resulting from it. First, I am against its constitutionality. I do not believe it is necessary and proper, in order to carry out the war-making power, to construct a Pacific railroad now. In the next place, I am against it on the score of expediency; and at the present time it does not seem to me that the proposition ought to be entertained at all.

In coming forward with these propositions, I will remark, we ought to come forward with the ways and means by which the money is to be raised to meet the liabilities we are about to incur. I lay it down as a safe rule of legislation, and especially in a free Government, that when you are going to create a great national debt, it should be first submitted to the people, and let them consider it. Public opinion has not passed upon this project. I know gentlemen may say the country is for it. Sir, the great mass of the people of the United States have never entertained the proposition in its true light. It has not been discussed; it has not been understood. They do not know the enormous extent to which the proposition leads, and consequently they are not for it when they do not understand it.

When you are going to create a great debt, State or national, the sound doctrine is first to submit it to the people. They have the taxes to pay; and after they have determined that the debt shall be created, when you create the debt you should provide the ways and means by which it is to be paid. How is this debt to be paid? Is there any provision for its payment in the bill? Where is the money to come from? It must either come by direct taxation from the people, or indirectly by the operation of your tariff, and your tariff system is now adjusted so that the receipts are falling short of the wants of the Government. Where is the interest of the $100,000,-000 to come from, or the $100,000,000 itself? Where is the $25,-000,000 proposed in this bill to come from? You get in debt and issue the obligations of the Government; Treasury notes, Government stocks, and high tariffs for protection, are to follow.

This Government was inaugurated in 1789, and since it has been in operation it has gone on and created debts, until now the debts of the State and Federal and municipal governments amount together to over $400,000,000. Look at the debt of Great Britain, nearly $4,000,000,000. At the same rate of creating indebtedness, before this country is half as old as Great Britain, we shall have a debt three times as large. We point our children to the injustice of the British system; we point them to the British national debt, and tell them that it is a means by which an aristocracy is sustained on money extorted from the hard earnings of the great mass of the people. Sir, we are in our swaddling clothes as a nation; and before we are one tenth as old as England, we will have as much debt in proportion as she has. Should we not provide for these things? Cannot we reason from cause to effect? Can we not see the inevitable result? We are alarmed and horrified at the debt of Great Britain, but our march is more rapid than hers was in the creation of a great public debt. The entire national debt of all the European Government is about $10,000,000,000. At the rate at which we are going, before we are as old as Great Britain we shall have a debt equal to that now owed by all the European Powers.

I ask, again, where is this money to come from? who is to pay it? Where is the wisdom of the Legislature in creating debts and providing no means by which they are to be paid? Is this the doctrine of Jefferson, who denied the right of the living to create debts, and hand them down as an inheritance to posterity? Is this the doctrine of Jefferson, who denied to the living, so far as soil was concerned, all title to it except the usufruct?[24] Is this the doctrine that has been taught by the apostles of Democracy? Is this the doctrine that has been taught by the strict constructionists? Is this the doctrine that has been taught by the great Democratic party as it once was in the United States? If so, I am free to confess that my understanding of the teachings of the Democratic party has been wrong. I know that parties have got somewhat jumbled up, so that, as the saying is, we can hardly tell one from t'other, or t'other from both; but I trust that there is enough pure Democracy left to form a nucleus around which a constitutional party may rally—a party that is for standing by the Constitution of the country, and for making such alterations in that instrument as the wants and necessities of the people may point out, and as are authorized by the Constitution itself. I have sometimes despaired, it is true, and thought that a pure, unadulterated Democrat, was rather a scarce article; and I confess it is a little refreshing to strike one now that is sound in all his fundamentals. It is to me like an oasis in the desert to a wayworn traveler, seeking a little water with which to quench his thirst. When I come across one of these true men of the people, whose sympathies and talents and energies are devoted to the amelioration and elevation of the great mass of the people, it is as refreshing to me as an oasis in the desert is to the wayworn traveler. I have almost thought, at some times, that a man of that description was about as hard to find as an honest man in olden times in the days of Diogenes, when in mid-day he lighted a lantern to go in search of an honest man. I hope that there are a few more sincere, pure Democrats left than there were honest men in his day, according to his version of honesty.

Mr. President, let us reject these propositions; let us kick them out of Congress; let us get to the legitimate legislation of the country; let us give the people protection and legislation within the prescribed limits of the Constitution. All the legislation that is necessary is little. The requirements of the Government are few. Let us direct our legislation in that way which conforms to the wants of the people, and not to speculation. Let us take our legislation in that direction that will protect the great mass of the people in their honest vocations; and, if we do that, we need not legislate half as much as we do. The great fault and difficulty is that we legislate too much; and one half our legislation is an impediment and obstruction thrown in the way of the laws of nature, preventing our people from conforming their action and conduct to great fundamental laws. Let your Government take as little from the people as possible; permit them to enjoy their own industry; protect them in their pursuits; let the people become rich, and let your Treasury keep poor. I am glad it is empty. I am not sure that I shall vote to borrow a dollar. I think it is a fortunate thing for the country that it is drained, that it is reduced; for the idea has got predominant here—I was going to say irrespective of party—that the way to get popular and the way to get power is by the expenditure of large sums of money. That is the channel in which popularity runs here.

I am not a military man; I wish I was a good one; but I have heard the idea advanced that if you want to reduce a garrison, starve them out, and you will bring them to submission. Retrenchment and reform can never be brought about in this Government, unless it is headed by the Administration. I am glad the necessity has come for retrenchment. I am glad the necessity has arrived for reduction in the expenditures of the Government. Let the people learn that the expenditures of this Government can be reduced by taking taxes off them, instead of increasing their taxes; that the wants of the Government can be met by beginning at the other end of the line, and by reducing, retrenching, lopping, cutting off, unnecessary expenditures of the Government. I honestly believe here to-day that instead of creating more debt, instead of imposing additional taxes on the people, instead of extorting more from their toil and from their sweat, this Government can be administered upon $50,000,000, in ordinary times, purer, better, and more efficiently than it is now upon seventy-five or eighty-one million dollars. The very depletion, the very reduction, would carry health, vigor, and honesty into the various departments of the Government; it would cut off sinecures; it would take off excrescences; it would remove hangers-on, dependents, who are swarming around the Government seeking for place and money and speculation.

The time has arrived for reform. We can see from the indications thrown out by the chairman of the Committee on Finance, in the resolutions that have been introduced, and we can see it from the indications in the President's message, and the depletion of the Treasury. We must begin at the right end of the line. I am in hopes that this depletion will be kept up, at least until the expenditures of this Government are brought down to that point at which they are honest, healthy, and economical. I know that sometimes when we get up and talk about expenditures, there are obstacles in our way. It may be said that I am a plebeian, and have made my way here from the ranks. Some gentlemen may say I contracted my prejudices there. I am a plebeian, and I am proud of it. I know there are others who can boast of more favored circumstances; that they have lived in the midst of affluence; that they have had parents who could extend to them all the facilities, all the comforts, and all the means seemingly necessary to give a man position in society in modern times. I know I cannot boast of these things; others may boast of them; I have no objection. All I regret is, that I had not a fair chance with them; but on the other hand, not to be egotistical, I thank God Almighty that he has endowed me with physical power, and with a tolerably healthy brain. I care more for the approval of my conscience, than for all this little, pettifogger flattering that runs around Senators, telling them "you have done this, and you have done that, and you are so well informed, you understood the subject," and all that sort of thing. I care not for that. The approval of the Author of my existence is far more flattering to me than all your fulsome stuff that may be heaped and brought about by influence and money.

It is very often said, "Oh, it is very easy to see why it is such a gentleman, such a Senator, or such a member is parsimonious; it is on account of his origin; he is contracted; he is limited in his views; he has not been raised so as to take a comprehensive and statesmanlike view of such things." Some proceed upon the idea that a man of this description is to be regarded as though he had been ensconced in a rock for a thousand years, like a toad that remains torpid and totally insensible of thought or action. The torpidity is on the other side; the stupidity is there, on account of the want of necessity to arouse to effort or action. While I am for an economical and rigid administration of the Government, I am not for a parsimonious administration. I am not for a narrow contracted administration; but I am for an honest and liberal administration, upon principles that will come up to and meet the wants of the country.

I have said more, Mr. President, than I intended to say. I have indicated, I think, pretty clearly that I am against this bill, that I shall vote against it, and, if necessary, I shall speak against it. When I start, if I get clearly under way, I am very apt to go through. In doing so, I repudiate that this is imposed upon me as a Democratic measure by the Cincinnati convention. I think this is a measure outside of a strict construction of the Constitution. I think it is inexpedient and wholly improper at the present time; and, this being my conviction, I leave the subject to the Senate.

[After Jefferson Davis assails Johnson's strict constructionist views, they turn to debate the cost of the railroad surveys. Davis remarks that he understands Johnson said that the railroad "was a bond to hold the union."]

Mr. JOHNSON, of Tennessee. I always make it a point, in answering a speech, to answer what was said. I think the Senator misunderstands me. I said it was argued, by some, that the construction of this railroad would be a great bond of union. I stated, in answer to that, that if the Union was going to be dissolved, the road would be no tie towards holding it together; that instead of its being a tie, if these States were prepared to be dissevered, the road would no more bind them together than a rope of sand.

[Davis refutes this argument, insisting that a transcontinental railroad would help to hold the states together, and, in the face of Johnson's attack, defends the expenditure for printing the route surveys. During the discussion, David Broderick of California criticizes Johnson for his opposition to railroad land grants, in view of his position on homesteads.]

Mr. JOHNSON, of Tennessee. All printing ordered by Congress is incident to, and resulting from, the action of Congress, and it is a necessary incident that has grown out of the surveys to get the information before the country; but let that pass.

The Senator took another position. I understood him to say that I had made an argument that this road should progress with settlement; and that I had treated one portion of the road as being a desert, sterile and barren. He wanted to know how I would carry settlement there. That was not my position. I assumed that, as far as the lands were good and the country was good, on the one slope and on the other, by the encouragement of agriculture settlements would go on, and, after a while, they would make the connection that was necessary between the settlements on each side. That was my argument. I did say that, if these lands were barren and unproductive, they would be worth nothing if you granted them to the company; and, if they were fertile and valuable lands, you would be granting too much. That is what I said, and say now.

Then the Senator takes up the constitutional question, and answers a position which I did not assume. I read the provisions giving Congress the power to declare war, and power to raise and maintain an army. I referred to that provision of the Constitution giving power to repel invasion and suppressing insurrection. I did say, though, that when the Army and Navy were called into actual service, the President of the United States had command of them. I say so yet. I say the Constitution makes him Commander-in-Chief of the Army and Navy, when they are called into actual service. If the President saw proper, he could go into the field and take the sword. So much for that.

Well, the Senator made a discrimination that perhaps, to minds as nicely balanced and as well trained as his, was perfectly clear, by which some ridicule was likely to follow. He asked, would I stand still and do nothing till war was declared? I read the provisions of the Constitution on this subject all together. It grants the power to declare war; and there is also an express grant of the power to raise an army; but what is the object of conferring this power? I put the question to the Senate, was it necessary as an incident to the exercise of the war power now to construct this road? What is there under the war power that now makes it necessary and proper to construct this road? That is the point. Is there anything? If it is necessary and proper to construct a road there, is it not equally necessary and proper to relieve the States from the burden that they have contracted and incurred in making the other links of the road? I can see no difference in principle as to the idea that you cannot make a road in a State, but can in a Territory. I confess I do not treat that argument with much seriousness. If it is necessary and proper to exercise any incident to carry the war power into effect, that power does not stop at the line between a State and Territory; you can exercise it anywhere; and if it is not necessary and proper to carry out the war power, you can exercise it in neither State nor Territory. That is my position.

But the Senator presses the idea that I deny the power to make a cannon or powder in advance of war. Is not that necessary to the very existence of the Government, and the proper perpetuation of the power in the Constitution? Is it necessary to construct a road? Is it necessary to buy provisions to sustain an army, even on the peace establishment, so far in advance of their being needed? Is it necessary to undertake works of agriculture to raise bread and meat all over the country? You might ask, "will you not make a barrel of corn, or will you not raise a bushel of wheat? We consider it necessary to have agriculture to sustain your army, to carry out the war power." Is not that a latitude that the framers of that sacred instrument never intended to be put upon it? What is the question before us? There is the constitutional power; and now look at the country and the condition of things, and say, is it necessary and proper to make this road as an incident to the war power? Mr. Buchanan says he is a strict-constructionist; and he says in his message, you should not exercise any power unless it is absolutely necessary to carry into effect an express grant. I ask the Senate, and I ask the country, is it necessary and proper, is it absolutely necessary, now to construct this road through a desert as a means to sustain and carry out the war power conferred in the Constitution of the United States? My honest convictions are that it is not.

But the gentleman, by way of being a little facetious, speaking of my reference to a change in the Constitution,[25] alluded to the number of candidates that might be before the country in reference, as I understood him, to a distinguished office.

Mr. DAVIS. I was answering you, sir; the office you spoke of.

Mr. JOHNSON, of Tennessee. If that policy was carried out, as I understood him—I speak the substance of what I understood—it might open the field to a pony race, with a number of pony candidates running. Well, if national conventions are the only means to rule off ponies, and bring forward great men, in the future I hope that all improper appliances will be omitted. Open the door for a pony race! I think the people of the different States are as competent to judge of their own citizens, and their qualifications and various merits, and their worth, as a national convention; and the chances are that they would be equally as pure and as good men as would be brought forward by a national convention or a congressional caucus. At this point, and I know I do it in a spirit of kindness, I assure the Senator I am willing to widen the field so that if he has any aspirations in that way, he may have a chance; I have none.

Mr. DAVIS. I have disclaimed in your favor already.

Mr. JOHNSON, of Tennessee. I increase your chance, particularly as I live in the South. But the idea seems to be, that you cannot come forward and discuss any great measure that has a tendency to popularize our free institutions, but you must be associated with the Presidency. That seems to have been the *summum bonum* of everything in this country. It is the climax of comparison and of aspiration; and whenever you make a move that has a tendency to popularize our free institutions, or carry the Government nearer to the people, it is said, "Oh! you are a candidate for the Presidency."

Mr. DAVIS. I ask the Senator now, as he is replying to me,

whether he did not bring in that himself, and whether my remarks were not in reply to him on that point?

Mr. JOHNSON, of Tennessee. Bring in what?

Mr. DAVIS. The whole subject of the mode of nominating a candidate for President.

Mr. JOHNSON, of Tennessee. Most assuredly I did; but I made no particular allusion to any set of individuals being candidates; the Senator did. That is the difference between us. I introduced the subject, and he alluded to the chances of particular individuals. That is all the difference. He brings cases up; I have a right to comment on those cases, in making a reply; and as I before told the Senator, I am not in his way. We have got to making Presidents in modern times, so that nobody knows who is safe. I do assure the Senator that I prefer to discharge my duty faithfully as an honest representative of the States or the people. Occupying that position—the Senate will pardon me for the expression, and I do not use it in a profane sense—when contrasted with being President of the United States, I say damn the Presidency; it is not worthy of the aspirations of a man who believes in doing good, and is in a position to serve his country by popularizing her free institutions.

The Presidency! I would rather be an honest man, an honest representative, than be President of the United States forty times. The Presidency is the absorbing idea, the great Aaron's rod that swallows up every other thing; and hence we see the best legislation for the country impaired, ruined, and biased. The idea of President-making ought to be scouted out of the Halls of Congress. Our legislation should be for the country, and let President-making alone. Let the people attend to that. Confer the great privilege, the constitutional right, upon the people to make their own Presidents, and not have them made by national conventions or by Congress; let the people make them themselves; and we shall have better Presidents, better Administrations, more economy, more honesty, more of every thing that tends to constitute an upright and correct Government.

But the Senator from California [Mr. Broderick] seems not to be satisfied with something that I said, and he wants to know what would become of the United States if it had not been for the six hundred millions of gold we had got from California. Now this was a country a good while before we got California, subjected to a great many trials, and went through the struggle of the Revolution which was consummated in 1815. He wants to know what we should have done—

Mr. BRODERICK. If the Senator will permit me one moment, to prevent him making a long speech on what I said, I will state it again. I stated this, that if the gold of California was withheld for fifty days, your banking institutions would go to pieces, as well as your manufacturing and commercial interests.

Mr. JOHNSON, of Tennessee. Well we had a good deal of manufacturing, a good deal of very successful banking and commerce, before California ever came into the Union.

Mr. SEWARD. Will the honorable Senator allow me to ask him to give way for a motion to adjourn?

Mr. JOHNSON, of Tennessee. I shall be done in two minutes. Where does the gold from California go to? While they dig in their gold-fields in California, we dig in our corn-fields, in our cotton-fields, and in our rice-fields, on this side of the Rocky Mountains. South Carolina, Georgia, Tennessee, Alabama, Mississippi, and other States, might ask, what would you do but for our cotton. Cotton is just as necessary in commerce as gold. All that gold, when it goes to New York or any other point, goes abroad and we have run through our mints in seven years six or seven hundred millions of gold.

Where did it go? Turn to your tables of exports, and there you find it went off with your bags of cotton, your hogsheads of tobacco, and tierces of rice. What would your country have done, but for rice, cotton, and tobacco? What would the country have done but for your manu[fac]tured articles? Gold is the peculiar product of California; cotton is the peculiar product of the South; hogs and horses are the peculiar products of the western States. You find that there is a reciprocity in trade. California brings her gold to the United States because she can do better with it here than anywhere else. If she could send it from San Francisco to England direct it would go there. Withhold gold from that point where it will command the greatest price! Withhold gold from going where it will command the greatest price! The Senator might as well attempt to lock up the winds or chain the waves of the ocean as to place gold beyond the influence of those laws which control the commercial world. Gold, like every other article of trade, will go where it is in the greatest demand. Gold will go where it gets the greatest price; so will cotton, tobacco, and every other article of commerce.

Let us reverse the argument, and ask what would California have done for flour, what would California have done for manufactured articles, if it had not been for the States on this side? What would she have done for iron? What would she have done for all those things that constitute her a great people? With the exception of gold, she would not have been much. While you are digging gold, you must have something to eat and to wear, and you send your gold off because you must use it to buy those articles somewhere else. That is all.

I did not intend to detain the Senate one third of the time I have. I merely wanted to answer the Senator's remarks.

Cong. Globe, 35 Cong., 2 Sess., 579–87.

1. The clamor for a transcontinental railroad had begun about 1845; after 1850, when the constitutional objections to government aid for a railroad were dead, the debate had shifted to the choice of a route. Although the 32nd Congress provided for surveys of possible routes, sectional rivalry prevented any agreement. The bill under consideration (S. 65) called for a road with San Francisco as the western terminus and a point between the mouths of the Big Sioux and the Kansas rivers as the eastern—within these limits, the exact location would be left to the contractors. Norman A. Graebner, Empire on the Pacific (New York, 1955), 95; Robert E. Riegel, The Story of the Western Railroads (Lincoln, Neb., 1926), 14; Robert R. Russel, Improvement of Communication with the Pacific Coast as an Issue in American Politics, 1783–1864 (Cedar Rapids, Iowa, 1948), 168, 186, 227; Cong. Globe, 35 Cong., 1 Sess., 1535.

2. Although the amendment, offered as a substitute for the original bill, did not stipulate location of the road, it was well known that Davis preferred the Gila route. Russel, Improvement of Communication, 223–24; Cong. Globe, 35 Cong., 2 Sess., 72–73.

3. Bell had proposed that bids be taken on three routes—northern, middle, and southern. Bidders were to specify aid and privileges required, rates to be charged the government, and the terms under which the government could, if it desired, take over the operation of the road. From this information, the "cheapest and most eligible and practicable" route could be ascertained by Congress. Ibid., 422.

4. Judah P. Benjamin (1811–1884), Louisiana senator, had been elected as a Whig (1853); reelected as a Democrat (1859), he withdrew in 1861 and became Confederate secretary of war and later secretary of state. After the war, he moved to Great Britain where he engaged in the practice of law. During the preceding week (January 19), Benjamin had spoken on the Pacific Railroad bill and its constitutionality. Refuting the argument that it could properly, or constitutionally, be referred to as a war measure, he suggested that the bill should be called a bill to increase California's population and the road acknowledged as a commercial road. BDAC, 542; DAB, II, 181–86; Robert D. Meade, Judah P. Benjamin, Confederate Statesman (New York, 1943); Simon I. Neiman, Judah Benjamin (Indianapolis, [1963]); Cong. Globe, 35 Cong., 2 Sess., 443–44.

5. Richardson, Messages, V, 526.

6. James F. Simmons (1795–1864), Rhode Island yarn-manufacturer, served in the state lower house (1828–41) and in the U. S. Senate (1841–47, 1857–62). Simmons' remarks were made on January 14. BDAC, 1602; Cong. Globe, 35 Cong., 2 Sess., 379.

7. Benjamin F. Hallett (1797–1862), Boston lawyer, political editor, and Democratic party manager, chaired the resolutions committee and wrote the party platform of 1856. DAB, VIII, 154–55; Official Proceedings of the National Democratic Convention . . . 1856 (Cincinnati, 1856), 14.

8. Ibid.

9. Ibid., 23.

10. Ibid., 27.

11. Willard Saulsbury (1820–1892), who had served as Delaware attorney general (1850–55), was U. S. senator (1859–71) and later state chancellor (1874–82). Ibid., 31; BDAC, 1563; DAB, XVI, 379.

12. William Shields of Lexington, delegate to the 1856 Democratic convention, became a member of the board of directors of the Missouri Valley Railroad Company in 1857. R. B. Oliver, "Missouri's First Railroad," *Missouri Historical Review*, XXVI (1931), 17; *Proceedings Democratic Convention, 1856*, p. 61.

13. *Ibid.*

14. *Ibid.*, 31, 61.

15. John C. Breckinridge.

16. *Ibid.*, 68.

17. Buchanan to Benjamin F. Washington, chairman, California Democratic Central Committee, September 17, 1856, John Bassett Moore, ed., *The Works of James Buchanan* (12 vols., New York, 1960), X, 93–94.

18. Charleston had recently been selected as the site of the Democratic convention of 1860.

19. William M. Gwin had summarized a bill which would authorize the President to contract for transportation of men and supplies by rail from the Missouri River to San Francisco. *Cong. Globe*, 35 Cong., 1 Sess., 1535.

20. Johnson appears to have drawn his figures from *Lippincott's Gazetteer* and from DeBow's *1850 Census, Compendium*, except for the population of Ohio which, according to DeBow, had been 1,980,329 in 1850. In the upcoming 1860 census it would be only 2,339,511, still short of Johnson's two and a half million. J. Thomas and T. Baldwin, eds., *A Complete Pronouncing Gazetteer, or Geographical Dictionary, of the World* (Philadelphia, 1855), 1997; DeBow, *1850 Census, Compendium*, 118; J. C. G. Kennedy, comp., *Population of the United States in 1860 . . . the Eighth Census* (Washington, D. C., 1864), 371.

21. Jefferson to John W. Eppes, June 24, 1813, Henry A. Washington, ed., *The Writings of Thomas Jefferson* (9 vols., Washington, 1853–54), VI, 136–38.

22. In April, 1858, during his argument against postponing the Pacific Railroad bill, Douglas had dwelt upon the commercial advantages of railroad over steamer transport. Pointing to the impairment of articles exposed to the tropics, he declaimed: "Let any man take one cup of tea that came from China to Russia overland, without passing twice under the equator, and he will never be reconciled to a cup of tea that has passed under the equator. The genuine article, that has not been manipulated and prepared to pass under the equator, is worth ten to one that which we receive here." *Cong. Globe*, 35 Cong., 1 Sess., 1646.

23. William T. Fitzgerald (1799–1864) of Stewart County, who had served in the Tennessee house (1825–27), was judge of the ninth judicial circuit (1845–61). In 1830 he defeated David Crockett for a congressional seat which he held until 1832, when Crockett displaced him. *BDAC*, 892; Philip M. Hamer, ed., *A History of Tennessee* (4 vols., New York, 1933), I, 284.

24. See Jefferson to Eppes, June 24, 1813, in Washington, *Writings of Jefferson*, VI, 136–37; also Jefferson to James Madison, September 6, 1789: "I set out on this ground, which I suppose to be self evident, '*that the earth belongs in usufruct to the living.*'" In the same letter he observed that no generation should "contract more debt than they may pay within their own age, or within the term of 19 years." Julian P. Boyd, ed., *The Papers of Thomas Jefferson* (18 vols. to date, Princeton, 1950–   ), XV, 392, 395.

25. In castigating the convention system and expressing his hope that "the time will come when the people . . . will have the constitutional right to elect their own President," Johnson had suggested that no limit be placed on the number of candidates and that, lacking a majority, the two highest names be resubmitted to popular vote. This proposition, retorted Davis, would result in a "pony race" in which "everybody who thinks he is fit to administer the Government" would be a candidate. *Cong. Globe*, 35 Cong., 2 Sess., 581, 585.

Amendment to Washington Passenger Railway Company Bill

January 29, 1859, Washington, D. C.; *Cong. Globe*, 35 Cong., 2 Sess., 679.

To H. R. 541—relating to construction of a railway through the District of Columbia—Johnson offers amendment restricting the company from issuing or circulating any medium other than money or legal currency and providing that "each of the stockholders . . . shall be liable in his individual capacity" for all debts incurred. [The amendment was adopted on February 5, 1859. *Cong. Globe*, 35 Cong., 2 Sess., 830–31.]

To Robert Johnson, Greeneville

Senate Chamber   Feb 3d 1859

My dear Son

I have received your letter with that of your mothers— I of Course was pained to hear how your brother was demeaning himself— I do not intend [to] Complain[.] I am prepared for a[n]y thing that m[a]y occur— I have done my duty and feel that I have nothing more incumbet on me as a father— God knows I have done all that I could to induce him to make a man of him self and have failed so far— Let it all pass and let the worst come— In your letter you say that you infer that I am opposed to your becoming a Candidate for the Legislature—[1] The letter I wrote to you was not intended to express an opinion the one w[a]y or the other; but intended to omitted the expression of a[n]y opinion whateve until I saw you in person which would be but a short time— I want you to think for your Self and to act accordingly— Of Course I would give my opinion when asked in reference to your future; but at the same time you must think for your self and with your self reliance determined what you may deem best— God knows I have no other object than to promote the [*sic*] my family— Think for your self and I will do what I can to sustain you— I will be at home as soon as the nature of the cas will permit— I am at a loss as to what to say to you now and will say nothing— I will write to you soon and, tell you all that has occured in referrence to several matters that the democratic party are deeply interested— I have writtn this in Confutsion and do not hardly know what I have written—   Your father

Andrew Johnson

ALS, MWiW-C.

1. Robert was elected to the Tennessee legislature in August, 1859.

Remarks on Railway for Pennsylvania Avenue[1]

February 7, 1859

Mr. JOHNSON, of Tennessee. I offer an amendment as an additional section:

And be it further enacted, That this act shall not take effect unless ratified by a majority of the legally-qualified voters of the city of Washington, at the annual election to be held for municipal officers on the first Monday in June next.

I believe the citizens of Washington are considered freemen. They have institutions among them, and I think the people of this city ought to have the same privileges that the people have in other communities. They should have, at least, the poor privilege of passing their judgment on the nature and character of the institutions they shall have among them. This bill may not technically, but it does practically, create a corporation, a monopoly, and confers upon it an important franchise, upon which, it seems to me, the people of the city of Washington should have an opportunity to pass.

Mr. BROWN.[2] I only rise to ask that nobody will reply to my friend from Tennessee, but let us vote. It is near five o'clock, and to-morrow we shall waste another day over this bill, unless we get through with it now.

Mr. MASON. According to my recollection, the amendment offered by the Senator from Tennessee is a new theory of this Government, not originating with that Senator, but originating within a very few years in some of the free States, as they call them—the idea that a law passed by the competent authority is afterwards to be submitted to the popular vote. That is the amendment offered by the Senator from Tennessee. Now, sir, I only wish to say this: that so far—

The PRESIDING OFFICER.[3] The Chair begs leave respectfully to suggest to Senators that conversation is so loud and so general in the Hall as to make it impracticable to proceed with the business before the body.

Mr. MASON. I wish to add only, that so far the judiciary have declared that such laws dependent on the popular will are no laws at all.

Mr. JOHNSON, of Tennessee. The gentleman from Virginia is always *au fait* on questions of this kind, and he seems to strike out the theory that is presented in this amendment; and he thinks it is not a very new one. It is not a new theory, Mr. President, that the people of this country are capable of self-government, and that they should have the right to determine the nature and character of their own institutions. In the State of Virginia, when the constitutional convention framed an organic law for the people of that State, did they not submit that constitution to the people for ratification or rejection?[4] I believe that is a slave State, and not a free State. I wonder whether most of the slave States of this Confederacy, as well as the free States, when they framed their organic laws, did not submit them to the people for ratification or rejection? Is there anything very alarming in that? Is this the theory that the gentleman is so terribly alarmed at, that the people in this country are capable of determining, and have a right to determine, the nature and character of their own institutions? The Senator tells us it is a theory of a free State. I have heard of a one-idea party; and now and then we come across one-idea individuals, persons who have a particular theory or idea that absorbs all others. This is common; most of us have our hobbies; but it is strange, passing strange, that no proposition can be presented here, I care not how small nor how large it is, without its being involved in the slavery question. Here, when it is proposed to confer a little privilege on the people of Washington, it is said to involve that great question, and it is charged that the idea had its origin in a free State. Sir, the principle has been practiced upon from the Declaration of Independence down to the present time, that the people are competent and capable of taking care of themselves. I hold that the people of the city of Washington have the same fundamental right, the same inherent right, to determine and pass upon the description of institutions which they will have amongst them that the people have in other communities.

I hope the amendment will be adopted. Has not Congress the power to confer legislative authority, as it were, on the municipal authorities of Washington? Cannot Congress confer power upon the corporation of Washington to grant licenses to construct roads? Can it not confer the power to incorporate companies in the District of Columbia? It seems to me that it can. If it can confer upon the municipal authorities the power to grant a license of this description, can it not make the existence of a law like this, dependent on the ratification of the people who are the source of power?

I have a word to say in reference to the suggestion made by the Senator from New Hampshire, [Mr. Clark,][5] with regard to the amendment which restrains this company, or association, or corporation, I care not by what name you call it, from issuing bank notes or checks or anything intended to circulate as money. The question is raised here between legal gentlemen in this body whether the bill does or does not create a corporation or a company. However that may be, one thing is clear—that the bill authorizes an association of persons to construct a railroad and to exercise certain privileges; and the query very naturally comes up, if you confer an express grant to do a particular thing, may they not, by construction, deem it necessary, as an incident to carry the express grant into effect, to issue promissory notes and put in circulation checks, as money, to enable this company to construct this road? If this company is not a corporation, my amendment does not affect these individuals, and does them no harm. If it is a corporation, the amendment is exactly right, and is offered in the right place. It can do no harm in any event; and lest there should be a certain construction given to the privileges to be exercised by this company, it restrains and defines what those privileges are.[6]

Cong. Globe, 35 Cong., 2 Sess., 862–63.

1. The House bill authorizing the construction of a railway through Washington was pending. Two days earlier Johnson's amendment relating to fares and debts had been adopted; other amendments were being debated when Johnson gained the floor to offer this one.

2. Albert G. Brown of Mississippi was chairman of the committee on the District of Columbia.

3. Solomon Foot of Vermont.

4. When Virginia revised its constitution in the Reform Convention of 1850–51, that document was passed upon by the voters. Charles H. Ambler, *Sectionalism in Virginia* (Chicago, 1910), 271.

5. Daniel Clark (1809–1891) had served intermittent terms in the New Hampshire legislature (1842–55) before election to the U. S. Senate (1857–66). Appointed U. S. district judge by Andrew Johnson in 1866, he served until his death. *BDAC*, 696–97; *DAB*, IV, 125–26.

6. The amendment was defeated, 35–5.

Resolutions on Government Expenditures

February 8, 1859, Washington, D. C.; *Cong. Globe*, 35 Cong., 2 Sess., 883–84.

Reintroduces resolution originally offered January 4 [see Remarks on Retrenchment], with request that President submit a budget "not exceeding $50,000,000 per annum, exclusive of the public debt and the interest thereon"; also reads letter from Buchanan to Baltimore citizens, February 23, 1852, advocating frugality in public expenditures.

Remarks on Governmental Expenditures[1]

February 12, 1859

Mr. JOHNSON, of Tennessee. I offer the following resolutions; and ask for their present consideration:

Resolved, That the President of the United States be, and he is hereby, requested to cause the heads of the various Executive Departments to submit estimates of the expenditures for the Government to the Thirty-

Sixth Congress upon a basis not exceeding $50,000,000 per annum, exclusive of the public debt, and the interest thereon.

Resolved, That so much of the President's second annual message as relates to a reduction of the expenditures of the Government of the United States, which is in the following words, to wit: "I invite Congress to institute a rigid scrutiny to ascertain whether the expenses of all the departments cannot be still further reduced, and I promise them all the aid in my power in pursuing the investigation," be referred to the Committee on Finance; and that said committee are hereby instructed, after first conferring with and obtaining all "aid" and information from the President and the heads of Departments as indicated in the President's message, to report a bill reforming, as far as possible, all abuses, if any, in the application of the appropriations made by Congress for the support of the various Departments, and which will reduce the expenses to an honest, rigid, economical administration of the Government.

[After some discussion, Trumbull of Illinois proposes an amendment to reduce army and navy expenses 50 percent, indicating opinion that the United States has no need for a large army and a strong navy.]

Mr. Johnson, of Tennessee. I rise for the purpose of making that motion to postpone;[2] but I will remark, before I make it, that this retrenchment resolution has been up now some two or three times. On one occasion before, it was within about one minute of being adopted; but in consequence of the announcement of the death of a member of the other House, it went over. It was up on another occasion, and was within a few minutes of being adopted, when a special order intervened.[3] It is now up, and can be adopted or rejected within five minutes. I am in hopes the Senate will dispose of the resolution, which will only take two or three minutes, and then we shall have an end of it.

It seems to me that the resolution contemplates all that the Senator from Illinois proposes in his amendment; and I suggest that he withdraw his amendment, and allow the proposition to be adopted, either appointing a select committee or referring the inquiry to the Committee on Finance; I care not which. I am in favor of this work being commenced, and I care not by what committee; but in commencing this work, I will say, in answer to what was said on the other side, I am not for beginning with the wafers and quills, pens and stationery, of members of Congress or any other department; but I want this work commenced in good faith, and I want us to get into the large veins of expenditure. I want the lancet to be put into the jugular vein. I am aware, as was remarked by the Senator from Illinois, that the principal expenditures of all Governments have been in the Army and Navy. They are the main arteries by which all Governments are bled to death; but there are extravagances and abuses, as I think, existing in other departments, as well as in the Army and Navy, and these resolutions are intended to embrace all, little and big; but I do not want to begin with the wafers and quills and pens. Let us begin with the leading expenditures of the Government, the principal departments. Let the work commence there, and these little incidental retrenchments will follow as a matter of course. I do not make the motion to interfere with the Senator from Maine; but I hope that, by general consent, the special order will go over for the present, and the resolution be adopted.

I will further remark, in reference to expenditures, that a short time since I was in conversation with the Secretary of War[4]—I did not receive the information officially, nor did I receive it privately; but he remarked to me on the subject of expenditures, notwithstanding he was justifying what he considered a reasonable and a liberal expenditure, as everybody is willing to concur, he stated to me that if he had a little legislative aid, he could take his Department and reduce the expenditures at least $14,000,000. Now, will we stand back and withhold this aid? Will we not come forward and take the Departments at their own proposition, when they say they can retrench? Will we, for this excuse, and for the other excuse, eternally postpone the beginning of this work? Now, for instance, there is a special order of a bill which can be postponed. Let it be laid aside; let the resolutions be adopted; and let the work begin. I know that a great deal of it cannot be done in the remaining weeks of this session; but let the work commence; let it go forth to the public that something has been done; let it go forward from session to session until the great result is accomplished. I hope the Senator from Maine will consent to let his bill go over for the present, and let us have action on the resolutions.

[A brief general discussion is followed by Johnson's motion to postpone consideration of Hamlin's lighthouse bill, the special order.]

Mr. JOHNSON, of Tennessee. If the Senate will indulge me, I will make a single remark further. There is always a difficulty in the way of considering this matter. It would be better to adopt the resolution in its original shape; and if the Committee on Finance cannot do anything during the present session, they can report that fact, and the country will receive their report in good faith, and so will the Senate. If that committee cannot progress in this work, how can its chairman?[5] The whole committee can progress with the work as well as the chairman; and I think you may as well refer it to that committee, and save all further trouble about it.

[The motion to postpone the lighthouse bill is agreed to and debate continues on Johnson's resolutions.]

Mr. JOHNSON, of Tennessee. We have come so near passing this resolution, that I shall have to move the postponement of the special order for a few minutes, so as to get clear of this question. I hope the Senate will act on it definitely. There are some things which I should like to say, but I refrain from doing so, for the purpose of having action. At this late period of the session, what we want is action, not long declamatory speeches of any character. I move to postpone the special order until we can have action on this resolution.

[Alfred Iverson of Georgia attempts to dissuade the Senate from postponing the private calendar.]

Mr. JOHNSON, of Tennessee. So far as the discussion is concerned beyond these resolutions, it has nothing to do materially with the points at issue. There may be charges preferred one way or the other, but they do not concern these resolutions, properly speaking. The resolutions contemplate retrenchment; their intention is to inaugurate a system of retrenchment and reform coextensive with the Government, to apply to every Department. They prefer no charge against this or any other Administration. There is an impression resting on the public mind, and on the mind of Congress, that there has been too much of the people's money expended; that its expenditure ought to be arrested; and the proper course is to ascertain if there has been an improper expenditure, and in what it consisted. For this purpose, let us appoint a committee who will go thoroughly and fully into the investigation. If there has been no improper expenditure; if there has not been too much money collected from the people and expended for improper purposes, the committee will report that fact to the country, and the people will then be satisfied that the Administration has not improperly expended their money. It is due to the Administration, it is due to the country, it is due to honesty itself, that there should be some indorsement of that kind. If the money has all been collected properly, and properly expended for the public good, let that fact come from the committee, and it will be an indorsement of what has been done; but if the money has not been properly expended, let the country know in what respects improper expenditure has taken place.

That is what these resolutions contemplate. They do not look at any particular Department, or at any particular point more than another. They strike out all improper expenditures, be they where they may. They are intended to inaugurate a new policy, coextensive with every department of the Government, embracing the small as well as the large items. My object is, first, to get at the leading extravagances of the Government wherever they exist.

I hope the Senate will postpone the special order for a few minutes, until these resolutions can be adopted. Why shall we get so near the consummation of a thing, the propriety of which all concede, without disposing of it? All admit that there has been too much money expended, and yet, when a proposition is made to ascertain the fact in the legitimate mode, there is one difficulty and another difficulty interposed; a special order intervenes now, and another special order on another occasion, and somehow or other we can never get action on the proposition. I hope we shall postpone the special order for a few minutes, for the purpose of disposing of these resolutions.

[Stephen R. Mallory of Florida questions what can be accomplished during this session by a committee investigating public expenditures.]

Mr. JOHNSON, of Tennessee. Allow me to suggest to the Senator from Florida that the resolutions can be adopted, and at the end of the session, if the committee are not able to make a report, they can state that fact to us. The first resolution contemplates action by the Executive Departments to make their estimates on a basis of expenditure not exceeding $50,000,000. That is not intended to be arbitrary or absolute; but we want to lay that down as a basis upon which they shall frame their estimates. If more is required for special purposes, they can easily say so; but I desire to have estimates presented to us upon the basis of an expenditure not beyond $50,000,000. I will here remark that this idea is not mine; it was suggested by the chairman of the Committee on Finance himself during the last session of Congress. He introduced a similar resolution then, but it was not pressed. I offer a resolution now embracing the same proposition. It is, in fact, the proposition of the Finance Committee. When the Finance Committee suggests the idea, when the President solicits investigation, when every Department seems to think it can retrench if Congress will come to its aid, why not let us extend the aid desired?

The Senator from Florida speaks of the private bills, and says that it is very important that they should be acted upon. I concede that; but there are public interests; there are public demands, involving millions upon millions of dollars, as well as the thousands involved in the claims of individuals. If either is to be neglected, which interest is to be neglected? Shall we neglect the interest of a few individuals, or shall we neglect the interest of the nation at large? Which is the most imperious? Which demands action at our hands— a vote on a few private bills, or a measure involving the interests of the whole country?[6]

Cong. Globe, 35 Cong., 2 Sess., 991–95 passim.

1. Johnson's penchant for economy had been expressed in a resolution introduced and discussed January 4, repeated two weeks later [Remarks on Governmental Expenditures, January 17], and expanded on February 8. Now reintroduced, although the day's order of business had been agreed upon, it would be debated without conclusive result.

2. Johnson refers to postponing the pending lighthouse bill introduced by Hamlin of Maine.

3. Allusions to events of January 17 and February 8.
4. John B. Floyd.
5. R. M. T. Hunter.
6. Johnson's efforts failed again at this time; however, on the final day of the session the first of the two resolutions was adopted, after he assured his colleagues, "It can do no earthly harm . . ." since it would merely set up a goal toward which the executive branch might work. *Cong. Globe*, 35 Cong., 2 Sess., 997, 1651, 1658–60.

From Lambert Gittings[1]

Baltimore February 21st 1859

The Honble Andrew Johnson
U. S. Senate Washington
    Dear Sir
    In the event of a mutual friend not having yet done so, may I beg permission to call your valued attention to the accompanying little pamphlet, upon the subject of the nomination as surgeon in the Army of Doctor James Simons[2] now before the Senate for confirmation—
    The friends of the nominee, in his absence, have had occasion to adopt this mode of calling the attention of honorable Senators to the subject, in consequence of the opposition heretofore manifested by the Chairman of the Military Committee when Secretary of War,[3] and their having learned casually of certain legal obsticles that have been agitated—
    The nomination seems to be a perfectly clear one in every aspect as I think you will find it upon examination consonant to the laws and practice of the Government for upwards of forty years in cases of restoration of injured officers and is based upon and in exact accordance with an express request of the Senate as will appear by reference to a resolution passed on the 3rd March 1857—[4] Asking then the favor of your kind cooperation in bringing it to a favorable close.

I am with high consideration &c   Your Obt Svt
                                     Lambert Gittings

LS, Johnson-Bartlett Col.
    1. Lambert Gittings (1806–*fl*1879), an affluent shipping and commission merchant of Baltimore and a Jacksonian Democrat, was writing in behalf of his son-in-law, Dr. James Simons. *Biographical Cyclopedia of Representative Men of Maryland and the District of Columbia* (Baltimore, 1879), 466.
    2. Simons (d. 1885), a South Carolinian appointed assistant army surgeon in 1839, was dismissed from service in January, 1856, after a court-martial on charges of "neglect of duty, and conduct unbecoming an officer." Accused of having left his post at Fort Riley, Kansas, during a cholera epidemic in August, 1855, he pleaded his own illness and exhaustion, his small daughter's cholera, and his having, in his medical capacity, ordered the troops and their families away from the post. Reinstated in October, 1856, he was now seeking Senate action to ensure that his recent promotion be made

retroactive to August, 1856, the time at which he would have been promoted had he not been out of the service. He argued that reinstatement implied a rejection of the validity of his dismissal and that, therefore, he should not suffer any loss in seniority or pension rights. On March 5, 1859, the Senate passed the pending resolution which confirmed him as surgeon, retroactive to August, 1856. During the Civil War he served with Union volunteers and was brevetted colonel in 1865. See correspondence in Personal Papers, Medical Officers and Physicians, Box 680, J. Simons, RG94, National Archives; *Senate Ex. Journal*, 35 Cong., Special Sess., 76; Heitman, *Register*, I, 388.

3. Jefferson Davis.

4. If passed, this resolution seems not to have been recorded. The nearest comparable legislation, passed on January 16, 1857, concerned the restoration of naval officers. *U. S. Statutes*, XI, 154.

To Robert Johnson, Greeneville

Washington City   Feb 22d 1859

My dear Son,

Your letter and that of your mothers were received by the Same mail— I was more than rejoiced to hear that Charles had recovered and was one time more attending to his business—

As to Mr Wm M Churchwell's[1] appointment I know nothing and if any Tenn delegation has been consulted about it I do not know who they were— Some say he is appointed merly as secret agent and others say that it is the entering wedge to the appointment of minister &c— If we have to Carry such men as he is in the next Canvass I fear we will be born down— And as to your accepting of any appointment which would place you under the Control of Wm M Churchwell is a proposition I hope you never have en[ter]tained— Infact I hope that you will give up holding any place in subor[di]nation to any one— It is quite as easy to be first as second in appointment[s] of this kind and the first place Can be obtained as readly as the second. I hope that you will never write another letter to any one on the Subject— I would occupy a place if I were in your position that would make others Court me instead of courting any body high or low. A little time and patience will enable you to accomplish the latter Course much easier than the former— I fear from all that I can hear that Maxwell will let Haynes run over him—[2] I regret that there is not more of Maxwell than there is— When he get[s] into a contest he Seems to evaporate and pass off in to thin air— If no one else will beat Haynes but powell he must Consent to run— For Haynes must be put down—[3] I know the man and know him to be unprincipled and a traitor— I have long since adopted the saying of the Roman in reference to Carthage—"Delenda est Carthago"—[4] If he succeeds now the district will not get Clear of him for years, and now is the time to do the work— I would be discreet in the Course

I took in regard to him— It is not worth while to take any stand until you see it indispensebl necessry— I will be at home in a short time where I can see and talk to you freely in reference to your own Course— I do not think that I will go to the [sic] Nashville during the setting of the convention—[5] If I go and anything should take place that is unfavorable to the Brown Clique[6] it will be charged to me[.] I presume that you will go and see how they manage the nominations &c— Nicholson is here and will stay until the adjournment—[7] I will be at home as soon as the nature of the case will permit— The impression is made here that John Bell will be nominated for the presidency by the K. N. Convention—[8] What will be the effect—[9]

ALS, CSmH-Misc. #8205.

1. William M. Churchwell, Knoxville lawyer, had just been appointed by Buchanan to a secret diplomatic mission to Mexico. Ruth Osborne Turner, The Public Career of William Montgomery Churchwell (M. A. thesis, University of Tennessee, 1954), 66–72. See also Johnson Papers, I, 622–23n.

2. Evidently William H. Maxwell had given some thought to seeking the nomination for Congress from the first district. Johnson may well have been accurate in his assessment of Maxwell's political personality, for the race on behalf of the Democrats was finally made by Landon C. Haynes.

3. It is clear that Johnson was eager to prevent Haynes's nomination as Democratic congressional candidate in the first district and was casting about for an alternative. Apparently his choice was Robert D. Powel (c1825–1861), one of the politically active sons of Judge Samuel Powel and editor of the Rogersville Sentinel, as well as delegate to the state Democratic convention, March 17, 1859. Several weeks later the district convention at Greeneville, with Johnson's expressed approval, selected Haynes, who was later defeated by the Opposition candidate, T. A. R. Nelson, a former Whig. Parson Brownlow hinted strongly that Johnson acquiesced in Haynes's nomination as a quid pro quo for Robert Johnson's election to the legislature. White, East Tenn. Journalism, 15; Nashville Union and American, March 18, 1859; James W. Bellamy, "The Political Career of Landon Carter Haynes," ETHS Publications, No. 28 (1956), 114–15; Knoxville Tri-Weekly Whig, June 30, 1859; Nashville Patriot, April 23, 1859.

4. Marcus Cato so hated and feared Carthage that he closed every debate with "Carthage must be destroyed (Delenda est Carthago)." Stevenson, Quotations, 2108.

5. The Democratic state convention nominated Isham G. Harris for reelection and adopted a resolution supporting the policies of the Buchanan administration but made no formal mention of a presidential nominee. Nashville Union and American, March 18, 1859.

6. The Middle Tennessee "Clique" associated with Aaron V. Brown, currently Buchanan's postmaster general, had long been at loggerheads with Johnson.

7. A. O. P. Nicholson, elected senator in 1857, was awaiting the close of the 35th Congress (and thus the end of Bell's term), in anticipation of an extra session.

8. Resorting to typical political mudslinging, Johnson accuses Bell of a flirtation with the Know-Nothings, although in actuality the December, 1858, Washington convention had been a gathering of various opposition men— a mixture of old-line Whigs and Know-Nothings from thirteen states—who had been exploring the possibility of a Union party and the nomination of a conservative candidate. Ultimately Bell became their nominee in 1860.

Arthur C. Cole, *The Whig Party in the South* (Washington, D. C., 1913), 331–32; New York *Tribune*, December 11, 1858; Edward Stanwood, *A History of the Presidency* (2 vols., New York, 1916), I, 288.

9. Perhaps the lack of a closing may be explained by the marginal notation: "I have written this letter in great confusion while the Senat is in session[.]"

To John L. Dawson, Brownsville, Pa.

Senate Chamber   Feb 23d 1859—

Hon John L. Dawson

Sir

Your letters of the 20th inst were recieved by this mornings mail— As suggested I showed your letter to the Hon John Slidel and he seemed to think that you were mistaken in reference to his Course heretofore on the Homestead bill— During the present congress he has opposed the bill with decided opposition—[1] The bill can be passed if we Can have a direct vote on the bill: but the great difficulty is in getting a direct vote on the passage of the bill— The chances are at the present time rather against the passage of the bill— I hope for success; but have my fears— I Have almost despared of congress ever passing any more laws for the benefit for the great mass of the people— They have but few sincere friends in the Senate of the U. S.— The ministry of Great Britain are more under the influence of the popular will than the Senate and do hope that the time will Come when the people Can be felt in the Senate and the public judgment obeyed— Inclosed you will find the vote on the bill referred to by you—[2] I wish that you were in the Senate[.] I feel will satisfied that the bill could be passed— It m[a]y be that it is not to pass until you take your seat in this body as one of Pennsylvania's Senators—[3] There is not much going on but the ordinary routine of business— There is now a Kansas debat going on upon the Civil and diplomatic appropriation bill,[4] which will do the democratic party no good as I think— It really seems that this question is never to have an end— I confess I am sick and tired of it and think that the proper Legislation of the count[r]y has been neglected long enough—

I have nothi[n]g of interest to write more than what you see in the news papers of the day—

Accept assurances of my high esteem and sincere frndship

Andrew Johnson

ALS, DLC-Jeremiah S. Black Papers.

1. Slidell's "decided opposition" is not evident in the *Congressional Globe*; indeed, as recently as February 3 he had presented, on behalf of New York

citizens, a homestead petition comparable to those being presented by Johnson. However, his support may have been something short of enthusiastic, for by April, 1860, he disclaimed any intentions of "factious opposition to the bill" and urged that it be discussed until it was resolved. When the measure passed the Senate on May 10, Slidell voted with the majority. *Cong. Globe*, 36 Cong., 1 Sess., 1661, 2043; Louis M. Sears, *John Slidell* (Durham, 1925), 153.

2. Dawson had probably inquired about the Senate vote of either February 17 or 19 on the motion to consider the homestead bill. In the first instance the Senate voted to consider, only to postpone consideration in favor of taking up the appropriation bill; in the second, it was rejected, 31–24. *Cong. Globe*, 35 Cong., 2 Sess., 1074, 1143.

3. Since there would be no Pennsylvania senatorial election until 1861, this anticipation of a seat for Dawson may be viewed in the light of a gesture acknowledging his yeoman service in behalf of a homestead measure during his terms in the House (1851–55).

4. Sectional issues had made it increasingly difficult to conduct even the most routine business. On February 22, the day before Johnson's letter, Hale of New Hampshire had injected into a debate on the appropriations bill a motion concerning the admission of Kansas. Not until March 3, the last day of the session, did the Senate pass this bill; even then it left the post office department in crisis by failing to include funds for its mounting deficit. *Ibid.*, 1222; Philip S. Klein, *President James Buchanan: A Biography* (University Park, Pa., 1962), 332.

To James Buchanan, Washington, D. C.

Senate Chamber,
Washington, Feby 25/59.

The President:

Sir,

Learning that the official term of the Hon. Samuel D. Lecompte,[1] as Chief Justice of the U. S. Dist. Court for the Territory of Kansas, will shortly expire, we take pleasure in cordially recommending his renomination for that office.[2] He has shown himself competent, honest & faithful to the Constitution, & has exhibited rare moral & physical courage, as well as patriotism, in resisting the efforts of the malcontents & anarchists who have endeavored to disorganize society & overthrow the lawful government of that Territory. We think the public interests of that Territory & of the Union will be best promoted by retaining him in his present position, & that superseding him would tend to encourage that spirit of insubordination which he has been so instrumental in suppressing.

We trust that you will appreciate his past services as we do & will send his name to the Senate as the proper person for the Chief Justiceship of the U. S. Dist. Court of the Territory of Kansas.

We have the honor to be, Most respectfully Yr. Obt. Svts.,

J. M. Mason[3]	C. C. Clay, Jr.,
Jas Alfred Pearce	R Toombs
A Kennedy	Jeffer. Davis.
J. P. Benjamin	R M T Hunter.
D. L. Yulee	James S. Green.
A. Iverson	Trusten Polk.
J. A Bayard	R. W Johnson.
James Chesnut, Jr.	W K Sebastian.
Andrew Johnson	Ben Fitzpatrick.
A G Brown	David S. Reid.
S. R. Mallory	Matt. Ward.

ALS, DNA-RG60, Appt. Papers: Kansas, 1853–1861, Samuel Lecompte. Written in the hand of Clement C. Clay, Jr.

1. For more than two years the winds of controversy had swirled around Samuel Lecompte (1814–1888), a founder of the proslavery stronghold of Lecompton and first chief justice of Kansas Territory. As the slavery agitation reached a high pitch in 1856, he added fuel to the fire by charging a grand jury to indict the members of the "free-state" government at Topeka; subsequently he was also blamed for the so-called "sack of Lawrence." Characterized by Allan Nevins as "bibulous, hot-tempered, partisan," Lecompte became an object of political attack in Congress as he became identified with the extreme southern faction in troubled Kansas. Efforts to remove him were ultimately successful when, despite the southern political backing shown by this and other petitions, he was replaced by John Pettit of Indiana in March, 1859. Yet when war came, Lecompte chose the Union, remaining in Kansas and becoming a Democratic member of the legislature (1867–68) before embracing Republicanism during the 1868 campaign. James C. Malin, "Judge Lecompte and the 'Sack of Lawrence,' May 21, 1856," *Kansas Historical Quarterly*, XX (1953), 465–94 *passim*, 553; George A. Root, "Ferries in Kansas: Part II—Kansas River," *ibid.*, II (1933), 344; Allan Nevins, *Ordeal of the Union* (2 vols., New York, 1947), II, 212–13, 434.

2. Nine months earlier, in May, 1858, when there was still a possibility that Kansas might soon achieve statehood, eighty-eight members of Congress —sixty-five representatives and twenty-three senators—had requested that Buchanan continue Lecompte as chief justice of Kansas Territory, and "in case Kansas shall become a state of the union, that he may be appointed District Judge of the U. States, for the same." James A. Stewart and others to James Buchanan, May 11, 1858, Appointment Papers, Kansas, 1853–1861, RG60, National Archives. It is interesting to observe that Johnson, often out of step with his southern colleagues over issues great and small, fell into line where this question of patronage was concerned.

3. Mason appended this note: "I must add, that having observed unremittingly, the trials to which this gentleman was subjected; & the courage, equanimity & success with which he overcame them under unspeakable difficulties, the Country owes to him its cordial support—"

Exchange Concerning Furniture for Committee Rooms[1]

March 2–3, 1859

Mr. JOHNSON, of Tennessee. I wish to call the attention of the Senator[2] to the person pointed out in this amendment to provide the furniture for the committee-rooms. It provides that "the superintendent of the Capitol extension[3] be directed to make a survey, and ascertain what articles of furniture will be needed, with the materials, designs, and dimensions of the same." It seems that the superintendent of the Capitol extension is to examine these rooms, make out a general design, and then procure furniture without regard to the committees, or any consultation with them or their chairmen, or anybody else. If the design is to furnish the committee-rooms in a manner corresponding with the useless and wasteful extravagance of public money that has been incurred in the building of these two wings of the Capitol, I think it is time it ought to be looked into.

It seems to me that we had better commit this matter to the care of the Secretary of the Senate or the Sergeant-at-Arms,[4] instead of the superintendent of the Capitol extension. Those officers, under the direction of the committees, can procure what furniture the committees need in their rooms. If, as the Senator from Virginia suggests, some of the committees want pine tables and pine shelves, let them have them. If other committees want furniture of a little better grade, let them have it. But, according to the original amendment, the superintendent is to make out a general plan for the furniture; and it is to carry out the general intention and design of this building, without consulting the convenience and interest of the committees, or their notions of economy or propriety. It seems to me, it is carrying the thing a little too far.

If I know myself, I have no unkind feelings towards the superintendent of this building; but it seems to me that Mr. Meigs has about as many jobs on hand as he can well attend to. He has the aqueduct, on which you are expending millions; he has the Capitol, on which you are expending millions; then the public grounds around the Capitol are to be placed in his hands, on which you have expended millions;[5] and now not even furniture can be procured for the committee-rooms unless Mr. Meigs makes out a general plan, without consulting the committees.

Mr. BRIGHT. I am quite sure the gentleman to whom the Senator refers does not desire to undertake the duty imposed on him by this amendment. I think it proper to state that I shall make no objection, for one, to substituting any other person whose name will satisfy the Senate.

Mr. JOHNSON, of Tennessee. I did not say that the superintendent desired an accumulation of more labor of a different character, and I do not think I intimated that he was seeking this appointment; but the amendment points him out, and makes it his duty to do this. It seems to me that an officer of this body, under the direction of the committees, could select the description of furniture they want; and then you would have your officer and the committees responsible. I repeat again, if members of the committees want cheap and economical furniture to satisfy their notions of republican simplicity— which is becoming rather an antiquated idea in this country—let them have it; if others want furniture a little more extravagant, let them have it. I move to strike out "the superintendent of the Capitol extension," and insert either the Secretary of the Senate, or the Sergeant-at-Arms, whichever will best suit the temper of the Senate.

The PRESIDING OFFICER. (Mr. Foot[6] in the chair.) The Senator will state his amendment definitely, not in the alternative.

Mr. JOHNSON, of Tennessee. I move to strike out "superintendent of the Capitol extension," and insert "Secretary of the Senate." The Secretary of the Senate, under the supervision of the Committee to Audit and Control the Contingent Expenses of the Senate, can do things properly, and the expenditure can be kept within reasonable and proper bounds.

[Jefferson Davis objects both to this amendment and to Mason's attempt to set a $10,000 upper limit on purchases. Answering Johnson's question as to the sum the committee deems proper, Bright replies that under the amendment furniture will be supplied by the lowest bidder.]

Mr. JOHNSON, of Tennessee. If I understand this amendment, I understand it very differently from the gentleman's speech. His speech comes up to my idea of requiring the selection of this furniture to be placed in the charge of somebody who will consult the taste of the committees. It seems to me that ought to be done. Let who will supply the rooms with furniture, the committees ought to be consulted as to the character and quality of it. His explanation, it seems to me, contemplates one thing, while the amendment contemplates another. The amendment seems to make it the duty of the superintendent to examine the rooms, make out a general design, and have furniture made according to the plan that he may lay down, without consulting the committees at all. He may, or may not, consult the committees, at his discretion. He is to make out his plan, prescribe the quantity and kind and quality of the furniture; and it is to be paid for, let it cost what it may.

There is one other suggestion that comes up in my mind, and there seems to me to be a contradiction so far as the Senator from Mississippi is concerned. In his first remarks I understood him as stating that the committees were not competent to select furniture suitable for their rooms, and that that was attributable to their being deficient in taste.

Mr. DAVIS. I did not arraign their taste generally. I took yourself and the Senator from Virginia as examples of men whom I would not take to select furniture for me.

Mr. JOHNSON, of Tennessee. I was not the person to select it, and the gentleman could not have selected me. I have made no such proposition, and intimated no such desire.

Mr. DAVIS. I was answering your remarks.

Mr. JOHNSON, of Tennessee. The committee to which I belong have no room in which to sit, and of course need no furniture; but the gentleman assumes as an argument, why my amendment should not be made, as I understand him, that the committees are not competent to select furniture suitable to their rooms on account of their being deficient in taste.

Mr. DAVIS. I did not say that, and I have just told you what I did say.

Mr. JOHNSON, of Tennessee. I think that is about the substance. I have no disposition to misrepresent. Then, in his last speech, the Senator rather concludes the committees might be competent, and this seems to me to be a contradiction.

Mr. DAVIS. I did not say any such thing.

Mr. JOHNSON, of Tennessee. I wish we had down what the Senator from Mississippi did say.

Mr. DAVIS. I suppose you might have heard what I said, sir.

Mr. JOHNSON, of Tennessee. I thought I did hear it.

Mr. DOOLITTLE.[7] I call the Senators to order. This conversation between Senators is out of order.

The PRESIDING OFFICER. The Senator from Tennessee will proceed.

Mr. JOHNSON, of Tennessee. I understood the Senator from Mississippi to assume, in the first place, that the committees were incompetent in consequence of their deficiency in taste to select furniture suitable to the committee-rooms.

Mr. DAVIS. My language did not justify you in any such understanding.

Mr. JOHNSON, of Tennessee. Well, what did the Senator say? I will stand corrected.

Mr. DAVIS. I have told you once.

Mr. JOHNSON, of Tennessee. What did the Senator say? I ask him again.

Mr. DAVIS. I told you once that I said, from your remarks and those of the Senator from Virginia, I was confirmed in the propriety of a proposition which had selected a particular person to choose this furniture, and not to refer it to the committees to select what furniture they should choose; for, from the two specimens, I did not consider that furniture would be well selected in that way. That was about the amount of it.

Mr. JOHNSON, of Tennessee. The explanation is, in substance, what I have stated. The Senator from Mississippi predicated his argument upon the statements made by the Senator from Virginia and myself; and, taking us as specimens, his conclusion was, that the committees were not competent, from the fact of their being deficient in taste, to select furniture suitable for their rooms. We have concluded just where we commenced.

["That is, you have concluded," remarks Davis; Robert Johnson of Arkansas, pleading for a vote, reminds the Senate of the lateness of the hour. To Andrew Johnson's protest that he has "not consumed time," the Arkansas Johnson replies that "the Senator started the difficulty" which has "wasted the spirits and strength of the gentlemen who have to sit this bill out." The Senate votes down both Andrew Johnson's amendment and Mason's motion to set a $10,000 limit and adopts Bright's motion for a $50,000 limit.]

Mr. JOHNSON, of Tennessee. I do not intend to occupy more than two minutes of the Senate's time; but I wish to call their attention to the provisions of this amendment. It declares:

The superintendent of the Capitol extension be directed to make a survey and ascertain what articles of furniture will be needed, with the materials, designs, and dimensions of the same; and that he be, and is hereby, authorized to publish the proper specifications and descriptions of the articles that may be required, and invite sealed proposals, to be made to him within thirty days from the date of the first publication of the same, for the manufacture and construction of the said articles of furniture, to be opened at the appointed time, in the presence of the bidders or other persons; and that a contract or contracts for such furniture shall be made with the lowest and best bidder, reference being had to the quality of the material, the superiority of workmanship, and the time in which the same shall be completed.

I will not say that it was the design of the drawers of this proposition to open the door for a speculation and a fraud; but, as I conceive it, it is susceptible of a fraud and speculation being practiced under it. For instance: it provides that proposals shall be published and bids received for furnishing rooms with furniture, and the superintendent is to judge of the quality of the furniture and the time in which it is to be delivered. It is very easy for a person wishing to make a contract with a particular man, to select him, and it will be in the power of the superintendent to rule them down to such time that he can practically confine the contract to the person whom he may select and upon whom he wishes to confer a benefit. We are told by the Senator from Indiana that he thinks $50,000 will be about half the amount that will be necessary to furnish the committee-rooms. Then, here is a door open for obtaining furniture to the amount of $100,000, leaving the officer to select his own man, and rule all others out. I do not wish to be understood as saying that this is the design of the drawers of the amendment; but in the manner in which it is drawn, it is susceptible of that practice being carried on under it, and it may result in that.

Mr. BRIGHT. Allow me to suggest to the Senator from Tennessee, that he propose an amendment which he thinks will remedy that difficulty.

Mr. JOHNSON, of Tennessee. I think it could be amended; but I have become so well satisfied that any amendment which restrains and restricts the expenditure of public money will not prevail in this body, that I have concluded to offer no amendment.

[On the following day Bright's original amendment is the order of business and Johnson has the floor.]

Mr. JOHNSON, of Tennessee. I move to amend the amendment by striking out all after its enacting clause, and inserting:

That the sum of $50,000 be, and the same is hereby, appropriated out of any money in the Treasury not otherwise appropriated, for the purchase of such furniture as may be required for the north Capitol extension, to be expended by the Secretary of the Senate under the direction of the committee to audit and control its contingent expenses.

I want it recorded now, that if the original amendment be adopted, the furniture for the various rooms, instead of costing $50,-000, will cost the Government over $300,000. As to the economy that has been heretofore evinced by the superintendent, I think we have evidence around us in this building to form a judgment. I know it is very easy to make remarks in reference to the taste of particular individuals, and when I talk of economy, it is not my intention that things shall be reduced to a point at which they do not comport with the Government, or the wants of those who have to enjoy them. I should like to see these rooms furnished suitably and properly, but, at the same time, economically. I am satisfied that if the rooms be furnished according to the original amendment, under the direction of the Superintendent of the Capitol extension, the furniture will cost over $300,000.

Mr. DAVIS. Who says so?

Mr. JOHNSON, of Tennessee. I am satisfied of it; and when we look at his economy in erecting the public buildings and in furnishing the other end of the Capitol, I think we may come to a conclusion as to what he will do in this case. We may judge what his action will be in the future from what it has been in the past. If it was necessary, I might call the attention of the Senate to a memorial which has been presented to Congress by an architect, who, as I understand, first prepared the plan of this building, and upon the basis of whose plan the extensions have been made. Take some items of expenditure that he gives, and I think we may have, at least, a vague idea of the kind of economy that would be carried into the furnishing of these rooms if it were left to the superintendent.[8]

I have no disposition, however, to consume unnecessarily the time of the Senate. It was remarked last night that the terms of the committee to audit the accounts will expire with the session. The Senate meets to-morrow again, however, and can then reorganize the committees. This is a committee under the control of the Senate to audit the accounts of one of its own officers—a gentleman who, I presume, has as good taste in selecting furniture as the superintendent. It is very strange that Senators upon committees, knowing the kind of desks and tables used in the committee-rooms, are not competent to direct an officer of their own making as to the kind of furniture they want for their committee-rooms, and be responsible to the Senate and the country for it; but, somehow or other, it seems we have got to such a pass that nothing can be done of the least importance about the Government unless it is placed under the charge of the military department. All the public buildings, it seems, must be carried on under that department, and we cannot even have the committee-rooms of the Capitol furnished now unless it is confided to the War Department. Your own committees and the Secretary of the Senate, it seems, are not competent to select the little articles of furniture suitable to their own rooms.

I hope my amendment will be adopted. I am satisfied, I repeat again, and want it remembered, that it will cost $300,000 if left to Mr. Meigs; and besides I shall not be surprised if there were to be a very fat contract under the original amendment.[9]

Cong. Globe, 35 Cong., 2 Sess., 1588, 1590, 1611.

1. In the course of considering the civil appropriations bill, Jesse Bright of Indiana (see *Johnson Papers*, I, 491n), chairman of the committee on public buildings and grounds, offered an amendment authorizing the Capitol superintendent to purchase furniture for the new Senate wing. Mason of Virginia dissented on grounds of economy, while others, including Stephen Mallory of Florida, spoke in support of the amendment.

2. Mallory, chairman of the naval affairs committee.

3. Captain Montgomery C. Meigs.

4. Asbury Dickens of North Carolina was secretary and Dunning R. McNair of Pennsylvania, sergeant-at-arms. *U. S. Official Register* (1859), 190.

5. Taken in a broad sense, the statement is not inaccurate. Though no figures for the expenditure on public grounds are readily available, the outlays for the Capitol extension alone had by 1861 reached nearly six million, and the final aqueduct cost between three and five million. Green, *Washington*, 203, 205; *Documentary History of the Capitol*, 786.

6. Solomon Foot of Vermont.

7. James R. Doolittle (1815–1897), New York-born Democrat who had moved to Wisconsin in 1851, left the party because of the repeal of the Missouri Compromise and was elected to the Senate as a Republican (1857–69).

One of Johnson's supporters after the war, he voted for acquittal during the impeachment proceedings. Rejoining the Democratic party, Doolittle ran unsuccessfully for governor; he spent his later years as law professor at the University of Chicago. *BDAC*, 822; *DAB*, V, 374–75.

8.   Charles B. Cluskey, a Washington architect who was one of the original competitors for the Capitol extension, had first submitted a petition in July, 1852, asking compensation for "labor and expense . . . incurred in making and preparing his plan, as well as the time spent in elucidating and giving his views generally on the subject" to government officials. Referred at that time to the Senate's committee on claims, the petition and accompanying documents were later referred to the committee on public buildings and grounds in January, 1854, August, 1856, and December, 1858. No favorable action was ever reported. Petitions and Memorials, Committee on Public Buildings and Grounds, 35 Cong., RG46, National Archives.

9.   Johnson's amendment was rejected, 29–19. *Cong. Globe*, 35 Cong., 2 Sess., 1611–12.

Resolution on Retrenchment[1]

March 3, 1859

On motion of Mr. JOHNSON, of Tennessee, the Senate resumed the consideration of the following resolution:

Resolved, That the President of the United States be, and he is hereby, requested to cause the heads of the various Executive Departments to submit estimates of the expenditures for the Government to the Thirty-Sixth Congress, upon a basis not exceeding $50,000,000 per annum, exclusive of the public debt, and the interest thereon.

[Bell of Tennessee offers an amendment to add the following sentence: "And that the committee also inquire into, and report, the causes which have mainly contributed to the great increase of the public expenditures."]

Mr. JOHNSON, of Tennessee. I would barely suggest that that amendment does not seem entirely germane to the resolution. I have no objection, however, to accepting the amendment; but I think if the information is obtained and presented to the country, as proposed by the amendment, it will be ascertained where the largest proportion of the expenditures have occurred. I think it will be traced back to Congress, as well as to the other departments. I have no objection to the amendment, if the Senator things it germane to the resolution.

[After Bell withdraws his amendment, the Senate accepts another offered by James Green of Missouri: "*Provided*, The same can be done without injury to the public service"; Jefferson Davis, opposing Johnson's resolution, avers that it would represent advice that the executive branch "have not asked."]

Mr. JOHNSON, of Tennessee. I merely wish to say—for it is not my intention to consume the time of the Senate—that the two resolutions originally introduced were based upon the propositions of the President himself.[2] We must all be satisfied that the retrenchment of the expenditures of this Government can never be carried out, as recent experiments prove conclusively, unless the Executive and the heads of Departments take the lead in this work. I want, so far as I am concerned, to hold them to the indications thrown out to the country, that the expenditures of the Government can be reduced. I can see no objection to the laying down any amount as a basis on which an estimate shall be made. They will make it on that basis, and indicate, at the same time, that this or that Department may want more than it authorizes them to make; and, of course, they will submit their regular estimates. This resolution will show what the expenditures will be by making $50,000,000, exclusive of the public debt and the interest thereon, the basis of the estimates to the next Congress of the United States. I hope the resolution will be adopted. It can do no earthly harm, and may do a great deal of good. It will do good thus far: it puts the Executive, and those who have assumed to the country that there can be retrenchment and that it ought to be commenced, in the lead; and, as faithful representatives of the States and people, let us give them all the aid we can.[3]

Cong. Globe, 35 Cong., 2 Sess., 1659–60.

1. During the last hours of the 35th Congress, the Senate agreed to consider Johnson's resolution, now introduced for the fourth time. *Cong. Globe*, 35 Cong., 2 Sess., 205, 402, 991, 1651, 1658.

2. In offering similar resolutions on January 4 and 17 and February 12, Johnson had cited Buchanan's second annual message (December 6, 1858), one-third of which was devoted to the subject of economy; he pointed out that the President had invited Congress "to institute a rigid scrutiny to ascertain whether the expenses of all the departments cannot be still further reduced." *Ibid.*, 402, 991; Richardson, *Messages*, V, 524.

3. The resolution was adopted—"Ayes twenty-one, noes not counted."

To John B. Floyd, Washington, D. C.

March 4, 1859, Washington, D. C.; LS, DNA–RG92, Let. Recd. from Sec. of War, Box No. 4.

Johnson and eight other Tennesseans, observing that the army appropriation bill of this date calls for the purchase of horses and mules, recommend Col. B. F. Cheatham "as a gentleman every way qualified to purchase such stock advantageously for the Government." In addition to having served in the Mexican War, he "has a full personal knowledge of the kinds of stock wanted for the service, while his long residence in the heart of a stock-raising country, gives him peculiar advantages for purchasing such as may be wanted for delivery at or near Fort Leavenworth."

From John B. Floyd

Hon. Andrew Johnson   War Department
" . A. O. P. Nicholson and others   March 8' 1859
Senate.

Gentlemen,

I have received your letter of the 4th instant, recommending Colonel B. F. Cheatham of Tennessee, as a gentleman every way qualified to purchase horses and mules for the use of the Army; and in reply have to say that, from present indications, I think it likely that instead of buying, we shall be compelled to sell a large quantity of stock now belonging to the Army.[1]

Under other circumstances it would give me great pleasure to meet your wishes in regard to Col. Cheatham. I am satisfied not only from your statements, but from those of others, that the interests of the Department in this respect might be safely and advantageously committed to his judgment and discretion.

Should an occasion arise for the purchase of animals, I will not forget your application in behalf of Colonel Cheatham.

Very respectfully Yr Obt. Servt.
John B. Floyd
Secretary of War.

LS, DNA-RG92, Let. Recd. from Sec. of War, Box No. 4; Copy, DNA-RG107, Copies Let. Sent, Vol. 41, p. 148.

1. Although $200,000 had been designated for the purchase of horses in the Army Appropriation Act of March 4, the same measure had reduced by $2,000,000 the war department budget; consequently, in an effort to avoid a deficiency, the department was obliged to sell at public auction all animals not absolutely essential. In fact, in December, 1859, "as a measure of economy and efficiency," Floyd recommended the purchase of camels for transporting men and supplies on the frontiers. *U. S. Statutes*, XI, 433; *Senate Ex. Doc.* No. 2, 36 Cong., 1 Sess., 3–9.

To Robert Johnson, Greeneville

Washington City   March 8.th 1859

My dear Son,

The Senate is now in Secret Session— It has this mo[me]nt been Communicated to the Senate privately that the P M Genl[1] has just died—which will detain the Senate some longer than was anticipated at first— Arons sad heart now ceases to beat and in fact is no more— Some of us are pressing the appointment of Geo W Jon[e]s

upon the President as the successor of A. V B.   I do most Sincerly
regret that he has died, for I wanted him to live and see the folly
of his Course and especially in So in regard to the P. O. Dept—[2]
I now think it very doubfull whether Mr Nicholson can be at the
convention—[3] If I am not at home in time for you to go to the
[convention] you had better be in readiness and go down— And
when you get there be Careful and prudent in all your moves— I
wish I could be there to talk to you about m[an]y things that I
cannot now put on paper—   There is [a] Stra[n]ge State of thi[n]gs
coming up that must be noted and studied— If you need mony you
must go to Mr Jon[e]s[?] or C Low[r]y[?] and get it— Put off lev'ng
home to the last day if I do not reach [home] Sooner than I now
think I will— Tell your mother the causes of my detention as I
have not written to her Since we have been conviened in executive
Session—[4] Nicholson says he wants you to attend the convention—

Your father   Andrew Johnson

ALS, DLC-JP.

   1. Aaron V. Brown.
   2. One detects a streak of vindictiveness in this reaction to the demise of
a political enemy. Undoubtedly Brown's "folly"—in Johnson's eyes—was the
inordinately large post-office deficit which had accrued during the Tennessean's incumbency. Roy F. Nichols, *The Disruption of American Democracy*
(New York, 1948), 244.
   3. Since he was in Nashville following Brown's funeral, Nicholson did attend the Democratic Convention. McGavock, *Pen and Sword*, 512.
   4. This special executive session, held March 5–10, was needed to confirm
a large backlog of appointments, take action on a number of treaties with the
Indians of the Pacific northwest, and deal with several other treaties, especially one with New Granada. *Senate Ex. Journal*, 35 Cong., Special Sess.,
passim.

To Bolivar Hagan [Memphis?]

April 8, 1859, Greeneville; ALS, DLC-JP2.

Has forwarded to Galloway and Campbell, owner-editors of the Memphis *Avalanche*, an order on Hagan for $100, "the amount I loaned you
while in Washington City now more than one year ago—" Hopes Hagan
can "call and pay it over to them at an early day—"

From Samuel Rhea

Blountville, Apl 13. [1859]

Dear Sir

Thus far we have had a very pleasant spring and although dry
and some what windy Vegitation is coming up pretty rapidly— I
will suggest to you on 2 items of Business—

1st.   The Bill[1] before you to give the soldiers of 1812 a pension of
$8 per mo—will be a heavy drag on our treasury. I would suggest
that if you were to give *now* $4 per mo; and after a while increase
it—the Bill would more likely pass—
2. We hope to get a double daily mail on our road— We need it
and it will be giving us $13,000 and cost us nothing— hope you
will do all you can for this line— And further, if we get it— Aud-
ley Gammon[2] son of Wm. is a candidate for Route Agent— I am
anxious he should get it. he is very capable—of steady moral habits
—and I know will give satisfaction— We would like you to help
him— You can *safely* recommend him——
    Our Country is healthy[.] prospect of fine fruit year is good—
Wishing you a pleasant time. I am yrs truly

                                                        Saml Rhea
Hon. A. Johnson

ALS, DLC-JP2.
    1. The bill failed in the Senate. Not until 1871 would a pension be pro-
vided for the veterans of the War of 1812 and their widows. *U. S. Statutes*,
XVI, 411.
    2. Audley [Odley?] Gammon (b. *c*1834). Marian K. Burgner, tr., *Popu-
lation Schedule of the United States Census of 1850 for Sullivan County, Tennessee* (Knoxville, 1963), 90.

To Charles H. Brainard,[1] Boston, Mass.

                                        Greeneville Tenn   April 23d 1859
Mr. C. H. Brainard
Dear Sir
    Your letter of the 15th inst was received by this mor[n]ings
mail—   I was not expecting you to take any further steps in reference to the likeness until you heard more from me on the Subject as
I had not fully determined on the full height or three fourths likeness when I saw you last and we then thought that the artist[2] could
even make, or take a better lik[e]ness than the one then taken and
I was to Call again and give another Sitting— It soo turned out that
I did not Call on the artist on account of being hurried off unexpect-
edly with the Co[r]pse of the P. M. Genl.[3] After this I had concluded
to wait until fall or winter and then have it all done as it should
be— As you have gone on and well nigh completed the likeness I
hope that it will *come up to your expectation* and that it will be pronounced a good likeness and a well executed job— These are the
two things that I most desired as you will remember when talking
to you on the subject. I trust that no incongruity will result from
making your likeness from two different pictures, and that it will

appear as though it had all been Copied from the same likeness— I have the fullest confidence that you will have it all done up right or you would not have proceede[d] with it as you have—

> I have the honor to be most respectfully &c
>
> Andrew Johnson

ALS, MB.

1. If the quality of his subjects is indicative, Charles H. Brainard (1817–1885) was an eminently successful print-publisher. In 1855 he published a *Portrait Gallery of Distinguished Americans* and in 1885 a biography of his friend, John Howard Payne. Boston *Evening Transcript*, February 5, 1885; see also Charles H. Brainard, *John Howard Payne, A Biographical Sketch, etc.* (Washington, D. C., 1885).

2. Brainard's artist was Francis D'Avignon (b. *c*1814), a French portrait painter, lithographer, and engraver, who had come to America in the early 1840's to work in New York (1844–59) and Boston (1859–60). George C. Groce and David H. Wallace, eds., *The New-York Historical Society's Dictionary of Artists in America, 1564–1860* (New Haven, 1957), 167.

3. When Aaron V. Brown, postmaster general from Tennessee, died March 8, Johnson, Nicholson, Congressman Savage, and Supreme Court Justice John Catron were designated to accompany the remains to Nashville. Johnson seems to have left the party in Greeneville. Nashville *Union and American*, March 12, 15, 1859.

From Charles H. Brainard

> 22½ Winter Street
>
> Boston April 27, 1859

Hon Andrew Johnson

Dear Sir

Your favor of the 23d inst is before me.

A few days since I sent you an early copy of your portrait, which I presume has reached you before this time. I am very confident that it will please you as it seems to me as near perfection as the lithographic art can make it.

I had the impression that you had fully determined upon the sise of the figure before I left Washington. At any rate you may be assured that the 3/4 length is the most desirable style for the picture, and one that is most generally approved.

I had a talk with the Artist at McClee's gallery[1] who told me that he did not think it possible to produce a better likeness than the smaller photograph which we examined in company with, Senator Donaldson[2] (I think.) My artist[3] has copied this but made a study from the larger head as that was more elevated and gave the figure a more commanding appearance. I deem the portrait one of the very best I have ever published. It is much admired here, and the editor of the Transcript, himself a good judge of art, has promised to notice it this evening.[4]

I have just published a portrait of Senator Douglas which is much admired, but many think yours is in some respects a better picture. My Artist worked a day longer on the face than he did on that of Douglas.

It is customary in drawing a portrait to make studies from more than one picture. I am getting up a portrait of Mr Bingham[5] of Ohio, which is to be of the size of yours, for which no less than *four* photographs are to be used. The head from one, the figure from another, and studies of the hair and drapery from others.

The print which I sent you was a proof. Before printing any more the stone will be lettered and your autograph transferred to it.

Hoping that the picture will be as satisfactory to yourself as it is to me I remain   Your friend & Serv't
                                                                   C H. Brainard

ALS, DLC-JP.

1. J. E. McClees, a daguerreotypist of Philadelphia, had opened a Washington studio on Pennsylvania Avenue. *Boyd's Washington and Georgetown Directory* (1858), xxv, 205.

2. Brainard meant Senator Nicholson, Johnson's Tennessee colleague.

3. Francis D'Avignon was a New York engraver who also worked for Mathew Brady. Josephine Cobb, "Mathew B. Brady's Photographic Gallery in Washington," Columbia Historical Society *Records*, LIII–LVI (1953–56), 31n.

4. Brainard includes a copy of the Boston *Transcript* notice: "NEW PORTRAITS. Two new portraits have been added to the large collection of Mr. Brainard. They are those of Hon. Andrew Johnson, U. S. Senator from Tennessee, and Hon. John Sherman, a Representative from Ohio. These portraits were drawn by D'Avignon, and are fully equal to the very best products of his crayon. That of Senator Johnson is a full length, in the style of the recent portrait of Douglas, and gives a spirited and accurate representation of a noble looking man, whose frank and open countenance bespeaks an honesty of purpose somewhat rare amongst the politicians of the present day." Along the margin of the clipping Brainard observes: "When the portrait is printed, with the lettering, I shall have it extensivel[y] noticed. In my judgement it is a bette[r] likeness than Sherman's[.]"

5. John A. Bingham (1815–1900) was a Republican representative from Ohio (1855–63, 1865–73) who later served as minister to Japan (1873–85) after having been one of the managers appointed by the House to conduct impeachment proceedings against Johnson. *BDAC*, 555.

From Bradley County Democrats

April 28, 1859, Cleveland; LS, DLC-JP.

Invitation, in the handwriting of John S. Brown and signed by eight men, to address the Bradley Democrats at the quarterly meeting of the county court next Monday "on the important questions now before the Country[.]"

From Sullivan County Democrats[1]

Bristol, Tenn., April 29th, 1859

Hon Andrew Johnson—Dear Sir—

The undersigned, believing they represent the general wish of the Democracy of Sullivan County, and the universally expressed desire of that portion of them residing near the Virginia border, respectfully request that you will address them at some early period, which may not conflict with your own convenience, (and which you will please to name,) at the town of Bristol,—upon those issues of national politics which are now the source of much variance of opinion between a portion of the Southern people— Believing that an expression of views from one like yourself, who not only participated in the proceedings of the last Congress, out of which many of the issues referred to grew, but who possesses in so eminent a degree the confidence and esteem of the Democracy of this country, would go far to strengthen us in combatting the fallacies with which an ingenious and active Opposition is seeking to prejudice our cause, we earnestly ask the benefit of your counsel; which will be of the more benefit at this time, when men of all parties are forming their opinions with regard to the principles at issue in the approaching election. We make this solicitation with the more freedom on account of the willingness you so patriotically expressed, in your late speech at Greenville,[2] to go where-ever, your party, in this respect, might require your services[.]

ALS, DLC-JP.

1. Signed by J. R. Anderson and eighteen others.
2. An unreported speech which Johnson delivered on April 19 at the Democratic convention in Greeneville. Nashville *Union and American*, April 20, 25, 1859.

To [Arthur] Crozier,[1] Knoxville

Private   Greeneville Tenn May 10th 1859—

Friend Crozier,

Your note from Knoxville was received— I was gratified to learn that you were again in our midst and feeling an interest in the wellfaire of democracy— I am free to say to you, that there has been a strange state of affairs in our ranks for the last two years both in Tennessee and in Washington, which has been doing us much injury as a party— Mr Buchanan from some Cause or other, has been

induced to beleive that two or three men in Tenn. Constitute the
entire democracy and has been acting accordingly—[2] If those [who]
have been assuming to be the democracy in the State, some of
whome you have alluded to in your letter are to be recognised as
such and they are infact to take control of the democratic party—I
for one would ask most respectfully to be excused from any further
Connexion with it— I would be far better to put the party into
Bankruptcy now and make a prorata distribution of its effects than
to pass into Such hands— [If] the party Cannot exist in Tennessee
without passing under the control of Mr Churchwell and his *ilk*, let
it be wound up, and the sooner the better for the party and its future
reputation—   it has some now then, it would have none—   You
need have no fears as to Mr. B's being the Candidate of the democratic party in 1860— I have no doubt of his aspiring to the nomination and so set his net in making his recommendations to the last
two Sessions of Congress; but it will be no go in my opinion—
Ho[we]ver, I do not think it of much importance who may be the
nominee, unless there is some reaction in the Black Republican feeling in the free states and more harmony in the democratic party—
For without both, defeat will be certain in the next presidential contest[.][3] I hope for better things; but my fears are strong at this time
— I was more than please to see Gov' Harris in his opening speech
at Nashville arraign Col Netherland[4] on various issues which I think
will [torn] if he will continue to press them [torn] keep Col Netherland on the defensive— On the contrary if we permit our selves to
be placed in the defensive and at the same time let the Clamor about
the public expenditures get fairly into the public mind, it [half-line
illegible] and perhaps defeat us in August— So far however I do
not think they have affected much with the charge of extravagance
in the administration of the Government—[5] In 1840, you will remember that the expenditures in reference to the presi[dent's] House
had [a won]derful influence and you remember also that [after] they
succeeded in putting the democracy down they in the first congress
voted a large sum to refurnish the Presd mansion[6] in much [the
same] style as that when Mr Vanburen was the occupant of the white
house— This ought to be brought up again for the purpose of showing their inconsistency— A list of the articles which were furnished
the white house after Genl Harrison's election was published in the
Nashville Union March the 23d 1841—which would be a good set
off to the list of items they are now publishing to the prejudice of the
democracy &c—[7] I would have been glad to see you and to have had
a full and free [illegible] in reference to [politics?] and your new
home &c—

If convenient, drop me a line what endorsed bonds can be had at in Nashville[8] or regular sixes and what amount and who f[illegible] I will be in Texas this fall[9] and will come and see you—

Please accept assurance of my high esteem and sincere friendship—

Andrew Johnson

ALS, TxDaHi.

1. In the light of comments later in this letter, it appears that Crozier, former state comptroller, had recently moved to Texas. White, *East Tenn. Journalism*, 13.

2. Probably a reference to the remnants of Aaron Brown's Nashville clique and more especially to Knoxvillian William M. Churchwell, recently returned from a special diplomatic mission to Mexico.

3. These fears materialized: the Republicans, united behind Lincoln, carried every northern state except New Jersey, while the Democrats, badly divided between Breckinridge and Douglas, lost the three border states of Kentucky, Virginia, and Tennessee to the Constitutional Union ticket, and failed to carry the South. Stanwood, *Presidency*, I, 295–97.

4. John Netherland (1808–1887), the opposition candidate, was a Rogersville Whig lawyer who had served in the state senate (1833–35) and in the legislature (1835, 1851–53). A Unionist, he took no active part in the war, but sat as a Democrat in the Constitutional Convention of 1870. William S. Speer, *Sketches of Prominent Tennesseans* (Nashville, 1888), 62–63; Oliver P. Temple, *Notable Men of Tennessee from 1833 to 1875* (New York, 1912), 159–65.

5. Johnson had spoken to this point in addressing the Democratic district convention at Greeneville early in April. In the brief excerpt which has survived, he observed: "It was sometimes charged that there was a wasteful extravagance in furnishing the new Hall of the House of Representatives. . . . The enlargement of the Capitol, and the consequent necessity of furnishing it at all, was *begun under Mr. Fillmore's administration*, and a large portion of the furniture purchased by a gentleman of this State one William Cullom, who was then Clerk of the *House*, elected by a "Know Nothing" House of Representatives with Mr. Speaker Banks at their head. This would serve to illustrate how these wholesole charges of waste and extravagance, *when squared by the truth of history, vanish into thin air;* and he warned the people when they heard such charges to understand them before they decided upon them." Greeneville *Democrat*, quoted in Knoxville *Tri-Weekly Whig*, April 28, 1859.

6. As amended by John W. Allen, Ohio Whig, the appropriation bill of March 3, 1841, had included $6,000 for "furniture for the President's House" —an item which gave the opposition press a field day. Democrats recalled that during the campaign of 1840 the Whigs had made much of Van Buren's sybaritic surroundings; at one point a Pennsylvanian delivered a lengthy speech which included an itemized list of all the White House furnishings and accommodations, down to the last chamber pot. The Nashville *Union* of March 18, 1841 (not March 23, as Johnson says), in a column headed "FIRST MOVE UNDER THE ECONOMIC ADMINISTRATION," observed that "The whig at the White House tells a very different story from that which was told by . . . stump speakers last summer" and called especial attention to "SIX THOUSAND DOLLARS WORTH OF FURNITURE FOR GEN. HARRISON'S ACCOMODATIONS!" *Cong. Globe*, 26 Cong., 2 Sess., 259–60; Robert G. Gunderson, *The Log Cabin Campaign* (Lexington, Ky., 1957), 101–5; Nashville *Union*, March 18, 1841.

7. Johnson probably refers to lists of Democratic extravagances being reprinted in the opposition press from a widely circulated tract, *What It Costs*

to Be Governed. Charging wholesale wastefulness and corruption in "every branch of the Government, that could be made to yield a farthing," the pamphlet indicted officials "from the President down" for raids upon the public treasury. Extracts and references to the publication had appeared in Nashville newspapers several days before Johnson wrote this letter. *What It Costs to Be Governed* ([Richmond, 1859]), *passim*; Nashville *Republican Banner*, May 5, 6, 7, 1859; Nashville *Patriot*, May 7, 9, 10, 1859.

8. Crozier had probably returned from Texas by way of Nashville. As former state comptroller, he undoubtedly kept himself informed on the bond market; Johnson may have relied upon his financial judgment when they were both in Nashville.

9. Johnson did not go to Texas that fall.

To [Senate Clerk, Washington, D. C.]

Greeneville Ten   May 18 59—

Dear Sir,

Will you prmit me one time mor to trouble you for some documets—Reports on finance for the years 1856–7 & 1857–8 three copies of each also the Secretier's report on Banks—March 3d 1857 Executive document No 87—and also one more copy of documt No 180[1] Feb 12th 1841, if it can be had— Presume that Mr Hedrick can furnish you with the reports on finance— The other docunts reached [me] in good time for which you will please accept my thanks—   Accept assurances of my esteem

Andrew Johnson

ALS, NN-T. H. Morrell Col.

1. Report of the secretary of the treasury showing the losses by the general government, and by the people of the United States, from the use of banks and bank paper. *Senate Doc*. No. 180, 26 Cong., 2 Sess.

Speech at Bristol [Democratic Version][1]

May 21, 1859

Commencing with the slavery issue, which in the present condition of parties, is really the pending and most dangerous one, he took the ground that negro slavery was neither a moral, social or political evil, but was right. That slavery of some sort grew naturally and inevitably out of the construction of society, and that negro slavery, as relieving us of the curse of white slavery, was a blessing rather than an evil. The more especially was this the case, as the negro, by his bondage, was elevated in the social scale; whereas in the absence of negro slavery there must be a class of whites degraded to the position of menials, whose condition in some states of society would be more oppressive than is the bondage of the negro in the

South. Slavery, then, being right, (the Senator argued,) we must defend it—not by a negative course—not by conservatism or compromises, as we are counselled to do by our Opposition friends—but by active resistance to the encroachments upon our federal rights by the aggressive party of the North, the Black Republicans, who under the leadership of Wm. H. Seward, are seeking control of the government, with the purpose of using its powers and its patronage for the extermination of negro slavery in the South. Senator Johnson was not a compromise man—he had not voted in Congress for all the compromise acts—he had not voted for any one of them because it was a compromise, but because it was right in itself. There could be no compromise without a sacrifice of *right* upon one side or the other. Virtue could not compromise with vice without losing its character. Falsehood was always willing to compromise with truth, and wrong with right, because falsehood and wrong must gain, and truth and right lose in proportion to the extent of the compromise.

Conservatism was another specious argument of the opponents of Democracy. What was conservatism? "A little more sleep, a little more slumber, a little more folding of the hands to sleep."[2] Conservatism simply meant a preserving of things as they are, and, as applied to this slavery issue, mounted in words to this: having compromised, and lost by the bargain, let us stick to it, until another compromise is made encroaching upon our right, and then, that being the bargain, let's stick to it again. The Democratic party, the Senator asserted, was not and could not be conservative—it was radical and progressive. No good had ever been done, no great principle ever established, by a conservative party.[3]

He next considered the currency question, and showed up the evils and fraud of the paper money system, with such apt and forcible illustrations as to make its ruinous tendency clear to every comprehension. Lastly, the Senator considered the clamor raised in this canvass about the expenditures of the government, and showed the insincerity of our opponents. He did not deem the mountebankism of their slop-tub charges worthy of serious notice; but he looked into the really useless and extravagant appropriations, which swelled the expenditures to millions; and, examining them item by item, showed that, with scarcely an exception, they had been passed by the opposition to Democracy. He thought the expenditures too large; so did Mr. Buchanan; so did other good Democrats. They thought the government ought to be administered on a basis of fifty millions a year. The Senate, at its last session, had passed a resolution, calling upon the President to direct the heads of departments to conform as near as possible to that basis, and the result was that the appropriations for the coming fiscal year were only forty-one millions of dollars. Adding to this for the Post Office deficiency, (which must be appropriated by the next Congress, but would be properly chargeable to the last,) twelve millions, and we have the expenditures reduced from upwards of seventy millions to fifty-three millions. This reduction was accomplished by the Democracy—they are, in good faith, carrying on the work of reform, in spite of the efforts of the Opposition to run up the expenditures.

Clipping, TKL-Bristol *Va. and Tenn. News*, May 25, 1859, in T. A. R. Nelson Scrapbook, VII, 16–17.

1. Johnson, although not a candidate in the coming August elections, agreed to speak in Bristol "on the political issues of the day," only to find Nathaniel Taylor, prominent East Tennessee Whig who had opposed him in the first district canvass of 1849, requesting permission to share the platform. Johnson, acquiescing, spoke for three hours; Taylor's two-and-one-half-hour speech followed. Since opposition papers of that day seldom reported speeches in any detail, this one is remarkable by being available in two versions. According to the Democratic reporter, "Mr. Johnson's speech was earnest, argumentative and statesmanlike . . . calculated to carry conviction to every hearer in whose breast a regard for the political rights of the South could prevail over a blind partizan prejudice"; whereas the Opposition correspondent, although conceding that it was "replete with all the cunning, that such a man as Andy possesses," nonetheless concluded that "TAYLOR gained a victory to day. . . . Johnson was completely used up." It may be noted that, although gubernatorial and congressional seats were at stake, the senator spoke only in general terms and not in behalf of specific candidates. Bristol *Va. and Tenn. News*, May 25, 1859, in T. A. R. Nelson Scrapbook (Knoxville Public Library), VII, 16–17.

2. A near-rendering of Prov. 6:10.

3. Here the editor reminded his readers that he was giving "the substance, not the language" of Johnson's remarks, and regretted that for lack of space he could not present "a tithe of the unanswerable points he made."

Speech at Bristol [Opposition Version]

May 21, 1859

He first discussed the question of slavery in the abstract, and labored desperately to show to his audience, that slavery was right from the nature of things. He consumed about an hour, in demonstrating a proposition, that no man South of Mason and Dixon's line, would attempt to controvert. The speaker, then took up the currency question: *a question, that the Democracy unite so cordially upon in Tennessee.*[1] The Senator said he was, and always had been a hard money man, and always expected to be; but, did not say what his party's position was on that subject. The truth is, Andy was with the currency question, like the murderer of the Duke of Clarence was with his conscience, when he said, "I'll not meddle with it; it is a dangerous thing."[2] The third question discussed by the Senator, was that of extravagant expenditures by the general government. And on this question, the Gov. come to a stand still several times before he could "draw out the thread of his argument." Really, I never heard such a lame effort from any democratic politician, in defence of the present administration. After the speaker had wound up himself on the questions referred to, he proceeded to deliver a eulogy upon the character of U. S. S. Johnson. This was decidedly the ablest part of the gentleman's elaborate speech. The "conclusion of the whole matter," was, (in substance,) Fellow-Citizens of the Good Old *Dimocratic* County of Swillivan! Be it known unto you and each one of you; that I, Andrew Johnson; U. S. S. from Tennessee, and Ex Gov. of the State aforesaid; and who has the honor this day to address you, am undeniably and unmistakably, *the* greatest man (in my own opinion) that ever walked terra firma: and further, the Charleston Convention will find in me the only suitable man for the Presidential nomination, &c., &c; *ad infinitum.*

Knoxville *Tri-Weekly Whig*, May 26, 1859.

1. This is a satirical reference to Democratic equivocation on the currency issue—an ambivalence reflected in the state convention's adoption of a resolution which recognized, but regretted, that paper money was so "deeply ingrafted into our pecuniary relations," and demanded reform. The *Tri-Weekly Whig* of March 24 sarcastically remarked that the convention "acted wisely and *took both* sides of the currency question. . . . They had seen that their party had acted both *for* and *against* paper money" throughout the state and "according to the interest of the banking facilities" in various counties. Campbell, *Banking*, 147n. See also The Tennessee Democracy on Banks and Currency, September 22, 1858.

2. Shakespeare, *Richard III*, Act I, sc. 4.

To Charles H. Brainard, Boston, Mass.

Greenville, Tenn., June 1st, 1859

Sir, I presume I have received all your letters, some of them it is true were detained on the road longer than the ordinary transit. I have also received the proof of copy of the portrait referred to in one of your letters, which came to hand of recent date. None of these reasons have been the cause of my not writing. When the letters and proof were received I was not able to write in consequence of being indisposed, and the telegraph was intended to stay all further proceeding until I was able to do so. I have always made it a rule to be —— and frank in all my affairs private and public. I am constrained to say that I was disappointed in the portrait. Most persons pronounce it a good picture but no likeness and say that it surely was not intended as a likeness. You will remember in all our interviews that I stated while I wanted the artistic part of it well done, that I was still more anxious to have an likeness. You will also remember that I called Senator Nicholson in to see the small likeness you had taken and he and I both concurred in the opinion that the face was *entirely too smoothe* and youthful in appearance and thereupon agreed to have another taken, and if that was not done the smoothness and youthfull appearance could be corrected from another which had been taken of smaller size.

It so turned out that I did not call any more and no other likeness was taken, and took it for granted from the confidence you had inspired me with that you would not proceed to have the portrait executed unless it was correctly done and as I desired it to be. The picture which was taken and the one which you said was the one by which the atitude or position "was so good" represented the right hand resting upon a desk or table. The proof you sent me represents the right hand extended some distance from the body and resting upon nothing, which really looks very awkward and unnatural. As to the hand resting upon a desk or table you spoke about and stated that the desk could be placed there as easily as the table. The name of the artist is placed where the table was and where the desk ought to be. I will forward by this Mail a small likeness which is pronounced by every person who has seen it, that it is a first rate likeness, which will when compared show very clearly that the objection I make is not a mere whim or notion. In fine the objection I have to the portrait is first, *the Smoothness and youthful* appearance of the face; second the awkward and unnatural position of the right hand without the desk or table, as now it is not far enough from the body to be the result of gesture, or close enough to be hanging natural and easy by the side. I will conclude without being more tedious, by saying that after you have compared the likeness I send you and a refference to all that transpired between you and myself, then if you are fully satisfied with the portrait and then the understanding in reference to its execution has been complied with, and will write me a letter, that you are, I will forward the money at an early day. So you have the whole affair in your own hands and whatever you say and do I will abide by. If, all the pictures are struck off like the proof you have sent me, you will please retain them until I order them for they will be of no use to me like the proof I have. Let me hear from you soon[.] I hope to be more prompt hereafter. Please return by mail the likeness I send you. Accept assurance of my respect, etc.

Andrew Johnson.

Curtis Guild, "Some Presidential Sidelights," Massachusetts Historical Society *Proceedings*, XLVII (1914), 477–78.

To James Buchanan, Washington, D. C.

June 1, 1859, Greeneville; ALS, DNA-RG59, Appl. & Recomm., 1853–1861, H. M. Watterson.

Recommends Harvey M. Watterson as minister to Nicaragua, should that post be vacated by resignation, or to some other post.

Deed to Greene County Property

June 5, 1859, Greeneville; Copy, Greene County Deed Book No. 30, pp. 194–95.

Robert M. Barton conveys to Johnson two tracts of land which Barton had purchased from Robert J. McKinney at public sale, February 20, 1857, and which are described as part of "the Dickson lands . . . on the south side of Greeneville." Lot No. 1, bordering Mrs. Payne's and Barton's properties, contains eight acres; lot No. 2, consisting of seven acres, is adjacent to lot No. 1 and "Barton's ridge."

To John B. Floyd, Washington, D. C.

June 8, 1859, Greeneville; ALS, *The Month at Goodspeed's Book Shop*, XXXVII (June, 1966), 252.

Requests discharge for Private N. B. McLin, who was a minor when he enlisted; encloses petition from Jonesboro citizens and a letter from the "afflicted mother [who] is in great distress of mind in consequence of the condition of her son—" [On June 11 Floyd reports that McLin is being discharged, according to Johnson's request.]

From John C. Rives[1]

Washington, 25th June, 1859

Hon Andrew Johnson
   Greenville, Tenn.
      Sir:
         You start in good luck, but may end in bad. I stayed in this City last night for the first time for several weeks, and received your letter of the 22nd instant early this morning, in time to see Mr Casey[2] before he went to his office. He says that your 3 per cent. U. S. Treasury notes[3] will be paid whenever they are presented at the Treasury, with interest up to that date. He does not know how-much Mr Cobb[4] gave for them in other Treas'y notes, and he doubts whether or not Mr Cobb knows now; but he, Mr Casey, thinks he will give others for them bearing 5½ or 5¾ per cent. interest. I

expect to learn within an hour or two from this time,—for I intend
to see Mr Cobb soon after he gets to his office, & shall keep this
letter open to let you know the result. I am sure he does not know
what he will do a week hence, for he will be regulated by the New-
York money market; it will be regulated, or greatly influenced by
the war rageing in Europe;[5] money holders there, if the war should
become general, will get scared & invest to a considerable extent in
our stocks; and, after all, much will depend, on our growng crops
& our selling more than we buy, for a while, at least. Those who are
called our wisest financiers here, will not tell you to-day, or cannot,
in decided terms, whether or not a general war in Europe will raise
or depress our Stocks. It would do one of the two things every body
knows; but one-half of our wise men will tell you that it would
operate one way, & the other half that it would have a direct contrary effect. So we go—more by luck & prudence, than by judgment.

I inclose the details of the money market in New-York, yesterday
evening. You will see that Tennessee Stocks have run up about 1:2
per cent. within the last two or three months. They will probably
run down 1 or 2 per cent. within the next three months, for the
"*bears*"—the moneyed men—will *pull them down* when they desire
to invest in them.

I intend to be in New-York the 1st of July; but I could invest for
you as well while here as I could in New York; for if I were there I
would go to Riggs & Cos[6] branch there & pay them ¼ per cent to do
the business for me. I have tried them for 10 or 15 years, & found
them trustworthy— I will go to see Cobb while this page is drying[.]

Well! I have been to see Cobb, and asked him what he thought
would be the effect on Stocks in the event of a general war in
Europe, or universal peace, and he seemed to think that a general
war in Europe would "depress Stocks" in this Country; but had not
confidence in his judgment, nor I neither.

He can let you have 5½ per cent for your money. He & Mr Casey
both thoug[ht] that Riggs would let you have 6's for ½ per cent
difference. I thought that he would do no such thing, unless as a
favor, which he would I was sure grant me on $2000. But to my
surprise Riggs said he would do it, that it made no difference to
him. & agreed to make the exchange for me, & ordered $2000, of
6's to be kept for me. It does not make any difference to a man who
does not intend to keep the 6's more than *one year*; but to a man who
intends to keep them two years, or more, it makes a considerable
in my opinion, & the longer he keeps them the greater the difference
will be in his favor. But I have not had the opportunity for judging
that he has had. Send your 3 per cents to me, or to Riggs & Co
direct, & [I] will see that it is attended to. If you shall conclude to

take Tennessee bonds, I will take the $2000 U S 6's on my own account[.]

Whatever you may wish done, I will do for you with great pleasure.

I see four numbers of my Cullom paper[7] under my table, & intend to send them to you, to send to the Knoxville District. I am too proud to send them, direct: Those I sent to you were for that purpose; but I did not so advise you, because I thought you were sensible enough to understand. Those which I shall now send to you, have been improved a little; but nothing has been struck out. I have not put in all I know; but it will come on during the trial of the four indictments,[8] which, now, I suppose will not come on until about the 1st of Jany. The main object of my paper was to place before the country part of the evidence in the Cullom case as not one in a million of the people would see the whole of the Committee's Report & the evidence.

The Members of the House are very mad because I brought up this subject by an article in the Globe of the 7th December 1857.[9] It was the main cause of their striking out of part of the appropriation for reporting the debats of the House. They expected to scare me off, & get the Senate to put it back. But I prevented that, & had the remainder stricken out. Cullom, Congress, & Corruption has got hold of the wrong man. When attacked I can neither be bought off nor scared off. Cullom has been here three weeks, & looks very ugly at me, & I look likewise at him. He is a perjured rogue, beyond a doubt in my mind, and I am all right as to truth & honesty. The poet says "Conscience makes cowards of us all."[10] I know it helps mightily to make me a brave man; or, at least, will keep me from cringing to any man, or to any set of men. You must be tired, & I will, therefore, have compassion on you, & stop writing.

I am, very respectfully
John C Rives

ALS, DLC-JP.

1. Rives, former member of Jackson's "Kitchen Cabinet" and a confidential friend of Johnson, edited both the *Congressional Globe* and the Washington *Globe*.

2. Samuel Casey of Kentucky was treasurer of the United States (1853–59). *Cong. Dir.* (1878), 229.

3. At this time Johnson held four of these notes, each worth $500, dated January 28, 1858, and payable one year after date. See Statement of Bonds, December 1, 1858.

4. Howell Cobb was Buchanan's secretary of the treasury.

5. The War of 1859, or the Austro-Franco-Sardinian War, April–July, 1859, was at its height as this letter was written.

6. Riggs and Company, banking and investment firm, had been established in the 1840's by William Wilson Corcoran and George Riggs. Green, *Washington*, I, 150, 264, 315.

7. On February 29, 1859, a special congressional committee appointed to investigate the accounts and conduct of former House clerk William Cullom exonerated him. Although Cullom (1810–1896), former Whig congressman from Tennessee (1851–55), was found negligent and careless in performing certain duties, there was no evidence to indicate that he was corrupt or dishonest. Rives, who had pushed the investigation in the *Globe*, printed on April 28, 1859, a lengthy review and rebuttal, which was excerpted and appeared in the Nashville *Union and American* over a period of several days in June. Rives probably refers to a reprint of this April 28 issue, but he may be alluding to a pamphlet which he printed for Robert Mayo, compiler of pension and bounty laws, entitled . . . *A Review of the report of Hon. Horace Maynard, Chairman of the Committee of investigation into the conduct and accounts of William Cullom . . . and an exposition of the frauds practiced on the Treasury . . . by the said William Cullom* (Washington, D. C., 1859). *Cong. Globe*, 35 Cong., 2 Sess., 1467; *House Report* No. 188, 35 Cong., 2 Sess.; *BDAC*, 762; Nashville *Union and American*, June 2, 3, 4, 1859.

8. These anticipated civil indictments evidently did not materialize.

9. The impetus to an investigation had been provided on this date when Rives published a lengthy exposition by Robert Mayo, along with an editorial, charging Cullom with attempting to defraud the government. Washington *Globe*, December 7, 1857.

10. Shakespeare, *Hamlet*, Act III, sc. 1.

From Isham G. Harris

                                        Nashville   July 7th 1859.

Hon Andrew Johnson,

My, Dear Sir,

From an interview with some of the Members of the Central Committee[1] I supposed that arrangements were made to get up barbecues in a number of the strong democratic Counties and invite you to address the people, I cannot learn that any thing has been done in this respect. If there have been no arrangements made to this effect I think it would be well for you to make a number of appointments in strong democratic Counties and make speeches in them before the election. The only thing we have to fear is inaction on the part of our friends, we are stronger than at any previous period in our history, but over Confidence and inaction may produce a result which will cause us to regret our lethergy. I am satisfied that we can increase our Majority if we can get the vote out.

The opposition are putting their volenteers in the field, and I shall be pleased to hear that you & Nicholson are out at the earliest day which You may find convenient.[2]

                        Very truly & Respectfully   Your friend
                                                Isham G Harris

I would suggest McMinn, Franklin, Lincoln, Marshall, Hickman, Dickson, Sumner and overton, and such other Counties as you may think proper, dispatch Central Committee the times and places that you can attend and they will arrange to give you a crowd.

                                                        Isham G. Harris

ALS, DLC-JP.

1. A fifteen-member central committee consisting of five representatives from each of the three grand divisions of Tennessee had been selected at the Democratic convention in Nashville, March 10, 1859. Nashville *Union and American*, March 11, 1859.

2. Although Senator Nicholson made several speeches in late July and early August, Johnson was conspicuously, even embarrassingly, absent. Nashville *Union and American*, July 30, August 1, 1859; Nashville *News*, July 14, 28, August 2, 1859; Nashville *Patriot*, July 28, 1859.

From John C. Rives

                                          Washington, 15th July, 1859.

Hon. Andrew Johnson
Greeneville, Tenn

Sir: I did not receive your letter of the 10th instant, until yesterday evening, after banking hours, when I could not procure a draft on New-York.

The money I borrowed from you on the 28th of last December had entirely escaped my memory, until it was refreshed by your letter. I hope you have not needed the money; only your modesty prevented your asking me for it. You now, ask me for it very modestly, by saying you wish it *"if convenient."*

Inclosed is a draft on New-York for $1910^{24}/100, the amount of my note for $1850, and interest from the 28th of December, 1858 until to-day. I find I should have added four days interest, to allow for the time it will take for the draft to reach you. Four days' interest is $1^{24}/100, which I inclose in postage stamps, which you do not need, but some of your constituents will need them.

I hope Harris will be re-elected Governor, & that Maynard[1] will be beaten for Congress. If the election shall result so thus far, I can very well bear the defeat of several members of the last Congress from Tennessee[.] I would rather lose all of them than Geo. W. Jones.[2] He would be worth more to the Government, in my opinion, than the whole of the Tennessee Delegation in the House of Reps, and half the Delegation in the Senate to boot,: I mean the *Nicholson half.*[3]   I am &C.

                                                        John C. Rives.

ALS, DLC-JP2.

1. Horace Maynard (1814–1882), a Massachusetts native, came to Knoxville to teach mathematics at the University of East Tennessee (1839–44). Admitted to the bar in 1844, he turned to politics, was elected to Congress,

first on an "Opposition" ticket and later as a Radical Republican (1857–63, 1866–75), and served as the state's wartime attorney general (1863–65), minister to Turkey (1875–80), and U. S. postmaster general (1880–81). Mary U. Rothrock, *The French Broad-Holston Country: A History of Knox County, Tennessee* (Knoxville, 1946), 453–54; *BDAC*, 1280; *DAB*, XII, 460–61.

2. Having served since 1843, when he and Johnson entered Congress, Jones had announced that he would not seek reelection in 1859. Fayetteville *Lincoln Journal*, March 24, 1859.

3. There are several possible explanations for Rives' disenchantment with Nicholson. Not only had they been rival Washington editors—Rives of the *Globe* and Nicholson of the *Union*—but also competitors for the post of Senate printer, won by Nicholson in 1855. Perhaps the feud came to a climax between 1857 and 1859, when Rives lost a bitter battle over government printing contracts to Cornelius Wendell, Nicholson's successor as *Union* editor. With considerable accuracy, Rives regarded Nicholson as Wendell's principal spokesman in the Senate. *Senate Report* No. 205, 36 Cong., 1 Sess., 106–15, 191–94, 200; *Cong. Globe*, 34 Cong., 1 Sess., 322.

From George W. Jones

Fayetteville Tennessee
August 9, 1859

Dear Sir,

Your favor of the 6th instant was received last night. I regret that Genl Milligan's letter to the editor of the Journal[1] has not yet reached him. The paper will be printed tomorrow, and the election will be held on Saturday next.

I have Spoken of Genl Milligan here as [a] gentleman of fine Capacity, excellent legal attainments, of good habits and morals, a Sound democrat and an honest man, who in my opinion, if elected would make an excellent Attorney General and Reporter for the State. It is my intention to vote for him. John W. Head Esqr,[2] was here the day the candidates for Governor Spoke in this place. The crowd was larger, and he made a good impression, and that was before even I was aware that Genl. Milligan was a Candidate. The vote in this county will be very light. No interest is manifested in the election or its result. I wish it was otherwise, but it cannot be helped. Well, the State and congressional elections are over, true, the exact results not Known. But admitting the most favorable result to the Democratic party which the few returns received indicate, the election of Governor Harris by a decreased majority, a Democratic minority in each branch of the Legislature and a delagation in Congress equally divided,[3] And the enquiry naturally presents itself what of principle has been gained or established? What good is to result to the great laboring, toiling, producing, and governed masses, by this Democratic triumph in Tennessee? Are these rights to be better protected, their burdens lightened and they secured in the quiet and peacefull enjoyment of all the products of their toil, except just so much of the proceeds thereof, as may be absolutely necessary for the proper and economical administration of that government established avowedly for their benefit? Alas for human deceit and credulity. I fear not. My observation and experience almost prompt me to Say I Know not. These are the Staple themes of most candidates during the canvass, Ambitious aspirants are profuse and liberal, in professions, promises and pledges, the people are confiding. Many of the chosen when in position act as they are acted. They seem to forget the people and their interests, by whose votes, they are empowered to inflict evils upon their benefactors, their creators.

The great error of the year and the canvas was committed by the Nashville Convention of March 17th which nominated Gov. Harris, in not clearly, explicitly and without doubt or equivocation, placing the democratic party in its true position upon the currency question, gold and Silver the legitimate currency of the Constitution.[4] As Mr. Webster said about 1811, "Gold and Silver is the law of the land at home and the law of the world abroad."[5]

THE CONSTITUTION IS THE TRUE DEMOCRATIC PLATFORM, and which is based upon *Individu[al] and State rights, a gold and silver Currency, an economical government, low taxes and no exclusive privileges.* And upon that platform the Democracy could have won the field in Tennessee on thursday last. But as it is they will I suppose have the honor and responsibility of administering the State government for the coming two years, and during the session of the Legislature just elected, will be perpetrated in the name of Democracy, the folly, absurdity and enormity of infusing a new and extended existence to those corrupt paper money manufactories, the Union and the Planters Bank. We can but exclaim, "Shake not thy gory locks at me. Thou Can'st not say I did it![”][6] Present my congratulations to Bob on his success.[7] But with my experience I would hesitate long before advising a young friend to launch his bark upon the boisterous and uncertain ocean of politics.

I should be very glad to see [you], and if I could know certainly when you will be in Nashville will endeavor to meet you, but would much prefer for you to come this way, the cars are now running within three miles of this place and on Friday the 19th instant, there is to be a great rail road jubilee here to celebrate the advent of the Horse of Iron into this our good town of Fayetteville. Can you not come and exchange congratulations with you[r] friends who will be pleased to meet you.[8] Come by all means.

Quiet retirement seems to agree with me. My health, I flatter myself is better than it has been for years, I have no regrets at being out of Congress. But, being out of employment—having nothing to do, is not altogether so pleasant. But I must make the best of it I can, and try to find some way to Keep off "THE BLUES" that is as much as possible.

With assurances of my best wishes for the success and happiness of you and yours,

You will believe me   Very truly Your friend
G. W. Jones

Hon Andrew Johnson
Greeneville   Tennessee

ALS, DLC-JP.

1. A reference to the *Lincoln Journal* of Fayetteville, a newspaper published from 1858 to 1860.

2. John W. Head (1821–1874), Sumner County lawyer, defeated Sam Milligan for attorney general of Tennessee in 1859 and served until the outbreak of the Civil War. He published three volumes of *Head's Reports* and in 1873 was a member of the state court of arbitration. Elected to the 44th Congress as a Democrat, he died before he could take his seat in 1875. *Cong. Dir.* (1903), 588; McGavock, *Pen and Sword*, 532n; Jay G. Cisco, *Historic Sumner County* (Nashville, 1909), 264.

3. Although Harris' majority was considerably less than his 11,000 vote margin in 1857, and only four of the ten congressmen elected were Democrats, the composition of the new legislature was safely Democratic—senate 14 to 9 and house 73 to 30. *Tenn. Official Manual* (1890), 170, 177; Nashville *Republican Banner*, August 11, 1859.

4. The previous fall, a Democratic committee of which Johnson was a member had drafted a statement against rechartering the banks and in favor of a "sound circulating medium, convertible at all times into gold and silver." See The Tennessee Democracy on Banks and Currency, September 22, 1858.

5. Jones exhibits a good memory for substance but a poor one for time. On February 28, 1816, during the course of debate on the re-establishment of a national bank, Webster was reported to have said: "Gold and silver currency . . . was the law of the land at home, and the law of the world abroad; there could, in the present state of the world, be no other currency." *Annals of Cong.*, 14 Cong., 1 Sess., 1092; Charles M. Wiltse to Andrew Johnson Project, August 11, 1971.

6. In addressing Banquo's ghost, Macbeth says, "Thou canst not say I did it: never shake Thy gory locks at me." Act III, sc. 4.

7. Robert Johnson had been successful in his bid for the state legislature.

8. The celebration went off as scheduled, but accounts give no evidence that Johnson attended. Nashville *Union and American*, August 21, 1859.

To [Harvey T. Phillips, Chattanooga][1]

Greeneville Tenn   August 15th/59

(*Strictly Confidential*)

My dear Sir

Your favor of the 13th inst was received in due Course of mail and Carefully read and the Subject matter of it duly Considered. In reply I Cannot do otherwise than be Candid and frank with you and in being So I am compelled to Say that I never was and never expect to be an aspirant to the presidency of the United States— I know however that there are Some who consider the presidency the Summit of all human greatness and honor and who have pursued it as the leading object of their ambition without regard to the first principles of the Government or measures that were consonant to them; in fact abandoning every thing to policy and mere questions of expediency, So as to enable them to accomplish their desired end.[2] If the presidency Could be conferred upon one who is not an aspirant as an incident flowing from the pursuit of correct principle and the Support of Sound measures Calculated in their bearing to promote our democratic form of Government and to advance the happiness, peace and prosperity of the whole people; it would then be desirable and acceptable, and in no other way— Principle and measures that are Sound and just in themselves Should be the objects pursued by evey honest statesman looking upon po[li]tical honor and preferment as mere Collaterals resulting from a faithful and consistent adhererance to them— *If* I *were* an aspirant upon the principles herein indicated, I feel well assured that I could not be nominated upon them by the Charleston convention, as parties now stand, and if nominated, Could not be elected in my opinion. The democratic party Cannot succeed in the next presidential Contest unless there is some reaction in public sentiment to the north on the question of Slavery and that is hardly to be expected during the next presidential Canvass involving the Subject of the highest importance to the whole South— Notwithstanding I feel and think that the chances in the next Contest are against the democratic party; I am Clear and decided in my own mind as to the propriety and Correctness of the South nominating a Candidate from a slave holding State — The idea that the South to Secure strength to the north must run a northern man is utopian— As parties now stand a Sothern man Can get as m[an]y votes in the free States as any Candidate in a free State who entertains the same opinions and sentiments— And if we are to be defeated it would be far better with a Southeren man as our standard bearer with issues distinctly made up and principles well defined and laid down So that the whole Country and especially the South might know what to depend upon in the future. I am for a Southern man as the standard bearer of the democracy let the Consequences be what they may— The South will lose nothing even in defeat, if She is only united, and if not united She will find out who are her enemies at home as well as in the nonslaveholding States; a fact the sooner it is developed the better for the whole Country and especially those North & South who have Spent their whole lives and all their energies in trying to Sustain the institution of

Slavery, in the South— The time has arrived when there should be no evasion; when there should be no deception practiced by either the north or the South, the one upon the other—in regard to the institution of Slavery— If the Goverment cannot be administered upon the principles as laid down in the Constitution and the institutions recognised by it mantained in their purity free from encroachment by the one or the other Sections, it is high time the great mass of the people understood it, so that the proper remedy Could be provided and that in due time— I have an abiding Confidence in their wisdom and descretion and in their determination to preserve the principles of this Government as develped in the Constitution of the United States—

I am aware as remarked in your letter that my name has been favorably mentioned through the press in various portions of the United States in Connection with the next presidency of the United States, and I will further add that it has not been brought about by any procurement of mine or that of my friends, which places me in a condition to appreciate it much higher than I otherwise would— Notwithstanding the favorable mention of the press as well as the reception of flattering and encouraging letters on the Subject, *I have never for one moment permitted* myself to entertain the *bewildering idea* of being an aspirant for presidential honors— It has been my determination as a public man to act upon principle and to serve the people with whatever efficiency I could in the faithful discharge of my duty as their Servent or agent, and feel that I have no right to disqualify myself as a faithful public Servent or agent by bearing [*sic*] of my own volition an aspirant for the presidency, and never shall—

According to my [o]bservation most public men, though usful, consistent and faithful before becoming aspirants for the first honors of the nation, have after fixing theirs eyes upon the presidency of the U. S. ceased longer to be worth a[n]y thing to the people as a faithful representative— Being president is the leadig notion and evey interest & energy of the mind is made to bend to the one single idea of being president of the U. S; A man who will abandon principle and the Support of Sound measures to attain the presidency ought not to be trusted by the people for he will betray them when ever there is an opportunity for doing So— And I fear the man who is honest and who is Controlled by principle and is willing to stand or fall upon measures that are right in themselves Cannot succeed in being brought before the people by national Conventions as they are gotten up in moderen times— For it does seem that the man who has most merit and strength before the people has the least chance befor a Convention as they are now Conducted by the respective parties of the Country— Of this though I shall not more complain and be prepared to takes things as they Come good, bad or indifferent—[3]

I have, I hope made my self understood in regard to my being a Candidate before the next Charleston Convention— I cannot and will not take any steps in placing my name before that or any other Convention which may be gotton up— If it goes there it must be the act of others not mine— If presidential honors ever *beset* my *path* it must be upon the principles laid down in the foregoing part of this letter *and none other*—

You will please accept my thanks for the kind maner in which you have been pleased to allude in your letter with respect to my name in Connection with the presidency and the interest you feel and seem willing to take in promoting my presidential aspirations if I had any—

I have the honor most respectfully &c—
Andrew Johnson

P. S. I hope you will pardon this incoherent Scrawl as it is with much difficulty that I write atall—
This letter was written some days since and supposed that I had mailed it; but was placed among some lose letters lying upon my table and was not discovered till this moment Sundy 20th—

ALS, Nathaniel E. Stein Col.

1. Harvey T. Phillips (b. *c*1824), a native of New York, was Chattanooga postmaster (1853–61) and the editor of the Chattanooga *Advertiser* during the late 1850's. 1860 Census, Tenn., Hamilton, 102; Zella Armstrong, *History of Hamilton County and Chattanooga, Tennessee* (2 vols., Chattanooga, 1940), I, 140; II, 142, 180; *Goodspeed's Hamilton*, 935.
2. A but thinly veiled allusion to Stephen A. Douglas, whose open candidacy for the nomination displeased Johnson.
3. A near rendering of "good—bad—indifferent or not indifferent" from Laurence Sterne, *Tristram Shandy*, Bk. III, ch. 2.

Real Estate Bond[1]

August 20, 1859

I Andrew Johnson bind myself to pay James F. Kirk[2] the Sum of one thousand Dollars— The condition of this obligation is Such, that whereas the Said James F. Kirk has this day purchased of me for Five hundred Dollars, for which he has executed his notes under Seal, one for two hundred Dollars, twelve months after date, from this day, and one for Three hundred Dollars, Twelve Months after date from this day, Said notes bearing interest from date, a lot or parcel of land Situated on Water Street in the town of Greeneville County of Greene & State of Tennessee, Known and designated in the plan of Said town as part of lot number Sixty eight, it being the Same whereon the Shop of Andrew Johnson, (and now occupied by Genl Sam Milligan as a Law Office) and the house in which Mrs. Whitesides[3] lived, now Stands, Beginning at the corner of the lot now owned by John A. and Joseph R. Brown on Main Cross Street, thence South Sixty nine degrees East to Water Street, thence with Said Street north twenty one degrees East four poles and eight links to a Stake—then North Sixty nine degrees west to the aforesaid John A and Joseph R Brown's lot, thence with Said lot to the Beginning—containing Seventeen poles more or less. Now if I should make or cause to be made to the Said James F. Kirk, his heirs or assigns a good and sufficient title in fee Simple with general warranty, to said lot or parcel of land, on the making of the last payment, then this obligation to be void. This 20th day of August 1859

Andrew Johnson

Test
Robt Johnson.

DS, Johnson-Bartlett Col.
    1. The property involved is the tailor shop lot which Johnson had purchased from the Jacob L. Wyrick estate in 1831. It is interesting to note that he seems to have paid only $51 for what he was now selling for $500, though a house may have been added.
    2. James Kirk (b. c1839) was a master shoemaker with personal wealth of $1300. 1860 Census, Tenn., Greene, 84.
    3. Sarah Whitesides (c1794–1854), Eliza Johnson's mother, had married John McCardle, Eliza's father, in 1809; after his death she became the wife of Moses L. Whitesides in 1833. Mrs. W. R. Hubbs, "The Genealogy of Andrew Johnson," November, 1958, 2–4, in Margaret Blanton Collection, University of Tennessee Library.

To Robert Johnson, Nashville

Greeneville Tenn   Oct 1st 1859—

My dear son
    Before you left for Nashvill I forgot to suggest to you the propriety of pressing upon Gov Harris the appointment of Major Mc-Gaughey[1] as one of the directors on the part of the State— I hope you will [go] at once and press his appointment[.] His term is about to expire and will be filled in a very short time— There is nothing new so far as I hear[.] Kingsly[2] as I understand this morning is about winding up— Mrs Cutler is about buying him out and McDannel has purchased the lot back he sold to him— I think when it is all closed up he Kingsly will be about closed out— His Career on the little Sum left him by his parents has been of Short duration

and not very brillian[t] at that— It would have been much better
for him to have started where he has ended without any thing and
have learned some sense— He is more an object of pitty than contempt— The town has reached its Swell at this time and will now
settle down upon its real basis as I think— Rambo[3] will wind up
next and that will be an end of him for the present and for this town
—[4] Little time will bring it all right— Do not forget the bonds I
spok to you about just before lea[v]ing—
  The family are all well—   Your father
                                                          Andrew Johnson
Robt Johnson Esqr   Nashville Tennessee

ALS, DLC-JP.
  1. Johnson's effort to have Major John McGaughey reappointed a director
of the East Tennessee and Virginia Railroad, a post he had held since 1851,
was apparently unsuccessful. James Holland, A History of Railroad Enter-
prises in East Tennessee (M. A. thesis, University of Tennessee, 1930), 215,
220, 418, 436; Nashville Union and American, October 26, 1859.
  2. Boswell J. Kingsly (b. c1837) was a Greeneville orphan who lived
with Mrs. Lucinda Cutler in 1850. 1850 Census, Tenn., Greene, 285.
  3. Probably John Rambo (b. c1833), originally a farmer in Sevier County, who was a merchant in several East Tennessee towns. Goodspeed's East
Tennessee, 1101.
  4. These two business failures may be seen as symptomatic of the levelling
off which Greeneville and other upper East Tennessee communities experienced after the completion of the East Tennessee and Virginia Railroad in
May, 1858.

From Robert Johnson

                                          Nashville Tenn   Oct 14th 1859
Dear Father,
  The State Fair opened last Monday, with a very small crowd—
I was out on Tuesday to hear Maury[1] deliver his address, there was
a large crowd in attendance, but they did not hear much of the
address, and I do not think it was anything extra, the idea of inviting
a Sailor, who has been on the high Seas since his boyhood, to deliver
an Agricultural address, at a state Fair, to say the least, is rediculous
— So far, my information is, that the Fair is a failure, I, have not
been out since Tuesday and cannot speak on my own Knowledge—
The Legislature is moving very slow— the members do not seem
inclined to work, and I am fearful there will not be much work done
soon[.] The public printing is exciting a good deal of uneasiness,
and at this time is in a considerable fog— The Memphis Appeal,
headed by J. Knox Walker,[2] as I am informed, is the formidable
competitor of the Union— The Douglass men are working hard to
get an entering wedge in— how successful they may be is uncertain

— the Democratic Members hold a meeting to-night to determine this question and also to nominate Comptroller, Secretary of State & Treasurer—

G. W. Bridges[3] of Athens is a Candidate for Comptroller and his chances are very flattering, and I believe will get the nomination[.] Ray[4] will be elected Secretary of State and McGregor[5] Treasurer— J. Lewis[6] of Knoxville is a candidate for Treasurer—

Dunnington has returned & seems to be very mad about Banks &C— I would not be surprised, if the Legislature Charter more Banks this session than at any previous one— even those members, that were above suspicion, are talking about compromise &c to save the unity & harmony of the party— Barksdale,[7] Guy,[8] of Hardeman, & myself stand out and I would not be surprised if we are the only ones that will hold out—

Britton[9] will vote any way, that he thinks is popular and I have no faith as to what he will do on any question— Jake Miller[10] is here, pressing the Legislature to repeal the act requiring Banks to pay out no bills but their own— Critz[11] introduced the Bill, and I presume [it] will pass— we are then back to the old *wild cat* system — Dunnington says he has lost confidence in all men and cannot rely on any person[.]

Excuse this, as the House is debating the question of the public printing and I have been interrupted at every line— Your friends are anxious to see you here[.]

no news—   Your son

                                                        Robt Johnson

ALS, DLC-JP.

1. Matthew Fontaine Maury (1806–1873) of Franklin was a naval officer whose writings on navigation and the sea had made him famous. Among his outstanding works were *A New Theoretical and Practical Treatise on Navigation*, *Wind and Current Chart of the North Atlantic* (Philadelphia, 1836), and *The Physical Geography of the Sea* (New York, 1855), the latter being the first textbook in modern oceanography. He served the Confederacy during the Civil War and spent his last years as a teacher at the Virginia Military Institute. *DAB*, XII, 429–31.

2. James Knox Walker (1818–1863), Memphis attorney and nephew and private secretary of President Polk, was a delegate from Shelby County to the Democratic convention at Nashville, January 18, 1860. When war came, he served as a colonel in the Confederate army. Nashville *Union and American*, January 19, 1860; *Goodspeed's Shelby*, 829.

3. George W. Bridges (1825–1873) of Athens, a district attorney general of Tennessee (1849–52, 1854–60), was an unsuccessful candidate for comptroller of the treasury in 1859, being defeated by the Democratic incumbent, James T. Dunlap. Elected to the 37th Congress, he was arrested by Confederates en route to Washington, but escaped in time to serve the last week of his term, after which he joined the Union army. In 1866 he was elected circuit judge of the fourth judicial district and served one year. *BDAC*, 596; McGavock, *Pen and Sword*, 439; *Tenn. Official Manual* (1890), 189.

4. J. E. R. Ray was elected secretary of state by the legislature in 1859. He served as a criminal judge in Shelby and later as a probate judge (1870–78). *Goodspeed's Shelby*, 815; *Tenn. Official Manual* (1890), 171.

5. W. F. McGregor, incumbent (1857–65), was reelected treasurer on October 29, 1859. *Ibid.*, 173; Nashville *Union and American*, October 30, 1859.

6. John F. J. Lewis (b. 1830), Knoxville lawyer and a Buchanan-appointed postmaster (1858–59), had been removed May 3, 1859. Principal editor of the Knoxville *Register* at this time, he later served in the Confederate army and was clerk of the county court (1874–86). *Goodspeed's Knox*, 995–96; Rothrock, *French Broad-Holston Country*, 538; Knoxville *Tri-Weekly Whig*, January 6, 13, April 9, 1859.

7. William H. Barksdale (c1835–1868), Sumner County lawyer, served in the Tennessee house (1859–61) and in the Confederate army (1861–64). Robison Biog. Data.

8. W. W. Guy (b. c1803), well-to-do Hardeman County farmer, with real estate worth $24,000 and personal property valued at $64,900, was in the Tennessee house (1859–61). 1860 Census, Tenn., Hardeman, 109.

9. James Britton, former sheriff (1840–46) and state senator, represented Greene County in the lower house (1859–61). *Goodspeed's East Tennessee*, 890; Temple, *Notable Men*, 51. See also *Johnson Papers*, I, 497n.

10. Jacob Miller, president of the Rogersville branch of the Bank of Tennessee, was probably the Jacob Miller (b. c1814) listed in the census with $14,000 personal and $12,000 real property. According to Brownlow, Miller was frequently "travelling back and forth from Hawkins to Nashville, on political business, at the expense of the bank." 1860 Census, Tenn., Hawkins, 201; Knoxville *Tri-Weekly Whig*, June 30, 1859.

11. Philip Critz of Hawkins County. See *Johnson Papers*, I, 33n.

From David F. Caldwell[1]

Greensboro N C Oct 15 59

Hon Andrew Johnston

Dear & much respected Sir; Your note of the 12 instant has been recieved, and I hasten to respond to the sam; When I wrote to the P M at greenvill I had received no answer to my letter, which had been written som four or five weeks. I could not account for your silence, but in two ways, 1st that you were absent, or, 2d that you did not care, or were desirous to have nothing more to do with me, in the way of corresponding. And I desired to know which of these motives, if [*sic*] influanced your action[.] For though I ranke myself above no honest man I am far from wishing to intrude myself upon the notice of any one[.] As you have delt frankely I have thus given you my motives for making the inquiry I did for your Post Master[.] I did not desire the *miserable Manuscript I sent you*[.] I wrote it in such great haste that on regaining it I am heartily ashamed of it— but the printed slip, I did not know how to get on with out, hence my annxiety for to recover it[.] I recieved your last letter & the communications, I mean the letter before the one received to day some four or five days since and I feel greatful to you for your kindness in returning them to me.

I am sory that you cannot see this matter in the light I do[.] I feel confident that I am right and if your next Legislature will but adopt & strictly adhead [adhere] to the system I proposed you will have no more *Bogus* Banks in Ten— The state & youre improvements will prosper and your people soon relieved from debt & heavy taxation—— I feel confident of this fact or I would not urge it upon you[.] I feel the more concerned about the matter, as I am seriously contemplating removing to Gibson county of your State, there to engage in the culivation of cotten & the practice of *the Law*[.] I dislike to sunder all the ties that bind me to my native state, but I have ma[n]y relatives and friends in Gibson who are doing well & press me strongly to emigrate and setel near them— assuring me that I can greatly benefit myself by so doing[.]² Under these circumstances I hope you will excuse me for troulig [troubling] you so much as I have done— I am so sure that I am right— that I cannot fail to be zelously efected when I look at the *Crisis* that will soon be upon your Legislature[.]³ If it were any thing else than chartering a Banke, it would not matter so much as if it did not suit the views of the Legislatur they could repeal the act when they conveaned again— but this is not the case by no means— what your Legislatur dose next winter will last through this generation & will tell for good or evil with great power[.] Wo[ul]d to *Heaven* all your people understood the great importance that attaches to the actions of there servants, touching this matter[.] I know they would ponder long before they would *submit* to having another bach of monopoly bogus banks chartered in your State[.] They are and will forever prove an unmitigated curse to any state[.] And I aver from my experiance that the stockholders in them where the Banks are chartered as yours & ours are, can controle all the financial affairs of the state throgh them that, they can not only accumilate great fortunes, but will certenly acquire influance enough to dictate to the Legislatur—& if they do not ultimately *break down* your Roads to purches them up like th[e]y did in Pensylvania⁴—it will be because they do not desire to exercise there power and capital in that way[.] But you are for a state sbutreasury. I am sory very sory my friend that you are anxious to place the Party in Tennesse on this platform. Pardon me for saying to you in all candor, that I honestly thinke it will prove most disasterous to the party[.] And I do hope you will ponder long before you take that, as I think, fatal step[.] Of course I cannot undertake to assign the reason, to you at the present time, that induces me to speake so confident on this point[.] But I am not prepared to say that the sub Treasury system would prove more disasterous than to continue the present monopoly Bogus system of Banking[.]

If you see Gov Harriss I hope you will prevale upon him to ponder long over the suggestions I have made— My observations my experiance & the time I have given to the investigation of this subject, I say it in all modesty, should induce him to give my suggestions some consideration— 1 A specie *Basis*— 2 State stocks, in R R compleated & in successful opperation, to be deposited with the P Treasry to double the amount of the capital of the Banke— 3 Then the liability clause—binding the individual property to double the [a]mount of the capital of the banke— 4 The Public Treasuer to register & counter sign all the notes of the Banke. Then limiting the divdends of the Banke & Roads to 7 per cent interest per Anum untill they the Road & Banke had each on hand a surplus fund of $100,000— This would give such confidence in the solvency of the Bankes & Roads as to throw up the stock in both far above par —& thus gradually but certenly advance the credit & prosperity of you[r] noble State—while at the same time, it would give you, A SOUND CONVERTABLE UNIFORM CURRENCY that would command a premium over the circulation of all the others in your State—as the R R Banks in Georgia during the last panic[.][5] Why is this I will try to explain[.] 1st Then the Banke is required to do as it would be done by[.] That is Besides the principal all banks require two suretes to sign all notes discounted and the rule is that the principle shall be solvent—the capital—and that each surety shall be worth double the amount loaned—the liabilty claus & the R R Stock— The Banks consiquently—in fact never when they adhear to this rule loose a debt— See my report as to the safty of Banking[.][6] So if the Legislature will require the capital to be paid in to the vaults of the Bank in spece—then require the stock in corporated roads to be deposited & the liabilty clause thus engrafted in the charter the public will see that the security is such that there is no chance for any creditor of the banke to loose a cent by it— And as Banks do not create public credit but live & thrive on it—it is all important to keep there credit up above par if we wish them to prosper and benifit the public[.] The Banks charterd thus would have the credit—to draw into ther valts all the money *as deposits*[.] This taken with the revenue of the roads would enable the Bank to discount to producers who brought in freight to the road freely[.] This would enable the Banks to draw upon the produce sent to market—especaly cotten &C and as there interest lay in this way— the Bankes would benefit the count[r]y by encouraging the Planter's Miners Manufactu[rer]s & Mecanics—with all others who produced or brought forward freight to the Road or roads— These positions cannot be successfully refuted—though all interested in the old Bogus corporations will cry out that the stocke in such banke cant or wont be taken[.] These have none— But it will be taken—but I must reluctanly close[.] If any member of your Legislature desires any aid I can give him if he will let me kno I will try & acomodat him if he will let me know it[.]

D. F. C

ALS, DLC-JP. Printed in Elizabeth Gregory McPherson, "Letters from North Carolina to Andrew Johnson," *North Carolina Historical Review*, XXVII (1950), 337–39.

1. It is difficult to understand why David F. Caldwell (1814–1898), an old-line Whig who had represented Guilford County in the house of commons (1848–58), was writing a friendly letter of advice to Johnson. Perhaps Caldwell, like other disillusioned Whigs, was flirting with the Democratic party. This letter seems designed not only to promote his pet banking ideas but also to be concerned with strengthening the Tennessee Democracy. With the coming of the war, Caldwell, a Unionist, held aloof from the Confederacy until drafted in 1864. During Reconstruction his posture was that of a moderate Republican. *North Carolina Manual* (1913), 634–35; David F. Caldwell to John Sherman, January 18, March 8, 1867, in James A. Padgett, "Reconstruction Letters from North Carolina," *North Carolina Historical Review*, XVIII (1941), 289–92, 294–97.

2. Caldwell did not remove to Tennessee.

3. With the collapse of many banks and the suspension of specie payment by others during the Panic of 1857, the demand for reform reached a peak during the gubernatorial campaign of 1859. Prior to 1860, Tennessee banks operated as purely speculative ventures, since the stockholders were not liable for losses. During periods of inflation banks issued paper currency far in excess of specie reserve; during depressions they could transfer their capital to various eastern banks and charge noteholders from 3 to 10 per cent premium to redeem their own notes. Pursuant to Governor Harris' campaign pledges, the General Assembly of 1859–60 enacted some genuine reforms. One law forbade banks to issue more than twice their specie reserve in currency or to circulate notes not payable at their own counters. A minimum capital requirement of $300,000 was set. Campbell, *Banking*, 147–49, 152–53.

4. During the administration of Governor James Pollock (1856–58), Pennsylvania sold all its state-owned railroads, canals, and other segments of its public works system to the Pennsylvania Railroad and the Philadelphia & Erie Railroad lines, an action which had reduced the state debt and eventually led to the repeal of state taxation. George P. Donehoo, ed., *Pennsylvania: A History* (7 vols., New York, 1926), III, 1407, 1412–13.

5. Although the Panic of 1857 caused many other banking institutions to suspend specie payment, the Central of Georgia Railroad and Banking Company had surpassed the earnings of other leading railroads, suggesting an over-all solvency. Amanda Johnson, *Georgia as Colony and State* (2 vols., Atlanta, 1938), I, 388, 410.

6. Caldwell, a member of the committee on corporations and currency during 1856–57, filed a minority report urging the passage of a bill to charter a "People's Bank"—a proposal on which the majority had reported unfavorably. Advocating the creation of a large state bank with branches over the state, he contended that "there is no other business, taking one year after another, that is so profitable as banking." A people's bank, he reasoned, would check irregularities, provide a sound currency, and avoid burdensome direct taxes. *North Carolina House of Commons Journal*, 1856–57, Doc. No. 29, pp. 1–7.

From David F. Caldwell

Greensboro N C Oct 18 59

Hon A Johnson

Dear Sir: Your favor of the 14th is just to hand and I hasten to respond to the same[.] I am truly *sorry* to find that a letter that I wrote to you in the *kindest spirit*—and particularly as an apology to you, for writing the letter of enquiry I did to your Post Master, should now call for an apolgy from me— I voluntary for the reasons stated in my last wrote you several letters[.] In one of these I enclosed you a printed communication which I requested to return to me when you had red it—stating at the time that I had no copy of it, and would soon have a demand for it[.] I waited for it for some time[.] it did not come in to hand[.] I then wrote you a polite note requesting you to return the same[.] I received no reply to that note[.] I then thinking you might like many other leading men, be from home or on a visit to a distant state I ventured to write to the P M to assertain whither you were absent as I suposed— I received no answer to my note to the P M[.] I then thinking my letters might have miscarried I concluded to wite to you again which note you answd & made every necessary explanation, and the other day all the manuscript, with the printed slips came safely to hand[.] I certenly have no cause to *complain* of you or your conduct[.] And I hope you will sensure me for nothing I have said or done as I certenly have not intended at any time to cast any blame on you— I thought at one time before I received your letter before the last, that there was so much trechery abroad in this land and *Wise* & *Donley* corrospondants[1] that you might be a little julus [jealous] of my position motives & honor and that such motives had caused you to pass by [my] letter & request in silence— That is the honest thought I ever entertained touching the matter— And had you entertaind such motives I could not under all the circumstans have blamed you[.] If the above is not sufficiently *explicit* and poligistic be kind enough to inform me in what point it is deficent[.] I will strive to amend it untill you shall in evey particular be *satisfied*[.] I will conclude if I can at any time or in any way be of any service to you or yours I shall be proud to serve you— And 'till then I beg to remain truly yours

D. F. Caldwell

Hon A Johnson
Greenvl Ten

ALS, DLC-JP. Printed in McPherson, "Letters to Andrew Johnson, " 339–40.

1. The unauthorized publication of private correspondence between Virginia Governor Henry A. Wise and Bernard Donnelly, a New York builder and supporter of the governor's presidential aspirations, had created a minor tempest in the Democratic party. Hopeful of widespread southern support at the upcoming Charleston convention, Wise was politically embarrassed by the wide dissemination of his letter, which condemned Douglas' platform as "a short cut to all the ends of Black Republicanism." Despite his attempts at explanation, Wise had ruined his chances at Charleston and heightened the atmosphere of suspicion and hostility in the party. New York *Herald*, August 4, 11, 1859; Nashville *Patriot*, August 9, 11, 1859; *Trow's New York City Directory* (1858–59), 221; Milton, *Eve of Conflict*, 373.

To Robert Johnson, Nashville

Greeneville Tenn   Oct 20th 1859

My dear Son,

Your letters dated 14th & 17th inst were both received by Tuesdys nights' mail and were read with Some interest— I was almost Surprised to find that the other Two divisions of the State had conceeded a[n]y of the appointments to the east end of the State— The Geologist[1] and a door keeper from Bradly[2] I think constitute the whole— A very liberal divide indeed, especially so when all the other appointments are considered— Dr Crawford I presume will make as good a Geolgist as Safford[3] if not better— If making out a report composed of unpronouncable Technicalities and Speculative theories is whats required Craford or Fout[4] will make first rate Geologists— In this point of view the appointment of Dr Crawford is a good one— The reports to the Legislature have been but little else than a mere report to print, filled up with matters of but little interest to the people at large— In fact the office ought to be abolished togeth[er] with that of the Commission of Roads and I would press their repeal[5] notwithstanding an E. T. man had obtained the appointment— It is an unnecessry expense upon the state and one from which the people derive no benefit— They will press the propriity of Comple[tin]g the survy and all that: but if the office of Geologist is never abolished until the survey is completed it will not be done until the Union is disolved— Robert, G. Payne Esqr, I see has introdu[ce]d a bill to increase the rate of interest from Six to ten percent,[6] to be greed upon at the time the money is loaned by the parties— I have but one word to Say in reference to the bill, and that is, I would support no bill changing the rate of intere[st] at this time— I know that there can be much said of such a measure: but it has to be said and the public mind prepared before the public mind would be reconciled to it, and especially so in this part of the State— The Argument is a strong one and hard to answer: why a person should not be allowed to sell his money for as much as it would bring in market as much so as he would his corn or wheat &c, and be Governed by the same law of Supply and demand— In argument to conceed the one is a concesion of the other— I am not sure that because wheat or corn should become scarce that the holder of it in strict justice has any right to take more than ordinay prices for it— the holder on account of its great scarcity has no right to extort more than a fair price from the bra[y]ing stomachs of a Suffering community than a remuniratig price, yet it is very often done— It is always safest to be first certain that the thing or principle we assume to Justify another by is right in itself and that it can [be] defended as such before an honest community— Infine I would let those who thought proper at the present increase the rate of interest— It is safe to go against it and might require a great deal [of] expla[na]tion of those who voted for it—

I would oppose the recharter of the Union & Planters Banks to the very last and all other corporations of like character— I would prepare a bill incorporating a compa[n]y to loan "Cash" or Gold & Silver at the same rate of interest proposed by the union & Planters Banks, and would show among other things that the present system of Banking was nothig more nor less than p[a]ying a premium of two percent for depreciated paper money to the exclusion of G[o]ld &c— I would there was enogh Gold & Silver to answer the purposes of the cou[n]try and then the Gold & Silver ought to be loaned instead of paper to the people— Your bill might be denominated a "Fiscal agent, to, aid in the managment of the finances of the state, to loan Gold & Silver, to receve the same on deposite and issue Certifficats therefor"—or some other caption indicating the purpose of the bill— I see in the last Bank report made by Col Johnson[7] to the Legislature that he is almost out in favor of a Bullion Bank as they are Some times called— See pages 12 & 13— The second paragraph from the top of page 13 he looks to the bank of the Tennessee being converted into a mere fi[s]cal agent of the state or the simple sub treasur system as recommended by the Secretry of the Treasuy[8] to the first Session of the last Congress— You will See also by refernce to the Bank report, that it is shown that the Bank has in Specie some 400,000 $ more than—circulation—
This fact shows that the State Bank could loan more hard money than it does in paper: if this is so, why not loan the Gold & Silver to the people and take there paper in— Col Johnson I see is dead against the two "Stock Banks["] and would no doubt be willing to unite with the hard mony men rathr than see them recharted, and would no

doubt prefer seeing the State Bank converted into and independnt Treasuy System or a Bullion Bank than to see them Succeed— If he and the "dependents" of the State Bank could be made to take a position of this kind it would greatly help the hard mony men in the Legislature— In connection with the hard money notion, I would call your attention to a letter of Mr Jefferson written to Mr Eppes in 1813[9] some 46 years ago in which he suggest[ed] the whole idea of a Bullion Bank— The whole letter is an instructive one and can be read with profit: but more especially the last paragraph of the letter, save one— See 6th vol page 247—Jeffersons works—[10] Infine upon the Subject of currency and Banks I hope that you will give it a carefull and thorough consideration—and then act upon principle and do it with firmness and boldness— If there is no other member in the Legislature who oppose Banks and the're foul appliances I hope you will be that man, let the consequences be what they m[a]y. As to Major Britton he has not sense enough to understand the question and if he did has not independence enough to act it out— So he is not fit for a guide in this nor any other question. Howe[ve]r it would be better if he could be controlled with out much trouble and thereby prevent conflict at home among your constituents— Theres is no fear of this question before the people and it would be as feeble in the hands of Britton as a[n]y other man in the State— Mr Jacob Miller is the last man that should exert influence with any body— He never was for [or] opposed to a[n]y thing upon principle: but on the contrary is alwys controlled by Some corrupt consideration— Neither the democratic nor the opposition party have any confidence in him and especially on the Bank question — Bank democrats and democrats who have Banks to control are very much like putting virtuous females in houses of illfame to protect their honesty and purity of character— They may enter virtuous women: but they never fail to come out prostitutes of the most accomplished order— Instead of removing any of the restrictions now placed upon the state and other banks I would put more upon theme and still more stringent in their character than they are now—

The Court is moving along slowly[.] nothing of much importance has been done that I now remember— I have heared little or no inquiry about the Legislature among the people— I do not to [sic] remember to have heard one single person s[a]y a word about the mess[a]ge—[11] I think the message a pretty good one as it is and would have been [a] most excellent one if [it] had taken the [public?] or open ground for a ha[r]d mony currency— On last night Miss Em Mulony and Mrs [sic] Rossenblat[12] eloped for the purpose of marrying and it is supposed they have accomplished it— Muley takes it pretty much as [a] Joke, Mrs Muley let on some as I understand, not to hard I imagine though— There has been some frost a few mor[nin]gs back[.]

Truly &c   Andrew Johnson

ALS, CSmH-Misc. #8206.

1. Apparently the Democratic caucus had agreed upon Dr. Sean P. Crawford (b. *c*1824), a Greeneville physician, as candidate for state geologist; but East Tennessee was denied even that appointment, since the office was abolished in February, 1860. 1860 Census, Tenn., Greene, 82; White, *Messages*, V, 213.

2. The "door keeper" was actually an assistant house clerk, John A. Campbell, of Bradley County. *Tenn. House Journal*, 1859–60, p. 8.

3. James M. Safford (1822–1907), state geologist (1854–60, 1871–1900), educated at Ohio State and Yale, taught at Cumberland University (1847–72) and the University of Nashville (1872–1900). He published widely on the geology of Tennessee; his official report of 1856 is considered perhaps the best of the contemporary state reports. *DAB*, XVI, 286–87.

4. George Foute, a Greeneville physician. See *Johnson Papers*, I, 333n.

5. Ten days earlier Robert Johnson had introduced "An act to abolish the office of Geologist and Mineralogist of the State." Ultimately the office was discontinued as the result of a measure originally introduced in the senate and supported principally by Democrats. A similar attempt to abolish the office of road commissioner failed. *Tenn. Acts*, 1859–60, Ch. XXIV; White, *Messages*, 209, 213; *Tenn. Senate Journal*, 1859–60, p. 42; *Tenn. House Journal*, 1859–60, pp. 158, 842.

6. Payne, former road commissioner now serving in the senate (1859–61), was successful in raising the permissible interest rate. *Tenn. Acts*, 1859–60, Ch. XLI.

7. Cave Johnson's report is in *Tenn. House Journal*, 1857–58, App. 3–13.

8. Howell Cobb.

9. Jefferson to John W. Eppes, November 6, 1813, in Washington, *Writings of Thomas Jefferson*, VI, 228–47.

10. A marginal notation, evidently prompted by this reference to Jefferson's writings, reads as follows: "What has become of the 1st & 2d vol of Jefferson's works—I cannot find them—"

11. Governor Isham G. Harris' message to the legislature, October 4, 1859. White, *Messages*, V, 100–132.

12. Emma (b. *c*1842), daughter of John Maloney, Greeneville innkeeper, and P. D. Rosenblatt, German-born silversmith and watchmaker, were living in Maloney's hotel in 1860. 1850 Census, Tenn., Greene, 278; 1860 Census, Tenn., Greene, 94; Greeneville *New Era*, July 8, 1865.

From Thomas H. Hopkins[1]

La Mesilla   New Mexico
Novr 22d. 1859.

Governor Andrew Johnson
Senitor in Congress:

My Dear Sir:

It is not all the Sophistry of big or little Politicians of these times as written & printed about Squatter Sovreignty or popular Sovreignty that induces me to write you now, nor is it your own more statesmanlike notions in nobly and Manly taking the great broad ground of *American Sovreignty* as I once heard you, and I was proud to hear you Say, Americans were alike Sovreign, whether Squating in the Territories, lying down in the states, or standing up in the Federal Capital;[2] it is that bold and fearless advocacy of the Sovreign rights of the whole American & Sovreign people, that places you high, and will place you higher in their good feelings and insure you their Support. I have always believed that the government was equally bound to protect the rights of a single citizen, as that citizen was bound to protect the government, that all those rights and duties were reciprical and mutual, but pardon a slight Digression.

I came out here in april 1857 with the appointment of a *Special Agency* of the P. O. Dept Signed by A V Brown P M Genl and Seal of the Department, dated 31st March 1857, and on the first of April a letter of Appointment Signed by H King first Asst P M Genl as *Local Mail* agent for New Mexico[.] I took the oath as Special Agent on the 1st day of April, yet in that oath of a special agent they use the word local Agent. my salary was fixed at $1600 per anum the pay of special agent, & in nearly all the official correspondence directed to me is as *special agent* two commissions but with but one Salary, and that agency given to me for four years, was discontinued at the End of two years, the discontinuance taking effect the 31 of March 1859— but my object as you will perceive is not so much to complain of that sort of protection, which last[ed] but half the time agreed upon as this[.] *Special Agents* are beside their Salary Entitled to per diem pay of $2 per day—not one Cent of which have I Ever received, and it may be said that Special agents are only Entitled to this when *ordered* on special service, then I reply that I was ordered on special service on the 4th day of April before I left Washington by a letter of Instructions from the office of the Chief Clerk;[3] directing me to aid in the recovery of the Stolen property taken by the thieves who it was reported had Robed the post office at Santa Fe in the month of February preceeding[.] in this my attention was constantly bestowed but all the property never recovered, but I insist I am entitled to the per diem pay during the time Employed in my agency in New Mexico, and anxiously desire you and Judge Nicholson to aid me in recovering this my due or get an order for its allowance.

Beside I anxiously desire you to get for me some good office here or Elsewhere, some place that would pay $2500 or $3000. I would be willing to take a Judgeship here, if made or if as is supposed that Judge Wm F Boone[4] District Judge of the third District of New

Mexico now on his way to his home in Philadelphia is not going to return, and who is Exceedingly unpopular & Justly so, said to be corrupt and I know to be Exceed[ing]ly Ignorant as to Law & its practices[.] if he is not to return I would be willing to take his place, however if any other Similar or better place, can be procured, I would of course feel under peculiar obligations to my friends for it. In fact a land office Register and receiver has been appointed and Established here at Sata Fe, and to speak honestly and frankly to an honest friend, there is not and never has been the slightest use for them but little of the public land has been Surveyed, perhaps the Surveys of none of it completed none ever reported or proclaimed for sale, and I am inclined to think it will be some time before there will be much use for Regesters and receivers of public moneys, yet I commenced to say they were here at salaries of $2500 per anum Each and nothing to do, and that the Register is the son of Hon Thos Green Davidson M. C. from La'[.] the young Man here Mr Wm A Davidson is always drunk in debt & Engaged in Every sort of disipation, if this office is to be kept up & young Davidson is to go out, I would be glad to have that office, and can give the best of securiety here. I am satisfied that not only the Bar but the whole people here would be pleased to see me have a Judgeship &c.

a third favor I wish to ask of you is to write to me at Santa Fe, N. M the place of my residence and to send me such Documents as you may think proper.

Now a word as to this Arizonia country. I have no certain information as to the population but from the best information I can get take it to be 10,000 or 12000. I have no doubt a good deal of it is fine pasture lands some of it pretty good agricultural land but the great source of wealth is its rich minerals for besides its gold & silver here is now in this town a large amt of crude copper ready for shipment and it is said to be the softest & best copper in the world, but the silver mines are most numerous & rich. I think upon the whole if the Govmt intends to purchase "Sonoro" or Chihuahua, soon, this Territory cannot be organized too soon, but if it is thought, that the expenses of a Territorial Government here now would be too great on the present condition of the Treasury, I do think that congress ought at least, to give these people two Judicial Districts & make the Judges Sit in the Supreme Court of New Mexico at Santa Fe, to which their appeals would be taken, and also a Surveyor General & have these rich lands surveyed soon as posible. please write me & send me some documents to Santa Fe—

And greatly oblige Your friend
Thos H Hopkins

ALS, DLC-JP.

1. Thomas H. Hopkins (b. c1806), native Kentucky lawyer, had represented Warren and Marion counties in the legislature (1841–43) and was a
delegate to the Nashville Convention of 1850. Several years earlier Johnson
had joined with others in recommending Hopkins' appointment as minister to
Guatemala. Unsuccessful in this application, he seems soon after to have been
given the post-office assignment. Thelma Jennings, A Reappraisal of the
Nashville Convention (Ph. D. dissertation, University of Tennessee, 1968),
495; Johnson and others to Lewis Cass, March 12, 1857, Johnson Papers, LC.

2. Although the source of this pithy statement has not been positively
identified, it is consonant with Johnson's sentiments expressed during the
presidential campaign of 1856 and subsequently in the Senate. See Speech at
Nashville, July 15, 1856, Johnson Papers, II, 418; Speech on Popular Sovereignty and Right of Instruction, February 23, 1858.

3. John Oakford of Pennsylvania. U. S. Official Register (1855), 1*.

4. Boone, a Maryland native who had received his appointment as a Pennsylvanian, was an associate justice of New Mexico Territory. Ibid. (1859),
172.

From Rae Burr Batten

                            [Philadelphia, Pa.]   Nov 23d 1859

Dear Friend

I suppose You have almost come to the Conclusion I have forgotten you—by my long Continued silence, indeed Govenor! I have
been suffering painfully, one of my eyes has been greatly inflamed,
and, untill this day, I have been unable to write to anyone—in fact
moderate light was painful and at times more than I Could bare, I
have been Compelled to keep my room, as the Doctor[1] found the air
greatly inflamed my eye— This, together with the severe illness,
then death, of Doctor's Grandma, has Caused my seeming neglect
toward You, our valued friend, Yes! often as we speak of You, and
would love dearly to have you visit us— the Children often speak
of you, and fear you will forget us— they are still going to school,
and they have really grown finely[.] Cicil is nearly the size of her
Ma and I think she very much resembles her Ma in face, and form,
tho I believe she will be as tall as her aunt Rae—

Helen has grown and resembles her father's family in face.—
they are certainly a great charge to Mother,[2] and they do really
feel very near, and dear, to her. she often says she knows no difference between them and her own children. I hope they may make
good, and useful women. for Mother is certainly very kind and in-
dulgent—and does by them a faithful [part?] [.] Mother desire's to
be kindly remembered to you, her health is good, and she tries hard
to renew her usual, or former excellent spirits. It seems since the
death of my dear Sister, she has lost in a measure that cheerful,

hopeful, disposition, and it was a long time before we could cause a smile to play upon her countenance. The entire family enjoy usual good health, Doctor included. he, and Ned,[3] are at this time practicing a piece upon the violin. I think Ned will in time make an excellent performer. he seems to have tallent. Mrs. Fidler[4] wishes to be remember to you— Yes! each and every member of the family join me in love to you—and hope you will write soon and inform us, how you are, and how your arm is getting, is it still painful? is Dr. [dear] Charles married yet? and how is Robert, is he still single? tell him he must not forget us, when he visits our City. we still reside 811 Race St. and would be most happy to see any of you— write us if you will still Continue in Washington. I hope soon to visit you at White House, and Call you President! remember me to all your family, and accept *Love from all to all.* write often, your letters are always most welcome— hoping this may find you enjoying excellent health, & spirits,

                                I Remain Truly   Mrs. Rae Batten

ALS, DLC-JP2.

1. A. Nelson Batten (b. *c*1831), Rae's husband, listed in the city directory as a "clerk, 19. N. 3d h 811 Race Street," appeared in the census as a New Jersey-born physician with $1,000 in personal estate. *McElroy's Philadelphia Directory* (1860), 46; 1860 Census, Pa., Philadelphia, 10th Ward, 74.

2. Hope Burr (b. *c*1797) was a native of New Jersey. *Ibid.*

3. Rae's brother, Edward Burr (b. *c*1840), was a watchmaker. *Ibid.*

4. Rae's sister, Helen E. Fidler, was the wife of a Philadelphia jeweler. In 1861 when she was left a widow with five children, she moved to 1002 Race Street, two blocks from her family. *Cohen's Philadelphia Directory* (1860), 320; *McElroy's Philadelphia City Directory* (1862), 205. See also Rae Burr Batten to Johnson, December 20, 1861, January 15, 1862, Johnson Papers, LC.

From Richard H. Jackson[1]

                                Vienna, Md   Nov. 28th. 1859[?]

Honl. William [*sic*] Johnson,[2]
U. S. S.   Washington D. C.
Sir

Not having the pleasure of your personal acquaintance, you will please excuse the liberty and freedom of this communication.

Having observed the Announcement of the death of Messrs Poindexter and Eastman[3] of the *Nashville Union*, and presuming that if its publication is continued an Editor will be in demand, permit [me] to suggest that I can be employed to conduct its Political Department. In this Connexion I would also state that I am here temporarily attending upon the settlement of a deceased father's Estate—have for several years resided in Ills.—and can present Any recommendation that may be required of me as a gentleman, a Scholar, a Demo-[c]rat, a lawyer, an Editor and political Essayist. Being desirous of removing further South, it would be agreeable to me to locate in Nashville in the aforegoing capacity. I am thirty years of age & without family—posess active, industrious habits, and am an experienced journalist,—am also thorougly acquainted with the general routine of the Printing Office.

Perhaps it may be advisable to state that I was the Democratic Candidate for Congress in the 1st. District of Ills. at the last Congressional Election in that State & was recommended by my friends in the North West generally, and by Senators Jones[4] of Iowa, & Fitch & Bright[5] of Indiana, and by Senator Slidell & others South for the Chief Justice of Arizonia when organized[.]

If there is any probability of the *Union & American* continuing to be published as a Southern Rights, National Democratic Journal, and its need of an Editor, you will please confer with me upon the subject,[6] and oblige   Very Resptly,   Your ob't Ser't
                                                          R. H. Jackson

P. S.

I have addressed you at Washington, thinking perhaps, it would reach you the Sooner.

                                                          R. H. J

ALS, DLC-JP2.

1. Richard H. Jackson (b. *c*1829), a Maryland native and anti-Lecompton Illinois Democrat, had just been roundly defeated in his bid for the congressional seat of Elihu B. Washburne. In 1865 Jackson was a treasury clerk and a leader of the "Johnson Departmental Club," a treasury-employee organization in support of the President, for which he was severely castigated on the House floor by Robert Schenck, January 9, 1867. In response, Jackson published a pamphlet, *To Robert E. Schenck* (Washington, D. C., 1867). *Cong Dir.* 1878), 686; *U. S. Official Register* (1866), 27; *Cong. Globe*, 39 Cong., 2 Sess., 376–77.

2. Endorsements on the envelope reveal that the letter went first to the office of R. W. Johnson of Arkansas and was then forwarded to Andrew.

3. G. G. Poindexter (1829–1859), a Virginia native and graduate of Cumberland Law School, purchased an interest in the Nashville *Union and American* and became its principal editor (1858). He was killed November 18, 1859, in the course of a duel; on the 23rd he was followed to the grave by his fellow-editor, E. G. Eastman. Clayton, *Davidson County*, 240; Nashville *Union and American*, November 19, 1859.

4. George Wallace Jones (1804–1896), Indiana-born delegate to Congress from Wisconsin and Michigan territories, served in the U. S. Senate from Iowa as a Democrat (1848–59) and later was minister to New Granada. *BDAC*, 1136; *DAB*, X, 172–73.

5. Johnson noted on the envelope, "Senators Bright and Fitch to be seen on the subject of an editor." Dr. Graham N. Fitch (1809–1892), native of New York State, had represented Indiana as a Democrat in the House (1849–53) and was now in the Senate (1857–61). *BDAC*, 891.

6. Jackson was unsuccessful in his application.

From Democrats in Tennessee Legislature

November 28, 1859, Nashville; Nashville *Union and American*, December 3, 1859.

Thirty-three signers "and others" request Johnson to deliver an address "on questions of national and domestic concern" during his stay in Nashville and "respectfully suggest to-morrow evening in the Hall of the House of Representatives" as the time and place. [Johnson is obliged to decline because of "the shortness of my stay, with the pressing necessity of my immediate return home. . . . "]

From Albert G. Graham

December 7, 1859, Jonesboro; ALS, DLC-JP2.

Asks Johnson to procure a temporary reappointment as clerk in the land office for his brother, Thomas B. Graham, "removed or rather allowed to resign . . . on the foolish ground that in 1857 I was opposed to the Democratic party in the Canvass in Tennessee." Observes, "With your acquaintance with the present Commissioner . . . I would suppose that you could without much, if any, inconvenience, obtain what I now request."

From J. G. M. Ramsey

[Knoxville]   December 7, 1859

(Private)

Hon. A. Johnson

Dear Sir

Mr. Charlton[1] the present Post Master at Knoxville has requested me to write to you in behalf of his confirmation before the U. S. Senate.

I promised to say that his official conduct has met the entire approbation of every one having business with him or the Post Office. I am familiar with the business men of all parties in Knoxville & have not heard the least complaint of Mr. Charlton[.] He is courteous & accomodating & I think is vigilant & attentive[.]

The Democracy of Knox County met on Monday to re-affirm our principles & appoint delegates to the State Convention[.] A resolution expressing our confidence & preference for you was presented by J. C. Ramsey[2] & after some discussion was adopted.[3] A Know Nothing Democrat made a speech against the resolution but it was carried.

I wrote some time since to Mr. Buchanan that although I was not seeking office I would like some position in the Public service in the South West (Texas) or elsewhere in which I could cultivate my taste for Aboriginal investigations—their languages—traditions—customs—history &c, &c. I took the liberty in my letter to refer the President to you for my character in science & other wise[.] He replied that there was at that time no vacancy but that I was sufficiently known at Washington. Will you be so kind as to enquire of the Secretary in the War Department or of the Interior whether in the Texas or Mexican Boundary service or some other a suitable vacancy exists.[4]   Yours Truly

J. G. M. Ramsey

Mecklinburg T.[5]   Dec. 7, 1859.

ALS, DLC-JP2.

1. Charles W. Charlton (1829–1889), Virginia native educated at Washington College and at Emory and Henry, was at one time a Methodist minister assigned to the Knoxville circuit. An owner of the Knoxville *Register*, he held various appointive offices, serving as postmaster at Knoxville (1859–61) and as Confederate commissioner of immigration for East Tennessee. After the war, he was affiliated with several newspapers. His major interest, however, was agriculture, and he advanced it in East Tennessee by bringing Jersey cattle from the East, introducing the first reaper, and becoming a promoter of the Granger movement. Rothrock, *French Broad-Holston Country*, 394–96.

2. John Crozier Ramsey (1824–1869) of Knoxville, son of J. G. M. Ramsey and district attorney for East Tennessee (1853–61), ran unsuccessfully for Congress (1859). A Confederate district attorney, he was captured in 1864 and imprisoned in Knoxville. When released on parole, he attempted to establish a law practice in Nashville, but was burdened with personal and family litigation until his death. David L. Eubanks, Dr. J. G. M. Ramsey of East Tennessee (Ph. D. dissertation, University of Tennessee, 1965), 39–48 *passim*.

3. When Knoxville Democrats met on December 5 to select delegates for the state convention, which in turn would appoint delegates to the Charleston convention, J. C. Ramsey offered a resolution endorsing Johnson, a man of "patriotism, ability, and statesmanship," one "who should be placed at the head of the Government at this peculiar and dangerous crisis," and one whom we should rejoice to see . . . receive the nomination as a candidate for the Presidency, at the Charleston Convention." Nashville *Union and American*, December 14, 1859.

4. Ramsey never received such an appointment.

5. Ramsey's home just outside of Knoxville.

From Thomas A. Devyr

Williamsburgh [N. Y.] December 9th 1859

Sir

When The 'National' (Land) 'Reform'. movement[1] was organized in New York City in 1844, nearly all the men engaged in it were *Democrats*. The writer of this conducted a Democratic paper in this suburb at the time;[2] and he made the inauguration speech of the movement at Croton Hall in March of that year.

By and by, it became apparent that the Democratic leaders, generally, viewed the new movement with no friendly eye; and as their hostility unfolded itself, it drove thousands of Democrats from under their banner, and over to the side of their opponents.

For the "Greely Whigs" made a show of favoring it—still more so did the Buffalo Platform men.[3] Indeed those impostors stole our thunder and our *name* in '48[.] Ours was the "Freesoil Party" up till that time. They deceived and drew from us nineteen twentieths of our men.[4]

This was because the Democratic Party had given our Democratic measure the "cold shoulder[.]" And for this crime the "Party" has been well-punished, and is likely to be punished still more.[5]

For they will not have the sense, even now, to proclaim a free home to every "enterprising citizen", and the comparative bagatelle of whether a slave shall work on the hither or thither side of a line will *continue* to swallow up public attention, and *lose* to your Presidential candidate such states as New York.

Sir— If now, at the "eleventh hour," The Democratic Statesmen would take up this redeeming law—pass it, and at the same time set all their papers and orators, inside of congress and out, to work to oppose this great primary principle to the little secondary principle of the Republicans, they w'd carry as many of the free states as w'd settle the national contest next year. For the Buffalo men, and their successors the Republicans, were and are Impostors. If the Democrats *were* indeed Democrats they could soon turn the tide against them. But being only impostors they will not accomplish anything[.]

If the government would lead on this movement in such a way as to arouse & enlist the enthusiasm that now lies hopeless and idle —and send that enthusiasm forth to combat this nigger delusion— the work would be done. If not—what will the end be?

Twenty three years ago, I published, in the North of Ireland, the pamphlet—of which, reprinted here, I send you a prospectus.[6] I removed to London for the purpose of forcing its views on public attention—was one of the foremost in the Chartist movement, and narrowly escaped to this country in 1840. I now *return to England*, to show my former compatriots that Universal Suffrage *does not*, simply and *per se*, secure good and economical government. That, when they get the upper hand, they must fix an, *inexorable limit* to the power of governments, local & national, to levy taxes—say for national a dollar a head for the population—for municipal 50 cents on $100 valuation,

AND NO MORE FOREVER!

God bless you! I would have little hope with me in crossing the Atlantic—hope for this country I mean—only for your action[7] in the Senate a day or two ago.

Your friend   Thomas Ainge Devyr.

Senator Andw Johnson of Tennessee

ALS, DLC-JP2.

1. The National Reform movement, the brainchild of George Henry Evans, drew members from the Working Men's and Equal Rights parties, the latter a group of radical New York Democrats called Locofocos. Meeting in the back of John Windt's New York printshop, the group launched their program for free homesteads, homestead exemptions, and land limitation to prevent monopoly. To publicize the movement, Evans and Windt published the *People's Rights*, later supplanted by the *Working Man's Advocate*. Aimed at allying eastern labor with western agrarianism, the movement hoped to help labor by siphoning off "redundant" population to western farms, thereby restoring the skilled worker to the position of an independent craftsman. Zahler, *Eastern Workingmen*, 36–37.

2. The Williamsburgh *Morning Post*.

3. Following the Democratic convention's nomination of Cass in 1848, northern anti-slavery Democrats, known in New York as "Barnburners," met in Buffalo and nominated Martin Van Buren. Joined by "Conscience Whigs" and some prominent land reformers, the movement, which became the Free-Soil party, adopted some of the ideas, but not the full program, of the land reformers. *Ibid.*, 97–98; James T. Adams, *Dictionary of American History* (5 vols., New York, 1940), II, 333–34.

4. The Free-Soilers split the New York Democratic party in the 1848 elections, with Van Buren drawing 120,000 votes to 114,000 for Cass and 218,000 for Taylor. Subsequently the "Barnburners" tended to return to the regular Democratic party. Zahler, *Eastern Workingmen*, 98; De Alva Stanwood Alexander, *A Political History of New York* (4 vols., New York, 1906–23), II, 130–44.

5. Devyr oversimplified the magnitude of the problems facing the Democrats, who had split into three factions—"softshells," "hardshells," and "Barnburners." While Pierce had carried the state in 1852, Buchanan lost it in 1856; in the years between, intraparty quarrelling was so intense that the Democrats lost the state elections in 1853 and 1855. David M. Ellis, *A History of New York* (Ithaca, 1957), 229–33.

6. Originally published in Belfast, *Our National Rights: A Pamphlet for the People: By One of Themselves* was reissued at Williamsburgh in 1842. There is no evidence that Devyr was successful in his efforts to reprint it at this time.

7. On December 8, Johnson had given notice of his intent to introduce a Homestead bill. *Cong. Globe*, 36 Cong., 1 Sess., 53.

From John E. Helms[1]

Knoxville, Ten, Dec. 9, 1859.

Dear Col:

I desired while you were at Nashville to have a private conversation with you in regard to a matter that affected, to some extent, the party of the State; but you were so thronged with company and

otherwise engaged that an oppertunity did not occur. I did not expect
at that time to return home before the adjournment, but it was rendered necessary for me to visit my family, and the first thing that
met my eye here was the reported proceedings of what is called a
Democratic meeting held here on the fifth instant. Of the proceedings I care not a fig; but there is an editorial accompanying the proceedings, as published in the Register, that I wish in the first place
to pronounce false in fact and intent,[2] and in the next place to withdraw every intimation or impression that I may have left upon your
mind, in the conversation held at Nashville, that the paper would
now be conducted with propriety for the good of the party.[3] From
the conversations I had had with the editor,[4] and especially from
the fact that he was a reasonable creature, and could himself form
as just an estimate of the choise of the people as any one I did not
expect so paltry an attempt to muzzle and stifle an expression of
public opinion as this exhibition in the Register. I repeat again, the
assertion that any man, save yourself, is the choice of any respectable number of the Democrats of this county is false. This editorial,
I believe is the suggestion, if not the product, of a man of the name
of Elliot,[5] whose insignificanse to the party is only equalled by his
insignificanse to the community, and while it can only injure the
assailants, and may not even cause a thought from you, I feel that
this explanation is no more than just to myself. I have just grounds
to complain myself of the treatment of these gentlemen, Lewis and
Newman and Ramsey,[6] in relation to the delegates to Nashville. I
requested the last thing I did when I left for Nashville, to be made
a delegate, as I expected to be there. But strange to say each of them
forgot my name, though Newman & Lewis had the names to report.

I was in hopes when the Legislature met of being elected a
Clerk, but of course could stand no chance by the side of an old line
Whig,[7] especially one who had proved Democratic speakers and
leaders liars on every stump they attempted to prove corruption
upon Cullom.[8] I shall return to Nashville to-morrow or next day, to
remain till January. Bob. Johnson and Russwurm[9] have promised
me an assistant's place in the House. I will remain in the Union office
till they want me. I have only seen the inside of the Register office
since my return to give the editor my opinion of his editorial. I found
Elliot, Newman and Ramsey present. I spoke plainly, and may be
severely. Ramsey was with me, but the fact that there was an argument at all on such a subject determined me to let no time pass before washing myself of an affilation with it until a change occurs. It
is sickly at best, and if it does not meet a sudden, it is sure of premature death.

What I desired particularly to see you upon at Nashville was in regard to the Union. Is there in [*sic*] no chance to get Maj. Milligan as Editor? They were (I mean prominent men in N.) Speaking and canvassing names to fill Poindexter's place when I left. I mentioned the name of Milligan several times to men who I hoped would repeat it. I also heard the names of John M. Bright, Clint Atkin[10] and Bate[11] of Sumner mentioned. Bate would do; but neither of the others would. Nor would Bate do as well as Miligan. My impression is that Douglas' friends will make an effort to get a place in the Union.

My present impression is, if I can make a few hundred dollars in Nashville and the Register[12] is for sale when I return that I will purchase it myself. I am confident that I could make it Democratic and a better reflector of Democratic sentiment than it is now, if not otherwise now acceptable.

I would be pleased to hear from you, in regard to Milligan or any thing else you may have time to write. I write hastily, with no time to condense. Direct to Nashville, if you write.

Truly Your Friend John E. Helms

Hon. A. Johnson—

ALS, DLC-JP.

1. Apparently Helms, former editor-owner of several Knoxville Democratic newspapers, was currently working on the Nashville *Union*, which had been left shorthanded since the death of its editors, G. G. Poindexter and E. G. Eastman, on November 18 and 23.

2. In reporting the meeting of the Knox County Democrats, the Knoxville *Register* erroneously stated that a resolution presented by John C. Ramsey, endorsing Johnson for the presidency, had failed of passage. The *Register* editorially explained that the resolutions committee felt that "Gov. Johnson had received too many substantial tokens of public confidence at the hands of the people of East Tennessee, to require, or even be flattered by the adoption of an *empty resolution!*" Yet, according to both J. G. M. Ramsey and the Nashville *Union and American*, Johnson had received the meeting's fulsome endorsement. Knoxville *Register*, quoted in Nashville *Patriot*, December 12, 1859; Nashville *Union and American*, December 14, 1859.

3. The *Register* changed editors so frequently during the first half of 1859 that Brownlow, in objecting to an article, complained: "There are so many persons writing editorials for the *Register*, that we have no idea as to who perpetrated the foregoing." Knoxville *Whig*, August 23, 1859.

4. George W. Bradfield (b. c1841), a Democrat of Clarke County, Virginia, became both publisher and editor of the *Register* during the fall. Helms's presumption that Bradfield was "a reasonable creature" is borne out by the observation of "Parson" Brownlow, "a constant reader," who called the *Register* under Bradfield "the most decent, dignified, and consistent Democratic paper published in Knoxville during the last twelve years." *Ibid.*, March 17, 1860; 1860 Census, Tenn., Knox, Knoxville, 1st district, 61.

5. Perhaps Henry Elliott, a 37-year-old lawyer, who appears to have been, as Helms observed, a minor political figure. *Ibid.*, 32.

6. For John F. J. Lewis see Letter from Robert Johnson, October 14, 1859. James Newman, brother of Taz and associate editor of the *Register*, was a minor politician; John Crozier Ramsey, district attorney and recently defeated congressional candidate, was active in local politics. Lewis and Newman had attended the opening of the legislature in October as repre-

sentatives of the *Register*. Knoxville *Whig*, January 6, 13, April 9, 1859; Eubanks, J. G. M. Ramsey, 42–43; Nashville *Union and American*, October 2, 1859.

7. Brownlow speculated whether the election of John McClarin (b. *c*1816), Irish-born merchant of Smith County, as principal clerk of the senate, was a reward for "turning Democrat?" He went on to point out that only one East Tennessean was favored with an appointment, which "was right upon the *spoils* principle," for "They done [*sic*] nothing for party, but allowed it to be routed 'horse, foot, and dragoons' in East Tennessee." 1860 Census, Tenn., Smith, 2; Knoxville *Tri-Weekly Whig*, October 8, 20, 1859.

8. McClarin, a friend and neighbor of William Cullom, former clerk of the House of Representatives accused of defrauding the government, had been his "righthand man" and strong defender. *Ibid.*

9. T. E. S. Russwurm of Rutherford County, later a Confederate cavalry officer and secretary of the constitutional convention of 1870, had recently been elected principal clerk of the house. Though Helms did not immediately obtain a house clerkship, he became acting clerk in January, when Russwurm took a leave of absence, and the following month was elected assistant clerk. *Tenn. House Journal*, 1859–60, pp. 6, 476, 747; *Tennesseans in the Civil War*, II, 352; *Journal of the Proceedings of the Convention of Delegates . . . to Make a New Constitution . . .* (Nashville, 1870), 9.

10. John D. C. Atkins.

11. William B. Bate (1826–1905), editor of *The Tenth Legion*, a newspaper he established in Gallatin following the Mexican War, had been in the Tennessee house (1849–51) and was attorney general for the Nashville district (1854–60). Subsequently a Confederate general, he became a Democratic governor (1883–87) and U. S. senator (1887–1905). *BDAC*, 525; White, *Messages*, VII, 1–3.

12. Helms did not buy the *Register* but eventually edited the Morristown *Gazette*. White, East Tenn. Journalism, 13.

From William M. Lowry

Greene Ten Decr 9/59

Gov Johnson
Dr Sir

enclosed is Col Fords[1] Recpt for 1 years Subscription to his paper[.] our Court adjourned Saturday night after I saw you. I had afirst rate Jury from all parts of E Ten. I found our freinds generally, of my Opinion that Johnson & Seymore[2] is the Tickit[.] in their primary meetings they will take ground for you. We ought to have some Concert of action. our primary meeting here on Monday, adjourned over untill 1st Monday, in January, when it will reassemble and brake ground. I had Considerable talk with Burch[.] I find in a Certain Continjency Burch would like to go on the State Electoral Ticket. I found when at Knoxville some feeling in favour of Haynes as one of the State electors & from a letter Haynes wrote me after the Election, I take it for granted that he is all right. if it would be of importance to have a good Speaker in the Charleston Convention how would Col Haynes do to go as a delegate for the State at large.[3] Ought our meeting to take ground and name our

prefference for State delegates to the Charleston Convention and also our prefference for one of the State Electors. I hope you will write to me fully and freely as any thing you say will be kept Strictly Confidential. We may then be able to give tone to matters here on 1st Monday in January when we appoint delegates to the Nashvill Convention. on my return home I found all well business brisk, yesterday and today is verry cold[.] every person Killing Pork. if you have any Suggestions to make let me know them as it is important to understand one another. So that we may act in concert. I have every Confidence in the final Success of any Ticket if we could get it fairly in the field. I am willing to do my part and more to bring it about. how would it do for Some of us here to open up a Correspondence with Hon H Seymore. if So give us his P. O. address. your freinds here are willing to Second any Movement that you might indicate, drop me a line Soon So that I get it before the 1st Monday in Jany[.] any thing you Say will be kept Strictly Confidential if mark Confidential[.]   in Haste Yr freind
                                                      Wm M Lowry.

ALS, DLC-JP2.

1. John W. Ford (b. c1799) published and edited a number of Tennessee newspapers, including the Sparta *Review*, the Warren *Register* (1832), and the McMinnville *Central Gazette*, and was McMinnville postmaster (c1845–49) before moving to Chattanooga, where he established the *Democratic Advertiser* in 1850. Selling the *Advertiser* in 1852, he started the weekly Hamilton *Vindicator*, which expired about a year later. At the time of this letter, as an attached receipt indicated, Ford was beginning the Hamilton *Reflector*, for which Johnson obtained a year's subscription at two dollars. White, East Tenn. Journalism, 20; John W. Ford & Sons Receipt, December, 1859, Johnson Papers, LC; Walter Womack, *McMinnville at a Milestone* (McMinnville, 1930), 83, 276–77.

2. Horatio Seymour (1810–1886), New York Democrat, was a member of the state assembly (1842, 1844, 1845), mayor of Utica (1842–43), and governor (1852–54, 1862–66). In 1860 the movement to nominate him as a compromise presidential candidate ended only with his withdrawal a few days prior to the Baltimore convention. As war governor of New York, he remained a power within the party and, when nominated for the presidency in 1868, did surprisingly well against Grant, losing by only 300,000 votes. Influential until his death, he assisted Samuel J. Tilden's drive against Boss Tweed during the 1870's. *DAB*, XVII, 6–9; Stewart Mitchell, *Horatio Seymour of New York* (Cambridge, Mass., 1938), *passim*.

3. Landon C. Haynes and W. C. Whitthorne were selected as delegates-at-large. Nashville *Union and American*, January 24, 1860.

From William W. Pepper[1]

                                    Springfield Tenn—12th Decr./59
(Private).

My Dear Sir

I had hoped to see you on your Late visit to Nashvill with a view of Confering with you generally, as well as Specially, in Reference to the matter About which I now Desire to Trouble you— As is known to you I have been for the Last Eight years Travelling as a Circuit Judge over one of the Longest & Roughest, Circuits in the State, the Salary yeilding a Bare Support, During which time, my wife has been from ill-health Past, going, so much so as to keep me in a state of Constant & unbroken Mise[r]y & Apprehinsion of her Death, & Such is the case now. in fact I Frequently Leave her to hold my Courts with Little hope of seeing her Again &c. the Perpetual Anxiety on her Account together with the Labors of my office have Pretty well worn me out. Now the Point with me is this. is there any chance, to get any sort of Position in France, or Itally, or other Country of Like Climate, So that I Could hope to Protract her Life a Few years, untill my Smaller Children get up a Litt[l]e, if so I would be more than Happy—& should feel myself yours for Life—

Whatever you can or will do for me in this matter will not be Forgotten, but Shall be to you & yours As Bread Cast upon the Waters;[2] Please write me & give me your Candid opinion, on the Subject;— who is to be the Democratic Candi[d]ate for President next year—. Could you not Favor me with a Birds Eye view of the Field of 1860 —from your Present Stand Point & in doing so do not, do yourself & Prospects injustice—for you Know full well How much Tenn. would be Delighted to support you for that or any other position— with the hope of Hearing from you soon—

I am Truly yours
W. W. Pepper

ALS, DLC-JP2.

1. Elected to the seventh judicial circuit in 1851, Judge Pepper held that office until his death on February 1, 1861, his hopes for a sinecure in a Mediterranean climate unrealized. Dan M. Robison, ed., "Andrew Johnson on the Dignity of Labor," *Tenn. Hist. Quar.*, XXIII (1964), 80.

2. Paraphrase of Eccles. 11:1.

Speech on Harper's Ferry Incident[1]

December 12, 1859

Mr. JOHNSON, of Tennessee. Mr. President, I regret that this resolution, when it was first introduced, could not have passed without discussion. It seemed to seek for information to which the country was entitled; and I was more than anxious that the country should be furnished with it, without looking at the question in a party aspect. But it has turned out differently, and I regret that it has. The discussion has taken a pretty wide range, involving party politics generally; and the range which it has taken has rendered it incumbent on me, occupying the position I do, to say a few words upon the resolution, and to answer some remarks that have fallen from Senators during this discussion. It is my intention to do it in a proper spirit, and I trust and hope I shall not be led beyond the boundary of propriety and courtesy.

Before I proceed, however, to the line of argument that I intend to present on this occasion, I wish to notice some few remarks which fell from the Senator from Illinois, [Mr. Trumbull;][2] and I intend, after noticing his remarks, to show that what has recently occurred at Harper's Ferry, in the shape of an insurrection, or invasion, or treason, or by whatever name you may think proper to call it, has been the legitimate result of certain teachings in this country.

In the discussion on Thursday last, the Senator from Illinois attempted to lay down the doctrine of the Republican party and to give his construction of that doctrine. In doing so he called our attention to their platform, which, he says, is a mere reiteration of the Declaration of Independence, (at least, that is his idea,) as it was formed by our fathers. To make myself intelligible and distinctly understood, I will read that portion of the platform which he quoted:

Resolved, That, with our republican fathers, we hold it to be a self-evident truth that all men are endowed with the inalienable right of life, liberty, and the pursuit of happiness, and that the primary object and ulterior design of our Federal Government is to grant these rights to all persons under its exclusive jurisdiction.[3]

As the discussion progressed, drawing deductions from this part of the platform, the Senator seemed to think—that was the tenor of his argument—that by reiterating the Declaration of Independence in this platform, they were embracing the doctrines laid down by Mr. Jefferson, and showing that he really meant to include persons of color in the Declaration, and that such was the understanding of our revolutionary fathers. I know that sometimes it has been said, and changes have been rung on it, that Mr. Jefferson, the apostle of Democracy and of liberty, laid down the doctrine that all men were created equal, that they had certain inalienable rights, that among these were life, liberty, and the pursuit of happiness. Now, it seems to me, that a party, an intelligent party that understands all the doctrines and principles of our Government, in this does great injustice to that instrument and to the framers of the Constitution of the United States. When we take the Declaration of Independence and connect it with the circumstances under which it was written, is there a man throughout the length and breadth of this broad Republic who believes for one instant that Mr. Jefferson, when he penned it, had the negro population in his mind? Notwithstanding, he says that "all men are created equal, and that they are by their Creator endowed with certain inalienable rights, that amongst these are life, liberty, and the pursuit of happiness," is there an intelligent man throughout the whole country, is there a Senator, when he has stripped himself of all party prejudice, who will come forward and say that he believes that Mr. Jefferson, when he penned that paragraph of the Declaration of Independence, intended it to embrace the African population? Is there a gentleman in the Senate who believes any such thing? Is there any one who will stake his reputation on the assertion that that is the correct interpretation of the Declaration of Independence? There is not a man of respectable intelligence who will hazard his reputation upon such an assertion. Why then indulge in this *ad captandum* discussion? Why try to delude and deceive the great mass of the people by intimating that Mr. Jefferson meant Africans or the African race? How were we situated when Mr. Jefferson penned the Declaration of Independence? Did he not own slaves? Did not most of the persons in the Congress which adopted the Declaration own Slaves, and after the Declaration was adopted, by way of giving a correct interpretation to it, what do we find incorporated in the Constitution of the United States? Were negroes then considered the persons who were embraced in the Declaration of Independence? Were they not considered as property? In fixing the representation, slaves were regarded as property, and only three fifths of them were to be counted, clearly recognizing that they were one of the forms of property, and not persons intended to be embraced in the Declaration of Independence, as contended by some. I think it is clear.

What more was provided in the Constitution of the United States, by way of giving a clear construction to the Declaration of Independence? It was provided that fugitives from labor should be restored to the States from which they escaped, upon demand being made.[4] Does that look as if this description of persons were embraced in the Declaration of Independence, and were considered equal to the white race? It is evident to my mind, and it must be so to everybody else, that Mr. Jefferson meant the white race, and not the African race. The Constitution gives it that interpretation. And his own acts, and those of his associates, when they were framing the Declaration of Independence, owning slaves, and afterwards passing laws and making wills which provided for their regular descent as property, confirm it. Then it seems to me that this does not avail the Senator much. But in the next resolution of the platform, which he read, it is declared:

That the Constitution confers upon Congress sovereign power over the Territories of the United States for their government, and that in the exercise of this power it is both the right and the imperative duty of Congress to prohibit in the Territories those twin relics of barbarism, polygamy and slavery.

The Republican platform declares, and the Senator from Illinois
argues, that the power of Congress being sovereign over the Territories, it can exclude slavery from the Territories. What do you
mean by sovereignty? I shall not undertake to define it on this occasion, but I will give my understanding of the power of Congress
over the Territories. I deny any such assumption as this platform
contains. I deny that any such power is conferred on the Federal
Government in reference to the Territories. It is not sovereign. This
Federal Government possesses no sovereign power. All its powers
are derivative and limited, and those that are not expressly granted
are reserved to the States respectively. Congress has no sovereign
power. All its powers are derived; it can exercise no single primitive
or original power. Where, then, does it get sovereign power in reference to a Territory of the United States? Where does it even get
sovereign power in reference to the District of Columbia? It has no
such power. The Congress of the United States may exercise exclusive and limited power, but not sovereign power. Its authority is
limited, it is defined, and I deny the assumption that the Federal
Government has sovereign power in reference to the Territories of
the United States.

But suppose, by way of testing the sincerity of the Republican
party, we proceed on the idea that the power of Congress is sovereign
in reference to the Territories, and that, in legislating for the Territories, Congress has the right to prescribe the qualifications of the
citizen who shall become an inhabitant or resident of the Territories.
Bear in mind their other doctrine that all men are created equal;
and let us try to ascertain, if we can, their consistency on this subject.
The Territories are filling up. Let me ask the Republican party, proceeding upon these two ideas, that all men are created equal, and
that the power of Congress is sovereign in the Territories, what will
you do with the black population when it goes into the Territories?
Now, we will test the practical operation of your doctrines. Let me
ask them, and I call upon them to answer me before the country, will
you let the free colored population that emigrates into the Territories stand on an equal footing with the white population? Let us
reduce your theory to practice, and see how it will operate. You say
that all men are created equal, and that the power of the Federal
Government is sovereign in the Territories. Will you, when the free
colored population goes into the Territories, make them equal in all
respects with the white population?

If you will not, why clamor so much about sovereignty over a
Territory; why clamor so much about all men being created equal?

Here is the touchstone. Let us see what you will do. Inform us whether, in filling up the Territories and making laws for the qualification and protection of their citizens, you will place the African on an equality with the white population? Come up and tell us. It is fair to put it to you. You have presented a theory; now let us know what your practice will be. Will you take that ground? Will you place the African population, or their descendants, or a mixed colored population of the African race, on an equality with the white man in the Territories over which you claim sovereign power? I believe the Senator's constituents in Illinois agree with me in the construction that I have given to the Declaration of Independence and the Constitution of the United States, in reference to the colored population. I think they themselves have interpreted this Declaration; and, if they have interpreted it wrongly, I want to know from him if he is prepared to commence the work in that quarter, and reduce his doctrines to practice. When we turn to the declaration of independence of Illinois, if I may so call it, what do we find? In the constitution of Illinois it is declared:

That the general, great, and essential principle of liberty and free government may be recognized and unalterably established, we declare:
Sec. 1. That all men are born equally free and independent, and have certain inherent and indefeasible rights; among which are those of enjoying and defending life and liberty, and of acquiring, possessing, and protecting property and reputation, and of pursuing their own happiness.[5]

This is the declaration of Illinois. Do the people of Illinois understand persons of color to be equal with white men? If they do, they have not combined, in the shape of a constitution or declaration of independence, their views and sentiments on the subject; and if the Senator entertains the views that he presented here the other day, I would suggest to him the propriety of going to the State of Illinois and commencing the work of reformation there by changing their organic law. Although they declare that all men are born equal in the State of Illinois, what do they do in their constitution? It shows that when our people speak of men being equals they do not include the African race, but regard them as an inferior race. Illinois says in her constitution that "the militia of the State of Illinois shall consist of all free male able-bodied persons, negroes, mulattoes, and Indians excepted"[6]—to do what? To perform militia duty, notwithstanding they declare that all men are born equal. Is not that a correct interpretation of the declaration in this case, as well as the Constitution is a correct interpretation of the Declaration of Independence in the other case? What more do we find in that constitution?

In all elections, all *white* male inhabitants above the age of twenty-one years, having resided in the State six months next preceding the election, shall enjoy the right of an elector.

The voters are white men, not free negroes. Notwithstanding in the declaration they say all men are born equal, yet here is a class of persons who they say are not equal to the white man, who shall not come to the ballot-box, shall not be found in the ranks mustering; and, as we go on and examine the constitution and laws, we find furthermore, and it will not be controverted by the Senator, that even these men who, they say, are born equal, are not permitted to come into a court of justice and be competent witnesses against a white man. They are not permitted to intermarry with the white race, under heavy penalties. They are not permitted to remain in any county without giving security that they, in the future, will not become chargeable on the poor list. Although these are the provisions of the constitution and laws of his own State, the Senator pathetically and eloquently repeats the words of the Declaration of Independence that all men are created equal. Look at his own constitution, look at his own laws, look at his own declaration of independence which uses the same language; and yet they say they are not equal, and that the negro race is not embraced and was not in the mind of the men who penned the Declaration of Independence.

So much for giving a literal construction to the Declaration of Independence. So much as to getting at what the Republican party would do who claim sovereign power over the Territories. You talk about a freeman, and yet this man who is free and equal, according to your idea of the subject, is not permitted to come into a court of justice as a competent witness against a white man, is not permitted to stand in the ranks as a man fit to muster, is not permitted to intermarry with a white, is not permitted to vote. What, then, does constitute a freeman? Oh, yes, I suppose he enjoys liberty. Liberty! Deprived of every privilege, he yet enjoys liberty! He is a freeman, and yet can exercise no franchise that pertains to a freeman! He is a worse slave, in fact, than the African who is in the South and in bondage; a great deal worse, for by these restraints and restrictions he is made a slave; he enjoys the shadow and the name of being a freeman, but is stripped of all the franchises that constitute a freeman. He is a slave, in fact, without a master; and I think his is a great deal worse condition than that of the slave who has a master.

In connection with this point, the Senator has thrown out another idea which I do not know whether I clearly apprehend or not. Of course that is my fault and not his. He says in another portion of his speech:

We will perpetuate free government, by continuing the principles that he advocated. But, sir, what beyond that? How has it come, from a gentleman upon that side of the House, to tell us we must not call ourselves Republicans, when they assume to call themselves Democrats? Democrats! And the illustration of your principle, democracy, is the supremacy of an aristocracy of slaveholders in this country. Any man can be a member of the Democratic party who will adopt your creed on the subject of the spread of slavery, and the upholding of slaveholding institutions in this country, which concern directly not one man in sixty of the population of this Union. That is the party that has arrogated to itself the name of "Democrat," and that reproaches us for calling ourselves Republicans. Democrats! A party that legislates for the interest of one out of sixty; forgetting the interest of four fifths of the families of the South to promote that of one fifth—free white men.[7]

If I understand him correctly, he proceeds upon the idea that anybody can be a Democrat who is in favor of the spread or the maintenance of slavery; he seems to lay that down as an essential or *sine qua non* of being a Democrat. Now, when we come to look at the broad principles of the Democratic party, we find that, so far as the institution of slavery is concerned, it constitutes a very small portion of the basis and principles on which they intend and expect to administer this Government, and have administered it heretofore; but the Democratic party assume to be a national party; the Democratic party assume to maintain the Constitution and all its guarantees as it is. They assume that this Constitution that was made and handed down to us by our forefathers, guaranties the institution of slavery wherever found within the United States. They, in advocating the Constitution of the country as it is, stand by this institution called slavery, it being recognized by the Constitution of the United States, which guaranties that it shall not be disturbed. Then the Democratic party stand on the Constitution of the country. They propose no innovation. They have made no advance on the North. They propose the introduction of no new institution, so far as the northern States are concerned; but they are disposed to stand by the Constitution of the country, as it has been handed down to them, willing and anxious to abide by its guarantees. Because a man in the North, who agrees that the institution is constitutional, who agrees that the southern States have constitutional guarantees, stands by an individual in the South maintaining these great constitutional rights, does that argue that he is in favor of the spread of African slavery; that he is for continuing it any more than the Constitution continues it? It seems to me not; and what the Senator lays down as the touchstone of the Democratic party, is not the basis of that party. It is a question now before the country, and has been one among other questions for a considerable length of time; and the time has well nigh arrived, I think, when Senators, North and

South, East and West, had better begin to look into it, and see where it is driving us.

In the remarks of the Senator from Illinois, which I just now quoted, there is another idea thrown out, seemingly not only to affect the people outside the slaveholding States, but to affect those inside the slaveholding States. It is said that the legislation of the South is for the benefit of one out of twenty [sic] of the southern people. We deny it. We say our legislation is in accordance with the Constitution and for the country, and not for one out of twenty or one out of sixty of the people. I have heard that idea suggested before. Is is intended to have its influence in the southern States. It is based on the old idea that a man who owns one hundred slaves stands equal to sixty white persons in political rights, by reason of the three-fifths clause of the Constitution. How does this matter really stand? Why will you not look at it on its true basis? Let us get at this legislation under the Constitution of the United States, and we will show that the Senator's argument is sophistry—pardon me for calling it by that name—that it is not sound in logic, that it is not sound in the premises, and, of course, not in the conclusion.

The Constitution of the United States provides for apportioning representation in the other House among the States, and declares that all the free population shall be included, Indians excepted; and it embraces three fifths of the slaves, who are to be added to the whole number of white persons. From this originates the idea that the man holding a hundred slaves stands equal to sixty white men at home. That is the argument, and it is intended to have a prejudice on the public mind. How does the matter stand? Is that the basis and is it the manner in which the thing operates practically in the States? Not at all. Under the Constitution of the United States, once in ten years the census is taken. That being done, laying down the basis that I have just stated, embracing three fifths of the slaves, Representatives are to be apportioned, to whom? Among the slaveholders? No. Where does the representation go? I want to be understood. Is it given to the slaveholders individually, or where does it go? Away with this sophistry, wrapped around with deception. The Representatives are to be apportioned among the several States, not among the individuals. You have fixed your basis of representation, and in the apportionment of representation it is to be apportioned among the several States. States are not known here in districts. States are not known here in detail, and especially so in apportioning the representation. You apportion the representation to the State—the sovereignty; and the sovereignty gets the benefit of the representation, and then it is that the Legislature is to prescribe the mode of electing those Representatives. What becomes of your idea of sixty to one? How many of the States used to elect their Representatives by general ticket, every qualified voter standing upon an equal footing? But, moreover, all the citizens of the States stand on an equal footing as to the benefit that their State has derived under the Constitution of the United States in this additional representation. The man that does not own a slave is permitted to come forward and participate in this additional representation as much as the slaveholder. Do you understand that? What then becomes of your idea of twenty or sixty to one?

Do not Illinois and all the other non-slaveholding States get the benefit of their free colored population in apportioning representation? After getting the benefit of your free colored population in representation, do you let them vote? Do you admit them into your courts as competent witnesses? Do you permit them to muster? No. Where, then, is this great injustice? Notwithstanding your clamor about all men being created equal, what is your practice? Your theory is one thing, and your practice is another. Suppose all the slaves in the southern States were free, how would the representation be?

We are told that we have a representation for three fifths of our negroes. Do not you get representation for all your negroes—all your slaves without masters? I mean the free negroes who are shorn of every franchise that constitutes a freeman. You get a full representation for all your free negroes, and yet you complain. How would the matter operate if all the negroes in the South were free? How would that affect this question of representation? We only get three fifths of our negroes represented now, according to the Constitution of the United States. Suppose you were to emancipate them all and make them all free, when you came to apportion the representation among the South, how would it be? Would it be three fifths or five fifths? What is three fifths of four million, assuming the slaves to be four million in number? The three fifths is two million four hundred thousand. What would two fifths be? One million six hundred thousand. Then, if your ratio were one hundred thousand, we have sixteen Representatives on the other floor less than we should have if all our negroes were free men of color. We can understand that. Instead of getting twenty-four Representatives for the blacks, we should have forty Representatives—sixteen more than we now have.

Where, then, is this great hardship to you; where is the wrong in the Constitution to you? You get a full representation for your negroes, who, I think, are slaves without masters, for they are deprived of all that constitutes freemen. Our slaves enjoy all the rights of freemen, with one or two exceptions; and to be deprived of these is an advantage to them in the relation which they occupy. Slavery, instead of being an element of political power to the South, is an element of political weakness in the national councils. Is not that easily seen and understood? Then, why try to poison the minds of your people? Why try to deceive them? Why not tell them that if all the slaves were free, instead of the power of the South being diminished in the Congress of the United States, she would have sixteen more Representatives? Why not tell them the truth? What becomes of all your sympathetic appeals, based upon the equality of black men and white men, when everybody sees and knows that the condition of a free colored man in the North is infinitely worse than that of the slave in the South? What, then, becomes of your argument of equality? There is nothing in it. Why can we not, as brothers in the same great Confederacy, approach each other with a disposition to understand our Constitution as it is, not with a view to get an advantage of the argument on the popular *ad captandum* slang which may be thrown out upon the country? Let us divest our minds of all prejudice, look at things as they are, and see the truth as it is. It is the want of understanding which gives rise to discussion; not the understanding of the question which causes argument. Let us understand the principles embraced in the Constitution as they are, and then we can approach each other as brothers of the same great family, and stand by our bond of union as it is. If the Constitution is wrong, and experience and time have proved it to be so, proceed in the manner pointed out in the instrument to revise or alter or abolish it; but do not let us do it by stealth and indirection.

I must notice one other paragraph of the speech of the honorable Senator from Illinois. He said:

Mr. President, I am satisfied that I am not understood by the Senator from Alabama. I say that the negro has the same natural rights that I have; and now I say it is not a crime, under all circumstances, to hold a negro in slavery.

Why does not the Senator, in the State of Illinois, place the negro, he being a freeman, on the same equal ground with himself?

[Trumbull, elaborating on "natural rights" and "political rights," declares that, while it is an abstract truth that men are equally endowed by nature, society in setting up political forms does discriminate.]

Mr. JOHNSON, of Tennessee. That is the precise point at which we come to ascertain those rights: it is when governments and societies are to be formed. Then we raise the question at once whether this description of individuals is equal to another description of individuals. The constitution of the Senator's own State assumes that all members of the white race, the race for whom they were making and forming government, were equal, and created equal. An African may be equal to his fellows in his own country, surrounded by his own kind of people, who are inferior to the white race; but, because he is transferred here, or happens to be born on this continent, he is not invested with the same rights with one of our race; he is not created equal in the very beginning. The distinction begins with the very germ itself. It depends entirely upon where he is born.

But I wish to ask the Senator a question. Assuming equality to be the rule in a natural state where there is no law, he assumes, then, that the black man is created with the same rights that the white man is. You assume that the power of the Federal Government is sovereign over a Territory. You now go into a community where there are no whites established. Will you, under this general idea of liberty, and this declaration that all men are created equal, in the organization of your territorial government under your sovereign power, make the negro equal to the white man? Will the Senator answer that?

[Trumbull answers that "under ordinary circumstances" he would not give "the same political rights either to females or to negroes that I would to the white male population."]

Mr. JOHNSON, of Tennessee. Mr. President, all that I want is, to get at the truth, and I want no fog or mystification about the subject. Do not understand me as assuming that the Senator is intentionally throwing fog about it. The fog may be on my part, not on his. But perhaps I can make my proposition understood by asking another question. If, for instance, the Territory of Arizona was colonized and filled up with a free colored population altogether, would the Senator be willing to admit it into the Union as a State on an equal footing with the other States of this Confederacy?

[Trumbull would not admit as a sovereign state "a community of negroes or of Indians either," preferring to separate the white and black races by removing the black race as it becomes free.]

Mr. JOHNSON, of Tennessee. I thank the Senator for the admission he has made, and I wish to press the matter a little further. I think we shall get together directly; I think we are traveling in converging lines, and we are traveling pretty much to the same conclusion. Suppose the four million slaves in the slave States were all emancipated, and were to fill up one of our Territories and apply for admission here, it seems to me the Senator's answer would apply to them as well as to the question I have put. If I am wrong in construing it so, he can correct me; but, in his last remarks, he has admitted what I set out to prove, which was opposed to the whole tendency of his argument and the doctrine he laid down a few days since, and what, it seems to me, according to my understanding, the honorable Senator has been denying. He admits to-day, in his explanation, that the Creator himself has made a difference between the black and the white race.

Mr. TRUMBULL. Not in their natural rights.

Mr. JOHNSON, of Tennessee. He says the difference begins with the very origin of man. If the Deity himself, according to the Senator's own admission, has made a difference between the races, how can they have been created with precisely the same equal rights and privileges? The difference began with the Deity. The Senator, in his last explanation, has conceded the whole ground; and all this clamor and claptrap about liberty, and men being created equal, falls to the ground, and the construction which should be put on the Declaration of Independence is clear and unobscured.

In speaking about the latter part of the second resolution of the platform of his party, which puts slavery and polygamy together as "twin relics of barbarism," the Senator, in reply to a suggestion of the Senator from Alabama, [Mr. Clay,][8] said:

> Mr. President, I will not cavil about the word "crime." I do not call it a crime in citizens of the South to hold slaves at all.
> Mr. Clay. Is not polygamy a crime?
> Mr. Trumbull. Polygamy is a crime under some circumstances, but not always a crime. I take it that polygamy is no crime in Turkey.

The Senator makes use of the word "crime," and says polygamy is not a crime under all circumstances; he says so in two parts of the speech. Mr. President, I am one of the last who should begin to discuss a question of ethics; but for myself, in early life—and I have practiced upon it since—I tried to lay down in my own mind certain great rules of right and wrong, truth and falsehood, vice and virtue. According to my judgment, and the teachings I have received, these things exist; and, in my view, a thing cannot be a crime in one place, and not a crime in another, according to circumstances. I do not believe that right and wrong are conventional. We know what the practice of the world is; in some nations one thing is practiced and tolerated by law and custom, and in another precisely the opposite. But does that disprove the great fundamental truth of the proposition upon which all religion, upon which all sound morals should rest, that there is a great principle of right which lies at the foundation of all things, and that the practices of this or that nation cannot change or vary it? What sort of a teaching is the Senator's to a nation? Nations must have morals, as well as individuals. Nations must have a high appreciation of the right, as well as individuals. If right and wrong, if truth and falsehood, if vice and virtue, are to be mere conventional terms, as morality or immorality may prevail in particular localities, where will this country and every other country go? Each individual will be a law unto himself, according to that system of ethics; and to one man polygamy will be right, and according to some other individual it will be wrong.

Are these the doctrines that are to be inculcated in this country? Are the pulpits and moralists to inculcate the idea that each man is to have his own system of morals; that each man must judge of right and of wrong; and that there is no rule, no fundamental rule, by which this great principle shall be determined? I repeat, that I hold that, according to my teachings, there is a great moral principle of right which lies at the foundation of all things; that it exists from eternity; that it began with the Deity himself, and will continue until the termination of His reign; that it reigns throughout all time as deep and as pervading as nature itself. Now, we are told in the Senate of the United States, in the presence of this intelligence, that polygamy may be right under some circumstances, and wrong under others.

The next question comes up, under what circumstances is it right? It is said to be right in Turkey; which is given as an illustration, and to be wrong here. If it is wrong, it violates a great truth, a great moral truth, and no set of circumstances can make it right. If my memory serves me right, I read the teaching or the doctrines of a professor called Hoffman, who, I think, wrote about the year 1598, just two hundred years before the Virginia resolutions were passed. I like to remember epochs, eras, and great events. He laid down the doctrine that truth was susceptible of division into two parts; and all that was true in philosophy was false in theology, and all that was true in theology was false in philosophy. This is a sort of paradox; and yet he founded a sect,[9] and many flocked to his standard, and inculcated the doctrines that he taught. It seems to me that system of ethics would suit the doctrines which have been recently inculcated, and which proclaim that, under the circumstances of Turkey, polygamy is precisely right; while, under the circumstances of the United States, is is precisely wrong. I suppose, according to that system, all that would be right in Turkey would be wrong in the United States, and all that would be right here would be wrong there. It seems to me, you might make another application of it, and say that all that is right in Republicanism is wrong in Democracy, and all that is right in Democracy is wrong in Republicanism—I mean modern Republicanism. I think we shall have to fall back on the teachings of Professor Hoffman, if the system of ethics recently inculcated is to be fastened on the country; but I trust and hope it will not.

So much for the honorable Senator from Illinois and his doctrines. I stated in the beginning that what I was saying in reference to the Senator from Illinois, was rather outside of the line of remark which I intended to make on the occasion. I stated that I should endeavor to show that the recent demonstrations made at Harper's Ferry had been the legitimate result of certain teachings for a great number of years in this country. I shall begin by calling the attention of the Senate and the country to doctrines promulgated in reference to the North and South prior to the year 1800, about ten years after the Federal Government was formed. I propose to read an extract from the fourth volume of Mr. Jefferson's works, an entry under the head of December 13, 1803:

> The Rev. Mr. Coffin of New England, who is now here soliciting donations for a college in Greene county, Tennessee, tells me that when he first determined to engage in this enterprise, he wrote a paper recommendatory of the enterprise, which he meant to get signed by clergymen, and a similar one for persons in a civil character, at the head of which he wished Mr. Adams to put his name, he being the President of the United States, and the application going only for his name, and not for a donation. Mr. Adams, after reading the paper and considering, said he saw no possibility of continuing the Union of the States; that their dissolution must necessarily take place; that he, therefore, saw no propriety in recommending to New England men to promote a literary institution in the South; that it was, in fact, giving strength to those who were to be their enemies; and, therefore, he would have nothing to do with it.[10]

Thus we find that prior to the year 1800, when a simple application was made to the elder Adams for the use of his name by a New England man, the Rev. Charles Coffin,[11] to solicit subscriptions to aid in building up an institution in the South, it was refused on the ground that the South would ultimately become, and was then in point of fact, the enemy of the North; and that as dissolution would finally take place, it was a bad investment for northern men to put their funds in southern institutions. I referred to this circumstance, which is familiar to me, as a beginning point, as a specimen brick of the building out of which this whole fabric has been reared against the South and southern institutions. In the Twenty-Seventh Congress, at the extra session, John Quincy Adams said, upon the celebrated 21st rule, prohibiting the reception of abolition petitions:

> He would say that, if the free portion of this Union were called upon to expend their blood and their treasure to support that cause which had the curse and the displeasure of the Almighty upon it, he would say that this same Congress would sanction an expenditure of blood and of treasure, for that cause itself would come within the constitutional action of Congress; that there would be no longer any pretension that Congress had not the right to interfere with the institutions of the South, inasmuch as the very fact of the people of a free portion of the Union marching to the support of the masters, would be an interference with those institutions; and that, in the event of a war (the result of which no man could

tell) the treaty-making power comes to be equivalent to universal emancipation.[12]

And do we not see the whole idea, to get up a foray, make a descent on a southern State, establish a provisional government, and if the Federal Government is called upon to interfere, under the treaty-making power, we will emancipate all your slaves? This idea has been longer inculcated than many are willing to believe. Mr. Adams's speech continues:

This was what he had then said; and he would add to it now, that, in his opinion, if the decision of this House, taken two days ago, should be reversed, and a rule established that the House would receive no petition on this subject, the people of the North would be *ipso facto* absolved from all obligation to obey any call from Congress.

Here is the whole doctrine laid down, broad and wide, upon which these recent depredations were to be committed. They have been the result of teachings like these. The idea was thrown out as to the manner in which the Federal Government could be caused to interpose, and how, by its interposition, under the treaty-making power, all the southern slaves were to be emancipated. This was what Mr. Adams said in the Twenty-Seventh Congress—sixteen years ago. About that time, in a letter written to the Abolitionists of Pittsburg, on the subject of anti-slavery societies, he said:

On the subject of abolition, abolition societies, anti-slavery societies, or the liberty party, I have never been a member of any of them. But, in opposition to slavery, I go as far as any of these; my sentiments, I believe, very nearly accord with theirs. That slavery will be abolished in this country, and throughout the world, I firmly believe. Whether it shall be done peaceably or by blood, God only knows; but it will be accomplished, I have no doubt; and, by whatever way, I say let it come.[13]

If it is to come by blood, let it come; that was his language then. Now, let me ask my brethren of the North, what are we to infer from teachings like these? We find that, before 1800, it was predicted by prominent, influential men, that this Union was not to stand; that the South was your enemy. In 1840, 1841, and 1842, we find the same doctrine reiterated by Mr. Adams the second. We find in the letter, which I have just read, that he says he firmly believes the end will come; and, by whatever means, even if it comes by blood, let it come. Are we prepared to submit to a state of things like this? Are we to hear these teachings year after year, and behold the recent developments, and say that we feel no apprehension? If I were to go into the speeches of Senators I could show you that the same idea and the same doctrine, in reference to a dissolution of these States, has been inculcated by the Senator from Massachusetts, [Mr. Wilson,] and the Senator from Ohio, [Mr. Wade.] We find the same doctrine promulgated by the Senator from New York [Mr.

Seward] in a remarkable speech delivered, not in this body, but before a portion of his constituents. I remarked before, that I presented a specimen brick, and I want to follow it up. I speak now of Mr. Seward as a politician, making a speech to the people at Rochester, as I have a right to do, and I shall not misrepresent him if I know it. In that speech, the honorable Senator from New York said:

Hitherto, the two systems have existed in different States, but side by side within the American Union. This has happened because the Union is a confederation of States. But in another aspect the United States constitute only one nation. Increase of population, which is filling the States out to their very borders, together with a new and extended net work of railroads and other avenues, and an internal commerce which daily becomes more intimate, is rapidly bringing the States into a higher and more perfect social unity or consolidation. Thus these antagonistic systems are continually coming into closer contact, and collision results.[14]

The Senator continues—I want to quote him fully and fairly, and not tear a portion of the speech from the context, and thus do him injustice:

Shall I tell you what this collision means? They who think that it is accidental, unnecessary, the work of interested or fanatical agitators, and therefore ephemeral, mistake the case altogether. It is an irrepressible conflict between opposing and enduring forces, and it means that the United States must and will, sooner or later, become either entirely a slaveholding nation, or entirely a free-labor nation. Either the cotton and rice fields of South Carolina and the sugar plantations of Louisiana will ultimately be tilled by free labor, and Charleston and New Orleans become marts for legitimate merchandise alone, or else the rye fields and wheat fields of Massachusetts and New York must again be surrendered by their farmers to slave culture, and to the production of slaves, and Boston and New York become once more markets for trade in the bodies and souls of men. It is the failure to apprehend this great truth that induces so many unsuccessful attempts at final compromise between the slave and free States, and it is the existence of this great fact that renders all such pretended compromises, when made, vain and ephemeral. Startling as this saying may appear to you, fellow-citizens, it is by no means an original or even a modern one.

The doctrine here proclaimed is, that there is an irrepressible conflict between slave labor and free labor. I hope the Senate will pardon me if I digress again from the line of my argument, to combat what, as I conceive, is a false proposition, which has no foundation in truth. The premises of the Senator are wholly incorrect; but, as long as the conclusions drawn from them are not combated, they have the same strength as if the premises were correct. Now, sir, is there, in fact, a conflict between slave labor and free labor? If I know myself, I want to be fair and honest on this subject; and as humble as I conceive myself to be, and as poor an estimate as I put on any argument of mine, I wish to God that I might to-day speak to the citizens of every free State in this Confederacy, and could get them, with unprejudiced minds, to look at this proposition as it is. What, sir; a conflict, an irrepressible conflict between free and slave labor! It is untrue. It is a mistaken application of an old principle to an improper case. There is a conflict always going on between capital and labor; but there is not a conflict between two kinds of labor. By sophistry and ingenuity, a principle which is conceded by all, is applied to a wrong case. There is a war always going on between capital and labor; but there is a material difference between two descriptions of labor, and a conflict between labor in the aggregate on the one hand and capital on the other.

Where is the conflict? We know that as far as labor and capital are concerned, labor is always trying to get as much capital for labor as it can; on the other hand capital is always trying to get as much labor for capital as it can. Hence there is an eternal warfare going on between capital and labor, labor wanting to absorb capital and capital wanting to absorb labor. Does that make a conflict between two kinds of labor? Not at all. Where is the conflict in the United States between slave labor and free labor? Is the slave who is cultivating the rice fields in South Carolina, is the slave who is following the plow in the rich and fertile plains of Mississippi, in competition with the man who is making boots and shoes in New York and Massachusetts? It there any conflict between their labor? Is there any conflict between the man who is growing mules and hogs and horses in the State of Ohio, and the man in the South who is raising cotton, rice, and tobacco with his slaves? The assumption is false, and upon these false premises a conclusion has been drawn which has deluded thousands of honest men in the country.

Instead of there being a conflict, an irrepressible conflict, between slave labor and free labor, I say the argument is clear and conclusive that the one mutually benefits the other; that slave labor is a great help and aid to free labor, as well as free labor to slave labor. Where does the northern man go, to a very great extent, with his manufactured articles? He goes to the South for a market, or the southern merchant goes to the North and buys them. With what does he buy them? Does he buy them with the product of labor that is in conflict with his labor? No. What then? He buys them with the product of cotton, of rice, of tobacco, and of sugar. Is that conflict? The fact that he can produce these articles with slave labor, enables him to get the means, and sometimes a superabundance of means, by which he can pay higher prices for articles raised in the North.

Again, when a man raises mules and hogs in the West and Southwest, and another man raises cotton in the South, by means of his slaves, is there, as I before inquired, any competition, any irrepressible conflict between them? None. It is not entitled, in point of fact, to be dignified with the appellation of an argument; it is sophistry, the product of ingenuity, calculated, if not intended, to deceive thousands of honest laboring minds. Sir, I had been vain enough to think that I could satisfy a northern man, strip him of his prejudices, that the southern man who has his capital invested in slave labor, is his best friend. Let us analyze this a little more, and see where it will carry us to. You talk about a slave aristocracy. If it is an aristocracy, it is an aristocracy of labor. What kind of aristocracy have you in the North? Capital and money. Which is the most odious in its operations—an aristocracy of money or an aristocracy of labor? Which is the most unyielding? Which is the most exacting? Every man has the answer in his own mind.

But to illustrate still further. The southern man puts his capital into labor. He commences the production of cotton, or any other product peculiar to slave labor. Is he not interested in obtaining the highest price for slave labor? His capital is in slave labor. His talent, his mind, and his influence are employed to make slave labor productive, and, at the same time, to make it yield the greatest amount in dollars and cents; and just in proportion as he can find new markets, devise more ways and means for consumption, and thereby increase the price, in the very same proportion he increases his means —to do what? Whenever you see cotton and the other great staple of the South run up in price, does not everything increase in price, does not every article manufactured at the North run up correspondingly? Thus the southern man, in obtaining the highest price for the product of his capital invested in labor, gets the means by which he pays the highest price for labor. He is interested in getting the highest price for his products, and by doing so he becomes enabled to pay the highest price for free labor, and he is the most reliable advocate and the best friend of the laboring man at the North. Who can contradict the proposition? He is interested in obtaining the highest prices, and he pays corresponding prices for everything that he consumes. Who gets the benefit of it?

As I said just now, there is a conflict going on between capital and labor. Do we not know that a man who has his thousand dollars invested in a slave producing cotton, is interested in the product of that labor, while the man who has his thousand dollars invested in money is interested in reducing the price of labor. Capital at the North is the oppressor of the laboring man. There is where the oppression is; there is where the irrespressible conflicts exists. It is between the dollars and cents of the North and the free labor of the North, not between slave labor and free labor.

If I were disposed, Mr. President,[15] I might press this point still

further. I have no doubt that in the event of a dissolution of this
Union, Great Britain would try for a time to make friendly terms
with the southern States, because it would be to her interest to do
so. The North manufactures and so does Great Britain. Her capital
does not consist in labor; it consists in money, which is always arrayed against labor. Leaving that out of view, however, the reason
why Great Britain is so deeply interested in the abolition of slavery
in the United States is plain, and it must be apparent to all who
would think about it. Her capital exists in money and stocks, as
the capital of the non-slaveholding States does. Capital in Great
Britain is arrayed against oppressed and downtrodden free labor.
In the United States, what do they behold? Three thousand two
hundred million dollars invested in labor. Put the four million slaves
of the South at $800 apiece, and the result is $3,200,000,000 invested in labor. Do you not see that that amount of capital is identified with labor, trying to extort from the moneyed capital of the
world high prices for the product of that labor? If Great Britain
could succeed in diverting the investment or abolishing it altogether,
what would she do? Suppose that $3,200,000,000 should go into
dollars and cents, do you not see that those who own the capital
would take sides with Great Britain, sustaining the moneyed aristocracy of the world against free labor, and extorting it at the lowest
prices possible? That is no sophistry. It is just the case. Cannot we
understand it? Hence, I repeat again, when you come to look at this
subject, the southern man, with his capital invested in slaves and
the products of slave labor, is the best and most reliable advocate
that the free laboring man at the North has. He is his true friend, and
can be relied upon, because he is interested, leaving every other consideration out of view.

To show that what I have argued to be true in theory, is also sustained by the practical operation of things, let me present to the
Senate a table which, I understand, has been compiled with some
care by an editor in St. Louis.[16] It shows that, not only in theory,
but in fact, is the slaveholder the best friend to free labor. This table
presents a comparative view of the wages received by different
classes of workmen and mechanics in the slaveholding and non-
slaveholding States:

FREE STATES. Per Day. Chicago, Illinois.			SLAVE STATES. Per Day. New Orleans, Louisiana.		
Painters	$1 50 to	$1 75	Painters	$2 00 to	$2 50
Bricklayers	1 75 to	2 00	Bricklayers	2 50 to	3 50
Stone Masons	1 50 to	2 00	Stone Masons	2 00 to	3 00
Carpenters	1 25 to	1 75	Carpenters	2 25 to	2 50
Plasterers	1 50 to	2 00	Plasterers	2 00 to	2 25
Laborers	50 to	1 00	Laborers	1 25 to	1 50

FREE STATES.

Per Day.

Pittsburg, Pennsylvania.

Painters	$1 50 to	$2 00
Bricklayers	1 75 to	2 00
Stone Masons	1 50 to	1 75
Carpenters	1 37 to	1 75
Plasterers	1 50 to	1 75
Laborers	75	—

Cincinnati, Ohio.

Painters	$1 50 to	$1 75
Bricklayers	2 00 to	2 50
Stone Masons	1 25 to	1 50
Carpenters	1 00 to	2 00
Plasterers	1 50 to	1 75
Laborers	75 to	1 00

Detroit, Michigan.

Painters	—	$1 50
Bricklayers	—	2 00
Stone Masons	—	1 50
Carpenters	—	1 75
Plasterers	—	1 50
Laborers	—	87

Columbus, Ohio.

Painters	$1 50	—
Bricklayers	2 00	—
Stone Masons	1 50	—
Carpenters	1 50 to	$2 00
Plasterers	1 75 to	2 00
Laborers	75 to	1 00

Buffalo, New York.

Painters	$1 50 to	$2 00
Bricklayers	1 50 to	2 00
Stone Masons	1 25 to	1 75
Carpenters	1 00 to	1 50
Plasters	1 70 to	1 75
Laborers	60 to	75

Lowell, Massachusetts.

Painters	$1 00 to	$1 75
Bricklayers	1 50 to	1 75
Stone Masons	1 50 to	2 00
Carpenters	1 25 to	1 75
Plasterers	1 00 to	1 25
Laborers	75 to	1 00

Bangor, Maine.

Painters	$1 50 to	$2 00
Bricklayers	50 to	2 00
Stone Masons	1 50 to	2 00
Carpenters	1 50 to	2 00
Plasterers	1 50 to	2 00
Laborers	75 to	1 00

Madison, Wisconsin.

Painters	$2 00	—
Bricklayers	2 00	—
Stone Masons	1 50	—
Carpenters	2 00	—
Plasterers	2 00	—
Laborers	50 to	75

SLAVE STATES.

Per Day.

Richmond, Virginia.

Painters	$1 75 to	$2 25
Bricklayers	2 00 to	3 00
Stone Masons	2 00 to	2 50
Carpenters	1 50 to	2 00
Plasterers	1 75 to	2 25
Laborers	1 00 to	1 50

Louisville, Kentucky.

Painters	$1 75 to	$2 00
Bricklayers	2 50 to	3 00
Stone Masons	1 75 to	2 00
Carpenters	1 75 to	2 50
Plasterers	2 00 to	2 25
Laborers	1 00 to	1 25

Galveston, Texas.

Painters	$1 75 to	$2 00
Bricklayers	2 75 to	3 00
Stone Masons	2 00 to	3 00
Carpenters	2 00 to	3 00
Plasterers	1 75 to	2 25
Laborers	1 25 to	1 50

Charleston, South Carolina.

Painters	$1 75 to	$2 00
Bricklayers	2 50 to	3 50
Stone Masons	2 00 to	2 50
Carpenters	2 50 to	2 75
Plasterers	2 00 to	2 50
Laborers	1 00 to	1 50

Little Rock, Arkansas.

Painters	$2 50 to	$3 50
Bricklayers	2 00 to	3 00
Stone Masons	2 00 to	2 50
Carpenters	2 00 to	5 00
Plasterers	2 50 to	3 00
Laborers	1 00 to	1 25

Norfolk, Virginia.

Painters	$1 75 to	$2 00
Bricklayers	2 00 to	2 50
Stone Masons	2 25 to	2 50
Carpenters	1 50 to	2 00
Plasterers	1 75	
Laborers	1 00 to	1 25

Memphis, Tennessee.

Painters	$2 00 to	$2 50
Bricklayers	2 00 to	3 00
Stone Masons	2 00 to	2 50
Carpenters	2 25 to	2 50
Plasterers	1 75 to	2 50
Laborers	1 00 to	1 50

Nashville, Tennessee.

Painters	$2 25 to	$2 50
Bricklayers	2 50 to	3 00
Stone Masons	2 00 to	3 50
Carpenters	2 25 to	2 50
Plasterers	2 00 to	2 50
Laborers	1 00 to	1 25

In view of these facts, why do gentlemen speak of an irrepressible conflict? The northern people are told, if you are not constantly on the alert; if you are not driving back the encroachments of the South, as an immovable rock resists the advancing waves, the South, in a very short time, will take possession of the rye fields of Massachu-

setts and the wheat fields of New York, and cultivate them with
slave labor. Is not that utopian? Is it not ideal—mere fancy, with no
truth, no reality, in it? When touched and analyzed, it vanishes into
thin air.

But, the Senator from New York goes on, still inculcating this
idea in reference to the South, the dissolution of the Union, and all
that:

> It is true that they [meaning our fathers] necessarily and wisely modi-
> fied this policy of freedom, by leaving it to the several States, affected as
> they were by differing circumstances, to abolish slavery in their own way
> and at their own pleasure, instead of confiding that duty to Congress,
> and that they secured to the slave States, while yet retaining the system
> of slavery, a three-fifths representation of slaves in the Federal Govern-
> ment, until they should find themselves able to relinquish it with safety.
> But the very nature of these modifications fortifies my position that the
> fathers knew that the two systems could not endure within the Union, and
> expected that, within a short period, slavery would disappear forever.
> Moreover, in order that these modifications might not altogether defeat
> their grand design of a Republic maintaining universal equality, they
> provided that two thirds of the States might amend the Constitution.

Three fourths he should have said. Two thirds may propose an
amendment; two thirds of the States can call a convention; three
fourths must ratify the amendment. But the idea is all we are after.
He says—and I want to do the Senator justice, as he is not present;
I read more of his speech than I would if he were here:

> It remains to say on this point only one word, to guard against mis-
> apprehension. If these States are to again become universally slave-
> holding, I do not pretend to say with what violations of the Constitution
> that end shall be accomplished.

He seems to indulge the idea that slavery is again to become universal. See the sophistry of it:

> On the other hand, while I do confidently believe and hope that my
> country will yet become a land of universal freedom, I do not expect that
> it will be made so otherwise than through the action of the several States
> coöperating with the Federal Government, and all acting in strict con-
> formity with their respective constitutions.

Is there not an idea under that? His language is "in strict conformity with their" (meaning the Federal and State Governments)
"respective Constitutions." He intimates that two thirds of the
States can amend the Constitution; that the North is to go on in
conformity with the Constitution until slavery shall be narrowed
down to less than one third or one fourth of the States, and then
amend the Constitution, and obliterate it at once. Is not that the
plain interpretation? Cannot we understand that? You talk about
southern men being alarmed. They are not alarmed, but they see the
advance; they see the encroaching doctrine; they see the principles

laid down by which an institution that is dear to them is to be up-rooted and blotted out of existence. Then ought you to think a south-ern man violent, and call him rash when he declares that he will not be willing to see this man, or some other man entertaining and ad-vocating precisely the same doctrines, administer this Government when it is to be administered to the destruction of the Constitution, and the destruction of the institution that is most dear to him. Call us fire-eaters! I am no fire-eater; I am not panic-stricken; but be-cause I am neither, should I be blind and not see the advance; should I be deaf, and not hear the roar of the approaching storm? Can we be mistaken? What is covered up there? You see he speaks of the idea of consolidation. He speaks of the manner of amending the Constitution. He refers to the time when he believes that freedom will universally prevail. Then what more does he say:

Having spent my manhood, though not my whole life, in a free State, no aristocracy of any kind, much less an aristocracy of slaveholders, shall ever make the laws of the land in which I shall be content to live. Having seen the society around me universally engaged in agriculture, manufac-tures, and trade, which were innocent and beneficent, I shall never be a denizen of a State where men and women are reared as cattle, and bought and sold as merchandise.

Ought a man who entertains these sentiments, and looks to the consummation of these ends, to be willing to rule a people under whose laws he says he would not be content to live? And he says, too, if this can be the case, "where liberty dwells, there is my coun-try." Can we be mistaken in the meaning of all this? Would not the promotion and elevation of men entertaining these doctrines, and who intend to carry out these principles, be contributing to the de-struction of the Constitution, and of the Union which is based upon it, and of the institutions which are secured and guarantied to the South?

I have already referred to John Quincy Adams's declaration, that, under the treaty-making power, in the event of an insurrection of the slaves, and the Federal Government should be called upon to interpose, this Government could emancipate the slaves. Then look at the doctrines of the speech from which I have just quoted. Now bring into power a man entertaining these sentiments, and send some more John Browns on their forays against the South; let this Gov-ernment in the hands of such a man be called upon for force to put them down, and where shall we stand? Are we prepared to submit to encroachments of this kind, and see them openly proclaimed by the elevation and installation into power of men entertaining such doctrines? I do not wish to be a panic maker; I do not wish to alarm anybody; I do not suppose I could alarm any one, if I were disposed to do so; but I tell gentlemen of the North and of the South that there is a state of things in the country that never existed before. There is no outburst, there is no passion, but there is deep decided feeling in the country; and the idea is obtaining too much currency that this Union is to be dissolved. That seems almost to be a foregone conclusion, and it has got to be, in the minds of many, a belief that it is simply a question of time.

Do we not see what the inevitable result of pressing such doctrines upon the country will be, in this state of the public feeling? For myself, I am no dissolutionist; I am no madcap on this subject. Because we cannot get our constitutional rights, I do not intend to be one of those who will violate the Constitution. When the time comes, if it ever does come, when it shall be necessary—and God forbid that it ever should come—I intend to place my feet upon that Constitution which I have sworn to support, and to stand there and battle for all its guarantees; and if the Constitution is to be violated, if this Union is to be broken up, it shall be done by those who are stealthily and insidiously making encroachments upon its very foundation. I intend to stand upon the Constitution to the very last, and I tell the North it is with them; they have the Union in their own hands, and if it is broken up, it will be their own work, not that of the South; for all we ask is the Constitution of the country and the fulfillment of its guarantees, and upon them we intend to stand, be the consequences what they may.

God forbid that the time should ever come when this country shall be involved in a servile or a civil war. I trust that that day may be postponed to some far-distant future; and I hope, in the sincerity of my heart, that that future may never arrive. I would rather see this people involved in hostility against every Power on the face of the civilized globe than to see it involved in civil and servile war. If blood is to be shed, be it so; but let it not be the blood of the people of these confederated States, fighting against each other. So far as I am concerned, I intend to stand by the Constitution and its guarantees as the ark of our safety, as the palladium of our civil and our religious liberty; I intend to cling to it as the shipwrecked mariner clings to the last plank when night and the tempest close around him. It is in other hands; it is not in ours. We are for the Constitution as it is; we intend to stand by it. But when the time shall come, if it ever does come, for dividing this Union, I ask my friends, North and South, where is the line to be drawn? The North, which is so rampant, so bent upon the idea of universal liberty, will surely not have the audacity or the impudence to come upon slave territory; they certainly will not approach as far south as this Capitol. Surely they will not want to embrace, in a government formed by them, the shaft that has been reared in this District in commemoration of the illustrious Washington.[17] Will they want to come that far south, and lay their hands upon all the pledges to the Union and the Constitution which compose that shaft reared in our immediate vicinity? Certainly not. Who will take our pledge; who will carry it away; who will first lay his impious hand for spoliation upon that tower? I felt almost like exclaiming, in the language so often used by the schoolboy, from Addison's old play of Cato, that teaches stern purity, unyielding honesty, and a high appreciation of right:

——————— Is there not some chosen curse,
Some hidden thunder in the stores of heaven,
Red with uncommon wrath, to blast the wretch
Who owes his greatness to his country's ruin? [18]

I feel, in the sincerity of my heart, like invoking the most withering anathemas upon the man who would lay his sacrilegious hand upon this glorious Union of these States; who would take our pledge of faith; who would take the block of marble deposited by Tennessee, which has inscribed upon its surface the sentiment of her illustrious son who now sleeps in his grave—"The Federal Union, it must be preserved."[19] Who will carry away that monument built by the contributions of the people? I imagine that about the time when that takes place, that old man to whom I have referred, that patriot soldier who sleeps in his honored grave, will rise, shake off the habiliments of the tomb, and forbid the act.

But, Mr. President, I resume the line of my argument. I commenced with the purpose of showing that the recent foray upon Harper's Ferry was the legitimate result of certain teachings to which I have referred. Look at the provisional government which was framed by those who carried on that expedition; look at their idea of getting up stampedes, and their expectation that when they struck the first blow a portion of the white population and the blacks would flock to their standard, and that they could maintain themselves there for a certain time, and then the Federal Government would be made an instrument for the overthrow of slavery. I think the act is a legitimate result of the teachings; and those who have taught and still teach their followers these doctrines, though they may not have intended it, are, in fact, responsible for it. It is the result of their teachings, it is their work; and now is the time to commence a reformation, and put forth different teachings on this subject.

But, Mr. President, Senators have undertaken to rebuke those of us who have spoken of John Brown's acts as theft, murder, and treason, and apologies are offered for the man who has committed such outrageous offenses. I picked up a newspaper not long since which, referring to the acts of John Brown, said that, if he passed from the prison to the scaffold, making no false step, his gallows would be more glorious than the cross; that Christ, in the depth of his agony, had asked that his cup might pass from his lips, but that John Brown has drank it to the dregs, and therefore John Brown and his gallows have become superior to Christ and his cross.[20] The idea was, that the coming and mission of Christ were a failure, and that John Brown and the gallows on which he was executed would be their modern cross and their Christ. Such is the blasphemy of these teachings. I once heard it said that fanaticism always ends in hell or in heaven. I believe it is true. It is one of those wild, maddening passions that take possession of the human heart, and that always carry it to excess. There is no medium, and there is no cure for it but a consumption of the passion itself. I have got another idea in ethics, and that is that there never was any people on the face of the earth greater than the god they worshiped; and if John Brown becomes the Christ, and his gallows the cross, God deliver me from such people as they, whether they are fanatics, Democratic or Republican, or any other description of persons—I care not by what name they are called.

I hoped, when this resolution was introduced, that it would be kept clear from party associations, and that it would pass with unanimity, without any apologies or excuses being lugged in for the acts complained of. We find, however, that Senators disclaim the acts of John Brown in one breath, and in another they hold out apologies and excuses for the man, saying that he showed himself a man of endurance, a man of philosophy, a man of tact, a man of sense; and when we speak of him as a thief and a robber and a murderer and a traitor, they declare that we should not say such things about John Brown. Those may make him a god who will, and worship him who can; he is not my god, and I shall not worship at his shrine.

The honorable Senator from Wisconsin, [Mr. Doolittle]—and I confess that I am surprised at him—after condemning the abstract offenses of murder and treason in old John Brown, went on to state:

Under what circumstances do you hear of him? One of his sons is taken by Captain Pate, bound with thongs, driven in front of horses on foot, without food or water, until from famishing he becomes a maniac; and he has never recovered from his insanity to this day. In presence of the house of old John Brown, another son of his, a but half-witted boy, is shot down. Then it is that we begin to hear of old John Brown as a leader of a band of free-State men in Kansas. Then it was that the iron entered into the old man's soul; and from that hour up to the moment of his death he swore eternal hostility, and from that hour was ready not only to give his own life, but to take the lives of other men, in order to give liberty to those who were enslaved.[21]

Accommodations in Hibernian Hall, Democratic Convention, Charleston, S. C.
From *Harper's Weekly*, May 5, 1860.

Andrew Johnson, Democratic hopeful, as enlarged
from the illustration at left.

A biographical sketch of Johnson in *Frank Leslie's Illustrated
Newspaper*, April 21, 1860.

(left)
Prominent southern presidential aspirants. Howell Cobb (top left); Jefferson
Davis (left center); James L. Orr (bottom left); Sam Houston (top center);
Robert M. T. Hunter (bottom center); Andrew Johnson (top right); James H.
Hammond (right center); Robert Toombs (bottom right). From *Frank Leslie's
Illustrated Newspaper*, April 21, 1860.

A view of the National Capitol, *c*1857, showing construction of the new dome.
Courtesy National Archives.

Now, what is that calculated to do? I will not assume what it was intended to do. I presume that the Senator's motive was entirely correct; but what effect is such language calculated to have? It is to heighten the idea of this old felon to every fanatic who may read it. Then it was, after these atrocities in his presence, that the iron entered the old man's soul! This is tendered as an excuse for John Brown having committed murder, treason, and robbery. The iron entered his soul! Then he became a stoic; then he became philosophic; then he became a patriot; then he became careless of consequences! Well, now suppose that these things had taken place in the manner the Senator seems to infer that they did occur. We assume this to be a Christian community, and if it was true that his sons were badly maltreated, was that any excuse for his violating all the laws of humanity and of God? He was in a Christian country; he had his remedy without resorting to the means to which he had recourse. We have all read that "Whoso sheddeth man's blood, by man shall his blood be shed."[22] And also, "Thou shalt not kill."[23] It seems we have some new-born Christians who are making John Brown their leader, who are trying to canonize him and make him a great apostle and martyr. Were these the elements of a Christian and a Christian martyr? How do the facts stand in this case? When was old man Brown's son killed, and when did he commit these atrocities? Even admitting the truth of the statement of the Senator from Wisconsin, they are not justifiable; but when we show that the facts are different, they are less so. The circumstances are stated in the evidence of Mr. Harris, which will be found in a report made by a committee of Congress, and republished in the Herald of Freedom of Kansas[24]—a paper that has at its head for President, the name of a Republican, Mr. Chase, of Ohio, and Mr. Banks, of Massachusetts, for Vice President:

The circumstances attending William Sherman's assassination are testified to by James Harris, of Franklin county, Kansas. Mr. Sherman was staying over night at the house of Harris, when, on the 24th of May, at about two o'clock, Captain John Brown and party came there, and after taking some property, and questioning Harris and others, Sherman was asked to walk out. Mr. Harris, in his affidavit, says: "Old man Brown asked Mr. Sherman to go out with him, and Sherman then went out with Brown. I heard nothing more for about fifteen minutes. Two of the 'northern army,' as they styled themselves, stayed with us until they heard a cap burst, and then these two men left. Next morning, about ten o'clock, I found William Sherman dead, in the creek near my house. I was looking for him; as he had not come back, I thought he had been murdered. I took Mr. William Sherman (body) out of the creek and examined it. Mrs. Whiteman was with me. Sherman's skull was split open in two places, and some of his brains were washed out by the water; a large hole was cut in his breast, and his left hand was cut off, except a little piece of skin on one side."[25]

This was the 24th of May. I will read from the same paper another extract:

When the news of the threatened siege of Lawrence reached John Brown, jr., who was a member of the Topeka Legislature, he organized a company of about sixty men and marched towards Lawrence. Arriving at Palmyra, he learned of the sacking of the town, and the position of the people. He reconnoitered for a time in the vicinity, but finally marched back towards Ossawatomie. The night before reaching that place, when only a few miles away, they camped for the night. Old John Brown, who, we believe, was with the party, singled out with himself, seven men. These he marched to a point eight miles above the mouth of Pottawatomie creek, and called from their beds, at their several residences, at the hour of midnight, on the 24th of May, Allen Wilkinson, William Sherman, William P. Doyle, William Doyle, and Drury Doyle. All were found the next morning, by the road side, or in the highway, some with a gash in their heads and sides, and their throats cut; others with their skulls split open in two places, with holes in their breasts, and hands cut off.

He seems to have had a great passion for cutting off hands:

No man in Kansas has pretended to deny that old John Brown led that murderous foray which massacred those men. Up to that period not a hair of old John Brown's head, or that of his sons, had been injured by the pro-slavery party.

It was not until the 30th of August, three months after the Pottawatomie massacre, that the attack was made on Ossawatomie by the pro-slavery forces, and Frederick Brown, a son of old John, was killed.[26]

To show all the facts in regard to the massacre of the 24th of May, I will read to the Senate the affidavits of some of the eye-witnesses of the transaction. Allen Wilkinson was a member of the Kansas Legislature—a quiet, inoffensive man. His widow, Louisa Jane Wilkinson, testified that on the night of the 24th of May, 1856, between the hours of midnight and daybreak, she thinks, a party of men came to the house where they were residing and forcibly carried her husband away; that they took him in the name of the "northern army," and that the next morning he was found about one hundred and fifty yards from the house, dead. Mrs. Wilkinson was very ill at the time of measles. She says further:

I begged them to let Mr. Wilkinson stay with me, saying that I was sick and helpless, and could not stay by myself. My husband also asked them to let him stay with me, until he could get some one to wait on me; told them that he would not run off, but he would be there the next day, or whenever called for; the old man who seemed to be in command looked at me, and then around at the children, and replied, "you have neighbors." I said, "so I have, but they are not here, and I cannot go for them." The old man replied, "it matters not," and told him to get ready. My husband wanted to put on his boots, and get ready, so as to be protected from the damp and night air, but they would not let him. They then took my husband away. * *

After they were gone I thought I heard my husband's voice in complaint. * * * Next morning, Mr. Wilkinson's body was found about one hundred and fifty yards from the house, in some dead brush. A lady who saw my husband's body said that there was a gash in his head and side. Others said he was cut in the throat twice.[27]

Mr. Doyle and his sons were murdered on the same night with Sherman and Wilkinson; and Mrs. Doyle's deposition gives this account of it:

The undersigned, Mahala Doyle, states on oath: I am the widow of the late James P. Doyle. We moved into the Territory—that is, my husband, myself, and children—moved into the Territory of Kansas some time in November, A. D. 1855, and settled upon Musketo creek, about one mile from its mouth, and where it empties into Pottawatomie creek, in Franklin county. On Saturday, the 24th of May, A. D. 1855 [*sic*], about eleven o'clock at night, after we had all retired, my husband, James P. Doyle, myself, and six children, five boys and one girl—the eldest is about twenty-two years of age; his name is William. The next is about twenty years of age; his name is Drury. The next is about seventeen years of age; his name is John. The next is about thirteen years of age; her name is Polly Ann. The next is about eight years of age; his name is James. The next is about five years of age; his name is Henry. We were all in bed, when we heard some persons come into the yard, and rap at the door, and call for Mr. Doyle, my husband. This was about eleven o'clock on Saturday night, of the 24th of May last. My husband got up and went to the door. Those outside inquired for Mr. Wilkinson, and where he lived. My husband said he would tell them. Mr. Doyle, my husband, and several came into the house, and said they were from the army. My husband was a pro-slavery man. They told my husband that he and the boys must surrender; they were then prisoners. The men were armed with pistols and large knives. They first took my husband out of the house; then took two of my sons—William and Drury—out, and then took my husband and these two boys (William and Drury) away. My son John was spared, because I asked them, in tears, to spare him.

In a short time afterwards I heard the report of pistols; I heard two reports. After which I heard moaning as if a person was dying. Then I heard a wild whoop. They had asked before they went away for our horses. We told them that our horses were out on the prairie. My husband and two boys, my sons, did not come back any more. I went out next morning in search of them, and found my husband and William, my son, lying dead in the road, near together, about two hundred yards from the house. They were buried the next day. On the day of the burying, I saw the dead body of Drury. Fear for myself and the remaining children, induced me to leave the home where we had been living. We had improved our claim a little. I left and went to the State of Missouri.

her
MAHALIA X DOYLE.
mark.

Witness: T. J. Goforth.

State of Missouri, *Jackson county*, ss.

On the 17th day of June, A. D. 1856, personally appeared before me, the subscriber, a justice of the peace in and for the county and State aforesaid, Mahala Doyle, whose name appears to the above and foregoing statement, and makes oath according to law, that the above and foregoing statement is true as therein set forth.

Given under my hand and seal the day and year above written.

[Seal.]   THOMAS J. GOFORTH,
                                 Justice of the Peace.[28]

John Doyle confirms the testimony of his mother generally, and I will only give a short portion of his testimony:

I found my father and brother William lying dead about two hundred yards from the house. I saw my brother lying dead on the ground, about one hundred and fifty yards from the house, in the grass near a ravine. His fingers were cut off, and his arms cut off. His head was cut open. There was a hole in his breast. William's head was cut open, and a hole was in his side. My father was shot in the forehead and stabbed in the breast. I have talked often with northern men in the Territory, and these men talk exactly like eastern and northern men talk—that is, their language and pronunciation were similar to those eastern and northern men with whom we have talked. An old man commanded the party. He was dark-complected, and his face was slim. We had lighted the candle, and about eight of them entered the house. There were some outside. The complexion of most of those eight whom I saw in the house were of a sandy complexion. My father and brothers were pro-slavery men, and belonged to the law and order party.[29]

Mrs. Doyle wrote a letter to Brown during his imprisonment, showing that she still regarded him as the murderer of her husband and children:

Chattanooga, Tennessee, *November* 20, 1859. John Brown. Sir: Although vengeance is not mine, I confess that I do feel gratified to hear that you were stopped in your fiendish career at Harper's Ferry with the loss of your two sons. You can now appreciate my distress in Kansas, when you then and there entered my house at midnight, and arrested my husband and two boys, and took them out of the yard, and in cold blood shot them dead in my hearing. You cannot say you done it to free our slaves; we had none, and never expected to own one; but has only made me a poor, disconsolate widow, with helpless children. While I feel for your folly, I do hope and trust you will meet your just reward. Oh, how it pained my heart to hear the dying groans of my husband and children. If this scrawl gives you any consolation you are welcome to it.

MAHALA DOYLE.

N. B. My son, John Doyle, whose life I begged of you, is now grown up, and is very desirous to be at Charlestown on the day of your execution; would certainly be there if his means would permit it, that he might adjust the rope around your neck, if Governor Wise would permit.

M. D.

To John Brown, *Commander of the army at Harper's Ferry, Charlestown, Jefferson county, Virginia. Care of Jailor, Charlestown.*[30]

Now, how do the facts stand? What becomes of the apology, what becomes of the excuse? They say that old Brown is not identified as the man who led the party that committed this massacre. Harris says John Brown came to the house; and the description of him given by young Doyle, in 1856, is exactly that given now. Three months after William Doyle and his two sons were murdered, three months after Sherman was murdered, his skull cut open in two places, and the stream had washed the brains out of his cranium —three months after that, John Brown's son was killed at Ossawatomie. Then, what becomes of this excuse? Why this apology for a man like this? Three long months after he had committed this fiendish act, his son lost his life at the battle of Ossawatomie. It was on that night, about eleven o'clock, as testified by Mrs. Doyle, as testified by her son, as testified by Harris, these men, innocent, unoffending men, were taken out, and in the midnight hour and in the forest and on the road side fell victims to the insatiable thirst of John Brown for blood. Then it was that these murders were committed, that hell entered his heart—not the iron his soul. Then it was that he shrank from the dimensions of a human being into those of a reptile. Then it was, if not before, that he changed his character to a demon who had lost all the virtues of a man. And you talk about sympathy for John Brown!

[Doolittle explains that he did not intend to justify Brown's actions, but rather that he wanted to call the Senate's attention "to the school in which John Brown was educated," referring to the earlier raid by David Atchison of Missouri into Kansas.]

Mr. JOHNSON, of Tennessee. I am very much obliged to the Senator for the explanation he has made; but he has only confirmed the statement of facts that I relied upon to strip old John Brown of all apology and excuse for his outrageous career and offenses. I stated that the murder of the three Doyles and of Sherman and Wilkinson was on the 24th of May, predicated on the affidavits of Mrs. Doyle, Mrs. Wilkinson, and Mr. Harris. The gentleman corrects me by reading from a book[31] that I suppose has been got up and made to sell, which says that old man Brown's son was arrested on the last day of May. I exhibited the fact that the murder was committed on the 24th of May, and to contradict my statement, he attempts to show that his son received this ill-treatment on the last day of May. Does that contradict what I said? Does that change the nature of the fact in the least? Not at all. Old John Brown and his comrades, midnight assassins, then imbrued their hands in blood, with the weapons that had been sent to them from the northern States, or that they took with them. The sight of this blood, and the exhibition of these weapons to his son, so maddened him that it set him crazy without the ill-treatment of any pro-slavery man. His heart had not become adamant; he was not so steeled to barbarity as his father was, and when he saw the weapons, and the blood that was crying to Heaven for justice, he became a maniac. Does that disprove anything that I said? The book says this was on the last day of May. The affidavits show that the murders were committed on the 24th. The Senator from Wisconsin reads from the same book in reference to Brown's other son, precisely what I said, that it was on the 30th of August he was killed, at the battle of Ossawatomie.

What, then, does the explanation amount to? Has the Senator corrected any fact that I stated? He seems to think that I misrepresented him. The Senate will bear me witness, and the report of what I have said will show, that I stated expressly that in one portion of his speech he had disclaimed any sympathy with the conduct of old John Brown at Harper's Ferry, in the abstract, and then I read that portion of his speech in reference to John Brown. Is that misrepresenting the Senator? I stated all that he had said, and he has furnished additional proof of the facts which I presented. These facts stand uncontradicted.

John Brown stands before the country a murderer. The enormity, the extraordinary ferociousness of the father set the son mad. The blood of these murdered men, not unlike that of sacrificed Abel, cried even from the tongueless caverns of the earth to him for pity, and to Heaven for justice; but his iron heart, not soul, refused to yield; but Heaven, in the process of time, has meted out to him justice on the gallows. Justice divine to punish sin moves slow, the slower is its pace, the surer is its blow.[32] It will overtake us if living; it will overtake us if dead. Justice has overtaken its victim, and he has gone to eternity with crimsoned hands, with blood upon his head.

But the Senator talks about the school in which John Brown was taught. Why, sir, John Brown, according to his own confession, had entertained these ideas for twenty years. John Brown did not go to Kansas to go to school. He went there as a teacher; and on the 24th of May, at the mid hour of night, from the wife and mother, he dragged the husband and two sons, and imbrued his hands in their blood. These were the doctrines that he went there to teach. He did not go there to be taught; but he went there as a teacher. These were his teachings. Imagine the cries and lamentations on the one hand, and the shrieks of the dying and the mutilated on the other. I think sometimes that I hear shrieks so loud, so wild, so clear, that even listening angels stoop from heaven to hear.[33] This is the man for whom an apology is offered. I did the Senator the justice to say that he disclaimed all sympathy with Brown, and yet I read what, in fact, was an apology. What furthermore did the Senator say? We have shown, and the fact is not controverted, that he murdered five human beings on the 24th of May. They have shown, in trying to answer this, that his son did not receive this ill-treatment from Captain Pate until the last day of May. We have shown that his other son was not killed until the 30th of August. Let us remember these facts, and come to the old man as being a thief and murderer. I want these modern fanatics, who have adopted John Brown and his gallows as their Christ and their cross, to see who their Christ is. The Senator says again:

> I regret that gentlemen, in speaking of this man Brown, should be pleased to speak of him as a robber, or a thief, or a vagabond, in the ordinary sense of the term. Sir, it is of the essence of robbery and theft that the robber or the thief who robs or steals should act from the desire of gain. Certainly no such charge can be made against this man, as that he was actuated by the lust of gain. He acted from far different motives. He sought to give liberty to the enslaved, and laid down his life for that purpose; freely and bravely did he do it.

That is, you may steal and commit theft if you do it to aid in the cause of the abolition of slavery. Have we any proof that this is so? What does Mrs. Wilkinson say in her affidavit? When John Brown and his comrades were there on the night of the 24th, when they took Wilkinson out and murdered him, just before they left they took his property and his only horse. I suppose they needed the horse to aid in the emancipation of slaves! Horse stealing is carried on to a great extent sometimes in a frontier country. Mrs. Doyle states that they inquired where their horse was, and were told it was out on the prairie. What took place at Harper's Ferry? They took Colonel Washington's silver and his watch.[34] What does he admit in his own confession? That he during the last winter had stolen, had kidnapped, and run off eleven slaves from the State of Missouri to Kansas. That is not stealing, though; I suppose that is not theft, that is not robbery; and we ought not to talk about this old man as stealing in the common acceptation of the term! What is it, I, ask the country, I ask the Senate, if it is not stealing, robbery, highway robbery? And yet these things are thrown out, perhaps not intended, but they do operate as an apology and excuse in the minds of many for the infamy, the murders, the thieving, the treacherous conduct of this old man Brown, who was nothing more than a murderer, a robber, a thief, and a traitor.

I think, Mr. President, that so far as John Brown is concerned, the facts which I have presented stand uncontroverted. The Senator has failed to touch them. He has not removed them, but has added strength and additional proof to what I said in reference to them. It was not my intention to consume this length of time, and I should not have said a single word on the subject if the resolutions could have been adopted without discussion, and especially so if a reference had not been made to John Brown not being a murderer and a thief, involving the reputation and character of some of the citizens of my own State.

There does seem to be a providential interposition in this affair. Brown murdered Doyle and his two sons. Doyle left a widow and four helpless children. Justice seemed to be a little tardy; but it kept constantly in pursuit of its victim, and but a short time since the man who murdered Doyle and his two sons, fell a victim, with his two sons, at Harper's Ferry. I do not say that this was a stroke of Providence; but it was a singular coincidence. He whose hands were red, crimson with the blood of a father and two sons, fell a victim at Harper's Ferry with his own two sons. It seems that divine Providence intended it as a rebuke, an illustration that justice will not only overtake its victim, but will mete out justice in a similar manner.

I think, Mr. President, that I have shown the tendency of the policy to which I have called attention. Whether it has been designed at all times by those who preached it or not, I shall not undertake to say; but I will say that the effect of that kind of teaching has been the result which is so evident; and I want to say now, in no spirit of boasting, to my friends East and West, North and South, that the time has arrived when these things ought to be stopped; the time has arrived when encroachments on the institutions of the South should cease; the time has arrived when the southern States and their institutions should be let alone; the time has arrived when you must either preserve the Constitution or you must dissolve this Union; the time has arrived when we have well nigh done making any appeals to you on the subject; but all we ask of you is, that, as brothers of the same great Confederacy, you will understand and carry out the Constitution as it is, and let us cease this bickering. Let us cease this agitation, and stand upon the Constitution as the common altar, and maintain all its guarantees, and swear by our fathers and the God who made us that the Constitution and its guarantees shall be preserved; and, in doing so, we shall preserve the Union; and in preserving the Union, we shall have peace and harmony, and the unexampled prosperity which has visited our country will continue to go on.

Cong. Globe, 36 Cong., 1 Sess., 100–107.

1. Three days before Congress convened on December 5, John Brown was executed following a seven-day trial for murder and criminal conspiracy in seizing the federal arsenal at Harper's Ferry. On the opening day, James Mason of Virginia introduced a resolution calling for a complete investigation of the Harper's Ferry incident—a resolution which dominated Senate discussions until its adoption on December 14. Not to be outdone, Lyman Trumbull, Illinois Republican, offered a resolution for an investigation of a December, 1855, raid upon a federal arsenal in Liberty, Missouri, carried out by proslavery forces interested in extending slavery to Kansas. Nevins, *Emergence of Lincoln*, II, 86–90, 95–97; *Cong. Globe*, 36 Cong., 1 Sess., 1, 5–15. For John Brown, see Stephen B. Oates, *To Purge This Land with Blood: A Biography of John Brown* (New York, 1970).

2. Lyman Trumbull (1813–1896) had held various Illinois state offices, including justice of the supreme court (1848–53), before being elected senator as an anti-Nebraska Democrat (1855–73). Joining the Republican party during the late 1850's, he later introduced several significant pieces

of legislation, among them the first two confiscation acts, the Freedmen's Bureau bill, and the nation's first Civil Rights bill, and fathered the Thirteenth Amendment. *BDAC*, 1730; Mark M. Krug, *Lyman Trumbull: Conservative Radical* (New York, 1965), *passim*.

3. Speaking December 8 on Mason's resolution, Trumbull had quoted this part of the 1856 Republican platform. *Cong. Globe*, 36 Cong., 1 Sess., 54; Porter and Johnson, *National Party Platforms*, 27.

4. Art. IV, Sec. 2.

5. Illinois Constitution of 1847, Declaration of Rights, Art. XIII, Sec. 1.

6. *Ibid.*, Militia, Art. VIII, Sec. 1.

7. *Cong. Globe*, 36 Cong., 1 Sess., 56.

8. Clement C. Clay.

9. Although he had many followers, Daniel Hoffmann seems not to have founded a sect. Samuel M. Jackson, ed., *The New Schaff-Herzog Encyclopedia of Religious Knowledge* (12 vols., New York, 1908–12), V, 309; see also *Johnson Papers*, II, 119n.

10. Anas, in Thomas Jefferson Randolph, ed., *Memoir, Correspondence, and Miscellanies from the Papers of Thomas Jefferson* (4 vols., Charlottesville, Va., 1839), IV, 516–17. Johnson had used this passage, as well as the following passages from John Quincy Adams' speech and letter, in his first speech before the House in January, 1844. See Speech on Gag Resolution, January 31, 1844, *Johnson Papers*, I, 142, 147n.

11. Coffin (1776–1853) was president of Greeneville College in 1803. *Ibid.*, 147n.

12. Adams' remarks were made on June 9, 1841. *Cong. Globe*, 27 Cong., 1 Sess., 38.

13. *Niles' Register*, December 2, 1843, p. 218. See also *Johnson Papers*, I, 148n.

14. A quotation from Seward's "Irrepressible Conflict" speech, made in Rochester, New York, October 25, 1858. New York *Times*, October 28, 1858.

15. Graham N. Fitch of Indiana was in the chair.

16. The original of these tables has not been discovered. Interestingly enough, J. D. B. DeBow, in printing a portion of these figures a year later, observed, "The following table was recently compiled by Senator Johnson of Tennessee, from information received in reply to a circular letter sent to points indicated." *DeBow's Review*, XXX (1861), 72.

17. The Washington monument, designed by Robert Mills, was at this date only 150 feet above ground. Construction, halted because of lack of funds in 1855, was not recommenced until after the Civil War. Green, *Washington*, I, 170–71, 204, 238.

18. Addison's *Cato*, Act I, sc. 1.

19. Andrew Jackson's retort to the Calhoun nullifiers in a Jefferson's birthday dinner toast, April 13, 1830.

20. While it is impossible to determine which newspaper Johnson may have read, many northern preachers and reformers likened John Brown and his gallows to the cross, and their words were widely reported in the press. The Reverend Edwin M. Wheelock of Dover, New Hampshire, went so far as to declare that "*the gallows from which John Brown ascends into Heaven, will be, in our politics, what the cross is in our religion. . . . To be hanged in Virginia is like being crucified at Jerusalem.*" Ralph Waldo Emerson, speaking at a meeting in Boston's Tremont Temple on November 8, referred to Brown as "the new saint awaiting martyrdom, and who, if he shall suffer, will make the gallows glorious like the cross." New York *Times*, November 29, 1859; James Ford Rhodes, *History of the United States from the Compromise of 1850* (9 vols., New York, 1906), II, 413.

21. Doolittle's remarks came during the December 7 debate on the Harper's Ferry incident. *Cong. Globe*, 36 Cong., 1 Sess., 35.

22. Gen. 9: 6.

23. Deut. 5: 17.

24. James Harris, who lived alongside Pottawatomie Creek in Kansas Territory, sent this affidavit to the House committee investigating affairs in Kansas. Published in Lawrence, the *Herald of Freedom* was an anti-slavery paper owned and edited by George Brown, a former Pennsylvanian. *House Report* No. 200 (commonly called the *Howard Report*), 34 Cong., 1 Sess., 1177–79; Mott, *American Journalism*, 286.

25. Although Johnson credited this entire passage to the *Herald of Freedom*, only the Harris affidavit had appeared in that paper, as a quotation from the *Howard Report*. Inasmuch as many eastern papers quoted copiously from the *Herald*, Johnson may have found this introductory material, as well as the other passages attributed to the *Herald*, in one of those journals. *Herald of Freedom*, November 19, 1859.

26. *Ibid.*, October 29, 1859.

27. *Howard Report*, 1180.

28. *Ibid.*, 1175–76. This is an inexact rendering of Mrs. Doyle's affidavit.

29. *Ibid.*, 1176–77.

30. This letter, allegedly written by Mahala Doyle, an illiterate, and widely circulated in the contemporary press, was among John Brown correspondence deposited by order of Governor Wise in the Virginia State Library, where it was uncovered in 1901 by the state librarian and published shortly thereafter. W. W. Scott, "The John Brown Letters," *Virginia Magazine of History and Biography*, IX (1901–2), 391; *ibid.*, X (1902–3), 31–32.

31. Doolittle quoted from John H. Gihon, *Gihon's History of Kansas* . . . ([Philadelphia, 1857?]).

32. An almost verbatim couplet from John Ford's *'Tis Pity She's a Whore*, Act IV, sc. 3, this verse had also appeared in Johnson's circular *To the Freemen of the First Congressional District of Tennessee*, October 15, 1845. *Johnson Papers*, I, 267.

33. Again Johnson employed a literary source which he had used earlier, taking even greater liberties with the passage than in his Speech on the Gag Resolution, January 31, 1844. Alexander Pope in "The Temple of Fame," ll. 274–75, refers to the music of the Muses: "So soft, though high, so loud, and yet so clear/ Ev'n list'ning angels leaned from heav'n to hear. . . ." *Ibid.*, 143.

34. Colonel Lewis Washington, a grandnephew of George Washington residing near Harper's Ferry, had been captured during the raid. Forced to surrender a sword and pistol belonging to his ancestor, he refused to give up his watch, and the raiders decided not to take the silver service. *Senate Report* No. 278, 36 Cong., 1 Sess., 32–33; Scott, "John Brown Letters," 388–89.

From Alfred Smith[1]

Mt Vernon Kentucky
Decr- 14th 1859.

Hon. Mr. Johnson
Washington D C
Dear Sir

I have been spoken to by Mr Henry Miller,[2] an Invalid pensioner of this Rockcastle County to write to you on his behalf— Mr Miller has a claim pending before Congress—for some time— he is a pensioner on account of a wou[n]d he recieved—while he was a Soldier from Tennessee in the war 1812— on account of Said wou[n]d his leg was amputated from his body— his claim is for back pay, at $96 per annum, commencing at the date of the Amputation in August 1817— Honl J. M. Elliott[3] passed his bill in the House Session before last—by over 100 majority; to pay Mr Miller $96—per annum, com[me]ncing the 30th August 1817 and terminating the date his name was placed on the pension list in 1852, the bill went to the Senate—and there Slep in the armes of the Committee. no report was even last Session made upon his claim—to give the Senate a chance to vote whether a majority was willing to pay this poor old Soldier or not. a bill in point became a law last Session, which paid a soldier of the war 1812 $2.68 cts per mnth, comencing 1816 and terminating in 1841 when his name was placed on the pension list. Still at the Same time Mr Millers bill was permitted to Sleep in the hands of the Committee— no more meritorious claim than Henry Millers and his papers show it. he has been totaly disabled ever Since the amputation of his leg in 1817— he is a very poor man, but an honerable one— he has a young wife with Some helpless children looking to him for support—& unless Congress will give him his back pay—he & his Family is b[o]und to Suffer— Mr Miller wishes to get your assistance. You will please examine his papers filed in the Senate—& should you conclude to assist this poor old Soldier—you will be gratefully remembered by Mr Miller & his friends— You will find a petition filed in the case Signed by 250 persons of this county — probably his petition was presented by Honl. Adison White,[4] while he was a member of Congress from Ky. certai[n]ly it is filed with the bill passed by Honl J M Elliott now filed in the Senate. Honl L W Powell[5] will present the Case— he Knows me well from reputation, as well as Genl J M McCalla—[6] if you have time I would like to receive a line from you[.]

Truly Yours &c
Alfred Smith

I will further add that I expect no compensation from Mr Miller for writting this letter.

A. Smith

If you conclude to help Mr Miller—you will Verry much oblige him. if you would Speak to Such of your friends to assist, as you may think necessary[.]

A. Smith

ALS, DLC-JP2.

1. Alfred Smith (b. c1829) was a farmer of Rockcastle, Kentucky. 1860 Census, Rockcastle, 29, courtesy of James R. Bentley (Filson Club) to Andrew Johnson Project, December 2, 1970.

2. Henry Miller of Kentucky had enlisted as a private soldier in the Tennessee militia, December, 1812, serving until February, 1814, when he received the injury which caused his invalidism. Granted a pension of eight

dollars per month in 1852, retroactive to August, 1847, he then sought to collect from the treasury, and later from Congress, pension arrears for the period 1817 to 1847. On December 15, 1857, the court of claims had adversely reported his petition, and on April 6, 1860, a House committee asked to be discharged from further consideration of the claim, since a bill for the general relief of such pensioners was then in preparation. *House Report* No. 106, 35 Cong., 1 Sess.; *House Report* No. 389, 36 Cong., 1 Sess.; *U. S. Statutes*, X, 765; *Cong. Globe*, 35 Cong., 1 Sess., 2715; *ibid.*, 36 Cong., 1 Sess., 810.

3. John M. Elliott (1820–1879) was a Kentucky Democratic congressman (1853–59), state representative (1847, 1861), a member of the Confederate Congress, circuit judge (1868–74), and judge of appeals (1876–79) until his assassination. *BDAC*, 855.

4. Addison White had been Whig representative from Kentucky (1851–53). *Ibid.*, 1801; *Johnson Papers*, II, 73n.

5. Lazarus W. Powell (1812–1867), a Kentucky Democratic senator (1859–65), had been state representative (1836) and governor (1851–55). *BDAC*, 1476.

6. John M. McCalla (c1785–1873), veteran of the War of 1812 and militia officer, was a Lexington, Kentucky, lawyer and Democratic party leader who had served as second auditor of the treasury (1845–49) and stayed on in Washington to practice law. George W. Ranck, *History of Lexington, Kentucky: Its Early Annals and Recent Progress* . . . (Cincinnati, 1872), 249; New York *Times*, March 2, 1873.

From Anselm L. Carden[1]

Union County, East Tennessee.
[December 15, 1859]

Honl. Andrew Johnson

Dr. Govenor, from our short acquaintance, in former times, I have thought propper to address you these lines. I am in hopes you are well & well doing. I have several favors to ask at your hands & hope it may be that you may have an opportunity to give me the desired assistance.

I will first inform you that I was in the War, of 1812. I served a tour at Norfolk Virginia in the 4th, Regiment Virginia Militia & that Samuel Hooker a private in our Company, (Capt Carters) was owing me, that he gave me a power of attorny for his pay, he died I think on the 24 of December 1814. I never have recived the pay, & will send you the old power, if you can git it. I will let you have your charge out of it, I also have a power of Attorny to draw the pay of John Murrow of said Company[.]

I will inform you that I drawed my 2 Land Warrants, And am poor & needy & was sick on while in the Army, I there contracted a disease, the (Piles,) & in my old age am very much infeebled & infirm[.] I do hope you will devise som plan whereby I may be enabled to draw a Pension &c. Your compliance if in your power will greatly help me &c.

I have another thought to suggest to you & truly hope you will assist me in that respect,— I inform you that at the organization of our Union County in 1856. I was elected as one of the Justices of the Peace, & am still acting, it is all the office I have, And I think that my qualification is high enough to take the Census in 1860.[2] And from your personal acquaintance with Mr. Lowery the Marshall for East Tennessee I trust that you can procure my appointment. there are, I am informed upwards of 20 applicants. I can send Mr. Lowery as good a recommendation as any that have sent on if necessary. I have not addressed Mr. Lowery.

You will please give me an answer and please send me any papers &c[.]

Address me at Loys' X Roads, &c Oblige

Yours Respectfully
Anselm L. Carden

N. B.

I truly think that if you will lend me your aid I can draw a pension. I shall not address Mr. Maynard[.] I took an active part in Genl. Ramsys'[3] election & as such I presume Mr. Maynard would attend to his friends first, I further think that if you would write to Mr. Lowery, & let him know that my name is on record in the War department & that I am old & poor, that he would give m[e] the appointment. Please write & send any Information you see propper.

Yours as ever   A. L. Carden
December 15th, 1859.—

ALS, DLC-JP2.

1. Anselm L. Carden (b. c1795–1875), North Carolina native and veteran of the War of 1812, was a Union County schoolteacher who had received two eighty-acre warrants—one in July, 1851, and the other in February, 1856. Ultimately, in 1871, he would be awarded a pension of $8 per month for his war service. 1850 Census, Tenn., Anderson, 104; 1860 Census, Tenn., Union, 83; Anselm L. Carden, Va. War of 1812, Pension and Bounty Land File, RG15, National Archives.

2. The census of 1860 was not taken by Carden, but by a William Owen.

3. Horace Maynard had recently defeated John Crozier Ramsey for Congress.

From Albert G. Graham

Jonesboro Tenn Dec: 15th 1859—

Sir:

When Maj. Brookins Campbell went on to Washington in 1853,[1] to Congress, he informed me that he would, whilst there, make out, and obtain his arrears of pay and allowances as a Quarter Master, whilst in the Mexican War. He claimed, if I recollect right, some $4,00.00 or $500 00 balance.

After his death his widow requested me to see about the matter, and whilst at W. C. sometime since I made inquiry at the 2d. Audr. office, and was informed that his a/c had been settled in full in 1848—or '49, and that the papers had been transmitted to you.

My impression is, that there is something yet unsettled in Maj. Bs. accounts in some way; or he would not certainly [have] made a claim where none existed, as he was a most scrupulously honest man, as far as I ever heard or knew. The case may yet be unfinished —and in the following condition: The 2d. Audr. has probably stated the a/c which went to the 2d. Compt. who has approved it, and furnished you with the certificate of that Dept., which you forwarded to Maj. B. and there the matter rested. *The money was never paid* as I suppose.

My object in writing to you is to request you to refer this letter first to the 2d. Audr, then the 2d Comptr, and then the Treas. U. S. for such information as will enable me to arrive at the proper conclusion in regard to the state of this claim; and to inform the widow of the nature and character of their [*sic*] rights.

By so doing you will oblige yrs &c

Hon Andrew Johnson U. S.   A G Graham
Washington City

ALS, DLC-JP2.

1. Campbell, Johnson's successor from the first congressional district, had gone to Washington for the meeting of the 33rd Congress but died on December 25, 1853, less than a month after the session began. See *Johnson Papers*, I, 159n.

From John Commerford

New York Dec 17—/59

Dear Sir— I see that you have again introduced the Homestead Bill. I am gratified that one at least of our Southern Senators continues to have some regard for the interest and welfare of his white fellow Citisens[.] I recur to this the more readily because it is urged, that the hostility which was displayed by the representatives beyond a certain *line* in the Senate last winter,[1] shows how little reliance can be placed upon such men to assist in the passage of a measure that is Calculated to benefit the people. I refer to this with a sense of sorrow inasmuch as such action upon the part of these Statesmen is used as an argument that they are averse to doing anything to alleviate the condition, or promote any object that will tend to provide a

better state of things for what they should consider the advancement
of their White brethern[.] It appears to me that the delegates of the
South in Congress had a sufficiency of difficulties to encounter in the
contest to secure those rights to which they are so justly entitled,
without seeking for fresher and more numerous foes in the multitude
who have asked for the passage of a Homestead Bill. I presume that
you are aware that had the latter measure have been passed, that the
result in the various elections in the different localties throughout the
Country would have been materialy changed[.] I know that the Republicans attribute their Success to other issues than the advocacy of
the distribution of the lands amongst the people; but I am satisfied
that they are mistaken and that their victories have proceeded from
the supposition that it was to the free representatives of the North to
which the working men were to hereafter look for the accomplishment of their wishes[.] By our correspondence with the people of the
States & Territories, we are furnished with the amplest evidence that
it has not been the question of Slavery, but that with them the greater
consideration, is how and by what means they are to realise permanent happiness by the obtaining [of] the guarentee of future and enduring industry[.]

In demanding the passage of a Homestead Bill you may think it
strange that I as a Land Reformer take a position that is correlative
with that which must be conceded to be the right of the South, in that
which the latter should exact from its partnership in the Union[.]
I maintain that the South is entitled to all the advantages that have,
or may accrue from the partnership into which they entered at the
organisation of this government[.] I do not believe that the offspring
of those who framed the government of the original States, or the
coming descendants of such offspring have the Constitutional power
to apportion limit, or dictate by setting bounds to the enjoyment of
the full possession of all the rights which were mutualy agreed to,
as also of these acquisitions of territory which since have been the
product of the joint means of those who may have become partners
and participators in the Still existing compact[.] In asking Congress
to pass a Bill whereby the lands shall be divided among the people
untill they are taken up, we merely ask of those who are the agents
of our aggregate partnership to give to us individualy that portion of
the inheritance which as fractional partners we wish to use for ourselves and families[.] I voted for Mr Buchanan in the expectation
that he was favorable to our measure, but I now believe I made a
serious mistake[.] I have made it a rule for the last twenty years to
not support any man or party, that was not in favor of giving the
lands to the people, and I am afraid that in the next Presidential

Contest I shall have to Cast my ballot for the Republican Candidate. If I do it will be upon the Land issue[.] With thousands of others I am forced to look forward to the interest of the laboring White population of this Continent, and if that there be other *issues* involved in the conflict I must array myself under that banner upon whose surface is inscribed "Aid & Protection to the toiling White laborers of this Continent[.]

After the manifestation made in the Senate of the last Session we Shall cease troubling the Senate or House with Petitions this Winter[.] This being our determination, but few Memorials will be presented from our City[.] We think that we have shown that the Northern Conservative interest is with us, and we are sick of the repetition that the Southern Oligarchy will never consent to the passage of any kind of Homestead Bill[.]

I wish that you could prevail upon your Southern Associates in the Senate to reverse this State of things by springing upon their detractors the exhibition of their full consent to the passage of it[.] If they would but so act they would in the accomplishment of this great purpose find accessions of thousands who now Stand inactive under the impression that they are the determined enemies of the progress of the White race[.] Fearing that my letter is already too long I beg leave to Subscribe   Myself Your Ob St
                                                            John Commerford

Hon Andrew Johnsen

P S In the above I speak for myself and not by the authority of the Association of which I have the honor to be President[.][2]

ALS, DLC-JP2.

1. Introduced by Galusha Grow of Pennsylvania, a homestead bill passed the House February 1, 1859, and was sent to the Senate, where southerners, aided by Vice President Breckinridge's deciding vote, forced its tabling. This had been a disillusioning experience for the Land Reformers, who increasingly thereafter looked to the Republican party for action. *Cong. Globe*, 35 Cong., 2 Sess., 1074–76.
2. Commerford was serving as president of the National Reform Association.

From Isaac Toucey

December 19, 1859, Washington, D. C.; Copy, DNA-RG45, Gen. Let. Bk. No. 61, p. 316.

Secretary of the navy, returning letters of Mrs. Martha Knox, explains that marine corps appointments, limited by law, are made only to fill vacancies, usually from states not represented in the corps; that no candidates will be selected for the naval academy until September, 1860, at which time the "10th District of Tennessee will be entitled to an appointment."

From George W. Foute[1]

Greeneville, Tenn.   Decr. 21.st 1859.

Dear Governor:

Supposing that Robert[2] will be in Washington before the enclosed letter could reach Annapolis, I must request that you will hand it to him; but if he should not call on you by next tuesday, please send it to the Post Office, as he may be disappointed in his anticipated visit to Washington.

I recd. your Speech upon Masons resolution,[3] this morning, for which I thank you. I have not yet had time to read it, but will do so soon.

I am extremely anxious to have a hive of those *new fashioned Bees*, which have lately been received by the Patent Office,[4] when the time comes for distributing them. Could such a thing be worked?

No news.   Yrs. truly,

Geo. W. Foute

ALS, DLC-JP2.

1. Greeneville physician.
2. Dr. Foute's son Robert (b. *c*1841) had entered the naval academy in 1858. Resigning in December, 1860, he became an officer in the Confederate navy and served on the ironclad *Virginia* (*Merrimac*) in the battle of Hampton Roads, had a special assignment abroad (1863–64), and was paroled at Appomattox. 1850 Census, Tenn., Greene, 280; U. S. Naval Academy Alumni Association, *Register of Alumni, Graduates and Former Cadets and Midshipmen* (Annapolis, 1962), 10; *CSA. Naval Register*, 64.
3. See Speech on Harper's Ferry Incident, December 12, 1859.
4. Probably "a mixed breed" of Italian bees, found "throughout Lombardy," which the agricultural division of the patent office purchased in 1859. Slightly larger than domestic strains, the new bees were expected to produce more than one hundred pounds of honey, once the hive reached maturity. Report of Commissioner of Patents, *House Ex. Doc.* No. 11, 36 Cong., 1 Sess., 543.

From James B. Lamb

Fayetteville, Tenne,   Decr. 21, '59

Dear Govr:

I have not written to, or heard from you in so long a time that I feel something like a strangar to you and you to me, but having just finished reading your late Speech in the Senate on the *Slavey question*[1]—that fruitful source of all our political troubles of late—I feel impelled to Say to you what I think of it,—(the speech) which is, that it is the *best speech* I have yet had the pleasure of reading on

that subject—that it is an able argument on the question generally, and a most triumphant reply to those Senators—particularly Mr. Trumbull—whom you specially noticed. It is indeed strange, very strange that arguments and facts so simple, and indisputable should never have been used before. I really felt surprised that such reasoning and such facts had not occurred even to *me*, much more [to] Earnest politicians whose constant employment is thinking on, and speaking on the question! If you can get your speech *read* by Northern people it is *bound* to do good, because I think them generally honest, and therefore with minds open to reason and conviction—
Can't we then manage to have this speech circulated amongst them? Can't it be published any how in all good democratic papers North— at least that portion treating of *Slavery* & *Slave labor*, leaving out, if they please, all about old Brown & Harpers Ferry— Is there any Democratic Committee now at Washington, and if so, can not their attention be called to this matter, if not so already? I would not tax your modesty to do this *good* thing—but others of influence. I wish I was known and had position that I might do *some good*!

What is to be the *end* of this awful Slavery question.—for it Strikes me the end, be it for weal or woe to the country, is near at hand—? I am entirely at a loss—clear out at Sea—in politics—I don't even know what *democrat* means now! For there don't seem to be much, if any, unanimity of Sentiment amongst the members of the party called by that name, either North or South—and I don't comprehend what *is* to be if *any thing*. So, I wish you would do what you used to Say to me—"Set down and tell us all you know".

You are aware our State Convention meets on the 18th prox— I expect to go down, but I don't know what we are, or *ought* to do —outside of appointing delegates to Charleston— What *sort* of Resolutions shall we adopt? Shall we say any thing about Squatter Sovereignty, Old Brown, "Irrepressible Conflict," &C, &C, or leave these and kindred subjects to *dignified silence*? Now, tell me candidly and frankly, for *my own eye* if you prefer it, what you think generally concerning *these things*. But, whether you do so or not, pray don't forget your humble constituent and Frnd,

J. B. Lamb.

Hon A. Johnson,
Washington City—

ALS, DLC-JP2.
    1. See Speech on Harper's Ferry Incident, December 12, 1859.

From J. K. P. Pritchard[1]

Jacksonport Arks
Dec 24th 1859

Dear Sir:

By this mail I send you a copy of the "Old Line Democrat"[2] one of the leading democratic papers in this State—wherein I have taken the liberty of nominating you, for the Vice Presidency of these United States[.]

You probably do not remember of ever having seen me, but I have heard you speak often— I was raised by John Allison[3] near Jonesborough E Tenn one of your warmest and most steadfast friends and supporters. I well remember your celebrated Canvass against Landon C Haynes as well as your Gubernatorial race against Hon Gus Henry. It gives me much pleasure to say to you that you have numerous friends in this State, who knew you in Tenn and who would willingly and cheerfully vote for you for President. It is with a full confidence (that I propose your name in the connection I have,) that you will get an expression of Arkansas—at least the Northern & Eastern portions of the State. I refer you to Col Henderson[4] of your city.

Respectfully   Your Obt. Servant
J. K. P. Pritchard

ALS, DLC-JP2.

1. J. K. P. Pritchard, who had apparently moved to Arkansas in the mid- or latter 1850's, served as a captain in the Confederate quartermaster corps, stationed at home in Jacksonport. *OR*, Ser. 1, XXII, 908–9.

2. The *Old Line Democrat* was a Little Rock newspaper published weekly, 1859–61. Winifred Gregory, *American Newspapers 1821–1936: Union List of Newspapers* (New York, 1936), 25.

3. John Allison (b. c1798) was a prosperous Washington County farmer living near Jonesboro. 1850 Census, Tenn., Washington, 240.

4. Probably Tift Henderson (b. c1796) of Greene County, a deputy marshal in 1850. 1850 Census, Tenn., Greene, 284.

From Joseph R. Anderson[1]

Bristol Decr 29/59

Hon Andrew Johnson
Dear Sir

I am in recpt of your kind favor contain[in]g notice from the Acting Comr Land Office of the retu[r]n of 5 more of my Land warrants that were stolen or rather perverted from my use. when I receved notice of the first two last March that was returned, I in complyance with the instructions made proof to all the warrants I had lost (12 in No) or 1280 Acres—and now am notified in these you Send to prove that the warrants are mine. this I can do by those I purchased them of except one person who has Since deied and then can prove that they were given to James W Bondurant & J. C. Goodwin[2] to locate for me as pr our agreement. This Contract was written by Mr Sherman of the House of G. W. Howard & Co[3] of Baltimore and by him I can make the proof they were mine when given them to locate—but He ommitted to put in, or fill up the transfer on the back of the warrants with my name in them, hence they were more easily perverted. the point I wish to arrive at is to know from some one in Washington conversant with this business whether, this want or lack of my name in the transfer when given to Bondurant gives the person to whom He Sold them to a claim better than mine. What has been the usual decisions in such cases[?] no doubt there are Similar cases come up before by those there who have been prosecuting claims for bounty Land. this omission on the part of Mr Sherman to put my name in the transfer is the only plea the Purchaser of my warrants could put in as any tenable ground, as an innocent purchaser, and this is what I wish to know, if in Such Cases, this last purchaser of warrants has the prior claims and if this position is Sustained it will be useless to go into litigation about them. but if proof only is required of me to show I am the original owner and the true owner at present, I can make it Satisfactory— Bondurant who perverts the use of them was acting only as my agent to locate them, and had no power at all to Sell, as his Recpt I hold will show. this is troubling you too much—I fear—but I have no one in Washington on whom I can more Safely rely for information than yourself— Soon as convenient please reply.

Respectfully Yr friend

Jos. R Anderson

ALS, DLC-JP2.

1. Joseph R. Anderson (1819–1888), founder of Bristol in 1852, had been a Blountville merchant, realtor, banker, and director of the East Tennessee and Virginia and the East Tennessee and Georgia railroads. A Democrat, he served intermittently as mayor or alderman of Bristol (1858–76) and was nominated for governor by the Prohibition party in 1888. Speer, *Prominent Tennesseans*, 208–10; Oliver Taylor, *Historic Sullivan: A History of Sullivan County, Tennessee* (Bristol, 1909), 305–7.

2. James W. Bondurant and J. C. Goodwin have not been identified.

3. George W. Howard, William C. Cole, Jr., J. H. Cole, and H. F. Schuman or Schurmann, the partners of George W. Howard & Company, were importers and dealers in dry goods. *Ferslen's Baltimore City Business Directory* (1859–60), 95; *Woods' Baltimore Directory* (1858–59), 341, 356.

From Mrs. Harriett E. Brown[1]

Washington   Texas   Dec 29 1859

Hon. Andrew Johnson,
Sir:

The ladies of Washington Texas, seeing the Growing necessity of literary instructions Particularly for young ladies in our state Haveing determined to build up a female school in this place which is named for and desired to be a monument to the immortal Washington, Not being able however to accomplish unaided what they desire concerning it. They are asking assistance from every state in the union. In our community many Tenniseesians reside and are perfectly Confident in the generosity which has throughout all the world Characterised their native state[.] they told us to appeal to Tennisseans and they would vouch we would be responded to not *only* by words of encouragement—but by liberal Contributions. Hearing of your goodness and generosity we are determined to request of you a donation feeling assured that our doing so will not be in vain. The names of the donors together with the amount of their donations will be framed and placed in the college their to remain as long as the Institution stands[.] As to the worthiness of this enterprise I refer you to Hon. John Hempill[2] Senator from Texas and Houstion Gov of the state the Rev J. E. Carns[3] Editor of the Christian advocate Galveston Texas and Mr McNair[4] Presbyterian Minister at Galveston[.] Hopeing to hear from you soon I remain very Respectfully

Harriett E. Brown

Address to Mrs.

ALS, DLC-JP2.

1. This correspondent has not been identified.
2. John Hemphill (1803–1862), South Carolina-born lawyer and editor, had moved to Texas in 1838 where he became chief justice of the state court (1846–58). Elected as a State Rights Democrat to the U. S. Senate (1859), he withdrew and was expelled (1861), dying in Richmond during the war. *BDAC*, 1038; *DAB*, XIII, 520–21.
3. The Reverend J. E. Carnes, a Methodist minister, former editor of the Vicksburg (Miss.) *Whig* (1848) and at this time editing the *Texas Christian Advocate*, served as a Confederate chaplain. "The Press of Mississippi," *DeBow's Review*, XXIX (1860), 505; *OR*, Ser. 1, LIII, 661; Earl W. Fornell, *The Galveston Era: The Texas Crescent on the Eve of Secession* (Austin, 1961), 282.
4. Daniel McNair (1806–1883), North Carolina-born Presbyterian minister, spent most of his early ministry in Mississippi and Louisiana before serving a Galveston church (1855–69). E. C. Scott, comp., *Ministerial Directory of the Presbyterian Church, U. S.* (Austin, 1942), 485.

1860

From Thomas A. Devyr

Williamsburgh New York—Jany 1st 1860

Sir

I take it as a good omen that I find myself writing to such a man on such a day and on such a subject.

That conflict is not "irrepressible".[1] Your Measure would put an end to it. So, at least, think some of the most intelligent and even *wealthy* men in this neighborhood. They have caused me to embody *their* views, as well [as] my own, in the accompanying Circular[.][2] They [*sic*] way in which they think, and desire to act on this matter, has deferred my departure for England. Could not some good be effected before the different Legislatures of the South? If *you* could spare time to speak before them I think it likely "Instructions" might reach Washington that would bring less or more of the Southern Senators to your side.[3]

This is a momentous subject[.] It now involves a new issue— the issue of *Peace* or *War*. We ought to "leave no stone unturned" therefore. If you can not go on this southern mission—somebody else might be sent. A less efficient man, might still be better than none.

The gentlemen to whom I have alluded, would, I think, find both the man and the money to defray his expenses, if they could count upon co-operation, and even the chance of a result.

Would you drop me half a line on this most important matter? *You, only,* have raised our hopes. The Republicans are insincere, and nothing w'd be more disappointing to them than the passage of this measure. I know them well. Better than any other man in these parts. They are the vicious old "Distribution" men[4]—shifting their sails only to catch the popular gale, but *without the least desire to enter port if they can help it*. This is not a *speculation* of mine. I have had crushing *experience* of it in the first years of the movement.

If you think any good could be done, a representative man would probably go on to Washington to concert action[.]

Your ranksman in the cause

Thos A Devyr

ALS, DLC-JP2.

1. This allusion to Seward's phrase, first used in his Rochester speech of September 25, 1858, confirms Allan Nevins' assertion that this "indiscreet interpretation of the crisis," implying, as it did to many, armed strife, had "leaped into the nation's consciousness." Devyr could count on his reader's acquaintance with the phrase, inasmuch as Johnson had recently referred to the phrase and speech in his Speech on Harper's Ferry Incident, December 12, 1859. Nevins, *Emergence of Lincoln*, I, 409.

2. Devyr's pamphlet, *The Homestead and the Union*, by "A Land Reformer," noted that Jefferson had laid down the "philosophic truth" that "the earth belongs in usufruct to the living," while Jackson had recommended that public lands be reserved for actual settlers. In abandoning these principles, the Democratic party had been greatly weakened, while the real strength of the Republican party lay in its support of a homestead policy. The Democracy should return to its original position on the matter; to do so would strengthen the party. At the same time the slavery issue would be resolved, for once homesteads were granted, the northerner would have no reason for encroaching upon cotton, rice, and sugar lands in the South, and the southerner no interest in "merely agricultural land" to the North. Pamphlets, 1854–1861, Johnson Papers, Series 2, LC.

3. During the early months of 1860 three states, Minnesota, Wisconsin, and New Jersey, forwarded resolutions asking passage of the homestead measure. There is no evidence that Johnson directly contributed to the shaping of these petitions, nor were any similar pressures forthcoming from the South as a result of Johnson's activity in response to Devyr's urging. In fact, the Tennessean made no speeches before state legislatures during these months. *Senate Journal*, 36 Cong., 1 Sess., 106, 334, 340.

4. The "Distribution Whigs" had favored the allocation among the states of the proceeds from the sale of public lands—a proposal which became one of the basic points in Henry Clay's political program, since it would provide the states with the funds necessary for the internal improvements he advocated. Moreover, it promised to decrease the federal revenues, which in turn would necessitate raising the tariff, a project which Clay also warmly supported. St. George L. Sioussat, "Andrew Johnson and the Early Phases of the Homestead Bill," *Mississippi Valley Historical Review*, V (1918), 256.

From George R. Powel[1]

Branch Bank   Rogersville T
Jany 2d 1860

Hon A Johnson
  Dear Sir
    I herewith Enclose two dollars to pay for 1 Copy of the States & Union for Doct A Carmichael[2]—Weekly and I want a Copy of Either the States & Union or Constitution[3] Sent to me, whichever you think is the best paper &c &c[.] I thank you for the Copy of your speech which I recd a few days ago, & read it with much gratification. I regard it without flattery the ablest production of your life—& the best argument on the points discussed that I have seen from any quarter—
    I do believe that the Union is in more peril than Ever before—

What are we to do with the infernal Scoundrels who are continually aggressing upon the rights of the South?—

The South Americans or Know Knothing are at their old tricks in the House,[4] Setting up the old worn out howl of dont agitate dont, agitate when insurection & agitation from the north are thunde[ri]ng at our very domicils— I write in great Haste[.] Let me hear from you. Your friend   Geo R Powel

ALS, DLC-JP2.

1. Powel was cashier of the Rogersville branch of the Bank of Tennessee. See *Johnson Papers*, II, 70n.

2. Archibald Carmichael (*c*1818–1861) was a Rogersville physician and trustee of the Rogersville Female Academy. WPA, Records of Hawkins County, Will Book No. I, 1797–1886 (Nashville, 1938), 85; Rogersville *Times*, June 26, 1851.

3. The Washington *States and Union*, founded in 1857 as the *States*, was a pro-southern organ which endorsed Douglas. A daily and weekly journal, it was the brainchild of Tennessean John P. Heiss, former partner of Thomas Ritchie in the Washington *Union*. The Washington *Constitution*, formerly the *Union*, continued to be the administration paper until its demise in 1861. Bryan, *National Capital*, II, 442–43, 462; Mott, *American Journalism*, 361n.

4. During the lengthy conflict over the selection of a House speaker, southern Democrats and Opposition congressmen, consisting of old-line Whigs and Americans, charged each other with abetting the election of a Black Republican. When the Democrats offered a resolution providing that no one who had endorsed Hinton R. Helper's *Impending Crisis of the South* be chosen, the Opposition countered that it was the duty of every good citizen to resist renewing slavery agitation and that no one should be elected whose political opinions did not conform to that sentiment. Such old-line Whigs as Nelson, Etheridge, Brabson, and Maynard of Tennessee, along with Anderson of Kentucky and Gilmer of North Carolina, deplored sectionalism and appealed for a national outlook. Following Nelson's December 7 speech, the *States and Union* printed such an abusive editorial that he regained the House floor on December 23 for a personal explanation. *Cong. Globe*, 36 Cong., 1 Sess., 47, 51, 211, 217, 233, 275, 286; Nashville *News*, December 14, 24, 1859, January 11, 1860.

From Memphis Typographical Union

January 2, 1860, Memphis; PI, DLC-JP2.

Printed invitation accompanied by printed letter requesting an expression of sentiment from Johnson if he is unable to attend a festival in honor of Benjamin Franklin, to be held January 17 at Specht's Saloon. [There is no evidence that Johnson attended.]

From David J. Carr[1]

                              Boons Creek Post Office, Tenn,   Jan 7   1860.
Hon Andrew Johnson,
    Dear Sir,
        I have just read your great Speech deliverd in th U. S. Senate Dec 12[2] On the Resolution to appoint a committee to investigate

th Harpers Ferry envation. I say great because it is conseeded that yo last effort is the greatest of your life. Will you do us the honor to send a few to your frinds in this Section of Old Washington. You have as many warm and devoted frinds here as you have in any other, and we would be much pleased to have the pleasure of reading your Speech. If you will send me a lot of them I will distribut them a mong my neighbors who do not tak a newspaper.

I wish one of your speech[es] was in the hand of evry voter in the U. S. I would not aske these spechial favors of you if the Democ-[rac]y had a Representa[ti]ve in Congress from this district. Mr Nelson is fluding all East Tennessee with his speech.[3] We do not want to read speeches in this section that gives aide & comfort to Black Repu[b]licans. As ever your friend

D. J. Carr

ALS, DLC-JP2.

1. David J. Carr (b. c1818), formerly Chattanooga postmaster (1845–52), was a merchant and postmaster at Boon's Creek, Washington County. *Goodspeed's Hamilton*, 892; *U. S. Official Register* (1859), *351; 1860 Census, Tenn., Washington, 51.

2. Speech on Harper's Ferry Incident, December 12, 1859.

3. In a speech of December 7, during the House debate over a speaker, Nelson had supported John A. Gilmer's resolution denouncing slavery agitation, endorsing Unionism, and stipulating that no candidate whose views failed to conform to these sentiments was to be chosen speaker. Condemning Hinton R. Helper's "infamous" book and deploring the undue publicity given it, Nelson arraigned slavery agitation, both North and South. He blamed the Democratic party for the strength of the Republican opposition, observing that Democratic platforms from 1840 to 1856 had been "silent as death" on the issue of slavery in the territories. To criticism of his association with the American party Nelson retorted that he was not only an American but a Whig, "opposed to the modern Democracy in every shape and under every form." *Cong. Globe*, 36 Cong., 1 Sess., 3, 20, 46–50.

From Sam M. Duncan

January 7, 1860, Nicholasville, Ky.; ALS, DLC-JP2.

Having "Read So many conflicting accounts concer[n]ing your early life that—I now feel a deep interst to learn the whole truth—and nothing else," Duncan wants a "History," including "the year and the place of your birth, also, your early life &c. How old were you when you . . . entered Public life . . . and commen[c]ed the Study of Law."

From Thomas A. Devyr

New York   Williamsburgh

January 8th 1860

To Senator Johnson

Sir— I think it probable that you have hardly time to read, much less reply to the amount of correspondence, which your distinguished position (in regard to the Homestead) crowds upon you. I do not feel much disappointed, therefore, at your failure to respond to my letter written a week ago. I suppose I am the more resigned because I have no personal expectations save the expectation of further sacrafice—an addition to what I have made so largely since, I, the hand that writes this, gave first voice to that movement which is now powerful enough to carry the hollow "Distribution" Whigs along on its stream.

I have a public duty to discharge and that done, a portion, at least, of my object is gained.

I send you a pamphlet[1] published some time since—published by men who have never sought public distinction—whose labors may be mistaken, but are undoubtedly meant for the public good.

I presume you are well aware that owing to the Anti-Rent movement[2] in our central counties the relation of God's children to God's earth has been more generally discussed, and is, I think, better understood in this than in any other state. I know the means by which the Whigs seduced and betrayed this element. I stood foremost in the gap against them at the time they accomplished this scheme—I suffered more in resisting them than *all* other men, Such men as Judge Parker[3] it is true, abeted them—but he paid for it at the last election. 20.000 copies of a document[4] written by me & embodying his evil deeds were circulated; and, I thank God, not without effect.

One great mistake I fear will now be fallen into by the Dem. leaders. They will probably think *Union Sentiment* will turn up strong enough to carry such states as this in next November. It does not strike them that as much *counter* sentiment may arise as will neutralize it. If John Brown and his band had been treated as madmen, it would have been all the better for the Union. But if the men who *crowd our churches and say grace before their meals*, once take it in their heads that Brown and his fellows were martrys—then the late shock & excitement will be as likely to work *against* the Union as in favor of it.

If, therefore, the Dem Party think this incident has made them strong enough to defy the friends of the Homestead, it is very likely they will find themselves mistaken.

Your fellow citizen
Thomas A Devyr

ALS, DLC-JP2.

1. Evidently another copy of *The Homestead and the Union*.

2. Devyr had fished in the troubled waters of the tenant farmers' revolt in eastern New York against the semifeudal patroon system, which had provoked nearly a century of sporadic agitation. Beginning anew with the death of Stephen Van Rensselaer in 1839 and the subsequent efforts of his heirs

to collect the back rent from his leaseholders, the antirent movement spread
over eastern New York, becoming an impetus for the liquidation of the old
estates and a stimulus for national land reform. Before they shifted to more
conventional political action after 1845, the antirenters resorted to petitions,
boycotts, associations, and violence, all aimed at reducing the rents, eliminating labor and produce obligations, and allowing the tenant to buy his
leasehold. Professional agitators like Devyr and Alvan Bolvay saw in this
movement an affirmation of the antimonopolistic ideals of their own National
Reformers. Newspapers, among them Devyr's *Anti-Renter*, took up the torch
for the tenants, whose cause was judged "a ringing protest by democratic
farmers against the aristocratic clique" that dominated old New York state.
David M. Ellis, *Landlords and Farmers in the Hudson-Mohawk Region:
1790–1850* (New York, 1967 [1946]), 225–312 *passim*.

3. Probably Judge Amasa J. Parker (1807–1890), whose decisions
against the antirent movement in strife-torn Delaware County helped break
the back of the insurrection as an extrapolitical force in September, 1845.
Parker had served as state assemblyman (1833–34) from Delaware County
and as congressman (1837–39) before moving to Albany, where he became
a circuit judge (1844–47) and supreme court justice (1847–55). Nominated by the Democrats for governor, he ran unsuccessfully in 1856 and
1858, losing the last time to the Republican Edwin D. Morgan; it is likely
that Devyr refers to this last election. By the early 1850's the antirent movement had lost its vigor as a political force because of the slavery issue and the
rapid liquidation of the leaseholds. *Ibid.*, 262, 266, 267; *BDAC*, 1424; Alexander, *Political History of New York*, II, 232–33, 250, 255.

4. This document has not been identified. Perhaps Devyr exaggerates his
role; the antirent question was apparently a dead issue and slavery dominated
the New York election of 1858—a fact contemporaries regarded as an ill
omen for 1860. Even local officials campaigned "as if the levying of an execution, the holding of an inquest, or the pocketing of fees, were to be affected
in any way by the position of the official on the Kansas question." *New York
Herald*, October 31, November 3, 1858.

From Cave Johnson

                                   Clarksville   8th. of Jany 1860

Private

Dear Sir,

I am now at home— I had to watch the "deliver over" [of] the
assets of the Bank[1] & had not leisure to thank you for the copy of
your speech in pamphlet which I recd & read with much pleasure
early last week— It has given your friends great pleasure & enlisted
the commendation of your bitterest opponents— We feel much anxiety at the aspect of affairs throughout the Country and I am asked
wherever I go, what is to be [the] result of the hostility between the
North and South? It is a difficult question for me to answer; whilst I
cannot but be apprehensive of danger I yet am unwilling to contribute to the alarm existing among us and usually answer by the expression of a hope, that the good common sense of the country will
finally control the demagogues & fanatics North & South— I do not
often agree with Wise yet I feel that we should unite with him, in

driving ⁺he *mad men North* & *South* out of *the country*, by *force* if necessary, rather suffer a ᵈissolve [*sic*] the Union; or attempt a Southern confederacy.² I regard such a result as the greatest calamity that could befal the country— I feel much anxiety too as to the working of our Convention on the 18th.—³ We have a *formidable* portion of our party, who seem inclined to take up Genl. Lane⁴ & our Gov.⁵ in view [*sic*] under the hope that success may be achieved by humbuggery & the personal popularity of both of them; and thus enable them to continue the patronage they now enjoy— what they will attempt is uncertain but with such counsellors as the Union Editors & the Post office clique⁶ we may fear a serious split in the ranks of the democracy— for the last two years, great anxiety has been felt for the establishment of a new Democratic paper that will advocate just principles & a fair dis[tri]bution of the offices & I may say with truth but for my opposition to it, it would have been done— I was apprehensive, that by so doing, our party would be divided & defeated, which I should regard as a great calamity to the country, especially after having battled for the ascendency more than twenty years— I am however out of all those contests but should not be less mortified at defeat than those who enjoy the offices & honors— I shall attend the convention under the hope of keeping down dissention in our ranks— many of your freinds are for urging *your name* as the candidate under the hope of crushing out the other—⁷ I suppose however our true policy will be, to avoid any nominations, to pass strong resolutions based upon your speech, to select our best and most prudent men to act as circumstances may dictate at Charleston. The chances seem to be, that the nomination will be given to no one who is an avowed candidate & whose pretensions are discussed— but I shall not be surprized, if the "powers that be" should use every exertion to keep me out of the convention— I shall not however grieve at any result as I neither expect or wish for any thing, with perhaps one exception; that suggested by you of taking your widdow⁸ the tour of Europe— I made my bow to her after you left but had no opportunity of ever alluding to the tour suggested by you[.]

I am sure you will be gratified to learn, that *your* Board⁹ delivered over the assets of the Bank, in proper order & to the entire satisfaction of the new Board & left the Bank in a better condition than ever before, having made for the State over $1,800,000 & with a loss of less than fifty thousand dollars in six years, & that made chiefly upon the recommendation *of politicians* who were most active iι having it dismissed— the new is composed principally of *the enemies* of the Bank¹⁰ without the *least experience* in banking except Genl A who has been under protest for many years & has proven himself execution proof[11] against all my activity & vigilance— I can boast of having collected more than $300,000 of the old suspended, which was regarded as lost when I went into the Bank & never borrowed or used a dollar of the money of the Bank for my individual benefit[.]

I suppose most of the Branch Boards will be dismissed & most of the experienced cashiers— Jacob McGavock[12] said when his opinion was asked of the New Board that he Supposed, it was the shortest cut to wind up the Bank[.] I have never known a high officer so utterly mistaken as to the true means of preserving the unity of his party in which he was more interested than any other person in the State, as our Governor— there is but little complaint openly made by our freinds from a desire to avoid any seeming misunderstanding among our freinds— the act now pending before the Legislature to drive the free negroes from the State[13] will cause much trouble, if it should become a law— Their Banking project[14] seems likely to lead in to re-charter of the Union & Planters Bank, & the chartering of Brokers & every body else who may happen to have a little money & will probably lead to a derangement of the currency worse than in 1857— Such are my fears & if so, we are prostrate for the next twenty years[.]

I am thinking of going to N. O. & Cuba, return by Charleston & pay Washington my last visit— I shall see the widdow next week & she may like such a trip better than to Paris[.]

I am very respectfully   Yr freind & servt
C Johnson

Hon Andrew Johnson
Washington City

ALS, DLC-JP2.

1. Cave Johnson, president of the Bank of Tennessee since 1854, was in the process of turning that institution over to his successor, Granville P. Smith.

2. Henry A. Wise, retiring governor of Virginia and aspirant for the Democratic presidential nomination, had become identified with determined resistance to northern subversion of southern rights and interests. At a Richmond reception for southern medical students returning from Philadelphia, he declared that he would not advocate secession but "If invasion shall ever again cross the Northern border of Virginia and I can get one hundred men . . . every black republican, every abolitionist, every Northern disunionist" would be driven into Canada. In his last message to the legislature, Wise recommended that Virginians, in lieu of stronger federal action, organize and arm "to defend ourselves, and to suppress sympathy in insurrections." New York *Herald*, December 26, 1859; Richmond *Enquirer*, December 6, quoted in Nashville *Patriot*, December 12, 1859.

3. These fears over the outcome of the state Democratic convention were not without reason, for the party, if not divided, was badly splintered— between those who advocated "Protection to Slavery" and those who stood for

"Douglas, Squatter Sovereignty," between Bank Democrats and "hard-money men," and between the supporters of Andrew Johnson and those of Isham G. Harris. Memphis *Appeal*, December 24, 1859; Nashville *News*, December 29, 1859; Nashville *Republican Banner*, January 19, 1860.

4. Joseph Lane (1801–1881), born in North Carolina and reared in Kentucky, went to Indiana at fifteen and in 1822 was elected to the lower house of the legislature. A member of the state senate (1841–46), he served in the Mexican War, was commissioned territorial governor of Oregon (1848), and in 1850 became territorial delegate to Congress, being re-elected three times before winning election to the Senate in 1859. In 1860 he was a candidate for the vice presidency on the Breckinridge ticket as an avowed secessionist. *DAB*, X, 579–80; James E. Hendrickson, *Joe Lane of Oregon* (New Haven, 1967), *passim*.

5. The supporters of Harris were anxious for his nomination as vice president, a course advocated by the Memphis *Appeal* in December. At the same time, the opposition press hinted that the Johnson and Harris factions were brewing trouble for each other. After the state convention the *Union and American* declared that Tennesseans wanted Johnson nominated for the presidency; if, however, a northern Democrat were chosen, then Harris should be put forward for vice president. Ultimately Lane became Breckinridge's running mate. Memphis *Appeal*, December 24, 1859; Nashville *News*, December 29, 1859; Nashville *Union and American*, January 20, 1860; see also Hendrickson, *Joe Lane*.

6. The *Union and American* was currently edited by John C. Burch, former state senator from Chattanooga, and F. C. Dunnington and J. O. Griffith, both of Columbia; Burch and Dunnington were Johnson supporters. The "Post office clique" represented remnants of the old Brown–Pillow Middle Tennessee Democracy. Samuel R. Anderson was Nashville postmaster and Granville P. Smith, general mail agent. Nashville *Union and American*, November, 1859–March, 1860; see Letter to Robert Johnson, January 23, 1858.

7. Isham G. Harris.

8. Cave Johnson, a widower, was probably referring to Mrs. Lizinka Campbell Brown (1820–1872), widow of James Percy Brown and daughter of George W. Campbell, U. S. minister to Russia (1818–21). Upon first meeting her some three years earlier, he had described her as "a blooming widdow of 35 with two children." A close social acquaintance of Andrew Johnson during his gubernatorial years, she married her cousin General Richard S. Ewell during the Civil War and afterward sought his release through petition to her former friend, President Johnson. *DAB*, VI, 230; Harriot S. Turner, "Recollections of Andrew Johnson," *Harper's Magazine*, CXX (1910), 168–76; Cave Johnson to James Buchanan, October 5, 1856, James Buchanan Papers, Historical Society of Pennsylvania; Jeannette T. Acklen, comp., *Tennessee Records* (2 vols., Nashville, 1933), I, 52.

9. During his first administration Harris left unchanged the Bank of Tennessee board of directors, headed by Cave Johnson and originally appointed by Andrew Johnson in October, 1853. Now, as an indication of the rifts developing within the Democratic party, he replaced "Johnson's" board with an entirely new group of directors. *Tenn. Senate Journal*, 1853, pp. 104–5; *ibid.*, 1855–56, pp. 84, 86; *ibid.*, 1857–58, p. 102; *ibid.*, 1859–60, p. 68.

10. The new board was composed of Granville P. Smith, Willo. Williams, James Johnson, William Stockell, Samuel R. Anderson, Edward S. Gardner, R. F. Nevins, all of Davidson County; M. C. H. Puryear of Williamson; E. A. Keeble of Rutherford; John F. Doak of Wilson; W. S. Massie of Cannon; Hugh H. Bradley of Smith; Elisha Oglesby of Macon; Thomas Boyers of Sumner; and Thomas Menees of Robertson. *Ibid.*

11. Samuel R. Anderson could thus rest in anonymity, "execution proof,"

because "protested accounts" were lumped together in one amount when reported by the bank. See *Johnson Papers*, II, 324, 325n.

12. Jacob McGavock (1790–1878) moved to Nashville from Virginia in 1807, served for the next fifty years as clerk in county, circuit, and U. S. circuit and district courts, and subsequently was clerk of the Confederate circuit and district courts. He acquired extensive holdings in Tennessee, Arkansas, and Kentucky, and married Louise, daughter of Felix Grundy. Randal, their oldest son, was prominent in Nashville affairs, serving as mayor in 1858. McGavock, *Pen and Sword*, *passim*.

13. Both senate and house passed separate bills to expel all free Negroes from Tennessee, but inability to agree upon one measure doomed the effort to failure. During the late 1850's a number of southern states considered legislation to ban free Negroes, but only Arkansas passed such a law, which was suspended early in 1861 after having been on the books less than two years. Orville W. Taylor, *Negro Slavery in Arkansas* (Durham, 1958), 257–58; John Hope Franklin, *From Slavery to Freedom* (New York, 1967), 221; White, *Messages*, V, 174–208.

14. Johnson had in mind two bills then before the legislature. One, rechartering the Union and Planters' banks with greatly liberalized benefits, passed the senate on February 8 and, with some amendments, the house on March 1; the other, designed "to encourage the use of private capital," allowed moneylenders to receive deposits, issue checks or bills of exchange, and discount notes and other securities. With amendments, this latter proposal was also enacted. *Tenn. Acts*, 1860, Chs. CVIII, CXXIX; *Tenn. State Journal*, 1859–60, pp. 436–38, 723; *Tenn. House Journal*, 1859–60, pp. 857, 1074.

From J[ohn?] L. Cox

January 9, 1860, Louisville; ALS, DLC-JP2.

Louisville postmaster extols Johnson's recent Speech on Harper's Ferry Incident, December 12, 1859, "As a great triump—of Constitutional—argument—and a just and withering denunciation of the sympathizers with that old felon—who murdered our inofensive Doyles in Kansas."

From Daniel P. Braden[1]

Springfield Tennessee
January 10th, 1860

Hon A. Johson
    of Tennessee

Dr. Sir, permit me to thank you for the very able Speach which you delivered in the Sennate of the U. S. on the 12 Dcr. last. It is praised by all parties, and is Said to be One of the very best, most degnified, and most convincing aurguments uppon the Subject that has yet been diliverd. As your personal and political friend, living in the Strong hold of the Oposition, my heart is rejoiced in Seeing and hearing Our principels and policeys So abley advocated; and hearing from the very lips of your most bitter political oponents, their acknowledgements of your great and noble effort, in convincing them of the true policeys of the South, as well as the preservation of The Federail Union.

I have thought for Severail years that Our Southern Delagation in Congress was not well posted up uppon the great Comercial policys that Should bind and link together this union in ties of recip[ro]cal benefits one Section of the union to the Other, for just as certain as one part of this Federail union comences domineering, and withholding Strick Justice towards her *Equal* part of this Confederacy when one Section of these united States because She may happen to have the mere majority, Shall Systamattically appropriate the Lions Shear to herself. I Say then if come it must, Tho I Pray God may forbid it let us Seperat let us part, but if forced to this last Extrimity let the South be fully able to convince the enlightened nations of this world that She was right in the Great and responsible undertaking[.]

We hold it here that African Slavry is an ordinance of God, and that it is a political blessing in the *U. S.* The right to hold Such property has been fully established by the Constitution of these *U. S.* and fully co[n]firmed by the U. S. Coarts and the right to recapture Such property when found in any State is clear and undisputiabl[.] Still the practice has been to raise a mob and there by to prevent you from taking your property, hav we not borne with Such insults year after year in the most meek manner.! is there not a point in human nature when forbarence ceaces to be a virtue When good policeys would point Out the law of Retaliation? Who has yet heard of a mob in the South going in defiance of Our laws uppon Bourd a Boston vessel in order to retaliate the rongs that has been committed in Boston uppon the property belonging to Some of Our Southern Citizens[?][2]

The Sane might be Said in trouth and Justice to Cincinatti, O.[3] and many Other Such places[.]

There is One thing certain when the South is Oppressed to her utmost indurence She will be fully able to vindicate her rights; She will become more united in her political policies, She will build up Manufactories, She will open up and build up more Sources of Exports and imports uppon her Own Sea Cost. The South does and will possess all the vital elements of Comerce and Manufacto[r]y[.] She possesses the best Soil, the Best Climate for the raw material or for the manufactured articel[.] in Short we are just opening up Our great resorces, the North has come to a Stand Still, a run of high protective tarriffs for more than forty years have made the money capital of Some quite aristocratic but I think Should they push their "Negro" views but a very little more they will be as Shorne of their locks as ever Samson was of his.

I think a few more Such developments as Browns Revelations,[4] would do more good for the South, than a twelve months Seshion of debates would do in Congress. "Old vanwincle" has awoke Out of his twenty years Sleep[.] "Wooden Clocks" "and yankee notions" are Stal[e.] "Northern school teachers" not in demand. Nothern Schools not to be patronized, The fact is a home policy is much talked of and I Say may God Speed it on.[5] But engough[.]

I hope Sir you may long enjoy the high Opinions of your friends as well as your enemys, I think you Stand more deservedly high in the Opinion of all parties in this Section of "Old Robertson" than you have ever done hertofore[.] Please excuse this my frank Comunication[.]

Very Respectfully yours,
D. P. Braden

ALS, DLC-JP2.

1. Daniel P. Braden (b. c1803), Kentucky native and Springfield tailor, was a member of the first board of county commissioners (1825). By 1860 he had accumulated a sizable estate and was listed in the census as a farmer. *Goodspeed's Robertson County*, 840, 842; 1860 Census, Tenn., Robertson, 1.

2. Braden's reference is to the celebrated Anthony Burns case of May, 1854, when a Boston mob led by Thomas Wentworth Higginson sought to prevent the return to Virginia of a runaway slave. Only with the assistance of eleven hundred soldiers and a revenue cutter were the authorities able to return Burns to his owner. Nevins, *Ordeal of the Union*, II, 150–52.

3. Although noted for its southern sympathies, Cincinnati had recently been the scene of a number of cases arising from the Fugitive Slave Law, thereby eliciting the ire of slaveowners. The latest incident involved a Negro, Lewis Early, who had escaped from Virginia in 1856; tried in March, 1859, and remanded to his owners, he was soon after spirited away by a Cincinnati abolitionist. Charles T. Greve, *Centennial History of Cincinnati and Representative Citizens* (2 vols., Cincinnati, 1904), I, 764–65.

4. Ostensibly a reference to attitudes revealed during the course of the John Brown trial of the preceding fall—a hatred of slavery and a determination to destroy it at all costs. The resulting alarm in the South played into the hands of southern extremists.

5. Such allusions to Rip Van Winkle and his "twenty years Sleep," to "Wooden Clocks and yankee notions" arraign the lassitude of the South and its chronic dependence upon northern products and northern ideas. Southerners had become increasingly conscious of their minority status, and this sense of regional unity, budding in the late 1840's, blossomed during the following decade into a heightened sectionalism which approached nationalism. Those who summered at Newport and Saratoga were urged to patronize southern spas; a variety of journals with an emphasis on things southern appeared; planters' meetings and commercial conventions promoted the development of southern industry and local resources; and there was strong sentiment for the training of teachers, the multiplication of schools, and the writing of textbooks with a southern flavor—all designed to provide "a southern education for southrons." Avery O. Craven, *The Growth of Southern Nationalism, 1848–1861* (Baton Rouge, 1953), 748–55; John S. Ezell, "A Southern Education for Southrons," *Journal of Southern History*, XVII (1951), 303–27.

From Michael Burns[1]

Nashville   January 10   1860

Honl A Johnston
    Dear Sir:
I received your speech on the Harpers Ferry Resolutions and read it attentively and will Say without any intention to flatter you that in my opinion It was the most able document I Ever read both as It regarded arguments and facts[.] I wish It was in the Hands of evry man North of Mason & Dixons line as I think If they had any Sense or Patriotism It would show them the course they are pusuing and its Consequences[.]
you will Excuse me for trespasing on your time in writing to you but I was so much pleased that I could not withhold Expressing my pleasure on the reading of it[.] I gave it to an opposition man to read who was much pleased with It[.] there is very little new here[.] the opposition wanted to get up a union Meeting[.] they wanted Hon C. Johnson to aid them to get It up[.] I as far as I could advised him to have Nothing to do with It as I have Evry Democrat I Seen and think It has fell through[.] there will be a Convention on the 18 to get delegates for the Charleston Convention[.] If [I] could Serve you It would afford me a plasure[.]

                                              your friend   M Burns

ALS, DLC-JP2.
    1. Michael Burns (b. 1813), a native of Ireland and a close friend of Johnson, arrived in Nashville in 1836 and established a successful saddlery business which became one of the leading mercantile houses in the city. When Johnson became governor in 1853, Burns was first made a director of the Bank of Tennessee and later of the Union Bank of Tennessee. Perhaps his most notable achievements, however, lay in his connection with the railroad interests of the state. Largely through his efforts as president (1861–67), the Nashville and Northwestern Railroad increased its mileage from some sixty miles of track until the line eventually stretched from Nashville to the Mississippi River; from 1865 to 1868, he was successful in resuscitating the depleted Nashville and Chattanooga Railroad. Burns was later president of the First National Bank of Nashville and a director of the Third National Bank and the National Commercial Insurance Company. Clayton, *Davidson County*, 381–83.

From Robert Johnson

Nashville   Jany   10th/60

Dear Father,
    I did not reach Nashville until Tuesday evening,[1] owing to the fact, that the train ran off the track about two miles this side of

Murfreesboro' and we had to stay there all night, which was not
altogether as pleasant as it might have been—but I am thankful it
was no worse, as no person was injured—

The Free negro bill[2] has been under consideration in the House
since Friday, and I think that perhaps we may get a vote on it tomorrow, but it is uncertain— The bill has been modified so as to hire
them out instead of selling them into Slavery, and in that form I am
rather inclined to think it will pass, though it is very doubtful, as
the Opposition are making an effort to unite their forces against it—[3]
John Bell has been attending the house regularly since it has been
under discussion[.]

Nicholson has written a letter to Genl Anderson, in which, (so I am
informed) he states that you do not desire the Democratic State
Convention to give an expression for you for the Presidency—[4] this
letter has been shown to some of your friends, and they are extremely
anxious to know whether it speaks your sentiments or not— Burch
and myself[5] have been discussing the matter tonight, and it is at his
suggestion that I write to know if there would be any objection from
you, to the Convention giving an expression— Burch thinks it ought
to be done, but is willing to defer to your judgment— if you think it
bad policy and would have an injurious effect, to do so, we would like
to know it[.] if on the contrary it would not; but rather advance your
claims &c we would like to be informed so that it can be done— The
convention meets on the 18th inst, and I hope you will let Burch or
myself know how you feel on the subject by that time, so that the
action of the Convention may be shaped accordingly— let me hear
from you—

Burch and myself are boarding at Col Torbetts,[6] and are getting
along finely, the only thing I regret is that I did not get here before[.]

I would like for you to send me the *Congressional Globe* from
the *beginning* of this session, as I want to be fully posted on the election of Speaker &c. And have it sent to me regularly, if convenient[.]

I wish you would send me a few copies of your speech— it is
spoken of on all sides in very complimentary terms— Hurt, (Op)[7]
from Madison told me that he had written to you about it—

Dr Richardson[8] sends his compliments for documents sent[.]

Excuse this as I write in haste. will write again in a few days—
better write to me on the Presidency—

R. Johnson

ALS, DLC-JP2.
1. Robert returned to his seat in the legislature two days late after the
holiday recess. *Tenn. House Journal*, 1859–60, p. 438.
2. See Letter from Cave Johnson, January 8, 1860, note 13.
3. A vote on the amended house bill No. 19 (Free Negro bill) was taken

January 12, with Robert Johnson voting in the affirmative. *Tenn. House Journal*, 1859–60, p. 486; see Letter to Robert Johnson, January 12, 1860.

4. Johnson's version of his conversation with Nicholson may be found in Letter to Robert Johnson, January 15, 1860.

5. John C. Burch, now of Davidson County, and Robert were both delegates to the state Democratic convention to be held January 18. Burch was an enthusiastic proponent of Johnson for President.

6. Granville C. Torbett, former state legislator from Monroe, state treasurer, now a Nashville lawyer, and sometime editor of the Nashville *Union and American*, had been selected to represent Blount County in the upcoming Democratic state convention. *Johnson Papers*, I, 80n; *Nashville Bus. Dir.* (1860–61), 270; Nashville *Union and American*, January 19, 1860.

7. Robert B. Hurt was an Opposition representative from Madison County (1859–61). Robison Biog. Data.

8. John W. Richardson (1809–1872), prominent physician and leading Rutherford County Whig, served in the state house (1843–47, 1851–53, 1857–59) and senate (1847–49, 1859–61). Robison, *Preliminary Directory, Rutherford*, 46; Carlton C. Sims, *A History of Rutherford County* (Murfreesboro, 1947), 135–36.

From Charles F. Sevier[1]

                        Rogersville   East Tenn   Jan 10th, 1860

Hon Andrew Johnson
Washington
Dear Sir

I made application to Mr Nelson[2] for a situation in the U. States Military Academy. I stated to him that I had received a letter, from an acquaintance at the Academy[.] he says it does not make any difference about living a certain time in a district although it is required by the Government, for there are members there who received their appointments from Territories and live in States, as I have not heard from him I do not know whether he has applied for one of the 10 appointments or not. I wrote with the expectation that he could make the arrangement with some Territorial member whose district is vacant and that I would go and make that district my residence. but in looking over the list of members I see they disagree with him in politics knowing that you have none at your disposal[.]

As it is my last attempt, I will be under many obligation[s] to you if you will use your influence in my behalf in getting a situation. I think I am qualified to pass both examination[s] for I commenced preparing at the age of 14 with the expectation [of] getting a situation when I become of age[.]   Your most Obedient
                                                               C F Sevier

Born Oct 16th 1842
5 feet, 10 in in heigth

I am very much obliged to you for the List of Regulation[s] you sent me[.]

ALS, DLC-JP2.

1. Charles F. Sevier (1842–1931), appointed to the U. S. Naval Academy in 1860, resigned to become a commodore in the Confederate navy, and was later a colonel in the Confederate army. Cora B. Sevier and Nancy S. Madden, *Sevier Family History* (Washington, D. C., 1961), 445.

2. Thomas A. R. Nelson.

To Robert Johnson, Nashville

Washington City Jany 12th 1860

Private

My dear Son,

On last night I was much gratified by the receipt of four phials of Arnolds' Union pills[1] and at once took too of them and this morning feel somewhat releived and hope to be entirely So in a few d[a]ys— There is no [e]llection for Speaker as yet and infact there Seems to be but little prospect of one at present— I hope there will be a change for the better before long or it will look like there is a dead lock in the Government— I see in the Union of the 7th inst that Barksdale has offered an amendment to his bill expelling free negroes from the State[2] which I think from a cursory reading puts the measure in a pretty good form and releives it from any thing like oppression or inhumanity to the free Colored man, and think that if I was in the Legislature that I would vote for a bill somthing like the amendment he has offered inleiu of the original bill— However this is a matter for your own judgement to determin— If they Could begotten Clear of without violating the great principles of humanity and Justice, it would be better for the Country and especially the Slave States— I think the bill in its present shape will drive them from the State in a few years— I would give them a reasonable time to get aw[a]y before the loaw Commenced operating—

The State Convention will now Soon come off— If Milligan Could be put on to attend the Charleston Convention as one of the delegates it would be gratifying to him and he would do as well as a[n]y one else and much better than Some who want to go there in that capacity—[3] There Seems to be quite a move alover [all over] the State to place Col Haynes[4] on the electoral ticket for the State at large in connection with Genl Atkins—[5] I would let it all pass, perhaps it is best at present— By noticing the proceed[in]gs of the different meetigs it is quite apparent that there is [a] new divession of the democracy wishing to come up in the State with the view of taking charge of affairs in the State in a few years: it is most Clear to me—

Knox Walker Esqr is now in Washington and will be there (that is at the Convention) for the purpose no doubt of promoting S. A. Douglas' pretentions for the presidency— He has been since my return to Washington on better terms of intimacy than at a[n]y former time and I think Sees as I do there is a third branch of democracy Coming up in the State and is prepared (which is natural and right to) take Care of himself and friends[.] Hence Johnson and his friends are not so obnoxios as heretofore— Walker will make no move as I understand to procure an expression from the Convention infavor of S. A. D. but will be desposed to act with my friends in the event there Should be a[n]y move made to obtain Such an expression in my behalf, and would no doubt in Case the Candidate for the Presidency was selected from the South give me a decided Support: But in the event the Candidate Comes from the north he by this move would expect to make Douglas' acceptable to the Johnson Democracy— Let this all be as it may, I do not think he is Coming to make a[n]y war upon me and hope that you will receive him kindly and courteously and here and understand what are his designs and if there is nithig [nothing] wrong in them and he wants to act with our frinds let him do so— Knox is a politician in the proper acceptation of the terme and is about as fair as most of them in trying to cary out their plans— In reference to Douglas I would not Say any hard things at present for it might So turn out that he might be the nominee and as against a B. Republican we might be Compelled to go for him, for at presnt he is the Strong man in the free States and will go into the convention the strong man of the party[.] what will be done there no one at this time Can tell— One word in referince to my Self— So far as any expression on the part of the convention which is to Sit on the 18th inst goes I do not care one fig about it, and will take no Step to procure Such an expression at this time— There are Some persons it is true to gratify their personal envy and Jealousy would like to defeat any thing that might be Calculated to give me Stand[in]g and consequence, either here in the Senate or before the Charleston convention, on this account if none other it would be a source of Some personal pride and gratification. But I intend to let matters take their Course[.] If Wa[l]ker and frinds are disposed to be my friend against my enemies, though it m[a]y be in the end to promote his own interest let him be so— There is nothing wrong it Seems to me, in one half of my enemies joining me to put down the other half, let them Come and as long as they act in good faith we will treat them as friends and allies and no longer— I do not want you to place your Self in any position

that would Subject you to the charge of being wanting in delacacy
in reference to your relation to me— I would be prudent and discret
in all that I did or Said in reference to my position— You have
already acquired Some Credit for discretion and good Common
Sense in going over the State and would now do nothig to lose it—

Harvy M. Waterson will be at the convention[.] he seems to be
my decided friend and perhaps will talk to you freely on matters
which are to Come off before the convention and Some which have
and are Coming off here— I have been trying to Serve him and
hope that I will Succeed in the end—

Turnner[6] is here and Commenced operations in the Land office— You will remember that when I first returned home after
his Comig to Greeneville that I had formed rather an unfavorable
opinion of him from a letter he wrote to me[.] I regret to Say that
Since I have Seen more of him that I have not had Cause to Change
it— Infine he is no account and has but ve[r]y little infomation of
any kind and worse than all I fear he is a man of very low instincts—
Let this all pass and hope for the better: but if [it] was to do over
again I would have nothing to do with him—

Accept assurances of the best wishes of a devoted fathers heart
                                                   Andrew Johnson

Robet Johnson Esqr
I do not know whethr you can read it or not for I can hardly write
this mornig atall this mor[nin]g and infact have not time to read the
letter over: So take as it is and guess at it the best w[a]y you can[.]

ALS, CSmH–Misc. #8207.
    1. Apparently Johnson had run out of his "sovereign" remedy for all
ailments.
    2. On October 6, 1859, William H. Barksdale, representative for Smith,
Sumner, and Macon counties (1859–60), had introduced a bill providing for
the expulsion by January 1, 1862, of all free Negroes aged twenty-one through
fifty with minors to be leased out until they became of age. Named chairman
of a new committee on free Negroes and slave population, he reported in mid-
November a substitute bill which specified such removal by May 1, 1861, and
provided trial and auction into slavery for violators. Still dissatisfied, in early
January, 1860, he offered on his own initiative an amended bill removing the
age qualification and specifying that it would be "unlawful for any free person of color" to remain in Tennessee after January 1, 1861. Included also
were provisions requiring freed Negroes to produce funds adequate for their
transportation to Liberia and six months' support. There was a clause excluding the aged (over forty-five), ill, and infirm. Adopted January 12, this substitute was sent to the senate, where an amendment was tacked on and the bill
failed a third reading. Despite repeated efforts the two houses failed to reach
an agreement, the whole matter being finally laid on the table in the house,
March 12. Throughout the parliamentary maneuvering, Robert Johnson supported the Barksdale revised bill which his father found acceptable. *Tenn.
House Journal*, 1859–60, pp. 237–38, 456–58, 486, 1033; White, *Messages*,
V, 174–80, 206–8.
    3. Named as one of the four delegates-at-large, Sam Milligan went to

Charleston and later to Baltimore. Hesseltine, *Three against Lincoln*, 288, 302; Nashville *Union and American*, January 19, 1860.

4. Landon C. Haynes was chosen a candidate for elector-at-large. *Ibid.*, January 20, 1860.

5. John D. C. Atkins, a delegate to the state Democratic convention from Henry County, declined the nomination as elector-at-large which then went to W. C. Whitthorne. *Ibid.*, January 20, 24, 1860.

6. Samuel S. Turner, a Georgia native, was coeditor of the Greeneville *Democrat* in 1859. The following year, while still acting as associate editor and Washington correspondent, he was also employed as a clerk in the interior department at a salary of $1,200. Greeneville *Democrat*, May 4, 1859, April 7, 1860; Knoxville *Whig*, June 6, 1860; *U. S. Official Register* (1861), 76.

From S. Yorke Atlee

January 14, 1860, Washington, D. C.; ALS, DLC-JP2.

Librarian of the treasury department congratulates Johnson on his "excellent speech on the Harper's Ferry Invasion," and invites him to attend the meeting of Federal [Masonic] Lodge No. 1, "of which I was Master 3 years."

To Robert Johnson, Nashville

Washington City   Jany 15th 1860

Confidential

My dear Son,

Your letter of the 10th inst[1] has just been received and read with Some Surprise, especially that portion of it in reference to Mr Nicholson— Some short time since in a conversation with Mr Nicholson I told him that I was not a Candidate for the presidency, yet I was for a Southern man and was infavor of our state convention expressing an opinion as to their first choice and after that to do the best they Could in convention in the event they Could not succeed in getting their first Choice— I told him also after refering to the relation which existed between him and myself and to what had been Said by others that there had been a bargain between us in regard to his ellection for Senator and my future prospects for the presidency— I told him I did not want him to feel under any obligations to me on account of any thing that had occurred with reference to his election as Senator but on the Contray, I wanted him to feel at liberty to do what ever seemed to Suit his feelings and judgment best. As to the State convention I told him I did not know what it would do, that I did not wish to occupy a positio[n] that would Cause a divession among our frinds or the democratic party and should therefore leave the matter in the hands of others to dispose of it as

they might deem best for the interest of the party[.] I also told him
that I was for the convention expressing an opinion infavor of Some
one whether it was for me or not—That we had a Choice and that
we ought to indicate our preference— In reply to this he stated,
that he "as a general rule was opposed to conventions expressing any
preference; but leave them free to do the best they Could; but in this
Case and at this time he was for the convention making a nomination;
for the reason among other things that it would nominate me, and
that, that would defeat the Douglas men and that he beleived I was
the only man that Could do it— I replied to him—that I wished he
was for me on some other account or ground than mere opposition
to, D, that I did not want my name used just to break some one else
down, that, that was a kind of strength I did not care much about,
that I had enemies enough already and that I had no dispos[i]tion
to be run for the purpose of making more enemies— In this conversation kindly and pleasantly I referred to his Course in 1856
when he in fact was desirious of ha[v]ing an expression for Mr
Peirce and Brown² wanted one for himself and found they Could not
obtain it, they both concluded it was *most judicious* to have *no expression atall*— My intention was to release Mr Nicholson from all
embarassment whatever and leave him to do as his own inclination
dictated— I told him a nomination by the convention would be a
source of some personal gratification if nothing more; but I should
leave matters to take their own Course &c— On last Friday morning, before H. M. Waterson started for Nashville I asked Mr Nicholson if he had been writing to any one in the state as to what Course
the convention should take in reference to a nomination &c— He
Replied readly and promptly, that he had not written a letter to any
one on the Subject and did not intend to [do] so— It seems that his
letter was there in Nashville before the 10th and this took place on
the 13th— I think I mentioned this to Waterson before he left the
Capitol— For to be Serious about it, I thought he ought to have
written to his friends and to have suggested the propriety of my
nomination; ha[v]ing been his friend under the Circumstances I
was— But lo and behold, he had written a letter the best Calculated to defeat it— In fact I think that little flair up at Knoxville³
in which his name was alluded to inspired him with the beleif that
he was the Choice of the people of the State for the Presidency—and
that *perhaps* by this course he could procure a nomination himself—
I fear Nicholson is by nature treacherous and by practice a liar—
If the matter is as you understand it, I shall have no further confidence in him— Infine my friends are authorised to do whatever
they think best. My own opinion is the convention ought to nominate
a candidate as their first Choice leaving the delegation in a condi-

tion [to] do whatever they m[a]y beleiv to be best after they have failed in their first choice— Before you receive this you and Whitthorne[4] will both have recd my letters— I did not know that Mr Nicholson had written a letter to any one on the Subject of my nomination—and if he has written one it was never showed to me or its Contents relateded— You will please relate the contents of this lette to Burch and say to him that the true policy is to nominate— I thought Sam Anderson[5] was my friend and would do whatever he could to promote my interest and especially the democratic party and if you think proper you m[a]y say so to him and that the democratic party in Tennessee ought to make a nomination; there are many reasons why it should be so at this time— Do nothing that is indiscret[.] if there is to be a rupture between Mr Nicholson and myself let all the facts be got right before there is a[n]y move made — I have sent you [this with] dispatch for if this does not go strait through it will not reach you until after until [sic] the convention is over—

Your father
Andrew Johnson

P. S. Tell Burch I rely much on his good common sense and judgment in this matter and that I have m[an]y thngs to S[a]y to him that will not do to put on paper if I ever had the time more to do so— More soon[.]

ALS, DLC-JP.

1. See Letter from Robert Johnson, January 10, 1860.
2. Aaron V. Brown.
3. At the Knoxville Democratic meeting, December 5, 1859, the committee on resolutions, reporting against a declaration in support of Johnson for the presidency, expressed the belief that such action would not embrace "the real sentiment" of Knoxville Democrats, many of whom "would prefer that the honor should fall upon Governor Isham G. Harris or Hon. A. O. P. Nicholson." Knoxville *Register*, quoted in Nashville *Patriot*, December 12, 1859.
4. Washington C. Whitthorne (1825–1891), Columbia lawyer and Johnson's personal representative at the Charleston Convention, had been a state senator (1855–58) and state representative and speaker (1859). After service in the Confederate cause, he became a Democratic congressman (1871–83, 1887–91) and briefly senator (1886–87). *BDAC*, 1810; John Trotwood Moore and Austin P. Foster, *Tennessee: The Volunteer State* (4 vols., Nashville, 1923), II, 249–50.
5. Samuel R. Anderson was at this time Nashville postmaster.

From Albert G. Graham

Jonesboro Tenn.   18 Jany '60.

Sir:

Enclosed I send you the application of Mr. Cornelius Hughes, now of Hawkins Co. but formerly of Greene Co. for an Increase of his pension.[1] Will you be so good as to present it to the Senate in due form, and have it appropriately referred?

Mr. Hughes says that when you were in Congress, (in the House) you had his pension allowed; and he wishes you to give such attention as you can afford from your other duties to his present application. The papers are drawn up in such form as, I think, will pass them thru without much trouble. His claim is but a small one; and if the law allowed it to be made at the pension office would be readily granted.[2]

Our people here are very impatient in regard to the non election of a speaker.[3] The ties which bind the government together at present appear to be very fragile— Indeed, the government might be said to be partially suspended. For the honor & credit of our Country, I hope this state of affairs will not long continue.

Nelson's friends here quote Hatton's speech,[4] in that part when Hatton's quotes from you, as sustaining Nelson's position in his recent speech. I cannot clearly see the inference; I think your remarks correct; but Nelson is certainly wrong.

I am, &c   A. G. Graham

ALS, DNA-RG46, 36 Cong., Pension Pet., Cornelius Hughes.

1. Cornelius Hughes (b. c1794), a farmer and veteran of the War of 1812, had sought an invalid pension based on two-thirds disability even before Johnson's first congressional term. Finally, in 1852, he was awarded a pension of $5.33⅓ per month and placed upon the pension rolls in Jonesboro. 1860 Census, Tenn., Hawkins, 164; *Johnson Papers*, I, 327, 653, 660, 671; War of 1812 Pension Files, Cornelius Hughes, RG15, National Archives.

2. It appears that Johnson was only partially successful in his efforts on Hughes's behalf, for although a private bill (S. 183) to increase the pension to $8 a month passed the Senate on April 7, it died in the House after a favorable recommendation from committee. *Cong. Globe*, 36 Cong., 1 Sess., 1569, 2187; *Alphabetical List of Private Claims . . . Thirty-second to Forty-first Congresses (House Misc. Doc.* No. 109, 42 Cong., 3 Sess.), 226.

3. A close division of congressional seats, coupled with heightened sectionalism and a desire to control committees, resulted in a deadlock in organizing the House until February 1, 1860, when William Pennington of New Jersey was finally elected speaker on the forty-fourth ballot. For nearly two months the country's legislative business was at a standstill. Nevins, *Emergence of Lincoln*, II, 112–24.

4. T. A. R. Nelson was currently under attack as disloyal to the South because of remarks in Congress on December 7, when he argued that the mere election of a Republican President or speaker was not sufficient cause for destroying the Union, unless some "overt act leading to peril of the South" was also committed. On January 13, during debate on the speaker election, Tennessee Congressman Robert Hatton sought to defend his fellow old-line Whig by using a quotation from Johnson which Hatton contended expressed a sentiment similar to that of Nelson, now so bitterly criticized by certain southern Democrats. In his Harper's Ferry speech of December 12, 1859, Johnson had declared: "Because we cannot get our constitutional rights, I do not intend to be one of those who will violate the Constitution." Thomas B. Alexander, *Thomas A. R. Nelson of East Tennessee* (Nashville, 1956), 64; *Cong. Globe*, 36 Cong., 1 Sess., 51, 442; James V. Drake, *Life of Gen. Robert Hatton* (Nashville, 1867), 208.

From Sam Milligan

Greeneville Ten   Jan. 18, 1860

Dear Governor,

I could not conveniently attend the State Convention, which meets today. The weather has been bad—the trains irregular, and my funds low—all of which combined to prevent me from going. Lowry went of course—M. L. Patterson,[1] and I think Bullen,[2] but as to him I am not sure, who will do up things after their own heart.

Yesterday I received your poetry in the "Traveler."[3] It is elegant. The sentiment elevated, and the language chaste and poetical. I will preserve it.

I have a notion if I can find time to write a letter or two on the Slavey question. I have been thinking about it, and with the lights now before me, I have come to the conclusion, that the "Old Public Functionary's" volcano,[4] will overwhelm the South, long before he can sprout a blue-eyed bean on the lava, ashes, and squalid scoriae of its present eruptions, much less cultivate a fruitful crop of the olive —the vine—and the corn. He thinks the agitation will burn out, or be displaced by other questions less threatening in their character. I can see no just ground for such a hope. The South has waited twenty five years for this result, and today, the question is more threatening than at any subsequent [sic] period of its history. How long must She wait? And what hope have her people that time will allay the fanaticism of the North. Already the territorial questions are nearly all settled, and compromise after compromise have been entered into, and as often failed to quiet the agitation, or to stay the aggressions of the North.

In addition to all this, nearly or quite all the leading protestant Churches have seperated, and organized seperate polit[i]es; and the affection of our section is thoroughly alienated from the other. What, under such circumstances, can we expect from delay? The answer must be—nothing! nothing! !

But what is the remedy? That is the question. Will empty eulogies on the union—the glorious union—save the Union? That is nonsense, and generly hypocritical twaddle. What then must be done? I answer:—*Demand from the North a restoration of the Constitutional rights, of which she has rob[b]ed the South, and a restoration of that equilibrium of political power which originally was incorporated into the government by the fathers of the republic.* How is this practicable? I know the South has not the power to enforce any such demand. But it is equally obvious unless the North grants it, the south can not maintain the institution of Slavey ten years longer.— Already the North has the power in a large majority of the State— the House of Representatives—the Electoral College, and soon will have it in all probability in the Senate, and by the admission of a few more free States, which must come in, She can alter and amend the Constitution at her pleasure. So the time never will be more favorable for the South to act than it is now.

But how are these lost constitutional rights to be restored, and this equilibrium of power regained? It must be done either by an amendment of the constitution, or by cutting up the Southern States so as at least to secure in the Senate that equilibrium of power which the South originally had. Nothing else will do it, and we had as well make the issue now as hereafter, for it will come sooner or later. This will test the sincerity of the "*Union-loving*" north, and drive the Souther[n] Opposition to take a decided position.

I am not for disolution of the Union, because that would end in revolution, and in no wise secure the South against northern aggressions. But it matters but little what we are for, we have no power in the South to do any thing, and can gain none by longer indulging the North. If there are true men in the North, they can not be injured by restoring to the South the Constitutional power to protect herself against the aggressions of their bad men. No harm Can result, in my opinion, to any portion of the Union by the adoption of this remedy, and I do not now see why any man who lovs the Union should be opposed to it.

The South speaks of disunion, and yet public men in her midst will tell her, she is too ultra—be qui[e]t, when a moments reflection will convence any sane mind, that qui[e]t will end in the distruction of all her domestic institutions. She must act— Act first to save the Constitution, and then her own honor next. How the latter will be done, I do not now decide. But I will say disunion will end in revolution, in which the North will suffer from her own citizens as much as we will from our slavs.

The foregoing is a sort of an out line of my Contemplated papers. Will it do? Is it sound doctrine? Let me hear from you, and send me all the documents you can find on the present state of parties—and the no. of square miles of slave and free territory if you can find it. All well— God bless you[.]

                                                          Sam Milligan

P. S. Give my very best regards to A. O. P. Nicholson, and tell him I would like to hear from him occasionally—

ALS, DLC-JP2.

1. Michael L. Patterson (1827–*fl*1887), a North Carolina native, taught school in Washington County before moving to Greeneville where he served as clerk of the circuit court (1856–62), clerk of the supreme court of the eastern division (1865–70), and clerk and master of the chancery court (1870–82). A Unionist during the war, he was a quartermaster in the 4th Tennessee infantry. *Goodspeed's Knox*, 1027.

2. Lloyd Bullen, former state senator. See *Johnson Papers*, I, 497n.

3. Efforts to locate this publication have proved fruitless.

4. In his third annual message, December 19, 1859, Buchanan, styling himself "an old public functionary whose service commenced in the last generation," compared the present state of affairs with former crises, which erupted and had their day and were like "volcanoes burnt out . . . upon whose lava and ashes . . . grow the peaceful olive, the cheering vine, and the sustaining corn." The sobriquet soon afterwards came to be used as a term of derision. Richardson, *Messages*, V, 553; George E. Shankle, *American Nicknames: Their Origin and Significance* (New York, 1955), 62.

From Washington C. Whitthorne

Nashville. Jany 19. 1860.

Private

Honl Andrew Johnson
Dear Sir:

I got your letter by Watterson[1] only the eveni[n]g before Convention met. I wish it had been earlier. Everything might have been smooth. As it was & in view of things as they were, it was smoothly done, but might have been better. Are you satisfied? I write hurriedly, but allow me to say, that Gov. Harris acted like a man, repudiated the idea that he was to be brought into conflict with you. Walker,[2] smoothed things, I beleive he acted in good faith to you here[.] He is not a delegate— I make no doubt that he is really for Douglass—but your friends have no right to complain of him here. His defeat as delegate is ascribable to other things, of which & other incidents I will write you. Give me your opinion of the convention, men & things. Shall I go to Charleston.[3] I would like to see you before then. I should as Elector like to do you[r] battles this summer & fall.

Yr friend. &c   Whitthorne

ALS, DLC-JP2.

1. It is unfortunate that this letter, which might have provided additional information about Johnson's ideas on convention strategy, has not been found.

2. J. Knox Walker.

3. Whitthorne was not originally chosen as a delegate to Charleston, but served in place of Dr. S. B. Moore of Hickman County. Nashville *Union and American*, April 26, 1860.

From Samuel R. Anderson

Nashville PO   Jany 21, 1860

Honl. A Johnson
Dr Sir

I am quite obliged to you, for your several favors, in the way of documents.

I have been trying to get a spare hour to write you ever since, you left our city but the press of business has prevented.

I, now, have very little to write you of interest, except the doings of Legislature, and the action of our late state Convention. I must refer you to the published proceeding of both for a correct understanding of what they have done. I would remark, that I fear the democratic cause will not gain much strength, by the doings of the Legislature— there seems to be a great want of unity of feeling among our friends, in that boddy. I hope for the best but have my fears. The Session will be a long one—[1]

I am pleased with the result, of the deliberations of the Convention, and especially so with there action in regard to the Presidency. As a matter of course we had some wild men in the Convention, and at one time, things looked very much like going rong, but after Sykes and Several others let off Steam,[2] things righted up, and went off harmoniously. The reccommendation of your name, as Tennessees favorite for the Presidency, was recevd. by the Convention, with old fashioned, Shouts, and applause.—[3] I thought I saw two or three men, whose faces looked twisted, and resembled a boy who had been eating green parcimons.— but the people, the great mass, was with the move, and if the Committee had failed to have reported your name, it would have been done by other members of the Convention— It was plain, that it was a fixed fact that your name was to be presented before the Country, as Tennessees choice for the Presidency— It has been done, and if we manage matters right, and our delegation to Charleston, use the influence, they will be entitled to, I believe your chances for the nomination will be first rate. The delegation from Tennessee can do a great deal to, advance or retard your chances. I am pleased with the platform— there is a small streak of the "Judicious taney"[4] in it, but still I suppose it will be favorably reced. North or South—

I see up to this writting, no organisation has been effected in the House. I hope our men will stand firm, and never consent or vote for a Black Republican.[5] I was pleased with your speech, and regard it, as the true ground to be assumed— I hope our friends will all act in the same way[.]

I hope to hear from you as often as Convenient[.] Give my respects to Nicholson Wright⁶ and others[.]

Yours very Respt   S R Anderson

ALS, DLC-JP2.

1. Meeting from October 3, 1859, until March 26, 1860, the 33rd General Assembly became the longest thus far in the history of the state. However, the trend in recent years had been toward significantly longer sessions: in 1851–52, and again in 1857–58, the assemblies lasted two weeks longer than those immediately preceding them; the current session exceeded that of 1857–58 by only a week.

2. William J. Sykes of Maury County, a leader of the proslavery faction, sought to maneuver voting procedures so that his faction could control the convention. Failing in this, he and Thomas Williams of Hickman, in an effort to amend the resolutions to make them more acceptable to the "ultras," succeeded in rejecting them on first reading, sending them back to committee from which they reemerged with two paragraphs more favorable to slavery protectionists. Nashville *Republican Banner*, January 19, 1860.

3. A resolution complimentary to Johnson and naming him as Tennessee's "first choice for the Presidency" was maneuvered through a reluctant resolutions committee by William Lowry and other Johnson supporters. Once on the floor of the convention the sailing was smoother, though an opposition paper reported that "Some irresponsible delegate in the crowd moved to strike out Johnson and insert Isham G. Harris, but his motion was not recognized by the chair [Johnson's friend G. W. Jones] and he dried up quick." Nashville *Union and American*, January 19, 20, 1860; Letter from William M. Lowry, January 27, 1860; Nashville *Republican Banner*, January 19, 1860.

4. The platform adopted by the Nashville convention endorsed Taney's Dred Scott decision as "a true and clear exposition of the powers reposed in Congress upon the subject of the Territories of the United States, and the rights guaranteed to the residents in the Territories." Evidently Anderson had some reservations about this stance. Nashville *Union and American*, January 19, 1860.

5. With the Harper's Ferry incident inflaming passions on both sides of the aisle, the House was unable to elect a speaker, a clerk, or a printer until February 1, when William Pennington, an innocuous Whig, was finally chosen speaker. Southern Democrats, unalterably opposed to a Black Republican, were not much more sympathetic to an old-line southern Whig. With all sorts of diversionary tactics, including dilatory motions and lengthy speeches, the southerners succeeded in paralyzing the House for nearly eight weeks. Nevins, *Emergence of Lincoln*, II, 116–24.

6. John V. Wright (1828–1908) of McNairy County was a lawyer, Democratic congressman (1855–61), Confederate colonel, and member of the first and second Confederate congresses. Settling in Columbia after the war, he was judge of the ninth circuit court (1877–78) before removing to Nashville, where he practiced law (1881–86). An unsuccessful candidate for governor (1880), he ended his career in Washington in the law division of the general land office (1887–1908). *BDAC*, 1852; Porter, *Tenn. Confed. Mil. Hist.*, 797–98.

From Thomas A. Devyr

Williamsburgh   Jany 21 1860

Sir—

I am unwilling to think that your neglect of my communications to you is a deliberate thing. That you do not think the soldiers of the great cause,[1] residing in this neighborhood, are worthy of notice.

Those soldiers want neither personal advantage, nor personal countenance, even, from you. They regarded you as their general-in-chief—and as such asked orders—instruction—advice from you. Were they wrong in their estimate? Are you *not* the General-in chief?

Your Obdt Servt
Thos A Devyr

Hon Andw Johnson. Senator

ALS, DLC-JP2.

 1. A reference to workers on behalf of the homestead, particularly those in the New York Land Reform movement.

From Robert Johnson

Nashville Jan'y 22nd [1860]

Dear Father,

Yours of 15th and 13th inst received, and I was somewhat surprised to learn that Nicholson had stated that he had not written to any person, as to what action the Convention Should take in regard to the Presidency— Mr George Gantt[1] told me that Nicholson had written to him, that you did not desire an expression in your favor &c. And I was also informed that the same had been written to Genl Anderson— And I am Satisfied that if it could have been done, no expression would have been permitted by the convention, as there was evidently an undercurrent from some quarter, I wont say where now at work, to stifle it, but the delegates were so overwhelmingly in your favor, that they themselves were smothered and driven from the field, and any open attempt would have been met with a perfect storm[.] Hunter Nicholson[2] has been about Nashville pretty often this winter, and at first was exceedingly friendly with me, but here of a late, "a change has come over the spirit of his dreams,"[3] and he has been very cool— on the day of the convention, after he saw that an expression was inevitable, he came to me, and said that perhaps some of his Fathers friends might make an effort to strike your name out and insert Nicholson's, and that if it was done, he wished me to know that it was not his Fathers desire, and there would be no conflict &c, and that he was for you— well, I thought it was entirely useless, as I do not believe there was any man that had the most remote idea of presenting his name, and whenever Mr Nicholson, gets from under the wing of your protection, he sinks, never to rise again— set that down as fixed— I would not let him know anything about what you have heard, and let it all pass, for "time at last sets all things even[.]"

Harris' friends acted very well, and were willing for the convention to give an expression—. J. Knox Walker acted in good faith as I believe, and did do some good with his Shelby delegation, he was extremely friendly and kind— Bill Carroll[4] one of his delegates to Charleston, pretends to be out and out for you— my opinion is that Knox thinks Douglas will throw his strength for you in the Convention and thereby secure your nomination— he will be at Washington in a few days—

Watterson can tell you all the particulars of the Convention, and you have seen the proceedings in the Union & American and no use in my writing details at this time— If you have any use for me, in any way, after the Legislature adjourns, let me know, and I will cheerfully go to work—and if you think it advisable for me to go to Washington before the meeting of the Charleston Convention, in order that you may give me your plans &c., I will go and do anything you may desire— I have a kind of presentiment that you can get the nomination by a little management—but enough of that—

What do you think of my *marrying* Miss Childress,[5] (Maj J. W. Childress' daughter) *provided* I can get her— she is a nice woman and no mistake[.]

I will write you again in a few days[.]

Have the *Congressional* Globe sent to the Union & American[.]

Whitthorne & Burch[6] think you ought to have your late speech circulated all over the north[.] Dunnington[7] worked hard for you at the Convention and deserves credit &c[.]

Your Son   R. J.

ALS, DLC-JP2.

1. George Gantt (1826–1897), Maury County lawyer and judge, served in the legislature (1849–50), was a lieutenant colonel in the Confederate army, and after 1865 was a member of the Memphis bar. Robison Biog. Data; Speer, *Prominent Tennesseans*, 521; *Goodspeed's Maury*, 759, 764.

2. Hunter Nicholson (1834–1901), son of A. O. P. Nicholson, was a Maury County delegate to the state convention. Associate editor of his father's paper, the Washington *Union*, and later editor of the Columbia *Herald* and the *Dixie Farmer*, he was a military aide to Governor Isham Harris and a Confederate officer. After the war he became the first professor of agriculture and horticulture at East Tennessee University (1869), switched to the chair of natural history, and briefly served as librarian before the reorganization of 1886 left him unemployed. He continued to live in Knoxville and edit agricultural journals. Patricia P. Clark, A. O. P. Nicholson of Tennessee: Editor, Statesman, and Jurist (M. A. thesis, University of Tennessee, 1965), 13–14; Stanley J. Folmsbee, *Tennessee Establishes a State University*, in *University of Tennessee Record*, LXIV (May, 1961), *passim*.

3. An inexact quotation from Byron's "The Dream," st. 5: "A change came o'er the spirit of my dream." W. Gurney Benham, *Cassell's Classified Quotations* (London, 1930), 59.

4. William H. Carroll (1820–fl1886), Memphis postmaster and son of ex-governor William Carroll, was a brigadier general in Tennessee's pro-

visional, later Confederate, army until his resignation in 1863. Porter, *Tenn. Confed. Mil. Hist.*, 300–301.

5. Robert Johnson never married. His reference is probably to Elizabeth (variously Betsy, Betty, or Bettie) Childress (b. *c*1843), a daughter of John W. Childress (1807–1884) of Rutherford County, a lawyer and James K. Polk's brother-in-law, whom Johnson nominated in 1853 for a directorship of the Bank of Tennessee. In 1859 Childress was serving as president of the Planters' Bank of Murfreesboro. Miss Childress later became the wife of Governor John C. Brown. *Ibid.*, 299; Speer, *Prominent Tennesseans*, 26–27; Deane Porch, comp., *Tombstone Inscriptions of Evergreen Cemetery* (Murfreesboro, 1965), 146.

6. Washington C. Whitthorne, the Tennessee house speaker, and John C. Burch, former speaker of the state senate and present editor of the Nashville *Union and American.*

7. Frank C. Dunnington.

From William B. Franklin[1]

Office Cap Extension
Jan. 25, 1860.

Dear Sir

Not finding you to-day at the Senate, I enclose you the Resolution which you handed me yesterday, and with it a House Doct[2] which I think covers much of the ground which would have to be travelled in answering the resolution.[3]

There has been, and is now, much difference of opinion among those capable of judging, as to the fitness of the New Dome to the Building.

My own opinion is that it is too large, and that no Dome ought to have been commenced until after the completion of the Wings. But, as you will observe from the letters of the Secretary of War (Mr. Davis) the work was authorized by Congress upon plans adopted by a Committee, without consultation with the Department.[4] In obedience to the Law the work was commenced, and has been prosecuted to its present State.

It is my opinion that notwithstanding the unfitness of the Dome to the Building, it will not be economical to Stop the work, or to reduce its size or height. I have no reason to doubt that the cost will come within the amount estimated, and I could with little trouble estimate very nearly what the cost will be.

The questions contained in the resolution as to the amounts of expansion & contraction, opening and rusting of the joints & bolts are very easily answered, but I do not think the answers will be of use. The Dome constructed of iron will last for centuries, if proper care to keep it well painted is taken, and this you are aware is necessary in any iron work.

The method of uniting the iron pieces is good and safe, and I am Sure there will be no danger of its falling when it is once erected. There is no similarity of condition to that of the Troy Depot, New York, which was a brick building surmounted by a wooden roof secured by iron rods, the fastenings of which rods broke.[5]

I think there would be no propriety in introducing pumice Stone in the construction of the Dome, and the resolution makes an assumption as to the cheapness of that material that the facts will not entirely warrant, for the expense of procuring the stone from Teneriffe,[6] and of working it after it was procured would be very great, greater I think than will be that of completing the Dome according to the present design. The danger of lightning is less in an iron Dome than it would be in one of any other material, I think.

The questions as to the amounts expended, & the persons to whom they were paid, with the contracts, papers, &c connected with the expenditures can all be answered & furnished from this office, and may give useful information to the Senate.

But if the object of the Resolution is merely to obtain information to guide Congress in ordering a change in the design for the Dome, I think it will be bad policy to adopt it, for I do not think any change would be economical, from the fact that the present work has gone too far to be changed without material loss and delay. I believe delay in these large works is a fruitful Source of expenditure and waste, and that it ought always to be avoided, even if by incurring it, we may sometimes make an alteration which at first sight appears beneficial.

Excuse this long letter, but I have thought that I could sooner place you in possession of the facts which induce me to think an alteration of the Dome injudicious, by this means, than by a personal interview.

I repeat however that all of the questions in the resolution can easily be answered, and some of the information would be useful to Congress. I do not however think that the design of the Dome ought to be changed.

If you conclude to offer the resolution, I would respectfully suggest that the proper channel for the information will be the War Department, and that the Resolution Should read "that the Secretary of War be requested to report to the Senate &c[.]" It will then be referred to me for a report.

I am very respectfully yours   W. B. Franklin
Cap Top Engs   in charge Cap Exetn &c.

Hon A. Johnson
U. S. Senate.

ALS, DLC-JP.

1. William B. Franklin (1823–1903) of Pennsylvania, a West Point graduate (1843) assigned to the corps of engineers, served in the Mexican War and superintended various construction projects before he succeeded Montgomery C. Meigs on November 1, 1859, as officer in charge of the Capitol extension, continuing in this capacity until 1861. A Union general, he was wounded in 1864 and saw no further active service. Soon after the close of the war, he became general manager of the Colt Fire Arms Manufacturing Company, Hartford, Connecticut, continuing until 1888. *DAB*, VI, 601–2.

2. *House Misc. Doc.* No. 65, 34 Cong., 1 Sess.

3. Johnson seems never to have introduced the resolution which had probably been prepared by Charles F. Anderson. Perhaps Franklin's arguments, based on economy, convinced him of the wisdom of abandoning them. Anderson's resolution called for a study to investigate the "propriety" of changing not only the height of the dome, but also the building materials used in its construction. On February 1, Jesse Bright of Indiana, chairman of the public buildings and grounds committee, introduced a more general resolution concerning the delayed construction of the dome, which was passed. *Cong. Globe*, 36 Cong., 1 Sess., 647, *passim; Senate Misc. Doc.* No. 29, 36 Cong., 1 Sess.; see also *Documentary History of the Capitol, passim.*

4. A reference to Jefferson Davis' letters of March 5, 10, 14, 1856, to the chairman of the House ways and means committee, in *House Misc. Doc.* No. 65, 34 Cong., 1 Sess., 1, 7, 8.

5. On December 30, 1859, the northeast corner and north end of the Troy, New York, Union Depot collapsed because of shrinkage in the iron girders, caused by extremely cold weather; the north half of the building was a complete wreck. Arthur James Weiss, *History of the City of Troy* . . . (Troy, 1876), 223, courtesy of Carol M. Dean (Troy Public Library) to Andrew Johnson Project, December 4, 1968.

6. Anderson's resolution suggested pumice stone instead of iron because it was "lighter, much more economical and a more durable material . . . impervious to decay, lightening or atmospheric action of any kind," and referred to its use in the Roman Pantheon. It could be obtained, he asserted, from "the Island of Teneriffe for the labor of sawing it into the required dimensions, and the cost of the carriage." Deposits of pumice from volcanoes were found on Tenerife, largest of the Canary Islands. Draft Resolution by Charles F. Anderson, n. d., Johnson Papers, LC.

From Charles F. Anderson[1]

Architects Studio   Washington D. C.
456 Eleventh St.
January 26th 1860—

For The Hon. Andrew Johnson. U. S. Senator.

Dear Sir

If you shall find it necessary, in sustaining the purport of the resolution appertaining to the construction of the new dome of the Capitol, you have the following facts[2] to refer to, showing the necessity of the cognoscence of Congress to the subject matter of the said resolution: —1st That I, in person, with the aid of sundry plans and sections, brought this matter under the notice of the Secretary of

War,[3] who refused to entertain the matter in any shape "even admitting it was all wrong and that I was all right" not wishing to bring Colonel Davis and the military of the United States on his back, but thought it "a very proper subject for Congress to investigate and decide on, as he was no architect and presumed no judgement in such matters but would endeavor to carry out their desires. He found certain plans and arrangements made and he had no idea of bringing himself into trouble by doing what he considered belonged to Congress.—

2ndly That I hold Captn. Franklyn's letter, in which he says he has no authority for interfering in any act already in progress, in connection with the works of the Capitol—

Now Sir, This Dome is a new matter, introduced by Mr. Walter[4] for his own private and personal object. His original plan, that was marked "REJECTED" by President Fillmore, had no such dome on it; nor had my plan, which was adopted such a dome on it, and if any remarks should arise from Col. Davis, who would feign give the public to imagin that it was Captn. Meigs[5] designed the Capitol, you have my assertions over my signature, to refer to, when you state, that it was I that furnished Captn. Meigs with the necessary plans and instructions, by which he took down Walter's work and carried out my design as well as his want of the knowledge of architecture enabled him[.] Mr. Walter seeing himself thourghly thrown overboard, then invented the scheme of a new and different dome of iron, and actually had himself connected with the bill to carry out the same,[6] which occurrence causes the difficulty just now, as he has set Captn. Meigs at defiance, and can set Captn. Franklyn, as he is, actually by Law, conductor of the erection of the Dome of the Capitol.—   This man, who is by trade a bricklayer and who could not produce a plan for the Capitol, has got into league with a foundry man in New York,[7] who actually employs and pays a lobby man, who resides in Washington at the National, to sustain this awful and notorious fraud, which is to cost millions—

This distructive and fraudulent act keeps Mr. Walter in connection with the Capitol, and makes a tremendous fortune for this N. York foundry man, who spends thousands in Washington to deceive and inveigle Congress into a participation with their acts, which must end in costing the nation disappointment, and the distruction of the center works of the Capitol & likely many lives[.]

I was appointed the examiner of this Mr. Walter's plans by President Fillmore at the suggestion of the Hon. Daniel Webster, when I found him to be thoroughly ignorant on the subject of scientific architecture, and therefore his acts and opinions are very doubtful, decidedly in a case like the present when the lives of thousands and the property of the nation is at risk, besides the shame of such a specimen of ignorance and botchery being perpetrated on the U. States just to establish some act, part or originality in the erection of the Capitol, by an individual who otherwise had nothing to do with the design of this Building, and to make a millionaire of an obscure stone and grate maker in New York.— If Congress will submit to such insulting and outrageous injustice, why let them and they'l repent it when it will be too late, like the factory at Lawrence[8] and the Railroad Terminus at Troy.—

Now Sir, Captn. Franklyn is also deprived of the power to interfere by this most injudicious act, which I'm informed was presented to Congress in such a wily shape as to evade their observation, or perception of the scheme.

Captn. Franklyn therefore declines to investigate this outrage as he has no power to interfere with an act of Congress.—unless he is authorised—

If you are called on for an authority in any one, or all of these assertions, I authorise and empower you to use this letter and my name in support of the same in or out of Congress, as they are facts that cannot be contradicted on investigation[.]

> I have the honor to be
> Your Humble Servt.
> Charles Fredk Anderson

LS, DLC-JP.

1. Charles F. Anderson of New York was one of four architects who won premiums in 1851 for their competitive designs for an extension adding wings and a dome to the Capitol building. Although Thomas U. Walter was appointed architect for the project, the government made extensive use of Anderson's ideas. A committee report of the Senate admitted as much, and a bill was reported in 1864 which would have recompensed him for his efforts. *Senate Report* No. 39, 38 Cong., 1 Sess., 1–8; *Documentary History of the Capitol*, 127–28.

2. See Memorandum from Charles F. Anderson, n.d. [January 26, 1860].

3. John B. Floyd.

4. Thomas U. Walter (1804–1887), a Philadelphia architect trained at the Franklin Institute, had designed the buildings for Girard College and the Philadelphia County prison before going to Washington in 1851 as architect in charge of the Capitol extension. A founder of the American Institute of Architects (1857), he later served as its president. *DAB*, XIX, 397–98; Glenn Brown, *History of the United States Capitol* (2 vols., Washington, D. C., 1903), II, 192–93. See also Homer T. Rosenberger, "Thomas Ustick Walter and the Completion of the United States Capitol," Columbia Historical Society *Records*, L (1948–50), 273–322.

5. Montgomery C. Meigs had been captain of engineers in charge of the Capitol extension.

6. A section of the civil and diplomatic appropriation bill for the fiscal year 1855–56 provided for the removal of the existing dome "and the construction of one upon the plan as designed by Thomas U. Walter, architect of the Capitol extension . . . one hundred thousand dollars." *U. S. Statutes*, X, 663. It was this unilateral congressional action which so annoyed Secretary of War Davis.

7. Undoubtedly Abram S. Hewitt (1822–1903), New York iron manufacturer, merchant, congressman (1874–86), and mayor (1886), who had
formed a partnership with Edward Cooper, son of Peter Cooper the inventor,
and established a foundry and rolling mill in New Jersey. Pioneering in iron
beams and girders, the company had a lucrative business in the 1850's, supplying structural iron for customhouses and other federal buildings, and was
one of the contractors for the Capitol extension. Allan Nevins, *Abram S.
Hewitt* (New York, 1935), 118, 132; Brown, *Capitol History*, II, 201;
Trow's New York City Directory (1859–60), 393.

8. Pemberton Mill, a five-story factory building in Lawrence, Massachusetts, had collapsed a fortnight earlier, reportedly from "mere weakness of
the walls, and their inability to support the structure." This catastrophe
caused many to question the conventional engineering methods used in the
larger new buildings. Washington *National Intelligencer*, January 13, 18,
1860.

Memorandum from Charles F. Anderson

[Washington, D. C.]
[January 26, 1860][1]

NEW DOME OF THE CAPITOL

The House report of 34th Congress, March /56 referred to the
Committee of Ways and Means, was evidently a stratagem got up
by Mr. Stanton[2] of Kentucky and Mr. Houston[3] the Chairman, to
give Walter[4] some permanent and legal position, in connection with
the works of the Capitol, as they were the actual persons who got
him employed by Mr. Fillmore, aided by Mr. Steward,[5] the Secretary of the Interior and for which service it was at the time reported
large sums of money were paid by the parties who were afterwards
contracting stone-cutters.   This report of /56 was got up to quash
the Senate report,[6] charging Mr. Walter with frauds; in the 11th
page of Audit report (1st case), the Commissioner of Public Buildings accuses Walter of paying $100,000 more than was necessary
for one contract of stone work to these men, and in his testimony
states that $50,000 must have been paid for this contract.

This Senate report was not returned to Congress after being printed
until the eve of their breaking up, but it was made the ground work
for employing Captn. Meigs[7] by President Pierces' administration
and placing the whole matter under the Secretary of War.

Captn. Meigs took down Walter's work but sustained him in the
position Mr. Fillmore placed him, but received from me the necessary plans and instructions in presence of Colonel Hickey,[8] which he
(Captn Meigs) acted on, with some differences, after Captn. Meigs
broke his arrangement with me by mantaining Walter with all this
botchery and fraud hanging over him, from under which Walter evidently crept by getting his friend Stanton to establish him by means

of this bill for a new cast iron dome, which was never contemplated in any of the designs.

This is done without compromising the Secretary of War. He is left out of this job, but acquiesces with Meigs in supporting it. None of them, can tell what it's to cost. Its appearance was unknown; the Executive, whose control the building was under, was not consulted and Mr. Walter alone is held responsible, who was bred a bricklayer and knew nothing of iron work.

It is idle for Col. Davis[9] to state that Walter was retained in office by act of Congress and independent of his control after all this robbery and botchery was proved by the Senate report of which General Houston of Texas was chairman as this very bill that gave control to Walter, was evidently sustained by Col. Davis and Meigs before the work was commenced, at the same time that military party, shifting the responsibility of such an architectural outrage on, *Walter and Stanton's* shoulders altogether, both of these men, being bricklayers by trade and brother workmen and the Committee of Ways and Means of which Mr. Houston, Walters friend, was chairman, being altogether inadequate to judge of such matters.

There is nothing tangible in this House report but a numerical flourish by Captn. Meigs as to the strength of the material that composes the old walls, merely the book results of experiments on record;[10] the whole in reality a mere puff to sustain Walter and the iron job, the stone contract having been all used up, Captn. Meigs having actually not only sustained, but doubled the frauds of which Walter was accused in the Report of the Senate Committee.

All this botchery and public robbery was allowed to go on. Mr. Fillmore refusing by letter to interfere with Walter. Mr. Pierce by letter referring the matter to Col. Davis. Col. Davis by letter refusing to interfere with Captn. Meigs[.] Captn. Meigs by letter sustaining Walter and holding himself responsible for his (Walter's) acts. Gov. Floyd[11] by letter, refusing to interfere with Mr. Walter or Captn. Meigs. The Senate Committee on Public Buildings at last session of Congress refusing to interfere lest it should interfere with the Executive power in this matter, and Secretary Floyd in reply to that states, that he would not interfere or bring the Army on his back, that Congress had the power to act, this building was for their use, he would not interfere with what he knew nothing about and that Congress might have it built just as they thought proper and that any thing I had to say I should lay before them. President Buchanan declined to interfere and Captn. Franklyn, the new superintendent, considers that he has no authority to interfere, his instructions are to carry out matters as he finds them, he declines therefore to investigate any improvements without authority and it is quite certain that he can have none from the executive unless it comes through Congress, and it is quite certain also that Secretary Floyd will refer any proposition made to him, as he did before, to Mr. Walter, who is the actual author of all this scandalous botchery and bare faced robbery.

When this unfortunate building is allowed to proceed and be literally mangled by men, ignorant of scientific architectural and who proved themselves incapable of originating it, and only proved themselves clever in swindling other men out of their knowledge and emptying the treasury by wanton and unnecessary expenditures of the public money.

These are facts that can defy contradiction and no doubt would have been long since remedied if the parties politically opposed to the present and past administration were made aware of them, but the subscriber being a man of too much principal and honor to embarass a form of government so widely spread and so competent to guide the destiny of the country, if only conducted by men of talent and honor, and which he has always strenuously supported heretofore the more regrets to see this fine building, as he himself qualifies as a professional and scientific architect should be made the medium for amassing wealth for a few contemptible [men?] that have millions who sacrifice their countries honor and means to gratify their miserable prejudices and fill their purses, making immense fortunes for the men that will act their tools[.] One man, a notorious proprietor of gambling houses in Washington,[12] boasts of having cleared over half a million by his connection with the stone work and nearly every other person in proportion yet the building is unfinished, thoroughly botched and has already cost over double what would have been necessary to erect such a structure.

Although Meigs and Walter fell out, both were afraid to speak and then, to avoid an exposure of such fraud and botchery Captn. Meigs is removed and matters are allowed to proceed in the usual way, no person having authority to interfere.—

Charles Frdk. Anderson   archt
Designer of the original Plan of the Capitol wing

DS, DLC-JP2.

1. Although printed here because of its relationship to the preceding documents, this memorandum was prepared "For the Honble A Johnson U S Senator—" with the endorsement "Remarks on the House Report. March 1856/ 34th Congress 1st Session/New Dome on the Capitol."

2. Richard H. Stanton (1812–1891), Virginia-born Democrat and brother of Tennessee Congressman Frederick P. Stanton, was a lawyer, editor of the Maysville (Kentucky) *Monitor* (1835–42), congressman (1849–55), Democratic presidential elector (1856), and district judge (1868–74). *BDAC*, 1645.

3. George S. Houston of Alabama.

4. Thomas U. Walter, architect of the extension of the Capitol.

5. Alexander H. H. Stuart.

6. In 1853 a special Senate investigating committee concluded that "great irregularities, and gross abuses and frauds" had accompanied the construction of the Capitol extension. Most of the complaints had come from disappointed contractors and discharged workers. Walter, against whom the charges had been placed, was vindicated by the attorney general in May, 1853, and remained as architect. As a result of the investigation Pierce assigned the extension construction to the war department. Three years later, responding to requests for additional appropriations, the House authorized a new examination of the Capitol construction. The resulting report, consisting of a series of letters from Secretary of War Davis, Superintendent Meigs, and Architect Walter to the chairman of the committee on ways and means, was referred to that committee on March 15, 1856, and ordered to be printed. If not designed to quash the earlier Senate report, the House document was certainly a defense of the present arrangement under the secretary of war. *Senate Report* No. 1, 33 Cong., Special Sess., 10–24, 78–190; *House Misc. Doc.* No. 65, 34 Cong., 1 Sess.; Brown, *Capitol History*, II, 124–28; *Documentary History of the Capitol*, 998–1004.

7. Montgomery C. Meigs.

8. William Hickey was the secretary of the Senate's chief clerk.

9. Jefferson Davis, secretary of war.

10. This slurring remark about Meigs appears to refer particularly to his letter to Jefferson Davis, November 8, 1856. *Ibid.*, 1000–1002.

11. John B. Floyd, secretary of war.

12. Probably Matthew G. Emery (1818–1901), a master mason, builder, and last mayor of Washington (1870–71) until the office was reestablished in 1967; he profited considerably from government contracts. Owner of a stone yard, he supplied granite for the Capitol extension. William Van Zandt Cox, "Matthew Gault Emery: The Last Mayor of Washington," Columbia Historical Society *Records*, XX (1917), 19–45; Brown, *Capitol History*, II, 201; *Boyd's Washington and Georgetown Directory* (1858), 106*, 249, 328; *Sen. Ex. Doc.* No. 20, 36 Cong., 1 Sess., 171, 180.

From William M. Lowry

Greeneville   Jany 27 1860

Hon A Johnson
   Dr Sir
      I returned some days ago from Nashville and have been intending dropping you afew lines ever since but on account of the press of business, have neglected it from time to time[.] We had the largest convention ever held in the State, good feeling and harmoney predominated throughout the meeting[.] you will observe from the proceedings that I was on the Committee of Resol. We hammered away at them all day and after reporting them they did not give general Satisfaction and were remanded back again.   after some little alteration we again reported to the house, all right this time.   after getting through with the Platform I told the Committee I had a Resol adopted by our meeting at Greenville recommending Gov Johnson for the Presidency that I would like for our Committee to adopt and report to the Convention.   to this some of our Committee objected

that we were only appointed a Committee to prepare a platform and that this Resol. was outside of that instructions. I told them that I did not wish to make it part of the platform, that I should insist on reporting the Resolution to the Convention, if this Committee refused to do so I had assurances from the Convention that they would pass. our Chairman then put it to the Committee whether we should report to [*sic*] Johnson Res to the House[.]   the Ayes and Noes were taken[.] the vote stood 14 for reporting and 6 against[.] So we carried it and reported it with the other Resolutions which were all Unanimously adopted[.] I am not all together pleased with our delegation to Charleston, getting Milligan for the State at large estoped Greene County from getting a District delegate. I presume if I had been as bold as some who were in attendance I could have thrust my self in. Knox Walker fought awfully for his man[.]   his great object was to get into the Charleston Convention as one of the delegates for the State at large.[1]   they made all sorts of pledges and promises[.] Watterson was yr freind and Seconded my moves handsomely. So did Wayne W Wallace[2] of Knox Co who resides at Concord Rd. Send him some documents. I have a good many little incidents that we will talk over when we meet. people generally well.   old man Morris[3] & McKee[4] are both verry low and I fear cannot live[.]

Yr freind   W M Lowry[5]

ALS, DLC-JP2.

1. Walker, whose candidate was Stephen A. Douglas, was unsuccessful in his efforts to be named a delegate to Charleston.

2. Wayne W. Wallace (b. c1818), Knox County Democratic lawyer, had run unsuccessfully for Congress in 1857. *Cong. Dir.* (1878), 527; 1860 Census, Tenn., Knox, 95.

3. John Morris (c1787–1860), a Greeneville coppersmith, died early in February. 1850 Census, Tenn., Greene, 279.

4. John McKee died the following day, January 28, at the age of seventy-seven.

5. Marginal endorsement: "*write me all the news.*"

From Blackston McDannel

January 27, 1860, Greeneville; ALS, Johnson-Bartlett Col.

Asks Johnson to check number and date of Missouri land warrant issued to David Robertson for War of 1812 service, inasmuch as the heirs have been offered $25.00 for their quitclaim; also requests "the *particulars* [from the pension or adjutant general's office] of Robertson's enlistment, as this may be necessary to establish the claim of the heirs in question."

From John M. Crosland

January 28, 1860, Philadelphia [Pa.]; ALS, DLC-JP2.

Sends Johnson "Song of the Union," a "National Anthem . . . to revive
the memories of the Past as a sure guide to the Patriotism of the future"
and asks him to endorse the sentiments expressed—"a Strict adherence
to the Constitution as it was, and the Union as it is!"

From Andrew McSweeney

January 28, 1860, [Washington, D. C.]; ALS, DLC-JP2.

Native Tennessean employed in the Washington navy yard until December 14, 1860, solicits aid in obtaining employment; "your identification
with the homestead bill giving a farm to any man a citizen" indicates that
"you are man of the people and sooner or later it will tell."

From Samuel Rhea[1]

Blountville Jany 28. 1860

Hon A. Johnson
    Dear Sir
        A particular friend of yours and mine, John Jackson,[2] be-
lieves he ought to have a pension and a Physician told me last night
that he was entitled to it— I think if I had the necessary blanks, I
could get it for him & save him 10 or 15 $ lawyers fee— He served
in the Creek war 1813—incurred the disease under which he labours
while in the service— It will I know be troublesome to you, but we
will take it as a kind favour if you will get from the Pension office &
send me, the necessary Blanks and law (if necessary) at your convenience— he is poor but worthy, who asks our aid— I am Sorry
that the House cant organize— where are we to land? in disunion? I
cant, I am unwilling to believe it— The Friends of Union must not
faulter— I have strong hope all will be well. My kindest regards[.]
                                        I am yrs truly   Saml Rhea

    Every 2 years Our pensioners have to pay, to 2 Physicians $5
each—to get their Pension renewed—[3] it seems to me that if the time
was extended to 5 years or even longer it would answer all purposes— I wish you would look at this— it is a small matter but *not so*
to many a poor Soldier—

                                                        S R
    Jos. Lynn,[4] My Brother inlaw is an applicant to Mr Lowry to be
Census Taker for Sullivan County— He is very capable—writes a

good hand—is needy—and will do the work *well*—(He is an old line Whig) — would you say "a word" for him to Mr Lowry if it comes in the way[.] you will oblige—a good many friends[.]   SR

ALS, DLC-JP2.

1. See *Johnson Papers*, I, 462n.
2. John Jackson (b. *c*1786) was a Virginia-born Sullivan County farmer. Burgner, *1850 Census, Sullivan*, 70.
3. According to an act of March 3, 1859, not only were affidavits of two surgeons or physicians required with all applications for pensions to invalids, but such affidavits must be submitted every two years for renewal of pensions, except those granted for total disability. Inasmuch as the law specified no definite fee for the examining physicians, it appears that the five-dollar fee was local practice. *U. S. Statutes*, XI, 439.
4. Joseph Lynn (b. *c*1813), listed as a clerk in the 1850 Census, did not get the appointment. Burgner, *1850 Census, Sullivan*, 26; Records of the Eighth Census, List of Marshals and Assistants, RG29, National Archives.

From Charles Johnson

Greeneville Jan 29th 1860

Dear Father

We have had for the last three weeks the most delightfull weather; a clear sky and a soft balmy air; but yet, with all this; there are those who have been visited with sickness, sorrow and death;— old man McKee died yesterday evening[.] on friday Moses Bowers[1] was burried; he lives 8 miles below here. Henry Feazel[2] I understand can not last but a few days;— Old Man Morris is sinking slowly and I hardly think he can last long; There seems to be quite a fatality with the old men of the county this winter.— in a few years there will be none of our business men left who managed our affairs 20 years ago;— how gradually radical changes come upon us,—how truthfully has the world been likened to a stage and all the men and women but players;[3] some play principal parts, others but Supernumeraries[.] Some play their parts well; while others are hissed from the stage;— but I did not commence this expecting to moralise; so I shall change my thesus. Mr Hoyal[4] called a few days since and said he wanted to pay $100, on his note; In absence of knowing just what you would do; but thinking that there could be no harm done I took it and gave him a receipt; I do not think he intended to pay it; but thought he would, tender it and no one would be authorised to receive it;— it was honored I think for he said he did not know when he could pay the bal; for he would have to borrow it too:

I will just make one suggestion,— I think were I in you[r] place I would sell *Sam*;[5] it does not suit him to stay in this country;— a few days since Mother sent him word to cut wood at Pattersons,—[6] he came up in the house and said, he would "be damed" if he wanted to cut wood there; and if you wanted to sell him you could just do so, just as soon as you pleased, he did not care a *dam*," You will see he is quite an independent gentleman and just to show his notions of himself and his rights, at another time he was asking Mother for his part of some money paid him for work[.] Mother remarked to him if he was as ready to pay others as he was to collect, he would do better; he replied that he did not get half enough no how;—that he ought to have *all* that he could make &c, well, it may be all right, but one thing is certain; I do not desire to own negroes; but if I did, they should know their place or I would not have them about me. do not understand me as, complaining at your course; not so; but it does seem the more attention, the more kindness you show a negrro, the less acount he is; they seem to misconstrue it;— but after all the negro to be of any value, must be subjugated; and they are the fewest number of men that are fit to have negroes; this is especially the case in E Tennessee[.] The negro must have a Master; and those who, use them severly seem to have the best slavs; but more of this again[.]

All are well   Your Son

Charles Johnson

ALS, DLC-JP2.

    1. Moses Bowers (*c*1798–1860) was a Virginia-born Greene County farmer. 1850 Census, Tenn., Greene, 590.

    2. Henry Feazel (b. *c*1782), a Pennsylvania-born Greene County farmer. *Ibid.*, 671.

    3. Shakespeare, *As You Like It*, Act II, sc. 7.

    4. Perhaps George Hoyal, from whom Johnson bought property in 1841. *Johnson Papers*, I, 30.

    5. Sam, born about 1830 and purchased by Johnson in 1842, proudly boasted that he was the latter's "first servant." Johnson's favorite slave, he was possessed of an independent nature and lordly attitudes—encouraged, no doubt, by the excessive indulgence of his master. In later years we are told that Sam's aristocratic feelings were revealed when, as a janitor of a local church, he regularly wore a silk hat and long-tailed coat; as late as 1901 he was living in Greeneville. Robert W. Winston, *Andrew Johnson: Plebeian and Patriot* (New York, 1928), 102–3; Margaret S. Royall, *Andrew Johnson—Presidential Scapegoat* (New York, 1958), 32.

    6. Johnson's son-in-law and daughter, David and Martha Patterson.

From Sam Milligan

Greeneville Ten   January 30. 1860

Dear Governor.

The scriptural quotation about which we were talking when you were at home I have since found— It seems that after Job's three comforters and Elihu had failed to convince him of his want of true wisdom, that the Lord spake to him out of the whirlwind, and propounded various *tight* questions to him. Among which was, where he was; when the corner stone of the earth was laid; *"when the morning stars sang together, and all the sons of God shouted for joy."*

Job ch. XXXVIII vers. 7—

But I did not sit down to write about Job, but politics. I am afraid our state convention has not done evey thing they should have done. My opinion is the delegates[1] are about as shabby a set as could have been conveniantly selected in the State, myself included in the number. They are not the right sort of men especially in E. Ten.

What do you think of the platform. I think they have substantially taken ground for a Slave Code,[2] but I suppose the delegates did not think of it—I mean part of them, but others did, and I imagine— *inter nos*—imposed upon the rest.

This platform led me to examine for the first time in my life carefully the much talked of "popular sovereignty question," and I must say, so far as I have any opinion at present about it, (I have not finished my investigations) I am inclined to the opinion: That a Territorial Government unrestrained except by the constitution, can as well legislate on the subject of slavery, and to the same extent, as it can upon any other species of property.

Slavery in the light of the constitution and the Dred Scott desision is *property*, and held by no other or different authority than a horse—an ox, a gun; and why not the Territorial Legislature exercise authority over it in the same way it does over other property in the Territory? I have not yet seen the reason. It is true that at common law, salvey [*sic*] did not exist in the form we find it in U.S.; and is dependant on the *written law* for its existance or non existance, yet this is true as to a thousand other things, which may or may not be property in a State or Territory, as the written law shall declair it.

Besides this, I have as yet not been able to see, how the people of a territory, acting to day, in the capacity of a Territorial Legislature, can not legislate upon the subject of Slavery, and the same people, acting tomorrow in the capacity of a convention to establish a constitution, can legislate upon it. Have they any more sovereignty in the one capacity, than the other? If they have where does it come from? Is there any thing in the actual transition state, from a Territory to a State, which communicates sovereignty to the citizen, which he did not have before? If there be, I have not seen it in my investigations thus far.

In writing this way, I am only after the constitutional question, and not to promote this or that interest; and in fact, I cant see much practical difference in the question. It may be in one sense the doctrine contended for by "the old public Functionary" would favor the south,[3] but if it be contrary to the constitution, it might in other things damage it more than in this it would benefit it. The South can not abandon the guarantees of the constitution. They are our only safeguard.

Write about the Charleston convention. All well. Old John McKee died Saturday evening— he is buried[.]

Yours truly   Sam Milligan

ALS, DLC-JP2.

1. The state Democratic convention which met in Nashville on January 18, 1860, selected four at-large delegates and alternates and two delegates from each of the ten districts in Tennessee to attend the nominating convention in Charleston. Milligan was one of the at-large delegates; other East Tennessee delegates included William H. Maxwell, John D. Riley, James W. Newman, W. E. B. Jones, William Wallace, and George W. Rowles. Randal McGavock disagreed with Milligan's assessment, feeling that the "delegates to Charleston are upon the whole very good—much better than usual, although not as good as hoped." Nashville *Union and American*, January 19, 1860; McGavock, *Pen and Sword*, 553.

2. Milligan probably has reference to the resolution which declared that "the federal government has no power to regulate the institution" but has the duty "to protect the rights of the owner . . . and to restore fugitives from labor." Turning away from a premise of congressional nonintervention in slavery in the territories, southern partisans were now pushing for positive protection of the institution by Congress, as is revealed in this resolution. Nashville *Union and American*, January 19, 1860.

3. In his recent message to Congress Buchanan had expatiated on the "final settlement" of the slavery question, asserting that "The right has been established of every citizen to take his property of any kind, including slaves, into the common Territories . . . and to have it protected there under the Federal Constitution." He further pontificated that "Neither Congress nor Territorial legislature nor any human power has any authority to annul or impair this vested right." Richardson, *Messages*, V, 554.

From Lizinka Campbell Brown

Nashville 2nd Feby   1860

Hon. Andrew Johnson

My dear Sir

Some weeks since I had the pleasure of giving to Mrs. Knox[1] your letter & the communication from the Secy. of the Navy enclosed to me for her— She was very much gratified at your kind and prompt attention to her wishes and would have written to tell you so but I assured her it was unnecessary and as you had plenty of official duty to attend to—to keep you busy would be rather an intrusion— Was I right? for I am rather doubtful about it remembering how fond you are of letter-writing—

I have to thank you for a copy of your speech in the Senate which I read with equal pleasure and profit and have heard universally spoken of as the best made in the Senate this session— one gentleman made an exception in favor of Lane's[2] which he said was better because shorter— As he is a man of sense I presume he had not read them both—

I received last night a "Cincinnati Commercial" containing an account of the glorification of our Legislature at Columbus & Cincinnati[3] and also a pretty severe article on the expulsion of citizens of Ohio from Kentucky & N. Carolina on account of their 'principles honestly entertained'[4] and the very pertinent question is asked—how citizens of Kentucky can be so friendly with Ohio editors &C on the soil of Ohio & banish them as soon as they have the power from the soil of Kentucky &c &c— I want to know what you think of all this feasting & merry making— Although your son was along I see no account of his making any Union speeches in Ohio—[5]

Gov. Harris was too much indisposed—(not physically I fancy as some young girls walking in the Capitol saw him in his room the afternoon the Legislature set out) but morally and politically to accompany the "Revellers" and Lieut. Gov. Newman[6] seems to have distinguished himself not a little in his place— Our State Senator Mr. Trimble[7] was also too much indisposed to travel—

The wife of one of our wealthiest men—a large southern planter and a life-long democrat—said yesterday that her husband was determined not to buy another negro—considering them now as uncertain property more especially from the general conduct of our Legislature—[8] The present exorbitant prices of slaves would be a conclusive reply to such apprehensions, were it not very evidently the policy of Kentucky—Tennessee Missouri & Virginia to keep up prices until the mass of them are taken South as is being now done with unexampled rapidity—

Of course being a woman, I do not pretend to understand these matters but I wish you would write me what you think of them—of the prospects of slavery? of the stability of the Union? and of the election of Pennington?[9] If you do this write me whether you choose your opinions to be known or not—

If I had not the excuse of indisposition I would not send so carelessly written a letter but will try to do better next time— Hattie[10] says that Bob Johnson did make a speech at Xenia but I thought it was in Kentucky but no matter he is young enough to repent of his political sins if he has committed any—

Remember *I* have not expressed any opinion about the conduct of the Legislature only written to you what rumor says—

Your Sincere friend
L. C. Brown

Our representative Mr East[11] was also indisposed to travel as I have just heard—& congratulates himself on the circumstance—

ALS, DLC-JP2.

1. Martha A. Knox, who operated a school in Nashville, had inquired concerning appointments in the marine corps. *Nashville Bus. Dir.* (1860–61), 208; Harriet C. Owsley, ed., *Guide to the Processed Manuscripts of the Tennessee Historical Society* (Nashville, 1969), 17; Letter from Isaac Toucey, December 19, 1859.

2. Lane's brief remarks of December 19, 1859, on the subject of slavery and territorial policy, affirmed his belief in the equality of the states in determining the settlement of the territories without interference from either Congress or territorial legislatures. Hendrickson, *Joe Lane*, 218–19; *Cong. Globe*, 36 Cong., 1 Sess., 185.

3. Upon completion of the Louisville and Nashville Railroad, celebrations attended by state and local legislators and dignitaries were staged in Nashville late in October, 1859, and in Louisville on January 24, 1860. From the latter city, members of both state legislatures, who, together with assorted hangers-on made a party of some six hundred, moved on to Cincinnati and Columbus, where further banquets, characterized by strong Unionist speeches and endless Union toasts, were held. As one might expect, the Tennessee legislators were extolled at length by the speakers, among them governors Dennison of Ohio and Magoffin of Kentucky. Nashville *Union and American*, January 27, 28, 29, 1860; Madison Bratton, "The Unionist Junket of the Legislatures of Tennessee and Kentucky in January, 1860," ETHS *Publications*, No. 7 (1935), 64–80; Cincinnati *Enquirer*, January 24, 26, 27, 29, 31, 1860.

4. On January 23, 1860, fifty prominent citizens met at Brooksville, Kentucky, and instructed several alleged abolitionists to leave Bracken and Madison counties by February 4 or be expelled by violent means. Those threatened —a minister, a schoolteacher, and sixteen other individuals—left the state peacefully before the deadline and were taken in by like-minded people in Ohio. In North Carolina several members of the American Missionary Society, including Daniel Worth, a Wesleyan Methodist minister, were being arrested and tried, charged with "circulating incendiary books . . . principally the 'Impending Crisis,' by Helper." The arrests began in late December, 1859; by the middle of January, 1860, six had been charged. As soon as it was learned that Worth had influenced a number of teachers in the common schools, the state press began to call for the purging of antislavery teachers. Indignant Charlotte citizens tarred and feathered a stonemason for espousing abolitionist views. *Ibid.*, February 1, 1860; Nashville *Gazette*, February 1, 3, 1860; New York *Tribune*, January 26, February 4, 1860; Guion Griffis Johnson, *Ante-Bellum North Carolina: A Social History* (Chapel Hill, 1937), 580–81.

5. The Nashville *Union and American*, January 29, 1860, reported: "Among the speeches made at Xenia [Ohio], were those by a son of U. S. Senator Johnson of Tennessee who is a member of the legislature of that state . . . ." See also Letter from Robert Johnson, February 5, 1860.

6. Tazewell W. Newman (1827–1867) of Franklin County, having served earlier in the house (1855–59), was now speaker of the senate (1859–61). The Opposition press tried in vain to correct northern press reports that Speaker Newman was lieutenant governor. Robison, *Preliminary Directory, Franklin*, 24; Nashville *News*, January 26, 1860; see also *Johnson Papers*, II, 480n.

7. John Trimble (1812–1884) of Nashville was a state Whig representative (1843–45) and senator (1845–47) who amassed a considerable estate through a lucrative law practice and then for several years occupied himself with "cultural self-improvement." Returning to politics in 1859, he served in the Tennessee senate until 1861, when he resigned because of his opposition to secession. Subsequently he was United States district attorney (1862–64), state senator (1865–67), and Republican congressman (1867–69). Clayton, *Davidson County*, 124–25; *BDAC*, 1728.

8. At the time of the legislature's debates on the Free Negro bill, the press

speculated about a possible decline in the value of slaves resulting from the sale of freedmen into bondage if they did not leave the state. However, many slaveowners and their representatives in the legislature opposed the bill as unconstitutional, unjust, and inhumane. Nashville *News*, December 23, 1859; Nashville *Republican Banner*, December 20, 21, 1859, January 5, 6, 10, 1860.

9. After a bitter contest which required forty-four ballots, William Pennington (1796–1862) had been chosen speaker on February 1. A former Whig governor of New Jersey (1837–43), elected to Congress (1859–61) by a "People's Party," and long a figure of controversy, Pennington, described by a contemporary as a "dolt" and an "old owl," was to prove, in the words of Allan Nevins, "one of the worst-equipped and most incompetent Speakers in the nation's history." *BDAC*, 1443; Nevins, *Emergence of Lincoln*, II, 124, 405.

10. Harriot (*c*1844–1932), Mrs. Brown's daughter, was later the wife of Capt. Thomas T. Turner, aide to General Richard S. Ewell. Turner, "Recollections," 168–76; Percy G. Hamlin, ed., *The Making of a Soldier: Letters of General R. S. Ewell* (Richmond, 1935), 143; *OR*, Ser. 1, XI, Pt. I, 607.

11. Edward H. East (b. 1830), a Nashville lawyer, served in the legislature (1859–61, 1875–77), as Tennessee's secretary of state during Johnson's military governorship, and as state chancellor (1870–72). Clayton, *Davidson County*, 395.

From William Henry Maxwell

Jonesboro E Ten   Feby 2d 1860

Private & Confidential

Dear Governor

I intended after my return home, after a calm review of all I saw and heard at Nashville to write to you, beleiving you had an interest in what transpired there. I thrill I had the honour to occupy there from the first, the position of one of your friends, premising this much only as to myself I will give a detail of facts which will make the points I aim at and then a few of my own Conclusions and then leave the whole for your own deliberation—

On the morning of my arrival after breakfast, I was introduced to Maj. Sam Walker[1] and, Col. Carrol[2] of Memphis[.] They asked for a private interview, of a few moments. Maj Walker asked me if the friends of Gov Johnson intended to insist, upon his nomination for the Presidency by the convention[.] I replied that I had had no opportunity to Confer with any person since my arrival and Could only speak for myself and my own Constituency. They had passed a resolution of preference for Gov. Johnson, that was my private feeling and at the proper time and in the proper way I expected to bring it before the Convention— Carroll replied, that he intended the moment it was introduced, to oppose it, for that Gov. Harris occupied, just as prominent, a position for the V. P, & his friends would press him &c &c— my replies were conciliatory & so we seperated— I should have stated that Knox Walker was on the

train with me but had not yet arrived as he had been left accidentally
at Stevenson. I had seen Waterson and from him learned that Knox
Walker had had an interview with you before leaving Washington
and was for you— I thought I would watch the corners as the
thing went up in the convention and act accordingly. I had, never
the honour before to be in one, but I knew I should keep sober, and
from the quantity of imbibing I saw going on I Concluded I should
take the points about as fast as the most of them— I thought from
the ripples in the Convention when your name was mentioned after
the first morning that bringing things up right we could carry any
proposition in which you were concerned over their heads without
the crack of a whip— In the mean time Knox Walker came and
Sam. Walker sought me and told me he was authorised, by Carroll
to say he withdrew the declartion he had made to me and they would
interpose no obstacle in your case— It soon became apparent that
Knox Walker wanted to be nominated as a delegate to the Charleston Convention & I was soon satisfied that there was a determination
on the part of *our folks*, to defeat him— So I thought I wd. strike
just one blow on my "own hook" and in the committee room, I went
for Knox[3] and against Quarles.[4] I had two objects to subserve in
this[.] one was to secure Knox' friends for Howard[5] and the other,
on the supposition that if they were Douglass men, they might be of
service at Charleston in the course of events. Knox was defeated but
I was greeted by his friends afterward most warmly as one of the
Democrats who were willing to be just to the 10th District.[6]

I told you at Greeneville long ago what I thought of Gov. Harris'
position toward you— He treated me with a dignified inoffensive,
indeference and I have not changed my opinion— Haynes friends
were jubilant at his success[7] which was most decided and look upon
his nomination for Governor as a foregone conclusion— I look
upon you as the most available man among all who have been named
for the contest at Charleston[.] But if it passes away & you are not
nominated—I suppose it is a waste of time for me to stop & tell you
that there is a strong party opposed to you in Tennessee & *yet alive*—
Col H—[8] called on Mrs Brown & Mrs Polk before leaving and gave
a dining at the St. Cloud to the Gov. and other distinguis[h]ed gentlemen of the state *including myself*[.]

I shall go to Charleston if able although I am illy prepared to
stand the expense— But when I look at the men, at the time, at all
the circumstances, I solemnly beleive that this is your time and any
friend you have ought to be there— Douglass can't be nominated
that is my opinion[.] He & his friends may pour out money like
water but It wont win. But I do think that just one *honest* move
will make him the next nominee of the Democratic Party. If he will

just say that his name shall not be used to promote discord at Charleston but that if he is not the choice there that he will go with all his forces into the field for the nominee, and then make that nominee a Southern man, Then he would come next. For by the time Bucks administration is through 4 years no man will be sick enough of love for it to prescribe for its sake any body—

I have one more thing to say by request and then I have done— Carroll, (who is P. M at Memphis I am not certain that I called him William correctly) took me to one side and requested me to write to you and say that evy d—d one of Harris's friends had gone against them in the convention and now when you or your friends had any call upon the 10th District that you would find a guard at Memphis always ready and always reliable— You will know better what all this means and what it is worth than I—

If it was not for the fever of the times and the pressure thereof I do not believe that Tennessee in the next canvass will do herself justice. If I heard a specimen of Whithornes powers[9] he wd not be a strong man in E Ten[.] Haynes pleases more men than he [carries?] but I hope all will be well— The reason I have not written sooner is that ever since my return I have been laid up with the worst cold I ever had[.]

If you have any thing to suggest or want any thing done—drop me a line[.]

Your friend   Wm Henry Maxwell

Jno Riley[10] was appointed to Charleston through Jac Miller[11] (who is an unmitigated nuisance and general humbug)[.] I found Jno: was fearful at Nashville that your nomination by the convention might *hurt your prospects*— I think Jno can manage Jacob[.] did you notice the resolutions of Hawkins?

W H M

If you think of it when talking to any one familiar with Charleston give me the name of a private boarding house or two— I think I shall take my wife & my time too[.] If I go[.][12]

ALS, DLC-JP2.
    1. Sam P. Walker, Shelby County lawyer, served as chancellor (1870–75) and as Memphis city attorney (1884–87). *Goodspeed's Shelby*, 815, 889; *Tenn. Official Manual* (1890), 184.
    2. William H. Carroll.
    3. Maxwell not only "went for" Walker, he actually nominated him. See Letter from Frank C. Dunnington, February 13, 1860.
    4. William A. Quarles (1825–1893), prominent Clarksville lawyer, Democratic elector (1852), and circuit court judge (1858–59), became president of the Memphis, Chattanooga, and Louisville Railway Company in 1858. He was also bank supervisor for the state and a delegate to the Democratic national conventions in 1856 and 1860. Siding with the Confed-

eracy, he held the rank of a general and served with distinction in several engagements. *Goodspeed's Montgomery*, 1086–87.

5. John K. Howard, who was named an alternate.

6. It appears that Maxwell was making a play for Memphis support for Johnson by establishing himself as an East Tennessean sympathetic to the West Tennesseans and their "mistreatment" by the Middle Tennessee stronghold of the party.

7. Landon C. Haynes had been chosen as a Democratic elector-at-large by the state convention.

8. Landon C. Haynes.

9. W. C. Whitthorne was the other elector-at-large.

10. John D. Riley (1816–1879), Virginia-born farmer, was a Hawkins County delegate to the state convention and attended the Charleston convention. Eleanor F. Morrissey, comp., *Portraits in Tennessee Painted before 1866: A Preliminary Checklist* ([Nashville], 1964), 107; 1860 Census, Tenn., Hawkins, 45.

11. Jacob Miller of Hawkins County.

12. Maxwell did attend the convention.

From Wyndham Robertson

February 3, 1860, Washington, D. C.; ALS, DLC-JP2.

Editor of New York *Daily News* asks for documents to circulate in New York City and state: "I intend, in my editorial Capacity, to leave no 'stone unturned' towards rescuing that great State from the controlling influence of Seward and his Compeers."

From John K. Howard

Lebanon, Tennessee
Sunday Feby. 5 1860

Confidential.

My Dear Sir:

I owe you an apology for not having before this, thanked you for your kind effort to secure me the appointment of visitor to the Military Academy.[1] For many reasons I am extremely desirous to receive the position. I know that you will do every thing you can to get it for me; and you know that I will *seek* for opportunity to show you that I am not ungrateful. I suppose you have received a full account of the proceedings of our late Convention. There happened several things not at all agreeable to me—One entirely personal. The contest for the nomination for Elector for the State was between Whitthorne & myself. The nomination was made by a Committee of two from each Congressional district. The vote stood 11 to 9. The Committee men from the 3d district were under a pledge to go for me; but shortly before the Committee met a few of the Delegation got together, my friends being absent, and instructed their Come. to vote for Whitthorne. The result was thus changed. It was a most unfair puzzle, in which, however, Whitthorne had nothing to do. In the whole matter he acted in a fair manly way.

The Delegation to Charleston, in my opinion will not reflect the wishes of the Democracy[.] Mr Ewing will be against you and will as I think, do all he can to cuffle you.[2] Quarles and Atkins,[3] both true men, will be for you as a *Politician*, but their hearts will not be in the matter. I have my doubts about the members from this District. The idea of making George W. Jones an Alternate and sending two men from his District utterly unknown as Politicians,[4] was a great outrage— Maj. Burford[5] will be for you first last and all the time. In the Committee on resolutions there was strong opposition to your nomination. I understand the vote was as follows:

For the resolution:

Lowry, Clarkson, Ramsey, Armstrong, Thompson, Watterson, Childress, Newman, Cummings, Key, Bridges, & Cox.

Against the resolution:

Bate, Gen. Pillow, T. M. Jones, Williams, Cave Johnson, A. Ewing D. Peters & Noe—[6]

Gen. Bate[7] was one of the Committee from this district. In my opinion there are not fifty men in the District who do not prefer you to any man living for President. I had prepared a resolution making a nomination "pure and simple," without any ifs or ands, and without connecting you with any other name, which I intended to offer with an exhortation, but it was deemed best to wait on the Committee. I am sorry now that I did not follow my own judgement. The resolution would have been adopted with such a shout as would have drowned all opposition— I shall go to Charleston. An 'alternate' has but little power, but something may 'turn up' so as to give me a vote. If the Tennessee Delegation stand firm I believe you may be nominated. But of course, you know more about the matter than any one not in Washington can. Write to me frankly what you think of your prospects. If you are nominated: I hardly need say, that I will go into the canvass with eagerness and ardor.

We are all very much obliged to you for your kindness in writing to George:[8]—and as for him, I think he believes he will go to you when he dies—

If it is not too much trouble, I wish you would learn positively from Gov. Floyd[9] if I am to be appointed.

Our family are all well: and send you their respects—

As ever, your friend
John K. Howard

Gov. Johnson

ALS, DLC-JP2.

1. Recommended by both Johnson and Nicholson, Howard was appointed a member of the sixteen-man board of visitors for West Point in 1860. Register of Cadet Applicants, Entry 242, RG94, National Archives.

2. Howard's assessment was inaccurate; Andrew Ewing, as Chairman of Tennessee's delegation, held most of the delegates to Johnson until he withdrew Johnson's name following the thirty-sixth ballot.

3. John D. C. Atkins.

4. William McClelland and R. M. Matthews were chosen as delegates to Charleston from the sixth district.

5. David Burford (1791–1864), North Carolina-born wealthy Smith County farmer, veteran of the War of 1812 and a major in the state militia, served in the state senate (1829–35) and as speaker in the 1833–35 session; he was a Smith County delegate to the 1860 Democratic state convention and a district representative to Charleston. Judge George W. Allen to Andrew Johnson Project, September 17, 1969; Nashville *Union and American*, January 19, 1860; 1860 Census, Tenn., Smith, 139.

6. John A. Nooe, a Memphis attorney. According to Gideon Pillow, the vote was a close 12–10, rather than Howard's report of 12–8. Milton, *Eve of Conflict*, 403, citing Gideon Pillow to Stephen A. Douglas, April 3, 1860.

7. William B. Bate.

8. George Howard, younger brother of John K. Howard, was a midshipman at the naval academy.

9. John Floyd, secretary of war.

From Robert Johnson

Nashville Feby 5th 1860.

My Dear Father

You have no doubt read in the newspapers an account of the excursion of the Kentucky and Tennessee Legislatures to Ohio, and it is unnecessary for me to give you any of the details— all were more than satisfied, and the trip will be long remembered by its participants as the *event* of their lives— The reception at Cincinnatti was a most magnificent affair—the most magnificent I expect that ever came off in the north west— The reception took place at the Opera house— it was crowded to its utmost capacity— we were welcomed by the Mayor & Judge Storer[1]—Gov McGoffin[2] of Ky. replied first—Mr Newman of Tennessee next— he made quite an appropriate speech,— it was well timed, and delivered in an impressive style— As he took his seat the crowd as one man, sprang to their feet and gave three cheers for Tennessee— The Lady's waved their hankerchiefs, and such a shout you never heard— My feelings at that moment are indescri[b]able, but great God how proud I felt — I was glad that I was a Tennessean, and in after years will look back upon that scene and day as the happiest of my life— I cannot even now recur to it, but an electric thrill passes through my veins— but in conclusion on this subject, I can say that Tennessee acquitted herself nobly—

I made a short speech at Zenia [*sic*] which was well received and complimented very highly—

So passed by the excursion to the Ohio Legislature— It is an indication as I believe of better days ahead—

I have a serious idea of *marrying* provided it meets with your approbation and you deem it advisable— it is an important step to take and I want your advice, upon the subject, as I know you will write what you think, and I am willing to be governed by your views— The young lady is about nineteen years old— she is intelligent, pretty, (not beautiful) amiable, and the sweetest girl I ever met—take her all in all, I have never yet seen her equal— She is of good family and has property in her own right to the amount of at least forty thousand Dollars—but I consider that the least of her qualifications— She is an orphan and I believe will marry me, if I ask her—[3]

I have made a frank and candid statement and hope you will do the same to me—as I desire it for my good and happiness—but let this be between ourselves[.]

I do not hardly think the Legislature will adjourn before the 15th of March—a great deal of business on the Calendar— I am afraid the Conventional interest bill[4] will pass the House[.]

I hope to hear from you soon[.]

Your Son   R. J.

ALS, DLC-JP2.

1. The mayor was Richard M. Bishop (1812–1893), Kentucky-born Cincinnati grocer, who served as city councilman (1857) and mayor (1859–61). A Union Democrat, he later became governor of Ohio (1878–79). Bellamy Storer (1796–1875), native of Maine, was a lawyer and law professor, a Whig congressman (1835–37), and judge of the superior court of Cincinnati (1854–72). Greve, *History of Cincinnati*, I, 655, II, 50; *BDAC*, 1664.

2. Beriah Magoffin (1815–1885), lawyer and state senator (1850), was elected governor in 1859. Although he believed in the right of secession, Magoffin sought to maintain the Union and thus supported attempts at compromise; only when these failed did he urge the legislature to call a convention to allow the people of Kentucky to decide the issue of secession. Unsuccessful in this effort, he proclaimed a short-lived neutrality for Kentucky, but its failure, coupled with his increasing obstructionism in the face of an expanding Unionist sentiment in the state, led to his forced resignation. After the war Magoffin returned to the legislature (1867–69). *DAB*, XII, 199–200.

3. Presumably the wealthy "orphan" was still Betty Childress, object of young Johnson's affections two weeks before, although, having lost only her mother (1851), she had both a father and step-mother living. See Letter from Robert Johnson, January 22, 1860.

4. Although rejected by the house on February 15, the Conventional Interest bill, fixing standard rates and stiffening the punishment for usury, was reconsidered and passed the next day. It received senate approval on February 21. Nashville *Union and American*, February 21, 22, 1860; *Tenn. Acts*, 1859–60, Ch. XLI.

From Joseph E. Bell[1]

Evert Farm Greene County Tennessee
8 February 1860

Hon Andrew Johnson U. S. S.

Very dear friend.   I received your speech of 12th December last,[2] 3 days ago. I thank you for the same. Trumbull, Doolittle and others, though called great, are, in my opinion, boys in logic, though Giants in wickedness— I have, for some time, looked upon the opposition, as a pack of hungry wolves, seeking whom they might devour. But lately, I view them as but little inferior to incarnate Demons. He that will apologize for John Brown, has no love for human happiness, for God or his creatures. He that dared to assert, that Brown & his gallows are superior to Christ and his Cross,[3] is lost forever to all sense of honor & human dignity— I am almost ready to look up to heaven, and ask why sleeps the thunder to the ground, and ask, where is the earthquake? Such persons are only fit to grace the walls of a prison or a madhouse— We have good reason to believe, that such persons have been educated by tract societies, total abstinence Societies, manumission Societies, Know-nothing societies & such institutions as have, whether designed or not, made more fools & fanatics than all the Ballrooms in America. The foray at Harper's ferry, is the beginning of the theories promulged from the pulpit as well as the halls of the national Councils, for many years. There are men engaged in John Brown's affair, who stand high as statesmen and scholars.[4] For fear that Brown would make disclosures, they praised, as a hero & worthy of a great name, that cold blooded murderer & base villian. Since his execution, they elevate him to a martyr: —and nothing but fear deters them from similar actions. I am sorry to learn that Congress is so much divided & doing nothing. You have my heart & hand & Prayers— I will be glad to receive any document you may think proper to send me. My address is Gourley's Bridge Tennessee (*I am informed* that there is a book written by Lambert A. Wilmer, called the Crimes and corruptions of the American Newspaper press, published by J. T. Lloyd of *Philadelphia*.[5]) If you can, without trouble, procure a copy & send it to me, I will pay all cost & charges & thank you also. My health is bad. I will support you as long as I live. I would rather read the speech you sent me, than all I ever saw from Congress before. Hon. T. A. R. Nelson sent me his speech. "*Montes parturient.*"[6] &C. God bless you.

Jos. E. Bell

You will, no doubt, be one among others, before the Charleston Convention[.] if so, I request that your name be not withdrawn, either by yourself or friends. I am afraid that the Black Republicans are the strongest; but am of opinion that you would get more votes than any other Democrat in the Union. I do hope that there is, or will be, men enough, having a love for our government, to stand up for him who is the sworn friend of the Union—whose public acts & private conduct, have never varied from the center of liberty. Although our statesmen, preachers and others, are enormously wicked, and deserve punishment, yet I do hope that the Lord will see some modern Noah, & spare the many for the sake of a few, or that, our nation, unlike Sodom, will number more than ten to save the Country.[7] God rules all things—we are safe or ruined just as he pleases. Put your trust in him who has hitherto led you by the hand and furnished you seats in high and honorable places. You have, no doubt, seen how men lean towards treason & civil war, yet pretend to be all for the Union— these, will soon be too large for concealment, and will be compelled to stop, or go on to ruin the country— But you know these things better than I do— I ask pardon. My request is, that you will always remember what cured Gehazi of despair—the vision of a mountain full of horses & chariots of fire.[8] (2 Kings 6. 15.17) The same God is our God. May we depend upon him for victory, and ever be found battling for the high ways of the Lord. O my old friend, may heaven shed upon you its richest blessing—put you in the Capitol & conduct you into the New Jerusalem— an eternal happy citizen of the paradise of God. Farewell—

Very Respectfully
Jos. E. Bell

ALS, DLC-JP2.

1. Joseph E. Bell (b. c1790) was a Virginia-born minister. 1860 Census, Tenn., Greene, 29.
2. Speech on Harper's Ferry Incident, December 12, 1859.
3. See *ibid.*
4. In the intense excitement which accompanied the John Brown raid and its aftermath, there were rumors of a fanatical plot to destroy the peculiar institution and indeed southern society itself. Prominent figures most commonly associated with such speculation were political abolitionists like Charles Sumner and Wendell Phillips, literary figures like Emerson and Thoreau, and, above all, a group of reformers identified by a modern biographer as "the Secret Six"—Thomas Wentworth Higginson, Samuel Gridley Howe, Theodore Parker, Franklin Sanborn, Gerrit Smith, and George Luther Stearns. Oates, *John Brown,* 238 and *passim.*
5. Lambert A. Wilmer (d. 1863), *Our Press Gang, or a Complete Exposition of the Corruptions and Crimes of the American Newspapers* (Philadelphia, 1859).
6. "Parturient montes, nascetur ridiculus mus"—"The mountains labor, and a ridiculous mouse is born." Horace, *Ars Poetica* 1. 139. Stevenson, *Quotations,* 1354.
7. A reference to the unique bargain in which the Lord promised Abra

ham that he would not destroy sinful Sodom if ten righteous inhabitants could be found there. Gen. 18:32.

8. To silence the troublesome prophecies of Elisha, the Syrians invaded Israel and encircled Dothan, the city where he and his servant Gehazi were sleeping. When Gehazi despaired at the sight of the Syrian force, his master prayed, "and, behold, the mountain *was* full of horses and chariots of fire round about Elisha," who thereupon escaped with his servant. II Kings 6:8–20.

From Sam Milligan

Greeneville Ten   February 8, 1860

Dear Governor,

As my letters only cost the trouble of reading them, you will excuse the number of them.

Recently Dugless and his friends have been flooding the whole Country with his speeches, letters &c— I take it they are going to make a most desperate effort to secure his nomination in the Charleston Convention. I see nothing in his recent speeches which to me are seriously objectionable, but his whole record is evedently a bad one. Besides, personally, I have no faith in the man, and could only be induced to support him, in or out of the convention, as a sort of last resort, yet I think it is obvious, he will have strength in the convention, and enough of it to make his influence an object. The question is, after it is demonstrated that he can not receive the nomination, as I now think it will be, Can any one secure the influence of his friends? Or will they withdraw from the convention and run him as an independent candidate? They would hardly dare to do the latter, as I can not see what they would hope to achieve by it; and if they do the former, is it not the policy to at least attempt to secure his influence?

I make these enquiries because—waiving all modesty for the present—you know, I would do any thing in my power, which is reasonable, to secure you[r] nomination; and what I am trying to ascertain is the best way to achieve that end. But I am so far removed from the seat of political power and influence, and so much engaged, that I am unable to decide, many questions which come up in my mind.

I do not know when good policy would dictate that your name should be brought forward. Should it be presented at first, or after a few ballotings have been had? This I suppose can only be determined by the circumstances of the case. In the Tennessee delegation I fear you have some enemies. Ewing I do not regard as your friend, still I think under the resolution of the convention, he will be tied up, and we can compel him to act right.

Now under all these circumstances what should be done? I would if you could find time be exceedingly glad if you would give me your own views; and should you do it, I assure you, you may regard them as communicated under the most sacred confidence. Who will the South press,—what are the feelings of her members of Congress. They seem to be divided and without plans or program[.] Is it their policy to go into the convention with no candidate upon whom they could consistently unite? I would like to know the man if he can be found, who will be the prominant opponent *at first* of Duglass; and them [*sic*] if that state of things could be brought about, I think it would be the policy of your friends to hold your name back, and affend neither side, until they wear themselves out, and as a compromise present your name. But this is a conjecture with out facts to predicate it upon. Let me hear from you.

I have found no leisure to write my slavey letters. I have gotten up a good many facts, and *think* I could make some valuable papers.

I read last night Roger A Pryor's[1] speech. He *aint* much. Some times send me a good speech, and when you make one about slavey justify it not by the *Bible*, but the *Laws of nature*; God made the earth for its inhabitants, and at the same time ordained that the race should gloryfy him, and that can only be done by civilization, and it can only be secured by laws, compelling *all* to do their duty, or act their part in the great family of the earth: So that if the *common interest* require either the lands (as of the indians) or the labor (as of the idle negro) of the vicious the idle or unproductive, the laws of civilization can take them for the good of the whole. "*Them's my sentiments.*"[2] Old John Morris is dead— L C Hays[3] has bought property in Knoxville, and going to move there, I understand. Your folks are well, and so are mine— No other news—

> Your[s] truly
> —Sam Milligan

ALS, DLC-JP2.

1. Roger Pryor (1828–1919), Virginia lawyer, editor, and congressman (1859–61), was special U. S. minister to Greece (1854–57); later he served in both the Confederate army and the Virginia Confederate legislature. Moving to New York after the war, he sat on a lower court (1890–94) before becoming a justice of the New York supreme court (1894–99) and referee of the appellate division (1912–19). His December 29 speech, made during the speaker-election debate, was a defense of the South's previous compliance with the Constitution and of its economic system. *BDAC*, 1485; *Cong. Globe*, 36 Cong., 1 Sess., 281–86.

2. Associated with Frank Bullock in Thackeray's *Vanity Fair*, I, Ch. 21.

3. Landon C. Haynes, twice defeated for Congress in the first district, may have been encouraged to move his political base to Knoxville as a consequence of his warm reception at the recent state Democratic convention, when he was named elector-at-large. At any rate, by early March he had established his legal practice there. Nashville *Union and American*, March 10, 1860.

From Jackson B. White

February 8, 1860, Nashville; ALS, DLC-JP2.

Davidson County legislator acknowledges receipt of "documents of the Pacific Rail Road surveying expedition. My daughter is very much pleased with the Books on the natural history of the country." Sends copy of his speech on the Free Negro bill pending before the legislature, and comments, "We will adjourn in March without having done much for the benefit of the state."

From William W. Wick[1]

Indianapolis   8 Feb. 1860

Sir.

I did not congratulate you upon your accession to the Senate, because that was a personal matter. I was glad however that one so proverbially, moderate, Calm, & yet decided should bring into the Senate an infusion of those good elements.

But Sir I do heartily tender you my Congratulations upon the fact that the Indiana Convention,[2] recently held, gave an earnest endorsement to your homstead plan, and did what could be done to annex it to the *expediency* platform of the Dem. party. I see you have put the ball in motion; and I do both hope and predict that you will remain in public life till you shall see the *idea* become a *fact*, sanctioned by a law, which, once made, will remain forever.

We are all for Douglas here in Indiana; yet I and others see, with pleasure, that your state has presented your name for the Presidency. Should that name come forward now, we can do better for it than for any other save one.

And it will not be forgotten, tho' even temporarily postponed.

As I grow old I become less loyal to Party, and to an administration; and more & more loyal to principle, right, and truth. What little of personal loyalty remained with me, the present administration has fully emancipated me from.

I love a man who is tolerant, and dislike a trimmer. One who is at once a trimmer himself, and yet intolerant towards those who dissent from *him*, is an abomination[.][3]

Very truly Your friend.[4]   W W Wick

ALS, DLC-JP2.

1. William W. Wick (1796–1868), Pennsylvania-born lawyer and jurist, filled a number of offices in Indiana before his election as a Democrat to Congress (1845–49). After serving as Indianapolis postmaster (1853–57), he returned to the practice of law. *BDAC*, 1811.

2. The Indiana Democratic convention, held January 11–13 to select delegates to Charleston, upheld the principle of a homestead for "all actual settlers." New York *Times*, January 14, 1860.

3. The word "trimmer," here applied to Buchanan, refers to one who does not adhere to a single set of opinions but instead fluctuates or holds a middle position appearing to favor both sides—in short, one who is guided by expediency. *Webster's Third International.*

4. In answer to this letter Johnson apparently sent a copy of his Speech on Harper's Ferry Incident, December 12, 1859, to which Wick responded enthusiastically, observing that although "one cannot catch the traitorous scamps . . . a persevering adherence to actual truth, free from Rhetorical flourishes, is the way to use them up." Wick to Johnson, February 18, 1860, Johnson Papers, LC.

From William M. Lowry

Greenv Ten Feby 9 1860

Gov Johnson
    Dr Sir
        enclosed is a Communication hastily thrown together[.] I wrote it in such away, that you might if you saw proper transmit it to the Comptroller for his action[.]¹ I thought If I sent it through you he would attend to it more promptly[.] in addition to what I say in the enclosed, I would ask if it would not be imposeing too much upon your time, that you would purchase me afee [*sic*] Book.² I presume some one about Washington has gotten up a Book of this Kind for Marshals, and that it is for sale in Washington. I am frequently at a loss to know what fees, I am entitled to, and have no doubt that I frequently neglect to charge Fees that I am honestly entitled to. we have but little local news that would interest you. what is the news about the Charleston Convention[?] how dose the Johnson stock range[?] high or low. I wish I could Controle things for a while. I am honest in the belief that you could be elected without doubt. If I mistake not I See that Gov Siblie³ of Minnesota is appointed one of the delegates to the Charleston Convention. I am glad of this[.] I wish you would give me his name and address as I would like to sound him in a prudent way.
Our local Elections are beginning to excite attention[.] lots and cards of candidates for every office[.] the good man only knows how it will terminate. will you go to Charleston at the time of the Convention. if you have any suggestions that I could further let me know them, in reference to census takers. I hardly know what to say, a man by being Marshal will get him self, pretty well known. I think I have recd and read 500 letters upon the subject. I shall endeavour to discharge the duties faithfully, and give as general satisfaction as I can[.] Our business pretty good[.] Produce verry high[.] Wheat

selling here at 125 to 130 p Bu Flour at 3 to 3 25 p 100 ct[.] let me hear from you often[.]

in Haste Yr freind   Wm M Lowry.

ALS, DLC-JP2.

1. Lowry's letter of February 9 to the first comptroller, William Medill, is unavailable; however, a copy of Medill's reply to Lowry by way of Johnson, is on file in the comptroller's records. Lowry apparently felt that the law of February 26, 1853, fixing fees and costs for marshals, had operated to his detriment in a case where, for one hundred miles of travel, he was able to collect only ten dollars (or ten cents per mile). But, as the comptroller explained, though the law might appear prejudicial in some cases, "the losses in one case" are often "made up by the profits in another," and it is assumed that Congress "contemplated" these inequities "when the maximum of fees was fixed upon." Medill to Lowry, February 17, 1860, First Comptroller's Office, Let. Sent, Vol. 71, pp. 252–54, RG217, National Archives.

2. Although a schedule of fees was included in "An Act to Regulate the Fees and Costs to be allowed Clerks, Marshals, and Attorneys of the Circuit and District Courts of the United States, and for other Purposes," which passed February 26, 1853, there is no evidence of a separate publication such as Lowry requests. U. S. Statutes, X, 164–67.

3. Henry H. Sibley (1811–1891), a native of Michigan and onetime fur trader, was territorial delegate from both Wisconsin (1848–49) and Minnesota (1849–53), as well as governor of Minnesota (1858–60). A Union brigadier general (1862–65), he was subsequently interested in banking, railroads, and other public corporations. Elected a delegate by the state Democratic convention held in St. Paul in January, he attended the Charleston convention. BDAC, 1599; New York Times, January 21, 1860; Charleston Courier, April 27, 1860.

To Robert Johnson, Nashville

Washington City   Feb 11th 1860

My dear Son,

Your letter dated the 5th inst and post marked the 7th was recieved by this morning's mail and was read with much pleasure— You Seem to be highly pleased with your trip to Kentucky and Ohio— I am gratified to learn that you were So well entertained and hope that it will prove as profitable to you at it has been interesting— I regret to hear that the Legislature will be in session So long for it will have a tendency to make it unpopular with the people and will Cause them to condemn all that will be done good and bad— While it occurs to me I would in the reciept of my per-diem be very careful not to take pay for any more time than I was empl[o]y[e]d as a Legislator— During my absence from Nashville in the Christmas holy days and off to Kentucky and Ohio on the Legislativ excursin I would not take one cent— It will be worth more to you in the future than it is now and would therefore not touch one dollar more than what I was honestly entitled to— Mr Jos. R. Anderson of Bristol wrote to me the other day that he had employed you to file a bill in chancery for him in reference to the location of some land warrants where there had been some fraud practiced &c and that he desired me to furnish you with all the information on the subject I might be able to procure from the land office— From the reading of his letter to me I think he is under the impression that the bill is to be filed in the State of Tenn— The bill will have to be filed where the persons who have practiced the fraud Can be made parties to the Suit— I am inclined to think that it would be better for Mr Anderson to emply Some one who resides where the parties are— However this is a matter between you and him[.] I do not know what he has written to you and of Course Can forme no Correct opinion as to what you should do in the premises— I think his idea was or is to have his business attended to for little or nothing— Let that be as it m[a]y I would dispose of it in that way which my interest dictated— I have seen nothing of your Bank Speech[1] as yet. I hope that you have not declined making it— For I thought you had a Collection of facts and figures that was worth throwing out to the Country— There is a bill now before Congress to prohibit the Banks of the district from iss[u]ing any thing in the shape of Circulatin less than twenty dollars[2] and I was in hopes that you would get your speech off in time for me to use some of the facts here in the discussion on the bill—[3] I have sent our Copy of the Congressional Globe to the Union as requested by you— I will have the Copy you want sent home— For if it was sent to Nashvill the nunbers [sic] m[an]y of them would be misplaced— I wish you would go to the Uni[o]n office and have the Triweekly Union sent to me at this place— I do not want the daily, also have the one sent to Greenevill stopped. it is not necessay to have it sent ther and here too— There is one numb[er] of it taken there by Patterso[n] and when you leave Nashville for home you Can have the triely weekly sent to you[r] address and I will pay for it— Last fall one year ago when I was in Nashville I Settled with them and requeste them to arrange the matter[4]

AL, DLC-JP. A fragment.

    1. On February 24, in a speech against rechartering the Union and Planters' banks, Robert gave "his views on the currency question, proclaiming his hostility to all banks of issue." Nashville *Union and American*, February 25, 1860.
    2. John Slidell of Louisiana had introduced such a bill on January 9. *Cong. Globe*, 36 Cong., 1 Sess., 375.
    3. Johnson did not speak to this issue and Slidell's measure died in committee.
    4. The last page of this letter is missing.

From Frank C. Dunnington

Columbia, Feb. 13, 1860.

Dear Governor.

Mrs. Dunnington desires to tax your liberality once more in the way of flower seeds, and as it will only cost you the writing of an order to the *Secretary of the flower Department*, just at the foot of the public grounds, I do not hesitate to communicate her wishes to you. You will find the list enclosed.

I have been very constantly engaged with business matters of various kinds since I saw you, but am now at home comparatively idle. I fear I shall become a confirmed dispeptic unless I go on to a farm or engage in some other *active* pursuit. I shall take no part in the next canvass unless we happen to get a candidate that suits me much better than I was suited in /56. I took a very deep interest in our recent State Convention and witnessed some very rich[?] things. Several days in advance the Memphis delegation, with Sam Walker, Bill Carroll & Judge King[1] at their head, were there. They manifested unusual interest in what was coming off—as much concerned as if there was a bank charter at stake or a bank board to be appointed and danger of their being left off. Knox had missed the connection somewhere & had not come up.[2] They soon wanted to know who had resolutions and what was the programe. They said they were for peace and harmony—all they desired was that the Convention should re-adopt the Cincinnati pla[t]form, approve in general terms the Dred Scott decision, and adjourn without expressing any preference as to a candidate. I told them that a good many of the Delegates believed that the Democracy of Tennessee had a choice and that it ought to be expressed and would likely test the question. They were very decidedly of the opinion that an attempt to do this would blow the Convention to the devil, and swore that if your name was put forward in that connection they would nominate Gov. Harris. I was amused at their newly-awakened admiration for Harris. I told Harris of his new friends and increasing prospects. He very promptly checked them, declaring his unwillingness to be used as such an instrument and in such hands. Their next proposition was to make Cave Johnson chairman of the Convention, but they readily assented to Jones. They were as thick as two in a bed with Haynes an hour after he got to town. He ought to move to Memphis. He would take well there. His happy adaptation to Memphis reminds of the anecdote of the young man who, having moved to Illinois, wrote back to his father, a professional office-seeker, to move out

there by all means *for d—d mean men got office there.* But, to the
Convention. It was agreed that Haynes & Andrew Ewing should be
the Electors for the State at large, (Andrew accepting reluctantly,) [3]
and that old Cave Gen. Pillow and Bob Payne or Knox should go for
the State at large to Charleston.[4] Philip Glenn[5] was unprovided for
but seemingly satisfied with the prospect of a good sweat & an immense amount of his loud talk. Bob Payne and Gen. Pillow, Cave
Johnson & Wm. Carroll, Andrew Ewing & Knox Walker, Judge
King and Mr. Hebb,[6] Pete Turney[7] & Co. were all working in glorious unison. Coming together from entirely different causes, they
seemed to be acted upon by a common sympathy. I appealed to Harris' friends and to your friends to stand fast together—admit of no
jealousies, or rivalry—and beat down the elements of disaffection
towards both. I am gratified to say that the immediate personal
friends of Gov. Harris toed the mark squarely, and I also know that
it was Harris' wish they should do so. I noticed that Knox was not
seen much during the exciting part of the proceedings, but when
the business of the Convention had been completed & we learned
what had been going on before the Committee on Delegates for the
State at large, it appeared that Knox, like Saul of Tarsus, had been
the subject of a suden and miraculous conversion to the "modern,
Andrew Johnson, Jacobs-lader, converging lines Democracy," and
had been struling to have himself appointed a delegate for the
State at large to Charleston, that he might be the chief instrument
of your nomination for the Presidency. At the very intimation that
he might be for Douglass, his representative man Mr. Farreley
[*sic*],[8] another new admirer of yours, swore roundly that he was not
for Douglass, and in proof of it he said Knox had been made the
confidential bearer of a letter from you to Bob.[9] And I am sorry to
say that your man Maxwell[10] put Knox in nomination. So the thing
worked. I will not bore you with any more of it. You should be satisfied to know that you have such additions to your long list of friends
in Tennessee. I regret very much, that Andrew Ewing managed to
get an appointment as delegate, as I have not heard of his conversion.
I understand he is for Guthrie.[11] We must manage to make Milligan,
Quarles and Atkins[12] the leaders of our delegation. I am for making
Ewing one of the Vice Presidents of the Convention. The man has
sunk himself deeper and deeper in my estimation every day since
you and me used to discuss his merits in a private way in /56-7.

Not being a delegate & not having much love for Conventions, I
don't think I shall go to Charleston. I don't know what your plans
are (if you have any,) but whenever I can contribute anything to
the advancement of sound men and sound principles you may feel

assured that I am ready to do so. Bob told me several times that he had a letter from you that he wished me to read, but he never brought it up. I should be glad to hear from you at any time, but would not have you tax yourself with a letter merely to be civil.

Your friend,   F. C. Dunnington.

N. B.

Walker brought with him from Washington a series of resolutions drawn up by Nicholson.[13] They were laid before the Committee on Resolutions, but I did not learn their purport. Did you see them?

ALS, DLC-JP2.

1. E. W. M. King (1808–1871) was district attorney general (1836–42), judge of the Shelby County criminal court (1843–53), county register, and a member of the Tennessee house (1857–59). *Tenn. Official Manual* (1890), 184, 191; 1860 Census, Tenn., Shelby, 6th district, 193; Robison Biog. Data.

2. J. Knox Walker of Memphis; see Letter from William H. Maxwell, February 2, 1860.

3. Ewing ultimately avoided serving as elector; he was replaced by Washington C. Whitthorne.

4. In the end, the delegates-at-large at Charleston were Sam Milligan, John D. C. Atkins, William A. Quarles, and Andrew Ewing.

5. Although chosen neither as an elector nor as a delegate to Charleston, Glenn appears to have made the most of the convention. A Whig paper observed, "The stentorian voice of the inevitable Philip Glenn, of Fayette, was heard, at one time, above the din and uproar, advocating the claims of Andrew Johnson for the Presidency, deprecating innovations and opposing the recommital of the resolutions." Nashville *Patriot*, January 19, 1860.

6. George V. Hebb (b. 1823), Maryland-born Lincoln County farmer of comfortable means, served in the Mexican War and in the Tennessee house (1853–55, 1859–61) as a Democrat. 1860 Census, Tenn., Lincoln, 73; Robison, *Preliminary Directory, Lincoln*, 21.

7. Peter Turney (1827–1903), son of former Senator Hopkins L. Turney, was a Winchester lawyer, state supreme court justice (1870–86), chief justice (1886–93), and governor (1893–97). When Tennessee seceded, Turney organized the first Tennessee Confederate regiment and served as its colonel throughout the war. White, *Messages*, VII, 451–53.

8. John P. Farrelly (c1831–1868), one of the Shelby County delegates, was a member of the Tennessee house (1859–61). Robison Biog. Data.

9. It is quite possible that Knox Walker, who had conferred with Johnson during an early-January visit to Washington, carried a letter, now lost, to Robert before the state convention met. Yet, in light of Johnson's clearly expressed caution in dealing with Walker, it is unlikely that he entrusted any particularly confidential advice or opinions to such a communication. Letters to Robert Johnson, January 12, 15, 1860.

10. William H. Maxwell of Jonesboro.

11. Senator James L. Guthrie of Kentucky.

12. Sam Milligan, William A. Quarles, and John D. C. Atkins.

13. Nicholson had drafted resolutions calling for guaranteed protection of slavery in those states where it existed as well as for a cessation of agitation in nonslaveholding states and deploring the existence of a sectional political party which violated the spirit of "comity" and "fraternal forbearance," thus endangered the Union. Perhaps Nicholson offered these proposals for consideration by the committee on resolutions. See Clark, A. O. P. Nicholson, App. G.

From Henry G. Wax[1]

Rogersville Feby 13th 1860

Hon A. Johnson
Dr Sir

I drop you a line to day, to inform you that Stephen A Douglas is sending Documents to every man in this country, & he is gaining ground every day. I fear he will get the nomination at Charleston. be on your Guard & see that you are not out Generaled. him & his friends are making de[s]perate efforts to procure his pasports, thro the convention. now is the time to work the wires,[2] & clear away the Brush, before the fight comes on, & then stand your ground while there is any thing to stand too is my motto. I think Tho. A. R. Nelson has sent every woman in Hawkins Co his speech[3] & nearly evry man too— I write this to let you know what is going on[.]

Respectfully Yours   H. G. Wax

ALS, DLC-JP2.

1. A Rogersville tinner with real and personal property valued at $2700, Wax (b. c1818) had been charged fifteen years earlier with an election bet, "to the evil example of all others . . . and against the peace and dignity of the State," and the sheriff was duly instructed to "take the body of Henry Wax" until he could be tried before the judge of the circuit court in Rogersville. The outcome of this incident is unknown. 1860 Census, Tenn., Hawkins, 11; WPA, Hawkins County Circuit Court Minutes, 1817–1845, pp. 87–88.

2. Probably a variation of "pull the wires," political slang which meant to exert all influence, to manipulate skillfully and even underhandedly, to attain desired ends. Mathews, *Americanisms*, II, 1881–82.

3. *Cong. Globe*, 36 Cong., 1 Sess., 46–48, 50–52; for discussion of Nelson's speech, see Letter from David J. Carr, January 7, 1860, note 3.

From Mortimer F. Johnson[1]

Tellico Plains, E. Tenn
February 15th 1860

Hon Andrew Johnson.

Dear Sir There is much solicitude felt in Tennessee upon the present Aspect of the Political Horison and every thing will depend upon the deliberations of the Councils of the Nation. The man who is to be the Nominee of the Charleston Convention will have to be selected with a view of Combining the greatest amount of Democratic strength without regard to sections and to determine this much depends upon the developements in the Congress between this and the time of holding the Convention[.] I was at Nashville as a member of the State Convention and must say I never saw a more dignified and solid representation in any State, and the delliberations were Characterised with great harmony, and unanimity of feeling. The sentiments of the Convention was strongly in favour of leaving the Delegation uninstructed so that they might in all things consult the greatest ammt. of good to the party. But the expression of its Choise was Spontaneous and I was rejoiced that it was an East Tennession and from the Mountains in which I live and which is as warmly attached to the union as any portion of our Country— I feel quite assured the State at no time has presented a more thorough political organization[.]

I allude to this subject because it is highly gratifying to all men who have large and abiding interests in the property and business of the Country and who have always been identified with the interests and success of the true principles of Democracy[.]

I feel some interests in the position of Hon Wm. H. Seward and should be gratified that you would send me his speech (if made) in the Senate Explanatory of his position and of his Rochester Speech[.][2] I presumed he was preparing it and it would not find its way into this region[.] In early times in New York, I knew him well and admire his Tallents But his position of latter years is not one to admire whether being North or South[.]

Allow me to call your attention to the subject of the Mail Contract for East Tenn. David Yulee[3] who has been the Chairman of the Post office Committee in the Senate is the Brother in law I believe of the P M Genl.[4] whose interests are in Louisville and Yulees in Florida[.] It is feared that with the[ir] influence The great Central Route through Tennessee to New Orleans may not be selected. But of this you will know all. I would simply say that now nearly all our Letters from Washington and New York Come by way of Nashville or Augusta and are 7 & 8 days in Coming[.]

Having been long familliar with the designs of Senator Yulee and having a personal acquaintance[5] I have reason to fear we may not get the great Southern Mail facilities by the best Route[.]

Allow me to assure of my solicitude for your health, and usefulness, and remain with Considerations of the highest esteem and regard Yours

                                                            M. F. Johnson

Permit me to say I became quite well acquainted with your son at Nashville and found him both active and Efficient in the best interests of the Country— My Father Hon. E. Johnson[6] desires me to Express to you his kindest wishes[.]

                                                            M. F. Johnson

ALS, DLC-JP2.

1. Mortimer F. Johnson (b. *c*1813), New York-born ironmaster, was postmaster at Tellico Plains and subsequently Confederate postmaster. 1850 Census, Tenn., Monroe, 241; Will T. Hale and Dixon L. Merritt, *A History of Tennessee and Tennesseans* (8 vols., Chicago, 1913), III, 592n.

2. Contrary to expectations, Seward did not in this session elaborate upon his "Irrepressible Conflict" speech delivered in Rochester, New York, October 28, 1858. His one major speech of the session, on February 29, dealt with the admission of Kansas. *Cong. Globe*, 36 Cong., 1 Sess., 910–14.

3. David L. Yulee (1810–1886), St. Augustine lawyer, delegate to Congress (1841–45), and U. S. senator from Florida (1845–51, 1855–61), was a planter and one of the earliest railroad promoters in the South. He served in the Confederate Congress throughout the war. *DAB*, XX, 638; *BDAC*, 1862.

4. Joseph Holt (1807–1894), Kentucky lawyer and Democrat, served as commissioner of patents (1857–59), postmaster general (1859–61), secretary of war (1861–62), and judge advocate of the army (1862–75). In the latter capacity he gained notoriety by his zealous prosecution of the Booth conspirators and of Henry Wirz, Confederate commandant at Andersonville. Holt and Yulee had married daughters of Charles A. Wickliffe of Kentucky. *DAB*, IX, 181–82.

5. This acquaintance with Yulee undoubtedly developed during the time M. F. Johnson spent in Florida between his flight from Rochester—where, according to Tellico Plains lore, he had killed a man in a duel—and his arrival in Tennessee early in the 1840's. Willard Yarbrough, "Historic Tellico Plains," Knoxville *News-Sentinel*, April 17, 1966.

6. Elisha Johnson (*c*1785–1866), New England-born engineer, onetime mayor of Rochester, New York, and proprietor of the Tellico Iron Works, owned real estate valued at $60,000. 1850 Census, Tenn., Monroe, 241; 1860 Census, Tenn., Monroe, 247; Reba Bayless Boyer, comp., *Monroe County, Tennessee, Records, 1820–1870* (2 vols., [Athens], 1969–70), II, 21.

From Louis G. Thomas[1]

Washington, D. C. Feb. 16th 1860.

Hon. Andrew Johnson,—

Sir,—my Sister-in-law, Mrs Shermer,[2] requested me to hand her address to you, inasmuch as you had promised to Send to her when finished, a copy of your Photograph likeness. She desired me to ask of you as a special favor, an *additional* copy, for a friend of hers, who is one of the leading Democrats of Philadelphia.

I trust Governor, that, while executing this commission of Mrs. Shermer, you will pardon me if in the space of these few lines, I obtrude upon your attention a Subject appertaining to myself.

I have made partial arrangements to go to Nashville, in your State, where a Situation in my business, (Bookbinding,) has been tendered me. Before going however, I desire to tarry in Washington until the Post master General shall have made Some appointments which have been contingent upon the passage of the Post office appropriation Bill.

Last year I caused to be filed in that Department, my letter of application for a Messengership, accompanied by recommendations from Mayor Berrett,[3] Marshal Selden,[4] and other distinguished gentlemen of our Party. (And while on the Subject, I may mention that two or three years ago, I was very highly recommended by Gen. Cass; by the Philadelphia Democratic delegation in Congress, as well as by a number of distinguished gentlemen of Washington, for a Clerkship in the "Department of the Interior." Those papers are on file in that Departt. I mention this to show that I have been recommended for a post under this administration—)

I have four young children in Philad. whither they were taken after the death of their mother. My business, Sir, for the last two years here has been very precarious and uncertain; almost rendering me incapable of providing for the Support of my family. Hence my desire to Secure Something more permanent.

Should I Secure the Situation of *Messenger* in the *Post office*, I would prefer it to going to *Tennessee*, as I would be nearer my children.

Having thus explained as briefly as possible, my position, I desire Sir, most respectfully, to ask of you whether you would be disposed to aid me, a Stranger to you, in the attainment of the object of my pursuit?

In connection with the influence already exerted in my favor, I feel confident that, if you would Speak a word for me personally to the Hon. Mr Holt,[5] P. M. G. I would receive an *immediate appointment*. I understand Sir, that it was the intention of the Department to appoint *temporary* Messengers, &c. to be made *permanent* upon the passage of the *Appropriation Bill*. As that Bill will probably be a *law* in a few days, doubtless the appointments will soon be made.

Be kind enough Governor, to pardon me for the liberty I have assumed in asking this favor at your hands, but Since I had occasion to See you at the Hotel, during my attendance upon Mrs. Shermer, I was impressed with the belief that I might approach you upon the subject. I concluded to put my petition to you in writing, as being possibly the least annoying to you.

With the highest respect, I subscribe myself your obedient Servant   Louis G. Thomas.

ALS, DLC-JP2.

1. Louis G. Thomas was a Washington bookbinder boarding at "331 5th West." *Boyd's Washington and Georgetown Directory* (1860), 146.

2. Mrs. Mary Shermer operated a dry goods store at 1222 Pine Street, Philadelphia. *Cohen's Philadelphia City Directory* (1860), 819.

3. Elected mayor of Washington in 1858, James G. Berret (1815–1901) served until 1861, when he became embroiled in a controversy with the military and was confined briefly in Fort Lafayette. Born in Baltimore, Ber-

ret had been in the Maryland house of delegates (1837–39) and had also served as clerk in the U. S. treasury (1835–48), chief pension clerk (1848–49), and Washington postmaster (1853–58). Allen C. Clark, "Richard Wallach and the Times of His Mayoralty," Columbia Historical Society *Records*, XXI (1918), 211–12; New York *Times*, April 15, 1901; Bryan, *History of the National Capital*, II, 430, 486–87.

4. William Selden (b. *c*1795), a native of Virginia and an extensive property-holder in Washington, was marshal of the District of Columbia (1858–61). For eleven years prior to 1850 he served as treasurer of the United States, and for four years thereafter headed the banking firm of Selden, Withers and Co. *Ibid.*, 386n, 442n; 1860 Census, Washington, D. C., 320.

5. Joseph Holt.

From Robert Johnson

Nashville   Feby 17th [1860]

Dear Father,

Your letter of 11th inst received this morning and I merely write to acknowledge its receipt—

The Bank question is made the special order in our house for next Thursday at which time I will make my speech. I have no doubt but what some six or eight Banks will be chartered and the country again flooded with a worthless currency— I have made some amendments to my speech that I think are good and will have some effect on the house—

The Conventional Interest Bill has passed both houses and as soon as the Senate concur with Some house amendments, will be the law of the land, and will do more to damn the Democratic party in Tennessee than all the measures enacted in ten years— I made a hard and desperate fight on it and had it defeated at one time, but four of my men faltered and refused to vote— it was carried in the house by *one* vote—[1]

Both houses agreed to adjourn 5th March—but the house cannot possibly get through its calendar by that time, in my opinion[.]

I will write you in a few days in regard to my marrying in full— and other things of interest— Mrs Hubbard[2] desires you to send her some *tea* seed or plants[3] and other seeds— Mrs Brown also—both send their respects— what do you think of Miss Hattie Brown—[4]

Nothing new—   Your Son   R. Johnson

ALS, DLC-JP2.

1. The Conventional Interest Bill, which became law on February 21, was rejected in the house on February 15, but passed on reconsideration the next day. Robert Johnson, who had voted against it, tried several diversionary motions—tabling, adjourning, calling the roll (twenty-four members did not answer)—all without effect. After a motion to reconsider, the house sustained the bill by one vote, sending it to the senate. *Tenn. House Journal*, 1859–60, pp. 731–34, 737–38; *Tenn. Acts*, 1859–60, Ch. XLI.

2. Mrs. J. T. Hubbard, wife of a dry goods merchant, was Lizinka C. Brown's aunt. *Nashville Bus. Dir.* (1860–61), 196; Cave Johnson to James Buchanan, November 9, 1856, James Buchanan Papers, Historical Society of Pennsylvania.

3. The idea of raising tea in the United States had received a strong impetus from Dr. Julius Smith's successful cultivation of the plant in Greenville, South Carolina, between 1848 and 1852. Favorable references appeared in reports to the commissioner of patents from 1855 on; by August, 1858, the federal government had began construction of a hothouse and garden in Washington to experiment with the imported plant. In order that interested individuals might attempt cultivation in their own regions, the patent office, aided by members of Congress, distributed seedlings during February and March, 1860, stipulating that "there will be but one consignment to each congressional district, and that to some intelligent and responsible person, selected with the assistance of the representative of the district." Report of the Commissioner of Patents for the Year 1855: Agriculture, *Senate Ex. Doc.* No. 20, 34 Cong., 1 Sess., xlii; Report of the Commissioner of Patents for the Year 1859: Agriculture, *House Ex. Doc.* No. 11, 36 Cong., 1 Sess., 1, 13.

4. Lizinka Brown's daughter, who was about sixteen.

From George Asbury[1]

Eugene City,   Lane Co. Oregon,
Feb'y 18th 1860.

Hon. Andrew Johnson,
Senate Chamber, Washington;

Dear Sir— As a native of the old North State, and a conservative Democrat, I venture to entrust you with a brief *exposé* of politics in this distant State of the Union. Your undoubted fealty of principle to the Constitution and the Union, your influence as a Democrat, and a settled faith in the ultimate success of your destiny as a politician incline me thus to address you.

The early settlers of Oregon were generally of Southern origin, and are now to be regarded as reliable Democrats; but having been remotely aloof from the political, battle fields of the past ten years, it cannot be expected that they understand the signs of the times with the perception of those who have fought those battles at the ballot-box. It is no matter for surprise, therefore, that many of them are likely to be beguiled into the ranks of the enemy. The New England or Abolition element in this State is composed of a class of reckless adventurers who for the most part have taken place in the ranks of the Democracy—march under the flag of Democracy—and claim to be Democrats—merely as spies in the Democratic Camp, and for the purpose of inflicting treacherous and secret stabs upon the party when opportunities present themselves. Thus far these men have managed to fill every State office in Oregon. Oregon is largely Democratic, but almost every office-holder in the State is opposed to the

Administration of Mr. Buchanan—claims to be a Democrat, yet opposes everything Democratic.[2] This is to be accounted for in the fact
that while the people of Oregon are honest and unsuspecting Democrats, every newspaper in the State is controlled and published by
Northern men, who in nine cases out of ten are Abolition adventurers, deeply dyed in the phrensy of hate and who use the name of
Democracy as a cloak to the deepest hatred to Democracy and the
people upon whom they subsist. These men and these newspapers
have almost managed to gain the custody of the Ark of Democracy
in Oregon. They denounce the Administration, they denounce Gen.
Lane, they utterly contemn and despise the people of Oregon—*who
to be sure are not politicans*—yet they lustily shout for Democracy.

Gen. Lane's nomination at Charleston is all that can save the
people of Oregon from the utter prostration of their inherent power
and a degrading thralldom to Yankee cunning. One half the *federal*
officers in Oregon are Republicans in disguise. Gen. L.'s nomination
will trim all the cob-webs out of Oregon politics, frustrate his *Democratic* enemies, and confirm the Democracy of Oregon in its proper
possessions and rights.

Aside from its importance to the people of Oregon, his nomination
will be endorsed by the people of the Union. You will pardon me
when I say that no man can be nominated at Charleston with the
same certainty of Success. His nomination will have the effect to
break up the Republican organization while it will open no field to
the Opposition. What say you to Lane and Cushing?[3]

As for yourself, my dear Sir, it is in your power to nominate Gen.
Lane; and, as your devoted admirer, I hope you will do so. Men *do
not* make themselves Presidents; the process by which men become
Presidents is one which time works upon them as *patients* to its action for right.

You will not doubt my sincerity when I say that I never saw Gen
Lane, am only a sojourner in Oregon, and have not the social, pecuniary, or political *status* to hope for office or official favor. Yet, in
political sagacity I claim to be behind no man, and do not hesitate to
indulge the prediction that his nomination will prove to be wise.

                                        Very respectfully Yours   George Asbury.
P. S   I write only to you.

ALS, DLC-JP2.

    1. Not identified.
    2. Perhaps the Oregon Democracy represented a microcosm of the
national party crisis: more or less united until 1859, the party was now
splintering ideologically over the slavery issue. Two of Senator Joseph Lane's
strongest supporters and political friends, James W. Nesmith, superintendent
of the Indian agency and controller of more patronage than any other state
officer, and Ashbel Bush, editor of the *Oregonian Statesman*, the state's most

powerful newspaper, became disenchanted with the Lane directives, thus precipitating a power struggle. After Lane had Nesmith replaced during 1859 for allegedly trying to buy the support of a disaffected Democrat with a job offer, the latter endorsed the alliance of Republicans with Douglas Democrats. At the same time, Bush became a follower of Douglas. It was with some difficulty that Lane manipulated the selection of proslavery delegates to the Charleston convention. Hendrickson, *Joe Lane,* 181ff; Robert W. Johannsen, *Frontier Politics and the Sectional Conflict* (Seattle, 1955), 96, 118.

3. Caleb Cushing (1800–1879), Massachusetts Democratic congressman (1835–43), commissioner to China (1843–45), and attorney general in Pierce's cabinet (1853–57), was chairman of the Charleston convention. President Johnson subsequently appointed him commissioner to codify the laws of the U. S. (1866–70), and following his service as U. S. counsel on the *Alabama* claims, Grant nominated him to the Supreme Court, but the Senate failed to confirm. Cushing ended his active career as minister to Spain (1874–77). *BDAC,* 768; *DAB,* IV, 623–30. See also Claude M. Fuess, *The Life of Caleb Cushing* (2 vols., New York, 1923).

From William H. Carroll

February 18, 1860, Memphis; ALS, DLC-JP2.

Son of former governor solicits Johnson's aid in procuring for "a very intelligent educated Irishman" an appointment as postal route agent—a move which would "materially strengthen the hold you already have with our foreign population."

From Charles Johnson

Greeneville   Feb. 19th 1860

Dear Father

This day I am thirty years old according to my understanding: Well, really it seems, that it has almost been a blank; but tis gone and can not be recalled therfor we should not trouble ourselves about that which we can not change; and it is equally true that we should not trouble ourselves about that which we can; ergo, we should not trouble ourselves at all; thats pretty good philosophy, but hard to practice. Some times I almost conclude that about one half our troubles are ideal;— we will conjure up all kinds of difficulties that we are to encounter, that have no other existence than in our own morbid imagination, or if they have, tis time enough to trouble ourselves when they Come upon us; St Paul understood that thing well,— "Fret not thyself" again he says, "eat drink and be merry for tomorrow ye die"[1] now he certainly means that we should enjoy life the best we can, make ourselves happy while we may; for the evils we can not avoid will come soon enough, and when they do come it will be time enough to fret;

He who is always looking on the dark side, and anticipating troubles from every quarter; increases his real troubles when they do come; while he who is always looking on the suny side, lessens his real troubles, and is at least happy in anticipation, of happiness, for I really belive that most of our happi[n]ess is in anticipation; the experience of the world I think proves this; ambition was neer satisfied; the attainmet of any cherished object fails to give contentment; in truth it seems only to increase our ability and desires;— Men are but children further along lifes voyage and what is true of them is equally true of children[.] See the happy child, the gaoal of whose ambition is the atainment of some childish project; which when attained fails to satify, but only increases the desire for greater attainments; and so it is through life; but no more of this now[.]

I am all alone now, Mother has gone to visit Mary.[2] will be gone some weeks[.] All are moving along about as usual[.] Circuit Court is now in session,—nothing of importance doing[.]

Bob, I understand contemplates changing his condition;—who the fortunate Lady is I know not; I received a letter from him a few days since but he made no mention of it to me; well that is a thing in which he must suit himself, it may or it may not be a judicious step, though it is an important one. If you would send us two or three hundred of your Speeches they Could be distributed to advantage[.] they are called for daily[.]

Your Son   Charles Johnson

Do you ever see any coppies of a paper published in Philadelphia Called the "American Baner, and working Mens Leader" edited by Theophilus Fiske[.][3] it is rather a novel paper and I think you would like it; Fiske is rather radical but advances some good things, if it is a permanet thing I would like to take it; perhaps you may know[.]

You must look over this scribbling this time as I write under disadvantages,

Charles Johnson

I enclose an article from the paper refered to,

ALS, DLC-JP2.

1. "Fret not thyself because of evil," or one of its several variations, is found in Prov. 24:19 and Ps. 37:1, 7, 8, not the writings of Paul. Jesus, in Luke 12:19, and Paul, in 1 Cor. 15:32, are both quoting the much older words of Isa. 22:13: ". . . let us eat and drink; for to-morrow we shall die."

2. Mary Johnson Stover lived in the Watauga Valley in Carter County.

3. Theophilus Fiske (c1802–1867), radical workingmen's leader, former Universalist minister, editor, author, and pamphleteer, was known for his anti-capitalist, "hard-money" writings. Coeditor of the Boston *Reformer* (1835) and editor-publisher of the *Democratic Expositor* (1844–46), he helped foster the development of the trades unions and industrial congresses of the 1840's. Disillusioned with the lack of progress and interest within the working classes, he gave up his *Expositor* and disappeared from the cause, only to reappear in the 1850's, with an "e" added to his name, as an editorial

writer for the Philadelphia *Argus* and, later, the *Pennsylvanian*. In 1856 he was a clerk in the Philadelphia navy yard. An early admirer of Calhoun and a defender of the South, he tried to revive the *Expositor* in 1860 to launch a compromise Democratic ticket headed by Andrew Johnson; failing in this effort, he eventually supported Douglas and the Union. Arthur M. Schlesinger, Jr., *The Age of Jackson* (Boston, 1946), 496; Elwyn B. Robinson, "The *Pennsylvanian*: Organ of the Democracy," *Pennsylvania Magazine of History and Biography*, LXII (1938), 351, 354; Mrs. Phyllis Whitman (Universalist Historical Society) to Andrew Johnson Project, March 8, 1971. See also Letter from Theophilus Fiske, August 6, 1860.

From George W. Rowles

February 20, 1860, Cleveland; ALS, DLC-JP2.

Has declined appointment as United States treasurer because "the office has too much pecuniary responsibility attached to it," but thanks Johnson for his "kind services in aiding to procure me the appointment."

From Anthony Ten Eyck[1]

Detroit Feby, 20, 1860

My dear Sir.

I enclose herewith a list of the No. of officers employed by the Govt in its various departments, arranged from the various States, from which they were appointed—compiled from the last "Blue book,"[2] two years ago, at your request. As it was prepared for you, & I have no use for it, & you may find it servicable in your Senatorial position, I have taken the liberty to send it to you—[3]

I improve this opportunity, also, to say a few words to you respecting the nomination to be made at Charleston, next April, for President—

If you have taken note at all of the expression of the public sentiment of the democratic masses, in the Northern & Northwestern States, you will have seen that that sentiment is almost universally & determinately in favor of Douglas[.]

That this is so you cannot wonder at, for Mr. Douglas has endeared himself in many ways to the democracy of the North & NWest, & possesses more of the elements of popularity with them than any other man in the country; besides he is the only man under whose banner they can hope to redeem their States from the blight & corruption of Black republicanism[.]

It is not to be disguised, & the gentlemen of position & influence in the South should not shut their eyes to the fact, that if Mr. Douglas is not the nominee of the Charleston Convention Mr. Seward is almost certain to be elected[.]

With any other candidate than Mr. Douglas we cannot hope to carry a single N'Western State, except perhaps Illinois— Let him be our nominee & I think I hazzard little in saying, that the democracy will redeem not only this State, (Michigan) but Ohio. Wis. Minn. & Iowa—

I cannot convey to you in words, the great anxiety our people, in this Section of the Country, entertain in regard to Mr. Douglas' nomination, or the enthusiasm which his nomination would inspire amongst the democracy— They all feel that such nomination, in connexion with the mal-administration of the Black Republicans since they have held power in our State Governments, would enable us to regain our State Administrations—to regain our democrati[c] Reps. in Congress—our State Legislatures, & U. S. Senators as soon as opportunity offers—& our County officers. All these have been lost within the last few years, & if the Charleston Convention will nominate Douglas, we can regain them all—

Our Northern & N'Western democratic majorities have been overturned & gone to the opposition, not because we were unfaithful to our democratic brethern of the South, or failed to aid them whenever they deemed our aid essential, but *precisely because we have stood by them every where*— Surely the Southern democracy should not distrust us now, or hesitate to yield to our wishes, when nothing can possibly be lost thereby, but when every thing is to be gained— With Douglas we can, in all human probablity, redeem this State— elect democratic State officers—three at least, of the four reps. in Congress—a majority of our Legislature, which will enable us to send a democrat to the Senate in place of Chandler[4]—& our County officers, which latter will give us a *prestage* & power that cannot be overcome for years—& what I believe true in this matter of this State—is true of all the N'Western States—& such a result, my dear Sir, will enable the democrats to settle this sectional controversy in their own way, & in a way that the South will be satisfied with, for they will have a potential voice in the matter— You see then this matter resolves itself into this—with the South it is a simple question of a President—with us of the N'West it is a question not only of President, but of all our State offices—Legislatures, members of Congress & Co. & Township offices— You ought to be willing to trust Douglas & the N'Western democracy— We have no hope of success with any other nominee for President— However much I may admire your own qualifications for that position, or those of Mr. Hunter, Mr. Cobb or Mr. Breckenridge,[5] & however much I might desire to see either in the Presidential Chair, or however much I might prefer either to Mr. Douglas, yet—knowing the feelings, views & wishes of the great masses of the democracy of the NWest-ern States, I should feel that the Charleston Convention were doing us the greatest possible wrong, & were throwing away the chance of electing a democratic President, if they nominated any other than Mr. Douglas[.]

I have written thus freely & frankly, because I know you to be a man of generous impulses & of excellent common sense, & because I believe, like myself, you love the democratic masses & would like to subserve their interests & aid them in carry out their wishes—

Our only real hope is with Southern gentlemen, who can & will see & appreciate our position— If you have any influence (& I know you have much) don't fail to exert it in our behalf, & that you can only do in the way indicated above[.]

Adopt at Charleston, the Cincinnati platform *intact*, without note or comment, if you please—& give us Douglas for our Candidate, & you will see such an enthusiasm enlisted in his behalf, throughout the NWest, that has not been seen since the days of Old Hickory, & that will sweep away the Black republican majorities as easily as you sweep cobwebs from the walls of your house— whatever your personal feelings may be respecting Mr. Douglas, I know you are too patriotic, & too devoted to the interests of the democratic masses, to let personal feelings control your public action— Believe me, my dear sir, the democracy of the N'Western States will not forget the Southern Statesman, who in this political emergency, will assist them to rid themselves of the political thraldom of the Black republican State Administrations— Asking your pardon for this extended epistle, I remain— Very respectfully & truly

Your friend   A. Ten Eyck

Hon. Andrew Johnson
U. S. Senate—

ALS, DLC-JP2.
    1. Anthony Ten Eyck (1810–1867), New York-born Detroit lawyer, was commissioner to Hawaii (1845–49), clerk of the Senate committee on public lands (1857–59), and, upon his return to Detroit, an alderman. He became deputy postmaster of Detroit (1860) and served in the Union army. Two months earlier Ten Eyck had asked Johnson to intercede in his behalf to regain his Senate clerkship. Ten Eyck to Johnson, December 12, 1859, Johnson Papers, LC; *NCAB*, XII, 259; Charles Lanman, *Biographical Annals of the Civil Government of the United States* (Washington, D. C., 1876), 420, 599.
    2. A reference to the biennial *U. S. Official Register*.
    3. The nature of Ten Eyck's letter reveals clearly that he was using this list, since lost, as an excuse to set before Johnson the viewpoint of the Northwest Democracy.
    4. Zachariah Chandler (1813–1879), a native of New Hampshire, moved to Detroit in 1833, becoming through trade, banking, and land speculation one of the richest men in Michigan. Mayor of Detroit (1851–52), a founder of the Republican party, and U. S. Senator (1857–75), he allied himself with the radical antislavery element of the party and, until the Democratic

landslide of 1874, was the undisputed state political boss—assisted, no doubt, by his generous dispensing of federal patronage. Chandler was secretary of the interior (1875–77) and returned to the Senate for a few months in 1879. *DAB*, III, 618; see also Wilmer C. Harris, *Public Life of Zachariah Chandler* (Lansing, 1917).

5. R. M. T. Hunter, Howell Cobb, and John C. Breckinridge.

From David M. Currin

Memphis, Feby. 21st, 1860.

Dear Sirs:

Rumours are rife on the streets here, to-day, that Col. Wm. H. Carroll, Post-master, is to be removed from his office.[1]

I trust that this is but a rumour:—First, I must confess, on personal considerations; for he and I were at school together, as boys; and though our relations, for the past two or three years, have not been so intimate as before; yet I have never met from him any other opposition than such as was open and manly, and he had a perfect right to offer, if his inclination, judgment, or notions as to what was due to party loyalty—(overlooking personal considerations)—so prompted him.

In the second place, as a mere question of local policy, I beleive the movement would be unfortunate.

I am one, who under no circumstances—(even though Mr. Douglass should be the nominee of a thousand Democratic Conventions) —could ever vote for him, for the presidency; while my *quondam political*, and still, personal friend, Carroll, is well known to have Douglass proclivities. In those proclivities—(which I cannot doubt are sincerely and honestly entertained)—I do not beleive that he has the sympathy of more than two dozen persons in this City and county. While the Democratic masses would probably, *tolerate* Douglass, and vote for him, if the Democratic nominee, on the low ground of *choice of evils*; yet scarcely any one here avows Douglass his *first* choice.

And hence, resting this matter upon mere considerations of party policy, I fear that the cause of what I conceive to be the right, would suffer from the change; because it would furnish factionists here, with a new text upon which they could declaim against the administration; and might, to some extent at least, build up for Douglass a strength he does not now possess, in this locality.

If there were any official delinquencies on the part of Carroll,— that would, of course, present a very different question. But I am informed, that none such are alleged; and, from my long acquaintance with him, I presume that none such exist. My own opinion is,—

(and I have lived here since March, 1846)—that Carroll has discharged the duties of his office, fully as well; to say the least of it, as any other incumbent who has occupied it, during the interval to which I have referred. Meantime, it should be remembered that its duties and responsibilities have been constantly increasing. I have presumed upon the acquaintance, personal and political, which exists between us, to intrude upon your attention what I, of course, feel to be a candid statement, in reference to the subject-matter of my letter.

Most respecty   Davd. M. Currin

Hons. Andrew Johnson
    A. O. P. Nicholson

ALS, DLC-JP2.

1. As rumored, Carroll's removal arose from his espousal of Douglas, a move which had provoked the Buchanan administration, but the *Avalanche* insisted that the removal, if accomplished, would be the result of local charges. Whatever the reason, Carroll was retired, and his successor, M. C. Galloway, editor of the *Avalanche*, named postmaster in July. Nashville *Gazette*, March 2, 1860; Memphis *Avalanche*, quoted in the *Gazette*, March 6, 1860; John M. Keating, *History of the City of Memphis, Tennessee* (3 pts., Syracuse, 1888), I, 444.

From James M. Crockett[1]

Richmond   Febuay 22 1860

Mr Andrew Johnson   sir   I Wente to New yark[.] I Expeced to gite Check For one Thousan Dallor Bute Faild to gite it[.] I donte know Whey it did not Com to hand[.] it Left me Wythaute mony[.] I draw one [on] orly [Otey?] & Saundes[2] of Lynchburg Va to gite mony[.] I gote twenty Dallors For Which I giv them a Drafte one you For twenty Dallors[.] I hop you Will pay at sight. I wante you to Rite to me Whire you wante me to Send you the mony[.] I Will pay it prompley[.] I hope you Will pay this Drafte prompley For me[.]

I am your Frend truley   J M Crockett
of Union Depot   Sullivan Co   Tennessee

ALS, DLC-JP2.

1. Probably either James Crockett (b. *c*1785), listed in 1850 as a Sullivan County farmer with real property valued at $1,000, or Jas. Crocket (b. *c*1818), also a Sullivan farmer, who appears to have lived near such Johnson friends as John Jackson and Valentine Bridleman (or Beidleman). Burgner, *Sullivan County, 1850 Census*, 71, 154.

2. Otey and Saunders may have been a Lynchburg business or banking firm at one time, since both surnames were prominent in antebellum Lynchburg finance and society. A John M. Otey who married in 1817 was a cashier of the bank and president of the city council. "Saundes" was possibly Dr. James Saunders, a surgeon in the War of 1812 and noted Virginian who

was a delegate to the constitutional conventions of 1829–30 and 1850–51 and who made a large fortune in tobacco. Rose Faulkner Yancey, *Lynchburg and Its Neighbors* (Richmond, 1935), 44, 378.

From Robert Johnson

House of Rep   Nashville Feby 22, [1860]

Dear Father

The opposition convention met here to day— a fair number of delegates in attendance— Bell nominated for the Presidency— Rev N. G. Taylor[1] and Bailey Peyton[2] appointed Electors for state at large— several speeches made—not much enthusiasm— I have no doubt but what the Union is now safe,—

I have just returned from Mrs Brown's where I have spent a pleasant evening— She and Mrs Hubbard are very anxious for you to send them some *Tea plants*, and anything else that may be of interest to them—

A rumor prevails here that Taz Newman and his brother James, are charged by the Pension Department with divers *forgeries*[3]— and my information is, which I get confidentially from Dunnington, that an order for the arrest of Taz Newman is now in the city— how true the charges may be, I know not, but am inclined to the opinion that so far as Taz Newman is concerned, that there is really no foundation for the suspicion— he denies knowing anything about the charges and denounces it as a base falshood, and says he will start to morrow for Washington to have the matter investigated— which I presume he will do— he will call on you to assist him, and I hope you will extend all the aid in your power to have the matter cleared up, for I do not believe the charges are true, but that the investigation has been set on foot by Mr Spence[4] & others for the purpose of breaking him down, as a few weeks ago in the Senate Newman denounced Spence in connection with the Exchange Bank in severe and bitter terms and that these charges are now made for the purpose of parying his blows and injure his character— in this though I may be mistaken— But I hope and trust it will all turn out right and that he may be triumphantly acquitted from all suspicion[.] I would like very much to hear from you in full on the subject of the Presidency and would also be pleased for you to write to Dunnington upon the subject, as he would be gratified to hear from you.

The Conventional Interest Bill has passed both houses and is now the law of the land— I voted against it all the time— The Senate rejected the Free Negro Bill[5] on yesterday—

I hardly think we will be able to adjourn on the 5th March. The

Bank question[6] is the special order for tomorrow, when I will make my speech—[7]

I will write again in a few days[.]   Yours truly
                                                             Robt Johnson

ALS, DLC-JP2.

1. Nathaniel G. Taylor, Johnson's opponent in the congressional canvass of 1849, was an ordained Methodist minister. Bellamy, "Landon C. Haynes," 106n.

2. Balie Peyton (1803–1878), Gallatin native, was a Whig attorney, party functionary, and congressman (1833–37). Declining a position in Tyler's cabinet, he moved to New Orleans in 1841 and became U. S. district attorney for the eastern district of Louisiana, aide-de-camp for General W. J. Worth during the Mexican War, and minister to Chile (1849–53). After serving as prosecuting attorney for San Francisco (1853–59), he returned to Gallatin, campaigned on behalf of the Bell-Everett Constitutional Union ticket, and sat in the state senate (1869–78). BDAC, 1450–51.

3. The Newman-Ramsey affair involved District Attorney John Crozier Ramsey's charges that senate speaker Tazewell W. Newman and his brother James W. had obtained pensions in 1853 by using fraudulent documents. Resigning as speaker, though the senate was in session, T. W. Newman traveled to Washington to demand an investigation; on being vindicated, he returned to his duties. Johnson received correspondence from both parties, and the Tennessee press widely circulated letters between the antagonists. The feud culminated in a shooting incident between Ramsey and James Newman in which both men were injured. Nashville News, March 7, 14, 1860; Nashville Union and American, March 2, 4, 8, 13, 24, 1860; Nashville Patriot, March 7, 1860; Eubanks, J. G. M. Ramsey, 46–47.

4. William Spence (c1812–1892), state senator (1865–67) and owner of the Exchange Bank of Tennessee at Murfreesboro, was accused of abetting J. C. Ramsey in prosecuting the Newmans because Taz Newman had charged Spence with swindling the state. The occasion for the speaker's attack was the consideration of a resolution that the state redeem certain Exchange Bank notes. Referring to the "stupendous fraud," Newman blamed Spence's bank for over-issuance of notes on bonds that were never deposited. Ibid., 44–45; Robison, Preliminary Directory, Rutherford, 55; Nashville Union and American, January 11, 1860.

5. On February 21, 1860, the state senate rejected house bill No. 19, which would have required that any free person of color who remained in Tennessee after January 1, 1861, be auctioned into slavery. Tenn. Senate Journal, 1859–60, pp. 522–23, 689.

6. S. 107, "to incorporate the capital stock of the Union and Planters' Banks," not only extended the lives of the two banks but also provided for an increase in their stock, for the establishment of additional branches, and for the privilege of issuing bank notes. Tenn. House Journal, 1859–60, p. 790; Tenn. Acts, 1859–60, Ch. CVIII.

7. Robert Johnson spoke on February 24, 1860.

From M. E. Wilcox[1]

                                          Graysville Ky, Fby. 22nd/60

Hon. Andrew Johnson
Washington D. C.

My Dear Sir,

Though I have been suffering, nay *prostrated*, for the last four months, with that most excrutiating of all diseases, Neuralgia, I have not yet ceased to feel an interest in public affairs. Such, at least, is the case during those intervals of quiet and ease which I sometimes have, and without which I could not long survive.

My object in writing you now is to obtain information upon a matter which, to some, might be regarded as of small significance, but upon which I, nevertheless, would like to be informed—to wit— have Messers Buchanan and Douglass effected a reconciliation, and upon such terms as to give to the latter the control of all appointments in the State of Illinois? If such is not the case, I am at a loss to account for the removal of Len. Faxon[2] as P. Master at Cairo and a Douglass-ite appointed in his place. That Faxon has been, all the while, a firm, unyielding supporter of the Administration his paper will abundantly show; while, at the same time, he has been openly hostile to the principles advocated by Mr. Douglass.

Then why the romoval?

If such a contract has been consumated as above intimated, it would seem that Mr. Douglass is to have the influence of the Administration in the Charleston Convention, or *vice versa*. While I rejoice at the growing prospects for *your* nomination by said convention, I would be unwilling to see you enter the *lists* against a man backed by the influence of the Executive, at least, unless such fact were publicly known to all the Delegates. The fact is, Douglass will not do, either for the North or the South; and his nomination will be tantamount to a defeat. What think you of *your* chances? The best indications, in your favor, that I see about here, are the increasing fears of the K. Nothing-Union—Oppositionists, who say, by the way, that your nomination for any office is equivelent to an election.

But enough of speculation for once.

Address me as above, where I am staying at present with my brother Dr. Wilcox[3] trying to get cured.

If you have a copy of your speech delivered some weeks since to dispose of, I would like to have it, as I have not yet seen it in any of my papers. Any other documents of interest which you may have at your disposal, I would be thankful to receive, provided the sending would not trespass too much upon you[r] time.

As ever your Friend   M. E. Wilcox

ALS, DLC-JP2.

1. M. E. Wilcox (b. *c*1823), had been a member of a Montgomery County committee which drafted resolutions in 1857 endorsing Johnson as presidential timber. 1850 Census, Tenn., Montgomery, 266; Clarksville *Jeffersonian*, April 8, 1857.

2. Leonard G. Faxon, son of Charles O. Faxon, founder of the Clarksville *Jeffersonian*, moved to Cairo, Illinois, where he edited the Democratic *City Times* (1851–55), the *Delta*, and the merged *Times and Delta* (1855–59);

he became postmaster in July, 1859. Franklin W. Scott, *Newspapers and Periodicals of Illinois, 1814–1879* (Springfield, 1910), 35; William P. Titus, *Picturesque Clarksville* (Clarksville, 1887), 225; *U. S. Official Register* (1859), *55.

3. C. L. Wilcox (b. c1805) had been a Montgomery County physician. With a wife and eight children to support, he apparently decided that his services would be more in demand in Kentucky and moved there sometime during the decade. 1850 Census, Tenn., Montgomery, 265.

From *"Clara"* [*Charlotte Clara Marling Cole*][1]

Birds Nest Cottage.—
Nashville—February 23rd 1860.

Honoured & dear Sir

emboldened by a complimentary remark of yours to a mutual friend (Robt Rains Esqr.)[2] regarding a few lines I wrote on the death of Gen'l Jackson—I take the liberty of enclosing to you the *prospectus*, of a vol. of *poems*, & I design publishing in a short time —for which I solicit your kindly influence, feeling confident—that the courteous gentlemanly leader of that *party* for whose principles —my *only Son* (& last child)—Sacrificed his invaluable life[3]—will nobly aid his *lonely* mother in thus endeavoring to secure a competency for the evening of a life, embittered with many Sorrows,— it is not as *charity*, my dear sir—I ask this,—far from it,—*none* of *my race ever did that*—& I think all who give me their name,—will be perfectly satisfied with the elegant and tasteful volume, they will receive in return for the price of subscription—

The vol. will be published in New-York under the careful direction of that eminent literary-critic *Park Benjamin*[4]—& other friends, —& in very handsome Style, with a few illustrations & a *portrait* of the *Authoress*—& I feel assured will give Satisfaction to my generous friends, & the public generally—& perhaps add one more leaf, tho but a simple one, to the budding garlands of Southern Literature—

I trust dear Sir—you will recieve this as it is intended as a mark of my high regard for your character, as a politician, & a gentleman,—& altho' we are *personally* unacquainted at present—I hope this will not always be the case as nothing would give me more pleasure than to welcome you on your return, to the hospitality of my little Cottage,—save that of Congratulating you in the *white house* as *president*, of our glorious republic.—

With sentiments of esteem & admiration for you in the various relations—you have occupied for many years—I am dear sir—most truly your friend

"Clara—"

ALS, DLC-JP2.

1. Charlotte Clara Marling Cole (1807–1883) of Nashville, mother of John L. Marling, is best remembered for *Clara's Poems*, published by J. B. Lippincott and Company of Philadelphia in 1861. The title page, which bears an engraving of Bird's Nest Cottage, tells the reader all—nay more—than he needs to know: *Clara's Poems; being, a collection of Miscellaneous Poetry, by "Clara," of Bird's Nest Cottage, Nashville, Tennessee. Also a few original Poems and Essays, by her son, the late Hon. John Leake Marling, and her lamented and talented daughter "Ada"; with an introductory notice by Rev. John T. Edgar, D. D., Pastor of the First Presbyterian Church, Nashville, Tennessee; to be dedicated to the pride of her sex, Mrs. James Knox Polk, of Nashville, Tennessee. Price—Two Dollars per volume.* Acklen, *Tenn. Records*, I, 9.

2. Felix R. Rains (1810–*fl*1880), for more than five years sheriff of Davidson County, was a businessman, director of the Bank of Tennessee, and prominent member of the Agricultural Association. Clayton, *Davidson County*, 463.

3. Marling, wounded in a political duel, had died of tuberculosis in 1856, soon after returning from two years as U. S. minister to Guatemala. *Johnson Papers*, II, 446–47n.

4. Park Benjamin (1809–1864), poet, editor, and critic, established the Norwich (Conn.) *Spectator* (1829–30), a short-lived weekly, and was associated (1834–39) with a number of literary publications until he founded the *Evening Signal* and the *New World* (1839). In his journals Benjamin published but few American works, practically none of which had any merit; most of his own poetry, virtually forgotten, has been scattered or lost. *DAB*, II, 187–88.

From William M. Lowry

Greenv Ten Feb 24 1860

Gov Johnson
Dr Sir

Yours enclosing, Mr Fords[1] letter Came duly to hand. you need not apologise for any Communication you may wish to make me and it will allways afford me pleasure to meet your views, where I can do So[.] in this Case Hon Saml A Smith[2] askd me to appoint Mr. Peters[3] while Ford was holding his office as route agent. Smith told me that Peters was his long tried boy friend and hoped I would give him the appointment[.] feeling under obligations to him I told him he might rely upon it at the proper time. this I presume he communicated to Peters and in good faith I cannot do otherwise than appoint him[.] I am free to Confess that all my Sympathy is with and for Ford—as I regard him as one of the original panel of Democracy in Tenns. the only hope I have for him is when you get to be President that he must have a good fat office[.]

I want you to go to New york in the Course of 2 or 3 weeks and have this day written my old friend B. M. Whitlock[4] Esq. to get an invitation up for you to make a national address which I presume he will do[.] if so. you must go, I have also made a Communication to the

Index.[5] a paper published at Richmond in your behalf and Sub-
scribed for his paper and presume he will publish it. is Gov Sibly.[6] a
delegate to the National Convention. I have just returnd from Rogersville[.] I was Courted in a small way, equal to the President of the
U S. We elected the old officers, G R Powell[7] told me he had a Communication from N[i]cholson[.] he agrees with me & says all you
want of an Election to the Presidency is a fair Start. our friend
N[i]cholson is in position to advance your prospects verry much.
Could we not fork him up to work[?] I have got so many letters to
write and So much other business that I hardly know what to do
first,   this is about the Close of court[.] every thing verry quiet. business first rate[.] our cash Sales and Collections for the two week of
court will be three thousand Dollars[.]

as ever   Yr friend
W. M. Lowry

ALS, DLC-JP2.
    1. The letter written by John W. Ford, editor of the Hamilton *Reflector*,
a pro-Johnson organ in Chattanooga, has not been found; it undoubtedly
concerned a request for a position as census taker, inasmuch as Lowry was
U. S. marshal in charge of these appointments.
    2. Samuel A. Smith (1822–1863), Cleveland, Tennessee, lawyer and
Democratic congressman (1853–59), was district attorney general (1845–
50), served briefly as commissioner of the general land office (1860), and
in 1861 was appointed agent to collect arms for the Confederate army.
BDAC, 1623.
    3. Joseph B. Peters (b. *c*1818), a farmer near Ooltewah, became census
taker for Hamilton County. Records of the Eighth Census: List of Marshals
and Assistants, RG29, National Archives; 1860 Census, Tenn., Hamilton, 57.
    4. Benjamin M. Whitlock was a New York merchant and southern sym-
pathizer, trading under the name of B. M. and E. A. Whitlock & Co., 13
Beekman Street. *Trow's New York City Directory* (1859–60), 907; *Wilson's
New York Directory of Co-Partnerships* (1859–60), 86; *Johnson Papers*, I,
535n.
    5. The *Virginia Index*, edited by Bennett M. DeWitt, was a Democratic
campaign newspaper published weekly and semiweekly in both Richmond
and Petersburg from January, 1859, through November, 1860. It was generally considered pro-Douglas. Signed "Tennessee" and dated February 24,
Lowry's communication urging Johnson's nomination at Charleston was subsequently reprinted in the Nashville *Union and American*, March 30, 1860.
Lester J. Cappon, *Virginia Newspapers, 1821–1835* (New York, 1936), 155.
    6. Henry H. Sibley of Minnesota.
    7. George R. Powel of Rogersville.

From Reuel Birdwell[1]

Cannon's Store Sevier Co. Ten
February 26th 1860

Hon Andrew Johnson. U, S, S
    Washington City D: C
        Dear Sir—Inclosed I send you $6—to pay for the Congres-
sional Globe & Appendix— You must excuse me for not sending it

sooner. I am greatly obliged to you for sending it and so promptly replying to my request[.]

The opposition seem to swallow Pennington very well Since it is said he paid Henry Clay's debts,[2] that I suppose was started to sugar-coat. the conduct of the opp in Congress who voted for him. We are looking with anxiety to the time of the Charleston Convention and are hoping that nomination will fall upon you. The opposition are in hopes it will fall upon Douglass so that their prospects will be better to carry Tenn as they think. Douglass must not get the nomination. If it falls on a Northern man it must be somebody else than Douglass—

Yours Respt   Reuel Birdwell

Cannon's Store   Ten

ALS, DLC-JP2.

1. Reuel Birdwell (b. *c*1818) was a Tennessee-born physician with personal and real property valued at $20,000. 1860 Census, Tenn., Sevier, 11.
2. Efforts to find evidence to support this rumor have proved unsuccessful.

From Kenton (Del.) Democratic Club

February 26, 1860, Kenton, Del.; ALS, DLC-JP2.

John P. Hickey, secretary, having been taught "in the School room to try to emulate the Example of Andrew, Johnson, of Tennessee, My respected preceptor having been a decided friend evidently of yours," requests copies of the Homestead and other speeches, as well as a "short history of your life." Envelope endorsement reads: "Homestead bill & Speeches to be Sent/Speech have been Sent—the other facts have not—Attended to."

From William G. Swan[1]

Knoxville Feby 27 1860

Private

Hon Andrew Johnson.

My dear Sir

You have already heard of the accusation, so far in the shape only of a public rumour against the Newman's. Taz. has gone to Washington and Cro. Ramsey[2] fears will deceive the Pension Commissioner. He Ramsey has asked me to write to you and say as I can that the evidences in Ramsey's possession in my judgment make a clear and unquestionable case of wrong doing.[3]

The Newmans are endeavoring to create the impression that the

hue and cry has been originated by A. R. Crozier & Spence,[4] and
under this pretence they seek shelter.

Can you not privately advise the Commis.

Yours truly   Wm G. Swan

ALS, DLC-JP2.

1. William G. Swan, a Knoxville lawyer. See *Johnson Papers*, II, 214n.
2. John Crozier Ramsey, the district attorney.
3. Despite early differences in party affiliation, William G. Swan, a onetime Whig turned Democrat, enjoyed close ties with the Ramsey family.
Dr. J. G. M. Ramsey, a fierce southern Democrat and father of John Crozier,
regarded Swan as "my personal friend" although "never a favorite political
friend, as I have often voted against him." William B. Hesseltine, ed., *Dr.
J. G. M. Ramsey: Autobiography and Letters* (Nashville, 1954), 101.
4. Arthur R. Crozier, young Ramsey's uncle, and William Spence.

From "Alabama"

Montgom[er]y Ala Feby 29th 1860

Sir

I had hoped that you had ere this abandoned your absured notions
of abolishinning the Western States by opening the doors to the
public Lands for those Northern fanantics by your wild Scheme of
Giving to Evy one of them a quarter section of Land by moving to
it[.] Now Sir dont you know that there are thousands of the help-
erits[1] who are only waiting the Consummation of your darling object
to be sent off to the West to Locate on the best Land, in the Terri-
torie[s] for the benefit of some Northern Aid Society[.] dont you
know that Evy foot of Land this rabble will take up by your help
will in a few years belong to the rich men of the North. if you do not
it is because you have not thought about it[.] so sure as the homestead bill passes & becomes a law so sure will the rich men of the
North own Evy foot of Land that is squandered by your bill— But
thanks to providence we have a President that knows his duty &
will use his veto—when Ever such a bill passes[.] Now Sir I see that
you are ambitious of doing Something that will brng your name before the world as of having done something to be Spoken of hereafter. If that is what you are up to I will suggest something that will
be remembered & will be appreciated by the whole American
people[.]

What I would suggest is this, That you Introduce and pass a
resol. that hereafter that Evy person Elected to any office of honor
or profit shall take and subscribe to an Oath to surport the Constitution of the United States *as Construed by the Supreme Court of the
United States*[.] Unless this is done there will always be a difficulty
in Constr[u]ing that instrument. One Senator will get up and make

a Speach and Give *his* Construction of the Constitution— Another will Get up and Give his Construction of the *same* and another will do likewise so you see unless the Constitution is made a fixed fact you had as well have none[.]

Let the Supreme Court say what the Constitution is and then you all swear to surport it[.] If you do this—peace and harmony will hereafter preval throughout o[u]r beloved Country— pass such a resol[ut]ion and your name will shine high above that of others who have tried for years for notariety.

Abandon your Homested humbug and Mount a Charger that will carry you through all the difficulties that have or may hapen to your or our Country[.] Let all swear to Surport the Constitution as Interpretd by the Supme Court and there will be no Conflict hereafter as to the Mean[in]g of that Instrument[.]

Pray for Wisdom to direct you in all your undertakings— if you will I am Certain your prayers will avail much[.]

Respectfully   Alabama[2]

ALS, DLC-JP2.

1. "Helperites" was a term of abuse applied to those who agreed with the views of Hinton R. Helper (1829–1909), the North Carolinian whose *Impending Crisis of the South* had appeared in 1856. Helper's thesis that the backwardness of the South resulted from Negro slavery and his warning that the system might be overthrown by a slave rebellion enraged southerners, who furiously attacked and condemned it. The *Impending Crisis* was widely read in the North; in 1860 an additional one hundred thousand copies were printed as a Republican campaign document. Hugh C. Bailey, *Hinton Rowan Helper, Abolitionist-Racist* (Tuscaloosa, Alabama [1965]), *passim.*

2. Johnson's endorsement reads: "From Some one who Signs himself Alabama— To be preserved—."

From Wyndham Robertson[1]

Washington 29th. Feb. 1860

Hon Andrew Johnson
My Dear Sir;

I shall have more telegraphic matter than usual to despatch to our paper to day, and beg that you will excues [*sic*] the liberty which I take in asking the loan of $10 until I can hear from New York.[2] I am somewhat excused by the fact that you have in the "Daily News" a zealous supporter.   Yours with great Regard

Wyndham Robertson
N. Y. Daily News

ALS, DLC-JP2.

1. No information has been discovered concerning the whereabouts of Wyndham Robertson, Jr., in the later 1850's. A son of former Governor Robertson of Virginia, he was at one time in Memphis before moving to

New Orleans, where he hoped to establish a Democratic newspaper. While in the Crescent City, he practiced law (1849–53); in 1852 his listing in the city directory was "Recorder's Office." By 1854 he had apparently left New Orleans. Wyndham Robertson, Jr., to Thomas Carter Reynolds, January 21, 1848, April 3, 1849, Misc. MSS., McClung Collection, Knoxville Public Library; *Cohen's New Orleans Directory* (1850), 141; *ibid.* (1852), 195.

2. There is no evidence that Johnson complied with this request, though the fact that it was made raises interesting speculations about the senator's relationships with the working press. See Letter from Wyndham Robertson, February 3, 1860.

From William B. McCamy[1]

Cleveland Tenn March 2nd/60

Hon Andrew Johnson,
Dear Sir.

Shortly my application will come before Congress asking a Pension as Volunteer Comp. I. of 5 Reg. of E Tenn Soldiers during the war with Mexico in 1848. It will have to originate in the House but wish your influence to get a Concurrence in the Senate— Then send it to Brabson[2] because he is from my dist.

The petition will warrant your hearty Concurrance, please see Subscribers & these men have known me at, before & since my enlistment—Certified by three [of] the best practicing Physicians in the Town of Cleveland & some of them have known me from my boyhood. Could [have] gotten a pension when returned from the service—but formerly having bin very stout then young & anxiously hoped to regain health defered the matter but since have bin revisited some ten years since my discharge with the former disease Called the Diarhea with General Debility—by reason of (Change in Climate) that I make my application unscrupulously & ask it because most of my time especially in Sumner [sic], am not able for business. Therefore ask it [as] a wright.

I Could have gotten more names certifying to the facts even two hundred should I have asked it but for Convinience dispensed with so many names, & further those assigned are the right sort of men & doubtless known to you & many of your honorable body[.] Therefore may I not hope for Success knowing that the States have ever bin mindful of the honest Soldier.

I remain very Respetfly &C
W. B. McCamy

N B. please See Col Underwood[3] now Representative in the House from Ga[.] Am personly acquainted with him. also written him on this Subject.

W B. McC

P S. I was born in Greene Co your adopted County son of Alexd McCamy, used to go to your shop with Pa. you then made his Coats[.] he always (though different in politics to us.) voted for Andy—even to the last race here for Governor. Says I why Continue thus to vote[?] my Son says he Andy is the right sort of a man—
He now lives no more, was (the) old man right[?]   go to the record.

W B. McCamy

ALS, DLC-JP2.
1. William B. McCamy (*c*1825–*c*1902), a private in Company "I" of the 5th Tennessee volunteers, was issued a pension under the Act of January 29, 1887, for "chronic diarrhea and back injury," incurred while in service from January to July, 1848. His application of 1860 apparently miscarried; on his declaration of May, 1887, there appears the notation, "no record of any prior application $13. Aug. 5/87." After 1860 he seems to have moved to Texas. William B. McCamy, Mexican War Pension File, RG15, National Archives.
2. Reese B. Brabson (1817–1863), Chattanooga Democrat, was admitted to the bar (1848), served in the state legislature (1851–53), and was now in Congress (1859–61). *BDAC*, 584.
3. John W. H. Underwood (1816–1888) of Georgia was solicitor general of the state's western judicial circuit (1843–47), member of the General Assembly (1857–59), and currently a Democratic congressman (1859–61). A brigade inspector in the Confederate army, he was subsequently judge of the superior court of Georgia (1867–69, 1873–82) and a member of the first tariff commission (1884). *Ibid.*, 1739.

From J. G. M. Ramsey

March 2, 1860, Knoxville; ALS, DLC-JP2.

Urges retention of son, John Crozier Ramsey, as district attorney: "*Official fidelity* will hardly be considered cause for removal— This is all that can be made out of his *vigilance* in preventing pension claims fraudulently obtained against the United States from continueing to be paid." [An allusion to young Ramsey's controversy with the Newman brothers.]

From Sam Milligan

At Home Sunday Evening [Greeneville]
March 4. 1860

Private

Dear Governor,
    This is the fourth of March— I wonder what the 4th of March 1861 will develop! I hope it will witness your inauguration as president of the United States!! But about that no one can possibly foretell. I think your prospects are brightening. Douglass is not making any head-way with the masses in the South. Thousands of them could not even in Tennessee be induced to support him. He

can not, I fear, if nominated carry Tennessee. But his influence in the Convention will be very powerful, and your friends have nothing to loose by keeping silent at present as to him. The North West, I believe with a little management can be induced to come to your support after they fail to get Douglass, and in my opinion that is the game to play. Could we secure the North West, for any Southern man, the whole South would wheel into line, and secure his nomination.

But you understand all this better than I do, and I will not waste paper in refering to it. What I wanted to say however is this: I have to day, for in deed I have had no other time, collected up a great many extracts of your speeches, messages &c &c—which I had a thought of throwing together in pamphlet form, and sending one to each delagate throughout the Union to the Charleston Convention.

I will take the materials with me round on the Circuit, and devote all the leisure time I may have to its preparation. I have no time to devote to such things, only as I steal it from my daily labor, and I have not money enough to print it deacently when I get it done, but this matter I have arranged.

I design using the extracts I once before grouped together, together with such others as I can gather up—[1]

I want you, if you please to send me, a copy of your resolution introduced into the Senate last year in relation to the expenditures,[2] together with such others extracts as you think will be useful to me— I might possibly find it but I have to go away in the morning before day to the Carter Court, and will not be back for 3 weeks, and really can not, I fear in time, get it up.

I think a point made on the subject of extravegance, just at this time, especially contrasted with the old public functionary's administration, and Judge Douglass' plundering propensities[3] would tell. I can use it successfully in connection with some extracts, which I have gotton from your message of 1853[.][4]

Send me all you gather up, and my wife will promptly forward them to me— I want to have it finished by the termination of the Blountville Court— If you can get a list of the delegates to the Convention send me that also. The paper will not hurt you I assure you that.

Our county election came off yesterday, and has resulted as follows—as far as heard from—M. L. Patterson elected Clerk of the Circuit Court—E W Headerick[5] County court clerk—James Davis[6] —Know Nothing Tax Collector—and James Bannon[7] or James Reeves[8] Sheriff— I have herd from all the County but three precincts—Smith's Biggs' and Warrensburg—and Reeves is 54 votes a head— I think he is elected. William McClelland[9] is defeated pretty badly— I am glad of that— Mercer[10] elected Trustee without opposition.

Dont fail send the resolution before mentioned—

You will see I signed a petition to you and Nicholson for the appointment of A. G. Graham Treasurer—[11] You know him as well as I do, and he has so recently supported me for Atto General I could not well avoid it, and at the same time knowing it would do no harm—   Yours truly   Sam Milligan—
Gov Johnson
U. S. Senate Washingto[n] City D C

ALS, DLC-JP2.

1. There is no evidence that Milligan ever carried through on this project.

2. On January 4, 1859, Johnson submitted a resolution calling for an investigation of departmental expenditures by the committee on finance, with a view to reporting a bill which would reduce expenditures "to an honest, rigid, economical administration." See Remarks on Retrenchment, January 4, 1859.

3. Although Douglas was relatively innocent of the more flagrant abuses of governmental extravagance during the Buchanan years, Milligan probably refers to the Illinois senator's earlier pursuit of federal subsidies in the form of land grants for the construction of not one, but three, railroads to the Pacific and other internal improvements, as well as to the "plundering propensities" of many Douglas supporters who took great advantage of whatever patronage came their way. For Johnson's outspoken view of Douglas, see Letter to David T. Patterson, April 4, 1852, *Johnson Papers*, II, 30–31. See also Nevins, *Ordeal of the Union*, II, 6–11, 87, 201–2.

4. Presumably Milligan had drawn his extracts, if they dealt with the general problem of government expenditures, from Johnson's comments on state support of internal improvements. Though he endorsed "a well regulated system of internal improvements," Johnson had warned that it should "not result in great loss and useless expenditure of the people's substance." *Johnson Papers*, II, 190.

5. E. W. Headrick (b. c1804) was clerk of the Greene County court for sixteen years (1852–68). *Goodspeed's East Tennessee*, 890; 1860 Census, Tenn., Greene, 90.

6. James Davis (b. c1814) was a Greene County farmer with $4,000 real and $1,000 personal property. *Ibid.*, 123.

7. Probably James Brannon. *Johnson Papers*, II, 66n.

8. James G. Reeves (b. c1824) was successful in his race for sheriff of Greene County (1860–66) and later served as a delegate to the Union meeting in Greeneville, June 17, 1861. 1860 Census, Tenn., Greene, 100; *Goodspeed's East Tennessee*, 890; Oliver P. Temple, *East Tennessee and the Civil War* (Cincinnati, 1891), 572.

9. William D. McLelland (b. c1822), a Greeneville tailor and later a farmer, was a delegate to the Union meetings in Knoxville and Greeneville, May and June, 1861. *Ibid.*; 1850 Census, Tenn., Greene, 278; 1860 Census, Tenn., Greene, 98.

10. Elbert F. Mercer (c1808–1887), farmer and carpenter, had been a deputy sheriff of Blount County and was serving as a trustee of Greene County (1858–68). *Ibid.*, 130; *Goodspeed's East Tennessee*, 890, 1253–54.

11. Graham, Jonesboro editor and strong Johnson supporter, did not get the appointment.

From William B. Franklin

Office U. S. Capitol Extension,
Washington, March 5th, 1860.

Sir:

I have the honor to acknowledge the receipt of your letter of the
1st instant, and submit herewith a statement of the estimated annual cost of fuel and oil and repairs for heating and ventilating the
North Wing of the Capitol, and the cost of lighting with gas[.]

The gas now used in the North Wing of the Capitol is paid for
by the Superintendent of Public Buildings and Grounds from the
appropriation for "lighting the Capitol, President's House, Capitol
grounds, Pennsylvania avenue, the Mall, and Georgetown," and is
therefore not a charge against the appropriation for the contingent
fund of the Senate. I have, however, included it in the estimate,
which is herewith enclosed.   Very respectfully,
                                                     Your obdt. servt.
                                                     W B. Franklin
                                          Capt of Topl. Engrs. in charge.

Hon. Andrew Johnson,
Chr. Com. to audit & control
contingent expenses of Senate.

Estimate of annual cost of maintenance of the gas, heating and ventilating,
            and water apparatus, North Wing, U. S. Capitol.

2,250,000 feet of gas, at $3.50 per 1,000 feet	7,875.00
800 tons of coal, at $5.00 per ton	4,000.00
65 cords of pine wood for kindling, at $4.00 per cord	260.00
70 gallons of best sperm oil, at $1.70 per gallon	119.00
500 pounds of cotton waste, at 16 cts per lb	80.00
300 sheets of emory cloth at 1½ cts. per sheet	4.50
48 papers of tripoli,[1] at 10 cts. per paper.	4.80
48 lbs. of brown soap, at 8 cts. per pound	3.84
12 brooms, at 37½ cts.	4.50
50 lbs. hemp packing, at 16 cts. per lb.	8.00
100 lbs. rubber packing at 60 cts. per lb.	60.00
Grate bars	200.00
Red and white lead, 10 cts. per lb.	25.00
6 shovels, at $1.00 each	6.00
Small articles, oil cans, feeders, sponges, leather bands, &c.	50.00
Repairs of gas and water pipes and fixtures which cannot be made by the permanent employe's [sic], such as repairs of water closets and plumbing	250.00

                                                   $12,950.64

Copy, Architect's Office, U. S. Capitol, Let. Bk. 9, pp. 1749–50.

1. Tripoli is a fine dustlike silica used chiefly as an abrasive for buffing
and polishing. *Encyclopaedia Britannica* (1971), XXII, 244.

From Robert Johnson

Nashville March 6th/60

Dear Father

We have been working for the last few days and I have neglected to some extent my other business in attending closely to the business before our house, for there are several important propositions pending, that have been postponed until now, in order that they might be rushed through at the close of the session, which I do not care about seeing done, as I am fully satisfied in my own mind that enough has already been done to destroy the little confidence that the people may have had in the Legislatures, without being guilty of the folly of rendering it odious—

The indebtedness of the people will be increased four per cent by the enactment into a law of the Bill to "amend the usury laws, and establish a conventional rate of Interest".[1] And in addition the country will be flooded with a worthless paper currency by the six Manufacturing Bank concerns that have been chartered[2]—but let all these things go— my skirts are clean and it cannot be said that I had any hand in it— my record is clean and I wash my hands of the whole affair— We will adjourn about Monday week—

Taz W. Newman has returned and was to-day re-elected Speaker of the Senate—[3] all I believe agree in saying that they consider him innocent of the charges preferred against him—

From all I can gather, the opinion I expressed to you directly after the state convention, is more fully confirmed, in regard to your nomination at Charleston, and I am well satisfied that the nomination can be effected, if properly managed— Newman seems very confident of your nomination and Avery[4] writes the Same thing to Genl Lea[5] of Haywood— if you will place your claims in the hands of the proper man at Charleston, all will work out right in my Judgment[.]

The opinion seems very prevalent here that that will be the result of the convention:

I have been expecting to hear from you on the subject, but as yet have received nothing— I would like very much to hear from you in full in regard thereto— If you need me, or my services at any time, command me, and I will cheerfully perform any duty assigned me— If I can do any good by going to Washington before the conventions assembles let me know and I will go— I will attend the convention and perhaps it would be well enough for me to know fully your

views— write in full— Payne[6] will attend the convention if you think
he could be of any service &c.

Nothing new   Your Son   R. Johnson

ALS, DLC-JP2.

    1. *Tenn. Acts*, 1859–60, Ch. XLI.

    2. Probably a reference to the incorporation of the banks of Clarksville,
Middle Tennessee (Lebanon), Frankland (Knoxville), Merchants' and Me-
chanics' (Memphis) and an extension of the Union and Planters' banks. Bills
chartering these establishments had all passed the house on March 1. *Tenn.
House Journal*, 1859–60, pp. 857, 860; *Tenn. Acts*, 1860, Chs. CVI, CVII,
CVIII.

    3. See Letter from Robert Johnson, February 22, 1860, note 4.

    4. William T. Avery (1819–1880), Tennessee lawyer and member of
the state legislature (1843–45), was at this time a Democratic congressman
from West Tennessee (1857–61). He later served as a Confederate officer
and as clerk of the Shelby County criminal court (1870–74). *BDAC*, 497.

    5. Benjamin J. Lea (1833–1894) was a lawyer who represented Hay-
wood County in the legislature (1859–61). Although he had moved to Shelby
County prior to the special session of 1861, Lea was allowed to retain his
seat. During the war he was a Confederate colonel. Robison Biog. Data;
Goodspeed's Haywood, 823; *Tenn. House Journal*, 1861, extra session, 3–4.

    6. Robert G. Payne was not a delegate. Campbell, *Tenn. Attitudes*, 237.

From William G. Swan

Knoxville March 6 1860

Hon Andrew Johnson
    My dear Sir

    Would you believe it that the Newmans are represented here
and at Nashville as saying that yourself and Mr. Nicholson have declared in Washington that if five or even three respectable men in
East Tennessee should ask the removal of Ramsey from the office of
District Attorney it would at once be done. Of course I give no credence to the rumor and only mention it to advise you that some movement may be on foot to replace him. In the affairs of the Newmans
he has discharged his whole duty—is right in everything and will
be fully sustained when an exposé is made as will be done in due
time. The Commissioner of Pensions[1] has acted very badly somehow or other in this business and one of the consequences will be
serious injury to the Democratic Party. I understand from the documentary and other proofs in Ramsey's possession whereof I speak
that no prosecution may be instituted by the Commissioner, yet as
Newman (Ex Speaker) has assailed Ramsey all the facts must
come out. If I did not know that Ramsey has done right in this whole
business I would not say so. I will not undertake to detail all the

facts to you. See to it that he is not assailed without an opportunity for a hearing and you will do no wrong.[2]

Yours Truly   Wm. G. Swan

ALS, DLC-JP2.

1. George C. Whiting (1816–1867) of Virginia began his career as clerk in the general land office (1838), advanced to chief clerk, and was currently commissioner of pensions (1857–61). Later he served as an adviser and assistant to the secretary of the interior. Lanman, *Biographical Annals*, 461.

2. For the Newman-Ramsey affair, see Letter from Robert Johnson, February 22, 1860.

From John L. Dawson[1]

Private   Brownsville March 7/60

My Dear Govenor

I did not succeede in having a resolution passed at Reading[2] for the Homestead Bill[.] The President is opposed to the measure, opposed my nomination for Govenor on account of my advocacy of & identity with the Same.— Again you unfortunately spoke to David Lynch[3] of Pittsburg so he said to bring it before the Convention— This was error Lynch being the Confidential *man* of the President— He *notified* me that it should not be endorsed.

I withdrew my name without a ballot, having previously been elected a delegate at large to the Charleston Convention. I will see you in Washington on my way South[.]

Your friend   John L. Dawson

Hon Andrew Johnston
Washington D. C.

ALS, DLC-JP2.

1. See *Johnson Papers*, II, 188n.

2. The Pennsylvania state Democratic convention was held at Reading, March 1, 1860. New York *Times*, March 2, 1860.

3. Johnson had committed a political blunder in trying to work through David Lynch, a minor politico and ardent Buchanan supporter from the early 1820's. Lynch had earlier served as Pittsburgh postmaster until removed by Tyler for misappropriation of government funds. An inept and untrustworthy public servant, thoroughly discredited by this time, he was the recipient of Buchanan's private charity rather than being rewarded with an important post after the election of 1856. Klein, *James Buchanan*, 281, *passim*.

From Tazewell W. Newman

Nashville   March 8th, 1860

Hon Andrew Johnson
Washington City D. C.

My Dear Sir   I reached home in Safety and have published all the evidence I had:[1] which in the opinion of evry one fixes the crime of Slander on Ramsey—and disgraces him for ever in the State—

The Senate on yesterday morning reelected me Speaker of the Senate which you will See in the Legislat[i]ve reports in the *Union*: and allow me again and again to thank you for your intrest in this matter— and shall be ever remembered—so by me[.]

My opinon now is that Tenessee will go into the Convention with a fixed determination to Stand by their recomendation through— "*Thick and Thin*"[.] And my advise to the deligates has been to enter into no entangling alliances with any one of any of the factions —either Administrative or Anti Administrative—Douglass or Anti Doglass Lecompton or Anti Lecompton—Popular Sovergnity or Anti *Popular Sovrignety*[.] Keep clean hands Should be the Watchword of evry Tennessee in the Coming Convention[.] Such will in my opinion will be their action[.]

We will adjourn on the 19th day of this month with perfect harmony in our party—evry man willing to Stand by the Nominee[.] No other news[.]

Your Friend   Taz. W. Newman

ALS, DLC-JP2.

1. The evidence here referred to was submitted to the press as a refutation of charges by J. C. Ramsey that James and Tazewell Newman, as pension agents, had defrauded the government on claims. Published in the Nashville *Union and American*, March 6, 1860, the evidence included Taz Newman's correspondence with the commissioner of pensions, February 27, 28, 1860; Ramsey's correspondence with the commissioner, February 10, 28, 1860; and James Newman's letter of March 2, 1860. From the date this refutation appeared until June 8, the *Union* was publishing notices to the public from one or the other of the parties in the dispute.

From James W. Newman

Knoxville Tennessee
March 9th, 1860

Hon A Johnson:
   Sir:
      Enclosed I send you a communication for the Commissioner of Pensions[.][1] You will greatly oblidge me by seeing that my requests are attend to. I have searched in vain among my own papers for evidences of what I request therein! I intend to make a full exposition of the *scoundrelism* of Gen Ramsey in this affair. I am particularly anxious to get a copy of my letter to the Comsr of Pensions in 1853 showing that I demanded the investigation you had.

In haste.   Very Respectfully
                                   James W. Newman.

[Endorsement]
I have enclosed the letter of Mr Newman to the Commissioner and

the request he makes of me— It is for you [to] determine as to the propriety of complying with his letter— I will not ask any thing on the part of the Com. which is not in strict Conformity with the rules of the office and do not [know] whether M Newmans request is or not—and have therefore made no request, Know[in]g that the Commissioner will do whatever is right in [the] premises—

        With much respect Andrew Johnson

Please return this letter—[2]

ALS, DLC-JP2.

1. Newman's letter to the commissioner was dated March 9. In his reply of March 28, the commissioner indicated that he was unable to find a letter from Newman dated 1853 but sent a copy of one "addressed by you for Taze. W. Newman" dated April 27, 1854. This correspondence, along with a letter of John Crozier Ramsey to the commissioner, December 2, 1853, is found in James Newman's card to the public printed in the Nashville *Union and American*, April 20, 1860. Apparently lost, Newman's 1853 letter did not appear in the printed correspondence.

2. On March 30, Pension Commissioner Whiting returned this March 9 letter to Johnson, in "compliance with your request. . . . I presume you did not want me to address you officially on the subject & as his other letter was addressed directly to me I have replied directly to him, but that you may see what I have said I send you herewith my answer, which when you have read, please seal & drop it in your mail. Have I done right?" Johnson Papers, LC.

From Hu Douglas[1]

               Nashville March 11th 1860

Private

Hon Andrew Johnson
Washington City
 Dear Sir

I have just returned from the North. It was my intention to have written you while there, prevented by the pressure of my business. I find a good feeling there towards you, of course among the Democrats. All however want a Northern Man. I took great pains to say to them that this was the time for a Southern Conservative, and that in you they had that man and more of the elements of success than any other that I knew. I took pains to Call them to your Course and to assure them that in a business view it was all important to calm the South. On my return here, I do not find our folks right[.] I have Conversed with some of the leaders and I learn that they are for giving you a Complimentary vote, at Charleston but all expect to have to go over to Dickinson of N.Y[.][2] They are down upon Douglas, and really not for you only through fear. from all I can learn I think that our Delegation to Charleston is an unfortunate Selection. I hope I am in error.

We have some other men aspiring that were turned down and I think disappointment renders them Cool, but afraid to show it.

I wish much that you had some men to be of the right stamp at the right time. You Should have Some to go from Washington to Charleston and to take up the matter after the different parties & Clicks have failed. You may rely upon Douglas as an important man, he should be treated kindly by us. I do not think he can get the nomination, but I would be glad to have a good feeling among your friends with the *house of Douglas.* There is a division in Va with Wise & Hunter, neither of whom can go through, in Ky between Guthrie[3] & Breckenridge. They will not be able to pass. No one from Louisiana Georgia South Carolina or Mississippi will pass[.] all of these will be opposed to Douglas. If Houston of Texas is held back, I think you ought to start with them Arkansas Missouri &C &C[.]

I have written this in a great hurry, take any Suggestions for what they are worth. I am much engaged with a large stock of guns. If I can Cut the stock down well, will go to Charleston, as much to watch & see the Course of yr friends from here as any thing else. talk not to me of NY Politicians, & tricksters. We have them here that are equal to any to be found any where.

If I could not go as a delegate & carry out my wishes I would not go at all, but they are afraid to oppose you altho at heart against you. I have *ever been your personal friend* but *almost* always *politically opposed* to you, and have *never been afraid to avow myself*[.] Watch the movements & check mate them if you can, you have always Succeeded and you have always had Some trouble with yr friends.

If you have time & any suggestions &C Command me.

Yrs Very Truly
Hu Douglas

oh the Democratic
Legislature of Ten [is] for
Banks Banks Banks[4]

ALS, DLC-JP2.

1. Hu Douglas, formerly of Greeneville and one of Johnson's early friends, was now a Nashville merchant. See *Johnson Papers,* I, 21n.

2. Daniel S. Dickinson (1800–1866), a Conservative Democrat of New York, was an unsuccessful aspirant for the presidential nomination at Charleston and was also considered for the vice-presidential nomination on the Union ticket in 1864. An attorney, he served as state senator (1837–40), U. S. senator (1845–51), state attorney general (1861–64), and attorney general for the southern district of New York (1865–66). *DAB,* V, 294–95.

3. James Guthrie (1792–1869), Kentucky lawyer, politician, and capitalist, had been a state legislator (1827–40) and secretary of the treasury (1853–57); subsequently he was a member of the Washington Peace Convention of 1861 and Democratic senator (1865–68). A favorite-son candi-

date at Charleston in 1860, Guthrie later adhered to the Union. *BDAC*, 983–84; *DAB*, VIII, 60–62.

4. On the subject of banks and banking, currently occupying much of the legislature's time, the Democrats remained sharply divided between the "softs" and "hards," between Bank Democrats and Anti-Bank Democrats. Nineteen banking bills were introduced and some reforms enacted, but, while the legislature was chartering additional banks, Governor Harris failed to get party support for his recommendation to liquidate the state bank. As one contemporary remarked on March 26, 1860, at the close of the session, "Many of the democratic members came here as hard as mettle on the subject of banks, and they have passed more bank charters than any previous body." McGavock, *Pen and Sword*, 563; White, *Messages*, V, 55, 139–40.

From J. H. C. Basham[1]

[Union City]   March 12th 1860

Mr Johnson   Sir   your speech came to hand in due time[.] it was just what I would have anticipated[.] I am fifty odd years of age[.] ever since I made myself known to you I have been cutting and splitting railes to repair my little homested a pleasing idear to you and I am in hopes your policy will place every poore man in the United States in the same independant situation[.] they then will be independant sovregns[.] a few words in self defence[.] Mr. Seward says thare is and irrepressible conflict between Slave labor and free labor[.] well I will suppose the idear to be correct for the sake of argument as false as it is— The first question is whare will that conflict commence[?] of course between the free Labour and the Slave labour of the Slave States[.] it is a matter that dont concern the free States[.] they are attending to the business of the non Slaveholders of the Slave States[.] well Sir we are competent and capeable of attending to our own business and we would thank them if they would attend to their own which is lying negro Stealing and murder in the first degree[.] Secondly if African Slave labor is a Sin and a National Curse whare should we expect the first complaint to arrise[?] certainly from the non Slave holders of the Slave States[.] if the non slave holders of the Slave States dont believe that african Slavery is a Sin and a National Curse has any man in the North any right to think So[?] we are certainly the best judges[.] all the offices of this County has been filled by non Slaveholders for the last thirty years[.] the actions of the Slave holders speaks just this much to me[.] we have the benefit of Slave labour and the non Slave holders must have the benefit of Office[.] I must confess that i have heard som murmering from the non Slave holder respecting the Slaveholder[.] if a non Slave holder helps a rich Slave holder to rool [roll] logs or raise a house and the Slave holder faile to Send him two or three hands in the place of one you frequently hear the non Slave holder complaine[.] we are certainly the last people that Should complain[.] Sir I have just examined the controversy[2] between Judge Douglass and Judge Black and Mr. Gwinn thrown in to leg for Judge Black[.] well Sir it reminds me of a debate between three brothers[.] they run it into a quarrel and was in the act of fighting two or three times[.] two of the Brothers contended that New Orleans was in the State of New orleans and the third Brother Swore that it was in the State of Mississippi[.] it is a one Sided affair a hide and hoop [whoop] play or game[.] Sir when you go to deliver a Speech why dont you do as Others hide yourself in Some magazene[?] you are a bold man[.] you come it face to face and why because you desire no advantage of your opponent[.] I am well aware what excuse Mr Douglass would make[.] he would Say that Colonel Paton[3] and Old Parson Brownlow[4] had been hid in the Mammoth of Kentucky for the last fifteen or twenty years and by so doing had no political Sins to answer for the Same length of time that the hideing business was a law of self-preservation but unfortunately for them John Bell has as many political Sins to answer for as any other man in these United States[.]

The fact is by compromeses the Goverment got So fare off from the constitution it was a hard matter to get back at one Step[.] the Democratice Party was Verry Sanguin to return to the Old Stamping ground which caused them to over look one clause in Mr. Douglasses Teretorial Bill[.] by pinning their faith to the coat tail of Mr. Douglass they all in one perticular fell into the pit[.] they were Supporting a Bill with one bad feature[.] the opposite Party was in-favour of a compromise that was unconstitutional in every Sense of the word[.] the idear of a compromise is and objection to the Constitution[.] it would take just five compromises by congress to compromise the Constitution out of existance[.] Mr. Clay was called the great American Compromiser[.] that was just as much as to Say That Mr. Clay was the greatest enemy that the constitution ever had in America[.] If that man ever did introduce a const[i]tutional measure I never had the knowledge to know it— I will illustrate Mr. Douglasses position[.] When the deposits was in that old Eurepeeian united States Bank the Deposits was a long way from home[.] well it took a long Stride to bring them back to their proper place[.] the first Step the Democratice Party made was to the State Banks[.] the attributes thare was a perfect failure and just So with Mr. Douglasses Teritorial Bill[.] The Second Step the Democratic Party made they brought the Deposits home and put the money into the Goverment Safe which is the indepenant Treasury of these United States[.] It just requires one more Step by the Democratice Party to bring back the Teritorial Bill to the Constitution of these United States

and then the Bill will work just like the Independant Treasury and
that works just like a charme[.] we must judge the Tree by its
fruit[.] the Constitution of the United States is the best and purest
Tree that ever has been produced[.] look at the fruit[.] Mr. Doug-
[las'] Bill has produced fruit of the Verry worst kind[.] So did the
State Banks[.] The priviledges and powers that the Constitution
grants to the Sovereign States Mr. Douglass applyes to a Teritory[.]
it appears to me that Mr. Douglass cannot discover the great difference of a Teritorial Legislature which is a law makeing power by
permission[.] Mr. Douglass Says it is their duty to ask congress
permision to elect delegates to a convention to frame a constitution
and all preparatory means to become and indepenant Sovregn
power which is and organised State[.] right whare the guardianship
cease[s] the Sovregn power takes holt and the Mother of Sovregn
attributes comes into existance[.] I ask whare did Mr. Douglass get
the attribute or in other words the baby before the mother was in
existance[.] the appeal to the Supreme Court is milk to feed the baby
with[.] he is trying to get congress to help him to find a wet nurse
and means to cloath his pet baby[.] The fact is the Baby had no
mother at the time Mr. Douglass forced it into existance[.] well I
will illustrate[.] I once had a five Dollar Bill handed to me on The
Owl Creek Bank of Ky, thare was no such Bank in existance[.] it
was not genuine and of course could not be a counterfeit[.] well
what was it[?] it was just like Mr. Douglasses attribute or baby[.]
if Mr. Douglass will name his baby that will enable me to get a
name for the Bill[.] thare is a great difference in a Legislature Legislating for the protection of Slave property in the Teritory and the
great priviledge of Legislating that property into a Teritory and
forceing it Out[.] Congress their guardean has not the power to do
it[.] It is out of the power of the Legislatures of the States to do it
which is proof that it belongs to the people[.] the attributes they all
combined which is the Sovergn power of the State not the Sovregn
power of a Teritory as Mr. Douglass Suposes[.] The power that Mr.
Douglass gives to a Teritorial Legislature on the Slave question
makes that Legislature the Supreme Law makeing power in the
United States and no man can deny it[.] Mr. Douglass Says the
President in his Lecomton Mesage Said Slavery went into Kansas
by Virtue of the Constitution and that made Kansas a Slave State
as much So as any other Slave State[.] he Says the Constitution is
silent on the Subject[.] the President could Say Silence gives consent[5] in his Nebraska mesage[.] he could Say Slavery did not go
into that Teritory by Virtue of the Constitution because Silence
gives consent[.][6] What is the Sovregn power of the Black Republican Party[?] Lying negro Stealing and murder in the first degree[.]

what are its attributes[?] Whigism Nonothin[g]ism and Opposi-
tionism[.] and what Spirit will that Party be governed by in the
canvass of 1860[?] the Spirit of Self love and why[?] the Apostle
Paul Says Self love is the damning Sin of the world[.] What I have
to Say in conclusion is that the Deligates from Tennessee to the
Charlston Convention Should be well instructed on these important
points which will enable the Convention to render unto Cezar the
things that belong to Cezar and unto God the things the [*sic*] belong
to God[.]

J. H. C. Basham

ALS, DLC-JP2.

1. Possibly Joseph Basham (b. *c*1809), an Obion County farmer. 1850
Census, Tenn., Obion, 704.

2. In an attempt to answer the critics of popular sovereignty, Stephen A.
Douglas published in *Harper's Magazine*, September, 1859, an article entitled "Popular Sovereignty in the Territories—the Dividing Line between
Federal and Local Authority." Coming as it did from the pen of a leading
politician, the article created something of a sensation and resulted in
Buchanan's selecting his attorney general, Jeremiah S. Black, to reply.
Black's answer, originally published in the Washington *Constitution*, led
to a war of words and pamphlets between Douglas and Black. In a speech
at Grassy Valley, California, during the summer of 1859, William Gwin,
chairman of the Senate Democratic caucus, took Douglas to task for his
stand, as revealed in the Freeport Doctrine, on slavery in the territories and
asserted that the Illinois senator's loss of the chairmanship of the territorial
committee after eleven years was evidence of the party's rejection of his
position. Douglas' reply, in a letter to the San Francisco *National*, later published as a pamphlet, and Gwin's answer kept the controversy alive during
the fall of 1859, further dividing the already troubled Democratic party.
"To the Editors of the San Francisco *National* [August 16, 1859]," Robert W.
Johannsen, ed., *The Letters of Stephen A. Douglas* (Urbana, 1961), 453–
66; New York *Times*, November 5, 1859; Milton, *Eve of Conflict*, 363,
386–90.

3. Samuel K. N. Patton (b. *c*1816), a Washington County Unionist and
member of the legislature (1859–61), was later colonel of the 8th Tennessee
cavalry, U. S. A. *Tennesseans in the Civil War*, I, 340; Robison Biog. Data.

4. William G. Brownlow, editor of the Knoxville *Whig*. See *Johnson
Papers*, I, 130n.

5. An expression from Goldsmith, *The Goodnatur'd Man*, Act III.

6. In his special message of February 2, 1858, requesting congressional
approval of the Lecompton Constitution, Buchanan alluded to the Dred Scott
decision and observed that under the Constitution "Kansas is . . . at this
moment as much a slave State as Georgia or South Carolina." Though
Douglas discussed the constitutional issues, both in the Senate and in his
Harper's article, he did not say specifically that "the Constitution is silent
on the Subject." Nor is it possible to identify a "Nebraska message," though
both Buchanan's first and second annual messages gave considerable attention
to the Kansas question. Richardson, *Messages*, V, 479.

To George W. Jones, Fayetteville

Washington City   Mar 13th 1860

Friend Jones

I have recieved and just read your historic account of the Compromise of 1850 as published in the Lincoln Journal—[1] It is concise, clear and conclusive, the most so of any explanation I have ever read on the Subject— You will please accept my thanks for the Copy you have Sent me and think I shall make good use of it in a short time—[2] You no doubt have Seen Davise's & Browns resolutions[3] in reference to the power of Congress over the Subject of Slavery in the Territories and the passage of a Slavry Coad &c[.] Davis is trying to Cut und[e]r Brown but infact is the Same thing— For my own part I can see no good that is to Come out of them at this time, except divission and distruction of the democratice party— As to laying down tenets for the democratic party in the Shape of abstract prnciples or the mere passage of resolutions by the Senate I think is not part of its official duty— If the Senate assumes the prerogative of putting the slav[er]y plank into the democratice platform which is to be adopted at Charleston I do not See any good reason why it should not make a whole and hand it over to the Convention in a complete and perfect forme and save the convention the trouble of perfor[m]i[n]g the work and then go one step farther and nominate the Candidate of the party and make the people take the nominee—without regard to his being acceptable or not— I confess that I am sick and tired of proceedings of this kind—

The whole Senate, both sides I think are aspirants for the presidency at this time and how m[an]y outside the Senat Lord only knows— And in the means employed to be president the interest and will of the people Seems to be the last thing thought of or consulted— Douglas and friends are making a desperate effort and he will go into the Convention stronger than any other one man—
Some here who assume to be posted up in matters of this kind say that he can not be nominated and if nominated cannot be elected, and that he will when he ascertains that fact become magnanimous from necessity and with draw from the Contest and dictate the nomination and leavi[n]g himself a liv[in]g Candidate with some chances of Success in 1864— That he would prefer a course of that kind to Success before the Convention in the spring and defeat before the people in november— If D. Cannot be nominated the nomination will fall upon some Southern man and that Southern man will be the man who can come nearest carrying Douglas' strength and who

is most acceptable to his friends in convention— The man, not the strongest man in the South but the man who can carry the South and is acceptable to the north western and northern democracy is the man in the South who will get the nomination if it falls upon a Southern man— My own opinion is now, that if the convention incorporate some new planks into the platform and the freinds of Douglas find he Cannot be nominated that they will with draw and make an independent nomination and run him upon their own hook—

Jefferson Davis of Miss' is burning up with ambition and is nearer Consumed by an internal heat than any man I ever saw except John Slidell of La— What Jeff will do if he is not nominated *God* only knows— Old Buck seems for the candidates by tu[r]ns, som time for one and then for another and so on— I think he is alwys for the weakest man until he seems to run up and then he is for the next weakest, hoping that they will be strong enough to defeat a nomination and that it will devolve on the convention to remominate him yet he disclaims it all the time—[4]

Seward I am satisfied will now be the nominee of the black republican party, if not the party will be broken up for the great bulk of it is for him— And they intend to make an extraordinary effort to Secure his election— I thought some little time back that they would be driven into the nomination of Som other Candidate but have Cha[n]ged that opinion now—

I hope you will go to the Convention. you can no doubt do much good there and might save the party from taking Some imprudent steps which might prove fatal—[5]

I have never seen the time when you were so much needed in the House of Rep's as at the present time,— I did not sit down to write you a letter but to thank you for the article referred to—

                              I *am your friend*   Andrew Johnson

ALS, PHi.

1. Jones' three-column article, much of it extracted from the *Congressional Globe* and entitled "The Truth of History: The Compromise Measures of 1850—What Were They?" appeared in the Fayetteville *Lincoln Journal*, March 8, 1860. *Cong. Globe,* 31 Cong., 1 Sess, 1463–73.

2. There is no evidence that Johnson used this article in preparing speeches during the ensuing spring.

3. On January 18 Albert G. Brown of Mississippi introduced resolutions on the territories and slavery. Two weeks later, Jefferson Davis offered resolutions similar insofar as the territorial question was concerned, but condemning sharply as a violation of the Constitution "any intermeddling" with the domestic institutions of the states and asserting that Negro slavery "as it exists in the fifteen States of this Union" is an "important portion of their domestic institutions." Brown's resolutions were apparently superceded by Davis's. On March 1 Davis withdrew his resolution, substituting another which retained his statement on the territorial question and slavery. After a number of postponements, the resolution was considered point by point on May 24 and 25, and the entire proposal approved; Johnson, surprisingly

enough in view of these comments, voted in the affirmative each time. *Cong. Globe*, 36 Cong., 1 Sess., 494, 658, 935, 2321–22, 2344–52.

4. For over a year Douglas supporters had attempted to create the impression that Buchanan hoped for a second term—a notion fostered even by the President's friends in an article in the Pittsburgh *Post*, July 19, 1859. Protesting his disinterest, Buchanan lent quiet support to several anti-Douglas candidates, at first backing the southern Unionist Howell Cobb of Georgia; however, when the Georgia Democratic convention refused on March 15 to support Cobb, the President placed his hopes on such men as Vice President Breckinridge, James Guthrie of Kentucky, or Joseph Lane of Oregon. Klein, *James Buchanan*, 340–41.

5. Though he served as president of the state convention in January, Jones was not among those selected to go to Charleston; nor is there any indication that he went as an observer.

From Charles W. Charlton

Knoxville Tennessee   March 15, 1860.

Hon. A. Johnson
Washington,
Dr Sir:

I send by this mail, in envelope, the last issue of the *"Knoxville Register"* that you may see its position *clearly* and *unequivocally* defined. The article signed *"Jackson"* is my own production, written with the hope that I could thus prevail upon him[1] to modify, at least, his views & feelings with reference to your claims to the Presidency. But, as you will discover, it is a *total failure*. I have, *again* and *again*, talked with him, upon this Subject, using every argument, in my power, to set him right. Once, I thought I had succeeded. It is the only paper, I believe, in the State, inimical to your nomination and its course has been so Stubborn and self-willed, that it has aroused my *profoundest Contempt*. Let it go. You do not *need* its support. Nor can it influence the Democracy of this region. The masses, everywhere, are for you, and if the fortunate day should arrive when your name shall be put forward as the nominee of the Charleston Convention, you will witness, throughout this noble State, whose redemption from the thraldom of Know Nothingism, was gloriously brought about by your own great force of character, a universal Shout in your favor.

Your friends are determined to stand by you in the Convention, and I am sanguine in the belief that you will secure the nomination[.]

(*Private*). I learned, a few days ago, through another party, but reliable, that Col. Churchwell[2] had written to a friend in this City that he regarded your chances [as] much more favorable than any one now spoken of. T. W. Newman circulated the same report on his return from Washington, and asserted, boldly, that you were certain of the nomination.

Your Home Sted Bill will injure you some, though, if properly understood, could not fail to do you good among the Masses. Will you do me the favor of giving me a *condensed Statement* of your views upon this subject as I would like to embody them in an article for the Register.[3] Do so, if you please, and that, too, at your earliest convenience.

Very Respectfully   C. W. Charlton

ALS, DLC-JP2.

1. A reference to George W. Bradfield, who purchased the Knoxville *Register* in 1859 and conducted it as a southern-rights organ, supporting first R. M. T. Hunter and then Breckinridge during the campaign. Bradfield particularly disliked the homestead idea and was generally unenthusiastic about "Andy Johnsonism." On March 7 he chaired a district meeting in Clinton at which those attending approved the "upright, independent, and zealous course of the *Register*, as conducted by its present able editor." Nashville *Union and American*, March 20, 1860; Nashville *Republican Banner*, February 29, 1860; White, East Tenn. Journalism, 8.

2. William M. Churchwell.

3. Apparently Charlton wrote the proposed article; the Nashville *Union* of April 8 reprinted from the *Register* a disquisition supporting Johnson and his homestead bill. See Letter from Charles W. Charlton, April 10, 1860.

From John C. Vaughn[1]

Sweet, Water Tenn
15th March 1860

Hon Andrew Johnston
    Dear Sir
        After my respects to you. The democracy of this Section of East Tennessee are becoming verry much dissatisfyed with the Course the Knoxville Register is taken towards you and many of us have determend to cut loose from it. have you saw the last two or three Nos. of that paper. They Ceartainly know or the Editor knows Mr Hunter has no chanse of the nomination at Charleston, and I do think your chanses are very good & are getting better evry day—
        What Course aught we to take towards the Register.[2] Let me hear from you[.]

Yours Very Respectfully   J C Vaughn

Will you be at Charleston the 23d Aprile. I beeing one of the allternates from this district, if the delligates go & I do also would I be admitted to a Seat in the Convention[?][3]

Yours   J C Vaughn

ALS, DLC-JP2.

1. John C. Vaughn (1824–1875), who opened the first hotel in Sweetwater in the 1850's, had served in the Mexican War and was later a Confederate brigadier and speaker of the state senate (1871–73). At this time he

was sheriff of Monroe County (1856–62). Porter, *Tenn. Confed. Mil. Hist.*, 339–41.

2. In April the *Union and American* reprinted from the Cleveland *Banner* a letter in which Vaughn denounced the course of the *Register* and its advocacy of R. M. T. Hunter, condemned the editor's "thrusts and cuts at Gov. Johnson" as "uncalled for," and predicted that the "course of the *Register* will read itself out of the Democratic party." Nashville *Union and American*, April 15, 1860.

3. Vaughn apparently did not go to the Charleston convention; however, he did attend the Baltimore convention and was one of the "seceders." Hesseltine, *Three against Lincoln*, 302.

From William F. Elliott

March 17, 1860, Nashville; ALS, DLC-JP2.

Nashville coachmaker expresses thanks for a "liberal supply of Documents," observing: "I know of no other Senator whom I would approach with such freedom and confidence of receiving attention. *It was done like Andrew Johnson* and in saying this I but express the feeling of fellowship or brotherhood felt towards you by the great body of the Democratic party."

Resolution Concerning Senate Messengers

March 17, 1860

Mr. JOHNSON, of Tennessee. I am instructed by the Committee to Audit and Control the Contingent Expenses of the Senate to offer the following resolution; and I ask the action of the Senate upon it now:

Resolved, That any vacancy now existing, or which shall hereafter occur, in the places of messengers of the Senate, by death, resignation, removal, or otherwise, such vacancy so existing or occurring shall not be filled by the appointment of other messengers, until it is so ordered by the Senate.

Mr. DAVIS. I should like to have some explanation of that resolution.

Mr. JOHNSON, of Tennessee. I will state, for the information of the Senator from Mississippi, that there are more messengers than are needed by the Senate, while we have not quite so many laborers as we need. My object is to dispense with the further appointment of messengers, and to leave the employment of laborers, if needed, under the control and subject to the order of the committee. These officers are not needed, and I am so informed by the Sergeant-at-Arms.[1] This resolution is offered at his request, and the committee, after considering it, have thought it best to dispense with the appointment of additional messengers, unless otherwise ordered by the Senate.[2]

Cong. Globe, 36 Cong., 1 Sess., 1194.

1. Dunning R. McNair (1797–1875), born in McNairstown, Pennsylvania, seems to have been a mail contractor in Louisville, Kentucky, before becoming sergeant-at-arms of the Senate (March 17, 1853–July 6, 1861). James B. McNair, *McNair, McNear, and McNeir Genealogies* (Chicago, 1923), 145–46; *BDAC*, 157, 173.

2. The resolution passed by unanimous consent. *Cong. Globe*, 36 Cong., 1 Sess., 1194.

From John L. Dawson

Brownsville   March 18/60

My Dear Govonor:

I wish you would send me a Copy of the Homestead Bill as you have reported it in the Senate.— The Amendments proposed by you[r] Committee as I read them in the telegrapick report are not objectionable, for the reason that they strip the bill of *pretexts* for its defeat. I hope you have retained the $10 consideration.[1] This will head off the Constitutional objection of Old Buck. Strip him of every pretext for a Veto.— The $10. Consideration keeps the measure within His pledge Contained in his inaugural address— examine this address & refer to it so as to clinch him.

The measure is decidedly popular here in Western Pennsylvania as it is everywhere else. The extract from Secty Thompson's report[2] as published in the Union or Constitution is to flat to offer as an objection— it does not present one good argument against the Bill— A much better argument could have been offered against the Swamp land acts & the frauds which have been practiced under them.

Your friend   John L. Dawson

Hon Andrew Johnston.

ALS, DLC-JP2.

1. In order to meet Buchanan's inaugural dictum that public lands ought to be available to "actual settlers . . . at moderate prices," the House homestead bill, passed March 12, 1860, called for a fee of ten dollars payable after five years' residence. Johnson's final version omitted the ten dollar clause and instead provided that the land be sold for twenty-five cents per acre; to his consternation, the President objected on the ground that the sum was too low. Richardson, *Messages*, V, 434, 609; Washington *Constitution*, March 14, 1860; Roy M. Robbins, *Our Landed Heritage* (Gloucester, Mass., 1960 [1942]), 181.

2. Extracts from Secretary of the Interior Jacob Thompson's annual report for 1859 appeared in the Washington *Constitution*, March 14, 1860. Lamenting that government land receipts had failed to reach anticipated levels, the secretary blamed the popular expectation that Congress "would pass a law making a gratuitous distribution of the public domain." To insure sufficient revenues from land sales, he proposed legislation requiring payment on all property within two years. Washington *Constitution*, March 14, 1860.

From Charles Johnson

Greeneville   March 18th [1860]

Dear Father

Your letters dated the 11th 12th & 14th have all come to hand and have been carefully read[.]

Mother is still in Carter, I am looking for her home this week!

The Atlas[1] you refer to in your first letter came to hand all safe and in good condition[.]

The proposition about selling to the C.P. Church[2] one of the lots refered to, I made to them,   they have not yet organised their building comittee who will have authority to make contracts; I think they are all pleased with the Miller lot, as it is the most eligible site in town; I think they have comand of about $200. in cash, if they buy their plan as I understand is for ten of them to join in the note; and I infer that they only want sufficient time to make their means available; You I presume will be at home in ample time to make all necessary arangemts, when too you can more thoroughly understand their designs[.]

The Kingsley house[3] has been sold,   Jo. D. Allen & Rumbaugh[4] are the fortunate purchasers; at $3000.

Our business[5] still continues good; we are selling but little on credit; we have now in New York about $1500, and enough here to pay what little we owe; If there was some other business that we could add to our present, that would double it; we I think could manage it equally well, but I am at a loss to know what it shall be[.] had we been able to have got an other more suitable house this Spring, I intended to have gone to N. York and improve and increase our present stock; but I see no opening even for renting an other house, Browns[6] ask $2.50 for their new Rooms but I presume we will not be entirely crowded out.

Cousin Andrew,[7] I have not seen for some days, he perhaps has made a brake for Texas; he told me some ten days since that he was going down to Evans x Roads but did not know what he would do there,   I think if he has gone there, it is to keep a Dog[g]ery;[8] this business seems more congenial to him than any other; he has never mentioned to me that he had no means; I suppose he expected me to app[r]oach him; I think perhaps it would be just as well to let him alone;— he has been very solicitous about "Aunt's" Coming home.

We are all in our usual health; with nothing unusual going on.

Your Son   Charles Johnson

ALS, DLC-JP2.

1. Possibly a copy of *Mitchell's New Universal Atlas* . . . (Philadelphia, 1857), or *Colton's Atlas of the World* . . . (2 vols., New York, 1856).

2. See Deed to Cumberland Presbyterians, July 20, 1860.

3. Probably a legacy of E. G. Kingsley (b. *c*1843), South Carolina-born clerk, who in 1860 claimed a personal estate of $15,000 and was living in the home of J. Bomar, a Greeneville merchant. 1860 Census, Tenn., Greene, 94.

4. Probably Joseph D. Allen (b. *c*1835), prosperous Greene County farmer with declared wealth of $24,000, and James H. Rumbaugh (b. *c*1833), a Greeneville merchant with $21,000 in real and personal property. *Ibid.*, 59, 91.

5. Charles was a partner with postmaster Elbert Biggs in a drug firm. For Biggs, see *Johnson Papers*, II, 391n.

6. John and Joseph Brown were Greeneville merchants. *Ibid.*, I, 36n.

7. Andrew Johnson, son of the senator's brother, William.

8. A saloon, or small grocery which sold liquors. Mathews, *Americanisms*, I, 501.

From M. E. Wilcox

Graysville Ky. Mar. 18th,/60

Hon. Andrew Johnson
Washington D. C.
My Dear Sir,

I trespass upon the Sabbath to impart an item of news which may prove interesting to you, at least, if you are a believer in the doctrine of ultra-mundane influences.

Being confined to my room, and "hard up"—excuse the expression—for something to read, I have been reading "Foot-falls on the verge of another World" by Mr. R. Dale Owen;[1] and have been impressed with the plausibility, if not probability, of the doctrine of, what is termed, "Spirit Rappings". Hence, what would otherwise have passed unheeded, now leaves *some* impression.

This much by way of prelude; and now for the news.

There is in this neighbourhood a young Lady, of good standing, residing with one of [the] wealthiest and most respectable families in Ky. who is both a "Spirit medium" and "Clarvointess".

She and the family with whome she resides are all anti-Johnson folks. Well, a few days since the young Lady, in a Clarvoint state saw, and described the persons and dress, of Old John Brown and his associates in crime in the spirit land; all of whom she recognized save one, who was heavy set, with a slouched broad brim hat on his head and a large, heavy, whip in his hand. Upon inquiry he (the unknown one) informed her that he was the Son of John Brown, and that, if permitted to live again on earth, instead of sympathising with the negroes, he would become an overseer and whale the rascals with the whip he held in his hand. Upon inquiry of Old Brown who was to be the next Democratic candidate for the Presidency, he unhesitatingly said "Andrew Johnson of Tenn"[.] Upon the suggestion of a gentleman present that he (Brown) did not know any more about that matter than he (the gentleman) did; Brown repeated that "Andrew Johnson would be the candidate". These answers were, what is termed, "spelled out" by raps at certain letters as the finger was passed over an Alphabet.

I will here state that said "Medium", a week before the last Presidential Election, told, with remarkable precision, the result of said election; both as to the states and the number of Electoral votes each candidate would get.

You now have the story for what it is worth. God grant it may not be a lying Spirit in this instance!

The only thing I particularly object to in the communication is the professed intimacy of John Brown with *our* affairs, and more especially making *you* his *pet*. Still I am willing that you shall be nominated, even though Old Brown did know all about it. What I have written above is fact; time must prove the truth of the communication.

Very Respectly, &C   M. E. Wilcox

I shall *believe* the "Spirit" until the contrary be proven[.]   M. E. W.

ALS, DLC-JP2.

1. Robert Dale Owen, *Footfalls on the Boundary of Another World* (London and Philadelphia, 1860), was an attempt to explain rationally some of the phenomena of spiritualism, a popular belief of the 1850's. As Owen observed in his preface, the book was "devoted to an inquiry whether occasional interference from another world in this can be reality or delusion." Richard W. Leopold, *Robert Dale Owen* (Cambridge, 1940), 232.

From Hu Douglas

Nashville March 19th 1860

Private

Hon Andrew Johnson
Washington City
My Dear Sir

I have your esteemed letter of the 14th Inst and have noted Contents with pleasure. I am glad to see that you have a correct idea of things as they stand here. You may rely upon it that the Democracy are for you, but the people are at *heart* for you, from no *selfish motives*[.] I have just called to see Mr Burch[1] and I am glad to see that he is alive on the Subject. I have told him that I feared some in the Camp & have discussed the merits of all fully. I have told him that many of our folks were first for you & then for Guthrie Dickinson Seymour or Breckinridge.[2] I have told him we should have no second choice & prudence & good management will secure us in the result. The idea of men telling me that they are of course for you but after you for Guthrie regarding him as the best man in the nation &C is all stuff[.] I would rather they would go at once for Guthrie, others are for Dickinson or Seymour. now this will not do[.] the former cannot carry N Y nor do I think the latter can if nominated. By the bye I would like your friends to Cultivate the friendship of Fernando Wood,[3] he is strong will do any man good that he supports. I have told Mr Burch that we ment to lay no claim to the Vice Presidency, that if we cant get you that we are for no Compromise but let the matter go. I have feared that our Govr Harris wanted the last. this would be *death* to your prospects[.] We ask for a Southern Conservative man for President, (And Johnson) we ask nothing more. I hope our friends will act prudent, and insist upon our rights—

I do think your speech[4] should be sent North & North West[.] it will do good. *You do not work nor have you working men*[.] I cant work for I have enough to do with Douglas in this way but I *told Burch that I was* willing to pay for some work if it *was done*[.] Mr Burch will be in Washington on Sunday, he will tell you about men &C. I am glad to learn from him that some of our folks will come up right, for all this I refer you to him—

We should insist that this is the time for a Southern man, that you are the *man* and urge it upon the Convention.

If possible I will be at Charleston[.] I wish they would move it to Balto.

I should be glad to hear from you at all times[.]

Believe me to be truly yr friend

Hu Douglas

ALS, DLC-JP2.

1. John C. Burch.

2. James Guthrie of Kentucky, Daniel S. Dickinson and Horatio Seymour of New York, and John C. Breckinridge of Kentucky.

3. Fernando Wood (1812–1881), a New York shipping merchant, was Democratic congressman (1841–43, 1863–65, 1867–81), dispatch agent for the state department at the port of New York (1844–47), and mayor of New York City (1855–58, 1861, 1862). During the Civil War, Wood at first supported the war effort, but soon joined Clement L. Vallandigham in organizing the "Peace Democrats." *DAB*, XX, 456–57; *BDAC*, 1843; see also Samuel A. Pleasants, *Fernando Wood of New York* (New York, 1948).

4. Johnson had made no major speech since his Harper's Ferry address in December; undoubtedly this was the speech that Douglas wished to circulate.

From Thomas J. Henley[1]

San Fran[c]isco Cal March 19. 60

Hon A Johnson

Dear Sir We cannot tell at this greate distance from the political centre what is to be the result of the Charleston Convention.

I see that Tennessee is instructed to vote for you for the Presidncy. I should be glad if this could be done, and you are the only man South that I can think that I belive could be elected. But I am of opinion that a man from the North will be selected by the Convention, this will of course bring the V. President from the South. Chiefly with reference to this I have given several of our deligates letters of introduction to you, and have talked with all of them in regard to placing you on the ticket for V President. If circumstances shall happen to favor your nomination they will go for you[.]

Your name would add greatly to our strength in this state[.]

Your views in regard to the disposition of the public lands—and other kindred subject—are overwhelmly popular in this state.

I dont know why it is but I have, a sort of presentment that you will be nominated at Charleston for V. P. I hope so.

Yours truly   Tho J. Henley,

ALS, DLC-JP2.

1. Thomas J. Henley (1810–1865), San Francisco postmaster (1860–64), had served in the Indiana house of representatives (1832–42) and in Congress as a Democrat (1843–49) before moving west in 1849. A member of the California legislature (1851–53), he had been superintendent of Indian affairs for California (1855–58). *BDAC*, 1042.

From Henry Watterson[1]

[Washington, D. C.]
States & Union Office.
March 19th '60

My Dear Gov;

I enclose my resignation,[2] which may be of service in supplying the vacancy with a successor. You will of course use it for that purpose, without ceremony.

In regard to the matter I mentioned to you yesterday I have on reflection concluded not to trouble you. I was under the impression that a transfer of the sort could be made very easily by the verbal request of yourself or Mr Etheridge.[3] I could, as a Southern man, make a formal application of the sort with but ill grace; and nothing but the extreme moneyed distress of father[4] could induce me to think of official position at all.

I think, that committing the "honors and emoluments of state" to

"the vile dust from whence, they sprung"[5]

I will retire from office like a philosopher, and go to honest work, like a man, not doubting that whilst the certain salery of the one would be more convenient, the necessity for activity in the latter will in the end, prove better for a fellow of my go-a-head propensities.

I thank you sincerely for your kind offers, and with the entreaty that you will not forget my friend Pillow—[6]

Remain Your friend   Henry Watterson

ALS, DLC-JP.

1. Henry Watterson (1840–1921), noted editor and son of Johnson's friend Harvey Watterson, was both a reporter on the Washington *States* and a clerk in the land office. A unionist, he embraced the Confederate cause when Tennessee seceded and after desultory army service became editor of the Chattanooga *Rebel*, which he turned into an army organ. In the postwar years he continued newspaper work, first in Cincinnati, then in Nashville, and finally in Louisville, where he remained for fifty years (1868–1918), making the *Courier-Journal* one of the nation's leading newspapers. *DAB*, XIX, 552–55; Joseph F. Wall, *Henry Watterson: Reconstructed Rebel* (New York, 1956), *passim*.

2. Attached is the notation, "H. M. Watterson's resignation as Clerk in the Land Office."

3. Emerson Etheridge. See Exchange with John Bell, February 24, 1858, note 10.

4. Harvey Watterson had lost heavily in the Panic of 1857; by 1859 the family had become dependent upon young Henry's income. Wall, *Henry Watterson*, 26.

5. Sir Walter Scott's *Lay of the Last Minstrel*, Canto IV, st. 1.

6. Probably Gideon J. Pillow's son, George M. (1839–1872), who may have been seeking a clerkship in Washington. Jill H. Garrett, ed., *Confederate Soldiers and Patriots of Maury County, Tennessee* (Columbia, 1970), 276.

From Sam Milligan

Court House Blountville

Confidential   March 20. 1860

Dear Governor,

Yesterday I received you[r] letter at this place, and also the Herald[1] and copy of the resolution desired.[2] At the same time, I received a long letter from Andrew Ewing on the presidential question. We have been corresponding ever since the State Convention. At first confidentially he was against you, but his two last letters show a most decided determination to support you most cordially. I do not by any means attribute his change to my letters, but to the force of public opinion. So it is, he is now all right, and seems anxious to promote your interest.[3]

You must permit me to lay aside all delicacy, and speak right out on this subject. It is now manifest that your prospects are brightening, and that too, without any efforts either on your part, or the part of your friends. It seems to be the spontaneous action of the people. If this be so, and it is directed a little by a cautious and prudent hand, it will not only nominate, but elect you.

Tennessee if she can only be supported by any other state firmly can do much to secure you nomination. If Kentuckey could be brought up firmly to your support, and those two States could play off a litle with Douglass' friend[s], so that when he is given up, they would come up to your support, the whole thing would be over. Cant you operate a little on Breckenridge, and Gutherie? It would be efforts in my opinion well directed.

Kentuckey secured, my next effort would be to secure North Carolina[.] She is your mother State, and I think on that account, as well as many others, could easily be brought to your support. You then have a safe nucleus. Three great southern states—all contiguous, and eminently conservative in their sentiments on the slavery question, could do the work.

If you could favorably impress some of the prominent men of these t[w]o States—N. C. & Kentucky; and these things could be judiciously managed in the Convention, I feel sanguine of Success—

I have concluded to make the artic[l]e[4] I spoke of in my last short and as comprehensive as possible. I now have all the materials for it, except I want to find something you have said on the Tariff which will do to read in Pennsylvania. The extracts I have suits me exactly, but if I can suit others I would like to do it.

I will also as soon as I can get home go to work on the other document,[5] and at least collect and arrange all the material in my power, and hold it in readiness for the occasions which I hope & believe will demand its publication.

I want to say one word on the platform. I am anxious to re-affirm the Cincinnati Platform,[6] and add nothing thereto unless it be the principles of the Dred Scott decision of the Supreme Court of the U. S.

I do not, I declare with modest difidence, like the Senatorial Caucus resolutions.[7] They have nothing in them but mischief, except a painful supper a bundance of words— Their adoption by the Charleston Convention of necessity, makes the democratic party Sectional, and at once burdens our Northern and N. Western friends with Sentiments which will do the south no good, and which the N & N. W. can not defend— We must not drive off the north, nor must We offend Douglass if it can possibly be avoided.

You speak of coming home[.] I do wish in my heart you would

do it. I feel at a great loss for facts. The field is too large for me to comprehend with the limited knowledge I have of men and things.

I am determined to go to Charleston if sickness or death does not prevent it, and do all I can to carry out our program— You speak of wishing me to go if you should come home— that you may rely on— Come home. It will pay. I am right sick to day, but will be better I think when my medicine works off[.] Write

Your friend   Sam Milligan

ALS, DLC-JP2.

1. In all probability Johnson had sent Milligan the March 9 issue of the New York *Herald*, in which Daniel Clark's Dover speech, to which Johnson took exception, was reported. See Exchange with Daniel Clark, March 27, 1860; Letter from William S. Pease, March 28, 1860.

2. Milligan had earlier asked for Johnson's resolution of January 4, 1859, calling for an investigation of departmental expenditures. See Letter from Sam Milligan, March 4, 1860.

3. At Charleston Ewing placed Johnson's name in nomination and worked to keep the Tennessee delegation behind him until his name was withdrawn. Hesseltine, *Three against Lincoln*, 98, 104.

4. This "article" was to be a campaign document on behalf of Johnson's nomination at the forthcoming Charleston convention. See Letter from Sam Milligan, March 4, 1860.

5. Milligan was preparing a collection of Johnson's speeches to be published as a campaign document in the event that Johnson received the Democratic nomination.

6. The Democratic Platform of 1856.

7. Southern Democratic senators had recently caucused and approved a series of resolutions, earlier introduced in the Senate by Jefferson Davis, which amounted to a "grim sectional manifesto" on all issues relating to slavery. Obviously, Johnson did not endorse the caucus stand. Nevins, *Emergence of Lincoln*, II, 179–80; Milton, *Eve of Conflict*, 411.

From George W. Buchanan[1]

Shelbyville   March 21st 1860

Hon Andrew Johnson.

Dr Sir   Mr Newman,[2] my brotherin law has detailed to me the many acts of kindness, and Efforts on your part to assist him, while at Washington,— Feeling a *powerful* interest [in] the matter— and *knowing* that he was inocent of any crime, I was satisfied that if he could have an investigation of the matter that he would vindicate himself— I was truly greatful to you as well as to your colleage Mr Nichelson for your unwearied assistance in the matter—and it has Endeared you to me more & more & your kindness will be Ever remembered by me and my family[.]

Your friend Ever   Geo. W. Buchanan

ALS, DLC-JP2.

1. George W. Buchanan (b. *c*1821–1868), originally from Franklin County, was a Bedford County Democrat who served in the legislature

(1849–51), was a delegate to the Nashville Convention of 1850, and campaigned as a presidential elector in the Confederate election of 1861. Robison, *Preliminary Directory, Bedford*, 9.

2. Charged with pension irregularities, Tazewell Newman, husband of Sarah Buchanan, had recently been in Washington trying to settle the matter. *Ibid., Franklin*, 24; see Letter from Robert Johnson, February 22, 1860.

Bill for Whiskey

[March 21, 1860?]

Hon Mr Johnson
Tennee
Dr Sir

I this day forw[ar]d 1 Doz delicate whiskey.

C $7.50
Bondd 37
————
$7.87

You will find this whiskey delicate— it is much approved of— I thank you for this order—& remain

address

Your resp Servt
A N Laurence[1]
Balto. March 21—[2]   Wash. City   D Cola.

DS, DLC-JP2.

1. Perhaps Col. Augustus N. Lawrence, who lived at 192 W. Madison Street in Baltimore during the late fifties and in 1860 moved to Washington, where his address was 83 Pennsylvania Avenue. *Woods' Baltimore Directory* (1856–57), 155; *ibid.* (1858–59), 255; *Boyd's Washington and Georgetown Directory* (1860), 101.

2. Endorsed by Johnson, "Paid the 27th to some men in the Capitol."

From Gibson County Democrats

Milan Depot M. & ORR[1] Ten
March 22/[60?]

Hon A. Johnson
Washington City D C
Dear Sir

we the pertetoner [petitioners] Livng in and around Milan Depot Tenn want a post office at this pleace and use this method to obtain it[.] Ther has ben Ssome one or two petition gone up from this place from the Op Party for a post office[.] we as Democrat[s] protess any one of them and want them all Defeated as they ar the Vailont [violent] Enamies of you and the adm. and we as Dmocts dmand that Mr George Peoples[2] of this Place be apointed and his apointmt will defeat the Op[.] pray us [*sic*] do us the kindness to See that he is appoint[ed.] he has been recom[mend]ed by Mr Craven[3] heretofore to the post Office D—patmet[.] We propose to be the bone and sinew of the Democratic party in this vicin[ity] and we refer you to Gen Adkins for the facts[.]

he Adkins will put his name to this petition and will Endoss us as being good and Fathfull Dmocrats[.][4] help us to defeet the Op petition and will Evr rmne [remain] Gratful[.]

| J P King[?] | J. Cunningham | L. Craven |
| Levi G Danner | Charles L Yancey | J. P Boyd[?] |

LS, DLC-JP2.

1. In 1858, with the construction of the Memphis and Ohio Railroad, the community of Shady Grove moved closer to the tracks; the new location became Milan Depot. Frederick Culp and Mrs. Robert E. Ross, *Gibson County, Past and Present* (Trenton, Tenn., 1961), 167.

2. George Peoples (b. *c*1805), Milan's first merchant and later postmaster, was a wealthy man who possessed real estate valued at $55,000 and personal property worth $77,275. 1860 Census, Tenn., Gibson, 291; *Goodspeed's Gibson*, 806; *U. S. Official Register* (1866), *347.

3. Swinburne Craven was the retiring postmaster. *Ibid.*

4. Former Congressman John D. C. Atkins, in an accompanying letter, endorsed Peoples' appointment and confirmed that the signers were "among the leading D[e]mocrats of Gibson Co." Atkins to Johnson, March 22, 1860, Johnson Papers, LC.

Remarks Concerning Senate Homestead Bill[1]

March 22, 1860

Mr. JOHNSON, of Tennessee. Mr. President,[2] I do not rise for the purpose of making a speech, but simply to make two or three remarks on the present position of the question before the Senate. The first bill that was introduced into the Senate at the present session was the homestead bill, which was presented at a very early day. It is bill No. 1. That bill was referred to the Committee on Public Lands; and, after mature consideration, they reported it back in its present shape, and it is now under consideration. The committee, I repeat, considered the bill maturely. Those members of the committee who voted in favor of it, being friends of the measure, being friends of the homestead principle disconnected from party considerations, reported that bill back, because they thought it had been put in the most acceptable shape, and in that shape in which it was most likely to receive the sanction of the country at the present time. It was then made a special order. The time arrived for its discussion in the Senate. It was continued a special order, and has been so continued from time to time up to the present moment. In the mean time, the House passed a bill on the same subject, and it was transmitted to the Senate. That bill was referred, as was remarked by the gentleman who has just taken his seat—the Senator from Arkansas—to the Committee on Public Lands. That bill was promptly considered by the committee with a view of getting it back before the Senate; and a friend of the measure,[3] as has been very correctly remarked, was authorized to report it. That friend of the measure has exercised due diligence in reporting it. This morning, after the morning hour had expired—no other time being presented for reporting the bill—by the courtesy of the Senate, and after the unfinished business had been taken up, it was reported back without displacing the regular order of business of the Senate.

The query now comes as to the propriety of postponing the Senate bill, which has been regularly introduced, regularly referred, maturely considered, and reported back in that shape believed to be most acceptable, and in that shape in which it was thought it would command the greatest strength, upon the reporting by the committee of the House bill with substantially the Senate bill as an amendment in lieu of it. It is proposed that that bill should be taken up, the regular business of the Senate postponed, and the House bill considered. I can see no substantial or good reason for it. I do not understand it to be discourteous or unparliamentary that we should proceed with our regular order of business, and especially when that order had been taken prior to the passage of the bill of the House. There are points of difference between the two bills, as was remarked by the Senator from Ohio.[4] If he wishes to test those points upon the Senate bill, it is very easy to offer them as amendments, or offer the House bill as a substitute in lieu of the Senate bill; and then we can have a fair test when the action of the Senate shall be had. I think it neither unparliamentary nor discourteous to the House of Representatives for the Senate to proceed regularly with the consideration of a bill that it has matured and made a special order.[5]

I regret, I will remark while I am up, to see this measure take a party direction.[6] It may be the feeling and the design of some to sustain it for the express purpose of making political capital before the country. I hope, though, that it is not. I shall speak for myself, and I think I am authorized to speak for others, when I say that they are for this great measure from principle, and not merely on account of what little capital can be made out of it in one direction or another. I repeat, I have been pained to see an attempt to give this measure a party direction. I have been pained to see men in different portions of the country seizing this measure and trying to incorporate it as part of their creed, for the purpose of affecting the public mind. If there are friends of the people in the Senate and in the other branch of Congress, let them be friends, and friends upon correct principles. If there are Senators here who believe that this is a great measure, calculated to ameliorate and elevate the condition of the common men and advance the great cause of civilization, let them stand by the great measure upon principle; not upon party, or the feeling or direction that may be given to it. All these movements, though they may be made with correct intentions, are calculated to weaken, to retard, and in the end to defeat, its final consummation.

I speak what I know, when I say that no bill can pass the Senate containing the provisions of the House bill.[7] Then, he who is a friend of the homestead proposition, when he can get the substance of that great proposition, when he can get all the essentials, all that is material in the bill now under consideration, it does seem to me is not acting in good faith when he takes that course, and gives the measure that direction that is likely to defeat it. If we cannot get what we most desire, let us take what comes the nearest to it. If we cannot get some of the details of the measure that may be desired by some, let us come forward and take the substance. Let us take the great principle; let us incorporate and place upon our statute-book this homestead principle, which will carry relief, which will ameliorate, as I remarked before, the condition of thousands, if not millions, of the people of the United States.

Why, then, should we not proceed regularly, and consider the proposition legitimately and regularly before the Senate? If the Senator simply wishes to test the strength of the two propositions; if he wishes to throw this side of the Chamber in opposition to some points that he conceives material in the House bill, for the purpose of effecting party objects, let him test it on the Senate bill. If we cannot get that which we most desire, let us take that which comes the nearest to it; leaving those who are desirous to pass the measure to stand on practical grounds, and where they properly belong.

The time has been, Mr. President, when this was no party measure. In 1846,[8] when it was introduced in the other wing of the Capitol, it was not looked upon as a party measure. Then Whigs and Democrats sustained it; and in 1852 it passed that body by a majority of two thirds.[9] In 1854 it was considered, debated, and finally put upon its passage, and passed by a similar majority.[10] But recently, it is true, some of the parties of the country have assumed to make it a tenet of their creed; but let me ask the Senator or member who started originally for this great measure upon principle—let me say to him who looked at the measure and its application to the toiling millions of the United States, and was for it upon great national principles—let me ask him, either on this side of the Chamber or on the other side of the Chamber, is he now going to be driven from its support, because some to whom he stands opposed in politics favor the measure?

I say for myself that I care not who sustains it; but, on the contrary, I am anxious to obtain support for this measure, come from what quarter it may. It is right in itself; it embraces a great principle; and I intend to pursue this principle, carry me where it will. I have learned in early life that, in the pursuit of a great principle, you never can reach a wrong conclusion. If this great measure is right in itself, I say the politician and the statesman is timid, and has not the moral courage which should accompany every man in high place, when he is driven from its support because some may assume to support it to whom he stands opposed in reference to their political creed. It is right in itself; it is a great measure, calculated to do great good. Why, then, should we abandon it? Why should we not act on it, without reference to its bearing on any particular action that may come off hereafter? I say, let the measure be passed now, or as soon as it can be considered; let it be placed on your statute-book as a law, and take it out of the hands of wrangling and contending and misrepresenting parties. It is above parties. Parties have scarcely aspired to the elevation of the principle involved in this measure. Parties too frequently, on both sides, forget the people, the interests of the great masses of the toiling millions of the United States who bear all, who produce all, who toil all, who pay all. Their rights and their interests are over-slaughed and neglected in many contests and conflicts that transpire between the parties of this country.

It was not my purpose, sir, to make a speech on this occasion. It was not my purpose, when I entered the Senate, to obtrude myself upon it, unless where I believed the importance of the measure with which I was connected, or the interests of my people, required me to speak. I hope, then, that we shall consider our own bill. If the Senators wish to test the sense of the Senate upon the leading points, it can be done. If this bill is rejected, the other bill can come up as a matter of course, and we can have the sense of the Senate upon it in that shape.

But while I am up, Mr. President, I may allude to the amendment that has been proposed.[11] Perhaps, however, I ought not to speak of that now. The question before us is simply a motion to postpone; but it seems to me that before the action of the Senate is had on the postponement, the suggestion made by the Senator from Alabama,[12] which is a good one, is entitled to consideration: that the two bills be read, and the comparative difference between them understood, so that the Senate can act understandingly. In reference to the amendment offered by the Senator from North Carolina to the Senate bill now under consideration, I do not know whether it be legitimate or not to discuss it now. Probably it is not, until the

Senate determines whether it will postpone the one measure and take up the other, and therefore I will not touch that point. All I desire, I will say to the friends of the homestead measure, is, that it will receive the sanction of the Senate and House of Representatives —feeling confident that, if we can pass the bill in such a shape as to indorse the policy, in a very short time Congress will cure all the defects that there may be in the original bill. I hope, therefore, that the Senate will proceed to consider the bill that is now before it.[13]

Cong. Globe, 36 Cong., 1 Sess., 1297–98.

1. Thomas L. Clingman, North Carolina Democrat, had moved to amend the pending Homestead bill, substituting instead a system of warrants donating one hundred and sixty acres to every head of a family and citizen over twenty-one. Meanwhile, a debate began on a motion of Benjamin F. Wade, Ohio Republican, to consider the House Homestead bill (H. R. 280) brought to the Senate that morning in place of the Senate measure (S. 1), Johnson's bill, first introduced on December 20, 1859. Robert Johnson, Arkansas Democrat and chairman of the committee on public lands, had just accused the Republicans of trying to make political capital of the bill. *Cong. Globe*, 36 Cong., 1 Sess., 1219, 1293–97.

2. Lafayette S. Foster (1806–1880) of Connecticut, lawyer, newspaperman, state assemblyman (1839–40, 1846–48) and unsuccessful gubernatorial candidate (1850, 1851), served as a Republican in the Senate (1855–67). *BDAC*, 908.

3. Earlier that day, Johnson himself had reported H. R. 280 with an amendment to substitute his own Senate bill after the enacting clause of the House measure. *Cong. Globe*, 36 Cong., 1 Sess., 1292.

4. Benjamin F. Wade (1800–1870), Massachusetts-born Ohio lawyer, was a member of the state senate (1837–38), judge of the third judicial court of Ohio (1847–51), a Whig and later Republican senator (1851–69). *BDAC*, 1759; Hans L. Trefousse, *Benjamin Franklin Wade: Radical Republican of Ohio* (New York, 1963), *passim*.

5. His determination, evident in these remarks, to have the Senate discuss his bill, rather than H. R. 280 amended by substitution of his bill, appears to reflect the concern of a shrewd politician eager to receive full credit for a long and hard-fought struggle to enact a homestead measure.

6. Inasmuch as southern Democrats had come to oppose violently any measure which seemed a threat to slavery, the Republicans had adopted the bill as their own; thus northern and western Democrats, at one time inclined toward the homestead, were confronted with the task of reconciling party and principle. Robbins, *Our Landed Heritage*, 178–80.

7. The House bill, in essence a Republican measure more liberal than the Senate version, had been approved (115–65) in the lower chamber without sectional debate on March 2, 1860. This measure, unlike the Senate bill, extended homestead privileges to those over twenty-one, as well as to heads of families, and gave aliens seeking to complete their naturalization an additional two years beyond the five required for homestead rights. Homesteading applied to any land subject to preemption; lands not sold after thirty-five years were to be ceded to the states in which they were located. *Ibid.*, 180.

8. During the early months of 1846 both Johnson and Felix G. McConnell of Alabama had introduced bills giving 160 acres of the public domain to settlers; both bills were sent to committee, where they died. *Cong. Globe*, 29 Cong., 1 Sess., 175, 473, 563; George M. Stephenson, *The Political History of the Public Lands from 1840–1862* (New York, 1967), 117.

9. An analysis of the votes on this measure, passed May 12, 1852, clearly sustains the claim that it was not a party matter: the "majority of two thirds"

(107–56) to which Johnson refers represented two-thirds of each party's voting members.

10. On March 6, 1854, the Democrats voted 72–52 for the measure and the Whigs, 35–19. Benjamin H. Hibbard, *A History of the Public Land Policies* (Madison, 1965), 371; John B. Sanborn, "Some Political Aspects of Homestead Legislation," *American Historical Review*, VI (1900), 31.

11. Clingman's amendment.

12. Clement C. Clay.

13. The ensuing discussion was inconclusive, and debate on the bill was postponed to Monday, March 26, when a further postponement was agreed upon. *Cong. Globe*, 36 Cong., 1 Sess., 1304, 1345.

From William N. Clarkson[1]

Mooresburg March 24th 1860

Hon Andrew Johnson—

Dear Sir

I understand that a petition has been sent to the Post office depart-mant asking the appointment of Robt Simpson[2] Post Master at this place in place of G. M. Etter[3] resigned. Mr Simpson is a rabbid Know Nothing, & many of your friends does not desire his appoint-ment, and are getting up a petition for C. J. Kountz—[4] I hope you will see the Post Master Genl and prevent the appointment of Simp-son untill the petition [for] Kountz reacheses Washington[.]

We have no news that would interest you. The Democracy of my portion of the State are arming themselves for the contest of 1860 and are in fine Sperits[.] I would Say who we are for the Presidency, but modesty forbids. Send me all needfull information such as docu-ments &c, and let me hear from you personally. By all means do not let Simpson be appointed Post Master at this place; we do not [want] the office in the hands of the opposition in the coming contest.

Very Respectfully   W. N. Clarkson

ALS, DLC-JP2.

1. William N. Clarkson (b. *c*1817), a railroad commissioner and Rogers-ville attorney with $15,650 in personal property, resided in Mooresburg. Hol-land, Railroad Enterprise, 387; 1860 Census, Tenn., Hawkins, 163.

2. Robert Simpson (b. *c*1820), Hawkins County Whig and Mooresburg merchant, received the appointment but served less than a month. He was later a Confederate cavalry officer. *Ibid.*, 165; WPA, Records of Hawkins County: Miscellaneous (Nashville, 1937), 33; Knoxville *Tri-Weekly Whig*, March 12, 1859; Herman J. Viola (National Historical Commission) to Andrew Johnson Project, September 12, 1968.

3. G. M. Etter (b. *c*1834), a tanner, had been postmaster for one year (April, 1859–April, 1860). *Ibid.*; 1860 Census, Tenn., Hawkins, 162.

4. Campbell J. Kountz (b. *c*1823), a farmer-saddler living in Moores-burg, succeeded Simpson on May 8, 1860, and served until November 1865. *Ibid.*;Viola to Johnson Project, September 12, 1968.

From Robert D. Powel

Rogersville March 24th 1860

Hon A Johnson
Dear Sir

   Inclosed I send you the petition of sundry citizens of Hawkins for
a post rout through Stanly vally[.]¹ you are well acquainted with the
country it passes over and I need not say any thing as to the propriety
of this rout[.] I find the deficiency in this matter very much in the
way of geting subscribers both in Hawkins and Hancock and to that
extent am personally interested and of course would be very glad on
my own account [if] the rout could be procured[.] It seems to me
there is a general deficiency in reference to this matter in E Ten as I
find every where[.] It is a drawback to the circulation of Newspapers
and general information[.] If this matter could be got through the
people of Stanly and Cove Valleys would be under great obligations
to you as they all seem to be no little interested in this matter. I find
Newspaper mangeing [*sic*] a poor business as to money making but
a fellow can console himself with the belief he is not altogether useless in his day and generation—If he be really a great nuisance[.]
doubtless Brownlow does[.] I am under some obigations to the thing
for I believe I would have kicked out before this time, If I had not
have got hold of something that drew my attention off from a subject
upon which I was brooding and still cant keep from it too much[.]
The vissit with Brownlow last summer furnished me no little amuse-
ment and when I can get any thing up that makes my goodly godly
folks look sideways or old George stired up about *Decency* and *good
taste* It is no little fun to me but such weekly drains as the tilt on the
4th of July I find is doing me no good[.]² If it is not too much to ask
of you, I would be glad [if] you would read the article and let me
know what you think of it as a moral ground of defence for slavery[.]
It may not be popular but I can look at the thing in no other light at
present[.] Wee can hope for nothing in this union untill there is a
revolution in sentiment in the North and common sense takes the
place of fool fanaticism[.] I think the question ought to be met on
moral ground, as I honestly think it can be and successfully fought
through[.] for that reason I am less interested as a matter of policy
in running a Northern man[.] If wee can make a successful tilt at
them by turning this moral weapon upon them and throwing a defence around the institution impregnable The battle would have been
fought and won to all intents and purposes. The question is shall this

unequivocal fight be made with a Southern man or a half compromise one be made to be renewed again with a Northern man or what Northern man carries with him the prestige of success so as to make sure of a Northern strength sufficient to elect him[.] Our folks here think Lane can do it but in my honest Judgement Lane is a Zachery[3] though I may be grossly mistaken having barely seen him[.] If It be as for one I am out and out against any such thing[.] I saw Zachery in his glory and I simply say defeat with a man a real man to any such degradation[.] The bitter opposition to Douglas is I think if any thing giving away but any thing of a union man I think could carry several of the Southern states against him. He could enlist no enthusiasm and would be merely supported as a choice of evils and a Devilish hard choice if a Union man was runing though I believe the mass of the party would support him if he was the nominee[.] I am satisfied in my mind if Douglas is the nominee The elements of opposition will coalesce and a moderate man be selected[.] The devil kicked up about the Union and the long and the short of the matter is Stephen's legs are too short and wee are beat most disgracefuly beat for in my opinion if the Democracy is beat in this election It is beat to all intents and purposes for all time to come[.] I therefore think the greatest possible care and circumspection should be used in the selection of a candidate[.] I am inclined to think the more I do think about the matter that wee had better face the music at once come out with a Southern man least objectionable in the North one they could make no Union tilt at and who was sound and reliable as to his record upon the subject of acconomy. I will simply say to you and mean to be frank in saying it that in my Judgement very few men unite these qualities in the South with any hope of success[.] I believe your chances very far superiour to any one and, I do think your claims should be earnestly and ardently pressed between this and the time the convention meets[.] I saw Milligan at Jonesborough and wee agreed between us to fix up a short biography and present as forcibly as wee could the bearing your record would have upon the points upon which the canvass must turn[.] I would be glad [if] you would send me any documents you can[.] I published the prospectus for the States[4] but I have not received a single paper[.]

Very respectfully yours &c   R D Powel.

ALS, DLC-JP2.

1. Although this petition is missing, it can be assumed that the proposed route ran between Rogersville and Jonesville, Kentucky, by way of Stanley and Cove valleys. *Geologic Atlas of the United States: Estillville Folio* (Washington, D. C., 1894), plate 1.

2. During the spring and summer of 1859, Powel and Brownlow carried on a lively journalistic duel characterized by heavy-handed satire and crude burlesque. Responding to Powel's sallies against "Billy Brownlow," the "Par-

son" portrayed his opponent as "a sort of *slobbering loose-mouthed* fellow" without the talent to write his own editorials. Since Powel and his brothers were associated with the Rogersville bank—long a *bête noir* of Brownlow— the latter charged that its funds had been misappropriated, that the bank directors, supposedly bankrupt, had been speculating in Negro slaves, and that the Tennessee and Virginia Railroad had been swindled on a loan. Finally, he insinuated that Powel had information concerning the origin of a mysterious fire on the Knoxville post-office square. During the canvass of that year, Brownlow continued to inveigh against the "dirty little Bank sheet" and its Locofoco editor, whom the "Parson" regarded as "the fool, tool, and ass of a desperate clique," dedicated only to political and personal gain. In consequence of Brownlow's peculiar talents, the Rogersville editor apparently came out second best in the war of words. Knoxville *Tri-Weekly Whig*, March 24, May 5, June 16, July 5, 1859.

3. While Powel may have had in mind several similarities between Joseph Lane and Zachary Taylor—both men had military, but not political, reputations and both possessed less ability than their supporters claimed—he was probably implying that Lane was undependable on the subject of slavery, even as Taylor had been. A slave owner whose silence on the subject during the campaign had won southern support, Taylor had subsequently disappointed slaveholders by his willingness to permit California's admission as a free state, contrary to what most southerners regarded as their sectional interest. Hendrickson, *Joe Lane*, 228; Holman Hamilton, *Zachary Taylor: Soldier in the White House* (New York, 1951), 224, *passim*.

4. Probably a reference to the Washington *States*, which had recently added *Union* to its name.

To Blackston McDannel, Greeneville

Washington City   Mar. 24th 1860

B. McDannel Esqr
Dear Sir

Your letter of the 22d was this moment received and read— The application of Nancy C. Parmon[1] for a land warrant is now before the Atty Genl[2] for his opinion as to the true Construction of the law under which the application was made—   The present Commission[er][3] thinks the Construction put upon the law by his predecessor is an erro[n]eous one; but does not feel authorised to disturb the construction of the former Commissioner—[4]   I took the Case to the Secretay of the Interior[5] and he was of the opinion also that the Commissione[r] had given a wrong opinion and thought the warrant ought to be issued; but would not agree to reverse the decision made in the pension office without the concurring opinion of the Atty Genl and then the Case was Submitted to him as before stated where the papers have been ever since—   The delay on his part has been Caused on account of Sickness[6] and the great press of business—   I have strong hopes that he will make a favorable decision— That is all there is of that—   In regard to warrants which have become valuless on account of the time having expired for their location, there is now a bill on its third re[a]ding in the Senate to extend the

time three years from the pass[a]ge of the law—[7]   So much for
that—   The tea plant referred to in your letter is ready for distribution in boxes Contain[in]g from 100 down to 25 plants, the freight
of the box to be paid by the person to whom it is sent—   The freight
by Aadams' express will Cost from $2- to $6- per box—   What Size
box will you have forwarded—   Write and let me know and I will
have it sent to you immediately—[8]

I do not think of a[n]y thing worth writing to you at this time
more than what you see in the papers of the day—   There is here
as evy where else much being said in reference to the next presidency—   Douglas' friends are very Sanguin of his nomination and
his opponents speak as possitive of his defeat and say he cannot be
elected if nominated—   There is one thing very certain at this time,
if Douglas is not nominated the nominee will be from the South and
the man who is most acceptable to D.S friends will be the man—[9]
However, I did not intend to bore you with a political letter and especially as you have become to some extent disgusted with politics—
I will do the best I can with your business and the other matter I
was talking to you about—

I am your friend   Andrew Johnson

ALS, DLC-JP2.

1. Probably Nancy (b. *c*1832), the wife of David Parmon, a farmer, and
the mother of a nine-year-old son. Mrs. Parmon wanted two 80-acre tracts,
rather than one warrant for 160 acres, "as they are better for sale or location." Application had already been made for one 80-acre tract and, subsequently, when a law extending the time to locate certain warrants was passed,
she filed application for an additional 80 acres. McDannel to Johnson, March
26, 1860, Johnson Papers, LC.

2. Jeremiah Black.

3. Samuel Smith of Tennessee.

4. Thomas A. Hendricks.

5. Jacob Thompson.

6. Attorney General Black suffered from poor health and was frequently
unable to discharge his duties. *DAB*, II, 312.

7. S. 199, a bill to authorize the location of certain warrants for bounty
lands and to extend for three years the location of such warrants, passed a
third reading April 24 and became law June 23, 1860. *Cong. Globe*, 36
Cong., 1 Sess., 1480; *ibid.*, App. 496; *U. S. Statutes*, XII, 90.

8. McDannel ordered the tea plants, "25 in a box." McDannel to Johnson,
March 26, 1860, Johnson Papers, LC.

9. As to Douglas' nomination, McDannel replied: "Douglass is not my
man. And if he should be the nominee, I will not vote for him." *Ibid.*

Exchange with Daniel Clark[1]

March 27, 1860

Mr. JOHNSON, of Tennessee. I rise, Mr. President to do what I
am not in the habit of doing in the Senate—make a personal explana-

tion. As I see the Senator from New Hampshire [Mr. Clark] in his seat, I desire to make an inquiry of him in regard to a speech purporting to have been made by him, as reported in the New York Herald of the 9th of this month. My attention was called to it the other day by a friend. It is a speech represented as having been made by him, in which there are certain allusions to the State that I have the honor in part to represent, and some allusions to myself. The speech purports to have been made at Dover, New Hampshire, March 7, and is reported by a correspondent of the Herald. The gentleman is reported to have said what I ask the Secretary to read.

The Secretary read as follows:

He commenced his address by saying that he desired to be heard, not for himself, but for his cause; that he always delighted to speak to laboring men, and that if he did not honor the working classes, he should cast reproach upon the father and mother whose memory he was proud to perpetuate. He was the son of a blacksmith; and while he blew the bellows at the forge, his father hammered out the son's education on the anvil. He had been that day through the Coheco print works, and while there, was introduced to an intelligent workman, with whom he offered to shake hands; but the man drew back, declaring that his hand was too dirty to give to a gentleman. He, [the speaker,] however, assured him that smut did not do a man any harm unless it penetrated to the soul. The soil of New England, he said, was rugged and sterile. She had no mines of coal, iron, copper, or tin, to increase her wealth; but she had what was better. She had free men and free hands; and with these she was able to excel more favored States, where the blight of slavery rested. Tennessee had both coal and copper, but she lacked the energy to develop her resources. If a man went there and asked the price of coal, it was always so much a bushel; they never thought of selling it by the cargo; and he had himself seen copper taken from the mines there and sent to New York to be smelted by the 'mud sills' of society, because there were not energy and enterprise enough in Tennessee to do it.* * * *

The idea of the South dissolving the Union was preposterous. Senator Johnson, of Tennessee, recently told him [Clark] that in the disturbances in that State in 1856, the people became highly alarmed, and that any politic man could have gone through the State, and the planters would have joined in driving all the slaves out of the State, because they were afraid of them. What, then, would be the helpless condition of Georgia and other southern States, should they once put themselves without the pale of the Union?[2]

Mr. JOHNSON, of Tennessee. I ask the Senator from New Hampshire if that is a correct report of his speech made at that place, or whether he made a speech there at all?

Mr. CLARK. Mr. President, I do not know why or for what reason anything I may have said in my State on the stump should be brought here into the Senate of the United States. I am entirely willing to meet the honorable Senator from Tennessee at any time or any place, and have any personal conversation with him, or give him any explanation he may demand or require in regard to what I said; but I really do not know why it should be brought here. I do not know what it has to do with the public business. That is all I have to say now, that I know of or think of. I shall be very happy to meet the Senator at any time on this matter, which, it seems to me, does not concern the Senate.

Mr. JOHNSON, of Tennessee. It seems to me, Mr. President, that here was a public declaration of statements, made on the authority of a Senator in his absence, and where he could not be heard. If it is a correct report of the Senator's speech on that occasion, I cannot see what hesitancy there should be in avowing it; or, if it is not, in disavowing it. I am in hopes that the Senator will say yea or nay, whether it is or is not.

Mr. CLARK. I am not disposed to say anything about it, because I do not understand that it belongs here. If the Senator is disposed to go into the public press, or go on the stump, I will answer him anywhere where it belongs.

Mr. JOHNSON, of Tennessee. A thing of this sort is exceedingly painful and unpleasant to me; but I shall take the privilege of replying to what is represented here as the Senator's speech, made at Dover, on the 7th of this month. I have called on the Senator courteously and politely, here in my place, either to avow it or disavow it. He declines to do either. I think, then, that I am authorized to infer that it is a correct report of what he said, and to treat it as such.

In reference to what the Senator has said, then, I am constrained to make the remark that, if he was familiar with the facts connected with the history of the State of Tennessee, her copper mines, and the energy of her people, he has said that which he must have known to be untrue; if he was not familiar with the facts, and did not understand them, he was not authorized to say what he did not know; and as he has declined to avow or disavow this report of his speech, he is at liberty to take either horn of the dilemma[.]

If that Senator had made himself familiar with the facts in relation to the copper mines in the State of Tennessee, to which he has alluded, he would have found that the principal mines were discovered in 1851[3]—nine years ago—in an almost inaccessible portion of the country, lying between two mountains, where they could scarcely be reached by a man on foot; and since the discovery of those mines, there has been a sufficient amount of enterprise and energy to dig down the hills, fill up the valleys, make good roads, and extract large amounts of ore from the mines. That does not seem to show a want of energy or enterprise; but, on the contrary, they have pursued this with, I may say, unusual energy and enterprise, until to-day, at those very copper mines at Ducktown, to which he has alluded, there are seven smelting furnaces in operation, running out many tons of pig metal every day. Does this show that the people there are wanting in energy and enterprise? It must be remembered that the ore has been discovered within a short time, and in an almost inaccessible portion of the country. I think, on the other hand, it argues a great deal for their enterprise.

Mr. President, it never has been, and it never will be, voluntarily my business to make invidious comparisons between one State and another; and if the Senator had pursued his investigation a little further before making his references to the energy and enterprise of the people of Tennessee, I do not think that he would, if he had regard to truth and accuracy, have made the statements that he did make. How does Tennessee compare even with the Senator's own State, where she was lugged in and referred to before an audience where she had no one to defend her and tell the true history of her case? Even when we turn back to 1850, and examine the statistics, what do we find? I am sorry to be compelled to go into this matter, but the course of the Senator seemed to require it. A friend of mine directed my attention to this speech of his, or I should not have seen it; and I was in hopes that the Senator, so soon as he got to see it himself, if he has seen it, would rise in his place and correct it.

When we turn to the comparative capacity and production resulting from the energy and enterprise of the people of the two States, how does the matter stand? We find, so far as farms are concerned— and the farms in our State are much larger than they are in New Hampshire—that in 1850 there were in the State of Tennessee 72,735 farms and plantations; in New Hampshire, 29,229; Tennessee having nearly treble the number of farms, and they of a much larger size. We had 5,175,173 acres of improved land; New Hampshire had 2,251,448; Tennessee having two and a half times as many acres improved. The cash value of farms in the State of Tennessee was $97,851,212, and it has been greatly increased since that time; in New Hampshire, $55,245,977. The value of farm implements and machinery in the State of Tennessee was $5,360,210; in New Hampshire, $2,314,125; more than double again. The number of persons engaged in agriculture was, in Tennessee, 227,739; in New Hampshire, 77,949; nearly four times as many. The number of persons engaged in mining in New Hampshire, where, according to the Senator, there is all the enterprise, was 13; in Tennessee, 103. The number of persons engaged in commerce, notwithstanding Tennessee is an interior State, and especially so when compared with the State of New Hampshire, was, in Tennessee, 2,217; New Hampshire, 1,379; Tennessee having almost double the number of New Hampshire. The number of persons engaged in manufacturing in Tennessee was 17,815; in New Hampshire, 17,826; nearly as many engaged in manufactures in Tennessee as in the State of New Hampshire. Then we come to the number of pounds of wool, and we have 1,364,378 pounds; New Hampshire, 1,108,476; even beating them in the production of wool. Then we come to cotton. We have 194,532 bales, at four hundred pounds to the bale; New Hampshire, none. This is the result of our enterprise.

Next we come to the number of bushels of wheat. The Senator seems wonderfully to object to bushels; he says that we talk there about bushels instead of cargoes. That is a mere arbitrary distinction. We can call them by any name we please so that we convey the idea, and that is the great object of language. Of wheat, we raised, in 1850, 1,619,386 bushels; New Hampshire, 185,658; Tennessee nearly ten times as much as New Hampshire. In corn, Tennessee had 52,276,223 bushels, (bushels again;) New Hampshire, 1,573,670; Tennessee nearly fifty times as much as New Hampshire. Of oats, (bushels again,) Tennessee had 7,703,086; New Hampshire, 973,-381; Tennessee eight times as many as New Hampshire. Of tobacco, we raised 20,148,932 pounds; the State of New Hampshire raised 50 pounds. Of cattle, Tennessee raised 750,762 head; New Hampshire, 26,910.[4] Of horses, asses, and mules, which are very common commodities, especially the asses, [laughter,] Tennessee raised 345,939; New Hampshire, 34,252; ten times as many. Of sheep, Tennessee had 811,591; New Hampshire, 384,756; nearly treble those of New Hampshire in value. Of swine, Tennessee raised 3,104,800; New Hampshire, 63,487. Of pig-iron, that people who have so little enterprise, and have to go away to the North to get any, produced 30,420 tons; while New Hampshire produced but 200. In its manufacture, Tennessee employed 1,822 hands; New Hampshire 10. The taxable property of the State of Tennessee in 1850 was $195,281,358, and her taxable property to-day is $300,000,000; while that of New Hampshire was $95,251,596.

Then let us come to railroads. In 1850, when our system was scarcely commenced, New Hampshire had 512 miles of railroad; Tennessee, 388. We have now over 1,100 miles, even beating New Hampshire upon the subject of railroads. Then, in making a comparison, I do not see why it was necessary—

Mr. MALLORY.[5] My friend from Tennessee will allow me to make an appeal to him. I gave way for the purpose of allowing him to make an explanation, and I appeal to him to make it as brief as possible.

Mr. JOHNSON, of Tennessee. I shall take but a few moments longer. So much for the energy, enterprise, and industry of Tennessee. I have no invidious remarks to make in reference to New Hampshire. It is not my place or my business to do it. But I wish to call attention to this other paragraph:

The idea of the South dissolving the Union was preposterous. Senator Johnson, of Tennessee recently told him [Clark] that in the disturbances in that State in 1856, the people became highly alarmed, and that any politic man could have gone through the State, and the planters would have joined in driving all the slaves out of the State, because they were afraid of them. What, then, would have been the helpless condition of Georgia and other southern States, should they once put themselves without the pale of the Union?

In the first place, I do not remember ever to have had a conversation with the Senator from New Hampshire upon that subject, and especially not during this session. If I had a conversation with him or with anybody else upon that subject, I know what I said. I know what I have ever said upon that subject. I know what I thought, I know what I felt, and I know that I never said that. I will state what I have said, but whether I ever said it in the hearing of the Senator from New Hampshire or not, I do not know. I do not remember to have had a conversation with him during the present session of Congress on that or any other subject. I have stated what I feared would be the result if the abolition and anti-slavery feeling were carried out to its consummation; and I have said, in speaking on that subject, that in 1856 [6] I had seen a spirit and a feeling manifested in the country that I had never seen before, which convinced me clearly and conclusively what the abolition agitation would eventuate in when it was pressed to its final ultimatum. I say that if the day ever does come when the effort is made to emancipate the slaves, to abolish slavery, and turn them loose on the country, the non-slaveholder of the South will be the first man to unite with the slaveholder to reduce them to subjugation again; and if one would be more ready to do so than the other, it would be the non-slaveholder. I have said that; and that if their resistance to subjugation were obstinate and stubborn, the non-slaveholder would unite with the slaveholder, and all this abolition philanthropy, all this abolition sympathy, when pressed to its ultimatum, would result in the extirpation of the negro race. That is what I said. It is what I felt, and what I saw, and what I know to be the feeling of the non-slaveholders in the slaveholding States to-day. Press this question to its ultimatum, and the non-slaveholder will unite, heart and hand, in subjugating the Africans, and if resistance be made, in extirpating the negro race; and that is where this question will end, notwithstanding all the sympathy and all the philanthropy that may be evinced, if the agitation be carried out successfully to its consummation.

If I said anything in the presence or hearing of anybody on that point, that is what I did say; and I repeat now, that the idea of there being any difference between the feelings of the slaveholders and non-slaveholders of the South on this question, is a mistaken one, a false one, as the demonstrations at Harper's Ferry proved most conclusively. When there was agitation in Tennessee, in 1856, I saw that the non-slaveholder was the readiest man to rise up and reduce the negro to subjugation; and he would join the master in extirpating, if necessary, this race from existence, rather than see them liberated and turned loose upon the country. Everything I said on this subject was to meet the fallacious and absurd idea that the non-slaveholders of the South would unite with the negroes against their masters.[7]

The propriety or the courtesy of taking a portion of a brother Senator's conversation, or picking up a portion of it overheard and using it, and referring to him by name in a public speech elsewhere, I will not undertake to discuss here. I leave that to those who think proper to indulge in that practice.[8]

Cong. Globe, 36 Cong., 1 Sess., 1366–68.

1. Johnson interrupted a routine discussion of a navy bill in order to direct this question to Clark.

2. This is the *Herald*'s report verbatim except for minor variations in spelling, capitalization, and punctuation.

3. Although copper was discovered in the Ducktown area in 1843, the first extensive mining began eight years later at the Hiwassee Mine. After a period of hard times during the middle years of the decade, the copper mines began to revive in 1858; by 1860 prosperity had returned. R. E. Barclay, *Ducktown Back in Raht's Time* (Chapel Hill, 1946), 44, 49, 77, 82; J. B. Killebrew, *Resources of Tennessee* (Nashville, 1874), 251–52.

4. A printer's error, this figure was actually 267,910. With one or two insignificant exceptions, Johnson's figures are accurate according to the census *Compendium*. DeBow, *1850 Census, Compendium*, 170, *passim*.

5. Stephen R. Mallory, chairman of the committee on naval affairs.

6. When Johnson was governor, in December, 1856, there was a general alarm about the possibility of slave insurrections. Considerable excitement was engendered, based more on rumor than fact; in Tennessee the actual uprising was confined mainly to the ironworks area in Montgomery and Stewart counties. Nevertheless, throughout the state, vigilante committees were organized, the movement of both slaves and free Negroes greatly restricted, and any of the latter found in a locality "without authority" were ordered to leave the state. An investigation apparently led Johnson to the conclusion that there was a concerted effort on the part of nonslaveholders, under the guise of repressing a threatened uprising, to anticipate instead the extermination of all the Negroes, at least in Tennessee. Nashville *Union and American*, December 14, 20, 28, 1856; see also Letter from Springfield Citizens, December 6, 1856, *Johnson Papers*, II, 456–57n.

7. Johnson's experiences in the alarming times of 1856 were cited by Senator James Doolittle in 1862 during debates concerning slavery and the attitudes of nonslaveholders toward Negroes. Doolittle, "upon the authority of Andrew Johnson, of Tennessee," told of the governor's being asked to supply arms to nonslaveholding whites: "For what purpose? To prevent an insurrection of the slaves? This was the alleged purpose; but he ascertained the fact to be that these men were conspiring to massacre the whole slave population in that section of the State, and he was compelled to call out the militia, not to prevent the negroes from rising in insurrection, but to prevent the whites from destroying them altogether." *Cong. Globe*, 37 Cong., 2 Sess., App. 84–85.

8. Clark replied that, given the occasion, he would repeat in the Senate the statements he had made in New Hampshire. "In the meantime," Johnson might "rest assured that I shall say nothing even then in disparagement of his State; and I will not dispute but that they raise more horses, asses, and mules, than we do." *Ibid.*, 36 Cong., 1 Sess., 1368.

From William S. Pease[1]

Herald Office
New York March 28th 1860

Dear Sir

I see by the telegraphic report of the proceedings in Congress yesterday, that you called upon Senator Clark of N. H, for an explanation of his Dover Speech as published in the New York Herald of the 9th inst. As I am the person who reported the Senator upon that occasion I have thought proper to furnish you with the Exact language used by the honorable gentleman upon that occasion, so far as they are personal to yourself. I give you his Exact Language as taken by me on the spot. "Senator Johnson himself told me that if the Union should be disolved the South could not hold thier slaves five years, for said he, during the insurrection among the Slaves in Tennessee in 1856, the planters became so much alarmed that any politic Man could have gone through the State and the planters would have joined him in an effort to drive the slaves out of the State." His remarks concerning the mineral wealth of Tennessee and the inability of the people to develop the same, were in the main reported *Verbatim*. That portions of his Dover Speech he repeated at Concord on 10th of the Same Month, and was done to show the supeority of the people of New Hampshire with free institutions, over the people of Tennessee with Slavery to clog thier energy. I reported all the Main features of Mr Clarks Dover Speech and gave the essence of all his remarks but in a condensed form. I now regret that I had not reported both his Dover and Concord Speeches more fully for I then thought and am now fully persuaded that the honorable gentleman was greatly mistaken in very many of the assertions which he then made. Among other statements that he made was one Concerning the Kidnapping of two Negro children while playing in the Streets of Washington and the frantic grief of thier aged Grand parent who urgently besought members of Congress to interfere and rescue the children from thier doom. He also related a Conversation between a Negro named Isaac and himself relative to the purchase of Isaacs Wife and children, who were owned by a lady in Washington or Vicinity and who refused to Sell Isaac his family although he was anxious to purchase them. This Isaac he represented as his boot black and fire builder, and the conversation as he alleges took place upon an occasion when the man was building his fire. I have given you these facts that you may know some of the Means Made use of by these Black Republicans to Keep alive the popular New England prejudice against Slavery, and also that you may be better prepared to receive Senator Clarks Explanation. You are at liberty to make any necessary use of my name in this matter that you choose, but I would prefer that it should not be used unless absolutely necessary[.]

I am Sir,   Very Respectfully Yours

Hon A Johnson)
William S Pease
U S Senate   )

ALS, DLC-JP.

1. Pease appears to have been the typically anonymous newspaperman of the emerging large-city press. The one biographical clue thus far discovered appears in a New York directory of 1862, where he is identified as "an editor" residing at 223 West 31st Street. *Trow's New York City Directory* (1862), 668.

From William M. Lowry

Greeneville Mar 29 1860

Hon A Johnson
    Dear Sir
        I presume you will think me a greate bore, yet as important events are ahead you must bare with me in my running random Correspondence. I enclose you a few lines from our worthy freind Genl Ramsey,[1] whoes opinion is worth looking at, and as Charleston has acted So badly,[2] I would My, Self, be glad to See the Convention moved. I have laid down to Wm H Maxwell My, Program. as I am not a delegate I Can only, act out Side. I want Maxwell to be the spokesman of the Tenns delegation and I tell him when Tenns is calld upon, for her vote that he as Chairman, Must get up and advance to the Middle of the Hall and get the eye of the Chairman and Nominate you in a speech of five Minuits. that Speech must be short and pithy and if done right no telling the effect that it will have.[3] I am not Satisfied with our delegation.[4] Nevertheless Burch tells me they will all vote for you, in Convention. I am Sorry, I could not have been present in the Committee on delegates[.]   at the time of their Meeting I was on the Committee on resolutions and it Seemed we never could agree[.]   this kept me from knowing what was going on with the Other Committees, Untill every thing was too late. I was down in Middle Tenns the other day. Meet with Burch and Campbell[5] of the Avalanch. I asked Campbell why he had not [run] up the Johnson flag[.]   he made many excuses and told me his first choice

was for Nicholson then you and that he would insert Gardenhires' letter,[6] and, some Other Communications in your behalf. I wish I could See you about a day, as I feel much interest in the next race. I think the Success of our principles depend much upon the man we Nominate. It wont, do to tell me that principle is every thing[.] We might have a man whoes *principles* were first rate but had no other element of Success about him, therefore as we have a man whoes principles are Correct and who has Other elements that will rally the Mass of the people let us take him. No news only that business is pretty good[.]

Yr freind   W M Lowry

ALS, DLC-JP2.

1. This letter from John Crozier Ramsey has not been found; it is also referred to in a letter from Ramsey to Johnson, March 30, 1860, LC.

2. The advertised hotel rates, along with promised crowded accommodations, caused a number of delegations, mainly Douglas supporters from the North, to appeal for a change in convention site. The Charleston Hotel, with a normal capacity of 300, planned for 1,000 guests, with charges of $5.00 per night to cover the expenses of moving furniture and "renting additional outhouses." Comparisons were made to the Cincinnati Convention of 1856, where high costs resulted in some delegates' having difficulty returning home. Memphis *Appeal*, March 25, 1860; New York *Tribune*, March 14, 1860; New York *Herald*, March 14, 18, 1860.

3. Ewing, as chairman of the Tennessee delegation, and not Maxwell, ultimately nominated Johnson far more prosaically than Lowry envisioned. According to the press report he perfunctorily announced, "The Democracy of Tennessee have requested their Delegates to put in nomination the Hon. Andrew Johnson of Tennessee." Charleston *Courier*, May 3, 1860.

4. Lowry first mentions his displeasure with the slate in his letter of January 27. See also letters from Samuel R. Anderson, January 21; from Sam Milligan, January 30; from William H. Maxwell, February 2; from John K. Howard, February 5, 1860.

5. Colin M. Campbell (d. 1860), who had represented Shelby County at the Nashville Democratic convention in January, 1860, was briefly coeditor and copublisher of the Memphis *Avalanche*, a strongly pro-southern organ. Nashville *Union and American*, January 19, 1860; Keating, *Memphis*, I, 445, II, 219.

6. A communication from "E. L. G.," dated March 17, appeared in the Nashville party organ on March 23. Carefully written, the letter attempted to touch all bases, extolling Johnson's credentials as "a national Democrat" in the mold of Jefferson, Madison, Monroe, Jackson, and Polk. Seen as "a favorite of the toiling millions," the once humble mechanic was now the peer of the world's greatest statesmen, unswerving in his devotion to principle— and, on the basis of his homestead legislation, eminently acceptable to North, South, and Northwest. E. L. Gardenhire (1815–1899), a party wheelhorse from White County, had practiced law in Carthage and Sparta. Elected to the state senate (1849–51), he represented Fentress, Overton, Jackson, White, and Van Buren counties. While editor of the Sparta *Mountain Democrat* (1856–57), he was a delegate to the 1856 Democratic national convention and a Buchanan elector. Judge of the fifth circuit court (1858–61), he joined the Confederacy and represented the fourth district in the first permanent Confederate Congress. A decade after the war he was returned to state office, first as a representative (1875–77) and then as a judge of the court of arbitration (1877), a temporary court designed to relieve the congested docket of the

Tennessee supreme court. Nashville *Union and American*, March 23, 1860; Speer, *Prominent Tennesseans*, 387–88; *Tenn. Official Manual* (1890), 177.

From Charles Skelton[1]

Trenton [New Jersey] March 29th, 1860

Hon. Andrew Johnson,
    Dear Sir,
Your esteemed favor has been received.
Our State Convention came off yesterday. The Delegates appointed are unpledged, but opposed to Dugless.[2] I have conversd with a majority of them and find them favorably disposed to your nomination.[3] I declined being a candidate for the appointment of delegate, as I found that I could harmonise and accomplish more by not coming in conflict with those who wanted to be delegates. Judge Naar[4] the Editor of the True American, was exceedingly anxious to be a delegate and as he was friendly to you I concluded to give way to him and others. I will continue to operate on our Delegates to the extent of my ability until the convention meets.
If we can get you nominated I pledge you New Jersey by a large majority.
With high esteem I remain

your friend   Charles Skelton

ALS, DLC-JP2.

1. Charles Skelton (1806–1879), Trenton physician, served as superintendent of schools (1848), Democratic congressman (1851–55), and member of the common council (1873–75). *BDAC*, 1607.

2. In view of this observation, it is interesting to note that in the 1860 election New Jersey alone among the free states gave electoral votes to Douglas, dividing them between Lincoln and Douglas, 4–3. Joseph N. Kane, *Facts about the Presidents* (New York, 1968), 103.

3. At the Charleston convention the New Jersey delegation gave its seven votes to Guthrie; at Baltimore, Douglas received two and a half votes, all New Jersey cast. Obviously, Skelton was overly sanguine about the favorable disposition of his colleagues toward Johnson. Hesseltine, *Three against Lincoln*, 99, 249.

4. David Naar (1800–1880), born on St. Thomas, Virgin Islands, settled in 1834 in Elizabeth, New Jersey, where he was elected mayor and presiding judge of the special court. After serving as a Democrat in the state assembly (1851–52), he moved to Trenton and became editor of the *True American*. Sympathetic to the South, he tried to organize pro-southern sentiment on the eve of the war. In 1867, as chairman of the Democratic state executive committee, he drafted the party's platform stand against Negro suffrage as embodied in the proposed fourteenth amendment. New York *Times*, February 25, 1880; Charles P. Smith, *New Jersey Political Reminiscences, 1823–1882*, Hermann K. Platt, ed. (New Brunswick, 1965), 109–10; Abner J. Gaines, "New Jersey and the Fourteenth Amendment," New Jersey Historical Society *Proceedings*, LXX (1952), 50.

From Lizinka Campbell Brown

Nashville 30th. March 1860

Hon Andrew Johnson
My dear Sir

I know it is you I am to thank for two boxes of Tea plants received by Adams' Express last monday— I have delayed acknowledging them hoping every evening to receive a letter from you on the subject — in truth I only conclude they are Tea plants from their appearance corresponding with descriptions we have read of them—never having seen any before— Two weeks since I received some plants by mail under your frank but they were dead— of those you sent me last year I have one grape vine flourishing & growing well[.] the rest I lost partly from neglect but principally from ignorance.

Before receiving these plants I was about writing to you of my gratification at the course of your son Robt. with regard to a bill before the Legislature in the defeat of which I took great & I think justifiable interest— It was that for converting the old Lunatic asylum into an Executive mansion,[1] and although manifestly a scheme of the property-holders in its vicinity to raise the value of such property by an expenditure of the money of the State was so skilfully advocated by highly respectable citizens that it passed the Senate and might have passed the H. of Representatives but for the opposition of Robt. Johnson, Mr. Hurt[2] & Dr. Kennedy—[3] Mr. Cooper[4] said—*after it failed*—it was atrocious—would have been a disgrace to the Legislature had it succeeded &c—but the Ewings[5] were so much interested in its favor that he promised And. Ewing not to oppose it— Independent was it not? Edwin Ewing, Jno. M. Bass,[6] Bilbow[7]—Currin McNairy[8] &c electioneered warmly for it & no one against it—except that the Medical College & County Court each offered to purchase the building but neither offer was brought before the Legislature the members from this county being in favor of the Lunatic Asylum bill— The electioneering here in this case with members of the Legislature was what you constantly witness in the Federal Capitol— They were invited out, feasted &c &c— By the way your son says I am the worst electioneer he ever saw—and I am afraid there is some truth in it but I fancy *you* never were fond of asking favors yet those who can make friends of every vain and Common mind have never soared so high— Perhaps one secret is that you have never asked personal or pecuniary favors and Friends and Foes alike confess that "Andrew Johnson is incorruptible." If I had been entirely disinterested in the case referred to that is if there had been no question of the State purchasing this place,[9] I could have "electioneered" far more freely & effectively but there are very few men from whom I could ask a personal favor—or receive one—without feeling in some degree humiliated— Perhaps you remember how hard I found it in the case of Capt. Ewell[10] yet then I thought the promotion asked for him no more than he deserved from Government although perfectly aware that the interest you and a few others took in the matter arose from your kind interest in my wishes—

What think you at Washington of the action of the Charleston Hotel-Keepers[11] & the course of the Mercury?[12] Is there not some political motive underlying the whole action or is it simple folly? At any rate it seems to me a striking indication of the difficulty or impossibility of disunion—and of our relying for importations of foreign goods on a people who would certainly double the price the moment they secured a monopoly—

Genl. Foote[13] was here the other evening and has made up his mind to Douglas or Disunion—no other man can save the Country by preventing the election of a Black republican—& therefore under the impulse of exalted patriotism the Ex-governor has attached himself to the fortunes of the Illinois senator—and spares neither flattery, promises nor threats (of disunion) to promote his cause— but so far as I have been able to ascertain the Governor's facile eloquence has so far succeeded only with the female portion of the community and Mrs. Polk, Mrs. Porter and Mrs. G. M. Fogg[14] are the converts of whom he chiefly boasts— In this country men—particularly such men as Gov. Foote—are fond of talking of the influence of women—but it seems to me such a complete mockery that the only thing to reconcile one to it is the reflection that from those to whom much is given, much will be required—and awful will be their responsibility who assist in moulding the destiny of nations— I need not tell you we look forward with intense interest to the nomination at Charleston and earnestly hope it will *not* be Douglas but will be one in whose support North & South can cordially unite—

Did I write you that Campbell Hattie[15] & I expect to go to Europe in July and perhaps remain a year or more— Mrs. Jno Bell has applied to rent our house during our absence and I have promised her a positive answer in a month— The nearer the time approaches the more reluctance I feel at going but I have resolved on it as the best thing for Campbell & Hattie & hope to have resolution to carry it out—[16]

I was sorry to hear such bad accounts of my friend "Isabel" but can believe her guilty of nothing but imprudence—and must confess that a worse excuse for even the slightest indiscretion than that man

Stuart[17] whom I met at Genl. Cass' could hardly be found— possibly this consciousness in Isabella might have thrown her off her guard against appearances which did as much injustice to her good taste as to more important qualities—

I am sorry to send so uninteresting a letter but have not been well this winter & am therefore more stupid than usual—

Your sincere friend   L. C. Brown

ALS, DLC-JP2.

1. Having passed the senate by a comfortable margin, the bill (S. 277), appropriating the old asylum property as a permanent site for the governor's mansion, encountered strong opposition in the lower house. Complicating the matter, the University of Nashville medical department held a lease on the land in question. Robert Johnson tried to block consideration of the bill by laying it on the table; when this motion failed, he offered a substitute measure authorizing division of the land into lots, streets, and alleys for sale at public auction. The opposition tabled Johnson's proposal, but after further maneuvering his supporters rallied to defeat the original bill on March 23, 30–25. Since the University's lease had six years remaining, possession of the asylum property would have been difficult, even had the bill succeeded. *Nashville News*, March 7, 25, 1860; *Tenn. House Journal*, 1859–60, pp. 1149–53.

2. Robert B. Hurt was a native of Halifax, Virginia, and represented Madison County (1859–61, 1875–77). Robison Biog. Data.

3. Thomas J. Kennedy (b. c1800), a physician, represented Giles County (1859–61). *Ibid.*

4. William F. Cooper (1820–1909), one of the compilers of the most recent *Tennessee Code*, was a Nashville lawyer and judge of the state supreme court (1861, 1878–86). A vice president of the American Bar Association (1879) and one of the great legal minds of his day, he edited a republication of supreme court reports, published *Tennessee Chancery Reports*, and re-edited numerous other legal works. John W. Green, *Lives of the Judges of the Supreme Court of Tennessee, 1796–1947* (Knoxville, 1947), 194–97.

5. Andrew and Edwin Ewing. Cooper was Andrew Ewing's law partner.

6. John M. Bass (1804–1878), several times mayor of Nashville and the president of the Union Bank, was a lawyer, merchant, and planter with extensive holdings in Louisiana and Arkansas. Clayton, *Davidson County*, 120; McGavock, *Pen and Sword*, 35; Owsley, *Guide to Manuscripts*, 27.

7. William N. Bilbo (c1815–1867), a Virginia-born Nashville lawyer, was a leader in the Know-Nothing party and a newspaperman serving on the staff of the Nashville *Gazette*; he was briefly proprietor of the paper (1856). McGavock, *Pen and Sword*, 337n; *Nashville Bus. Dir.* (1860–61), 128; Josephus C. Guild, *Old Times in Tennessee* (Nashville, 1878), 498; 1850 Census, Tenn., Davidson, 281.

8. Probably R. C. McNairy (b. c1818) a wealthy Nashville dry goods merchant. 1860 Census, Tenn., Davidson, Nashville, 5th ward, 161; *Nashville Bus. Dir.* (1860–61), 232.

9. Her own home across the street from the state capitol was later requisitioned and used by Johnson as military governor. Turner, "Recollections of Andrew Johnson," 172.

10. Richard S. Ewell (1817–1872), West Point graduate (1840) who served in the Mexican War and on the frontier, resigned from the army in 1861 to become a Confederate cavalry officer under Stonewall Jackson. After the loss of a leg in 1862, he married Lizinka Brown, his widowed cousin, during his convalescence. Returning to the field, he was captured on the retreat toward Appomattox and held at Fort Warren for three months before being released; he spent his remaining years on his wife's farm in Spring Hill,

Tennessee. *DAB*, VI, 229–30; also see Hamlin, *Letters of General R. S. Ewell.*

11. A reference to the high prices and condescending manner of the Charleston hotel-keepers who seemed determined not only to profit greatly from the convention but also "to confine the convention to the silk-stocking Democracy." New York *Tribune*, March 20, 1860.

12. In the face of mounting criticism of Charleston as the convention site, the *Mercury*, owned by fire-eater Robert Barnwell Rhett, had responded by attacks on the northern, and especially northwestern, Democracy. The Charleston paper averred, "It is greatly desired that their number [the 'hangers-on' present at all conventions] may be reduced [as a result of high prices] . . . . If Mr. Douglas and his friends desire a Northern convention let them call one." *Ibid.*, March 19, 1860.

13. Henry S. Foote (1804–1880) was a lawyer, U. S. senator (1847–52), and governor of Mississippi (1852–54). After a four-year sojourn in California, he returned East, moving near Nashville in 1859. He served in the first and second Confederate congresses and later became superintendent of the mint at New Orleans (1878–80). *BDAC*, 902; *DAB*, V, 500–501.

14. The ladies were Sarah Childress Polk, widow of James K. Polk; Felicia Ann Grundy Eakin Porter (1820–1889), daughter of Felix Grundy, also a widow; and Mrs. Godfrey M. Fogg (d. 1881), the wife of a leading Nashville businessman and civic leader. McGavock, *Pen and Sword, passim*; Acklen, *Tenn. Records*, I, 91.

15. Campbell and Hattie were Mrs. Brown's children. Campbell Brown (1840–1893) served as General Ewell's aide during the Civil War and later became a prosperous Maury County dairy farmer. *Ibid.*, 276; Hamlin, *Letters of General R. S. Ewell*, 133; Tennessee Bureau of Agriculture, *Forty-fifth Biennial Report* (Nashville, 1964), 271.

16. See Letter from Lizinka Campbell Brown, June 12, 1860.

17. The participants in this "indiscretion" probably were Isabella Cass (Baroness von Limburg), daughter of Secretary of State Lewis Cass, and Charles E. Stuart, Democratic senator from Michigan. Frank B. Woodford, *Lewis Cass: The Last Jeffersonian* (New Brunswick, 1950), 296.

From John Crozier Ramsey

Knoxville Ten March 30th [1860]

Dear Sir

I have been wanting to write to you for some time—but I have been absent for a week or two attending Court—and then I have had the *Newman controversy* on hand also— I suppose you have read both sides of the case—and knowing them as you did before—I expect you had your opinion formed— since my communications have been published[1]—public sentiment is now sett[l]ed down that they are *both guilty*.

I am very much surprised at the course of the Register in regard to yourself— their is but one opinion here (and I might say all over the State) and that is for you—and yet we have a paper misrepresenting the will of our party—[2] Can you account for it? We cant help it here—but from this on up to the time of the meeting of the Convention—we intend to have communications weekly favoring your nomination and by that means to kill off to some extent the edi-torial influance the paper may have[.]

I wrote to Mr Lowry a few days ago giving him my opinion that I thought that it would be greatly to your interest to have the place for the meeting of the convention changed to Baltimore. In the ex-treme South the [*sic*] some are opposed to you on account of your Homestead bill—and at Charleston the outside pressure (which has its influence) might be against you—but at Baltimore the outside feeling would be in your favor—   Aside from this Charleston is rather an arristocratic place any how—   If you should agree with me you might suggest to your friends the propriety of changing the convention. A friend of mine from Madisonville has written me the following letter which I send you—[3]   that is the only information I have of an effort to have me removed—and I am disposed to doubt that Newman or his friends would try it—   If I should be entitled to more credit for one official act than another—it should be given to me for my action in the exposure of the fraud and forgery in the Newman case. If any thing of the kind is going on I hope you will see that no injustice is done me and that no one misrepresents me. I have done nothing wrong and have only discharged my official duty[.] Let me hear from you soon[.]

Yours truly   J. C. Ramsey

ALS, DLC-JP2.

1. See Nashville *Union and American*, March 6, 8, 1860; see also Letter from Robert Johnson, February 22, 1860.

2. The editorial statements of George Bradfield, owner-editor of the Knoxville *Register*, ostensibly a Democratic paper, were a continuing embar-rassment to Johnson's Knoxville supporters. See Letter from John E. Helms, December 9, 1859, and letters from Charles W. Charlton, March 15, April 10, 1860.

3. Ramsey enclosed a confidential letter from H. A. Hood of Madisonville, warning that there was a movement on foot to have Ramsey removed as at-torney general for East Tennessee. Hood to Ramsey, March 28, 1860, John-son Papers, LC.

Resolution on Improvements in the Capitol[1]

March 30, 1860

Mr. JOHNSON, of Tennessee. Some days ago, it will be remem-bered, I offered a resolution, by instruction of the Committee to Audit and Control the Contingent Expenses of the Senate, for the purpose of authorizing that committee to have the committee-rooms of the Senate furnished, and such lights provided as should be deemed ad-visable and expedient. I hope the Senate will take up the resolution and pass it. I think it will save many thousands of dollars to the Government.

The motion was agreed to; and the following resolution, submitted by Mr. JOHNSON, of Tennessee, on the 21st of March, was read:

Resolved, That the Committee to Audit and Control the Contingent Expenses of the Senate be, and they are hereby, authorized to have the north wing of the Capitol fitted up with the necessary fixtures for gas (in conformity with the general style of those in the south wing) in the passage, corridors, committee, office and other rooms; and also to provide the committee and other rooms with such other furniture as, in their judgment, is necessary; and that the cost thereof be paid out of the contingent fund of the Senate.

The VICE PRESIDENT.[2] This is the second reading of the resolution. It must go through the same forms as a bill. It is now before the Senate as in Committee of the Whole, and open to amendment.

Mr. MASON.[3] I would ask the honorable chairman of the committee, whether there has been any estimate of the cost of the furniture and fixtures which it is proposed to purchase. There is no statement in the resolution of the amount required.

Mr. JOHNSON, of Tennessee. I will say to the Senator that the Secretary[4] has been going on and purchasing furniture and furnishing the rooms, as required by the members of committees. The Secretary is now indisposed, and cannot attend to such business, and the accounts have all to be submitted to the Committee on Contingent Expenses. The resolution authorizes—it does not direct—that committee to have it done. Of course they will examine the prices, and know what everything is to cost the Government before allowing the expenditure. It is not directory, but simply to authorize them to do so if, in their judgment, it is required.[5]

Cong. Globe, 36 Cong., 1 Sess., 1443.

1. Johnson resubmitted his resolution, originally offered on March 21, but not considered then because Senators Cameron and Mason had voiced objections, causing the resolution to be laid over. *Cong. Globe*, 36 Cong., 1 Sess., 1277.

2. John C. Breckinridge.

3. James Mason of Virginia.

4. Asbury Dickens.

5. With the present Congress saddled by "extravagant bills," Chandler of Michigan moved an amendment aimed at forcing acceptance of the lowest bid on the gas contract. After assurances from Johnson and Powell of Kentucky that the committee would accept the best bid, since "the committee have universally acted on that principle during the session," Chandler withdrew his amendment and the resolution passed. *Cong. Globe*, 36 Cong., 1 Sess., 1443.

From William C. Scruggs[1]

Marshalls Ferry Ten April 3rd 1860

Hon Andrew Johnson

Dr Sir Enclosed you will find a Letter that I wish you to give it [sic] To the Revd Wm. McLain Fin Sec A. C. S[2] as I do not know how to direct it [.] I am not acquainted with the usual way of Sending Letters to Liberia[.] The Boy Alfred was liberated by Hugh Cain Senr[.][3] He landed at Monrovia in December[.] He is dissatisfied and wants to return[.] I told him before he left the only condition that he could come back upon that He would have to go into Slavery[.] Please enquire and inform me how I can arrange to have money deposited to pay his passage and Rail Road fees to this place[.] I own his wife & children[.] his wife is very willing for him to return[.] He promised her he would do so if he did not like the country[.] I thought best to write to you upon the Subject not knowing how the Secretary might view the thing[.] you can manage the thing for me as you may think best[.] I want the boy to come back[.] He lived with me about eight years and I know him to be a good Boy[.] I have written to him that the money will be ready in Baltimore by the time the ship returns to pay his passage &c and you can if necessary assure the Secretary that the money will be ready and I will deposit the funds in any Bank or other place that I may be directed[.] If any thing has been done about Thos Glassgow Pension[4] please inform me[.] The said Thos. now thinks you one of the greatest men in the nation but heretofore has universally voted against you[.] Everything is working well for the Democracy & Should you be honored with the nomination at Charleston I feel certain that Tennessee will give you more votes than upon any former occasion[.]

Yours very Respectfully   Wm C. Scruggs

ALS, DLC-JP2.

1. William C. Scruggs (b. c1811) was a Tennessee-born merchant with real estate valued at $15,000. 1860 Census, Tenn., Grainger, 42.

2. As governor, Johnson had corresponded with McLain, secretary of the American Colonization Society, concerning passage to Liberia for an emancipated slave, Hector, and his family and had commissioned Robert as agent to transport freed Negroes to ports of embarkation. See *Johnson Papers*, II, 360, 377, 380, 445, 447, 451.

3. Probably Hugh Cain, Sr., of Hawkins County, who died about 1850. Worth S. Ray, *Tennessee Cousins* (Baltimore, 1966), 128.

4. Probably Thomas Glassgo [Glasgow?] (b. c1783), a Virginia-born Grainger countian of modest means in 1860. On March 23, 1860, Tennessee Congressman William B. Stokes reported a private bill (H. R. 466) granting an invalid pension to Thomas Glasgow; however, the Senate committee on

pensions reported the bill adversely on June 14, and no further action was taken. 1860 Census, Tenn., Grainger, 8; *Cong. Globe*, 36 Cong., 1 Sess., 1336, 2955.

From James C. Luttrell[1]

Knoxville Tenn April 5th, 1860.

Hon Andrew Johnson
   Washington D. C.
     Dear Sir

On yesterday I received a letter from Mr Maynard[2] informing me that the "River Bill"[3] which I spoke to you about when in Washington had passed the House and had gone to the Senate. I will be much obliged to you if you will look into the matter at once and get it pushed through the Senate at as an [*sic*] early day as possible. The claim is a just one and ought to have been paid five years ago. Your attention to this for me will place me under many obligations to you as I really need the amount due me very much, and hope you may get the matter along easily. Would be much pleased to hear from you soon.

Very truly yours   James C. Luttrell

ALS, DLC-JP2.

1. James C. Luttrell (1813–1878), Knoxville Whig lawyer, served as county register (1848–56), postmaster (1849–53), state comptroller (1855–58), and mayor (1854, 1859–67). A Unionist during the war, he later became a Democrat and was elected to the state senate (1869–71). Rothrock, *French Broad-Holston Country*, 440.

2. Horace Maynard, second district congressman.

3. On August 30, 1852, Congress appropriated $50,000 for the improvement of the Tennessee River. When these funds were exhausted in 1854, no further appropriation was made and the work ceased. Money was owed to the project's engineer and foreman, as well as to a number of citizens, including Luttrell and Charles W. Charlton, Knoxville postmaster, who had furnished powder and supplies. The bill (H. R. 89) to settle these accounts passed the House on March 30, 1860, was agreed to without amendments by the Senate, and received Buchanan's signature on June 12. *Cong. Globe*, 36 Cong., 1 Sess., 1462, 1466, 2797, 2840, 2896; Charlton to Johnson, April 3, 1860, Johnson Papers, LC.

Exchange with James S. Green[1]

April 5, 1860

Mr. JOHNSON, of Tennessee. Mr. President, so far as my views go with reference to the homestead question, I am willing to give them now or at any other time. What I mean by a homestead is to put a man into the possession of a certain amount of soil that he may call his home; and, so far as the Federal Government is concerned, to protect him from any forced sale or execution so long as the title remains here. Then I proceed upon the idea that if the States have not already provided for it, they will commence the policy where the Federal Government ceases; that they will, by State legislation, secure to each individual a certain amount of soil that he may call his own. You may denominate it a homestead—the abiding place of his wife and children—or whatever name you think proper. The advocates of this bill do not assume any power on the part of the Federal Government to come into conflict with State authority; but while the title remains in the Federal Government, until the settler complies with the condition of the law, it is intended to guaranty and protect him in the enjoyment of the land against any debt or contract made prior to the title passing from the Federal Government to him, presuming that the States where this land lies, and where the individuals are, will pursue the same policy and carry out the same principle of justice. The same popular sentiment that induces the Federal Government to adopt the policy here, will induce the States to take up and carry it out. That is what I mean by the homestead measure.

Mr. GREEN. He says "the same popular sentiment." That discloses a wonderful amount of information. I understand—

Mr. JOHNSON, of Tennessee. Permit me, in addition, to say, so far as securing homesteads is concerned, that it is very hard for a State or the Federal Government to secure one of its citizens in the enjoyment of that which never existed. There is one thing very clear; neither the State nor the Federal Government can secure a man in the enjoyment of a home, if he never possesses one. If he gets one, it must be subject to the operation of the laws under which he lives.

Mr. GREEN. I understand that, Mr. President. He says, "the same popular sentiment." There is a wonderful amount of meaning in that. I see why it is that the trees bend to the gushing wind. I see why it is that individuals bow to what they suppose to be popular sentiment. Popular sentiment! Sir, I will stand by the Constitution of the country against popular sentiment. I will stand up for justice, against the gushing wind. I will stand up for what is right, even if public sentiment is against it. Now, sir, is it right, or wrong, in this Federal Government, to do this?

Mr. JOHNSON, of Tennessee. By permission of the honorable Senator, I will say that, in assuming any position I may assume here, I do not act in contravention of the Constitution of the United States. I stand here as the advocate of popular sentiment, in conformity with the organic law and the laws that are made in pursuance of it. I believe the homestead proposition is right; I believe it is constitutional; and in standing by it, I believe I stand by the Constitution, and thereby reflect popular sentiment in accordance with its provisions.

[Green remarks that the Homestead bill would discourage "industry, enterprise, and energy" by attempting to equalize the condition of the citizens. Intimating that popular sentiment for a measure can have ulterior motives, he asserts that when the people are wrong, they must be opposed.]

Mr. JOHNSON, of Tennessee. Who are to be the judges?

Mr. GREEN. Good sense and honesty.

Mr. JOHNSON, of Tennessee. Who is to exercise that—the people or the Senate?

Mr. GREEN. The Senate—the people sending them here.

Mr. JOHNSON, of Tennessee. I say the people.

[Reaffirming his position that the Senate should exercise judgment, Green expresses fear that the states would abuse the federal Homestead law once the land and settler became subject to state law. Further, he questions the wisdom of tax exemption on public lands sold as homesteads.]

Mr. JOHNSON, of Tennessee. The Senator makes his proposition very broad. It seems to me that the Government is generally in a better condition to do without what is due it than an individual is; and if we exempt a homestead from the payment of a debt between man and man in the same neighborhood, it would seem to me that the Federal Government is competent to get along without collecting taxes from the homesteads of the settlers. I repeat to the Senator, I would exempt the homestead that gives a man's wife and children, and himself, an abiding place, from the payment of all taxes to the Government, State or Federal.

Mr. GREEN. Is that the law of Tennessee?

Mr. JOHNSON, of Tennessee. I say the homestead there is exempt from the payment of any description of debt, either to the State or individuals.[2]

[Here Green asserts that "a State may do certain things which the Federal government cannot do."]

Mr. JOHNSON, of Tennessee. I would ask the Senator if most of the States do not exempt their public buildings, their burial grounds, their churches, and their benevolent institutions from taxes? Is not that the custom in all the States?[3]

Mr. GREEN. True; exactly as I say. I say the States have a right to do it, and most of them do; but this Federal Government cannot do the same thing. Can we sell a piece of land, or give away a piece of land, and say it shall never be subject to taxation, and that the party occupying it shall never be subjected to the payment of taxes upon it?

Mr. JOHNSON, of Tennessee. I would ask the honorable Senator if the public lands now lying in the States are subject to taxation?[4]

Mr. GREEN. They are not subject to taxation, because there is a special compact made that they should not be until they were sold. But for that compact, it might be so; but when they are sold—

Mr. BENJAMIN. I would remind the Senator also of the fact, that the General Government gave a large quantity of land to the States in exchange for that.

Mr. GREEN. Yes, sir; we gave the sixteenth section, and in some cases the thirty-sixth section; we gave seventy-two sections for public buildings; we gave the salt springs, and six sections surrounding them, and various other land grants, and five per cent. of the proceeds, as a consideration for not taxing them.

Mr. JOHNSON, of Tennessee. Really, I want to be informed on this subject.

Mr. GREEN. You shall be.

Mr. JOHNSON, of Tennessee. Does the Senator concede that the States have authority to tax the public lands lying within their limits?

Mr. GREEN. When you get through, I will answer.

Mr. JOHNSON, of Tennessee. Has not that power been denied again and again? It has been a matter of agreement in the admission of a State, one of the conditions on which she could get in, that she would not tax the public lands. Has the power to tax them ever been conceded and acknowledged on the part of this Government?[5]

Cong. Globe, 36 Cong., 1 Sess., 1554–55.

1. James S. Green (1817–1870), Virginia-born lawyer who settled in Missouri, served as a Democrat in Congress (1847–51), chargé d'affaires to Colombia (1853–54), and senator (1857–61). During the course of the previous day, Green, apprehensive that the pending homestead bill would not be fully carried out in the various states having public lands, had proposed, as a substitute for the House homestead bill, that the government, instead of initiating a new public land sale system, extend existing preemption laws to allow two years to pay for land. *BDAC*, 970; *DAB*, VII, 549–50; *Cong. Globe*, 36 Cong., 1 Sess., 1535, 1553–54.

2. As Green later observes, Johnson is wrong. Although homesteads worth up to five hundred dollars were "exempt from attachment and execution, for the debts of every such housekeeper or head of a family," the *Tennessee Code* stated clearly that such homesteads were subject to sale, "for all State, county and corporation taxes, legally assessed thereon." Return J. Meigs and William F. Cooper, comps., *Code of Tennessee Enacted by the General Assembly of 1857–58* . . . (Nashville, 1858), 430, 431.

3. As a general rule, religious, educational, and charitable institutions, public buildings and property, monuments and cemeteries have not been taxed by the state. The *Tennessee Code* authorized such exemptions, and other states likewise shielded their religious and public service institutions from taxation, either by law, custom, court decision, or constitutional decree. *Ibid.*, 172; Carl Zollmann, *American Civil Church Law*, in Columbia University *Studies in History, Economics and Public Law*, LXXVII (New York, 1917), 236–84.

4. According to the Ordinance of 1787, "no tax shall be imposed on lands the property of the United States." A modification of this sweeping exemption came during the period from 1802 until 1820, when new states were obliged to agree not to tax public lands until five years after purchase. Although with the passage of time the issue became almost a moot question, Congress, clarified the matter on January 26, 1847, by passing a law allowing states to tax all lands sold by the United States from the day of sale. Ordinance of 1787, Art. 4; Robbins, *Our Landed Heritage*, 157; *U. S. Statutes*, IX, 118.

5. In answer, Green affirmed that federal lands are subject to taxation the moment the title passes from the United States, and he correctly observed that homesteads in Tennessee were subject to state taxation. Advocating the cession of public lands to the states, he attacked the current graduation law as encouraging fraud and speculation and denounced the idea of federal homesteads as reflecting an "agrarian principle" that threatened southern interests. The session ended inconclusively.

From Reuben H. Long[1]

Memphis Ap 6th 1860

Hon Andrew Johnson
    Dear Sir
Although personally unknown to you I have a feeling of gratitude on account of your unwavering devotion to the homestead measure. The mechanics and laboring men of our country will remember you when the Wigfalls[2] and men of his stripe are lost in oblivion. I am a carpenter by trade and will say that the Memphis mechanics fare about as well as they do in most cities, but our situation is far from enviable. Wages range here from 2. to 2.50 pr day, but then the expenses incident to housekeeping absorb all a mans earnings. Rents here for the class of houses that Mechanics occupy range from $15 to $25 pr month, and provisions in proportion, so that even here where mechanics and laborers are paid punctually and fair wages, our condition is verry precarious, and there is no remedy that I can see but in a homestead law. I hear men say every day "What is the poor mechanic to do[?] he labors hard from year to year deprived of the comforts of life and without hope for a home in declining years?" for it is out of the question now for a poor man to think about getting property in the cities of our country.
It is not worth while to review the arguments used in opposition to the homestead bill; nor even to notice the charge that is made against you as aiding the abolitionists in your advocacy of this measure, but there is one thing certain that the white man and the free man needs some legislation and his interests and wants demand attention as well, if not more than the everlasting negro question.
    Praying that the Lord may strengthen you in your advocacy of this measure I subscribe myself an humble mechanic

R H Long

P. S. any documents you may have to spare would be gratefully received[.]

Reuben H Long

ALS, DLC-JP2.

1. Reuben H. Long (b. c1828) was a Virginia-born carpenter. 1850 Census, Tenn., Shelby, 43; *Memphis City Business Directory* (1855–56), 142.

2. Louis T. Wigfall (1816–1874), South Carolina-born Texas senator (1859–61), served in the Seminole War in Florida (1835), was admitted to the bar (1839), and moved to Texas (1848) where he was a state representative (1849–50) and senator (1857–60) before election to the U. S. Senate in December, 1859. A flamboyant and vigorous spokesman for southern rights—and ultimately for secession—the new senator had recently harangued his associates in what his biographer calls "the most disorganized speech of his senatorial career, a four-hour extemporaneous filibuster" replete with caustic comment against Johnson and the homestead idea, making loyal friends of both indignant. Withdrawing from the Senate early in 1861, Wigfall served in the Confederate army and Congress. *BDAC*, 1813; *DAB*, XX, 187–88; *Cong. Globe*, 36 Cong., 1 Sess., 1298–1302; Alvey L. King, *Louis T. Wigfall: Southern Fire-eater* (Baton Rouge, 1970), 88.

From George V. Hebb

Mulberry, Lincoln Co Ten
April 7th, 1860.

Dear Sir

Some days ago I Enclosed a letter from our Legislature to Mr Nicholson recommending me to the President for the appointment of Superintendent of Indian Affairs for the Territory of Utah—
I should be under lasting obligation—if you would, do me the kindness to join in the recommendation to the President— I need not say any more to you on this Subject—as our acquaintance has been of old standing & you know whether my Energy, & Experience in both Civil & Military would suit the position I ask—
You are aware that I was two years & six months in the Army—on the Rio Grande & in the City of Mexico—
I am aware that at this time your position is such that you could not take an active part in this matter— You must urge our delegation on for me & make them put it through[.] I understand there will be two appointments of this sort to make—one for Utah & one for Washington Territory (superintendent)[.] Sebastion[1] of Arkansas could do me a great deal of good in this case as he is chaiman of the Committee on Indian affairs[.] I am well acquainted with him[.] his first appointment in Arkansas he received from my Father-in-law Col. Yell[.][2] get him Enlisted in the Cause[.] Arkansas will not ask for the place as she already has one superintendent & six or Eight *Agencies*— I have no news of interest— Bob.[3] was in Lincoln last

week & promised to spend his time with me while here but the
fair sex took posession of him[.] I saw Geo. W. Jones, three days
ago. I urged it upon him the importance of his going to Charleston.
he has partly promised— I must see him again & make him go—⁴
he could be of great service to you[.] I so stated it to him & a
friend who can be of service—& will not put himself to some inconvenience is no true friend[.] Jones of course feels as anxious for your
Success at Charleston as any man in Tennessee—feeling sure with
such a Ticket we need not dread the contest—

Excuse haste   Your friend

To the Hon Andrew Johnson Geo. V. Hebb

ALS, DLC-JP2.

    1. William K. Sebastian, senator from Arkansas.

    2. Archibald Yell (1797–1847) moved to Tennessee from North Caro-
lina as a youth, campaigned in the Creek War, the War of 1812, and the
Mexican War, practiced law in Lincoln County, was judge of Arkansas Territory (1832–35), Democratic congressman from Arkansas (1836–39,
1845–46), and governor (1840–44). He was killed at Buena Vista in 1847.
Goodspeed's Bedford, 1189; *BDAC*, 1856–57.

    3. Robert Johnson.

    4. Despite Hebb's pressure, Jones did not go to Charleston.

From William M. Lowry

Greeneville Ten Apl 7 1860

My Dear Sir

    as the business of the day is over I seat my Self to have a verry
Short talk with my old freind[.] in the first place I Enclose you a
letter from our Mutual freind Dr Ramsey¹ that you may See what the
old man is about in the event of your Nomination[.] then it will be
necessary to get up a number one paper here. I have written to Some
of the Tennessee delegation recommending Maxwell as their Chairman[.]² if you felt disposed and thought it would not be indelicate
you might do Something in that way, through our freinds Nicholson,
Wright, & Smith.³ I sent some Communications to the Daybook, &
Richmond Index⁴ upon the Subject of the Presidency Some days ago
with a request that they publish the Same. I See that Hunters⁵ freinds
are making a Strong push for him. of all the public men spoken of,
I regard him as the Weakest[.] I look upon him however as a good
sound National Man and if Nominated would rejoice at his Election[.] I would like much [if] I could be at Washington to hear the
under Current. I trust however that all things may work out for the
best. If you leisure drop me a line. If I Can pull any string[s], that
will beanifit my freind let me know where to Strike. I am going down

to Knoxville next week[.] if I hear any thing, may write you, tho as the time of the Meeting of the Convention is now so near I presume nothing will turn up to effect any thing. We have had remarkably fine weather the last week[.] all Nature is putting on her beauty, and lovelyness, business verry fine. and the wheat prospect much better than anticipated[.] a freind of ours in Sevier County sent me a list of names[6] to whom he would be obliged if you would Send them Some Documents along from time to time.   in Haste

Yr freind

Hon A Johnson   Wm. M. Lowry.
Washington City

ALS, DLC-JP2.
    1. J. G. M. Ramsey suggested that, in view of the *Register*'s activities, Johnson's friends should take steps to establish a paper in Knoxville. He pledged his cooperation and that of "the other Democrats in Knox except those of the Newman School—6 or perhaps 6 & ½—" Ramsey to Lowry, April 5, 1860, Johnson Papers, LC.
    2. Lowry's advice was not followed; Andrew Ewing was named chairman.
    3. A. O. P. Nicholson, John V. Wright, Samuel A. Smith.
    4. The Norfolk (Va.) *Day Book*, originally established by John R. Hathaway as a "neutral" daily, was published from October, 1857, to July, 1880. Suppressed by the Union forces during the Civil War, it was revived as a Republican paper. Cappon, *Va. Newspapers*, 135. For Richmond (Va.) *Index*, see Letter from William M. Lowry, February 24, 1860.
    5. R. M. T. Hunter.
    6. Not located.

From George W. Jones

Fayetteville Tennessee   April 8, 1860.
Hon Andrew Johnson
Dear Sir;
    Upon reading the Editorial in Union and American in which Col Gentry[1] was represented as an opponent of the Homestead measure, I turned to the Journal and Globe, and furnished the facts and votes prepared and copied from the records, from which the Editor made the very excellent article in the Union and American of yesterday, and which I send herewith enclosed.[2] From the vote of May 12, 1852 he omitted the name of A. G. Brown,[3] of Miss, who was then in the House and voted for the bill— From the Same vote the name of Wm. M. Churchwell of Tennessee is omited. These two omissions supplied, to correct the facts and I think the article an excellent one.
                                    Your friend   G. W. Jones
[Enclosure][4]
    In the estimation of some gentlemen, it is a crying evil and awfully unconstitutional, for the free born, and Citizens of the United States

by birth rights, to govern themselves in the Territories and introduce or exclude—protect or neglect Slavery, and the exercise of which is deemed by some rigidly patriotic as Cause sufficient, to dismember this fair fabric of government and resolve society into its original elements. But a gentleman[5] of the good old Commonwealth of Virginia, Can marry a wife, be elected to Congress, appointed Governor of a Territory, the legislature of that Territory passes a bill divorces him from his wife he left in Virginia, he marries another woman and returns to Washington, and not a word is said against the exercise of such power by such Territory, in dissolving the most sacred of all human alliances and which for near sixteen hundred years of the Christain era was held by the Mother Church, she still so holds, to be indissoluble. The Washington Star a few weeks Since Stated that Dr. Strother[6] of Washington, City, who had previously married Rhoda Gaines the daughter of Genl E. P. Gaines, had seperated from his wife, and was then in Kansas, for the purpose of procuring a divorce from his wife. And that he had before leaving Washington, procured letters from Senators, Mason, Crittenden and others to aid him in effecting his purposes.[7]

ALS, DLC-JP2.

1. Meredith P. Gentry, Tennessee Whig congressman (1839–43, 1845–53).

2. In an editorial published on April 4, the Johnson organ had accused Gentry of opposing the homestead bill; three days later, thanks to Jones's prompt vigilance, it corrected itself. Gentry had voted for the Johnson-sponsored bill (H. R. 7) which passed the House on May 12, 1852. The correction was an important one, for it furnished an argument to refute the Opposition's efforts to link Johnson's homestead proposals with Republicanism. Indeed, on every possible occasion the *Union and American* presented Opposition stalwarts Gentry, Gustavus A. Henry, John Bell, and even Millard Fillmore, as friends of homestead legislation. *Cong. Globe*, 32 Cong., 1 Sess., 1351; *House Journal*, 32 Cong., 1 Sess., 705; Nashville *Union and American*, April 4, 7, 1860.

3. Albert G. Brown.

4. Although Jones makes no reference to it, the following comment on the inconsistency of views regarding the power of a territorial legislature was apparently part of this letter.

5. Fayette McMullen, Virginia congressman, was appointed governor of Washington Territory in 1857. Once in Olympia, he applied through the legislature for a divorce, which was granted January 25, 1858. In July, soon after his marriage to Miss Mary Wood of Olympia, McMullen was removed for incompetence. He later served in the Confederate Congress. Ralph R. Knapp, "Divorce in Washington," *Pacific Northwest Quarterly*, V (1911), 121. See also *Johnson Papers*, I, 633n.

6. Robert S. Strother married Miss Whitney, daughter of Myra (Clark) Whitney Gaines, wife of General Edmund P. Gaines. John B. Nicklin, "The Strother Family," *Tyler's Historical and Genealogical Magazine*, XI (1929–30), 185.

7. This disquisition on the sanctity of marriage vows came from a man who was by this time firmly committed to bachelorhood.

To Robert Johnson, Greeneville

                                        Washington City   April 8th 1860

My dear Son,

   Your letter has been received and read— In reference to the Charleston Convention I have but little to Say as to what would be the proper Course for you to pursue— As to my nomination at Charleston there is little or no hope if I even desired it, which I do not unless it could be attained in a proper manner which is a thing that Cannot be done in my opinion— There will be evey possible appliance brought to bear upon the convention foul and fair that is believed will have any influence whatever— If you think you can do any good by going and desire to go, I would go and see the matter through and take such a hand as delacacy and propriety dictated and no more— My intention has been alalong[*sic*] to come home before the convention Sit for the purpose of seeing Genl Milligan & Maxwell in person: but find now that it will be impossible to do so— The Homestead is now before Senate and under discussion and will continue So until it is disposed of, which I hope will be next week: but it m[a]y continue longer and [I] must stay of course and see it disposed of— I think we shall pass it in some shape— I wish you would say to Genl Milligan that as matters now stand I cannot come home as I expected to in time [to] see him before the convention— As to being posted up there is no points here that are not understood there that are worth understanding— Evey day of [*sic*] or two there is some new phase presented in reference to some of the candidates— There is but one way to be posted up and that is to understand the leading eliments which are involved and then to give them a proper direction— The delegation from Tenn ought to go into the convention firm and united, prepared to stand by the nomination the State has made[1] without being offensive to any other candidate— Douglas and friends seem at present very sanguin of his nomination— They Claim more than his posative [strength] and then imagine by some sort of expediency that other strength can be brought over to his support and that by some sort of hook or by crook he will get through— He Douglas no doubt will go into the convention the Strong man as the matter now stands and after making a fair effort should fail and then with draw from the contest he can if he will dictate the nomination: hence the importance of occupying an acceptable position to him and friends— It is said by some that if he can rally one half of the convention in his Support,[2] that they intend to sit the convention out or have him nominated.— I do not vouch for the truth of this statement: but there is one thing very certain; that they will go into convention determined to make a desperate fight and there is no telling what extrems they go to— But our delegation should go there and see how the matters stand with the other delegations and ascertain whether the Douglas men are so wedded to him that they will go for no one else— It m[a]y be when his assumed strength is understood that they are not prepared to go so far as some suppose and that after giving him afair [*sic*] trial will support some other man with as much willingness as Mr Douglas— Infine there is no knoing much about it in these Corrupt times— I heard it said yesterday that Bright[3] of Indiana had the delegation of that State in his pocket notwithstanding they were Douglas men and then others say that John Slidell of La has bright in his pocket, so it would seem then that Indiana would be for Slidell & Bright— I do not believe it myself and think there is no truth in it— I hope you will consult Mr Milligan before and after you get there as to the proper course to pursue— If we could have definite action on the Homestead Bill by next Fridy I would still come home so that I could consult freely and fully with Milligan on the subject and especially as to the action of the delegation in the last resort— If you & Milligan will go I will pay the expense of both— It is asking too much of him to lose his time and bear the expense when I know he would not go if it was not on my account— He went to the convention held at Cincinnati[4] more to promote my interest than any thing else— If I come home I will have as much money as will pay the expense[.] if not and the money is needed before you go from me you must Call on Mr Jones for same— If not let it stand until you see me— Think it all over and do what you think the occasion requires and with [the] result I will be content— You can say to Mr Milligan at this moment I have nothing to suggest more than what would naturally occur to him with the elements all before him—

Enclosed you will find the letter of Mr Walter Willis[5] accepting for the C[umberland] Presbeterian Church my offer of the Miller property—[6] I wrote a letter to your brother in which I proposed that they might have the House and lot at $1200 and a reasonabl time to pay it in— There was no definite time specified if my memory serves me aright— I also stated that I would Subscribe $100 toward building the Church, which of course would be deducted out of the price of the House and Lot when the last paymt was made— Consult with your brother and he can show you the lettr and tell you all that has transpired between him and them on the Subject— In Willis' letter he says nothing about when the money is to be paid— Of course I want the paymints made as soon as convenient— I have made this statement for the purpose of having them a little made [sic] if I do not come home at the time expected— You can state to Mr Willis that [if] I do not come home soon [enough] for them that you will fix all the papers and send them here for signature and that th[e]y m[a]y consider the Contract Closed &C—

Mr Boyce[7] I presume has never paid any rent yet and nevr will I imagine[.] I want [to] get Clear of it some how or oth[er.] it will be burned up Some of these nights and that will be the last of it— Robertson[8] will pay none, so it is not ve[r]y productive and I fear never will be—

A few d[a]ys Since I received a long letter from Mrs L. C. Brown[9] and among other things [she] made a v[er]y kind allusion to you in regard to the defeat of th[e] bill authorizing the purchase of the Asylum for a Governor's mansion— She wrote to me that she would start to Europe in July and would be gone perhaps a year or more and that Mrs John Bell desired to rent her house until her return and desired to know my opinion &c.— I advised her not to go [to] Europe until this Sumer come [a] year and not to rent her House & lot to Mrs Bell and I am inclined to thing [sic] it will have some influence with her—[10] time will tell— Tell Charles he must write to me— I received a letter from your Siste[r] and She and the childrn are well[.] In her letter she said reck[o]n you had changed your notion about marrying; that it was pretty near time[.] Let that all pass for the present[.]

Your father   Andrew Johnson

ALS, DLC-JP.

1. Johnson had been nominated in January at the state Democratic convention.

2. Although subject to decision by each national convention, the two-thirds rule had been regularly adopted by the Democratic party since the 1830's. Stanwood, *Presidency*, 161–212 *passim*.

3. Jesse D. Bright.

4. The Democratic National Convention of 1856.

5. Walter Willis (b. c1826), a Greeneville carpenter with real estate worth $800 and personal assets valued at $200. 1860 Census, Tenn., Greene, 86.

6. Edmund B. Miller (b. c1818) was a Greeneville tailor. His property, acquired by Johnson in 1854 and 1857, contained a store, tailor shop, and printing office, and was located at the northwest corner of First Cross and Main streets. 1850 Census, Tenn., Greene, 277; *Johnson Papers*, II, 232, 513; see Deed to Cumberland Presbyterians, July 20, 1860.

7. Probably William Boyce (b. c1827), Greeneville silversmith and widower with three small children. The Maryland-born craftsman, son of William Boyce (b. c1803), declared only $150 personalty in 1860, apparently having fallen on hard times. 1860 Census, Tenn., Greene, 88.

8. H. G. Robertson, editor of the Greeneville *Democrat*, lived only two doors away from Boyce, Johnson's other delinquent tenant. Since the *Democrat* beat the drums for Johnson and the party, the senator apparently was

reluctant to press for the rent, despite the editor's rather comfortable circumstances of $1,000 real and $3,000 personal property. *Ibid.*

9. Lizinka C. Brown.

10. For Mrs. Brown's subsequent rental negotiations with Mrs. Bell, see Letter from Lizinka C. Brown, June 12, 1860.

From Ralph R. Gurley[1]

Coln Office Washington   April 9th 1860

My dear Sir,

I think Mr Schruggs [*sic*][2] had best write to Rev Wm McLain Financial Secretary of the Society, requesting him to grant a return passage to the man he mentions. The cost of passage will be $35. & probably twenty or thirty more to get to Tennessee. Mr McLain might be authorized on the arrival of the man in Baltimore to draw for the sum due on some Bank in Tennessee, or Baltimore[.]

With great respect   I have the honor   Dr Sir

Yours faithfully   R R Gurley

Hon A. Johnson
U. S. Senate

ALS, Copy, DLC-Am. Col. Soc. Papers, Let. Bk., Vol. 8, p. 134.

1. Ralph R. Gurley (1797–1872), Connecticut-born philanthropist, became an agent for the American Colonization Society in 1822 and successfully served as its secretary, vice president, and life director. As secretary he was in charge of plannning and outfitting expeditions, regulating the stateside affairs of Liberia, and editing the Society's organs, *African Repository* and *Annual Reports*. After a visit to the colony, he wrote the biography of the unofficial acting governor, Jehudi Ashmun. An unordained Presbyterian minister, Gurley was a popular preacher among Negro congregations around Washington. *DAB*, VIII, 56–57.

2. See Letter from William C. Scruggs, April 3, 1860.

From Charles W. Charlton

Post Office   Knoxville Tenn
April 10. 1860

Hon. Andrew Johnson
Washington D. C.
Dr Sir:

I promptly called upon the Editor of the Register,[1] & asked him to publish the speech of Mr Nicholson,[2] as also your own, but he as promptly *declined*, upon the ground that neither of you sent your speeches to him! I would suggest that you send him those speeches, *at once*.

I much regret the course of the Register, as it *stands alone* in the

State. It is loosing ground every day & must continue to do so, so long as it remains antagonistic to your claims.

The Union & American has taken a bold & decided stand in your behalf. My own impression is that your chances are brightening every day. I now hear men speaking of it, favorably, who heretofore, thought there was no prospect.

It has become current in this community, as well as in the upper counties, that, if the friends of Douglass cannot carry *him*, they intend uniting upon you.

Maj. Ramsey[3] & myself will continue to furnish matter for the Register, from week to week. The Editor has never yet refused to publish anything of this sort at any time.

Very Respectfully   C. W. Charlton

ALS, DLC-JP2.
   1. George W. Bradfield.
   2. On March 19, following Johnson's motion to consider the bill, Nicholson, at Johnson's request, had delivered a speech on the homestead. *Cong. Globe*, 36 Cong., 1 Sess., 1219–23.
   3. See Letter from John Crozier Ramsey, March 30, 1860.

From Hiram F. Cummins[1]

Paris Tenn   April 10th 1860

Gov Johnson
   Dr Sir

I heard a report at Nashville a few days since, which I think proper to contradict as there is no truth in it.

It has been spoken of in *private* circles, that W. A. Quarles & Genl Atkins[2] will not Support you for the nomination, at Charleston.

Gov, I travelled with Atkins & Quarles to Nashville, we were delegates to the state Convention, & all of us agreed to Support your nomination and did so, when *some* who now have *fears & doubts* flinched in that body. I know Quarles & Atkins will stand by you at Charleston at "all hazzards & to the last Extremity."[3]

As a member of the Committee on resolutions & to appoint Delegates I know the position of those comprising, those Committees & who voted for your recommendation in Committee.

As I profess to be a friend to your nomination, I am unwilling that Either of my frieds should be placed in opposition to your nomination, unless they really occupy that position. I hope you will not consider this note out of place, for we all are warming up. Col Buck Travis,[4] will canvass the state should you secure the nomination.

Very Respectfully   Your obt St   H. F. Cummins

ALS, DLC-JP2.

1. Hiram F. Cummins (1818–1897), Kentucky-born editor of the pro-southern Paris *Weekly Sentinel*, was mayor of Paris (1852) and a member of the Tennessee house (1861–63). Edythe Whitley, *Tennessee Genealogical Records: Henry County "Old Time Stuff"* (Nashville, 1968), 9, 10, 73, 82, 102; Roger A. Van Dyke, A History of Henry County, Tennessee, through 1865 (M. A. thesis, University of Tennessee, 1966), 58, 80; Robison, *Preliminary Directory, Henry*, 15–16.

2. William A. Quarles and John D. C. Atkins.

3. Johnson had earlier used this phrase in his Speech on Popular Sovereignty and Right of Instruction, February 23, 1858.

4. William E. Travis (b. *c*1825) of Henry County, a brother-in-law of Governor Isham G. Harris, served in the house (1853–57, 1877–79) and in the senate (1857–59), was a colonel of the county militia at the outbreak of the war, and raised the 5th Tennessee infantry regiment, CSA. Robison, *Preliminary Directory, Henry*, 54–55.

From Hu Douglas

Nashville Apl 10th 1860

Hon And Johnson

My Dear Sir

I inclose you some Slips,[1] I recd from my friend W. H Hennessey[2] Esqr of N.Y[.]

Mr Hennessey is a partner of one of the best wholesales Houses in NY, and a reliable Gentleman but a devoted friend of Mr Wood[.][3] read the inclosed. I wish you would send him some of yr speeches &C[.]

I have written to him that you are the man for the times and that I wanted his friend Wood to take this view of the case. If he will Come up to the mark he Can do you great good. I will try to be at Charleston & I think Wood & Mr. Hennessey will be there.[4]

Yr friend   Hu Douglas

ALS, DLC-JP2.

1. The enclosed editorial, "A Man for the Times," from the New York *News*, April 6, 1860, observes that although Fernando Wood has been favorably spoken of for the Charleston nomination, he is not a candidate but will support the nominee. A second article credits Wood with contributing to the reduction of the Republican vote in Connecticut.

2. Probably William E. Hennessy, a Chambers Street merchant. *Trow's New York Directory* (1859–60), 388.

3. Fernando Wood.

4. If Hennessy was at Charleston, he went with the Wood delegation, which was not seated.

From Robert Johnson

Greeneville Ten   April 10th 1860

Dear Father

I was glad to receive your letter of 8th inst this morning and merely write to acknowledge its receipt— I will leave at one O'clock for Carter County as I have not been to Mary's for over two years.

Milligan and myself will Start to Charleston Wednesday or Thursday week— I have an abiding faith and a presentiment that the Convention will nominate you— I have never yet been deceived in any presentiment I have had and am as Confident of the truth of the present one, as the Sun will sink behind the western hills this evening— It may all be fancy, but still I feel that there is a some thing within me that teaches and foretelds the result as unerringly as the hourglass does the passing hours— *mark it down*— "the Stars have said it"—[1]

I will return from Mary's Friday or Saturday[.]

Your Son   Robt Johnson

ALS, DLC-JP2.

1. Although this expression cannot be precisely identified, it may derive from "The stars, that in their courses roll, Have much instruction given"; from Isaac Watts, *The Excellency of the Bible*. Stevenson, *Quotations*, 158.

From O. P. Baer

April 11, 1860, Richmond, Ind.; ALS, DLC-JP2.

Geologist requests volumes IX and X of Pacific railroad report. Johnson endorses it: "Will Mr. Headrick [sic] be kind enough to send this gentlem[a]n a patent office report of the latest date and write on the document, that I have more orders for the Pacific Rail report than I Can Supply and ofCourse [sic] cannot Comply with resquest [sic][.]"

From Washington C. Whitthorne

Columbia Te. Apl. 11. 1860

Private)

Honl. Andrew Johnson

Dear Sir:

Nothing but sickness of myself or family, or the absence of funds will prevent me from attending the Charleston Convention. my calculation is to leave Nashville upon Wednesday next. I am no delegate, but am anxious to see how matters are "done up". If our

General assembly had not continued its session so long, I would have visited Washington as was my purpose. I regret that of the delegates at Charleston from other states I shall know nothing, I might else do some good. Will you do me the favor, if you have time, to enclose me letters of introduction to friends, you may have outside of Tennessee. Direct to me at Charleston[.] I will be there about 21st.

I should have been glad to have seen you prior to this, because I am apprehensive that you are mistaken as to certain men in Tennessee. but a few days will tell, suffice to say that I do not believe Gov. Harris or his friends will at all attempt anything that is not exactly right. I wrote a letter to the Editor of the Indianapolis Sentinel,[1] which I learn was published with some comments. I have not seen the paper. Have you? Was it conceived rightly?

If you think, I can aid you at Charleston, do not neglect to furnish me with the letters I have suggested[.]   I am very truly yours.

W. C. Whitthorne

Cant you get Nicholson[2] to go down?

ALS, DLC-JP2.

1. The Indianapolis *Sentinel* (formerly *Indiana State Sentinel*) was a daily newspaper edited at this time by Joseph J. Bingham. Gregory, *Union List of Newspapers*, 153; *Indianapolis City Directory* (1860–61), 37.
2. Nicholson did not attend any of the conventions.

Speech on Amendment to Homestead Bill[1]

April 11, 1860

Mr. JOHNSON, of Tennessee. Mr. President, when I came here, at the beginning of this session, it was not my intention to speak upon the homestead proposition; I had spoken again and again upon it in years gone by, and there is very little new that I can now say on the subject; but since it has been introduced in the Senate during the present session the debate and the direction of the measure seem to be somewhat strange; and especially the direction that the discussion took yesterday.[2] On account of this, I feel it to be incumbent on me to say a few words in reference to the homestead, and the position that some Senators occupy on the question. It has been, I think, somewhat remarkable, that, since the discussion came up on this subject during the present session, Tennessee should be singled out as the object of attack, and her Senators particularly, in connection with this subject. There has been an unwarrantable and uncalled-for attempt made to associate this measure, and the position of Tennessee upon it, with certain principles that are advocated in the country with which she has no sympathy.

The Senator from Virginia [Mr. Mason] yesterday seemed to be enlightened—at least he so stated—upon listening to the speech of the Senator from Wisconsin, [Mr. Doolittle.] He said that Senator had shed a flood of light on this subject; that he had given a phase to this question that was peculiarly interesting, and one which the country would understand. He repeated that the Senator from Wisconsin had shed a flood of light on the subject; thereby meaning, I presume, the connection or the association of the slavery question with the homestead proposition. I confess that on the one hand I was gratified, while on the other, I was extremely mortified. I was gratified to hear the Senator from Virginia—who has on one or two occasions assumed, as it were, to be the custodian of the interests and policy of the State of Tennessee—confess, for once at least since I have been in the Senate, that he had had a flood of light shed on his mind; for I do not think any other occasion has presented itself when he would have made the acknowledgment. I incline to think that Tennessee can now, as she has in times gone by, either in the councils of the nation or in the battle-field, take care of her own interest, without calling upon the Senator from Virginia to do it.

We have been driven round and round upon the slavery question; round and round the giddy circle of slavery agitation we have gone, until our heads are reeling and our stomachs are sick, and almost heaving. The agitation of the slavery question seems to be a subject that is always to be introduced here, I care not what is before the Senate. While I was gratified, as I remarked, to hear the Senator from Virginia—who speaks in oracular language when he does speak, as if all should not only hear, but obey him—on the other hand I was mortified when I heard the speech made yesterday by the Senator from Wisconsin, connecting and involving this with the slavery question. I think they have no connection, and they should be kept separate and distinct. As I remarked on a former occasion, I look on the homestead proposition as rising above all party or sectional questions. I look upon this measure as one in conformity with the Constitution of the United States; in conformity with the genius and spirit of the Government; a measure carrying out the great objects for which the public lands were acquired. I look upon it, besides, as coming up to that great idea of philanthropy and Christianity which is enjoined upon us all in our legislative, as well as in our private capacity.

But yesterday the Senator from Wisconsin must involve in this discussion the negro question; and then, in reply, the Senator from Virginia must give us a dissertation on the same subject, administer a rebuke to the State of Tennessee, and assume to know where she stood, and what her opinions and her doctrines were. Sir, she has never disguised her opinions or her doctrines, and she does not disguise them now. It really seems to me that if some member of this body was to introduce the ten commandments for consideration, and they were to receive consideration and discussion, somebody would find a negro in them somewhere; the slavery agitation would come up. The chances are, that if they were introduced by a northern man, he would argue that they had a tendency to diminish the area of slavery, to prevent the increase of the slave population, and in the end perhaps to abolish slavery; while on the other hand, if some Senator from the South was to introduce the Lord's prayer, somebody would see a negro in it somewhere. It would be argued just as the question might be presented—either upon the ten commandments or the Lord's prayer—that the result would be a tendency to promote and advance slavery, on the one hand, or on the other, to diminish or abolish it. Is it not time that the legislation of the country was directed to something else, and that some other things were considered? I do believe that the country, North and South, is becoming sick and tired of the constant agitation of the slavery question, to the exclusion of all others; and I do trust and hope, in God's holy name, that there is a public judgment and public spirit in the country that will rise above this agitation, and the purposes for which it has been kept up.

But the Senator from Virginia informed us that he had had a flood of light shed on him. I repeat that I was highly gratified to hear him say so, and I recur to it now more from the fact of being gratified at it than anything else. He seemed to rise and come forward into the discussion with that kind of renewed energy, information, and light that Paul had when he was traveling from Jerusalem to Damascus, and was struck blind with the refulgence of light thrown on his mind; but Paul inquired of the Lord what he would have him to do. Whether the conduct of the Senator from Wisconsin has had the same influence on the Senator from Virginia, I will not undertake to say; but if it was improper and dangerous to associate the homestead measure with Black Republicanism, as it is commonly called, or the Republican party, I will say—for I do not use the term in derision— would it not really be dangerous and objectionable to receive a flood of light from a Republican? One of that party has shed light on this occasion, as the Senator from Virginia admits. Will the Senator receive light from such a source?

But when we come to examine the homestead proposition, where do we start with it? I want the Senator's attention. We start with it in 1791, under the administration of General Washington, and I think he was from the Old Dominion. In 1791, the first homestead proposition was introduced, and, in the language of the law, it was enacted:

That four hundred acres of land be given to each of those persons who, in the year 1783, were heads of families at Vincennes, or the Illinois country, or the Mississippi and who, since that time, have removed from one of the said places to the other; but the Governor of the Territory northwest of the Ohio is hereby directed to cause the same to be laid out for them at their own expense, &c.[3]

That law makes use of the word "give", and it received the approval of General Washington. I think that is tolerably good company. Tennessee is willing to be associated with Washington, and especially upon homestead propositions. That law was approved by the immortal Washington. I think he was about as great a man as any of the modern lights; and so far as I am concerned, I prefer following in the lead of the larger, instead of what I consider the lesser, lights. What next do we find on this subject? Mr. Jefferson recommended, in one of his messages to the Congress of the United States, the homestead policy.[4] In the administrations of Washington and Jefferson, this policy was inaugurated by this Government. I prefer to follow the lead and to be associated with Washington and Jefferson, than the lights that now shine from the Old Dominion. There are forty-four precedents of laws approved and sanctioned by various Presidents, running through every Administration, from Thomas Jefferson down to the present time, carrying out the same principle. Where did this policy have its origin? Where did it start? Its very germ commenced with Virginia, and it has been followed up and brought down to the present time. But, without dwelling on all the cases, I will refer to what was done in 1850. The fourth section of "An act to create the office of surveyor general of public lands in Oregon, and to provide for the survey, and to make donations to settlers on the said public lands," approved in 1850, is in these words:

Sec. 4. *And be it further enacted,* That there shall be, and hereby is, granted to every white settler or occupant of the public lands, American half-breed Indians included, above the age of eighteen years, being a citizen of the United States, or having made a declaration according to law of his intention to become a citizen, or who shall become a resident thereof on or before the 1st day of December, 1850, and who shall have resided upon and cultivated the same for four consecutive years, and who shall otherwise conform to the provisions of this act, the quantity of one half section, or three hundred and twenty acres of land, if a single man, and if a married man, or if he shall become married within one year from the 1st day of December, 1850, the quantity of one section, or six hundred and forty acres, one half to himself, and the other half to his wife, to be held by her in her own right. *Statutes at Large*, vol. 9, p. 497.

There is a homestead bill. There is a grant of six hundred and forty acres to a married man, and three hundred and twenty acres to a single man, not being the head of a family, but twenty one years of age. That was passed in 1850. I should like to know where the vigilant and watchful Senator from Virginia was when that law passed. I presume that this flood of light had not been shed. He did not see its bearings and tendencies as he seems to understand and see them now. How did the Senator vote upon that question? I suppose the Senator knows, for surely a measure so important, and embracing principles so sacred and vital, could not have passed through this body without the Senator knowing how he recorded his vote. Where was this faithful sentinel that should have been standing upon the watch-tower, and should have sounded the alarm and aroused the people of the United States to the dangerous inroads that were being made on their rights and institutions? Where was he? Did he speak? Did he say "yea" or "nay," either by speech or vote? No; but he sat with his arms folded, and allowed this "infamous measure," this "agrarian measure," that was to work such dangerous influences upon certain institutions of the country, to pass without saying either yea or nay.[5]

There was one homestead proposition passed in 1850. Yesterday I quoted a law passed in 1854,[6] and it seemed to be a little difficult for Senators to understand it. One Senator understood it one way, and another understood it another. Sometimes it is a good plan to examine, and see how a thing is. One said that the law of 1854 was to give homesteads in New Mexico; and if they were given in New Mexico, and not in Kansas, that would change the principle![7] Now, I should like to know the difference in principle. But let us see how the thing stands. I read one section from the act of 1850; and, before I could get to read another section, the Senator from Missouri [Mr. GREEN] took the floor, and made an issue with me; and then the Senator from Virginia resumed the floor, and did not permit me to read another section, and make it understood. The act of 1854 is entitled "An act to establish the offices of surveyor general of New Mexico, Kansas, and Nebraska, to grant donations to actual settlers therein, and for other purposes." Well, what do we find in the second section of that act?

Sec. 2. *And be it further enacted*, That, to every white male citizen of the United States, or every white male above the age of twenty-one years, who has declared his intention to become a citizen, and who was residing in said Territory prior to the 1st day of January, 1853, and who may be still residing there, there shall be, and hereby is, donated one quarter section, or one hundred and sixty acres of land. And to every white male citizen of the United States, or every white male above the age of twenty-one years, who has declared his intention to become a citizen, and who shall have removed, or shall remove to and settle in said Territory between the 1st day of January, 1853, and the 1st day of January, 1858, there shall, in like manner, be donated one quarter section, or one hundred and sixty acres, on condition of actual settlement and cultivation for not less than four years. *Statutes at Large*, vol. 10, p. 308.

There is a clear and distinct grant; but the answer was that it was not a homestead, because the grant was made in New Mexico. Would there be any difference, in principle, between holding out inducements to go into New Mexico to free homes, and holding out inducements to anywhere else? What is the difference? Even in regard to New Mexico, where there was a prospect of slavery, here was a bill passed inviting settlers to go into the Territory and take the land free; and to carry out this very disastrous idea in reference to slavery that the Senator from Virginia speaks of. And where was he? Yesterday, when we referred to it, the Journal was produced to show that there was no vote taken on it; and the answer to the principle and the inconsistency I was exhibiting was, that "donated" was bad English, as if thereby to escape from the inconsistency in which the Senator was involved.

Mr. MASON. I think if the Senator heard me, he will recollect that I said I did not remember how I had voted upon that law, but the probability was that I had voted for it; but so far from attempting to escape from any responsibility as to my vote, I distinctly declared that it was a matter of not the slightest consequence to me, so far as that policy was concerned, how I voted, and that I presumed I voted for it.

Mr. JOHNSON, of Tennessee. Well, it is a homestead proposition, embracing the precise idea of this measure and going to a greater extent, being more enlarged than the bill now under consideration. The Senator sat by and permitted a bill to pass, so obnoxious and so disastrous, as he now says, especially in reference to the slavery interest, and that, too, with his great literary qualifications, when the bill not only established the homestead policy, but he actually permitted it to pass in bad grammar.

Mr. MASON. That was wrong, I admit. [Laughter.]

Mr. JOHNSON, of Tennessee. But let us travel on a little further. That was in New Mexico. Next we come right over into Kansas, now in the midst of the Emigrant Aid Society, and see how it operates when we get over into Kansas. We find this is the law now providing for preemptions there—I read from the same law which I have just quoted:

Sec. 12. *And be it further enacted*, That all the lands to which the Indian title has been, or shall be, extinguished within said Territories of Nebraska and Kansas, shall be subject to the operations of the preëmption act of 4th September, 1841, and under the conditions, restrictions, and stipulations therein mentioned: *Provided, however*, That where unsurveyed lands are claimed by preëmption, notice of the specific tracts shall be filed within three months after the survey has been made in the field, &c. *Statutes at Large*, vol. 10, p. 310.

These acts were referred to by the Senator from Ohio [Mr. Pugh] the other day. He was referring to them in the range of precedents, in the speech that he made on this subject vindicating the measure against the objections that were made both as to its expediency and constitutionality. He referred to this as one of the precedents, and made an argument (permit me to say here in parenthesis) that cannot be answered. Some may attempt, as some have attempted, to answer it; but it cannot be answered. Why try to associate the measure with prejudices that may exist North or South? If it is unconstitutional, come up and meet it on constitutional grounds. If it is inexpedient and dangerous, show it to be so. But here is a preëmption granted, in Kansas, and when? In 1854, at the time of all the alarm in reference to emigrant aid societies. Where was the vigilant, sleepless sentinel then? Where was he who came forth with such power and eloquence yesterday, after receiving that new flood of light—from a Republican source, too?

In 1850 a homestead was granted. In 1854, in the midst of the excitement about emigrant aid societies, an act was passed granting homesteads and preëmptions to young men who were not heads of families. Anybody could go into Kansas, and squat down upon land. Inducements were held out for them to run in. Where was this sentinel that has now become so alarmed, and who wants to know how Tennessee can stand up by such a proposition? Was he here, and did not understand the measure? Was he here understanding it, and standing upon the watch-tower as the faithful sentinel, and did not sound the alarm? Was he here, and did not say to those inside the citadel that the enemy was at the gate? If he was, and knew it to be so, I ask why a sentinel of that kind, entertaining the views he does in reference to this subject, when he saw such a dangerous encroachment upon the institution peculiar to the South, did not sound the alarm? Failing to do so, knowing how the facts stand, he is no longer entitled to the confidence of those who placed him here. If he was here, and had not sagacity or acumen enough to see it, or if his mind was not so constructed as to go from cause to effect, and look a little into the distance, and see the operation of this preëmption law; and if he has not been enlightened until he has received light from Republicans, his mind is dark, and not to be trusted. A Sentinel, standing on the watchtower, to have eyes and not see, ears and not hear, a tongue and not speak,[8] deserves to be taken down, and another put in his place. Sir, think of the mariner who is placed on deck, when he descries in the distance the approaching storm, or the man who is familiar with the forest, and hears the roaring of the trees—an indication of the whirlwind—and will be so listless, so indifferent, as not to sound the alarm that danger is approaching. I say he is an unworthy and unfaithful sentinel.

When the Senator talks about the representatives of Tennessee, or Kentucky, or any other States, I desire to know where he was when these things were being done? Did he vote? It seems some gentlemen thought yesterday that they got him out of the dilemma, because he did not vote. When a bill is before the Senate, and it passes and no objection is made, it is understood that it receives the sanction of the body—it has at least the tacit consent of all—and every member here is committed to the passage of the bill. If there was all this danger, would it not have been the duty of the Senator to rise in his place, sound the alarm, call for the yeas and nays, and let the country know where all parties stood?

Then we see where the Senator stood in 1854, and where he stood in 1850. Now, let us follow this history a little further, and see where it will carry us. What is the proposition now before the Senate? It is to grant a homestead. It is true the Senator from Missouri, [Mr. GREEN,] became very learned the other day in reference to the term "homestead," as though there was anything in the christening of a child. The long and short of the bill is, to grant a man a homestead, embracing so many acres. That is the object of it. I do not care whether you call it a homestead or by any other name. The substance is what we want. It is a home, an abiding place for a man, his wife and children; and I think if we take the ordinary meaning, as given by our lexicographers, "homestead" is the proper name. It embraces the building and the inclosure about it, which is commonly denominated a homestead. As to the idea that it must be made perpetual, there is nothing in it. Homesteads can be changed as well as anything else. Then the bill provides that men shall get homes at low rates, reasonable prices; that it shall be placed in the power of every one to get a home; and it is not to be taken out of that which belongs to anybody else. There was a homestead bill before the Senate in 1854—a time of great excitement and danger. To that bill Mr. Hunter, then and now a Senator from Virginia, offered an amendment, and in his amendment there was one section which I will read:

Sec. 9. *And be it further enacted*, That the person applying for the benefit of the eighth section of this act shall, upon application to the register of the land office in which he or she is about to make such entry, make affidavit before the said register that he or she is the head of a family, or is twenty-one years of age, and that such application is made for his or her exclusive use and benefit, and those specially mentioned herein, and not either directly or indirectly for the use or benefit of any other person or persons whomsoever; and upon making the affidavit as herein required, and filing it with the register, he or she shall thereupon be permitted to enter the quantity of land specified: *Provided, however*,

That no certificate shall be given or patent issued therefor, until the expiration of five years from the date of such entry, and until the person or persons entitled to the land so entered shall have paid for the same twenty-five cents per acre, or if the lands have been in market more than twenty years, twelve and a half cents per acre.[9]

This was an amendment offered by Mr. HUNTER to the homestead bill of 1854, which passed the House of Representatives by nearly a majority of two thirds; and the Journal gives the vote upon it, which I will read:

On the question to agree to the said amendment as amended,
It was determined in the affirmative—yeas 34, nays 13.
On motion of Mr. Adams,
The yeas and nays being desired by one fifth of the Senators present,
Those who voted in the affirmative are:
Messrs. Adams, Atchison, Benjamin, Bright, Brodhead, Brown, Butler, Cass, Clay, Dodge of Wisconsin, Dodge of Iowa, Douglas, Evans, Fitzpatrick, Geyer, Gwin, Houston, Hunter, James, Johnson, Jones of Iowa, Mallory, MASON, Pettit, Rusk, Sebastian, Shields, Slidell, Stuart, Thompson of Kentucky, Thomson of New Jersey, Toombs, Toucey, and Walker.[10]

Before we had not the Senator's vote, but we had his tacit consent; but here stands the vote of the gentleman who is arraigning Tennessee, to reduce the price of the public land, and let a man have it at twelve and a half cents an acre, according to a proposition introduced by his own colleague. Where does he stand now? I think Tennessee will compare at least favorably with the Old Dominion in that particular. But again:

On motion of Mr. Fitzpatrick, to amend the amendment proposed by Mr. Hunter, by inserting after the word "acre," in the first section, sixteenth line, "and all lands which shall have been offered at public sale, and shall remain unsold thirty years thereafter, shall be reduced to a price of twelve and a half cents an acre;"[11]

the yeas and nays were again called; and the Senator from Virginia a second time recorded his vote to reduce the price of the land to twelve and a half cents an acre. Then came the question on the final passage of the bill:

The bill (H. R. No. 37) to grant a homestead of one hundred and sixty acres of the public lands to actual settlers, was read the third time, as amended; and having been further amended, by unanimous consent, on the motion of Mr. Pettit, the title was amended; and,
On the question, Shall the bill pass?
It was determined in the affirmative—yeas 36, nays 11.
On motion of Mr. Weller,
The yeas and nays being desired by one fifth of the Senators present,
Those who voted in the affirmative are:
Messrs. Adams, Atchison, Bright, Brodhead, Brown, Butler, Cass, Chase, Clay, Dodge of Wisconsin, Dodge of Iowa, Douglas, Evans, Fitzpatrick, Geyer, Gwin, Hamlin, Houston, Hunter, James, Johnson, Jones of Iowa, Mallory, MASON, Pettit, Rusk, Sebastian, Shields, Slidell,

Stuart, Sumner, Thomson of New Jersey, Toombs, Toucey, Walker, and Weller.[12]

The Senator was enlightened a little yesterday: I want to enlighten him more today. I doubt very much if he remembers exactly what he did on all of these questions sometimes, and the refreshing of the memory is of no disadvantage to any of us. I think that his speech yesterday came with no very good grace from a Senator with this sort of a record. How do you stand when you talk about the influence on the slavery question? Does not reducing land to twelve and a half cents induce settlement? What is the proposition under consideration? It is to reduce the price to twelve and a half cents an acre in one bill, and in the other to ten dollars for the whole one hundred and sixty acres, and paying office fees. Where is the difference in principle? Where is the enormity of the one that does not exist in the other? Where is the danger to the institution of slavery growing out of the adoption of the one measure that does not grow out of the other?

Virginia, under a system of bounty land warrants to her revolutionary soldiers and others, has received nearly two million five hundred thousand acres of land;[13] and when we stand with Virginia, and, commencing with Washington, with every Administration to the present time, are we to be arraigned and taunted with our association? When and where did the preëmption policy start? Did it not start with General Jackson? When and where did the graduation policy start? Did it not start with General Jackson? Is not Tennessee standing now where she stood then? What is the homestead policy? It is a part and parcel of the same great idea of carrying the public lands into the possession of every man that will take them and make a proper use of them. We stand where Washington stood. We stand where Jefferson stood. We stand where all the Democratic Administrations have stood, and even where the Senator himself has heretofore stood.

Where does the gentleman get his association, and what is it for? Instead of relying on the argument of the question, he tries to associate with it a prejudice with which he thinks it can be struck with much more ease and force than by meeting the question upon argument. Virginia is to rebuke Tennessee on this subject, talking about making free States! Is Virginia to rebuke any other State in this Confederacy in reference to free States? Go back to the ordinance of 1787, first brought forward by Mr. Jefferson in 1784; go back to the surrender of public lands in the Northwest, which I never conceded were Virginia's more than any other State's—but let that be as it may, I will not argue it now; she assumed that they were hers; but the surrender of her territory resulted in the creation of five free

States, all now admitted into this Confederacy with their Senators on this floor. Is Virginia to rebuke Tennessee, alarmed at the creation of free States? Those States have fallen from your hands. Are you dissatisfied with them? Do you want to turn them out of the Union? Tennessee prefers to follow principle, understanding that, in the pursuit of correct principle, we can never reach a wrong conclusion; and although some become alarmed and are carried off by the *ad captandum* slang of the day, Tennessee intends to stand on principle, and intends to pursue it unalterably and unswervingly, as her own noble rivers that come rushing from her mountains' sides, and make their way down her valleys and through her plains in their majestic career to the great father of waters. Here Tennessee intends to stand firm upon principle—as firm and unyielding as her own native mountains, with their craggy and projecting brows, rock-ribbed, and as ancient as the sun. She does not stand here to be rebuked by any State, or the Senators from any State. Now, as heretofore, in the field or in the council chamber, she can take care of herself. Gentlemen taunt us with an association with the Republican party, because the Republican party is showing a little sagacity, being pretty hard pressed for capital, and setting out as privateers, picking up whatever they can find that is profitable. They find that a measure and a great principle that has been advocated by the Democratic party for years is popular; that the public judgment is recorded for it.

In 1846, when this measure was inaugurated in its present substantial shape, was it inaugurated by that party? It was before the party had an existence. It was pressed amid the taunts and the jeers of individuals, until the public judgment laid hold of it; and, in 1852, in compliance with that public judgment, the House of Representatives, on the 12th day of May, passed it by a fraction less than a two-thirds vote. It is a Democratic measure, not a Republican. Do we know so little of ourselves, do we stand so little upon principle, that because Republicans come forward and assume a measure we are for, we are to be scared off and let them take it? Do we not understand ourselves better than that? In 1854, it was brought up by a Democratic member,[14] and passed the House of Representatives by a two-thirds vote, and came to the Senate. In the last Congress it passed the House again, and came to the Senate. The public judgment has ratified it again and again, and will the Senate not yield to the high behests of an enlightened public judgment? We are told here that the Senate is to be obeyed, and not the people; that the Senate is to be obeyed, and not the States. Whom does this Government belong to, and for whose use was it created? Was the Government created for the people, or the people for the Government? I hold that the Government was created for the people; that this Federal Government is the creature of the States; and when they have spoken and declared their solemn judgment, it is the duty of the Senate to obey. Look at the votes in the House of Representatives in 1852 and 1854. There was no party test then on this measure. Whigs and Democrats, Americans and every other class, voted for it, and some of all classes voted against it;[15] but, all at once, it has got a "nigger" in it—slavery has crept into the question—and now it takes a new phase.

Sometimes the measure is met upon constitutional grounds. I do not pretend at all to be a constitutional lawyer; but there are some propositions that are so plain that anybody can understand them. I say the distinction is broad and clear between the power of the Federal Government over its revenues and over its public lands. Congress has power to lay and collect taxes, duties, imposts, and excises, to pay the debts and provide for the common defense and general welfare. When duties and debts have been laid, when taxes have been collected and paid into the Treasury, Congress then has specific and definite powers in reference to their appropriation. But in reference to the public lands, the power is in a separate clause and the words are different. It may dispose of the public lands for the purpose of obtaining revenue; and being disposed of for revenue, that revenue when obtained must be appropriated under the restraints and restrictions of the Constitution. It is not worth while to be very metaphysical, or to draw very nice distinctions; but in this matter the distinction is broad. Congress has the power "to dispose of and make all needful rules and regulations respecting the territory or other property belonging to the United States." "Dispose of" it for what purpose? What does the Government acquire territory for? Is it to lie vacant and dormant? Is it to remain unproductive? What is the great object of acquiring territory? When you acquire territory that is unpopulated, you have not only the power, but, in obedience to the object for which it was acquired, it is your duty to pass laws that will encourage and induce the settlement of that territory. Has not that been the practice? The fathers of the Republic looked at it in that way, and gave it that construction. I say it is the duty of the Government to adopt those means that will induce settlement, to populate an unsettled territory.

I will say here, that I do not believe this Government can dispose of the territory for other than governmental purposes; but it can dispose of it for some governmental purposes for which it cannot dispose of the public money. I know that this sort of argument is sometimes made: "You get money, you buy land, and you give the land away." That does not affect the broad provisions of the Constitution at all. If the land is acquired by treaty, whether you pay money or not, it then passes under the general provision "to dispose of the territory." If we acquire territory must we have back precisely what we pay for that territory? If the argument be sound in one case it is equally sound in the other. Where are the great and patriotic men who have gone to the battle-field and perished at the cannon's mouth? Can we get them back? Where are the great men that now sleep in a foreign land, who fell in deadly conflict with a foreign foe, beneath the crimsoned spear, and went to their long, narrow home, with no winding sheet save their tent-blankets, which were saturated with their blood? Can you get them back? If you must have back what you offered up for this territory, you must get these men; get back the fathers of those orphans that are left in the land; get back the husbands of these widows who have been made poor and destitute, before you talk about getting back the dollars and cents. Where would you get the material out of which to coin this blood?

Who, then, is entitled to this public domain? Are not the descendants of those who shed their blood and offered up their lives on the altar of their country, entitled to a little piece of ground upon which they can make their support? Whose land is it? Is it the Government's? If the land is the Government's, whom does the Government belong to? It belongs to the people. The Government is the agent: and it has no right to withhold from the great mass of the people that which is theirs.

Mr. WIGFALL. Will the Senator allow me to ask him what he means by the people? I ask him seriously, because I want a reply.

Mr. JOHNSON, of Tennessee. I would rather the Senator would not interrupt me. He can reply after I am through. I am asked what I mean by the people. I think it is a term well understood and comprehended by everybody in this country, if not by the Senator. I do not deal in technicalities. I speak in a broad sense. When I say the people, I mean that material that constitutes the Government, the bone and sinew; that portion of the community that produce all, that sustain all, that do all the fighting, and win all the victories.

But we have had brought into this discussion agrarianism, and this is said to be an agrarian measure.[16] Why, sir, it begins where agrarianism ends; and instead of going down the line, it ascends. It does not propose to take away what belongs to anybody else and give to the people; but the whole proposition is simply to enable the rightful owner, the man who has made the sacrifice, either by himself directly or his ancestor, or somebody connected with him, to go forward and do—what? Take somebody else's? No; but to take a portion of that which belongs to him, to take a part of that which is his. The public lands belong to the people; and, as I before remarked, they were acquired by their blood and treasure, and they are entitled to participate in their benefit. How many quarter sections of public land have you in the United States? According to a table I have had made out at the Land Office, we have seven million quarter sections.[17] How many heads of families are there in the United States? Do you discriminate by this bill? No, but you say to the rich and to the poor, to all, "Go and take a quarter section of land." You discriminate against none.

Thus each individual is left, at his own option, to go and take a part of that which belongs to all. I said there were seven million quarter sections. How many qualified voters are there in the United States? There are not more than four million, if my memory serves me right; and if you give a quarter section to each head of a family— as everybody belongs to one family or another—the head getting it would confer a benefit through the families. What is your whole voting population? Not over four million. Then you have three million quarter sections left, after giving to each qualified voter in the United States a quarter section, which is a little over one half of what belongs to him. Is that anybody's else? Is that agrarian? Did you ever hear of a Government being overturned by the people having property? It is for the want of it. I want to let the great mass of the owners of this property come forward and take a part of that which belongs to them, and for which they have shed their blood. Is it agrarianism to permit a man to take possession of that which is his? Does that take from anybody else anything that belongs to him?

Then, what injustice is done to the old States? Is there any? As to the idea of doing them injustice, by filling up the new States and increasing their political power, there is nothing in it. Suppose the population remains in the old States: when you apportion Representatives, do you not give them Representatives in proportion to population? It is true, making new States as Virginia has made five, so far as the Senate is concerned, has an effect on political power; but a man in a new State will not count more than he will in an old State.[18] It does not affect the other branch a single scintilla, so far as that goes.

But a word as to agrarianism and the Gracchi. There are a few persons who have learned to talk about the French Revolution and the Jacobins, and the Red Republicans and the Gracchi, and the agrarians and all that, and they get up a terrific idea, and make everybody fear that there is something terrible in the measure. It is learned and literary and classical to repeat these things, and gentlemen are constantly talking about them and losing sight of the great principle, of the great object to be accomplished, of ameliorating the condition of the great mass of the people out of that which belongs to them. You may talk about Tiberius and Caius Gracchus, but there were never two men more slandered in all the tide of history. I wish to

God we had some men in this day possessing their spirit and their courage and their energy. When was Rome in her palmiest days? When she acquired large accessions of territory, and her territory was populated by her citizens; while the great mass of the people had homes, the Roman eagle carried terror into every continent that was invaded by her. That was the time when Roman citizens were most respected.

Under the Licinian law, every Roman citizen was qualified to share in the possession of newly-acquired public land, to an extent not exceeding five hundred jugers.[19] This applied only to the public domain. That stood the law for a long number of years; but gradually they commenced violating it; and when all the lands, public and private, passed into the hands of a few, Rome sank into a rotten aristocracy on the one hand, and what was denominated at that day a populace, or what we call a rabble, on the other. One class owned the lands and were corrupt; the other class were poor and servile; they were shut out of homes; and when Rome had decayed to her very core, when her greatness was gone, when she was perishing, the Gracchi came forward and attempted to do—what? To take away the land belonging to others? No; but their effort was to restore Rome back to the Licinian law, which had never been repealed, and had only been trampled under foot by arbitrary power, by usurpation. That was what the Gracchi attempted to do; and, for making their attempt to do this, they were overthrown. On a certain occasion in Rome, when Tiberius Gracchus was making his speech, as history bears me out in saying, this dependent rabble that would do anything for a few six pences and grog, instigated by a factious Senate and aristocracy, knocked him down and killed him with one of the pieces of timber that constituted the rostrum on which he stood. That is the way Tiberius Gracchus fell. The Roman Senate united with the rabble and murdered and annihilated the man that was trying to stand by the people. Yes, and that, too, in the season of the year when those who lived in the rural districts were not accessible to Rome, and could not get there. It was in harvest time, when they were at a distance. That man was there struggling for them, advocating and sustaining their rights, and they were in their harvest fields, and a corrupt Senate joined the rabble and murdered the people's man. Niebuhr, in his Lectures on Roman History, thus describes it:[20]

[The passage inserted here elaborates upon the account of Roman history presented in the preceding paragraph.]

I have said that the Gracchi sought only to restore the Licinian law, under which Rome prospered. To show what was the policy of Rome in her most prosperous days, I will read a portion of one of the old Roman lays, translated and published by Macaulay:

For Romans in Rome's quarrel
  Spared neither land nor gold,
Nor son nor wife, nor limb nor life,
  In the brave days of old.

Then none was for a party,
  Then all were for the state;
Then the great man helped the poor,
  And the poor man loved the great;
Then lands were fairly portioned;
  Then spoils were fairly sold:
Then Romans were like brothers
  In the brave days of old.[21]

Mr. President, I have trespassed now longer than I intended to trespass on the Senate, but there are a few other facts that I will advert to. It seems to be conceded by all who have paid any attention to the operations of this Government, that now is the time to prevent the state of things that we have been speaking of, which occurred in Rome. While the public lands belong to the people, hold out reasonable inducements for people to go and settle on them and become cultivators of the soil. Who is it that is willing to suspend and hang the destinies of this Republic upon cities? I for one am not; and unless the present tendency of things is arrested, and arrested now—and the policy of this bill will arrest it and result in a different system—I fear the consequences, and I fear this Government will go as Rome went. We are in our swaddling clothes; we have scarcely reached man's estate; yet these spots of decay are visible, and the tendency of the pernicious policy that has been pursued must be observed by all. What then is our true policy? Build up your rural districts; build up the mechanics' shops. Let the productions of agriculture go hand in hand with mechanism. Let each man have a home, and when your elections come around he is a freeman, he is an independent man; he goes to the ballot-box and votes his own vote, and not the vote of his landlord or his master. Build up these districts, and there you will have virtue; there you will have honesty in private as well as public affairs, for after all, the people of the rural districts are to be trusted. Into their hands this Government must go. It is their interest to do right in all governmental affairs. It being their interest to do right, they can be relied upon and confided in implicitly. They expect no office. They do not live by politics, but they live by their labor, and they want the best government, the purest government that they can get. Go there amidst your rural population; there is industry, there is virtue, and intelligence; and I might speak of them in the language of a celebrated author:

Unlearned, he knew no schoolman's subtle art
No language but the language of the heart;
By nature honest, by experience wise,
Healthy by temperance and exercise.[22]

That is the population to sustain this Government. It is a population to rely upon. If you do not, your government is gone. Why, then, do the Senate resist this state of things being brought about? Why will the Senate of the United States longer stand up in opposition to an enlightened public judgment that has been rendered on this question three several times? I trust in God that the time will come when the Senate, instead of being chosen by the Legislatures of the respective States, will be chosen by the people of the several States, and then they will feel and know their relative position to the people that constitute the State. I hope that time will come; I trust it may. It is districts like those I have been describing, represented on the principles I have just referred to, that constitute States. These are the men and the description of men who are necessary and proper to make a virtuous, intelligent, and patriotic State; a State capable of governing itself—men like these "who know their rights, and knowing, dare maintain."[23]

The bill before the Senate meets another objection that has been urged; and that is, that the public lands should be made to pay for themselves. I have no scruples upon that question myself; but there has been a disposition to place the bill beyond the reach of constitutional scruples, beyond the reach of questions as to expediency, and beyond the reach of the exercise of the veto power. I do not speak *ex cathedra* on this point; I do not speak advisedly at all; but I have heard it thrown out in the way of taunt, perhaps with a view of frightening some, that it would receive the Executive veto. I do not believe it; and I will give you one reason why I do not believe it. Look at this bill. It provides for the settler defraying the expenses, paying the office fees; and it holds out a reasonable inducement to settlers, and imposes the condition of the settlement and cultivation for five years. It is not a bill for paupers, for miserable lazzaroni, for persons from lazar-houses,[24] for vagabonds, not for what are denominated some times poor people in one sense; but it is for men who have arms, who have muscles, who have sinews, and who have willing hearts to work. What business would a vagabond have on one hundred and sixty acres? A vagrant is a man running about, unsettled, with no particular abiding place. To fix a man down and set him to work is the precise opposite of vagabondism. Because a man is poor, because he has not got a convenient or sufficient amount of this world's means, that does not make him a loafer; and the fact that a man is poor is no crime.[25] If being poor was a crime, and I was before you as my judge upon trial, and the charge was read to me, and I was asked to put in my plea, I should have to plead that I was guilty; that I was a great criminal; that I had been born a criminal; and that I had lived a criminal a large portion of my life. Yes, I have wrestled with poverty, the gaunt and haggard monster; I have met it in the day and night; I have felt his withering approach and his blighting influence; but did I feel myself a criminal? No; I felt that I was chastened, and that I was an honest man, and that I would rescue myself from the grasp of the monster. But there is sin; and there is more sin committed sometimes in becoming poor than almost anything else. We are told upon high authority that the drunkard and the glutton shall see poverty;[26] but because it is affixed as a penalty, that does not make it a crime. It may be the penalty of committing crime.

Then, on the other hand, we see some start from poverty and commit a great deal of sin in getting rich. Poverty is no crime. If every man is criminal in this country who is poor, the country is full of criminals, and we have not got enough places of confinement to contain them. I demur; I put in a plea of not guilty, on behalf of the poor men of the country, and say they are not criminal. A man can be poor and honest. Sometimes poverty drives a man to commit a sin, and that sin may be criminal; but poverty itself is no crime. It is a great inconvenience and a great misfortune; but if poverty is a crime, where are the ten thousand, yea, the millions of little boys that are thrown on the world? Where is this rising population? Three out of every four are poor; and are they all criminals? Suppose they are poor; they have got muscles and bones and will, and by this measure we say to every man: "Notwithstanding you have not got $200, go and take your one hundred and sixty acres of land; take care of your wife and children; educate your boys; build up your school-houses; have your stock about you, and become a free and independent man." Even on the score of revenue, it will be an advantage to the Treasury. When a man is poor, he buys little. You increase his means of buying, and he buys more; and the Government, in bestowing one hundred and sixty acres of land, increases the occupant's means to buy; and, in a few years, by the operation of your tariff on the articles used for the consumption of his family, the Government will be remunerated twenty times, even in dollars and cents. Is that all? No. He is a better citizen; he is a more elevated man, better calculated to perform all the duties of a sovereign.

It is said that this is giving away the public lands greatly below what they cost. When I turn to a report made by a distinguished man of Virginia, for I have been dealing in Virginia authorities all day, I find that up to 1850, Mr. Stuart, who was then Secretary of the Interior, made this estimate:

That this matter may be correctly understood, and the value of these lands as a source of revenue be properly appreciated, I beg leave to state that, by a careful examination, it is ascertained that the entire area of the public domain, exclusive of the lands in Oregon, California, New Mexico, Utah, the Indian and Nebraska Territories, was four hundred and twenty-four million one hundred and three thousand seven hundred and fifty acres.

About one fourth of this land has been sold, and the purchase money received for it amounts to........................$135,339,092

The cost of the whole of these lands, including
    the amount paid to France for Louisiana, to
    Spain for the Floridas, and amount paid for
    extinguishing the Indian title...........$61,121,717

A portion only of these lands has been
    surveyed, the cost of which, in-
    cluding salaries of surveyers
    general and clerks, and expenses
    attending the surveys, was............. 6,369,838

Less than half the land surveyed has been sold,
    and the whole cost of selling and managing
    the same, including every expense not
    previously charged, is................. 7,466,324

Aggregate outlay of every kind.................... 74,957,879

Net profit to the Government....................$60,381,213[27]

Since 1850 there has been received from the public lands about thirty-seven millions. Where is the balance? Where is the deficit? The measure before you provides for the settlement of each alternate, leaving the remaining sections to be entered, either at $1 25 or $2 50. Add the twelve and a half cents proposed to be charged to the $1 25 and you get more than Mr. Stuart himself says was the cost of the public lands. He says twenty cents is the average cost. There were $60,000,000 of profits in 1850, and now $37,000,000 more, making $97,000,000 profit from the public lands. What right, then, have you to withhold from the man who shed his blood, and from his children, a part of that which is his? Have you any right to do it? I demand it in the name of the American people; I demand it in the name of the Constitution; I demand it in the name of justice, as being in conformity to the spirit and genius of our Government.

When we begin to press this measure, there are various other measures brought forward. One is to give all the lands to the States. The enlightened statesman, Mr. Calhoun, some years ago, brought forward a proposition to surrender all the lands to the States.[28] I remember it well. Mr. Calhoun did not want to electioneer at all! He was above that sort of thing! Yet, when he wanted to concede the power to make internal improvements, he could change the name of a river to a great inland sea,[29] and then it became constitutional. An extraordinary statesman! I do not question that he was an extraordinary statesman. Mr. Calhoun had some peculiar notions about government; and if he were now living, he and all the men in the United States could not put a Government into successful and practical operation under the system he laid down.[30] He was a logician; he could reason from premise to conclusion with unerring certainty, but he was as often wrong in taking his premises as anybody else. Admit his premises, and you were swept off by the conclusion; but look at his premises, and he was just as often wrong as any other statesman; and I think Mr. Calhoun was more of a politician than a statesman. Mr. Calhoun never possessed that class of mind that enabled him to found a great party. He founded a sect; and if he had been a religionist, he would have been a mere sectarian. He would never have gone beyond founding a sect peculiar to himself. His mind was metaphysical and logical, and he was a great man in his peculiar channel; but he might be more properly said to have founded a sect than a great national party.

I have been for the preëmption and graduation policy; I have been for the homestead policy; I have been in favor of confining the future sales of public lands to actual settlers, and to them in limited quantities. I have looked forward to the day when, after these measures were fixed on the country, the homestead consummating the policy that has been heretofore inaugurated, the result in a few years would be a surrender of the public lands to the States; and I look on these measures as merely preliminary; and it is an object I have long desired, for I want the powers of this Federal Government circumscribed; I want it kept in its proper orbit, and I want to withdraw the operations of the Federal Government, as far as possible, without the limits of the States. The preemption, graduation, and homestead policy is nothing but the preliminary, the prelude to an ultimate surrender of the land to all the States in which it lies. I want to make myself understood as to what my policy is.

But, not to be vain or egotistic, or to claim anything from the Democratic party, I want to repeat, in conclusion, that this is emphatically a Democratic measure—inaugurated by the Democracy; and the Republican party have only shown their sagacity, as I remarked before, in one sense, in coming forward and trying to appropriate that which they know meets the approbation of the popular heart. They show their good sense in it; but because they will now go for my measure, or for a Democratic measure, I shall not turn against it.

Looking on this as a great measure, involving great principles and great results in the future, I say let us stand up for it; let us forget party; let us go for it as a measure to advance and elevate the condition of the great mass of the people. Why cannot we rally around it as a common altar, and proclaim to the nation that it is above party, and that it is intended to perpetuate the Union, and the Government as they have been? But I want to come down to the last Democratic authority on this subject. I hold in my hand a document that was issued in 1857. The paragraph that I will call the attention of the Senate to is this:

No nation in the tide of time has ever been blessed with so rich and noble an inheritance as we enjoy in the public lands. In administering this important trust, whilst it may be wise to grant portions of them for the improvement of the remainder, yet we should never forget that it is our cardinal policy to reserve these lands, as much as may be, for actual settlers, and this at moderate prices. We shall thus not only best promote the prosperity of the new States and Territories, by furnishing them a hardy and independent race of honest and industrious citizens, but shall secure homes for our children and our children's children, as well as for those exiles from foreign shores who may seek in this country to improve their condition, and to enjoy the blessings of civil and religious liberty. Such emigrants have done much to improve[31] the growth and prosperity of the country. They have proved faithful both in peace and in war. After becoming citizens, they are entitled, under the Constitution and laws, to be placed on a perfect equality with native-born citizens; and in this character they should ever be kindly recognized.

Would it not seem that the bill now under consideration was drafted with an eye to the propositions here laid down, a portion of the lands being appropriated for the improvement of the remainder, and the balance being, as far as possible, reserved to actual settlers, and as homes for our children and our children's children; and at the same time opening the door to the exiles of other countries to come here and cultivate these lands? I may say that there is bread and work for all. Let them all come, and comply with the law. Who was it that made use of the language I have just read? A Republican? No. Who was it? James Buchanan, in his inaugural address on the 4th of March, 1857. It would seem that this bill covered precisely the ground laid down in that inaugural address. Hence I infer that the President of the United States will not veto this measure. I hope he will not, in the event of its passage. I feel satisfied that we can and will pass the proposition in some shape. What shape it will be, I cannot tell; but, in conclusion, let me say to the friends of the homestead proposition, who have been engaged in this warfare a long time—for the present proposition commenced in 1846—it is now near its completion; let us stand by it, let us put it upon the statute-book in some shape. Once upon the statute-book, there will never be power to recall it. The people will come up to those who are struggling in their behalf, and there will never be a Senate here who will take it off the statute-book. Shall I make the appeal to the friends of the measure—after having fought this battle for fifteen or sixteen long years—now, when we are in sight of the very conclusion, do not let us divide and become distracted among ourselves, and let the measure fall to the ground? Let us meet each other in a spirit of compromise, holding to the substance; holding to the great principle that runs through the bill; not falling out about little details or immaterial points; but now, as we have got so near to the final attainment, let us consummate this great measure. Shall we stop here, and like the Dead Sea fruit, let it turn to ashes,[32] or shall we stand firm and consummate this great measure?[33]

Cong. Globe, 36 Cong., 1 Sess., 1650–55.

1. The Senate, acting as a committee of the whole, resumed consideration of the homestead bill (H. R. 280). On behalf of the committee on public lands, Johnson withdrew an earlier amendment submitted by that committee in lieu of the House measure and offered a second amendment which, like the first, was to be a substitute for the original House bill. Briefly summarized, Johnson's new amendment provided that family heads might enter one quarter section of unoccupied public land which, after five years' occupancy, could be purchased at 12½¢ an acre. Aliens, provided they declared their intentions to become U. S. citizens as required by naturalization laws, had the same rights as citizens. No part of the bill should be construed to impair existing pre-emption or graduation laws. Settlers residing on surveyed land as yet unmarketed had two years to purchase one quarter section; those living on unsurveyed lands for at least three months had two years after the land had been surveyed in which to purchase a quarter section. Within two years after receipt of the plots, the President would place on sale all other surveyed or unsurveyed lands, excluding any reserved by the government for special purposes. *Cong. Globe*, 36 Cong., 1 Sess., 1649–50.

2. Endorsing the House version of the homestead bill, James R. Doolittle of Wisconsin had anticipated that it would encourage settlement, bind the continent together, eliminate Mormonism, and allow the southern white to escape the immoral and unprofitable plantation system. In an angry rejoinder, James M. Mason of Virginia attacked the measure as a Republican ploy, a large-scale emigrant aid society, and an encouragement to pauperism. He chided Johnson for sponsoring a bill praised as a means of excluding the slave population and concluded with a defense of slavery as the best condition for both races. *Ibid.*, 1629–37.

3. "An Act for granting lands to the inhabitants and settlers at Vincennes, and the Illinois country, in the territory northwest of the Ohio, and for confirming them in their possessions," approved March 3, 1791. *Annals of Cong.*, 1 Cong., 3 Sess., 2413–15.

4. While it is true that Jefferson espoused the idea that the "earth is given as a common stock for man to labor and live on," the homestead allusion is rather less clear in his annual messages. In his first annual message, following a reference to the increase in population since the earlier census, he noted that "we contemplate this rapid growth and the prospect it holds up to us [with a view] to the settlement of the extensive country still remaining vacant"; in his sixth, he made reference "to the early settlement of the most exposed and vulnerable parts of the country." Richardson, *Messages*, I, 327, 410; Hibbard, *Public Land Policies*, 2, 143.

5. Although there was no roll-call record of the final vote on the Oregon Public Land Bill of 1850, Mason, throughout the discussion, had sought to avoid giving land to settlers: "I doubt the justice and propriety of giving them [public lands] away at all. But if they are to be given to actual settlers as a donation, it seems to me that this donation should at least be restricted to citizens of the United States." This restrictive position was further reflected in his amendment to exclude aliens who had declared their intention to become citizens and in his vote on an amendment to extend the free land principle to all public lands. *Cong. Globe*, 31 Cong., 1 Sess., 1845–48.

6. The day before, Johnson had quoted from an act setting up land policies and procedures for New Mexico, Kansas, and Nebraska. Enacted July 22, 1854, the law "donated one quarter section" to every white male,

twenty-one or older, who was a citizen or had declared his intentions of becoming one, and who resided in the territory or might settle there between January 1, 1853, and January 1, 1858. *Ibid.*, 36 Cong., 1 Sess., 1635; *U. S. Statutes*, X, 308.

7. Mason had justified the donation of public land in New Mexico as a means of attracting a white population, thereby relieving the government of "the still greater burden of defending them by a soldiery." Such a consideration, he argued, did not apply to Kansas. *Cong. Globe*, 36 Cong., 1 Sess., 1636.

8. This appears to be a Johnsonism pieced together from Ps. 135:16–17 —"eyes have they, but they see not/ They have ears, but they hear not" and from Cicero, *De Natura Deorum*, Bk. II, Ch. 56, sec. 40: "the eyes like sentinels." Stevenson, *Quotations*, 597.

9. *Senate Journal*, 33 Cong., 1 Sess., 534–35.

10. *Ibid.*, 541.

11. *Ibid.*, 537.

12. *Ibid.*, 543.

13. This figure approximates the original reserve set aside in Ohio for Virginia Revolutionary bounty grants at the time the state ceded her western territories. In actuality, the amount of land granted by the U. S. for Virginia bounties was nearly 6,300,000 acres and required thirty-four acts, aside from special legislation, to satisfy these claims. Payson J. Treat, *The National Land System, 1785–1820* (New York, 1910), 338–39; Hibbard, *Public Land Policies*, 123n.

14. Johnson refers to H. R. 37 introduced by John L. Dawson of Pennsylvania on December 5, 1853, and passed in the House, March 6, 1854, by a 107 to 53 vote. It failed of adoption when the House refused to reconsider the bill with Senate amendments. *House Journal*, 33 Cong., 1 Sess., 91, 458, 1302; *Cong. Globe*, 33 Cong., 1 Sess., 4–5, 549.

15. While Johnson is essentially correct in noting that the votes of 1852 and 1854 were not partisan, since both Whigs and Democrats voted for and against, it was already a sectional issue. In 1854 only three southern congressmen voted for it, while the newer and western states overwhelmingly supported it, and the vote was about equally divided in the North Atlantic states; moreover, the Democrats split, 72 for and 52 against, the Whigs, 35–19. Hibbard, *Public Land Policies*, 366–71.

16. In the mid-nineteenth century, "agrarianism" carried the imputation of land expropriation and social leveling. See *Johnson Papers*, I, 572n.

17. Once again, even as in his Speech on Homestead Bill, May 20, 1858, Johnson drew from the tables which Land Commissioner Hendricks had earlier prepared for him.

18. This assertion overlooks the inordinate political per capita weight in the Senate enjoyed by new states with smaller populations.

19. Here Johnson draws on Barthold Niebuhr's study of Roman history which he had borrowed from the Library of Congress prior to his May, 1858, speech. The Licinian law (367 B.C.) instituted by Gaius Licinius Calvus Stalo, tribune and consul of the plebeians, sought to prevent anyone from acquiring more than 350 acres of the new public domain. The juger represented .622 of an acre. Niebuhr, *History of Rome*, II, 279; Borrower's Ledger, 1857–59, Library of Congress Archives, LC, 146; Frank C. Bourne, *A History of the Romans* (Boston, 1966), 84.

20. With only minor variations in spelling, capitalization, and punctuation, the extract which follows may be found in Lecture LXXVIII. Interestingly enough, the passage in question is marked in pen and red crayon in the 1849 edition of Niebuhr's *Rome* in the Library of Congress; it may be the same volume that Johnson borrowed. Niebuhr, *History of Rome*, II, 289, 290–91.

21. "Horatius," st. 31, in *Lays of Ancient Rome*. Stevenson, *Quotations*, 202.

22. Alexander Pope, *Epistle to Dr. Arbuthnot*, l. 398. *Ibid.*, 238.

23. William Jones, "An Ode in Imitation of Alcoeus." *Ibid.*, 1917.

24. Lazzaroni are Italian beggers; a lazar house is a hospital for the contagiously ill, generally lepers. *Webster's Third International.*

25. On April 4, one week before Johnson spoke, Louis Wigfall of Texas, in a lively exchange on the Senate floor, had attacked the homestead measure as one "providing for pauperism." He had gone on to declare, "I know it is popular to talk about poor men, but I tell you that poverty is a crime. A man who is poor has sinned, [laughter;] there is a screw loose in his head somewhere. [Laughter.]" It is clear that Johnson was hoping in this section of his speech to make political capital with the poor. That he succeeded and that Wigfall's remarks had stung to the quick some of the working poor may be seen in the comments on Johnson's defense of the poor and the Texan's condemnation found in the Letter from James Bennett, April 8, 1860, which follows. *Cong. Globe*, 36 Cong., 1 Sess., 1535.

26. Prov. 23:21.

27. These figures are from the report of the commissioner of the land office, Justin Butterfield, and are included in Secretary of the Interior Alexander H. H. Stuart's report to Congress. *Senate Ex. Doc.* No. 2, 31 Cong., 2 Sess., 5.

28. Introduced in 1837, Calhoun's cession bill was also offered in 1841 as an amendment to Crittenden's distribution bill. Stephenson, *History of the Public Lands*, 33, 47; *Cong. Debates*, 24 Cong., 2 Sess., 729; *Cong. Globe*, 26 Cong., 2 Sess., 90, 91.

29. An allusion to the "Inland Sea" idea expressed by Calhoun in his keynote address at the Memphis Railroad Convention of 1845. Although he did not use the term itself, Calhoun conceived of the Mississippi and its tributaries as a body of water such as the term suggested. Gerald Capers, *John C. Calhoun—Opportunist: A Reappraisal* (Gainesville, Fla., 1960), 230; Richard K. Crallé, ed., *Works of John C. Calhoun* (6 vols., New York, 1854–57), VI, 273–84.

30. Johnson refers to Calhoun's concept of government by "rule of concurrent majority" rather than by absolute numerical majority. By this theory each major sectional interest must be given the power of vetoing legislation; issues are settled only by agreement of a majority of both major and minor interests. He also suggested the possibility of the creation of a dual executive —one elected by the North and one by the South—with independent veto power. Capers, *Calhoun*, 245–47.

31. According to Richardson's *Messages*, V, 434, Buchanan in his inaugural used the words "to promote" rather than "to improve."

32. A reference to an apple-like fruit, growing on the shores of the Dead Sea, which has a bitter taste and seeds resembling ashes. Two literary works, Byron, *Childe Harold's Pilgrimage*, Canto 3, st. 34, and Milton, *Paradise Lost*, Bk. X, 560, make reference to the fruit. Stevenson, *Quotations*, 452.

33. Mason denied any inconsistency in his votes on the Orgeon bill or graduation and his vote on the homestead, refuted Johnson's view that those measures had embodied the homestead principle, contended that he had always been opposed to the "system of making gratuities of the public lands," and asserted that his opposition to the House bill was based on his fears that the lands would be confined to settlers from free states to the exclusion of those from slave states. Calling the Tennessee senator "too sensitive," Mason admitted he had not expected the "wrath" exhibited—"a wrath to which that of Achilles, celebrated in Homeric verse, would hardly be compared." Following these remarks, Wigfall attacked Johnson for accusing southerners of making a party issue of the measure. After considerable discussion, the Senate acted favorably on Albert G. Brown's motion to recommit both Senate and House bills, together with all their amendments, to the committee on public lands, with instructions to report back to the Senate on the next Tuesday.

From James Bennett[1]

Brooklyn 12th April 1860

Hon Sir,

pardon this intrusion by a stranger, but perceiving by your speech in the senate on the homestead bill that you are the friend of the poor man, i could not resist the temptation to address you these few lines, to express my feelings for so nobly advocating the cause of the poor (or as Mr Wigfall call[s] us criminals)[.] sir, if that gentleman, or any of the opponents of the bill knew what it is to be very poor the[y] would not think poverty such a very great crime. Sir i have served in the constitution frigate under Commodore Thomas Mc Donough,[2] and in the guerriere frigate under Commodore C B Thomson,[3] and am neither pauper nor loafer, but although an old man am both able and willing to work if i could get it, Sir i have been earnestly watching and praying for the passage of your homestead bill that myself and children might be able to enjoy a bit of land that we might call our own, so that we should no more be turned out in the street because we could not pay our rent as was the case with us last winter, not because we are lazy, or indolent, or intemperate, but the want of employment. Sir if it should please the Almighty god to grant you sucess in getting the bill passed, myself and eight children will fall on our knees and pray for you that when you shall have finished your carrier [sic] on this earth our Heavenly Father shall welcome you in to the heavenly kingdom with well done though [sic] good and faithful servant. although it may be considerd great presumption in a poor old sailer to address a senator, i belive your goodness of heart will prompt you to forgive such presumption[.]   may god bless you and every one that is the friend of the poor will always be the prayer of   your very humble servant

James Bennett
No 60 south street
New York

To the Hon Senator Johnson   of tennessee
ALS, DLC-JP2.

1. James Bennett is not readily identifiable; during these years in Brooklyn a boatman, fisherman, and sailmaker, none of whom lived at No. 60 South Street, all bore this name. *Lain's Brooklyn Directory* (1859–60), 25; *ibid.* (1860–61), 26.

2. Thomas MacDonough (1783–1825), U. S. naval officer, served in the wars with Tripoli and more prominently in the War of 1812, in which his squadron won the battle of Plattsburgh, fought on Lake Champlain. *DAB*, XII, 19–21.

3. Charles C. B. Thompson was a midshipman on the *Nautilus* during

the Barbary Wars, and during the War of 1812 commanded the sloop of war *Louisiana* at the siege of New Orleans, where he distinguished himself by training raw recruits as sailors and greatly assisting General Jackson. At one time MacDonough had commanded the *Guerrière*. United States Office of Naval Records, *Naval Documents Relating to the United States Wars with the Barbary Powers* (6 vols., Washington, D. C., 1940), II, 421; Edgar S. McClay, *A History of the United States Navy from 1775 to 1898* (2 vols., New York, 1898), I, 618, 621; Wilburt S. Brown, *The Amphibious Campaign for West Florida and Louisiana, 1814–1815* (University, Ala., 1969), 116–17; *DAB*, XII, 20.

From Thomas T. Gosnell

April 12, 1860, Ringgold, Ga.; ALS, DLC-JP2.

A Georgia Democrat, who despairs of receiving any documents from the Georgia congressional delegation and is "indebted to T. A. R. Nelson & Wm B. Stokes for all the congressional documents I have recd this session," would like copies of recent speech of Alabama Congressman Jabez L. M. Curry; is "gratified to hear your name spoken of in Connection with the Nomination at Charleston," and knows no one who "would receive a better vote, in this Stronghold of Democracy in Georgia (the 5th District)[.]"

From Clement C. Clay, Jr.

130 Penn. Av.
Washington Apl 13. 1860

Hon. A. Johnson:

My Dear Sir,

Since I saw you, I went over an amendment[1] offerred, I think, by you, in which Section 4 is materially changed by striking out the word *Contracted*, in the original bill; which obviates my objections in the main.[2] I, also, agreed with Hon. Robt Johnson[3] on a slight alteration that would make it altogether satisfactory. I enclose what I prepared to offer.

For the reasons I suggested, I would advise putting the amount to be paid at 25 cents per acre. wh[ich] would pay the gov't what the land cost, or quite do it, & take away the objection that it was giving it away.

I would strike out in 2d Sec. the words "and have not alienated the same or any part thereof"—wh[ich] requires proof of a negative, that could hardly be honestly made.

I would strike out the proviso of that section, as it proposes to direct the distribution of the proceeds of the land among *minor* children, where, according to the laws of the state, *all* the children would claim, wh[ich] may be objected to as invading the rights of the state. I think you might concede that without impairing the merits of the bill; for the minors would still get their share.

I do not like including foreigners; but would be quite reconciled to your original proposition, confining it to those *who had declared their intention*, at the date of the approval of this bill, of becoming citizens &c.

I think all lands under 25 cents should be ceded, without cost, to the states in wh[ich] they lie, because I can prove by figures that they will not for their sale, under existing laws at that price, & that the United States would gain by such cession; but I will take the 12½ cent lands, if I can get no more.

I trust you can so modify yr. bill as to preserve the principles & purposes that we hold in common, & shall be happy, in that case, to yield it a cordial support.

I am, very truly yrs.,
C. C. Clay, Jr.[4]

ALS, DLC-JP.

1. The "amendment" to the homestead bill pending before the Senate was in reality a different bill containing twelve sections. Section 4 had originally prohibited the use of the land to satisfy debts contracted *before* the issuance of the patent; Johnson's amendment simply provided that the land could not be used to satisfy debts until after the patent was issued. *Cong. Globe*, 36 Cong., 1 Sess., 1508, 1650.
2. On April 9, Clay had proposed as a substitute for the homestead bill "a bill to cede the public lands within the limits of the land States on certain conditions therein mentioned." Given a number (S. 389), the bill was printed and referred to the committee on public lands but never reached the Senate floor, for on May 26, when the committee asked to be discharged from further consideration of S. 389, the Senate concurred. *Ibid.*, 1619, 2372.
3. Robert W. Johnson of Arkansas, chairman of the committee on public lands.
4. The envelope endorsement reads: "Mr. Dooly [James F. Dooley, a Senate messenger] will please deliver as soon as possible[.]" *U. S. Official Register* (1859), 190.

From George E. Pugh

[Washington, D. C.]
Friday, April 13th, 1860.

Dear Sir:

My ear has been so much inflamed, since day before yesterday, that I could not attend the sessions of the Senate.

I am now engaged in reconstructing your amendment so as to prevent any evasion of its purpose by speculators—and to embrace two or three other propositions of the same charactor. I will meet you in the room of the Committee on Public lands at eleven o'clock to morrow, and we can examine it carefully and in detail.

Yours truly   G. E. Pugh

Hon. A. Johnson   U. S. Senate.

ALS, DLC-JP2.

From Joseph B. Heiskell[1]

Rogersville Junction
April 14 1860

Dear Sir,

I find great anxiety here among our people for the immediate transfer of the mail to the Rail-Road. We have the utmost confidence that when you take it in hand it will not fail, and calculate with certainty upon getting it now. As to the present Contract the state of things is this. Mr Blair[2] the Contracter has sub let his contract to a Mr Rhea,[3] a hard working man who was to keep it until the road was pushed to the river.[4] It is now within ¾ of a mile and their iron has given out. (probably by a load being left somewhere). so that it will be some time (a month perhaps) before this link is filled, in the mean time the R Road carries all the passengers, and Rhea is ruined if he has to carry the mail from Russellville. He is exceedingly anxious for the change. He expects to obtain Blairs consent & to make application for the change himself— The only post office on the old route between Russellville & Rogersville is St Clair; and you will see that Fain[5] proposes at the [rate of] $1000 to carry this mail, 2 or 3 times a week. You will certainly save a worthy & industrious man, from undeserved ruin if you can get Mr Rhea released, and I hope you will succeed in the effort[.]

Very Respectfully   J B Heiskell

Hon A Johnson

ALS, DLC-JP2.

1. Joseph B. Heiskell (1823–1913), a native of Knoxville, practiced law in Madisonville and later in Rogersville, where he had extensive real estate holdings. Elected to the state senate (1857–59), he chaired the committee on the *Code* adopted during the 32nd session. Subsequently he represented the first Tennessee district in the Confederate Congress; when federal army units occupied Rogersville in August, 1864, he was captured, along with Albert G. Watkins, a former U. S. congressman. Regarded as dangerous by Military Governor Johnson, Heiskell spent the remainder of the war in prison camps in Tennessee, Kentucky, and Ohio. Moving to Memphis during Reconstruction, he served as chairman of the judiciary committee in the Constitutional Convention of 1870 and held the office of attorney general and reporter for the state (1870–78). Robison Biog. Data; Porter, *Tenn. Confed. Mil. Hist.*, 534–35; *Tenn. Official Manual* (1890), 194; John B. Brownlow to O. P. Temple, January 2, 1892, Temple Papers, University of Tennessee.

2. William P. Blair of Jonesboro, whose bid of $790 for a "2-horse hack" received the contract for the route between Rogersville and Bulls Gap. Leaving Rogersville daily except Sunday at 1:00 p.m., the mail was to arrive at Bulls Gap, fifteen miles away, by 7:00 p.m. It left Bulls Gap at 6:00 a.m., arriving at Rogersville by 12 noon. Blair was also awarded the Jonesboro to Blountville route and the Jonesboro to Gotts' Cross Roads. These contracts

ran from July, 1858, to June, 1862. Ray, *Tennessee Cousins*, 37; *House Ex. Doc.* No. 109, 35 Cong., 2 Sess., 94, 97, 98.

3. Probably the Robert Rhea who had unsuccessfully bid $1,425 per annum for the Rogersville to Bulls Gap route. He had also lost his bid on the route from Russellville to Sneedville. *Ibid.*, 94, 99.

4. The Rogersville and Jefferson Railroad, incorporated in 1852, was a fourteen-mile spur of the East Tennessee and Virginia Railroad extending from near Bulls Gap to Rogersville. Grading had begun in 1857; by 1860 it was still unfinished, although the bridge over the Holston River had been authorized. Holland, *Railroad Enterprise*, 302–4.

5. Richard G. Fain (1811–1878), a "clerk" with $3,500 real and $7,000 personal property, was president of the Rogersville and Jefferson Railroad. *Ibid.*, 396; 1860 Census, Tenn., Hawkins, 108.

From John H. Keyser[1]

New York April 14th 1860

Mr Andrew Johnson
Dear Sir

When a man performes a noble act it is some satisfaction to know how it is Received by his friends. Your timely Rebuke to the enemys of the Homestead Bill and your masterly defense of our cherished principles in the debate in the Senate on Wensday is gratefully Received by the friends of the measure here and by none more than by myself— you Said more practical truths than has been spoken in the senate during its session— The course being pursued by the democratic party is Rapidly alienating all the friends of land Reform from the party and the Republicans are dilegently stealing the thunder[.] It formed a large portion of the capital [*sic*] of the Republican capital in the last canvass in connecticut[2] while the Democrats following their false leaders at Washington either ignored or were silent upon this vital question— It is becoming *the* element of strength with the Republican party in wining over the germans in this city and will prove much more powerful in the west[.]

Hoping to See and converse with you on the subject soon I Remain as ever

Yours truly   John H Keyser

P S—I have writen Mr Greely asking him to notice your Remarks in the Senate as they deserve— He will do so if he deems it politic towards the Republican party—[3] He has done more than any one to Engraft the measure into the creed of the Republican when it should legitimately have ben a leading Democratic measure[.]

ALS, DLC-JP2.

1. John H. Keyser, associated with the National Reform movement, was a New York plumber and agent for furnaces and ranges. *Trow's New York City Directory* (1860–61), 465; Zahler, *Eastern Workingmen*, 154; *Johnson Papers*, II, 56, 57n.

2. On April 2, 1860, the Republicans scored a tremendous victory in

Connecticut, electing the governor, 13 of 20 senators, and 142 of 231 representatives. New York *Tribune*, April 4, 1860.

3. Keyser's request fell on deaf ears; Greeley, because of his Republican partisanship, ignored the Tennessee senator's efforts on behalf of homestead legislation. When Johnson's bill was finally passed, the *Tribune* editor scorned it as a "half-loaf . . . with regard to Free Homesteads." *Ibid.*, June 21, 1860; Jeter A. Isely, *Horace Greeley and the Republican Party, 1853–1861* (Princeton, 1947), 291.

From Fredrica R. Lambert[1]

[Washington, D. C.]   April 14, 1860

Gov. Johnson,

Dr. Sir,

You will please permit me to remind you of your promise to call and see a suite of delightfully situated rooms I desired you to take—in the event of your making a change from your present location—

I pray Dr. Sir you will call, even should you not wish them yourself— you may know some one among your friends wanting a pleasant spring and summer residence to whom you would be so kind as to recommend them—

I beg that you will pardon this trespass upon your time, and attention[.] circumstances of an imperative nature impels me, Necessity compels me to rent my rooms—hence I deem further apology not requisite since I believe you to be the embodiment of all the higher elements which constitute a good and great man—ready to sympathise with women in trouble. By taking my rooms you would relieve me of great pecuniary embarrassment, and my troubled heart of many aching pangs of anxiety— I beg you will call at the earliest moment possible—and let me know by bearer of this when to expect you[.] my number is 578 H st between 4th and 5 sts[.] In haste I am yours with much respect—

April 14th 1860   Mrs F R Lambert

ALS, DLC-JP2.

1. Mrs. Fredrica Lambert was a thirty-seven-year-old Washington widow with a son of seventeen. She is not listed in *Boyd's Washington Directory*. 1860 Census, Washington, D. C., 263.

From William B. Franklin

Office U. S. Capitol Extension,
Washington, April 16, 1860

Dear Sir:

A man named James Smith,[1] employed upon the Senate heating and ventilating apparatus, has requested me to make known to you his desire for an increase of wages, and his reasons therefor, having stated to me that he had spoken to you on the subject.

I know that he is a good workman, and that he has the lowest rate of those employed on the apparatus[.] He gets $45 per month, while those on the next higher rate, who I think are not worth as much as he is, get $60 per month.

There is no necessity for the employment of any more men, and it would, I suspect, produce ill feeling among those now employed were Smith's wages increased, and those of one of them cut down on that account.

Smith's rate might be increased to $60 per month instead of $45, with the understanding that when a vacancy occurs among the $60 men, (of whom there would then be three.) the person who is appointed to fill it should get but $45 per month.

Or, the matter might remain as it is until a vacancy happens among the $60 men, when Smith might be promoted to that, thus having the rates just as they are now. This latter arrangement will cost less, but will not be so well for Smith, who I think ought to have his wages increased, if possible.

Very respectfully,   Your obdt. Servant
W. B. Franklin
Capt. of Topl. Engineers,
In charge of Capitol Extn.

Hon. Andrew Johnson,
Chairman of Committee to audit and
control contingent expenses of the Senate.

Copy, Architect's Office, U. S. Capitol, Let. Bk. 9, pp. 1869–70.

1. Although it is impossible to determine which of the thirteen James Smiths listed in the 1860 Washington directory was the subject of Franklin's concern, it is likely that he was the James Smith employed as a coal heaver at the Capitol in 1858 and that he was one of the laborers paid $1.50 per day who, in 1860, sought to become firemen at $2.00 a day. *Boyd's Washington and Georgetown Directory* (1860), 139; *Senate Ex. Doc.* No. 20, 36 Cong., 1 Sess., 109; U. S. Senate, Committee Reports, 36 Cong., RG46, National Archives.

From Edward D. Tippett[1]

Washington City April 16 1860

Honored Sir

Will you be so kind as to read the within enclosed *printed* petition,[2] to Congress; of 1860, written by me, at the time, Rushia commenced the war with Turky; and long before England and France concentrated their power, against Rushia in favour of Turkey;

2000 copies went out, as a *prediction*; *sir*; all has been fulfiled, *but one.* I am looking out for all. But sir; a word to you; please read the *prose*, and then the *poetry*; see, if I do not deserve my rights.

Senator; *this 'government'* promised me, the money; to make practical test, of the Balloon; as stated. They righteously owe me $2000; in one claim, I can prove it by John Tyler. They righteously owe me, another claim; by, *violation of contract.* It has been tried before the *Court of Claims,* see, *printed report,* by the *senate;* refered to Committee on Claims, by *senator Clay;*[3]

Now sir, I close;! this government will never prosper; until justice is Paid to the line, and judgment to the plainted. Give me my rights, and I will honor this nation. Please send me, my pamphlet, when you have perused it; *I have but 2 left.*

Your Friend

Edward D Tippett

Clay and *Fitspatrick*[4] are my *friends*;
I think! If they are not, I am greatly
decived; at least, I am not Crazy, as
Outsiders wish to make me.[5]

Please direct to Georgetown D C

ALS, DLC-JP2.

1. Edward D. Tippett (b. *c*1789), sometime schoolmaster, clerk, inventor, and crank, was a frequent petitioner for government favors. In June, 1833, he secured a temporary clerkship in the adjutant general's office, with the rank of sergeant, under an enlistment for three years unless sooner discharged. Tippett was assigned to copying letters, but while attentive and willing to attend to business, he proved incompetent and was discharged in August, 1834. For years thereafter he hounded the war department and Congress with a claim which sought compensation for the period from his discharge to the expiration of his enlistment—a claim the war department termed "preposterous." Congress agreed. On March 23, 1838, he memorialized Congress for financial aid to perfect and introduce a safety steam boiler, but although the request was considered at intervals for the next twenty years, it seems never to have been acted upon. In 1859 Tippett carried his case to the court of claims, where it was rejected. In February, 1860, he petitioned for a grant of bounty lands, on the ground of participation in the battle of Bladensburg in the War of 1812; the Senate committee on public lands found him ineligible. *House Ex. Doc.* No. 281, 25 Cong., 2 Sess.; *Senate Doc.* No. 106, 29 Cong., 1 Sess.; *House Report* No. 8, 35 Cong., 1 Sess.; *Court of Claims Report* No. 233, 36 Cong., 1 Sess.; *Senate Report* No. 64, 36 Cong., 1 Sess.

2. According to the petition, the Tyler administration had appropriated money for further research on a gigantic self-propelled machine which Tippett had visualized, but the coming of a new administration had deprived him of the funds. His next discovery, a "practical principle of Balloon Navigation," was also destined for obscurity, for while the Polk administration was temporarily interested, the fall of the castle of San Juan de Ulloa to Scott ended interest in the practical application of his researches, and again the granting of money had been deferred. Pamphlet, *Historical Review of Passing Events, Deeply Interesting. In Prose and Poetry. By Edward D. Tippett. Author of the Navigation Balloon.* 4 pp., n.p., n.d., Johnson Papers, LC.

3. Clement C. Clay, Jr., of Alabama.

4. Benjamin Fitzpatrick, the other Alabama senator.

5. In his endorsement Johnson agrees with the "Outsiders," observing: "From A, Crazey man By the name Tippet."

Remarks Introducing New Homestead Bill[1]

April 17, 1860

Mr. JOHNSON, of Tennessee. Mr. President, I do not rise for the purpose of making a speech or trespassing on the time of the Senate more than a few moments; but, in making the report which I made, the impression seemed to rest on the minds of some Senators that the House bill No. 280 and the Senate bill No. 1, with all the amendments, were in the committee. These propositions were all referred to the committee; and the committee, after careful and mature consideration of all the propositions, prepared the bill which they have now reported as an independent proposition, and the instruction to me was to report the independent proposition in lieu of all the measures that were referred to the committee, which was to take their place on the table and to accompany the report of the committee, and they are now upon the table.

Mr. President, there were many propositions brought forward. We had the House bill and the Senate bill before us. The Senate bill had been under consideration, and had been made the special order; it had been debated, and had gone over from day to day. The House bill was then taken up, and various propositions were offered by several Senators. They were all referred to the committee, on the motion of the chairman. I think I can speak with truth and sincerity when I say, that the committee took up all these propositions, and considered them with deliberation and care, and scrutiny. They have passed this bill through an ordeal to which, in all my experience of legislation, I have never seen a bill subjected. It is true my experience is not as much as that of some others; but I have witnessed a good deal of legislation, and I have been on committees. I know the spirit and feeling that were manifested when this subject was referred back to the Committee on Public Lands on the motion of its chairman. There has been but one single purpose, and that was to embrace the homestead idea proper, and embrace in the bill principles that are pertinent to the homestead measure, and bring it back to the Senate in such a shape as it was believed would meet the approbation of all the departments of the Government. The precise shape it has now assumed will be more fully explained by others, in a very short time, for I do not intend to occupy the attention of the Senate. It will accommodate both parties, on this and the other side of the Chamber. The object of it was to establish and carry out the homestead principle, irrespective of party influence, or the policy that might be proposed by the respective parties on this question; and I want to say, in this connection, that the bill now is in a shape in which the genuine friends of the homestead proposition have put it. It is true that, on some of the details, which will be more fully explained by others, there was a little difference of opinion; but there was no difference in the committee on the great principle running through the whole bill.

The intention was, I repeat, for I want it distinctly understood, not to take advantage of this or that party; but to place it on its true ground; to put it in such a shape that it would receive the sanction of the Senate, of the House of Representatives, and of the Executive of the United States. Those who are real friends to the homestead proposition do not desire to see the bill vetoed. Those who are friends to the homestead proposition do not desire to see it rejected in either House; they are anxious for it to take that shape and form which will make it acceptable to all departments of the Government, and that was the leading idea and consideration with the committee in the preparation of this proposition.

As to the difference between this bill and the original Senate bill and the House bill, which were both referred to the committee, I shall not speak. I shall leave that to the chairman[2] on whose motion the recommitment was made. In compliance with the order of the Senate, the report has been made here to-day. As to the differences between the proposition now under consideration, and the two bills and all the amendments that were referred, I shall leave to the chairman to explain, who will, I do not say it unmeaningly, explain it to the Senate more satisfactorily than I can; and there is another member of the committee, on the other side of the Chamber, who understands it,[3] and I take this occasion to say, not because the Senators are present, that those two Senators have worked in good faith, and in a spirit of compromise, with a fixed determination to put the proposition in a shape to be acceptable to the country, and to establish a great principle, and establish a system in connection with the public lands. Those two gentlemen are entitled to the credit and respect of the country. I bear this tribute to them, humble as I am, whether it be worth anything to them or not. Those gentlemen have engaged their hearts and their souls in this matter; and there has been a magnanimity on the part of the chairman and of the gentleman in the Opposition on the other side, to whom I have referred, that has commended them, and the country ought to know the part they have borne in the consummation of this great measure. I will not do it here. There are things that I can and will say, when the proper occasion arises, in reference to those gentlemen, who have made a sacrifice, notwithstanding they are antipodes in politics, to secure the consummation of a great idea, and the establishment of a great principle, which, I believe, will have a more beneficial influence on our present land system than everything that has been adopted anterior to it.

I hope that, when explanations are made by the chairman pointing out the leading differences between the various propositions, the Senate, after so much time has been consumed; after so much expectation has been created; after the excitement that has pervaded the whole country, will keep this proposition under consideration until it is disposed of. The public mind is entitled to it. It ought to have definite action; and I trust and hope that the Senate will keep the subject under consideration until it is disposed of in one way or the other. I do not wish to consume the time of the Senate; and I will give way for the chairman, who has taken the part he has, and who is entitled to the commendation of the whole country, irrespective of party, on this subject, to explain the differences in the bills.[4]

Cong. Globe, 36 Cong., 1 Sess., 1749–50.

1. Two bills, one from the Senate (S. 1) and the other from the House (H. R. 280), both pertaining to homestead legislation, had been referred to the Senate committee on public lands. After considering the merits of both proposals, the committee instructed Johnson to report a third (S. 416) in lieu of the others. After various objections over procedure and technicalities were withdrawn, the bill passed on second reading and was before the committee of the whole when he made these remarks.

2. Committee chairman Robert W. Johnson of Arkansas had moved to recommit to the committee on public lands both bills and all amendments with instructions to report to the Senate on Tuesday, April 17. Following Andrew Johnson's brief statement, the senator from Arkansas spoke at some length, explaining the rationale of the new bill. *Cong. Globe*, 36 Cong., 1 Sess., 1659, 1750–53.

3. James Harlan, Iowa Republican, was also a floor manager of S. 416.

4. After Robert Johnson's explanation of the committee's action, the bill was set aside, to be taken up the following day.

From Samuel Jenkins[1]

Philada April 18' 1860

Dear Sir

It has given me much pleasure to find that you as a Senator from So noble a State as Tennessee are in favour of the homestead law one of the most if not the most Important measures that has ever been brought before congress[.]

though a native of Wales I arrived in this City July 18 1801 being then 12 years old[.]   my brother Jonathan S Jenkins[2] later Judge in California and Recently U S-consul at Apia in the Island of Upolu was then 6 but we Still are well acquainted with our native language and he with Several others Especially the Spanish[.]

My present object in addressing you is to give Some facts not generally known in Connection with the history of Britain in the matter of
homestead, and homestead Exemption laws. how far these laws
prevailed in Britain Perhaps it is now past finding out.   but as the
anc[i]ent history of Wales and the fact that it was til 1283 an Independent or Rather 3 Independent States and the Judiciary Independent of that of England. and the control of the English Parliament
till. the Legislative union in 1544 we know Exactly what was the
nature of our ancient government[.] I published about 8 years ago a
book[3] of 326 pages 12 mo. in which I presented "the Triads of the
Social State" and Sent a copy to the Hon Lewis Cass, but as I have
only one copy left I cannot (much as it would gratify me to do so)
Send you a copy. Indeed the one I have is the property of one of my
sons who boards at home, as I gave away my own last copy.   there
are 248 Triads on the Social Condition of Wales.   this makes 744.
particulars[.]   from these and other Important documents. I have in
the Welsh language it is plain that the Rights of men in the Social
State were better defined and more Strictly guarded than they were
in any other Country at the Cotemporary Period. I have been among
the active men of this City but never joined in the Slavery discussion
as I have always considered that the matter was conceded to the
Several States in the Constitution of the United States. In fact it is
a grand Error in those Citizens of the Non Slaveholding States to
Suppose that they are Responsible for its Existence be it Right or
wrong—

The Welsh National Motto was—"The Truth against the World"
the land was all public domain. Every Citizen having a family was
Entitled in virtue of Natural Right to a free homestead of 5 acres of
land[.]   ministers of Religion both Druidical and Christian had 5
acres more as the Privilege of their Caling. the object being as Stated
in the Triads "to make Truth manifest and to Prevail with Peace
over disorder and violence[.]"   the Legislative power was in a National Constitutional assembly the members of which were Elected
by all the Citizens of the male gender as soon as they had a Beard
and all of the gentler Sex who were married[.]   a beardless Swain
or a maiden had no vote—

masons Smiths and Carpenters were also Entitled to 5 additional
acres in all—10. So also Bards & ovates,[4] teachers of youth &c but
Simple laborers had only 5 by Natural Right. Chiefs and Representatives had good Estates during office, Called their "Plowlands." it
was to get these as their own that Induced many of the Rascals to aid
Edward the first of England or Remain Neutral when that able
monarch made war upon the Brave Llywellen Prince of Gwyndd—

which was a part of North Wales. Contain[in]g about 2000 Square miles[.] he was also nominally Prince of Wales. As in case of war in which the Confederate States were Engaged he was Commander in Chief Called Pendragon or head Dragon of Wales— but after the death of that virtuous Prince all the Chiefs united in Rejecting the English laws and the power of Parliament hence not a cents of taxes was Paid till the act of union (with their own Consent) in 1544. See the Speech of Lord Chatham[5] a short time before his death in which he Justifies the Americans in Refusing to pay taxes on the authority of Parliament in which they had no Representatives from the Example of Wales which never paid any till they had Such, but after that Paid their taxes as freely as any.

It was at the time that the Principality became dependent on the Crown of England in 1283 that the Homestead Right was lost by the Welsh for the king as king of Wales as well as of England gave the public domain to the Chiefs who had aided or connived at his ambitious Project of Conquering Wales. though it never was in the strict sense Conquered— the Prince of Powys the middle Principality fought in the Ranks of the English and the Prince of South Wales was neutral— there were a number of Chieftens beside the 3 "golden Banded chiefs"— although there were 3 principal tribes one of these consisted of 15 sub tribes and in all probably not less than 40 in all Wales. Each of these tribes had its territory. The difference between the welsh tribes and the Scottish Clans, was that the Scotch Lairds were absolute, having the Power of life and death over the members of their Clans. The Welsh Chiefs were Elected by all the Bearded men and married Women—and their Power was very limitted and as they were Elected from certain family connections and might abuse their authority—a family Representative was Elected from Each Subtribe who had an Equal Plowland with the Chief and he was also Commander of the military Except when in camp or in Actual Service in which case they were subject to the Pendragon[.] these family Representatives were Elected from the whole body of Citizens[.] there were laws to Exempt from levy or Sale on any Claim of debt or fine all wearing apparel house furniture —the harp, books, tools of trade, Cattle and grain because "it was unjust in the law to unman the man or to uncall the Calling"— an armed man, dared not Enter a dwelling house where there was a woman till he had put off his armour outside of the door and given them into the custody of the man of the house[.] the lady was queen of her dwelling and to this day the Gray mare is about as good a horse[6] as any in Welsh houses. and their churches are mostly on the congregation order where the ladies as well as the bipeds who claim to be lords of this planet, have the Right to vote on all matters—for not over one in 13 of the population pretend to be attached to the Established church.

No law was Ever Enacted in Wales on matters of opinion hence there never was a drop of blood Shed there while the ancient laws Remained on account of Religious belief and not a word in the laws or history about Witchcraft[.] nothing was punished but overt acts. they had nine forms of oaths in giving Evidence and if a man believed that his grand mothers night cap or the beard of Mahomet was the most Sacred of all things they would have made him Swear by it as Taffy[7] did not care how they Swore So that he got at the truth. the Jurisprudence of Wales was perfect So Say "Philadelphia Lawyers"[8] who Read the Triads in my book— they add that the Rules of their courts were more correct than those of ours now in this State as Injustice is often done here by Ruling out Evidence that would have been Received in the welsh courts[.] this accounts for the advance of Britain and her colonies in the knowledge of human Rights &c those free mountaineers were never brought into any Species of deep oppression for the Supremacy of the pope was never admitted in the Civil State: the papists stood legally Just as they do now in this country, Except in Marys Reign of 5 years, in which 3 men were burnt in Wales the native laws having been Superceded by the Semi-barbarous laws of England by the act of union in 1544. the people of the U States have made a most Important advance in Political Science but leaving Slavery out of the question there is much yet to do. in fact the Slave has a Right to live and a place to live in, and that in the Right of his Master but the free man who has no homestead does not live on this planet by any Right[.] he only lives on Suffrance by paying dues for it and failing to pay may be turned into the Road with his helpless offspring and taken up there as a vagrant. I wish that the people of the North would turn their attention to the multitudes of poor families in our large cities who live huddled up in Confined Courts and alleys—and cease to make Jacks of themselves about the negroes in the South. I have been for many years trying to Enlighten the public mind on the Subject of Social order. and if Congress pass the homestead law I hope that in less than ten years Some plan of association will be devised Superior in many Respects to the present State of Society viz the land to be held by the association and Each member having his quota during life and all children wither there be one or a dozen in a family to have Equal claims on the body for a Share of the domain[.]

Yours with Much Respect   Samuel Jenkins
112 North 6th Street

Hon. Senator Johnson of Tennessee

[Marginal notation]

I am happy to learn that Revd Mr Roberts[9] a distinguished Independent minister is attracting the welsh to the hilly parts of Tennessee[.] it is the Right place and they the Right people for a Countrey of hills and vallies and abounding in minerals[.] A Rich level country would be only a grave yard for them[.]

ALS, DLC-JP2.

1. Samuel Jenkins (b. 1789) was one of eleven children of the Reverend J. S. Jenkins, who came to Philadelphia from Wales in 1801. At this time a fire and garden hose dealer, Samuel Jenkins had long been an exponent of Welsh nationalism; in 1832 he attempted to found a Welsh colony in Tioga County, north-central Pennsylvania, offering land to immigrants at three dollars an acre. *McElroy's Philadelphia City Directory* (1860), 483; Alan Conway, ed., *The Welsh in America* (Minneapolis, 1961), 72–73.

2. Jonathan Jenkins (b. 1795) was, like his brother, a resident of Philadelphia except for sojourns in Mexico and Cuba and a brief consulship at Apia (1856–57). Jonathan Jenkins to W. L. Marcy, February 11, 1856, in Correspondence Record Book, U. S. Consulate Apia, Consular Post Records, RG84, National Archives.

3. Samuel Jenkins, *Letters on Welsh History: To Which is Added Many of the Triads* (Philadelphia, 1852.)

4. A special class of Welsh poets schooled in bardic lore. *Webster's Third International.*

5. In his speech in defense of the colonies, delivered on January 14, 1766, William Pitt (Lord Chatham) saw Parliament as supreme over America in every respect "except that of taking their money out of their pockets without their consent," and compared the situation with that of Wales, "that never was taxed by parliament, till it was incorporated." *The Parliamentary History of England, from the Earliest Period to the Year 1803* (36 vols., London, 1806–1820), XVI, 104, 108.

6. The "grey mare is the better horse" is an old English proverb conveying the idea that the wife rules the husband; it perhaps originated, according to Macaulay, "in the preference generally given to the grey mares of Flanders over the finest coach horses of England." William Smith, *The Oxford Dictionary of English Proverbs* (Oxford, 1948), 267; Stevenson, *Quotations*, 929.

7. Slang for Welshman. *Webster's Third International.*

8. A term originating in late eighteenth-century Great Britain, meaning a shrewd attorney—one well versed in the fine points of the law. Mathews, *Americanisms*, II, 1230.

9. Samuel Roberts (1800–1885), Welsh-born reformer and Congregational minister, came to Tennessee in 1857 to establish a colony for those of his countrymen who wished to escape English landlords and Anglican clergy and at the same time gain a freehold. The tract purchased for the colonists on the Cumberland Plateau lay mostly in Scott and Morgan counties. Plagued both by lawsuits over land titles and by the Civil War, the settlement never really flourished, although Roberts remained until 1867, returning to Wales only after his efforts to obtain a railroad into the area failed. Conway, *Welsh in America*, 112–17; see also Wilbur S. Shepperson, *Samuel Roberts: A Welsh Colonizer in Civil War Tennessee* (Knoxville, 1961).

From Samuel J. Pooley[1]

Liberty Corner[2] Somerset County,
New Jersey, April 18th 1860.

to Hon. Andrew Johnson
Washington,
My dear sir,

I have just arisen, from a perusal, of an abstract of [a] speech, delivered by you, in United States Senate, upon 11th Inst, on the 'Homestead bill[.]' If said speech passes into pamphlet form, will you be so kind as to send a copy to my address, by so doing, you will confer, quite a favor on me— Senators, Mason & Wigfall's, objections to said measure, cannot nor will not, be well received, by the great mass of the people.

There is an evident tendency, by certain Senators, to follow up the policy, as set by President Pierce, to contribute the public lands in the main, to Railway Contractors, or Corporators of Railroads. deeply deeply did I regret on noticeing President Pierce's policy on this subject, and his miserable apology,[3] for the same—That I ever uttered a word, in advocacy of his Election, or gave my vote for him, at the polls. many, & many a hardworking Farmer and Mechanic, purchaseing lands, under this policy from 'Railway Corporators,' will have exhausted their energies, before such lands, become ultimately free, from mortgages, interest &c,

President Pierce was very anxious, to leave a clean record behind him, on his retirement from the Presidential chair, but I have no doubt whatever, that the genius of history, at least in the particular, indicated, will deign to gratify his desire,

I have always held the executive (Buchanan) to be favorable to the 'Homestead principle', Indeed he could not have arisen, to the honorable position, which he now holds, nor have won the confidence & esteem of the Democracy of Pennsylvania, had he held, counter principles on the subject,

The principle, as promulged by you, in the debate, 'That Tennessee, will never fail in her fidelity to the American Union' (I quote from memory), doing both you & your noble state a great honor indeed, the ashes, of Gen. Jackson, would assume, their mortall[?] character, and rising from the Tomb, & with a voice of thunder, vow it not so, "That the Union must, & shall be preserved,"

Yours very Respectfully   Samuel James Pooley

ALS, DLC-JP2.

1. Samuel J. Pooley (c1805–c1883), New York-born New Jersey farmer, with his brother Joseph (b. c1803) and a nine-year-old mulatto boy, Thomas

J. Jackson, constituted a household in the 1860 census. Each of the Pooleys had real property valued at $1,500 and personal, $200. 1860 Census, N. J., Somerset, Warren Township, 697.

2. Liberty Corner was a small Somerset County village, consisting of "1 temperance tavern, 2 stores, a grist and saw mill, about 20 dwellings, and a Presbyterian church. . . ." John N. Barber, *Historical Collections of New Jersey* . . . (New Haven, 1868), 443.

3. In reality, Pierce displayed little enthusiasm for providing public lands to assist railroad building. That portion of his second annual message which Pooley calls a "miserable apology" is remarkable for its equivocation, containing, among other observations, the statement that "If . . . it is necessary that the aid of the General Government be primarily given, the policy will present a problem so comprehensive in its bearings and so important to our political and social well-being as to claim in anticipation the severest analysis." Roy F. Nichols, *Franklin Pierce: Young Hickory of the Granite Hills* (Philadelphia, 1931), 372–73, 403; Haney, *Congressional History of Railways*, II, 17; Richardson, *Messages*, V, 290–91.

From Joseph L. Williams[1]

Washington City 18th April [1860]

Dear Sir,

This will be handed to you by my friend Wilmer Marsh;[2] a young man possessing the highest qualifications for any subordinate position in the public offices & who, by reason of that very fact, is, as you may well suppose, very sure of being overlooked. His very superior qualifications as an Accountant and, as a business man, will not render him the less qualified to fill a *Sinecure* about the Senate; one of which, I am advised, is now vacant, by reason of a death some weeks since.

He would make a first rate fellow to colonize on the public lands under your Homestead Bill; but, inasmuch as the Virginia 'chivalry',[3] may postpone you too long, in the enactment of that measure, Mr. Marsh would be willing to have the pay of the Sinencure referred to, provided he can have the countenance & aid of some of the Senators.

It has occurred to me, that you might be willing to afford some aid in the premises to an energetic & industrious young man, who deserves, tho' such an one is not apt generally to receive here so much consideration as the Lazy Drones who usually frequent & smell around the public places of this City.

Respectfully & truly yrs

Hon Mr Johnson—   Joseph L. Williams
U. S. Senate.

ALS, DLC-JP2.

1. Joseph L. Williams (1810–1865), former Whig congressman (1837–43) from Knoxville, son of John Williams, senator (1814–23), and member of a prominent North Carolina and East Tennessee family, was a Washington,

D. C., lawyer whom Lincoln later appointed a U. S. district court judge in Dakota Territory. *BDAC*, 1823.

2. Perhaps S. W. Marsh, of Pennsylvania, subsequently a clerk in the treasury department. *U. S. Official Register* (1863), 19.

3. Mason of Virginia had recently been in the forefront of opposition to the homestead bill.

Remarks on Immigrants and Homestead Bill[1]

April 19, 1860

Mr. JOHNSON, of Tennessee. I do not intend to consume the time of the Senate. When we come to examine this bill in this respect, I think it will be conceded by all that it is an improvement on the existing laws. By our preëmption laws any foreigner, who has made a declaration of intention to become a citizen, can go and locate on the public lands. There is no restraint whatever. And, in addition to this, by filing his declaratory certificate, he can enter it at the Government price, without ever becoming a citizen of the United States. If there is anything in the argument made by those who are opposed to the fifth section, the system as it stands—the law as it now is—is much worse than the provision here proposed. The fifth section of the bill proposes—what? If you are now a resident of any State or Territory, or shall hereafter become a resident of any State or Territory, having filed your declaration of intention to become a citizen, you make an entry of land; and if, before the expiration of the five years, you shall become a citizen, then the Government passes its title to you.[2]

It is very easy to talk about jail-birds, and foreigners, and paupers, and all that description of thing; but when we come to examine our naturalization law, it must be clear to all who understand anything about it that that description of persons cannot become citizens of the United States. What does your naturalization law require? Does it not require the man to take an oath renouncing all allegiance to any foreign prince or potentate; and that he believes, in effect, in our form of government; that he adheres to the Constitution; and, in addition to that, must he not go before a court, and show, by proof satisfactory to the court, that he is a man of good moral character, and attached to your institutions? Then, this bill first requires— what? He shall declare an intention to become a citizen, and he shall actually become a citizen of the United States, before the patent can pass; and before he can become a citizen, he must prove to the courts that he is a man of good moral character. What becomes of all that idea about paupers and loafers and jailbirds?

But I do not know, Mr. President, that a man gains anything by his particular place of birth. It is true that we, by our education, and perhaps from some instinct, have attachments for our place of birth.

This is all well enough. I like to see it; but what is the objection to allowing England and Ireland and Scotland and Russia and Prussia and Austria and France and all the Powers of the earth, if they think proper, to grow men, and lose the time, and incur the expense of raising them, and send able-bodied men here, men that are grown with muscles and sinews, ready to be brought in contact with the soil, which is to result in production and adding to the national wealth? These men come of their own free will, after having compared the character of our institutions with their own. If they, of their own good will, voluntarily come to the United States, preferring our form of government, and complying with all its conditions, I do not think there is any very great objection to it.

When we come to examine this feature, there, we find, is one of the great secrets of the vast and rapid and vigorous progress of the country. It is, that other countries have produced labor; that other countries have consumed the time in which the labor was to be grown; that other countries have incurred the expense of raising it; and after this was done, it was transferred to us ready to commence the work of production. That is one of the great secrets of the rapid advancement of this country. I do not know that a man is entitled to claim any very great credit because he was simply born in the United States. Many of us are here because we cannot help ourselves. It is not a matter of choice, but a matter of necessity. Then I do not see why a man should be discriminated against who is a man of good moral character, who has bones and sinews and the will to produce and to work, merely because he was born in another land. I do not know that the objection is valid against him when he comes here and proposes to comply with all our laws. When we compare this provision of the bill with former laws, as I before remarked, we find that it is a safer and better provision, admitting the validity of the arguments offered by those who are against it, than the present system; for it says that the title shall be passed to no one until he becomes a citizen of the United States; and no man can be a citizen of the United States until he has proved that he is a person of good moral character.

We talk about the legislation of our fathers on this subject. They have legislated wisely, and we have profited by it. This is carrying out precisely the same idea on which they commenced, and on which the Government has progressed. It used to be the good old doctrine of this Republic or the democracy, or by whatever name you think proper to call it, to say to all those men who make good citizens, "Come—yes, come, and take protection beneath our stripes and our stars; come, and participate with us in this feast of liberty and of freedom that we enjoy." These used to be the doctrines of Jefferson, and of Madison, and of Washington, and the fathers who have been before us. I say, if you love the nature and character of our free institutions better than you do your own, where you are downtrodden and oppressed, and where the heel of the tyrant stands on the neck of the oppressed, come and comply with our laws. I would even go further, and in the language of the philanthropist, I would say, that the world is my home, and every honest man is my brother.

This is a better law than the one we now have. It restricts, and restrains, and confines it to those who must be good citizens, who must be men of good moral character, before they can enjoy the benefit of the provisions of this bill. I do not see why we should discriminate between the man who is now a resident and one who may come in to-morrow, and fix his residence, and in five years become a citizen. There can be no difference. If this policy is wrong, when you are holding out an invitation to foreigners to come, then I say your whole land system is based on an invitation to foreigners to come. You offer them cheap land for an inducement; you offer them the elective franchise; you offer them freedom; you extend to them equality and justice, which they do not get in their own lands. If the doctrine now advanced is to be carried out, you must abolish your land system, or run your land up to such exorbitant prices that these men coming into the country cannot acquire it. If we carry on our system and foreigners do come, had they not better be passed into those pursuits that are industrial; which will result in adding to the capacity, the power, and greatness of the country? It seems to me that we should do so. But I do not intend to consume the time of the Senate in the discussion of this proposition. I do hope we shall get a vote on the various amendments and end the subject.

[Although he considers it better than the existing law, Davis argues that the bill without the Crittenden amendment would be "a land bribe" to foreigners, since it makes no distinction between those already in the United States and those who may enter in the future. Fitzpatrick of Alabama first requests an adjournment to allow more time to study the bill and then moves to proceed to the consideration of executive business.]

Mr. Johnson, of Tennessee. I hope the Senate will not proceed to the consideration of executive business. We are nearly through this bill, and the idea that there has not been time to consider the proposition is rather novel. This bill has been under consideration for about fourteen years. Now, after discussing it during nearly all this session, in both Houses of Congress, to get up and put in a plea that we must postpone it because we do not understand it, does not seem to me well founded; and I hope that the friends of the measure will press it to a point where we can have action on it. The Senate has provided that when it adjourns over to-day, it shall adjourn substantially for ten days, and then there will be another adjournment; and when, I ask, in the name of common sense and high Heaven, will there be time for this bill to be acted on? In the early part of the session we would not consider it; in the middle part of the session there was other business so pressing that we could not take it up, and then, on the heel of a temporary adjournment, we must go to other business, and let this bill be overslaughed. Can we never do any legislation for the country, for the people? It seems to me the time has arrived when we should quit sporting with this bill, and with the country; and if we are not prepared to act on it now, we never shall be. Every single proposition contained in this bill has been before the country, in one form or other; has been discussed, and is understood in the public mind; and it is now too late in the day, it seems to me, to plead that we are not prepared to act on this measure.[3]

Cong. Globe, 36 Cong., 1 Sess., 1800–1801.

1. In response to efforts by Graham Fitch of Indiana and others to amend the homestead bill, Johnson asked that it be approved without amendment, declaring that changes could be made after it became law. When questioned by James W. Grimes of Iowa, he explained that the bill empowered the secretary of the interior to establish guidelines ensuring that those settlers who were not heads of households would not be subject to discrimination, as Grimes had feared. The ensuing discussion among Crittenden, Johnson of Arkansas, and Jefferson Davis revolved around the question of extending the homestead privilege to aliens.

2. Crittenden's amendment would have denied land to future immigrants by limiting the benefits of the homestead to those who were already residents and had made application for citizenship at the passage of the act. *Cong. Globe*, 36 Cong., 1 Sess., 1797.

3. After some deliberation the Senate agreed to consider the bill on Wednesday, May 2.

From Rae Burr Batten

Philadph April 20th, 1860

Hon Andrew Johnson
    Dear Friend

Although it has been a long time, since we have received a letter from you, but recollecting, your aversion, to waiting for formal replies, I again, take the liberty, of trespassing upon your valuable time, as I flatter myself, that pressing business matters, has prevented, us from receiving the ever welcome letter, of so valued a friend.— and now Governor, I must be allowed, to cast my vote, and tender my most heartfelt congratulations, as your name, is so frequently spoken of here, in connexion with the Charleston Convention. Governor, if it be your wish to gain this honorable position and I pray it may, there Can be no sutch word as fail.

My husband has just brought me a paper[1] containing quite a correct likeness of you so much So, that all the family recognised it at once, and when showed to Cicile and Helen, they both exclaimed Oh! Aunty! it is a likeness of our dear friend Governor Johnson.—

And in the event do not think me (altho I cannot enter the field) too extravagant when I pledge you our keystone state, and without asking permission! allow, me, to Quote a sentance from my husband with a sound Consistent democrat as nominee, the democratic Party must be not only victorious, but cast sutch a withering gloom, over the so Called, republican party, that there will not be a spark of vitality left to reanimate them, and that man is Governor, Andrew Johnson. I find my letter is becoming somewhat lengthy and I fear tiresome, and having other anda's [sic] to add I will close by saying the family are all well, except myself, I have been seriously ill—but with sutch good nursing and kind attention hope soon to be myself again. today being my first to sit up, I concluded my first pleasure would be to write you—

Cicile and Helen are well and going to school[.] they are growing nicely and bid fair to make fine women[.] they both send much Love to you and would dearly love to see you— Cicile they say grows so like her Ma— she is almost as tall as her Ma[.] we all desire to be kindly remembered to all your family particularly Dr. Charles, & Robert,

and with many wishes for your health and happiness, and a hope that we may have the pleasure of seeing you Soon I bid you adieu.

Remaining Truly   Mrs. Rae Batten
811 Race St

Hon Andrew Johnson

ALS, DLC-JP2.

1. In *Frank Leslie's Illustrated Newspaper* of April 21, a sketch of Johnson appears, along with portraits of other southern hopefuls for the Democratic nomination; included are Howell Cobb, Jefferson Davis, James L. Orr, Sam Houston, Robert M. T. Hunter, James Hammond, and Robert Toombs. *Frank Leslie's Illustrated Newspaper*, April 21, 1860, p. 327. See illustration following page 342.

From Thomas Lane, Jr.[1]

April 20 1860
Greenville Tenn

Mr A Johnson

Dear Sir after my last respecks to you I would say that I sent 18 duplicats of the location of my land warents to Washing Citey a short time back and requested that the[y] would send me my Pattens her[e] to me at this place and the sent them back to me her and said that the had sent my Pattens to spring fiald Mo and I then sent the duplicats to spring fieald Mo and requested that the Regester of Land office to send me my Pattens her at this place and he returnd 17 Pattens and 1 duplicate and it noted on the bottom with red ink this pattent not receved at this office[.]   you will confer a faver on me by taken this duplicate to the offise and get the patten for it and Send it to me and you will oblige

Your frend   Thomas Lane Jr

ALS-JP2.

1. Probably Thomas Lane (b. c1818), a well-to-do Greeneville tanner and merchant with $6,200 real and $18,800 personal property. 1850 Census, Tenn., Greene, 276; *ibid.*, 1860, p. 87.

From Gilbert B. Towles[1]

Washington April 20th/60

Hon Andrew Johnson
Sir;

You must excuse me for taking the liberty of addressing you this communication, but as it is in reference to legislative business having an important bearing upon the interests and rights of a large class of people called "inventors" and patentee's", I would respectfully call your attention and invoke your favorable consideration of the enclosed remonstrance protesting against the passage of a certain section in the Patent Bill[2] pending before the Senate, and as one of the "class of people," I have deemed it proper to say that the proposed section abolishing the right of an appeal from adverse decisions of the Commissioner of Patents to the Judges of the Circuit Court of the D. Columbia is a direct deprivation of the rights and privileges of inventors heretofore granted of long existence and from the very incipiency of the Patent Statute itself through a number of years found to have worked and administered satisfaction and Justice to all without any complaint, and if any, it should emanate from the *people*, to whom their sacred rights and interests should be consulted in measures of reform and proposed changes; now it is not to be supposed that an Officer of the Government exercising the functions of his Office can with that nicety and exactness discriminate and decide legally questions arising from Patent Cases, involving an expense labor an[d] ingenuity on the part of a large body of inventors, would nor could they be satisfied with such decisions until, decided by a Judicial body competent to render impartial Justice and to subserve their rights and privileges as to give the utmost and implicit

confidence in the integrity of their decisions to which an Officer of
the Government might otherwise be presumed to be liable to be
biased one way or the other.

Attached to this enclosed protest are the names of Inventors,
Patentee's and Agents representing a local sentiment, irrespective
also, of those representing the Sentiments of a large body of Inventors and others throughout the country[.]

I have the honor to be—

Very Respectfully   Your Obedient Servant
Gilbert B. Towles

P. S. A—copy of the inclosed will be presented to the Senate in due
time.

ALS, DLC-JP2.

1. Gilbert B. Towles, a draughtsman, boarded at 490 H Street. *Boyd's
Washington and Georgetown Directory* (1860), 148.

2. The enclosed printed protest with twenty-one signatories remonstrated
against Section 2 of a substitute patent bill, approved by the Senate on April
13, which provided for a board of three examiners-in-chief to handle appeals
involving adverse decisions of the examiners. Appeals from this board could
be taken to the commissioner of patents, whose decision was final. The House
deferred action until the next session, when the bill, without the "no appeal"
provision, finally became law March 2, 1861. *Cong. Globe*, 36 Cong., 1 Sess.,
1699, 2835; *ibid.*, 2 Sess., 1431; *U. S. Statutes*, XII, 246–47.

From Zadoc T. Willett[1]

U. S. Mil Academy
West Point N Y. April 20th '60

Hon Andrew Johnson.

My Dear Sir.

The news of the passage in the House, of an amendment fixing
the term of study at this Institution at four years have just reached
us—[2]

We are deeply grateful to you for your support of the amendment when it was offered in the Senate—[3] We are so fearful of its
fate in the Senate that I am constrained to again trouble you— We
hope that you will still assist us—

Mr Nicholson voted against the amendment before—Can you not influence him to vote for it this time?

The circumstances were not fairly stated when the matter was first
brought before the Senate— We attribute our defeat to Mr Davis—[4]
He stated that there never had been any changes in the term— its
Course was changed in 1854, 1856 and lastly April '59[.] He also
said that a Board composed of distinguished officers & civilians was
at that time in session to determine upon the relative merits of the

four & five year terms— That Board was sent here for a different purpose entirely— Every single one of that Board were strongly in favor of a four year course, but had not the liberty to recommend the change— Please help us and we will be everlastingly indebted to you—[5]

Very Respectfully   Yr obt Servant
Z. T. Willett

Hon A Johnson
U. S. S

ALS, DLC-JP2.

1. Admitted to West Point in 1857, Zadoc T. Willett (c1839–1862) of Washington County did not graduate with his class, probably because he left during the troubled months of early 1861; for he was in East Tennessee during May and June, when Company B of the 19th Tennessee infantry, of which he became captain, was being organized. Willett was killed at the battle of Shiloh. West Point Alumni Foundation, *Register of Graduates and Former Cadets* (New York, 1953), 190; John B. Lindsley, *The Military Annals of Tennessee: Confederate . . .* (Nashville, 1886), 380; *Tennesseans in the Civil War*, I, 214–15; 1850 Census, Tenn., Washington, 115.

2. Since 1854, with the exception of a six-month period in 1858–59, the academy had been experimenting with a five-year curriculum initiated by Superintendent Robert E. Lee. Both cadets and congressmen expressed dissatisfaction with this arrangement; on at least two occasions efforts were made to withhold appropriations in order to bring about a reinstatement of the four-year program. The day before this letter was written, the House, under the guise of increasing the army for Indian service on the frontier, had approved an appropriation bill amendment which returned the academy to the former curriculum. Stephen E. Ambrose, *Duty, Honor, Country: A History of West Point* (Baltimore, 1966), 141; *Cong. Globe*, 36 Cong., 1 Sess., 1809–10, 1813.

3. When the proposal to revert to the four-year curriculum was before the Senate on March 14, Johnson and Nicholson had taken opposing positions in a vote of 31–15 against the change. *Ibid.*, 1146.

4. Jefferson Davis' advocacy of the five-year program was long standing, since this innovation had been instituted while he was secretary of war; when the Senate debated the question in March, he had been among the most vigorous opponents of a return to the four-year system. *Ibid.*, 1142, 1145–46.

5. Willett and his fellow cadets were to be disappointed, for in June, 1860, Congress approved the recommendation of a committee headed by Davis that the additional year be retained. However, the coming of the war ended the experiment. Ambrose, *Duty and Honor*, 141; *U. S. Statutes*, XII, 23.

From Clement C. Clay, Jr.

April 22, 1860, Washington, D. C.; ALS, DLC-JP2.

Endorses efforts of Gilbert M. Wight, Washington furniture dealer, to get contract for furnishing new wing of Capitol.

To Robert Johnson, Charleston, S. C.

Washington City   April 22d 1860

Private

My dear Son,

Since my last letter to you[1] I have become Satisfied that Douglas must be nominated and Tennessee Should take that position which will Contribute most to her present and future Success— If she is defeated for the first, the query Comes up if it would not be better to take that positin which will give her the inside track four yers hence— There Could be so Safer positin to Secure the first place four years hence than Second place on the ticket now— It would infact Say to the Country that the Second man now must be the first four yers hence— This I Say to you and no one else you see the force of th[e] positio— If Tennessee Could Succeed now with the Second place, it would place her in the field four years hence with much assurance of Success and at the Same time be passing one of her Citizens through all the gradations of office from the lowest to highest which would be a very remarkable fact to record in history— As the matter is now before my mind I do not See how Douglas' nomination is to be Successfully resisted without great injury to the party and perhaps its overthrow— Hence the importance of Tennessee being on good terms with the north west— If She Can be first of Course She ought to Stand firme, if not take the next best Stand which will make her first four years hence— I have said enough on this point and will not Say more now— I hope you will be prudent and Say no foolish thigs which Can be used against you or me— There will be much importance attached to a[n]y thing you may Say from the relation the Son occupies to the father— If the whole affair is man[a]ged right if Tenn is not now first She can be Second and first next time without a doubt— You Should mix freely with the delegates from the north west and See how th[e]y feel in regard to Ten[.] I have evy assurance that it is of the most favorable character—

I saw on[e] of the delegates here the other d[a]y from Indiana and he told he was anxious to make your acquaintance— His name is Wilson[2] and is native of Grene Co and knew me before he went to Indiana. hunt him up and he will introdu[c]e you to the rest of the delegates from that State—

If a[n]y th[in]gs occurs I will write—

Your father   Andrew Johnson

ALS, CSmH–Misc. #8208.

1. We cannot be certain that the "last letter" is the one of April 8, printed above. Indeed it would be interesting to know whether Johnson, in

an intervening communication, had revealed some of the considerations which led him to reassess Douglas' strength, as well as his own prospects. In the earlier communication, he clearly contemplated a dark-horse candidacy; in this letter, his strategy looks toward cooperation with the Little Giant so as to win second place on the 1860 ticket, in anticipation of first place in 1864.

2. Henry K. Wilson was the county auditor for Sullivan County, Indiana. *Hawes' Indiana State Gazetteer and Business Directory* (1858–59), 357.

From Robert Johnson

Charleston Apl. 23 18[60]

To Hon Andrew Johnson

Howard[1] here Vice Quarles[.] delegation firm as a rock, all right[.]

Robt Johnson

Tel, DLC-JP2.

1. John K. Howard, an alternate delegate, attended in place of William A. Quarles.

From William M. Lowry

Greenv Ten Apl 23 1860

Gov Johnson

Dr Sir

this is the beginning of the big day and event at Charleston. I presume you have Your mind made up and your Course Chalked out; yet the advice of one no matter how humble, may be of Service Some times. in the event of your Nomination by the Convention, I do not think it in cumbent on you to resign your Seat as senator[.] in fact I do not think you aught by any means to resign, this is My advice. I told Genl Milligan when he left to pull every String he could for Johnson[.] if you could not be Nominated then for Breckenridge as the Next Choice of the Democracy of Tenn. I am surprised at the Course of the Memphis Avalanch.[1] it has done Much to give tone to things in Alabama Arkansas Missisipi & Texas: I think it has acted badly and aught to have stood up manfully for Tennessees Nomination. tell Breckenridge if you cannot come in then he has one friend in Tennessee in the person of your humble Servant[.] I have allways admired him. I suppose you have heard of the fight at Knoxville between Jim Newman & Ramsey. Newman went into Ramseys office with a big Stick to flog him alive[.] the first pass he made was to brake Ramseys left Arm and the next pass Ramsey shot him in his left Arm braking it and inflicting as I under stand a very dangerous wound[.][2]

in Haste   Yr friend   W M Lowry

ALS, DLC-JP2.

1. The Memphis *Avalanche*, founded in 1858 by M. C. Galloway, a southern extremist, had come out for the nomination of Joseph Lane of Oregon. Between 1862 and 1866, the *Avalanche* ceased publication; in 1870, it merged with the *Appeal*. Keating, *Memphis*, II, 218–19; III, 133–34.

2. Lowry's account coincides with the report in the contemporary press, which also noted a significant disparity in the size of the contestants, since Newman weighed 210 pounds to Ramsey's 125! Newman was to have been a delegate to the Charleston convention. Nashville *Gazette*, April 25, 26, 1860; see Letter from Robert Johnson, February 22, 1860.

From Robert Johnson

Charleston Apl 25 1860

To Hon Andrew Johnson

Indications very favorable resolutions will be reported in the morning[.] Wood delegates from New York rejected[.][1]

Robt Johnson

Tel, DLC-JP2.

1. Two New York delegations appeared at Charleston. The one headed by Mayor Fernando Wood of New York City curried favor with southern delegates; but it was the Douglas faction which gained the seats. Eyeing the presidential nomination, Wood hoped that in a deadlocked convention he might be considered a northerner acceptable to the South. Hesseltine, *Three against Lincoln*, 21, 31, 34; Nichols, *Disruption of Democracy*, 259.

From Hu Douglas

Charleston Apl. 26th 1860

My Dear Sir

I have been here since Monday Morn[in]g, and hav closely watched the movements as far as I could. It was my intention to have written you evey day, but really I am now and have been at a sea all the time and fear that I will not be able to get to land.

My fears in regard to my delegation as expressed in a former letter[1] hav thus far been realized to the fullest extent, and I have only to say that a more unfortunate selection both for the Demcratic [party] and yourself Could not have been made. It is needless for me to persenate [*sic*] them; this will doutless be done by more efficient hands, But really I am at a loss to know what they Came here for— surely not for the Cause [of] the party or the individual they were expected to represent—more again—

They have not yet been able to make a platform & I fear that they will not be able to make one that all Can Stand upon—

It Seems to me that some Southern Men will be satisfied with nothg, short of a desolution of the union, and act as though they feel that they are here for that purpose.

I have begged my folks to be prudnt & Conser[v]ative—but Some go as far as the farthest. We have Ultra men in ET in Middle & Wst Ten.[2]

A desolution of the Union &C is talked of as freely here by these people as [if] they were Conver[sing?] in regard to Cotton Tobacco or Trade,   all are down upon Douglas[.] I Cant believe that he Can get the Nomination if any is made—and I have much to hope from this quarter—but really there is so little policy, & prudence with our Delegation that I am alarmed—

I will probaly stay to see it out & will write you again—

Keep all to yrself that I write, no good Can be effected by a differt Course—

Yr friend Hu Douglas

Hon Andrew Johnson
Washington D. C.

ALS, DLC-JP2.

1. Writing in March, Douglas had referred to the "unfortunate Selection" of delegates. See Letter from Hu Douglas, March 11, 1860.

2. Douglas probably had in mind such men as John D. C. Atkins and William H. Wall, both of Paris, James Connor of Ripley, and John D. Riley of Rogersville—all regarded as extremists by another of Johnson's friends. See Letter from W. E. B. Jones, May 15, 1860.

From Mortimer F. Johnson

[April 26, 1860], Tellico Plains; ALS, DLC-JP2.

Postmaster requests copy of *Exploration of the Valley of the Amazon* by William L. Herndon and Lardner Gibbon [*Senate Ex. Doc. No. 36, 32 Cong., 2 Sess.*] and thanks the senator for forwarding a copy of Nicholson's speech on the homestead bill. If Johnson "should be selected as the *man*" at Charleston, "it would gratify the Heart of every true Democrat in Tennessee."

From Daniel W. McCauley[1]

April 27, 1860

Hon. Andrew Johnson   of Tenn.
Dear Sir.

I was in company with a party of gentlemen last evening & the conversation turned on the relative positions of the Democrats & Republicans[.] One of the number remarked that some years ago free Negroes voted in Tenn & North Carolina.[2] I told him he was mistaken, he was certain he was correct[.] I told him I would investigate the matter. I do not believe the assertion & will not until I have undoubted authority. There is no one better posted about Tenn. than yourself. & you will confer a favor on me by giving the information I desire.

Yours Very Respectfully

Danl. W. McCauley
23 Nth 4th St.   Philada.

Phila April 27/60.

ALS, DLC-JP.

1. McCauley was a Philadelphia liquor dealer. *Cohen's Philadelphia City Directory* (1860), 576.

2. Under the original state constitutions free Negroes had been allowed to vote in both Tennessee and North Carolina. However, opposition grew, and in 1834 the new Tennessee constitution deprived the free Negro of the vote; a year later North Carolina followed suit. William K. Boyd, *History of North Carolina* (New York, 1919), 220; Stanley J. Folmsbee, Robert E. Corlew, and Enoch L. Mitchell, *History of Tennessee* (4 vols., New York, 1960), I, 478.

From Charles W. Charlton

Knoxville Tenn   April 28, 1860.

Hon. A. Johnson
Washington D. C.
Dr Sir: —

I hope you will pardon me for calling your attention to our claim now before Congress.[1] If you can possibly do anything for us, it would be, at least, on my part, properly appreciated. I know that *one* of the parties, interested (Brownlow) is not friendly disposed towards you, yet I am Satisfyed that this would not prevent you from aiding the ballance in obtaining their just rights. Col. Luttrell, who, aside from Brownlow, is the only one opposed to you in politics, is, by no means, unfriendly Towards you. He speaks in high terms of you, both as a man, and as a Statesman.

We have nothing yet from Charleston. Of course you are posted at Washington. You have, doubtless, heard of Ramsey's & Newman's affray. Since this, Newman has appeared in a long card,[2] in which, I think, he has clearly vindicated himself. And this is the impression of the Community.

Respectfully &C   C. W. Charlton

ALS, DLC-JP2.

1. See Letter from James C. Luttrell, April 5, 1860.

2. James W. Newman's April 14 card, nearly two columns long, includes letters from George C. Whiting, March 28, 1860; John Crozier Ramsey to

Commissioner of Pensions, December 2, 1853; James W. Newman to Commissioner of Pensions, April 27, 1854; and Newman to Sam Morrow, April 12, 1858, concerning money used for "Crow" Ramsey's campaign and the charges against the Newmans. Nashville *Union and American*, April 20, 1860. See also Letter from James W. Newman, March 9, 1860, note 1.

From Samuel J. Pooley

Liberty Corner Somerset County, New Jersey,
April the 28, 1860—

to   Hon. Andrew Johnson
Washington
My good sir,

Your kind favor, (as per request) of copy of speech, delivered by you in the Senate of the United States, on the 12th Inst.,[1] on the subject of the "Homestead bill," came safely & duly to hand. Be pleased to accept my best acknowledgments for the same—

I shall avail myself in an early moment, by reading it, & I confidently promise myself that in its perusal, I shall be both gratified & instructed.

I perceive that Senators Mason & Wigfall take exception, to the principles of your bill, Thus indirectly repudiating a Cardinal & long cherished principle of the democracy. I must say, but it is with perfect respect to these Senators, that because the Republicans may adopt a measure of democratic policy, first mooted & upheld by the democracy, That it will never be considered by the Democrats, that the principle is wrong or unsound, because taken up by them, and made a part of their platform of principles, even if a Mason, or a Wigfall, may hold a contrary view in the premises.
Indeed it is not difficult to perceive the germ of a sectional cast, or bearing of these gentlemen in the matter at issue. These gentlemen, should first trim their own Lamps, before complaining of the lights, of others[.] Again in plain language, I am not prepared to take the political orthodoxy in the matter refered to above, from Either of these gentlemen, for my rule & government of Action, whatever is clearly Constitutional, whatever measures are in perfect accord, with our governmental system, of states & of United States, That enlarges the blessings of liberty, among the people, without infringing upon the fundamental or organic laws of the Country, above all, tending to their perpetuation & lasting benefit to our posterity, shall have my countenance & support let it come from what quarter it may, our Country first & always, is my motto. I am a democratic republican in principle, & not a partisan, have for the last fourty years, held to

the principles of government, as defined & set forth in "Jefferson's Inaugurel Address of 1801," & never will I countenance any interpolation, in Opposition to those principles set up in our Platform let it be done, or come from what quarter it may, my principles are settled & fixed proud to acknowledge that they have Washington Jefferson Madison, & Jackson, for their authors & advocates; our Country has prospered under them, in peace & in war. if we are true to ourselves, our country, liberty & our posterity, we will stand by them, as against all opposition—

Yours Very Respectfully,
Samuel James Pooley

ALS, DLC-JP2.
    1. The speech was actually delivered on April 11.

From Washington C. Whitthorne

Charleston Apl 29 1860

To Hon Andrew Johnson
Have you declared for Douglas in the event of the adoption of the minority report?[1] Six or more states will withdraw[.] what ought Tennessee to do.

W. C. Whittehorne

Tel, DLC-JP2.
    1. The minority report, the product of northern and western Democrats, reaffirmed the Cincinnati Platform of 1856, recognized the Supreme Court as final authority on slavery, and in all else agreed with the majority report. Tennesseans favored the latter, which specified that neither Congress nor the territorial legislatures had the power to abolish or prohibit slavery in the territories. Hesseltine, *Three against Lincoln*, 45–47.

To Washington C. Whitthorne,[1] Charleston, S. C.

[Apr. 29?, 1860]

Hon W. C. Whitthorne
I would [hold] on, and acquiesce in the nomination—   Nicholson, Wright and Avery concurring—

Andrew Johnson

Tel, draft, DLC-JP2.
    1. The original draft of this telegram began with the following clause: "If five or six southern states seceed. . . ." On second thought, or perhaps in consultation with those fellow-Tennesseans in Washington whom Johnson mentioned as concurring with him, he decided that this proviso was not necessary—that under any circumstance party loyalty was to prevail.

From Rae Burr Batten

[Philadelphia, Pa.]
Monday April 30th./60—

Hon Andrew Johnson
    Dear Friend

Your most welcome letter, was received, and perused, with much pleasure, and we have been looking the past week, for a visit from you— indeed, we were quite disappointed when Sabbath evening arrived, and no Governor here.— however, I hope we shall be allowed the pleasure, of seeing you ere long,— be assured, one, and all, would be most happy, to see our dear friend, the Governor!—
You write of sending some Books, Documents,—&c to Doctor![1] to which You received no acknowledgments, I assure You Governor! — we have never received a book, or paper, but the once, and that was directly after—your return from Philada. the documents, you then send to my husband he, as well [as] myself!—acknowledged— altho' the book you spoke of sending to me, was not among the number— however we were both grateful, to You; for Your kind remembrance. Brother Benjamin,[2] received many from You, both documents, and other interesting, books. which he informed me he had made known to You, in fact— We are all Quite well, except myself, I am improving as fast, as could be expected, my dear husband, proposes to take me out riding tomorrow, it being my first leave of my room, I trust ere long, to be enjoying, my usual good health. the *children* each, send much love to you, feel Quite disappointed, with *the rest!* at Your not coming last week. they are both well, and going to School, You will scarcely know Cicile!— we think her so changed—
Mother send the best wishes of her heart, Father,[3] has entirely recovered, and looks well, he too, is anxious to see the Govenor!— Mrs. Fidler's health has not been as good as usual, she sends Love, also each, and every member of the family, join me in love, not forgetting Dr. Charles, and Robert, with whom "we were much pleased. with a hope of hearing from You soon, and that we may soon have the pleasure of seeing, you. and that You may be enjoying health, I Remain Yours

                                With Respect   Mrs. Rae Batten

ALS, Johnson-Bartlett Col.

    1. Her husband, "Doctor" A. Nelson Batten.
    2. Benjamin J. Burr (b. *c*1830), native of New York, was a merchant tailor at 33 S. 8th with a residence at 811 Race Street. *McElroy's Philadel-*

phia City Directory (1860), 121; 1860 Census, Pa., Philadelphia, 10th Ward, 74.
3. Benjamin Burr, born in New Jersey about 1793, was listed as a "Gentleman" in the 1860 census. *Ibid.*

From Charles W. Charlton

Post Office   Knoxville Tenn
April 30, 1860.

Hon Andrew Johnson
Washington City   D. C.
Dr Sir:

I am more & more convinced of the pressing necessity of having an organ at this point wholly devoted to your desires. It is a question, tobesure, I have not stired, nor do I think it, altogether, prudent to do so at the present time. Of its importance, however, I have not a single doubt. This must be either done, or the present Editor of the Register[1] must be *killed off*, or else, his *constant harping* upon the villainous character of the Homestead, must, sooner or later, poison, to some extent, the public mind against you. You must, yourself, see the tendency of this thing, and to throttle the matter, *at once*, without any Ceremony, or Circumlocution, I would respectfully insist upon the adoption of some measures, whereby the matter can be reached. Of course the whole thing must be submitted to your own sagacity and judgement, and for you to inaugurate such a policy as will, effectually, Consumate this desirable end. *At least*, it is worthy of your Considerate attention. The *man* is *against you*. His opposition to you is *severe* and *determined*. And, to day, if you were the nominee of the Charleston Convention, he would *vote* against you. This is my deliberate opinion, based upon frequent conversations I have had with him, and the undisguised Conduct of his paper.

Excuse me for the liberty I have thus taken with you in making these suggestions[.] I have done so in good faith with the hope that something might be done to *gag* this Slanderous impughner of your motives, and to get him out of the way. When he bought the Register he was regarded as unwavering in his attachment & devotion to his party, and every one thought he was the Man for the place.

Very Respectfully   C. W. Charlton

ALS, DLC-JP2.
1. George Bradfield.

From Irving College Logician Society

April 30, 1860, Irving College [Warren County]; ALS, DLC-JP2.

Corresponding Secretary Jno. A. Campbell informs Johnson of his election to the society, "the Members believing you to be a Man, that will Stand by and defend the rights of the South, and as a conservative man, who will give to every portion of this glorious Union, its Constitutional rights." [Johnson's endorsement requests Joseph Headrick, superintendent of Senate folding room, to send the secretary "any documents I have to Spare— Send the[m] one copy of the Congressional Globe—"]

From William H. Carroll

Charleston May 2 1860

To Hon A. Johnson
We have withdrawn you.[1] Douglas has majority ought we support him.

W. H. Carroll

Tel, DLC-JP2.
1. Johnson's name was withdrawn after the thirty-sixth ballot. Nineteen of Tennessee's twenty-four delegates, each of whom cast a half-vote, then shifted to Guthrie; three continued to back Johnson; two, Carroll and Mc-Clanahan, turned to Douglas. Nashville *Union and American.* May 6, 1860.

From William M. Lowry

May 2, 1860, Greeneville; ALS, DLC-JP2.

Endorses James M. Rankin's efforts to get a post office appointment for C. J. Kountz and observes, "up to this writing We have nothing tangable from the Charleston Convention[.] I fear it is to end in a general muss[.]"

From James M. Rankin[1]

Russellville May 2th [*sic*], 1860

Hon A. Johnson
    Dear Sir
        I learn that the opposition folks at Mooresburg have secretly managed through a *Milk* & *Cider* Democrat[2] to have Col Robt Simpson[3] of that place appointed Post Master at Red Bridge Hawkins Co[.] I am requested by some of the citizens of that place to call your

attention to this appointnt an[d] ask you to give your influence for Mr C. J. Kountz[4] who is responsible and well qualified to make a good PM[.] A pet[i]tion will be sent you perhaps this mail, as it is important that our Lette[r] Offices should all be filed with good and reliable working Democrats[.] I hope that you will give your influence for the appointment of our friend C J Kountz. Col Robt Simpson is its true a clever good fellow but a violent Know Nothing or opposition man and one that wo[r]ks for his party[.]

Your attention to this at once will greatly oblige your friends[5] in this section[.]

Your friend   J. M. Rankin

ALS, DLC-JP2.

1. James M. Rankin (b. c1825), a Russellville merchant, was a Jefferson County delegate to the state convention in Nashville in January, 1860. 1860 Census, Tenn., Jefferson, 110; Nashville *Union and American*, January 7, 1860.
2. Possibly an updating of "milk-and-water," an expression used several decades earlier to mean weak and devoid of energy: "Change the milk-and-water style of your last memorial; assume a bolder tone." *Journal of Congress* (1823), IV, 209, quoted in Richard H. Thornton, *An American Glossary* (2 vols., Philadelphia, 1912), II, 580.
3. Simpson, held the post only a month, from April 10 to May 8, 1860. See Letter from William N. Clarkson, March 24, 1860.
4. Campbell J. Kountz was immediately appointed postmaster of Red Bridge (now Mooresburg), serving from May 8, 1860, to November, 1865. *Ibid.*
5. Lowry was among those endorsing Kountz.

To William H. Carroll, Charleston, S. C.

W. H. Carroll Esqr   May 3, 1860

The delegation present, with all the facts before them are better prepared to determine what Course to pursue than I am.

Andrew Johnson

Washington City   May 3d 1860

Tel, draft, DLC-JP2.

From Elizabeth A. R. Linn[1]

Washington City, May-4- 1860
National Hotel

Much honored, & Dear Sir

I cannot take, my departure for Missouri, without again expressing, my *deep felt* gratitude, for your kindly interest, for an unfortunate Widow. I will take delight in stating to the Noble hearted Missourians, that you are not only, the greatly gifted Statesman, of whom they have heard so much, but that you possess, such a Noble, kind heart, that you must secure, the confidence and warmest regard, of all that become acquainted with you—

May I not indulge, the hope, that you will give me, your powerful influence, in obtaining my Money,[2] from the *contingent* expenses, of the Senate, when the Money is there, to be paid. if I do not get it I will be compeled to sell my dear little home, in Missouri, it is passing strange, how bitter & malignant, Mr. Secretary Dickens, is against me[.] My Husbands[3] influence many Years since with his half Brother, Gov- Dodge,[4] & his Nephew Genl A C Dodg,[5] with *Their Votes alone*, saved Mr Dickens from being removed from the Office, that he still continues to hold, in the, U. S Senate, but Mr Dickens could not forgive Dr Linn, for opposing his three Daughters, getting a thousand Dollars each one, of them, annually for Coloring Maps, for the Senate, which both Dr Linn, & Col Benton,[6] with all the other Senators thought *intirely unnecessary*, & after the Ladies, had for some years, enjoyed the Revenue of three thousand Dollars a Year, for their Coloring Maps, for the Senate, by Dr Linns suggestion, their work, was dispensed with, & from that moment, Mr Dickens became the *secrete* Enemy of my dear Husband, & has tried to injure myself & Children, ever since the Dr. death, & certainly to some extent, did in a most *under handed manner*, injur my dear departed Son—Col. W A Linn, two years since in a matter of business before Congress—[7] Pardon me dear Sir for encroaching my affairs on your valuable time, but as a gallant Son, of the West, I am confident that the Chivalry of your Character, will prompt you to aid the Widow of *one*, that was ever the Widows, & the Orphan Friend— Mr Dickens tried, to deceive me Yesterday, by Signing the most *equivocal* Paper, that I ever read—

All, that ever loved, my dear departed Husband, in Missouri and that I believe is her entire Population—will feel grateful to you, for your friendly attention, to the Widow, of their *Model States Man*, Dr Lewis, F Linn—

With the highest esteem, & respect
Sincerely & most *gratefully* Yours
Elizabeth. A. R. Linn

Honl Senator Andrew Johnson
Washington City
Will you, please my noble Friend, to receive the information contained in this letter, coming in confidence *from me*[.] I do not wish to render the *Old Gentleman* more bitter against me, although he injured my dear departed Son— Mr Fitzpatrick[8] has Called, to see

me, & given me all that the necessary, power, to bind Mr D— to do my justice[.] in this Act, I see you[r] kindly influence—
Honl. Andrew Johnson
Member of The. U. S. Senate
Washington City   D C

ALS, DLC-JP2.

1. Elizabeth A. Relfe, widow of Lewis F. Linn whom she married in 1818. *DAB*, XI, 282.

2. On March 20, 1860, the Senate adopted a resolution to pay to Mrs. Linn the mileage due her late husband for his attendance at the special sessions in 1837 and 1841; the sum, which would be $2,672, was to come from the chamber's contingent fund. However, Asbury Dickens, secretary of the Senate, refused on the grounds that there was not enough money in the contingent fund to cover such a debt and that the Senate had no authority to use the fund for that purpose. Dickens was sustained by that body, which had learned to its embarrassment that no senator had received mileage for attending any special session between 1818 and 1845. Later, at Johnson's insistence, the Senate attempted to make amends to Mrs. Linn by attaching an amendment to the appropriations bill for sundry civil expenses of the government ending June 30, 1862. This rider was incorporated into the act and became law March 2, 1861. *Senate Journal*, 36 Cong., 1 Sess., 276; *Cong. Globe*, 36 Cong., 1 Sess., 1249, 2227–28; *Senate Journal*, 36 Cong., 2 Sess., 233, 294; *Cong. Globe*, 36 Cong., 2 Sess., 699–702, 918, 1138–40; *U. S. Statutes*, XII, 219.

3. Lewis F. Linn (1795–1843), Missouri Democratic senator (1833–43), studied medicine in Louisville, Kentucky, served as a surgeon in the War of 1812, completed his medical studies in Philadelphia, and established a practice in St. Genevieve, Missouri, becoming noted for his work with Asiatic cholera. As senator, Linn was a leader in the revival of interest in Oregon, and for the last five years of his life regularly called for its "reoccupation" as a check upon the designs of England. *DAB*, XI, 282; *BDAC*, 1222.

4. Henry Dodge (1782–1867), Wisconsin Democratic senator (1848–57), was twice governor of Wisconsin Territory (1836–41, 1845–48) and territorial delegate to Congress (1841–45). Dodge's mother, Nancy Hunter Dodge, was a widow when she married Lewis Linn's father, Asahel Linn. *Ibid.*, 819; *DAB*, XI, 282.

5. Augustus C. Dodge (1812–1883) was Iowa territorial congressman (1840–46) and senator (1848–55). After serving as minister to Spain (1855–59), he was an unsuccessful candidate for governor (1859) and held minor political posts thereafter. *Ibid.*, V, 344; *BDAC*, 819.

6. Thomas Hart Benton (1782–1858), a North Carolinian, moved to Nashville and was state senator in 1809. Following service in the War of 1812, he moved to St. Louis, becoming editor of the *Missouri Enquirer* and a successful attorney. After three decades in the U. S. Senate (1821–51), he served briefly in the House (1853–55). Benton, a powerful political figure, espoused "hard money" and a liberal land policy for settlers; but his outspoken opposition to the annexation of Texas and to the proslavery forces within the Democracy led to his virtual expulsion from the party and his rapid political decline. *Ibid.*, 546; *DAB*, II, 210–13; see also Elbert B. Smith, *Magnificent Missourian: The Life of Thomas Hart Benton* (Philadelphia, 1958).

7. William A. Linn (d. 1859) of Missouri was a second lieutenant of infantry during the Mexican War, serving from March 4, 1847, until he was mustered out in July, 1848. Mrs. Linn probably alludes to Dickens' indifference or even antagonism toward her son's efforts to persuade Congress to

assume the cost of litigation arising out of his activities as an army officer. Linn had become indebted for legal services to Thomas C. Reynolds, a St. Louis lawyer; after his death this fee was one of the liens against his estate. On June 23, 1860, Congress voted to discharge the debt, but the bill was too late for the President's signature. When the issue was brought up in the second session, it became law on December 22, 1860. Heitman, *Register*, I, 634; *Cong. Globe*, 36 Cong., 1 Sess., 3277, 3283; *ibid.*, 2 Sess., 83, 160; *U. S. Statutes*, XII, 877.

8. Probably Benjamin Fitzpatrick, Alabama senator.

From Sam Milligan

Confidential

Greeneville Ten
May 7, 1860

Dear Governor,

I have a crippled hand so I can scarsely write at all, and bad as I write it is done with great pain. But I can not avoid attempting to write a few lines to you, and you may feel assured that in all my life long, I never attempted to write to you under so much agitation and painful feelings. Things at Charleston did not by any means go off as I desired, and I fear they resulted to your prejudice. I went there with a single idea, and that was to prevent a disruption of the democratic party if possible, and to promote your interest, and I feel that I have accomplished neither.

When I reached Charleston I found as I thought directly, it was morally impossible for that convention to nominate Judge Duglas— and that if he should be nominated he could not get a large portion of the Southern States in the election. It was also manifest that his friends were your friends, and when Duglas was out of the way, his friends would come to your support— Under this State of facts, I conceived the true policy of your friends to be to adhere patiently & persistantly to your support, and in that way, to offend neither the North or the South. This our delegation agreed to do until such time, as it became apparent longer persistance would be unavailing. But to this proposition, I could not get them to stand when the fight came on. They all professed great devotion to your interest, but some of them, be came excited, and greatly affected with the *fire eating* influence that surrounded us, and had it not been for Andrew Ewing, myself and One or two others, I am firmly of the opinion our delegation would have withdrawn with the other ceceeding states. But we assumed the bold ground that we would not with draw unless other circumstances arose that would force us out. But this broke the unity of our action, and threw all our excitable material beyond all control. We however held them all on, except Carrol and McClanahan[1] who deserted us after a few ballots, and went to Douglas.

After some 30 or 35 ballots Avant & McGavoch[2] broke off, and then we called the delegation together, and I addressed them at length on the propriety of standing firm, which was seconded by Ewin[g], Whitthorn and others. I told them that I did not desire to see you frittered away one by one—that we could in that way have no chance of achieving any thing, and we would not only render ourselves ridiculous, but injure you. To this they all agreed, but when we again entered the Convention, a part of them—Judge Rools[3] &c— again flew off and declaired they would vote only once more under the arangement, and then vote for the strongest Southern man, which was Mr Guthrie[.]

Before this I had talked with all your friends out side—Hugh Douglass and others, and they advised that it would be best, rather than have you frittered away in your own State to with draw your name temporarily with the view of bringing it forward again. This was done with the announcement that it was with out any consultation with you— Then the delegation cast their vote for Gutherie.[4] I feel now as then, this was all wrong, and unjust to your future prospects, but I could not see how under the captious state of things that existed in our delegation any thing better could be done. It was not as I desired—and I even now feel deeply pained on account of it.

The truth is, I feel sure Guthrie can not be nominated, and I believe the movement operated to conciliate his friends, and soften the South towards you. It may however have the opposite effect on Duglas' friends, but they are so identified with your interest that circumstances will drive them into your support much more easily than the south could be brought to Mr Douglas or any one representing his wing of the party. But all this aside, your friends lie in the North and, North West, and it is to them you must look for support— This is true at present, but there will spring up at Baltimore a great union party with which Tennessee—Va. Ky. N. C. now stands closely identified; and I do believe, by a little consert of action with Mr Duglas and the conser[v]ative men in those states, your nomination at Baltimore is by no means improbable—

In Ten. I can see Gov Harris hand wielded against you; and that accounts for so much hesitation in our delegation. I must say that Ewing has stood much more firmly to you than I anticipated. I think it grows out of the fact, that he sees Harris' position and in the future, desires to seek protection under your wing of the party— But more about this when I see you— Whitthorn, & Burch will write to you.

I will soon write again more at length so soon as the Chancery Court is over here—

I want to hear from you very soon. If I can serve you even to the protecting of your reputation I will go to Baltimore, and even to Washington, and see you face to face.

I really fear the election is lost in any event, and if so, the extreme South is responsible for it.

Write to me only a line or two, and let me know what ought to be done, and how I can best serve you and the country[.]

Excuse this letter—for it has been written with pain both of the heart and my lame hand, and in the midst of the confusion of a crowded Court House—

Your friend   Sam Milligan

P. S. I suggested to some of our middle Ten friends to get the papers there to lead off on the idea of calling the people together on the 1st Monday of June to appoint electors, and to speak out on this question of Union or disunion—5

S. M.

I have not written half I desire to tell you[.]

ALS, DLC-JP2.

1. William H. Carroll and Sam McClanahan.
2. James M. Avent (1816–1895) was a prominent Murfreesboro lawyer. John McGavock (1815–1893), graduate of the University of Nashville (1837) and wealthy Williamson County farmer, had been appointed by Johnson a director of the bank of Tennessee, a post he held for eight years. According to the newspaper report, McClanahan and Carroll voted consistently for Douglas after seven ballots, while McGavock broke after the thirteenth. Deane Porch, tr., *1850 Census of Rutherford County* (Nashville, 1967), 364; Porch, *Evergreen Cemetery*, 141; *Goodspeed's Williamson*, 996; McGavock, *Pen and Sword*, 474n; Nashville *Union and American*, May 6, 1860.
3. George W. Rowles (1808–1867), Cleveland attorney, was a veteran officeholder. John M. Wooten, *A History of Bradley County* (Cleveland, 1949), 147–48; *Johnson Papers*, I, 413n.
4. James Guthrie of Kentucky, former secretary of the treasury, received 65½ votes on the fifty-seventh and final ballot to Douglas' 151½. Johnson received 12 votes, 11 from Tennessee and one from Minnesota, through the first 29 ballots, then 11 until Ewing withdrew his name after the 36th. *Proceedings of the National Democratic Convention at Charleston . . .* (Washington, D. C., 1860), *passim*.
5. Ratification meetings to support the Breckinridge-Lane ticket were held on the first Monday in July, not June, in Nashville and in Wilson, Robertson, Lincoln, Dickson, Stewart, Smith, and Henry counties. Nashville *Union and American*, July 3, 6, 7, 12, 14, 1860.

From Robert Johnson

Greeneville Tennessee   May 8th 1860

Dear Father,

I returned from Charleston last Friday, and was glad to get home safe and sound— I left there on Monday and came by way of Columbia and Greeneville So. Ca. and enjoyed the trip very much, and would have been better pleased if I could have been so situated as to have been perfectly free and unencumbered, but as it was, I had Charles along with me, who, commenced a spree a day or two after we reached Charleston— I done my best to Keep him from going, but go he would, and the only thing I then could do was to watch him and keep him straight if possible— I failed in that, and the only Course left me was to get him home, and in that I came very near failing, and it was a mere accident that I found him and got him started—but so [be] it, I started with him and got him about straight before reaching home, and was congratulating myself that there would be no more of it, but I was doomed to be disappointed, for no sooner had he got home, than he went to drinking and is still at it, and I presume will not quit until it compels him to— I regret it very much, but it cannot be remedied now, and [we] will have to make the best of it—

Mother and myself would have started to Washington this week, if he had kept straight, but as it is, we cannot say when we will get off, but I hope in a short time—.[1]

How long will you want me to stay at Washington— have you any work you want done while I am there, if so have it ready and I will attend to it[.]

The Charleston Convention was a general row, and injured the Democratic party more than any thing that has happened to it for years— I was sorry to see the Southern States permit such a man as W. L. Yancey[2] of Ala. lead them by the nose, wheresoever he saw proper— I would have had more independence than that, and if I had wanted a leader, I would have selected a different man—but he, in the opinion of some is a *very great* man—in my Judgement he is no man at all—

Some of the Tennessee delegates were stricken with the fire-eating movement and were ready to go off with the Others—but better Counsel prevailed. Andrew Ewing worked manfully and I must say deserves credit for his conduct— he stood up for you all the time—and was a much better friend, than some whose pretensions were greater— Jones[3] (of Overton) stood square out and fought nobly—but I will give you all the particulars on sight—

Excuse this writing as I am very unwell and scarcely able to sit up— yesterday I was very sick[.]

I would be glad to hear from you in a short time[.]

Your Son   Robt Johnson

ALS, DLC-JP2.

1. Before the end of the month Robert, his mother, and young Andrew (Frank) made the trip to Washington. Sam Milligan to Robert Johnson,

May 28, 1860; Charles Johnson to Robert Johnson, June 3, 1860, Johnson
Papers, LC.
   2. William L. Yancey. See *Johnson Papers*, I, 185n.
   3. W. E. B. Jones.

From Washington C. Whitthorne

                                    Columbia Tennessee, May 8, '60
Honl. Andrew Johnson.
   Dear Sir: I reached Charleston on thursday eve[nin]g preceding the meeting of the Convention, a good many delegates had assembled. I found the Douglass men confident of his nomination, as
well as determined to leave no stone unturned to effect [it]. They
would listen to no effort at compromise of any character. And my
impression then was, & is confirmed by reflection, that the hectoring
was altogether upon that side—But to the narrative. It was first
reported that you were willing, if not pledged, to run upon th D.
ticket as V.P. But it was soon discovered there was no authority for
this, it was being hourly reported that Tennessee, would within a
few ballots vote for Douglass. Such reports continued until within a
few hours of the adjournment, nothwithstanding the constant con-
tradictions which came after. I must beleive these reports injured
the influence of Tennessee. I found the North West delegates very
favorably inclined toward you, as well as some from New Jersey &
Pennsylvania, but with them it was Douglas first last and all the
time.
   In our State Caucus, it was early resolved by 22 out of the 24
delegates to abide by you until Millegan said stop, or it was de-
monstrable there was no further necessity of voting for you. Messrs
Carrol and McClanahan from the first claimed the right to vote in-
dependtly[.] Their whole course had demonstrated they were Douglass men, and accordingly upon the 7th Ballot, I beleive, they went
for him. Upon the 13th. Ballot you recd. one vote from Minnesota.
(Mr. A. J. Edgerton[1] of Mantorville Dodge Co.) who held out.
Upon adjournment at about 30th. Ballot upon Wednesday, our delegation was bro't together for consultation there having been a manifestation upon [the] part of McGavock, Avent, Robb & Jones[2] of
Giles to change their votes. Millegan & myself agreed that if there
was a movement to drop off, that it would be better to withdraw
entirely. At the consultation, I was called in from my room,[3] and
learned that it was being discussed, (the propriety of dropping your
name.) I gave my own opinion that it was better to keep on voting
for you, because that could give no offence, whilst I could not see any
good to be effected by voting for any one just then. I understood this

to be agreed upon & left. When the Convention met, I did not get in
for some 15 minutes, in which time your name had been withdrawn
& the vote of the State was just then cast for Guthrie. The reason for
which, I learned to be, that George Sanders[4] had received a dispatch
from Mr. Clingman[5] saying that you & others beleved that Douglass
having received a majority of the votes was entitled to the nomination, which dispatch being circulated induced some gentlemen to
vote for another than yourself. And the "flying off" having commenced Millegan thought it was proper to consent to the withdrawal
of your name with the understanding that if no "good" was accomplished the Delegation would return. Had I voted it would not have
been Guthrie or Douglass. Nothwithstanding any appearance to the
contrary, I regard McGavock & Avent as good friends of yours particularly Mc.G. They were alarmed at the aspect of things & simply
ready to do anything to produce harmony. Atkins[6] acted fairly
squarely & faithfully as your friend, as *I know*. The delegation were
opposed to Douglass as they ought to have been in my opinion, but
they were not offensive in their opposition. As I said Douglass
friends were confident of his nomination at the outset, and when they
found that it could not be done in a full convention, I beleive that if
not purposely, at least consultingly forced the Southern States to
withdraw, hoping thereby to secure Douglass' nomination by
2/3rds. of the remaining vote. When however, Tenn. Va. Md. N.C.
& Ky saw that this could be done by a purely sectional vote, which
of itself more effectually than the secession of the Gulf States, would
denationalize the party, they insisted upon the construction given to
that rule.[7] This being done there was no hope for Mr. Douglass'
nomination, unless it was suspended, which no doubt was contemplated, if Mr. D. recd. the 2/3rds. of the vote given, to secure
which, by a clap trap movement many supposed the Sanders dispatch fabricated. The feeling in the convention was deep, but respectful, pertinacious but not violent. Douglass could prevent, but
could not succeed. An individual had pocketed the party. However
with good enough feeling they adjourned and I hope when they
meet at Baltimore that harmony and success may attend their
deliberations.
I yesterday made a speech here,[8] and told off [*sic*] encouraging
harmony good feelings, and bidding them be of good cheer &c. &c.
In which I stated my own position to be, that I was not for Ds. nomination, did not beleive he would further press his claims, or if
pressed that he would be nominated, but yet if nominated, con-
formably to Democratic usage and the question being between
Sewardism, Bellism, & Douglasism I would support Douglass, nothwithstanding I disagreed with his so called Squatter or popular sov-

ereignty notions, & argued to show that Squatter Sovereignty was better than Wilmot-proviso-ism. The masses of the people are against Douglass in this section of the State. They are not only against him, but warmly so, and whilst a majority of the party would support him, if nominated, yet we would hopelessly loose the State. The labor of years would be thrown away, & certain defeat overtake us. More than one half the Democrats I have met since my return. I have seen them from several counties declare they will not vote for Douglass. If the fate of the Democratic party in Tennessee be worth anything to us, it is our solemn duty to prevent it if possible[.] That you may know the feeling here in Maury, I mention the names of a half dozen or more who declared upon yesterday, they would not vote for D. (Ask Nicholson or Thomas as to their character) viz Munford Smith, R B. Moore, Fayette Wilkes, Dr. Corcoran⁹ Ezra Hardison, Benoni Grisham, James N. Scribner, Lee Bullock & so on to hundreds. But if our party says *Death*, I am willing to face it, as death to us here in Tennessee most assuredly it would be. Shall we barter Tennessee for Iowa & Michigan[?] Shall we swap certainties for uncertainties—. Our opposition friends are the highest elated fellows you ever saw.

Nothwithstanding I have written you so strongly against the nomination of Douglass, I am to day accused by some of both parties, with having made a Douglass speech upon yesterday, a speech preparing the public mind for his nomination. Let me hear from you.

If I had the time & the money, I would go on to Baltimore.¹⁰

Very truly your friend   W. C. Whitthorne

I recd. your letter but not till Wednesday of the Convention[.]
I also recd. your dispatch.

ALS, DLC-JP2.

1. Alonzo J. Edgerton (1827–1896), Dodge County, Minnesota, lawyer and state senator (1858, 1859), served in the Minnesota volunteers during the Civil War. Railroad commissioner (1871–75), and again state senator (1877–78), he was appointed as a Republican to fill a vacancy in the Senate (1881), later becoming chief justice of the supreme court of Dakota Territory and United States judge in the newly admitted state of South Dakota. *BDAC*, 846.

2. Alfred Robb (1818–1862), a delegate to Charleston and Baltimore, was a Clarksville lawyer and member of the state lower house (1861–62). A lieutenant colonel in the 49th Tennessee infantry, CSA, he was mortally wounded at Fort Donelson in February, 1862. Thomas M. Jones, a Pulaski attorney, was a delegate to Charleston. Robison, *Preliminary Directory, Montgomery*, 52; James McCallum, *A Brief Sketch of the Settlement and Early History of Giles County* (Pulaski, 1928), 16.

3. Whitthorne, although neither an elected delegate nor an alternate, served in place of Dr. S. B. Moore of Hickman, a delegate who had been unable to make the trip. Nashville *Union and American*, April 26, 1860.

4. George Sanders (1812–1873), Kentucky-born political and financial promoter, was a leader in the "Young America" movement, editor of the

Democratic Review (Washington, D. C.), and later a Confederate agent. A member of the Douglas campaign organization, Sanders was assigned the duty of soliciting support from wavering delegations at the convention. In 1856 he had been instrumental in the Buchanan nomination and as a reward had received the rich post of navy agent at New York. *DAB*, XVI, 334–35; Milton, *Eve of Conflict*, 431; Hesseltine, *Three against Lincoln*, 8, 14–15.

5. This dispatch has not been found. For Thomas L. Clingman, see *Johnson Papers*, I, 185n, 518n.

6. John D. C. Atkins. See Exchange with John Bell, February 24, 1858, note 11.

7. Following the bolt of the deep southern states, the Virginia, North Carolina, Kentucky, and Tennessee delegations caucused and resolved to remain in the convention but to put forth a plan intended to insure Douglas' defeat. The strategy called for the chairman to rule that a two-thirds vote of the theoretical full convention strength, rather than two-thirds of the remaining delegates, would be required for nomination. Thus 202 out of 303 votes would be needed, whereas only 248 votes remained in the convention. Since Douglas would have to get five-sixths of this vote, it became impossible for him to win. Milton, *Eve of Conflict*, 443.

8. At least one Tennessee paper considered Whitthorne's remarks of May 7 a qualified endorsement of Douglas. Nashville *Patriot*, May 10, 1860.

9. Probably William C. Cockrinn (b. *c*1813), a Maryland-born physician with $7,000 real property in 1850. Deane Porch, *1850 Census, Maury County, Tennessee* (Nashville, 1966), 309.

10. Whitthorne did go to Baltimore. Nashville *Union and American*, June 22, 1860.

Remarks on Homestead Bill[1]

May 10, 1860

Mr. JOHNSON, of Tennessee. I do not rise, sir, for the purpose of making a speech; but more for the purpose of trying to press action on this bill. I think the time has arrived when we should vote. It is not my intention to consume the time of the Senate in making a speech; but there are one or two things that I will say in answer to the Senator from Minnesota [Mr. WILKINSON][2] on the pending amendment. He seems to think that this bill will do very little good; that it amounts to nothing; that it substantially confines the settlers under it to the knobs and swamps and the sterile land. It seems to me that there is a very large proportion of public land entered at $1 25, and at less prices, as rich and productive as any lands in the world. A very large proportion of the receipts into the Treasury are from one dollar and twenty-five cent, one dollar, seventy-five cent, fifty cent, and twenty-five cent lands. Some of these lands are valuable, rich, and productive. The bill proceeds on the basis of allowing lands which are subject to private entry to be taken by actual settlers. It makes no discrimination; it gives all an equal privilege on the lands subject to private entry, to make their entry, comply with the provisions of law, and get their one hundred and sixty acres of land, or less.

The Senator seems to think that it discriminates against the original settler. Suppose this bill does not pass: he stands precisely as he has stood; he has no relief. If the bill passes, it does not make his condition any worse. But the query comes up, do we not better the settler's condition by the passage of the bill? In the first place, a large portion of those to whom the Senator alludes have been in the enjoyment of the land some five or six years. He says that they are hard pressed for payment. The sales of the lands have been continued from time to time. Many of those persons, perhaps, are hard pressed; but what does the bill do? It says to those persons who are now occupants, "You shall have two years longer to perfect your title, and pay your $1 25 an acre." It seems to me that would be some relief, and do some good to the settler who is not now in a condition to pay his money.

There is another thing to be considered in connection with this. These people have been on the land for five or six years, and the proposition is to give them a credit of two years more[.] They have gone in advance of other settlers, and selected the pick and cream of the land. The bill says to them, "Now, after you have selected your land, the rich sections of the country, you shall have two years longer to pay for these good pieces at the rate of $1 25 an acre." It seems to me that the bill does some good in that point of view, so far as those settlers are concerned. But even reduce it to the hardest extremity, and suppose that, at the expiration of two years, there should be any occupant who cannot pay his $200 for one hundred and sixty acres: what does this bill say to him? "If you are not able to comply with the contract that you made with the Government as a preëmptor, at the end of two years, come under the homestead provision, and get one hundred and sixty acres." So, instead of its operating as a hardship against the settler, it is giving him two chances where he only has one, and gives an extension of the time to pay his money.

It did not [sic] seem to me, and I do not say it in any unkindness, that the Senator from Minnesota was indulging in a little extravagance in his argument. This bill gives the settler a double chance. He has gone on the land in advance, and selected the best and most fertile portions of it. We say now to him, "take two years longer to pay, and if you cannot pay your $200 at that time, go and be on an equality with all others." It does not discriminate against them at all, but places them on an equality. It still gives them another advantage. After they have gone on the public lands, and got one hundred and sixty acres of the richest and fattest land that the country affords, they can pay up their $200, and then go and take another one hundred and sixty acres, under this bill. Surely I do not think the Senator understood the practical operation of the bill, or he would not have made the argument he has on the present occasion. The man who entered on land under the present law impliedly promised to pay the Government a certain amount upon certain conditions; a contract was made, and this bill was intended not to be retrospective or in favor of any existing contracts, but to leave the laws that were in existence to operate as they were designed to do; and then, if they were any hardship to those persons who cannot comply with their provisions, they can come forward and take one hundred and sixty acres under the provisions of the bill. If the argument be true that you must provide for these cases, and that your law must be retrospective, what will become of those men who have paid in their money? Is the Senator prepared to go to the Treasury and refund it? You have as much right to do it in the one case as the other. If you release these individuals from their contract, go and take from the Treasury and pay back the money that has been paid in for the land.

Thus we see that this bill operates equally on all. It really discriminates against none; but if there is a discrimination, it is in favor of those who are now occupying the soil as proprietors. If I know myself, I will go as far in things of this sort as any one; but the great object of the committee, and of the honest and sincere supporters of this bill, has been to place it in a shape in which it would receive the sanction of the various departments of the Government, and ultimately be placed on the statute-book, and become the law of the land. By the passage of this bill, is not the great principle attained? Will not the great object have been accomplished? Will you not have introduced a perfect system, and that, too, before any hardship can result by the operation of any existing law? It gives Congress and the country time to see how it will operate; and if the preemptors who are now upon the public lands require more legislation, there will be time for it. You will have another session of this Congress. Two years from the passage of the bill will carry you to the close of the first session of the incoming Congress. Then here are two sessions of Congress for experience, to suggest every improvement that should be made in this bill, and extend whatever relief should be extended to this portion of the settlers on the public lands. It does seem to me that it would better their condition, and carry out, to a very great extent, the very object that the Senator from Minnesota seems to desire.

Now let me ask every sincere and honest friend of this bill to stand by it; and I believe there are some such. I will say here, that I fear there are those who want to see this bill defeated and the Democracy responsible for that defeat. They clamor at the very top of their voices in favor of the hardy pioneer and the occupant settler; but yet they would prefer to see this bill defeated and let them be stripped of their homes for the purpose of party aggrandizement, rather than pass this bill and quiet the question and take it away from the respective parties of the country. If we are for the policy, if we are sincere in it, let us take what we can get; let us put it upon the statute-book; let it become a law; and I repeat again, as time and experience shall suggest the alterations that ought to be made, they can be made, and before the expiration of the two years allowed to the preëmptor, or the five years to the individual who takes the land under the homestead provision of the bill, there will be ample time for such alterations as may be necessary to be made.

But the Senator speaks of speculators buying up the land. If the Senator would join with us, and help to pass this bill, and not incumber it and follow it up with General Jackson's policy of bringing the lands into market and disposing of them only to actual settlers, and to them in limited quantities—by the homestead followed by those concomitant propositions—the great scheme that should be practiced in this country would be secured. Why not then be consistent and come up to the support of the best land system, in my judgment, ever inaugurated since the Government commenced?

Now, sir, let us vote on the various propositions, and do it understandingly. There has been ample time to mature and consider every proposition. Let us vote. I appeal to friends on this side of the House and on the other side of the House to let us vote. We have talked enough. Yesterday I feared that we had talked the bill to death. Now I beg the Senate to let us vote.[3]

Cong. Globe, 36 Cong., 1 Sess., 2037–38.

1. As the Senate discussed the Homestead bill, Morton S. Wilkinson of Minnesota began a lengthy discourse on its shortcomings, declaring that its only advantage came from the extension of time given to pay for land already occupied; otherwise, it threatened to leave the actual settlers with "the worthless swamp lands" and "the knobs and hills," while wealthy speculators engrossed the more valuable lands. Johnson took the floor following a rambling argument between Wilkinson and Wigfall of Texas.

2. Morton S. Wilkinson (1819–1894), New York-born lawyer, was a member of the first Minnesota territorial legislature (1849), a Republican senator (1859–65), congressman (1869–71), and state senator (1874–77). *BDAC*, 1816–17.

3. After rejecting several amendments, the Senate passed the bill on the same day, 44–8. *Cong. Globe*, 36 Cong., 1 Sess., 2043.

From W. S. Crouch[1]

Chillicothe Mo   May 12 1860

Hon A Johnson
    Verry Dear Sir
    I hope you will not consider it an intrusion for me to trouble you with a line. There is considerable talk here about who is going to get the nomination at Baltimore, and there is a diversity of opinion, and among persons mentioned for that place ricently I here your name mentioned, and in no instance but what you seem to occupy a verry favorable position among a great many persons of this State, all who I have met and herd speak on the Subject, Seems to think that you would be more acceptable than allmost any other man, after looking over all the ground, it Seems that you ought to be up and doing or your frends, in the evennt, that Douglass is withdraw[n] at Balt— it seems to me your chanc is a good one. I hope to Se his name withdraw[n]. You will excuse me for writing this, but hoping it might be a word of encourgemt is the appoligey I offer you. I wish you would Send me a coppy of the States[2] if you think it a good papr[.] I have not Seen it for Some time.

Except my best wishes for your Suckcess
I reman yours   Truly
W. S. Crouch[3]

ALS, DLC-JP2.
1. W. S. Crouch was a general merchant at Chillicothe. *Missouri State Gazetteer and Business Directory* (1860), 55.
2. A pro-southern Washington newspaper, originally *States and Union*, it had a brief existence (1857–61). Gregory, *Union List of Newspapers*, 91.
3. Johnson's endorsement reads: "Please Send this man a patent office report"

From Samuel J. Pooley

Monticello, near Liberty Corner Somerset Co
New Jersey May the 14 1860—

to   Hon. Andrew Johnson
Washington
My good sir
    I was fearful, immediately on hearing that the Cincinnatti Convention had fixed the Convention, for 1860, at Charleston, South Carolina, that, the "Diplomats" of that locality would in all probability take measures to push there crotchets to extremes. I have not been disappointed in my anticipations[.]

The evident intentions of those gentlemen is now, to make up a ticket, anterior to the meeting of the Convention at Baltimore, & to put the Candidates before the Country among others on there favorite & distracting issues. Extremism & abolitionism are equally obnoxious to me, both are inimical to the best interests of the country, & letter & spirit of the Organic laws. I trust my friend that, the event will show, as I doubt not it will, that ultraism unenacted[?] by law, finds no favor of fearful import, in the south, as it most assuredly does not, nor will not find it, in the north;

I deeply regret that the practice of the platform were ever introduced among us. Its effects at Charleston recently, should admonish us, to scout it as one in deadly hostility to the peace, spirit & genius of our institutions. The Executive, Legislative, & Judicial, departments of the government, should be preserved in there fullest strength, & purity, no fanatic or outside influence, should be permitted to pervert, them, from there legitimate & true purpose, of Union & of government, without this, our government, must necessarily become corrupted & terminate into one consolidated system. The Oath of Office enjoins on the incumbent executive the faithful fulfillment of his Official duties, & other responsibilities attached thereto, this and a due caution expressed, in the selection, of the gentlemen for the post, that he possesses undoubted qualifications for the position, are here, all that we can reasonably & in [any] case ask for. Of cou[r]se the Candidate, to be appointed at Baltimore will come before the Country on a Platform[.] I have no hesitation in saying on this point, (altho regretting the practice) Mr. Samuels[1] of Iowa, is the best one, & should be adopted by the body, refered to. This of course, is said with perfect repect to the Opinions of others.

Yours Very Respectfully
Samuel James Pooley

ALS, DLC-JP2.

1. Benjamin M. Samuels, a Douglas Democrat, was an Iowa delegate to the Charleston convention. Defeated for governor in 1857, and for Congress in 1860, he was the Iowa representative on the committee on resolutions and platforms at Charleston; signing the minority report, he became the group's spokesman. Louis Pelzer, "The History of Political Parties in Iowa from 1857 to 1860," *Iowa Journal of History and Politics*, VII (1909), 185, 216, 229; Hesseltine, *Three against Lincoln*, 30, 46, 60, 61.

From Shelby County Democrats

May 14, 1860, Memphis; ALS, DLC-JP2.

James Hamilton and others invite Johnson to address a Memphis mass meeting May 31 of Democrats "favorable to the principle enunciated in the Majority Platform which was rejected by the Charleston Convention, and who sympathize with the Course of those delegates who withdrew from said Convention, as well as the assembling of the Proposed Convention at Richmond Va on the 11th June prox."

From William P. Bond

May 15, 1860, Brownsville; ALS, DLC-JP2.

Expresses interest in Johnson's appointment to the select committee investigating claims of American citizens for spoliations committed by the French prior to 1801. Bond's wife is a granddaughter of John Proudfit of Norfolk, Virginia, who had been "an actual sufferor."

From William E. B. Jones

Livingston Tennessee
May 15th 1860

Gov Andrew Johnson
    Dear Sir
        I take pleasure in writing you as one of your devoted friends a confidential letter which will give you knowledge you might not otherwise acquire[.]
I was at Charleston and done honestly all I could for you[.] These were your only true friends at Charleston Gen Milligan Wm H Maxwell James M Sheid David Burford John R Howard Mathews and McClellan[d] of 6th District W C Whitthorn Dr Thos Menees and myself[.]
Carrol & McClanahan were for Douglass first all the time then you[.] Gen[?] Adkins [Atkins] & Waul [Wall?] & Conner his pets were for Gen Lane & I G Harris[.] McGavoch Avent & Robb were for Guthrie partly influenced by J D Winston[.]
Thos Lyon G W Rowles and Mr Wallace were for R M T Hunter[.] John Riley from Hawkins became such a fool fire eater he was for nobody[.]
I considered you were betrayed & withdraw[n] by the overpowering influence of men who were pretended friends and the timidity of a majority of your real friends[.] Therefore I voted for you after the balance of the delegation consented to withdraw your name and would have done so until the close of the convention at Charleston only I thought it was placing you in a false position to say that only one twenty fourth of the Democracy of Tennessee were for you[.]
I forgot to mention that Ewing was really for Dickinson[.]
I saw no use in abandoning you while Douglass whas getting three fifths of the number of votes cast in convention against the field[.]
I was confident if Douglass was withdrawn you would be nominated

as the whole Northwest were for you[.] This could be yet if the
Delegates from Tennessee were true to Tennessee & you her favorite
son at Baltimore[.] My country is warm for you and next for
Douglass[.]

We want to beat Black republicanism and also John Bell & Everett
in november next and I now write to you as a true friend to ask your
advice as a friend in confidence what is best to be done at Baltimore
because if I am well I will be there[.]¹ Write me all you see proper
to disclose and it shall be entirely confidential[.] Send me such
speeches & documents as are use full to a politician[.] Accept my
thanks for past favors and allso my highest assurances of regard for
you as a man[.]

Yours Respectfully   Wm E B Jones

ALS, DLC-JP2.

1. Jones went to Baltimore, where he did not join the Tennessee bolters
but, along with Watterson, Carroll, and three others, remained to cast three
Tennessee votes for Douglas, while seven more stayed to cast four and a half
votes for Guthrie. Hesseltine, *Three against Lincoln*, 243, 250.

From Tazewell W. Newman

Winchester Tenn
Apl [May]¹ 15th, 1860

Hon Andrew Johnson
Washington City D. C.

My Dear Sir   There is a bill before the Senate from the House of
Rep, No. 98., "To Liquidate the unadjusted contracts of the Tennessee river improvement[.]"² by examing this bill, and pressing its
passage you will Confer a very great favor. (provided you think it is
proper to pass the bill)   the claim is for the Servaces of my father
and others—on the improvement— by refferance to report No. 2 accompany[ing] the House Bill, from the Committee on claims you can
gain more information in regard to the justice of the Bill than by any
thing I can *write*.

As for the political prospects of our party in Tennessee they are
any thing but pleasing, we are splitting up into factions—and look
but with little hope to Baltamore³ for Settlement—   I have been urging the party here to Stand by the regular organization of the party
—which will be done by the Masses here. Bell⁴ cannot carry Tennessee against any one nominated at *Baltamore*.

If Mr Duglass would withdraw his name from the Convention
placing it on high ground for the good of the party—and the Safety
of the Country he would at this time immortalize himself with the
party, and in my opinion, the party could unite on any other man &

again reorganize with Strong hopes of victory. I hope this will be the Course persued[.] if not our party will be rent in two in Tennessee—completly desorganized and demoralized. while I shall support the nominee of the Batamore Convention many here will stand by the Richmond Nominations[.][5] Write me in regard to the hopes the prospects and chances of the party and what is the best course to persue—, and urge on the people for they are unionist and do not know what course to persue.

Your Friend   And Obt. Servt. &c.
Taz. W Newman

ALS, DLC-JP2.

1. From the contents, it is clear that Newman has misdated his letter.
2. This measure, authorizing payment of contracts made under an 1852 act for Tennessee River improvements, passed, June 12, 1860. *U. S. Statutes*, XII, 29.
3. The Baltimore convention convened on June 18; withdrawals began on the fifth day, with the seceders, mainly southern delegations, meeting in Maryland Institute Hall the next day. The original Baltimore convention proceeded to nominate Douglas, while the seceders chose Breckinridge. Hesseltine, *Three against Lincoln, passim*.
4. Bell had been nominated on May 10 at the Baltimore National Constitutional Union Convention. *Ibid.*, 134.
5. The Richmond Constitutional Democratic Convention of southern delegations meeting on June 11 did not select candidates; a second convention on June 26 reaffirmed the Baltimore nominees, Breckinridge and Lane. *Ibid.*, 178–84, 277–78.

From Jeptha Fowlkes[1]

Continental Hotel Phila.
May 19. 1860.

Private

Hon. A. Johnson:

My dear Sir:

I shall be in Washington City Monday— I have a good deal to communicate to you— The Baltimore nomination a failure.[2] It enlists no particular interest here or in N. Y! Maj Henry[3] is here—many[?] enlisted but arousing few in this Crusade v.s. Democracy &c! If, occasion offers, remember to strengthen me, with Senator Douglass! I have to-day, written him, *significantly*! His speech, considered by most whom I hear speak of it, as a masterly & triumphant vindication of himself for Consistancy & sound Democracy!

You are prominent with the people—often spoken of—& possess great *latent* strength! But it is with you as with Douglass, opposed by politicians & aspirants to office! You & Douglass should be & must be friends, if true to yourselves & the country! It is, evidently, the policy of Tennessee to affiliate with North-West! Why, then, should

THEIR FORCES, not coalesce & unite, in their leading & prominent MEN? to "form & fashion" the destiny of the Country?

Yr. friend.   J. Fowlkes—

ALS, DLC-JP2.

1. Jeptha M. Fowlkes (1806–1864), Virginia-born physician who settled in Memphis in 1835, was president of the Farmers' and Merchants' Bank until its failure in 1847; subsequently he was editor of the Memphis *Avalanche* (1861–63). An investor in Arkansas real estate, he was also active in Southern Pacific Railroad promotion. During the war he was a peace commissioner from the Confederacy to East Tennessee. Memphis *Commercial Appeal*, August 13, September 20, 1949; S. R. Bruesch, "Early Medical History of Memphis," West Tenn. Hist. Soc. *Papers*, No. 2 (1948), 42–43.

2. The National Constitutional Union convention, composed of former Whigs and others alarmed at the divisive atmosphere of the times, met in Baltimore, May 9–10, and nominated John Bell of Tennessee for President and Edward Everett of Massachusetts for Vice President. Hesseltine, *Three against Lincoln*, 134–37.

3. Probably Gustavus A. Henry, who had served as vice president for Tennessee at the Constitutional Union convention and had made a rousing Union speech in response to Bell's nomination. *Ibid.*, 135–37.

From William M. Lowry

Greeneville Ten May 19 1860

Gov Johnson
    Dear Sir
        I herewith enclose you a list of my assistants[1] in the different counties of E Tenn[.] they are men on whom you may rely, and to whom you might send some Public Documents. What is to become of the Democratic Party, (to us, Mr. Yancy)[2] since its disruption at Charleston. I am not one of those who have said I would not vote for Douglass, if he were Nominated[.] I would go for him or any Other good sound man[.] yet I must think in the present disorganised State of things Mr Douglass Could hardly do Justice to himself to permit his name to stand before the Country, as a Candidate because if he is Elected it must be done by the South and it seems the South is verry reluctant to take him up. I am utterly opposed to the action of some of our Democratic friends in with drawing from the Convention[.] this wont do. the Democracy of the Union must stand together[.] I was at Chattanooga the other day and found but few to side with Mr. Yancy. I told our friends that in their District Electoral Convention that they must sustain the course of the Tennessee delegation at Charleston. I have not yet Seen their proceedings. I hope the Richmond Convention will prove a failure, and that our friends may rally at Baltimore with the proper sperit. if Mr Douglass Could only withdraw from the Contest and bide his time I think it would have a good effect at harmonizing our folks. I am

now Closely engaged with my census[.] I find it a verry troublisome
and difficult business. My Court Comes on next week at Knoxville[.]³
I fear We will have some difficulty in Selecting our Elector. the
Nomination of Bell I consider a farce. I presume from the Start he
is making that he intends to Stump the Union[.]⁴ if I could advise
him I would tell him to stay at home as of all the Public Men I know
he is the poorest Man to Show off: let me hear from you on recpt of
this as I am behind the news. Not much news[.] We have had fine
rains for the last week or two[.] the Wheat Crop is not promising[.]
the business of the town is good and people cheerful and in good
sperits[.] present my kind regards to my friend Hon Mr Nicholson,
to whom I am under obligations for a number of Public documents
lately, and accept for your self, the kind regards of your freind &
obt Sevt

Wm M Lowry

ALS, DLC-JP2.

1. Lowry, as marshal for East Tennessee, had charge of taking the 1860
census and in this capacity appointed forty-one census takers, including his
own son, John, Johnson's son-in-law, Daniel Stover, and Dr. J. G. M. Ramsey's son, Francis. Records of the Eighth Census: List of Marshals and Assistants, RG29, National Archives.

2. Perhaps an ironic allusion to Yancey's tactics at Charleston. See also
Letter from Robert Johnson, May 8, 1860.

3. As marshal, Lowry was the arresting officer for cases tried in the eastern district court, which sat in Knoxville.

4. At this time, Bell had not made much of a "start"; his formal acceptance
letter was not drafted until May 21, two days after Lowry wrote. Following
his nomination on May 10, he journeyed to Philadelphia, where he was welcomed by some six thousand people. On May 18 a Nashville newspaper quoted
Bell as saying at Philadelphia that he believed the majority of Republicans
and Democrats were Union-loving and devoted to the Constitution; from this
statement one might infer that he hoped to attract dissidents from both parties.
Parks, *John Bell*, 356–58; Nashville *Union and American*, May 18, 1860.

From Albert G. Graham¹

Jonesboro Tenn May 23rd 1860.

(Private & Confidential.)

Hon: Andw. Johnson,
Washington City, D. C.

Dear Sir—

The recent disturbance in the harmony of the Democratic party
at Charleston is very much to be regretted; and should it not be
healed by some proper and just measures at Baltimore in the approaching Convention, the permanency of the party as a national
organization is rather doubtful; and in the fall of the party, the

Union goes to pieces. I feel quite sure of this; and as a patriot, I am anxious to contribute my mite to avert this threatened calamity.

As an evidence that these apprehensions are not unfounded, I would refer you to the tone of various of the organs of the opposition in the South. A few of them have jeered and taunted the Democracy at their misfortunes at Charleston, but the more sensible and reflecting of them look upon the matter with alarm, and they are apprehensive that the breach in the party will not be healed at Baltimore; and if not there, the Country & the Union is endangered by the bitter sectional strife such an anomaly in the history of the party would occasion.

If the matter is viewed thus by our opponents, with what alarm should we look upon it ourselves? A serious disruption of the party, and the breaking up of the only national organization in the Country, would to my mind forbode the dissolution of the Union—a prospect which no true patriot can for a moment look upon without being seized with a feeling of horror. For my part, I would rather lose my right arm, or my right eye; nay even life itself—rather than such a calamity should occur.

Senator Douglas' recent speech[2] in the Senate has certainly presented to my mind his position on the territorial—Slavery question in a more favorable light than I had been in the habit of regarding it. He may be in error; but if so, the error undoubtedly existed in the Cincinnati platform too, and in its cotemporaneous exposition. Buchanan's letter of acceptance, his inaugural address, Breckinridge's address at Lexington,[3] and the resolves of divers Conventions in the South, and the speeches and letters of distinguished democrats,[4] as quoted in that Speech, go to show most conclusively that if Douglas is wrong *now*, he has only followed an error inaugurated in 1856. The majority at Charleston of the party were willing, and actually did endorse these sentiments; and I hold that the policy is a good one which follows the lead of a majority—I care not of what party.

The Black Reps. seem to entertain the idea that Douglas will be the nominee of the Democracy by their putting forth Mr. Lincoln,[5] his old competitor, hoping to carry Ills. and some of the North Western states on the strength gained by him in his contest with Mr. Douglas in 1858. But whether Mr. D. is nominated or not, it is very evident that his friends in the north are so much devoted to him that the nomination of another man would be the signal for the success of Lincoln; for it seems to be conceded that Douglas is the only champion who can successfully cope with him in the northern states. Even if Douglas and his friends should bolt—(which I think they would not do—) it would not be worse than the ultra-Southern Democrats have already done.

My object however in writing to you was not to discuss these questions. Suffice it to say that whilst I have not been altogether satisfied with Douglas' career for the past four years, if he was nominated fairly, I would cheerfully sustain him, & believe, if elected, he would make a good national president—which is all that the South, or any body else, ought to ask, or expect.

Your Tenn. friends, in which number I wish to be placed, have urged your name for the position of presidential Candidate. I believe that your nomination would satisfy the Douglasites much more than that of any other Southern man; but it is very evident that even they would not support you in Convention, unless there was shown less opposition to them in the ballots. But for many reasons, I think the nomination of any Southern man at this time extremely hazardous; and the stake is too great to hazard so much. A ticket that would carry, as I think, is what we ought to seek for; & that ticket can be found, as I believe in the names of Douglas for Prest. & Johnson for V. Prest. On such a ticket, the Democracy could carry 3/4ths. of the Electoral College.

My understanding is that when approached upon the subject, you have not only uniformly declined the use of your name, not only for Prest., but for V. Prest. If the former were attainable, I assure you there lives no man in this region who would more cheerfully work for that object at this time than I would; but I think it extremely hazardous, even if a nomination could be secured. But how about the latter?

I was assured by a leading Douglas man (Mr. Montgomery) [6] that your nomination for V. Prest. would be made on the first ballot, if you would consent to it. Such consent, it is presumed, carries with it the idea that the Tenn. Delegates shall vote for Douglas for Prest.; hoping in this way that other southern states will follow this lead, & thus secure the requisite 2/3rds. I have conversed with various of your friends here—persons whom I know are your friends, and whom you would recognize as such—and I think their uniform opinion is that if this could be effected you should interpose no objections.

I am writing pretty freely to you; but I hope you will excuse it. It is best for a man to speak plain—even if what he has to say is unpalatable.

The position of the V. Prest. is by no means undesirable. It is perhaps the most honorable in the nation, having less of responsibility than that of Prest., and less to do than that of any other position with equal salary. As such, the V. Prest. becomes Prest. on the death of the incumbent; the term is for four years, with double the Salary of a Senator;[7] his labors are merely nominal; the sins of an administration are never imputed to him, whilst its honors are not infrequently attached to his name; his official position brings him in contact with all classes of politicians in the Union, and he can without any imputation of interested motives make friends among all classes; and if he desires it, may become the most formidable candidate in the field for the next Canvass for the Presidency. Upon these subjects I need not enlarge. Your own mind and experience of public affairs, are so much greater than mine than [*sic*] it is great presumption in my saying what I have.

I would however remark that your nomination and acceptance of the office of V. Prest. would not only give you the advantages that I have pointed out for a nomination for the next Canvass (in 1864) but the Admn. of Douglas would certainly feel bound to sustain you also for that position with all its power.

I think I express the wishes of your friends here in the foregoing. They may be indifferent in number, & perhaps in influence; but I hope you will pardon the freedom I have taken in communicating them. The honor of being V. Prest. is surely no mean honor—and it is undoubtedly a safe stepping stone to a higher one.

I saw, & conversed with divers Douglas men, & they confirmed what Mr. Montgomery said; and I think they, as well as the Country, regard such a ticket as inevitable. Mr. M. you will remember was Douglas' Coadjutor in the House on the Lecompton question;[8] and is perhaps as much in his confidence as any man living. And allow me to remark just here that I write these remarks to you on my own responsi[bi]lity; and in the promptings of no man whatever. I informed Major Crouch[9] and a few other friends here that I would write to you, & what were my views; and they approved my intention; but I have been induced, solely, to write to you in consequence of what I deem the imminent peril of the affairs of the Democracy, which I regard those of the nation.

It would indeed be unjust to you for me to suppose that you took no interest in the present aspects of our Country's Condition. It has been doubtless the main ingredient of your thoughts for weeks; I have thought of it too, & I have presented my remedy before you. I believe if D. & J. were nominated at Balto. even on the minority platform, as adopted at Charleston, we could carry ¾ths of the electoral College. Any other nomination for Prest. would create an unheard of uproar north—and I think the Condition of parties now are so precarious & imminent that I do not wish to risk the democracy to such an exciting scene as would follow Douglas' defeat at Balto. I may err in my views—and things may not be as bad as they seem— I hope to God they are not—but they so appear to me.

I again ask pardon for thus addressing you with so much freedom; and if I have forfeited your good opinion, or wishes in any thing I have said, I assure you, it was from no want of respect, or of a proper appreciation of your eminent abilities.

I am, Very Respy   Yr obt svt.   A. G. Graham

ALS, DLC-JP2.

1. Graham, a Johnson supporter, was the editor of the Democratic Jonesboro *Union*. See *Johnson Papers*, II, 98n.

2. On May 15 and 16, 1860, Douglas clarified his position on slavery in the territories and stressed his support of the Cincinnati Platform of 1856, which had disapproved of federal interference with the institution. *Cong. Globe*, 36 Cong., 1 Sess., App. 301–6.

3. In accepting the Democratic nomination in 1856, Buchanan acknowledged that each state was free to legislate independently concerning the establishment or abolition of slavery—a principle which he also stressed in his inaugural. Breckinridge, speaking in Lexington, Kentucky, on June 10, 1856, similarly declared his support of the noninterference plank of the Cincinnati platform. Moore, *Works of Buchanan*, X, 83; Richardson, *Messages*, V, 431–32; Cincinnati *Enquirer*, June 13, 1856.

4. In an effort to marshal evidence that the bulk of the Democracy had long stood for nonintervention with slavery in the territories, Douglas cited resolutions of the Florida and Georgia legislatures in 1847 and of the latter in 1854, as well as speeches and public letters of such party stalwarts as Yancey, Davis, Brown, Pierce, and many others. *Cong. Globe*, 36 Cong., 1 Sess., App. 301–16.

5. Lincoln had been nominated at Chicago on May 18. Hesseltine, *Three against Lincoln*, 171.

6. William Montgomery (1818–1870), Pennsylvania Democratic congressman (1857–61), was not a candidate for reelection in 1860, although he unsuccessfully sought renomination in 1866. A strong Douglas supporter, Montgomery knocked down a "Buchaneer" who attacked him in Baltimore. *BDAC*, 1347; Milton, *Eve of Conflict*, 471, 473.

7. The salary differential between senators and the vice president amounted to a third rather than a half. By an 1856 law, senators received $6,000; since 1853, the vice president had been receiving $8,000. *U. S. Statutes*, X, 212; XI, 48.

8. In 1858 Montgomery had attempted to steer through the House an amendment to the Senate's Kansas bill whereby the Lecompton Constitution would have been resubmitted to the people. Milton, *Eve of Conflict*, 291, 431, 469, 473; *Cong. Globe*, 35 Cong., 1 Sess., 1192–99.

9. William H. Crouch, wealthy Jonesboro farmer. See *Johnson Papers*, I, 418n.

From Joseph Powell

May 24, 1860, Greenville, S. C.; ALS, DLC-JP2.

Requests appointment in Indian agency or some other department as reward for thirty years' service "to the Union and to democratic principles"; comments that "politics are pretty hot—in South Carolina just now —But the *Union is in no danger at all*—these mad-Cap-disunionists in the South will consume themselves, and the Sooner the better. I Suppose that the Richmond and Baltimore conventions will meet and agree to disagree and this will be the end of all conventions of the kind for all future time—it is most devoutly to be hoped for at least for the peace of the Country."

From J. E. S. Blackwell[1]

Knoxville Tenn May 28th 1860.

Hon Andrew Johnson
Washington D. C.

Dear Sir

Several years ago, Congress appropriated Fifty Thousand Dollars for the improvement of the Tennessee River above the "Suck"[2] extending to Knoxville. This work was put in charge of Col. McClelland[3] of the U. S. Army as Engineer in chief. my self and others were appointed by the Secretary of War as assistants. We devoted nearly two years faithfully to this work, until the appropriation was expended and the further improvement of the River was suspended. At the time the work was stopped there was not enough of the appropriation left to pay all that was due by about Five or Six Thousand Dollars, consequently we, the Assistants of Col McClelland, got nothing for our services for nearly of all [sic] the last year[.] after paying off the Laborers employed on the several works there was none of the appropriation left, indeed there was not quite enough for that, this deficiency being advanced by one of the assistants.

In one month after the work was suspended Col McClelland, the Engineer in Chief, and who had chief control of the work, *died* before he had time to make a full report of his operations in reference to this matter and hence the difficulty in regard to our pay as Assistant Engineers,— had Col. McClelland not *died* we would not of [sic] had any difficulty in getting our pay, would have received it as soon as the facts could have been reported by him to the proper department. Our only chance since his death was to apply to Congress which we did some three or four years ago, and in the early part of this Session the House of Representatives passed a Bill for our relief[4] which has been before the Senate for sometime.

We have been deprived of the use of this money justly due us for more than six years, and, I assure you, that every one of us absolutely need it.

Can I under the circumstances, and as a personal and political friend of yours, one who has stood up for you in all your struggles in Tennessee appeal to you in my behalf in this matter, to ask you to call up this Bill in the Senate at once and have it passed? If called up I apprehend there would be no opposition, I at least have assurances there would be none, to it,—in the House there was none. As Congress is approaching to a close it is necessary that whatever is done should be done quickly—at once, for if the Bill be suffered to lie upon the table and expire with the Session our work will all be to do over again, and we deprived of our money justly due us still longer and which we ought to have had more than six years ago. It is a small matter to the government, but one of importance to us, and I hope as a friend of yours, and being the Senator from our division of the State that you will at once call up this matter, take it in hand and push it through the Senate. I would be much obliged to hear from you in regard to this matter *soon*, and any other topic you may choose to write about.[5]

Very truly your friend
J E S Blackwell

ALS, DLC-JP2.

1. J. E. S. Blackwell was a Knoxville saddler. *Williams' Knoxville Directory* (1859–60), 37.

2. The stretch of thirty miles of treacherous water on the Tennessee just below Chattanooga, originally known as the Narrows and more recently as the Grand Canyon, was often locally referred to as the "Suck," the name given by early boatmen to the first of the downstream obstacles. Tennessee State Planning Commission, *The Tennessee River Gorge: A Report to the 1961 General Assembly* (Nashville, 1961), 8; Donald Davidson, *The Tennessee* (2 vols., New York, 1946), II, 12.

3. John McClellan (*c*1805–1854), a native of Pennsylvania and brother of George B. McClellan, was a West Point graduate (1826), served in the Mexican War, and died of cholera in Knoxville in August, 1854. *Goodspeed's Knox*, 844; *West Point Register* (1953), 160.

4. On February 16, 1860, H. R. 89 was introduced to liquidate the unadjusted contracts for the Tennessee River improvement project. Reported out of committee on March 30, the proposal passed. *Cong. Globe*, 36 Cong., 1 Sess., 810, 1462–63.

5. On May 18, 1860, the Senate committee on claims reported H. R. 89 with a recommendation for passage. When Lyman Trumbull of Illinois objected, further consideration was postponed until, with Johnson's help, it was again taken up on June 8 and approved. *Ibid.*, 2168, 2750.

From Jeptha Fowlkes

Memphis Ten. May 28/60.

Private

Hon. A. Johnson
My dear Sir:

I find the friends of Senator Douglass firm & fastly attached to his fortunes! I seen gentlemen from Ark. & Mississippi, who insist the people are for Douglass—& that, "the war" on him, is, by political aspirants for Presidency! Your friends hope to See you nominated if Douglass be not at Baltimore— Your course & Senator Nicholson's, so far, as I can learn, is, *universally* approved! I shall return in a day or so—

Yr. friend,   J. Fowlkes.

P. S. It is insisted that Benjamin's Speech[1] is made by Slidell & Bright, in fact—it has not made much impression, so far as I can learn here! On the cars & *here*, the war on Douglass is not held to be a war of principle—but from "the calculations of rivalry"— Inter nos—I simply give facts which I pick up—

ALS, DLC-JP2.

1. Louisiana Senator Judah P. Benjamin's May 22 speech in reply to Douglas attacked the "Little Giant" on the popular sovereignty doctrine, defended the bolters at Charleston, and charged that the Illinois senator, interested solely in his own candidacy, had both reneged on his bargain to abide by the decisions of the Supreme Court and split the party. This vigorous attack was in line with the campaign being waged by Senators Slidell of Louisiana and Bright of Indiana, two administration spokesmen determined to see that Douglas did not receive the presidential nomination. Both were at Charleston, "working the wires." Slidell, according to Murat Halstead, was "the power behind the throne," with the "special mission . . . to see that Stephen A. Douglas is not nominated for the Presidency." Bright was a leader of the Indiana anti-Douglas delegation upon which the administration vainly pinned its hope of capturing the northwest Democracy from Douglas. *Cong. Globe*, 36 Cong., 1 Sess., 2233–41; Murat Halstead, quoted in Sears, *John Slidell*, 162–63; Nevins, *Emergence of Lincoln*, II, 201–2.

From University of Georgia Demosthenian Society

May 28, 1860, Athens, Ga.; ALS, DLC-JP2.

Harrison Wells, corresponding secretary of the society, informs Johnson of his election to honorary membership.

From William M. Lowry

Greenv Ten May 29 1860

Gov Johnson
Dear Sir

I recd the enclosed letter from N Gammon[1] to day, (and wishing to say to our freind Blackwell If he Should here after make enquiry of me) that I had written you herewith enclose you Mr Gammon letter that will explain to you what is wanted[.] I know nothing, of the merits of this claim, and if I did would not expect to influence your Coarse in the matter[.] All that I can say is that Mr. Blackwell is a verry worthy man[.] If all those associated with him in this claim[2] were as correct a man as he is I would be better Satisfyed with Seeing it pass. I was at Knoxville attending court last week and Seen a good many of our freinds and found a diversity of opinion amongst our freinds as to who Should be the Candidate of the Democracy, for the Presidency. Some are advocating the importance of Sending delegates to Richmond, in fact I Should not be Surprised if some delegates attend that Convention from Tennessee[.] this I think all wrong. if We expect to suceede in the next Canvass, we must stand United. I fear that this Douglass furor has gone So far that it will be impossible to Unite our forces. the more I think about it the more I am Convinced that Judge Douglass aught under the Circumstances to decline the Contest and at once Announce the fact and let a new man be braught forward. I am free to admit that I Could cheerfully vote for Judge Douglass if he were the Candidate of our Party yet a number of verry indiscreet freinds and news papers both North and South are so committed that I do not See how they could come up to his Support and that it would be an uphill business to get him along in the South, the nomination of Mr Bell falls below what I had anticipated. No enthusiasm[.] No excitement. I was fearful they would nominate Genl Houston and when it was announced that Bell was the, Nominee I felt releived as I think Bell can rally no excite-ment[.] in fact I do not think he can get a State in the Union particu-larly, if our freinds make a judicious Nomination at Baltimore. I thought probably the Nomination of Bell might bring your Name more prominantly before the Country. I had one or two talks with Maj Lyons,[3] who told me he would attend the Baltimore Conven-tion[.] he thinks with me that if you Could once get fairly before the Country, that you Could be elected. I am pleased to see that the RRoads have reduced the fare from this to Baltimore[.][4] I hear of a number talking of going[.] I hope and trust that its deliberations may result in harmonizeing the various Conflicting elements and once more unite and harmonize the invincible Democracy of the Union when triumph and victory will be Certain.

with much regard   Yr freind & Obt Servt.
Wm M Lowry.

ALS, DLC-JP2.

1. Nathan Gammon, earlier a Jonesboro merchant and now clerk of the U. S. court in Knoxville, had written Lowry on behalf of Blackwell on May 28, 1860, the same day the latter wrote Johnson. Johnson Papers, LC; *Wil-liams' Knoxville Directory* (1859–60), 53; see also *Johnson Papers*, I, 418n.

2. Lowry refers to Charles W. Charlton and James C. Luttrell, both of Knoxville. See Letter from James C. Luttrell, April 5, 1860; Charles W. Charlton to Andrew Johnson, Johnson Papers, LC.

3. Thomas M. Lyon (b. *c*1825), a Knox County farmer with personal property worth $500 in 1860, was a delegate to the Charleston convention but does not appear in the list of delegates at Baltimore. 1860 Census, Tenn., Knox, 234; Nashville *Union and American*, June 22, 1860.

4. The Nashville and Chattanooga Railroad announced on May 29, 1860, that it was offering half-fare tickets to convention delegates bound for Balti-more. The normal fare from Nashville to Baltimore was $25.75. *Ibid.*, May 29, 1860.

From Joseph S. Wilson[1]

General Land Office
June 2d 1860

Hon A. Johnson
U S. Senate

Sir

In reply to your note of this morning as to the "amount of land that will fall to the States under the Graduation Act of 1854 at the expiration of thirty years," that is land in the fourth[?] class at 12½¢ per Acre.[2] I have the honor to enclose herewith a statement showing by estimate the acres on the 1 Jany 1860 in each of the States subject to entry at 12½¢ pr acre[.]

For details of the law the public lands have been in market as well as the quantity classified according to the Graduation Act of Aug. 4 1854, I respectfully refer you to Ex Doct No 13[3] 1st Sess 34 Congress[.]

Very respectfully   Your obt Servt
Jos Wilson   Commissioner

Estimate of the area of public lands in each of the States on the 1st January 1860 remaining unsold after having been liable to entry for thirty years[.][4]

Ohio	5,000 Acres		Missouri	1,037,000 Acres
Indiana	5,000 "		Florida	— 000 "
Illinois	30,000 "		Alabama	4,900,000 "
Michigan	56,000 "		Louisiana	903,000 "
Wisconsin	— 000 "		Mississippi	2,872,000 "
Iowa	— 000 "		Minnesota	— 000 "
Arkansas	2,408,000 "			

Copy, DNA-RG49, Misc. Let. Sent (M25).

1. Joseph S. Wilson of Washington, D. C., was a career civil servant in the land office of the department of the interior. Appointed principal clerk of private land claims in 1851, he had risen by 1860 to the position of chief clerk of the land office and later served as interim commissioner (1860–61) and commissioner (1866–71). *U. S. Official Register* (1851), 135; Lanman, *Biographical Annals*, 471.

2. For Johnson's discussion of graduation policy, see Speech on Amendment to Homestead Bill, April 11, 1860.

3. *House Ex. Doc.* No. 13, 34 Cong., 1 Sess.; "An Act to Graduate and Reduce the Price of the Public Lands to actual Settlers and Cultivators," August 4, 1854, *U. S. Statutes*, X, 574.

4. Johnson quotes these figures in his Speech on Homestead Bill Veto, June 23, 1860.

From Ferdie McClelland[1]

At home June 3d 1860

Hon Andrew Johnson
    Sir

You will remember I visited Washington a few months since, and asked your assistance in procuring me an appointment to West Point, which appointment I failed to get. Since that time I have been studying in my own room, to the improvement of my education, as well as acquiring general information, which course I expect to pursue. My aspirations are all-most entirely political, and I have chosen your character as a model, hoping to be profited by the example, which your perseverence, & decision of character or determination of purpose, have afforded me, in which respects I am deficient.

The object of my letter is simply to ask you to send me a photograph of yours, of as large size as is convenient. By doing this you will oblige an admirer of your character as well as a private political friend[.]

Respectfully   Ferdie McClelland
Address ⎱ Cornersville
        ⎰ Giles Ct Tenn

ALS, DLC-JP2.
1. Probably F. S. McClelland, a private in Company "G," later "B," 3rd Tennessee infantry (Clack's), CSA. *Tennesseans in the Civil War*, II, 270.

From William M. Lowry

Office of Lowry & Eason,
Greeneville, Tenn. June 4 1860

Hon A Johnson
Dear Sir

one of my assistants Capt J C Vaughn writes me that Judge Rowles will not attend the Baltimore Convention and that he is the alternate and wishes to know if I can give him leave of absence. he is your friend and wishes to go to advance the Johnson interest. I have written him that I want him to go, that if the Census is completed early in August I presume it will be in time[.] he can go and return in some 10 days and I think complete his work pretty early in August. I have written the Hon Mr Kennedy[1] Census office to know the longest time that can be given the assistants to complete their work[.] have not heard from him yet[.] My men are all at work and I flatter my self they will do it up promptly. If I understand the law authorizes the Census takers untill 1st Nov to complete their work, tho in all the instructions and intimations I get from the Department they desire it done in a much shorter time and I have impressed it upon my assistants that they must complete their work by 1st August[.]

We held a Demo Meeting to day appointing delegates to a District Convention to nominate a Demo Candidate for Elector[.] We also endorsed the course of the Tennessee delegation in the Charleston Convention in still clinging to the old Ship and not jumping out into the whirl wind. We had a pretty large attendance and more enthusiasm than we generally have at our little County Meeting[.] We recommended no one for Elector tho the feeling was very decided for Maxwell[.][2] the oppo[sition] had a Meeting here the Week I was at Knoxville selecting their Elector and nominated Bradford[3] of Jefferson. I am told their speakers were awfully abusive of Democratic Men and Measures. I notice in the papers this morning that the President had appointed Wm. M Churchell a Minister to Guatemala[.] I presume it was a missprint and that it was ment for Wm M Churchwell[.] if so I regret it and think it a verry unfortunate appointment and one that the real Democracy condems and one that will be hard to defend[.][4] I must think the President has been badly imposed upon[.] however in all this I may be mistaken as probably the Tennessee delegation seconded the move, yet I can hardly think that you did as you & I have talkd this thing over heretofore and agreed in Sentiment[.] We have many accidents upon our road. this morning on the up Train some 7 miles this side of Knoxville We had a bad accident[.][5] the Cars run off and killed Grant the Engineer and Dempsy[?] the fireman[.] I am debating the pro[s]pects of my going to the Convention, were it not that my assistants are writing me every mail about instructions &c I would not hesitate a moment, tho I am no delegate Could act as a Lobby Member. I am against abandoning the Demo Ship[.] If I cannot get all I want I am willing to take what I can get, and cling to the old vessel in the hope that here-after by working manfully at our post We may get our vessel righted and once more upon a Smooth Sea. this is County Court day. Next week Circuit Court[.] More people & strangers about than I have Seen and business first rate[.] We have never had so fine a business[.] it is work work all the time[.] it has been so long since I have heard from you that I have allmost forgot your hand[.] Write[.]

                                        Yr friend   Wm M Lowry

ALS, DLC-JP2.

1. Joseph C. G. Kennedy (1813–1887) was superintendent of both the seventh (1850) and eighth (1860) censuses. Following a European tour in 1851 to examine statistical systems in other countries, he helped organize the First International Statistical Congress which met in Brussels in 1853 and was secretary of the U. S. commission to the World's Fair in London in 1857. *DAB*, X, 335.

2. William Henry Maxwell.

3. William M. Bradford (*c*1827–1895), a Jefferson County merchant and state senator (1859–61), declined the appointment made on May 26; J. W. Deaderick of Jonesboro was later selected. Robison Biog. Data; Nashville *Republican Banner*, June 5, 1860; Nashville *Patriot*, July 23, August 26, 1860.

4. Churchwell was objectionable to Lowry and his friends not only because he was a Bank Democrat, but also because he belonged to the faction, unfriendly to Johnson, which controlled the Knoxville *Register*. Nominated for the Guatemalan post, Churchwell declined; it was rumored that Johnson and Nicholson would have opposed the appointment in the Senate. Knoxville *Whig*, March 17, 1860; Turner, William Montgomery Churchwell, 75–79.

5. On Sunday night, June 3, at Caswells, seven miles east of Knoxville, torrential rains washed out a culvert, causing a train to derail. While no passengers were seriously hurt, Donald Grant, engineer, and Mr. Moody, fireman, were killed, and the locomotive "Jefferson" was completely wrecked. Knoxville *Whig*, June 9, 1860.

From Washington C. Whitthorne

Columbia Te June 5 '60

Gov. Andrew Johnson.

Dear Sir:

Yr acknowledgment of receipt of mine of 8th. ult came duly to hand. I now think it more than probable that I will be in Washington in about ten days. I have seen no reason to change my opinion as to things in Tennessee since I last wrote you. Bell's nomination is recd. very coldly, and the only consolation derived by the KNs.[1] in the present attitude of affairs, is from our disorganization[.] Their only hope of life & dignity is Douglass nomination. But of these things, when I see you, if I come on as I hope to do. What think you of Genl. P's letter, recently published.[2] He endorses the opinions of Judge Taney, yet endorses Douglass. Oil & water! Is it not better to say Douglass is wrong at once & take him as the best under the circumstances if we have it to do.

Very truly yours W. C. Whitthorne

ALS, DLC-JP.

1. Whitthorne and others took satisfaction in equating the Bell-Everett Constitutional Union party with the old Know-Nothing movement.

2. In a letter dated May 28, 1860, addressed to dissident Democrats from the Charleston convention, Gideon J. Pillow attempted to reconcile Douglas' position on popular sovereignty with Chief Justice Taney's Dred Scott deci-

sion. Pointing out that the Supreme Court had denied the national government the power to regulate slavery in the territories, Pillow argued that consequently the people of potential states might determine whether they wished to be free or slave; therefore, Douglas' policy was not in conflict with Taney's decision. Nashville *Union and American*, June 8, 1860.

From Blackston McDannel

June 6, 1860, Greeneville; ALS, DLC-JP2.

Requests a document relative to the claims of Nancy C. Parman, and, inquiring about price of land warrants in Washington, observes: "I am opposed to the homestead, until I sell off my warrants, and then I dont care a damn.—Will it pass soon?"

From Hugh Graham[1]

Tazewell East Tennessee.
[June 7, 1860]

Hon. A. Johnson
Senate U. S.

Dear Sir.   Your labors in the Senate Homestead Bill &C have not had much time to send out many public documents.

Please send me Mr. Benjamins speech[2] in reply to Mr. Douglass in the Senate. I would thank you also for copies of the Coast Survey, Maps of these New Territories & specially for a copy of the Indian (last) Report from the Indian Bureau. Any of these are interesting to the home reader, and we can only look for them from the members & Senators of Congress, who will take the trouble & be at the kindness to send them to us.

The Baltimore Convention, 18th, will soon come on & you will doubtless be there.[3] But few events, for many years has created so much anxiety everywhere & doubts exist if they will again divide & make a wider split than that at Charleston. I sincerely hope, as a man of much influence, that you will use all your influence & power to promote peace & harmony, & nominate some good man that all can unite on, & let Platform go.

My Dear Sir, another division in the Democratic ranks will be fatal to our party. Now in my 75th year I greatly desire to see the sceptre continued & held by good Democratic Presidents as long as I live; all of which I ardently hope, by wise & united counsels at Baltimore.

My best wishes for your good health, & safe return to your family in Tennessee.

Hu Graham.

P. S. For the last two weeks we have scarcely had more than two dry days together & much of the rain fell heavy accompanied with hail, but not any storms that I have heard, in East Tennessee. What little wheat is left, will I fear be injured by the rust.

By the present Census the Southern States will greatly loose.[4] A large number of families have left for their summer tour before the first of June and no heads of families reports strangers to the Census taker after or at this time.

H. G.

ALS, DLC-JP2.

1. Hugh Graham (b. c1785), a native of Ireland, was a pioneer settler of Claiborne County and a Tazewell merchant of some means, possessing nearly $40,000 in real and personal property. 1860 Census, Tenn., Claiborne, 176; Goodspeed's East Tennessee, 849, 1211.

2. Speech of May 22, 1860. Cong. Globe, 36 Cong., 1 Sess., 2233–41.

3. Johnson, preoccupied with the recent veto of the homestead bill, prudently stayed in Washington during the convention.

4. As early as April, 1860, the New York Times predicted an overall net loss for the South and a loss of one congressional seat for Tennessee—a prediction reprinted in the Nashville Union and American of April 17. Actually, Tennessee lost two seats, although her total population increased by over one hundred thousand. Nichols, Disruption of Democracy, 453; DeBow, 1850 Census, Compendium, 61, 82, 83, 102; Kennedy, 1860 Census, Population, 465.

From Lamson Goodnow & Company

June 8, 1860, New York, N.Y.; ALS, DLC-JP2.

Asks the senator, on behalf of several companies interested in hardware, to present the enclosed petition objecting to the proposed tariff increase on steel and to move its reference to the committee on finance. [Johnson apparently ignored this petition.]

From William K. Heiskell[1]

Abingdon Va June 8, 1860

My Dear Sir

A vacancy occurring by the death of Judge Daniel[2] of the United States Supreme Court and a possibility of Judge Brockenborough,[3] the present Judge of the District Court of the United States receiving that appointment or promotion.

I take the liberty of, addressing you as an acquaintance, & friend, upon the subject.

In the event Judge Brockenborough should (be promoted) receive the appointment as associate Judge on the Supreme Bench, May I be permitted to ask your aid and assistance in advancing the

interest & claims of my friend John W. Johnston[4] Esqr. than whom
there is no superior as a Jurist in our section of the state[.]

Mr Johnston is a Democrat & one of the most reliable at that, he
is one of the cleverest men living, and one of the few Lawyers that
attends well truly and strictly to his cases, and has the energy &
will to attend strictly & closely to his business[.]

Individually it would suit me best that he should remain where
he is, but he has such high claims as a jurist, gentleman, & in every
capacity in life I must ask your kind aid & assistance in getting this
appointment[.]

I say appointment, yet there may be no vacancy, for if Judge
Brockenborough is not put upon the Supreme bench there will be
no vacancy, but I write this early that every thing may be upon the
way, in the event the vacancy in the Dist Court should occur[.]

Mr Wigfall a senator from Texas was a class mate of Mr J & will
no doubt give you any information in relation to Mr J, early history,
so will Mr Boyce[5] of the Ho of Rep.

A letter yesterday from our mutual friend Lowrey says "Tennessee is right side up." I suppose politically[.]

Very Truly   Yr Friend & Obt Sevt
Wm. King Heiskell

ALS, DLC-JP2.

1. William K. Heiskell, sheriff (1860–62, 1864–65) of Washington
County, Virginia, had been a member of the Virginia house of delegates
(1852–53, 1855). Lewis P. Summers, *History of Southwest Virginia* (Richmond, 1913), 818, 830.

2. Peter V. Daniel (1784–1860), a Stafford County Democrat, studied
law under Edmund Randolph, became a member of the Virginia legislature
(1809), served on the privy council (1812–35), and was judge of the U. S.
district court before becoming a Supreme Court justice (1841–60). *DAB*,
V, 69.

3. John W. Brockenbrough (1806–1877) of Lexington, Virginia, did
not succeed Daniel. Judge of the U. S. court for western Virginia (1846–60),
Brockenbrough represented his state at the Peace Conference of 1861, served
in the Confederate Congress, and after the war became head of the newly
created law school at Washington and Lee. Oren F. Morton, *A History of
Rockbridge County, Virginia* (Staunton, Va., 1920), 246–47.

4. John W. Johnston (1818–1889) of Abingdon was Commonwealth's
attorney (1845), state senator (1847–49, 1869–82), Confederate receiver
for the southwestern district of Virginia, circuit judge (1867–69) and practiced law in Washington, D. C., where for a time he acted as attorney for the
Northern Pacific Railroad. Lyon G. Tyler, ed., *Encyclopedia of Virginia Biography* (5 vols., New York, 1915), IV, 539–41.

5. William W. Boyce (1819–1890) of Winnsborough, South Carolina,
served as a State Rights Democrat in Congress (1853–60), was a member
of the Confederate Congress (1861–64), and for several years after 1866
practiced law in Washington, D. C. *BDAC*, 582.

From Thomas J. Usrey[1]

Fayetteville Ark June 8th/60

Hon A. Johnson
Dear Sir

Since your name was placed before the people of U States for the Presidency your position on many important [issues which] have agitated the public mind for years past have been variously represented[.] On the 'Homestead Bill' you have been wilfully misrepresented, by certain persons adherents of what [is] known as the Johnsonian Faction. The Clique is headed by R. H. Johnson,[2] Democratic Candidate for Governor of Ark. The foregoing statement is made for purpose of explaining the following request that you Send me if Convenient your Inaugural of Oct 1853, Speech on the Harper Ferry foray & the Speech de[li]vered on the presentation of the Bell Resolutions condemning the course of Mr. Bell[.]

As I shall commence the publication of a Democratic party [newspaper] in this city as soon as the necessary arrangements can be completed,[3] I will embrace every opportunity [of] placing right before the masses of North West Arkansas. You have many friends in this part of the West. One fourth of this people have heard you on the stump in old Tenn[.] You will doubtless recognize in the Signature of the undersigned a resident (of formerly) Alexandria in Dekalb, also Sparta[.]

I am with high regard   Your friend &c
T. J. Usrey

ALS, DLC-JP2.

1. Thomas J. Usrey (b. *c*1831), listed as a physician in the 1860 census, was a DeKalb County delegate to the Nashville Democratic convention of 1856 but had moved to Arkansas. Nashville *Union and American*, January 10, 1856; John L. Ferguson, Arkansas state historian, to Andrew Johnson Project, October 8, 1970.

2. Richard H. Johnson (1826–1891), brother of Senator Robert W. Johnson, was nominated for governor in 1860 by questionable methods and subsequently defeated. The principal issue in the campaign was the "Johnson Family" rule of the state from 1836 to 1860. *DAB*, X, 118; Josiah H. Shinn, *Pioneers and Makers of Arkansas* (Baltimore, 1967 [1908]), 205.

3. The Fayetteville *Democrat*, a weekly, was printed from August 10, 1860, until sometime in 1861. Gregory, *Union List of Newspapers*, 23; Ferguson to Johnson Project, October 22, 1970.

From Lizinka Campbell Brown

Nashville 12th June 1860

To Hon: Andrew Johnson
My dear Sir

I have delayed answering your last letter first because I have been suffering from that sort of ill-health which makes any exertion painful, and next I have been waiting to be able to tell you Mrs. Bell had released me from my promise to rent her this house—[1] in this however I have been disappointed— She made a suggestion that the number of servants' children rendered the price I asked rather unreasonable & I wrote her a note that I would decline renting so early as the 1st. July & notified Mr. Watson[2] the house would be for rent during the summer—but Mrs Bell came up yesterday & reminded me she had applied first—had been much disappointed &c & if it was rented at all claimed the refusal of it— I could not without acting unhandsomely evade it & so the matter stands— I have not promised to rent it to her at any particular time but to let her have the refusal after we are gone— This is a small matter amid the National questions to which your attention is now turned but as you seemed to take some interest in it I prefer your knowing exactly how it is managed.

A great deal of interest is of course felt here about the Conventions at Richmond and Baltimore— Every one is alive to the immense importance of harmony in the Democratic party but I do not see how it is to be obtained— The prejudice in the South against Douglas is very great and I suppose he possesses little of the heroism which induces a man to sacrifice his personal advancement to the good of his country—and yet in his case the sacrifice would be only apparent— Young as he is he could well afford to wait four years and were he now to withdraw his name in favor of a more universally acceptable candidate it seems to me he would be nominated by acclaim in 1864 and carried into the presidency with an enthusiasm such as we have not seen since the days of Jackson— I wish I had seen more of Douglas when in Washington— He is certainly one of the foremost men of the age and whether or not he becomes President he wields immense power—

We expect to leave here in about a month for a twelve month's sojourn in Europe— I am so much the slave of habit & association that I dread the change very much—but think it cannot but be of advantage to Campbell and Harriot to see something for themselves of the habits & customs of other countries & thus learn the better to appreciate their own—notwithstanding the abuses which have crept into every department of our Government not excepting the War Department— It is a striking comment on Mr Buchanan's declining to appoint Capt. Ewell[3] Pay master on account of the number of Pay masters from Virginia & the Superior services of Capt. Rhett[4] —that he has since appointed two civilans from Virginia Pay masters — I wish he knew we are aware of it—and consequently sympathize with the Covode committee[5] in their success at ferretting out abuses — but I expect you are tired of this stupid letter so will bore you no longer[.]

Your Sincere friend   L. C. Brown

ALS, DLC-JP2.

1. See Letter from Lizinka Campbell Brown, March 30, 1860.
2. Probably Samuel Watson (1807–1876), a Massachusetts native who came to Nashville in 1849; he was a lawyer and civic leader, serving as a trustee of both the University of Nashville (1867) and the Peabody Education Fund, as president of the state teachers' association (1870), and as a member of the state board of education (1875). McGavock, *Pen and Sword*, 376n.
3. Richard S. Ewell, her cousin and future husband.
4. Thomas G. Rhett (1821–1878) of South Carolina, a graduate of West Point (1845) and a major general in the Confederate army, was at this time a paymaster in the war department. *U. S. Official Register* (1859), 112; Barnwell Rhett Heyward, "The Descendants of Col. William Rhett of South Carolina," *South Carolina Historical and Genealogical Magazine*, IV (1903), 59.
5. As much to embarrass Buchanan as to ascertain the truth, the House on March 5, 1860, appointed a committee, chaired by "Honest John" Covode of Pennsylvania, to investigate the administration's use of money, patronage, or other means to influence local elections or congressional legislation. Hearings, which began in late March and lasted until early June, revealed irregularities, patronage abuse, bribery, and incompetence on the part of administration officials. Nevins, *Emergence of Lincoln*, II, 196–200.

From John J. Hofman

June 12, 1860, Massillon, Ohio; ALS, DLC-JP2.

Postmaster and news dealer, requesting copies of speeches, complains: "In this District we are represented by a Black Republican (Mr Edgerton) consequently get nothing but Republican speeches except it be speeches of Mr Dougless[*sic*] & his especial friends[.]"

To Blackston McDannel, Greeneville

Senate Chamber June 12th 1860

B. McDannel Esqr

I have just returned from the pension offic with the enclosed certificate which is bette than the mode you propose— You Can proceed upon this as you would with the other proof— You Can attach this certificate to the warrant or if you will Send the warrant to me the Commission will place the certificate on the face of the warrant —either of the three modes as I understand from the Commission— It would be perhaps bette to make the assign[men]t in the w[a]y you have been accustomd to do—

You ought to tell Nancy Carolin Parmon that you have had about as much trouble as her forty acree warrant is worth, where as She will be [sic] hardly be willing to pay you any thing for your trouble — Let this all pass for what it is worth— I feel well paid in the Success I met with in h[a]ving the decision of the Commission reversed— I hope it will do Nancy Some good—[1]

What will become of the presidency next mondy no one Can tell —[2] all seems to be Confusion and doubt— And unless there is some strai[gh]t[en]ing up with the democratic party and the introduction of harmony, defeat will follow as certain as the nomination is made[.] I fear the Chances are against us under the most favorable Circumstances and with distruction and abitter contest among our own frinds makes defeat absolutely certain—

I have a promise from the Secretary of the Interior[3] of one appointment in [the] census bureau when the appointmts are made— Congress will adjourn on the 28th I think and not before—

As ever your frind   Andrew Johnson

ALS, DLC-JP.

1. The claim of Nancy C. Parmon, minor heir of William Jones, was validated by the attorney general under the Bounty Act of 1850 and she received a warrant for forty acres. See George G. Whiting to Andrew Johnson, May 25, 1860, Johnson Papers, LC.

2. The adjourned Democratic convention was scheduled to meet in Baltimore on Monday, June 18.

3. Jacob Thompson of Mississippi. See *Johnson Papers*, I, 303n.

From Thomas A. Rogers

June 14, 1860, Quarryville; ALS, DLC-JP2.

Requests a patent office report and observes: "It is hoped that the Democracy will settle their differences at Baltimore and unite on some man that will be acceptable to all. I think Douglas is the strongest man we can run, tho' some have doubts of his fidelity to the south. If I understand his views on the slavery question rightly I think he is right as I believe in his doctrine of 'non intervention and popular sovereignty.' "

From Joseph S. Wilson

General Land Office   June 15 1860

Hon Andrew Johnson
U. S. Senate
Sir,

In reply to your note of this morning[1] I have the honor to state that no tabular statement has been prepared showing in detail the extent of the amount of land remaining unsold and subject to private entry.

Our estimate of 80000 000 [eighty million] Acres was a round one, land above the aggregate of offerings & sales of other disposals[.]

Very respectfully   Your Obt Sert
Jos Wilson   Comm

Copy, DNA-RG49, Misc. Let. Sent (M25).

1. Evidently Johnson was continuing his efforts to accumulate data to be used in support of the homestead bill. See Letter from Joseph Wilson, June 2, 1860.

To Sam Milligan, Baltimore, Md.

Washington City, June 18, 1860.

Gen. Samuel Milligan: —Dear Sir: —Whilst deeply thankful to you and your associate delegates in the National Convention for your support of my name as a candidate for the Presidency, endorsing and reflecting therein the honor done me by the State Convention of the Democracy of Tennessee, an honor and distinction given my name, by the people whom I have served and whose confidence is worthy of the best efforts and highest ambition of any man, yet in this hour of peril to the harmony and integrity of the Democratic party—in this hour of serious apprehension for the future welfare and perpetuity of our government, I cannot and will not suffer my name to add to the difficulties and embarrassment of my friends.

I feel that it is incumbent upon you, upon me, that everything that can honorably and consistently be done, should be done by us to secure unity and harmony of action, to the end that correct principles may be maintained, the preservation of the only national organization remaining continued, and, above all, that the Union, with the blessings, guaranties, and protection of its constitution, be perpetuated forever.

That the Tennessee delegation may so act, and that in no contingency they may find themselves embarrassed by the action of our State in regard to myself, I desire through you to request that they will not present my name to the Convention at Baltimore,[1] and to each of them tender my regards. I have the honor to be, &c.,

Andrew Johnson

Nashville *Union and American*, June 21, 1860; also found in New York *Times*, June 20, 1860.

1. Johnson's name was never brought before the ill-starred Baltimore convention which limped along from its opening on June 18 until June 23 when the anti-Douglas faction seceded. The same day each group nominated its slate—Breckinridge and Lane; Douglas and H. V. Johnson—and adjourned. Hesseltine, *Three against Lincoln, passim.*

Conference Committee Report on Homestead Bill[1]

June 19, 1860

Mr. JOHNSON, of Tennessee, from the committee of conference on the disagreeing votes of the two Houses on the bill (S. No. 416) to secure homesteads to actual settlers on the public domain, and for other purposes, made the following report:

The committee of conference on the disagreeing votes of the two Houses on the bill (S. No. 416) to secure homesteads to actual settlers on the public domain, and for other purposes, having met, and after a free and full conference, they have agreed to recommend, and do recommend, to the respective Houses, as follows:

That the House of Representatives do recede from its amendment to the bill of the Senate, and agree to the said bill of the Senate, (S. No. 416,) with the following amendments:

Section one, line eleven, strike out the word "and."

Section one, lines twelve and thirteen, strike out the words, "and become subject to private entry."

Section one, line nineteen, after the word "register," insert the words, "or receiver of said land office."

Section one, at the end thereof, insert:

Provided, That nothing in this section shall be so construed as to embrace, or in any way include, any quarter section, or fractional quarter section, of land upon which any preëmption right has been acquired prior to the passage of this act: *And provided further*, That all entries made under the provisions of this section upon lands which have not been offered for public sale, shall be confined to and upon sections designated by odd numbers.

Section seven, at the end thereof insert:

Provided further, That all persons who are preëmptors on the date of the passage of this act, shall, upon the payment to the proper authority of sixty-two and one half cents per acre,[2] if paid within two years from the passage of this act, be entitled to a patent from the Government, as now provided by the existing preëmption laws.

Strike out section eight.[3]

Section ten, line nine, after the word "time," insert the words, "after an actual settlement of six months, and."

And that the Senate do agree to the same.

ANDREW JOHNSON,
SIMON CAMERON,
Managers on the part of the Senate.
SCHUYLER COLFAX,
WILLIAM WINDOM,
Managers on the part of the House.[4]

Mr. JOHNSON, of Tennessee. I move a concurrence in the report of the committee of conference.

Mr. GWIN. I hope the Senator from Tennessee will permit it to lie over and be printed, and take a vote on it when the Senate is full. It is a very important question; and we have had a great deal of discussion about it. I am rather disposed, so far as I am concerned, to agree with the committee of conference; but I think we had better have a full vote on it. The Senate is not full;[5] and I think the Senator will accomplish his object entirely by letting it be printed and lie over until to-morrow.

Mr. LANE. Let him explain it.

Mr. GWIN. I have no objection to that at all.

Mr. JOHNSON, of Tennessee. I think the bill is well understood; and it is growing late in the session. There have been three committees of conference upon it; and I do not think the Senate will have any objection to what has been agreed upon. There are no material changes from the Senate bill. If the subject is not understood by the reading of the amendments, and if it is necessary to make any explanation, I will do it; but the bill has been before the Senate for a long time, and is well understood by both Houses; and I hope the Senator will not insist on the motion to postpone, and have it printed.[6]

Cong. Globe, 36 Cong., 1 Sess., 3159.

1. On May 21, 1860, Illinois Congessman Lovejoy's motion that the House teminate consideration of the Senate Homestead bill and substitute its own version passed by an overwhelming margin. However, the Senate refused to accept the substitute bill and three conference committees were required to resolve the differences. Johnson, who served on all three committees, here reports these recommendations for the third and final committee. *Cong. Globe*, 36 Cong., 1 Sess., 2221–22, 2462, 2813–14, 2846, 2862, 2955, 2998, 3038, 3159; Stephenson, *History of the Public Lands*, 210–11.

2. The Senate bill had provided that preëmptioners then on public lands could remain two years before being required to purchase the property at $1.25 per acre, thus in effect barring them from the benefits of the Homestead bill. *Ibid.*, 211.

3. Section eight would have benefited speculators by requiring the President to bring all public lands into market within two years. *Ibid.*

4. Notable for their absence from the committee report are the signatures of Senator Benjamin Fitzpatrick of Alabama and Representative M. R. H.

Garnett of Virginia, the two other southerners on the six-man conference committee. See Wigfall's comments in Speech on Homestead Bill Veto, June 23, 1860.

5. Thirty-eight of sixty-six senators were present and voting at the time. *Cong. Globe*, 36 Cong., 1 Sess., 3159.

6. When Joseph Lane of Oregon proposed that the measure be brought to a vote, it passed, 36–2. *Ibid.*

From J. C. Burch, F. C. Dunnington, and W. C. Whitthorne

Baltimore   June 22 1860.

To Hon Andrew Johnson
    34 Missouri Ave[1]
Our Senators and Representative[s] are earnestly requested to come here early to-morrow[.]

Burch Dunnington & Whittehorne

Tel, DLC-JP2.

1. Although Johnson normally stayed at the St. Charles Hotel, he may, because Mrs. Johnson and Robert were visiting Washington, have been temporarily residing in this Missouri Avenue boardinghouse run by Mary R. Stewart, a widow. *Boyd's Washington and Georgetown Directory* (1860), 93, 99, 142.

From William H. Carroll

Balt. twentythird. [June 23, 1860]

Hon. And. Johnson. Washn.

Your friends request your immediate presence. If not shall we act.

Wm. H. Carroll.

Tel, DLC-JP2.

From Sam Milligan and Frank C. Dunnington

Balto. Twentythird. [June 23, 1860]

Hon. Andrew Johnson, U. S. S. Washn.

If the withdrawing delegations from the moderate states north and south should recommend your name for the presidency would you object.

Samuel Millican.   F. C. Dunnington.

Tel, DLC-JP2.

Speech on Homestead Bill Veto[1]

June 23, 1860

Mr. JOHNSON, of Tennessee. Notwithstanding the veto message upon this homestead bill is a long one, and presents many arguments and statements as reasons for the veto, I am free to say that the message has not wrought the slightest change in my mind. The fact of these reasons being sent here by the President of the United States, it is true, entitles them to consideration; but their solidity and soundness are to be examined just the same as if they had been presented by anybody else; and the mere fact of a President of the United States vetoing a bill makes no change in my mind as to its propriety and constitutionality, unless he presents reasons and arguments which, if presented by others, would have the same effect. Now, to a correct understanding of this bill, and especially of what was done in the committee of conference, I will make a plain statement of facts.

The first section of the Senate bill, as it was originally, required all persons provided for in the bill, in making their entries, to be confined to land which had been surveyed and offered at public sale. The House bill extended to all land, whether surveyed or unsurveyed. The two bills differed in that respect. Further, the first section of the Senate bill confined its benefits to heads of families, and the House bill extended to all persons over twenty-one years of age. The Senate bill requires the President of the United States to bring all land into market within two years from the date of the survey or filing of the approved plats of survey with the proper officer. This was another difference. There was still a fourth difference. The tenth section of the bill, as it now stands, the eleventh section of the original Senate bill, provided that, at the expiration of thirty years, the lands unsold that had graduated down to the price of twelve and a half cents an acre should be surrendered to the States within which they lie.

These were the four leading points of difference between the House amendment and the Senate bill. A committee of conference[2] was raised. They conferred freely and frankly. The House committee insisted upon all persons twenty-one years of age being included. They insisted on the bill applying to all lands which had been surveyed, whether offered at public sale or not. They insisted on striking out the eighth section, which provided for bringing the lands into market within two years, and on striking out the eleventh section.

Finally, the committee on the part of the Senate agreed to let in persons twenty-one years of age, provided the House would let the other portion of the section stand, which confined it to the surveyed lands subject to sale at private entry. We agreed further, that, if they would let the eleventh section stand, we would strike out the eighth section of the bill. This, however, was not acceded to.

We had two committees of conference, and they could not agree. We got a third committee, and I am free to say here that I then came forward with a proposition in reference to the first section, proposing to confine it to heads of families, and to make one half of the unoffered lands subject to the operation of this bill. I further proposed that, if the House committee would agree to let the eleventh section remain in the bill, we would agree to strike out the eighth section. I made this proposition, however, on the express condition that I was not to be bound by it until I came into the Senate and consulted with friends on this side of the House as to the propriety of it. I made that a condition precedent, and I consulted with Senators on this side before I ventured even to accede to my own proposition; and after a full and free consultation here with them, receiving their sanction and countenance, I went back to the committee, and it was agreed upon; and the bill now stands in that shape.

Mr. Wigfall.[3] I desire to ask the Senator a question, as a matter of information, because these things go to the public. I should like to know of the Senator from Tennessee with whom he consulted on this side. Surely I, for one, was not consulted.

Mr. Johnson, of Tennessee. I consulted with several on this side.

Mr. Wigfall. There were very few, I think, because most of us were opposed to the whole thing.

Mr. Johnson, of Tennessee. Does the gentleman dispute my word?

Mr. Wigfall. No, sir; but you said you consulted with Senators here; and I should like to know how many there were.

Mr. Johnson, of Tennessee. I consulted with Senator Bright; I consulted with Senator Fitch; I consulted with Senator Polk; I consulted with Senator Davis; I consulted with Senator Nicholson, and some three or four others on this side of the House—I do not remember all with whom I consulted. Senator Fitzpatrick was on the committee.[4]

Mr. Wigfall. The Senator gives eight out of thirty-six.

Mr. Johnson, of Tennessee. I have stated the differences between the Senate bill and the House amendment. Finally, the House gave up the provision including young men of twenty-one years of age, and we conceded that the bill should apply to half of all the lands which had been surveyed and have not been offered at public sale, confining it to the sections designated by odd numbers. We can understand that. There are between fifty-six and fifty-seven million acres of lands which have been surveyed, and ready to be brought into market. By confining it to the odd-numbered sections, we subject just one half the land to the operation of the bill, which had not been offered at public sale; and one strong reason for doing it was, that, in Minnesota, in Iowa, in California, and in Wisconsin, there were comparatively no lands that had been offered, and hence none upon which the Senate bill would operate. We agreed by the compromise on these two points, to apply the bill to the odd sections, which would include just one half the lands in those States where there had been none offered. It does not seem to me that there is anything unfair in that. The eighth section of the Senate bill provided that the President of the United States should, within two years, bring the lands into market. I am free to say that I thought it required the President of the United States to bring too much land into market within two years, and the House insisted on this being stricken out. About sixty million acres are now ready for market. I think, in fact, the eighth section would bring too much public land into market in so short a time; and therefore I was willing to give up the eighth section, on condition that the House would let us retain the eleventh section, which ceded the lands to the States at the expiration of thirty years, when they had graduated down to twelve and a half cents an acre.

Now, looking at the Senate bill as it passed this body, and the bill as reported by the committee of conference, I wish to know where has any principle been deviated from? I do not think any Senator can show it. I have not read the veto message, and only heard it read at the Clerk's desk; but I do not see that the President intimates, in any part of the message, that he would ever approve of any bill granting homesteads to actual settlers, on the principle laid down in this bill. Is there any intimation given in the message that he would approve the homestead proposition in any other shape? On the other hand, is not the inference clear and conclusive, from the general tone and tenor of the message, that he would veto any and every bill which incorporated the homestead principle?

I have shown the immaterial alteration made by the conference committee in the first section of the bill, so far as principle is concerned; and we see how important it is to men who are in the new States where there are no lands that have been offered at public sale. Then, I think, when we struck out the eighth section, and thus refused to bring into market, within two years, sixty million acres, to pass into the hands of speculators, we did not depart from the principle of the original bill, and especially when we retained the eleventh section, which surrendered to the States a large quantity of public lands; and for the information of some I will state what amount of land that section would cause to be surrendered to the States. I have before me a statement made out on the 2d instant, showing the exact number of acres which each State would get under that section?

Estimate of the area, on the 1st of January, 1860, of public lands in each of the States remaining unsold, after having been liable to entry for thirty years:

States.	Acres.
Ohio	5,000
Indiana	5,000
Illinois	30,000
Michigan	56,000
Wisconsin	—
Iowa	—
Arkansas	2,408,000
Missouri	1,037,000
Florida	—
Alabama	4,900,000
Louisiana	903,000
Mississippi	2,872,000
Minnesota	—
Total	12,216,000[5]

Thus we see that the southern States get much the larger proportion of land under this section. While Wisconsin, Iowa, and Minnesota get nothing, Arkansas and Missouri and Alabama and Mississippi get millions of acres. I think this shows that there was no design in this respect to be unjust to the South. I think, in view of this fact, there is nothing unjust or unfair in saying that, in those States where no land has been offered at public sale, their citizens may have the privilege of going on one half and reserving the other half for the Government to derive revenue from.

How has the President of the United States brought his mind to the conclusion that it is unconstitutional to surrender the public lands to the States in which they lie, and thereby withdraw the jurisdiction of the Federal Government without their limits, and inaugurate the system by which the jurisdiction of the Federal Government would cease? How this power can be questioned now is a matter of some astonishment, when the principle has been recognized from the origin of the Government to the present time. In making grants to individuals, corporations, Territories, and States, for internal improvement, educational, and agricultural purposes, it has been conceded by nearly every Administration in the new States for schools, and in nearly all the old ones for other purposes where the public lands lie. We have seen forty million transferred to the States in the shape of swamp lands, twenty-four million to aid in the work of internal improvement;[6] but with the President of the United States, it has all at once become unconstitutional, after the public lands have been in market for thirty years, and graduated to twelve and a half cents per acre, scarcely defraying the expense of keeping the land offices open in the respective States, to be unconstitutional to surrender them to the States in which they lie. Is there no means by which the Federal Government can get clear of these lands? Does the Constitution prohibit the Government from surrendering them to the people or the States? The argument upon the unconstitutionality by the President against surrendering the lands is simply absurd, not to say ridiculous, after the long-established usage of the Government, receiving the sanction of nearly every President of the United States. The policy of granting lands to individuals by the Government as homesteads was approved by Washington, sanctioned by Jefferson, and cherished by the immortal Jackson, whose names and memories will compare, in my opinion, most favorably with that of the present Administration. General Jackson earnestly looked forward to the day when the public lands would cease to be a source of public revenue, and pass into the hands of the honest cultivator. It was his anxious desire for the time to come when every head of a family in the United States would be domicilated, and have an abiding place for his wife and for his children. Whether considerations so national, so humane, so Christian, have ever penetrated the brain of one whose bosom has never yet swelled with emotions for wife or children, is for an enlightened public to determine.[7]

There is another point with reference to preëmptors.[8] There is a large number of preëmptors on the public lands, and the sales have been suspended again and again. Why? Because these men went upon the lands and they were unable to pay. Fifty-six million acres have been kept out of the market because the preëmptors were required to prove up their claims, and pay, before the sale could take place, under the law as it now stands. Then it was important to grant relief to them. It was important to have the public lands placed in such a position that we could derive revenue from them. Then what is done in this bill? We declare that these preëmptors shall have two years longer to prove up and pay before the Government puts the land into market for sale; and in addition to that, by way of inducement, by way of raising revenue, by way of stimulant to those who are on these lands, and who have subjected themselves to the hardships and privations of frontier life, we say to them, "if, within two years, you pay sixty-two and a half cents an acre, the Government shall issue a patent to you, as now provided by the preëmption laws." The sales of these lands have been postponed until the annual receipts from your public lands are only $1,700,000.[9] By extending this relief to the preëmptors, and giving them two years, you enable the Executive, without oppressing anybody, to bring into the market sixty million acres of land at his own discretion, and raise revenue from it, and fill the coffers of the nation. Is there anything very hard in that, anything wrong, anything unfair in principle?

Where, then, is the departure, as the honorable Senator from Arkansas seems to intimate, from the general tenor of his speech, from any principle laid down in the original bill?[10] There is none. The committee on the part of the Senate acted in good faith, and they consulted with their compeers here before they even ventured to make the proposition which was finally reported, and concurred in by the Senate. This reduction to sixty-two and a half cents an acre was confined to the preëmptors at the date of the passage of the law, and did not extend to those who might go hereafter. You can inaugurate no new system in reference to your public lands, unless there be a change of price from the present existing system. If this bill passes, getting the preëmptors out of the way, stopping the clamor, giving the Executive the privilege of bringing the lands into market, it will increase the revenue the incoming year. I do not see that there is any departure from the principle in holding out a stimulant to those who are upon the lands, to pay up within two years. It is suggested that there are twelve million acres in Minnesota. If every acre of it were preëmpted, and these men would pay up within two years, you would bring into your coffers many million dollars from the public lands in the State of Minnesota.

My worthy friend from Arkansas supported this bill originally with a commendable zeal—a zeal which I and others admired. He has made to-day an argument to justify himself in sustaining this veto, which holds out no expectation or intimation that the President will ever approve of a homestead bill upon any principle. But my honorable friend himself offered this amendment to the bill which I originally introduced:

That every actual settler upon offered or unoffered lands shall be entitled henceforth to enter his one quarter section of land at fifty cents per acre, if graduated to a lower rate, at the graduated price, upon proof that he has lived upon the same at least three months, and upon making oath that he enters the same for the purpose of actual residence: *Provided*, That he shall also make oath that he has never at any previous time had the benefit of this act, and comply with such regulations for the due and proper execution of this act as shall be prescribed by the Secretary of the Interior.[11]

His amendment applied indiscriminately to surveyed and unsurveyed lands, and provided, not for getting sixty-two and a half cents an acre, but fifty cents an acre. In what respect have I, as one of this committee of conference, departed from the principles laid down by himself; and now, after having offered this amendment, and standing by the original Senate bill, how can he come forward to justify and sustain the Executive veto? I do not see how my worthy friend can desert us at this stage. I do not see how he can abandon a great measure that he has advocated upon principle, and has exerted all his influence towards consummating, just because the President of the United States thinks proper to withhold his signature. I always have a respect for a man who fills the place of the President of the United States, irrespective of party, and it would be very natural for me to have more respect for a President of my own party than for any one of opposite politics. But does the fact of the President's speaking change the nature and character of great principles and truths? Does it make wrong right, or right wrong? If there is a great fundamental principle in this measure connected with Government and the great cause of humanity, the fact that he withholds his approval does not change my opinion; but if there were forty Presidents, with forty assistants, to write out vetoes,[12] I would still stand by this bill, and give it the sanction of my vote and support.

But, sir, the Executive calls our attention to quite a discovery which he seems to have made in the bill. I cannot believe that he has examined the bill with care. I do not think he has read it as he ought to have read it, I presume for the very good reason that there is a great press of bills on his attention and consideration at the close of a long session of Congress, and he has not had time to do it. I infer that it has been on account of the want of time that he has not read and understood this measure. He speaks of the sixth section of the bill. Now, mark the first section:

That any person who is the head of a family, and a citizen of the United States, shall, from and after the passage of this act, be entitled to enter one quarter section of vacant and unappropriated public lands, or any less quantity, to be located in a body, in conformity with the legal subdivisions of the public lands, after the same shall have been surveyed, upon the following conditions: that the person applying for the benefit of this act shall, upon application to the register of the land office in which he or she is about to make such entry, make affidavit before the said register or receiver of said land office that HE OR SHE IS THE HEAD OF A FAMILY, AND IS ACTUALLY SETTLED on the quarter section, or other subdivision not exceeding a quarter section, proposed to be entered.

But this idea about poor "foreigners," somehow or other, bewilders and haunts the imagination of a great many, who imagine that if you can get in a foreigner somewhere, everybody is to be ruined. I am not exactly as wild on that subject as some may think I am; but one thing is very clear, so far as foreigners are concerned, that, unless we have prohibitory laws, unless we have a system by which their immigration to this country is prevented, the faster we can plant them on land, and engage them in industrial pursuits, the better for them, the better for the country, the better for humanity, the better for the advance of civilization. Remember that the first section provides that the beneficiary of the bill must be the head of a family and a citizen of the United States, and an actual settler, and that he must do certain things. Then the sixth section provides:

And be it further enacted, That if any person, now or hereafter, a resident of any one of the States or Territories, and not a citizen of the United States, but who, at the time of making such application for the benefit of this act, shall have filed a declaration of intention, as required by the naturalization laws of the United States, and shall have become a citizen of the same before the issuing of the patent, as provided for in this act, such person shall be entitled to "all the rights conferred by this act."

What rights? If you are the head of a family and a citizen of the United States, you are entitled to all the benefits conferred by this act; and so, too, the foreigner who is the head of a family may obtain land. All the flourishes on this point, all the figures of rhetoric put forth in the veto message vanish into thin air, have no basis, when you come to examine the bill itself.

The President could not, in the hasty reading he gave the bill, have compared the provisions of the first section with those of the sixth, which admits the foreigner to all the benefits conferred by the first section, conditioned that he does two things; one is, to declare his intention to become a citizen; and the other is, he must become such before the patent issues to him from the United States. Now, what are the conditions to be complied with in the first section. They are as follows:

That the person applying for the benefit of this act shall, upon application to the register of the land office in which he or she is about to make such entry, make an affidavit before the said register or receiver of said land office, that he or she is the head of a family, and is actually settled on the quarter section proposed to be entered, and that such application is made for his or her use and benefit, &c.

Upon this comparison of the two provisions, it must be obvious to all that, notwithstanding the foreigner complied with the two conditions in the sixth section, he could enter no land under the provisions of the first section, until he took the oath that he was the head of a family. On the contrary, if he had been the head of a family, he could not enter land under the first section until he complied with the requirements of the sixth, which requires, before making his entry, that he shall declare his intention to become a citizen, and before the issuance of the patent by the Government must have complied with all the forms of the naturalization laws, and, in fact, be a citizen of the United States. And the allusion to Chinese entering lands under the provisions of this bill, is another proof that the President had not given the subject the consideration he should have done; for the courts of California have declared in unmistakable terms that the Chinese cannot become citizens of the United States under our naturalization laws,[13] and cannot, therefore, entitle themselves to any of the benefits conferred by this bill upon the citizens of the United States.

I am constrained to say that I look upon this objection to the bill as a mere quibble on the part of the President, and as being hard-pressed for some excuse in withholding his approval of the measure; and his allusion to foreigners in this connection looks to me more like the *ad captandum* of the mere politician or demagogue, than a grave and sound reason to be offered by the President of the United States in a veto message upon so important a measure as the homestead bill. The President, though, in the conclusion of his argument seems to think that it was an "inadvertence;" substantially admitting, after his argument, that the bill meant no such thing as he assumed in his message. Is there a Senator here, or an intelligent man throughout the whole country, after reading this bill, that would believe for one moment that the Secretary of the Interior or any other officer of the Government, in the execution of this law, would put such a construction upon it as that put by the President of the United States in the veto message now before us for consideration? This objection is too palpable and too far-fetched to require further comment from me or any one else who is at all disposed to give language its plain and obvious meaning. I look upon this allusion as a mere appeal to a prejudice which exists in reference to the foreign population of this country. If the argument of the President in reference to foreigners in connection with the homestead measure is sound, it is equally strong against our whole land system, which now offers cheap land from one dollar and twenty-five cents to twelve and a half cents per acre, and nothing to prohibit foreigners from entering those lands at those prices without even becoming citizens of the United States. Our preëmption laws now permit all persons who are twenty-one years of age, and all persons of foreign birth, upon a simple declaration of intention, to become preëmptors, and to acquire their titles as such. All this seems not to have entered the President's mind heretofore. Hence his veto message is, in fact, an argument against our whole land system. I will here submit, without further argument, this portion of the veto message to the judgment of an enlightened public.

But the main argument of the President, his principal battery, is directed to the tenth section of the bill, which surrenders the land to the States in which it lies, after the lapse of thirty years. Most of the land to be surrendered to the States by that section, as I have already shown, will go to the southern States. The Executive has discovered all at once that that is an infraction of the Constitution of the United States. How wonderfully constitutional we get at times! It is entirely constitutional to grant millions upon millions of acres to aid in the construction of railroads;[14] but when it comes to granting an alternate quarter section to the honest pioneer, the hardy man of the forest, upon which he may make a support for his wife and his little ones, the Constitution blazes up before him and interposes an impenetrable and insurmountable barrier. If you will turn to the report of your Secretary of the Interior, you will find that forty million acres called swamp lands have been surrendered to the States, for which patents have been issued. That was not unconstitutional; but when it comes to giving land to the man who is poor, who is dependent upon his own muscular power for the support of himself and his family, the Constitution cannot be got over. When it comes to granting land by the wholesale and appropriating millions of acres for other purposes, the Constitution is so broad that you can drive a six-horse team and wagon clear through it anywhere. We have granted twenty-four million acres to aid in the construction of railroads; this all seemed to be constitutional. There was a proposition before the last Congress to grant alternate sections to a railroad two thousand miles long, running from the valley of the Mississippi to San Francisco, on the Pacific coast.[15] This grant was to run twenty miles on each side of the road, which would make a solid belt of land two thousand miles long and twenty miles wide—making more than an average sized State of the Confederacy. This was proposed to be given in one single grant, to aid in the construction of a railroad; and in addition to that, twenty-five million more, in Government scrip, to induce the company, I suppose, to accept a grant of public land amounting to forty thousand square miles. Here is a proposition to pass through the Constitution a grant of land, as before remarked, two thousand miles long, twenty miles wide, with $25,000,000 as an inducement; and the President of the United States thinks this all constitutional and expedient under the war-making power of the Constitution. But there is no provision in the Constitution which opens wide enough to let an honest settler have one hundred and sixty acres at twenty-five cents per acre. In the one case the road is necessary for the transportation of men and munitions of war. It would seem that populating a country, and thereby increasing its productions, is as clearly constitutional, under the war-making power, as it is to have a railroad to transport them upon after they are produced. It is as necessary to have men and provisions, to the successful prosecution of a war, as it is to have a railroad to transport them upon. The railroad and the war-making power of the Constitution would be entirely useless and unmeaning without men and provisions to sustain the country in its hour of peril. The homestead, in fact, constitutes, in part, the true basis of the war power, and is as constitutional under the war-making power as the construction of railroads by the aid of the Federal Government.

If this bill be unconstitutional, there is no bill that could be passed which is constitutional. As to the cost of the lands, if you will turn to the report of the Secretary of the Interior you will find that their cost is put down at twenty-two and a half cents an acre, and that the public lands, as far back as 1850, had yielded $60,000,000 more than they cost the Government. One hundred and seventy-three million dollars have been received from the public lands—extorted from the sons of the West in the forest. Will not the President take into account that there will still be preëmptors; that there will still be purchasers of land? The lowest price under this bill is twenty-five cents per acre; and if the land goes to public sale it will bring $1 25. Surely, then, the average will be far above twenty-two and a half cents, which is the cost of the lands to the Government. Certainly, the President has not examined the statistics of the question. I say, in my place, that if he had understood it, he would not have made such a statement as he has made in his message; and if he did not understand it, he had no right to state to the American people that which he did not know.[16]

It seems to me that it must be evident that this bill is a revenue measure. Here are fifty-six million acres to be offered at public sale according to the discretion of the Executive, and those who will enter land at $1 25 an acre can do so. Many acres will yet be sold; for there will be many men who do not want to be settlers, but who will make investments in the public lands if you hold out inducements to settlement; because, just in proportion as the settlements increase and cultivation increases, in the same proportion you enhance the value of the land, and increase the inducement to make investments of money in the public domain.

I have often heard that this world is all a fleeting show;[17] that it is constantly changing; men are changing. These are changing and revolutionary times. It seems to me that the President of the United States, in his inaugural address, gave us a slight glimpse of a homestead; but to-day, in his veto message, the curtains are all let down,

everything is darkness and doubt, and he does not leave even a gleam
to come from beyond that would indicate that he is for any sort of a
homestead measure. In his inaugural address he used this remarkable language:

No nation in the tide of time has ever been blessed with so rich and
noble an inheritance as we enjoy in the public lands. In administering
this important trust, whilst it may be wise to grant portions of them for
the improvement of the remainder, yet we should never forget that it is
our cardinal policy to reserve these lands, as much as may be, for actual
settlers, and this at moderate prices.

Does not this bill dispose of the lands to actual settlers at moderate prices? In framing it, this very paragraph of the President's
inaugural address was kept in view. He proceeds:

We shall thus not only best promote the prosperity of the new States
and Territories by furnishing them a hardy and independent race of
honest and industrious citizens, but shall secure homes for our children,
and our children's children, as well as for those exiles from foreign shores
who may seek in this country to improve their condition and to enjoy the
blessings of civil and religious liberty.

Then the foreigners did not rise before his imagination in terrific
proportions; but he was for inducing them to come here:

Such emigrants have done much to promote the growth and prosperity
of the country. They have proved faithful both in peace and in war. After
becoming citizens, they are entitled, under the Constitution and laws, to
be placed on a perfect equality with native-born citizens; and in this
character they should ever be kindly recognized.

Is there anything in this homestead bill that this paragraph does
not cover? "Oh, consistency! thou art a jewel"[18] much to be admired,
but rarely to be found. Perhaps the President is too far advanced in
life now to undertake the difficult task of explaining and defending
his inconsistencies; but the fact that he is inconsistent, and changes
his opinion with reference to a great measure and a great principle
is no reason why a Senator or Representative, who has acted understandingly, upon his own deliberate judgment, on a measure that
has been discussed for fifteen years, in Congress and before the
people, should change his opinion. The President of the United
States presumes—yes, sir, I say presumes—to dictate to the American people and to the two Houses of Congress, in violation of the
spirit, if not the letter, of the Constitution, that this measure shall
not become a law. Why do I say this? I ask, is there any difference in
the spirit of the Constitution whether a measure is sanctioned by a
two-thirds vote before its passage or afterwards? When a measure
has been vetoed by the President, the Constitution requires that it
shall be reconsidered and passed by a two-thirds vote, in order to
become a law. But here, in the teeth of the Executive, there was a

two-thirds vote in favor of this bill. The vote was thirty-six to two in this body. The two Houses have said that this bill is constitutional and right. In the other House, reflecting the popular sentiment of the nation, the vote was one hundred and twelve to fifty-one—ten more than the two-thirds majority which the Constitution requires; and when there is a two-thirds vote for a measure, I say it is against the spirit of the Constitution for the Executive to say, "no; you shall not have this measure; I will take all the chances of vetoing it."

I am one of those who have always been the advocate of the veto power under the Constitution.[19] When bare majorities have passed bills, it is a salutary check to arrest what may be called hasty and intemperate legislation. I have advocated its exercise, though seldom and cautiously, in that view; but, sir, when, according to the spirit, if not according to the exact letter of the Constitution, a measure has been passed by a two-thirds vote of both Houses, after a discussion of fifteen years, showing that it is not hasty or improvident legislation—I say, respect to the public judgment of the nation, respect to both Houses of Congress, should have been a great inducement to the Executive to approve such a bill.

I have shown, I think, that the facts and figures and arguments presented by the Executive give way when compared with the reality. All the fabric which he has reared gives way at the touch of truth and sound argument. It is not my intention to consume the time of the Senate further. I desired to present the facts which I have presented. I have read a paragraph from the President's inaugural address. I read it while I was laboring on this bill, and I had it constantly in my mind, and I was determined, as far as I was concerned, to put the measure in a shape that would be clearly covered by that paragraph.

In these revolutionary times it is hard to tell where we are going, and it is, perhaps, difficult for each individual to know his precise locality. I started for this bill upon principle; I supported it upon principle; I voted for it upon principle, and I intend to follow it to its conclusion, let it carry me where it may; for in the pursuit of a correct principle I feel well assured that I can never reach a wrong conclusion. Whether the President differs from me or concurs with me, I do not intend to bear either to the right or to the left, but my course is onward and direct. I hope the Senate and House of Representatives, who have sanctioned this bill by a more than two-thirds majority, will, according to the Constitution, exercise their privilege and power and let the bill become the law of the land, according to the high behest of the American people.

If I were disposed to take up the revenue part of the subject, I could show most conclusively that this bill would enhance the revenues of the Government. I have on previous occasions demonstrated, as clearly as anything can be proved in arithmetic, that if you take a million heads of families and put them upon a million quarter sections of land, if you only thereby added to their capacity to buy goods to the amount of fifty dollars' worth per family more than they now buy, it would increase your revenue $16,800,000 per annum. That would be the operation of their consumption under your present tariff system. Increase their ability to buy, and your revenue will be largely enhanced, because the more they buy the more they pay under the tariff. By taking a million men without homes, and putting them upon a million quarter sections now without cultivators, the result will be to bring more into your Treasury annually, under the operation of your tariff, than you have derived from your whole land system, from its commencement to the present time. I shall say no more on the subject, but refer the President of the United States and the country to a statement of the facts in my speech of May 20, 1858, which I deem conclusive and unanswerable as regards the revenue to be derived from the public lands:

[Johnson repeats verbatim the argument from his May 20 speech that the Homestead bill is a revenue measure, inasmuch as those who live on the land produce, and in producing, become consumers. By increasing a man's ability to buy, the government gains in tariff revenue. With his usual array of figures, Johnson shows that by placing one million families on one-sixth of the public land, the government would gain $17,000,000 in revenue.]

Mr. President,[20] I shall now merely express the sincere hope that the Senate will act upon the measure, and that it will become the law of the land without further delay. The Senate having twice passed the bill by more than a two-thirds majority, I trust that it will not now recede from its high position upon so important a measure upon the mere dictation of the President; but prove to the country and the world that it has a high appreciation of the public judgment, regardless of the arbitrary exercise of the veto power.[21]

Cong. Globe, 36 Cong., 1 Sess., 3267–70.
1. The compromise homestead bill, passing both houses on June 19 with overwhelming majorities, was vetoed by the President and returned to the Senate on the 23rd. Efforts to postpone further consideration of the bill until December were defeated and, after extended remarks by Johnson of Arkansas, Andrew Johnson took the floor. For veto message, see Richardson, *Messages*, V, 608–14.
2. It is not easy to discover from Johnson's ensuing remarks in which of the several conference committees the discussions and changes occurred. Early in June, when neither house could agree on the other's bill, a conference committee was appointed (Senators Johnson of Tennessee, Johnson of Arkansas, and Harlan of Iowa; Representatives Galusha Grow of Pennsylvania, James H. Thomas of Tennessee, and Owen Lovejoy of Illinois). When this committee failed to resolve differences, a new committee was selected (Sena-

tors Johnson of Tennessee, Doolittle of Wisconsin, and Brown of Mississippi; Representatives Colfax of Indiana, J. L. M. Curry of Alabama, and Aldrich of Minn.). Upon the failure of this effort, yet a third committee (Senators Johnson of Tennessee, Fitzpatrick of Alabama, and Cameron of Pennsylvania; Representatives Colfax, Garnett of Virginia, and Windom of Minnesota) was named. On June 19, when Johnson reported that agreement had at last been reached on the wording of the bill, which remained substantially the same as the original Senate enactment, the upper house passed the bill, 36–2. *Cong. Globe*, 36 Cong., 1 Sess., 2462, 2846, 2862, 2955, 3038, 3159; *Senate Journal*, 36 Cong., 1 Sess., 623, 657, 710–11; Stephenson, *History of the Public Lands*, 210–11.

3. Louis Wigfall of Texas.

4. Jesse Bright, Indiana; Graham N. Fitch, Indiana; Trusten Polk, Missouri; Jefferson Davis, Mississippi; A. O. P. Nicholson, Tennessee. Benjamin Fitzpatrick of Alabama, though on the conference committee, did not sign the report.

5. These figures were prepared by the general land office at Johnson's request. Letter from Joseph S. Wilson, June 2, 1860.

6. Since the federal government felt it impractical to reclaim swamplands on a national scale, Congress in 1850 began to turn over that portion of the public domain to the states for improvement by means of "levees and drains." By 1859, some 42,381,274.67 acres had been distributed to the states. Meanwhile, other federal grants were made to internal improvements, especially railroads, in the belief that such grants would promote the development of the interior, facilitate the carrying of government traffic at reduced rates, and raise the value of the remaining public lands. On this basis, some 27,876,772 acres had been transferred to the railroads by 1860. Hibbard, *Public Land Policies*, 269–70; *Senate Ex. Doc*. No. 2, 36 Cong., 1 Sess., 176; Haney, *Congressional History of Railways*, II, 14.

7. In his chagrin at the veto of his cherished Homestead, Johnson resorts to the time-honored, if regrettable, practice of the stump speaker and injects Buchanan's bachelor estate, a personal and private consideration, into a public debate. In 1819, the young Pennsylvania politician had been engaged to Ann Coleman, the daughter of one of the country's wealthiest iron magnates. When the rumor circulated that Buchanan was more infatuated with the Coleman fortune than with the young heiress, she broke off the engagement and died soon afterward. Though not indifferent to women and their charms, Buchanan never undertook the responsibilities of matrimony. Klein, *James Buchanan*, 28–32.

8. Buchanan complained that the homestead bill would give an advantage to existing preemptors, who would be required to pay only 62½¢ per acre, compared to future preemptors, who would be assessed $1.25 per acre. He saw "no reason or justice in this discrimination." *Cong. Globe*, 36 Cong., 1 Sess., 3264; Richardson, *Messages*, V, 613.

9. Revenue from public lands during the fiscal year 1858–59 had been $1,756,687.30. *Senate Ex. Doc*. No. 2, 36 Cong., 1 Sess., 205, 211.

10. In his remarks urging delay in considering the President's veto, Robert Johnson of Arkansas, at the same time that he referred to his Tennessee namesake as "the very father of the homestead measure," had sharply criticized the intransigence of the House conferees in insisting on certain changes which would make the bill less acceptable to the Senate and bring almost inevitable rejection by the President. He further declared that the homestead bill would have led to diminishing federal revenues, inasmuch as the 62½¢-per-acre price for the present preemptors would eventually have to be extended to future settlers, thereby compounding the revenue loss to the government. *Cong. Globe*, 36 Cong., 1 Sess., 3264–67.

11. On April 3, 1860, Johnson of Arkansas gave notice of his intention to propose an amendment to S. 1 to grant to any person who was the head of a family, and a citizen of the United States, a homestead of one hundred and

sixty acres of land out of the public domain, upon condition of occupancy and cultivation of the same for the period therein specified. The amendment was ordered printed, but does not appear in either the *Congressional Globe* or the *Senate Journal. Ibid.*, 1502, 1508.

12. There is no evidence that anyone other than Buchanan, who was served by one private secretary—at this time his nephew James Buchanan— wrote the veto. G. Ticknor Curtis, *Life of James Buchanan* (2 vols., New York, 1883), II, 237.

13. In 1854, the California supreme court ruled in People *v.* Hall that Chinese were of ethnic origin similar to that of Indians and thus not qualified to testify for, or against, a white man in court. Thereafter, this racial defini- tion was applied to a 1790 federal statute limiting naturalization to "free white persons." In actuality the interpretation affected few Chinese, since most did not then desire to become citizens. This device was used for almost one hundred years, until it was repealed by federal law in 1952. Walton Bean, *California: An Interpretive History* (New York, 1968), 165.

14. Of the 27,876,772 acres granted to railroads prior to the Civil War, 19,679,179 had been given during the last two years of Pierce's administra- tion. No congressional railroad grants were made during Buchanan's term; thus the President's position was not tested. However, he remained basically conservative in regard to the public domain. His endorsement of the Pacific Railroad project was based more on political expediency—to win California's vote—than on constitutionality, and even more on national security—a road was necessary for the defense of the West Coast; therefore it was constitu- tional and an exercise of his power as commander-in-chief, with authority to raise and support military forces. Klein, *James Buchanan*, 259, 263–64, 346; Haney, *Congressional History of Railways*, II, 14, 18, 59; Richardson, *Mes- sages*, V, 456–57.

15. On December 13, 1858, Congress began deliberation on S. 65, a bill to provide assistance in building a Pacific railroad. The proposal would have given to the builders twenty sections of land for each mile built, ten on each side of the roadbed in alternating sections. In its final form, the bill lacked any provision for granting land, but simply advocated the construction of three routes—one northern, one central, and one southern. Although approved 31–20 by the Senate on January 27, 1859, the measure did not pass the House. *Cong. Globe*, 35 Cong., 2 Sess., 50, 629, 634; Haney, *Congressional History of Railways*, II, 60–61. See also Speech on Transcontinental Rail- roads, January 25, 1859.

16. Johnson's strictures are echoed by a modern historian of the public lands, who observes that it was "perhaps the most irrational, ill-conceived and amazingly inaccurate veto message that has ever emanated from an American president." Paul M. Gates, *50 Million Acres* (Ithaca, N. Y., 1953), 89.

17. Thomas Moore, "This World Is All a Fleeting Show," st. 1.

18. "Consistency, thou art a jewel" is a proverb of unknown origin. Stev- enson, *Quotations*, 304.

19. As early as 1842, and again in 1848, Johnson had defended the veto power, whether exercised by state or national executive. See Speech on Elec- tion of Senators, The Veto Power, and Other Matters, October [5], 1842, and Speech on Veto Power and Responsibility for War With Mexico, August 2, 1848. *Johnson Papers*, I, 91–96, 444–49; see also *ibid.*, II, 150, 154.

20. Lafayette Foster of Connecticut.

21. Although the bill had originally passed the Senate, 44–8, the vote this time, 28–18, lacked the two-thirds majority necessary to override the veto. *Senate Journal*, 36 Cong., 1 Sess., 458, 757.

From Stephen A. Douglas

[Washington, D. C.]
June 30th 1860

Dr Sir

The Bearer of this note, Mr Dodson of the firm of Clagett and Dodson[1] of this city will call upon you in regard to some business in their line connected with furnishing the Capitol. They are old & respectable merchants of this city, well known to the whole community and I have no doubt would deal fairly & justly with the government. I refer you to Mr Dickens, Secy of the Senate for their character. Mr Dodson desires to see you as chairm[a]n of the Committee on contingent expenses, & I ask for him a fair hearing which I know you will give him.[2]

Very truly yours   S A Douglas

Hon Andrew Johnson

ALS, DLC-JP2.

1. James B. Dodson was a partner in the firm of Clagett and Dodson, dry goods merchants. Darius Clagett (1792–1860), a Georgetown merchant, who, early in 1838, opened a dry goods store at the corner of Pennsylvania Avenue and Ninth Street, "the largest and handsomest store on Pennsylvania Avenue," was the other partner, and the firm was now located at 4 Market "space." Brice McAdoo Clagett, "Three Generations of Clagetts in Georgetown and Washington, 1751–1860," Columbia Historical Society *Records*, LXIII (1963), 70–78; Bryan, *National Capital*, II, 196; *Boyd's Washington and Georgetown Directory* (1860), 65.

2. Johnson received a similar recommendation from John Slidell who averred that Clagett and Dodson "are gentlemen of excellent standing in this community & as I am informed & believe have always supported the democratic ticket in municipal elections." Slidell to Johnson, June 30, 1860, Johnson Papers, LC.

From Horatio G. Wright[1]

Engineer Department
Washington   July 6   1860

Hon Andrew Johnson
U S Senate
Sir

I have the honor to return herewith the letter of Mr C W. S. Wilkinson[2] which you left at the Department this morning & in reference thereto to present the following brief history of Mr Wilkinson's connection with the Mili Academy[.]

It appears from the records of this office that he was appointed a conditional Cadet in 1859 to report at West Point between the 1st & 20th June of that year; that failing to pass the examination preparatory to admission in that month he was granted a re-examination on or about the 29h of August following when he was admitted[.]

At the ensuing semi-annual examination in Jany 1860, he was declared deficient by the Academic Board in the two branches comprised in the course of study up to that time viz, mathematics & English studies, and was recommended for discharge. This recommendation was approved with the privilege of resigning: and this privilege he availed himself of, by tendering his resignation, which was accepted[.]

The vacancy in his district was filled by the appointment in Febr. last of John C New;[3] but as he failed in his initiatory examination in June, being declared "not proficient" in reading, "writing including othrography", the district is again vacant. Following the long established custom however, it can be filled only, upon the nomination of the Representative in Congress from that district[.]

very respectfully &c   H. G. Wright
Capt of Engrs. In charge

Copy, DNA-RG94, Military Academy Let., Entry 206.

1. Horatio G. Wright (1820–1899), Connecticut-born army officer, taught French and engineering at West Point and served with distinction during the Civil War, retiring from service as brigadier general and chief of engineers. Mark M. Boatner, *The Civil War Dictionary* (New York, 1959), 949–50.

2. Charles W. S. Wilkinson was nothing if not persistent. Subsequent to this letter, Congressman Robert Hatton once again nominated him and he was appointed August 22, 1860. He did not graduate but served in the Confederate cavalry. Register of Cadet Applicants, Entry 242, RG94, National Archives; *Tennesseans in the Civil War*, II, 432.

3. John Coffee New, captain of Company "A," 18th Tennessee infantry, CSA. *Ibid.*, I, 222.

From Hiram S. Bradford[1] and Fred. S. DeWolfe[2]

Brownsvill[e] July 11, 1860

Honl Andrew Johnson
Dear Sir

Gloom settles on us in the Memphis district. You must come to our grand barbecue on 21 inst (Saturday). Your voice could rally every man. Indeed we speak the truth. In the name of our god and Country come. We intend to have a tremendous demonstration. In this last stand for Constitutional freedom will you not help us hold up our hands! We know your power here. Come at all hazzards and roll back the tide. You can strike terror to the enemies of the Constitution and secure Tennsse [for] Breckenridge & Lane.

(write [illegible])

Respectfully H. S. Bradford
Fred. S Dewolfe[3]

ALS, DLC-JP.

1. Hiram S. Bradford (b. *c*1830), a farmer with real estate valued at
$17,500 and personal assets of $28,000, was a state representative (1857–
59), a Breckinridge elector, an assistant adjutant general in the Confederate
army, and a leading merchant in Brownsville after the war. Robison Biog.
Data; *Goodspeed's Haywood*, 826; 1860 Census, Tenn., Haywood, 57.

2. Fred S. DeWolfe (b. *c*1833), a Tennessee-born lawyer, was the enu-
merator for Brownsville in the 1860 census. *Ibid.*, 35.

3. Johnson did not attend the barbecue. Nashville *Republican Banner*,
August 1, 1860.

From John C. Burch

Nashville June [July]¹ 12 1860

Dear Governor

I am glad that you have returned home and I am also glad to
learn from the Greeneville Democrat that there is a probability of
your soon entering upon the Canvass. The Manifesto of the Douglas
National Committee² puts an end [to] every hope of compromise or
reconciliation. We must either make a struggle or submit to a severe
thrashing from the Bellites. The news we receive from all portions
of the state [is] in the highest degree encouraging. The Democracy
were never so enthusiastic this early in the canvass. We do not think
that the Douglas defection can seriously injure us. The violence of
Foote & the Memphis faction³ will work their own ruin. I know not
what course George Jones may pursue on his return. I learn that
there is no danger in his district except in Lincoln. They have held a
Breckinridge & Lane ratification meeting there & every thing passed
off well. The friends there & here think it would be in the highest
degree beneficial for you to make a speech there soon. Will you not
do so?⁴ A few speeches from you would have a telling effect in determining the wavering. The Douglas & Bell men have continued
busily to circulate the report that you were for Douglas & thus
caused many of your friends to doubt the course they should pursue.
I think the Douglas men will have a ticket composed of such men as
Foote, Ed. Yerger,⁵ Knox Walker, Bill Carroll & the like.⁶ If you
could possibly make a few speeches before the electoral candidates
get into the field. Allow me to suggest Washington Rhea Co[un]ty,
Pikeville Bledsoe Coty, Dunlap Sequachee Coty Marion, Jasper
County & then over to Dechard or Fayetteville. If you will consent
to take the field let me know & suggest your places & I will make the
arrangements for getting the crowds & also for conveyances for you.
I think a few blows from you would settle the matter beyond a perad-
venture. Let it be done before there is any bold position taken by the

Douglasites. I feel very much the importance of this step. Hence it
is that I take the liberty of *urging* it upon you.

Truly Your friend   Jno. C. Burch

ALS, DLC-JP.

1. The contents of this letter show clearly that it was written July, not
June, 12: inasmuch as Congress did not adjourn until June 28; Johnson was
not in Greeneville until after that date; the Baltimore conventions did not meet
until June 18, so there were no candidates by June 12; and George W. Jones
made a tour of the North after the convention, not before.

2. This committee met in Washington following the Baltimore convention and on June 30, in response to rumors of an impending union of Douglas
and Breckinridge electors, drafted and published a statement repudiating
such an arrangement. Nashville *Union and American*, July 12, 1860.

3. William Carroll, former Memphis postmaster, and Knox Walker, along
with Henry S. Foote and two converts to Douglas Democracy, John P. Pryor,
former editor of the Memphis *Eagle and Enquirer*, and Edwin M. Yerger, recent Whig candidate for Congress, were active in Douglas' campaign in Memphis. *Ibid.*

4. Johnson did not enter the campaign until late September; there is no
evidence that he visited Lincoln County.

5. Edwin M. Yerger (c1819–fl1871), former Whig and congressional
candidate, was a Memphis lawyer and onetime chancellor. Keating, *Memphis*,
II, 78–79; 1860 Census, Tenn., Shelby, Memphis, 5th Ward, 66.

6. None of those named were electors. Besides Watterson and Polk, the
at-large candidates, the Douglas electors were James Britton (Greene),
G. W. Bridges (McMinn), G. F. G. Galbreath (Jackson), T. J. S. John
(Cannon), J. N. McCutchan (Franklin), O. A. Nixon (Hickman), J. R.
McCann (Davidson), Wm. P. Caldwell (Weakley), and W. T. Brown
(Shelby). Memphis *Appeal*, August 3, 1860.

Deed to Cumberland Presbyterians[1]

July 20, 1860

I, Andrew Johnson of the town of Greeneville, County of Greene and
State of Tennessee, have this day bargained and sold, and do hereby
transfer and convey unto Rev. John P. Holtsinger,[2] Lewis F. Self[3]
Thomas Davis[4] and Thomas Lane Jr.[5] they being the members of
the Session of the Greeneville, congregation of the Cumberland
Presbyterian Church, and their Successors, for ever in Trust for the
use and benefit of the congregation of the said Cumberland Presbyterian Church in the town of Greeneville, for and in consideration
of Twelve hundred dollars a lot or parcel of ground, situated in the
town of Greeneville County and State aforesaid, lying on main
Street, opposite West, & Brothers Store[6] and constituting the corner
lot, formed by main and first cross, street, on which is situated a two
story frame building, formerly occupied as a Store and Tailor Shop
by E. B. Miller the upper story of which is now occupied as a printing office,[7] also one small frame building situated in the rear of said
building and containing an oblong of twenty two feet on main street

and sixty feet back parallel with first cross street, it being the lot, or parcel of land conveyed to James Britton Jr.[8] and Edmund B. Miller in common by Jacob Howard[9] of the town of Lebanon County of Wilson, and State aforesaid on the 9th. day of July 1853,[10] containing thirteen hundred and twenty square feet more or less, and bounded as near as can be ascertained without an actual survey as follows. Beginning at the corner of main and first cross street a North East, direction, twenty two feet to a stake thence back nearly at a right angle with main Street a north West direction sixty feet to a stake, thence Nea[r]lly at a right angle with the last line aforesaid a south west direction out to the cross Street aforesaid twenty two feet thence down or with said cross street a south east course, sixty feet to the beginning on main Street, To have and to hold the same to the said Rev. John P. Holtsinger, Lewis F. Self, Thomas Davis and Thomas Lane Jr. the Session aforesaid, and their Successors forever—

[usual assurances of ownership and relinquishment of claim]

In Testimony whereof I have hereunto set my hand and seal, this the 20th. day of July, one thousand eight hundred and Sixty[.]
Witness
James Britton Jr. }
W. D. McLelland }

Andrew Johnson

Greene County Deed Bk. No. 31, pp. 88–89.

1. Organized in 1843 under the leadership of the Reverend Isaac S. Bonham, the Greeneville Cumberland Presbyterians had erected a small wooden structure in the southwestern part of the town. With the purchase of Johnson's property, the church built a new brick edifice. *Goodspeed's East Tennessee*, 888.

2. John P. Holtsinger (b. c1820), the incumbent minister, was Johnson's personal friend who drove him to Cumberland Gap when the senator was escaping from East Tennessee in 1861. Following the war he received his reward in an appointment as a district collector of internal revenue, June, 1866. 1860 Census, Tenn., Greene, 95; Register of Presidential Appointments, 1865–1869, Part II, Johnson Papers, Series 6B, LC, 127; conversation with Richard Doughty, Greeneville, December 16, 1971.

3. Lewis Self (1817–1907), a Greeneville tailor, had been a journeyman in Johnson's shop. One of the founders and original elders of the Cumberland Presbyterian Church, he was a Unionist who served as a regimental quartermaster during the war. After the war Johnson appointed him Greeneville postmaster, and he was elected to the state senate for one term (1869–71). Genealogical data from Mrs. C. Haynes Barnes (Helen Self Barnes), Knoxville.

4. Thomas Davis (b. c1819), a Greene County farmer, was another of the original elders. 1860 Census, Tenn., Greene, 132; *Goodspeed's East Tennessee*, 888.

5. Thomas Lane, Jr., was also a charter member and original elder. *Ibid.*

6. Probably William (b. c1817), Edward (b. c1832) and Richard West (b. c1836), all listed as merchants in the 1860 Census. 1860 Census, Tenn., Greene, 88.

7. The occupant was H. G. Robertson, editor of the Greeneville *Democrat*.

8. James Britton was currently direct representative from Greene to the state legislature. See *Johnson Papers*, I, 497n.

9. Jacob Howard had formerly lived in Greeneville. See *ibid.*, 215n.

10. Johnson had acquired this property in two steps, buying Britton's half-interest in May, 1854, and Miller's in December, 1857, after a public sale the preceding June. Deed to Greeneville Town Lot, May 27, 1854; Deed to Greeneville Property, December 26, 1857, *ibid.*, II, 232, 513.

To George C. Whiting, Washington, D. C.

Greeneville Tenn   July 23d 1860

Hon Geo C. Whiting
Commiss'r of Pensions.

Sir,

Enclosed please find the Amended Declaration and other papers of Jeremiah Harrison,[1] Claiming Bounty Land Under act of 28th Sept. 1850—[2] By reference to Copies of two letters from department enclosed,[3] you will see that Mr Harrison's Declaration for Land bounty was filed prior to 22d Sept 1851 under above named act, and that the same was refused upon the ground that he had already received 320 acres &c. The accompanying certified copies of two discharges show that there were two Jeremiah Harrison's who served in the 39th reg't.

I am acquainted with Jeremiah Harrison of Greene County Tennessee and I am fully satisfied that he is the man who performed the 12 months service—there can be no question as to who performed this service[.] I am also acquainted with the witnesses to wit, Jacob Broyles, John K. Harrison and Michael George,[4] whose affidavits are herewith enclosed, and have no doubt as to their statements[.] They are men of good standing and respectability in this Community whose statements are entitled to full faith and credit[.]

As Mr Harrison's case has been delayed and kept in suspense for about nine years, and he has failed to obtain his rights through an unintentional error of the Department—by confounding the two Jeremiah Harrison's with the one person, I think it not unreasonable to ask an immediate re-examination of his papers and that if found to be entitled to issue his warrant for 160 acres as soon as possible, as the old man is frail and life uncertain—

There can be no doubt of his having performed the 12 months service and is entitled to a warrant for 160 acres. I Know Harrison personally and all the parties and am well satisfied there is no mistake about it[.]

very respectfully   Your Ob't Ser't
Andrew Johnson

L, DNA-RG15, War of 1812 Pensions, Jeremiah Harrison [Letter written and signed by Robert Johnson?].

1. Jeremiah Harrison (b. 1785), a Greene County farmer, enlisted in November, 1813, for one-year service in the Indian wars and was thus entitled to a bounty land warrant. After first confusing two Jeremiah Harrisons who had served in the same regiment but in different years, the pension office finally approved Harrison's claim, only to have Third Auditor R. J. Atkinson inform Johnson that Harrison's bounty had already been awarded in 1854 to a Minerva Harrison, apparently the heir of the other Jeremiah, who had subsequently lived in Alabama. Along with this letter Johnson filed the requisite "Amendatory Declaration," clarifying and fully establishing the Greene Countian's claim. Johnson's old friend Blackston McDannel was the agent pressing the case. R. J. Atkinson to Andrew Johnson, July 2, 1860, Jeremiah Harrison, War of 1812 Pension Files, RG15, National Archives.

2. The 1850 bounty law authorized the issuance of military land grants to veterans of the War of 1812 and all Indian wars since 1790. Robbins, *Our Landed Heritage*, 156.

3. J. D. Wilson [clerk, for commissioner] to B. McDannel, September 22, 1851; S. Cole [clerk, for commissioner] to B. McDannel, September 9, 1852, Harrison, War of 1812 Pension Files, RG15, National Archives.

4. Jacob Broyles (b. *c*1793) and John K. Harrison (b. *c*1796), a half-brother of Jeremiah, were Greene County farmers. Michael George (b. *c*1794), a Pennsylvania-born farmer, was a neighbor of the Harrison brothers. 1850 Census, Tenn., Greene, 393, 458.

From Washington C. Whitthorne

Nashville Te.   July 24. '60

Honl. Andrew Johnson.

Dear Sir:

For the last week, I have been in Nashville, looking over "old documents," to me, a most exceeding tedious work. At Baltimore Gus Henry in accepting the nomination of the Opposition, termed John Bell "slow and cautious",[1] his record establishes the truth of this proposition as well as hypocrisy & inconsistency; Since my return, I have made several speeches, I have heard from all parts of the State, and beleive I am pretty well *posted*, and am more sanguine than when I left you in Washington City. At Memphis & in that portion of the State, we will lose. There is some defection here, some in Overton, & in lower East Tennessee. Taking all Middle Tennessee together there will not be, unless things are altered one thousand democratic votes cast for Douglass. I do not suppose it will equal that in East Tennessee and in West Tennessee not enough to lose us the State,[2] while I am satisfied that there are men of the opposition who will vote with us. If we prosecute the canvass with vigor, and organization we can beat the "allied army." Were it not supposed that the foreign vote would be cast for Douglass, I do not beleive, that an effort would be made by the Douglassites[.]

I saw Jones as he returned,[3] he was here at the time, but did not speak at the *Douglass* meeting—[4] I did not have much talk with him, thought it best not to do so,— I am satisfied that he will not enter the canvass unless provoked severely— *He* is fully aware of the effects of a diversion. I have seen and talked with several gentlemen from old *Lincoln*, and she will come up all right.[5] I have not seen Nicholson since his return but learn that he will canvass a large portion of the State. I learn from Gov. Harris, that such is his intention, or rather to go out when he is invited. I am afraid Gov. H. would find himself embarrassed by his Nashville proposition.[6]

Sometime since, I wrote to Col Haynes[7] to meet me here to agree upon the plan of canvass &c. In his reply he stated that he was engaged in Courts &c. that he could not then come down, at [the] same time infor[m]ing that it was probable that Col. Taylor[8] had stated that possibly he would not canvass as Elector, and inasmuch as Col Haynes & myself had agreed, that I should go with Taylor— I have found myself somewhat embarrassed in making a list of appointments as well as determining the points of the canvass. I think all of our forces ought to be now in the field—but—Col. Taylor & the Douglassites embarrass us. But I have fixed my own plan of the canvass, which in short I submit to you, for your judgment. Rapidly tracing the history of the Slavery question, & the organization and existence of the Black republican organization, its aims & purposes. I declare that we but flank ourselves in opposition thereto. That four parties challenge the popular verdict. The Black republican seeks by all means, particularly by Congress to exclude us from the enjoyment of the Common territories whilst Mr. Douglass denies the power of Congress to exclude yet claims the power for the Creature of Congress, notwithstanding its injustice & the decision of the Supreme Court. Mr. Bell & his party fold their arms and ignore &c. and that it remains our duty true to the ancient faith of the Democratic party, and its history to maintain the equality of the citizen & the several States. That this *equality* the proclamation of equality establishes the verity of our adherence to the party. This is but the general plan. In reference to "popular sovereignty" I have to say, that I am for the people govering, but that their voice must be governed by the Constitution, otherwise the weak, the poor, the humble, whether regarded as States or individuals, are at the mercy of the Strong—the rich and powerful. That the moment that you proclaim any other idea, the blessings of a written form of govement are gone &c &c. From the small experiments I have thus far made, I am thoroughly satisfied, that those gentlemen who have the arts of oratory &c. can make this canvass a telling one. I wish I had them[.] I can see what can be done, & regret my inability to do it[.] But I submit my plan of the argument for your criticism.

Excuse the frankness with which I ask it, but do me the favor to advise equally so.

Allow me at same time to say to you that I think you can do the party more good than any other man in the State, and that looking at every thing, I would advise you to enter into it.[9] From the general and universal expression I have heard, among the people I Know that there is more anxiety to hear you than all of us put together. In view of every thing, personally or politically, whether success awaits us or not, it will be well, if you can make speeches throughout the State. As I have already said I am sanguine. With but two words, carried out fully, we can win[.] "Organization & Information." Col Wm H Carrol is in Nashville and upon Saturday, the Douglass convention is to be holden[.] Foote[10] it is said will be back at the time. My own guess is that Carroll & Foote will be the electors for the State at Large.[11]

I shall be glad to hear from you as soon as you can conveniently [reply], because I shall start out as soon as I can, & want your views, as to the canvass.

                                   Yr friend   W. C. Whitthorne

ALS, DLC-JP.

1. In his speech supporting the nomination of John Bell at the Constitutional Union convention, Gustavus A. Henry, chairman of the Tennessee delegation, compared the candidate to George Washington, describing both as slow and cautious individuals. Nashville *Republican Banner*, May 16, 1860.

2. Whitthorne underestimated Douglas' appeal: official returns showed his vote to be 7,548 in West Tennessee, 2,183 in Middle Tennessee, and 1,599 in East Tennessee. Inasmuch as Bell carried the state by only 4,367, the Democratic vote for Douglas clearly deprived Breckinridge of the victory. Campbell, *Tenn. Attitudes*, 285–87.

3. Following the Baltimore convention, George W. Jones had spoken in the North on behalf of Douglas' candidacy. Nashville *Patriot*, July 9, 1860.

4. Douglas Democrats met July 7 in Nashville to endorse the Douglas-Johnson ticket. Nashville *Union and American*, July 10, 1860.

5. In the fall elections Lincoln County cast a resounding vote of 2,442 for Breckinridge, with only 517 for Bell and 293 for Douglas. Campbell, *Tenn. Attitudes*, 286.

6. At a meeting of Davidson County Democrats held on June 30 to ratify the choice made by the bolters' convention, Harris was selected to chair the meeting. In his remarks he observed that, while he personally preferred Breckinridge and Lane and would support them to the end of the campaign, should it "clearly appear that the vote of Tennessee could not benefit Mr. Breckinridge, but could enable Judge Douglas to defeat Lincoln," he would "regard it as the duty of patriotism to choose between them, and . . . advise the Democratic electors chosen by the people of Tennessee to vote for Judge Douglas." Though the Harris proposition might have been embarrassing at this time, with the passions aroused at Baltimore not as yet subsided, the same course of action was suggested two months later, perhaps at Johnson's prompting, by James Britton of Greeneville, a Douglas elector. Nashville *Union and American*, July 1, 1860. See Speech at Winchester, September 29, 1860, note 6.

7. Landon C. Haynes and Whitthorne were state electors-at-large for Breckinridge. Nashville *Union and American*, January 19, 1860.

8. Nathaniel G. Taylor was a Bell elector-at-large. Nashville *Patriot*, July 23, 1860.

9. Johnson had returned home after Congress adjourned June 28, but, pleading ill health, he refrained from extensive canvassing until late in September.

10. Henry S. Foote.

11. The Douglas convention to choose electors met on July 28 and selected William H. Polk and Harvey M. Watterson as electors-at-large. Milton, *Eve of Conflict*, 498.

From Davidson County Democrats

July 28, 1860, Nashville; ALS, DLC-JP.

John A. Fisher, president of the Democratic Central Club, invites Johnson to speak and encloses request signed by more than nine hundred Democrats who "remembering with pleasure your successful advocusy of the cause of Equal rights, and equal priviledges, in the ever memorable Canvass of 1855, and beleiving that the present canvass presents issues equally vital to the Native, and foreign born Citizen, both in the States and in the Territories, would be pleased to hear an address from you at Nashville . . . and earnestly hope that you will not only address your fellow citizens here but at every other prominent point in the State."

To Abraham L. Gammon[1] [Blountville]

Private

Greeneville Tenn
July 31st 1860

Dear Sir

Your esteemed favor of the 21st inst was received in due Course of mail— I fear that it will be out of my power to be with you on the 9th of August[.][2] Immediately after reaching Tenn I was compelled to leave on Some business which detained me Some time and after my return I was taken sick and for Some time confined to my bed and was Scarcely able to Speak at a ratification meeting in this place on the 21st— If I Can come I will; but do not now think it will be reasonably possible for me to be there at the time appointed for your ratification meeting— You will no doubt have more Speakers than will have an opportunity to Speak. So there will be nothing lost by my absense—

The present position of the democratic party is [*sic*] before the Country is to be deeply regreted and unless there is much done between now and the election to arrest the Current which is Setting against us in the free States and dividing us in the Slave States, defeat is inevitable in Tennessee and the nation— Thank God that I am not responsible for the division and distruction of democracy— Its disruption and overthrow is no fault of mine— I have labored day and night to prevent the present State of things— But while I am in no way responsible for the blunders of Some and the designs of others in bringing about the present deplorable Condition of the party, I am more than willing to do all in my power mental or physical to restore peace and harmony in our ranks in the State and out of it and thereby Save the party from a permanent disruption which will end in breaking up the confederacy— While my hopes are Strong that there is no party that is in favor of desolving the Union *my fears are great* that it is So—   For my part I intend to fighting in the Union not outside of it—   If there are any who are tired of Staying in the Union let them go out—   If it is to be broken up let Tennessee keep her Self in the right, and then when the impious work is done She will not be held responsible for the disapointed hopes of the friends of free Govnmt throughout the Civilized world, nor will the blame of millions attach to her Shield[.] I repeat I [am] will[in]g to do all in my power to Save the party in the State and the whole Country and the Consciousness of having Contributed Somthing toward redeem[in]g democracy and placing the Govmnt under its Control will be ample reward for me—   It will require a great effort to Save the State as matters now Stand[.]

> I have the honor to be most Sincerely
> Andrew Johnson

ALS, NjMoW.

1. Abraham L. Gammon (1812–1872), a Sullivan County farmer and merchant, was a member of the legislature (1857–59) and mail agent. Robison Biog. Data.

2. A Democratic meeting to ratify the Breckinridge-Lane ticket met in Blountville on July 25; there is no record of a subsequent meeting on August 9. Nashville *Union and American*, July 29, 1860.

From Theophilus Fiske

> *Private and Confidential.*
> Office of the "Democratic Expositor" [?]
> Washington Aug. 6, 1860.

My Dear Sir,

I have determined to make one energetic effort to save our party and our country from the hands of the fanatics who seem bent upon the destruction of both. I have run up the following ticket at the head of my columns—

> For President
> Andrew Johnson
> of Tennessee.

> For Vice President
> Thomas H. Seymour[1]
> of Connecticut.

The ticket has been received with unbounded enthusiasm since it was announced the day before y[esterday?]. It is one that will ensure [a] triumphant victory in Novem[ber if] the factious disorganisers can *both* be made to withdraw and we can unite our party upon it. At any rate it is worth a persevering, energetic effort— if we can save our country from falling under abolition rule, it will be a blessing beyond all price.

By this mail I send you a few copies of my paper which has already obtained an immense circulation and is increasing at the rate of a 1000 per week.

In great haste   Your True friend

Hon. A. Johnson.   Theophilus Fiske

ALS, Johnson-Bartlett Col.

1. Thomas H. Seymour (1807–1868), Democratic congressman (1843–45) and an officer under Scott in the Mexican War, was minister to Russia (1853–58). Absent during much of the antislavery agitation, Seymour returned sympathetic to the South, becoming a leader of the "Peace Democrats"; their unsuccessful gubernatorial candidate in 1863, in 1864 he received thirty-eight votes on the first ballot for the presidential nomination. *DAB*, XVII, 11–12; *BDAC*, 1584.

Receipt for Curbing

Received of Andrew Johnson Forty dollars and forty five cents in full for account of Kirbing furnished by R. W. Hopper[1] and placed in front of his house in Green[ev]ille[.]

Henry A. Farnsworth[2]

August 6th 1860.

RS, Johnson-Bartlett Col.

1. Not identified.
2. Henry A. Farnsworth (b. c1804) was a wealthy Greene County farmer. 1860 Census, Tenn., Greene, 106.

From Breckinridge Democrats

[August 10, 1860], Nashville; Nashville *Union and American*, August 10, 1860.

Washington C. Whitthorne and 719 others ask Johnson, Isham G. Harris, and A. O. P. Nicholson to speak at Nashville and throughout the state. [Though carrying different signatures, this document is identical with the invitation from Davidson County Democrats, July 28, 1860.]

From Hawkins County Democrats

Rogersville August 11th 60

Hon A Johnson
Dear Sir

We are informed Mr Neilson[1] is to make a speech here saturday[.] We think it at this time essentially necessary some one should
be here that can successfully meet him[.] The idea of giving away
and allowing the Opposition all the advantage of a start in the contest we think the very worst of policy[.] It is settled beyond question
a desperate strugle must be made to carry Tennessee and as there is
but little hope but to throw the election in the house and in the event
the house does not make an election the vote of Tennessee may be
necessary to bring Lane before the senate so leaving the importance
of the next state election out of the question every thing may depend
upon carrying Tennessee and that depends no little upon starting out
right and keeping up the fire from now till the election[.] Key[2]
made us a good speech last week but there was not crowd enough
out[.] We are satisfied a speech from you at this time would unite
and rouse the party more effectually than from any one else[.] Let
us know by return mail if you can come[.] We will have hand bills
struck off and get out the Democracy in full force[.]

Respectfully Your friends
J W McCord[3]

LS, Johnson-Bartlett Col.

1. Thomas A. R. Nelson was a Bell elector. Since the issues of the Knoxville *Whig* from July 28 to August 18, 1860, are missing, a report of this
meeting, if held, is not available.

2. David M. Key (1824–1900), Greeneville native and Chattanooga lawyer, campaigned as elector for the Breckinridge-Lane ticket. A Confederate
officer, he subsequently served as chancellor of the third district (1870–75),
was appointed Johnson's successor in the Senate (1875–77), and became
postmaster general in Hayes's cabinet (1877–81). *BDAC*, 1161; *DAB*, X,
361–62.

3. Signed by McCord and twenty-seven others.

From Warren County Democrats

August 13, 1860, McMinnville; ALS, Johnson-Bartlett Col.

Committee invites Johnson to address "a grand rally" on August 24;
hopes for an affirmative answer, "as we have given your name as one of
the speakers."

From George W. Jones

Fayetteville Tennessee Augt. 15, 1860.

Dear Johnson

Your favor of the 11th instant has been received and read with deep interest. The Democratic party upon which [rest?] all my hopes of good to the world through human government has been distracted, disrupted, broken up—destroyed. Thank God I am not responsible for it— nevertheless the fact is so, and so far as the result and effects of its destruction are concerned it matters but little by whom and by what means it was done. No one I am satisfied in all the Country is more deeply pained and mortified in consequence of it than I am. I have endeavored for nearly twenty five years of my life to advocate, defend and vindicate the Democratic party and its cherished principles. I had withdrawn from the public service, with as I believed the approbation, of an intelligent, patriotic and confiding constituency, of my acts and services as their representative. And in this I doubt not I was correct. But, now, I find those friends with whom I so long acted and harmonized upon principles and measures, best calculated to promote and insure to the whole Country, the benefits and blessings, for the enjoyment of which, our government the best ever devised by man was designed by the purests patriots that ever lived, divided and arrayed against each other. Some it is true agreeing with me as to principle, and the men to carry them out under the circumstances, but the majority I doubt not on the opposite side in the present case. I had determined before my return home not to take any part in the Ca[n]vass for several reasons. I was satisfied that in this Country I did not concur in opinion with the majority of my friends and former Constituents. They think if I cannot go with them that I should not take part against them. Some of those who agree with me think that I should by all means take the Stump and vindicate my principles. But that would only tend to widen the breach, and embitter many of my old friends against me, without the slightest hope or prospect of doing any good to the Cause or the Country. Douglas never was a favorite of mine. I never desired his nomination as a choice. But he now stands as I believe fairly and squarely upon the great Democratic principle of non-interference by Congress with the question of slavery, and the right of the people in Territories and States to form and regulate their domestic institutions in their own way subject only to the Constitution of the United States. For these principles I have voted and spoken. I acted upon my honest convictions. I cannot abandon them without loosing my self respect. I must adhere to them let the consequences be what they may.

You have seen me low down, very, but never so low as I am now. I see not one ray of light or gleam of hope in the future. I feel as if I had already outlived my time. I know not that I can bear up under it. And yet I trust that an All Wise Providence will not desert or abandon our beloved Country in this the day and hour of her greatest Calamity. But that He will bring order out of Confusion, and so direct things by His Wisdom as to perpetuate its blessings.

I read your letter to the Editor of the "Journal."[1] I requested him before not to criticise you as he did in his issue of the 2d instant.[2] He has ever been one of your most sincere friends and ardent supporters. You were his model of a statesman, and a peoples man. He inferred your change upon popular sovreignty, upon your vote for the Davis resolutions in the Senate and your determination to advocate the Election of Breckinridge upon the Platform upon which he was nominated. That platform he regards as in direct antagonism to non-interference and popular sovreignty. That one of the resolutions is strongly Federal, in virtually asserting the people have no sovreignty until it is conferred on them by the General government in the admission as a state into the Union. The resolutions in my opinion are the opposite of the Cincinnati Platform.[3]

Under present circumstances there is not the least possibility of the election of either Breckinridge or Douglas by the people. Lincoln is the only man who has any chance of election by the Electoral College in my opinion. And he will be elected by the Electors unless Douglas can get votes enough in the free states to defeat him. But from the appearances there, is but little prospect of that. The friends of Breckinridge and Douglas seem determined to make the contest in every state almost north and south. In this state there can be no hope of carrying it for Douglas, and if the contest is continued almost as little of carrying it for Breckinridge. At this time I do not believe that either could get the vote of Tennessee. Can anything be done? I fear there cannot. I do not believe there can be. The Democratic party is in ruins, and the Government tending to disunion and revolution.[4]

I shall be glad to hear from you at any and all times. I hope your health is good and also that of your family. Present my respects to Mrs J. and believe as ever very truly and sincerely

Your friend
G. W. Jones

When do you expect to speak in Nashville?

ALS, Johnson-Bartlett Col.

1. In an effort to persuade Charles A. French, editor of the Fayetteville *Lincoln Journal*, to moderate his criticism of Johnson, Jones evidently had read to him Johnson's letter (now lost) which appears to have set forth the senator's views of current issues.

2. The *Lincoln Journal*, a weekly, contains nothing about Johnson on August 2; perhaps Jones meant the issue of the preceding week, July 26, when the Douglas organ took issue with the Breckinridge definition of sovereignty, which held that sovereignty commenced only *after* the settlers formed a constitution. Editor French chided Johnson for now embracing this view, inasmuch as he earlier had argued, in his Nashville address of July 15, 1856, that a citizen carried his sovereignty with him into the territories, asserting that "the Federal Government can impart no sovereignty to the citizens of a territory." *Lincoln Journal*, July 26, 1860; Speech at Nashville, July 15, 1856, *Johnson Papers*, II, 395–433.

3. Jefferson Davis' resolutions of February, 1860, finally voted on in May, specifically rejected popular sovereignty by calling for congressional protection of slavery in all the territories, whereas the Cincinnati platform came out for congressional noninterference, leaving the way open for popular sovereignty. Breckinridge was running on the Cincinnati platform significantly modified by specification that during the territorial period all citizens must be protected in their property, including slavery. Further, the Breckinridge platform announced that the right of sovereignty commenced only when the state constitution was formed. Nevins, *Emergence of Lincoln*, II, 179; Porter and Johnson, *National Party Platforms*, 25, 31; *Cong. Globe*, 36 Cong., 1 Sess., 658, 2321–22, 2350–52.

4. In view of subsequent events, Jones's analysis of the political prospect is remarkable for its accuracy.

From John E. Helms

Knoxville, Tenn., Aug. 16./60

Hon. A. Johnson:

Dear Governor:

Since writing to you yesterday, Bradfield[1] has informed me that he will not sell his establishment until after the present canvass is concluded, even if he does then. He is evidently acting under the advice and directions of his few friends here—Wallace, Elliott,[2] &c.

I have a proposition from the Lamar House proprietors[3] to take charge of their office and books. I have agreed to accept until something better turns up, or until I venture upon an enterprize myself. From present signs of the times, I am at a loss what to do. My brother is in the country, and I do not know what to indicate as my idea for the future without an understanding with him.

There is a report on the streets today, (which I have been unable to trace to a responsible party) that Breckinridge and Douglas are off the track and a new ticket on.— one report says you head the new ticket—another that Dickinson,[4] is the man[.]

The only objection Bradfield has to selling now, he says, is the absence of any thing to do.

Have you any suggestion to make in regard to the matter as it stands?

Truly Your Friend   John E Helms

ALS, Johnson-Bartlett Col.

1. George W. Bradfield, editor of the Knoxville *Register*, a Democratic, but anti-Johnson, organ.

2. Probably Wayne W. Wallace, earlier an unsuccessful congressional candidate, and Henry Elliott, a minor politico and writer for the *Register*.

3. James M. Bridges & Co. were the proprietors of the Lamar House, located on the southwest corner of Gay Street and Cumberland Avenue. *Williams' Knoxville Directory* (1859–60), 61.

4. Daniel Dickinson, senator from New York.

To A. O. P. Nicholson, Columbia

PRIVATE.   Greenville, Tenn., August 23rd, 1860.

My dear friend:

Your letter of the 13th inst. was received yesterday and is postmarked Columbia instead of Nashville— I received a letter of invitation from the democratic club of Nashville and for me to fix the time.[1] I replied that I would do so; but at the time of writing could fix no time with anything like reasonable certainty on account of the precarious condition of my health; but would give them notice when I could do so. I have since seen an invitation published in the Union to N. H. & J.[2] without any time being set for the meeting and without references as to who was to fix the time and, of course, could not assume the right to fix the date for the meeting without regard to the others who were invited. My intention was to have been in Nashville and in Columbia if I had not met you N. before now, but my health would not admit of it, and think now I will be there some time next week.

As to making a list of appointments at this time I cannot do it and do not feel willing to do so until I see you in person, for I want to consult with you freely and fully as to the appointments and other matters connected with it. I shall not be at Cleveland on the 28th as suggested in your letter. It will not be in my power to accompany yourself, Harris and Ewing to the western part of the State. Would it not make the impression for so many *"distinguished"* persons all at once to pounce down upon their portion of the State that there was great danger and alarm on the part of the democracy and do more harm that [*sic*] good—(a mere suggestion).

Whitthorne has been with us and has more than sustained himself and has gone far beyond the most sanguine expectations of the democracy, and it has been admitted in many instances by the opposition that he is completely demolishing his competitors and especially Taylor.[3] You may rest assured that he is making reputation in this part of the State of the right kind, which will be of use to him hereafter and at the same time inspiring the democracy with much confidence. His speech here caused some of the Douglass men to fall into line, and if he pursues the same conciliatory course will, I think, pretty much wind up the Douglassites in this end of the State.

My dear friend, if the State is saved to the democracy, the work has yet to be done, for as matters now stand, the State is lost, if I am not mistaken. Things look gloomy to me at this time and how it will end no one can tell.

Give my best respect to Mrs. Nicholson.   As Ever,

ANDREW JOHNSON.

Printed in "Documents," *Tennessee Historical Magazine*, IX (1925), 81–82. Original at that time in possession of Judge W. C. Whitthorne, Columbia, Tennessee.

1. See Letter from Davidson County Democrats, July 28, 1860.
2. A. O. P. Nicholson, Isham Harris, and Andrew Johnson. See Letter from Breckinridge Democrats, August 10, 1860.
3. W. C. Whitthorne, elector-at-large on the Breckinridge ticket, was engaged in a canvass with other electors, including Nathaniel G. Taylor, a Bell-Everett elector.

To Nashville Democrats

Greenville, Aug. 28, 1860.

Gentlemen: —Your letter of the 21st inst.,[1] inviting me to attend and address a mass meeting to be held on the 3d of September, has been received. Since my return from Washington my health has been so irregular that it has been out of my power to make and fill any appointments for public speaking, and so far I have made but one.[2] However, my health of late has been improving, and if I find I can be with you on the day designated for your meeting with reasonable assurance of being able to address the people, I will be there and participate in the proceedings of the day.

With very great respect, your ob't. serv't,

ANDREW JOHNSON

Messrs. F. C. Dunnington, John B. Hays, and others.

Nashville *Union and American*, September 8, 1860.
1. Not found.
2. After speaking in Greeneville, July 21, Johnson did not appear again in the canvass until he went to Nashville on September 27, when his speech was but briefly reported; however, the scanty evidence indicates that his performance two days later at Winchester conveys the tenor of his Nashville remarks. Nashville *Union and American*, July 28, 29, 1860; Nashville *Republican Banner*, October 2, 1860.

From the Democracy of Northern Mississippi

August 29, 1860, Sardis, Miss.; ALS, Johnson-Bartlett Col.

Calvin Foster and others, representing "the friends of Breckinridge and Lane," invite Johnson to address a giant rally at Sardis on September 19, and pledge a cordial welcome. "The distinguished part you played in the memorable contest with KnowNothingism is still fresh in our minds and the honest yeomanry of the country are naturally anxious to hear the man who whipped *Sam* upon his favorite Battle ground and did more than any other to crush out this monstrous humbug from the land."

Speech at Winchester[1]

September 29, 1860

The first part of his speech was devoted to Conventions. He said Conventions were ridiculous mockeries[2]—not ridiculous, perhaps, but to say the least, not very solemn mockeries, but after a Convention we found ourselves engaged in the ridiculous business of ratifying what had been done.

Said the Convention was disrupted at Baltimore, and the consequence is *we* have two candidates in the field. The difficulties of the democratic party commenced with the secession at Charleston. If the delegates had remained in the Convention two days longer, the difficulty would have been settled. Breckinridge or Douglas, or some other good man, would have been nominated, and then we should have had no difficulty. With a united democracy we could have beat our opponents without difficulty. The division at Charleston seemed to be upon principle, but at Baltimore upon a mere preliminary question.[3] The Convention split, and there was no regular nomination— *no* nomination made according to the usages of the party. The nomination of one was as regular as the other. The Convention played out, and was disrupted. We have two candidates, said he, neither of them regularly nominated. This is not the fault of the people, but of the leaders. Instead of doing what they were sent to do, they did just what they were sent not to do. They have brought us into difficulty and confusion. *I am proud to say I have no hand in it —the blood is not upon my skirts.*[4] I did it not, but I come forward to *extenuate* my party, *if possible*. Instead of fighting our enemies, we are engaged in the humiliating business of fighting each other. Not *much* disunion here,[5] but *you are more fortunate than we are in other places*. He submitted the Britton proposition,[6] and said it had been denounced as infamous, and as being his trick. It comes (said the Governor) from Mr. Britton, a Douglas man of respectability and character, but it has been attacked by the itinerant politician of Nashville—the man whose jurisdiction seems to be from Maine to California.[7] Some say, however, there is a question of great importance —of serious difficulty—between Breckinridge and Douglas, and here the Governor defined squatter sovereignty and popular sovereignty —said he was for the latter, but not the former.[8] Says the Supreme Court, in the Dred Scott case, expressed an opinion upon two points, though it *decided* but one—that was, that Scott was an African, and had no *status* in court. The court then gave its opinion upon the other point—the territorial question. The Governor then took pains to show that Douglas was for standing by the decision of the Supreme Court. If it had been made he stood by it, or when it should be made he would stand by it. He referred to Douglas' speech in answer to Jeff. Davis upon this point.[9] Mr. Douglas asks, "What are we quarreling about?" and I ask, says the Governor, should we split upon little minor differences, and break up the party? Here the Governor read the following extract from Mr. Breckinridge's speech to the Kentucky Legislature upon the question of popular sovereignty.

A large portion of the Democracy of the North differ from the Democracy of the South on one or two well known questions of legislative action, but they unite thoroughly on all the other vital questions that convulse the country, and on the determination of which its peaceful resistence may hang. The first duty of all who love their country is to overthrow the Republican party, and with this conviction I should be untrue to Kentucky if I did not plead for the union of all opposed to that dangerous organization; and to fall to pieces on questions of less magnitude than its defeat, is to surrender to its domination and all the fatal consequences that may ensue.[10]

Here the Governor made a strong appeal to all, whether for or against popular sovereignty, to come together, saying, shall we go to war among ourselves upon these questions for the purpose of defeating ourselves and electing Mr. Bell? In discussing this question the speaker again came back to the Convention, and triumphantly asked, in going out of the Convention did you get any *protection*?— any slave territory?—any Southern right? What did you get? You say you got *principle—principle*—and will fight for principle, and if we can't get that the world must be turned-up!

A principle, said the speaker, without the power to enforce it is nothing— to assert a right that cannot be enforced, said the speaker, is folly. He here enforced his argument by what Burke said to the British Parliament after the revolution, that by the assertion of a principle which could not be enforced, the government had lost thirteen colonies,—the Convention was thus broken up upon a mere abstract right. It was like the case of a fellow making a great fuss and noise and getting up a family quarrel upon his right to shear a wolf—[11] why can't we all unite? Mr. Bell was an old fossil, and could have been crushed at the start without trouble if the Democracy had been united, but now, we will have enough to do *when united,* to beat him.

The speaker here turned upon Mr. Bell's record, and stated the points against him without elaborating them; devoted sometime to the Mexican war policy of Mr. Bell, traced the history of parties, and concluded (perhaps from spiritual mediation) that Harrison and Taylor were taken off to save the country.[12] He said the talk about disunion was to alarm, and warmed up on Knownothingism.

Nashville *Republican Banner*, October 2, 1860.

1. Having made his entry into the Breckinridge campaign in an unreported speech in Nashville two days earlier, Johnson moved on to Winchester where his remarks were reported to the Bell-Everett organ, the *Republican Banner*, by A. S. Colyar, a Bell supporter who shared the Winchester platform with Johnson and whose statements, according to the editor, H. K. Walker, were "entitled to *implicit credence.*" It is interesting to note that Walker, in assessing this speech, felt that Johnson was "determined not to go down in the Breckinridge boat. Though at present a sort of way passenger, his baggage is not checked through, and he evidently intends to jump off in time to save his bacon." Certainly as Colyar reports it, the speech appears to reflect ambivalence and some evidence of "a plague on both your houses" attitude toward the supporters of both Democratic candidates. Nashville *Republican Banner*, October 2, 1860.

2. Conventions, like caucuses before them, were anathema to Johnson. He frequently argued against the expensive machinery and the undemocratic methods of both the convention system and the electoral college. Although he seldom indicated what method he would substitute for selecting party candidates, undoubtedly it would have involved greater rank-and-file participation, for the entire tenor of his approach to government was to carry decision-making back to the voter, clearly revealed in his long-advocated constitutional amendments for direct election of the President and U. S. senators. For one of his proposals concerning the choice of presidents, see Speech on Transcontinental Railroads, January 25, 1859, p. 224.

3. At Charleston the adoption of a slave-code plank was the issue; the trouble in the Baltimore convention arose over the seating of delegates. The credentials committee submitted two reports: the majority, pro-Douglas, proposed to admit many newcomers and exclude most of the Charleston bolters; the minority provided for the seating of all the original delegates from the southern states. The bolters left because they refused to accept the majority report. Nevins, *Emergence of Lincoln*, II, 269.

4. Possibly an expression derived from "and their blood shall be sprinkled upon my garments." Isa. 63:3.

5. Franklin County, of which Winchester is the county seat, was very definitely pro-Breckinridge: the November vote was Bell, 388; Breckinridge, 1,526; Douglas, 26. Campbell, *Tenn. Attitudes*, 286.

6. James Britton of Greeneville, a Douglas elector, proposed the fusion of the Douglas and Breckinridge tickets in order to defeat Bell in Tennessee; if the combined effort carried the state, the electoral vote would be cast for the Democratic candidate who had the greatest chance of election. The Nashville *Patriot* accused Johnson, "that distinguished professor of the mesmeric art," along with Nicholson, of contriving the fusion by dispatching his son Robert to East Tennessee for a conference with Britton. When the latter hurried to Nashville, even to the same hotel where Johnson stayed, he "showed whose chestnuts he was to pull out of the ashes." Nashville *Union*

and American, September 20, 1860; Nashville *Patriot,* September 25, 1860.

7. Probably a reference to Henry S. Foote, an enthusiastic Douglas man, whose previous career had taken him from Mississippi to California, as well as into the Senate, and who was aggressively defending Douglas' candidacy against all detractors.

8. In this campaign a sharp differentiation between these terms was made. "Squatter sovereignty" was equated with the Cass-Douglas doctrine that the people of a territory had the right through territorial legislation to determine the question of slavery; whereas "popular sovereignty" implied that the issue of slavery could be decided only upon application for statehood. The latter definition, embraced by the South and bolstered by the Dred Scott decision, considered the territorial legislature a creature of Congress and therefore bound to the principle of nonintervention, except for the requirement that all property, including slaves, be protected. Nashville *Union and American,* September 8, 14, 1860; Knoxville *Whig,* August 18, 1860; Emerson D. Fite, *The Presidential Campaign of 1860* (New York, 1911), 98–99.

9. Douglas, in a Senate speech of May 15 and 16, 1860, regarding the Davis resolutions and the Dred Scott controversy, had argued, "If the decision is made, it is the law of the land, and we are all bound by it. If the decision is not made, then what right have you to pass resolutions here prejudging the question, with a view to influencing the views of the court?" *Cong. Globe,* 36 Cong., 1 Sess., App. 311.

10. This is probably extracted from Breckinridge's speech before the Kentucky house of representatives on December 21, 1859, following his election as United States senator. Although the exact paragraph has not been located, the tone of this passage resembles other excerpts which received wide publicity during the canvass, appearing in both Breckinridge and Bell organs. Nashville *Union and American,* July 18, 1860; Nashville *Patriot,* July 18, 1860.

11. Speaking in the House of Commons on November 27, 1781, Edmund Burke dilated upon the folly of waging a war for the maintenance of rights— for the assertion of a principle which had cost Britain "thirteen provinces, four islands, a hundred thousand men, and more than seventy millions of money." In the course of his strictures, he likened this dogged insistence upon "rights" to the reasoning employed in shearing a wolf: "there is excellent wool on the back of a wolf, and therefore he must be sheared. What! shear a wolf? . . . Have you considered the trouble? How will you get this wool? Oh, I have considered nothing, and I will consider nothing, but my right." [J. Wright, ed.], *The Speeches of Edmund Burke, in the House of Commons, and in Westminster-Hall* (4 vols., London, 1816), II, 288–89.

12. From the viewpoint of an ardent Democrat like Johnson, the fact that both these Whig presidents died in office represented nothing less than divine intervention to save the country from Whiggery.

Speech at Fayetteville[1]

October 1, 1860

He stated in the beginning that he was not before them to indulge in highly wrought and flowery exordiums, &c., but to speak to them as he always had done, frankly—honestly. He was now just where he was twenty years ago, battling for the great principles of Democracy. John Bell as then was battling against these great principles. Here Mr. J. traced the history, rise, fall and progress of parties in this country, and showed what the great Democratic party had done as well as the other parties. The congressional caucus system failed to meet the wants of the people, and they did away with that, and so would they do when the present National Convention system failed, as he thought they ou[gh]t to do. See how the thing is working. We sent delegates to the Convention to give us *one* candidate and they gave us *two*, the very thing we did not want them to do.

Who could say that the nominations of either of these disrupted conventions was per se binding on any one? The people should do for themselves everything they could and not employ agents. There was an old adage, "If you want a thing done send some one to do it, but if you want it done well do it yourself."— In our divisions what should we do? Take John Bell, a thing laid on the shelf?—a thing that was but is not, who was instructed out of his seat in the Senate by the people of Tennessee?[2] Surely not. We have had in our ranks since there has been two democratic candidates in the field crimination and recrimination, but such things ought not to be. We ought unitedly to fight the opposition—Lincoln a Black Republican, and Bell nearly one. Who does not know in Tennessee that 49 out of every 50 Democrats are for Breckinridge? Why divide, then, on minor differences, and give away the State to John Bell? Two of the Douglas Electors in East Tennessee have proposed to unite on the Breckinridge Electors,[3] and let them cast the electoral vote for Breckinridge or Douglas as may be best. The Douglas paper at Nashville[4] was down on it very severely—styled it a *trick—a trick!* To save the State of Tennessee from Know Nothing misrule—to save the Democratic party, is a *trick! Strange!*

Suppose there is a difference in the Democratic party on the subject of squatter sovereignty, popular sovereignty, or whatever you please to call it; is not the difference still greater between the Democratic party and any other party?

Douglas and Breckinridge agree that they will abide by the decision of the Supreme Court. (That is, to say nothing of Douglas' Freeport speech.) Mr. J. explained fully the meaning of Squatter Sovereignty and Popular Sovereignty. Squatter Sovereignty could not be right for it was unconstitutional, for the constitution was plain that private property could not be taken away without compensation, which thing would have to be done if Squatter Sovereignty prevailed. Of course the Government should protect its property as well as its persons; to say otherwise would be only to say an absurdity. If it could and would not do this, it would be no government at all, a thing he would dislike much to say of his country, in the prosperity and advancement of which he had so rejoiced. Mr. J. had no quarrel for Douglas men. He would not, he could not fight his brother Democrats. But he was ready and willing as he had always been, to go it might and main against the opposition.

> John Bell had *wired* in and *wired* out
> Till it left the mind in doubt
> As to whether the *snake* that made the track
> Was going North or coming back.[5]

He had shown himself in some of his votes in reference to the Territories obtained by the treaty of Guadalupe Hidalgo, to be a regular straight Squatter Sovereignty man;[6] and *they say* he is against it. What has John Bell ever done for the people? Who has he ever been for but John Bell? He opposed the extravagance of the administration, yet voted himself for every extravagant measure, and advocated a policy that would overwhelm our nation in so great a debt that she would not without a miracle ever pay it.—[7] John Bell has sanctioned the outrages of the Know Nothings, and particularly the bloody work at Louisville,[8] and that too after it was done and he had had time to reflect upon it in all of its enormity. Mr. J's description of that bloody scene was graphic and touching. The old mexiam that "Honesty was the best policy," was true he honestly believed; and exhorted the party to stand firm and true, and it would all come out right.

He thanked the people profoundly and gratefully for what they had done for him, and he only had to regret that he had not had more ability to serve them. He knew and felt conscious that he had been honest and faithful, carrying out in all cases the measures he had advocated before the people.

Fayetteville *Observer*, October 4, 1860.

1. Johnson's appearance in Lincoln County was before a "very large crowd assembled at the court-house" to hear him. Fayetteville *Observer*, October 4, 1860.

2. The Democratically controlled legislature not only elected Johnson to the U. S. Senate in 1857, but also chose Nicholson to succeed Bell, whose term did not expire until 1859. Hoping to unseat Bell before the end of his term, the Tennessee legislature instructed the state's senators to support the admission of Kansas under the Lecompton Constitution. Bell defied the instructions and kept his seat until his term expired. Parks, *John Bell*, 318ff; see also Speech on Popular Sovereignty and the Right of Instruction, February 23, 1858.

3. The letter in which James Britton set forth the proposal for a Democratic fusion ticket was endorsed by his fellow Douglas-Johnson elector, W. H. Malone of Knoxville. However, even before Johnson made this speech, Malone had repudiated his support, having discovered that according to Britton's plan, the Douglas electors statewide would be expected to step aside, leaving the Breckinridge electors to receive all the Democratic votes with the mandate to cast the state's electoral ticket for whichever candidate had the best chance to win. Malone had expected that the Breckinridge electors would withdraw in West Tennessee, where Douglas had his greatest strength, and the Douglas electors in East Tennessee, where Breckinridge was far stronger.

Nashville *Union and American*, September 20, 1860; Nashville *Republican Banner*, September 27, 1860.

4. The Nashville *Democrat*, a Douglas organ, was established by William Carroll in July, 1860.

5. See Speech on Popular Sovereignty and the Right of Instruction, February 23, 1858, note 21.

6. It is impossible to find evidence that Bell's votes during the crisis of 1850 marked him as a sympathizer with squatter sovereignty. Failing to get an extension of the Missouri Compromise line, which would have protected slavery in most of the new territory acquired from Mexico, he did not cast a recorded vote on the New Mexico-Utah Territorial Act. In the early phase of the debate on the admission of California, he had suggested a compromise that would carve another slave state out of Texas, thus retaining the balance principle, and at the same time allow the remaining territory from the Mexican Cession to be admitted as either free or slave, depending on the decision of its inhabitants. Perhaps it was this proposal, later repudiated by Bell, which Johnson and other southern critics attempted to use in 1860 to associate him with squatter sovereignty. Parks, *John Bell*, 244-46, 256-61.

7. Probably a reference to Bell's opposition to homestead legislation and his support of federal grants to private railroad companies. *Ibid.*, 435-37.

8. On August 5, 1855, a serious riot developed in Louisville between Know-Nothings, who were participating in a "No-Popery" campaign, and the German sector of town. Twenty men were killed and several hundred wounded. Condoning the action, Bell declared in a Knoxville speech, September 22, 1855, that native Americans should stand up against foreigners, for it "is better that a little blood shall sprinkle the pavements and side-walks of our cities now, than that these streets should be drenched with blood hereafter." Ray A. Billington, *The Protestant Crusade, 1800–1860* (New York, 1938), 421–22, 450.

To Robert Johnson, Greeneville

Tullahoma Tenn   Oct 4th 1860—

My dear Son,

Your letter was recieved at Fayettevill on Mondy ev[en]ing remailed from Nashville— I was with Jones Some two d[a]ys— He Says he [is] taking no part: but I found the people of Lincoln v[er]y much inclined to support Douglas, yet I think there is decided reaction going on in favor of B and think that in the end there will be a pretty full vote for B— I made a Speech[1] there and m[an]y of the Dougles Supporters Came forwarde and told me that they approved of my Course and would fall into the Support of B— Davidson poor fellow was Shot on Saturdy night while I was there, and died on Sundy about 12 oclok—and on mondy I attended his funerl o[b]sequies—[2] Nicholson and my Self Spoke here on yesterdy to about three thousan people and all went off well— Nicholson tells me that Harris was not So well pleased with his visit to E. Tenn— I presum the Crowds were not large enogh— He is a very Small man at most and the more he is brought in Contact with the people the more apparent it will be— Nicholson tells me that it [has] been determined to hold a mass meeting in Greenevill[.] if that is So, it ought not to be a half meeting: but [a] full one and no pains Spared to have a turn out— If a basket dinner is determined upon, be liberal in the Subscribtion to gettig it up— Fall Branch meeting[3] might be [the occasion?] to give more time if there is not enough to have it at Greeneville before the mee[t]ing at Fall Branch— And after the meeting at Fall if it Suited the convenience of [all] parties have a mass meeting at Bristol— If there is a[n]y alteration made as to appoi[n]t[ment]s there Should be due notice givn of it— Tell Charles if [he] expects to get his man Breckinridge through he must be pretty active and do all that he Can— Tell him I have bought some bonds but Could not get the kind I wanted[.] I was Compelled to buy regular Six's at 90 in [sic] the 1,00— In this part of the State democracy Seems to be in good condition and fine Spirits— If the West Tenn Can [be] Straitened out the State Can be Carried and E. Tenn warmed[?] up— I told Britton[4] when he left me in Nashville that I would writt to him if any thing turned up worthy of writing about— Tell [him] there has been nothig more than what he has Seen [in] the papers and I therefore deamed it unnecessay to write to him and you may Say to him that his proposition is approved of by the rank & file evy where of both parties and if he had just Stood up to it he had made himself a great man with the democracy—[5] As you State in your letter th people of Greene ought to be Stirred up and there ought [to] be Steps taken to do it— Tell Frank[6] to be a good boy and go to School and learn all that he Can[.]

As ever &c   Andrew Johnson

I leave for Nashville in an hour—

ALS, DLC-JP.

1. See Speech at Fayetteville, October 1, 1860.

2. James M. Davidson, the "Irish Orator" of Fayetteville, was shot on Saturday, September 29, by James Carty; the dispute arose over Davidson's handling of Carty's money when the latter was drunk. Johnson's matter-of-fact reporting of this tragedy is a little surprising in view of Davidson's having been a long-time political associate and having shared the platform with Johnson at his recent speech in Nashville on September 21. Nashville *Republican Banner*, October 2, 1860; Nashville *Union and American*, September 20, 1860

3. Fall Branch, a small community fifteen miles northwest of Jonesboro in Washington County, was the site of a mass meeting scheduled for October 31. *Ibid.*, October 6, 1860.

4. James Britton.

5. Johnson clearly felt that Britton, having introduced a proposal for combining the Douglas and Breckinridge tickets, should have pressed with more vigor for a Democratic fusion against Bell. Although Watterson, Polk, Carroll, and other Douglas men were unfavorable, Johnson, because he himself saw fusion as a way to insure Democratic victory, was convinced that the average Democratic voter was receptive to the plan. The opposition press had

from the first asserted that the Britton proposal had originated with his more famous Greeneville friend. Nashville *Patriot*, September 25, 1860.

6. Johnson's youngest son, Andrew Johnson, Jr.

Speech at Memphis [*Two Versions*][1]

October 16, 1860.

I

He announced himself as not so much the advocate of any particular man or candidate, as of measures and principles, remarking at the same time that his present position in addressing a divided Democracy was exceedingly "embarrassing," as he found himself battling against known and tried political friends.

He entered into a full history of the convention system, acknowledging that it has never had his approval, and thought 1860 the period of its downfall and decay. Their only object from the era of their establishment, had been to concentrate public opinion upon some one man so as to prevent a multiplicity of candidates being in the field.

He denounced the Yanceyites[2] for seceding from the national convention at Charleston and Baltimore, saying that they ought to have staid in those Conventions and battled there for Southern rights. He said that the Democratic party had been disrupted at the latter place, *not upon principles*, but upon a mere preliminary question of organization. Politicians, party leaders, office holders and office-seekers had brought about this division, and he was not himself any way connected with, or responsible for it—he washed his hands of the result.

Gov. Johnson also defined the difference which he understood to exist between *popular* and *squatter* sovereignty. Giving the same definition to the latter that is attached to it by Senator Douglas, he made a most egregious and novel error in explaining the signification of the former—which he thought meant the power of the people of a territory to form their own domestic institutions, when they come to form a State constitution. He generously vindicated Mr. Douglas from the unfounded imputation of favoring the doctrine of *squatter sovereignty* as he had stated it. Douglas, he said, had promised and pledged himself to stand upon the adjudication of the Supreme Court when that tribunal should decide the vexed question of territorial powers, but did not believe as yet that it had been settled. He himself thought that the "principle" had really been decided in the case of Dred Scott, though no such case as that contemplated in the Kansas-Nebraska bill had ever directly come up before the court.[3] He said that the members of the Democratic party were free, under present circumstances, to vote as they chose, but at the same time counseled them to support Breckinridge in the South and Douglas in the North—remarking that if he lived in any State where the friends of the latter were in the majority, he would support him for the purpose of defeating Lincoln and Bell.

Gov. Johnson concluded with an announcement that he for one would never follow Yancey out of the Union,[4] but intended to fight for the South and her rights *within its limits*.

II

Andy is wild for Breckinridge.[5] He abused Bell all the way through; said Bell was not fit to be trusted, and that he had acted so treacherous towards the South that he deserved not the respect of southern people. He begged Douglas' friends to "fuse with him (Andy) and save the State from the Lincoln-Bellites."

Andy was wonderfully wrothy because the cotton States seceded at Charleston. He believes Andy Johnson would have been nominated on the Cincinnati platform if Yancey had not led the Alabama delegation out of the convention and thereby enticed the other States to follow. He said it was foolish to contend for a right that "could not be enjoyed." He was opposed to every doctrine that is not practicable. [Immense applause.] Said these "actors on high principle reminded him of the madman, who, acting on the principle that the human kind are superior to the brute creation, and had a right to control them, determined he would exercise his right to shear a wolf, and accordingly set out on a journey to the desert for that purpose, and sacrificed himself in a fruitless attempt to exercise a worthless right."

He said "Ike Cook and his followers in Illinois,[6] and the Bell men too, could not, if acting in good faith against Lincoln, vote against Douglas in that State;" and paid some high compliments to Douglas. Said "Douglas was fighting in the midst of the enemy, with a zeal that put to shame the ablest efforts of the slaveholders themselves;" said he "supported Breckinridge because he believed he was the strongest man South." Johnson soon discovered that there was not an omnibus load of Breckites in his audience. In the commencement he put out a feeler to test the sentiment of his hearers; for here in Memphis it is admitted by all parties that the secession candidate will not poll two hundred and fifty votes.[7] He declared that the "secession at Charleston was brought about by designing demogogues for ignoble purposes," which brought down the house in such a manner that it was some moments before silence could be restored, and the speaker allowed to proceed.[8] Every few moments he implored in the most piteous manner the friends of Douglas to "come and fuse," and finally expressed the hope that the "people would rise in their majesty and compel the electors when they cast their vote to vote altogether for the strongest man, and defeat the seceding and dishonest politicians, as well as the Republicans of the North."

Memphis *Appeal*, October 17, 27, 1860.

1. Both of these accounts come from Douglas newspapers. It is probable that a fuller and more sympathetic account appeared in the Memphis *Avalanche*, the Breckinridge paper, but it is not extant. According to the *Appeal* editor, "The Hon. Andrew Johnson was first introduced and spoke for over two hours," and was followed by A. O. P. Nicholson, also campaigning for Breckinridge. Memphis *Appeal*, October 17, 1860.

2. Although one cannot be certain that Johnson used this term to describe the seceders at both Democratic conventions, he was obviously critical of these, his fellow Breckinridge supporters, in this most unorthodox of campaigns.

3. As written into the Kansas-Nebraska Act, the "principle" nullifying the Missouri Compromise and prohibiting territorial legislatures from deciding on the question of slavery was in effect upheld by the Supreme Court in the Dred Scott decision. Settlement of the slavery issue in a territory would be delayed until application for statehood was made and a constitution drafted. Nevins, *Emergence of Lincoln*, I, 90–95.

4. Clearly, Johnson was embarrassed by the disunionist bedfellows with whom he found himself in the Breckinridge campaign.

5. This version originally appeared in the Missouri *Republican*, a St. Louis Democratic paper which was supporting Douglas' candidacy, and was reprinted in the Memphis *Appeal*, October 27, 1860. William H. Taft, *Missouri Newspapers* (Columbia, 1964), 57, 63.

6. Isaac Cook, Chicago postmaster and bitter Douglas foe, had unsuccessfully attempted to seat an anti-Douglas faction at the Charleston convention. Hesseltine, *Three against Lincoln*, 21, 31, 34, 39.

7. Breckinridge would run a poor third in Shelby County, receiving only 744 votes to 2,959 for Douglas and 3,048 for Bell. Campbell, *Tenn. Attitudes*, 287.

8. In an audience largely Douglas in its sympathies the response to any condemnation of those who had left the Charleston convention to avoid being party to Douglas' nomination could not but arouse great enthusiasm.

From Moreau Brewer[1]

Brownsville. Tenn.   Nov'r 8th 1860.

Hon. Andrew Johnson:

Dear Sir,

After my sincere compliments, allow me to say that I hope you will pardon the liberty I take of addressing you on a subject of interest only to myself. For several years I have been connected with the Democratic press—have stuck to it and advocated the men and measures of the party with what zeal and ability I possessed. In the year '56 at Jackson I edited "The Madisonian"[2] voting for and supporting the claims of Buchanan & Breckinridge. Amid all the detraction showered upon that administration, the treachery of some, and lukewarmness of others, I haven't failed or faltered in its defense. When the deplorable division occurred in our party, I thought it the duty of all true Democrats to rally under the flag of Breckinridge, and went into the "Atlas"[3] office in this place to advocate and help sustain that ticket. But the owner of that concern has discontinued it and I find myself out of employment with little or no prospect of a situation in this section. I have a wife and child to take care of and cannot afford to remain idle or unemployed. Previously to my engagement to edit the "Atlas" here, I had exhausted every means and effort to procure a situation.

I address you seeking your aid and influence, because I know you have more influence with those in authority than any man in the State. I am making an effort to procure a clerkship at Washington. The Secretary of the Interior has numerous Clerkships at his disposal (on the Census work) and with such recommendation as you might be pleased to give me, I feel sure that I could succeed. I feel qualified to discharge the duties of any clerkship they may give me at Washington, and will have every incentive to do so that a man could have. For a corroboration of the foregoing statements I can refer to Wm. T. Avery, H. S. Bradford, our elector, or any leading Democrat in West Tenn. It is only the direst necessity that impels me to address you this letter—and you may be fully assured that whatever you are so kind as to do for me in the matter will ever be most gratefully remembered. During this canvass and the preceeding ones I have always endeavored to refute and repel the newspaper slanders and falsehoods levelled at your character. This I did from a sense of duty to the party and its most trusted and able leader. Again, trusting that the embarrassed circumstances in which I find myself will be with you, a sufficient apology for this letter, I remain, very truly

Your friend & fellow citizen,
Moreau Brewer.[4]

ALS, DLC-JP.

1. Moreau Brewer (b. c1825) of Yorkville, a sometime editor, was part owner and editor (1847–49) of the Trenton *Star Spangled Banner*, a Whig organ. *Goodspeed's Gibson*, 804; 1860 Census, Tenn., Gibson, 175.

2. Not to be found in Gregory's *Union List of Newspapers*, the *Madisonian* apparently was of short duration; only the issue of June 20, 1857, is listed among Tennessee newspapers in the state library.

3. The Brownsville *Atlas*, a weekly published in 1859–60, survives only in one issue, that of July 18, 1860. Gregory, *Union List of Newspapers*, 653.

4. Apparently Brewer was unsuccessful in his bid for a clerkship. Moreau Brewer to Andrew Johnson, February 22, 1875, Johnson Papers, LC.

From George H. Finley

November 8, 1860, Ormes Store, Cumberland County; ALS, DLC-JP.

Former county judge solicits Johnson's aid in obtaining "an appointment of Mail Ageant [*sic*] on Some one of the Rail Road lines leading out from Chattanooga," and observes that "there is a great Excitement as to the Political Condition of our Country[.] how it will determin is not known but hope for the bet[t]er."

Speech at Union Meeting, Greeneville[1]

November 24, 1860

He vindicated the resolutions[2] with an ability characteristic of the man—showing most conclusively that they embodied the doctrines of the Constitution. He came down upon the Black Republican party for their efforts to *nullify the Fugitive Slave Law*, by the enactment of laws in most of the Northern States to obstruct the execution of the same. He then took up the docrine of seperate State secession, and said that while he was free to admit that the South had just cause of complaint, he did not think the Constitution made any provision for a State to go out of the Union, short of that inherent right in all people to resort to revolution when peacable remedies fail and grievances become intolerable. The Constitution when ratified by the "*original thirteen*" States, and by every State that has come into the Federal Union since that time, was ratified, in the language of one of the resolutions, *without condition or reservation and forever.* He thought the better course for the South to pursue, was a course of moderation, and demand her rights in the Union and not out of it.[3]

Greeneville *Democrat*, November 27, 1860.

1. As anti-Union sentiment mounted in the South following Lincoln's election on November 6, moderate leaders of all parties became alarmed and began to cooperate in an effort to exorcise the spectre of disunion. Symbolic of the new alignments, Johnson and his longtime Whig rival, T. A. R. Nelson, participated in a Union meeting in Greeneville where they spoke in favor of resolutions advocating "*a union of equal States, with equality of rights in those States*," as the editor of the Greeneville *Democrat* described them. Adopting a somewhat different tack, Thomas D. Arnold urged the meeting to go on record as supporting the Lincoln administration within the framework of the peaceful ballot. According to the *Democrat*, Arnold's objections to the more moderate orientation of the resolutions "disappeared before the convincing and terse logic of the Governor, more rapidly than the morning dew before the rising sun." Nevertheless he did not endorse them. Greeneville *Democrat*, November 27, 1860.

2. After a sharp debate between Johnson and Arnold, the group concurred on fourteen resolutions, agreeing that Congress had no right to interfere with slavery in the territories, that the Supreme Court was the final

arbiter of territorial cases involving slavery, and that the government must protect slave property in the territories. Upholding the principle of popular sovereignty, the gathering deplored the sectional character of the recent presidential election and condemned the personal-liberty laws. Nevertheless the Greene Countians opposed secession until all other means of redress had been exhausted, believing that secession without the consent of other states would be revolution. The prospect of a civil war, they declared, was more odious than a conflict with all the major world powers. Certain that the ascendancy of Black Republicanism was temporary and resolving never to abandon the friends of the Union in the North, the group affirmed that the "glorious Constitution, with all of its solemn guarantees, good enough for Washington and Jackson, is good enough for us and our children." Nashville *Union and American*, November 24, December 5, 1860.

3. The report in the *Democrat* concluded, "The Governors speech was altogether very conservative, steering clear of the *fanaticism of the North*, and the *secession of the South*." Greeneville *Democrat*, November 27, 1860.

From J. H. C. Basham

[Union City]
December 1st 1860

Mr. Johnson   for the love of my count[r]y I feel a disire as weak as they are to advance my idears a little farther[.] The Laws of God are Laws of preserfation[.] If mankind would ovserve Them Laws they would superceed the neaseesity of all others[.] The disobedience of man forced out all laws of protection[.] The intention of all delegated Law makeing powers were for protection[.] No delegated power or their creatures have the right to pass a law of prohibition[.] when they pass bank laws or bankrupt laws they over reach their power[.]   they are laws of temtation the verry opposite of the laws of God[.] The first question to be asked is[:]   Is the constitution of the united States a Slave constitution or is it a freesoil constitution[?] The fugitive clause proves to any sane man that it is a Slave constitution[.] That is a plane law to protect that species of property[.] Secondly can any sane man believe that the Slave States ever would have consented to the confederacy if the constitution had of failed to recognise Slave property as property[?] That proves the fact to any intiligent mind that the decision of the supreme court in the dred scott case was correct[.] Mr. Douglass in his controversy with Judge Black[1] said Mr. Buchannan in his Kansas message said that Slave property went into Kansas by Virtue of the constitution[.]   if that be a fact Illinoise is just as much a slave State as Ky.   well that was a plaine matter of fact[.] I can take Slave property to Illinoise[.] The local laws of the state will deprive me of that property[.] I then take and [*sic*] Appeal to the supreme court of the United States[.]   that court is bound to refund back my property with damages and the strong arme of goverment is bound to protect me and my property

on any Teriatory in the United States[.] And why the constitution
recognises Slave property as property and in the eye of the constitution evey foot of Teritory in the United States is Slave teritory[.]
Mr. Douglass said a Teritorial Legislature had the right to pass a
law to prohibt a Turk from comeing into the teritory with his twenty
wifes and the Massachusetts man from bringing in his black wife[.]
A law to prevent a Turk from bring[i]ng in his twenty wifes is to
protect the Teritory from the sin of bigamy and on the other hand
to protect the teritory of the sin of amalgamation just simple [*sic*]
a law of protection and not prohibition[.]   does the constitution
recognise bigamy or amalgamation as property[?]   no Sir the idear
is just as weak as squatter priviledges "not Sovringnty is its self"[.]
Well Sir I am bound to render unto cezar the things that belong [to]
cezar[.] I confess Mr. Douglas stuck as close to his Squatter prive-
ledges as grim death did to the ded nigger[.] he swore befor the
Election should go into the house he would throw it to Lincoln[.]
well he don so when he Voted against Kansas[.]   he said he had
taken a through ticket bagage and all and when he went out of the
Democratic Party he would go with his own accord and take all he
could with him and when he got over the river he would cut down
the bridges and sink the boats so they never can get back again[.]
well he has carryed out his rule or ruin policy and they say gone over
to the black Republican camps[.] That party are well aware that
Mr. Douglass proved traitor to the Democratic Party[.] That party
can never have confidence in the man[.]   he cant take up thare and
when he comes to the river Sticks [*sic*] Old carion [*sic*] the ferryman[2] will say Sir you have a through ticket[.] I am bound to set you
across[.] you cant take up here[.] In the name of God whare will the
man find repose[?]

Well Sir as i have flew the track[3] I will say a few words for the
consolation of Mr. John Bell[.] The first campaign paper from the
Bell committe gave his Kansas Speech they say in full[.] Mr. Bell
says I know the Missouri compromise is unconstitutional[.] I know
the repeal is constitutional[.] my friend[s] say if I Vote against the
repeal I will repent it all the days of my life[.] the South was forced
into that restriction[.] I confess my weakness so fare [*sic*] as to say
that I have frequently Voted on Bills of miner importance to gratafy
my friends contrary to my better informed judgeme[n]t[.] the great
bugaboo is with me what will be the result if we blow up that unconstitutional compromise[?]   Genl. Butler in a late speech in Massachusetts[4] not [k]nowing or careing what Mr. Bell said says he
when Mr. Douglass introduced that repeal I thought at the time that
it was one of the most imprudent steps that a man could take to aggi-
tate the slave question at that time[.] that Mr. Douglass was well

aware of one fact [.] That every man that had respect for his oath was bound to Vote for the repeal of an unconstitutional restriction Bells oath forceing him to Vote against the repeal[.] well Sir just such legislatures as I have been nameing would ruin any Goverment[.] Well Sir I will now come to the point[.] as well as i can recollect thirteen of the Nothern States have passed free liberty Bills for the purpose of defeating the constitution in the fugitive protection for slave property treason[able] in their nature a law to justify men of one state in stealing property of men of and other state and why all this[?] they [k]no[w] the fact that the Constitution is slave[.] the South have the constitution and the Law on their side and the only chance they have to carry out freesoilism is to rebell against those Laws by treason purgery in congress in the teritories by John Browns spikes and murder in the first degree[.] Murder in Virginue [sic] and in Texas sticnine [strychnine] fire and blood[.][5] a member of congress after he takes the oath to suport the constitution and then boast that he is bound by a higher law certainly in the eye of God he is a purged [perjured] man[.] What do they mean by a higher law[?] is it the law of freedom or the law of God[?] is spilling the blood of the innocent freedom[?] God forbid[!] does God require them to use stricnine powder lead fire and every means of distruction the life of innocent Women & children to fulfill his Law[?] God forbid any such hypocracy[.] I say Sir thare is a way to try the sincerity. If african slavery is such a monster of sin as to cause all this certainly the southern people ar the most wicked people on Earth[.] under such circumstances I would advise the North to seceed from a slave constitution and set up for themselves with a freesoil constitution[.] the South will not only grant them the priviledge of secession but they will aid them in keeping house divide all the meanes of goverment and the waste Teritory agreeable to population[.] the great sin of slavery in the South will be taken off their shoulders[.] God will release them then of the great sin of Affrican slavery and certainly they then will be the freest and of course the happyest people on the face of the globe[.] If the North is not willing to be made a happy people "do unto others as you would wish for them to do unto you["] well then will you permit the South to seceede in peace[?]

If the North objects to the Souths seceding in peace well what does that prove[?] it proves that they have the good sence to know that they move br[e]athe and have their being by Affrican labour and that the Southern States are their best friends and know they cannot live without them and best of all is the constitution is the best will that was ever made by any set of Farthers[.] Sir I have read of England paying millions to slave owners for property[.] I will assure you I have never read or heard of a nation or Party that would pass Laws to autherise one man to steal or take another mans property by force without recompence and cloath their sins with garments of relegion[.] If Affrican slavery is a sin whare was the Ademic [Adamic] transgression[?] your eye is now looking at Old Massachusetts— Massachusetts was only the agent of Affrica in carrying out the sin[.] Can it be possible in this enlighten Nation the City of reffuge[6] for the poore of all Nations I say can it be possible That thare has a party arrision thats to govern this Nation more degraded than any other Party that has ever been put on record[?] Sir I am fifty odd years of age[.] I never owned a slave[.] I never expect to be master of one and yet I have never objected to Affrican slavery[.] every tub has to set on its own bottom[.][7] it is a sin "if a sin" that a nonslaveholder is not responsible for[.] we expect to account to God for our own sins and not the sins of others[.] we have lernt and important lesson and that is to attend to our own business and let other persons business alone— happyness is the object of every man and i can safely say the slaves of the South are the Happyest people that inhabits the globe[.] Thare is and old man servant in this neighbourhood ninety years of age that has not experienced as much trouble in life as old John Brown experienced in twenty four hours— free labour is one hundred percent higher in the slave states than it is in the North[.] The slave holders gets the benefit of slave labour the non slave holder receives all the benefit of Office[.] we are the free men[.] we can emigrate to any state[.] The slave holder is confined to the slaves states[.] If the slave holder were to take abolition advice and set their slaves at liberty the non slaveholder of the South would slaughter them in twelve months[.] self preservation the first law of nature[8] would force us to commit the deede[.] they would steel every thing we could make and starve us to death if we did not act in self defince[.] Sir thare is many of them that would even dare to steal a meeting house[.] I have a near neighbours that was raised in new Jersey[.] he was twenty six years of age when he left[.] he has been a citizen of nearly every southern state[.] he says the people of the South are a highminded honerable people and that they never can live with the people of the North[.] his reasons are that three fourths of the people of the North believe in witch craft and if one Old Woman was suspicioned for being a witch and she was to say Affrican slavery was a sin it would throw the whole North in a full blaze for negro freedom[.] as for myself I believe thare is as many good sound patriotic constitutional men in the North as there is in the South[.] Sir I have been talking all this time about things I did not wish to talk about[.] Mr. Lincoln is elected president on a freesoil platform[.] how to sware in a presi-

dent to support a slave constitution standing on a freesoil platforme
gets me. as genl Butler said i can take water and molasses put them
together and make vinegar but how to make molasses out of Vinegar
is a something I never lernt[.] I could see verry plane how to sware
him out[.] it is a brand new page on American history[.] after Mr.
Van burin was released of his oath he turned freesoil[.] It was the
duty of his party to have made some amendments to the constitution
before they made the platforme[.] if he recommends freesoil measures it is the duty of congress to take him before the supreme
court[.] all of the teritory that Virginue gave to the United States
for free States came in by the will of Virginue (Ky) came in and
Tennessee by Virtue of the constitution and why their constitutions
recognise slave property as property which makes them cons[ti]tu-
tional states[.] Lueasaanner [sic] came in by purchase a slave state
which made her constitutional[.] Texas came in by annexation with
a slave constitution which made her constitutional[.] Oregon and
others came in by the will of the people with freesoil constitutions
contrary to the true sperit of the constitution of these united States[.]
If every member of congress will pay that respect for their oath that
is their duty to do thare can never another Free state come into this
confederacy through that body[.] That is proof they must come in
some other way and how[?] by Teritorial priviledges[?] no[.] by
popular priviledges[?] no[.] by congress a delegated law makeing
power, no[.] They must come in by the sovregn power of a state
what I call popular sovregnty not teritorial Priviledges as some
suppose[.] whare dos a teritorial Legislature obtain that power to say
free or slave[?] whare does a teritorial convention and other creature of congress obtain that power from[?] can water rise higher
than its fountain[?] no[.] The question must be reserved for the
sovregn power. it has allmost becme a kowlidge [sic] of instinct in
the minds of the people[.] they stick sovregn to a teritorial legislature others stick sovregn to a Teritorial convention others stick
sovregn to congress a delegated law makeing power agents only for
the sovregn powers and the best of it is the Black Republicans have
stuck sovregn to the buck negro by a freesoil Law[.] Mr. Brackin-
ridge in his late Ashland speech said the people of a state had the
right to settle the slave question[.] That is correct but the people of
a state is not the people of a Teritory[.] thare is the eror[.] Mr.
Lincoln says he wants all the new states to come in free after they
become sovregn[.] if they then should change their constitution to
slave he could not see how he could object[.] settle the teritory by
non slaveholders [with] no interest in slave labour[.] if they be-
[c]ome insane after they become a sovregn power should Change
their constitution which would be a Maricle[.] A power independant

of him as president he could not see how he could object[.] The idear
is certainly the weakest that any man has ever expressed on the subject[.] Them fre[e]soil letters written to congress the first struggle
with Kansas are sufficient evidence to satisfy any man saying take
us in for God sake we dont wish for Kansas to blow up the goverment take us in and make us a free and independant people[.] we
can then attend to our own business and we never can before— we
must look at the extreme of parties to get their true position[.]
Thare is two verry noted charactors in this country[.] The southern
fire eator and Northern fanatic[.] the southern fier eater is a red hot
constitutional man[.] did a fier eater ever ask the North to come
farther south than the constitution[?] no never— a Northern fanatic is a man that can take the oath to support the constitution put
his foot on it turn round and spit in the face of the supreme court of
the United States and bloated with treason at that— Every man
that has any knowledge [of] politics are satisfyed that popular
sovregnty of state has the right to change or alter their constitution
which makes it as plaine as one fact can be made— That no other
power aggreeable to equity or justice can posess or can distroy that
right that only belongs to a sovregn state—and not Teritorial priviledges or congressional intervention whare no sovregnty exist—
Thare is no sovregnty in a Teritory while in a Teritorial capasity[.]
The great e[rr]or is many persons believe that the people of a Teritory possess sovregnty which is not the case[.] It should be hands
off Teritorial Legislature hands off Teritorial convention hands off
Congress— Take holt [sic] ye sovregn power— Sir if that fire
brand has to pass through the Teritory and then [be] thrown into
congress by a Teritorial convention or legislature the sooner this
Union dissolves the better— The question to be asked every man
in the United States is this— what will be the consequences if the
slave question is reserved and handed to the proper power— The
answer is peace in the Teritories peace in congress and peace to
these United States[.] The members of congress would love each
other[.] Sewards irrepressible conflict would ceace and you would
never hear again the question of power aggitated by congress
again[.] They would say let us first attend to our commercial affairs
secondly The Pacific Rail road and thirdly how shal we obtain Cuba
and whare the blessing would end God only knows for I do not[.] I
will venture to say if the States were dissolved and one side propose
to the other to reserve the slave question for the sovregn or popular
sovregnty of the State that they would be sure to unite again[.] Mr.
Johnson you said you would stick to the last plank of the reck of
State[.] I love your conservatism because I love my country[.] Confession of Truth is unto salvation[.] The Apostle John says God is

Truth[.] it is the only act that man can do that is noble[.] it is simple confessing God and he says when i am for you who can be against[?] Truth will prevail[.] all Partyes are wrong that confession will distroy party feelings and sectional prejudices[.] it will then be come one come all and help me to throw that Vexed question to whare it belongs and save my beloved count[r]y[.] The measure is and attribute of the Law of God[.] Teritorial priviledges and congressional intervention are Laws of temtation[.]

                                                                J H C Basham

Sir I forgot to say in conclusion as I am a non Slaveholder you can use this letter in any way you may think best[.] I allways feel ressponsible for any thing I do or say[.] I am no secret man[.] I can say for the non slave holders of the slave States that they never will degrade themselves so fare as [to] equalise themselves with free negroes[.] If Affrican slavery is a sin it is a moral religious question and not a question of Law and Politics[.] a Resolution by congress to reserve the slave question for the sovergn[ty] of the state or the popular sovregnty of same will forever suffice[.] I have advanced the Idear to many of all Parties and I will assure you it dont require one moments reflection[.]

                                                your friend   J. H. C. B.

ALS, DLC-JP.

1. Jeremiah S. Black (1810–1883) of Pennsylvania, U. S. attorney general (1857–60) and secretary of state (1860–61), assisted Buchanan in his attempts to maintain unity within the party. When Douglas attacked administration policy, Black engaged him in a pamphlet war, denouncing his views on squatter sovereignty on the grounds that territorial legislatures could never make laws in violation of the Fifth Amendment. Black upheld the legality of the Lecompton Constitution, but when Lincoln's election made secession imminent, Black took the position that federal property should be protected and urged the adequate garrisoning of federal forts in the South. With the end of his service in the Cabinet, he resumed the practice of law in York, Pennsylvania, remaining influential in politics until his death. *DAB*, II, 310–13; see also William N. Brigance, *Jeremiah Sullivan Black: A Defender of the Constitution and the Ten Commandments* (Philadelphia, 1934).

2. In Greek mythology, Charon was the ferryman who transported the souls of the properly buried dead across the river Styx into Hades. For his services, he required a fee of an obolus or other small coin. Catherine B. Avery, ed., *New Century Classical Handbook* (New York, 1962), 1034.

3. A term meaning to depart from a usual or prescribed course. In 1847, a congressman was "accused of flying the track on the creed of the Democratic Party." Mathews, *Americanisms*, II, 1756.

4. In the elections of 1860 Benjamin F. Butler was the candidate of the Breckinridge Democrats for the Massachusetts governorship; this speech may have been delivered in his canvass. Robert S. Holzman, *Stormy Ben Butler* (New York, 1954), 24–25.

5. Following John Brown's raid in October, 1859, excitement spread throughout the South. Near hysteria reigned in portions of Texas; strange fires of an incendiary character occurred in Dallas and other north Texas cities; rumors were rife that the fires were the work of abolitionists and that

mass poisonings and slave uprisings were planned. Rupert N. Richardson, *Texas: The Lone Star State* (New York, 1943), 244.

6. Num. 35:6.

7. Variations of this proverb appear in a number of literary works, among them Charles Macklin, *The Man of the World*, Act I, sc. 2, and John Bunyan, *The Pilgrim's Progress*, Pt. I. Burton E. Stevenson, *The MacMillan Book of Proverbs, Maxims, and Famous Phrases* (New York, 1968), 2397.

8. Samuel Butler, *Remains*, II, 27.

From J. Rufus Smith[1]

Hillsboro   Hill Co. Texas,
1 Decr 1860

Hon Andrew Johnson
Senate Chamber—
Dear Sir—
Often, while I lived in Loudon & since I moved here, I have recd various valuable documents under your frank— I hope you will occasionally—while I am out here herding my sheep—think of my address & send such documents, speeches &c, as will keep me up with the threatning Storm—

I take pleasure in reading the Sceintific works eminating from the Smithsonian Institute— Also send something to E. C. Zolli-coffer[2]—Hillsboro Texas— He is a Cozin to F. K[3]—but went for Breckenridge & is a good man—but has been an old whig—

Your freind   J. Rufus Smith

Send a Document to
Snead Harris[4]—an old Democrat from Tenn—& your devoted friend— I have given him Several of your Speeches—(To Hillsboro)

ALS, DLC-JP.

1. J. Rufus Smith (b. *c*1823), Hill County farmer, declared $10,300 in personal property on the eve of the war. 1860 Census, Texas, Hill, 65.

2. E. C. Zollicoffer (b. *c*1823) was a wealthy Texas farmer with $30,000 worth of real and personal property in 1860. *Ibid.*, 45.

3. Felix K. Zollicoffer, Tennessee Whig politician, editor, and later Confederate general. *DAB*, XX, 659–60.

4. Sneed Harris (b. *c*1806), Tennessee-born farmer, claimed property valued at $17,000 in 1860. 1860 Census, Texas, Hill, 62.

From William P. Johnson[1]

Columbia Texas   December the 2—1860

Dear Brother
I now Sit down to wright you a fue lines and I hardly know how to commence[.] my familys helth is generly good except my own which

is not good nor has it bin for a long time and I feare it will never be good a gain but I do the best I can and keep Sober all the time[.] Texas is no place for a one Eyed man a bout know [now.] there is an Election on tomorow to Elect Delagates to go to Austin to form a convention² to make a constitution for the State of Texas and to suseed from the union of the States at all hazerds regardless of all concequences of property or life[.] the lone [picture of a star] is the go here and there [is] not one in ten of the tite larks³ that knows the value of a country or what it cost tho I am braught to think verry seriously on the mater[.] I have a beloved Wife and five helpless children in Texas with me that I think will stand a good chance to be bucherd by they [sic] Negrows for if the force of Texas I mean the white force was put in to requisition it is not a surficent and safe patrole over the Negrows in the State[.] The sensus taker told me when he took my little William⁴ that he was the two thousanth white person he had taken in this county and that he had taken four thousand Negrows two weks before and allmost all he had to take was Negrows, and the Mexicans are tickling in there Sleaves[.] as soon as an out brake shall take place in our East then they with the Indians and fugitive Negrows will come in on the west and over run the country but I am here and will make the best of the affair that I can[.] I morn for my country[.] it is lost to a certainty[.] there is rogues a nuff [sic] in the North and South to distroy the kingdom of Heaven and there is at least at this time 500 fuss makers in Texas that expects to be President of the Southern Confedracy[.] we have men here waring the Star on ther hats and on the left lappell of there coats that dos not know what they are wareing it for and if some of them dont mind they will get there necks cracked and a bout that time the people will hunt these dear fellows that has made the rumpus and try the strenth of hemp and live Oake limbs[.] the busness of the vigelance will be changed[.] there has bin several men hung in Texas for mere expresion of Opinion and people of Other States will not allways bare it but when the worst comes to the worst I am a mung [sic] those that will defend my Wife and children to the last drop of my Blood[.] I have a Good Shot Gun and a good yoarger [jaeger?]⁵ and a plenty of buck shot and balls[.] I have got my wife practiceing with the Shot Gun and I am a tolrable shot [at] a hundred[.] yet I can kill only a Goo[se] or a turkey yet and I believe that I can kill a Negrow or a mean white man with a good gun and there is no scarcety of mean men in Texas[.] the arastocracy is the vigilence and they better deserve to be hung than the devel does to be in hell[.] they are usurpers of the common law and I believe traters to the goverment of the United States[.] they complain of grevence that they have not had to bare but we have

Some aspiring chaps here that if they Say one thing and do a nother
they will Suffer buckrum[.][6]   the people has bin guld as long as they
intend to bare guling and those men that gows to Austin had beter
be on there peas and cues[7] or they may fall in to the hands of a different vigelence from that of the arestockracy in to viglence of the
Sober steady thinking Country loving people and they never do
rong at eny time and had the peopl have bin left to think for them
selves there would have bin non of this National Turmoil a bout
Sesion and abolition but men that deserve the rope if they do not
mind will find one in the hands of the proper persons and they will
execute justice to all indiscriminatly with out favour to person or
party[.] these are some of the feelings as well as I can learn by
hering them talk[.] this count[r]y is in bad State of feeling you may
depend at this time[.] now my Brother these are facts or the mase of
the people is not to [be] believed[.]   in and a bout our little town the
old Texas flag is flying throu[gh] the top of a live Oak in our little
vilage and the polititions say they will die under it but there is not
much Spunk whare it does not pay pritty well[.]   now I come to some
thing that concerns you and me as Brothers[.] I have no good news
to wright but I hope you will answer my letter and let me here from
you and your family[.] as I never expect to see you in this life makes
[me] more anxious to here from you[.] you certainly can tak time to
wright to me twice a year and let me here from you[.] give Our
Love to Sister and your children and if you know eny thing of my
son Andw let me here of him[.] I hope he is doing well for him
Self[.]
Elezebeth and Olive[8] sends there Love to there uncle and Aunt and
cusins[.]   it is now 12 oclock at night and the rain is faling fast[.] I
must come to a close[.]   good by for the present[.] I shall look for an
answer soon[.] I remain your Brother in that bond that [n]othing
but Death can Sever[.]

                                        William, P. Johnson
          to his Brother Andrew Johnson
P. S. I have no complaint to make[.] I would rather die than make
one complaint to man on the face of Gods Green Earth[.]

ALS, DLC-JP; also printed in Andrew F. Muir, ed., "William P. Johnson,
Southern Proletarian and Unionist," *Tenn. Hist. Quar.*, XV (1956), 330–38.

   1. William P. Johnson (1803–1865), Andrew's older brother, was born
in Raleigh, North Carolina. Apprenticed to a printer about 1812, and somewhat later to a tailor, he ultimately became a carpenter. Sometime after his
arrival in Tennessee in 1826, William married Sarah Giddings McDonough
(1816–1882), a native of Tennessee, who, during years of wandering in
search of a prosperity which never came, bore him ten children. (For his
progeny, see *Johnson Papers*, I, App. I.) As late as 1842 the Johnsons were
living in Georgia; from 1845 to 1851 they were definitely in Alabama, and
in 1857 they appeared in Columbia, Texas, where William seems to have

accepted as final his failure to acquire a homestead of his own. During the war he remained Unionist in sympathy but served neither side. In July, 1865, he was appointed surveyor of the port of Velasco, but his good fortune was short lived, for in October the accidental discharge of a gun during a hunting expedition and the gangrene which followed resulted in his death. Andrew F. Muir, ed., "William P. Johnson, Southern Proletarian and Unionist," *Tenn. Hist. Quar.*, XV (1956), 330–38; Winston, *Andrew Johnson*, 12–14, 21.

2. In the excitement which followed Lincoln's election, secessionist elements in Texas agitated for a convention to consider the state's relationship to the Union. Various local meetings, notably one of Travis County citizens on November 17, called for elections to select delegates for such a convention. Apparently Brazoria County held its election on December 3. Larry J. Gage, "The Texas Road to Secession and War," *Southwestern Historical Quarterly*, LXII (1958), 202.

3. The titlark is a small singing bird, also described as a pipit. *Webster's Third International.*

4. William (b. 1857) was the youngest child.

5. "Jaeger," or "yager," a rifle with a short barrel and large bore.

6. "Buckram," as used here, appears to carry the old English connotation of "non-existent persons"; in short, the "aspiring chaps," candidates for the state secession convention, may well be displaced politically if they do not measure up to the expectations of union-loving Texans. John S. Farmer and W. E. Henley, comps., *Dictionary of Slang & Its Analogues* (New York, 1966), 400.

7. An expression derived from an old tavern custom of hanging up a slate marked P. and Q., with the customers' names written beneath, and check marks for the pints and quarts consumed. Stevenson, *Quotations*, 1637.

8. Elizabeth (b. *c*1842) and Olive (b. *c*1845) were among William's ten children.

From Amos David[1]

Somerville   Tennessee, Decr. 3d.   1860.

Dear Sir,

In view of the danger to the union of these United States, now upon us, I look forward with great anxiety, to the forthcoming Message from President Buckhannon, as well as to the action of the present congress; without Some Early, and decisive Step taken towards a radical change in the Manner of Electing a President, I greatly fear there will be an erreparrable disruption of the Union; I will respectfully suggest a plan, which if carried into effect, would in my opinion, go far towards removing the Cause of Complaint, to wit, let each State, Elect one of his citizens as a *Candidate* for the Presidency. Send up to the President of the U. S. Senate, a duly authinticated Certificate of such Election,   Let the President of the Senate appoint a Committee of that body, who shall take the names of the Candidates, So Elected, and in the presence of the Senate, *draw by lot*, from those names, No. 1 for President of the U. S., No. 2 for Vice President, and the next seven lowest numbers, to form the Cabinet, the President Elect, to appoint them to the s[e]veral Bureaus, as he may think best;

Such a course would take all the *Political gass* out of the abboli-
tion cloud, Which now hangs so darkly over us, that being effected,
the cloud would disperse: Surely the Executive, and Congress, will
find some remedy some means to avert the threatened deadly blow
to our union, and that immediately; after the "Ides of March" the
"Rubicon" will have been passed:

Yours With Respect. Amos David
of Somerville Tennessee

Hon. A Johnson.
U. S. Senate

ALS, DLC-JP.
    1. Amos David (b. *c*1793), a native of Virginia, was a Fayette County
farmer. 1860 Census, Tenn., Fayette, 14.

From Fisk Kirkpatrick

December 5, 1860, Hilham [Overton County]; ALS, DLC-JP.

Asks assistance in locating land patent for 10,000 acres in Florida or
Mississippi "given under the signet of King George" to Sir William Har-
coart for services in the French and Indian War. Purchased by Samuel
Denton, of Overton County, and bequeathed to his widow, the patent and
accompanying papers were entrusted to Senator Hopkins Turney and are
now apparently misplaced. "I will say to you if you will aid me & I succeed you will be rewarded."

From Samuel Williams[1]

Trenton Decr 5th 1860

Hon Andrew, Johnson
    Dear sir   yours of the [blank] is recd together with a coppy of
the Resolutions passed at Greenville on the 24th Novr[.][2] I have examined the resolutions of the Committy carefully and shown them
to a good many leading men of both Partys all of whome most
cordially and heartily approve the Resolutions in all their parts, and
we are dilighted to see East Tennessee taking this sound conservative position[.] we believe it will have a good effect through the state
and in the neighbouring states[.] I feel satisfyed that 9 out of 10 in
our community of all parties will fully endorse those resolutions[.]
we have a few here who are for secession not now right out but
using all the arguments in their favour to give that side the secis-
sionests strength[.]   they appeal to the Passions and attempt [to] excite the popular mind relating grievances in there most aggrivated
form and pretending to be disgusted with the Idea of ocupying
the position of what they call Submissionists but I feel sure that the
masses of our people are not to be alarmed by taunts and have the

nerve to do right even if in doing that they should find it necessary to behave in a peaceable dignified and prudent manner while we would rather revolutionise the government than to submit to degridation yet secession or Revolution we all believe would be ruin[.] we believe it utterly impossible that it can be peaceable[.] the navigation of the Mississippi River Carrying the produse of the Free states through the slave states could never be carryed on peaceably & with war or without would come heavy Taxes[.]   then the enquiry why this[?] Answer the difficultys of the slavry question[.] then the non slave holder says this money is being raised to protect one species of property in which he has no interest and consequently he ought not to be burthened or in convenienced about it[.] when pressed on him he resists it first to avoid paying the Tax and finally stands out against the Institution itself[.] it is easy to see where it leads[.] our people regard this secession movement as a road full of Troubles & none can regret that it is so more than us or be more aroused not to rush into Revolution but to avoid it[.]   we know that he who may excite the popular mind & bring on the conflict will have no power to quiet the contending elements & restore Peace[.] we hope that our apprehensions and fears of the results are higher than they ought to be but certainly the right time to avert an evil is before it has gone too far[.] I again say we are highly gratifyed to see your part of the state ocupying what we believe to be the right ground[.]   enclosed I send you a coppy of Resolutions passed at a meeting of our citizens on the 19th inst[.][3] I had intended & still intend not to interfere with Politi[c]s but seeing that the meeting was coming on & some of the Admire[r]s of Yancy in our County were very much disposed to follow him I determined to go into the meeting and as far as in me lay privent a secession movement being made[.] I drew the 1st five of the Resolutions[.] I drew them hastily but you will see they are not for secession[.] Mr Freeman[4] of our Town &. L. W. Taliaferro[5] opposed the resolutions generally declareing for the south and [a]gainst secession but the large crowd present were nearly unanimous for them as you will see from a tourn half sheet of a paper not now being able to get a resolution paper, with them in it & this being the only paper published here[.][6] Let me close by appoligising for the ligth [length] of my letter without more substance in it[.]

I remain very   Truly yours &c
S. Williams

ALS, DLC-JP.
    1. Samuel Williams (c1811–1864), was at mid-century judge of the 15th judicial circuit, composed of Gibson and other counties. Opposed to secession, he moved his family to Carbondale, Illinois, when Tennessee with-

drew from the Union. Culp and Ross, *Gibson County*, 261; 1860 Census, Tenn., Gibson, 137.

2. See Speech at Union Meeting, Greeneville, November 24, 1860, note 2.

3. The November 19 Trenton resolutions took cognizance of the South's grievances and fears—concern over the election of Lincoln, consciousness of problems inherent in the threatening secession of coastal states, commitment to defense of southern rights against any impairment—yet all within the context of devotion to the Constitution and adherence to the Union, reiterated in each of the several paragraphs of complaint. It represented a skillful walking of the tightrope of sectional loyalty and federal unity. Memphis *Appeal*, November 27, 1860.

4. Thomas Jones Freeman (1827–1891), a Trenton lawyer, moved to Brownsville in 1861 and subsequently served as colonel of the 22nd Tennessee regiment, CSA. After the war, he became associate justice, then chief justice, of the Tennessee supreme court; later he was the first dean of the University of Tennesse Law School at Knoxville. Culp and Ross, *Gibson County*, 266–67.

5. Although Williams clearly indicates that Taliaferro's initials were L. W., a careful search has failed to reveal anyone so named in Gibson County. The nearest possibility is a Virginia-born J. A. Talliaferro (b. *c*1802) a wealthy banker with real and personal property valued at $88,366. 1860 Census, Tenn., Gibson, 136.

6. Probably the Trenton *Southern Standard*, a weekly established in 1856 and still being published in 1862, but not presently available. Gregory, *Union List of Newspapers*, 663.

To Robert Johnson, Greeneville

Washington City
Dec 6th 1860—

My dear Son,

Your letter of the 3d inst was recieved on Tuesday e[ven]ing, coming directly through in some 26 hours— When I first Came to Congress it took letters sometimes two weeks to get through and never less than six or seven days— what a change there is in mail facilities as well as travil— I was of the opinion that Genl Milligan would think the bond valid whether it was drawn by Judge McKenney[1] or not— I have no doubt of the bond being drawn by McKinny myself— It is not material who drew the bond so that it is valid and the signers good for the amount they are bound for— Mr. Sherfy[2] hauled some seven loads of wood for me shortly before leaving home for which I was to pay him fifty cents per load, amounting to $3.50— His Cow as I understand from some has been runing in the pasture all Summer, it ought to be worth something— Sutch pasturage as that is worth $2 00 per month at least— But if he objects to paying a[n]y thing for it, pay him the $3.00 and let the matter stand— You or Charles try and get Boyce's not[e][3] for something at least— It ought to be for $100, but do not be particular about it so that he will giv his note for something— I ow the drugstore $4 00 and forgot to Call and pay it before I left home[.] I hope you will Call and pay it— It m[a]y not be so much, but pay it what ever it is— Times, monitary and political look gloomy, evey thing seems to portend evile— There are some of the states or their leaders at least prefere a desolution to any adjustment of the difficulties between the States— At this moment no one can tell what the result will be— The middle or border states hold a meeting this mo[rn]ing[4] for the purpose of Consulting as to what Course they would take in the invent [event] the Cotton States preciptate a disolution of the Country— I find there is some notion among the border states of setting up for themselves in case of a disruption— The determination of the ultra men at this time is to involve the middle states at once upon the question of Coersion and thereby Carry them along— I will write to you as soon as there is any thing developed that is tangible— Tell Genl Milligan I will write to him as soon as there is any thing to write about more than what he sees in the papers—

As ev[er]   Andrew Johnson

ALS, DLC-American Academy of Arts and Letters, Box 5, J-L.

1. Robert J. McKinney. See *Johnson Papers*, I, 33n.
2. Samuel Sherfy (b. *c*1808), Virginia-born "waggoner," on the eve of the war claimed about $800 in personal and real property. 1860 Census, Tenn., Greene, 75.
3. William Boyce was Johnson's delinquent tenant. See Letter to Robert Johnson, April 8, 1860.
4. No record of such a gathering has been found in contemporary accounts. On the following day a caucus of northern and border state Democrats, including Douglas of Illinois, Crittenden of Kentucky, Pearce of Maryland, Bayard of Delaware, Bigler of Pennsylvania, and others, proposed a convention of border states to devise an arbitrary settlement, comparable to the Missouri Compromise. Further, a southern caucus of varying composition met three nights during the long weekend—"one of the most fateful in the entire history of the Republic," according to a modern historian— which began the Thursday Johnson wrote this letter. Evidently Johnson attended only the Saturday, December 8, caucus, when all southern senators save Iverson of Georgia were present. Apparently the principal result of these sessions was to make clear how divided the representatives of the South were on the impending question of secession; neither fire-eaters nor moderates could claim that they spoke for the South. Nichols, *Disruption of Democracy*, 395–98; New York *Herald*, December 8, 9, 10, 1860.

From William Sharswood[1]

Sharswood St.—Philadelphia, 8th, Dec. 1860.

My Dear Sir;

I have the honor to inclose the rude prospectus of my work,[2] from which You may find that the University of the South has been enrolled amongst those entitled to receive a copy. I should be pleased to learn to whom such deposits would most properly be addressed, as I presume the University has not as yet obtained its quarters.[3]

I should be pleased to learn a word in relation to the prospects of that Institution, as I hold myself open for a chair of science, and I was made acquainted of this opportunity from two distinguished gentlemen.

My work is being produced con luce[4] by the Imperial Printing Establishment of Austria. The prospectus abounds in typographical errors, in addition to which certain parts of the design have been changed.

In the hope of your receiving my petition of pardon for thus addressing my enquiries, may You, in the mean time, receive the sentiments of my highest esteem.

William Sharswood, Ph. Dr. (Jena)

ALS, DLC-JP.

1. William Sharswood (b. 1836), a native of Philadelphia, was graduated from the University of Pennsylvania in 1856 and received a Ph. D. from the University of Saxony, Jena, Germany, in 1859. In addition to various scientific writings, he was the author of a play, *Elenore, a Drama* (Philadelphia, 1862), reissued as *The Troth* (Philadelphia, 1865). S. Austin Allibone, *A Critical Dictionary of English Literature and British and American Authors* (2 vols., Philadelphia, 1874), II, 2059; *Appleton's Cyclopaedia*, V, 483–84.

2. Although he later published *The Miscellaneous Writings of William Sharswood* (Philadelphia, 1862), he was at this time trying to obtain subscribers for *Studia Physica*, a work published in Vienna as a series of monographs. *Ibid.*

3. Intent upon founding an American Oxford for the sons of southern aristocrats, Episcopal Bishop Leonidas Polk laid the cornerstone of the University of the South at Sewanee, Tennessee, on October 10, 1860. By December the fledgling academic community had become imbued with secessionism and Polk, the moving spirit behind the college, soon became a Confederate lieutenant general. Razed by Federal troops in 1863, the institution was finally able to open in September, 1868. Arthur B. Chitty, Jr., *Reconstruction at Sewanee: The Founding of the University of the South and Its First Administration, 1857–1872* (Sewanee, 1954), 62–66, 71–72, 115, 121; Charles E. Thomas, *Sewanee: The Oxford of America* (Sewanee, 1932), 3.

4. Perhaps a reference to a style of type perfected by Louis Luce, an eighteenth-century French print designer and typesetter. Hugh Williamson, *Methods of Book Design* (London, 1956), 91.

From Sam Milligan

Greeneville Ten.
December 13, 1860

Dear Governor:

I still have the fate of the Republic greatly at heart; and can not look with any complacency upon a disolution of the Union. I think I fully appreciate the wrongs and insults, which for a series of years, have been inflicted upon the South. I feel that they are all unjust, and many of them in direct conflict with the Constitution of the U. S. But for my life, I can not believe, any of them—, or even all together, are sufficient to justify a disruption of the Confederacy. The remedy is too extreme for the disease, and more likely to kill than to cure the patient.[1]

But how is the *fanaticism* to be arrested? I say *fanaticism*, because, I can call it nothing else. The facts are not sufficient to justify the belief, that this whole movement is the result of voluntary patriotism, honestly springing up in the hearts of an oppressed and injured people, and in good faith, endeavoring to throw off oppression, and redress political grievances, which are no longer honorably to be born. Nothing of this sort of true patriotism, and genuin philanthropy to the people, enters into the present excitement. And I am fully of the opinion, if this day, evry grievance complained of by the South was removed, that the fanaticism would not be in the slightest degree abated.

If I am right in this conclusion, it follows, that the redress of present grievances is not the thing sought by the South; and the remedy for the evils of the times is not to be found in additional constitutional guarantees, or the repeal of the personal liberty Acts in the North.

What is the trouble then, and what the remedy? Alienation of feelings And an utter want of confidence between the people of the North and the South, it seems to me, is the most fearful difficulty under which the country at present, labors. How this estrangement and want of Confidence have been produced, is too obvious to require remark, further than to say:— The responsibility lies at the door of the Northern fanatics. But the evil is the groath of time, and the remedy, in like manner, must be slow, and to some extent uncertain. Time alone can restore confidence and fraternal feeling between the two extremes.

But the imergency will not admit of delay. The evil Carries with it its own remeedy[2]—The disease its own antidote. Let disunion come, if come it must,—but if it can be averted, that only proves there is no evil in the government, which justifys the remeedy proposed.— Let South Carolina and the New England States, if they desire, with such other fanatical states as wish, absolve their allegiance to the Confederacy, and form such government as they desire. Let them make the experiment, and enjoy or suffer the legitimate fruits of their wisdom or their folly. But let the border slave states and the middle free States, with such others, North & South, as are conservative enough, to carry their people, unite, and form one grand Central Republic, on the *old Constitution*, just as it is, with, if need be, additional guarantees securing slave property, and the rights of the owners in the Territories & then elect a new president, and go forward with a firm and a just administration.

This plan preserves our ancient and beloved form of Government, and in the heart of our great country, sets up an over shadowing power, which if justly administered, will reunite all the rebellious States under the old banner, and upon the old constitution.

Our people must be divided into parties, and this plan furnishes the bases of parties in all the seceding States. They will all leave the Confederacy with a nucleus around which a Union party will soon grow into power; and as time wears out the memory of the present grievances in the South, and demonstrates the folly of the North, One by one, these rebellious states will naturally fall back, and again take shelter under the ample folds of the glorious old Constitution.

There is nothing in the way of the practicability of a great Central republic, unless it might be the unwillingness of Louisana to go into it. Should she favor it, and I can not see why she would not, that will secure the mouth of the Mississippi river, and at the same time nearly the entire North West. New York & Pennsylvania could not withhold their adhesion from it, and that would, at once give to such a republic complete control of all, or nearly all the available power that now exists in the present government.

Experiment and time can alone correct the errors of an infatuated people, who have grown rich and powerful under the very government which they now wish to tear down over their heads. They will, I fear, accomplish it, and with it their own distruction. It is said, and truly said—That whom God determines to destroy, he first makes mad.[3] On such minds reason has no power. But it is the part of wisdom, as well as the highest duty of patriotism, in such a crisis, to save the Constitution, and its eternal principles of true government from the general ruin. The madness that rules the hous, will pass away, and returning reason bring back the wanderers under its broad aegis again.

Well Johnson—I have had a bad head ache all day, and this afternoon, have had to wear a way the day in boring you with a long letter. If it wearies you, burn it up, but if not read it, and put your head to work on it.

I did intend to say something about the Functionary's message,[4] but that must be defered. It is right in Some things, and wrong in others. Mr Attony General Black is not, I am thinking as sound a Lawyer as I supposed—[5]

Let me hear from you if you have time, and send me your speech when you make it.

Your family are all well—

Yours very truely   Sam Milligan

ALS, DLC-JP.

1. An observation found in many authors, usually in the more succinct "The remedy is worse than the disease." Francis Bacon, *Essays: Of Seditions;* Juvenal, *Satires,* XVI, 31; Le Sage, *Gil Blas,* Bk. XII, ch. 8, and many other works. Stevenson, *Quotations,* 1287.

2. Probably a corruption of "there is no evil in the world without a remedy." Jacopo Sannazaro, *Ecologa Octava. Ibid.,* 584.

3. From an old Greek maxim, "whom the gods destroy, they first make mad." *Ibid.,* 1232.

4. Milligan refers to Buchanan's fourth annual message, delivered December 3, 1860. Richardson, *Messages,* V, 626–53.

5. At about the time Buchanan was drafting his December message to Congress, his attorney general, Jeremiah Black, issued a dogmatic legal opinion proclaiming the "Union is necessarily perpetual"; thus no state "can lawfully withdraw or be expelled from it." Doubtlessly this statement was upsetting to those fence-straddling southerners who had yet to take a firm stand on secession. Brigance, *Jeremiah Sullivan Black,* 89.

Joint Resolution for Amendments on Presidential, Senatorial, and Judicial Selection[1]

December 13, 1860

Mr. JOHNSON, of Tennessee. I offer the following joint resolution, and ask that it be read:

The Secretary read it, as follows:

Joint resolution (S. No. 48) proposing amendments to the Constitution of the United States.

Whereas the fifth article of the Constitution of the United States provides for amendments thereto in the manner following, viz: "Congress, whenever two thirds of both Houses shall deem it necessary, shall propose amendments to this Constitution, or, on the application of the Legislatures of two thirds of the several States, shall call a convention for proposing amendments, which, in either case, shall be valid to all intents and purposes, as part of this Constitution, when ratified by the Legislatures of three fourths of the several States, or by conventions in three fourths thereof, as the one or the other mode of ratification may be proposed by the Congress: *Provided,* That no amendment which may be made prior to the year 1808 shall in any manner affect the first and fourth clauses in the ninth section of the first article; and that no State, without its consent, shall be deprived of its equal suffrage in the Senate:" Therefore,

Be it resolved by the Senate and House of Representatives of the

United States of America in Congress assembled, (two thirds of both Houses concurring,) That the following amendments to the Constitution of the United States be proposed to the Legislatures of the several States, which, when ratified by the Legislatures of three fourths of the States, shall be valid to all intents and purposes as part of the Constitution:

That hereafter, the President and Vice President of the United States shall be chosen by the people of the respective States, in the manner following: Each State shall be divided, by the Legislature thereof, into districts, equal in number to the whole number of Senators and Representatives to which such State may be entitled in the Congress of the United States; the said districts to be composed of contiguous territory, and to contain, as nearly as may be, an equal number of persons entitled to be represented under the Constitution, and to be laid off, for the first time, immediately after the ratification of this amendment, and afterwards, at the session of the Legislature next ensuing the apportionment of representatives by the Congress of the United States, that, on the first Thursday in August, in the year 1864, and on the same day every fourth year thereafter, the citizens of each State who possess the qualifications requisite for electors of the most numerous branch of the State Legislatures, shall meet within their respective districts, and vote for a President and Vice President of the United States;[2] and the person receiving the greatest number of votes for President, and the one receiving the greatest number of votes for Vice President, in each district, shall be holden to have received one vote; which fact shall be immediately certified by the Governor of the State, to each of the Senators in Congress from such State, and to the President of the Senate and the Speaker of the House of Representatives. The Congress of the United States shall be in session on the second Monday in October, in the year 1864, and on the same day on every fourth year thereafter; and the President of the Senate, in the presence of the Senate and House of Representatives, shall open all the certificates, and the votes shall then be counted. The person having the greatest number of votes for President, shall be President, if such number be equal to a majority of the whole number of votes given; but if no person have such majority, then a second election shall be held on the first Thursday in the month of December then next ensuing, between the persons having the two highest numbers for the office of President; which second election shall be conducted, the result certified, and the votes counted, in the same manner as in the first; and the person having the greatest number of votes for President, shall be President. But, if two or more persons shall have received the greatest, and an equal number of votes, at the second

election, then the person who shall have received the greatest number of votes in the greatest number of States, shall be President. The
person having the greatest number of votes for Vice President, at
the first election, shall be Vice President, if such number be equal
to a majority of the whole number of votes given; and if no person
have such majority, then a second election shall take place between
the persons having the two highest numbers, on the same day that
the second election is held for President; and the person having the
highest number of the votes for Vice President, shall be Vice President. But if there should happen to be an equality of votes between
the persons so voted for at the second election, then the person having
the greatest number of votes in the greatest number of States, shall
be Vice President. But when a second election shall be necessary in
the case of Vice President, and not necessary in the case of President,
then the Senate shall choose a Vice President from the persons
having the two highest numbers to the first election, as is now
prescribed in the Constitution: *Provided*, That the President to be
elected in the year 1864 shall be chosen from one of the slaveholding
States, and the Vice President from one of the non-slaveholding
States; and in the year 1868, the President shall be chosen from
one of the non-slaveholding States, and the Vice President from one
of the slaveholding States, and so alternating the President and
Vice President every four years between the slaveholding and non-
slaveholding States during the continuance of the Government.[3]

Sec. 2. *And be it further resolved*, That article one, section three,
be amended by striking out the word "Legislature," and inserting
in lieu thereof the following words, viz: "persons qualified to vote
for members of the most numerous branch of the Legislature," so
as to make the third section of said article, when ratified by three
fourths of the States, read as follows, to wit:

The Senate of the United States shall be composed of two Senators from each State, chosen by the persons qualified to vote for the
members of the most numerous branch of the Legislature thereof,
for six years, and each Senator shall have one vote.

Sec. 4. *And be it further resolved*, That article three, section one,
be amended by striking out the words "good behavior," and inserting
the following words, viz: "the term of twelve years." And further,
that said article and section be amended by adding the following
thereto, viz: "and it shall be the duty of the President of the United
States, within twelve months after the ratification of this amendment by three fourths of all the States, as provided by the Constitution of the United States, to divide the whole number of judges, as
near as may be practicable, into three classes. The seats of the
judges of the first class shall be vacated at the expiration of the

fourth year from such classification; of the second class, at the expiration of the eighth year; and of the third class, at the expiration of the twelfth year, so that one third may be chosen every fourth year thereafter."

The article, as amended, will read, as follows:

ARTICLE III.

Sec. 1. The judicial power of the United States shall be vested in one Supreme Court, and in such inferior courts as the Congress from time to time may ordain and establish. The judges, both of the supreme and inferior courts, shall hold their offices during the term of twelve years, and shall, at stated times, receive for their services a compensation, which shall not be diminished during their continuance in office. And it shall be the duty of the President of the United States, within twelve months after the ratification of this amendment by three fourths of all the States, as provided by the Constitution of the United States, to divide the whole number of judges, as near as may be practicable, into three classes. The seats of the judges of the first class shall be vacated at the expiration of the fourth year from such classification; of the second class, at the expiration of the eighth year; and of the third class, at the expiration of the twelfth year, so that one third may be chosen every fourth year thereafter: *Provided, however,* That all vacancies occurring under the provisions of this section shall be filled by persons, one half of whom shall be chosen from the slaveholding States, and the other half with persons chosen from the non-slaveholding States, so that the Supreme Court will be equally divided between the slaveholding and the non-slaveholding States.[4]

Mr. JOHNSON, of Tennessee. That committee[5] not having been appointed, though I presume it will be appointed, I ask that the resolution lie on the table, and be printed, with a view, at the proper time, to refer it to that committee.[6]

Cong. Globe, 36 Cong., 2 Sess., 82–83; DNA-RG46, 36A-B4, S. 48 Joint Res.

1. These amendments are virtually the same as those which Johnson had introduced in the House on February 21, 1851, reiterating ideas incorporated in his Biennial Legislative Messages of 1853 and 1855. This time, however, he sought not merely to make federal officials more reflective of the popular will but to introduce certain changes designed to protect southern interests in the Union by requiring that the presidency be alternated between North and South and that judicial posts be equitably divided between the sections.

2. In view of the subsequent proviso that President and Vice President be from different sections, Johnson here omitted the constitutional clause included in his earlier version: "one of whom at least shall not be an inhabitant of the same State with themselves."

3. This proviso, not found in earlier versions, was clearly intended to ease the growing crisis of the Union.

4. Here again, with the sectional controversy in mind, Johnson added to his original proposals.

5. The Senate had been discussing the establishment of a committee "to inquire into the present condition of the country"; on December 18 this became the Committee of Thirteen.

6. The motion was agreed to.

Resolution Proposing "Unamendable" Amendments Affecting Slavery[1]

December 13, 1860

Mr. JOHNSON, of Tennessee. I introduce the following resolution, with a view of referring it at the proper time:

Resolved, That the select committee of thirteen be instructed to inquire into the expediency of establishing, by constitutional provision: 1. A line running through the territory of the United States, not included within the States, making an equitable and just division of said territory, south of which line slavery shall be recognized and protected as property, by ample and full constitutional guarantees, and north of which line it shall be prohibited. 2. The repeal of all acts of Congress in regard to the restoration of fugitives from labor, and an explicit declaration in the Constitution, that it is the duty of each State for itself to return fugitive slaves when demanded by the proper authority, or pay double their cash value out of the treasury of the State. 3. An amendment of the Constitution, declaring that slavery shall exist in navy-yards, arsenals, &c., or not, as it may be admitted or prohibited by the States in which such navy-yards, arsenals, &c., may be situated. 4. Congress shall never interfere with slavery in the District of Columbia, so long as it shall exist in the State of Maryland, nor even then, without the consent of the inhabitants and compensation to the owners. 5. Congress shall not touch the representation of three fifths of the slaves, nor the inter-State trade, coastwise or inland. 6. These provisions to be unamendable, like that which relates to the equality of the States in the Senate.

I move that the resolution lie on the table for the present, and be printed.[2]

Cong. Globe, 36 Cong., 2 Sess., 82–83.

1. This resolution follows immediately Johnson's Joint Resolution for Amendments on Presidential, Senatorial, and Judicial Selection. By the opening of the second session of the 36th Congress, the need for compromise on slavery was manifest, and nearly two hundred constitutional amendments were introduced seeking to define the position of the institution in the Union. In most cases these proposals carried a clause making them unamendable. Herman V. Ames, *The Proposed Amendments to the Constitution of the United States*, American Historical Association, *Annual Report* (1896), II, 194–95.

2. Johnson's resolution was referred to the Committee of Thirteen on December 21. Ten days later Lazarus Powell of Kentucky reported that, after consideration of proposals by Johnson, Jefferson Davis of Mississippi, Joseph Lane of Oregon, and Henry M. Rice of Minnesota, the committee had "not been able to agree upon any general plan of adjustment." *Senate Journal*, 36 Cong., 2 Sess., 60, 66–67; *Cong. Globe*, 36 Cong., 2 Sess., 182.

From R. A. Bennett

December 15, 1860, Gallatin; ALS, DLC-JP.

Gallatin attorney seeks Johnson's views "in regard to the dangerous and perilous times," commenting that "our people are very much perplexed, they love the union but cannot think of remain[in]g in the Confed[e]racy without a guarantee . . . that there will be no more aggressions upon her constitutional rights and a respect on the part of the north for the Compact which holds us together."

From John M. Seely[1]

Maysville Kentucky Decm 15/60

My Dear Frind

I have this day red the resolutions you perposed in the Senate a few days ago[.]

they not only harmonise with my full feeling apon the present cri[s]is of our National affairs but they are universally aproved of By Every true frind to our national welfare in this city and the Sourounding country on this Side the ohio River while they are bitterly repudiated on the other Side. I hope and all our true frinds hope you may be Successfull in your Efforts to Secure the passage not only [of] one but all of them,   you can tell our freind More[2] of Congress, from this District that we are beset on all Sides in this his district with Black Republicans even of the Bench of the Judiciarry[.][3] you may rest asured we Live in fear and drad of the consequences of any Longer Depending upon the emty promises of our northern nighbous unless Secured by Such Statuary enactments as will insue our Safty in person and property beyound any cavile or Latitudinou construction,

I am in this county only for the present working my way to Memphis as I have determind to Locate ther and Endevour to Identify my self and family with the Best intrests of the Citizens of Tennesse, in the pesuite of My professin[.]

I have determind to try to arive ther about the first of Febuary. If I can Rais the Means to do So[.]   tims are Very Dull here but I am advised I can precu [procure] abundant of Employment in Memphis and the Sourounding Count[r]y[.]

Thre is a great want of confidence here in the General way of Business[.] Some Down the River and South of the ohio there is desidedly a more healthy complexion in Business affairs[.] in cincinatti there never has been Such Stagnation in the History of her Existance as a City[.]⁴

The whole of which has originated upon a fanatical disposition of a Large portion of her Business population to Force upon us as their nighbous a course of unconstitutional op[pr]essions and gr[ie]vances wich we in our Soving [Sovereign] capasity are totally unwilling and unable to accord to and maintain as a Soving people and the Garrantees awarded to us by the Constitution and as an Inheritanc of our fourfathers,

I Shal hope to here from you as Soon as circumstancs will permit[.] Excuse the freedom of the Epistle and belive me Dear Sir

Respectfully and truly Your frind and Ob. Servant

John M. Seely

If any thing of momnt Should transpire in your Hon. Boddy relative to the pesent national affai[r]s I wold be happy to ricve a coppy from you[.]

Dir[e]ct to Maysville K   John M, Seely

ALS, DLC-JP.

1. John M. Seely was a "mechanic" who prior to 1862 moved to Crittenden County, Arkansas, about ten miles from Memphis. In 1862 he appeared as a witness for a merchant, Asa Hodges, accused of treason against the Confederacy. Seely to Johnson, January 20, 1861, Johnson Papers, LC; OR, Ser. 2, II, 1553.

2. Laban T. Moore (1829–1892), a lawyer of Louisa, Kentucky, was elected to Congress (1859–61) on the American party ticket. During the war he raised a Union regiment, serving briefly as its colonel (Nov., 1861–Jan., 62); after the war he became a Democrat and state senator (1881). BDAC, 1351.

3. No evidence has been found to substantiate this charge.

4. Cincinnati suffered the same economic troubles that plagued other financial and commercial centers in the uncertain period following Lincoln's election. Blaming the depression on the Republicans, one editor complained that "It is a poor consolation to the laboring masses who have been thrown out of employment that through their distress and sufferings the Republican party expects to benefit the Negro." The business reversal, characterized by discounted currency, falling markets, and declining trade with the South, had destroyed public confidence in the paper of even the strong banks. The Enquirer bleakly observed that "business is dead"; unless the outlook changed rapidly, the editor expected the worst panic in history. Cincinnati Enquirer, November 27, 28, December 7, 1860.

From B. B. Trousdale[1]

Corinth Miss. 17th. December 1860

Dr. Sir

We notice that on the 13th Inst. You introduced in the Senate of
the United States a series of resolutions looking to amendments of
the Constitution with a view of settleing the difficulties existing between the slaveholding and non Slave holding States[.] we would
Suggest to you that your rosolutions (if they are correctly reported)
do not cover the whole ground.   if those dificulties can be settled by
amendments to the Constitution the Negro must be wiped out of
having any share, *or vote*, in the election of electors for President &
vice President of the United States or for members of Congress in
all the states of the Confederecy.   if this is not done there is no reasonable probability that the people of the slave holding States would
ratify the amendments.   in addition to this no person should be per-
mited to vote either for Electors or for Members of Congress except
native born and naturalized citizens of the United States. candor
compels me to say to you that the majority of the people in the cotton
growing States seem to have calmly come to the conclusion that it
is a duty which they owe to themselves and their posterity to Sunder
all political connection with the people of the non slave holding
States.   the people of the cotton growing States believe that the people of the free States are the greatest enimies they have on the face
of the earth, instead of being as they Should be their best friends.
the people believe also that by Sundering all political connection
with the northern States that it would produce a State of prosperity
in the planting States surpassing any thing that has ever occured by
keeping out of the country Millions of dollars worth of goods which
is continually being sent here from the Northern States duty free and
inducing the people to spend all their surplus earnings for goods
instead of laying out their money in useful and substancial improvements.   such opinions as those Stated above being honestly entertained, and for good reasons, You can see how dificult a task it will
be to induce the people of the Cotton growing states to consent to
remain in the present confedracy of States.

this government was made by white men, and for white men[.]
the Negro had no part or lot in making it, and the Constitution left
the Negro where GOD placed him in a subordinate condition, therefore the negro should have no share in the machinry of the Federal
Government either in voting for law makers or any other department.   if the Pharisee's and hypocrites of the Churches, and the per-

jured Scoundrels who passed the personal liberty bills in some of
the non Slave holding states wish to have the wisdom of the negro
to aid them in carrying on their State governments that is their own
business, but we are opposed to negroes voting in any State for any
one connected with the Machinery of the Federal government.

verry respectfully

B. B. Trousdale

Hon. And. Johnson

ALS, DLC-JP.

1. Bryan B. Trousdale (b. c1800), born in North Carolina, was a wealthy
Corinth trader. In 1860 his accumulated holdings amounted to $39,000.
1860 Census, Miss., Tishomingo, 468.

From James Monroe[1]

New York Dec. 18—1860

Sir: —

The conservative citicens of New York are about to convene for
the purpose of forming an Anti-Abolition Association,[2] the object
of which is to counteract the pernicious and false theories & influences of Abolitionism, by means of lectures and documents.

The public mind is now in condition to place such an Association
upon a permanent & commanding basis, and to support it in its collateral endeavour to bring about a compromise of the exciting
questions of the day, which will prove satisfactory to all parties
interested.

Mr Elisha Whittlesey[3] of Ohio, whose services in behalf of the
Republic are well known & appreciated throughout its lenght [sic]
and breadth, has consented, by letter to act as President of the
Association.

Your views in regard to the practicality of this movement are
solicited in reply, to be laid before the prominent conservativs of this
city, at a meeting to be held at the Laforge House[4] upon Wednesday
evening Dec 26 1860[.]

Yours Respectfully   James Monroe

Box 4570   N. Y   P. O.

Hon. Johnson of Tenn.
Washington D. C.

ALS, DLC-JP.

1. James Monroe (1799–1870) of New York was a nephew of President
Monroe. A graduate of West Point (1815), he served in the army until
1832, when he entered politics in New York City, becoming alderman (1833),
Whig congressman (1839–41), and state senator (1852–55). Monroe was
one of the earliest members of the Union Club of New York City; on the eve

of the conflict he visited Richmond, where he made public speeches in an attempt to avert war. *BDAC*, 1345; *Appleton's Cyclopaedia*, IV, 362.

2. While the precise organization to which Monroe refers has not been identified, the variety of associations which appeared in New York City during the war years suggests the existence there of ample conservative sentiment on this issue. The American Society for Promoting National Unity was formed in March, 1861, for the purpose of propagating a conservative view of slavery based on the assumption that all men are not equal. Its first president was Samuel F. B. Morse, its major weapons the pen and the lectern. Many of its members were also founders of the Anti-Abolition Rights Association (1863). Other organizations with an anti-Negro bias included the Democratic States Rights Union Association, formed in the summer of 1861, and the Young Men's Democratic Association (1862). Basil Leo Lee, *Discontent in New York City, 1861–1865* (Washington, D. C., 1943), 28, 230, 232.

3. See *Johnson Papers*, II, 469n.

4. After South Carolina's secession on December 20, a wave of indignation swept New York City's business community, which had heretofore sympathized with the South. Under these conditions, it is probable that Monroe's proposed meeting was canceled; no evidence of such a gathering has been found in New York newspapers. Philip S. Foner, *Business and Slavery: The New York Merchants and the Irrepressible Conflict* (Chapel Hill, 1941), 239.

Appendix

Andrew Johnson in the Senate[1]
1857–60

35 CONGRESS, 1 SESSION
December, 1857–June, 1858

Journal	Globe	Date	Subject
6	1	Dec. 7, 1857	Takes oath of office.
40	38	Dec. 16	Named member of standing committees on public lands and District of Columbia.
61–62	135	Dec. 22	Presents memorial of W. S. Munday, J. Knox Walker, and others, members of Tennessee legislature, asking protection for overland mail route through Arizona; referred to committee on post offices and post roads.
63	135	Dec. 22	* Remarks on Introducing Homestead Bill (S. 25); referred to committee on public lands.
79	186	Jan. 5, 1858	Moves Jesse Wyatt be given permission to withdraw petition and papers; so ordered.
102	264	Jan. 13	Presents petition of Fayette County, Indiana, citizens asking for a homestead law; referred to committee on public lands.
122	354	Jan. 21	Reports, from committee on public lands, homestead bill; moves to postpone further consideration until Feb. 8.
126	377	Jan. 25	Presents petition of New York citizens asking for homestead bill; referred to committee on public lands.
166	566	Feb. 4	Presents petition of Terryville, Conn., citizens asking that public lands be reserved for settlers; referred to committee on public lands.
175	623	Feb. 9, 1858	Presents numerous memorials from citizens in Connecticut, Kentucky, New York, and Wisconsin, asking for a homestead bill. Moves memorials be tabled; agreed to.
178	640	Feb. 10	Presents petition of New York citizens asking that public lands "be laid out in farms or lots for the free and exclusive use of actual settlers only"; tabled; also, thirty-six petitions of Luzerne County, Pennsylvania, citizens asking that public lands be confined to settlers; tabled.

1. The data in this Appendix are drawn from the *Journal of the Senate* and the *Congressional Globe*. Asterisks indicate items printed in Volumes II or III.

Journal	Globe	Date	Subject
186	697	Feb. 15	Presents memorial of Walter James asking compensation for horse lost during War of 1812; referred to committee on claims; also, three petitions of Lee County, Iowa, citizens, and two petitions of Wisconsin citizens asking that public lands cease to be a source of revenue and be confined to actual settlers; tabled.
	737–41	Feb. 17	* Speech on Maintaining Federal Authority in Utah. [Includes an amendment which is in effect a substitute for pending army increase bill (S. 79).]
	757–58, 760 766–68	Feb.18	* Exchanges Concerning Volunteer Forces.
203	783	Feb. 19	Presents petition of Apollo Herold and others [Oswego, N. Y.] asking that public lands no longer be considered a source of revenue; tabled.
	806–13	Feb. 23	* Speech on Popular Sovereignty and Right of Instruction.
	830–39	Feb. 24	* Exchange with John Bell.
	867	Feb. 25	Suggests substitute bill for increasing army be modified to raise 3,000 instead of 4,000 men.
	875	Feb. 25	Moves to amend an omission in substitute bill to increase army; agreed to.
219	876	Feb. 25	Votes for army bill (S. 79) to increase the military establishment; rejected.
	876–77	Feb. 25	Remarks on Tennessee resolutions and admission of Kansas under Lecompton Constitution.
222	900	Mar. 1	Presents petition of West Manchester, Pennsylvania, citizens asking that public lands not constitute a source of revenue; tabled; also, four petitions of Wisconsin citizens asking that public lands no longer be sold for revenue and be reserved only for settlers; tabled; also, resolution from Tennessee legislature favoring amendment of postage laws to allow "persons sending public documents or newspapers to indorse upon them their names"; referred to committee on post offices and post roads.
253	1119	Mar. 15	Presents petition of Fort Dodge, Iowa, citizens and two petitions of Wisconsin citizens asking that public lands no longer be considered a source of revenue and the land be confined to actual settlers; tabled.

Journal	Globe	Date	Subject
271	1187	Mar. 19	Presents petition of citizens of Washington County, Texas, asking that public lands no longer be considered a source of revenue and that occupancy be confined to actual settlers; tabled.
	1187	Mar. 19	Suggests bill for relief of Dr. Charles Maxwell (H. R. 216) be referred to committee; bill passes Senate.
280	1264-65	Mar. 23	Votes for bill (S. 161) to admit Kansas; passed.
	1299	Mar. 24	Explains his vote on Minnesota statehood bill.
	1326-27	Mar. 25	* Remarks on State Representation in Congress.
290	1401	Mar. 29	Presents petition of Detroit citizens asking that public lands no longer be considered a source of revenue and be confined to settlers; tabled.
308	1433	Apr. 1	Votes for army bill (H. R. 313) providing mounted volunteer regiments for Texas frontier; passed.
310	1438	Apr. 2	Presents papers relating to claim of Levi Johnson and Mary Burchfield concerning Samuel Slaughter's right to bounty land; referred to committee on pensions.
	1461-62 1467-69	Apr. 5	* Remarks on Amendment to Washington Police Bill (S. 232).
	1471	Apr. 5	Moves to recommit Washington police bill; rejected.
318	1473	Apr. 5	Votes against Washington police bill (S. 232) establishing auxiliary guard to protect public and private property; passed.
	1491-92 1513-14	Apr. 6-7	* Remarks on Voting Qualifications.
326	1516	Apr. 7	Votes for bill (S. 86) to admit Minnesota; passed.
	1579	Apr. 14	Asserts calendar of Senate business could be handled more efficiently if taken in its regular order.
403	1899	Apr. 30	Votes for report of conference committee on English bill to admit Kansas (S. 161); accepted.
	1912-13	May 3	* Remarks on Senate Calendar.
409	1914	May 3	Votes for Indian appropriation bill (H. R. 5); passed.
419	1963	May 5	Votes against bill (H. R. 62) appropriating money for military academy; passed.
447	2101	May 13	Moves to postpone civil appropriation bill for year ending June 30, 1859, and to consider the homestead bill in its stead; not agreed to.

Journal	Globe	Date	Subject
	2102	May 13	* Remarks on Taking up Homestead Bill.
	2124	May 14	Expresses "gratification" to R. M. T. Hunter of Virginia for allowing something other than appropriation bills to be considered.
462	2159	May 15	Named to committee on contingent expenses.
464	A.372–77	May 15	* Speech on School Funds for District of Columbia.
476	2202	May 18	Moves to postpone further consideration of Oregon statehood bill in order to take up homestead bill; not agreed to.
477	2209	May 18	Votes for bill (S. 239) to admit Oregon; passed.
	2230	May 19	Opposes delay in consideration of special orders.
486	2239	May 19	Votes for bill (S. 10) repealing all laws giving bounties to vessels employed in cod fishing; passed.
	2239	May 19	* Amendments to Homestead Bill.
	2265–73	May 20	* Speech on Homestead Bill.
	2306–7	May 22	Comments on homestead bill.
	2353	May 24	Opposes special action to consider loan bill.
	2422–24	May 27	Moves to refer resolution paying account of N. C. Towle to committee on contingent expenses; motion withdrawn.
531	2424–26	May 27	States that homestead bill has been under consideration since 1846 and that Senate should act now. Moves to reconsider vote to postpone bill until next session; motion entered.
	2526–27	May 31	Urges postponing adjournment in order to spend more time on public business.
	2570	June 1	Offers amendment to appropriate money for courthouse and post office at Memphis; withdraws amendment.
576	2588–90	June 1	* Remarks on Public Works Appropriations for Washington.
578	2627	June 2	Presents petition of Wisconsin citizens asking that public lands no longer be a source of revenue and be reserved for settlers; tabled.
601–2	2676–77	June 3	Moves to amend civil appropriation bill (H. R. 200) by omitting appropriations for improvement of the mall and for Capitol extension; rejected.
	2677	June 3	Votes against civil appropriation bill; passed.
	2804	June 8	Opposes army appropriation bill (H. R. 243); pairs with Hammond of South Carolina; passed.
668	2895	June 10	Votes for post office appropriation bill (H. R. 556); passed.

Journal	Globe	Date	Subject
	2993–94	June 12	Asks discussion of his motion (May 27) to reconsider vote postponing homestead bill; motion held not in order.
703	3001–2	June 12	* Exchange on Widows' Pensions.
714	3039	June 14	Votes against conference committee report on post office appropriation bill (H. R. 556); accepted.
719	3042–44	June 14	* Remarks on Origin of Homestead Bill.

35 CONGRESS, 2 SESSION
December, 1858–March, 1859

Journal	Globe	Date	Subject
40	10	Dec. 9, 1858	Makes appearance in Senate chamber several days after session begins.
43–44	45	Dec. 13	Named member of standing committees on public lands, District of Columbia, and audit and control of Senate contingent expenses.
77	139	Dec. 20	Moves to reconsider adverse report (No. 327) of committee to audit and control expenses regarding binders of 34th Congress *Globe* and Appendix; agreed to. Moves report be recommitted; agreed to.
103	205	Jan. 4, 1859	Submits resolution that "so much of the report of the Secretary of the Interior as relates to the compensation of the United States district attorneys, marshals, and clerks of the courts, be referred to the Committee on the Judiciary;" agreed to.
103	205–6 208–9	Jan. 4	* Remarks on Retrenchment.
111	232	Jan. 6	Presents Memphis city council resolution favoring "establishment of an inspection district and the erection of a marine hospital;" referred to committee on commerce.
118	276	Jan. 10	Presents petition of Micajah Owen, soldier of War of 1812; referred to committee on pensions.
122	285	Jan. 10	Votes against French spoliations bill (S. 45); passed.
124	303	Jan. 11	Presents petition of Joel M. Smith, Nashville pension agent, "praying a per centage on his disbursements"; referred to committee on pensions.
125	303	Jan. 11	Presents petition of Paterson, New Jersey, citizens asking that public lands be "laid out in farms for the free and exclusive use of actual settlers;" tabled.

Journal	Globe	Date	Subject
151	402–3 405	Jan. 17	* Remarks on Governmental Expenditures.
	406	Jan. 17	Declines to serve as chairman of committee to investigate governmental expenditures.
172	507	Jan. 21	Introduces bill (S. 521) to provide compensation to certain pension agents; referred to committee on pensions.
	537	Jan. 24	Objects to second reading of joint resolution on Capitol extension; sustained.
	577	Jan. 25	Moves to reconsider his resolution for retrenchment of government expenses; denied.
	579–87	Jan. 25	* Speech on Transcontinental Railroads.
223	634	Jan. 27	Votes against Pacific railroad bill (S. 65) authorizing action related to contracts, plans, and routes; passed.
236	679	Jan. 29	* Amendment to Washington Passenger Railway Company Bill.
238	686	Jan. 31	Presents memorial of National Land Reform Association asking change in system of disposing of public lands; tabled; also, memorial of citizens of Tennessee [Jonesboro] asking passage of pension bill for soldiers of War of 1812; referred to committee on pensions.
264	805	Feb. 4	Reports, from committee on public lands, House homestead bill (H. R. 72).
273	830	Feb. 5	Submits amendment first offered Jan. 29; agreed to.
278	857	Feb. 7	Opposes agricultural colleges bill (H. R. 2) donating land to states and territories for agriculture and mechanical arts; pairs with Stuart of Michigan; passed.
281	862–63	Feb. 7	* Remarks on Railway for Pennsylvania Avenue.
287	883–84	Feb. 8	* Resolutions on Government Expenditures.
290	885	Feb. 8	Votes against bill (H. R. 541) establishing railway on Pennsylvania Avenue; rejected.
299	921	Feb. 10	Presents petition of "citizens of the United States" [New York] asking law to prevent "further traffic in, and monopoly of, the public lands"; tabled.
308	991–95	Feb. 12	* Remarks on Governmental Expenditures.
	A.147–48	Feb. 14	Remarks on resolution concerning seating of Indiana senators [Graham N. Fitch and Jesse D. Bright].
311	1011	Feb. 14	Presents petition of New York

Journal	Globe	Date	Subject
			citizens asking that public lands be set aside for settlers only; tabled.
	1074	Feb. 17	Comments on House homestead bill.
	1141	Feb. 19	Explains refusal to vote for any more special orders.
	1143	Feb. 19	Moves that Senate take up homestead bill; not agreed to.
352	1179	Feb. 21	Votes against consular and diplomatic appropriation bill (H. R. 666); passed.
361	1238	Feb. 23	Presents petition of Marlborough, Tenn., citizens asking mail route from Paris to Sandy Bridge; referred to committee on post offices and post roads.
366	1275	Feb. 23	Votes against general appropriation bill (H. R. 711); passed.
	1275	Feb. 23	Urges Senate not to take up post route bill (S. 874); Senate adjourned.
379	1326	Feb. 25	Votes for bill (H. R. 874) establishing certain post roads; passed.
	1352	Feb. 25	Asks action on Cuba question to clear way for homestead bill.
392	1405	Feb. 26	Votes against army appropriation bill (H. R. 667); passed.
396	1433	Feb. 28	Moves to print amended Senate homestead bill for comparison with House bill; agreed to.
415	1520	Mar. 1	Votes against post office appropriation bill (H. R. 872); passed.
420	1531	Mar. 1	Votes for naval appropriation bill (H. R. 712); passed.
	1588, 1590, 1611	Mar. 2–3	* Exchange Concerning Furniture for Committee Rooms.
457	1633–34	Mar. 3	Votes against civil appropriation bill (H. R. 713); passed.
	1651	Mar. 3	Asks unanimous consent to consider resolution on retrenchment; objection, hence not considered.
479	1659–60	Mar. 3	* Resolution on Retrenchment; adopted.

35 CONGRESS, SPECIAL SESSION
March, 1859

Journal	Globe	Date	Subject
486	1685	Mar. 4, 1859	Presents credentials of A. O. P. Nicholson, newly elected Tennessee senator.
488	1686	Mar. 5	Named to committees on public lands, District of Columbia; made chairman of committee to audit and control contingent expenses.

36 CONGRESS, 1 SESSION
December, 1859–June, 1860

Journal	Globe	Date	Subject
	53	Dec. 8, 1859	Gives notice of intent to introduce a homestead bill.
	100–107	Dec. 12	* Speech on Harper's Ferry Incident.
	143	Dec. 14	Denies saying that Wilson of Massachusetts and Wade of Ohio had made disunion speeches; said rather that "their teachings would finally result in the dissolution of the Union."
14	190	Dec. 20	Introduces homestead bill (S. 1); tabled until committees appointed.
15	198	Dec. 21	Named to committees on public lands, District of Columbia; made chairman, committee to audit and control contingent expenses.
20	199	Dec. 21	Moves to refer homestead bill to committee on public lands; so ordered.
28	223	Dec. 22	Presents additional papers in support of payment to George W. Farmer for marking out and opening road [1816] from Reynoldsburg to Chickasaw Old Town; referred to committee on claims.
69–70	387	Jan. 10, 1860	Presents petition of "citizens of the United States" [New York City] asking for homestead bill; referred to committee on public lands; also, pension petition of Nathaniel Rye, soldier of 1812; referred to committee on pensions.
93	551	Jan. 23	Presents memorial of Cornelius Hughes, Hawkins County, asking increase in pension; referred to committee on pensions.
103	622	Jan. 30	Presents petition of Fernando Wood, mayor of New York City, and others, asking for a homestead bill; referred to committee on public lands. Moves petition and papers of William R. West, alias Mooney, be referred to committee on pensions; so ordered.
165	789	Feb. 15	Votes for bill (S. 35) abolishing franking privilege; passed.
188	874	Feb. 24	Moves to refer to committee on public lands papers relating to claims of Levi Johnson and Mary Burchfield; so ordered.
189	874	Feb. 24	Reports, with amendments, from committee on public lands, homestead bill (S. 1), which Senate then considers as a committee of whole. Moves bill

Journal	Globe	Date	Subject
			be made special order for next Thursday; so ordered.
205	942	Mar. 1	Moves to make homestead bill special order for next Wednesday; agreed to.
228	1021	Mar. 7	Moves to postpone homestead bill till next day; agreed to.
231	1047–48	Mar. 8	Moves to make homestead bill special order for next Tuesday; agreed to.
247	1119–20	Mar. 13	Moves, with remarks, to make homestead bill special order for next Thursday; agreed to.
250	1129	Mar. 13	Votes against bill (S. 53) amending act establishing Court of Claims; passed.
262	1194	Mar. 17	* Resolution Concerning Senate Messengers.
269	1217	Mar. 19	Presents petition from New York citizens asking for homestead bill; tabled.
273	1219, 1223	Mar. 19	Moves Senate proceed with consideration of homestead bill (S. 1); agreed to. After debate on bill, moves to make it special order for coming Wednesday; agreed to.
280	1276–77	Mar. 21	Moves to postpone bill (S. 230) regarding Spanish treaty of 1819 so that homestead bill can be considered; agreed to. Moves to take up homestead bill; agreed to. Following debate, submits resolution that committee on contingent expenses make improvements in Capitol at their discretion; tabled.
284	1292	Mar. 22	Comments on amendment to Washington market house bill. Reports, from committee on public lands, homestead bill (H. R. 280) with an amendment substituting S. 1 for the House measure. Moves amendment be printed, and bill placed on calendar; agreed to.
	1297–98	Mar. 22	* Remarks Concerning Senate Homestead Bill.
	1301 1303–4	Mar. 22	Engages in acrimonious exchange with Wigfall of Texas.
295	1345	Mar. 26	Votes against bill (S. 84) for establishing telegraph to West Coast; passed.
297	1352	Mar. 26	Votes for bill (S. 45) providing for sale of arms to states and territories; passed.
	1366–68	Mar. 27	* Exchange with Daniel Clark.
322	1443	Mar. 30	* Resolution on Improvements in the Capitol.
339	1505–7	Apr. 3	Moves to postpone all prior orders so Senate can take up homestead bill (S. 1); agreed to.
	1554–55	Apr. 5	* Exchange with James S. Green.
	1619	Apr. 9	Urges action on homestead bill.

Journal	Globe	Date	Subject
	1629	Apr. 10	Presents prospective amendment to homestead bill and asks that it be printed.
	1635	Apr. 10	Exchange with James Mason concerning Mason's earlier votes for donation of land and present opposition to homesteads.
383	1649	Apr. 11	Withdraws, on behalf of committee on public lands, amendment previously reported in lieu of House bill and offers new amendment instead.
	1650–56	Apr. 11	* Speech on Amendment to Homestead Bill.
407	1748	Apr. 17	Introduces, as an "independent proposition" from the committee on public lands, a homestead bill (S. 416) drawn from other bills (S. 1 and H. R. 280) and amendments. Moves that bill be printed; agreed to.
	1749–50	Apr. 17	* Remarks Introducing New Homestead Bill.
	1796–97	Apr. 19	Answers questions about homestead measure.
415	1800–1801	Apr. 19	* Remarks on Immigrants and Homestead Bill.
428	1958	May 4	Named to select committee on bill (S. 428) concerning "claims of American citizens for spoliations committed by the French prior to the 31st day of July, 1801" (*Cong. Globe*, May 8).
	1971–72	May 8	Moves postponement of Jefferson Davis' resolutions *re* slavery in the territories; no action.
	1996, 2003	May 9	Urges Benjamin F. Wade of Ohio to withdraw amendment to homestead bill.
	2037–38	May 10	* Remarks on Homestead Bill.
458	2043	May 10	Votes for homestead bill (S. 416) securing homesteads for actual settlers; passed.
	2043–44	May 10	Opposes alteration in title of homestead bill.
500	2268	May 23	Votes against concurrence with House amendment substituting S. 299 for similar bill relative to naval pay regulations and increases; accepted.
504	2309	May 24	Votes for bill (S. 464) amending an act *re* slave trade; passed.
508–10 512–18	2321–22 2350–52	May 24–25	Votes for resolutions offered by Senator Jefferson Davis affirming rights of slave states; adopted.
539	2462	May 30	Named to conference committee on homestead bill.
540	2474	May 30	Votes against Indian war debts bill (S. 11) providing payment of debts incurred by Washington and Oregon territories during Indian hostilities of 1855–56; passed.

Journal	Globe	Date	Subject
	2750	June 8	Supports Tennessee river improvement bill (H. R. 89).
615	2813	June 11	Presents conference committee report on homestead bill.
623	2862	June 12	Moves to consider House amendment to Senate homestead bill (S. 416); named to conference committee.
	2865	June 12	Offers amendment providing funds for committee to audit and control contingent expenses; agreed to.
639	2888	June 12	Votes against civil appropriation bill (H. R. 501); passed.
656–57	2955	June 14	Presents conference committee report on House amendment to Senate homestead bill; no agreement. Moves further conference; named to conference committee.
682	3055	June 16	Presents petition of Charles H. Lane and other Washington citizens asking passage of House bill to incorporate Metropolitan Gas Company; tabled.
710–11	3159	June 19	* Conference Committee Report on Homestead Bill.
711		June 19	Votes for conference committee report on homestead bill (S. 416); passed.
	3187, 3193	June 20	Comments on bill for retrenchment of government expenses.
	3267–70	June 23	* Speech on Homestead Bill Veto.
757	3272	June 23	Votes against final passage of homestead bill so he may call for reconsideration of vote; bill defeated. Moves reconsideration; postponed to next day.
767	3281	June 23	Reports, from committee on public lands, bill (H. R. 337) for relief of Elizabeth Smith of Coffee County; passed.
769	3293	June 25	Reports, from committee on public lands, bill (H. R. 812) to amend an act "granting public lands in alternate sections to State of Mississippi, to aid in the construction of railroads in said State"; passed.
771	3295	June 25	Reports, from committee to audit and control contingent expenses, resolution regarding pay of late Senator Broderick of California, and moves discharge of committee; agreed to.
773	3297	June 25	Reports, from committee to audit and control contingent expenses, resolution regarding pay of clerks of standing committees; passed [June 27].

36 CONGRESS, SPECIAL SESSION
June, 1860

Journal	Globe	Date	Subject
	3304	June 27	Announces pairing with Hannibal Hamlin of Maine for duration of executive session.
	3308	June 28	Objects to discussion of printing additional copies of Pacific Railroad survey.

36 CONGRESS, 2 SESSION
December, 1860–March, 1861

Journal	Globe	Date	Subject
	23	Dec. 10, 1860	Named member of committees on public lands, to audit and control contingent expenses, and the District of Columbia.
	23	Dec. 10	Moves that bill (H. R. 24) securing homesteads for actual settlers on public domain be referred to committee on public lands; agreed to.
41	82–83	Dec. 13	* Joint Resolution for Amendments on Presidential, Senatorial, and Judicial Selection (S. 48); read and passed to second reading.
41	83	Dec. 13	* Resolution Proposing "Unamendable" Amendments Affecting Slavery; ordered printed.
49–50	117	Dec. 18	Moves consideration of his joint resolution (S. 48); agreed to.

[The remainder of this calendar will be forthcoming in Volume IV.]

Index

Primary identification of a person is indicated by an italic *n* following the page reference. Identifications found in *Johnson Papers*, Volumes I and II, are indicated by a Roman numeral and page number in parentheses immediately following the name.

Abolition, abolitionists, abolitionism, 331–32, 375n, 417, 495, 598, 679, 683, 690, 700; equated with "white basis," 86; expelled from Ky. and N. C., 408, 409n; homestead as aid to, 449, 512; and John Brown, 348–49, 417–18n; in Ore., 433; petitions, 62, 63, 75, 331–32; slave trade in D. C., 62–63, 73n, 75; *see also* Sectionalism; Slavery

Adam: as a tailor, xix, 160

Adams, John: on dissolution of the Union, 331

Adams, John Quincy: funeral expenses of, 211n; on slavery, 339; speech on abolition petitions, quoted, 331–32

Adams, Stephen, 185, 190n; votes of, 75, 532

Adams' Express, 490, 501

Addison, Joseph: quotations from, 130n, 232, 341

Africa: emigrants from and voting rights, 100, 103; post sought in, 181

African, 323; *see also* Negro

Agrarianism: defined, 168n, 546n; discussed, 143–44, 536–38; homestead and, xix, xx, 512n

Agricultural colleges: Johnson opposes bill for, 708

Agriculture: and mechanism, 539; in N. H., 493; in Tenn., 493; Vattel on, 133–34

Agriculturists, 146, 164

"Alabama": from, 449–50

Alabama: constitution, 89n, 152, 168n; delegates at Charleston, 670; public lands unsold, 612, 630; RR grants, 149; slaveholders, 160; swamp lands, 149; unsold lands, 148, 149; and "white basis," 87, 89n

Aldrich, Cyrus: on homestead conference committee, 640n–41n

Alfred (liberated slave), 507

Aliens: and homestead, 545n, 565–68n, 634–35, 638; and voting qualifications, 105, 107n

Allen, John W., 276n

Allen, Joseph D., 472, 473n

Allen, William (I, 164n): on democracy, 157; vote of, 75

Allison, John, 361n

American Banner and Working Mens Leader, 436

American Colonization Society: Johnson's correspondence with, 507n, 520

American party: *see* Constitutional Union party; Know-Nothings; Opposition party

Anderson, Charles F., 397n; from, 395–97; memorandum from, 398–400; resolution of, *re* Capitol dome, 393, 394, 395n

Anderson, Joseph R., 274n, 362n, 423–24; employs Robert Johnson as legal counsel, 423–24; from, 361–62

Anderson, Samuel R. (II, 325n), 41, 197; as bank director, 370–71, 372n; from, 389–90; and Johnson's candidacy, xxv, 377, 384, 391

Anti-Abolition Association: in N. Y., 700

Anti-Rent movement: in N. Y., 368, 369n

Appointments, presidential: recommendations and requests, 180–81, 259–60, 282, 430–31, 513, 607; *see also* Patronage

Appropriations: for army, 15, 17–19, 34, 208, 216, 268, 709, 713; bills under consideration, 110, 112n, 114, 115n, 258, 259, 430, 709; for completion of aqueduct, 170, 174, 178; congressional, 135, 207–8, 278–79, 535; Johnson's amendment on, defeated, 180n; for Capitol, 173–74, 178, 397n, 401n, 455; for D. C., 93, 95–97, 116–17, 120, 121, 122, 128–29, 129n; for furnishing White House, 276n; for mall, 174, 177, 178; for military academy, 572n; for navy, 208, 709; for Pacific RR, 217, 228–29; for Pacific RR surveys, 233; for post office, 259n, 709; for public buildings and works, 170, 174; reduction in, urged, 176, 210; for Senate furniture, 262, 264, 265; to states, 175; for Tenn. River improvement, 508n, 608; for visit of Amin Bey, 27, 40; *see*

Military academy (West Point): applications and appointments to, 30, 378, 613, 643–44; appropriation bill for, 705; board of visitors to, 413, 415n; term of, 571, 572n

Military bounty lands: Act of 1850, claims under, 648, 705; land grants and warrants for, 354, 489, 490n, 533, 622, 649; reserved for Va. veterans, 546n; *see also* Public lands

Militia system: Johnson's support of, 23

"Milk & cider" Democrat, 582

Miller, Edmund B., 519n; property of, sold to Johnson, 472, 518, 647, 648n

Miller, Henry, 353n; invalid pension claim for, 352–53

Miller, Jacob, 295, 296n, 303, 412

Miller, Washington D., 180, 181n

Milligan, Sam (I, 114n), 204n, 574, 590, 599; appointment for, 6; on congressional race, 204; considered for Nashville *Union* editor, 7, 8n, 315; delegate to Charleston, xxv, 379, 381n, 402, 426, 517–18, 523; from, 386–87, 405–7, 419–20, 452–54, 477–79, 586–88, 626, 689–92; and Johnson's candidacy, 419, 453, 454n, 478, 488, 518; legal services of, 293, 687, 688; on prospects of disunion, 689–91; reports on state convention, 406; runs for state attorney general, 287; to, 623–24

Mills, Robert, 351n

Mining: in Tenn., 492, 493, 496n; in N. H., 493

Minnesota, 67; bill for admission of, debated, 89–91, 91n, 100, 130n; Charleston delegates from, 422, 423n, 590; Douglas' candidacy in, 438; Johnson's vote on statehood for, 69, 705; legislature of, and homestead measure, 365n; RR grants in, 149; representation in Congress, 89–91; suffrage and voting rights in, 102, 103, 105; unsold public lands in, 149, 612, 629, 630

Mississippi, 116, 461, 574; Johnson invited to speak in, 661; labor in, 334; RR grants in, 149; support for Douglas in, 609; swamp and unsold public lands in, 148, 149, 612, 630; "white basis" and representation in, 89n, 91n

Mississippi Democrats: from, 661

Mississippi River: as an "Inland Sea," 547n; wartime navigation of, 686, 691

Missouri: attitude of, toward Johnson's nomination, 461, 597; fails

Missouri (*cont.*) to apportion districts, 91n; land warrant in, 402; price of slaves in, 408; RR grants in, 149; swamp and unsold public lands in, 149, 612, 630

Missouri Compromise: Bell's position on, 79, 85, 109n, 667n; extension of, 48, 72n; Johnson on, 64; and Kansas-Nebraska bill, 675–76; repeal of, 44, 47–48, 49, 50, 59, 72n, 75, 76, 266n, 671n

Missouri *Republican* (St. Louis): Douglas paper, 671n

Money: stock market and war in Europe, 283; *see also* Paper currency

Monopolies and corporations: Johnson's opposition to, xix, xxii, 167, 226–28, 248

Monroe, James, 499n

Monroe, James, (1799–1870), 700n; from, 700

Montgomery, William, 605, 606, 607n

Moody, Mr., 615n

Moore, Laban T., 697, 698n

Moore, Dr. S. B., 388n, 592n

Moore, Sydenham, 181

Mooresburg, 582; postmaster appointment at, 486

Morals and morality: Johnson on, 329–30, 342

Mormons and Mormonism, 38–39; and homestead bill, 545n; in Utah, 11–34

Morris, Gouverneur: on property, 152

Morris, John, 402n, 420

Morrow, Sam, 578n

Morse, Samuel F. B., 701n

Morton, Cecelia (Cicile), 4n, 307, 569, 580

Morton, Helen, 4n, 307, 569

Moses: quotations from, used in homestead argument, xix, 133, 134

Mott, Dr. Valentine, 4n

"Mudsills" of society: *see* Society

Mulattoes: excluded from Ill. Militia, 322

Munday, W. S.: memorial of, 703

Municipal debts, 234, 236

Murfreesboro: train derailment at, 376–77

Murrow, John, 354

Naar, David, 500n

Nashville: Democratic convention in, xxv, 257, 317, 390n, 407n, 410, 651; Democratic factions in, 276n, 370, 372n, 376; Democratic papers in, 370, 372, 424, 667; Johnson's invitations to speak and speeches in, xxvi, 74–

Nashville (*cont.*)
75, 84, 310, 314, 317, 652, 654, 657, 659, 660n, 663n; labor in, 337; merchants in, 376n; postmaster, 372n, 384n; RR celebrations in, 409n; state fair in, 294
Nashville & Chattanooga RR, 376n; bonds of, 197–98; reduces fare to convention, 611n
Nashville convention (1860): *see* Tennessee Democratic convention
Nashville *Daily World*, 71n
Nashville *Democrat*, 667n; opposes fusion, 665
Nashville Democrats: to, 660
Nashville & Northwestern RR: building of, 376n
Nashville *Patriot*: Bell quoted from, 76; on Johnson, 663n
Nashville *Republican Banner*: quoted, 663n
Nashville *Union and American*, 191, 196, 294, 379, 424, 459, 515; on banking report, 195n; editors of, 8n, 204n, 372n, 393n; new editor sought for, 7, 309n, 315; reports on Robert Johnson's speech, 409n; supports Johnson's candidacy, xxv, 372n, 447n, 516n, 521
National debt: for Indian wars, 712; Johnson on, 234–35, 238, 250
National Reform Association: agitates for homestead, 11n, 358n, 369n, 708; Johnson presents petition from, 708; in New York City, 311, 313n, 358
Natural rights: Johnson's discourse on, 328–29
Naturalization: and homestead, 527, 545, 550, 634; laws, 102, 105–6; restrictions of, 565, 635, 642n; and suffrage, 100; *see also* Aliens
Naval academy: appointments to, 30, 358
Navy: appropriations for, 208, 709; expenditures of, 18–19; pay regulations in, 712; reduction in, urged, 251
Navy department: reduces expenses, 211n
Nebraska: land policies in, 545n; surveyor general for, 528; territory of, 45, 542; unsold public lands in, 149, 529–30
Nebraska bill: *see* Kansas-Nebraska Act
Negroes, 56, 100, 174; and congressional representation, 162, 320; doctrine of equality of, denied, 319–20, 327, 328–29; and Declaration of Independence, 319–20; education of, in public schools, 130n; insurrections of, feared, 682; Charles Johnson on, 404–5; kidnapped in D. C., 497; Republican party and, 698n; status

Negroes (*cont.*)
of, in Ill., 322–23; suffrage rights for, opposed, 699–700; threatened destruction of, 495, 496n; *see also* Free Negroes; Slaves
Nelson, T. A. R. (I, 159*n*), 378, 549, 673n; as Bell elector, 655n; in Congress, 257n, 366n, 367, 385n, 417, 428
Nesmith, James W., 434n, 435n
Netherland, John, 275, 276*n*
New, John Coffee, 644*n*
New England: material wealth of, 491; prejudice against slavery, 498
New Hampshire: commerce in, 493; compared with Tenn., xxiii, 497; fails to apportion districts, 91n; manufacturing and mining in, 493–94; size of, 49
New Jersey: 1860 election in, 500n; and homestead measure, 365n; size of, 49; state Democratic convention, 500; supports Johnson, 590
New Mexico, 44, 72n, 306, 529, 542; land policies in, 546n; mail agent in, 305; size of, 49; surveyor general for, 528; territorial bill for, 48, 50, 667n; unsold public lands in, 149
New Orleans, 92, 95, 231; battle of, 41; labor in, 336
New York, 461; Charleston delegation of, 522, 575; election (1858) in, 369n, (1860), 475; labor in, 334, 491; in middle confederacy, 691; population and size of, 227; tenant farmers' struggle in, 368n
New York City, 283, 472; conservatism in, 701n; crime in, 92, 168n; homestead petitions from, 703, 708, 710, 711; Johnson plans trip to, 3, 4; land reformers in, 311, 391n; pauperism in, 142, 143, 159, 168n; reaction in, to S. C. secession, 701n
New York *Herald*, 477, 479n; Daniel Clark's speech in, 479n, 491, 496n, 497
New York *News*, 193, 413; supports Johnson, 450; on Wood's candidacy at Charleston, 522n
New York *Times*: predicts southern loss of congressional seats, 617n
Newman, James, 314, 315n, 515n, 574, 577; charged with pension forgeries, 442, 443n, 459–60, 504, 505, 575n; as delegate to Charleston, 407n; from, 459
Newman, Tazewell, 170, 409*n*; charges against, on pension frauds, 442, 443n, 448, 457, 459, 460n, 480n, 504, 574, 577; from, 458–59, 600–1; state sen-

Pillow, George M., 477n
Pillow, Gideon (II, 351n), 7, 41, 426; letter of, to dissident Democrats, 615; on popular sovereignty and the Dred Scott decision, 615n; against endorsing Johnson, 414, 415n
Pitt, William (Lord Chatham), 560, 562n
Pittsburgh: abolitionists in, 332; labor in, 337
Planters' Bank, 457n; increase in stock, 442, 443n; recharter of, 302, 371, 373n
Plasterers: wages for, 336–37
Plebeian: Johnson as, 239
Poindexter, G. G., 8n, 309n; death of, 308, 315
Polk, James K. (I, 32n), xxiii, 499n
Polk, Leonidas, 689n
Polk, Sarah Childress (Mrs. James K.) (II, 260n), 411, 446n, 502
Polk, Trusten, 205n, 628; on homestead, 641n; recommendations by, 181, 260
Polk, William H. (II, 229n): Douglas elector, 652n, 668n
Pollock, James, 299n
Polygamy, 329; Johnson on, 26, 27, 39; in N. Y., 28; Republican platform on, 56, 321; in Turkey, 27, 39
Pooley, Samuel J., 563n; from, 563, 578–79, 597–98
Pope, Alexander: quotation from, 146, 352n
Popular sovereignty: Breckinridge quoted on, 662; as contrasted with "squatter" sovereignty in 1860 election, 650, 657, 658n, 662, 664n, 665, 669, 675, 678, 680; Douglas' position on, 76, 372n, 463–64, 465n, 610n, 615n–16n, 622, 664n, 669; and Dred Scott decision, 615n–16n, 664n; Greeneville resolution on, 674n; Johnson's position on, 59–60, 74, 305, 657; Milligan's opinion of, 406–7; principle of, in Kansas-Nebraska bill, 49–50, 52, 55–56, 76; Republican platform (1856) on, 56; Tenn. delegates on, 459; see also Squatter sovereignty
Population, 137, 540; of cities, 142; homestead and, 147; in relation to federal expenditures, 121, 122, 207–8; in Tenn., 227
Porter, Felicia Ann Grundy Eakin, 502, 504n
Post office department: applications for appointments to, 431, 480–81, 486, 582, 673; appropriations for, 259n, 279, 430, 706, 709; draft from, 202; laws and regulations of, 11, 704; mail con-

Post office department (cont.)
tracts, 429, 551n–52n; route agents, 199–200, 271, 435, 487, 488n; special agents, 305
Postmaster general: see Brown, Aaron V.; Holt, Joseph
Postmasters: removed by Buchanan, 441n, 444
Pottawatomie massacre, 344–50
Poverty: equated with crime, 541, 548; Johnson on, 540–41
Powel, George R. (II, 70n): from, 365–66, 447
Powel, Robert D., 257n; as congressional candidate, 256; from, 487–88; journalistic duel with Brownlow, 488n; supports Johnson, 488
Powel, Samuel, 257n
Powell, Joseph: from, 607
Powell, Lazarus W., 353, 354n, 506n; reports from Committee of Thirteen, 697n
Preemption policy, 533; and foreigners, 565, 635; Johnson for, 543; laws relating to, 529–30, 635; not impaired by homestead bill, 545n; see also Homestead bill
Preemptors: and homestead provisions, 594, 595, 624, 625n, 631–32, 635, 637, 641n
President: appointment powers of, 30–32, 94, 99n; changes proposed in election of, 684, 699; Johnson on office of, xxiv, 204, 242–43, 290–91; Johnson's proposals for election of, xxviii, 189–90, 223–24, 242, 246n, 663n, 693–94, 714; support of a southerner for, 460, 466, 475, 487–88; wartime power of, 33, 216, 241
Price, Benjamin, 194n; from, 193–94
Pritchard, J. K. P., 361n; from, 361
Property: as basis of congressional representation, 152–53; as foundation of society, 154, 158; slaves considered as, 86, 166, 320, 406, 674; and taxes, 126–27
Protestant churches: division of, 386
Proudfit, John, 599
Prussia: emigrants from, 566
Pryor, John P.: Douglas supporter, 646n
Pryor, Roger, 420n
Public buildings, commissioner of, 398
Public lands, 111, 117, 135–36, 306, 512n, 537, 539, 547n, 559, 563, 565; Buchanan on disposal of, xxi, 471n, 544, 640; disposition of, 54, 111, 132, 135, 547n, 557, 558; estimated unsold, 5–6, 149, 623, 630–31; Johnson on federal trusteeship of, 178–79; legislation relating to, 527–30, 531–33,

Public lands (*cont.*)
545n, 612; ownership of, 539; for Pacific RR, 218, 226, 636–37; price of, 629, 635; RR grants from, estimated, 6, 138, 148, 167n; sale of and revenue from, 137, 138, 139–41, 145, 365n, 449, 471n, 511n, 535, 540–42, 543, 549–50, 550n, 631, 637, 641n; speculation in, 10, 550, 596n; state taxes on, 510, 512n; surveys of, 628–29; surveyors general of, 527, 542; transferred to states for internal improvements, 631; *see also* Homestead bill; Military bounty lands; Preemption policy; Preemptors
Public printing, 29n
Pugh, George E., 182, 183, 184n; from, 550; and homestead, 530
"Pull the wires," 428
Puryear, M. C. H.: appointed bank director, 372n

Quarles, William A., 412n, 574n; as delegate to Charleston, 411, 426; as Johnson supporter, 414, 522

Railroads: and banking, 298; construction of, through D. C., 247–50; federal land grants to, 6, 138, 147, 148, 167n, 454n, 563, 636, 641n, 642n, 667n; in N. H., 494; and postal contracts, 551, 673; reduce fare for conventions, 611; state construction of, 230, 234, 241, 299n; in Tenn., 288, 294n, 376n, 409n, 489n, 494; transcontinental, speech on, 214–45n; *see also* Pacific RR; individual RR
Rains, Felix R., 445, 446n
Rambo, John, 294n
Ramsey, Francis, 603n
Ramsey, J. G. M. (II, 214n), 449n, 603n; from, 310–11, 452; supports Johnson's candidacy, 514, 515n
Ramsey, John Crozier (I, 317n), 311n, 498; defeated for Congress, 355n; from, 504–5; and Newman affair, 443n, 448, 449n, 457, 458–59, 460n, 505, 574, 577; rumored removal of, as attorney general, 452, 505n; supports Johnson's candidacy, 310, 314, 315n, 414, 504–5, 521, 521n
Ramsey, W. B. A. (II, 185n), 197, 198
Rankin, Anthony: claim of, 212
Rankin, James M., 582, 583n; from, 582–83
Ray, J. E. R., 295, 296n
Reagan, John H., 181
Reapportionment: congressional, 693; of legislature, 86, 89n; *see also* Con-

Reapportionment (*cont.*)
gressional redistricting; "White basis"
Red Bridge: postmaster for, 582
Red Republicanism, 166, 537
Reed, William B., 30n
Reeves, James G., 453, 454n
Reid, David S. (II, 64n): House colleague of Johnson, 211n; recommendations by, 181, 260
Republican party, 418, 438, 439, 662, 671; blamed for depression, 698n; in Conn., 552, 552n–53n; and 1860 elections, 275, 276n; and homestead, xviii, xx, xxi, 312, 357, 358, 364, 365n, 485n, 526, 534, 543, 552, 578; House speaker's election and, 366n, 367, 389, 390n; in Ore., 434, 435n; platform (1856), quoted, 56, 319, 320–21; platform (1860), 650; Seward's leadership of, 196, 278, 467; and slavery, xxii, 278, 319, 323, 464–65, 498, 673, 698n
Retrenchment: and army bill, 16, 19, 26, 34; as issue in 1859 canvass, 278–79; President and, 206, 207, 209, 238, 250, 278, 454n; urged in congressional appropriations and federal expenditures, xxii, 122, 170–71, 174–76, 206–7, 209–10, 211n, 212–14, 234, 238–39, 250–54, 267–68, 278–79, 454n, 506n, 708; *see also* Appropriations; Federal expenditures
Revenue: and homestead bill, 111, 179n, 637, 639–40; Edmund Burke on, 17; from sale of public lands, 137, 138, 140–41, 142, 471n, 535, 641n; sources of, 169n, 237
Revolution: right of, 673, 686
Revolutionary War, 40, 51, 81n; bounty land grants to veterans of, 533, 546n
Rhea, Robert: mail contractor, 551, 552n
Rhea, Samuel (I, 462n): from, 270–71, 403–4
Rhett, Robert Barnwell, 504n
Rhett, Thomas G., 621n
Rhode Island: size of, 49
Richardson, John W., 378n
Richmond (Va.): labor in, 337; reception for southern medical students, 371n
Richmond (Va.) *Index*, 514
Richmond Democratic Convention: reaction to, in Tenn., 599, 601, 602, 610–11, 620; reaffirms nominations of Breckinridge and Lane, 601n
Riggs, George, 284n
Riggs and Company: D. C. banking firm, 283, 284n

Senate, U. S. reports (*cont.*)
naval affairs (expenditures), 209; select committee (on retrenchment), 212–13; special committee investigating frauds and abuses in Capitol construction, 401n; of Thirteen, 696n, 697n; on territories, 66, 67
reports and recommendations brought by Johnson from committees: to audit and control expenses (clerks and messengers) 470–71n, 713, (construction workers' wages) 553–54, (improvements in Capitol) 455, 505–6n, (Mrs. Lynn's claim) 584, 585n; conference committee on homestead bill, 470, 624–25, 641n, 713; on public lands and homestead, 8n, 481, 545n, 547n, 556, 558n
resolutions by Johnson: for amendments on presidential, senatorial, judicial selection, 692–95; on Capitol improvements, 505–6, 711; on governmental expenditures, 250–51, 454n, 479n, 708; on retrenchment, 206, 212, 250–51, 267–68n; concerning Senate messengers, 470, 711; on Harper's Ferry incident, 350n; proposing "unamendable" amendments affecting slavery, 696
speeches by Johnson: on amendment to homestead, 524–45, 712; on Harper's Ferry incident, 318–50, 710; on homestead bill, 132–67, 703, 706; on homestead veto, 612n, 627–40, 714; on maintaining federal authority in Utah, 11–29, 704; on popular sovereignty and right of instruction, 43–71, 704; on school funds for D. C., 115–29, 706; on transcontinental RR, 214–45, 703
See also Appendix, Andrew Johnson in the Senate, 703–14
Sevier, Charles F., 379n; from, 378–79
Sevier, David D., 200, 201
Sevier County, 515
Seward, William H., xviii, xxii, 26, 34, 53, 132n, 187, 244, 413; called author of homestead, 185–88; and D. C. school funds, 122, 123; "higher law" speech of, 72n; "irrepressible conflict" speech of, xxii, 332–33, 338, 351n, 365n, 429, 430n, 462, 679; in N. Y. politics, 413; as Republican leader and candidate, 196, 278, 437, 467; on slavery, 338; vote of, 75
Seymour, Horatio, 316, 317n; Tenn. support of, 475
Seymour, Thomas H., 654n; recommended for vice president, 653

Shakespeare: quotations from, 73n, 88n, 121, 130n, 279, 284, 285n, 288, 289n, 404
Sharswood, William, 689n; from, 688–89
Sheep: in N. H. and Tenn., 494
Sheid, James M., 599
Shelby County: 1860 election in, 671n
Shelby County Democrats, 392n; from, 598–99; *see also* Memphis Democrats
Sherfy, Samuel, 687, 688n
Sherman, John, 273n
Sherman, William: murdered by John Brown, 343, 344, 346, 347
Sherman: *see* Schurmann, H. F.
Shermer, Mary, 430, 431n
Shields, James: votes of, 75, 532
Shields, William, 221, 246n
Shorter, Eli S., 181
Sibley, Henry H., 422, 423n, 447
Silver, 288, 306; as monetary standard, 195, 289n, 302
Simmons, James F., 34, 219, 245n; recommendation by, 181
Simons, James, 255n
Simpson, Robert, 486n, 582
Skelton, Charles, 500n; from, 500
Slaughter, Samuel: bounty land claim of, 705
Slave labor, xix–xx, 161, 162, 163, 164, 420, 676, 677; in conflict with free labor, xxii, 333, 338, 462–63, 691; Johnson on, 335–36
Slave states, xxviii, 247n, 686; Democratic party in, 652; proposal to elect President from, 694, 695n; secession of, justified, 699; *see also* South
Slave trade, 696, 712; abolished in D. C., 62–63, 64, 73n; illegal incidents of, 180n
Slaveowners: as aristocracy, 335, 339; conflict between nonslaveholders and, 462–63; in 1850 census, 169n; and free Negro bill, 409n–10n; nonslaveholder support of, 495; number of, 161, 164, 169n
Slavery: John Q. Adams on, 332; attitude of nonslaveholders toward, 165, 462–64, 495, 496, 677, 679, 680, 686; Buchanan's message on, quoted, 407n; Constitution on, 291, 324, 338–39, 675, 676; Davis' resolutions on, 467n, 479n, 658n; Democratic platform on, 367n, 466, 478; in D. C., 62–63, 696; doctrine of noninterference with, 44, 49, 50, 409n, 622, 696; free Negro bill and, 377, 381n, 409–10, 442, 443n; and homestead, 133, 166, 357, 365n, 485n, 525–26, 533, 534, 535, 545; Johnson on, xviii, xix–xx,

The Papers of Andrew Johnson

Monticello, the type chosen for this series, is a Linotype design based on the first successful American face, which was cut by Archibald Binny at Philadelphia in 1796. The clean legibility of Monticello, especially in the smaller sizes, suits it admirably for a series in which documentation is extensive.

Volume 3 of *The Papers of Andrew Johnson* was composed and printed by Heritage Printers, Inc., Charlotte, North Carolina. Bound by Kingsport Press, Inc., Kingsport, Tennessee. Illustrations were printed by offset lithography on paper made by the Mohawk Paper Mills, Cohoes, New York; text paper was manufactured by the P. H. Glatfelter Co., Spring Grove, Pennsylvania. Arkwright-Interlaken, Inc., Fiskeville, Rhode Island, supplied cloth for the binding. The book was designed by Hugh Bailey and Helen Orton.

THE UNIVERSITY OF TENNESSEE PRESS